U.S.
ENVIRONMENTAL
LAWS

BNA Environmental Services

Air & Water Pollution Control

Chemical Regulation Reporter

Chemical Substances Control

Environment Reporter

Hazardous Materials Transportation

Index to Chemical Regulation

International Environment Reporter

Noise Regulation Reporter

Right-To-Know Planning Guide

Sewage Treatment Construction Grants Manual

Toxics Law Reporter

For orders or information, contact:

BNA Customer Service Center
9435 Key West Avenue
Rockville, MD 20850-3397

or call the BNA Response Center toll free:

(800) 372-1033

U.S. ENVIRONMENTAL LAWS

1988 Edition

Prepared by the
BNA Editorial Staff

The Bureau of National Affairs Inc., Washington, D.C.

The Bureau of National Affairs Inc.
Washington, D.C. 20037

Library of Congress Cataloging-in-Publication Data

United States:
  U.S. environmental laws.

  1. Environmental law — United States. I. Bureau of
National Affairs (Washington, D.C.)   II. Title.
KF3775.A3   1988   344.73'046   87-37348
ISBN 0-87179-568-X   347.30446

Printed in the United States of America

International Standard Book Number: 0-87179-568-X

CONTENTS

Foreword xxxiii
  by Wallis E. McClain, Jr.
Preface xxxv
  by William D. Ruckelshaus

Part 1. Text of Major Environmental Laws

1. National Environmental Policy Act 3
   Introduction 3
   Text of The National Environmental Policy Act 6

2. Comprehensive Environmental Response, Compensation, and Liability
   Act of 1980 14
   Introduction 14
   Text of Comprehensive Environmental Response, Compensation, and
   Liability Act of 1980 18

3. Toxic Substances Control Act 145
   Introduction 145
   Text of Toxic Substances Control Act 147

4. Federal Insecticide, Fungicide, and Rodenticide Act 227
   Introduction 227
   Text of Federal Insecticide, Fungicide, and Rodenticide Act 229

5. The Resource Conservation and Recovery Act 276
   Introduction 276
   Text of Resource Conservation and Recovery Act 280

6. Clean Air Act 419
   Introduction 419
   Text of Clean Air Act 423

7. Clean Water Act 584
   Introduction 584
   Text of Federal Water Pollution Control Act, as amended by the
   Clean Water Act of 1977 (commonly referred to as Clean Water
   Act) 587

8. Emergency Planning and Community Right-To-Know Act of 1986
   792
   Introduction 792
   Text of Emergency Planning and Community Right-To-Know Act of
   1986 794

Part 2. Summaries of Related Environmental Laws ─────────────

9. The Endangered Species Act 827
   Summary 827

10. Marine Mammal Protection Act 832
    Summary 832

11. Port and Tanker Safety Act 838
    Summary 838

12. Safe Drinking Water Act 841
    Summary 841

13. Noise Control Act 850
    Summary 850

14. Intervention on the High Seas Act 854
    Summary 854

15. National Ocean Pollution Planning Act 857
    Summary 857

16. Marine Protection, Research, and Sanctuaries Act 859
    Summary 859

17. Outer Continental Shelf Lands Act 864
    Summary 864

Section-by-Section Finding List

(References are to relevant sections of the act.)

Title	*Section*		*Page*
		The National Environmental Policy Act (P.L. 91–190, effective January 1, 1970; as last amended by P.L. 94–83, approved August 9, 1975)	6
42	4321.	Congressional declaration of purpose	6
		Subchapter I. Policies and goals	6
	4331.	Congressional declaration of national environmental policy;	6

Title	Section		Page
42	4332.	Cooperation of agencies; reports; availability of information; recommendations; international and national coordination of efforts	7
	4333.	Conformity of administrative procedures to national environmental policy	9
	4334.	Other statutory obligations of agencies	9
	4335.	Efforts supplemental to existing authorizations	10

Subchapter II. Council on Environmental Quality — 10

	4341.	Reports to Congress; recommendations for legislation	10
	4342.	Establishment; membership; Chairman; appointments	10
	4343.	Employment of personnel, experts and consultants	11
	4344.	Duties and functions	11
	4345.	Consultation with the Citizens' Advisory Committee on Environmental Quality and other representatives	12
	4346.	Tenure and compensation of members	12
	4346a.	Travel reimbursement by private organizations and federal, state, and local governments	12
	4346b.	Expenditures in support of international activities	12
	4347.	Authorization of appropriations	13

Comprehensive Environmental Response, Compensation, and Liability Act of 1980 (P.L. 96–510, approved December 11, 1980; as last amended by P.L. 99–499, approved October 17, 1986 — 18

Subchapter I. Hazardous Substances Releases, Liability, Compensation — 18

| | 9601. | Definitions | 18 |

Title	Section		Page
42	9602.	Designation of additional hazardous substances and establishment of reportable released quantities; regulations	26
	9603.	Notification requirements respecting released substances	27
	9604.	Response authorities	29
	9605.	National contingency plans; preparation, contents, etc.	48
	9606.	Abatement action	53
	9607.	Liability	54
	9608.	Financial responsibility	64
	9609.	Civil penalties	67
	9610.	Employee protection	70
	9611.	Uses of fund	71
	9612.	Claims procedure	78
	9613.	Civil proceedings	80
	9614.	Relationship to other law	85
	9615.	Presidential delegation and assignment of duties or powers and promulgation of regulations	86
	9616.	Schedules	86
	9617.	Public participation	87
	9618.	High priority for drinking water supplies	89
	9619.	Response action contractors	89
	9620.	Federal facilities	93
	9621.	Cleanup standards	99
	9622.	Settlements	106
	9623.	Reimbursement to local governments	116
	9624.	Methane recovery	117
	9625.	Certain special study wastes	117
	9626.	Indian Tribes	118

Subchapter II. Hazardous Substance Response Revenue Act of 1980

			119
		Part A. Hazardous Substance Response Trust Fund	119
	9631—9633.	[Repealed]	119
		Part B. Post-closure Liability Trust Fund	119
	9641.	[Repealed]	119

Title	*Section*		*Page*
42		**Subchapter III. Miscellaneous provisions**	119
	9651.	Reports and studies	119
	9652.	Effective dates, savings provision	125
	9653.	Repealed	126
	9654.	Applicability of federal water pollution control funding, etc., provisions	126
	9655.	Legislative veto of rule or regulation	126
	9656.	Transportation of hazardous substances; listing as hazardous material; liability for release	127
	9657.	Separability of provisions	127
	9658.	Actions under state law for damages from exposure to hazardous substances	128
	9659.	Citizens' suits	129
	9660.	Research, development, and demonstration	130
	9660a.	Grant program	138
	9661.	Love Canal property acquisition	138
	9662.	Limitation on contract and borrowing authority	140
		Subchapter IV. Pollution Insurance	140
	9671.	Definitions	140
	9672.	State laws; scope of title	141
	9673.	Risk retention groups	141
	9674.	Purchasing groups	143
	9675.	Applicability of securities laws	144
		Toxic Substances Control Act (P.L. 94-469, approved October 11, 1976; as last amended by P.L. 99-519, approved October 22, 1986)	147
		Subchapter I. Control of Toxic Substances	147
15	2601.	Findings, policy, and intent	147
	2602.	Definitions	148
	2603.	Testing of chemical substances and mixtures	150
	2604.	Manufacturing and processing notices	159
	2605.	Regulation of hazardous chemical substances and mixtures	168
	2606.	Imminent hazards	175

Title	Section		Page
15	2607.	Reporting and retention of information	177
	2608.	Relationship to other federal laws	180
	2609.	Research, development, collection, dissemination, and utilization of data	182
	2610.	Inspections and subpoenas	183
	2611.	Exports	184
	2612.	Entry into customs territory of the United States	185
	2613.	Disclosure of data	186
	2614.	Prohibited acts	188
	2615.	Penalties	189
	2616.	Specific enforcement and seizure	190
	2617.	Preemption	191
	2618.	Judicial review	192
	2619.	Citizens' civil actions	194
	2620.	Citizens' petitions	196
	2621.	National defense waiver	197
	2622.	Employee protection	198
	2623.	Employment effects	199
	2624.	Studies	200
	2625.	Administration	201
	2626.	Development and evaluation of test methods	204
	2627.	State programs	204
	2628.	Authorization of appropriations	205
	2629.	Annual report	206

Subchapter II. Asbestos hazard emergency response   206

	2641.	Congressional findings and declaration of purpose	206
	2642.	Definitions	207
	2643.	Environmental Protection Agency regulations	209
	2644.	Requirements upon failure of EPA to promulgate regulations	214
	2645.	Submission of management plan to State Governor	216
	2646.	Contractor and laboratory accreditation	217
	2647.	Enforcement	220
	2648.	Emergency authority	222
	2649.	Preemption	223

Title	Section		Page
15	2650.	Liability insurance for asbestos contractors and local educational agencies	224
	2651.	Discrimination by State or local educational agency	225
	2652.	Asbestos Ombudsmen	225
	2653.	Study of asbestos-containing material in public buildings	225
	2654.	Transitional rules	226

Federal Insecticide, Fungicide, and Rodenticide Act   229

(P.L. 92–516, approved October 21, 1972; as last amended by P.L. 98–620, approved November 8, 1984)   229

Subchapter I. Insecticides   229

| 7 | 121–134. | Repealed | 229 |

Subchapter II. Environmental Pesticide Control   229

	136.	Definitions	229
	136a.	Registration of pesticides	235
	136b.	Use of restricted use pesticides; certified applicators	245
	136c.	Experimental use permits	246
	136d.	Administrative review; suspension	247
	136e.	Registration of establishments	252
	136f.	Books and records	252
	136g.	Inspection of establishments, etc.	253
	136h.	Protection of trade secrets and other information	254
	136i.	Standards applicable to pesticide applicators	257
	136j.	Unlawful acts	257
	136k.	Stop sale, use, removal, and seizure	260
	136l.	Penalties	261
	136m.	Indemnities	262
	136n.	Administrative procedure; judicial review	263
	136o.	Imports and exports	263

Title	Section		Page
7	136p.	Exemption of federal agencies	265
	136q.	Disposal and transportation	265
	136r.	Research and monitoring	265
	136s.	Solicitation of comments; notice of public hearings	266
	136t.	Delegation and cooperation	266
	136u.	State cooperation, aid, and training	266
	136v.	Authority of states	267
	136w.	Authority of Administrator .	268
	136w–1.	State primary enforcement responsibility	273
	136w–2.	Failure by the state to assure enforcement of state pesticide use regulation	274
	136w–3.	Identification of pests; cooperation with Department of Agriculture's program	274
	136w–4.	Annual report	274
	136x.	Severability	275
	136y.	Authorization for appropriations	275

Resource Conservation and Recovery Act

(P.L. 94–580, approved October 21, 1976; as last amended by P.L. 99–499, approved October 17, 1986)   280

Subchapter I. General Provisions   280

42	6901.	Congressional findings	280
	6901a.	Congressional findings: used oil recycling	282
	6902.	Objectives	282
	6903.	Definitions	283
	6904.	Government cooperation	287
	6905.	Application of act and integration with other acts	288
	6906.	Financial disclosure	289
	6907.	Solid waste management information and guidelines	290

**Subchapter II. Office of Solid Waste;
Authorities of the Administrator**   291

	6911.	Office of Solid Waste and Interagency Coordinating Committee	291
	6912.	Authorities of administrator	292

Title	Section		Page
42	6913.	Resource Conservation and Recovery Panels	293
	6914.	Grants for discarded tire disposal	293
	6914a.	Labeling of lubricating oil	293
	6915.	Annual report	294
	6916.	General authorization	294
	6917.	Office of Ombudsman	295

Subchapter III. Hazardous Waste Management   295

	6921.	Identification and listing of hazardous waste	295
	6922.	Standards applicable to generators of hazardous waste	303
	6923.	Standards applicable to transporters of hazardous waste	304
	6924.	Standards applicable to owners and operators of hazardous waste treatment, storage, and disposal facilities	305
	6925.	Permits for treatment, storage, or disposal of hazardous waste	320
	6926.	Authorized state hazardous waste programs	330
	6927.	Inspections	332
	6928.	Federal enforcement	335
	6929.	Retention of state authority	338
	6930.	Effective date	339
	6931.	Authorization of assistance to states	340
	6933.	Hazardous waste site inventory	341
	6934.	Monitoring, analysis, and testing	342
	6935.	Restrictions on recycled oil	344
	6936.	Expansion during interim status	345
	6937.	Inventory of federal agency hazardous waste facilities	346
	6938.	Export of hazardous waste	347
	6939.	Domestic sewage	349
	6939a.	Exposure information and health assessments	350

Subchapter IV. State or Regional Solid Waste Plans   352

	6941.	Objectives of subtitle	352
	6942.	Federal guidelines for plans	352
	6943.	Requirements for approval of plans	353

Title	Section		Page
42	6944.	Criteria for sanitary landfills; sanitary landfills required for all disposal	355
	6945.	Upgrading of open dumps	356
	6946.	Procedure for development and implementation of state plan	357
	6947.	Approval of state plan; federal assistance	359
	6948.	Federal assistance	360
	6949.	Rural communities assistance	364
	6949a.	Adequacy of certain guidelines and criteria	365

Subchapter V. Duties of the Secretary of Commerce in Resource and Recovery — 365

	6951.	Functions	365
	6952.	Development of specifications for secondary materials	366
	6953.	Development of markets for recovered materials	366
	6954.	Technology promotion	366
	6955.	Nondiscrimination requirement	366
	6956.	Authorization of appropriations	367

Subchapter VI. Federal Responsibilities — 367

	6961.	Application of federal, state, and local law to federal facilities	367
	6962.	Federal procurement	368
	6963.	Cooperation with the Environmental Protection Agency	371
	6964.	Applicability of solid waste disposal guidelines to executive agencies	372

Subchapter VII. Miscellaneous Provisions — 373

	6971.	Employee protection	373
	6972.	Citizens' suits	375
	6973.	Imminent hazard	378
	6974.	Petition for regulations; public participation	379
	6975.	Separability	380
	6976.	Judicial review	380
	6977.	Grants or contracts for training projects	381
	6978.	Payments	382
	6979.	Labor standards	382

Title	Section		Page
42	6979a.	Interim control of hazardous waste injection	383
	6979b.	Law enforcement authority	384

Subchapter VIII. Research, Development, Demonstration, and Information — 384

	6981.	Research, demonstration, training, and other activities	384
	6982.	Special studies; plans for research, development, and demonstrations	387
	6983.	Coordination, collection, and dissemination of information	394
	6984.	Full-scale demonstration facilities	396
	6985.	Special study and demonstration projects on recovery of useful energy and materials	397
	6986.	Grants for resource recovery systems and improved solid waste disposal facilities	398
	6987.	Authorization of appropriations	400

Subchapter IX. Regulation of Underground Storage Tanks — 400

	6991.	Definitions and exemptions	400
	6991a.	Notification	402
	6991b.	Release detection, prevention, and correction regulations	403
	6991c.	Approval of state programs	411
	6991d.	Inspections, monitoring, and corrective action	413
	6991e.	Federal enforcement	415
	6991f.	Federal facilities	416
	6991g.	State authority	416
	6991h.	Study of underground storage tanks	417
	6991i.	Authorization of appropriations	418

Clean Air Act

(P.L. 84–159, approved July 14, 1955; as last amended by P.L. 98–213, approved December 8, 1983) — 423

Title	Section		Page
		Subchapter I. Air Pollution Prevention and Control	423
		Part A. Air Quality and Emission Limitations	423
42	7401.	Congressional findings and declaration of purposes	423
	7402.	Cooperative activities	424
	7403.	Research, investigation, training, and other activities	424
	7404.	Research relating to fuels and vehicles	427
	7405.	Grants for support of air pollution planning and control programs	429
	7406.	Interstate air quality agencies; program cost limitations	431
	7407.	Air quality control regions	431
	7408.	Air quality criteria and control techniques	433
	7409.	National primary and secondary ambient air quality standards	436
	7410.	State implementation plans for national primary and secondary ambient air quality standards	438
	7411.	Standards of performance for new stationary sources	449
	7412.	National emission standards for hazardous air pollutants	457
	7413.	Federal enforcement procedures	459
	7414.	Recordkeeping, inspections, monitoring, and entry	470
	7415.	International air pollution	472
	7416.	Retention of state authority	472
	7417.	Advisory committees	473
	7418.	Control of pollution from federal facilities	473
	7419.	Primary nonferrous smelter orders	474
	7420.	Noncompliance penalty	478
	7421.	Consultation	483
	7422.	Listing of certain unregulated pollutants	484
	7423.	Stack heights	485
	7424.	Assurance of adequacy of state plans	486
	7425.	Measures to prevent economic disruption or unemployment	486
	7426.	Interstate pollution abatement	488

Title	Section		Page
42	7427.	Public notification	489
	7428.	State boards	489

Part B. Ozone Protection — 490

	7450.	Congressional declaration of purpose	490
	7451.	Congressional findings and definitions	490
	7452.	"Halocarbon" and "stratosphere" defined	491
	7453.	Studies by Environmental Protection Agency	491
	7454.	Research and monitoring by other agencies	493
	7455.	Progress of regulation	494
	7456.	International cooperation	494
	7457.	Regulations	495
	7458.	Other provisions unaffected	495
	7459.	State authority	495

Part C. Prevention of Significant Deterioration of Air Quality — 495

Subpart I. Clean Air — 496

	7470.	Congressional declaration of purpose	496
	7471.	Plan requirements	496
	7472.	Initial classifications	497
	7473.	Increments and ceilings	497
	7474.	Area redesignation	499
	7475.	Preconstruction requirements	502
	7476.	Other pollutants	506
	7477.	Enforcement	507
	7478.	Period before plan approval	507
	7479.	Definitions	508

Subpart II. Visibility Protection — 509

| | 7491. | Visibility protection for federal class I areas | 509 |

Part D. Plan Requirements for Nonattainment areas — 513

	7501.	Definitions	513
	7502.	Nonattainment plan provisions	513
	7503.	Permit requirements	515
	7504.	Planning procedures	516
	7505.	Environmental Protection Agency grants	517
	7506.	Limitations on certain federal assistance	517
	7507.	New motor vehicle emission standards in nonattainment areas	518
	7508.	Guidance documents	518

Title	Section		Page
		Subchapter II. Emission Standards for Moving Sources	518
		Part A. Motor Vehicle Emission and Fuel Standards	518
42	7521.	Emission standards for new motor vehicles or new motor vehicle engines	518
	7522.	Prohibited acts	530
	7523.	Actions to restrain violations	532
	7524.	Penalties	532
	7525.	Motor vehicle and motor vehicle engine compliance testing and certification	532
	7541.	Compliance by vehicles and engines in actual use	537
	7542.	Records and reports	541
	7543.	State standards	541
	7544.	State grants	542
	7545.	Regulation of fuels	543
	7546.	Low-emission vehicles	548
	7547.	Fuel economy improvement from new motor vehicles	551
	7548.	Study of particulate emissions from motor vehicles	552
	7549.	High altitude performance adjustments	552
	7550.	Definitions for Part A	553
		Part B. Aircraft Emission Standards	554
	7571.	Establishment of standards	554
	7572.	Enforcement of standards	555
	7573.	State standards and controls	555
	7574.	Definitions	556
		Subchapter III. General Provisions	556
	7601.	Administration	556
	7602.	Definitions	556
	7603.	Emergency powers	558
	7604.	Citizen suits	559
	7605.	Representation in litigation	561
	7606.	Federal procurement	561
	7607.	Administrative proceedings and judicial review	562
	7608.	Mandatory licensing	567
	7609.	Policy review	568

Title	Section		Page
42	7610.	Other authority not affected	568
	7611.	Records and audit	568
	7612.	Cost studies	569
	7613.	Additional reports to Congress	570
	7614.	Labor standards	570
	7615.	Separability of provisions	571
	7616.	Sewage treatment grants	571
	7617.	Economic impact assessment	572
	7618.	Financial disclosure; conflicts of interest	573
	7619.	Air quality monitoring	575
	7620.	Standardized air quality modeling	576
	7621.	Employment effects	576
	7622.	Employee protection	577
	7624.	Cost of vapor recovery equipment	579
	7625.	Vapor recovery for small business marketers of petroleum products	580
	7625-1	Exemptions for certain territories	581
	7625a.	Statutory construction	581
	7626.	Authorization of appropriations	582

Subchapter IV. Noise Pollution 582

	7641.	Noise abatement	582
	7642.	Authorization of appropriations	583

Federal Water Pollution Control Act, as amended by the Clean Water Act of 1977 (commonly referred to as Clean Water Act)

(P.L. 92–500, approved October 18, 1972; as last amended by P.L. 100–4, approved February 4, 1987   587

Subchapter I. Research and Related Programs 587

33	1251.	Congressional declaration of goals and policy	587
	1252.	Comprehensive programs for water pollution control	589
	1253.	Interstate cooperation and uniform laws	591

Title	*Section*		*Page*
33	1254.	Research, investigations, training, and information	591
	1255.	Grants for research and development	600
	1256.	Grants for pollution control programs	602
	1257.	Mine water pollution control demonstrations	604
	1258.	Pollution control in Great Lakes	605
	1259.	Training grants and contracts	606
	1260.	Application for training grant or contract; allocation of grants or contracts	607
	1261.	Award of scholarships	608
	1262.	Definitions and authorizations	609
	1263.	Alaska village demonstration projects	610
	1264.	Lake Tahoe study	611
	1265.	In-place toxic pollutants	612
	1266.	Hudson River PCB reclamation demonstration project	612
	1267.	Chesapeake Bay	612
	1268.	Great Lakes	614
		Subchapter II. Grants for Construction of Treatment Works	618
	1281.	Congressional declaration of purpose	618
	1282.	Federal share	623
	1283.	Plans, specifications, estimates, and payments	625
	1284.	Limitations and conditions	628
	1285.	Allotment of grant funds	632
	1286.	Reimbursement and advanced construction	640
	1287.	Authorization of appropriations	642
	1288.	Areawide waste treatment management	643
	1289.	Basin planning	652
	1290.	Annual survey	652
	1291.	Sewage collection systems	652
	1292.	Definitions	653
	1293.	Loan guarantees for construction of treatment works	654
	1294.	Pubic information and education on recycling and reuse of wastewater, use of land treatment, and reduction of wastewater volume	655
	1295.	Requirements for American materials	655
	1296.	Determination of priority of projects	655
	1297.	Guidelines for cost-effectiveness analysis	656

Title	Section		Page
33	1298.	Cost effectiveness	656
	1299.	State certification of projects	657

Subchapter III. Standards and Enforcement — 657

	1311.	Effluent limitations	657
	1312.	Water quality related effluent limitations	671
	1313.	Water quality standards and implementation plans	671
	1314.	Information and guidelines	677
	1315.	State reports on water quality; transmittal to Congress	685
	1316.	National standards of performance	686
	1317.	Toxic and pretreatment effluent standards	688
	1318.	Records and reports; inspections	692
	1319.	Enforcement	693
	1320.	International pollution abatement	703
	1321.	Oil and hazardous substance liability	705
	1322.	Marine sanitation devices	718
	1323.	Federal facilities pollution control	723
	1324.	Clean lakes	725
	1325.	National Study Commission	728
	1326.	Thermal discharges	729
	1327.	Financing study	729
	1328.	Aquaculture	730
	1329.	Nonpoint Source Management Programs	730
	1330.	National Estuary Program	738

Subchapter IV. Permits and Licenses — 742

	1341.	Certification	742
	1342.	National pollution discharge elimination system	745
	1343.	Ocean discharge criteria	755
	1344.	Permits for dredged or fill material	755
	1345.	Disposal or use of sewage sludge	763

Subchapter V. General Provisions — 766

	1361.	Administration	766
	1362.	Definitions	767
	1363.	Water Pollution Control Advisory Board	769

Title	Section		Page
33	1364.	Emergency powers	770
	1365.	Citizens' suits	771
	1366.	Appearance	772
	1367.	Employee protection	773
	1368.	Federal procurement	774
	1369.	Administrative procedure and judicial review	775
	1370.	State authority	777
	1371.	Authority under other laws and regulations	778
	1372.	Labor standards	779
	1373.	Public health agency coordination	779
	1374.	Effluent standards and Water Quality Information Advisory Committee	779
	1375.	Reports to Congress	780
	1376.	Authorization of appropriations	783
	1377.	Indian tribes	783

Subchapter VI. Title VI—State Water Pollution Control Revolving Fund   786

	1381.	Grants to states for establishment of revolving funds	786
	1382.	Capitalization grant agreements	786
	1383.	Water pollution control revolving loan funds	787
	1384.	Allotment of funds	789
	1385.	Corrective action	789
	1386.	Audit, reports, and fiscal controls: intended use plan	790
	1387.	Authorization of appropriations	791

Emergency Planning and Community Right-To-Know Act of 1986   794

(P.L. 99-499, approved October 17, 1986)

Subchapter I. Emergency Planning and Notification   794

	11001.	Establishment of State commissions, planning districts, and local committees	794
	11002.	Substances and facilities covered and notification	796
	11003.	Comprehensive emergency response plans	797

Title	Section		Page
33	11004.	Emergency notification	799
	11005.	Emergency training and review of emergency systems	801

Subchapter II. Reporting Requirements 802

	11021.	Material safety data sheets	802
	11022.	Emergency and hazardous chemical inventory forms	804
	11023.	Toxic chemical release forms	807

Subchapter III. General Provisions 814

	11041.	Relationship to other law	814
	11042.	Trade secrets	814
	11043.	Provision of information to health professionals, doctors, and nurses	818
	11044.	Public availability of plans, data sheets, forms, and follow-up notices	820
	11045.	Enforcement	820
	11046.	Civil actions	823
	11047.	Exemption	825
	11048.	Regulations	825
	11049.	Definitions	825
	11050.	Authorization of appropriations	826

The Endangered Species Act

		(P.L. 93-205, approved December 28, 1973; as last amended by P.L. 98-327, approved June 25, 1984)	827
16	1531.	Congressional findings and declaration of purposes and policy	827
	1532.	Definitions	827
	1533.	Determination of endangered species and threatened species	827
	1534.	Land acquisition	827
	1535.	Cooperation with states	828
	1536.	Interagency cooperation	828
	1537.	International cooperation	828
	1537a.	Convention implementation	829
	1538.	Prohibited acts	829

Title	Section		Page
16	1539.	Exceptions	829
	1540.	Penalties and enforcement	830
	1541.	Endangered plants	830
	1542.	Authorization of appropriations	830
	1543.	Construction with Marine Mammal Protection Act of 1972	831

Marine Mammal Protection Act

(P.L. 92-522, approved October 21, 1972; as last amended by P.L. 98-364, approved July 17, 1984)   832

Subchapter I. Generally   832

	1361.	Congressional findings and declaration of policy	832
	1362.	Definitions	832

Subchapter II. Conservation and Protection of Marine Mammals   832

	1371.	Moratorium on taking and importing marine mammals and marine mammal products	832
	1372.	Prohibitions	833
	1373.	Regulations on taking of marine mammals	833
	1374.	Permits	833
	1375.	Penalties	834
	1376.	Seizure and forfeiture of cargo	834
	1377.	Enforcement	834
	1378.	International program	834
	1379.	Transfer of management authority	834
	1380.	Marime mammal research grants	835
	1381.	Commercial fisheries gear development	835
	1382.	Regulations and administration	835
	1383.	Application to other treaties and conventions	835
	1384.	Authorization of appropriations	836

Subchapter III. Marine Mammal Commission   836

	1401.	Establishment	836

Title	Section		Page
16	1402.	Duties of commission	836
	1403.	Committee of scientific advisors on marine mammals	836
	1404.	Reports	836
	1405.	Coordination with other federal agencies	837
	1406.	Administration	837
	1407.	Authorization of appropriations	837

Port and Tanker Safety Act

		(P.L. 95-474, approved October 17, 1978)	838
33	391a(1).	Statement of policy	838
	391a(2).	Definitions	838
	391a(3).	Applicability	838
	391a(4).	Exceptions	838
	391a(5).	Fish processing vessels	838
	391a(6).	Regulatory authority	838
	391a(7).	Minimum standards	839
	391a(8).	Evidence of compliance	839
	391a(9).	Personnel and manning standards for vessels of the United States	839
	391a(10).	Tankerman requirements	839
	391a(11).	Personnel and manning standards for foreign vessels	839
	391a(12).	Modifications	839
	391a(13).	Prohibited acts	839
	391a(14).	Enforcement	840
	391a(15).	Inspection	840
	391a(16).	Marine safety information system	840
	391a(17).	Lightering	840
	391a(18).	Tank washings	840

Safe Drinking Water Act

	(P.L. 93-523, approved December 16, 1974; as last amended by P.L. 99-339, approved June 19, 1986)	841

Title	Section		Page
		Subchapter XII. Safety of Public Water Systems	841
		Part A. Definitions	841
42	300f.	Definitions	841
		Part B. Public Water Systems	841
	300g.	Coverage	841
	300g-1.	National drinking water regulations	841
	300g-2.	State primary enforcement responsibility; regulations; notice and hearing; publication in Federal Register; applications	842
	300g-3.	Failure of state to ensure enforcement of drinking water regulations	842
	300g-4.	Variances	842
	300g-5.	Exemptions	842
	300g-6.	Prohibitions on use of lead pipes, solder, or flux	843
		Part C. Protection of Underground Sources of Drinking Water	843
	300h.	Regulations for state programs	843
	300h-1.	State primary enforcement responsibility	843
	300h-2.	Enforcement of program	844
	300h-3.	Interim regulation of underground injections	844
	300h-4.	Optional demonstration by states relating to oil or natural gas	844
	300h-5.	Regulation of state programs	844
	300h-6.	Sole source aquifer demonstration program	845
	300h-7.	State programs to establish wellhead protection areas	845
		Part D. Emergency Powers	845
	300i.	Emergency powers	845
	300i-1.	Tampering with public water systems	845
		Part E. General Provisions	845
	300j.	Assurances of availability of adequate supplies of chemicals necessary for treatment of water	845
	300j-1.	Research, technical assistance, information, training of personnel	846
	300j-2.	Grants for state programs	846
	300j-3.	Special project grants and guaranteed loans	846
	300j-3a.	Grants to public sector agencies	847
	300j-3b.	Contaminant standards or treatment technique guidelines	847

Title	Section		Page
42	300j–4.	Records and inspections	847
	300j–5.	National Drinking Water Advisory Council	847
	300j–6.	Federal agencies	848
	300j–7.	Judicial review	848
	300j–8.	Citizens' civil actions	848
	300j–9.	General provisions	848
	300j–10.	Appointment of scientific, etc., personnel by administrator of EPA for implementation of responsibilities, compensation	849
	300j–11.	Indian tribes	849

Noise Control Act

(P.L. 92–574, approved October 18, 1972; as last amended by P.L. 95-609, approved November 8, 1978) — 850

	4901.	Congressional findings and statement of policy	850
	4902.	Definitions	850
	4903.	Federal programs	850
	4904.	Identification of major noise sources	850
	4905.	Noise emission standards for products distributed in commerce	851
	4906.	Omitted	851
	4907.	Labeling	851
	4908.	Imports	851
	4909.	Prohibited acts	851
	4910.	Enforcement	852
	4911.	Citizens' suits	852
	4912.	Records, reports, and information	852
	4913.	Quiet communities, research, and public information	852
	4914.	Development of low-noise-emission products	853
	4915.	Judicial review	853
	4916.	Railroad noise emission standards	853
	4917.	Motor carrier noise emission standards	853
	4918.	Authorization of appropriations	853

Intervention on the High Seas Act

(P.L. 93-248, approved February 5, 1974; as last amended by P.L. 97-164, approved October 1, 1982) — 854

Title	Section		Page
33	1471.	Definitions	854
	1472.	Grave and imminent danger from oil pollution casualties to coastline or related interests of United States; federal nonliability for federal preventive measures on the high seas	854
	1473.	Consultations and determinations respecting creation of hazards to human health, etc.; criteria for determinations respecting grave and imminent dangers of major harmful consequences to the United States coastline or related interests	854
	1474.	Federal intervention actions	854
	1475.	Consultation procedure	855
	1476.	Emergencies	855
	1477.	Responsible measures; considerations	855
	1478.	Personal, flag state, and foreign state considerations	855
	1479.	Federal liability for unreasonable damages	855
	1480.	Notification by Secretary of State	855
	1481.	Violations; penalties	855
	1482.	Consultation for nomination and nomination of experts, negotiators, etc.; proposal of amendments to list of substances other than convention oil; presidential acceptance of amendments	856
	1483.	Foreign government ships; immunity	856
	1484.	Interpretation and administration; other right, duty, privilege or immunity, and other remedy unaffected	856
	1485.	Rules and regulations	856
	1486.	Revolving fund for federal actions and activities	856
	1487.	Effective date	856

National Ocean Pollution Planning Act

(P.L. 95-273, approved May 8, 1978; as last
amended by P.L. 97-375, approved
December 21, 1982)   857

Title	Section		Page
33	1701.	Findings and purposes	857
	1702.	Definitions	857
	1703.	Comprehensive federal plan relating to ocean pollution	857
	1704.	Comprehensive ocean pollution program in the administration	858
	1705.	Financial assistance	858
	1706.	Interagency cooperation	858
	1707.	Dissemination of information	858
	1708.	Effect on other laws	858
	1709.	Authorization of appropriations	858

Marine Protection, Research, and Sanctuaries Act

(P.L. 92–532, approved October 23, 1972; as last amended by P.L. 99–499, approved October 17, 1986)   859

Chapter 27. Ocean Dumping   859

33	1401.	Congressional finding, policy, and declaration of purpose	859
	1402.	Definitions	859

Subchapter I. Regulation   859

	1411.	Prohibited acts	859
	1412.	Dumping permit program	859
	1412a.	Dumping of sewage sludge and industrial waste	860
	1413.	Dumping permit program for dredged material	860
	1414.	Permit conditions	860
	1415.	Penalties	860
	1416.	Relationship to other laws	861
	1417.	Enforcement	861
	1418.	Regulations	861
	1419.	International cooperation	861
	1420.	Authorization of appropriations	861
	1421.	Annual report to Congress	861

Title	Section		Page
16		**Subchapter II. Research**	862
	1441.	Monitoring and research program; reports to Congress	862
	1442.	Research program respecting possible long-range effects of pollution, overfishing, and man-induced changes of ocean ecosystems	862
	1443.	Cooperation with public authorities, agencies, and institutions, and private agencies and institutions, and individuals	862
	1444.	Authorization of appropriations	862
	1445.	Removal of heavy metals and other toxic organic materials from sewage sludge of city of New York; study, etc.	862
		Chapter 32. Marine Sanctuaries	863
	1431.	Definitions	863
	1432.	Designation of sanctuaries	863
	1433.	Penalties	863
	1434.	Authorization of appropriations	863

Outer Continental Shelf Lands Act

		Page
(Chapter 345, Section 2, 67 Stat. 462, approved August 7, 1953; as last amended by P.L. 97–212, approved June 30, 1982)		864
Chapter 29		864

Title	Section		Page
		Subchapter III. Outer Continental Shelf Lands	864
43	1331.	Definitions	864
	1332.	Congressional declaration of policy	864
	1333.	Laws and regulations governing lands	864
	1334.	Administration of leasing	864
	1335.	Validation and maintenance of prior leases	865
	1336.	Controversies over jurisdiction; agreements; payments; final settlement or adjudication; approval of notice concerning oil and gas operations in Gulf of Mexico	865
	1337.	Grant of leases by Secretary	865
	1338.	Disposition of revenues	866

Title	Section		Page
43	1339.	Refunds; filing time limitation; certification of repayment; necessity of report to Congress	866
	1340.	Geological and geophysical explorations	866
	1341.	Reservation of lands and rights	866
	1342.	Prior claims as unaffected	867
	1343.	Annual report by Secretary to Congress	867
	1344.	Outer continental shelf leasing program	867
	1345.	Coordination and consultation with affected state and local governments	867
	1346.	Environmental studies	868
	1347.	Safety and health regulations	868
	1348.	Enforcement of safety and environmental regulations	868
	1349.	Citizens' suits, jurisdiction, and judicial review	868
	1350.	Remedies and penalties	869
	1351.	Oil and gas development and production	869
	1352.	Oil and gas information program	869
	1353.	Federal purchase and disposition of oil and gas	870
	1354.	Limitations on export of oil or gas	870
	1355.	Restrictions on employment of former officers or employees of the Department of the Interior	870
	1356.	Documentary, registry, and manning requirements	870

Subchapter I. Offshore Oil Spill Pollution Fund — 870

	Chapter 36.		870
	1811.	Definitions	870
	1812.	Offshore oil pollution compensation fund	871
	1813.	Claims for economic loss from oil pollution	871
	1814.	Scope of liability	871
	1815.	Financial responsibility	871
	1816.	Notification, designation, and advertisement	871
	1817.	Claims settlement	871
	1818.	Subrogation	872
	1819.	Jurisdiction and venue	872
	1820.	Relationship to other state or federal laws	872
	1821.	Oil discharge prohibition	872
	1822.	Penalties	872

Title	Section		Page
43	1823.	Authorization of appropriations	872
	1824.	Annual report	872

Subchapter II. Fisherman's Contingency Fund — 873

	1841.	Definitions	873
	1842.	Fishermen's contingency fund	873
	1843.	Duties and powers of Secretary	873
	1844.	Burden of proof	873
	1845.	Claims procedure	873
	1846.	Annual report	873
	1847.	Repealed	874

Subchapter III. Miscellaneous Provisions — 874

	1861.	Report to Comptroller General on shut-in and flaring oil and gas wells; submission of findings and recommendations to Congress	874
	1862.	Natural gas distribution	874
	1863.	Unlawful employment practices; regulations	874
	1864.	Disclosure of financial interests by officers and employees of the Department of the Interior	874
	1865.	Investigation of reserves of oil and gas in outer continental shelf	874
	1866.	Relationship to existing law	874

FOREWORD

The Bureau of National Affairs Inc. is pleased to present this second edition of *U.S. Environmental Laws*, incorporating major changes to several key federal environmental statutes. The new edition also contains the text of a major new federal statute concerning the community's right to know about emissions of toxic substances.

Since the publication of the first edition of *U.S. Environmental Laws*, Congress enacted the Superfund Amendments and Reauthorization Act of 1986 (P.L. 99-499), which significantly tightened requirements under the Comprehensive Environmental Response, Compensation, and Liability Act (superfund law) and made major changes to the Resource Conservation and Recovery Act (RCRA).

In addition, Title III of the Superfund Amendments and Reauthorization Act (SARA) established the Emergency Planning and Community Right-To-Know Act, an important new law that deals with routine and accidental (emergency) emissions of toxic substances into the environment.

The texts of the superfund law and RCRA as published within this volume have been amended to reflect the changes made by SARA. Title III of SARA is published as a free-standing act—42 U.S.C. 11001-11050.

The other major change reflected in this new edition is the amended Clean Water Act. Congress in 1987 overrode a presidential veto and enacted the amendments, which reach far beyond the Water Act's original focus on municipal sewage and industrial waste water. In addition to providing for a new federal-state program to control non-point source pollution, the amended law clamps down on pollution of the nation's waterways by toxic substances; directs the Environmental Protection Agency to solve pollution problems in estuaries; bolsters U.S. efforts to comply with the Great Lakes Water Quality Agreement; and makes several other important changes.

This new volume includes the texts of eight environmental statutes of Titles 7, 15, 33, and 42 of the U.S. Code. It also includes summaries of nine other important federal statutes.

The appropriate U.S. Code title and section numbers of these statutes can be located in the finding list following the table of contents. The original public law section numbers of these laws are included in brackets throughout the text.

The environmental laws included in this volume are current through March 1988. Congressional efforts to amend the Clean Air Act are continuing at this time. Most observers consider that it will be very difficult—but nonetheless possible—to agree on a bill before the 100th Congress adjourns.

This second edition is the result of the diligent efforts of the BNA editorial staff. In particular, the efforts of Cheryl Drew, editor for BNA's Books Division, are greatly appreciated. Thanks also to Jeffrey Kimmel, Peyton Sturges, and Miriam Ozer of the legal staff of *Environment Reporter*, and to the entire staff of *Environment Reporter* for their work on the introductions to the texts of the statutes—Mary Houghton, William Kelly, Jeffrey Johnson, Wevonneda Minis, Barbara Musfeldt, and James Stimson.

Wallis E. McClain, Jr.
Managing Editor
  Environment Reporter
Washington, D.C.

March 1988

PREFACE

The statutes collected in this volume, the environmental laws of the United States, are at the same time a monument to twenty years of work towards a cleaner and safer environment and a source of substantial contention and perplexity among both lawmakers and the general public. These statutes often appear to be working at cross-purposes to one another; there are even apparent conflicts of intent within the same statute. This suggests that our nation has not yet settled unequivocably on what we want our environmental protection effort to do. But I also believe that some of the confusion is rooted in the legal-philosophical parentage of the laws themselves.

Our environmental statutes arise from at least three separate legal traditions. The first of these is public health protection and it extends back to remote antiquity. There were Babylonian laws against the adulteration of bread and there were restrictions on the burning of coal in medieval England. Laws of quarantine and laws regarding the disposal of biological wastes are common in many societies. In America, until around 1970, this tradition was embodied in local ordinances regarding dumping, drinking water, open burning, and sewage treatment.

The second tradition derives from common law antecedents pertaining to property damage and personal injury. If you dump poison in a stream, and my cow drinks it and dies, I can bring suit against you for damages. Until recently, it had been very hard for private citizens to bring suit against firms for damages resulting from the normal operation of industrial plants.

But beginning in the 1950's, the number of such suits, and their success, began to increase, perhaps owing to greater public awareness of chemical hazards or to the apparently greater toxicity of the emissions of industry in the post-war period. We may, in fact, trace the tortuous history of the Clean Air Act back to a suit brought by the Martins family of Troutdale, Oregon, against the Reynolds Company. The Martins claimed that fluoride emissions from the Reynolds plant were poisoning their dairy cattle and injuring their own health. The major issue then (as it is now) was specifying the relation between the exposure and the health damage it may have caused. Responding to this issue, the state of Oregon set up a scientific panel to make such determinations and passed laws giving the state the right to sue in order to stop air pollution where it was deemed injurious to its citizens.

Other states felt obliged to do the same, including Washington, some of whose residents were suing the same plant. Much of the impetus for establishing national rules about what was safe in the air thus may have come from the prospect of the chaos that could have resulted from the nation's industrial plants attempting to comply with dozens of different standards for the same pollutant, or worse, the prospect of industry shopping around for locations in states that were prepared to set the weakest standards.

The third tradition is a complex one and particularly American. It arises out of the conservation ethic, as exemplified early in this century by the preservation work of Roosevelt and Pinchot, and more recently by the new ecological consciousness. The older notion that America is a kind of earthly paradise being consumed by the base greed of its inhabitants was reinforced by the broader observation that the entire ecosphere is vulnerable to human activity. The publication of *Silent Spring*, together with reports of oil spills, burning rivers, nuclear fallout, and so on, generated a crisis atmosphere, which, (also in the American tradition) produced a political movement demanding Federal government action. Obviously, the thinking went, the market economy cannot be trusted to control its own externalities of production. National planning was proposed and, to an extent, accepted as the solution.

These traditions, variously compounded, are expressed in the nine major environmental statutes, which are administered in whole or in part by a single organization, the Environmental Protection Agency. The fact that there are *nine* statutes, and that they derive from mixed legal traditions provides no little trouble to the Agency in their execution. Public health protection is rather a different business from preserving environmental values; establishing and administering a national plan (to clean the air, for example) is in some conflict with the need to establish an equitable solution for a particular area where, say, people are in danger of being hurt by emissions from an economically important industrial facility.

These conflicts tend to be exacerbated by the paradoxical nature of the American political consciousness. On the one hand, we want problems solved, and we have learned to look to government to solve them. On the other, we want it done with as little personal inconvenience or sacrifice as possible. For example, we are ideological "liberals" when we demand vigorous clean air programs, and operational "conservatives" when we resist inspection and maintenance programs for automobiles to achieve clean air. The execution of our environmental statutes over the past fifteen years reflects this paradox. If you read the environmental laws literally—especially the Clean Air and Clean Water Acts—you are reading a recipe for a quite radical reordering of American society. In fact, nothing of the sort has happened. To note one of many instances, our attempt to impose transportation plans on metropolitan areas to meet Clean Air Act standards failed in the mid-70s, as no doubt it would today. In real-world situations, Americans balance environmental values against other values, as does the Environmental Protection Agency, whether or not the law specifically allows it to so declare publicly.

Have these laws worked? Yes and no. The environment is certainly cleaner than it was, and *much* cleaner than it would have been had these laws not been passed. But the laws have not straightened out the conflicts inherent in their different philosophical antecedents. For example, the public health ethic demands that we take a protective stance in response to the *probability* that some exposure will result in an adverse health effect. This demand runs counter to the common law tradition that before we impose an economic penalty we establish the actuality of harm, or at least balance the equities in each particular case.

Most important, the laws do not recognize that the different compartments of the environment — air, water, and land — are interconnected. Pollution moves easily among these compartments, either naturally or through the operation of pollution control apparatus. The ecological ethic built into these statutes mandates that each compartment be rendered pure, although in practical terms this can only be done at the expense of the other compartments. Pollution has to go somewhere, but the laws typically assume it away, or assume that, somehow, technologies can be developed that do not pollute at all.

This promise of an end to pollution is contained in each of our environmental laws. It is a noble goal, but it renders the laws less effective in fact than they could be, if a keener sense of the need to distinguish the important from the trivial were built into their basic structure.

Thus a gulf has developed between the expectations of environmental clean-up presented in much of the legislative language in this book and what we have been able to accomplish. This gulf can only contribute to the decline of faith in the ability of our democratic polity to solve its problems. One hopes, therefore, that the reader will regard these laws as works in progress. There will always be a tension between the economics of an industrial society and the health of its citizens and their environment. Oddly enough, as we become healthier and live longer, and thus as each life becomes more precious, we worry more about the imperfections of our protective machinery and any lapses noted from the illusion of perfect safety become more intolerable. This intolerance, however, interferes with the practical execution of environmental law. Of course we need goals, especially given the propensity of our civilization to live as if each generation were the last. But what we have yet to learn in environmental law is how to keep our eyes on the horizon without stumbling on the thickets around our feet.

William D. Ruckelshaus

March 1986

1

Text of Major Environmental Laws

1 • National Environmental Policy Act

INTRODUCTION

In drafting the National Environmental Policy Act (NEPA) in 1969, Congress said the U.S. government should "use all practicable means . . . to create and maintain conditions in which man and nature can exist in productive harmony."

The statute, which was signed into law on January 1, 1970 by President Richard Nixon, established a framework for the government to assess the environmental effects of its major actions. It requires federal agencies to prepare "environmental impact statements" assessing the environmental effects of proposed projects and requests for legislation. The Act also created the President's Council on Environmental Quality (CEQ), a three-member advisory group that advises the President and is required to prepare an annual environmental quality report for Congress.

Until the Environmental Protection Agency (EPA) was organized and staffed, a process which was not completed until late 1971, the CEQ served as the principal U.S. environmental policy-making body and the source of major environmental legislation, according to Alvin L. Alm, CEQ's first staff director and former deputy EPA administrator. The council laid the legislative base for many of the earliest environmental laws, developing Administration legislative proposals for what later became the Clean Water Act; the Federal Insecticide, Fungicide, and Rodenticide Act; the Noise Control Act; the Ocean Dumping Act; the Resource Recovery Act; the Safe Drinking Water Act; the Surface Mining Control and Reclamation Act; and the Toxic Substances Control Act.

Gus Speth, CEQ chairman during the Carter Administration, said the council's 1978 revision and codification of NEPA guidelines was an important milestone, for the first time providing specific regulations for federal agencies to follow in preparing environmental impact statements.

The council continues to monitor federal agencies' compliance with NEPA and in April 1985 was considering whether to recommend changes in the language carrying out the portion of the statute that specifies when a worst-case analysis must be performed as part of the environmental impact statement (EIS) process.

The council also serves as mediator of disputes among federal agencies over environmental issues, most recently over the Presidential Parkway in Atlanta and the Tennessee-Tombigbee Waterway.

The EPA, as the administrator of federal pollution control programs, does not have to comply with the Act, but it reviews environmental impact statements prepared by other agencies and makes comments and recommendations on the projects proposed. According to EPA statistics, federal agencies have prepared more than 22,000 draft, final, and supplemental environmental impact statements since the Act took effect. In one year, an additional 66,000 environmental assessments were carried out by federal agencies to comply with CEQ guidelines under NEPA, according to Jan Shaw, a staff member in EPA's Office of Federal Activities.

In requiring government agencies to prepare environmental impact statements, the Act also created a governmental duty that has been the subject of more than 1,800 lawsuits in the 15 years since it was enacted, according to CEQ statistics. CEQ General Counsel Dinah Bear told The Bureau of National Affairs (BNA) that the majority of the lawsuits filed in most years since 1970 to enforce the environmental assessment requirement have challenged government decisions not to prepare an EIS. The exception was in 1983, when the majority of the lawsuits filed under NEPA challenged the adequacy of the impact statements prepared, Bear said.

The number of environmental statements prepared annually has declined fairly steadily from an average of nearly 2,000 in the early 1970s to 591 in 1984, according to EPA. The total dropped from 1,802 in 1976 to 1,568 in 1977, when President Jimmy Carter ordered CEQ to reduce the paperwork imposed as a result of the statute's requirements, and the annual total declined steadily through the Carter Administration to 998 in 1980.

To carry out Carter's directive, the council set up a "cooperative agency" system to avoid duplication in preparing environmental statements, according to Shaw. In some cases, the CEQ impact statement regulations reduced the number of statements prepared by directing that segments of projects or similar actions be studied in one EIS, she said.

Under the Reagan Administration, the number of impact statements has declined further, dropping to less than 600 in 1984, according to EPA statistics. One cause for this decline, Shaw said, was a decision by the Department of Housing and Urban Development in 1982 to prepare impact statements only for projects with more than 2,500 units. Previously, HUD prepared environmental statements for all projects with more than 500 units, she said. The department wrote from 400 to 500 impact statements annually under the previous threshold, but the number has dropped to about 10 a year now, according to Shaw.

In addition, EPA has prepared fewer environmental impact statements as Reagan's directive to delegate federal programs to the states has been carried out, the agency staff member told BNA. For example, Shaw said, states are not required to prepare impact statements for new source permits under the national pollutant discharge elimination system or for sewage treatment construction grants administered by the states under authority delegated by EPA.

In addition, Shaw said, after years of experience with NEPA, federal agencies have refined and expanded their lists of categorical exclusions, which are actions the agencies take regularly and have determined as a class will not have a major effect on the environment.

At the Interior Department, efforts to enforce NEPA, along with increasing public environmental awareness and enactment of subsequent environmental statutes, has helped the Interior Department to become more attuned to environmental concerns in managing U.S. natural resources, according to Rep. Morris Udall (D-Ariz). Udall called NEPA a "landmark piece of legislation" that helped bring Interior and other federal agencies into the "modern world" of environmental awareness, although he said the department's compliance with the statute has been reluctant at times.

Conservation Foundation President William Reilly said the Alaska oil pipeline project during the 1970s exemplifies how NEPA helped allow "a whole new constituency, the environmentalists, to play a substantive part in [Interior] decision-making." Rather than just "throwing together a couple of papers," the department prepared extensive studies, including environmental damage mitigation plans in response to environmentalists' concerns, before the pipeline project was completed, he said.

Recently, EPA challenged a federal agency's proposal to limit the scope of its environmental reviews under NEPA. The Army Corps of Engineers proposed changes in its list of categorical exclusions, along with a change in its EIS guidelines that would limit its review to the segment of a project only for which a permit is sought. Now, corps impact statements assess the potential environmental effects of an entire project even when the Army is required to issue a permit for only part of the planned development.

EPA, acting under Section 309 of the Clean Air Act and Section 1504 of CEQ's environmental impact statement regulations, asked the council in March 1985 to mediate the dispute concerning the corps' proposed changes. EPA claims that the change would hamper its program to review significant environmental effects of proposed federal actions under the Clean Air Act and NEPA.

Lynton Caldwell, an Indiana University public and environmental policy professor who helped the Senate Interior Committee draft NEPA in 1969, told BNA that the corps proposal could be part of a trend to restrict the scope of the statute. "Most people in federal agencies have accepted the process" of environmental reviews under the Act, but some federal officials, "particularly in the military agencies," have not, he said.

However, Caldwell told BNA that he believes the EIS process has been "institutionalized" because the public wants environmental issues to be considered in setting public policy. Even if the law were repealed, federal agencies would continue to assess the potential environmental effects of their proposed actions because the public expects them to do so, he said.

The National Environmental Policy Act

(P.L. 91–190, effective January 1, 1970; as last amended by P.L. 94–83, approved August 9, 1975)

§ 4321. Congressional declaration of purpose

[Sec. 2] The purposes of this Act are: To declare a national policy which will encourage productive and enjoyable harmony between man and his environment; to promote efforts which will prevent or eliminate damage to the environment and biosphere and stimulate the health and welfare of man; to enrich the understanding of the ecological systems and natural resources important to the Nation; and to establish a Council on Environmental Quality.

Subchapter I. Policies and goals

§ 4331. Congressional declaration of national environmental policy

[Sec. 101] (a) The Congress, recognizing the profound impact of man's activity on the interrelations of all components of the natural environment, particularly the profound influences of population growth, high-density urbanization, industrial expansion, resource exploitation, and new and expanding technological advances and recognizing further the critical importance of restoring and maintaining environmental quality to the overall welfare and development of man, declares that it is the continuing policy of the Federal Government, in cooperation with State and local governments, and other concerned public and private organizations, to use all practicable means and measures, including financial and technical assistance, in a manner calculated to foster and promote the general welfare, to create and maintain conditions under which man and nature can exist in productive harmony, and fulfill the social, economic, and other requirements of present and future generations of Americans.

(b) In order to carry out the policy set forth in this Act, it is the continuing responsibility of the Federal Government to use all practicable means, consistent with other essential considerations of national policy, to improve and coordinate Federal plans, functions, programs, and resources to the end that the Nation may—

(1) fulfill the responsibilities of each generation as trustee of the environment for succeeding generations;

(2) assure for all Americans safe, healthful, productive, and esthetically and culturally pleasing surroundings;

(3) attain the widest range of beneficial uses of the environment without degradation, risk to health or safety, or other undesirable and unintended consequences;

(4) preserve important historic, cultural, and natural aspects of our national heritage, and maintain, wherever possible, an environment which supports diversity and variety of individual choice;

(5) achieve a balance between population and resource use which will permit high standards of living and a wide sharing of life's amenities; and

(6) enhance the quality of renewable resources and approach the maximum attainable recycling of depletable resources.

(c) The Congress recognizes that each person should enjoy a healthful environment and that each person has a responsibility to contribute to the preservation and enhancement of the environment.

§ 4332. Cooperation of agencies; reports; availability of information; recommendations; international and national coordination of efforts

[Sec. 102] The Congress authorizes and directs that, to the fullest extent possible: (1) the policies, regulations, and public laws of the United States shall be interpreted and administered in accordance with the policies set forth in this Act, and (2) all agencies of the Federal Government shall—

(A) utilize a systematic, interdisciplinary approach which will insure the integrated use of the natural and social sciences and the environmental design arts in planning and in decisionmaking which may have an impact on man's environment;

(B) identify and develop methods and procedures, in consultation with the Council on Environmental Quality established by title II of this Act, which will insure that presently unquantified environmental amenities and values may be given appropriate consideration in decisionmaking along with economic and technical considerations;

(C) include in every recommendation or report on proposals for legislation and other major Federal actions significantly affecting the quality of the human environment, a detailed statement by the responsible official on—

(i) the environmental impact of the proposed action,

(ii) any adverse environmental effects which cannot be avoided should the proposal be implemented,

(iii) alternatives to the proposed action,

(iv) the relationship between local short-term uses of man's environment and the maintenance and enhancement of long-term productivity, and

(v) any irreversible and irretrievable commitments of resources which would be involved in the proposed action should it be implemented.

Prior to making any detailed statement, the responsible Federal official shall consult with and obtain the comments of any Federal agency which has jurisdiction by law or special expertise with respect to any environmental impact involved. Copies of such statement and the comments and views of the appropriate Federal, State, and local agencies, which are authorized to develop and enforce environmental standards, shall be made available to the President, the Council on Environmental Quality and to the public as provided by section 552 of title 5, United States Code, and shall accompany the proposal through the existing agency review processes;

(D) Any detailed statement required under subparagraph (C) after January 1, 1970, for any major Federal action funded under a program of grants to States shall not be deemed to be legally insufficient solely by reason of having been prepared by a State agency or official, if:

(i) the State agency or official has statewide jurisdiction and has the responsibility for such action,

(ii) the responsible Federal official furnishes guidance and participates in such preparation,

(iii) the responsible Federal official independently evaluates such statement prior to its approval and adoption, and

(iv) after January 1, 1976, the responsible Federal official provides early notification to, and solicits the views of, any other State or any Federal land management entity of any action or any alternative thereto which may have significant impacts upon such State or affected Federal land management entity and, if there is any disagreement on such impacts, prepares a written assessment of such impacts and views for incorporation into such detailed statement.

The procedures in this subparagraph shall not relieve the Federal official of his responsibilities for the scope, objectivity, and content of the entire statement or of any other responsibility under this Act; and further, this subparagraph does not affect the legal sufficiency of statements prepared by State agencies with less than statewide jurisdiction.

(E) study, develop, and describe appropriate alternatives to recommended courses of action in any proposal which involves unresolved conflicts concerning alternative uses of available resources;

(F) recognize the worldwide and long-range character of environmental problems and, where consistent with the foreign policy of the United States, lend appropriate support to initiatives, resolutions, and programs designed to maximize international cooperation in anticipating and preventing a decline in the quality of mankind's world environment;

(G) make available to States, counties, municipalities, institutions, and individuals, advice and information useful in restoring, maintaining, and enhancing the quality of the environment;

(H) initiate and utilize ecological information in the planning and development of resource-oriented projects; and

(I) assist the Council on Environmental Quality established by title II of this Act.

§ 4333. Conformity of administrative procedures to national environmental policy

[Sec. 103] All agencies of the Federal Government shall review their present statutory authority, administrative regulations, and current policies and procedures for the purpose of determining whether there are any deficiencies or inconsistencies therein which prohibit full compliance with the purposes and provisions of this Act and shall propose to the President not later than July 1, 1971, such measures as may be necessary to bring their authority and policies into conformity with the intent, purposes, and procedures set forth in this Act.

§ 4334. Other statutory obligations of agencies

[Sec. 104] Nothing in Section 102 or 103 shall in any way affect the specific statutory obligations of any Federal agency (1) to comply with criteria or standards of environmental quality, (2) to coordinate or consult with any other Federal or State agency, or (3) to act, or refrain from acting contingent upon the recommendations or certification of any other Federal or State agency.

§ 4335. Efforts supplemental to existing authorizations

[Sec. 105] The policies and goals set forth in this Act are supplementary to those set forth in existing authorizations of Federal agencies.

Subchapter II. Council on Environmental Quality

§ 4341. Reports to Congress; recommendations for legislation

[Sec. 201] The President shall transmit to the Congress annually beginning July 1, 1970, an Environmental Quality Report (hereinafter referred to as the "report") which shall set forth (1) the status and condition of the major natural, manmade, or altered environmental classes of the Nation, including, but not limited to, the air, the aquatic, including marine, estuarine, and fresh water, and the terrestrial environment, including, but not limited to, the forest dryland, wetland, range, urban, suburban, and rural environment; (2) current and foreseeable trends in the quality, management and utilization of such environments and the effects of those trends on the social, economic, and other requirements of the Nation; (3) the adequacy of available natural resources for fulfilling human and economic requirements of the Nation in the light of expected population pressures; (4) a review of the programs and activities (including regulatory activities) of the Federal Government, the State and local governments, and nongovernmental entities or individuals, with particular reference to their effect on the environment and on the conservation, development and utilization of natural resources; and (5) a program for remedying the deficiencies of existing programs and activities, together with recommendations for legislation.

§ 4342. Establishment; membership; Chairman; appointments

[Sec. 202] There is created in the Executive Office of the President a Council on Environmental Quality (hereinafter referred to as the "Council"). The Council shall be composed of three members who shall be appointed by the President to serve at his pleasure, by and with the advice and consent of the Senate. The President shall designate one of the members of the Council to serve as Chairman. Each member shall be a person who, as a result of his training, experience, and attainments, is exceptionally well qualified to analyze and interpret environmental trends and information of all kinds; to appraise programs and activities of the Federal Government in the light of the policy set forth in title I of this Act; to be conscious of and responsive to the scientific, economic, social, esthetic, and cultural needs and interests of the Nation; and to formulate and recommend national policies to promote the improvement of the quality of the environment.

§ 4343. Employment of personnel, experts and consultants

[Sec. 203] (a) The Council may employ such officers and employees as may be necessary to carry out its functions under this Act. In addition, the Council may employ and fix the compensation of such experts and consultants as may be necessary for the carrying out of its functions under this Act, in accordance with section 3109 of title 5, United States Code (but without regard to the last sentence thereof).

(b) Notwithstanding section 3679(b) of the Revised Statutes (31 U.S.C. 665(b)), the Council may accept and employ voluntary and uncompensated services in furtherance of the purposes of the Council.

§ 4344. Duties and functions

[Sec. 204] It shall be the duty and function of the Council—
(1) to assist and advise the President in the preparation of the Environmental Quality Report required by section 201;
(2) to gather timely and authoritative information concerning the conditions and trends in the quality of the environment both current and prospective, to analyze and interpret such information for the purpose of determining whether such conditions and trends are interfering, or are likely to interfere, with the achievement of the policy set forth in title I of this Act, and to compile and submit to the President studies relating to such conditions and trends;
(3) to review and appraise the various programs and activities of the Federal Government in the light of the policy set forth in title I of this Act for the purpose of determining the extent to which such programs and activities are contributing to the achievement of such policy, and to make recommendations to the President with respect thereto;
(4) to develop and recommend to the President national policies to foster and promote the improvement of environmental quality to meet the conservation, social, economic, health, and other requirements and goals of the Nation;
(5) to conduct investigations, studies, surveys, research, and analyses relating to ecological systems and environmental quality;
(6) to document and define changes in the natural environment, including the plant and animal systems, and to accumulate necessary data and other information for a continuing analysis of these changes or trends and an interpretation of their underlying causes;
(7) to report at least once each year to the President on the state and condition of the environment; and

(8) to make and furnish such studies, reports thereon, and recommendations with respect to matters of policy and legislation as the President may request.

§ 4345. Consultation with the Citizens' Advisory Committee on Environmental Quality and other representatives

[Sec. 205] In exercising its powers, functions, and duties under this Act, the Council shall—

(1) consult with the Citizens' Advisory Committee on Environmental Quality established by Executive Order numbered 11472, dated May 29, 1969, and with such representatives of science, industry, agriculture, labor, conservation organizations, State and local governments, and other groups, as it deems advisable; and

(2) utilize, to the fullest extent possible, the services, facilities, and information (including statistical information) of public and private agencies and organizations, and individuals, in order that duplication of effort and expense may be avoided, thus assuring that the Council's activities will not unnecessarily overlap or conflict with similar activities authorized by law and performed by established agencies.

§ 4346. Tenure and compensation of members

[Sec. 206] Members of the Council shall serve full time and the Chairman of the Council shall be compensated at the rate provided for Level II of the Executive Schedule Pay Rates (5 U.S.C. 5313). The other members of the Council shall be compensated at the rate provided for Level IV of the Executive Schedule Pay Rates (5 U.S.C. 5315).

§ 4346a. Travel reimbursement by private organizations and federal, state, and local governments

[Sec. 207] The Council may accept reimbursements from any private nonprofit organization or from any department, agency, or instrumentality of the Federal Government, any State, or local government, for the reasonable travel expenses incurred by an officer or employee of the Council in connection with his attendance at any conference, seminar, or similar meeting conducted for the benefit of the Council.

§ 4346b. Expenditures in support of international activities

[Sec. 208] The Council may make expenditures in support of its international activities, including expenditures for: (1) international travel; (2) activities in implementation of international agreements; and (3) the support of international exchange programs in the United States and in foreign countries.

§ 4347.   Authorization of appropriations

[Sec. 209] There are authorized to be appropriated to carry out the provisions of this Act not to exceed $300,000 for fiscal year 1970, $700,000 for fiscal year 1971, and $1,000,000 for each fiscal year thereafter.

2 • Comprehensive Environmental Response, Compensation, and Liability Act of 1980

INTRODUCTION _____

Hazardous waste, largely a byproduct of the synthetic organic chemical revolution of post-World War II America, followed air and water pollution control in gaining the attention of the public and environmental regulators. Although Congress gave the Environmental Protection Agency (EPA) authority to regulate hazardous waste in 1976, the chemical contamination of homes in the Love Canal area of Niagara Falls, N.Y., in 1978 was the event that stirred the national consciousness, spurring EPA to accelerate rules to carry out that task.

In 1980, Congress passed Public Law 96–510, the "superfund law" or, more properly, the Comprehensive Environmental Response, Compensation, and Liability Act, which authorized $1.6 billion to finance the cleanup of Love Canal and other abandoned dumpsites. The act, a logical complement to the provisions in the Resource Conservation and Recovery Act for the safe treatment and disposal of wastes, allows the EPA to recover cleanup costs. It established the Post-Closure Liability Trust Fund, which is financed by a tax on the receipt of hazardous waste at a qualified hazardous waste disposal facility. The cleanup fund established by the act, formally called the Hazardous Substance Response Trust Fund, is financed by a tax on crude oil (delivered to a refinery or imported into the United States) and chemicals feedstocks.

The concept of a "superfund" to pay for cleaning up abandoned hazardous waste sites originated with a proposal by the large oil companies to finance a fund to pay for the cleanup of oil spills from their supertankers. The spills had aroused outrage and caused tremendous environmental damage worldwide. In return for their contributions to the cleanup fund, the oil companies wanted to be released from liability for damages. "It was to be a superfund to clean up spills from supertankers," a Senate aide recalled. Although that idea was never taken up, in December 1980, Congress responded to the public's demand for hazardous waste cleanup with the passage of the "superfund."

In the spring of 1983, congressional charges of mismanagement of the hazardous waste program and allegations of conflict of interest became the center of a controversy that resulted in the resignations or firings of more than 20 top EPA officials, including Administrator Anne Gorsuch Burford. Democrats contended the issue demonstrated the administration's indifference to environmental concerns. In the midst of the controversy, public concern about hazardous waste was heightened when high levels of dioxin were found at Times Beach, Mo., forcing a government buyout of the town and the relocation of 2,400 families.

Burford's immediate successor, William D. Ruckelshaus, changed EPA's superfund policies to speed cleanup. Yet it was the judgment of many, including many in Congress, that EPA had been given a powerful tool in CERCLA, but because there had been so few completed cleanups, something was not working the way they had envisioned in 1980. Congressional efforts to strengthen the law culminated in the signing of the Superfund Amendments and Reauthorization Act of 1986 (P.L. 99-499), which increased the amount of money in the fund from the original $1.6 billion to $8.5 billion over five years.

SARA preserves the 1980 act's basic concept of liability. The message remains: liability was and remains strict, joint and several. On the House floor just before the House passed SARA in October 1986, Rep. John D. Dingell (D-Mich) said, "Nothing in this legislation is intended to change the application of the uniform federal rule of joint and several liability enunciated in the *Chem-Dyne* case and followed by a number of other federal courts." The case referred to is one of the basic judicial articulations of the strict, joint and several liability issue as applied to superfund cases (*U.S. v. Chem-Dyne*, DC SOhio, No. C-1-82-840, Oct. 11, 1983; 19 ERC 1953).

That is perhaps the government's most powerful tool. All it has to do is establish a link to a superfund site and it can seek to recover cleanup costs from a potentially responsible party. However, because litigation can be a protracted process in even the best of situations, Congress also decided it had to improve the settlement procedures. As a way of enticing parties to enter voluntary settlements, Congress gave settlors protection against contribution actions by nonsettling parties and also insulated them against being sued by the federal government in a "covenant not to sue." The amendments also codified an "innocent landowner" defense to liability.

EPA's control over settlement negotiations with PRPs was strengthened by SARA. Only information placed in the administrative record may be used to challenge the agency's choice of remedy at a superfund site.

In addition, the agency was given authority to use mixed funding — use of money from the fund to supplement contributions from settling PRPs. The first preauthorized mixed funding agreements came in the summer of 1987 at the Motco site in Texas and the Harvey and Knotts site in Delaware. Congress also established a unique concept in the "non-binding allocation to responsibility," under which EPA may decide to make a preliminary allocation of responsibility among parties as a way of achieving a quick settlement. Such settlements arrived at through the NBAR process, according to the amendments, "shall not be admissible as evidence in any proceeding, and no Court shall have jurisdiction to review the non-binding permanent allocation of responsibility."

There is a new statutory authorization of *de minimis* settlements by parties who may be able to "buy" their way out of the cleanup process because of their limited involvement. The idea is to facilitate the settlement process and also to use the revenues gained from the de minimis parties to entice other PRPs to settle.

SARA also established a strong preference for permanent remedies at superfund sites and set schedules for beginning cleanup work and studies. EPA must, under the amended law, begin cleanup activities at a minimum of 375 superfund sites by 1991. The agency also must begin 275 remedial investigation and feasibility studies by October 1989. If that deadline is missed, it must start another 175 RI/FSs by October 1990 and another 200 by October 1991.

The Agency for Toxic Substances and Disease Registry must now, in addition to performing health assessments at superfund sites, list the hazardous substances found at superfund sites, prepare toxicological profiles of those substances, and research health effects.

In 1987, EPA issued a number of memoranda and guidances for its regional administrators to use in superfund decision-making. Although these guidances and memoranda do not have the same status as regulations, they are important in that they set agency policy in dealing with such issues as settlements and enforcement. These memoranda and guidances include interim guidelines for preparing nonbinding preliminary allocations of responsibility, interim guidance on de minimis waste contributors, a memorandum on covenants not to sue, guidance on applicable or relevant and appropriate requirements, and a memorandum guiding regional administrators on the use of mixed funding.

The agency generated considerable opposition from environmentalists with its interim guidance on ARARs. EPA had decided that the agency's maximum contaminant levels, as opposed to the more restrictive maximum contaminant level goals, should apply to ground water cleanups at superfund sites.

In its comments, dated October 12, 1986, on the guidance, the Sierra Club noted that the legislative history of SARA required that SARA's "overriding standard" of protecting human health or the environment be met before considerations of cost-effectiveness are addressed. "At its worst," the Sierra Club said, "the Interim Guidance contains policies which flout the clear meaning and intent of SARA. At its best, the document will so confuse anyone who tries to use it to make cleanup decisions that it will prove an ineffective influence on the agency's ongoing decision-making."

The agency also came under fire in late 1987 for the application of its policy on disposal of superfund wastes offsite. The U.S. District Court for Kansas said EPA's application of the policy has made it "so vague and ambiguous as to provide private parties no guidance on how to follow it" (*Chemical Waste Management Inc. v. EPA*, DC Kan, No. 87-2411-S, Nov. 5, 1987; 26 ERC 1781).

Although, to date, not many court decisions have come down specifically interpreting the amended law, one such action involved states' immunity from suits. The U.S. Court of Appeals for the Third Circuit ruled that SARA makes it clear that the doctrine of sovereign immunity does not shield a state against claims for cleaning up hazardous waste contamination for which it bears responsibility (*U.S. v. Union Gas*, CA 3, No. 85-1177, Nov. 3, 1987; 26 ERC 1769).

Comprehensive Environmental Response, Compensation, and Liability Act of 1980

(P.L. 96–510, approved December 11, 1980; as last amended by P.L. 99–499, approved October 17, 1986)

Subchapter I. Hazardous Substances Releases, Liability, Compensation

§ 9601. Definitions

[Sec. 101] For purpose of this title—

(1) The term "act of God" means an unanticipated grave natural disaster or other natural phenomenon of an exceptional, inevitable, and irresistible character, the effects of which could not have been prevented or avoided by the exercise of due care or foresight.

(2) The term "Administrator" means the Administrator of the United States Environmental Protection Agency.

(3) The term "barrel" means forty-two United States gallons at sixty degrees Fahrenheit.

(4) The term "claim" means a demand in writing for a sum certain.

(5) The term "claimant" means any person who presents a claim for compensation under this Act.

(6) The term "damages" means damages for injury or loss of natural resources as set forth in section 107(a) or 111(b) of this Act.

(7) The term "drinking water supply" means any raw or finished water source that is or may be used by a public water system (as defined in the Safe Drinking Water Act) or as drinking water by one or more individuals.

(8) The term "environment" means (A) the navigable waters, the waters of the contiguous zone, and the ocean waters of which the natural resources are under the exclusive management authority of the United States under the Magnuson Fishery Conservation and Management Act of 1976, and (B) any other surface water, ground water, drinking water supply, land surface or subsurface strata, or ambient air within the United States or under the jurisdiction of the United States.

(9) The term "facility" means (A) any building, structure, installation, equipment, pipe or pipeline (including any pipe into a sewer or publicly owned treatment works), well, pit, pond, lagoon, impoundment, ditch, landfill, storage container, motor vehicle, rolling stock, or aircraft, or (B) any site or area where a hazardous substance has been deposited, stored, disposed of, or placed, or otherwise come to be located; but does not include any consumer product in consumer use or any vessel.

(10) The term "federally permitted release" means (A) discharges in compliance with a permit under section 402 of the Federal Water

Pollution Control Act, (B) discharges resulting from circumstances identified and reviewed and made part of the public record with respect to a permit issued or modified under section 402 of the Federal Water Pollution Control Act and subject to a condition of such permit, (C) continuous or anticipated intermittent discharges from a point source, identified in a permit or permit application under section 402 of the Federal Water Pollution Control Act, which are caused by events occurring within the scope of relevant operating or treatment systems, (D) discharges in compliance with a legally enforceable permit under section 404 of the Federal Water Pollution Control Act, (E) releases in compliance with a legally enforceable final permit issued pursuant to section 3005 (a) through (d) of the Solid Waste Disposal Act from a hazardous waste treatment, storage, or disposal facility when such permit specifically identifies the hazardous substances and makes such substances subject to a standard of practice, control procedure or bioassay limitation or condition, or other control on the hazardous substances in such releases, (F) any release in compliance with a legally enforceable permit issued under section 102 of section 103 of the Marine Protection, Research, and Sanctuaries Act of 1972, (G) any injection of fluids authorized under Federal underground injection control programs or State programs submitted for Federal approval (and not disapproved by the Administrator of the Environmental Protection Agency) pursuant to part C of the Safe Drinking Water Act, (H) any emission into the air subject to a permit or control regulation under section 111, section 112, title I part C, title I part D, or State implementation plans submitted in accordance with section 110 of the Clean Air Act (and not disapproved by the Administrator of the Environmental Protection Agency), including any schedule or waiver granted, promulgated, or approved under these sections, (I) any injection of fluids or other materials authorized under applicable State law (i) for the purpose of stimulating or treating wells for the production of crude oil, natural gas, or water, (ii) for the purpose of secondary, tertiary, or other enhanced recovery of crude oil or natural gas, or (iii), which are brought to the surface in conjunction with the production of crude oil or natural gas and which are reinjected, (J) the introduction of any pollutant into a publicly owned treatment works when such pollutant is specified in and in compliance with applicable pretreatment standards of section 307(b) or (c) of the Clean Water Act and enforceable requirements in a pretreatment program submitted by a State or municipality for Federal approval under section 402 of such Act, and (K) any release of source, special nuclear, or byproduct material, as those terms are defined in the Atomic Energy Act of 1954, in compliance with a legally enforceable license, permit, regulation, or order issued pursuant to the Atomic Energy Act of 1954.

(11) The term "Fund" or "Trust Fund" means the Hazardous Substance Superfund established by section 9507 of the Internal Revenue Code of 1986.

(12) The term "ground water" means water in a saturated zone or stratum beneath the surface of land or water.

(13) The term "guarantor" means any person, other than the owner or operator, who provides evidence of financial responsibility for an owner or operator under this Act.

(14) The term "hazardous substance" means (A) any substance designated pursuant to section 311(b)(2)(A) of the Federal Water Pollution Control Act, (B) any element, compound, mixture, solution, or substance designated pursuant to section 102 of this Act, (C) any hazardous waste having the characteristics identified under or listed pursuant to section 3001 of the Solid Waste Disposal Act (but not including any waste the regulation of which under the Solid Waste Disposal Act has been suspended by Act of Congress), (D) any toxic pollutant listed under section 307(a) of the Federal Water Pollution Control Act, (E) any hazardous air pollutant listed under section 112 of the Clean Air Act, and (F) any imminently hazardous chemical substance or mixture with respect to which the Administrator has taken action pursuant to section 7 of the Toxic Substances Control Act. The term does not include petroleum, including crude oil or any fraction thereof which is not otherwise specifically listed or designated as a hazardous substance under subparagraphs (A) through (F) of this paragraph, and the term does not include natural gas, natural gas liquids, liquefied natural gas, or synthetic gas usable for fuel (or mixtures of natural gas and such synthetic gas).

(15) The term "navigable waters" or "navigable waters of the United States" means the waters of the United States, including the territorial seas.

(16) The term "natural resources" means land, fish, wildlife, biota, air, water, ground water, drinking water supplies, and other such resources belonging to, managed by, held in trust by, appertaining to, or otherwise controlled by the United States (including the resources of the fishery conservation zone established by the Fishery Conservation and Management Act of 1976), any State or local government, any foreign government, any Indian tribe, or, if such resources are subject to a trust restriction on alienation, any member of an Indian tribe.

(17) The term "offshore facility" means any facility of any kind located in, on, or under, any of the navigable waters of the United States, and any facility of any kind which is subject to the jurisdiction of the United States and is located in, on, or under any other waters, other than a vessel or a public vessel.

(18) The term "onshore facility" means any facility (including, but not limited to, motor vehicles and rolling stock) of any kind located in, on,

or under, any land or nonnavigable waters within the United States.

(19) The term "otherwise subject to the jurisdiction of the United States" means subject to the jurisdiction of the United States by virtue of United States citizenship, United States vessel documentation or numbering, or as provided by international agreement to which the United States is a party.

(20)(A) The term "owner or operator" means (i) in the case of a vessel, any person owning, operating, or chartering by demise, such vessel, (ii) in the case of an onshore facility or an offshore facility, any person owning or operating such facility, and (iii) in the case of any facility, title or control of which was conveyed due to bankruptcy, foreclosure, tax delinquency, abandonment, or similar means to a unit of State or local government, any person who owned, operated, or otherwise controlled activities at such facility immediately beforehand. Such term does not include a person, who, without participating in the management of a vessel or facility, holds indicia of ownership primarily to protect his security interest in the vessel or facility.

(B) In the case of a hazardous substance which has been accepted for transportation by a common or contract carrier and except as provided in section 107(a)(3) or (4) of this Act, (i) the term "owner or operator" shall mean such common carrier or other bona fide for hire carrier acting as an independent contractor during such transportation, (ii) the shipper of such hazardous substance shall not be considered to have caused or contributed to any release during such transportation which resulted solely from circumstances or conditions beyond his control.

(C) In the case of a hazardous substance which has been delivered by a common or contract carrier to a disposal or treatment facility and except as provided in section 107(a)(3) or (4) (i) the term "owner or operator" shall not include such common or contract carrier, and (ii) such common or contract carrier shall not be considered to have caused or contributed to any release at such disposal or treatment facility resulting from circumstances or conditions beyond its control.

(D) The term "owner or operator" does not include a unit of State or local government which acquired ownership or control involuntarily through bankruptcy, tax delinquency, abandonment, or other circumstances in which the government involuntarily acquires title by virtue of its function as sovereign. The exclusion provided under this paragraph shall not apply to any State or local government which has caused or contributed to the release or threatened release of a hazardous substance from the facility, and such a State or local government shall be subject to the provisions of this Act in the same manner and to the same extent, both procedurally and substantively, as any nongovernmental entity, including liability under section 107.

(21) The term "person" means an individual, firm, corporation, association, partnership, consortium, joint venture, commercial entity, United States Government, State, municipality, commission, political subdivision of a State, or any interstate body.

(22) The term "release" means any spilling, leaking, pumping, pouring, emitting, emptying, discharging, injecting, escaping, leaching, dumping, or disposing into the environment, (including the abandonment or discarding of barrels, containers, and other closed receptacles containing any hazardous substance or pollutant or contaminant) but excludes (A) any release which results in exposure to persons solely within a workplace, with respect to a claim which such persons may assert against the employer of such persons, (B) emissions from the engine exhaust of a motor vehicle, rolling stock, aircraft, vessel, or pipeline pumping station engine, (C) release of source, byproduct, or special nuclear material from a nuclear incident, as those terms are defined in the Atomic Energy Act of 1954, if such release is subject to requirements with respect to financial protection established by the Nuclear Regulatory Commission under section 170 of such Act, or, for the purposes of section 104 of this title or any other response action, any release of source byproduct, or special nuclear material from any processing site designated under section 102(a)(1) or 302(a) of the Uranium Mill Tailings Radiation Control Act of 1978, and (D) the normal application of fertilizer.

(23) The terms "remove" or "removal" means the cleanup or removal of released hazardous substances from the environment, such actions as may be necessary taken in the event of the threat of release of hazardous substances into the environment, such actions as may be necessary to monitor, assess, and evaluate the release or threat of release of hazardous substances, the disposal of removed material, or the taking of such other actions as may be necessary to prevent, minimize, or mitigate damage to the public health or welfare or to the environment, which may otherwise result from a release or threat of release. The term includes, in addition, without being limited to, security fencing or other measures to limit access, provision of alternative water supplies, temporary evacuation and housing of threatened individuals not otherwise provided for, action taken under section 104(b) of this Act, and any emergency assistance which may be provided under the Disaster Relief Act of 1974.

(24) The terms "remedy" or "remedial action" means those actions consistent with permanent remedy taken instead of or in addition to removal actions in the event of a release or threatened release of a hazardous substance into the environment, to prevent or minimize the release of hazardous substances so that they do not migrate to cause substantial danger to present or future public health or welfare or the environ-

ment. The term includes, but is not limited to, such actions at the location of the release as storage, confinement, perimeter protection using dikes, trenches, or ditches, clay cover, neutralization, cleanup of released hazardous substances and associated contaminated materials, recycling or reuse, diversion, destruction, segregation of reactive wastes, dredging or excavations, repair or replacement of leaking containers, collection of leachate and runoff, onsite treatment or incineration, provision of alternative water supplies, and any monitoring reasonably required to assure that such actions protect the public health and welfare and the environment. The term includes the costs of permanent relocation of residents and businesses and community facilities where the President determines that, alone or in combination with other measures, such relocation is more cost-effective than and environmentally preferable to the transportation, storage, treatment, destruction, or secure disposition offsite of hazardous substances, or may otherwise be necessary to protect the public health or welfare; the term includes offsite transport and offsite storage, treatment, destruction, or secure disposition of hazardous substances and associated contaminated materials.

(25) The terms "respond" or "response" means remove, removal, remedy, and remedial action, all such terms (including the terms "removal" and "remedial action") include enforcement activities related thereto.

(26) The terms "transport" or "transportation" means the movement of a hazardous substance by any mode, including pipeline (as defined in the Pipeline Safety Act), and in the case of a hazardous substance which has been accepted for transportation by a common or contract carrier, the term "transport" or "transportation" shall include any stoppage in transit which is temporary, incidental to the transportation movement, and at the ordinary operating convenience of a common or contract carrier, and any such stoppage shall be considered as a continuity of movement and not as the storage of a hazardous substance.

(27) The terms "United States" and "State" include the several States of the United States, the District of Columbia, the Commonwealth of Puerto Rico, Guam, American Samoa, the United States Virgin Islands, the Commonwealth of the Northern Marianas, and any other territory or possession over which the United States has jurisdiction.

(28) The term "vessel" means every description of watercraft or other artificial contrivance used, or capable of being used, as a means of transportation on water.

(29) The terms "disposal", "hazardous waste", and "treatment" shall have the meaning provided in section 1004 of the Solid Waste Disposal Act.

(30) The terms "territorial sea" and "contiguous zone" shall have the meaning provided in section 502 of the Federal Water Pollution Control Act.

(31) The term "national contingency plan" means the national contingency plan published under section 311(c) of the Federal Water Pollution Control Act or revised pursuant to section 105 of this Act.

(32) The terms "liable" or "liability" under this title shall be construed to be the standard of liability which obtains under section 311 of the Federal Water Pollution Control Act.

(33) The term "pollutant or contaminant" shall include, but not be limited to, any element, substance, compound, or mixture, including disease-causing agents, which after release into the environment and upon exposure, ingestion, inhalation, or assimilation into any organism, either directly from the environment or indirectly by ingestion through food chains, will or may reasonably be anticipated to cause death, disease, behavioral abnormalities, cancer, genetic mutation, physiological malfunctions (including malfunctions in reproduction) or physical deformations, in such organisms or their offspring; except that the term "pollutant or contaminant" shall not include petroleum, including crude oil or any fraction thereof which is not otherwise specifically listed or designated as a hazardous substance under subparagraphs (A) through (F) of paragraph (14) and shall not include natural gas, liquefied natural gas, or synthetic gas of pipeline quality (or mixtures of natural gas and such synthetic gas).

(34) The term "alternative water supplies" includes, but is not limited to, drinking water and household water supplies.

(35)(A) The term "contractual relationship", for the purpose of section 107(b)(3), includes, but is not limited to, land contracts, deeds or other instruments transferring title or possession, unless the real property on which the facility concerned is located was acquired by the defendant after the disposal or placement of the hazardous substance on, in, or at the facility, and one or more of the circumstances described in clause (i), (ii), or (iii) is also established by the defendant by a preponderance of the evidence:

> (i) At the time the defendant acquired the facility the defendant did not know and had no reason to know that any hazardous substance which is the subject of the release or threatened release was disposed of on, in, or at the facility.

> (ii) The defendant is a government entity which acquired the facility by escheat, or through any other involuntary transfer or acquisition, or through the exercise of eminent domain authority by purchase or condemnation.

> (iii) The defendant acquired the facility by inheritance or bequest.

In addition to establishing the foregoing, the defendant must establish that he has satisfied the requirements of section 107(b)(3)(a) and (b).

> (B) To establish that the defendant had no reason to know, as provided in clause (i) of subparagraph (A) of this paragraph, the defendant must have undertaken, at the time of acquisition, all

appropriate inquiry into the previous ownership and uses of the property consistent with good commercial or customary practice in an effort to minimize liability. For purposes of the preceding sentence the court shall take into account any specialized knowledge or experience on the part of the defendant, the relationship of the purchase price to the value of the property if uncontaminated, commonly known or reasonably ascertainable information about the property, the obviousness of the presence or likely presence of contamination at the property, and the ability to detect such contamination by appropriate inspection.

(C) Nothing in this paragraph or in section 107(b)(3) shall diminish the liability of any previous owner or operator of such facility who would otherwise be liable under this Act. Notwithstanding this paragraph, if the defendant obtained actual knowledge of the release or threatened release of a hazardous substance at such facility when the defendant owned the real property and then subsequently transferred ownership of the property to another person without disclosing such knowledge, such defendant shall be treated as liable under section 107(a)(1) and no defense under section 107(b)(3) shall be available to such defendant.

(D) Nothing in this paragraph shall affect the liability under this Act of a defendant who, by any act or omission, caused or contributed to the release or threatened release of a hazardous substance which is the subject of the action relating to the facility.

(36) The term "Indian tribe" means any Indian tribe, band, nation, or other organized group or community, including any Alaska Native village but not including any Alaska Native regional or village corporation, which is recognized as eligible for the special programs and services provided by the United States to Indians because of their status as Indians.

(37)(A) The term "service station dealer" means any person—

(i) who owns or operates a motor vehicle service station, filling station, garage, or similar retail establishment engaged in the business of selling, repairing, or servicing motor vehicles, where a significant percentage of the gross revenue of the establishment is derived from the fueling, repairing, or servicing of motor vehicles, and

(ii) who accepts for collection, accumulation, and delivery to an oil recycling facility, recycled oil that (I) has been removed from the engine of a light duty motor vehicle or household appliances by the owner of such vehicle or appliances, and (II) is presented, by such owner, to such person for collection, accumulation, and delivery to an oil recycling facility.

(B) For purposes of section 114(c), the term "service station dealer" shall, notwithstanding the provisions of subparagraph (A), include any government agency that establishes a facility solely for the purpose of accepting recycled oil that satisfies the criteria set forth in subclauses (I) and (II) of subparagraph (A)(ii), and, with respect to recycled oil that satisfies the criteria set forth in subclauses (I) and (II), owners or operators of refuse collection services who are compelled by State law to collect, accumulate, and deliver such oil to an oil recycling facility.

(C) The President shall promulgate regulations regarding the determination of what constitutes a significant percentage of the gross revenues of an establishment for purposes of this paragraph.

(38) The term "incineration vessel" means any vessel which carries hazardous substances for the purpose of incineration of such substances, so long as such substances or residues of such substances are on board.

§ 9602. Designation of additional hazardous substances and establishment of reportable released quantities; regulations

[Sec. 102] (a) The Administrator shall promulgate and revise as may be appropriate, regulations designating as hazardous substances, in addition to those referred to in section 101(14) of this title, such elements, compounds, mixtures, solutions, and substances which, when released into the environment may present substantial danger to the public health or welfare or the environment, and shall promulgate regulations establishing that quantity of any hazardous substance the release of which shall be reported pursuant to section 103 of this title. The Administrator may determine that one single quantity shall be the reportable quantity for any hazardous substance, regardless of the medium into which the hazardous substance is released. For all hazardous substances for which proposed regulations establishing reportable quantities were published in the Federal Register under this subsection on or before March 1, 1986, the Administrator shall promulgate under this subsection final regulations establishing reportable quantities not later than December 31, 1986. For all hazardous substances for which proposed regulations establishing reportable quantities were not published in the Federal Register under this subsection on or before March 1, 1986, the Administrator shall publish under this subsection proposed regulations establishing reportable quantities not later than December 31, 1986, and promulgate final regulations under this subsection establishing reportable quantities not later than April 30, 1988.

(b) Unless and until superseded by regulations establishing a reportable quantity under subsection (a) of this section for any hazardous substance as defined in section 101(14) of this title, (1) a quantity of one pound, or (2) for those hazardous substances for which reportable quantities have been established pursuant to section 311(b)(4) of the Federal Water Pollution Control Act, such reportable quantity, shall be deemed that quantity, the release of which requires notification pursuant to section 103(a) or (b) of this title.

§ 9603. Notification requirements respecting released substances

[Sec. 103] (a) Any person in charge of a vessel or an offshore or an onshore facility shall, as soon as he has knowledge of any release (other than a federally permitted release) of a hazardous substance from such vessel or facility in quantities equal to or greater than those determined pursuant to section 102 of this title, immediately notify the National Response Center established under the Clean Water Act of such release. The National Response Center shall convey the notification expeditiously to all appropriate Government agencies, including the Governor of any affected State.

(b) Any person—

(1) in charge of a vessel from which a hazardous substance is released, other than a federally permitted release, into or upon the navigable waters of the United States, adjoining shorelines, or into or upon the waters of the contiguous zone, or

(2) in charge of a vessel from which a hazardous substance is released, other than a federally permitted release, which may affect natural resources belonging to, appertaining to, or under the exclusive management authority of the United States (including resources under the Fishery Conservation and Management Act of 1976), and who is otherwise subject to the jurisdiction of the United States at the time of the release, or

(3) in charge of a facility from which a hazardous substance is released, other than a federally permitted release, in a quantity equal to or greater than that determined pursuant to section 102 of this title who fails to notify immediately the appropriate agency of the United States Government as soon as he has knowledge of such release or who submits in such a notification any information which he knows to be false or misleading shall, upon conviction, be fined in accordance with the applicable provisions of title 18 of the United States Code or imprisoned for not more than 3 years (or not more than 5 years in the case of a second or subsequent conviction), or both. Notification received pursuant to this subsection or information obtained by the exploitation of such notification shall not be used against any such person in any criminal case, except a prosecution for perjury or for giving a false statement.

(c) Within one hundred and eighty days after the enactment of this Act, any person who owns or operates or who at the time of disposal owned or operated, or who accepted hazardous substances for transport and selected, a facility at which hazardous substances (as defined in section 101(14)(C) of this title) are or have been stored, treated, or disposed of shall, unless such facility has a permit issued under, or has been accorded interim status under, subtitle C of the Solid Waste Disposal Act, notify the Administrator of the Environmental Protection Agency of the existence of such facility, specifying the amount and type of any hazardous substance to be found there, and any known, suspected, or likely releases of such substances from such facility. The Administrator may prescribe in greater detail the manner and form of the notice and the information included. The Administrator shall notify the affected State agency, or any department designated by the Governor to receive such notice, of the existence of such facility. Any person who knowingly fails to notify the Administrator of the existence of any such facility shall, upon conviction, be fined not more than $10,000, or imprisoned for not more than one year, or both. In addition, any such person who knowingly fails to provide the notice required by this subsection shall not be entitled to any limitation of liability or to any defenses to liability set out in section 107 of this Act: *Provided, however,* That notification under this subsection is not required for any facility which would be reportable hereunder solely as a result of any stoppage in transit which is temporary, incidental to the transportation movement, or at the ordinary operating convenience of a common or contract carrier, and such stoppage shall be considered as a continuity of movement and not as the storage of a hazardous substance. Notification received pursuant to this subsection or information obtained by the exploitation of such notification shall not be used against any such person in any criminal case, except a prosecution for perjury or for giving a false statement.

   (d)(1) The Administrator of the Environmental Protection Agency is authorized to promulgate rules and regulations specifying, with respect to—
   (A) the location, title, or condition of a facility, and
   (B) the identity, characteristics, quantity, origin, or condition (including containerization and previous treatment) of any hazardous substances contained or deposited in a facility;
the records which shall be retained by any person required to provide the notification of a facility set out in subsection (c) of this section. Such specification shall be in accordance with the provisions of this subsection.
   (2) Beginning with the date of enactment of this Act, for fifty years (thereafter or for fifty years after the date of establishment of a record (whichever is later), or at any such earlier time as a waiver if obtained under paragraph (3) of this subsection, it shall be unlawful for any such person knowingly to destroy, mutilate, erase, dispose of, conceal, or otherwise render unavailable or unreasonable or falsify any records identified in paragraph (1) of this subsection. Any person who violates this paragraph shall, upon conviction, be fined in accordance with the applicable provisions of title 18 of the United States Code or imprisoned for not more than 3 years (or not more than 5 years in the case of a second or subsequent conviction), or both.
   (3) At any time prior to the date which occurs fifty years after the date of enactment of this Act, any person identified under paragraph (1) of this subsection may apply to the Administrator of the Environmental Protection Agency for a waiver of the provisions of the first sentence of paragraph (2) of this subsection. The Administrator is authorized to

grant such waiver if, in his discretion, such waiver would not unreasonably interfere with the attainment of the purposes and provisions of this Act. The Administrator shall promulgate rules and regulations regarding such a waiver so as to inform parties of the proper application procedure and conditions for approval of such a waiver.

(4) Notwithstanding the provisions of this subsection, the Administrator of the Environmental Protection Agency may in his discretion require any such person to retain any record identified pursuant to paragraph (1) of this subsection for such a time period in excess of the period specified in paragraph (2) of this subsection as the Administrator determines to be necessary to protect the public health or welfare.

(e) This section shall not apply to the application of a pesticide product registered under the Federal Insecticide, Fungicide, and Rodenticide Act or to the handling and storage of such a pesticide product by an agricultural producer.

(f) No notification shall be required under subsection (a) or (b) of this section for any release of a hazardous substance—

(1) which is required to be reported (or specifically exempted from a requirement for reporting) under subtitle C of the Solid Waste Disposal Act or regulations thereunder and which has been reported to the National Response Center, or

(2) which is a continuous release, stable in quantity and rate, and is—

(A) from a facility for which notification has been given under subsection (c) of this section, or

(B) a release of which notification has been given under subsections (a) and (b) of this section for a period sufficient to establish the continuity, quantity, and regularity of such release:

Provided, That notification in accordance with subsections (a) and (b) of this paragraph shall be given for releases subject to this paragraph annually, or at such time as there is any statistically significant increase in the quantity of any hazardous substance or constituent thereof released, above that previously reported or occurring.

§ 9604. Response authorities

[Sec. 104] (a)(1) Whenever (A) any hazardous substance is released or there is a substantial threat of such a release into the environment, or (B) there is a release or substantial threat of release into the environment of any pollutant or contaminant which may present an imminent and substantial danger to the public health or welfare, the President is authorized to act, consistent with the national contingency plan, to remove or arrange for the removal of, and provide for remedial action relating to such hazardous substance, pollutant, or contaminant at any time (including its removal from any contaminated natural resource), or take any other response measure consistent with the national contingency plan which the President deems necessary to protect the public health or welfare or the environment. When the President determines that such action will be done properly and promptly by the owner or operator of the facility or vessel or by any other responsible party, the President may allow such person to carry out the action, conduct the remedial investigation, or conduct the feasibility study in accordance with section 122. No remedial investigation or feasibility study (RI/FS) shall be authorized except on a determination by the President that the party is qualified to conduct the RI/FS and only if the President contracts with or arranges for a qualified person to assist the President in overseeing and reviewing the conduct of such RI/FS and if the responsible party agrees to reimburse the Fund for any cost incurred by the President under, or in connection with, the oversight contract or arrangement. In no event shall a potentially responsible party be subject to a lesser standard of liability, receive preferential treatment, or in any other way, whether direct or indirect, benefit from any such arrangements as a response action contractor, or as a person hired or retained by such a response action contractor, with respect to the release or facility in question. The President shall give primary attention to those releases which the President deems may present a public health threat.

(2) Any removal action undertaken by the President under this subsection (or by any other person referred to in section 122) should, to the extent the President deems practicable, contribute to the efficient performance of any long term remedial action with respect to the release or threatened release concerned.

(3) The President shall not provide for a removal or remedial action under this section in response to a release or threat of release—

   (A) of a naturally occurring substance in its unaltered form, or altered solely through naturally occurring processes or phenomena, from a location where it is naturally found;

   (B) from products which are part of the structure of, and result in exposure within, residential buildings or business or community structures; or

   (C) into public or private drinking water supplies due to deterioration of the system through ordinary use.

(4) Notwithstanding paragraph (3) of this subsection, to the extent authorized by this section, the President may respond to any release or threat of release if in the President's discretion, it constitutes a public health or environmental emergency and no other person with the authority and capability to respond to the emergency will do so in a timely manner.

(b)(1) Whenever the President is authorized to act pursuant to subsection (a) of this section, or whenever the President has reason to believe that a release has occurred or is about to occur, or that illness, disease, or complaints thereof may be attributable to exposure to a hazardous substance, pollutant, or contaminant and that a release may have occurred or be occurring, he may undertake such investigations, monitoring, surveys, testing, and other information gathering as he may deem necessary or appropriate to identify the existence and extent of the release or threat thereof, the source and nature of the hazardous substances, pollutants or contaminants involved, and the extent of danger to the public health or welfare or to the environment. In addition, the President may undertake such planning, legal, fiscal, economic, engineering, architectural, and other studies or investigations as he may deem necessary or appropriate to plan and direct response actions, to recover the costs thereof, and to enforce the provisions of this Act.

(2) The President shall promptly notify the appropriate Federal and State natural resource trustees of potential damages to natural resources resulting from releases under investigation pursuant to this section and shall seek to coordinate the assessments, investigations, and planning under this section with such Federal and State trustees.

(c)(1) Unless (A) the President finds that (i) continued response actions are immediately required to prevent, limit, or mitigate an emergency, (ii) there is an immediate risk to public health or welfare or the environment, and (iii) such assistance will not otherwise be provided on a timely basis, or (B) the President has determined the appropriate remedial actions pursuant to paragraph (2) of this subsection and the State or States in which the source of the release is located have complied with the requirements of paragraph (3) of this subsection, or (C) continued response action is otherwise appropriate and consistent with the remedial action to be taken, obligations from the Fund, other than those authorized by subsection (b) of this section, shall not continue after $2,000,000 has been obligated for response actions or 12 months has elapsed from the date of initial response to a release or threatened release of hazardous substances.

(2) The President shall consult with the affected State or States before determining any appropriate remedial action to be taken pursuant to the authority granted under subsection (a) of this section.

(3) The President shall not provide any remedial actions pursuant to this section unless the State in which the release occurs first enters into a contract or cooperative agreement with the President providing assurances deemed adequate by the President that (A) the State will assure all future maintenance of the removal and remedial actions provided for the expected life of such actions as determined by the President; (B) the State will assure the availability of a hazardous waste disposal facility acceptable to the President and in compliance with the requirements of subtitle C of the Solid Waste Disposal Act for any necessary offsite storage, destruction, treatment, or secure disposition of the hazardous substances; and (C) the State will pay or assure payment of (i) 10 per centum of the costs of the remedial action, including all future maintenance, or (ii) 50 percent (or such greater amount as the President may determine appropriate, taking into

account the degree of responsibility of the State or political subdivision for the release) of any sums expended in response to a release at a facility, that was operated by the State or a political subdivision thereof, either directly or through a contractual relationship or otherwise, at the time of any disposal of hazardous substances therein. For the purpose of clause (ii) of this subparagraph, the term "facility" does not include navigable waters or the beds underlying those waters. The President shall grant the State a credit against the share of the costs for which it is responsible under this paragraph for any documented direct out-of-pocket non-Federal funds expended or obligated by the State or a political subdivision thereof after January 1, 1978, and before the date of enactment of this Act for cost-eligible response actions and claims for damages compensable under section 111 of this title relating to the specific release in question: *Provided, however,* That in no event shall the amount of the credit granted exceed the total response costs relating to the release. In the case of remedial action to be taken on land or water held by an Indian tribe, held by the United States in trust for Indians, held by a member of an Indian tribe (if such land or water is subject to a trust restriction on alienation), or otherwise within the borders of an Indian reservation, the requirements of this paragraph for assurances regarding future maintenance and cost-sharing shall not apply, and the President shall provide the assurance required by this paragraph regarding the availability of a hazardous waste disposal facility.

(4) The President shall select remedial actions to carry out this section in accordance with section 121 of this Act (relating to cleanup standards).

(5)(A) The President shall grant a State a credit against the share of the costs, for which it is responsible under paragraph (3) with respect to a facility listed on the National Priorities List under the National Contingency Plan, for amounts expended by a State for remedial action at such facility pursuant to a contract or cooperative agreement with the President. The credit under this paragraph shall be limited to those State expenses which the President determines to be reasonable, documented, direct out-of-pocket expenditures of non-Federal funds.

(B) The credit under this paragraph shall include expenses for remedial action at a facility incurred before the listing of the facility on the National Priorities List or before a contract or cooperative agreement is entered into under subsection (d) for the facility if—

(i) after such expenses are incurred the facility is listed on such list and a contract or cooperative agreement is entered into for the facility, and

(ii) the President determines that such expenses would have been credited to the State under subparagraph (A) had the expenditures been made after listing of the facility on such list and after the date on which such contract or cooperative agreement is entered into.

(C) The credit under this paragraph shall include funds expended or obligated by the State or a political subdivision thereof after January 1, 1978, and before December 11, 1980, for cost-eligible response actions and claims for damages compensable under section 111.

(D) The credit under this paragraph shall include 90 percent of State expenses incurred at a facility owned, but not operated, by such State or by a political subdivision thereof. Such credit applies only to expenses incurred pursuant to a contract or cooperative agreement under subsection (d) and only to expenses incurred after December 11, 1980, but before the date of the enactment of this paragraph.

(E) In the case of expenditures made after the date of the enactment of this paragraph, the President may require prior approval of each item of expenditure as a condition of granting a credit under this paragraph.

(F) Credits granted under this paragraph for funds expended with respect to a facility may be used by the State to reduce all or part of the share of costs otherwise required to be paid by the State under paragraph (3) in connection with remedial actions at such facility. If the amount of funds for which credit is allowed under this paragraph exceeds such share of costs for such facility, the State may use the amount of such excess to reduce all or part of the share of such costs at other facilities in that State. A credit shall not entitle the State to any direct payment.

(6) For the purposes of paragraph (3) of this subsection, in the case of ground or surface water contamination, completed remedial action includes the completion of treatment or other measures, whether taken onsite or offsite, necessary to restore ground and surface water quality to a level that assures protection of human health and the environment. With respect to such measures, the operation of such measures for a period of up to 10 years after the construction or installation and commencement of operation shall be considered remedial action. Activities required to maintain the effectiveness of such measures following such period or the completion of remedial action, whichever is earlier, shall be considered operation or maintenance.

(7) During any period after the availability of funds received by the Hazardous Substance Superfund established under subchapter A of chapter 98 of the Internal Revenue Code of 1954 from tax revenues or appropriations from general revenues, the Federal share of the payment of the cost of operation or maintenance pursuant to paragraph (3)(C)(i) or paragraph (6) of this subsection (relating to operation and

maintenance) shall be from funds received by the Hazardous Substance Superfund from amounts recovered on behalf of such fund under this Act.

(8) The President is authorized to undertake or continue whatever interim remedial actions the President determines to be appropriate to reduce risks to public health or the environment where the performance of a complete remedial action requires recontracting because of the discovery of sources, types, or quantities of hazardous substances not known at the time of entry into the original contract. The total cost of interim actions undertaken at a facility pursuant to this paragraph shall not exceed $2,000,000.

(9) Effective 3 years after the enactment of the Superfund Amendments and Reauthorization Act of 1986, the President shall not provide any remedial actions pursuant to this section unless the State in which the release occurs first enters into a contract or cooperative agreement with the President providing assurances deemed adequate by the President that the State will assure the availability of hazardous waste treatment or disposal facilities which—

(A) have adequate capacity for the destruction, treatment, or secure disposition of all hazardous wastes that are reasonably expected to be generated within the State during the 20-year period following the date of such contract or cooperative agreement and to be disposed of, treated, or destroyed,

(B) are within the State or outside the State in accordance with an interstate agreement or regional agreement or authority,

(C) are acceptable to the President, and

(D) are in compliance with the requirements of subtitle C of the Solid Waste Disposal Act.

(d)(1)(A) A State or political subdivision thereof or Indian tribe may apply to the President to carry out actions authorized in this section. If the President determines that the State or political subdivision or Indian tribe has the capability to carry out any or all of such actions in accordance with the criteria and priorities established pursuant to section 105(a)(8) and to carry out related enforcement actions, the President may enter into a contract or cooperative agreement with the State or political subdivision or Indian tribe to carry out such actions. The President shall make a determination regarding such an application within 90 days after the President receives the application.

(B) A contract or cooperative agreement under this paragraph shall be subject to such terms and conditions as the President may prescribe. The contract or cooperative agreement may cover a specific facility or specific facilities.

(C) Any State which expended funds during the period beginning September 30, 1985, and ending on the date of the enactment of this subparagraph for response actions at any site included on the

National Priorities List and subject to a cooperative agreement under this Act shall be reimbursed for the share of costs of such actions for which the Federal Government is responsible under this Act.

(2) If the President enters into a cost-sharing agreement pursuant to subsection (c) of this section or a contract or cooperative agreement pursuant to this subsection, and the State or political subdivision thereof fails to comply with any requirements of the contract, the President may, after providing sixty days notice, seek in the appropriate Federal district court to enforce the contract or to recover any funds advanced or any costs incurred because of the breach of the contract by the State or political subdivision.

(3) Where a State or a political subdivision thereof is acting in behalf of the President, the President is authorized to provide technical and legal assistance in the administration and enforcement of any contract or subcontract in connection with response actions assisted under this title, and to intervene in any civil action involving the enforcement of such contract or subcontract.

(4) Where two or more noncontiguous facilities are reasonably related on the basis of geography, or on the basis of the threat, or potential threat to the public health or welfare or the environment, the President may, in his discretion, treat these related facilities as one for purposes of this section.

(e)(1) Any officer, employee, or representative of the President, duly designated by the President, is authorized to take action under paragraph (2), (3), or (4) (or any combination thereof) at a vessel, facility, establishment, place, property, or location or, in the case of paragraph (3) or (4), at any vessel, facility, establishment, place, property, or location which is adjacent to the vessel, facility, establishment, place, property, or location referred to in such paragraph (3) or (4). Any duly designated officer, employee, or representative of a State or political subdivision under a contract or cooperative agreement under subsection (d)(1) is also authorized to take such action. The authority of paragraphs (3) and (4) may be exercised only if there is a reasonable basis to believe there may be a release or threat of release of a hazardous substance or pollutant or contaminant. The authority of this subsection may be exercised only for the purposes of determining the need for response, or choosing or taking any response action under this title, or otherwise enforcing the provisions of this title.

(2) Any officer, employee, or representative described in paragraph (1) may require any person who has or may have information relevant to any of the following to furnish, upon reasonable notice, information or documents relating to such matter:

(A) The identification, nature, and quantity of materials which have been or are generated, treated, stored, or disposed of at a vessel or facility or transported to a vessel or facility.

(B) The nature or extent of a release or threatened release of a hazardous substance or pollutant or contaminant at or from a vessel or facility.

(C) Information relating to the ability of a person to pay for or to perform a cleanup.

In addition, upon reasonable notice, such person either (i) shall grant any such officer, employee, or representative access at all reasonable times to any vessel, facility, establishment, place, property, or location to inspect and copy all documents or records relating to such matters or (ii) shall copy and furnish to the officer, employee, or representative all such documents or records, at the option and expense of such person.

(3) Any officer, employee, or representative described in paragraph (1) is authorized to enter at reasonable times any of the following:

(A) Any vessel, facility, establishment, or other place or property where any hazardous substance or pollutant or contaminant may be or has been generated, stored, treated, disposed of, or transported from.

(B) Any vessel, facility, establishment, or other place or property from which or to which a hazardous substance or pollutant or contaminant has been or may have been released.

(C) Any vessel, facility, establishment, or other place or property where such release is or may be threatened.

(D) Any vessel, facility, establishment, or other place or property where entry is needed to determine the need for response or the appropriate response or to effectuate a response action under this title.

(4)(A) Any officer, employee or representative described in paragraph (1) is authorized to inspect and obtain samples from any vessel, facility, establishment, or other place or property referred to in paragraph (3) or from any location of any suspected hazardous substance or pollutant or contaminant. Any such officer, employee, or representative is authorized to inspect and obtain samples of any containers or labeling for suspected hazardous substances or pollutants or contaminants. Each such inspection shall be completed with reasonable promptness.

(B) If the officer, employee, or representative obtains any samples, before leaving the premises he shall give to the owner, operator, tenant, or other person in charge of the place from which the samples were obtained a receipt describing the sample obtained and, if requested, a portion of each such sample. A copy of the results of any analysis made of such samples shall be furnished promptly to the owner, operator, tenant, or other person in charge, if such person can be located.

(5)(A) If consent is not granted regarding any request made by an officer, employee, or representative under paragraph (2), (3), or (4), the

President may issue an order directing compliance with the request. The order may be issued after such notice and opportunity for consultation as is reasonably appropriate under the circumstances.

(B) The President may ask the Attorney General to commence a civil action to compel compliance with a request or order referred to in subparagraph (A). Where there is a reasonable basis to believe there may be a release or threat of a release of a hazardous substance or pollutant or contaminant, the court shall take the following actions:

(i) In the case of interference with entry or inspection, the court shall enjoin such interference or direct compliance with orders to prohibit interference with entry or inspection unless under the circumstances of the case the demand for entry or inspection is arbitrary and capricious, an abuse of discretion, or otherwise not in accordance with law.

(ii) In the case of information or document requests or orders, the court shall enjoin interference with such information or document requests or orders or direct compliance with the requests or orders to provide such information or documents unless under the circumstances of the case the demand for information or documents is arbitrary and capricious, an abuse of discretion, or otherwise not in accordance with law.

The court may assess a civil penalty not to exceed $25,000 for each day of noncompliance against any person who unreasonably fails to comply with the provisions of paragraph (2), (3), or (4) or an order issued pursuant to subparagraph (A) of this paragraph.

(6) Nothing in this subsection shall preclude the President from securing access or obtaining information in any other lawful manner.

(7)(A) Any records, reports, or information obtained from any person under this section (including records, reports, or information obtained by representatives of the President) shall be available to the public, except that upon a showing satisfactory to the President (or the State, as the case may be) by any person that records, reports, or information, or particular part thereof (other than health or safety effects data), to which the President (or the State, as the case may be) or any officer, employee, or representative has access under this section if made public would divulge information entitled to protection under section 1905 of title 18 of the United States Code, such information or particular portion thereof shall be considered confidential in accordance with the purposes of that section, except that such record, report, document or information may be disclosed to other officers, employees, or authorized representatives of the United States concerned with carrying out this Act, or when relevant in any proceeding under this Act.

(B) Any person not subject to the provisions of section 1905 of title 18 of the United States Code who knowingly and willfully divulges or discloses any information entitled to protection under this subsection shall, upon conviction, be subject to a fine of not more than $5,000 or to imprisonment not to exceed one year, or both.

(C) In submitting data under this Act, a person required to provide such data may (i) designate the data which such person believes is entitled to protection under this subsection and (ii) submit such designated data separately from other data submitted under this Act. A designation under this paragraph shall be made in writing and in such manner as the President may prescribe by regulation.

(D) Notwithstanding any limitation contained in this section or any other provision of law, all information reported to or otherwise obtained by the President (or any representative of the President) under this Act shall be made available, upon written request of any duly authorized committee of the Congress, to such committee.

(E) No person required to provide information under this Act may claim that the information is entitled to protection under this paragraph unless such person shows each of the following:

(i) Such person has not disclosed the information to any other person, other than a member of a local emergency planning committee established under title III of the Amendments and Reauthorization Act of 1986, an officer or employee of the United States or a State or local government, an employee of such person, or a person who is bound by a confidentiality agreement, and such person has taken reasonable measures to protect the confidentiality of such information and intends to continue to take such measures.

(ii) The information is not required to be disclosed, or otherwise made available, to the public under any other Federal or State law.

(iii) Disclosure of the information is likely to cause substantial harm to the competitive position of such person.

(iv) The specific chemical identity, if sought to be protected, is not readily discoverable through reverse engineering.

(F) The following information with respect to any hazardous substance at the facility or vessel shall not be entitled to protection under this paragraph:

(i) The trade name, common name, or generic class or category of the hazardous substance.

(ii) The physical properties of the substance, including its boiling point, melting point, flash point, specific gravity, vapor density, solubility in water, and vapor pressure at 20 degrees celsius.

(iii) The hazards to health and the environment posed by the substance, including physical hazards (such as explosion) and potential acute and chronic health hazards.

(iv) The potential routes of human exposure to the substance at the facility, establishment, place, or property being investigated, entered, or inspected under this subsection.

(v) The location of disposal of any waste stream.

(vi) Any monitoring data or analysis of monitoring data pertaining to disposal activities.

(vii) Any hydrogeologic or geologic data.

(viii) Any groundwater monitoring data.

(f) In awarding contracts to any person engaged in response actions, the President or the State, in any case where it is awarding contracts pursuant to a contract entered into under subsection (d) of this section, shall require compliance with Federal health and safety standards established under section 301(f) of this Act by contractors and subcontractors as a condition of such contracts.

(g)(1) All laborers and mechanics employed by contractors or subcontractors in the performance of construction, repair, or alteration work funded in whole or in part under this section shall be paid wages at rates not less than those prevailing on projects of a character similar in the locality as determined by the Secretary of Labor in accordance with the Davis-Bacon Act. The President shall not approve any such funding without first obtaining adequate assurance that required labor standards will be maintained upon the construction work.

(2) The Secretary of Labor shall have, with respect to the labor standards specified in paragraph (1), the authority and functions set forth in Reorganization Plan Numbered 14 of 1950 (15 F.R. 3176; 64 Stat. 1267) and section 276c of title 40 of the United States Code.

(h) Notwithstanding any other provision of law, subject to the provisions of section 111 of this Act, the President may authorize the use of such emergency procurement powers as he deems necessary to effect the purpose of this Act. Upon determination that such procedures are necessary, the President shall promulgate regulations prescribing the circumstances under which such authority shall be used and the procedures governing the use of such authority.

(i)(1) There is hereby established within the Public Health Service an agency, to be known as the Agency for Toxic Substances and Disease Registry, which shall report directly to the Surgeon General of the United States. The Administrator of said Agency shall, with the cooperation of the Administrator of the Environmental Protection Agency, the Commissioner of the Food and Drug Administration, the Directors of the National Institute of Medicine, National Institute of Environmental Health Sciences, National Institute of Occupational Safety and Health, Centers for Disease Control, the Administrator of the Occupational Safety and Health Administration, the Administrator of the Social Security Administration, the Secretary of

Transportation, and appropriate State and local health officials, effectuate and implement the health related authorities of this Act. In addition, said Administrator shall—

(A) in cooperation with the States, establish and maintain a national registry of serious diseases and illnesses and a national registry of persons exposed to toxic substances;

(B) establish and maintain inventory of literature, research, and studies on the health effects of toxic substances;

(C) in cooperation with the States, and other agencies of the Federal Government, establish and maintain a complete listing of areas closed to the public or otherwise restricted in use because of toxic substance contamination;

(D) in cases of public health emergencies caused or believed to be caused by exposure to toxic substances, provide medical care and testing to exposed individuals, including but not limited to tissue sampling, chromosomal testing where appropriate, epidemiological studies, or any other assistance appropriate under the circumstances; and

(E) either independently or as part of other health status survey, conduct periodic survey and screening programs to determine relationships between exposure to toxic substances and illness. In cases of public health emergencies, exposed persons shall be eligible for admission to hospitals and other facilities and services operated or provided by the Public Health Service.

(2)(A) Within 6 months after the enactment of the Superfund Amendments and Reauthorization Act of 1986, the Administrator of the Agency for Toxic Substances and Disease Registry (ATSDR) and the Administrator of the Environmental Protection Agency (EPA) shall prepare a list, in order of priority, of at least 100 hazardous substances which are most commonly found at facilities on the National Priorities List and which, in their sole discretion, they determine are posing the most significant potential threat to human health due to their known or suspected toxicity to humans and the potential for human exposure to such substances at facilities on the National Priorities List or at facilities to which a response to a release or a threatened release under this section is under consideration.

(B) Within 24 months after the enactment of the Superfund Amendments and Reauthorization Act of 1986, the Administrator of ATSDR and the Administrator of EPA shall revise the list prepared under subparagraph (A). Such revision shall include, in order of priority, the addition of 100 or more such hazardous substances. In each of the 3 consecutive 12-month periods that follow, the Administrator of ATSDR and the Administrator of EPA shall revise, in the same manner as provided in the 2 preceding sentences, such list to include not fewer than 25 additional hazardous substances per revision. The Administrator of ATSDR and the Administrator of EPA shall not less often than once every year thereafter revise such list to include additional hazardous substances in accordance with the criteria in subparagraph (A).

(3) Based on all available information, including information maintained under paragraph (1)(B) and data developed and collected on the health effects of hazardous substances under this paragraph, the Administrator of ATSDR shall prepare toxicological profiles of each of the substances listed pursuant to paragraph (2). The toxicological profiles shall be prepared in accordance with guidelines developed by the Administrator of ATSDR and the Administrator of EPA. Such profiles shall include, but not be limited to each of the following:

(A) An examination, summary, and interpretation of available toxicological information and epidemiologic evaluations on a hazardous substance in order to ascertain the levels of significant human exposure for the substance and the associated acute, subacute, and chronic health effects.

(B) A determination of whether adequate information on the health effects of each substance is available or in the process of development to determine levels of exposure which present a significant risk to human health of acute, subacute, and chronic health effects.

(C) Where appropriate, an identification of toxicological testing needed to identify the types or levels of exposure that may present significant risk of adverse health effects in humans.

Any toxicological profile or revision thereof shall reflect the Administrator of ATSDR's assessment of all relevant toxicological testing which has been peer reviewed. The profiles required to be prepared under this paragraph for those hazardous substances listed under subparagraph (A) of paragraph (2) shall be completed, at a rate of no fewer than 25 per year, within 4 years after the enactment of the Superfund Amendments and Reauthorization Act of 1986. A profile required on a substance listed pursuant to subparagraph (B) of paragraph (2) shall be completed within 3 years after addition to the list. The profiles prepared under this paragraph shall be of those substances highest on the list of priorities under paragraph (2) for which profiles have not previously been prepared. Profiles required under this paragraph shall be revised and republished as necessary, but no less often than once every 3 years. Such profiles shall be provided to the States and made available to other interested parties.

(4) The Administrator of the ATSDR shall provide consultations upon request on health issues relating to exposure to hazardous or toxic substances, on the basis of available information, to the Administrator of EPA, State officials, and local officials. Such consultations to

individuals may be provided by States under cooperative agreements established under this Act.

(5)(A) For each hazardous substance listed pursuant to paragraph (2), the Administrator of ATSDR (in consultation with the Administrator of EPA and other agencies and programs of the Public Health Service) shall assess whether adequate information on the health effects of such substance is available. For any such substance for which adequate information is not available (or under development), the Administrator of ATSDR, in cooperation with the Director of the National Toxicology Program, shall assure the initiation of a program of research designed to determine the health effects (and techniques for development of methods to determine such health effects) of such substance. Where feasible, such program shall seek to develop methods to determine the health effects of such substance in combination with other substances with which it is commonly found. Before assuring the initiation of such program, the Administrator of ATSDR shall consider recommendations of the Interagency Testing Committee established under section 4(e) of the Toxic Substances Control Act on the types of research that should be done. Such program shall include, to the extent necessary to supplement existing information, but shall not be limited to—

  (i) laboratory and other studies to determine short, intermediate, and long-term health effects;

  (ii) laboratory and other studies to determine organ-specific, site-specific, and system-specific acute and chronic toxicity;

  (iii) laboratory and other studies to determine the manner in which such substances are metabolized or to otherwise develop an understanding of the biokinetics of such substances; and

  (iv) where there is a possibility of obtaining human data, the collection of such information.

(B) In assessing the need to perform laboratory and other studies, as required by subparagraph (A), the Administrator of ATSDR shall consider—

  (i) the availability and quality of existing test data concerning the substance on the suspected health effect in question;

  (ii) the extent to which testing already in progress will, in a timely fashion, provide data that will be adequate to support the preparation of toxicological profiles as required by paragraph (3); and

  (iii) such other scientific and technical factors as the Administrator of ATSDR may determine are necessary for the effective implementation of this subsection.

(C) In the development and implementation of any research program under this paragraph, the Administrator of ATSDR and the Administrator of EPA shall coordinate such research program implemented under this paragraph with the National Toxicology Program and with programs of toxicological testing established under the Toxic Substances Control Act and the Federal Insecticide, Fungicide and Rodenticide Act. The purpose of such coordination shall be to avoid duplication of effort and to assure that the hazardous substances listed pursuant to this subsection are tested thoroughly at the earliest practicable date. Where appropriate, consistent with such purpose, a research program under this paragraph may be carried out using such programs of toxicological testing.

(D) It is the sense of the Congress that the costs of research programs under this paragraph be borne by the manufacturers and processors of the hazardous substance in question, as required in programs of toxicological testing under the Toxic Substances Control Act. Within 1 year after the enactment of the Superfund Amendments and Reauthorization Act of 1986, the Administrator of EPA shall promulgate regulations which provide, where appropriate, for payment of such costs by manufacturers and processors under the Toxic Substances Control Act, and registrants under the Federal Insecticide, Fungicide, and Rodenticide Act, and recovery of such costs from responsible parties under this Act.

(6)(A) The Administrator of ATSDR shall perform a health assessment for each facility on the National Priorities List established under section 105. Such health assessment shall be completed not later than December 10, 1988, for each facility proposed for inclusion on such list prior to the date of the enactment of the Superfund Amendments and Reauthorization Act of 1986 or not later than one year after the date of proposal for inclusion on such list for each facility proposed for inclusion on such list after such date of enactment.

(B) The Administrator of ATSDR may perform health assessments for releases or facilities where individual persons or licensed physicians provide information that individuals have been exposed to a hazardous substance, for which the probable source of such exposure is a release. In addition to other methods (formal or informal) of providing such information, such individual persons or licensed physicians may submit a petition to the Administrator of ATSDR providing such information and requesting a health assessment. If such a petition is submitted and the Administrator of ATSDR does not initiate a health assessment, the Administrator of ATSDR shall provide a written explanation of why a health assessment is not appropriate.

(C) In determining the priority in which to conduct health assessments under this subsection, the Administrator of ATSDR, in consultation with the Administrator of EPA, shall give priority to those facilities at which there is documented evidence of the release of hazardous substances, at which the potential risk to human health appears highest, and for which in the judgment of the Administrator of ATSDR existing health assessment data are inadequate to assess the potential risk to human health as provided in subparagraph (F). In determining the priorities for conducting health assessments under this subsection, the Administrator of ATSDR shall consider the National Priorities List schedules and the needs of the Environmental Protection Agency and other Federal agencies pursuant to schedules for remedial investigation and feasibility studies.

(D) Where a health assessment is done at a site on the National Priorities List, the Administrator of ATSDR shall complete such assessment promptly and, to the maximum extent practicable, before the completion of the remedial investigation and feasibility study at the facility concerned.

(E) Any State or political subdivision carrying out a health assessment for a facility shall report the results of the assessment to the Administrator of ATSDR and the Administrator of EPA and shall include recommendations with respect to further activities which need to be carried out under this section. The Administrator of ATSDR shall state such recommendation in any report on the results of any assessment carried out directly by the Administrator of ATSDR for such facility and shall issue periodic reports which include the results of all the assessments carried out under this subsection.

(F) For the purposes of this subsection and section 111(c)(4), the term "health assessments" shall include preliminary assessments of the potential risk to human health posed by individual sites and facilities, based on such factors as the nature and extent of contamination, the existence of potential pathways of human exposure (including ground or surface water contamination, air emissions, and food chain contamination), the size and potential susceptibility of the community within the likely pathways of exposure, the comparison of expected human exposure levels to the short-term and long-term health effects associated with identified hazardous substances and any available recommended exposure or tolerance limits for such hazardous substances, and the comparison of existing morbidity and mortality data on diseases that may be associated with the observed levels of exposure. The Administrator of ATSDR shall use appropriate data, risk assessments, risk evaluations and studies available from the Administrator of EPA.

(G) The purpose of health assessments under this subsection shall be to assist in determining whether actions under paragraph (11) of this subsection should be taken to reduce human exposure to hazardous substances from a facility and whether additional information on human exposure and associated health risks is needed and should be acquired by conducting epidemiological studies under paragraph (7), establishing a registry under paragraph (8), establishing a health surveillance program under paragraph (9), or through other means. In using the results of health assessments for determining additional actions to be taken under this section, the Administrator of ATSDR may consider additional information on the risks to the potentially affected population from all sources of such hazardous substances including known point or nonpoint sources other than those from the facility in question.

(H) At the completion of each health assessment, the Administrator of ATSDR shall provide the Administrator of EPA and each affected State with the results of such assessment, together with any recommendations for further actions under this subsection or otherwise under this Act. In addition, if the health assessment indicates that the release or threatened release concerned may pose a serious threat to human health or the environment, the Administrator of ATSDR shall so notify the Administrator of EPA who shall promptly evaluate such release or threatened release in accordance with the hazard ranking system referred to in section 105(a)(8)(A) to determine whether the site shall be placed on the National Priorities List or, if the site is already on the list, the Administrator of ATSDR may recommend to the Administrator of EPA that the site be accorded a higher priority.

(7)(A) Whenever in the judgment of the Administrator of ATSDR it is appropriate on the basis of the results of a health assessment, the Administrator of ATSDR shall conduct a pilot study of health effects for selected groups of exposed individuals in order to determine the desirability of conducting full scale epidemiological or other health studies of the entire exposed population.

(B) Whenever in the judgment of the Administrator of ATSDR it is appropriate on the basis of the results of such pilot study or other study or health assessment, the Administrator of ATSDR shall conduct such full scale epidemiological or other health studies as may be necessary to determine the health effects on the population exposed to hazardous substances from a release or threatened release. If a significant excess of disease in a population is identified, the letter of transmittal of such study shall include an assessment of other risk factors, other than a release, that may, in the judgment of the peer review group, be associated with such disease, if such risk factors were not taken into account in the design or conduct of the study.

(8) In any case in which the results of a health assessment indicate a potential significant risk to human health, the Administrator of ATSDR shall consider whether the establishment of a registry of exposed persons would contribute to accomplishing the purposes of this subsection, taking into account circumstances bearing on the usefulness of such a registry, including the seriousness or unique character of identified diseases or the likelihood of population migration from the affected area.

(9) Where the Administrator of ATSDR has determined that there is a significant increased risk of adverse health effects in humans from exposure to hazardous substances based on the results of a health assessment conducted under paragraph (6), an epidemiologic study conducted under paragraph (7), or an exposure registry that has been established under paragraph (8), and the Administrator of ATSDR has determined that such exposure is the result of a release from a facility, the Administrator of ATSDR shall initiate a health surveillance program for such population. This program shall include but not be limited to—

(A) periodic medical testing where appropriate of population subgroups to screen for diseases for which the population or subgroup is at significant increased risk; and

(B) a mechanism to refer for treatment those individuals within such population who are screened positive for such diseases.

(10) Two years after the date of the enactment of the Superfund Amendments and Reauthorization Act of 1986, and every 2 years thereafter, the Administrator of ATSDR shall prepare and submit to the Administrator of EPA and to the Congress a report on the results of the activities of ATSDR regarding—

(A) health assessments and pilot health effects studies conducted;

(B) epidemiologic studies conducted;

(C) hazardous substances which have been listed under paragraph (2), toxicological profiles which have been developed, and toxicologic testing which has been conducted or which is being conducted under this subsection;

(D) registries established under paragraph (8); and

(E) an overall assessment, based on the results of activities conducted by the Administrator of ATSDR, of the linkage between human exposure to individual or combinations of hazardous substances due to releases from facilities covered by this Act or the Solid Waste Disposal Act and any increased incidence or prevalence of adverse health effects in humans.

(11) If a health assessment or other study carried out under this subsection contains a finding that the exposure concerned presents a significant risk to human health, the President shall take such steps as may be necessary to reduce such exposure and eliminate or substantially

mitigate the significant risk to human health. Such steps may include the use of any authority under this Act, including, but not limited to—

(A) provision of alternative water supplies, and

(B) permanent or temporary relocation of individuals.

In any case in which information is insufficient, in the judgment of the Administrator of ATSDR or the President to determine a significant human exposure level with respect to a hazardous substance, the President may take such steps as may be necessary to reduce the exposure of any person to such hazardous substance to such level as the President deems necessary to protect human health.

(12) In any case which is the subject of a petition, a health assessment or study, or a research program under this subsection, nothing in this subsection shall be construed to delay or otherwise affect or impair the authority of the President, the Administrator of ATSDR, or the Administrator of EPA to exercise any authority vested in the President, the Administrator of ATSDR or the Administrator of EPA under any other provision of law (including, but not limited to, the imminent hazard authority of section 7003 of the Solid Waste Disposal Act) or the response and abatement authorities of this Act.

(13) All studies and results of research conducted under this subsection (other than health assessments) shall be reported or adopted only after appropriate peer review. Such peer review shall be completed, to the maximum extent practicable, within a period of 60 days. In the case of research conducted under the National Toxicology Program, such peer review may be conducted by the Board of Scientific Counselors. In the case of other research, such peer review shall be conducted by panels consisting of no less than three nor more than seven members, who shall be disinterested scientific experts selected for such purpose by the Administrator of ATSDR or the Administrator of EPA, as appropriate, on the basis of their reputation for scientific objectivity and the lack of institutional ties with any person involved in the conduct of the study or research under review. Support services for such panels shall be provided by the Agency for Toxic Substances and Disease Registry, or by the Environmental Protection Agency, as appropriate.

(14) In the implementation of this subsection and other health-related authorities of this Act, the Administrator of ATSDR shall assemble, develop as necessary, and distribute to the States, and upon request to medical colleges, physicians, and other health professionals, appropriate educational materials (including short courses) on the medical surveillance, screening, and methods of diagnosis and treatment of injury or disease related to exposure to hazardous substances (giving priority to those listed in paragraph (2)), through such means as the Administrator of ATSDR deems appropriate.

(15) The activities of the Administrator of ATSDR described in this

subsection and section 111(c)(4) shall be carried out by the Administrator of ATSDR, either directly or through cooperative agreements with States (or political subdivisions thereof) which the Administrator of ATSDR determines are capable of carrying out such activities. Such activities shall include provision of consultations on health information, the conduct of health assessments, including those required under section 3019(b) of the Solid Waste Disposal Act, health studies, registries, and health surveillance.

(16) The President shall provide adequate personnel for ATSDR, which shall not be fewer than 100 employees. For purposes of determining the number of employees under this subsection, an employee employed by ATSDR on a part-time career employment basis shall be counted as a fraction which is determined by dividing 40 hours into the average number of hours of such employee's regularly scheduled workweek.

(17) In accordance with section 120 (relating to Federal facilities), the Administrator of ATSDR shall have the same authorities under this section with respect to facilities owned or operated by a department, agency, or instrumentality of the United States as the Administrator of ATSDR has with respect to any nongovernmental entity.

(18) If the Administrator of ATSDR determines that it is appropriate for purposes of this section to treat a pollutant or contaminant as a hazardous substance, such pollutant or contaminant shall be treated as a hazardous substance for such purpose.

(j)(1) The President is authorized to acquire, by purchase, lease, condemnation, donation, or otherwise, any real property or any interest in real property that the President in his discretion determines is needed to conduct a remedial action under this Act. There shall be no cause of action to compel the President to acquire any interest in real property under this Act.

(2) The President may use the authority of paragraph (1) for a remedial action only if, before an interest in real estate is acquired under this subsection, the State in which the interest to be acquired is located assures the President, through a contract or cooperative agreement or otherwise, that the State will accept transfer of the interest following completion of the remedial action.

(3) No Federal, State, or local government agency shall be liable under this Act solely as a result of acquiring an interest in real estate under this subsection.

§ 9605. National contingency plans; preparation, contents, etc.

[Sec. 105] (a) Within one hundred and eighty days after the enactment of this Act, the President shall, after notice and opportunity for public comments, revise and republish the national contingency plan for the removal of oil and hazardous substances, originally prepared and published pursuant to section 311 of the Federal Water Pollution Control Act, to reflect and effectuate the responsibilities and powers created by this Act, in addition to those matters specified in section 311(c)(2). Such revision shall include a section of the plan to be known as the national hazardous substance response plan which shall establish procedures and standards for responding to releases of hazardous substances, pollutants, and contaminants, which shall include at a minimum:

(1) methods for discovering and investigating facilities at which hazardous substances have been disposed of or otherwise come to be located;

(2) methods for evaluating, including analyses of relative cost, and remedying any releases or threats of releases from facilities which pose substantial danger to the public health or the environment;

(3) methods and criteria for determining the appropriate extent of removal, remedy, and other measures authorized by this Act;

(4) appropriate roles and responsibilites for the Federal, State, and local governments and for interstate and nongovernmental entities in effectuating the plan;

(5) provision for identification, procurement, maintenance, and storage of response equipment and supplies;

(6) a method for and assignment of responsibility for reporting the existence of such facilities which may be located on federally owned or controlled properties and any releases of hazardous substances from such facilities;

(7) means of assuring that remedial action measures are cost-effective over the period of potential exposure to the hazardous substances or contaminated materials;

(8)(A) criteria for determining priorities among releases or threatened releases throughout the United States for the purpose of taking remedial action and, to the extent practicable taking into account the potential urgency of such action, for the purpose of taking removal action. Criteria and priorities under this paragraph shall be based upon relative risk or danger to public health or welfare or the environment, in the judgment of the President, taking into account to the extent possible the population at risk, the hazard potential of the hazardous substances at such facilities, the potential for contamination of drinking water supplies, the potential for direct human contact, the damage to natural resources which may affect the human food chain and which is associated with any release or threatened release, the contamination or potential contamination of the ambient air which is associated with the release or threatened release, State preparedness to assume State costs and responsibilities, and other appropriate factors;

(B) based upon the criteria set forth in subparagraph (A) of this paragraph, the President shall list as part of the plan national priorities among the known releases or threatened releases throughout the United States and shall revise the list no less often than annually. Within one year after the date of enactment of this Act, and annually thereafter, each State shall establish and submit for consideration by the President priorities for remedial action among known releases and potential releases in that State based upon the criteria set forth in subparagraph (A) of this paragraph. In assembling or revising the national list, the President shall consider any priorities established by the States. To the extent practicable, the highest priority facilities shall be designated individually and shall be referred to as the "top priority among known response targets", and, to the extent practicable, shall include among the one hundred highest priority facilities one such facility from each State which shall be the facility designated by the State as presenting the greatest danger to public health or welfare or the environment among the known facilities in such State. A State shall be allowed to designate its highest priority facility only once. Other priority facilities or incidents may be listed singly or grouped for response priority purposes;

(9) specified roles for private organizations and entities in preparation for response and in responding to releases of hazardous substances, including identification of appropriate qualifications and capacity therefor and including consideration of minority firms in accordance with subsection (f); and

(10) standards and testing procedures by which alternative or innovative treatment technologies can be determined to be appropriate for utilization in response actions authorized by this Act.

The plan shall specify procedures, techniques, materials, equipment, and methods to be employed in identifying, removing, or remedying releases of hazarodus substances comparable to those required under section 311(c)(2) (F) and (G) and (j)(1) of the Federal Water Pollution Control Act. Following publication of the revised national contingency plan, the response to and actions to minimize damage from hazardous substances releases shall, to the greatest extent possible, be in accordance with the provisions of the plan. The President may, from time to time, revise and republish the national contingency plan.

(b) Not later than 18 months after the enactment of the Superfund Amendments and Reauthorization Act of 1986, the President shall revise the National Contingency Plan to reflect the requirements of such amendments. The portion of such Plan known as "the National Hazardous Substance Response Plan" shall be revised to provide procedures and standards for remedial actions undertaken pursuant to this Act which are consistent with amendments made by the Superfund Amendments and Reauthorization Act of 1986 relating to the selection of remedial action.

(c)(1) Not later than 18 months after the enactment of the Superfund Amendments and Reauthorization Act of 1986 and after publication of notice and opportunity for submission of comments in accordance with section 553 of title 5, United States Code, the President shall by rule promulgate amendments to the hazard ranking system in effect on September 1, 1984. Such amendments shall assure, to the maximum extent feasible, that the hazard ranking system accurately assesses the relative degree of risk to human health and the environment posed by sites and facilities subject to review. The President shall establish an effective date for the amended hazard ranking system which is not later than 24 months after enactment of the Superfund Amendments and Reauthorization Act of 1986. Such amended hazard ranking system shall be applied to any site or facility to be newly listed on the National Priorities List after the effective date established by the President. Until such effective date of the regulations, the hazard ranking system in effect on September 1, 1984, shall continue in full force and effect.

(2) In carrying out this subsection, the President shall ensure that the human health risks associated with the contamination or potential contamination (either directly or as a result of the runoff of any hazardous substance or pollutant or contaminant from sites or facilities) of surface water are appropriately assessed where such surface water is, or can be, used for recreation or potable water consumption. In making the assessment required pursuant to the preceding sentence, the President shall take into account the potential migration of any hazardous substance or pollutant or contaminant through such surface water to downstream sources of drinking water.

(3) The President shall not be required to reevaluate, after the date of the enactment of the Superfund Amendments and Reauthorization Act of 1986, the hazard ranking of any facility which was evaluated in accordance with the criteria under this section before the effective date of the amendments to the hazard ranking system under this subsection and which was assigned a national priority under the National Contingency Plan.

(4) Nothing in paragraph (3) shall preclude the President from taking new information into account in undertaking response actions under this Act.

(d) Any person who is, or may be, affected by a release or threatened release of a hazardous substance or pollutant or contaminant, may petition the President to conduct a preliminary assessment of the hazards to public health and the environment which are associated with such release or threatened release. If the President has not previously conducted a preliminary assessment of such release, the President shall, within 12 months after the receipt of any such petition, complete such assessment or provide an explanation of why the assessment is not appropriate. If the preliminary assessment indicates that the release or threatened release concerned may pose a threat to human health or the environment, the President shall promptly evaluate such release or threatened release in accordance with the hazard ranking system referred to in paragraph (8)(A) of subsection (a) to determine the national priority of such release or threatened release.

(e) Whenever there has been, after January 1, 1985, a significant release of hazardous substances or pollutants or contaminants from a site which is listed by the President as a "Site Cleaned Up To Date" on the National Priorities List (revised edition, December 1984) the site shall be restored to the National Priorities List, without application of the hazard ranking system.

(f) In awarding contracts under this Act, the President shall consider the availability of qualified minority firms. The President shall describe, as part of any annual report submitted to the Congress under this Act, the participation of minority firms in contracts carried out under this Act. Such report shall contain a brief description of the contracts which have been awarded to minority firms under this Act and of the efforts made by the President to encourage the participation of such firms in programs carried out under this Act.

(g)(1) This subsection applies to facilities—
   (A) which as of the date of enactment of the Superfund Amendments and Reauthorization Act of 1986 were not included on, or proposed for inclusion on, the National Priorities List; and
   (B) at which special study wastes described in paragraph (2), (3)(A)(ii) or (3)(A)(iii) of section 3001(b) of the Solid Waste Disposal Act are present in significant quantities, including any such facility from which there has been a release of a special study waste.
(2) Pending revision of the hazard ranking system under subsection (c), the President shall consider each of the following factors in adding facilities covered by this section to the National Priorities List:
   (A) The extent to which hazard ranking system score for the facility is affected by the presence of any special study waste at, or any release from, such facility.
   (B) Available information as to the quantity, toxicity, and concentration of hazardous substances that are constituents of any special study waste at, or released from such facility, the extent of or potential for release of such hazardous constituents, the exposure or potential exposure to human population and the environment, and the degree of hazard to human health or the environment posed by the release of such hazardous constituents at such facility. This subparagraph refers only to available information on actual concentrations of hazardous substances and not on the total quantity of special study waste at such facility.
(3) Nothing in this subsection shall be construed to limit the authority of the President to remove any facility which as of the date of enactment of the Superfund Amendments and Reauthorization Act of 1986 is included on the National Priorities List from such List, or not to list any facility which as of such date is proposed for inclusion on such list.
(4) Nothing in this Act shall be construed to preclude the expenditure of

monies from the Fund for gathering and analysis of information which will enable the President to consider the specific factors required by paragraph (2).

§ 9606. Abatement action

[Sec. 106] (a) In addition to any other action taken by a State or local government, when the President determines that there may be an imminent and substantial endangerment to the public health or welfare or the environment because of an actual or threatened release of a hazardous substance from a facility, he may require the Attorney General of the United States to secure such relief as may be necessary to abate such danger or threat, and the district court of the United States in the district in which the threat occurs shall have jurisdiction to grant such relief as the public interest and the equities of the case may require. The President may also, after notice to the affected State, take other action under this section including, but not limited to, issuing such orders as may be necessary to protect public health and welfare and the environment.

(b)(1) Any person who, without sufficient cause, willfully violates, or fails or refuses to comply with, any order of the President under subsection (a) may, in an action brought in the appropriate United States district court to enforce such order, be fined not more than $25,000 for each day in which such violation occurs or such failure to comply continues.

(2)(A) Any person who receives and complies with the terms of any order issued under subsection (a) may, within 60 days after completion of the required action, petition the President for reimbursement from the Fund for the reasonable costs of such action, plus interest. Any interest payable under this paragraph shall accrue on the amounts expended from the date of expenditure at the same rate as specified for interest on investments of the Hazardous Substance Superfund established under subchapter A of chapter 98 of the Internal Revenue Code of 1954.

(B) If the President refuses to grant all or part of a petition made under this paragraph, the petitioner may within 30 days of receipt of such refusal file an action against the President in the appropriate United States district court seeking reimbursement from the Fund.

(C) Except as provided in subparagraph (D), to obtain reimbursement, the petitioner shall establish by a preponderance of the evidence that it is not liable for response costs under section 107(a) and that costs for which it seeks reimbursement are reasonable in light of the action required by the relevant order.

(D) A petitioner who is liable for response costs under section 107(a) may also recover its reasonable costs of response to the extent that it can demonstrate, on the administrative record, that the President's decision in selecting the response action ordered was arbitrary and capricious or was otherwise not in accordance with law. Reimbursement awarded under this subparagraph shall include all reasonable response costs incurred by the petitioner pursuant to the portions of the order found to be arbitrary and capricious or otherwise not in accordance with law.

(E) Reimbursement awarded by a court under subparagraph (C) or (D) may include appropriate costs, fees, and other expenses in accordance with subsections (a) and (d) of section 2412 of title 28 of the United States Code.

(c) Within one hundred and eighty days after enactment of this Act, the Administrator of the Environmental Protection Agency shall, after consultation with the Attorney General, establish and publish guidelines for using the imminent hazard, enforcement, and emergency response authorities of this section and other existing statutes administered by the Administrator of the Environmental Protection Agency to effectuate the responsibilities and powers created by this Act. Such guidelines shall to the extent practicable be consistent with the national hazardous substance response plan, and shall include, at a minimum, the assignment of responsibility for coordinating response actions with this issuance of administrative orders, enforcement of standards and permits, the gathering of information, and other imminent hazard and emergency powers authorized by (1) sections 311(c)(2), 308, 309, and 504(a) of the Federal Water Pollution Control Act, (2) sections 3007, 3008, 3013, and 7003 of the Solid Waste Disposal Act, (3) sections 1445 and 1431 of the Safe Drinking Water Act, (4) sections 113, 114, and 303 of the Clean Air Act, and (5) section 7 of the Toxic Substances Control Act.

§ 9607. Liability

[Sec. 107] (a) Notwithstanding any other provision or rule of law, and subject only to the defenses set forth in subsection (b) of this section—

(1) the owner and operator of a vessel or a facility,

(2) any person who at the time of disposal of any hazardous substance owned or operated any facility at which such hazardous substances were disposed of,

(3) any person who by contract, agreement, or otherwise arranged for disposal or treatment, or arranged with a transporter for transport for disposal or treatment, of hazardous substances owned or possessed by such person, by any other party or entity, at any facility or incineration vessel owned or operated by another party or entity and containing such hazardous substances, and

(4) any person who accepts or accepted any hazardous substances for transport to disposal or treatment facilities, incineration vessels or sites

selected by such person, from which there is a release, or a threatened release which causes the incurrence of response costs, of a hazardous substance, shall be liable for—

(A) all costs of removal or remedial action incurred by the United States Government or a State or an Indian tribe not inconsistent with the national contingency plan;

(B) any other necessary costs of response incurred by any other person consistent with the national contingency plan;

(C) damages for injury to, destruction of, or loss of natural resources, including the reasonable costs of assessing such injury, destruction, or loss resulting from such a release; and

(D) the costs of any health assessment or health effects study carried out under section 104(i).

The amounts recoverable in an action under this section shall include interest on the amounts recoverable under subparagraphs (A) through (D). Such interest shall accrue from the later of (i) the date payment of a specified amount is demanded in writing, or (ii) the date of the expenditure concerned. The rate of interest on the outstanding unpaid balance of the amounts recoverable under this section shall be the same rate as is specified for interest on investments of the Hazardous Substance Superfund established under subchapter A of chapter 98 of the Internal Revenue Code of 1954. For purposes of applying such amendments to interest under this subsection, the term "comparable maturity" shall be determined with reference to the date on which interest accruing under this subsection commences.

(b) There shall be no liability under subsection (a) of this section a person otherwise liable who can establish by a preponderance of the evidence that the release or threat of release of a hazardous substance and the damages resulting therefrom were caused solely by—

(1) an act of God;

(2) an act of war;

(3) an act or omission of a third party other than an employee or agent of the defendant, or than one whose act or omission occurs in connection with a contractual relationship, existing directly or indirectly, with the defendant (except where the sole contractual arrangement arises from a published tariff and acceptance for carriage by a common carrier by rail), if the defendant establishes by a preponderance of the evidence that (a) he exercised due care with respect to the hazardous substance concerned, taking into consideration the characteristics of such hazardous substance, in light of all relevant facts and circumstances, and (b) he took precautions against foreseeable acts or omissions of any such third party and the consequences that could foreseeably result from such acts or omissions; or

(4) any combination of the foregoing paragraphs.

(c)(1) Except as provided in paragraph (2) of this subsection, the liability under this section of an owner or operator or other responsible person or each release of a hazardous substance or incident involving release of hazardous substance shall not exceed—

    (A) for any vessel, other than an incineration vessel, which carries any hazardous substance as cargo or residue, $300 per gross ton, or $5,000,000, whichever is greater;

    (B) for any other vessel, other than an incineration vessel, $300 per gross ton, or $500,000, whichever is greater;

    (C) for any motor vehicle, aircraft, pipeline (as defined in the Hazardous Liquid Pipeline Safety Act of 1979), or rolling stock, $50,000,000 or such lesser amount as the President shall establish by regulation, but in no event less than $5,000,000 (or, for releases of hazardous substances as defined in section 101(14)(A) of this title into the navigable waters, $8,000,000). Such regulations shall take into account the size, type, location, storage, and handling capacity and other matters relating to the likelihood of release in each such class and to the economic impact of such limits on each such class; or

    (D) for any incineration vessel or any facility other than those specified in subparagraph (C) of this paragraph, the total of all costs of response plus $50,000,000 for any damages under this title.

  (2) Notwithstanding the limitations in paragraph (1) of this subsection, the liability of an owner or operator or other responsible person under this section shall be the full and total costs of response and damages, if (A)(i) the release or threat of release of a hazardous substance was the result of willful misconduct or willful negligence within the privity or knowledge of such person, or (ii) the primary cause of the release was a violation (within the privity or knowledge of such person) of applicable safety, construction, or operating standards or regulations; or (B) such person fails or refuses to provide all reasonable cooperation and assistance requested by a responsible public official in connection with response activities under the national contingency plan with respect to regulated carriers subject to the provisions of title 49 of the United States Code or vessels subject to the provisions of title 33 or 46 of the United States Code, subparagraph (A)(ii) of this paragraph shall be deemed to refer to Federal standards or regulations.

  (3) If any person who is liable for a release or threat of release of a hazardous substance fails without sufficient cause to properly provide removal or remedial action upon order to the President pursuant to section 104 or 106 of this Act, such person may be liable to the United States for punitive damages in an amount at least equal to, and not more than three times, the amount of any costs incurred by the Fund as a result of such failure to take proper action. The President is

authorized to commence a civil action against any such person to recover the punitive damages, which shall be in addition to any costs recovered from such person pursuant to section 112(c) of this Act. Any moneys received by the United States pursuant to this subsection shall be deposited in the Fund.

(d)(1) Except as provided in paragraph (2), no person shall be liable under this title for costs or damages as a result of actions taken or omitted in the course of rendering care, assistance, or advice in accordance with the National Contingency Plan ("NCP") or at the direction of an onscene coordinator appointed under such plan, with respect to an incident creating a danger to public health or welfare or the environment as a result of any releases of a hazardous substance or the threat thereof. This paragraph shall not preclude liability for costs or damages as the result of negligence on the part of such person.

(2) No State or local government shall be liable under this title for costs or damages as a result of actions taken in response to an emergency created by the release or threatened release of a hazardous substance generated by or from a facility owned by another person. This paragraph shall not preclude liability for costs or damages as a result of gross negligence or intentional misconduct by the State or local government. For the purpose of the preceding sentence, reckless, willful, or wanton misconduct shall constitute gross negligence.

(3) This subsection shall not alter the liability of any person covered by the provisions of paragraph (1), (2), (3), or (4) of subsection (a) of this section with respect to the release or threatened release concerned.

(e)(1) No indemnification, hold harmless, or similar agreement or conveyance shall be effective to transfer from the owner or operator of any vessel or facility or from any person who may be liable for a release or threat of release under this section, to any other person the liability imposed under this section. Nothing in this subsection shall bar any agreement to insure, hold harmless, or indemnify a party to such agreement for any liability under this section.

(2) Nothing in this title, including the provisions of paragraph (1) of this subsection, shall bar a cause of action that an owner or operator or any other person subject to liability under this section, or a guarantor, has or would have, by reason of subrogation or otherwise against any person.

(f)(1) In the case of an injury to, destruction of, or loss of natural resources under subparagraph (C) of subsection (a) liability shall be to the United States Government and to any State for natural resources within the State or belonging to, managed by, controlled by, or appertaining to such State and to any Indian tribe for natural resources belonging to, managed by, controlled by, or appertaining to such tribe, or held in trust for the benefit of such tribe, or belonging to a member of such tribe if such resources are subject to a trust restriction on alienation: *Provided, however,* That no liability to the United

States or State or Indian tribe shall be imposed under subparagraph (C) of subsection (a), where the party sought to be charged has demonstrated that the damages to natural resources complained of were specifically identified as an irreversible and irretrievable commitment of natural resources in an environmental impact statement, or other comparable environment analysis, and the decision to grant a permit or license authorizes such commitment of natural resources, and the facility or project was otherwise operating within the terms of its permit or license, so long as, in the case of damages to an Indian tribe occurring pursuant to a Federal permit or license, the issuance of that permit or license was not inconsistent with the fiduciary duty of the United States with respect to such Indian tribe. The President, or the authorized representative of any State, shall act on behalf of the public as trustee of such natural resources to recover for such damages. Sums recovered by the United States Government as trustee under this subsection shall be retained by the trustee, without further appropriation, for use only to restore, replace, or acquire the equivalent of such natural resources. Sums recovered by a State as trustee under this subsection shall be available for use only to restore, replace, or acquire the equivalent of such natural resources by the State. The measure of damages in any action under subparagraph (C) of subsection (a) shall not be limited by the sums which can be used to restore or replace such resources. There shall be no double recovery under this Act for natural resource damages, including the costs of damage assessment or restoration, rehabilitation, under acquisition for the same release and natural resource. There shall be no recovery under the authority of subparagraph (C) of subsection (a) where such damages and the release of a hazardous substance from which such damages have resulted have occurred wholly before the enactment of this Act.

(2)(A) The President shall designate in the National Contingency Plan published under section 105 of this Act the Federal officials who shall act on behalf of the public as trustees for natural resources under this Act and section 311 of the Federal Water Pollution Control Act. Such officials shall assess damages for injury to, destruction of, or loss of natural resources for purposes of this Act and such section 311 for those resources under their trusteeship and may, upon request of and reimbursement from a State and at the Federal officials' discretion, assess damages for those natural resources under the State's trusteeship.

(B) The Governor of each State shall designate State officials who may act on behalf of the public as trustees for natural resources under this Act and section 311 of the Federal Water Pollution Control Act and shall notify the President of such designations. Such State officials shall assess damages to natural resources for the purposes of this Act and such section 311 for those natural resources under their trusteeship.

(C) Any determination or assessment of damages to natural resources for the purposes of this Act and section 311 of the Federal Water Pollution Control Act made by a Federal or State trustee in accordance with the regulations promulgated under section 301(c) of this Act shall have the force and effect of a rebuttable presumption on behalf of the trustee in any administrative or judicial proceeding under this Act or section 311 of the Federal Water Pollution Control Act.

(g) For provisions relating to Federal agencies, see section 120 of this Act.

(h) The owner or operator of a vessel shall be liable in accordance with this section under maritime tort law and as provided under section 114 of this Act notwithstanding any provision of the Act of March 3, 1851 (46 U.S.C. 183ff) or the absense of any physical damage to the proprietary interest of the claimant.

(i) No person (including the United States or any State or Indian tribe) may recover under the authority of this section for any response cost or damages resulting from the application of a pesticide product registered under the Federal Insecticide, Fungicide, and Rodenticide Act. Nothing in this paragraph shall affect or modify in any way the obligations or liability of any person under any other provision of State or Federal law, including common law, for damages, injury, or loss resulting from a release of any hazardous substance or for removal or remedial action or the costs of removal or remedial action of such hazardous substance.

(j) Recovery by any person (including the United States or any State or Indian tribe) for response costs or damages resulting from a federally permitted release shall be pursuant to existing law in lieu of this section. Nothing in this paragraph shall affect or modify in any way the obligations or liability of any person under any other provision of State or Federal law, including common law, for damages, injury, or loss resulting from a release of any hazardous substance or for removal or remedial action or the costs of removal or remedial action of such hazardous substance.

(k)(1) The liability established by this section or any other law for the owner or operator of a hazardous waste disposal facility which has received a permit under subtitle C of the Solid Waste Disposal Act, shall be transferred to and assumed by the Post-closure Liability Fund established by section 232 of this Act when—

    (A) such facility and the owner and operator thereof has complied with the requirements of subtitle C of the Solid Waste Disposal Act and regulations issued thereunder, which may affect the performance of such facility after closure; and

    (B) such facility has been closed in accordance with such regulations and the conditions of such permit, and such facility and the surrounding area have been monitored as required by such regulations and permit conditions for a period not to exceed five years after closure to demonstrate that there is no substantial likelihood that any migration offsite or release from confinement of any hazardous substance or other risk to public health or welfare will occur.

(2) Such transfer of liability shall be effective ninety days after the owner or operator of such facility notifies the Administrator of the Environmental Protection Agency (and the State where it has an authorized program under section 3006(b) of the Solid Waste Disposal Act) that the conditions imposed by this subsection have been satisfied. If within such ninety-day period the Administrator of the Environmental Protection Agency or such State determines that any such facility has not complied with all the conditions imposed by this subsection or that insufficient information has been provided to demonstrate such compliance, the Administrator or such State shall so notify the owner and operator of such facility and the administrator of the Fund established by section 232 of this Act, and the owner and operator of such facility shall continue to be liable with respect to such facility under this section and other law until such time as the Administrator and such State determines that such facility has complied with all conditions imposed by this subsection. A determination by the Administrator or such State that a facility has not complied with all conditions imposed by this subsection or that insufficient information has been supplied to demonstrate compliance, shall be a final administrative action for purposes of judicial review. A request for additional information shall state in specific terms the data required.

(3) In addition to the assumption of liability of owners and operators under paragraph (1) of this subsection, the Post-closure Liability Fund established by section 232 of this Act may be used to pay costs of monitoring and care and maintenance of a site incurred by other persons after the period of monitoring required by regulations under subtitle C of the Solid Waste Disposal Act for hazardous waste disposal facilities meeting the conditions of paragraph (1) of this subsection.

(4)(A) Not later than one year after the date of enactment of this Act, the Secretary of the Treasury shall conduct a study and shall submit a report thereon to the Congress on the feasibility of establishing or qualifying an optional system of private insurance for postclosure financial responsibility for hazardous waste disposal facilities to which this subsection applies. Such study shall include a specification of adequate and realistic minimum standards to assure that any such privately placed insurance will carry out the purposes of this subsection in a reliable, enforceable, and practical manner. Such a study shall include an examination of the public and private incentives, programs, and actions necessary to make privately placed insurance a practical and effective option to the financing system for the Postclosure Liability Fund provided in title II of this Act.

(B) Not later than eighteen months after the date of enactment of this

Act and after a public hearing, the President shall by rule determine whether or not it is feasible to establish or qualify an optional system of private insurance for postclosure financial responsibility for hazardous waste disposal facilities to which this subsection applies. If the President determines the establishment or qualification of such a system would be infeasible, he shall promptly publish an explanation of the reasons for such a determination. If the President determines the establishment or qualification of such a system would be feasible, he shall promptly publish notice of such determination. Not later than six months after an affirmative determination under the preceding sentence and after a public hearing, the President shall by rule promulgate adequate and realistic minimum standards which must be met by any such privately placed insurance, taking into account the purposes of this Act and this subsection. Such rules shall also specify reasonably expeditious procedures by which privately placed insurance plans can qualify as meeting such minimum standards.

(C) In the event any privately placed insurance plan qualifies under subparagraph (B), any person enrolled in, and complying with the terms of, such plan shall be excluded from the provisions of paragraphs (1), (2), and (3) of this subsection and exempt from the requirements to pay any tax or fee to the Post-closure Liability Fund under title II of this Act.

(D) The President may issue such rules and take such other actions as are necessary to effectuate the purposes of this paragraph.

(5) Notwithstanding paragraphs (1), (2), (3), and (4) of this subsection and subsection (j) of section 111 of this Act, no liability shall be transferred to or assumed by the Post-Closure Liability Trust Fund established by section 232 of this Act prior to completion of the study required under paragraph (6) of this subsection, transmission of a report of such study to both Houses of Congress, and authorization of such a transfer or assumption by Act of Congress following receipt of such study and report.

(6)(A) The Comptroller General shall conduct a study of options for a program for the management of the liabilities associated with hazardous waste treatment, storage, and disposal sites after their closure which complements the policies set forth in the Hazardous and Solid Waste Amendments of 1984 and assures the protection of human health and the environment.

(B) The program referred to in subparagraph (A) shall be designed to assure each of the following:

    (i) Incentives are created and maintained for the safe management and disposal of hazardous wastes so as to assure protection of human health and the environment.

(ii) Members of the public will have reasonable confidence that hazardous wastes will be managed and disposed of safely and that resources will be available to address any problems that may arise and to cover costs of long-term monitoring, care, and maintenance of such sites.

(iii) Persons who are or seek to become owners and operators of hazardous waste disposal facilities will be able to manage their potential future liabilities and to attract the investment capital necessary to build, operate, and close such facilities in a manner which assures protection of human health and the environment.

(C) The study under this paragraph shall include assessments of treatment, storage, and disposal facilities which have been or are likely to be issued a permit under section 3005 of the Solid Waste Disposal Act and the likelihood of future insolvency on the part of owners and operators of such facilities. Separate assessments shall be made for different classes of facilities and for different classes of land disposal facilities and shall include but not be limited to—

(i) the current and future financial capabilities of facility owners and operators;

(ii) the current and future costs associated with facilities, including the costs of routine monitoring and maintenance, compliance monitoring, corrective action, natural resource damages, and liability for damages to third parties; and

(iii) the availability of mechanisms by which owners and operators of such facilities can assure that current and future costs, including post-closure costs, will be financed.

(D) In carrying out the responsibilities of this paragraph, the Comptroller General shall consult with the Administrator, the Secretary of Commerce, the Secretary of the Treasury, and the heads of other appropriate Federal agencies.

(E) In conducting the study under this paragraph, the Comptroller General shall consider various mechanisms and combinations of mechanisms to complement the policies set forth in the Hazardous and Solid Waste Amendments of 1984 to serve the purposes set forth in subparagraph (B) and to assure that the current and future costs associated with hazardous waste facilities, including post-closure costs, will be adequately financed and, to the greatest extent possible, borne by the owners and operators of such facilities. Mechanisms to be considered include, but are not limited to—

(i) revisions to closure, post-closure, and financial responsibility requirements under subtitles C and I of the Solid Waste Disposal Act;

(ii) voluntary risk pooling by owners and operators;

(iii) legislation to require risk pooling by owners and operators;

(iv) modification of the Post-Closure Liability Trust Fund previously established by section 232 of this Act, and the conditions for transfer of liability under this subsection, including limiting the transfer of some or all liability under this subsection only in the case of insolvency of owners and operators;

(v) private insurance;

(vi) insurance provided by the Federal Government;

(vii) coinsurance, reinsurance, or pooled-risk insurance, whether provided by the private sector or provided or assisted by the Federal Government; and

(viii) creation of a new program to be administered by a new or existing Federal agency or by a federally chartered corporation.

(F) The Comptroller General shall consider options for funding any program under this section and shall, to the extent necessary, make recommendations to the appropriate committees of Congress for additional authority to implement such program.

(l)(1) All costs and damages for which a person is liable to the United States under subsection (a) of this section (other than the owner or operator of a vessel under paragraph (1) of subsection (a)) shall constitute a lien in favor of the United States upon all real property and rights to such property which—

(A) belong to such person; and

(B) are subject to or affected by a removal or remedial action.

(2) The lien imposed by this subsection shall arise at the later of the following:

(A) The time costs are first incurred by the United States with respect to a response action under this Act.

(B) The time that the person referred to in paragraph (1) is provided (by certified or registered mail) written notice of potential liability.

Such lien shall continue until the liability for the costs (or a judgment against the person arising out of such liability) is satisfied or becomes unenforceable through operation of the statute of limitations provided in section 113.

(3) The lien imposed by this subsection shall be subject to the rights of any purchaser, holder of a security interest, or judgment lien creditor whose interest is perfected under applicable State law before notice of the lien has been filed in the appropriate office within the State (or county or other governmental subdivision), as designated by State law, in which the real property subject to the lien is located. Any such purchaser, holder of a security interest, or judgment lien creditor shall be afforded the same protections against the lien imposed by this subsection as are afforded under State law against a judgment lien

which arises out of an unsecured obligation and which arises as of the time of the filing of the notice of the lien imposed by this subsection. If the State has not by law designated one office for the receipt of such notices of liens, the notice shall be filed in the office of the clerk of the United States district court for the district in which the real property is located. For purposes of this subsection, the terms "purchaser" and "security interest" shall have the definitions provided under section 6323(h) of the Internal Revenue Code of 1954.

(4) The costs constituting the lien may be recovered in an action in rem in the United States district court for the district in which the removal or remedial action is occurring or has occurred. Nothing in this subsection shall affect the right of the United States to bring an action against any person to recover all costs and damages for which such person is liable under subsection (a) of this section.

(m) All costs and damages for which the owner or operator of a vessel is liable under subsection (a)(1) with respect to a release or threatened release from such vessel shall constitute a maritime lien in favor of the United States on such vessel. Such costs may be recovered in an action in rem in the district court of the United States for the district in which the vessel may be found. Nothing in this subsection shall affect the right of the United States to bring an action against the owner or operator of such vessel in any court of competent jurisdiction to recover such costs.

§ 9608. Financial responsibility

[Sec. 108] (a)(1) The owner or operator of each vessel (except a non-self-propelled barge that does not carry hazardous substances as cargo) over three hundred gross tons that uses any port or place in the United States or the navigable waters or any offshore facility, shall establish and maintain, in accordance with regulations promulgated by the President, evidence of financial responsibility of $300 per gross ton (or for a vessel carrying hazardous substance as cargo, or $5,000,000, whichever is greater to cover the liability prescribed under paragraph (1) of section 107(a) of this Act). Financial responsibility may be established by any one, or any combination, of the following: insurance, guarantee, surety bond, or qualification as a self-insurer. Any bond filed shall be issued by a bonding company authorized to do business in the United States. In cases where an owner or operator owns, operates, or charters more than one vessel subject to this subsection, evidence of financial responsibility need be established only to meet the maximum liability applicable to the largest of such vessels.

(2) The Secretary of the Treasury shall withhold or revoke the clearance required by section 4197 of the Revised Statutes of the United States of any vessel subject to this subsection that does not have certification furnished by the President that the financial responsibility provisions of paragraph (1) of this subsection have been complied with.

(3) The Secretary of Transportation, in accordance with regulations

issued by him, shall (A) deny entry to any port or place in the United States or navigable waters to, and (B) detain at the port or place in the United States from which it is about to depart for any other port or place in the United States, any vessel subject to this subsection that, upon request, does not produce certification furnished by the President that the financial responsibility provisions of paragraph (1) of this subsection have been complied with.

(4) In addition to the financial responsibility provisions of paragraph (1) of this subsection, the President shall require additional evidence of financial responsibility for incineration vessels in such amounts, and to cover such liabilities recognized by law, as the President deems appropriate, taking into account the potential risks posed by incineration and transport for incineration, and any other factors deemed relevant.

(b)(1) Beginning not earlier than five years after the date of enactment of this Act, the President shall promulgate requirements (for facilities in addition to those under subtitle C of the Solid Waste Disposal Act and other Federal law) that classes of facilities establish and maintain evidence of financial responsibility consistent with the degree and duration of risk associated with the production, transportation, treatment, storage, or disposal of hazardous substances. Not later than three years after the date of enactment of the Act, the President shall identify those classes for which requirements will be first developed and publish notice of such identification in the Federal Register. Priority in the development of such requirements shall be accorded to those classes of facilities, owners, and operators which the President determines present the highest level of risk of injury.

(2) The level of financial responsibility shall be initially established, and, when necessary, adjusted to protect against the level of risk which the President in his discretion believes is appropriate based on the payment experience of the Fund, commercial insurers, courts settlements and judgments, and voluntary claims satisfaction. To the maximum extent practicable, the President shall cooperate with and seek the advice of the commercial insurance industry in developing financial responsibility requirements. Financial responsibility may be established by any one, or any combination, of the following: insurance, guarantee, surety bond, letter of credit, or qualification as a self-insurer. In promulgating requirements under this section, the President is authorized to specify policy or other contractual terms, conditions, or defenses which are necessary, or which are unacceptable, in establishing such evidence of financial responsibility in order to effectuate the purposes of this Act.

(3) Regulations promulgated under this subsection shall incrementally impose financial responsibility requirements as quickly as can reasonably be achieved but in no event more than 4 years after the date of promulgation. Where possible, the level of financial responsi-

bility which the President believes appropriate as a final requirement shall be achieved through incremental, annual increases in the requirements.

(4) Where a facility is owned or operated by more than one person, evidence of financial responsibility covering the facility may be established and maintained by one of the owners or operators, or, in consolidated form, by or on behalf of two or more owners or operators. When evidence of financial responsibility is established in a consolidated form, the proportional share of each participant shall be shown. The evidence shall be accompanied by a statement authorizing the applicant to act for and in behalf of each participant in submitting and maintaining the evidence of financial responsibility.

(5) The requirements for evidence of financial responsibility for motor carriers covered by this Act shall be determined under section 30 of the Motor Carrier Act of 1980, Public Law 96–296.

(c)(1) In the case of a release or threatened release from a vessel, any claim authorized by section 107 or 111 may be asserted directly against any guarantor providing evidence of financial responsibility for such vessel under subsection (a). In defending such a claim, the guarantor may invoke all rights and defenses which would be available to the owner or operator under this title. The guarantor may also invoke the defense that the incident was caused by the willful misconduct of the owner or operator, but the guarantor may not invoke any other defense that the guarantor might have been entitled to invoke in a proceeding brought by the owner or operator against him.

(2) In the case of a release or threatened release from a facility, any claim authorized by section 107 or 111 may be asserted directly against any guarantor providing evidence of financial responsibility for such facility under subsection (b), if the person liable under section 107 is in bankruptcy, reorganization, or arrangement pursuant to the Federal Bankruptcy Code, or if, with reasonable diligence, jurisdiction in the Federal courts cannot be obtained over a person liable under section 107 who is likely to be solvent at the time of judgment. In the case of any action pursuant to this paragraph, the guarantor shall be entitled to invoke all rights and defenses which would have been available to the person liable under section 107 if any action had been brought against such person by the claimant and all rights and defenses which would have been available to the guarantor if an action had been brought against the guarantor by such person.

(d)(1) The total liability of any guarantor in a direct action suit brought under this section shall be limited to the aggregate amount of the monetary limits of the policy of insurance, guarantee, surety bond, letter of credit, or similar instrument obtained from the guarantor by the person subject to liability under section 107 for the purpose of satisfying the requirement for evidence of financial responsibility.

(2) Nothing in this subsection shall be construed to limit any other State or Federal statutory, contractual, or common law liability of a guarantor, including, but not limited to, the liability of such guarantor for bad faith either in negotiating or in failing to negotiate the settlement of any claim. Nothing in this subsection shall be construed, interpreted, or applied to diminish the liability of any person under section 107 of this Act or other applicable law.

§ 9609. Civil penalties

[Sec. 109] (a)(1) A civil penalty of not more than $25,000 per violation may be assessed by the President in the case of any of the following—
  (A) A violation of the requirements of section 103 (a) or (b) (relating to notice).
  (B) A violation of the requirements of section 103(d)(2) (relating to destruction of records, etc.).
  (C) A violation of the requirements of section 108 (relating to financial responsibility, etc.), the regulations issued under section 108, or with any denial or detention order under section 108.
  (D) A violation of an order under section 122(d)(3) (relating to settlement agreements for action under section 104(b)).
  (E) Any failure or refusal referred to in section 122(l) (relating to violations of administrative orders, consent decrees, or agreements under section 120).
(2) No civil penalty may be assessed under this subsection unless the person accused of the violation is given notice and opportunity for a hearing with respect to the violation.
(3) In determining the amount of any penalty assessed pursuant to this subsection, the President shall take into account the nature, circumstances, extent and gravity of the violation or violations and, with respect to the violator, ability to pay, any prior history of such violations, the degree of culpability, economic benefit or savings (if any) resulting from the violation, and such other matters as justice may require.
(4) Any person against whom a civil penalty is assessed under this subsection may obtain review thereof in the appropriate district court of the United States by filing a notice of appeal in such court within 30 days from the date of such order and by simultaneously sending a copy of such notice by certified mail to the President. The President shall promptly file in such court a certified copy of the record upon which such violation was found or such penalty imposed. If any person fails to pay an assessment of a civil penalty after it has become a final and unappealable order or after the appropriate court has entered final judgment in favor of the United States, the President may request the Attorney General of the United States to institute a

civil action in an appropriate district court of the United States to collect the penalty, and such court shall have jurisdiction to hear and decide any such action. In hearing such action, the court shall have authority to review the violation and the assessment of the civil penalty on the record.

(5) The President may issue subpoenas for the attendance and testimony of witnesses and the production of relevant papers, books, or documents in connection with hearings under this subsection. In case of contumacy or refusal to obey a subpoena issued pursuant to this paragraph and served upon any person, the district court of the United States for any district in which such person is found, resides, or transacts business, upon application by the United States and after notice to such person, shall have jurisdiction to issue an order requiring such person to appear and give testimony before the administrative law judge or to appear and produce documents before the administrative law judge, or both, and any failure to obey such order of the court may be punished by such court as a contempt thereof.

(b) A civil penalty of not more than $25,000 per day for each day during which the violation continues may be assessed by the President in the case of any of the following—

(1) A violation of the notice requirements of section 103 (a) or (b).

(2) A violation of section 103(d)(2) (relating to destruction of records, etc.).

(3) A violation of the requirements of section 108 (relating to financial responsibility, etc.), the regulations issued under section 108, or with any denial or detention order under section 108.

(4) A violation of an order under section 122(d)(3) (relating to settlement agreements for action under section 104(b)).

(5) Any failure or refusal referred to in section 122(l) (relating to violations of administrative orders, consent decrees, or agreements under section 120).

In the case of a second or subsequent violation the amount of such penalty may be not more than $75,000 for each day during which the violation continues. Any civil penalty under this subsection shall be assessed and collected in the same manner, and subject to the same provisions, as in the case of civil penalties assessed and collected after notice and opportunity for hearing on the record in accordance with section 554 of title 5 of the United States Code. In any proceeding for the assessment of a civil penalty under this subsection the President may issue subpoenas for the attendance and testimony of witnesses and the production of relevant papers, books, and documents and may promulgate rules for discovery procedures. Any person who requested a hearing with respect to a civil penalty under this subsection and who is aggrieved by an order assessing the civil penalty may file a petition for judicial review of such order with the United States Court of

Appeals for the District of Columbia Circuit or for any other circuit in which such person resides or transacts business. Such a petition may only be filed within the 30-day period beginning on the date the order making such assessment was issued.

(c) The President may bring an action in the United States district court for the appropriate district to assess and collect a penalty of not more than $25,000 per day for each day during which the violation (or failure or refusal) continues in the case of any of the following—

(1) A violation of the notice requirements of section 103 (a) or (b).

(2) A violation of section 103(d)(2) (relating to destruction of records, etc.).

(3) A violation of the requirements of section 108 (relating to financial responsibility, etc.), the regulations issued under section 108, or with any denial or detention order under section 108.

(4) A violation of an order under section 122(d)(3) (relating to settlement agreements for action under section 104(b)).

(5) Any failure or refusal referred to in section 122(l) (relating to violations of administrative orders, consent decrees, or agreements under section 120).

In the case of a second or subsequent violation (or failure or refusal), the amount of such penalty may be not more than $75,000 for each day during which the violation (or failure or refusal) continues. For additional provisions providing for judicial assessment of civil penalties for failure to comply with a request or order under section 104(e) (relating to information gathering and access authorities), see section 104(e).

(d) The President may pay an award of up to $10,000 to any individual who provides information leading to the arrest and conviction of any person for a violation subject to a criminal penalty under this Act, including any violation of section 103 and any other violation referred to in this section. The President shall, by regulation, prescribe criteria for such an award and may pay any award under this subsection from the Fund, as provided in section 111.

(e) Notwithstanding any other provision of law, any executive agency may use competitive procedures or procedures other than competitive procedures to procure the services of experts for use in preparing or prosecuting a civil or criminal action under this Act, whether or not the expert is expected to testify at trial. The executive agency need not provide any written justification for the use of procedures other than competitive procedures when procuring such expert services under this Act and need not furnish for publication in the Commerce Business Daily or otherwise any notice of solicitation or synopsis with respect to such procurement.

(f) Action taken by the President pursuant to this section shall not affect or limit the President's authority to enforce any provisions of this Act.

§ 9610. Employee protection

[Sec. 110] (a) No person shall fire or in any other way discriminate against, or cause to be fired or discriminated against, any employee or any authorized representative of employees by reason of the fact that such employee or representative has provided information to a State or to the Federal Government, filed, instituted, or caused to be filed or instituted any proceeding under this Act, or has testified or is about to testify in any proceeding resulting from the administration or enforcement of the provisions of this Act.

(b) Any employee or a representative of employees who believes that he has been fired or otherwise discriminated against by any person in violation of subsection (a) of this section may, within thirty days after such alleged violation occurs, apply to the Secretary of Labor for a review of such firing or alleged discrimination. A copy of the application shall be sent to such person, who shall be the respondent. Upon receipt of such application, the Secretary of Labor shall cause such investigation to be made as he deems appropriate. Such investigation shall provide an opportunity for a public hearing at the request of any party to such review to enable the parties to present information relating to such alleged violation. The parties shall be given written notice of the time and place of the hearing at least five days prior to the hearing. Any such hearing shall be of record and shall be subject to section 554 of title 5, United States Code. Upon receiving the report of such investigation, the Secretary of Labor shall make findings of fact. If he finds that such violation did occur, he shall issue a decision, incorporating an order therein and his findings, requiring the party committing such violation to take such affirmative action to abate the violation as the Secretary of Labor deems appropriate, including, but not limited to, the rehiring or reinstatement of the employee or representative of employees to his former position with compensation. If he finds that there was no such violation, he shall issue an order denying the application. Such order issued by the Secretary of Labor under this subparagraph shall be subject to judicial review in the same manner as orders and decisions are subject to judicial review under this Act.

(c) Whenever an order is issued under this section to abate such violation, at the request of the applicant a sum equal to the aggregate amount of all costs and expenses (including the attorney's fees) determined by the Secretary of Labor to have been reasonably incurred by the applicant for, or in connection with, the institution and prosecution of such proceedings, shall be assessed against the person committing such violation.

(d) This section shall have no application to any employee who acting without discretion from his employer (or his agent) deliberately violates any requirement of this Act.

(e) The President shall conduct continuing evaluations of potential loss of shifts of employment which may result from the administration or enforcement of the provisions of this Act, including, where appropriate, investigating threatened plant closures or reductions in employment allegedly resulting from such administration or enforcement. Any employee who is discharged, or laid off, threatened with discharge or layoff, or otherwise discriminated against by any person because of the alleged results of such administration or enforcement, or any representative of such employee, may request the President to conduct a full investigation of the matter and, at the request of any party, shall hold public hearings, require the parties, including the employer involved, to present information relating to the actual or potential effect of such administration or enforcement on employment and any alleged discharge, layoff, or other discrimination, and the detailed reasons or justification therefore. Any such hearing shall be of record and shall be subject to section 554 of title 5, United States Code. Upon receiving the report of such investigation, the President shall make findings of fact as to the effect of such administration or enforcement on employment and on the alleged discharge, layoff, or discrimination and shall make such recommendations as he deems appropriate. Such report, findings, and recommendations shall be available to the public. Nothing in this subsection shall be construed to require or authorize the President or any State to modify or withdraw any action, standard, limitation, or any other requirement of this Act.

§ 9611. Uses of fund

[Sec. 111] (a) For the purposes specified in this section there is authorized to be appropriated from the Hazardous Substances Superfund established under subchapter Λ of chapter 98 of the Internal Revenue Code of 1986 not more than $8,500,000,000 for the 5-year period beginning on the date of enactment of the Superfund Amendments and Reauthorization Act of 1986, and such sums shall remain available until expended. The preceding sentence constitutes a specific authorization for the funds appropriated under title II of Public Law 99-160 (relating to payment to the Hazardous Substances Trust Fund). The President shall use the money in the Fund for the following purposes:

(1) Payment of governmental response costs incurred pursuant to section 104 of this title, including costs incurred pursuant to the Intervention on the High Seas Act.

(2) Payment of any claim for necessary response costs incurred by any other person as a result of carrying out the national contingency plan established under section 331(c) of the Clean Water Act and amended by section 105 of this title: *Provided, however,* That such costs must be approved under said plan and certified by the responsible Federal official.

(3) Payment of any claim authorized by subsection (b) of this section and finally decided pursuant to section 112 of this title, including those costs set out in subsection 112(c)(3) of this title.

(4) Payment of costs specified under subsection (c) of this section.

(5) The cost of grants under section 117(e) (relating to public participation grants for technical assistance.)

(6) Payment of not to exceed $15,000,000 for the costs of a pilot program for removal, decontamination, or other action with respect to lead-contaminated soil in one to three different metropolitan areas.

The President shall not pay for any administrative costs or expenses out of the Fund unless such costs and expenses are reasonably necessary for and incidental to the implementation of this title.

(b)(1) Claims asserted and compensable but unsatisfied under provisions of section 311 of the Clean Water Act, which are modified by section 304 of this Act may be asserted against the Fund under this title; and other claims resulting from a release or threat of release of a hazardous substance from a vessel or a facility may be asserted against the Fund under this title for injury to, or destruction or loss of, natural resources, including cost for damage assessment: *Provided, however,* That any such claim may be asserted only by the President, as trustee, for natural resources over which the United States has sovereign rights, or natural resources within the territory or the fishery conservation zone of the United States to the extent they are managed or protected by the United States, or by any State for natural resources within the boundary of that State belonging to, managed by, controlled by, or appertaining to the State, or by any Indian tribe or by the United States acting on behalf of any Indian tribe for natural resources belonging to, managed by, controlled by, or appertaining to such tribe, or held in trust for the benefit of such tribe, or belonging to a member of such tribe if such resources are subject to a trust restriction on alienation.

(2)(A) No natural resource claim may be paid from the Fund unless the President determines that the claimant has exhausted all administrative and judicial remedies to cover the amount of such claim from persons who may be liable under section 107.

(B) As used in this paragraph, the term "natural resource claim" means any claim for injury to, or destruction or loss of, natural resources. The term does not include any claim for the costs of natural resource damage assessment.

(c) Uses of the Fund under subsection (a) of this section include—

(1) The costs of assessing both short-term and long-term injury to, destruction of, or loss of any natural resources resulting from a release of a hazardous substance.

(2) The costs of Federal or State or Indian tribe efforts in the restoration, rehabilitation, or replacement or acquiring the equivalent of any natural resources injured, destroyed, or lost as a result of a release of a hazardous substance.

(3) Subject to such amounts as are provided in appropriation Acts, the costs of a program to identify, investigate, and take enforcement and abatement action against releases of hazardous substances.

(4) Any costs incurred in accordance with subsection (m) of this section (relating to ATSDR) and section 104(i), including the costs of

epidemiologic and laboratory studies, health assessments, preparation of toxicologic profiles, development and maintenance of a registry of persons exposed to hazardous substances to allow long-term health effect studies, and diagnostic services not otherwise available to determine whether persons in populations exposed to hazardous substances in connection with a release or a suspected release are suffering from long-latency diseases.

(5) Subject to such amounts as are provided in appropriation Acts, the costs of providing equipment and similar overhead related to the purposes of this Act and section 311 of the Clean Water Act, and needed to supplement equipment and services available through contractors or other non-Federal entities, and of establishing and maintaining damage assessment capability, for any Federal agency involved in strike forces, emergency task forces, or other response teams under the national contingency plan.

(6) Subject to such amounts as are provided in appropriation Acts, the costs of a program to protect the health and safety of employees involved in response to hazardous substance releases. Such program shall be developed jointly by the Environmental Protection Agency, the Occupational Safety and Health Administration, and the National Institute for Occupational Safety and Health and shall include, but not be limited to, measures for identifying and assessing hazards to which persons engaged in removal, remedy, or other response to hazardous substances may be exposed, methods to protect workers from such hazards, and necessary regulatory and enforcement measures to assure adequate protection of such employees.

(7) Costs incurred by the President in evaluating facilities pursuant to petitions under section 105(d) (relating to petitions for assessment of release).

(8) The costs of contracts or arrangements entered into under section 104(a)(1) to oversee and review the conduct of remedial investigations and feasibility studies undertaken by persons other than the President and the costs of appropriate Federal and State oversight of remedial activities at National Priorities List sites resulting from consent orders or settlement agreements.

(9) The costs incurred by the President in acquiring real estate or interests in real estate under section 104(j) (relating to acquisition of property).

(10) The cost of carrying out section 311 (relating to research, development, and demonstration), except that the amounts available for such purposes shall not exceed the amounts specified in subsection (n) of this section.

(11) Reimbursements to local governments under section 123, except that during the 5-fiscal-year period beginning October 1, 1986, not more than 0.1 percent of the total amount appropriated from the Fund may

be used for such reimbursements.

(12) The costs of grants under section 126(g) of the Superfund Amendments and Reauthorization Act of 1986 for training and education of
workers to the extent that such costs do not exceed $10,000,000 for
each of the fiscal years 1987, 1988, 1990, and 1991.

(13) The cost of any awards granted under section 109(d).

(14) The cost of carrying out the study under subsection (f) of section 118
of the Superfund Amendments and Reauthorization Act of 1986
(relating to lead poisoning in children).

(d)(1) No money in the Fund may be used under subsection (c)(1) and (2)
of this section, nor for the payment of any claim under subsection (b) of this
section, where the injury, destruction, or loss of natural resources and the
release of a hazardous substance from which such damages resulted have
occurred wholly before the enactment of this Act.

(2) No money in the Fund may be used for the payment of any claim
under subsection (b) of this section where such expenses are associated
with injury or loss resulting from long-term exposure to ambient
concentrations of air pollutants from multiple or diffuse sources.

(e)(1) Claims against or presented to the Fund shall not be valid or paid in
excess of the total money in the Fund at any one time. Such claims become
valid only when additional money is collected, appropriated, or otherwise
added to the Fund. Should the total claims outstanding at any time exceed
the current balance of the Fund, the President shall pay such claims, to the
extent authorized under this section in full in the order in which they were
finally determined.

(2) In any fiscal year, 85 percent of the money credited to the Fund under
title II of this Act shall be available only for the purposes specified in
paragraphs (1), (2), and (4) of subsection (a) of this section. No money
in the Fund may be used for the payment of any claim under
subsection (a)(3) or subsection (b) of this section in any fiscal year for
which the President determines that all of the Fund is needed for
response to threats to public health from releases or threatened
releases of hazardous substances.

(3) No money in the Fund shall be available for remedial action, other
than actions specified in subsection (c) of this section, with respect to
federally owned facilities; except that money in the Fund shall be
available for the provision of alternative water supplies (including the
reimbursement of costs incurred by a municipality) in any case
involving groundwater contamination outside the boundaries of a
federally owned facility in which the federally owned facility is not the
potentially responsible party.

(4) Paragraphs (1) and (4) of subsection (a) of this section shall in the
aggregate be subject to such amounts as are provided in appropriation
Acts.

(f) The President is authorized to promulgate regulations designating one or more Federal officials who may obligate money in the Fund in accordance with this section or portions thereof. The President is also authorized to delegate authority to obligate money in the Fund or to settle claims to officials of a State or Indian tribe operating under a contract or cooperative agreement with the Federal Government pursuant to section 104(d) of this title.

(g) The President shall provide for the promulgation of rules and regulations with respect to the notice to be provided to potential injured parties by an owner and operator of any vessel, or facility from which a hazardous substance has been released. Such rules and regulations shall consider the scope and form of the notice which would be appropriate to carry out the purposes of this title. Upon promulgation of such rules and regulations, the owner and operator of any vessel or facility from which a hazardous substance has been released shall provide notice in accordance with such rules and regulations. With respect to releases from public vessels, the President shall provide such notification as is appropriate to potential injured parties. Until the promulgation of such rules and regulations, the owner and operator of any vessel or facility from which a hazardous substance has been released shall provide reasonable notice to potential injured parties by publication in local newspapers serving the affected area.

(h) [Repealed]

(i) Except in a situation requiring action to avoid an irreversible loss of natural resources or to prevent or reduce any continuing danger to natural resources or similar need for emergency action, funds may not be used under this Act for the restoration, rehabilitation, or replacement or acquisition of the equivalent of any natural resources until a plan for the use of such funds for such purposes has been developed and adopted by affected Federal agencies and the Governor or Governors of any State and by the governing body of any Indian tribe having sustained damage to natural resources belonging to, managed by, controlled by, or appertaining to such tribe, or held in trust for the benefit of such tribe, or belonging to a member of such tribe if such resources are subject to a trust restriction on alienation, having sustained damage to natural resources within its borders, belonging to, managed by or appertaining to such State, and by the governing body of any Indian tribe having sustained damage to natural resources belonging to, managed by, controlled by, or appertaining to such tribe, or held in trust for the benefit of such tribe, or belonging to a member of such tribe if such resources are subject to a trust restriction on alienation, after adequate public notice and opportunity for hearing and consideration of all public comment.

(j) The President shall use the money in the Post-closure Liability Fund for any of the purposes specified in subsection (a) of this section with respect to a hazardous waste disposal facility for which liability has transferred to such fund under section 107(k) of this Act, and, in addition, for payment of any claim or appropriate request for costs of response, damages, or other compensation for injury or loss under section 107 of this Act or any other State or Federal law, resulting from a release of a hazardous substance from such a facility.

(k) In each fiscal year, the Inspector General of each department, agency, or instrumentality of the United States which is carrying out any authority of this Act shall conduct an annual audit of all payments, obligations, reimbursements, or other uses of the Fund in the prior fiscal year, to assure that the Fund is being properly administered and that claims are being appropriately and expeditiously considered. The audit shall include an examination of a sample of agreements with States (in accordance with the provisions of the Single Audit Act) carrying out response actions under this title and an examination of remedial investigations and feasibility studies prepared for remedial actions. The Inspector General shall submit to the Congress an annual report regarding the audit report required under this subsection. The report shall contain such recommendations as the Inspector General deems appropriate. Each department, agency, or instrumentality of the United States shall cooperate with its inspector general in carrying out this subsection.

(l) To the extent that the provisions of this Act permit, a foreign claimant may assert a claim to the same extent that a United States claimant may assert a claim if—

(1) the release of a hazardous substance occurred (A) in the navigable waters or (B) in or on the territorial sea or adjacent shoreline of a foreign country of which the claimant is a resident;

(2) the claimant is not otherwise compensated for his loss;

(3) the hazardous substance was released from a facility or from a vessel located adjacent to or within the navigable waters or was discharged in connection with activities conducted under the Outer Continental Shelf Lands Act, as amended (43 U.S.C. 1331 et seq.) or the Deepwater Port Act of 1974, as amended (33 U.S.C. 1501 et seq.); and

(4) recovery is authorized by a treaty or an executive agreement between the United States and foreign country involved, or if the Secretary of State, in consultation with the Attorney General and other appropriate officials, certifies that such country provides a comparable remedy for United States claimants.

(m) There shall be directly available to the Agency for Toxic Substances and Disease Registry to be used for the purpose of carrying out activities described in subsection (c)(4) and section 104(i) not less than $50,000,000 per fiscal year for each of fiscal years 1987 and 1988, not less than $55,000,000 for fiscal year 1989, and not less than $60,000,000 per fiscal year for each of fiscal years 1990 and 1991. Any funds so made available which are not obligated by the end of the fiscal year in which made available shall be returned to the Fund.

(n)(1) For each of the fiscal years 1987, 1988, 1990, and 1991, not more than $20,000,000 of the amounts available in the Fund may be used for the purposes of carrying out the applied research, development, and demonstration program for alternative or innovative technologies and training program authorized under section 311(b) (relating to research, development, and demonstration) other than basic research. Such amounts shall remain available until expended.

(2) From the amounts available in the Fund, not more than the following amounts may be used for the purpose of section 311(a) (relating to hazardous substance research, demonstration, and training activities):

(A) For the fiscal year 1987, $3,000,000.

(B) For the fiscal year 1988, $10,000,000.

(C) For the fiscal year 1989, $20,000,000.

(D) For the fiscal year 1990, $30,000,000.

(E) For the fiscal year 1991, $35,000,000.

No more than 10 percent of such amounts shall be used for training under section 311(a) in any fiscal year.

(3) For each of the fiscal years 1987, 1988, 1989, 1990, and 1991, not more than $5,000,000 of the amounts available in the Fund may be used for the purposes of section 311(d) (relating to university hazardous substance research centers).

(o) Not later than 90 days after the enactment of this subsection, the President shall develop and implement procedures to adequately notify, as soon as practicable after a site is included on the National Priorities List, concerned local and State officials and other concerned persons of the limitations, set forth in subsection (a)(2) of this section, on the payment of claims for necessary response costs incurred with respect to such site.

(p)(1) The following sums are authorized to be appropriated, out of any money in the Treasury not otherwise appropriated, to the Hazardous Substance Superfund:

(A) For fiscal year 1987, $212,500,000.

(B) For fiscal year 1988, $212,500,000.

(C) For fiscal year 1989, $212,500,000.

(D) For fiscal year 1990, $212,500,000.

(E) For fiscal year 1991, $212,500,000.

In addition there is authorized to be appropriated to the Hazardous Substance Superfund for each fiscal year an amount equal to so much of the aggregate amount authorized to be appropriated under this subsection (and paragraph (2) of section 221(b) of the Hazardous Substance Response Revenue Act of 1980) as has not been appropriated before the beginning of the fiscal year involved.

(2) The amounts authorized to be appropriated under paragraph (1) of this subsection in a given fiscal year shall be available only to the extent that such amount exceeds the amount determined by the

Secretary under section 9507(b)(2) of the Internal Revenue Code of 1986 for the prior fiscal year.

§ 9612. Claims procedure

[Sec. 112] (a) No claim may be asserted against the Fund pursuant to section 111(a) unless such claim is presented in the first instance to the owner, operator, or guarantor of the vessel or facility from which a hazardous substance has been released, if known to the claimant, and to any other person known to the claimant who may be liable under section 107. In any case where the claim has not been satisfied within 60 days of presentation in accordance with this subsection, the claimant may present the claim to the Fund for payment. No claim against the Fund may be approved or certified during the pendency of an action by the claimant in court to recover costs which are the subject of the claim.

(b)(1) The President shall prescribe appropriate forms and procedures for claims filed hereunder, which shall include a provision requiring the claimant to make a sworn verification of the claim to the best of his knowledge. Any person who knowingly gives or causes to be given any false information as a part of any such claim shall, upon conviction, be fined in accordance with the applicable provisions of title 18 of the United States Code or imprisoned for not more than 3 years (or not more than 5 years in the case of a second or subsequent conviction), or both.

(2) The President may, if satisfied that the information developed during the processing of the claim warrants it, make and pay an award of the claim, except that no claim may be awarded to the extent that a judicial judgment has been made on the costs that are the subject of the claim. If the President declines to pay all or part of the claim, the claimant may, within 30 days after receiving notice of the President's decision, request an administrative hearing.

(3) In any proceeding under this subsection, the claimant shall bear the burden of proving his claim.

(4) All administrative decisions made hereunder shall be in writing, with notification to all appropriate parties, and shall be rendered within 90 days of submission of a claim to an administrative law judge, unless all the parties to the claim agree in writing to an extension or unless the President, in his discretion, extends the time limit for a period not to exceed sixty days.

(5) All administrative decisions hereunder shall be final, and any party to the proceeding may appeal a decision within 30 days of notification of the award or decision. Any such appeal shall be made to the Federal district court for the district where the release or threat of release took place. In any such appeal, the decision shall be considered binding and conclusive, and shall not be overturned except for arbitrary or capricious abuse of discretion.

(6) Within 20 days after the expiration of the appeal period for any

administrative decision concerning an award, or within 20 days after the final judicial determination of any appeal taken pursuant to this subsection, the President shall pay any such award from the Fund. The President shall determine the method, terms, and time of payment.

(c)(1) Payment of any claim by the Fund under this section shall be subject to the United States Government acquiring by subrogation the rights of the claimant to recover those costs of removal or damages for which it has compensated the claimant from the person responsible or liable for such release.

(2) Any person, including the Fund, who pays compensation pursuant to this Act to any claimant for damages or costs resulting from a release of a hazardous substance shall be subrogated to all rights, claims, and causes of action for such damages and costs of removal that the claimant has under this Act or any other law.

(3) Upon request of the President, the Attorney General shall commence an action on behalf of the Fund to recover any compensation paid by the Fund to any claimant pursuant to this title, and, without regard to any limitation of liability, all interest, administrative and adjudicative costs, and attorney's fees incurred by the Fund by reason of the claim. Such an action may be commenced against any owner, operator, or guarantor, or against any other person who is liable, pursuant to any law, to the compensated claimant or to the Fund, for the damages or costs for which compensation was paid.

(d)(1) No claim may be presented under this section for recovery of the costs referred to in section 107(a) after the date 6 years after the date of completion of all response action.

(2) No claim may be presented under this section for recovery of the damages referred to in section 107(a) unless the claim is presented within 3 years after the later of the following:

(A) The date of the discovery of the loss and its connection with the release in question.

(B) The date on which final regulations are promulgated under section 301(c).

(3) The time limitations contained herein shall not begin to run—

(A) against a minor until the earlier of the date when such minor reaches 18 years of age or the date on which a legal representative is duly appointed for the minor, or

(B) against an incompetent person until the earlier of the date on which such person's incompetency ends or the date on which a legal representative is duly appointed for such incompetent person.

(e) Regardless of any State statutory or common law to the contrary, no person who asserts a claim against the Fund pursuant to this title shall be deemed or held to have waived any other claim not covered or assertable against the Fund under this title arising from the same incident, transaction, or set of circumstances, nor to have split a cause of action. Further, no person asserting a claim against the Fund pursuant to this title shall as a result of any determination of a question of fact or law made in connection with that claim be deemed or held to be collaterally estopped from raising such question in connection with any other claim not covered or assertable against the Fund under this title arising from the same incident, transaction, or set of circumstances.

(f) Where the President has paid out of the Fund for any response costs or any costs specified under section 111(c) (1) or (2), no other claim may be paid out of the Fund for the same costs.

§ 9613. Civil proceedings

[Sec. 113] (a) Review of any regulation promulgated under this Act may be had upon application by any interested person only in the Circuit Court of Appeals of the United States for the District of Columbia. Any such application shall be made within ninety days from the date of promulgation of such regulations. Any matter with respect to which review could have been obtained under this subsection shall not be subject to judicial review in any civil or criminal proceeding for enforcement or to obtain damages or recovery of response costs.

(b) Except as provided in subsections (a) and (h) of this section, the United States district courts shall have exclusive original jurisdiction over all controversies arising under this Act, without regard to the citizenship of the parties or the amount in controversy. Venue shall lie in any district in which the release or damages occurred, or in which the defendant resides, may be found, or has his principal office. For the purposes of this section, the Fund shall reside in the District of Columbia.

(c) The provisions of subsections (a) and (b) of this section shall not apply to any controversy or other matter resulting from the assessment of collection of any tax, as provided by title II of this Act, or to the review of any regulation promulgated under the Internal Revenue Code of 1954.

(d) No provision of this Act shall be deemed or held to moot any litigation concerning any release of any hazardous substance, or any damages associated therewith, commenced prior to enactment of this Act.

(e) In any action by the United States under this Act, process may be served in any district where the defendant is found, resides, transacts business, or has appointed an agent for the service of process.

(f)(1) Any person may seek contribution from any other person who is liable or potentially liable under section 107(a), during or following any civil action under section 106 or under section 107(a). Such claims shall be brought in accordance with this section and the Federal Rules of Civil Procedure, and shall be governed by Federal law. In resolving contribution claims, the court may allocate response costs among liable parties using such equitable factors as the court determines are appropriate. Nothing in this subsection shall diminish the right of any person to bring an action for contribution in the absence of a civil action under section 106 or section 107.

(2) A person who has resolved its liability to the United States or a State in an administrative or judicially approved settlement shall not be liable for claims for contribution regarding matters addressed in the settlement. Such settlement does not discharge any of the other potentially liable persons unless its terms so provide, but it reduces the potential liability of the others by the amount of the settlement.

(3)(A) If the United States or a State has obtained less than complete relief from a person who has resolved its liability to the United States or the State in an administrative or judicially approved settlement, the United States or the State may bring an action against any person who has not so resolved its liability.

(B) A person who has resolved its liability to the United States or a State for some or all of a response action or for some or all of the costs of such action in an administrative or judicially approved settlement may seek contribution from any person who is not party to a settlement referred to in paragraph (2).

(C) In any action under this paragraph, the rights of any person who has resolved its liability to the United States or a State shall be subordinate to the rights of the United States or the State. Any contribution action brought under this paragraph shall be governed by Federal law.

(g)(1) Except as provided in paragraphs (3) and (4), no action may be commenced for damages (as defined in section 101(6)) under this Act, unless that action is commenced within 3 years after the later of the following:

(A) The date of the discovery of the loss and its connection with the release in question.

(B) The date on which regulations are promulgated under section 301(c).

With respect to any facility listed on the National Priorities List (NPL), any Federal facility identified under section 120 (relating to Federal facilities), or any vessel or facility at which a remedial action under this Act is otherwise scheduled, an action for damages under this Act must be commenced within 3 years after the completion of the remedial action (excluding operation and maintenance activities) in lieu of the dates referred to in subparagraph (A) or (B). In no event may an action for damages under this Act with respect to such a vessel or facility be commenced (i) prior to 60 days after the Federal or State natural resource trustee provides to the President and the potentially responsible party a notice of intent to file suit, or (ii) before selection of the remedial action if the President is diligently proceeding with a remedial investigation and feasibility study under section 104(b) or section 120 (relating to Federal facilities). The limitation in the preceding sentence on commencing an action before giving notice or before selection of the remedial action does not apply to actions filed on or before the enactment of the Superfund Amendments and Reauthorization Act of 1986.

(2) An initial action for recovery of the costs referred to in section 107 must be commenced—

(A) for a removal action, within 3 years after completion of the removal action, except that such cost recovery action must be brought within 6 years after a determination to grant a waiver under section 104(c)(1)(C) for continued response action; and

(B) for a remedial action, within 6 years after initiation of physical on-site construction of the remedial action, except that, if the remedial action is initiated within 3 years after the completion of the removal action, costs incurred in the removal action may be recovered in the cost recovery action brought under this subparagraph.

In any such action described in this subsection, the court shall enter a declaratory judgment on liability for response costs or damages that will be binding on any subsequent action or actions to recover further response costs or damages. A subsequent action or actions under section 107 for further response costs at the vessel or facility may be maintained at any time during the response action, but must be commenced no later than 3 years after the date of completion of all response action. Except as otherwise provided in this paragraph, an action may be commenced under section 107 for recovery of costs at any time after such costs have been incurred.

(3) No action for contribution for any response costs or damages may be commenced more than 3 years after—

(A) the date of judgment in any action under this Act for recovery of such costs or damages, or

(B) the date of an administrative order under section 122(g) (relating to de minimis settlements) or 122(h) (relating to cost recovery settlements) or entry of a judicially approved settlement with respect to such costs or damages.

(4) No action based on rights subrogated pursuant to this section by reason of payment of a claim may be commenced under this title more than 3 years after the date of payment of such claim.

(5) Notwithstanding any other provision of this subsection, where a payment pursuant to an indemnification agreement with a response action contractor is made under section 119, an action under section 107 for recovery of such indemnification payment from a potentially responsible party may be brought at any time before the expiration of 3 years from the date on which such payment is made.

(6) The time limitations contained herein shall not begin to run—

(A) against a minor until the earlier of the date when such minor reaches 18 years of age or the date on which a legal representative is duly appointed for such minor, or

(B) against an incompetent person until the earlier of the date on which such incompetent's incompetency ends or the date on which a legal representative is duly appointed for such incompetent.

(h) No Federal court shall have jurisdiction under Federal law other than under section 1332 of title 28 of the United States Code (relating to diversity of citizenship jurisdiction) or under State law which is applicable or relevant and appropriate under section 121 (relating to cleanup standards) to review any challenges to removal or remedial action selected under section 104, or to review any order issued under section 106(a), in any action except one of the following:

(1) An action under section 107 to recover response costs or damages or for contribution.

(2) An action to enforce an order issued under section 106(a) or to recover a penalty for violation of such order.

(3) An action for reimbursement under section 106(b)(2).

(4) An action under section 310 (relating to citizens suits) alleging that the removal or remedial action taken under section 104 or secured under section 106 was in violation of any requirement of this Act. Such an action may not be brought with regard to a removal where a remedial action is to be undertaken at the site.

(5) An action under section 106 in which the United States has moved to compel a remedial action.

(i) In any action commenced under this Act or under the Solid Waste Disposal Act in a court of the United States, any person may intervene as a matter of right when such person claims an interest relating to the subject of the action and is so situated that the disposition of the action may, as a practical matter, impair or impede the person's ability to protect that interest, unless the President or the State shows that the person's interest is adequately represented by existing parties.

(j)(1) In any judicial action under this Act, judicial review of any issues concerning the adequacy of any response action taken or ordered by the President shall be limited to the administrative record. Otherwise applicable principles of administrative law shall govern whether any supplemental materials may be considered by the court.

(2) In considering objections raised in any judicial action under this Act, the court shall uphold the President's decision in selecting the response action unless the objecting party can demonstrate, on the administrative record, that the decision was arbitrary and capricious or otherwise not in accordance with law.

(3) If the court finds that the selection of the response action was arbitrary and capricious or otherwise not in accordance with law, the court shall award (A) only the response costs or damages that are not inconsistent

with the national contingency plan, and (B) such other relief as is consistent with the National Contingency Plan.

(4) In reviewing alleged procedural errors, the court may disallow costs or damages only if the errors were so serious and related to matters of such central relevance to the action that the action would have been significantly changed had such errors not been made.

(k)(1) The President shall establish an administrative record upon which the President shall base the selection of a response action. The administrative record shall be available to the public at or near the facility at issue. The President also may place duplicates of the administrative record at any other location.

(2)(A) The President shall promulgate regulations in accordance with chapter 5 of title 5 of the United States Code establishing procedures for the appropriate participation of interested persons in the development of the administrative record on which the President will base the selection of removal actions and on which judicial review of removal actions will be based.

(B) The President shall provide for the participation of interested persons, including potentially responsible parties, in the development of the administrative record on which the President will base the selection of remedial actions and on which judicial review of remedial actions will be based. The procedures developed under this subparagraph shall include, at a minimum, each of the following:

(i) Notice to potentially affected persons and the public, which shall be accompanied by a brief analysis of the plan and alternative plans that were considered.

(ii) A reasonable opportunity to comment and provide information regarding the plan.

(iii) An opportunity for a public meeting in the affected area, in accordance with section 117(a)(2) (relating to public participation).

(iv) A response to each of the significant comments, criticisms, and new data submitted in written or oral presentations.

(v) A statement of the basis and purpose of the selected action.

For purposes of this subparagraph, the administrative record shall include all items developed and received under this subparagraph and all items described in the second sentence of section 117(d). The President shall promulgate regulations in accordance with chapter 5 of title 5 of the United States Code to carry out the requirements of this subparagraph.

(C) Until such regulations under subparagraphs (A) and (B) are promulgated, the administrative record shall consist of all items developed and received pursuant to current procedures for selection of the response action, including procedures for the participation of interested parties and the public. The development of an administrative record and the selection of response action under this Act shall not include an adjudicatory hearing.

(D) The President shall make reasonable efforts to identify and notify potentially responsible parties as early as possible before selection of a response action. Nothing in this paragraph shall be construed to be a defense to liability.

(l) Whenever any action is brought under this Act in a court of the United States by a plaintiff other than the United States, the plaintiff shall provide a copy of the complaint to the Attorney General of the United States and to the Administrator of the Environmental Protection Agency.

§ 9614. Relationship to other law

[Sec. 114] (a) Nothing in this Act shall be construed or interpreted as preempting any State from imposing any additional liability or requirements with respect to the release of hazardous substances within such State.

(b) Any person who receives compensation for removal costs or damages or claims pursuant to this Act shall be precluded from recovering compensation for the same removal costs or damages or claims pursuant to any other State or Federal law. Any person who receives compensation for removal costs or damages or claims pursuant to any other Federal or State law shall be precluded from receiving compensation for the same removal costs or damages or claims as provided in this Act.

(c)(1) No person (including the United States or any State) may recover, under the authority of subsection (a)(3) or (a)(4) of section 107, from a service station dealer for any response costs or damages resulting from a release or threatened release of recycled oil, or use the authority of section 106 against a service station dealer other than a person described in subsection (a)(1) or (a)(2) of section 107, if such recycled oil—

(A) is not mixed with any other hazardous substance, and

(B) is stored, treated, transported, or otherwise managed in compliance with regulations or standards promulgated pursuant to section 3014 of the Solid Waste Disposal Act and other applicable authorities.

Nothing in this paragraph shall affect or modify in any way the obligations or liability of any person under any other provision of State or Federal law, including common law, for damages, injury, or loss resulting from a release or threatened release of any hazardous substance or for removal or remedial action or the costs of removal or remedial action.

(2) Solely for the purposes of this subsection, a service station dealer may presume that a small quantity of used oil is not mixed with other hazardous substances if it—

(A) has been removed from the engine of a light duty motor vehicle or household appliances by the owner of such vehicle or appliances, and

(B) is presented, by such owner, to the dealer for collection, accumulation, and delivery to an oil recycling facility.

(3) For purposes of this subsection, the terms "used oil" and "recycled oil" have the same meanings as set forth in sections 1004(36) and 1004(37) of the Solid Waste Disposal Act and regulations promulgated pursuant to that Act.

(4) The effective date of paragraphs (1) and (2) of this subsection shall be the effective date of regulations or standards promulgated under section 3014 of the Solid Waste Disposal Act that include, among other provisions, a requirement to conduct corrective action to respond to any releases of recycled oil under subtitle C or subtitle I of such Act.

(d) Except as provided in this title, no owner or operator of a vessel or facility who establishes and maintains evidence of financial responsibility in accordance with this title shall be required under any State or local law, rule, or regulation to establish or maintain any other evidence of financial responsibility in connection with liability for the release of a hazardous substance from such vessel or facility. Evidence of compliance with the financial responsibility requirements of this title shall be accepted by a State in lieu of any other requirement of financial responsibility imposed by such State in connection with liability for the release of a hazardous substance from such vessel or facility.

§ 9615. Presidential delegation and assignment of duties or powers and promulgation of regulations

[Sec. 115] The President is authorized to delegate and assign any duties or powers imposed upon or assigned to him and to promulgate any regulations necessary to carry out the provisions of this title.

§ 9616. Schedules

[Sec. 116] (a) It shall be a goal of this Act that, to the maximum extent practicable—

(1) not later than January 1, 1988, the President shall complete preliminary assessments of all facilities that are contained (as of the date of enactment of the Superfund Amendments and Reauthorization Act of 1986) on the Comprehensive Environmental Response, Compensation, and Liability Information System (CERCLIS) including in each assessment a statement as to whether a site inspection is necessary and by whom it should be carried out; and

(2) not later than January 1, 1989, the President shall assure the

completion of site inspections at all facilities for which the President has stated a site inspection is necessary pursuant to paragraph (1).

(b) Within 4 years after enactment of the Superfund Amendments and Reauthorization Act of 1986, each facility listed (as of the date of such enactment) in the CERCLIS shall be evaluated if the President determines that such evaluation is warranted on the basis of a site inspection or preliminary assessment. The evaluation shall be in accordance with the criteria established in section 105 under the National Contingency Plan for determining priorities among release for inclusion on the National Priorities List. In the case of a facility listed in the CERCLIS after the enactment of the Superfund Amendments and Reauthorization Act of 1986, the facility shall be evaluated within 4 years after the date of such listing if the President determines that such evaluation is warranted on the basis of a site inspection or preliminary assessment.

(c) If any of the goals established by subsection (a) or (b) are not achieved, the President shall publish an explanation of why such action could not be completed by the specified date.

(d) The President shall assure that remedial investigations and feasibility studies (RI/FS) are commenced for facilities listed on the National Priorities List, in addition to those commenced prior to the date of enactment of the Superfund Amendments and Reauthorization Act of 1986, in accordance with the following schedule:

(1) not fewer than 275 by the date 36 months after the date of enactment of the Superfund Amendments and Reauthorization Act of 1986, and

(2) if the requirement of paragraph (1) is not met, not fewer than an additional 175 by the date 4 years after such date of enactment, an additional 200 by the date 5 years after such date of enactment, and a total of 650 by the date 5 years after such date of enactment.

(e) The President shall assure that substantial and continuous physical on-site remedial action commences at facilities on the National Priorities List, in addition to those facilities on which remedial action has commenced prior to the date of enactment of the Superfund Amendments and Reauthorization Act of 1986, at a rate not fewer than:

(1) 175 facilities during the first 36-month period after enactment of this subsection; and

(2) 200 additional facilities during the following 24 months after such 36-month period.

§ 9617. Public participation

[Sec. 117] (a) Before adoption of any plan for remedial action to be undertaken by the President, by a State, or by any other person, under section 104, 106, 120, or 122, the President or State, as appropriate, shall take both of the following actions:

(1) Publish a notice and brief analysis of the proposed plan and make

such plan available to the public.

(2) Provide a reasonable opportunity for submission of written and oral comments and an opportunity for a public meeting at or near the facility at issue regarding the proposed plan and regarding any proposed findings under section 121(d)(4) (relating to cleanup standards). The President or the State shall keep a transcript of the meeting and make such transcript available to the public.

The notice and analysis published under paragraph (1) shall include sufficient information as may be necessary to provide a reasonable explanation of the proposed plan and alternative proposals considered.

(b) Notice of the final remedial action plan adopted shall be published and the plan shall be made available to the public before commencement of any remedial action. Such final plan shall be accompanied by a discussion of any significant changes (and the reasons for such changes) in the proposed plan and a response to each of the significant comments, criticisms, and new data submitted in written or oral presentations under subsection (a).

(c) After adoption of a final remedial action plan—

(1) if any remedial action is taken,

(2) if any enforcement action under section 106 is taken, or

(3) if any settlement or consent decree under section 106 or section 122 is entered into,

and if such action, settlement, or decree differs in any significant respects from the final plan, the President or the State shall publish an explanation of the significant differences and the reasons such changes were made.

(d) For the purposes of this section, publication shall include, at a minimum, publication in a major local newspaper of general circulation. In addition, each item developed, received, published, or made available to the public under this section shall be available for public inspection and copying at or near the facility at issue.

(e)(1) Subject to such amounts as are provided in appropriations Acts and in accordance with rules promulgated by the President, the President may make grants available to any group of individuals which may be affected by a release or threatened release at any facility which is listed on the National Priorities List under the National Contingency Plan. Such grants may be used to obtain technical assistance in interpreting information with regard to the nature of the hazard, remedial investigation and feasibility study, record of decision, remedial design, selection and construction of remedial action, operation and maintenance, or removal action at such facility.

(2) The amount of any grant under this subsection may not exceed $50,000 for a single grant recipient. The President may waive the $50,000 limitation in any case where such waiver is necessary to carry out the purposes of this subsection. Each grant recipient shall be required, as a condition of the grant, to contribute at least 20 percent of the total of costs of the technical assistance for which such grant is made. The President may waive the 20 percent contribution require-

ment if the grant recipient demonstrates financial need and such waiver is necessary to facilitate public participation in the selection of remedial action at the facility. Not more than one grant may be made under this subsection with respect to a single facility, but the grant may be renewed to facilitate public participation at all stages of remedial action.

§ 9618.   High priority for drinking water supplies

[Sec. 118] For purposes of taking action under section 104 or 106 and listing facilities on the National Priorities List, the President shall give a high priority to facilities where the release of hazardous substances or pollutants or contaminants has resulted in the closing of drinking water wells or has contaminated a principal drinking water supply.

§ 9619.   Response action contractors

[Sec. 119] (a)(1) A person who is a response action contractor with respect to any release or threatened release of a hazardous substance or pollutant or contaminant from a vessel or facility shall not be liable under this title or under any other Federal law to any person for injuries, costs, damages, expenses, or other liability (including but not limited to claims for indemnification or contribution and claims by third parties for death, personal injury, illness or loss of or damage to property or economic loss) which results from such release or threatened release.

(2) Paragraph (1) shall not apply in the case of a release that is caused by conduct of the response action contractor which is negligent, grossly negligent, or which constitutes intentional misconduct.

(3) Nothing in this subsection shall affect the liability of any person under any warranty under Federal, State, or common law. Nothing in this subsection shall affect the liability of an employer who is a response action contractor to any employee of such employer under any provision of law, including any provision of any law relating to worker's compensation.

(4) A state employee or an employee of a political subdivision who provides services relating to response action while acting within the scope of his authority as a governmental employee shall have the same exemption from liability (subject to the other provisions of this section) as is provided to the response action contractor under this section.

(b)(1) The defense provided by section 107(b)(3) shall not be available to any potentially responsible party with respect to any costs or damages caused by any act or omission of a response action contractor. Except as provided in subsection (a)(4) and the preceding sentence, nothing in this section shall affect the liability under this Act or under any other Federal or State law of any person, other than a response action contractor.

(2) Nothing in this section shall affect the plaintiff's burden of establishing liability under this title.

(c)(1) The President may agree to hold harmless and indemnify any response action contractor meeting the requirements of this subsection against any liability (including the expenses of litigation or settlement) for negligence arising out of the contractor's performance in carrying out response action activities under this title, unless such liability was caused by conduct of the contractor which was grossly negligent or which constituted intentional misconduct.

(2) This subsection shall apply only with respect to a response action carried out under written agreement with—
   (A) the President;
   (B) any Federal agency;
   (C) a State or political subdivision which has entered into a contract or cooperative agreement in accordance with section 104(d)(1) of this title; or
   (D) any potentially responsible party carrying out any agreement under section 122 (relating to settlements) or section 106 (relating to abatement).

(3) This subsection shall not be subject to section 1301 or 1341 of title 31 of the United States Code or section 3732 of the Revised Statutes (41 U.S.C. 11) or to section 3 of the Superfund Amendments and Reauthorization Act of 1986. For purposes of section 111, amounts expended pursuant to this subsection for indemnification of any response action contractor (except with respect to federally owned or operated facilities) shall be considered governmental response costs incurred pursuant to section 104. If sufficient funds are unavailable in the Hazardous Substance Superfund established under subchapter A of chapter 98 of the Internal Revenue Code of 1954 to make payments pursuant to such indemnification or if the Fund is repealed, there are authorized to be appropriated such amounts as may be necessary to make such payments.

(4) An indemnification agreement may be provided under this subsection only if the President determines that each of the following requirements are met:
   (A) The liability covered by the indemnification agreement exceeds or is not covered by insurance available, at a fair and reasonable price, to the contractor at the time the contractor enters into the contract to provide response action, and adequate insurance to cover such liability is not generally available at the time the response action contract is entered into.
   (B) The response action contractor has made diligent efforts to obtain insurance coverage from non-Federal sources to cover such liability.
   (C) In the case of a response action contract covering more than one

facility, the response action contractor agrees to continue to make such diligent efforts each time the contractor begins work under the contract at a new facility.

(5)(A) Indemnification under this subsection shall apply only to response action contractor liability which results from a release of any hazardous substance or pollutant or contaminant if such release arises out of response action activities.

(B) An indemnification agreement under this subsection shall include deductibles and shall place limits on the amount of indemnification to be made available.

(C)(i) In deciding whether to enter into an indemnification agreement with a response action contractor carrying out a written contract or agreement with any potentially responsible party, the President shall determine an amount which the potentially responsible party is able to indemnify the contractor. The President may enter into such an indemnification agreement only if the President determines that such amount of indemnification is inadequate to cover any reasonable potential liability of the contractor arising out of the contractor's negligence in performing the contract or agreement with such party. The President shall make the determinations in the preceding sentences (with respect to the amount and the adequacy of the amount) taking into account the total net assets and resources of potentially responsible parties with respect to the facility at the time of such determinations.

(ii) The President may pay a claim under an indemnification agreement referred to in clause (i) for the amount determined under clause (i) only if the contractor has exhausted all administrative, judicial, and common law claims for indemnification against all potentially responsible parties participating in the clean-up of the facility with respect to the liability of the contractor arising out of the contractor's negligence in performing the contract or agreement with such party. Such indemnification agreement shall require such contractor to pay any deductible established under subparagraph (B) before the contractor may recover any amount from the potentially responsible party or under the indemnification agreement.

(D) No owner or operator of a facility regulated under the Solid Waste Disposal Act may be indemnified under this subsection with respect to such facility.

(E) A person retained or hired by a person described in subsection (e)(2)(B) shall be eligible for indemnification under this subsection only if the President specifically approves of the retaining or hiring of such person.

(6) For purposes of section 107, amounts expended pursuant to this subsection for indemnification of any person who is a response action contractor with respect to any release or threatened release shall be

considered a cost of response incurred by the United States Government with respect to such release.

(7) The President shall promulgate regulations for carrying out the provisions of this subsection. Before promulgation of the regulations, the President shall develop guidelines to carry out this section. Development of such guidelines shall include reasonable opportunity for public comment.

(8) The Comptroller General shall conduct a study in the fiscal year ending September 30, 1989, on the application of this subsection, including whether indemnification agreements under this subsection are being used, the number of claims that have been filed under such agreements, and the need for this subsection. The Comptroller General shall report the findings of the study to Congress no later than September 30, 1989.

(d) The exemption provided under subsection (a) and the authority of the President to offer indemnification under subsection (c) shall not apply to any person covered by the provisions of paragraph (1), (2), (3), or (4) of section 107(a) with respect to the release or threatened release concerned if such person would be covered by such provisions even if such person had not carried out any actions referred to in subsection (e) of this section.

(e) For purposes of this section—

(1) The term "response action contract" means any written contract or agreement entered into by a response action contractor (as defined in paragraph (2)(A) of this subsection) with—

(A) the President;

(B) any Federal agency;

(C) a State or political subdivision which has entered into a contract or cooperative agreement in accordance with section 104(d)(1) of this Act; or

(D) any potentially responsible party carrying out an agreement under section 106 or 122;

to provide any remedial action under this Act at a facility listed on the National Priorities List, or any removal under this Act, with respect to any release or threatened release of a hazardous substance or pollutant or contaminant from the facility or to provide any evaluation, planning, engineering, surveying and mapping, design, construction, equipment, or any ancillary services thereto for such facility.

(2) The term "response action contractor" means—

(A) any—

(i) person who enters into a response action contract with respect to any release or threatened release of a hazardous substance or pollutant or contaminant from a facility and is carrying out such contract; and

(ii) person, public or nonprofit private entity, conducting a field demonstration pursuant to section 311(b); and

    (iii) Recipients of grants (including sub-grantees) under section 126 for the training and education of workers who are or may be engaged in activities related to hazardous waste removal, containment, or emergency response under this Act; and

  (B) any person who is retained or hired by a person described in subparagraph (A) to provide any services relating to a response action.

  (3) The term "insurance" means liability insurance which is fair and reasonably priced, as determined by the President, and which is made available at the time the contractor enters into the response action contract to provide response action.

(f) Response action contractors and subcontractors for program management, construction management, architectural and engineering, surveying and mapping, and related services shall be selected in accordance with title IX of the Federal Property and Administrative Services Act of 1949. The Federal selection procedures shall apply to appropriate contracts negotiated by all Federal governmental agencies involved in carrying out this Act. Such procedures shall be followed by response action contractors and subcontractors.

§ 9620. Federal facilities

[Sec. 120] (a)(1) Each department, agency, and instrumentality of the United States (including the executive, legislative, and judicial branches of government) shall be subject to, and comply with, this Act in the same manner and to the same extent, both procedurally and substantively, as any nongovernmental entity, including liability under section 107 of this Act. Nothing in this section shall be construed to affect the liability of any person or entity under sections 106 and 107.

  (2) All guidelines, rules, regulations, and criteria which are applicable to preliminary assessments carried out under this Act for facilities at which hazardous substances are located, applicable to evaluations of such facilities under the National Contingency Plan, applicable to inclusion on the National Priorities List, or applicable to remedial actions at such facilities shall also be applicable to facilities which are owned or operated by a department, agency, or instrumentality of the United States in the same manner and to the extent as such guidelines, rules, regulations, and criteria are applicable to other facilities. No department, agency, or instrumentality of the United States may adopt or utilize any such guidelines, rules, regulations, or criteria which are inconsistent with the guidelines, rules, regulations, and criteria established by the Administrator under this Act.

  (3) This subsection shall not apply to the extent otherwise provided in this section with respect to applicable time periods. This subsection shall

also not apply to any requirements relating to bonding, insurance, or financial responsibility. Nothing in this Act shall be construed to require a State to comply with section 104(c)(3) in the case of a facility which is owned or operated by any department, agency, or instrumentality of the United States.

(4) State laws concerning removal and remedial action, including State laws regarding enforcement, shall apply to removal and remedial action at facilities owned or operated by a department, agency, or instrumentality of the United States when such facilities are not included on the National Priorities List. The preceding sentence shall not apply to the extent a State law would apply any standard or requirement to such facilities which is more stringent than the standards and requirements applicable to facilities which are not owned or operated by any such department, agency, or instrumentality.

(b) Each department, agency, and instrumentality of the United States shall add to the inventory of Federal agency hazardous waste facilities required to be submitted under section 3016 of the Solid Waste Disposal Act (in addition to the information required under section 3016(a)(3) of such Act) information on contamination from each facility owned or operated by the department, agency, or instrumentality if such contamination affects contiguous or adjacent property owned by the department, agency, or instrumentality or by any other person, including a description of the monitoring data obtained.

(c) The Administrator shall establish a special Federal Agency Hazardous Waste Compliance Docket (hereinafter in this section referred to as the "docket") which shall contain each of the following:

(1) All information submitted under section 3016 of the Solid Waste Disposal Act and subsection (b) of this section regarding any Federal facility and notice of each subsequent action taken under this Act with respect to the facility.

(2) Information submitted by each department, agency, or instrumentality of the United States under section 3005 or 3010 of such Act.

(3) Information submitted by the department, agency, or instrumentality under section 103 of this Act.

The docket shall be available for public inspection at reasonable times. Six months after establishment of the docket and every 6 months thereafter, the Administrator shall publish in the Federal Register a list of the Federal facilities which have been included in the docket during the immediately preceding 6-month period. Such publication shall also indicate where in the appropriate regional office of the Environmental Protection Agency additional information may be obtained with respect to any facility on the docket. The Administrator shall establish a program to provide information to the public with respect to facilities which are included in the docket under this subsection.

(d) Not later than 18 months after the enactment of the Superfund Amendments and Reauthorization Act of 1986, the Administrator shall take steps to assure that a preliminary assessment is conducted for each facility on the docket. Following such preliminary assessment, the Administrator shall, where appropriate—

(1) evaluate such facilities in accordance with the criteria established in accordance with section 105 under the National Contingency Plan for determining priorities among releases; and

(2) include such facilities on the National Priorities List maintained under such plan if the facility meets such criteria.

Such criteria shall be applied in the same manner as the criteria are applied to facilities which are owned or operated by other persons. Evaluation and listing under this subsection shall be completed not later than 30 months after such date of enactment. Upon the receipt of a petition from the Governor of any State, the Administrator shall make such an evaluation of any facility included in the docket.

(e)(1) Not later than 6 months after the inclusion of any facility on the National Priorities List, the department, agency, or instrumentality which owns or operates such facility shall, in consultation with the Administrator and appropriate State authorities, commence a remedial investigation and feasibility study for such facility. In the case of any facility which is listed on such list before the date of the enactment of this section, the department, agency, or instrumentality which owns or operates such facility shall, in consultation with the Administrator and appropriate State authorities, commence such an investigation and study for such facility within one year after such date of enactment. The Administrator and appropriate State authorities shall publish a timetable and deadlines for expeditious completion of such investigation and study.

(2) The Administrator shall review the results of each investigation and study conducted as provided in paragraph (1). Within 180 days thereafter, the head of the department, agency, or instrumentality concerned shall enter into an interagency agreement with the Administrator for the expeditious completion by such department, agency, or instrumentality of all necessary remedial action at such facility. Substantial continuous physical onsite remedial action shall be commenced at each facility not later than 15 months after completion of the investigation and study. All such interagency agreements, including review of alternative remedial action plans and selection of remedial action, shall comply with the public participation requirements of section 117.

(3) Remedial actions at facilities subject to interagency agreements under this section shall be completed as expeditiously as practicable. Each agency shall include in its annual budget submissions to the Congress a review of alternative agency funding which could be used to provide for the costs of remedial action. The budget submission shall also

include a statement of the hazard posed by the facility to human health, welfare, and the environment and identify the specific consequences of failure to begin and complete remedial action.

(4) Each interagency agreement under this subsection shall include, but shall not be limited to, each of the following:

    (A) A review of alternative remedial actions and selection of a remedial action by the head of the relevant department, agency, or instrumentality and the Administrator or, if unable to reach agreement on selection of a remedial action, selection by the Administrator.

    (B) A schedule for the completion of each such remedial action.

    (C) Arrangements for long-term operation and maintenance of the facility.

(5) Each department, agency, or instrumentality responsible for compliance with this section shall furnish an annual report to the Congress concerning its progress in implementing the requirements of this section. Such reports shall include, but shall not be limited to, each of the following items:

    (A) A report on the progress in reaching interagency agreements under this section.

    (B) The specific cost estimates and budgetary proposals involved in each interagency agreement.

    (C) A brief summary of the public comments regarding each proposed interagency agreement.

    (D) A description of the instances in which no agreement was reached.

    (E) A report on progress in conducting investigations and studies under paragraph (1).

    (F) A report on progress in conducting remedial actions.

    (G) A report on progress in conducting remedial action at facilities which are not listed on the National Priorities List.

With respect to instances in which no agreement was reached within the required time period, the department, agency, or instrumentality filing the report under this paragraph shall include in such report an explanation of the reasons why no agreement was reached. The annual report required by this paragraph shall also contain a detailed description on a State-by-State basis of the status of each facility subject to this section, including a description of the hazard presented by each facility, plans and schedules for initiating and completing response action, enforcement status (where appropriate), and an explanation of any postponements or failure to complete response action. Such reports shall also be submitted to the affected States.

(6) If the Administrator, in consultation with the head of the relevant department, agency, or instrumentality of the United States, determines that remedial investigations and feasibility studies or remedial

action will be done properly at the Federal facility by another potentially responsible party within the deadlines provided in paragraphs (1), (2), and (3) of this subsection, the Administrator may enter into an agreement with such party under section 122 (relating to settlements). Following approval by the Attorney General of any such agreement relating to a remedial action, the agreement shall be entered in the appropriate United States district court as a consent decree under section 106 of this Act.

(f) The Administrator and each department, agency, or instrumentality responsible for compliance with this section shall afford to relevant State and local officials the opportunity to participate in the planning and selection of the remedial action, including but not limited to the review of all applicable data as it becomes available and the development of studies, reports, and action plans. In the case of State officials, the opportunity to participate shall be provided in accordance with section 121.

(g) Except for authorities which are delegated by the Administrator to an officer or employee of the Environmental Protection Agency, no authority vested in the Administrator under this section may be transferred, by executive order of the President or otherwise, to any other officer or employee of the United States or to any other person.

(h)(1) After the last day of the 6-month period beginning on the effective date of regulations under paragraph (2) of this subsection, whenever any department, agency, or instrumentality of the United States enters into any contract for the sale or other transfer of real property which is owned by the United States and on which any hazardous substance was stored for one year or more, known to have been released, or disposed of, the head of such department, agency, or instrumentality shall include in such contract notice of the type and quantity of such hazardous substance and notice of the time at which such storage, release, or disposal took place, to the extent such information is available on the basis of a complete search of agency files.

(2) Notice under this subsection shall be provided in such form and manner as may be provided in regulations promulgated by the Administrator. As promptly as practicable after the enactment of this subsection but not later than 18 months after the date of such enactment, and after consultation with the Administrator of the General Services Administration, the Administrator shall promulgate regulations regarding the notice required to be provided under this subsection.

(3) After the last day of the 6-month period beginning on the effective date of regulations under paragraph (2) of this subsection, in the case of any real property owned by the United States on which any hazardous substance was stored for one year or more, known to have been released, or disposed of, each deed entered into for the transfer of such property by the United States to any other person or entity shall

contain—
(A) to the extent such information is available on the basis of a complete search of agency files—
   (i) a notice of the type and quantity of such hazardous substances,
   (ii) notice of the time at which such storage, release, or disposal took place, and
   (iii) a description of the remedial action taken, if any, and
(B) a covenant warranting that—
   (i) all remedial action necessary to protect human health and the environment with respect to any such substance remaining on the property has been taken before the date of such transfer, and
   (ii) any additional remedial action found to be necessary after the date of such transfer shall be conducted by the United States.

The requirements of subparagraph (B) shall not apply in any case in which the person or entity to whom the property is transferred is a potentially responsible party with respect to such real property.

(i) Nothing in this section shall affect or impair the obligation of any department, agency, or instrumentality of the United States to comply with any requirement of the Solid Waste Disposal Act (including corrective action requirements).

(j)(1) Site specific presidential orders.—The President may issue such orders regarding response actions at any specified site or facility of the Department of Energy or the Department of Defense as may be necessary to protect the national security interests of the United States at that site or facility. Such orders may include, where necessary to protect such interests, an exemption from any requirement contained in this title or under title III of the Superfund Amendments and Reauthorization Act of 1986 with respect to the site or facility concerned. The President shall notify the Congress within 30 days of the issuance of an order under this paragraph providing for any such exemption. Such notification shall include a statement of the reasons for the granting of the exemption. An exemption under this paragraph shall be for a specified period which may not exceed one year. Additional exemptions may be granted, each upon the President's issuance of a new order under this paragraph for the site or facility concerned. Each such additional exemption shall be for a specified period which may not exceed one year. It is the intention of the Congress that whenever an exemption is issued under this paragraph the response action shall proceed as expeditiously as practicable. The Congress shall be notified periodically of the progress of any response action with respect to which an exemption has been issued under this paragraph. No exemption shall be granted under this paragraph due to lack of appropriation unless the President shall have specifically requested such appropriation as a part of the budgetary process and the Congress shall have failed to make available such requested appropriation.

(2) Notwithstanding any other provision of law, all requirements of the Atomic Energy Act and all Executive orders concerning the handling of restricted data and national security information, including "need to know" requirements, shall be applicable to any grant of access to classified information under the provisions of this Act or under title III of the Superfund Amendments and Reauthorization Act of 1986.

§ 9621. Cleanup standards

[Sec. 121] (a) The President shall select appropriate remedial actions determined to be necessary to be carried out under section 104 or secured under section 106 which are in accordance with this section and, to the extent practicable, the national contingency plan, and which provide for cost-effective response. In evaluating the cost effectiveness of proposed alternative remedial actions, the President shall take into account the total short- and long-term costs of such actions, including the costs of operation and maintenance for the entire period during which such activities will be required.

(b)(1) Remedial actions in which treatment which permanently and significantly reduces the volume, toxicity or mobility of the hazardous substances, pollutants, and contaminants is a principal element, are to be preferred over remedial actions not involving such treatment. The offsite transport and disposal of hazardous substances or contaminated materials without such treatment should be the least favored alternative remedial action where practicable treatment technologies are available. The President shall conduct an assessment of permanent solutions and alternative treatment technologies or resource recovery technologies that, in whole or in part, will result in a permanent and significant decrease in the toxicity, mobility, or volume of the hazardous substance, pollutant, or contaminant. In making such assessment, the President shall specifically address the long-term effectiveness of various alternatives. In assessing alternative remedial actions, the President shall, at a minimum, take into account:

(A) the long-term uncertainties associated with land disposal;
(B) the goals, objectives, and requirements of the Solid Waste Disposal Act;
(C) the persistence, toxicity, mobility, and propensity to bioaccumulate of such hazardous substances and their constituents;
(D) short- and long-term potential for adverse health effects from human exposure;
(E) long-term maintenance costs;
(F) the potential for future remedial action costs if the alternative remedial action in question were to fail; and
(G) the potential threat to human health and the environment associated with excavation, transportation, and redisposal, or containment.

The President shall select a remedial action that is protective of human health and the environment, that is cost effective, and that utilizes permanent solutions and alternative treatment technologies or resource recovery technologies to the maximum extent practicable. If the President selects a remedial action not appropriate for a preference under this subsection, the President shall publish an explanation as to why a remedial action involving such reductions was not selected.

(2) The President may select an alternative remedial action meeting the objectives of this subsection whether or not such action has been achieved in practice at any other facility or site that has similar characteristics. In making such a selection, the President may take into account the degree of support for such remedial action by parties interested in such site.

(c) If the President selects a remedial action that results in any hazardous substances, pollutants, or contaminants remaining at the site, the President shall review such remedial action no less often than each 5 years after the initiation of such remedial action to assure that human health and the environment are being protected by the remedial action being implemented. In addition, if upon such review it is the judgment of the President that action is appropriate at such site in accordance with section 104 or 106, the President shall take or require such action. The President shall report to the Congress a list of facilities for which such review is required, the results of all such reviews, and any actions taken as a result of such reviews.

(d)(1) Remedial actions selected under this section or otherwise required or agreed to by the President under this Act shall attain a degree of cleanup of hazardous substances, pollutants, and contaminants released into the environment and of control of further release at a minimum which assures protection of human health and the environment. Such remedial actions shall be relevant and appropriate under the circumstances presented by the release or threatened release of such substance, pollutant, or contaminant.

(2)(A) With respect to any hazardous substance, pollutant or contaminant that will remain onsite, if—

  (i) any standard, requirement, criteria, or limitation under any Federal environmental law, including, but not limited to, the Toxic Substances Control Act, the Safe Drinking Water Act, the Clean Air Act, the Clean Water Act, the Marine Protection, Research and Sanctuaries Act, or the Solid Waste Disposal Act; or

  (ii) any promulgated standard, requirement, criteria, or limitation under a State environmental or facility siting law that is more stringent than any Federal standard, requirement, criteria, or limitation, including each such State standard, requirement, criteria, or limitation contained in a program approved, authorized or delegated by the Administrator under a statute cited in subparagraph (A), and that has been identified to the President by the State in a timely manner, is legally applicable to the hazardous substance or pollutant or contaminant concerned or is relevant and appropriate under the circumstances of the release or threatened release of such hazardous substance or pollutant or contaminant, the remedial action selected under section 104 or secured under section 106 shall require, at the completion of the remedial action, a level or standard of control for such hazardous substance or pollutant or contaminant which at least attains such legally applicable or relevant and appropriate standard, requirement, criteria, or limitation. Such remedial action shall require a level or standard of control which at least attains Maximum Contaminant Level Goals established under the Safe Drinking Water Act and water quality criteria established under section 304 or 303 of the Clean Water Act, where such goals or criteria are relevant and appropriate under the circumstances of the release or threatened release.

(B)(i) In determining whether or not any water quality criteria under the Clean Water Act is relevant and appropriate under the circumstances of the release or threatened release, the President shall consider the designated or potential use of the surface or groundwater, the environmental media affected, the purposes for which such criteria were developed, and the latest information available.

(ii) For the purposes of this section, a process for establishing alternate concentration limits to those otherwise applicable for hazardous constituents in groundwater under subparagraph (A) may not be used to establish applicable standards under this paragraph if the process assumes a point of human exposure beyond the boundary of the facility, as defined at the conclusion of the remedial investigation and feasibility study, except where—

(I) there are known and projected points of entry of such groundwater into surface water; and

(II) on the basis of measurements or projections, there is or will be no statistically significant increase of such constituents from such groundwater in such surface water at the point of entry or at any point where there is reason to believe accumulation of constituents may occur downstream; and

(III) the remedial action includes enforceable measures that will preclude human exposure to the contaminated groundwater at any point between the facility boundary and all known and projected points of entry of such groundwater into surface water

then the assumed point of human exposure may be at such known and projected points of entry.

(C)(i) Clause (ii) of this subparagraph shall be applicable only in cases where, due to the President's selection, in compliance with subsection (b)(1), of a proposed remedial action which does not permanently and significantly reduce the volume, toxicity, or mobility of hazardous substances, pollutants, or contaminants, the proposed disposition of waste generated by or associated with the remedial action selected by the President is land disposal in a State referred to in clause (ii).

(ii) Except as provided in clauses (iii) and (iv), a State standard, requirement, criteria, or limitation (including any State siting standard or requirement) which could effectively result in the statewide prohibition of land disposal of hazardous substances, pollutants, or contaminants shall not apply.

(iii) Any State standard, requirement, criteria, or limitation referred to in clause (ii) shall apply where each of the following conditions is met:

(I) The State standard, requirement, criteria, or limitation is of general applicability and was adopted by formal means.

(II) The State standard, requirement, criteria, or limitation was adopted on the basis of hydrologic, geologic, or other relevant considerations and was not adopted for the purpose of precluding onsite remedial actions or other land disposal for reasons unrelated to protection of human health and the environment.

(III) The State arranges for, and assures payment of the incremental costs of utilizing, a facility for disposition of the hazardous substances, pollutants, or contaminants concerned.

(iv) Where the remedial action selected by the President does not conform to a State standard and the State has initiated a law suit against the Environmental Protection Agency prior to May 1, 1986, to seek to have the remedial action conform to such standard, the President shall conform the remedial action to the State standard. The State shall assure the availability of an offsite facility for such remedial action.

(3) In the case of any removal or remedial action involving the transfer of any hazardous substance or pollutant or contaminant offsite, such hazardous substance or pollutant or contaminant shall only be transferred to a facility which is operating in compliance with section 3004 and 3005 of the Solid Waste Disposal Act (or, where applicable, in compliance with the Toxic Substances Control Act or other applicable Federal law) and all applicable State requirements. Such substance or pollutant or contaminant may be transferred to a land disposal facility only if the President determines that both of the following requirements are met:

(A) The unit to which the hazardous substance or pollutant or contaminant is transferred is not releasing any hazardous waste, or constituent thereof, into the groundwater or surface water or soil.

(B) All such releases from other units at the facility are being controlled by a corrective action program approved by the Administrator under subtitle C of the Solid Waste Disposal Act.

The President shall notify the owner or operator of such facility of determinations under this paragraph.

(4) The President may select a remedial action meeting the requirements of paragraph (1) that does not attain a level or standard of control at least equivalent to a legally applicable or relevant and appropriate standard, requirement, criteria, or limitation as required by paragraph (2) (including subparagraph (B) thereof), if the President finds that—

(A) the remedial action selected is only part of a total remedial action that will attain such level or standard of control when completed;

(B) compliance with such requirement at that facility will result in greater risk to human health and the environment than alternative options;

(C) compliance with such requirements is technically impracticable from an engineering perspective;

(D) the remedial action selected will attain a standard of performance that is equivalent to that required under the otherwise applicable standard, requirement, criteria, or limitation, through use of another method or approach;

(E) with respect to a State standard, requirement, criteria, or limitation, the State has not consistently applied (or demonstrated the intention to consistently apply) the standard, requirement, criteria, or limitation in similar circumstances at other remedial actions within the State; or

(F) in the case of a remedial action to be undertaken solely under section 104 using the Fund, selection of a remedial action that attains such level or standard of control will not provide a balance between the need for protection of public health and welfare and the environment at the facility under consideration, and the availability of amounts from the Fund to respond to other sites which present or may present a threat to public health or welfare or the environment, taking into consideration the relative immediacy of such threats.

The President shall publish such findings, together with an explanation and appropriate documentation.

(e)(1) No Federal, State, or local permit shall be required for the portion of any removal or remedial action conducted entirely onsite, where such remedial action is selected and carried out in compliance with this section.

(2) A State may enforce any Federal or State standard, requirement,

criteria, or limitation to which the remedial action is required to conform under this Act in the United States district court for the district in which the facility is located. Any consent decree shall require the parties to attempt expeditiously to resolve disagreements concerning implementation of the remedial action informally with the appropriate Federal and State agencies. Where the parties agree, the consent decree may provide for administrative enforcement. Each consent decree shall also contain stipulated penalties for violations of the decree in an amount not to exceed $25,000 per day, which may be enforced by either the President or the State. Such stipulated penalties shall not be construed to impair or affect the authority of the court to order compliance with the specific terms of any such decree.

(f)(1) The President shall promulgate regulations providing for substantial and meaningful involvement by each State in initiation, development, and selection of remedial actions to be undertaken in that State. The regulations, at a minimum, shall include each of the following:

(A) State involvement in decisions whether to perform a preliminary assessment and site inspection.

(B) Allocation of responsibility for hazard ranking system scoring.

(C) State concurrence in deleting sites from the National Priorities List.

(D) State participation in the long-term planning process for all remedial sites within the State.

(E) A reasonable opportunity for States to review and comment on each of the following:

(i) The remedial investigation and feasibility study and all data and technical documents leading to its issuance.

(ii) The planned remedial action identified in the remedial investigation and feasibility study.

(iii) The engineering design following selection of the final remedial action.

(iv) Other technical data and reports relating to implementation of the remedy.

(v) Any proposed finding or decision by the President to exercise the authority of subsection (d)(4).

(F) Notice to the State of negotiations with potentially responsible parties regarding the scope of any response action at a facility in the State and an opportunity to participate in such negotiations and, subject to paragraph (2), be a party to any settlement.

(G) Notice to the State and an opportunity to comment on the President's proposed plan for remedial action as well as on alternative plans under consideration. The President's proposed decision regarding the selection of remedial action shall be accompanied by a response to the comments submitted by the State, including an explanation regarding any decision under subsection (d)(4) on compliance with promulgated State standards. A copy of such response shall also be provided to the State.

(H) Prompt notice and explanation of each proposed action to the State in which the facility is located.

Prior to the promulgation of such regulations, the President shall provide notice to the State of negotiations with potentially responsible parties regarding the scope of any response action at a facility in the State, and such State may participate in such negotiations and, subject to paragraph (2), any settlements.

(2)(A) This paragraph shall apply to remedial actions secured under section 106. At least 30 days prior to the entering of any consent decree, if the President proposes to select a remedial action that does not attain a legally applicable or relevant and appropriate standard, requirement, criteria, or limitation, under the authority of subsection (d)(4), the President shall provide an opportunity for the State to concur or not concur in such selection. If the State concurs, the State may become a signatory to the consent decree.

(B) If the State does not concur in such selection, and the State desires to have the remedial action conform to such standard, requirement, criteria, or limitation, the State shall intervene in the action under section 106 before entry of the consent decree, to seek to have the remedial action so conform. Such intervention shall be a matter of right. The remedial action shall conform to such standard, requirement, criteria, or limitation if the State establishes, on the administrative record, that the finding of the President was not supported by substantial evidence. If the court determines that the remedial action shall conform to such standard, requirement, criteria, or limitation, the remedial action shall be so modified and the State may become a signatory to the decree. If the court determines that the remedial action need not conform to such standard, requirement, criteria, or limitation, and the State pays or assures the payment of the additional costs attributable to meeting such standard, requirement, criteria, or limitation, the remedial action shall be so modified and the State shall become a signatory to the decree.

(C) The President may conclude settlement negotiations with potentially responsible parties without State concurrence.

(3)(A) This paragraph shall apply to remedial actions at facilities owned or operated by a department, agency, or instrumentality of the United States. At least 30 days prior to the publication of the President's final remedial action plan, if the President proposes to select a remedial action that does not attain a legally applicable or relevant and appropriate standard, requirement, criteria, or limitation, under the authority of subsection (d)(4), the President shall provide an opportunity for the State to concur or not concur in such selection. If the State concurs, or does not act within 30 days, the remedial action may proceed.

(B) If the State does not concur in such selection as provided in subparagraph (A), and desires to have the remedial action conform to such standard, requirement, criteria, or limitation, the State may maintain an action as follows:

  (i) If the President has notified the State of selection of such a remedial action, the State may bring an action within 30 days of such notification for the sole purpose of determining whether the finding of the President is supported by substantial evidence. Such action shall be brought in the United States district court for the district in which the facility is located.

  (ii) If the State establishes, on the administrative record, that the President's finding is not supported by substantial evidence, the remedial action shall be modified to conform to such standard, requirement, criteria, or limitation.

  (iii) If the State fails to establish that the President's finding was not supported by substantial evidence and if the State pays, within 60 days of judgment, the additional costs attributable to meeting such standard, requirement, criteria, or limitation, the remedial action shall be selected to meet such standard, requirement, criteria, or limitation. If the State fails to pay within 60 days, the remedial action selected by the President shall proceed through completion.

(C) Nothing in this section precludes, and the court shall not enjoin, the Federal agency from taking any remedial action unrelated to or not inconsistent with such standard, requirement, criteria, or limitation.

§ 9622.   Settlements

[Sec. 122] (a) The President, in his discretion, may enter into an agreement with any person (including the owner or operator of the facility from which a release or substantial threat of release emanates, or any other potentially responsible person), to perform any response action (including any action described in section 104(b)) if the President determines that such action will be done properly by such person. Whenever practicable and in the public interest, as determined by the President, the President shall act to facilitate agreements under this section that are in the public interest and consistent with the National Contingency Plan in order to expedite effective remedial actions and minimize litigation. If the President decides not to use the procedures in this section, the President shall notify in writing potentially responsible parties at the facility of such decision and the reasons why use of the procedures is inappropriate. A decision of the President to use or not to use the procedures in this section is not subject to judicial review.

(b)(1) An agreement under this section may provide that the President will reimburse the parties to the agreement from the Fund, with interest, for certain costs of actions under the agreement that the parties have agreed to perform but which the President has agreed to finance. In any case in which the President provides such reimbursement, the President shall make all reasonable efforts to recover the amount of such reimbursement under section 107 or under other relevant authorities.

(2) The President's decisions regarding the availability of fund financing under this subsection shall not be subject to judicial review under subsection (d).

(3) If, as part of any agreement, the President will be carrying out any action and the parties will be paying amounts to the President, the President may, notwithstanding any other provision of law, retain and use such amounts for purposes of carrying out the agreement.

(4) In the case of a completed remedial action pursuant to an agreement described in paragraph (1), the Fund shall be subject to an obligation for subsequent remedial actions at the same facility but only to the extent that such subsequent actions are necessary by reason of the failure of the original remedial action. Such obligation shall be in a proportion equal to, but not exceeding, the proportion contributed by the Fund for the original remedial action. The Fund's obligation for such future remedial action may be met through Fund expenditures or through payment, following settlement or enforcement action, by parties who were not signatories to the original agreement.

(c)(1) Whenever the President has entered into an agreement under this section, the liability to the United States under this Act of each party to the agreement, including any future liability to the United States, arising from the release or threatened release that is the subject of the agreement shall be limited as provided in the agreement pursuant to a covenant not to sue in accordance with subsection (f). A covenant not to sue may provide that future liability to the United States of a settling potentially responsible party under the agreement may be limited to the same proportion as that established in the original settlement agreement. Nothing in this section shall limit or otherwise affect the authority of any court to review in the consent decree process under subsection (d) any covenant not to sue contained in an agreement under this section. In determining the extent to which the liability of parties to an agreement shall be limited pursuant to a covenant not to sue, the President shall be guided by the principle that a more complete covenant not to sue shall be provided for a more permanent remedy undertaken by such parties.

(2) If an agreement has been entered into under this section, the President may take any action under section 106 against any person who is not a party to the agreement, once the period for submitting a proposal under subsection (e)(2)(B) has expired. Nothing in this section shall be construed to affect either of the following:

(A) The liability of any person under section 106 or 107 with respect to any costs or damages which are not included in the agreement.

(B) The authority of the President to maintain an action under this Act against any person who is not a party to the agreement.

(d)(1)(A) Whenever the President enters into an agreement under this section with any potentially responsible party with respect to remedial action under section 106, following approval of the agreement by the Attorney General, except as otherwise provided in the case of certain administrative settlements referred to in subsection (g), the agreement shall be entered in the appropriate United States district court as a consent decree. The President need not make any finding regarding an imminent and substantial endangerment to the public health or the environment in connection with any such agreement or consent decree.

(B) The entry of any consent decree under this subsection shall not be construed to be an acknowledgment by the parties that the release or threatened release concerned constitutes an imminent and substantial endangerment to the public health or welfare or the environment. Except as otherwise provided in the Federal Rules of Evidence, the participation by any party in the process under this section shall not be considered an admission of liability for any purpose, and the fact of such participation shall not be admissible in any judicial or administrative proceeding, including a subsequent proceeding under this section.

(C) The President may fashion a consent decree so that the entering of such decree and compliance with such decree or with any determination or agreement made pursuant to this section shall not be considered an admission of liability for any purpose.

(2)(A) At least 30 days before a final judgment is entered under paragraph (1), the proposed judgment shall be filed with the court.

(B) The Attorney General shall provide an opportunity to persons who are not named as parties to the action to comment on the proposed judgment before its entry by the court as a final judgment. The Attorney General shall consider, and file with the court, any written comments, views, or allegations relating to the proposed judgment. The Attorney General may withdraw or withhold its consent to the proposed judgment if the comments, views, and allegations concerning the judgment disclose facts or considerations which indicate that the proposed judgment is inappropriate, improper, or inadequate.

(3) Whenever the President enters into an agreement under this section with any potentially responsible party with respect to action under section 104(b), the President shall issue an order or enter into a decree setting forth the obligations of such party. The United States district court for the district in which the release or threatened release occurs may enforce such order or decree.

(e)(1) Whenever the President determines that a period of negotiation under this subsection would facilitate an agreement with potentially responsible parties for taking response action (including any action described in section 104(b)) and would expedite remedial action, the President shall so notify all such parties and shall provide them with information concerning each of the following:

- (A) The names and addresses of potentially responsible parties (including owners and operators and other persons referred to in section 107(a)), to the extent such information is available.
- (B) To the extent such information is available, the volume and nature of substances contributed by each potentially responsible party identified at the facility.
- (C) A ranking by volume of the substances at the facility, to the extent such information is available.

The President shall make the information referred to in this paragraph available in advance of notice under this paragraph upon the request of a potentially responsible party in accordance with procedures provided by the President. The provisions of subsection (e) of section 104 regarding protection of confidential information apply to information provided under this paragraph. Disclosure of information generated by the President under this section to persons other than the Congress, or any duly authorized Committee thereof, is subject to other privileges or protections provided by law, including (but not limited to) those applicable to attorney work product. Nothing contained in this paragraph or in other provisions of this Act shall be construed, interpreted, or applied to diminish the required disclosure of information under other provisions of this or other Federal or State laws.

(2)(A) Except as provided in this subsection, the President may not commence action under section 104(a) or take any action under section 106 for 120 days after providing notice and information under this subsection with respect to such action. Except as provided in this subsection, the President may not commence a remedial investigation and feasibility study under section 104(b) for 90 days after providing notice and information under this subsection with respect to such action. The President may commence any additional studies or investigations authorized under section 104(b), including remedial design, during the negotiation period.

- (B) Persons receiving notice and information under paragraph (1) of this subsection with respect to action under section 106 shall have 60 days from the date of receipt of such notice to make a proposal to the President for undertaking or financing the action under section 106. Persons receiving notice and information under paragraph (1) of this subsection with respect to action under section 104(b) shall have 60 days from the date of receipt of such notice to make a proposal to the President for undertaking or financing the action under section 104(b).

(C) If an additional potentially responsible party is identified during the negotiation period or after an agreement has been entered into under this subsection concerning a release or threatened release, the President may bring the additional party into the negotiation or enter into a separate agreement with such party.

(3)(A) The President shall develop guidelines for preparing nonbinding preliminary allocations of responsibility. In developing these guidelines the President may include such factors as the President considers relevant, such as: volume, toxicity, mobility, strength of evidence, ability to pay, litigative risks, public interest considerations, precedential value, and inequities and aggravating factors. When it would expedite settlements under this section and remedial action, the President may, after completion of the remedial investigation and feasibility study, provide a nonbinding preliminary allocation of responsibility which allocates percentages of the total cost of response among potentially responsible parties at the facility.

(B) To collect information necessary or appropriate for performing the allocation under subparagraph (A) or for otherwise implementing this section, the President may by subpoena require the attendance and testimony of witnesses and the production of reports, papers, documents, answers to questions, and other information that the President deems necessary. Witnesses shall be paid the same fees and mileage that are paid witnesses in the courts of the United States. In the event of contumacy or failure or refusal of any person to obey any such subpoena, any district court of the United States in which venue is proper shall have jurisdiction to order any such person to comply with such subpoena. Any failure to obey such an order of the court is punishable by the court as a contempt thereof.

(C) The nonbinding preliminary allocation of responsibility shall not be admissible as evidence in any proceeding, and no court shall have jurisdiction to review the nonbinding preliminary allocation of responsibility. The nonbinding preliminary allocation of responsibility shall not constitute an apportionment or other statement on the divisibility of harm or causation.

(D) The costs incurred by the President in producing the nonbinding preliminary allocation of responsibility shall be reimbursed by the potentially responsible parties whose offer is accepted by the President. Where an offer under this section is not accepted, such costs shall be considered costs of response.

(E) Where the President, in his discretion, has provided a nonbinding preliminary allocation of responsibility and the potentially responsible parties have made a substantial offer providing for response to the President which he rejects, the reasons for the rejection shall be provided in a written explanation. The President's decision to reject such an offer shall not be subject to judicial review.

(4) If the President determines that a good faith proposal for undertaking or financing action under section 106 has not been submitted within 60 days of the provision of notice pursuant to this subsection, the President may thereafter commence action under section 104(a) or take an action against any person under section 106 of this Act. If the President determines that a good faith proposal for undertaking or financing action under section 104(b) has not been submitted within 60 days after the provision of notice pursuant to this subsection, the President may thereafter commence action under section 104(b).

(5) Nothing in this subsection shall limit the President's authority to undertake response or enforcement action regarding a significant threat to public health or the environment within the negotiation period established by this subsection.

(6) When either the President, or a potentially responsible party pursuant to an administrative order or consent decree under this Act, has initiated a remedial investigation and feasibility study for a particular facility under this Act, no potentially responsible party may undertake any remedial action at the facility unless such remedial action has been authorized by the President.

(f)(1) The President may, in his discretion, provide any person with a covenant not to sue concerning any liability to the United States under this Act, including future liability, resulting from a release or threatened release of a hazardous substance addressed by a remedial action, whether that action is onsite or offsite, if each of the following conditions is met:

(A) The covenant not to sue is in the public interest.

(B) The covenant not to sue would expedite response action consistent with the National Contingency Plan under section 105 of this Act.

(C) The person is in full compliance with a consent decree under section 106 (including a consent decree entered into in accordance with this section) for response to the release or threatened release concerned.

(D) The response action has been approved by the President.

(2) In the case of any person to whom the President is authorized under paragraph (1) of this subsection to provide a covenant not to sue, for the portion of remedial action—

(A) which involves the transport and secure disposition offsite of hazardous substances in a facility meeting the requirements of sections 3004 (c), (d), (e), (f), (g), (m), (o), (p), (u), and (v) and 3005(c) of the Solid Waste Disposal Act, where the President has rejected a proposed remedial action that is consistent with the

National Contingency Plan that does not include such offsite disposition and has thereafter required offsite disposition; or

(B) which involves the treatment of hazardous substances so as to destroy, eliminate, or permanently immobilize the hazardous constituents of such substances, such that, in the judgment of the President, the substances no longer present any current or currently foreseeable future significant risk to public health, welfare or the environment, no byproduct of the treatment or destruction process presents any significant hazard to public health, welfare or the environment, and all byproducts are themselves treated, destroyed, or contained in a manner which assures that such byproducts do not present any current or currently foreseeable future significant risk to public health, welfare or the environment,

the President shall provide such person with a covenant not to sue with respect to future liability to the United States under this Act for a future release or threatened release of hazardous substances from such facility, and a person provided such covenant not to sue shall not be liable to the United States under section 106 or 107 with respect to such release or threatened release at a future time.

(3) A covenant not to sue concerning future liability to the United States shall not take effect until the President certifies that remedial action has been completed in accordance with the requirements of this Act at the facility that is the subject of such covenant.

(4) In assessing the appropriateness of a covenant not to sue under paragraph (1) and any condition to be included in a covenant not to sue under paragraph (1) or (2), the President shall consider whether the covenant or condition is in the public interest on the basis of such factors as the following:

(A) The effectiveness and reliability of the remedy, in light of the other alternative remedies considered for the facility concerned.

(B) The nature of the risks remaining at the facility.

(C) The extent to which performance standards are included in the order or decree.

(D) The extent to which the response action provides a complete remedy for the facility, including a reduction in the hazardous nature of the substances at the facility.

(E) The extent to which the technology used in the response action is demonstrated to be effective.

(F) Whether the Fund or other sources of funding would be available for any additional remedial actions that might eventually be necessary at the facility.

(G) Whether the remedial action will be carried out, in whole or in significant part, by the responsible parties themselves.

(5) Any covenant not to sue under this subsection shall be subject to the

satisfactory performance by such party of its obligations under the agreement concerned.

(6)(A) Except for the portion of the remedial action which is subject to a covenant not to sue under paragraph (2) or under subsection (g) (relating to de minimis settlements), a covenant not to sue a person concerning future liability to the United States shall include an exception to the covenant that allows the President to sue such person concerning future liability resulting from the release or threatened release that is the subject of the covenant where such liability arises out of conditions which are unknown at the time the President certifies under paragraph (3) that remedial action has been completed at the facility concerned.

(B) In extraordinary circumstances, the President may determine, after assessment of relevant factors such as those referred to in paragraph (4) and volume, toxicity, mobility, strength of evidence, ability to pay, litigative risks, public interest considerations, precedential value, and inequities and aggravating factors, not to include the exception referred to in subparagraph (A) if other terms, conditions, or requirements of the agreement containing the covenant not to sue are sufficient to provide all reasonable assurances that public health and the environment will be protected from any future releases at or from the facility.

(C) The President is authorized to include any provisions allowing future enforcement action under section 106 or 107 that in the discretion of the President are necessary and appropriate to assure protection of public health, welfare, and the environment.

(g)(1) Whenever practicable and in the public interest, as determined by the President, the President shall as promptly as possible reach a final settlement with a potentially responsible party in an administrative or civil action under section 106 or 107 if such settlement involves only a minor portion of the response costs at the facility concerned and, in the judgment of the President, the conditions in either of the following subparagraph (A) or (B) are met:

(A) Both of the following are minimal in comparison to other hazardous substances at the facility:

(i) The amount of the hazardous substances contributed by that party to the facility.

(ii) The toxic or other hazardous effects of the substances contributed by that party to the facility.

(B) The potentially responsible party—

(i) is the owner of the real property on or in which the facility is located;

(ii) did not conduct or permit the generation, transportation, storage, treatment, or disposal of any hazardous substance at the facility; and

        (iii) did not contribute to the release or threat of release of a hazardous substance at the facility through any action or omission.

        This subparagraph (B) does not apply if the potentially responsible party purchased the real property with actual or constructive knowledge that the property was used for the generation, transportation, storage, treatment, or disposal of any hazardous substance.

(2) The President may provide a covenant not to sue with respect to the facility concerned to any party who has entered into a settlement under this subsection unless such a covenant would be inconsistent with the public interest as determined under subsection (f).

(3) The President shall reach any such settlement or grant any such covenant not to sue as soon as possible after the President has available the information necessary to reach such a settlement or grant such a covenant.

(4) A settlement under this subsection shall be entered as a consent decree or embodied in an administrative order setting forth the terms of the settlement. In the case of any facility where the total response costs exceed $500,000 (excluding interest), if the settlement is embodied as an administrative order, the order may be issued only with the prior written approval of the Attorney General. If the Attorney General or his designee has not approved or disapproved the order within 30 days of this referral, the order shall be deemed to be approved unless the Attorney General and the Administrator have agreed to extend the time. The district court for the district in which the release or threatened release occurs may enforce any such administrative order.

(5) A party who has resolved its liability to the United States under this subsection shall not be liable for claims for contribution regarding matters addressed in the settlement. Such settlement does not discharge any of the other potentially responsible parties unless its terms so provide, but it reduces the potential liability of the others by the amount of the settlement.

(6) Nothing in this subsection shall be construed to affect the authority of the President to reach settlements with other potentially responsible parties under this Act.

(h)(1) The head of any department or agency with authority to undertake a response action under this Act pursuant to the national contingency plan may consider, compromise, and settle a claim under section 107 for costs incurred by the United States Government if the claim has not been referred to the Department of Justice for further action. In the case of any facility where the total response costs exceed $500,000 (excluding interest), any claim referred to in the preceding sentence may be compromised and settled only with the prior written approval of the Attorney General.

(2) Arbitration in accordance with regulations promulgated under this

subsection may be used as a method of settling claims of the United States where the total response costs for the facility concerned do not exceed $500,000 (excluding interest). After consultation with the Attorney General, the department or agency head may establish and publish regulations for the use of arbitration or settlement under this subsection.

(3) If any person fails to pay a claim that has been settled under this subsection, the department or agency head shall request the Attorney General to bring a civil action in an appropriate district court to recover the amount of such claim, plus costs, attorneys' fees, and interest from the date of the settlement. In such an action, the terms of the settlement shall not be subject to review.

(4) A person who has resolved its liability to the United States under this subsection shall not be liable for claims for contribution regarding matters addressed in the settlement. Such settlement shall not discharge any of the other potentially liable persons unless its terms so provide, but it reduces the potential liability of the others by the amount of the settlement.

(i)(1) At least 30 days before any settlement (including any settlement arrived at through arbitration) may become final under subsection (h), or under subsection (g) in the case of a settlement embodied in an administrative order, the head of the department or agency which has jurisdiction over the proposed settlement shall publish in the Federal Register notice of the proposed settlement. The notice shall identify the facility concerned and the parties to the proposed settlement.

(2) For a 30-day period beginning on the date of publication of notice under paragraph (1) of a proposed settlement, the head of the department or agency which has jurisdiction over the proposed settlement shall provide an opportunity for persons who are not parties to the proposed settlement to file written comments relating to the proposed settlement.

(3) The head of the department or agency shall consider any comments filed under paragraph (2) in determining whether or not to consent to the proposed settlement and may withdraw or withhold consent to the proposed settlement if such comments disclose facts or considerations which indicate the proposed settlement is inappropriate, improper, or inadequate.

(j)(1) Where a release or threatened release of any hazardous substance that is the subject of negotiations under this section may have resulted in damages to natural resources under the trusteeship of the United States, the President shall notify the Federal natural resource trustee of the negotiations and shall encourage the participation of such trustee in the negotiations.

(2) An agreement under this section may contain a covenant not to sue under section 107(a)(4)(C) for damages to natural resources under the trusteeship of the United States resulting from the release or threat-

ened release of hazardous substances that is the subject of the agreement, but only if the Federal natural resource trustee has agreed in writing to such covenant. The Federal natural resource trustee may agree to such covenant if the potentially responsible party agrees to undertake appropriate actions necessary to protect and restore the natural resources damaged by such release or threatened release of hazardous substances.

(k) The provisions of this section shall not apply to releases from a vessel.

(l) A potentially responsible party which is a party to an administrative order or consent decree entered pursuant to an agreement under this section or section 120 (relating to Federal facilities) or which is a party to an agreement under section 120 and which fails or refuses to comply with any term or condition of the order, decree or agreement shall be subject to a civil penalty in accordance with section 109.

(m) In the case of consent decrees and other settlements under this section (including covenants not to sue), no provision of this Act shall be construed to preclude or otherwise affect the applicability of general principles of law regarding the setting aside or modification of consent decrees or other settlements.

•

§ 9623. Reimbursement to local governments

[Sec. 123] (a) Any general purpose unit of local government for a political subdivision which is affected by a release or threatened release at any facility may apply to the President for reimbursement under this section.

(b)(1) The President is authorized to reimburse local community authorities for expenses incurred (before or after the enactment of the Superfund Amendments and Reauthorization Act of 1986) in carrying out temporary emergency measures necessary to prevent or mitigate injury to human health or the environment associated with the release or threatened release of any hazardous substance or pollutant or contaminant. Such measures may include, where appropriate, security fencing to limit access, response to fires and explosions, and other measures which require immediate response at the local level.

(2) Reimbursement under this section shall not supplant local funds normally provided for response.

(c) The amount of any reimbursement to any local authority under subsection (b)(1) may not exceed $25,000 for a single response. The reimbursement under this section with respect to a single facility shall be limited to the units of local government having jurisdiction over the political subdivision in which the facility is located.

(d) Reimbursements authorized pursuant to this section shall be in accordance with rules promulgated by the Administrator within one year after the enactment of the Superfund Amendments and Reauthorization Act of 1986.

§ 9624. Methane recovery

[Sec. 124] (a) In the case of a facility at which equipment for the recovery or processing (including recirculation of condensate) of methane has been installed, for purposes of this Act:

(1) The owner or operator of such equipment shall not be considered an "owner or operator", as defined in section 101(20), with respect to such facility.

(2) The owner or operator of such equipment shall not be considered to have arranged for disposal or treatment of any hazardous substance at such facility pursuant to section 107 of this Act.

(3) The owner or operator of such equipment shall not be subject to any action under section 106 with respect to such facility.

(b) Subsection (a) does not apply with respect to a release or threatened release of a hazardous substance from a facility described in subsection (a) if either of the following circumstances exist:

(1) The release or threatened release was primarily caused by activities of the owner or operator of the equipment described in subsection (a).

(2) The owner or operator of such equipment would be covered by paragraph (1), (2), (3), or (4) of subsection (a) of section 107 with respect to such release or threatened release if he were not the owner or operator of such equipment.

In the case of any release or threatened release referred to in paragraph (1), the owner or operator of the equipment described in subsection (a) shall be liable under this Act only for costs or damages primarily caused by the activities of such owner or operator.

§ 9625. Certain special study wastes

[Sec. 125] (a) This section shall apply only to facilities which are not included or proposed for inclusion on the National Priorities List and which contain substantial volumes of waste described in section 3001(b)(3)(A)(i) of the Solid Waste Disposal Act. As expeditiously as practicable, the President shall revise the hazard ranking system in effect under the National Contingency Plan with respect to such facilities in a manner which assures appropriate consideration of each of the following site-specific characteristics of such facilities:

(1) The quantity, toxicity, and concentrations of hazardous constituents which are present in such waste and a comparison thereof with other wastes.

(2) The extent of, and potential for, release of such hazardous constituents into the environment.

(3) The degree of risk to human health and the environment posed by

such constituents.

(b) Until the hazard ranking system is revised as required by this section, the President may not include on the National Priorities List any facility which contains substantial volumes of waste described in section 3001(b)(3)(A)(i) of the Solid Waste Disposal Act on the basis of an evaluation made principally on the volume of such waste and not on the concentrations of the hazardous constituents of such waste. Nothing in this section shall be construed to affect the President's authority to include any such facility on the National Priorities List based on the presence of other substances at such facility or to exercise any other authority of this Act with respect to such other substances.

§ 9626. Indian tribes

[Sec. 126] (a) The governing body of an Indian tribe shall be afforded substantially the same treatment as a State with respect to the provisions of section 103(a) (regarding notification of releases), section 104(c)(2) (regarding consultation on remedial actions), section 104(e) (regarding access to information), section 104(i) (regarding health authorities) and section 105 (regarding roles and responsibilities under the national contingency plan and submittal of priorities for remedial action, but not including the provision regarding the inclusion of at least one facility per State on the National Priorities List).

(b) Should the President determine that proper remedial action is the permanent relocation of tribal members away from a contaminated site because it is cost effective and necessary to protect their health and welfare, such finding must be concurred in by the affected tribal government before relocation shall occur. The President, in cooperation with the Secretary of the Interior, shall also assure that all benefits of the relocation program are provided to the affected tribe and that alternative land of equivalent value is available and satisfactory to the tribe. Any lands acquired for relocation of tribal members shall be held in trust by the United States for the benefit of the tribe.

(c) The President shall conduct a survey, in consultation with the Indian tribes, to determine the extent of hazardous waste sites on Indian lands. Such survey shall be included within a report which shall make recommendations on the program needs of tribes under this Act, with particular emphasis on how tribal participation in the administration of such programs can be maximized. Such report shall be submitted to Congress along with the President's budget request for fiscal year 1988.

(d) Notwithstanding any other provision of this Act, no action under this Act by an Indian tribe shall be barred until the later of the following:

(1) The applicable period of limitations has expired.

(2) 2 years after the United States, in its capacity as trustee for the tribe, gives written notice to the governing body of the tribe that it will not

present a claim or commence an action on behalf of the tribe or fails to present a claim or commence an action within the time limitations specified in this Act.

Subchapter II. Hazardous Substance Response Revenue ⸻

Part A
Hazardous Substances Superfund

[§§ 9631–9633 Repealed by Sec. 517(c)(1) of P.L. 99-499, the Superfund Amendments and Reauthorization Act of 1986.]

Part B
Post-closure Liability Trust Fund

[§ 9641 Repealed by Sec. 514(b) of P.L. 99-499, the Superfund Amendments and Reauthorization Act of 1986.]

Subchapter III. Miscellaneous Provisions

§ 9651. Reports and studies

[Sec. 301] (a)(1) The President shall submit to the Congress, within four years after enactment of this Act, a comprehensive report on experience with the implementation of this Act, including, but not limited to—

(A) the extent to which the Act and Fund are effective in enabling Government to respond to and mitigate the effects of releases of hazardous substances;

(B) a summary of past receipts and disbursements from the Fund,

(C) a projection of any future funding needs remaining after the expiration of authority to collect taxes, and of the threat to public health, welfare, and the environment posed by the projected releases which create any such needs;

(D) the record and experience of the Fund in recovering Fund disbursements from liable parties;

(E) the record of State participation in the system of response, liability, and compensation established by this Act;

(F) the impact of the taxes imposed by title II of this Act on the Nation's balance of trade with other countries;

(G) an assessment of the feasibility and desirability of a schedule of taxes which would take into account one or more of the following: the likelihood of a release of a hazardous substance, the degree of hazard and risk of harm to public health, welfare, and the environment resulting from any such release, incentives to proper handling, recycling, incineration, and neutralization of hazardous wastes, and disincentives to improper or illegal handling or disposal of hazardous materials, administrative and reporting burdens on Government and industry, and the extent to which the tax burden falls on the substances and parties which create the problems addressed by this Act. In preparing the report, the President shall consult with appropriate Federal, State, and local agencies, affected industries and claimants, and such other interested parties as he may find useful. Based upon the analyses and consultation required by this subsection, the President shall also include in the report any recommendations for legislative changes he may deem necessary for the better effectuation of the purposes of this Act, including but not limited to recommendations concerning authorization levels, taxes, State participation, liability and liability limits, and financial responsibility provisions for the Response Trust Fund and the Post-closure Liability Trust Fund;

(H) an exemption from or an increase in the substances or the amount of taxes imposed by section 4661 of the Internal Revenue Code of 1954 for copper, lead, and zinc oxide, and for feedstock when used in the manufacture and production of fertilizers, based upon the expenditure experience of the Response Trust Fund;

(I) the economic impact of taxing coal-derived substances and recycled metals.

(2) The Administrator of the Environmental Protection Agency (in consultation with the Secretary of the Treasury) shall submit to the Congress (i) within four years after enactment of this Act, a report identifying additional wastes designated by rule as hazardous after the effective date of this Act and pursuant to section 3001 of the Solid Waste Disposal Act and recommendations on appropriate tax rates for such wastes for the Post-closure Liability Trust Fund. The report shall, in addition, recommend a tax rate, considering the quantity and potential danger to human health and the environment posed by the disposal of any wastes which the Administrator, pursuant to subsection 3001(b)(2)(B) and subsection 3001(b)(3)(A) of the Solid Waste Disposal Act of 1980, has determined should be subject to regulation under subtitle C of such Act, (ii) within three years after enactment of this Act, a report on the necessity for and the adequacy of the revenue raised, in relation to estimated future requirements, of the Post-closure Liability Trust Fund.

(b) The President shall conduct a study to determine (1) whether adequate private insurance protection is available on reasonable terms and conditions to the owners and operators of vessels and facilities subject to liability under section 107 of this Act, and (2) whether the market for such insurance is sufficiently competitive to assure purchasers of features such as a reasonable range of deductibles, coinsurance provisions, and exclusions.

The President shall submit the results of his study, together with his recommendations, within two years of the date of enactment of the Act, and shall submit an interim report on his study within one year of the date of enactment of this Act.

(c)(1) The President, acting through Federal officials designated by the National Contingency Plan published under section 105 of this Act, shall study and, not later than two years after the enactment of this Act, shall promulgate regulations for the assessment of damages for injury to, destruction of, or loss of natural resources resulting from a release of oil or a hazardous substance for the purposes of this Act and section 311(f)(4) and (5) of the Federal Water Pollution Control Act. Notwithstanding the failure of the President to promulgate the regulations required under this subsection on the required date, the President shall promulgate such regulations not later than 6 months after the enactment of the Superfund Amendments and Reauthorization Act of 1986.

(2) Such regulations shall specify (A) standard procedures for simplified assessments requiring minimal field observation, including establishing measures of damages based on units of discharge or release or units of affected area, and (B) alternative protocols for conducting assessments in individual cases to determine the type and extent of short- and long-term injury, destruction, or loss. Such regulations shall identify the best available procedures to determine such damages, including both direct and indirect injury, destruction, or loss and shall take into consideration factors including, but not limited to, replacement value, use value, and ability of the ecosystem or resource to recover.

(3) Such regulations shall be reviewed and revised as appropriate every two years.

(d) The Administrator of the Environmental Protection Agency shall, in consultation with other Federal agencies and appropriate representatives of State and local governments and nongovernmental agencies, conduct a study and report to the Congress within two years of the date of enactment of this Act on the issues, alternatives, and policy considerations involved in the selection of locations for hazardous waste treatment, storage, and disposal facilities. This study shall include—

(A) an assessment of current and projected treatment, storage, and disposal capacity needs and shortfalls for hazardous waste by management category on a State-by-State basis;

(B) an evaluation of the appropriateness of a regional approach to siting and designing hazardous waste management facilities and the identification of hazardous waste management regions, interstate or intrastate, or both, with similar hazardous waste management needs;

(C) solicitation and analysis of proposals for the construction and operation of hazardous waste management facilities by nongovernmental entities, except that no proposal solicited under terms of this subsection shall be analyzed if it involves cost to the United States Government or fails to comply with the requirements of subtitle C of the Solid Waste Disposal Act and other applicable provisions of law;

(D) recommendations on the appropriate balance between public and private sector involvement in the siting, design, and operation of new hazardous waste management facilities;

(E) documentation of the major reasons for public opposition to new hazardous waste management facilities; and

(F) an evaluation of the various options for overcoming obstacles to siting new facilities, including needed legislation for implementing the most suitable option or options.

(e)(1) In order to determine the adequacy of existing common law and statutory remedies in providing legal redress for harm to man and the environment caused by the release of hazardous substances into the environment, there shall be submitted to the Congress a study within twelve months of enactment of this Act.

(2) This study shall be conducted with the assistance of the American Bar Association, the American Law Institute, the Association of American Trial Lawyers, and the National Association of State Attorneys General with the President of each entity selecting three members from each organization to conduct the study. The study chairman and one reporter shall be elected from among the twelve members of the study group.

(3) As part of their review of the adequacy of existing common law and statutory remedies, the study group shall evaluate the following:

(A) the nature, adequacy, and availability of existing remedies under present law in compensating for harm to man from the release of hazardous substances;

(B) the nature of barriers to recovery (particularly with respect to burdens of going forward and of proof and relevancy) and the role such barriers play in the legal system;

(C) the scope of the evidentiary burdens placed on the plaintiff in proving harm from the release of hazardous substances, particularly in light of the scientific uncertainty over causation with respect to—

   (i) carcinogens, mutagens, and teratogens, and

   (ii) the human health effects of exposure to low doses of hazardous substances over long periods of time;

(D) the nature and adequacy of existing remedies under present law in providing compensation for damages to natural resources from the release of hazardous substances;

(E) the scope of liability under existing law and the consequences, particularly with respect to obtaining insurance, of any changes in such liability;

(F) barriers to recovery posed by existing statutes of limitations.

(4) The report shall be submitted to the Congress with appropriate recommendations. Such recommendations shall explicitly address—

(A) the need for revisions in existing statutory or common law, and

(B) whether such revisions should take the form of Federal statutes or the development of a model code which is recommended for adoption by the States.

(5) The Fund shall pay administrative expenses incurred for the study. No expenses shall be available to pay compensation, except expenses on a per diem basis for the one reporter, but in no case shall the total expenses of the study exceed $300,000.

(f) The President, acting through the Administrator of the Environmental Protection Agency, the Secretary of Transportation, the Administrator of the Occupational Safety and Health Administration, and the Director of the National Institute for Occupational Safety and Health shall study and, not later than two years after the enactment of this Act, shall modify the national contingency plan to provide for the protection of the health and safety of employees involved in response actions.

(g)(1) The Comptroller General of the United States, in consultation with the persons described in paragraph (2), shall undertake a study to determine the insurability, and effects on the standard of care, of the liability of each of the following:

(A) Persons who generate hazardous substances: liability for costs and damages under this Act.

(B) Persons who own or operate facilities: liability for costs and damages under this Act.

(C) Persons liable for injury to persons or property caused by the release of hazardous substances into the environment.

(2) In conducting the study under this subsection, the Comptroller General shall consult with the following:

(A) Representatives of the Administrator.

(B) Representatives of persons described in subparagraphs (A) through (C) of the preceding paragraph.

(C) Representatives (i) of groups or organizations comprised generally of persons adversely affected by releases or threatened releases of hazardous substances and (ii) of groups organized for protecting the interests of consumers.

(D) Representatives of property and casualty insurers.

(E) Representatives of reinsurers.

(F) Persons responsible for the regulation of insurance at the State level.

(3) The study under this section shall include, among other matters, an evaluation of the following:

(A) Current economic conditions in, and the future outlook for, the commercial market for insurance and reinsurance.

(B) Current trends in statutory and common law remedies.

(C) The impact of possible changes in traditional standards of liability, proof, evidence, and damages on existing statutory and common law remedies.

(D) The effect of the standard of liability and extent of the persons upon whom it is imposed under this Act on the protection of human health and the environment and on the availability, underwriting, and pricing of insurance coverage.

(E) Current trends, if any, in the judicial interpretation and construction of applicable insurance contracts, together with the degree to which amendments in the language of such contracts and the description of the risks assumed, could affect such trends.

(F) The frequency and severity of a representative sample of claims closed during the calendar year immediately preceding the enactment of this subsection.

(G) Impediments to the acquisition of insurance or other means of obtaining liability coverage other than those referred to in the preceding subparagraphs.

(H) The effects of the standards of liability and financial responsibility requirements imposed pursuant to this Act on the cost of, and incentives for, developing and demonstrating alternative and innovative treatment technologies, as well as waste generation minimization.

(4) The Comptroller General shall submit a report on the results of the study to Congress with appropriate recommendations within 12 months after the enactment of this subsection.

(h)(1) On January 1 of each year the Administrator of the Environmental Protection Agency shall submit an annual report to Congress of such Agency on the progress achieved in implementing this Act during the preceding fiscal year. In addition such report shall specifically include each of the following:

(A) A detailed description of each feasibility study carried out at a facility under title I of this Act.

(B) The status and estimated date of completion of each such study.

(C) Notice of each such study which will not meet a previously published schedule for completion and the new estimated date for completion.

(D) An evaluation of newly developed feasible and achievable permanent treatment technologies.

(E) Progress made in reducing the number of facilities subject to review under section 121(c).

(F) A report on the status of all remedial and enforcement actions undertaken during the prior fiscal year, including a comparison to remedial and enforcement actions undertaken in prior fiscal years.

    (G) An estimate of the amount of resources, including the number of work years or personnel, which would be necessary for each department, agency, or instrumentality which is carrying out any activities of this Act to complete the implementation of all duties vested in the department, agency, or instrumentality under this Act.

(2) Consistent with the authorities of the Inspector General Act of 1978 the Inspector General of the Environmental Protection Agency shall review any report submitted under paragraph (1) related to EPA's activities for reasonableness and accuracy and submit to Congress, as a part of such report a report on the results of such review.

(3) After receiving the reports under paragraphs (1) and (2) of this subsection in any calendar year, the appropriate authorizing committees of Congress shall conduct oversight hearings to ensure that this Act is being implemented according to the purposes of this Act and congressional intent in enacting this Act.

§ 9652. Effective dates, savings provision

[Sec. 302] (a) Unless otherwise provided, all provisions of this Act shall be effective on the date of enactment of this Act.

(b) Any regulation issued pursuant to any provisions of section 311 of the Clean Water Act which is repealed or superseded by this Act and which is in effect on the date immediately preceding the effective date of this Act shall be deemed to be a regulation issued pursuant to the authority of this Act and shall remain in full force and effect unless or until superseded by new regulations issued thereunder.

(c) Any regulation—
(1) respecting financial responsibility,
(2) issued pursuant to any provision of law repealed or superseded by this Act, and
(3) in effect on the date immediately preceding the effective date of this Act shall be deemed to be a regulation issued pursuant to the authority of this Act and shall remain in full force and effect unless or until superseded by new regulations issued thereunder.

(d) Nothing in this Act shall affect or modify in any way the obligations or liabilities of any person under other Federal or State law, including common law, with respect to releases of hazardous substances or other pollutants or contaminants. The provisions of this Act shall not be considered, interpreted, or construed in any way as reflecting a determination, in part or whole, of policy regarding the inapplicability of strict liability, or strict liability doctrines, to activities relating to hazardous substances, pollutants, or contaminants or other such activities.

§ 9653.   Repealed

§ 9654.   Applicability of federal water pollution control funding, etc., provisions

[Sec. 304] (a) * * *

(b) One-half of the unobligated balance remaining before the date of the enactment of this act under subsection (k) of section 311 of the Federal Water Pollution Control act and all sums appropriated under section 504(b) of the Federal Water Pollution Control Act shall be transferred to the Fund established under title II of this Act.

(c) In any case in which any provision of section 311 of the Federal Water Pollution Control Act is determined to be in conflict with any provisions of this Act, the provisions of this Act shall apply.

§ 9655.   Legislative veto of rule or regulation

[Sec. 305] (a) Notwithstanding any other provision of law, simultaneously with promulgation or repromulgation of any rule or regulation under authority of title I of this Act, the head of the department, agency, or instrumentality promulgating such rule or regulation shall transmit a copy thereof to the Secretary of the Senate and the Clerk of the House of Representatives. Except as provided in subsection (b) of this section, the rule or regulation shall not become effective if—

(1) within ninety calendar days of continuous session of Congress after the date of promulgation, both Houses of Congress adopt a concurrent resolution, the matter after the resolving clause of which is as follows: "That Congress disapproves the rule or regulation promulgated by the _____ dealing with the matter of _____, which rule or regulation was transmitted to Congress on _____", the blank spaces therein being appropriately filled; or

(2) within sixty calendar days of continuous session of Congress after the date of promulgation, one House of Congress adopts such a concurrent resolution and transmits such resolution to the other House, and such resolution is not disapproved by such other House within thirty calendar days of continuous session of Congress after such transmittal.

(b) If, at the end of sixty calendar days of continuous session of Congress after the date of promulgation of a rule or regulation, no committee of either House of Congress has reported or been discharged from further consideration of a concurrent resolution disapproving the rule or regulation and neither House has adopted such a resolution, the rule or regulation may go into effect immediately. If, within such sixty calendar days, such a committee has reported or been discharged from further consideration of such a resolution, or either House has adopted such a resolution, the rule or regulation may go into effect not sooner than ninety calendar days of continuous session of Congress after such rule is prescribed unless disapproved as provided in subsection (a) of this section.

(c) For purposes of subsections (a) and (b) of this section—

(1) continuity of session is broken only by an adjournment of Congress sine die; and

(2) the days on which either House is not in session because of an adjournment of more than three days to a day certain are excluded in the computation of thirty, sixty, and ninety calendar days of continuous session of Congress.

(d) Congressional inaction on, or rejection of, a resolution of disapproval shall not be deemed an expression of approval of such rule or regulation.

§ 9656.   Transportation of hazardous substances; listing as hazardous material; liability for release

[Sec. 306] (a) Each hazardous substance which is listed or designated as provided in section 101(14) of this Act shall, within 30 days after the enactment of the Superfund Amendments and Reauthorization Act of 1986 or at the time of such listing or designation, whichever is later, be listed and regulated as a hazardous material under the Hazardous Materials Transportation Act.

(b) A common or contract carrier shall be liable under other law in lieu of section 107 of this Act for damages or remedial action resulting from the release of a hazardous substance during the course of transportation which commenced prior to the effective date of the listing and regulation of such substance as a hazardous material under the Hazardous Materials Transportation Act, or for substances listed pursuant to subsection (a) of this section, prior to the effective date of such listing. *Provided, however,* That this subsection shall not apply where such a carrier can demonstrate that he did not have actual knowledge of the identity or nature of the substance released.

§ 9657.   Separability of provisions

[Sec. 308] If any provision of this Act, or the application of any provision of this Act to any person or circumstance, is held invalid, the application of such provision to other persons or circumstances and the remainder of this Act shall not be affected thereby. If an administrative settlement under section 122 has the effect of limiting any person's right to obtain contribution from any party to such settlement, and if the effect of such limitation would constitute a taking without just compensation in violation of the fifth amendment of the Constitution of the United States, such person shall not be entitled, under other laws of the United States, to recover compensation from the United States for such taking, but in any such case, such limitation on the right to obtain contribution shall be treated as having no force and effect.

§ 9658. Actions under state law for damages from exposure to hazardous substances

[Sec. 309] (a)(1) In the case of any action brought under State law for personal injury, or property damages, which are caused or contributed to by exposure to any hazardous substance, or pollutant or contaminant, released into the environment from a facility, if the applicable limitations period for such action (as specified in the State statute of limitations or under common law) provides a commencement date which is earlier than the federally required commencement date, such period shall commence at the federally required commencement date in lieu of the date specified in such State statute.

(2) Except as provided in paragraph (1), the statute of limitations established under State law shall apply in all actions brought under State law for personal injury, or property damages, which are caused or contributed to by exposure to any hazardous substance, or pollutant or contaminant, released into the environment from a facility.

(3) Nothing in this section shall apply with respect to any cause of action brought under section 107 of this Act.

(b) As used in this section—

(1) The terms used in this section shall have the same meaning as when used in title I of this Act.

(2) The term "applicable limitations period" means the period specified in a statute of limitations during which a civil action referred to in subsection (a)(1) may be brought.

(3) The term "commencement date" means the date specified in a statute of limitations as the beginning of the applicable limitations period.

(4)(A) Except as provided in subparagraph (B), the term "federally required commencement date" means the date the plaintiff knew (or reasonably should have known) that the personal injury or property damages referred to in subsection (a)(1) were caused or contributed to by the hazardous substance or pollutant or contaminant concerned.

(B) In the case of a minor or incompetent plaintiff, the term "federally required commencement date" means the later of the date referred to in subparagraph (A) or the following:

(i) In the case of a minor, the date on which the minor reaches the age of majority, as determined by State law, or has a legal representative appointed.

(ii) In the case of an incompetent individual, the date on which such individual becomes competent or has had a legal representative appointed.

§ 9659. Citizens' suits

[Sec. 310] (a) Except as provided in subsections (d) and (e) of this section and in section 113(h) (relating to timing of judicial review), any person may commence a civil action on his own behalf—

(1) against any person (including the United States and any other governmental instrumentality or agency, to the extent permitted by the eleventh amendment to the Constitution) who is alleged to be in violation of any standard, regulation, condition, requirement, or order which has become effective pursuant to this Act (including any provision of an agreement under section 120, relating to Federal facilities); or

(2) against the President or any other officer of the United States (including the Administrator of the Environmental Protection Agency and the Administrator of the ATSDR) where there is alleged a failure of the President or of such other officer to perform any act or duty under this Act, including an act or duty under section 120 (relating to Federal facilities), which is not discretionary with the President or such other officer.

Paragraph (2) shall not apply to any act or duty under the provisions of section 311 (relating to research, development, and demonstration).

(b)(1) Any action under subsection (a)(1) shall be brought in the district court for the district in which the alleged violation occurred.

(2) Any action brought under subsection (a)(2) may be brought in the United States District Court for the District of Columbia.

(c) The district court shall have jurisdiction in actions brought under subsection (a)(1) to enforce the standard, regulation, condition, requirement, or order concerned (including any provision of an agreement under section 120), to order such action as may be necessary to correct the violation, and to impose any civil penalty provided for the violation. The district court shall have jurisdiction in actions brought under subsection (a)(2) to order the President or other officer to perform the act or duty concerned.

(d)(1) No action may be commenced under subsection (a)(1) of this section before 60 days after the plaintiff has given notice of the violation to each of the following:

(A) The President.

(B) The State in which the alleged violation occurs.

(C) Any alleged violator of the standard, regulation, condition, requirement, or order concerned (including any provision of an agreement under section 120).

Notice under this paragraph shall be given in such manner as the

President shall prescribe by regulation.

(2) No action may be commenced under paragraph (1) of subsection (a) if the President has commenced and is diligently prosecuting an action under this Act, or under the Solid Waste Disposal Act to require compliance with the standard, regulation, condition, requirement, or order concerned (including any provision of an agreement under section 120).

(e) No action may be commenced under paragraph (2) of subsection (a) before the 60th day following the date on which the plaintiff gives notice to the Administrator or other department, agency, or instrumentality that the plaintiff will commence such action. Notice under this subsection shall be given in such manner as the President shall prescribe by regulation.

(f) The court, in issuing any final order in any action brought pursuant to this section, may award costs of litigation (including reasonable attorney and expert witness fees) to the prevailing or the substantially prevailing party whenever the court determines such an award is appropriate. The court may, if a temporary restraining order or preliminary injunction is sought, require the filing of a bond or equivalent security in accordance with the Federal Rules of Civil Procedure.

(g) In any action under this section, the United States or the State, or both, if not a party may intervene as a matter of right. For other provisions regarding intervention, see section 113.

(h) This Act does not affect or otherwise impair the rights of any person under Federal, State, or common law, except with respect to the timing of review as provided in section 113(h) or as otherwise provided in section 309 (relating to actions under State law).

(i) The terms used in this section shall have the same meanings as when used in title I.

§ 9660. Research, development, and demonstration

[Sec. 311] (a)(1) The Secretary of Health and Human Services (hereinafter in this subsection referred to as the Secretary), in consultation with the Administrator, shall establish and support a basic research and training program (through grants, cooperative agreements, and contracts) consisting of the following:

(A) Basic research (including epidemiologic and ecologic studies) which may include each of the following:

(i) Advanced techniques for the detection, assessment, and evaluation of the effects on human health of hazardous substances.

(ii) Methods to assess the risks to human health presented by hazardous substances.

(iii) Methods and technologies to detect hazardous substances in the environment and basic biological, chemical, and physical methods to reduce the amount and toxicity of hazardous substances.

(B) Training, which may include each of the following:
    (i) Short courses and continuing education for State and local health and environment agency personnel and other personnel engaged in the handling of hazardous substances, in the management of facilities at which hazardous substances are located, and in the evaluation of the hazards to human health presented by such facilities.
    (ii) Graduate or advanced training in environmental and occupational health and safety and in the public health and engineering aspects of hazardous waste control.
    (iii) Graduate training in the geosciences, including hydrogeology, geological engineering, geophysics, geochemistry, and related fields necessary to meet professional personnel needs in the public and private sectors and to effectuate the purposes of this Act.

(2) The Director of the National Institute for Environmental Health Sciences shall cooperate fully with the relevant Federal agencies referred to in subparagraph (A) of paragraph (5) in carrying out the purposes of this section.

(3) A grant, cooperative agreement, or contract may be made or entered into under paragraph (1) with an accredited institution of higher education. The institution may carry out the research or training under the grant, cooperative agreement, or contract through contracts, including contracts with any of the following:

(A) Generators of hazardous wastes.

(B) Persons involved in the detection, assessment, evaluation, and treatment of hazardous substances.

(C) Owners and operators of facilities at which hazardous substances are located.

(D) State and local governments.

(4) In making grants and entering into cooperative agreements and contracts under this subsection, the Secretary shall act through the Director of the National Institute for Environmental Health Sciences. In considering the allocation of funds for training purposes, the Director shall ensure that at least one grant, cooperative agreement, or contract shall be awarded for training described in each of clauses (i), (ii), and (iii) of paragraph (1)(B). Where applicable, the Director may choose to operate training activities in cooperation with the Director of the National Institute for Occupational Safety and Health. The procedures applicable to grants and contracts under title IV of the Public Health Service Act shall be followed under this subsection.

(5) To assist in the implementation of this subsection and to aid in the coordination of research and demonstration and training activities

funded from the Fund under this section, the Secretary shall appoint an advisory council (hereinafter in this subsection referred to as the "Advisory Council") which shall consist of representatives of the following:

(A) The relevant Federal agencies.

(B) The chemical industry.

(C) The toxic waste management industry.

(D) Institutions of higher education.

(E) State and local health and environmental agencies.

(F) The general public.

(6) Within nine months after the date of the enactment of this subsection, the Secretary, acting through the Director of the National Institute for Environmental Health Sciences, shall issue a plan for the implementation of paragraph (1). The plan shall include priorities for actions under paragraph (1) and include research and training relevant to scientific and technological issues resulting from site specific hazardous substance response experience. The Secretary shall, to the maximum extent practicable, take appropriate steps to coordinate program activities under this plan with the activities of other Federal agencies in order to avoid duplication of effort. The plan shall be consistent with the need for the development of new technologies for meeting the goals of response actions in accordance with the provisions of this Act. The Advisory Council shall be provided an opportunity to review and comment on the plan and priorities and assist appropriate coordination among the relevant Federal agencies referred to in subparagraph (A) of paragraph (5).

(b)(1) The Administrator is authorized and directed to carry out a program of research, evaluation, testing, development, and demonstration of alternative or innovative treatment technologies (hereinafter in this subsection referred to as the "program") which may be utilized in response actions to achieve more permanent protection of human health and welfare and the environment.

(2) The program shall be administered by the Administrator, acting through an office of technology demonstration and shall be coordinated with programs carried out by the Office of Solid Waste and Emergency Response and the Office of Research and Development.

(3) In carrying out the program, the Administrator is authorized to enter into contracts and cooperative agreements with, and make grants to, persons, public entities, and nonprofit private entities which are exempt from tax under section 501(c)(3) of the Internal Revenue Code of 1954. The Administrator shall, to the maximum extent possible, enter into appropriate cost sharing arrangements under this subsection.

(4) In carrying out the program, the Administrator may arrange for the use of sites at which a response may be undertaken under section 104

for the purposes of carrying out research, testing, evaluation, development, and demonstration projects. Each such project shall be carried out under such terms and conditions as the Administrator shall require to assure the protection of human health and the environment and to assure adequate control by the Administrator of the research, testing, evaluation, development, and demonstration activities at the site.

(5)(A) The demonstration assistance program shall include the following:

   (i) The publication of a solicitation and the evaluation of applications for demonstration projects utilizing alternative or innovative technologies.

   (ii) The selection of sites which are suitable for the testing and evaluation of innovative technologies.

   (iii) The development of detailed plans for innovative technology demonstration projects.

   (iv) The supervision of such demonstration projects and the providing of quality assurance for data obtained.

   (v) The evaluation of the results of alternative innovative technology demonstration projects and the determination of whether or not the technologies used are effective and feasible.

   (B) Within 90 days after the date of the enactment of this section, and no less often than once every 12 months thereafter, the Administrator shall publish a solicitation for innovative or alternative technologies at a stage of development suitable for full-scale demonstrations at sites at which a response action may be undertaken under section 104. The purpose of any such project shall be to demonstrate the use of an alternative or innovative treatment technology with respect to hazardous substances or pollutants or contaminants which are located at the site or which are to be removed from the site. The solicitation notice shall prescribe information to be included in the application, including technical and economic data derived from the applicant's own research and development efforts, and other information sufficient to permit the Administrator to assess the technology's potential and the types of remedial action to which it may be applicable.

   (C) Any person and any public or private nonprofit entity may submit an application to the Administrator in response to the solicitation. The application shall contain a proposed demonstration plan setting forth how and when the project is to be carried out and such other information as the Administrator may require.

   (D) In selecting technologies to be demonstrated, the Administrator shall fully review the applications submitted and shall consider at least the criteria specified in paragraph (7). The Administrator shall select or refuse to select a project for demonstration under this subsection within 90 days of receiving the completed application for such project. In the case of a refusal to select the project, the Administrator shall notify the applicant within such 90-day period of the reasons for his refusal.

(E) The Administrator shall propose 10 sites at which a response may be undertaken under section 104 to be the location of any demonstration project under this subsection within 60 days after the close of the public comment period. After an opportunity for notice and public comment, the Administrator shall select such sites and projects. In selecting any such site, the Administrator shall take into account the applicant's technical data and preferences either for onsite operation or for utilizing the site as a source of hazardous substances or pollutants or contaminants to be treated offsite.

(F) Within 60 days after the selection of the site under this paragraph to be the location of a demonstration project, the Administrator shall establish a final demonstration plan for the project, based upon the demonstration plan contained in the application for the project. Such plan shall clearly set forth how and when the demonstration project will be carried out.

(G) Each demonstration project under this subsection shall be performed by the applicant, or by a person satisfactory to the applicant, under the supervision of the Administrator. The Administrator shall enter into a written agreement with each applicant granting the Administrator the responsibility and authority for testing procedures, quality control, monitoring, and other measurements necessary to determine and evaluate the results of the demonstration project. The Administrator may pay the costs of testing, monitoring, quality control, and other measurements required by the Administrator to determine and evaluate the results of the demonstration project, and the limitations established by subparagraph (J) shall not apply to such costs.

(H) Each demonstration project under this subsection shall be completed within such time as is established in the demonstration plan.

(I) The Administrator may extend any deadline established under this paragraph by mutual agreement with the applicant concerned.

(J) The Administrator shall not provide any Federal assistance for any part of a full-scale field demonstration project under this subsection to any applicant unless such applicant can demonstrate that it cannot obtain appropriate private financing on reasonable terms and conditions sufficient to carry out such demonstration project without such Federal assistance. The total Federal funds for any full-scale field demonstration project under this subsection shall not exceed 50 percent of the total cost of such project estimated at the time of the award of such assistance. The Administrator shall not expend more than $10,000,000 for assistance under the program in any fiscal year and shall not expend more than $3,000,000 for any single project.

(6) In carrying out the program, the Administrator shall initiate or cause to be initiated at least 10 field demonstration projects of alternative or innovative treatment technologies at sites at which a response may be undertaken under section 104, in fiscal year 1987 and each of the succeeding three fiscal years. If the Administrator determines that 10 field demonstration projects under this subsection cannot be initiated consistent with the criteria set forth in paragraph (7) in any of such fiscal years, the Administrator shall transmit to the appropriate committees of Congress a report explaining the reasons for his inability to conduct such demonstration projects.

(7) In selecting technologies to be demonstrated under this subsection, the Administrator shall, consistent with the protection of human health and the environment, consider each of the following criteria:

(A) The potential for contributing to solutions to those waste problems which pose the greatest threat to human health, which cannot be adequately controlled under present technologies, or which otherwise pose significant management difficulties.

(B) The availability of technologies which have been sufficiently developed for field demonstration and which are likely to be cost-effective and reliable.

(C) The availability and suitability of sites for demonstrating such technologies, taking into account the physical, biological, chemical, and geological characteristics of the sites, the extent and type of contamination found at the site, and the capability to conduct demonstration projects in such a manner as to assure the protection of human health and the environment.

(D) The likelihood that the data to be generated from the demonstration project at the site will be applicable to other sites.

(8) In carrying out the program, the Administrator shall conduct a technology transfer program including the development, collection, evaluation, coordination, and dissemination of information relating to the utilization of alternative or innovative treatment technologies for response actions. The Administrator shall establish and maintain a central reference library for such information. The information maintained by the Administrator shall be made available to the public, subject to the provisions of section 552 of title 5 of the United States Code and section 1905 of title 18 of the United States Code, and to other Government agencies in a manner that will facilitate its dissemination; except, that upon a showing satisfactory to the Administrator by any person that any information or portion thereof obtained under this subsection by the Administrator directly or indirectly from such

person, would, if made public, divulge—

(A) trade secrets; or

(B) other proprietary information of such person,

the Administrator shall not disclose such information and disclosure thereof shall be punishable under section 1905 of title 18 of the United States Code. This subsection is not authority to withhold information from Congress or any committee of Congress upon the request of the chairman of such committee.

(9) The Administrator is authorized and directed to carry out, through the Office of Technology Demonstration, a program of training and an evaluation of training needs for each of the following:

(A) Training in the procedures for the handling and removal of hazardous substances for employees who handle hazardous substances.

(B) Training in the management of facilities at which hazardous substances are located and in the evaluation of the hazards to human health presented by such facilities for State and local health and environment agency personnel.

(10) For purposes of this subsection, the term "alternative or innovative treatment technologies" means those technologies, including proprietary or patented methods, which permanently alter the composition of hazardous waste through chemical, biological, or physical means so as to significantly reduce the toxicity, mobility, or volume (or any combination thereof) of the hazardous waste or contaminated materials being treated. The term also includes technologies that characterize or assess the extent of contamination, the chemical and physical character of the contaminants, and the stresses imposed by the contaminants on complex ecosystems at sites.

(c) The Administrator may conduct and support, through grants, cooperative agreements, and contracts, research with respect to the detection, assessment, and evaluation of the effects on and risks to human health of hazardous substances and detection of hazardous substances in the environment. The Administrator shall coordinate such research with the Secretary of Health and Human Services, acting through the advisory council established under this section, in order to avoid duplication of effort.

(d)(1) The Administrator shall make grants to institutions of higher learning to establish and operate not fewer than 5 hazardous substance research centers in the United States. In carrying out the program under this subsection, the Administrator should seek to have established and operated 10 hazardous substance research centers in the United States.

(2) The responsibilities of each hazardous substance research center established under this subsection shall include, but not be limited to, the conduct of research and training relating to the manufacture, use, transportation, disposal, and management of hazardous substances and publication and dissemination of the results of such research.

(3) Any institution of higher learning interested in receiving a grant under this subsection shall submit to the Administrator an application in such form and containing such information as the Administrator may require by regulation.

(4) The Administrator shall select recipients of grants under this subsection on the basis of the following criteria:

(A) The hazardous substance research center shall be located in a State which is representative of the needs of the region in which such State is located for improved hazardous waste management.

(B) The grant recipient shall be located in an area which has experienced problems with hazardous substance management.

(C) There is available to the grant recipient for carrying out this subsection demonstrated research resources.

(D) The capability of the grant recipient to provide leadership in making national and regional contributions to the solution of both long-range and immediate hazardous substance management problems.

(E) The grant recipient shall make a commitment to support ongoing hazardous substance research programs with budgeted institutional funds of at least $100,000 per year.

(F) The grant recipient shall have an interdisciplinary staff with demonstrated expertise in hazardous substance management and research.

(G) The grant recipient shall have a demonstrated ability to disseminate results of hazardous substance research and educational programs through an interdisciplinary continuing education program.

(H) The projects which the grant recipient proposes to carry out under the grant are necessary and appropriate.

(5) No grant may be made under this subsection in any fiscal year unless the recipient of such grant enters into such agreements with the Administrator as the Administrator may require to ensure that such recipient will maintain its aggregate expenditures from all other sources for establishing and operating a regional hazardous substance research center and related research activities at or above the average level of such expenditures in its 2 fiscal years preceding the date of the enactment of this subsection.

(6) The Federal share of a grant under this subsection shall not exceed 80 percent of the costs of establishing and operating the regional hazardous substance research center and related research activities carried out by the grant recipient.

(7) No funds made available to carry out this subsection shall be used for acquisition of real property (including buildings) or construction of any building.

(8) Administrative responsibility for carrying out this subsection shall be

in the Office of the Administrator.
 (9) The Administrator shall allocate funds made available to carry out this subsection equitably among the regions of the United States.
 (10) Not less than five percent of the funds made available to carry out this subsection for any fiscal year shall be available to carry out technology transfer activities.

(e) At the time of the submission of the annual budget request to Congress, the Administrator shall submit to the appropriate committees of the House of Representatives and the Senate and to the advisory council established under subsection (a), a report on the progress of the research, development, and demonstration program authorized by subsection (b), including an evaluation of each demonstration project completed in the preceding fiscal year, findings with respect to the efficacy of such demonstrated technologies in achieving permanent and significant reductions in risk from hazardous wastes, the costs of such demonstration projects, and the potential applicability of, and projected costs for, such technologies at other hazardous substance sites.

(f) Nothing in this section shall be construed to affect the provisions of the Solid Waste Disposal Act.

(g) The Administrator shall ensure, to the maximum extent practicable, an adequate opportunity for small business participation in the program established by subsection (b).

§ 9660a. Grant program

[Sec. 311] (a)(1) Grants for the training and education of workers who are or may be engaged in activitities related to hazardous waste removal or containment or emergency response may be made under this subsection.
 (2) Grants under this subsection shall be administered by the National Institute of Environmental Health Sciences.
 (3) Grants shall be awarded to nonprofit organizations which demonstrate experience in implementing and operating worker health and safety training and education programs and demonstrate the ability to reach and involve in training programs target populations of workers who are or will be engaged in hazardous waste removal or containment or emergency response operations.

§ 9661. Love Canal property acquisition

[Sec. 312] (a) The Administrator of the Environmental Protection Agency (hereinafter referred to as the "Administrator") may make grants not to exceed $2,500,000 to the State of New York (or to any duly constituted public agency or authority thereof) for purposes of acquisition of private property in the Love Canal Emergency Declaration Area. Such acquisition shall include (but shall not be limited to) all private property within the

Emergency Declaration Area, including non-owner occupied residential properties, commercial, industrial, public, religious, non-profit, and vacant properties.

(b) No property shall be acquired pursuant to this section unless the property owner voluntarily agrees to such acquisition. Compensation for any property acquired pursuant to this section shall be based upon the fair market value of the property as it existed prior to the emergency declaration. Valuation procedures for property acquired with funds provided under this section shall be in accordance with those set forth in the agreement entered into between the New York State Disaster Preparedness Commission and the Love Canal Revitalization Agency on October 9, 1980.

(c) The Administrator shall not provide any funds under this section for the acquisition of any properties pursuant to this section unless a public agency or authority of the State of New York first enters into a cooperative agreement with the Administrator providing assurances deemed adequate by the Administrator that the State or an agency created under the laws of the State shall take title to the properties to be so acquired.

(d) The Administrator shall enter into a cooperative agreement with an appropriate public agency or authority of the State of New York under which the Administrator shall maintain or arrange for the maintenance of all properties within the Emergency Declaration Area that have been acquired by any public agency or authority of the State. Ninety (90) percent of the costs of such maintenance shall be paid by the Administrator. The remaining portion of such costs shall be paid by the State (unless a credit is available under section 104(c)). The Administrator is authorized, in his discretion, to provide technical assistance to any public agency or authority of the State of New York in order to implement the recommendations of the habitability and land-use study in order to put the land within the Emergency Declaration Area to its best use.

(e) The Administrator shall conduct or cause to be conducted a habitability and land-use study. The study shall—
 (1) assess the risks associated with inhabiting of the Love Canal Emergency Declaration Area;
 (2) compare the level of hazardous waste contamination in that Area to that present in other comparable communities; and
 (3) assess the potential uses of the land within the Emergency Declaration Area, including but not limited to residential, industrial, commercial and recreational, and the risks associated with such potential uses.
The Administrator shall publish the findings of such study and shall work with the State of New York to develop recommendations based upon the results of such study.

(f) For purposes of section 111 [and 221(c) of this Act], the expenditures authorized by this section shall be treated as a cost specified in section 111(c).

(g) The provisions of this section shall not affect the implementation of other response actions within the Emergency Declaration Area that the Administrator has determined (before enactment of this section) to be necessary to protect the public health or welfare or the environment.

(h)(1) The terms "Emergency Declaration Area" and "Love Canal Emergency Declaration Area" mean the Emergency Declaration Area as defined in section 950, paragraph (2) of the General Municipal Law of the State of New York, Chapter 259, Laws of 1980, as in effect on the date of the enactment of this section.

> (2) As used in subsection (a), the term "private property" means all property which is not owned by a department, agency, or instrumentality of—
> (A) the United States, or
> (B) the State of New York (or any public agency or authority thereof).

§ 9662. Limitation on contract and borrowing authority

[Sec. 313] Any authority provided by [the Superfund Amendments and Reauthorization Act], including any amendment made by [SARA], to enter into contracts to obligate the United States or to incur indebtedness for the repayment of which the United States is liable shall be effective only to such extent or in such amounts as are provided in appropriation Acts.

Subchapter IV. Pollution Insurance

§ 9671. Definitions

[Sec. 401] As used in this title—
(1) The term "insurance" means primary insurance, excess insurance, reinsurance, surplus lines insurance, and any other arrangement for shifting and distributing risk which is determined to be insurance under applicable State or Federal law.
(2) The term "pollution liability" means liability for injuries arising from the release of hazardous substances or pollutants or contaminants.
(3) The term "risk retention group" means any corporation or other limited liability association taxable as a corporation, or as an insurance company, formed under the laws of any State—
> (A) whose primary activity consists of assuming and spreading all, or any portion, of the pollution liability of its group members;
> (B) which is organized for the primary purpose of conducting the

activity described under subparagraph (A);

(C) which is chartered or licensed as an insurance company and authorized to engage in the business of insurance under the laws of any State; and

(D) which does not exclude any person from membership in the group solely to provide for members of such a group a competitive advantage over such a person.

(4) The term "purchasing group" means any group of persons which has as one of its purposes the purchase of pollution liability insurance on a group basis.

(5) The term "State" means any State of the United States, the District of Columbia, the Commonwealth of Puerto Rico, Guam, American Samoa, the Virgin Islands, the Commonwealth of the Northern Marianas, and any other territory or possession over which the United States has jurisdiction.

§ 9672. State laws; scope of title

[Sec. 402] (a) Nothing in this title shall be construed to affect either the tort law or the law governing the interpretation of insurance contracts of any State. The definitions of pollution liability and pollution liability insurance under any State law shall not be applied for the purposes of this title, including recognition or qualification of risk retention groups or purchasing groups.

(b) The authority to offer or to provide insurance under this title shall be limited to coverage of pollution liability risks and this title does not authorize a risk retention group or purchasing group to provide coverage of any other line of insurance.

§ 9673. Risk retention groups

[Sec. 403] (a) Except as provided in this section, a risk retention group shall be exempt from the following:

(1) A State law, rule, or order which makes unlawful, or regulates, directly or indirectly, the operation of a risk retention group.

(2) A State law, rule, or order which requires or permits a risk retention group to participate in any insurance insolvency guaranty association to which an insurer licensed in the State is required to belong.

(3) A State law, rule, or order which requires any insurance policy issued to a risk retention group or any member of the group to be counter-signed by an insurance agent or broker residing in the State.

(4) A State law, rule, or order which otherwise discriminates against a

risk retention group or any of its members.

(b)(1) Nothing in subsection (a) shall be construed to affect the applicability of State laws generally applicable to persons or corporations. The State in which a risk retention group is chartered may regulate the formation and operation of the group.

(2) Subsection (a) shall not apply to any State law which requires a risk retention group to do any of the following:

(A) Comply with the unfair claim settlement practices law of the State.

(B) Pay, on a nondiscriminatory basis, applicable premium and other taxes which are levied on admitted insurers and surplus line insurers, brokers, or policyholders under the laws of the State.

(C) Participate, on a nondiscriminatory basis, in any mechanism established or authorized under the law of the State for the equitable apportionment among insurers of pollution liability insurance losses and expenses incurred on policies written through such mechanism.

(D) Submit to the appropriate authority reports and other information required of licensed insurers under the laws of a State relating solely to pollution liability insurance losses and expenses.

(E) Register with and designate the State insurance commissioner as its agent solely for the purpose of receiving service of legal documents or process.

(F) Furnish, upon request, such commissioner a copy of any financial report submitted by the risk retention group to the commissioner of the chartering or licensing jurisdiction.

(G) Submit to an examination by the State insurance commissioner in any State in which the group is doing business to determine the group's financial condition, if—

(i) the commissioner has reason to believe the risk retention group is in a financially impaired condition; and

(ii) the commissioner of the jurisdiction in which the group is chartered has not begun or has refused to initiate an examination of the group.

(H) Comply with a lawful order issued in a delinquency proceeding commenced by the State insurance commissioner if the commissioner of the jurisdiction in which the group is chartered has failed to initiate such a proceeding after notice of a finding of financial impairment under subparagraph (G).

(c) The exemptions specified in subsection (a) apply to—

(1) pollution liability insurance coverage provided by a risk retention group for—

(A) such group; or

(B) any person who is a member of such group;

(2) the sale of pollution liability insurance coverage for a risk retention group; and

(3) the provision of insurance related services or management services for a risk retention group or any member of such a group.

(d) A State may require that a person acting, or offering to act, as an agent or broker for a risk retention group obtain a license from that State, except that a State may not impose any qualification or requirement which discriminates against a nonresident agent or broker.

§ 9674. Purchasing groups

[Sec. 404] (a) Except as provided in this section, a purchasing group is exempt from the following:

(1) A State law, rule, or order which prohibits the establishment of a purchasing group.

(2) A State law, rule, or order which makes it unlawful for an insurer to provide or offer to provide insurance on a basis providing, to a purchasing group or its member, advantages, based on their loss and expense experience, not afforded to other persons with respect to rates, policy forms, coverages, or other matters.

(3) A State law, rule, or order which prohibits a purchasing group or its members from purchasing insurance on the group basis described in paragraph (2) of this subsection.

(4) A State law, rule, or order which prohibits a purchasing group from obtaining insurance on a group basis because the group has not been in existence for a minimum period of time or because any member has not belonged to the group for a minimum period of time.

(5) A State law, rule, or order which requires that a purchasing group must have a minimum number of members, common ownership or affiliation, or a certain legal form.

(6) A State law, rule, or order which requires that a certain percentage of a purchasing group must obtain insurance on a group basis.

(7) A State law, rule, or order which requires that any insurance policy issued to a purchasing group or any members of the group be countersigned by an insurance agent or broker residing in that State.

(8) A State law, rule, or order which otherwise discriminates against a purchasing group or any of its members.

(b) The exemptions specified in subsection (a) apply to the following:

(1) Pollution liability insurance, and comprehensive general liability insurance which includes this coverage, provided to—

(A) a purchasing group; or

(B) any person who is a member of a purchasing group.

(2) The sale of any one of the following to a purchasing group or a member of the group:

    (A) Pollution liability insurance and comprehensive general liability coverage.

    (B) Insurance related services.

    (C) Management services.

(c) A State may require that a person acting, or offering to act, as an agent or broker for a purchasing group obtain a license from that State, except that a State may not impose any qualification or requirement which discriminates against a nonresident agent or broker.

§ 9675. Applicability of securities laws

[Sec. 405] (a) The ownership interests of members of a risk retention group shall be considered to be—

(1) exempted securities for purposes of section 5 of the Securities Act of 1933 and for purposes of section 12 of the Securities Exchange Act of 1934; and

(2) securities for purposes of the provisions of section 17 of the Securities Act of 1933 and the provisions of section 10 of the Securities Exchange Act of 1934.

(b) A risk retention group shall not be considered to be an investment company for purposes of the Investment Company Act of 1940.

(c) The ownership interests of members in a risk retention group shall not be considered securities for purposes of any State blue sky law.

3 • Toxic Substances Control Act

INTRODUCTION

In 1976, after five years of effort dating from a 1971 report of the Council on Environmental Quality (CEQ), Congress enacted the Toxic Substances Control Act (TSCA) (PL 94-469) and passed to the Environmental Protection Agency (EPA) a new system for identifying and evaluating environmental and health effects of existing chemicals and any new substances entering the U.S. market.

The law's intent was to complete the chain of federal environmental protection statutes enacted piecemeal between 1970, when EPA was created, and 1976. In contrast to laws designed to improve and protect the quality of water, air, and natural resources, TSCA was designed as a gap-filling law and empowered EPA to evaluate the safety of raw materials. It gave the agency broad authority to control chemical risks that could not be dealt with under other environmental statutes.

The term "toxic" in the title of the law is a misnomer, referring not only to threats of acute poisoning but also to long-term, chronic effects on people and the environment. Such effects include cancer, genetic damage, birth defects, or bioaccumulation in the food chain with deleterious effects.

Section 5 of TSCA requires any company planning to manufacture or import a new chemical to submit to EPA a premanufacture notice containing information on the identity, use, anticipated production or import volume, workplace hazards, and disposal characteristics of the substance. A "new" chemical is one not included in an inventory list of chemicals already in production, drawn up under authority of TSCA. EPA has 90 days to consider the notice and approve production. If the agency anticipates problems, it may require additional data before manufacture or import may begin. Also under Section 5, the agency may prohibit or control any "significant new use" of a chemical listed in the inventory.

EPA may move to ban production of any new or existing chemical under Section 6 of TSCA, or to control the conditions under which the substance can be made. In the years since enactment, several of the environmental concerns that spawned TSCA have been subjected to extensive regulations under Sections 5 and 6, among them poly-chlorinated biphenyls (PCBs), chlorofluorocarbons, and many new chemicals. However, other substances of concern remain uncontrolled, most notably asbestos, the environmental hazard said to be the major impetus for Congress to enact the statute.

In 1986, the agency began planning to bring new substances created through genetic engineering under the TSCA regulatory programs. The first regulations, under Section 5, are expected to be proposed in late 1987 or early 1988.

Under Section 8 of TSCA, EPA has broad powers to collect information about chemicals. Production, use, exposure, and risk data may be collected from producers and importers under Section 8(a), and under Section 8(d) the agency can require manufacturers and processors to report unpublished health and safety studies on listed chemicals. Companies are required to collect allegations of adverse reactions and keep records of them. And, under Section 8(e) firms must report to EPA any time they receive information that a substance may pose a significant risk to humans or the environment.

The law gives EPA the authority to require manufacturers and processors of a chemical to conduct toxicological tests on the substance. The agency in 1984 began issuing final rules to require health, environmental, or chemical fate studies, as well as guidelines for conducting the tests.

The agency negotiated with chemical firms to obtain testing data voluntarily until a federal court in 1984 struck down the practice, which bypassed the two or more years needed to complete a formal rulemaking (*Natural Resources Defense Council v. Environmental Protection Agency*, 21 ERC 1625, 21 ERC 1919). In June 1986, EPA issued an interim final rule that allows it to negotiate enforceable consent agreements for testing under Section 4 of the act. EPA and the manufacturer of 3,4-dichlorobenzotrifluoride signed the first such agreement in June 1987.

In recent years, the agency has begun to use the law's authorities for programs throughout the agency and in other federal agencies. In May 1987, EPA proposed a rule that would would gather testing data the agency needs to regulate 73 substances as hazardous wastes under the Resource Conservation and Recovery Act (RCRA). The agency and industry in late 1987 were negotiating a consent agreement for the testing of nonylphenol to collect information for EPA's solid waste and water regulatory programs as well as the Food and Drug Administration.

Despite the agency's slow start in using TSCA to control exposure to harmful substances, Congress has not amended the law substantially in the 11 years since enactment. Conforming amendments were included in revisions to RCRA in 1984. Also in 1986, Congress enacted the Asbestos Hazard Emergency Response Act as Title II of TSCA. This new law requires school systems to inspect for and abate asbestos hazards found in school buildings. The only amendments to the law believed politically viable in the 100th Congress would extend this asbestos abatement program to public or commercial buildings.

This leaves the EPA in search of ways to make the law more useful in protecting the public from harmful substances. Agency officials have concentrated in recent years on developing generic regulatory schemes that would make it easier for the government to collect information and impose manufacturing controls. Streamlining procedures under TSCA would allow them to move more quickly against substances they believe pose a risk and to demand data to help them investigate suspect chemicals.

Toxic Substances Control Act

(P.L. 94–469, approved October 11, 1976; as last amended by P.L. 99–519, approved October 22, 1986)

Subchapter I. Control of Toxic Substances

§ 2601. Findings, policy, and intent

[Sec. 2] (a) The Congress finds that—

(1) human beings and the environment are being exposed each year to a large number of chemical substances and mixtures;

(2) among the many chemical substances and mixtures which are constantly being developed and produced, there are some whose manufacture, processing, distribution in commerce, use, or disposal may present an unreasonable risk of injury to health or the environment; and

(3) the effective regulation of interstate commerce in such chemical substances and mixtures also necessitates the regulation of intrastate commerce in such chemical substances and mixtures.

(b) It is the policy of the United States that—

(1) adequate data should be developed with respect to the effect of chemical substances and mixtures on health and the environment and that the development of such data should be the responsibility of those who manufacture and those who process such chemical substances and mixtures;

(2) adequate authority should exist to regulate chemical substances and mixtures which present an unreasonable risk of injury to health or the environment, and to take action with respect to chemical substances and mixtures which are immiment hazards; and

(3) authority over chemical substances and mixtures should be exercised in such a manner as not to impede unduly or create unnecessary economic barriers to technological innovation while fulfilling the primary purpose of this Act to assure that such innovation and commerce in such chemical substances and mixtures do not present an unreasonable risk of injury to health or the environment.

(c) It is the intent of Congress that the Administrator shall carry out this Act in a reasonable and prudent manner, and that the Administrator shall consider the environmental, economic, and social impact of any action the Administrator takes or proposes to take under this Act.

§ 2602. Definitions

[Sec. 3] As used in this Act:

(1) the term "Administrator" means the Administrator of the Environmental Protection Agency.

(2)(A) Except as provided in subparagraph (B), the term "chemical substance" means any organic or inorganic substance of a particular molecular identity, including—

(i) any combination of such substances occurring in whole or in part as a result of a chemical reaction or occurring in nature, and

(ii) any element or uncombined radical.

(B) Such term does not include—

(i) any mixture,

(ii) any pesticide (as defined in the Federal Insecticide, Fungicide, and Rodenticide Act) when manufactured, processed, or distributed in commerce for use as a pesticide,

(iii) tobacco or any tobacco product,

(iv) any source material, special nuclear material, or byproduct material (as such terms are defined in the Atomic Energy Act of 1954 and regulations issued under such Act),

(v) any article the sale of which is subject to the tax imposed by section 4181 of the Internal Revenue Code of 1954 (determined without regard to any exemptions from such tax provided by section 4182 or 4221 or any other provision of such Code), and

(vi) any food, food additive, drug, cosmetic, or device (as such terms are defined in section 201 of the Federal Food, Drug, and Cosmetic Act) when manufactured, processed, or distributed in commerce for use as a food, food additive, drug, cosmetic, or device.

The term "food" as used in clause (vi) of this subparagraph includes poultry and poultry products (as defined in sections 4(e) and 4(f) of the Poultry Products Inspection Act), meat and meat food products (as defined in section 1(j) of the Federal Meat Inspection Act), and eggs and egg products (as defined in section 4 of the Egg Products Inspection Act).

(3) The term "commerce" means trade, traffic, transportation, or other commerce (A) between a place in a State and any place outside of such State, or (B) which affects trade, traffic, transportation, or commerce described in clause (A).

(4) The terms "distribute in commerce" and "distribution in commerce" when used to describe an action taken with respect to a chemical substance or mixture or article containing a substance or mixture mean to sell, or the sale of, the substance, mixture, or article in commerce; to introduce or deliver for introduction into commerce, or the introduction or delivery for introduction into commerce of, the substance, mixture, or article; or to hold, or the holding of, the substance, mixture, or article after its introduction into commerce.

(5) The term "environment" includes water, air, and land and the interrelationship which exists among and between water, air, and land and all living things.

(6) The term "health and safety study" means any study of any effect of a chemical substance of mixture on health or the environment or on both, including underlying data and epidemiological studies, studies of occupational exposure to a chemical substance or mixture, toxicological, clinical, and ecological studies of a chemical substance or mixture, and any test performed pursuant to this Act.

(7) The term "manufacture" means to import into the customs territory of the United States (as defined in general headnote 2 of the Tariff Schedules of the United States), produce, or manufacture.

(8) The term "mixture" means any combination of two or more chemical substances if the combination does not occur in nature and is not, in whole or in part, the result of a chemical reaction; except that such term does include any combination which occurs, in whole or in part, as a result of a chemical reaction if none of the chemical substances comprising the combination is a new chemical substance and if the combination could have been manufactured for commercial purposes without a chemical reaction at the time the chemical substances

comprising the combination were combined.

(9) The term "new chemical substance" means any chemical substance which is not included in the chemical substance list compiled and published under section 8(b).

(10) The term "process" means the preparation of a chemical substance or mixture, after its manufacture, for distribution in commerce—

(A) in the same form or physical state as, or in a different form or physical state from, that in which it was received by the person so preparing such substance or mixture, or

(B) as part of an article containing the chemical substance or mixture.

(11) The term "processor" means any person who processes a chemical substance or mixture.

(12) The term "standards for the development of test data" means a prescription of—

(A) the—

(i) health and environmental effects, and

(ii) information relating to toxicity, persistence, and other characteristics which affect health and the environment,

for which test data for a chemical substance or mixture are to be developed and any analysis that is to be performed on such data, and

(B) to the extent necessary to assure that data respecting such effects and characteristics are reliable and adequate—

(i) the manner in which such data are to be developed,

(ii) the specification of any test protocol or methodology to be employed in the development of such data, and

(iii) such other requirements as are necessary to provide such assurance.

(13) The term "State" means any State of the United States, the District of Columbia, the Commonwealth of Puerto Rico, the Virgin Islands, Guam, the Canal Zone, American Samoa, the Northern Mariana Islands, or any other territory or possession of the United States.

(14) The term "United States", when used in the geographic sense, means all of the States.

§ 2603. Testing of chemical substances and mixtures

[Sec. 4] (a) If the Administrator finds that—

(1)(A)(i) the manufacture, distribution in commerce, processing, use, or disposal of a chemical substance or mixture, or that any combination of such activities, may present an unreasonable risk of injury to health or the environment.

(ii) there are insufficient data and experience upon which the effects of such manufacture, distribution in commerce, processing, use, or disposal of such substance or mixture or of any combination of such activities on health or the environment can reasonably be determined or predicted, and

    (iii) testing of such substance or mixture with respect to such effects is necessary to develop such data; or

(B)(i) a chemical substance or mxiture is or will be produced in substantial quantities, and (I) it enters or may reasonably be anticipated to enter the environment in substantial quantities or (II) there is or may be significant or substantial human exposure to such substance or mixture,

    (ii) there are insufficient data and experience upon which the effects of the manufacture, distribution in commerce, processing, use, or disposal of such substance or mixture or of any combination of such activities on health or the environment can reasonably be determined or predicted, and

    (iii) testing of such substance or mixture with respect to such effects is necessary to develop such data; and

(2) in the case of a mixture, the effects which the mixture's manufacture, distribution in commerce, processing, use, or disposal or any combination of such activities many have on health or the environment may not be reasonably and more efficiently determined or predicted by testing the chemical substances which comprise the mixture;

the Administrator shall by rule require that testing be conducted on such substance or mixture to develop data with respect to the health and environmental effects for which there is an insufficiency of data and experience and which are relevant to a determination that the manufacture, distribution in commerce, processing, use, or disposal of such substance or mixture, or that any combination of such activities, does or does not present an unreasonable risk of injury to health or the environment.

(b)(1) A rule under subsection (a) shall include—

    (A) identification of the chemical substance or mixture for which testing is required under the rule,

    (B) standards for the development of test data for such substance or mixture, and

    (C) with respect to chemical substances which are not new chemical substances and to mixtures, a specification of the period (which period may not be unreasonable duration) within which the persons required to conduct the testing shall submit to the Administrator data developed in accordance with the standards referred to in subparagraph (B).

In determining the standards and period to be included, pursuant to subparagraph (B) and (C), in a rule under subsection (a), the Administrator's considerations shall include the relative costs of the various test protocols and methodologies which may be required under the rule and the reasonable foreseeable availability of the facilities and personnel needed to perform the testing required under the rule. Any such rule may require the submission to the Administrator of preliminary data during the period prescribed under subparagraph (C).

(2)(A) The health and environmental effects for which standards for the development of test data may be prescribed include carcinogenesis, mutagenesis, teratogenesis, behavioral disorders, cumulative or synergistic effects, and any other effect which may present in unreasonable risk of injury to health or the environment. The characteristics of chemical substances and mixtures for which such standards may be prescribed include persistence, acute toxicity, subacute toxicity, chronic toxicity, and any other characteristic which may present such a risk. The methodologies that may be prescribed in such standards include epidemiologic studies, serial or hierarchical tests, in vitro tests, and whole animal tests, except that before prescribing epidemiologic studies of employees, the Administrator shall consult with the Director of the National Institute for Occupational Safety and Health.

(B) From time to time, but not less than once each 12 months, the Administrator shall review the adequacy of the standards for development of data prescribed in rules under subsection (a) and shall, if necessary, institute proceedings to make appropriate revisions of such standards.

(3)(A) A rule under subsection (a) respecting a chemical substance or mixture shall require the persons described in subparagraph (B) to conduct tests and submit data to the Administrator on such substance or mixture, except that the Administrator may permit two or more of such persons to designate one such person or a qualified third party to conduct such tests and submit such data on behalf of the persons making the designation.

(B) The following persons shall be required to conduct tests and submit data on a chemical substance or mixture subject to a rule under subsection (a):

    (i) Each person who manufactures or intends to manufacture such substance or mixture if the Administrator makes a finding described in subsection (a)(1)(A)(ii) or (a)(1)(B)(ii) with respect to the manufacture of such substance or mixture.

    (ii) Each person who processes or intends to process such substance or mixture if the Administrator makes a finding described in subsection (a)(1)(A)(ii) or (a)(1)(B)(ii) with respect to the processing of such substance or mixture.

    (iii) Each person who manufactures or processes or intends to manufacture or process such substance or mixture if the Administrator makes a finding described in subsection (a)(1)(A)(ii) or (a)(1)(B)(ii) with respect to the distribution in commerce, use, or disposal of such substance or mixture.

(4) Any rule under subsection (a) requiring the testing of and submission of data for a particular chemical substance or mixture shall expire at

the end of the reimbursement period (as defined in subsection (c)(3)(B)) which is applicable to test data for such substance or mixture unless the Administrator repeals the rule before such date; and a rule under subsection (a) requiring the testing of and submission of data for a category of chemical substances or mixtures shall expire with respect to a chemical substance or mixture included in the category at the end of the reimbursement period (as so defined) which is applicable to test data for such substance or mixture unless the Administrator before such date repeals the application of the rule to such substance or mixture or repeals the rule.

(5) Rules issued under subsection (a) (and any substantive amendment thereto or repeal thereof) shall be promulgated pursuant to section 553 of title 5, United States Code, except that (A) the Administrator shall give interested persons an opportunity for the oral presentation of data, views, or arguments, in addition to an opportunity to make written submissions; (B) a transcript shall be made of any oral presentation: and (C) the Administrator shall make and publish with the rule the findings described in paragraph (1)(A) or (1)(B) of subsection (a) and, in the case of a rule respecting a mixture, the finding described in paragraph (2) of such subsection.

(c)(1) Any person required by a rule under subsection (a) to conduct tests and submit data on a chemical substance or mixture may apply to the Administrator (in such form and manner as the Administrator shall prescribe) for exemption from such requirement.

(2) If, upon receipt of an application under paragraph (1), the Administrator determines that—

(A) the chemical substance or mixture with respect to which such application was submitted is equivalent to a chemical substance or mixture for which data has been submitted to the Administrator in accordance with a rule under subsection (a) or for which data is being developed pursuant to such a rule, and

(B) submission of data by the applicant on such substance or mixture would be duplicative of data which has been submitted to the Administrator in accordance with such rule or which is being developed pursuant to such rule,

the Administrator shall exempt, in accordance with paragraph (3) or (4), the applicant from conducting tests and submitting data on such substance or mixture under the rule with respect to which such application was submitted.

(3)(A) If the exemption under paragraph (2) of any person from the requirement to conduct tests and submit test data on a chemical substance or mixture is granted on the basis of the existence of previously submitted test data and if such exemption is granted during the reimbursement period for such test data (as prescribed by subparagraph (B)), then (unless such person and the persons referred to in clauses (i) and (ii) agree on the amount and method of reimbursement) the Administrator shall order the person granted the exemption to provide fair and equitable reimbursement (in an amount determined under rules of the Administrator)—

(i) to the person who previously submitted such test data, for a portion of the costs incurred by such person in complying with the requirement to submit such data, and

(ii) to any other person who has been required under this subparagraph to contribute with respect to such costs, for a portion of the amount such person was required to contribute.

In promulgating rules for the determination of fair and equitable reimbursement to the persons described in clauses (i) and (ii) for costs incurred with respect to a chemical substance or mixture, the Administrator shall, after consultation with the Attorney General and the Federal Trade Commission, consider all relevant factors, including the effect on the competitive position of the person required to provide reimbursement in relation to the person to be reimbursed and the share of the market for such substance or mixture of the person required to provide reimbursement in relation to the share of such market of the persons to be reimbursed. An order under this subparagraph shall, for purposes of judicial review, be considered final agency action.

(B) For purposes of subparagraph (A), the reimbursement period for any test data for a chemical substance or mixture is a period

(i) beginning on the date such data is submitted in accordance with a rule promulgated under subsection (a), and

(ii) ending—

(I) five years after the date referred to in clause (i), or

(II) at the expiration of a period which begins on the date referred to in clause (i) and which is equal to the period which the Administrator determines was necessary to develop such data,

whichever is later.

(4)(A) If the exemption under paragraph (2) of any person from the requirement to conduct tests and submit test data on a chemical substance or mixture is granted on the basis of the fact that test data is being developed by one or more persons pursuant to a rule promulgated under subsection (a), then (unless such person and the persons referred to in clauses (i) and (ii) agree on the amount and method of reimbursement) the Administrator shall order the person granted the exemption to provide fair and equitable reimbursement (in an amount determined under rules of the Administrator)—

(i) to each such person who is developing such test data, for a portion of the costs incurred by each such person in complying with such rule, and

(ii) to any other person who has been required under this
subparagraph to contribute with respect to the costs of complying with such rule, for a portion of the amount such person
was required to contribute.

In promulgating rules for the determination of fair and equitable
reimbursement to the persons described in clauses (i) and (ii) for costs
incurred with respect to a chemical substance or mixture, the Administrator shall, after consultation with the Attorney General and the
Federal Trade Commission, consider the factors described in the
second sentence of paragraph (3)(A). An order under this subparagraph shall, for purposes of judicial review, be considered final agency
action.

(B) If any exemption is granted under paragraph (2) on the basis of
the fact that one or more persons are developing test data
pursuant to a rule promulgated under subsection (a) and if after
such exemption is granted the Administrator determines that no
such person has complied with such rule, the Administrator shall
(i) after providing written notice to the person who holds such
exemption and an opportunity for a hearing, by order terminate
such exemption, and (ii) notify in writing such person of the
requirements of the rule with respect to which such exemption
was granted.

(d) Upon the receipt of any test data pursuant to a rule under subsection
(a), the Administrator shall publish a notice of the receipt of such data in the
Federal Register within 15 days of its receipt. Subject to section 14, each
such notice shall (1) identify the chemical substance or mixture for which
data have been received; (2) list the uses or intended uses of such substance
or mixture and the information required by the applicable standards for the
development of test data; and (3) describe the nature of the test data
developed. Except as otherwise provided in section 14, such data shall be
made available by the Administrator for examination by any person.

(e)(1)(A) There is established a committee to make recommendations to
the Administrator respecting the chemical substances and mixtures to which
the Administrator should give priority consideration for the promulgation of
a rule under subsection (a). In making such a recommendation with respect
to any chemical substance or mixture, the committee shall consider all
relevant factors, including—

(i) the quantities in which the substance or mixture is or will be
manufactured,
(ii) the quantities in which the substance or mixture enters or will
enter the environment,
(iii) the number of individuals who are or will be exposed to the
substance or mixture in their places of employment and the
duration of such exposure,
(iv) the extent to which human beings are or will be exposed to the

substance or mixture,

(v) the extent to which the subsance or mixture is closely related to a chemical substance or mixture which is known to present an unreasonable risk of injury to health or the environment,

(vi) the existence of data concerning the effects of the substance or mixture on health or the environment,

(vii) the extent to which testing of the substance or mixture may result in the development of data upon which the effects of the substance or mixture on health or the environment can reasonably be determined or predicted, and

(viii) the reasonably foreseeable availability of facilities and personnel for performing testing on the substance or mixture.

The recommendations of the committee shall be in the form of a list of chemical substances and mixtures which shall be set forth, either by individual substance or mixture or by groups of substances or mixtures, in the order in which the committee determines the Administrator should take action udner subsection (a) with respect to the substances and mixtures. In establishing such list, the committee shall give priority attention to those chemical substances and mixtures which are known to cause or contribute to or which are suspected of causing or contributing to cancer, gene mutations, or birth defects. The committee shall designate chemical substances and mixtures on the list with respect to which the committee determines the Administrator should, within 12 months of the date on which such substances and mixtures are first designated, initiate a proceeding under subsection (a). The total number of chemical substances and mixtures on the list which are designated under the preceding sentence may not, at any time, exceed 50.

(B) As soon as practicable but not later than nine months after the effective date of this Act, the committee shall publish in the Federal Register and transmit to the Administrator the list and designations required by subparagraph (A) together with the reasons for the committee's inclusion of each chemical substance or mixture on the list. At least every six months after the date of the transmission to the Administrator of the list pursuant to the preceding sentence, the committee shall make such revisions in the list as it determines to be necessary and shall transmit them to the Administrator together with the committee's reasons for the revisions. Upon receipt of any such revision, the Administrator shall publish in the Federal Register the list with such revision, the reasons for such revision, and the designations made under subparagraph (A). The Administrator shall provide reasonable opportunity to any interested person to file with the Administrator written comments on the committee's list, any revision of such list by the committee, and designations made by the committee, and shall make such comments available to the public. Within the 12–month period beginning on the date of the first inclusion on the list of a chemical substance or mixture designated by the committee under subparagraph (A) the Administrator shall with respect to such chemical substance or mixture either initiate a rulemaking proceeding under subsection (a) or if such a proceeding is not initiated within such period, publish in the Federal Register the Administrator's reason for not initiating such a proceeding.

(2)(A) The committee established by paragraph (1)(A) shall consist of eight members as follows:

    (i) One member appointed by the Administrator from the Environmental Protection Agency.

    (ii) One member appointed by the Secretary of Labor from officers or employees of the Department of Labor engaged in the Secretary's activities under the Occupational Safety and Health Act of 1970.

    (iii) One member appointed by the Chairman of the Council on Environmental Quality from the Council or its officers or employees.

    (iv) One member appointed by the Director of the National Institute for Occupational Safety and Health from officers or employees of the Institute.

    (v) One member appointed by the Director of the National Institute of Environmental Health Sciences from officers or employees of the Institute.

    (vi) One member appointed by the Director of the National Cancer Institute from officers or employees of the Institute.

    (vii) One member appointed by the Director of the National Science Foundation from officers or employees of the Foundation.

    (viii) One member appointed by the Secretary of Commerce from officers or employees of the Department of Commerce.

  (B)(i) An appointed member may designate an individual to serve on the committee on the member's behalf. Such a designation may be made only with the approval of the applicable appointing authority and only if the individual is from the entity from which the member was appointed.

    (ii) No individual may serve as a member of the committee for more than four years in the aggregate. If any member of the committee leaves the entity from which the member was appointed, such member may not continue as a member of the committee, and the member's position shall be considered to be vacant. A vacancy in the committee shall be filled in the same manner in which the original appointment was made.

    (iii) Initial appointments to the committee shall be made not later than the 60th day after the effective date of this Act. Not later than the 90th day after such date the members of the committee shall hold a meeting for the selection of a chairperson from among their number.

(C)(i) No member of the committee, or designee of such member, shall accept employment or compensation from any person subject to any requirement of this Act or of any rule promulgated or order issued thereunder, for a period of at least 12 months after termination of service on the committee.

    (ii) No person, while serving as a member of the committee, or designee of such member, may own any stocks or bonds, or have any pecuniary interest, of substantial value in any person engaged in the manufacture, processing, or distribution in commerce of any chemical substance or mixture subject to any requirement of this Act or of any rule promulgated or order issued thereunder.

    (iii) The Administrator, acting through attorneys of the Environmental Protection Agency, or the Attorney General may bring an action in the appropriate district court of the United States to restrain any violation of this subparagraph.

(D) The Administrator shall provide the committee such administrative support services as may be necessary to enable the committee to carry out its function under this subsection.

(f) Upon the receipt of—

(1) any test data required to be submitted under this Act, or

(2) any other information available to the Administrator,

which indicates to the Administrator that there may be a reasonable basis to conclude that a chemical substance or mixture presents or will present a significant risk of serious or widespread harm to human beings from cancer, gene mutations, or birth defects, the Administrator shall, within the 180–day period beginning on the date of the receipt of such data or information, initiate appropriate action under section 5, 6, or 7 to prevent or reduce to a sufficient extent such risk or publish in the Federal Register a finding that such risk is not unreasonable. For good cause shown the Administrator may extend such period for an additional period of not more than 90 days. The Administrator shall publish in the Federal Register notice of any such extension and the reasons therefor. A finding by the Administrator that a risk is not unreasonable shall be considered agency action for purposes of judicial review under chapter 7 of title 5, United States Code. This subsection shall not take effect until two years after January 1, 1977.

(g) A person intending to manufacture or process a chemical substance for which notice is required under section 5(a) and who is not required under a rule under subsection (a) to conduct tests and submit data on such substance may petition the Administrator to prescribe standards for the development of test data for such substance. The Administrator shall by order either grant or deny any such petition within 60 days of its receipt. If the petition is granted, the Administrator shall prescribe such standards for such substance within 75 days of the date the petition is granted. If the petition is denied, the Administrator shall publish, subject to section 14, in the Federal Register the reasons for such denial.

§ 2604. Manufacturing and processing notices

[Sec. 5] (a)(1) Except as provided in subsection (h), no person may—
  (A) manufacture a new chemical substance on or after the 30th day after the date on which the Administrator first publishes the list required by section 8(b), or
  (B) manufacture or process any chemical substance for a use which the Administrator has determined, in accordance with paragraph (2), is a significant new use,
  unless such person submits to the Administrator, at least 90 days before such manufacture or processing, a notice, in accordance with subsection (d), of such person's intention to manufacture or process such substance and such person complies with any applicable requirement of subsection (b).
  (2) A determination by the Administrator that a use of a chemical substance is a significant new use with respect to which notification is required under paragraph (1) shall be made by a rule promulgated after a consideration of all relevant factors, including—
  (A) the projected volume of manufacturing and processing of a chemical substance,
  (B) the extent to which a use changes the type or form of exposure of human beings or the environment to a chemical substance,
  (C) the extent to which a use increases the magnitude and duration of exposure of human beings or the environment to a chemical substance, and
  (D) the reasonably anticipated manner and methods of manufacturing, processing, distribution in commerce, and disposal of a chemical substance.
  (b)(1)(A) If (i) a person is required by subsection (a)(1) to submit a notice to the Administrator before beginning the manufacture or processing of a chemical substance, and (ii) such person is required to submit test data for such substance pursuant to a rule promulgated under section 4 before the submission of such notice, such person shall submit to the Administrator such data in accordance with such rule at the time notice is submitted in accordance with subsection (a)(1).

(B) If—
  (i) a person is required by subsection (a)(1) to submit a notice to the Administrator, and
  (ii) such person has been granted an exemption under section 4(c) from the requirements of a rule promulgated under section 4 before the submission of such notice,

such person may not, before the expiration of the 90 day period which begins on the date of the submission in accordance with such rule of the test data the submission or development of which was the basis for the exemption, manufacture such substance if such person is subject to subsection (a)(1)(A) or manufacture or process such substance for a significant new use if the person is subject to subsection (a)(1)(B).

(2)(A) If a person—
  (i) is required by subsection (a)(1) to submit a notice to the Administrator before beginning the manufacture or processing of a chemical substance listed under paragraph (4), and
  (ii) is not required by a rule promulgated under section 4 before the submission of such notice to submit test data for such substance,

such person shall submit to the Administrator data prescribed by subparagraph (B) at the time notice is submitted in accordance with subsection (a)(1).

(B) Data submitted pursuant to subparagraph (A) shall be data which the person submitting the data believes show that—
  (i) in the case of a substance with respect to which notice is required under subsection (a)(1)(A), the manufacture, processing, distribution in commerce, use, and disposal of the chemical substance or any combination of such activities will not present an unreasonable risk of injury to health or the environment, or
  (ii) In the case of a chemical substance with respect to which notice is required under subsection (a)(1)(B), the intended significant new use of the chemical substance will not present an unreasonable risk of injury to health or the environment.

(3) Data submitted under paragraph (1) or (2) shall be made available, subject to section 14, for examination by interested persons.

(4)(A)(i) The Administrator may, by rule, compile and keep current a list of chemical substances with respect to which the Administrator finds that the manufacture, processing, distribution in commerce, use, or disposal, or any combination of such activities, presents or may present an unreasonable risk of injury to health or the environment.
  (ii) In making a finding under clause (i) that the manufacture, processing, distribution in commerce, use, or disposal of a chemical substance or any combination of such activities pre-

sents or may present an unreasonable risk of injury to health or the environment, the Administrator shall consider all relevant factors, including—

(I) the effects of the chemical substance on health and the magnitude of human exposure to such substance; and

(II) the effects of the chemical substance on the environment and the magnitude of environmental exposure to such substance.

(B) The Administrator shall, in prescribing a rule under subparagraph (A) which lists any chemical substance, identify those uses, if any, which the Administrator determines, by rule under subsection (a)(2), would constitute a significant new use of such substance.

(C) Any rule under subparagraph (A), and any substantive amendment or repeal of such a rule, shall be promulgated pursuant to the procedures specified in section 553 of title 5, United States Code, except that (i) the Administrator shall give interested persons an opportunity for the oral presentation of data, views, or arguments, in addition to an opportunity to make written submissions, (ii) a transcript shall be kept of any oral presentation, and (iii) the Administrator shall make and publish with the rule the finding described in subparagraph (A).

(c) The Administrator may for good cause extend for additional periods (not to exceed in the aggregate 90 days) the period, prescribed by subsection (a) or (b) before which the manufacturing or processing of a chemical substance subject to such subsection may begin. Subject to section 14, such an extension and the reasons therefor shall be published in the Federal Register and shall constitute a final agency action subject to judicial review.

(d)(1) The notice required by subsection (a) shall include—

(A) insofar as known to the person submitting the notice or insofar as reasonably ascertainable, the information described in subparagraphs (A), (B), (C), (D), (F), and (G) of section 8(a)(2), and

(B) in such form and manner as the Administrator may prescribe, any test data in the possession or control of the person giving such notice which are related to the effect of any manufacture, processing, distribution in commerce, use, or disposal of such substance or any article containing such substance, or of any combination of such activities, on health or the environment, and

(C) a description of any other data concerning the environmental and health effects of such substance, insofar as known to the person making the notice or insofar as reasonably ascertainable.

Such a notice shall be made available, subject to section 14, for examination by interested persons.

(2) Subject to section 14, not later than five days (excluding Saturdays, Sundays and legal holidays) after the date of the receipt of a notice

under subsection (a) or of data under subsection (b), the Administrator shall publish in the Federal Register a notice which—

(A) identifies the chemical substance for which notice or data has been received;

(B) lists the uses or intended uses of such substance; and

(C) in the case of the receipt of data under subsection (b), describes the nature of the tests performed on such sustance and any data which was developed pursuant to subsection (b) or a rule under section 4.

A notice under this paragraph respecting a chemical substance shall identify the chemical substance by generic class unless the Administrator determines that more specific identification is required in the public interest.

(3) At the beginning of each month the Administrator shall publish a list in the Federal Register of (A) each chemical substance for which notice has been received under subsection (a) and for which the notification period prescribed by subsection (a), (b), or (c) has not expired, and (B) each chemical substance for which such notification period has expired since the last publication in the Federal Register of such list.

(e)(1)(A) If the Administrator determines that—

(i) the information available to the Administrator is insufficient to permit a reasoned evaluation of the health and environmental effects of a chemical substance with respect to which notice is required by subsection (a); and

(ii)(I) in the absence of sufficient information to permit the Administrator to make such an evaluation, the manufacture, processing, distribution in commerce, use, or disposal of such substance, or any combination of such activities, may present an unreasonable risk of injury to health or the environment, or

(II) such substance is or will be produced in substantial quantities, and such substance either enters or may reasonably be anticipated to enter the environment in substantial quantities or there is or may be significant or substantial human exposure to the substance,

the Administrator may issue a proposed order, to take effect on the expiration of the notification period applicable to the manufacturing or processing of such substance under subsection (a), (b), or (c), to prohibit or limit the manufacture, processing, distribution in commerce, use, or disposal of such substance or to prohibit or limit any combination of such activities.

(B) A proposed order may not be issued under subparagraph (A) respecting a chemical substance (i) later than 45 days before the expiration of the notification period applicable to the manufacture or processing of such substance under subsection (a), (b), or (c), and (ii) unless the Administrator has, on or before the issuance of the proposed order, notified, in writing, each manufacturer or processor, as the case may be, of such substance of the determination which underlies such order.

(C) If a manufacturer or processor of a chemical substance to be subject to a proposed order issued under subparagraph (A) files with the Administrator (within the 30-day period beginning on the date such manufacturer or processor received the notice required by subparagraph (B)(ii) objections specifying with particularity the provisions of the order deemed objectionable and stating the grounds therefor, the proposed order shall not take effect.

(2)(A)(i) Except as provided in clause (ii), if with respect to a chemical substance with respect to which notice is required by subsection (a), the Administrator makes the determination described in paragraph (1)(A) and if—

    (I) the Administrator does not issue a proposed order under paragraph (1) respecting such substance, or

    (II) the Administrator issues such an order respecting such substance but such order does not take effect because objections were filed under paragraph (1)(C) with respect to it,

the Administrator, through attorneys of the Environmental Protection Agency, shall apply to the United States District Court for the District of Columbia or the United States district court for the judicial district in which the manufacturer or processor, as the case may be, of such substance is found, resides, or transacts business for an injunction to prohibit or limit the manufacture, processing, distribution in commerce, use, or disposal of such substance (or to prohibit or limit any combination of such activities).

    (ii) If the Administrator issues a proposed order under paragraph (1)(A) respecting a chemical substance but such order does not take effect because objections have been filed under paragraph (1)(C) with respect to it, the Administrator is not required to apply for an injunction under clause (i) respecting such substance if the Administrator determines, on the basis of such objections, that the determinations under paragraph (1)(A) may not be made.

(B) A district court of the United States which receives an application under subparagraph (A)(i) for an injunction respecting a chemical substance shall issue such injunction if the court finds that—

    (i) the information available to the Administrator is insufficient to permit a reasoned evaluation of the health and environmental effects of a chemical substance with respect to which notice is required by subsection (a); and (ii)(I) in the absence of sufficient information to permit the Administrator to make such an evaluation, the manufacture, processing, distribution in commerce, use, or disposal of such substance, or any combination of such activities, may present an unreasonable risk of injury to health or the environment, or

(II) such substance is or will be produced in substantial quantities, and such substance either enters or may reasonably be anticipated to enter the environment in substantial quantities or there is or may be significant or substantial human exposure to the substance.

(C) Pending the completion of a proceeding for the issuance of an injunction under subparagraph (B) respecting a chemical substance, the court may, upon application of the Administrator made through attorneys of the Environmental Protection Agency, issue a temporary restraining order or a preliminary injunction to prohibit the manufacture, processing, distribution in commerce, use, or disposal of such a substance (or any combination of such activities) if the court finds that the notification period applicable under subsection (a), (b), or (c) to the manufacturing or processing of such substance may expire before such proceeding can be completed.

(D) After the submission to the Administrator of test data sufficient to evaluate the health and environmental effects of a chemical substance subject to an injunction issued under subparagraph (B) and the evaluation of such data by the Administrator, the district court of the United States which issued such injunction shall, upon petition, dissolve the injunction unless the Administrator has initiated a proceeding for the issuance of a rule under section 6(a) respecting the substance. If such a proceeding has been initiated, such court shall continue the injunction in effect until the effective date of the rule promulgated in such proceeding or, if such proceeding is terminated without the promulgation of a rule, upon the termination of the proceeding, whichever occurs first.

(f)(1) If the Administrator finds that there is a reasonable basis to conclude that the manufacture, processing, distribution in commerce, use, or disposal of a chemical substance with respect to which notice is required by subsection (a), or that any combination of such activities, presents or will present an unreasonable risk of injury to health or environment before a rule promulgated under section 6 can protect against such risk, the Administrator shall, before the expiration of the notification period applicable under subsection (a), (b), or (c) to the manufacturing or processing of such substance, take the action authorized by paragraph (2) or (3) to the extent necessary to protect against such risk.

(2) The Administrator may issue a proposed rule under section 6(a) to apply to a chemical substance with respect to which a finding was

made under paragraph (1)—

(A) a requirement limiting the amount of such substance which may be manufactured, processed, or distributed in commerce,

(B) a requirement described in paragraph (2), (3), (4), (5), (6), or (7) of section 6(a), or

(C) any combination of the requirements referred to in subparagraph (B).

Such a proposed rule shall be effective upon its publication in the Federal Register. Section 6(d)(2)(B) shall apply with respect to such rule.

(3)(A) The Administrator may—

(i) issue a proposed order to prohibit the manufacture, processing, or distribution in commerce of a substance with respect to which a finding was made under paragraph (1), or

(ii) apply, through attorneys of the Environmental Protection Agency, to the United States District Court for the District of Columbia or the United States district court for the judicial district in which the manufacturer, or processor, as the case may be, of such substance, is found, resides, or transacts business for an injunction to prohibit the manufacture, processing, or distribution in commerce of such substance.

A proposed order issued under clause (i) respecting a chemical substance shall take effect on the expiration of the notification period applicable under subsection (a), (b), or (c) to the manufacture or processing of such substance.

(B) If the district court of the United States to which an application has been made under subparagraph (A)(ii) finds that there is a reasonable basis to conclude that the manufacture, processing, distribution in commerce, use, or disposal of the chemical substance with respect to which such application was made, or that any combination of such activities, presents or will present an unreasonable risk of injury to health or the environment before a rule promulgated under section 6 can protect against such risk, the court shall issue an injunction to prohibit the manufacture, processing, or distribution in commerce of such substance or to prohibit any combination of such activities.

(C) The provisions of subparagraphs (B) and (C) of subsection (e)(1) shall apply with respect to an order issued under clause (i) of subparagraph (A); and the provisions of subparagraph (C) of subsection (e)(2) shall apply with respect to an injunction issued under subparagraph (B).

(D) If the Administrator issues an order pursuant to subparagraph (A)(i) respecting a chemical substance and objections are filed in accordance with subsection (e)(1)(C), the Administrator shall seek an injunction under subparagraph (A)(ii) respecting such substance unless the Administrator determines, on the basis of such objections, that such substance does not or will not present an unreasonable risk of injury to health or the environment.

(g) If the Administrator has not initiated any action under this section or section 6 or 7 to prohibit or limit the manufacture, processing, distribution in commerce, use, or disposal of a chemical substance, with respect to which notification or data is required by subsection (a)(1)(B) or (b), before the expiration of the notification period applicable to the manufacturing or processing of such substance, the Administrator shall publish a statement of the Administrator's reasons for not initiating such action. Such a statement shall be published in the Federal Register before the expiration of such period. Publication of such statement in accordance with the preceding sentence is not a prerequisite to the manufacturing or processing of the substance with respect to which the statement is to be published.

(h)(1) The Administrator may, upon application, exempt any person from any requirement of subsection (a) or (b) to permit such person to manufacture or process a chemical substance for test marketing purposes—

    (A) upon a showing by such person satisfactory to the Administrator that the manufacture, processing, distribution in commerce, use, and disposal of such substance, and that any combination of such activities, for such purposes will not present any unreasonable risk of injury to health or the environment, and

    (B) under such restrictions as the Administrator considers appropriate.

(2)(A) The Administrator may, upon application, exempt any person from the requirement of subsection (b)(2) to submit data for a chemical substance. If, upon receipt of an application under the preceding sentence, the Administrator determines that—

    (i) the chemical substance with respect to which such application was submitted is equivalent to a chemical substance for which data has been submitted to the Administrator as required by subsection (b)(2), and

    (ii) submission of data by the applicant on such substance would be duplicative of data which has been submitted to the Administrator in accordance with such susbection.

the Administrator shall exempt the applicant from the requirement to submit such data on such substance. No exemption which is granted under this subparagraph with respect to the submission of data for a chemical substance may take effect before the beginning of the reimbursement period applicable to such data.

(B) If the Administrator exempts any person, under subparagraph (A), from submitting data required under subsection (b)(2) for a chemical substance because of the existence of previously submitted data, and if such exemption is granted during the reimbursement period for such data, then (unless such person and the persons referred to in clauses (i) and (ii) agree on the amount and method of reimbursement) the Administrator shall order the person granted the exemption to provide fair and equitable reimbursement (in an amount determined under rules of the Administrator)—

    (i) to the person who previously submitted the data on which the exemption was based, for a portion of the costs incurred by such person in complying with the requirement under subsection (b)(2) to submit such data, and

    (ii) to any other person who has been required under this subparagraph to contribute with respect to such costs, for a portion of the amount such person was required to contribute.

In promulgating rules for the determination of fair and equitable reimbursement to the persons described in clauses (i) and (ii) for costs incurred with respect to a chemical substance, the Administrator shall, after consultation with the Attorney General and the Federal Trade Commission, consider all relevant factors, including the effect on the competitive position of the person required to provide reimbursement in relation to the persons to be reimbursed and the share of the market for such substance of the person required to provide reimbursement in relation to the share of such market of the persons to be reimbursed. For purposes of judicial review, an order under this subparagraph shall be considered final agency action.

(C) For purposes of this paragraph, the reimbursement period for any previously submitted data for a chemical substance is a period—

    (i) beginning on the date of the termination of the prohibition, imposed under this section, on the manufacture or processing of such substance by the person who submitted such data to the Administrator, and

    (ii) ending—

        (I) five years after the date referred to in clause (i), or

        (II) at the expiration of a period which begins on the date referred to in clause (i) and is equal to the period which the Administrator determines was necessary to develop such data,

    whichever is later.

(3) The requirements of subsections (a) and (b) do not apply with respect to the manufacturing or processing of any chemical substance which is manufactured or processed, or proposed to be manufactured or processed, only in small quantities (as defined by the Administrator by rule) solely for purposes of—

(A) scientific experimentation or analysis, or

(B) chemical research on, or analysis of such substance or another substance, including such research or analysis for the development of a product,

if all persons engaged in such experimentation, research, or analysis for a manufacturer or processor are notified (in such form and manner as the Administrator may prescribe) of any risk to health which the manufacturer, processor, or the Administrator has reason to believe may be associated with such chemical substance.

(4) The Administrator may, upon application and by rule, exempt the manufacturer of any new chemical substance from all or part of the requirements of this section if the Administrator determines that the manufacture, processing, distribution in commerce, use, or disposal of such chemical substance, or that any combination of such activities, will not present an unreasonable risk of injury to health or the environment. A rule promulgated under this paragraph (and any substantive amendment to, or repeal of, such a rule) shall be promulgated in accordance with paragraphs (2) and (3) of section 6(c).

(5) The Administrator may, upon application, make the requirements o subsections (a) and (b) inapplicable with respect to the manufacturing or processing of any chemical substance (A) which exists temporarily as a result of a chemical reaction in the manufacturing or processing of a mixture or another chemical substance, and (B) to which there is no, and will not be, human or environmental exposure.

(6) Immediately upon receipt of an application under paragraph (1) or (5) the Administrator shall publish in the Federal Register notice of the receipt of such application. The Administrator shall give interested persons an opportunity to comment upon any such application and shall, within 45 days of its receipt, either approve or deny the application. The Administrator shall publish in the Federal Register notice of the approval or denial of such an application.

(i) For purposes of this section, the terms "manufacture" and "process" mean manufacturing or processing for commercial purposes.

§ 2605. Regulation of hazardous chemical substances and mixtures

[Sec. 6] (a) If the Administrator finds that there is a reasonable basis to conclude that the manufacture, processing, distribution in commerce, use, or disposal of a chemical substance or mixture, or that any combination of such activities, presents or will present an unreasonable risk of injury to health or the environment, the Administrator shall by rule apply one or more of the following requirements to such substance or mixture to the extent necessary to protect adequately against such risk using the least burdensome requirements:

(1) A requirement (A) prohibiting the manufacturing, processing, or distribution in commerce of such substance or mixture, or (B) limiting

the amount of such substance or mixture which may be manufactured, processed, or distributed in commerce.

(2) A requirement—

    (A) prohibiting the manufacture, processing, or distribution in commerce of such substance or mixture for (i) a particular use or (ii) a particular use in a concentration in excess of a level specified by the Administrator in the rule imposing the requirement, or

    (B) limiting the amount of such substance or mixture which may be manufactured, processed, or distributed in commerce for (i) a particular use or (ii) a particular use in a concentration in excess of a level specified by the Administrator in the rule imposing the requirement.

(3) A requirement that such substance or mixture or any article containing such substance or mixture be marked with or accompanied by clear and adequate warnings and instructions with respect to its use, distribution in commerce, or disposal or with respect to any combination of such activities. The form and content of such warnings and instructions shall be prescribed by the Adminstrator.

(4) A requirement that manufacturers and processors of such substance or mixture make and retain records of the processes used to manufacture or process such substance or mixture and monitor or conduct tests which are reasonable and necessary to assure compliance with the requirements of any rule applicable under this subsection.

(5) A requirement prohibiting or otherwise regulating any manner or method of commercial use of such substance or mixture.

(6)(A) A requirement prohibiting or otherwise regulating any manner or method of disposal of such substance or mixture, or of any article containing such substance or mixture, by its manufacturer or processor or by any other person who uses, or disposes of, it for commercial purposes.

    (B) A requirement under subparagraph (A) may not require any person to take any action which would be in violation of any law or requirement of, or in effect for, a State or political subdivision, and shall require each person subject to it to notify each State and political subdivision in which a required disposal may occur of such disposal.

(7) A requirement directing manufacturers or processors of such substance or mixture (A) to give notice of such unreasonable risk of injury to distributors in commerce of such substance or mixture and, to the extent reasonably ascertainable, to other persons in possession of such substance or mixture or exposed to such substance or mixture, (B) to give public notice of such risk of injury, and (C) to replace or repurchase such substance or mixture as elected by the person to which the requirement is directed.

Any requirement (or combination of requirements) imposed under this subsection may be limited in application to specified geographic areas.

(b) If the Administrator has a reasonable basis to conclude that a particular manufacturer or processor is manufacturing or processing a chemical substance or mixture in a manner which unintentionally causes the chemical substance or mixture to present or which will cause it to present an unreasonable risk of injury to health or the environment—

    (1) the Administrator may by order require such manufacturer or processor to submit a description of the relevant quality control procedures followed in the manufacturing or processing of such chemical substance or mixture; and

    (2) if the Administrator determines—

        (A) that such quality control procedures are inadequate to prevent the chemical substance or mixture from presenting such risk of injury, the Administrator may order the manufacturer or processor to revise such quality control procedures to the extent necessary to remedy such inadequacy; or

        (B) that the use of such quality control procedures has resulted in the distribution in commerce of chemical substances or mixtures which present an unreasonable risk of injury to health or the environment, the Administrator may order the manufacturer or processor to (i) give notice of such risk to processors or distributors in commerce of any such substance or mixture, or to both, and, to the extent reasonably ascertainable, to any other person in possession of or exposed to any such substance, (ii) to give public notice of such risk, and (iii) to provide such replacement or repurchase of any such substance or mixture as is necessary to adequately protect health or the environment.

A determination under subparagraph (A) or (B) of paragraph (2) shall be made on the record after opportunity for hearing in accordance with section 554 of title 5, United States Code. Any manufacturer or processor subject to a requirement to replace or repurchase a chemical substance or mixture may elect either to replace or repurchase the substance or mixture and shall take either such action in the manner prescribed by the Administrator.

(c)(1) In promulgating any rule under subsection (a) with respect to a chemical substance or mixture, the Administrator shall consider and publish a statement with respect to—

    (A) the effects of such substance or mixture on health and the magnitude of the exposure of human beings to such substance or mixture,

    (B) the effects of such substance or mixture on the environment and the magniture of the exposure of the environment to such substance or mixture,

    (C) the benefits of such substance or mixture for various uses and the availability of substitutes for such uses, and

(D) the reasonably ascertainable economic consequences of the rules, after consideration of the effect on the national economy, small business, technological innovation, the environment, and public health.

If the Administrator determines that a risk of injury to health or the environment could be eliminated or reduced to a sufficient extent by actions taken under another Federal law (or laws) administered in whole or in part by the Administrator, the Administrator may not promulgate a rule under subsection (a) to protect against such risk of injury unless the Administrator finds, in the Administrator's discretion, that it is in the public interest to protect against such risk under this Act. In making such a finding the Administrator shall consider (i) all relevant aspects of the risk, as determined by the Administrator in the Administrator's discretion, (ii) a comparison of the estimated costs of complying with actions taken under this Act and under such law (or laws), and (iii) the relative efficiency of actions under this Act and under such law (or laws) to protect against such risk of injury.

(2) When prescribing a rule under subsection (a) the Administrator shall proceed in accordance with section 553 of title 5, United States Code (without regard to any reference in such section to sections 556 and 557 of such title), and shall also (A) publish a notice of proposed rulemaking stating with particularity the reason for the proposed rule; (B) allow interested persons to submit written data, views, and arguments, and make all such submissions publicly available; (C) provide an opportunity for an informal hearing in accordance with paragraph (3); (D) promulgate, if appropriate, a final rule based on the matter in the rulemaking record (as defined in section 19(a), and (E) make and publish with the rule the finding described in subsection (a).

(3) Informal hearings required by paragraph (2)(C) shall be conducted by the Administrator in accordance with the following requirements:

(A) Subject to subparagraph (B), an interested person is entitled—

   (i) to present such person's position orally or by documentary submissions (or both), and

   (ii) if the Administrator determines that there are disputed issues of material fact it is necessary to resolve, to present such rebuttal submissions and to conduct (or have conducted under subparagraph (B)(ii) such cross-examination of persons as the Administrator determines (I) to be appropriate, and (II) to be required for a full and true disclosure with respect to such issues.

(B) The Administrator may prescribe such rules and make such rulings concerning procedures in such hearings to avoid unnecessary costs or delay. Such rules or rulings may include (i) the imposition of reasonable time limits on each interested person's oral presentations, and (ii) requirements that any cross-examination to which a person may be entitled under subparagraph (A) be conducted by the Administrator on behalf of that person in such manner as the Administrator determines (I) to be appropriate, and (II) to be required for a full and true disclosure with respect to disputed issues of material fact.

(C)(i) Except as provided in clause (ii), if a group of persons each of whom under subparagraphs (A) and (B) would be entitled to conduct (or have conducted) cross-examination and who are determined by the Administrator to have the same or similar interests in the proceeding cannot agree upon a single representative of such interests for purposes of cross-examination, the Administrator may make rules and rulings (I) limiting the representation of such interest for such purposes, and (II) governing the manner in which such cross-examination shall be limited.

(ii) When any person who is a member of a group with respect to which the Administrator has made a determination under clause (i) is unable to agree upon group representation with the other members of the group, then such person shall not be denied under the authority of clause (i) the opportunity to conduct (or have conducted) cross-examination as to issues affecting the person's particular interests if (I) the person satisfies the Administrator that the person has made a reasonable and good faith effort to reach agreement upon group representation with the other members of the group and (II) the Administrator determines that there are substantial and relevant issues which are not adequately presented by the group representative.

(D) A verbatim transcript shall be taken of any oral presentation made, and cross-examination conducted in any informal hearing under this subsection. Such transcript shall be available to the public.

(4)(A) The Administrator may, pursuant to rules prescribed by the Administrator, provide compensation for reasonable attorneys' fees, expert witness fees, and other costs of participating in a rulemaking proceeding for the promulgation of a rule under subsection (a) to any person—

(i) who represents an interest which would substantially contribute to a fair determination of the issues to be resolved in the proceeding, and

(ii) if—

(I) the economic interest of such person is small in comparison to the costs of effective participation in the proceeding by such person, or

(II) such person demonstrates to the satisfaction of the Administrator that such person does not have sufficient resources adequately to participate in the proceeding without compensation under this subparagraph.

In determining for purposes of clause (i) if an interest will substantially contribute to a fair determination of the issues to be resolved in a proceeding, the Administrator shall take into account the number and complexity of such issues and the extent to which representation of such interest will contribute to widespread public participation in the proceeding and representation of a fair balance of interests for the resolution of such issues.

(B) In determining whether compensation should be provided to a person under subparagraph (A) and the amount of such compensation, the Administrator shall take into account the financial burden which will be incurred by such person in participating in the rule-making proceeding. The Administrator shall take such action as may be necessary to ensure that the aggregate amount of compensation paid under this paragraph in any fiscal year to all persons who, in rulemaking proceedings in which they receive conpensation, are persons who either—

(i) would be regulated by the proposed rule, or

(ii) represent persons who would be so regulated,

may not exceed 25 per centum of the aggregate amount paid as compensation under this paragraph to all persons in such fiscal year.

(5) Paragraph (1), (2), (3), and (4) of this subsection apply to the promulgation of a rule repealing, or making a substantive amendment to, a rule promulgated under subsection (a).

(d)(1) The Administrator shall specify in any rule under subsection (a) the date on which it shall take effect, which date shall be as soon as feasible.

(2)(A) The Administrator may declare a proposed rule under subsection (a) to be effective upon its publication in the Federal Register and until the effective date of final action taken in accordance with subparagraph (B), respecting such rule if—

(i) the Administrator determines that—

(I) the manufacture, processing, distribution in commerce, use, or disposal of the chemical substance or mixture subject to such proposed rule or any combination of such activities is likely to result in an unreasonable risk of serious or widespread injury to health or the environment before such effective date; and

(II) making such proposed rule so effective is necessary to protect the public interest; and

(ii) in the case of a proposed rule to prohibit the manufacture, processing, or distribution of a chemical substance or mixture because of the risk determined under clause (i)(I), a court has in an action under section 7 granted relief with respect to such risk associated with such substance or mixture.

Such a proposed rule which is made so effective shall not, for purposes of judicial review, be considered final agency action.

(B) If the Administrator makes a proposed rule effective upon its publication in the Federal Register, the Administrator shall, as expeditiously as possible, give interested persons prompt notice of such action, provide reasonable opportunity, in accordance with paragraphs (2) and (3) of subsection (c), for a hearing on such rule, and either promulgate such rule (as proposed or with modifications) or revoke it; and if such a hearing is requested, the Administrator shall commence the hearing within five days from the date such request is made unless the Administrator and the person making the request agree upon a later date for the hearing to begin, and after the hearing is concluded the Administrator shall, within ten days of the conclusion of the hearing, either promulgate such rule (as proposed or with modifications) or revoke it.

(e)(1) Within six months after the effective date of this Act the Administrator shall promulgate rules to—

(A) prescribe methods for the disposal of polychlorinated biphenyls, and

(B) require polychlorinated biphenyls to be marked with clear and adequate warnings, and instructions with respect to their processing, distribution in commerce, use, or disposal or with respect to any combination of such activities.

Requirements prescribed by rules under this paragraph shall be consistent with the requirements of paragraphs (2) and (3).

(2)(A) Except as provided under subparagraph (B), effective one year after the effective date of this Act no person may manufacture, process, or distribute in commerce or use any polychlorinated biphenyl in any manner other than in a totally enclosed manner.

(B) The Administrator may by rule authorize the manufacture, processing, distribution in commerce or use (or any combination of such activities) of any polychlorinated biphenyl in a manner other than in a totally enclosed manner if the Administrator finds that such manufacture, processing, distribution in commerce, or use (or combination of such activities) will not present an unreasonable risk of injury to health or the environment.

(C) For the purposes of this paragraph, the term "totally enclosed manner" means any manner which will ensure that any exposure of human beings or the environment to a polychlorinated biphenyl will be insignificant as determined by the Administrator by rule.

(3)(A) Except as provided in subparagraphs (B) and (C)—

    (i) no person may manufacture any polychlorinated biphenyl after two years after the effective date of this Act, and

    (ii) no person may process or distribute in commerce any polychlorinated biphenyl after two and one-half years after such date.

(B) Any person may petition the Administrator for an exemption from the requirements of subparagraph (A), and the Administrator may grant by rule such an exemption if the Administrator finds that—

    (i) an unreasonable risk of injury to health or environment would not result, and

    (ii) good faith efforts have been made to develop a chemical substance which does not present an unreasonable risk of injury to health or the environment and which may be substituted for such polychlorinated biphenyl.

An exemption granted under this subparagraph shall be subject to such terms and conditions as the Administrator may prescribe and shall be in effect for such period (but not more than one year from the date it is granted) as the Administrator may prescribe.

(C) Subparagraph (A) shall not apply to the distribution in commerce of any polychlorinated biphenyl if such polychlorinated biphenyl was sold for purposes other than resale before two and one half years after the date of enactment of this Act.

(4) Any rule under paragraph (1), (2)(B), or (3)(B) shall be promulgated in accordance with paragraphs (2), (3), and (4) of subsection (c).

(5) This subsection does not limit the authority of the Administrator, under any other provision of this Act or any other Federal law, to take action respecting any polychlorinated biphenyl.

§ 2606. Imminent hazards

[Sec. 7] (a)(1) The Administrator may commence a civil action in an appropriate district court of the United States—

    (A) for seizure of an imminently hazardous chemical substance or mixture or any article containing such a substance or mixture,

    (B) for relief (as authorized by subsection (b)) against any person who manufactures, processes, distributes in commerce, or uses, or disposes of, an imminently hazardous chemical substance or mixture or any article containing such a substance or mixture, or

    (C) for both such seizure and relief.

A civil action may be commenced under this paragraph notwithstanding the existence of a rule under section 4, 5, or 6 or an order under section 5, and notwithstanding the pendency of any administrative or judicial proceeding under any provision of this Act.

(2) If the Administrator has not made a rule under section 6(a) immediately effective (as authorized by subsection 6(d)(2)(A)(i)) with respect

to an imminently hazardous chemical substance or mixture, the Administrator shall commence in a district court of the United States with respect to such substance or mixture or article containing such substance or mixture a civil action described in subparagraph (A), (B), or (C) of paragraph (1).

(b)(1) The district court of the United States in which an action under subsection (a) is brought shall have jurisdiction to grant such temporary or permanent relief as may be necessary to protect health or the environment from the unreasonable risk associated with the chemical substance, mixture, or article involved in such action.

(2) In the case of an action under subsection (a) brought against a person who manufactures, processes, or distributes in commerce a chemical substance or mixture or an article containing a chemical substance or mixture, the relief authorized by paragraph (1) may include the issuance of a mandatory order requiring (A) in the case of purchasers of such substance, mixture, or article known to the defendant, notification to such purchasers of the risk associated with it; (B) public notice of such risk; (C) recall; (D) the replacement or repurchase of such substance, mixture, or article; or (E) any combination of the actions described in the preceding clauses.

(3) In the case of an action under subsection (a) against a chemical substance, mixture, or article, such substance, mixture, or article may be proceeded against by process of libel for its seizure and condemnation. Proceedings in such an action shall conform as nearly as possible to proceedings in rem in admiralty.

(c)(1)(A) An action under subsection (a) against a person who manufactures, processes, or distributes chemical substance or mixture or an article containing a chemical substance or mixture may be brought in the United States District Court for the District of Columbia or for any judicial district in which any of the defendants is found, resides, or transacts business; and process in such an action may be served on a defendant in any other district in which such defendant resides or may be found. An action under subsection (a) against a chemical substance, mixture, or article may be brought in any United States district court within the jurisdiction of which the substance, mixture, or article is found.

(B) In determining the judicial district in which an action may be brought under subsection (a) in instances in which such action may be brought in more than one judicial district, the Administrator shall take into account the convenience of the parties.

(C) Subpoenas requiring attendance of witnesses in an action brought under subsection (a) may be served in any judicial district.

(2) Whenever proceedings under subsection (a) involving identical chemical substances, mixtures, or articles are pending in courts in two or more judicial districts, they shall be consolidated for trial by order of any such court upon application reasonably made by any party in

interest, upon notice to all parties in interest.

(d) Where appropriate, concurrently with the filing of an action under subsection (a) or as soon thereafter as may be practicable, the Administrator shall initiate a proceeding for the promulgation of a rule under section 6(a).

(e) Notwithstanding any other provision of law, in any action under subsection (a), the Administrator may direct attorneys of the Environmental Protection Agency to appear and represent the Administrator in such an action.

(f) For the purposes of subsection (a), the term "imminently hazardous chemical substance or mixture" means a chemical substance or mixture which presents an imminent and unreasonable risk of serious or widespread injury to health or the environment. Such a risk to health or the environment shall be considered imminent if it is shown that the manufacture, processing, distribution in commerce, use, or disposal of the chemical substance or mixture, or that any combination of such activities, is likely to result in such injury to health or the environment before a final rule under section 6 can protect against such risk.

§ 2607. Reporting and retention of information

[Sec. 8] (a)(1) The Administrator shall promulgate rules under which—
- (A) each person (other than a small manufacturer or processor) who manufactures or processes or proposes to manufacture or process a chemical substance (other than a chemical substance described in subparagraph (B)(ii)) shall maintain such records, and shall submit to the Administrator such reports, as the Administrator may reasonably require, and
- (B) each person (other than a small manufacturer or processor) who manufactures or processes or proposes to manufacture or process—
  - (i) a mixture, or
  - (ii) chemical substance in small quantities (as defined by the Administrator by rule) solely for purposes of scientific experimentation or analysis or chemical research on, or analysis of, such substance or another substance, including any such research or analysis for the development of a product,

    shall maintain records and submit to the Administrator reports but only to the extent the Administrator determines the maintenance of records or submission of reports, or both, is necessary for the effective enforcement of this Act.

The Administrator may not require in a rule promulgated under this paragraph the maintenance of records or the submission of reports with respect to changes in the proportions of the components of a mixture unless the Administrator finds that the maintenance of such records or the submission of such reports, or both, is necessary for the effective enforcement of this Act. For purposes of the compilation of the list of chemical substances required under subsection (b), the Administrator shall promulgate rules pursuant to this subsection not later than 180 days after the effective date of this Act.

(2) The Administrator may require under paragraph (1) maintenance of records and reporting with respect to the following insofar as known to the person making the report or insofar as reasonably ascertainable:

(A) The common trade name, the chemical identity, and the molecular structure of each chemical substance or mixture for which such a report is required.

(B) The categories or proposed categories of use of each such substance or mixture.

(C) The total amount of each such substance and mixture manufactured or processed, reasonable estimates of the total amount to be manufactured or processed, the amount manufactured or processed for each of its categories of use, and reasonable estimates of the amount to be manufactured or processed for each of its categories of use or proposed categories of use.

(D) A description of the byproducts resulting from the manufacture, processing, use, or disposal of each such substance or mixture.

(E) All existing data concerning the environmental and health effects of such substance or mixture.

(F) The number of individuals exposed, and reasonable estimates of the number who will be exposed, to such substance or mixture in their places of employment and the duration of such exposure.

(G) In the initial report under paragraph (1) of such substance or mixture, the manner or method of its disposal, and in any subsequent report on such substance or mixture, any change in such manner or method.

To the extent feasible, the Administrator shall not require under paragraph (1), any reporting which is unnecessary or duplicative.

(3)(A)(i) The Administrator may by rule require a small manufacturer or processor of a chemical substance to submit to the Administrator such information respecting the chemical substance as the Administrator may require for publication of the first list of chemical substances required by subsection (b).

(ii) The Administrator may by rule require a small manufacturer or processor of a chemical substance or mixture—

(I) subject to a rule proposed or promulgated under section 4, 5(b)(4), or 6, or an order in effect under section 5(e), or

(II) with respect to which relief has been granted pursuant to a civil action brought under section 5 or 7,

to maintain such records on such substance or mixture, and to submit to the Administrator such reports on such substance or mixture, as the Administrator may reasonably require. A rule under this clause requiring reporting may require reporting with respect to the matters referred to in paragraph (2).

(B) The Administrator, after consultation with the Administrator of the Small Business Administration, shall by rule prescribe standards for determining the manufacturers and processors which qualify as small manufacturers and processors for purposes of this paragraph and paragraph (1).

(b)(1) The Administrator shall compile, keep current, and publish a list of each chemical substance which is manufactured or processed in the United States. Such list shall at least include each chemical substance which any person reports, under section 5 or subsection (a) of this section, is manufactured or processed in the United States. Such list may not include any chemical substance which was not manufactured or processed in the United States within three years before the effective date of the rules promulgated pursuant to the last sentence of subsection (a)(1). In the case of a chemical substance for which a notice is submitted in accordance with section 5, such chemical substance shall be included in such list as of the earliest date (as determined by the Administrator) on which such substance was manufactured or processed in the United States. The Administrator shall first publish such a list not later than 315 days after the effective date of this Act. The Administrator shall not include in such list any chemical substance which is manufactured or processed only in small quantities (as defined by the Administrator by rule) solely for purposes of scientific experimentation or analysis or chemical research on, or analysis of, such substance or another substance, including such research or analysis for the development of a product.

(2) To the extent consistent with the purposes of this Act, the Administrator may, in lieu of listing, pursuant to paragraph (1), a chemical substance individually, list a category of chemical substances in which such substance is included.

(c) Any person who manufactures, processes, or distributes in commerce any chemical substance or mixture shall maintain records of significant adverse reactions to health or the environment, as determined by the Administrator by rule, alleged to have been caused by the substance or mixture. Records of such adverse reactions to the health of employees shall be retained for a period of 30 years from the date such reactions were first reported to or known by the person maintaining such records. Any other record of such adverse reactions shall be retained for a period of five years from the date the information contained in the record was first reported to or known by the person maintaining the record. Records required to be maintained under this subsection shall include records of consumer allegations of personal injury or harm to health, reports of occupational disease or injury, and reports or complaints of injury to the environment submitted to the manufacturer, processor, or distributor in commerce from any source. Upon request of any duly designated representative of the Administrator, each person who is required to maintain records under this subsection shall permit the inspection of such records and shall submit copies of such records.

(d) The Administrator shall promulgate rules under which the Administrator shall require any person who manufactures, processes, or distributes in commerce or who proposes to manufacture, process, or distribute in commerce any chemical substance or mixture (or with respect to paragraph (2), any person who has possession of a study) to submit to the Administrator—

(1) lists of health and safety studies (A) conducted or initiated by or for such person with respect to such substance or mixture at any time, (B) known to such person, or (C) reasonably ascertainable by such person, except that the Administrator may exclude certain types of categories of studies from the requirements of this subsection if the Administrator finds that submission of lists of such studies are unnecessary to carry out the purposes of this Act; and

(2) copies of any study contained on a list submitted pursuant to paragraph (1) or otherwise known by such person.

(e) Any person who manufactures, processes, or distributes in commerce a chemical substance or mixture and who obtains information which reasonably supports the conclusion that such substance or mixture presents a substantial risk of injury to health or the environment shall immediately inform the Administrator of such information unless such person has actual knowledge that the Administrator has been adequately informed of such information.

(f) For purposes of this section, the terms "manufacture" and "process" mean manufacture or process for commercial purposes.

§ 2608. Relationship to other federal laws

[Sec. 9] (a)(1) If the Administrator has reasonable basis to conclude that the manufacture, processing, distribution in commerce, use, or disposal of a chemical substance or mixture, or that any combination of such activities, presents or will present an unreasonable risk of injury to health or the environment and determines, in the Administrator's discretion, that such risk may be prevented or reduced to a sufficient extent by action taken under a Federal law not administered by the Administrator, the Administrator shall submit to the agency which administers such law a report which describes such risk and includes in such description a specification of the activity or combination of activities which the Administrator has reason to believe so presents such risk. Such report shall also request such agency—

(A)(i) to determine if the risk described in such report may be prevented or reduced to a sufficient extent by action taken under such law, and

(ii) if the agency determines that such risk may be so prevented or reduced, to issue an order declaring whether or not the activity or combination of activities specified in the description of such risk presents such risk; and

(B) to respond to the Administrator with respect to the matters described in subparagraph (A).

Any report of the Administrator shall include a detailed statement of the information on which it is based and shall be published in the Federal Register. The agency receiving a request under such a report shall make the requested determination, issue the requested order, and make the requested response within such time as the Administrator specifies in the request, but such time specified may not be less than 90 days from the date the request was made. The response of an agency shall be accompanied by a detailed statement of the findings and conclusions of the agency and shall be published in the Federal Register.

(2) If the Administrator makes a report under paragraph (1) with respect to a chemical substance or mixture and the agency to which such report was made either—

(A) issues an order declaring that the activity or combination of activities specified in the description of the risk described in the report does not present the risk described in the report, or

(B) initiates, within 90 days of the publication in the Federal Register of the response of the agency under paragraph (1), action under the law (or laws) administered by such agency to protect against such risk associated with such activity or combination of activities.

the Administrator may not take any action under section 6 or 7 with respect to such risk.

(3) If the Administrator has initiated action under section 6 or 7 with respect to a risk associated with a chemical substance or mixture which was the subject of a report made to an agency under paragraph (1), such agency shall before taking action under the law (or laws) administered by it to protect against such risk consult with the Administrator for the purpose of avoiding duplication of Federal action against such risk.

(b) The Administrator shall coordinate actions taken under this Act with actions taken under other Federal laws administered in whole or in part by the Administrator. If the Administrator determines that a risk to health or the environment associated with a chemical substance or mixture could be eliminated or reduced to a sufficient extent by actions taken under the authorities contained in such other Federal laws, the Administrator shall use such authorities to protect against such risk unless the Administrator determines, in the Administrator's discretion, that it is in the public interest to protect against such risk by actions taken under this Act. This subsection shall not be construed to relieve the Administrator of any requirement imposed on the Administrator by such other Federal laws.

(c) In exercising any authority under this Act, the Administrator shall not, for purposes of section 4(b)(1) of the Occupational Safety and Health Act of 1970, be deemed to be exercising statutory authority to prescribe or enforce standards or regulations affecting occupational safety and health.

(d) In administering this Act, the Administrator shall consult and coordinate with the Secretary of Health and Human Services and the heads of any other appropriate Federal executive department or agency, any relevant independent regulatory agency, and any other appropriate instrumentality of the Federal Government for the purpose of achieving the maximum enforcement of this Act while imposing the least burdens of duplicative requirements on those subject to the Act and for other purposes. The Administrator shall, in the report required by section 30, report annually to the Congress on actions taken to coordinate with such other Federal departments, agencies, or instrumentalities, and on actions taken to coordinate the authority under this Act with the authority granted under other Acts referred to in subsection (b).

§ 2609. Research, development, collection, dissemination, and utilization of data

[Sec. 10] (a) The Administrator shall, in consultation and cooperation with the Secretary of Health and Human Services and with other heads of appropriate departments and agencies, conduct such research, development, and monitoring as is necessary to carry out the purposes of this Act. The Administrator may enter into contracts and may make grants for research, development, and monitoring under this subsection. Contracts may be entered into under this subsection without regard to sections 31 U.S.C. 3324(a) and (b) and 41 U.S.C. 5.

(b)(1) The Administrator shall establish, administer, and be responsible for the continuing activities of an interagency committee which shall design, establish, and coordinate an efficient and effective system, within the Environmental Protection Agency, for the collection, dissemination to other Federal departments and agencies, and use of data submitted to the Administrator under this Act.

(2)(A) The Administrator shall, in consultation and cooperation with the Secretary of Health and Human Services and other heads of appropriate departments and agencies design, establish, and coordinate an efficient and effective system for the retrieval of toxicological and other scientific data which could be useful to the Administrator in carrying out the purposes of this Act. Systematized retrieval shall be developed for use by all Federal and other departments and agencies with responsibilities in the area of regulation or study of chemical substances and mixtures and their effect on health or the environment.

(B) The Administrator, in consultation and cooperation with the Secretary of Health and Human Services may make grants and enter into contracts for the development of a data retrieval system described in subparagraph (A). Contracts may be entered into under this subparagraph without regard to sections 31 U.S.C. 3324(a) and (b) and 41 U.S.C. 5.

(c) The Administrator shall coordinate, with the Assistant Secretary for Health of the Department of Health and Human Services, research undertaken by the Administrator and directed toward the development of rapid, reliable, and economical screening techniques for carcinogenic, mutagenic, teratogenic, and ecological effects of chemical substances and mixtures.

(d) The Administrator shall, in consultation and cooperation with the Secretary of Health and Human Services, establish and be responsible for research aimed at the development, in cooperation with local, State, and Federal agencies, of monitoring techniques and instruments which may be used in the detection of toxic chemical substances and mixtures and which are reliable, economical, and capable of being implemented under a wide variety of conditions.

(e) The Administrator shall, in consultation and cooperation with the Secretary of Health and Human Services, establish research programs to develop the fundamental scientific basis of the screening and monitoring techniques described in subsections (c) and (d), the bounds of the reliability of such techniques, and the opportunities for their improvement.

(f) The Administrator shall establish and promote programs and workshops to train or facilitate the training of Federal laboratory and technical personnel in existing or newly developed screening and monitoring techniques.

(g) The Administrator shall, in consultation with the Secretary of Health and Human Services and other heads of appropriate departments and agencies, establish and coordinate a system for exchange among Federal, State, and local authorities of research and development results respecting toxic chemical substances and mixtures, including a system to facilitate and promote the development of standard data format and analysis and consistent testing procedures.

§ 2610. Inspections and subpoenas

[Sec. 11] (a) For purposes of administering this Act, the Administrator, and any duly designated representative of the Administrator, may inspect any establishment, facility, or other premises in which chemical substances or mixtures are manufactured, processed, stored, or held before or after their distribution in commerce and any conveyance being used to transport chemical substances, mixtures, or such articles in connection with distribution in commerce. Such an inspection may only be made upon the presentation of appropriate credentials and of a written notice to the owner, operator, or agent in charge of the premises or conveyance to be inspected. A separate notice shall be given for each such inspection, but a notice shall not be required for each entry made during the period covered by the inspection.

Each such inspection shall be commenced and completed with reasonable promptness and shall be conducted at reasonable times, within reasonable limits, and in a reasonable manner.

(b)(1) Except as provided in paragraph (2), an inspection conducted under subsection (a) shall extend to all things within the premises or conveyance inspected (including records, files, papers, processes, controls, and facilities) bearing on whether the requirements of this Act applicable to the chemical substances or mixtures within such premises or conveyances have been complied with.

(2) No inspection under subsection (a) shall extend to—
   (A) financial data,
   (B) sales data (other than shipment data),
   (C) pricing data,
   (D) personnel data, or
   (E) research data (other than data required by this Act or under a rule promulgated thereunder),
   unless the nature and extent of such data are described with reasonable specificity in the written notice required by subsection (a) for such inspection.

(c) In carrying out this Act, the Administrator may by subpoena require the attendance and testimony of witnesses and the production of reports, papers, documents, answers to questions, and other information that the Administrator deems necessary. Witnesses shall be paid the same fees and mileage that are paid witnesses in the courts of the United States. In the event of contumacy, failure, or refusal of any person to obey any such subpoena, any district court of the United States in which venue is proper shall have jurisdiction to order any such person to comply with such subpoena. Any failure to obey such an order of the court is punishable by the court as a contempt thereof.

§ 2611. Exports

[Sec. 12] (a)(1) Except as provided in paragraph (2) and subsection (b), this Act (other than section 8) shall not apply to any chemical substance, mixture, or to an article containing a chemical substance or mixture, if—
   (A) it can be shown that such substance, mixture, or article is being manufactured, processed, or distributed in commerce for export from the United States, unless such substance, mixture, or article was, in fact, manufactured, processed, or distributed in commerce, for use in the United States, and
   (B) such substance, mixture, or article (when distributed in commerce), or any container in which it is enclosed (when so distributed), bears a stamp or label stating that such substance, mixture, or article is intended for export.
   (2) Paragraph (1) shall not apply to any chemical substance, mixture, or article if the Administrator finds that the substance, mixture, or article

will present an unreasonable risk of injury to health within the United States or to the environment of the United States. The Administrator may require, under section 4, testing of any chemical substance or mixture exempted from this Act by paragraph (1) for the purpose of determining whether or not such substance or mixture presents an unreasonable risk of injury to health within the United States or to the environment of the United States.

(b)(1) If any person exports or intends to export to a foreign country a chemical substance or mixture for which the submission of data is required under section 4 or 5(b), such person shall notify the Administrator of such exportation or intent to export and the Administrator shall furnish to the government of such country notice of the availability of the data submitted to the Administrator under such section for such substance or mixture.

(2) If any person exports or intends to export to a foreign country a chemical substance or mixture for which an order has been issued under section 5 or a rule has been proposed or promulgated under section 5 or 6, or with respect to which an action is pending, or relief has been granted under section 5 or 7, such person shall notify the Administrator of such exportation or intent to export and the Administrator shall furnish to the government of such country notice of such rule, order, action, or relief.

§ 2612. Entry into customs territory of the United States

[Sec. 13] (a)(1) The Secretary of the Treasury shall refuse entry into the customs territory of the United States (as defined in general headnote 2 to the Tariff Schedules of the United States) of any chemical substance, mixture, or article containing a chemical substance or mixture offered for such entry if—

(A) it fails to comply with any rule in effect under this Act, or

(B) it is offered for entry in violation of section 5 or 6, a rule or order under section 5 or 6, or an order issued in a civil action brought under section 5 or 7.

(2) if a chemical substance, mixture, or article is refused entry under paragraph (1), the Secretary of the Treasury shall notify the consignee of such entry refusal, shall not release it to the consignee, and shall cause its disposal or storage (under such rules as the Secretary of the Treasury may prescribe) if it has not been exported by the consignee within 90 days from the date of receipt of notice of such refusal, except that the Secretary of the Treasury may, pending a review by the Administrator of the entry refusal, release to the consignee such substance, mixture, or article on execution of bond for the amount of the full invoice of such substance, mixture, or article (as such value is set forth in the customs entry), together with the duty thereon. On failure to return such substance, mixture, or article for any cause to the custody of the Secretary of the Treasury when demanded, such

consignee shall be liable to the United States for liquidated damages equal to the full amount of such bond. All charges for storage, cartage, and labor on and for disposal of substances, mixtures, or articles which are refused entry or release under this section shall be paid by the owner or consignee, and in default of such payment shall constitute a lien against any future entry made by such owner or consignee.

(b) The Secretary of the Treasury, after consultation with the Administrator, shall issue rules for the administration of subsection (a) of this section.

§ 2613. Disclosure of data

[Sec. 14] (a) Except as provided by subsection (b), any information reported to, or otherwise obtained by, the Administrator (or any representative of the Administrator) under this Act, which is exempt from disclosure pursuant to subsection (a) of section 552 of title 5, United States Code, by reason of subsection (b)(4) of such section, shall, notwithstanding the provisions of any other section of this Act, not be disclosed by the Administrator or by any officer or employee of the United States, except that such information—
(1) shall be disclosed to any officer or employee of the United States—
  (A) in connection with the official duties of such officer or employee under any law for the protection of health or the environment, or
  (B) for specific law enforcement purposes;
(2) shall be disclosed to contractors with the United States and employees of such contractors if in the opinion of the Administrator such disclosure is necessary for the satisfactory performance by the contractor of a contract with the United States entered into on or after the date of enactment of this Act for the performance of work in connection with this Act and under such conditions as the Administrator may specify;
(3) shall be disclosed if the Administrator determines it necessary to protect health or the environment against an unreasonable risk of injury to health or the environment; or
(4) may be disclosed when relevant in any proceeding under this Act, except that disclosure in such a proceeding shall be made in such manner as to preserve confidentiality to the extent practicable without impairing the proceeding.
In any proceeding under section 552(a) of title 5, United States Code, to obtain information the disclosure of which has been denied because of the provisions of this subsection, the Administrator may not rely on section 552(b)(3) of such title to sustain the Administrator's action.

(b)(1) Subsection (a) does not prohibit the disclosure of—
  (A) any health and safety study which is submitted under this Act

with respect to—

(i) any chemical substance or mixture which, on the date on which such study is to be disclosed has been offered for commercial distribution, or

(ii) any chemical substance or mixture for which testing is required under section 4 or for which notification is required under section 5, and

(B) any data reported to, or otherwise obtained by, the Administrator from a health and safety study which relates to a chemical substance or mixture described in clause (i) or (ii) of subparagraph (A).

This paragraph does not authorize the release of any data which discloses processes used in the manufacturing or processing of a chemical substance or mixture or, in the case of a mixture, the release of data disclosing the portion of the mixture comprised by any of the chemical substances in the mixture.

(2) If a request is made to the Administrator under subsection (a) of section 552 of title 5, United States Code, for information which is described in the first sentence of paragraph (1) and which is not information described in the second sentence of such paragraph, the Administrator may not deny such request on the basis of subsection (b)(4) of such section.

(c)(1) In submitting data under this Act, a manufacturer, processor, or distributor in commerce may (A) designate the data which such person believes is entitled to confidential treatment under subsection (a), and (B) submit such designated data separately from other data submitted under this Act. A designation under this paragraph shall be made in writing and in such manner as the Administrator may prescribe.

(2)(A) Except as provided by subparagraph (B), if the Administrator proposes to release for inspection data which has been designated under paragraph (1)(A), the Administrator shall notify, in writing and by certified mail, the manufacturer, processor, or distributor in commerce who submitted such data of the intent to release such data. If the release of such data is to be made pursuant to a request made under section 552(a) of title 5, United States Code, such notice shall be given immediately upon approval of such request by the Administrator. The Administrator may not release such data until the expiration of 30 days after the manufacturer, processor, or distributor in commerce submitting such data has received the notice required by this subparagaph.

(B)(i) Subparagraph (A) shall not apply to the release of information under paragraph (1), (2), (3), or (4) of subsection (a), except that the Administrator may not release data under paragraph (3) of subsection (a) unless the Administrator has notified each manufacturer, processor, and distributor in commerce who submitted such data of such release. Such notice shall be made in writing by certified mail at least 15 days before the release of such data, except that if the Administrator determines that the release of such data is necessary to protect against an imminent, unreasonable risk of injury to health or the environment, such notice may be made by such means as the Administrator determines will provide notice at least 24 hours before such release is made.

  (ii) Subparagraph (A) shall not apply to the release of information described in subsection (b)(1) other than information described in the second sentence of such subsection.

  (d)(1) Any officer or employee of the United States or former officer or employee of the United States, who by virtue of such employment or official position has obtained possession of, or has access to, material the disclosure of which is prohibited by subsection (a), and who knowing that disclosure of such material is prohibited by such subsection, willfully discloses the material in any manner to any person not entitled to receive it, shall be guilty of a misdemeanor and fined not more than $5,000 or imprisoned for not more than one year, or both. Section 1905 of title 18, United States Code, does not apply with respect to the publishing, divulging, disclosure, or making known of, or making available, information reported or otherwise obtained under this Act.

  (2) For the purposes of paragraph (1), any contractor with the United States who is furnished information as authorized by subsection (a)(2), and any employee of any such contractor, shall be considered to be an employee of the United States.

  (e) Notwithstanding any limitation contained in this section or any other provision of law, all information reported to or otherwise obtained by the Administrator (or any representative of the Administration) under this Act shall be made available, upon written request of any duly authorized committee of the Congress, to such committee.

§ 2614. Prohibited acts

[Sec. 15] It shall be unlawful for any person to—
(1) fail or refuse to comply with (A) any rule promulgated or order issued under section 4, (B) any requirement prescribed by section 5 or 6, or (C) any rule promulgated or order issued under section 5 or 6, or (D) any requirement of subchapter II of this chapter or any rule promulgated or order issued under subchapter II of this chapter;
(2) use for commercial purposes a chemical substance or mixture which such person knew or had reason to know was manufactured, processed, or distributed in commerce in violation of section 5 or 6, a rule or order under section 5 or 6, or an order issued in action brought under section 5 or 7;
(3) fail or refuse to (A) establish or maintain records, (B) submit reports,

notices, or other information, or (C) permit access to or copying of records, as required by this Act or a rule thereunder; or

(4) fail or refuse to permit entry or inspection as required by section 11.

§ 2615. Penalties

[Sec. 16] (a)(1) Any person who violates a provision of section 15 shall be liable to the United States for a civil penalty in an amount not to exceed $25,000 for each such violation. Each day such a violation continues shall, for purposes of this subsection, constitute a separate violation of section 15.

(2)(A) A civil penalty for a violation of section 15 shall be assessed by the Administrator by an order made on the record after opportunity (provided in accordance with this subparagraph) for a hearing in accordance with section 554 of title 5, United States Code. Before issuing such an order, the Administrator shall give written notice to the person to be assessed a civil penalty under such order of the Administrator's proposal to issue such order and provide such person an opportunity to request, within 15 days of the date the notice is received by such person, such a hearing on the order.

(B) In determining the amount of a civil penalty, the Administrator shall take into account the nature circumstances, extent, and gravity of the violation or violations and, with respect to the violator, ability to pay, effect on ability to continue to do business, any history of prior such violations, the degree of culpability, and such other matters as justice may require.

(C) The Administrator may compromise, modify, or remit, with or without conditions, any civil penalty which may be imposed under this subsection. The amount of such penalty, when finally determined, or the amount agreed upon in compromise, may be deducted from any sums owing by the United States to the person charged.

(3) Any person who requested in accordance with paragraph (2)(A) a hearing respecting the assessment of a civil penalty and who is aggrieved by an order assessing a civil penalty may file a petition for judicial review of such order with the United States Court of Appeals for the District of Columbia Circuit or for any other circuit in which such person resides or transacts business. Such a petition may only be filed within the 30-day period beginning on the date the order making such assessment was issued.

(4) If any person fails to pay an assessment of a civil penalty—

(A) after the order making the assessment has become a final order and if such person does not file a petition for judicial review of the order in accordance with paragraph (3), or

(B) after a court in an action brought under paragraph (3) has entered a final judgment in favor of the Administrator, the Attorney General shall recover the amount assessed (plus interest at currently prevailing rates from the date of the expiration of the 30-day period referred to in paragraph (3) or the date of such final judgment, as the case may be) in an action brought in any appropriate district court of the United States. In such an action, the validity, amount, and appropriateness of such penalty shall not be subject to review.

(b) Any person who knowingly or willfully violates any provision of section 15 shall, in addition to or in lieu of any civil penalty which may be imposed under subsection (a) of this section for such violation, be subject, upon conviction, to a fine of not more than $25,000 for each day of violation, or to imprisonment for not more than one year, or both.

§ 2616. Specific enforcement and seizure

[Sec. 17] (a)(1) The district courts of the United States shall have jurisdiction over civil actions to—
  (A) restrain any violation of section 15,
  (B) restrain any person from taking any action prohibited by section 5 or 6 or by a rule or order under section 5 or 6,
  (C) compel the taking of any action required by or under this Act, or
  (D) direct any manufacturer or processor of a chemical substance or mixture manufactured or processed in violation of section 5 or 6 or a rule or order under section 5 or 6 and distributed in commerce, (i) to give notice of such fact to distributors in commerce of such substance or mixture and, to the extent reasonably ascertainable, to other persons in possession of such substance or mixture or exposed to such substance or mixture, (ii) to give public notice of such risk of injury, and (iii) to either replace or repurchase such substance or mixture, whichever the person to which the requirement is directed elects.
  (2) A civil action described in paragraph (1) may be brought—
  (A) in the case of a civil action described in subparagraph (A) of such paragraph, in the United States district court for the judicial district wherein any act, omission, or transaction constituting a violation of section 15 occurred or wherein the defendant is found or transacts business, or
  (B) in the case of any other civil action described in such paragraph, in the United States district court for the judicial district wherein the defendant is found or transacts business.
In any such civil action process may be served on a defendant in any judicial district in which a defendant resides or may be found.

Subpoenas requiring attendance of witnesses in any such action may be served in any judicial district.

(b) Any chemical substance or mixture which was manufactured, processed, or distributed in commerce in violation of this Act or any rule promulgated or order issued under this Act or any article containing such a substance or mixture shall be liable to be proceeded against, by process of libel for the seizure and condemnation of such substance, mixture, or article, in any district court of the United States within the jurisdiction of which such substance, mixture, or article is found. Such proceedings shall conform as nearly as possible to proceedings in rem in admiralty.

§ 2617. Preemption

[Sec. 18] (a)(1) Except as provided in paragraph (2), nothing in this Act shall affect the authority of any State or political subdivision of a State to establish or continue in effect regulation of any chemical substance, mixture, or article containing a chemical substance or mixture.

(2) Except as provided in subsection (b)—

(A) if the Administrator requires by a rule promulgated under section 4 the testing of a chemical substance or mixture, no State or political subdivision may, after the effective date of such rule, establish or continue in effect a requirement for the testing of such substance or mixture for purposes similar to those for which testing is required under such rule; and

(B) if the Administrator prescribes a rule or order under section 5 or 6 (other than a rule imposing a requirement described in subsection (a)(6) of section 6) which is applicable to a chemical substance or mixture, and which is designed to protect against a risk of injury to health or the environment associated with such substance or mixture, no State or political subdivision of a State may, after the effective date of such requirement, establish or continue in effect, any requirement which is applicable to such substance or mixture, or an article containing such substance or mixture, and which is designed to protect against such risk unless such requirement (i) is identical to the requirement prescribed by the Administrator, (ii) is adopted under the authority of the Clean Air Act or any other Federal law, or (iii) prohibits the use of such substance or mixture in such State or political subdivision (other than its use in the manufacture or processing of other substances or mixtures).

(b) Upon application of a State or political subdivision of a State the Administrator may by rule exempt from subsection (a)(2), under such conditions as may be prescribed in such rule, a requirement of such State or political subdivision designed to protect against a risk of injury to health or the environment associated with a chemical substance, mixture, or article containing a chemical substance or mixture if—

(1) compliance with the requirement would not cause the manufacturing, processing, distribution in commerce, or use of the substance, mixture, or article to be in violation of the applicable requirement under this Act described in subsection (a)(2), and

(2) the State or political subdivision requirement (A) provides a significantly higher degree of protection from such risk than the requirement under this Act described in subsection (a)(2) and (B) does not, through difficulties in marketing, distribution, or other factors, unduly burden interstate commerce.

§ 2618. Judicial review

[Sec. 19] (a)(1)(A) Not later than 60 days after the date of the promulgation of a rule under section 4(a), 5(a)(2), 5(b)(4), 6(a), 6(e), or 8, or under subchapter II of this chapter, any person may file a petition for judicial review of such rule with the United States Court of Appeals for the District of Columbia Circuit or for the circuit in which such person resides or in which such person's principal place of business is located. Courts of appeals of the United States shall have exclusive jurisdiction of any action to obtain judicial review (other than in an enforcement proceeding) of such a rule if any district court of the United States would have had jurisdiction of such action but for this subparagraph.

(B) Courts of appeals of the United States shall have exclusive jurisdiction of any action to obtain judicial review (other than in an enforcement proceeding) of an order issued under subparagraph (A) or (B) of section 6(b)(1) if any district court of the United States would have had jurisdiction of such action but for this subparagraph.

(2) Copies of any petition filed under paragraph (1)(A) shall be transmitted forthwith to the Administrator and to the Attorney General by the clerk of the court with which such petition was filed. The provisions of section 2112 of title 28, United States Code, shall apply to the filing of the rulemaking record of proceedings on which the Administrator based the rule being reviewed under this section and to the transfer of proceedings between United States courts of appeals.

(3) For purposes of this section, the term "rulemaking record" means—

(A) the rule being reviewed under this section;

(B) in the case of a rule uner section 4(a), the finding required by such section, in the case of a rule under section 5(b)(4), the finding required by such section, in the case of a rule under section 6(a) the finding required by section 5(f) or 6(a), as the case may be, in the case of a rule under section 6(a), the statement required by section 6(c)(1), and in the case of a rule under section 6(e), the findings required by paragraph (2)(B) or (3)(B) of such section, as the case may be;

(C) any transcript required to be made of oral presentations made in

proceedings for the promulgation of such rule;
- (D) any written submission of interested parties respecting the promulgation of such rule; and
- (E) any other information which the Administrator considers to be relevant to such rule and which the Administrator identified, on or before the date of the promulgation of such rule, in a notice published in the Federal Register.

(b) If in an action under this section to review a rule the petitioner or the Administrator applies to the court for leave to make additional oral submissions or written presentations respecting such rule and shows to the satisfaction of the court that such submissions and presentations would be material and that there were reasonable grounds for the submissions and failure to make such submissions and presentations in the proceeding before the Administrator, the court may order the Administrator to provide additional opportunity to make such submissions and presentations. The Administrator may modify or set aside the rule being reviewed or make a new rule by reason of the additional submissions and presentations and shall file such modified or new rule with the return of such submissions and presentations. The court shall thereafter review such new or modified rule.

(c)(1)(A) Upon the filing of a petition under subsection (a)(1) for judicial review of a rule, the court shall have jurisdiction (i) to grant appropriate relief, including interim relief, as provided in chapter 7 of title 5, United States Code, and (ii) except as otherwise provided in subparagraph (B), to review such rule in accordance with chapter 7 of title 5, United States Code.
- (B) Section 706 of title 5, United States Code, shall apply to review of a rule under this section, except that—
  - (i) in the case of review of a rule under section 4(a), 5(b)(4), 6(a), or 6(e), the standard for review prescribed by paragraph (2)(E) of such section 706 shall not apply and the court shall hold unlawful and set aside such rule if the court finds that the rule is not supported by substantial evidence in the rulemaking record (as defined in subsection (a)(3)) taken as a whole;
  - (ii) in the case of review of a rule under section 6(a), the court shall hold unlawful and set aside such rule if it finds that—
    - (I) determination by the Administrator under section 6(c)(3) that the petitioner seeking review of such rule is not entitled to conduct (or have conducted) cross-examination or to present rebuttal submissions, or
    - (II) a rule of, or ruling by, the Administrator under section 6(c)(3) limiting such petitioner's cross-examination or oral presentations,

    has precluded disclosure of disputed material facts which was necessary to a fair determination by the Administrator of the rulemaking proceeding taken as a whole; and section 706(2)(D) shall not apply with respect to a determination, rule, or ruling

referred to in subclause (I) or (II); and
(iii) the court may not review the contents and adequacy of—
  (I) any statement required to be made pursuant to section 6(c)(1), or
  (II) any statement of basis and purpose required by section 553(c) of title 5, United States Code, to be incorporated in the rule

  except as part of a review of the rulemaking record taken as a whole.

  The term "evidence" as used in clause (i) means any matter in the rulemaking record.

(C) A determination, rule, or ruling of the Administrator described in subparagraph (B)(ii) may be reviewed only in an action under this section and only in accordance with such subparagraph.

(2) The judgment of the court affirming or setting aside, in whole or in part, any rule reviewed in accordance with this section shall be final, subject to review by the Supreme Court of the United States upon certiorari or certification, as provided in section 1254 of title 28, United States Code.

(d) The decision of the court in an action commenced under subsection (a), or of the Supreme Court of the United States on review of such a decision, may include an award of costs of suit and reasonable fees for attorneys and expert witnesses if the court determines that such an award is appropriate.

(e) The remedies as provided in this section shall be in addition to and not in lieu of any other remedies provided by law.

§ 2619. Citizens' civil actions

[Sec. 20] (a) Except as provided in subsection (b), any person may commence a civil action—

(1) against any person (including (A) the United States, and (B) any other governmental instrumentality or agency to the extent permitted by the eleventh amendment to the Constitution) who is alleged to be in violation of this Act or any rule promulgated under section 4, 5, or 6 or order issued under section 5 to restrain such violation, or

(2) against the Administrator to compel the Administrator to perform any act or duty under this Act which is not discretionary.

Any civil action under paragraph (1) shall be brought in the United States district court for the district in which the alleged violation occurred or in which the defendant resides or in which the defendant's principal place of business is located. Any action brought under paragraph (2) shall be brought in the United States District Court for the District of Columbia, or the United States district court for the judicial district in which the plaintiff is domiciled. The district courts of the United States shall have jurisdiction over suits brought under this section, without regard to the amount in controversy or the citizenship of the parties. In any civil action under this subsection process may be served on a defendant in any judicial district in which the defendant resides or may be found and subpoenas for witnesses may be served in any judicial district.

(b) No civil action may be commenced—

(1) under subsection (a)(1) to restrain a violation of this Act or rule or order under this Act—

    (A) before the expiration of 60 days after the plaintiff has given notice of such violation (i) to the Administrator, and (ii) to the person who is alleged to have committed such violation, or

    (B) if the Administrator has commenced and is diligently prosecuting a proceeding for the issuance of an order under section 16(a)(2) to require compliance with this Act or with such rule or order or if the Attorney General has commenced and is diligently prosecuting a civil action in a court of the United States to require compliance with this Act or with such rule or order, but if such proceeding or civil action is commenced after the giving of notice, any person giving such notice may intervene as a matter of right in such proceeding or action; or

(2) under subsection (a)(2) before the expiration of 60 days after the plaintiff has given notice to the Administrator of the alleged failure of the Administrator to perform an act or duty which is the basis for such action or, in the case of an action under such subsection for the failure of the Administrator to file an action under section 7, before the expiration of ten days after such notification.

Notice under this subsection shall be given in such manner as the Administrator shall prescribe by rule.

(c)(1) In any action under this section, the Administrator, if not a party, may intervene as a matter of right.

(2) The court, in issuing any final order in any action brought pursuant to subsection (a), may award costs of suit and reasonable fees for attorneys and expert witnesses if the court determines that such an award is appropriate. Any court, in issuing its decision in an action brought to review such an order, may award costs of suit and reasonable fees for attorneys if the court determines that such an award is appropriate.

(3) Nothing in this section shall restrict any right which any person (or class of persons) may have under any statute or common law to seek enforcement of this Act or any rule or order under this Act or to seek any other relief.

(d) When two or more civil actions brought under subsection (a) involving the same defendant and the same issues or violations are pending in two or more judicial districts, such pending actions, upon application of such defendants to such actions which is made to a court in which any such action is brought, may, if such court in its discretion so decides, be consolidated for trial by order (issued after giving all parties reasonable notice and opportunity to be heard) of such court and tried in—

(1) any district which is selected by such defendant and in which one of such actions is pending.

(2) a district which is agreed upon by stipulation between all the parties to such actions and in which one of such actions is pending, or

(3) a district which is selected by the court and in which one of such actions is pending.

The court issuing such an order shall give prompt notification of the order to the other courts in which the civil actions consolidated under the order are pending.

§ 2620. Citizens' petitions

[Sec. 21] (a) Any person may petition the Administrator to initiate a proceeding for the issuance, amendment, or repeal of a rule under section 4, 6, or 8 or an order under section 5(e) or (6)(b)(2).

(b)(1) Such petition shall be filed in the principal office of the Administrator and shall set forth the facts which it is claimed establish that it is necessary to issue, amend, or repeal a rule under section 4, 6, or 8 or an order under section 5(e), 6(b)(1)(A), or 6(b)(1)(B).

(2) The Administrator may hold a public hearing or may conduct such investigation or proceeding as the Administrator deems appropriate in order to determine whether or not such petition should be granted.

(3) Within 90 days after filing of a petition described in paragraph (1), the Administrator shall either grant or deny the petition. If the Administrator grants such petition, the Administrator shall promptly commence an appropriate proceeding in accordance with section 4, 5, 6, or 8. If the Administrator denies such petition, the Administrator shall publish in the Federal Register the Administrator's reasons for such denial.

(4)(A) If the Administrator denies a petition filed under this section (or if the Administrator fails to grant or deny such petition within the 90-day period) the petitioner may commence a civil action in a district court of the United States to compel the Administrator to initiate a rulemaking proceeding as requested in the petition. Any such action shall be filed within 60 days after the Administrator's denial of the petition or, if the Administrator fails to grant or deny the petition within 90 days after filing the petition, within 60 days after the expiration of the 90-day period.

(B) In an action under subparagraph (A) respecting a petition to initiate a proceeding to issue a rule under section 4, 6, or 8 or an order under section 5(e) or 6(b)(2), the petitioner shall be provided an opportunity to have such petition considered by the court in a de novo proceeding. If the petitioner demonstrates to the satisfaction of the court by a preponderance of the evidence that—

(i) in the case of a petition to initiate a proceeding for the issuance of a rule under section 4 or an order under section 5(e)—

(I) information available to the Administrator is insufficient to permit a reasoned evaluation of the health and environmental effects of the chemical substance to be subject to such rule or order; and

(II) in the absence of such information, the substance may present an unreasonable risk to health or the environment, or the substance is or will be produced in substantial quantities and it enters or may reasonably be anticipated to enter the environment in substantial quantities or there is or may be significant or substantial human exposure to it; or

(ii) in the case of a petition to initiate a proceeding for the issuance of a rule under section 6 or 8 or an order under section 6(b)(2), there is a reasonable basis to conclude that the issuance of such a rule or order is necessary to protect health or the environment against an unreasonable risk or injury to health or the environment;

the court shall order the Administrator to initiate the action requested by the petitioner. If the court finds that the extent of the risk to health or the environment alleged by the petitioner is less than the extent of risks to health or the environment with respect to which the Administrator is taking action under this Act and there are insufficient resources available to the Administrator to take the action requested by the petitioner, the court may permit the Administrator to defer initiating the action requested by the petitioner until such time as the court prescribes.

(C) The court in issuing any final order in any action brought pursuant to subparagraph (A) may award costs of suit and reasonable fees for attorneys and expert witnesses if the court determines that such an award is appropriate. Any court, in issuing its decision in an action brought to review such an order, may award costs of suit and reasonable fees for attorneys if the court determines that such an award is appropriate.

(5) The remedies under this section shall be in addition to, and not in lieu of, other remedies provided by law.

§ 2621. National defense waiver

[Sec. 22] The Administrator shall waive compliance with any provision of this Act upon a request and determination by the President that the requested waiver is necessary in the interest of national defense. The

Administrator shall maintain a written record of the basis upon which such waiver was granted and make such record available for in camera examination when relevant in a judicial proceeding under this Act. Upon the issuance of such a waiver, the Administrator shall publish in the Federal Register a notice that the waiver was granted for national defense purposes, unless, upon the request of the President, the Administrator determines to omit such publication because the publication itself would be contrary to the interests of national defense, in which event the Administrator shall submit notice thereof to the Armed Services Committees of the Senate and the House of Representatives.

§ 2622. Employee protection

[Sec. 23] (a) No employer may discharge any employee or otherwise discriminate against any employee with respect to the employee's compensation, terms, conditions, or privileges of employment because the employee (or any person acting pursuant to a request of the employee) has—

(1) commenced, caused to be commenced, or is about to commence or cause to be commenced a proceeding under this Act;

(2) testified or is about to testify in any such proceeding; or

(3) assisted or participated or is about to assist or participate in any manner in such a proceeding or in any other action to carry out the purposes of this Act.

(b)(1) Any employee who believes that the employee has been discharged or otherwise discriminated against by any person in violation of subsection (a) of this section may, within 30 days after such alleged violation occurs, file (or have any person file on the employee's behalf) a complaint with the Secretary of Labor (hereinafter in this section referred to as the "Secretary") alleging such discharge or discrimination. Upon receipt of such a complaint, the Secretary shall notify the person named in the complaint of the filing of the complaint.

(2)(A) Upon receipt of a complaint filed under paragraph (1), the Secretary shall conduct an investigation of the violation alleged in the complaint. Within 30 days of the receipt of such complaint, the Secretary shall complete such investigation and shall notify in writing the complainant (and any person acting on behalf of the complainant) and the person alleged to have committed such violation of the results of the investigation conducted pursuant to this paragraph. Within ninety days of the receipt of such complaint the Secretary shall, unless the proceeding on the complaint is terminated by the Secretary on the basis of a settlement entered into by the Secretary and the person alleged to have committed such violation, issue an order either providing the relief prescribed by subparagraph (B) or denying the complaint. An order of the Secretary shall be made on the record after notice and opportunity for agency hearing. The Secretary may not enter into a settlement terminating a proceeding on a complaint without the participation and consent of the complainant.

(B) If in response to a complaint filed under paragraph (1) the Secretary determines that a violation of subsection (a) of this section has occurred, the Secretary shall order (i) the person who committed such violation to take affirmative action to abate the violation. (ii) such person to reinstate the complainant to the complainant's former position together with the compensation (including back pay), terms, conditions, and privileges of the complainant's employment, (iii) compensatory damages, and (iv) where appropriate, exemplary damages. If such an order issued, the Secretary, at the request of the complainant, shall assess against the person against whom the order is issued a sum equal to the aggregate amount of all costs and expenses (including attorney's fees) reasonably incurred, as determined by the Secretary, by the complainant for, or in connection with, the bringing of the complaint upon which the order was issued.

(c)(1) Any employee or employer adversely affected or aggrieved by an order issued under subsection (b) may obtain review of the order in the United States Court of Appeals for the circuit in which the violation, with respect to which the order was issued, allegedly occurred. The petition for review must be filed within sixty days from the issuance of the Secretary's order. Review shall conform to chapter 7 of title 5 of the United States Code.

(2) An order of the Secretary, with respect to which review could have been obtained under paragraph (1), shall not be subject to judicial review in any criminal or other civil proceeding.

(d) Whenever a person has failed to comply with an order issued under subsection (b) (2), the Secretary shall file a civil action in the United States district court for the district in which the violation was found to occur to enforce such order. In actions brought under this subsection, the district courts shall have jurisdiction to grant all appropriate relief, including injunctive relief and compensatory and exemplary damages.

(e) Subsection (a) of this section shall not apply with respect to any employee who, acting without direction from the employee's employer (or any agent of the employer), deliberately causes a violation of any requirement of this Act.

§ 2623. Employment effects

[Sec. 24] (a) The Administrator shall evaluate on a continuing basis the potential effects on employment (including reductions in employment or loss of employment from threatened plant closures) of—

(1) the issuance of a rule or order under section 4, 5, or 6, or

(2) a requirement of section 5 or 6.

(b)(1) Any employee (or any representative of an employee) may request the Administrator to make an investigation of—

>(A) discharge or layoff or threatened discharge or layoff of the employee, or

>(B) adverse or threatened adverse effects on the employee's employment,

allegedly resulting from a rule or order under section 4, 5, or 6 or a requirement of section 5 or 6. Any such request shall be made in writing, shall set forth with reasonable particularity the grounds for the request, and shall be signed by the employee, or representative of such employee, making the request.

>(2)(A) Upon receipt of a request made in accordance with paragraph (1) the Administrator shall (i) conduct the investigation requested, and (ii) if requested by any interested person, hold public hearings on any matter involved in the investigation unless the Adminstrator, by order issued within 45 days of the date such hearings are requested, denies the request for the hearings because the Administrator determines there are no reasonable grounds for holding such hearings. If the Administrator makes such a determination, the Administrator shall notify in writing the person requesting the hearing of the determination and the reasons therefor and shall publish the determination and the reasons therefor in the Federal Register.

>(B) If public hearings are to be held on any matter involved in an investigation conducted under this subsection—

>>(i) at least five days' notice shall be provided the person making the request for the investigation and any person identified in such request,

>>(ii) such hearings shall be held in accordance with section 6(c) (3), and

>>(iii) each employee who made or for whom was made a request for such hearings and the employer of such employee shall be required to present information respecting the applicable matter referred to in paragraph (1)(A) or (1)(B) together with the basis for such information.

(3) Upon completion of an investigation under paragraph (2), the Administrator shall make findings of fact, shall make such recommendations as the Administrator deems appropriate, and shall make available to the public such findings and recommendations.

(4) This section shall not be construed to require the Administrator to amend or repeal any rule or order in effect under this Act.

§ 2624. Studies

[Sec. 25] (a) The Administrator shall conduct a study of all Federal laws administered by the Administrator for the purpose of determining whether and under what conditions, if any, indemnification should be accorded any person as a result of any action taken by the Administrator under any such law. The study shall—

(1) include an estimate of the probable cost of any indemnification programs which may be recommended;

(2) include an examination of all viable means of financing the cost of any recommended indemnification; and

(3) be completed and submitted to Congress within two years from the effective date of enactment of this Act.

The General Accounting Office shall review the adequacy of the study submitted to Congress pursuant to paragraph (3) and shall report the results of its review to the Congress within six months of the date such study is submitted to Congress.

(b) The Council on Environmental Quality, in consultation with the Administrator, the Secretary of Health, Education, and Welfare, the Secretary of Commerce, and the heads of other appropriate Federal departments or agencies, shall coordinate a study of the feasibility of establishing (1) a standard classification system for chemical substances and related substances, and (2) a standard means for storing and for obtaining rapid access to information respecting such substances. A report on such study shall be completed and submitted to Congress not later than 18 months after the effective date of enactment of this Act.

§ 2625. Administration

[Sec. 26] (a) Upon request by the Administrator, each Federal department and agency is authorized—

(1) to make its services, personnel, and facilities available (with or without reimbursement) to the Administrator to assist the Administrator in the administration of this Act; and

(2) to furnish to the Administrator such information, data, estimates, and statistics, and to allow the Administrator access to all information in its possession as the Administrator may reasonably determine to be necessary for the administration of this Act.

(b)(1) The Administrator may, by rule, require the payment of a reasonable fee from any person required to submit data under section 4 or 5 to defray the cost of administering this Act. Such rules shall not provide for any fee in excess of $2,500 or, in the case of a small business concern, any fee in excess of $100. In setting a fee under this paragraph, the Administrator shall take into account the ability to pay of the person required to submit the data and the cost to the Administrator of reviewing such data. Such rules may provide for sharing such a fee in any case in which the expenses of testing are shared under section 4 or 5.

(2) The Administrator, after consultation with the Administrator of the Small Business Administration, shall by rule prescribe standards for

determining the persons which qualify as small business concerns for purposes of paragraph (1).

(c)(1) Any action authorized or required to be taken by the Administrator under any provision of this Act with respect to a chemical substance or mixture may be taken by the Administrator in accordance with that provision with respect to a category of chemical substances or mixtures. Whenever the Administrator takes action under a provision of this Act with respect to a category of chemical substances or mixtures, any reference in this Act to a chemical substance or mixture (insofar as it relates to such action) shall be deemed to be a reference to each chemical substance or mixture in such category.

(2) For purposes of paragraph (i):

(A) The term "category of chemical substances" means a group of chemical substances the members of which are similar in molecular structure, in physical, chemical, or biological properties, in use, or in mode of entrance into the human body or into the environment, or the members of which are in some other way suitable for classification as such for purposes of this Act, except that such term does not mean a group of chemical substances which are grouped together solely on the basis of their being new chemical substances.

(B) The term "category of mixtures" means a group of mixtures the members of which are similar in molecular structure, in physical, chemical, or biological properties, in use, or in the mode of entrance into the human body or into the environment, or the members of which are in some other way suitable for classification as such for purposes of this Act.

(d) The Administrator shall establish in the Environmental Protection Agency an identifiable office to provide technical and other nonfinancial assistance to manufacturers and processors of chemical substances and mixtures respecting the requirements of this Act applicable to such manufacturers and processors, the policy of the Agency respecting the application of such requirements to such manufacturers and processors, and the means and methods by which such manufacturers and processors may comply with such requirements.

(e)(1) Except as provided under paragraph (3), each officer or employee of the Environmental Protection Agency and the Department of Health, Education, and Welfare who—

(A) performs any function or duty under this Act, and

(B) has any known financial interest (i) in any person subject to this Act or any rule or order in effect under this Act, or (ii) in any person who applies for or receives any grant or contract under this Act,

shall, on February 1, 1978, and on February 1 of each year thereafter, file with the Administrator or the Secretary of Health, Education, and

Welfare (hereinafter in this subsection referred to as the "Secretary"), as appropriate, a written statement concerning all such interests held by such officer or employee during the preceding calendar year. Such statement shall be made available to the public.

(2) The Administrator and the Secretary shall—

    (A) act within 90 days of the effective date of this Act—

        (i) to define the term "known financial interest" for purposes of paragraph (1), and

        (ii) to establish the methods by which the requirement to file written statements specified in paragraph (1) will be monitored and enforced, including appropriate provisions for review by the Administrator and the Secretary of such statements; and

    (B) report to the Congress on June 1, 1978, and on June 1 of each year thereafter with respect to such statements and the actions taken in regard thereto during the preceding calendar year.

(3) The Administrator may by rule identify specific positions with the Environmental Protection Agency, and the Secretary may by rule identify specific positions with the Department of Health, Education and Welfare, which are of a nonregulatory or nonpolicymaking nature, and the Administrator and the Secretary may by rule provide that officers or employees occupying such positions shall be exempt from the requirements of paragraph (1).

(4) This subsection does not supersede any requirement of chapter 11 of title 18, United States Code.

(5) Any officer or employee who is subject to, and knowingly violates, this subsection or any rule issued thereunder, shall be fined not more than $2,500 or imprisoned not more than one year, or both.

(f) Any final order issued under this Act shall be accompanied by a statement of its basis and purpose. The contents and adequacy of any such statement shall not be subject to judicial review in any respect.

(g)(1) The President, by and with the advice and consent of the Senate, shall appoint an Assistant Administrator for Toxic Substances of the Environmental Protection Agency. Such Assistant Administrator shall be a qualified individual who is, by reason of background and experience, especially qualified to direct a program concerning the effects of chemicals on human health and the environment. Such Assistant Administrator shall be responsible for (A) the collection of data, (B) the preparation of studies, (C) the making of recommendations to the Administrator for regulatory and other actions to carry out the purposes and to facilitate the administration of this Act, and (D) such other functions as the Administrator may assign or delegate.

(2) The Assistant Administrator to be appointed under paragraph (1) shall be in addition to the Assistant Administrators of the Environ-

mental Protection Agency authorized by section 1(d) of Reorganization Plan No. 3 of 1970.

§ 2626.   Development and evaluation of test methods

[Sec. 27] (a) The Secretary of Health, Education, and Welfare, in consultation with the Administrator and acting through the Assistant Secretary for Health, may conduct, and make grants to public and nonprofit private entities and enter into contracts with public and private entities for, projects for the development and evaluation of inexpensive and efficient methods (1) for determining and evaluating the health and environmental effects of chemical substances and mixtures, and their toxicity, persistence, and other characteristics which affect health and the environment, and (2) which may be used for the development of test data to meet the requirements of rules promulgated under section 4. The Administrator shall consider such methods in prescribing under section 4 standards for the development of test data.

(b) No grant may be made or contract entered into under subsection (a) unless an application therefor has been submitted to and approved by the Secretary. Such an application shall be submitted in such form and manner and contain such information as the Secretary may require. The Secretary may apply such conditions to grants and contracts under subsection (a) as the Secretary determines are necessary to carry out the purposes of such subsection. Contracts may be entered into under such subsection without regard to sections 31 U.S.C. 3324(a) and (b) and 41 U.S.C. 5.

(c)(1) The Secretary shall prepare and submit to the President and the Congress on or before January 1 of each year a report of the number of grants made and contracts entered into under this section and the results of such grants and contracts.

(2) The Secretary shall periodically publish in the Federal Register reports describing the progress and results of any contract entered into or grant made under this section.

§ 2627.   State programs

[Sec. 28] (a) For the purpose of complementing (but not reducing) the authority of, or actions taken by, the Administrator under this Act, the Administrator may make grants to States for the establishment and operation of programs to prevent or eliminate unreasonable risks within the States to health or the environment which are associated with a chemical substance or mixture and with respect to which the Administrator is unable or is not likely to take action under this Act for their prevention or elimination. The amount of a grant under this subsection shall be determined by the Administrator, except that no grant for any State program may exceed 75 per centum of the establishment and operation costs (as determined by the Administrator) of such program during the period for which the grant is made.

(b)(1) No grant may be made under subsection (a) unless an application therefor is submitted to and approved by the Administrator. Such an application shall be submitted in such form and manner as the Administrator may require and shall—

(A) set forth the need of the applicant for a grant under subsection (a),

(B) identify the agency or agencies of the State which shall establish or operate, or both, the program for which the application is submitted,

(C) describe the actions proposed to be taken under such program,

(D) contain or be supported by assurances satisfactory to the Administrator that such program shall, to the extent feasible, be integrated with other programs of the applicant for environmental and public health protection,

(E) provide for the making of such reports and evaluations as the Administrator may require, and

(F) contain such other information as the Administrator may prescribe.

(2) The Administrator may approve an application submitted in accordance with paragraph (1) only if the applicant has established to the satisfaction of the Administrator a priority need, as determined under rules of the Administrator, for the grant for which the application has been submitted. Such rules shall take into consideration the seriousness of the health effects in a State which are associated with chemical substances or mixtures, including cancer, birth defects, and gene mutations, the extent of the exposure in a State of human beings and the environment to chemical substances and mixtures, and the extent to which chemical substances and mixtures are manufactured, processed, used, and disposed of in a State.

(c) Not later than six months after the end of each of the fiscal years 1979, 1980, and 1981, the Administrator shall submit to the Congress a report respecting the programs assisted by grants under subsection (a) in the proceeding fiscal year and the extent to which the Administrator has disseminated information respecting such programs.

(d) For the purpose of making grants under subsection (a) there are authorized to be appropriated $1,500,000 for each of the fiscal years 1982 and 1983. Sums appropriated under this subsection shall remain available until expended.

§ 2628. Authorization of appropriations

[Sec. 29] There are authorized to be appropriated to the Administrator for purposes of carrying out this Act (other than sections 27 and 28 and subsections (a) and (c) through (g) of section 10 thereof) $58,646,000 for the fiscal year 1982 and $62,000,000 for the fiscal year 1983. No part of the funds appropriated under this section may be used to construct any research laboratories.

§ 2629. Annual report

[Sec. 30] The Administrator shall prepare and submit to the President and the Congress on or before January 1, 1978, and on or before January 1 of each succeeding year a comprehensive report on the administration of this Act during the preceding fiscal year. Such report shall include—

  (1) a list of the testing required under section 4 during the year for which the report is made and an estimate of the costs incurred during such year by the persons required to perform such tests;
  (2) the number of notices received during such year under section 5, the number of such notices received during such year under such section for chemical substances subject to a section 4 rule, and a summary of any action taken during such year under section 5(g);
  (3) a list of rules issued during such year under section 6;
  (4) a list, with a brief statement of the issues, of completed or pending judicial actions under this Act and administrative actions under section 16 during such year;
  (5) a summary of major problems encountered in the administration of this Act; and
  (6) such recommendations for additional legislation as the Administrator deems necessary to carry out the purposes of this Act.

Subchapter II. Asbestos hazard emergency response

§ 2641. Congressional findings and declaration of purpose

[Sec. 201] (a) The Congress finds the following:
  (1) The Environmental Protection Agency's rule on local educational agency inspection for, and notification of, the presence of friable asbestos-containing material in school buildings includes neither standards for the proper identification of asbestos-containing material and appropriate response actions with respect to friable asbestos-containing material, nor a requirement that response actions with respect to friable asbestos-containing material be carried out in a safe and complete manner once actions are found to be necessary. As a result of the lack of regulatory guidance from the Environmental Protection Agency, some schools have not undertaken response action while many others have undertaken expensive projects without knowing if their action is necessary, adequate, or safe. Thus, the danger of exposure to

asbestos continues to exist in schools, and some exposure actually may have increased due to the lack of Federal standards and improper response action.

(2) There is no uniform program for accrediting persons involved in asbestos identification and abatement, nor are local educational agencies required to use accredited contractors for asbestos work.

(3) The guidance provided by the Environmental Protection Agency in its "Guidance for Controlling Asbestos-Containing Material in Buildings" is insufficient in detail to ensure adequate responses. Such guidance is intended to be used only until regulations required by this title become effective.

(4) Because there are no Federal standards whatsoever regulating daily exposure to asbestos in other public and commercial buildings, persons in addition to those comprising the Nation's school population may be exposed daily to asbestos.

(b) The purpose of this subchapter is —

(1) to provide for the establishment of Federal regulations which require inspection for asbestos-containing material and implementation of appropriate response actions with respect to asbestos-containing material in the Nation's schools in a safe and complete manner;

(2) to mandate safe and complete periodic reinspection of school buildings following response actions, where appropriate; and

(3) to require the Administrator to conduct a study to find out the extent of the danger to human health posed by asbestos in public and commercial buildings and the means to respond to any such danger.

§ 2642. Definitions

[Sec. 202] For purposes of this subchapter—

(1) The term "accredited asbestos contractor" means a person accredited pursuant to the provisions of section 2646 of this title.

(2) The term "Administrator" means the Administrator of the Environmental Protection Agency.

(3) The term "asbestos" means asbestiform varieties of—

    (A) chrysotile (serpentine),

    (B) crocidolite (riebeckite),

    (C) amosite (cummingtonite-grunerite),

    (D) anthophyllite,

    (E) tremolite, or

    (F) actinolite.

(4) The term "asbestos-containing material" means any material which contains more than 1 percent asbestos by weight.

(5) The term "Guidance for Controlling Asbestos-Containing Material in

Buildings", means the Environmental Protection Agency document with such title as in effect on March 31, 1986.

(6) The term "friable asbestos-containing material" means any asbestos-containing material applied on ceilings, walls, structural members, piping, duct work, or any other part of a building which when dry may be crumbled, pulverized, or reduced to powder by hand pressure. The term includes non-friable asbestos-containing material after such previously non-friable material becomes damaged to the extent that when dry it may be crumbled, pulverized, or reduced to powder by hand pressure.

(7) The term "local educational agency" means—

    (A) any local educational agency as defined in section 198 of the Elementary and Secondary Education Act of 1965 (20 U.S.C. 3381),

    (B) the owner of any private, nonprofit elementary or secondary school building, and

    (C) the governing authority of any school operated under the defense dependents' education system provided for under the Defense Dependents' Education Act of 1978 (20 U.S.C. 921 et seq.).

(8) The term "most current guidance document" means the Environmental Protection Agency's "Guidance for Controlling Asbestos-Containing Material in Buildings" as modified by the Environmental Protection Agency after March 31, 1986.

(9) The term "non-profit elementary or secondary school" means any elementary or secondary school (as defined in section 2854 of Title 20) owned and operated by one or more nonprofit corporations or associations no part of the net earnings of which inures, or may lawfully inure, to the benefit of any private shareholder or individual.

(10) The term "public and commercial building" means any building which is not a school building, except that the term does not include any residential apartment building of fewer than 10 units.

(11) The term "response action" means methods that protect human health and the environment from asbestos-containing material. Such methods include methods described in chapters 3 and 5 of the Environmental Protection Agency's "Guidance for Controlling Asbestos-Containing Materials in Buildings".

(12) The term "school" means any elementary or secondary school as defined in section 2854 of Title 20.

(13) The term "school building" means—

    (A) any structure suitable for use as a classroom, including a school facility such as a laboratory, library, school eating facility, or facility used for the preparation of food,

    (B) any gymnasium or other facility which is specially designed for athletic or recreational activities for an academic course in physical education,

(C) any other facility used for the instruction of students or for the administration of educational or research programs, and

(D) any maintenance, storage, or utility facility, including any hallway, essential to the operation of any facility described in subparagraphs (A), (B), or (C).

(14) The term "State" means a State, the District of Columbia, the Commonwealth of Puerto Rico, Guam, American Samoa, the Northern Marianas, the Trust Territory of the Pacific Islands, and the Virgin Islands.

§ 2643. Environmental Protection Agency regulations

[Sec. 203] (a) Within 360 days after October 22, 1986, the Administrator shall promulgate regulations as described in subsections (b) through (i) of this section. With respect to regulations described in subsections (b), (c), (d), (e), (f), (g), and (i) of this section, the Administrator shall issue an advanced notice of proposed rulemaking within 60 days after October 22, 1986, and shall propose regulations within 180 days after such date. Any regulation promulgated under this section must protect human health and the environment.

(b) The Administrator shall promulgate regulations which prescribe procedures, including the use of personnel accredited under section 2646(b) or (c) of this title and laboratories accredited under section 2646(d) of this title, for determining whether asbestos-containing material is present in a school building under the authority of a local educational agency. The regulations shall provide for the exclusion of any school building, or portion of a school building, if (1) an inspection of such school building (or portion) was completed before the effective date of the regulations, and (2) the inspection meets the procedures and other requirements of the regulations under this subchapter or of the "Guidance for Controlling Asbestos-Containing Materials in Buildings" (unless the Administrator determines that an inspection in accordance with the guidance document is inadequate). The regulations shall require inspection of any school building (or portion of a school building) that is not excluded by the preceding sentence.

(c)(1) The Administrator shall promulgate regulations which define the appropriate response action in a school building under the authority of a local educational agency in at least the following circumstances:

(A) Circumstances in which friable asbestos-containing material or its covering is damaged, deteriorated, or delaminated.

(B) Circumstances in which friable asbestos-containing material or its covering is significantly damaged, deteriorated, or delaminated.

(C) Circumstances in which —

(i) friable asbestos-containing material is in an area regularly used by building occupants, including maintenance personnel, in the course of their normal activities, and

(ii) there is a reasonable likelihood that the material or its covering will become damaged, deteriorated, or delaminated.

    (D) Circumstances in which —

        (i) friable asbestos-containing material is in an area regularly used by building occupants, including maintenance personnel, in the course of their normal activities, and

        (ii) there is a reasonable likelihood that the material or its covering will become significantly damaged, deteriorated, or delaminated.

(2) In promulgating such regulations, the Administrator shall consider and assess the value of various technologies intended to improve the decisionmaking process regarding response actions and the quality of any work that is deemed necessary, including air monitoring and chemical encapsulants.

(d)(1) The Administrator shall promulgate regulations describing a response action in a school building under the authority of a local educational agency, using the least burdensome methods which protect human health and the environment. In determining, the least burdensome methods, the Administrator shall take into account local circumstances, including occupancy and use patterns within the school building and short- and long-term costs.

(2) In the case of a response action for the circumstances described in subsection (c)(1)(A) of this section, methods for responding shall include methods identified in chapters 3 and 5 of the "Guidance for Controlling Asbestos-Containing Material in Buildings."

(3) In the case of a response action for the circumstances described in subsection (c)(1)(B) of this section, methods for responding shall include methods identified in chapter 5 of the "Guidance for Controlling Asbestos-Containing Material in Buildings".

(4) In the case of a response action for the circumstances described in subsection (c)(1)(C), of this section, methods for responding shall include methods identified in chapters 3 and 5 of the "Guidance for Controlling Asbestos-Containing Material in Buildings", unless preventive measures will eliminate the reasonable likelihood that the asbestos-containing material will become damaged, deteriorated, or deliminated.

(5) In the case of a response action for the circumstances described in subsection (c)(1)(D) of this section, methods for responding shall include methods identified in chapter 5 of the "Guidance for Controlling Asbestos-Containing Material in Buildings", unless preventive measures will eliminate the reasonable likelihood that the asbestos-containing material will become significantly damaged, deteriorated, or delaminated.

(6) For purposes of this section, the term "preventive measures" means actions which eliminate the reasonable likelihood of asbestos-containing material becoming damaged, deteriorated, or delaminated, or

significantly damaged, deteriorated, or delaminated (as the case may be) or which protect human health and the environment.

(e) The Administrator shall promulgate regulations requiring the implementation of response actions in school buildings under the authority of a local educational agency and, where appropriate, for the determination of when a response action is completed. Such regulations shall include standards for the education and protection of both workers and building occupants for the following phases of activity:

(1) Inspection.

(2) Response Action.

(3) Post-response action, including any periodic reinspection of asbestos-containing material and long-term surveillance activity.

(f) The Administrator shall promulgate regulations to require implementation of an operations and maintenance and repair program as described in chapter 3 of the "Guidance for Controlling Asbestos-Containing Materials in Buildings" for all friable asbestos-containing material in a school building under the authority of a local educational agency.

(g) The Administrator shall promulgate regulations to require the following:

(1) An identification of the location of friable and non-friable asbestos in a school building under the authority of a local educational agency.

(2) Provisions for surveillance and periodic reinspection of such friable and non-friable asbestos.

(3) Provisions for education of school employees, including school service and maintenance personnel, about the location of and safety procedures with respect to such friable and non-friable asbestos.

(h) The Administrator shall promulgate regulations which prescribe standards for transportation and disposal of asbestos-containing waste material to protect human health and the environment. Such regulations shall include such provisions related to the manner in which transportation vehicles are loaded and unloaded as will assure the physical integrity of containers of asbestos-containing waste material.

(i)(1) The Administrator shall promulgate regulations which require each local educational agency to develop an asbestos management plan for school buildings under its authority, to begin implementation of such plan within 990 days after October 22, 1986, and to complete implementation of such plan in a timely fashion. The regulations shall require that each plan include the following elements, whenever relevant to the school building:

(A) An inspection statement describing inspection and response action activities carried out before October 22, 1986.

(B) A description of the results of the inspection conducted pursuant to regulations under subsection (b) of this section, including a description of the specific areas inspected.

(C) A detailed description of measures to be taken to respond to any friable asbestos-containing material pursuant to the regulations promulgated under subsections (c), (d), and (e) of this section, including the location or locations at which a response action will be taken, the method or methods of response action to be used, and a schedule for beginning and completing response actions.

(D) A detailed description of any asbestos-containing material which remains in the school building once response actions are undertaken pursuant to the regulations promulgated under subsections (c), (d), and (e) of this section.

(E) A plan for periodic reinspection and long-term surveillance activities developed pursuant to regulations promulgated under subsection (g) of this section, and a plan for operations and maintenance activities developed pursuant to regulations promulgated under subsection (f) of this section.

(F) With respect to the person or persons who inspected for asbestos-containing material and who will design or carry out response actions with respect to the friable asbestos-containing material, one of the following statements:

   (i) If the State has adopted a contractor accreditation plan under section 2646(b) of this title, a statement that the person (or persons) is accredited under such plan.

   (ii) A statement that the local educational agency used (or will use) persons who have been accredited by another State which has adopted a contractor accreditation plan under section 2646(b) of this title or is accredited pursuant to an Administrator-approved course under section 2646(c) of this title.

(G) A list of the laboratories that analyzed any bulk samples of asbestos-containing material found in the school building or air samples taken to detect asbestos in the school building and a statement that each laboratory has been accredited pursuant to the accreditation program under section 2646(d) of this title.

(H) With respect to each consultant who contributed to the management plan, the name of the consultant and one of the following statements:

   (i) If the State has adopted a contractor accreditation plan under section 2646(b) of this title, a statement that the consultant is accredited under such plan.

   (ii) A statement that the contractor is accredited by another State which has adopted a contractor accreditation plan under section 2646(b) of this title or is accredited pursuant to an Administrator-approved course under section 2646(c) of this title.

(I) An evaluation of resources needed to successfully complete response actions and carry out reinspection, surveillance, and operation and maintenance activities.

(2) A local educational agency may require each management plan to

contain a statement signed by an accredited asbestos contractor that such contractor has prepared or assisted in the preparation of such plan, or has reviewed such plan, and that such plan is in compliance with the applicable regulations and standards promulgated or adopted pursuant to this section and other applicable provisions of law. Such a statement may not be signed by a contractor who, in addition to preparing or assisting in preparing the management plan, also implements (or will implement) the management plan.

(3)(A) The regulations shall require that each local educational agency which has inspected for and discovered any asbestos-containing material with respect to a school building shall attach a warning label to any asbestos-containing material still in routine maintenance areas (such as boiler rooms) of the school building, including—

    (i) friable asbestos-containing material which was responded to by a means other than removal, and

    (ii) asbestos-containing material for which no response action was carried out.

(B) The warning label shall read, in print which is readily visible because of large size or bright color, as follows: "CAUTION: ASBESTOS. HAZARDOUS. DO NOT DISTURB WITHOUT PROPER TRAINING AND EQUIPMENT."

(4) A local educational agency may submit a management plan in stages, with each submission of the agency covering only a portion of the school buildings under the agency's authority, if the agency determines that such action would expedite the identification and abatement of hazardous asbestos-containing material in the school buildings under the authority of the agency.

(5) A copy of the management plan developed under the regulations shall be available in the administrative offices of the local educational agency for inspection by the public, including teachers, other school personnel, and parents. The local educational agency shall notify parent, teacher, and employee organizations of the availability of such plan.

(6) Each plan developed under this subsection shall be submitted to the State Governor under section 2645 of this title.

(j) Changes may be made in the regulations promulgated under this section only by rule in accordance with section 553 of Title 5. Any such change must protect human health and the environment.

(k) Any change made in the "Guidance for Controlling Asbestos-Containing Material in Buildings" shall be made only by rule in accordance with section 553 of Title 5, unless a regulation described in this section dealing with the same subject matter is in effect. Any such change must protect human health and the environment.

(l)(1) In the administration of this subchapter, any function, duty, or other responsibility imposed on a Governor of a State shall be carried out by the

Secretary of Defense with respect to any school operated under the defense dependents' education system provided for under the Defense Dependents' Education Act of 1978 (20 U.S.C. 921 et seq.).

(2) The Secretary of Defense, in cooperation with the Administrator, shall, to the extent feasible and consistent with the national security, take such action as may be necessary to provide for the identification, inspection, and management (including abatement) of asbestos in any building used by the Department of Defense as an overseas school for dependents of members of the Armed Forces. Such identification, inspection, and management (including abatement) shall, subject to the preceding sentence, be carried out in a manner comparable to the manner in which a local educational agency is required to carry out such activities with respect to a school building under this subchapter.

(m) The Administrator, upon request by a Governor and after notice and comment and opportunity for a public hearing in the affected State, may waive some or all of the requirements of this section and section 2644 of this title with respect to such State if it has established and is implementing a program of asbestos inspection and management that contains requirements that are at least as stringent as the requirements of this section and section 2644 of this title.

§ 2644. Requirements upon failure of EPA to promulgate regulations

[Sec. 204] (a)(1) If the Administrator fails to promulgate within the prescribed period—

(A) regulations described in section 2643(b) of this title (relating to inspection);

(B) regulations described in section 2643(c), (d), (e), (f), (g), and (i) of this title (relating to responding to asbestos); or

(C) regulations described in section 2643(h) of this title (relating to transportation and disposal);

each local educational agency shall carry out the requirements described in this section in subsection (b) of this section; subsections (c), (d), and (e) of this section; or subsection (f) of this section; respectively, in accordance with the Environmental Protection Agency's most current guidance documents.

(2) If the Administrator has promulgated regulations described in paragraph (1)(A), (B), or (C) within the prescribed period, but the effective date of such regulations has been stayed by a court for a period of more than 30 days, a local educational agency shall carry out the pertinent requirements described in this subsection in accordance with the Environmental Protection Agency's most current guidance document.

(3) The requirements of this section shall be in effect until such time as

the Administrator promulgates the pertinent regulations or until the stay is lifted (as the case may be).

(b)(1) Except as provided in paragraph (2), the local educational agency, within 540 days after October 22, 1986, shall conduct an inspection for asbestos-containing material, using personnel accredited under section 2646(b) or (c) of this title and laboratories accredited under section 2646(d) of this title, in each school building under its authority.

(2) The local educational agency may exclude from the inspection requirement in paragraph (1) any school building, or portion of a school building, if (A) an inspection of such school building (or portion) was completed before the date on which this section goes into effect, and (B) the inspection meets the inspection requirements of this section.

(c) The local educational agency shall, within 720 days after October 22, 1986 develop and begin implementation of an operation and maintenance plan with respect to asbestos-containing material, including friable asbestos-containing material.

(d)(1) The local educational agency shall—
    (A) develop a management plan for responding to asbestos-containing material in each school building under its authority and submit such plan to the Governor under section 2645 of this title within 810 days after October 22, 1986,
    (B) begin implementation of such plan within 990 days after October 22, 1986, and
    (C) complete implementation of such plan in a timely fashion.

(2) The management plan shall—
    (A) include the elements listed in section 2643(i)(1) of this title, including an inspection statement as described in paragraph (3) of this section,
    (B) provide for the attachment of warning labels as described in section 2643(i)(3) of this title,
    (C) be prepared in accordance with the most current guidance document,
    (D) meet the standard described in paragraph (4) for actions described in that paragraph, and
    (E) be submitted to the State Governor under section 2645 of this title.

(3) The local educational agency shall complete an inspection statement, covering activities carried out before October 22, 1986, which meets the following requirements:
    (A) The statement shall include the following information:
        (i) The dates of inspection.
        (ii) The name, address, and qualifications of each inspector.
        (iii) A description of the specific areas inspected.
        (iv) A list of the laboratories that analyzed any bulk samples of asbestos-containing material or air samples of asbestos found

in any school building and a statement describing the qualifications of each laboratory.

(v) The results of the inspection.

(B) The statement shall state whether any actions were taken with
respect to any asbestos-containing material found to be present,
including a specific reference to whether any actions were taken
in the boiler room of the building. If any such action was taken,
the following items of information shall be included in the
statement:

(i) The location or locations at which the action was taken.

(ii) A description of the method of action.

(iii) The qualifications of the persons who conducted the action.

(4) The ambient interior concentration of asbestos after the completion of
actions described in the most current guidance document, other than
the type of action described in sections 2643(f) of this title and
subsection (c) of this section, shall not exceed the ambient exterior
concentration, discounting any contribution for any local stationary
source. Either a scanning electron microscope or a transmission
electron microscope shall be used to determine the ambient interior
concentration. In he absence of reliable measurements, the ambient
exterior concentration shall be deemed to be—

(A) less than 0.003 fibers per cubic centimeter if a scanning electron
microscope is used, and

(B) less than 0.005 fibers per cubic centimeter if a transmission
electron miscroscope is used.

(5) A copy of the management plan shall be available in the administrative offices of the local educational agency for inspection by the public,
including teachers, other school personnel, and parents. The local
educational agency shall notify parent, teacher, and employee organizations of the availability of such plan.

(e) The local educational agency shall provide for the protection of
building occupants during each phase of activity described in this section.

(f) The local educational agency shall provide for the transportation and
disposal of asbestos in accordance with the most recent version of the
Environmental Protection Agency's "Asbestos Waste Management Guidance" (or any successor to such document).

§ 2645. Submission of management plan to State Governor

[Sec. 205] (a) Within 720 days after Oct. 22, 1986 (or within 810 days if
there are no regulations under section 2643(i) of this title) a local educational agency shall submit a management plan developed pursuant to regulations
promulgated under section 2643(i) of this title (or under section 2644(d) of
this title if there are no regulations) to the Governor of the State in which the
local educational agency is located.

(b) Within 360 days after Oct. 22, 1986, the Governor of each State —
(1) shall notify local educational agencies in the State of where to submit their management plans under this section, and
(2) may establish administrative procedures for reviewing management plans submitted under this section.
   If the Governor establishes procedures under paragraph (2), the Governor shall designate to carry out the reviews those State officials who are responsible for implementing environmental protection or other public health programs, or with authority over asbestos programs, in the State.

(c)(1) The Governor may disapprove a management plan within 90 days after the date of receipt of the plan if the plan —
(A) does not conform with the regulations under section 2643(i) of this title (or with section 2644(d) of this title if there are no regulations),
(B) does not assure that contractors who are accredited pursuant to this subchapter will be used to carry out the plan, or
(C) does not contain a response action schedule which is reasonable and timely, taking into account circumstances relevant to the speed at which the friable asbestos-containing material in the school buildings under the local educational agency's authority should be responded to, including human exposure to the asbestos while the friable asbestos-containing material remains in the school building, and the ability of the local educational agency to continue to provide educational services to the community.

(2) If the State Governor disapproves a plan, the State Governor shall explain in writing to the local educational agency the reasons why the plan was disapproved and the changes that need to be made in the plan. Within 30 days after the date on which notice is received of disapproval of its plan, the local educational agency shall revise the plan to conform with the State Governor's suggested changes. The Governor may extend the 30-day period for not more than 90 days.

§ 2646. Contractor and laboratory accreditation

[Sec. 206] (a) A person may not —
(1) inspect for asbestos-containing material in a school building under the authority of a local educational agency,
(2) prepare a management plan for such a school, or
(3) design or conduct response actions, other than the type of action described in sections 2643(f) and 2644(c) of this title, with respect to friable asbestos-containing material in such a school,
unless such person is accredited by a State under subsection (b) of this section or is accredited pursuant to an Administrator-approved course under subsection (c) of this section.

(b)(1)(A) Within 180 days after October 22, 1986, the Administrator, in consultation with affected organizations, shall develop a model contractor accreditation plan for States to give accreditation to persons in the following categories:

> (i) Persons who inspect for asbestos-containing material in school buildings under the authority of a local educational agency.
>
> (ii) Persons who prepare management plans for such schools.
>
> (iii) Persons who design or carry out response actions, other than the type of action described in sections 2643(f) and 2644(c) of this title, with respect to friable asbestos-containing material in such schools.

(B) The plan shall include a requirement that any person in a category listed in paragraph (1) achieve a passing grade on an examination and participate in continuing education to stay informed about current asbestos inspection and response action technology. The examination shall demonstrate the knowledge of the person in areas that the Administrator prescribes as necessary and appropriate in each of the categories. Such examinations may include requirements for knowledge in the following areas:

> (i) Recognition of asbestos-containing material and its physical characteristics.
>
> (ii) Health hazards of asbestos and the relationship between asbestos exposure and disease.
>
> (iii) Assessing the risk of asbestos exposure through a knowledge of percentage weight of asbestos-containing material, friability, age, deterioration, location and accessibility of materials, and advantages and disadvantages of dry and wet response action methods.
>
> (iv) Respirators and their use, care, selection, degree of protection afforded, fitting, testing, and maintenance and cleaning procedures.
>
> (v) Appropriate work practices and control methods, including the use of high efficiency particle absolute vacuums, the use of amended water, and principles of negative air pressure equipment use and procedures.
>
> (vi) Preparing a work area for response action work, including isolating work areas to prevent bystander or public exposure to asbestos, decontamination procedures, and procedures for dismantling work areas after completion of work.
>
> (vii) Establishing emergency procedures to respond to sudden releases.
>
> (viii) Air monitoring requirements and precedures.
>
> (ix) Medical surveillance program requirements.
>
> (x) Proper asbestos waste transportation and disposal procedures.
>
> (xi) Housekeeping and personal hygiene practices, including the

necessity of showers, and procedures to prevent asbestos exposure to an employee's family.

(2) Each State shall adopt a contractor accreditation plan at least as stringent as the model plan developed by the Administrator under paragraph (1), within 180 days after the commencement of the first regular session of the legislature of such State which is convened following the date on which the Administrator completes development of the model plan. In the case of a school operated under the defense dependents' education system provided for under the Defense Dependents' Education Act of 1978 (20 U.S.C. 921 et seq.), the Secretary of Defense shall adopt a contractor accreditation plan at least as stringent as that model.

(c)(1) Within 180 days after October 22, 1986, the Administrator shall ensure that any Environmental Protection Agency-approved asbestos training course is consistent with the model plan (including testing requirements) developed under subsection (b) of this section. A contractor may be accredited by taking and passing such a course.

(2) A person who —

(A) completed an Environmental Protection Agency-approved asbestos training course before October 22, 1986, and

(B) passed (or passes) an asbestos test either before or after October 22, 1986,

may be accredited under paragraph (1) if the Administrator determines that the course and test are equivalent to the requirements of the model plan developed under subsection (b) of this section. If the Administrator so determines, the person shall be considered accredited for the purposes of this subchapter until a date that is one year after the date on which the State in which such person is employed establishes an accreditation program pursuant to subsection (b) of this section.

(3) The Administrator, in consultation with affected organizations, shall publish (and revise as necessary) —

(A) a list of asbestos courses and tests in effect before October 22, 1986, which qualify for equivalency treatment under paragraph (2), and (B) a list of asbestos courses and tests which the Administrator determines under paragraph (1) are consistent with the model plan and which will qualify a contractor for accreditation under such paragraph.

(d)(1) The Administrator shall provide for the development of an accreditation program for laboratories by the National Bureau of Standards in accordance with paragraph (2). The Administrator shall transfer such funds as are necessary to the National Bureau of Standards to carry out such program.

(2) The National Bureau of Standards, upon request by the Administrator, shall in consultation with affected organizations —

> (A) within 360 days after October 22, 1986, develop an accreditation program for laboratories which conduct qualitative and semi-quantitative analyses of bulk samples of asbestos-containing material, and
>
> (B) within 720 days after October 22, 1986, develop an accreditation program for laboratories which conduct analyses of air samples of asbestos from school buildings under the authority of a local educational agency.

(3) A laboratory which plans to carry out any such analysis shall comply with the requirements of the accreditation program.

(e)(1) A school which is an applicant for financial assistance under section 505 of the Asbestos School Hazard Abatement Act of 1984 [20 U.S.C.A. §4011] is not eligible for such assistance unless the school, in carrying out the requirements of this subchapter —

> (A) uses a person (or persons) —
>
> > (i) who is accredited by a State which has adopted an accreditation plan based on the model plan developed under subsection (b) of this section, or
> >
> > (ii) who is accredited pursuant to an Administrator-approved course under subsection (c) of this section, and
>
> (B) uses a laboratory (or laboratories) which is accredited under the program developed under subsection (d) of this section.

(2) This subsection shall apply to any financial assistance provided under the Asbestos School Hazard Abatement Act of 1984 for activities performed after the following dates:

> (A) In the case of activities performed by persons, after the date which is one year after October 22, 1986.
>
> (B) In the case of activities performed by laboratories, after the date which is 180 days after the date on which a laboratory accreditation program is completed under subsection (d) of this section.

§ 2647. Enforcement

[Sec. 207] (a) Any local educational agency —

(1) which fails to conduct an inspection pursuant to regulations under section 2643(b) of this title or under section 2644(b) of this title,

(2) which knowingly submits false information to the Governor regarding any inspection pursuant to regulations under section 2643(i) of this title or knowingly includes false information in any inspection under section 2644(d)(3) of this title, or

(3) which fails to develop a management plan pursuant to regulations under section 2643(i) of this title or under section 2644(d) of this title,

is liable for a civil penalty of not more than $5,000 for each day during which the violation continues. Any civil penalty under this subsection shall be assessed and collected in the same manner, and subject to the same provisions, as in the case of civil penalties assessed and collected under section 2615 of this title. For purposes of this subsection, a "violation" means a failure to comply with respect to a single school building. The court shall order that any civil penalty collected under this subsection be used by the local educational agency for purposes of complying with this subchapter. Any portion of a civil penalty remaining unspent after compliance by a local educational agency is completed shall be deposited into the Asbestos Trust Fund established by section 5 of the Asbestos Emergency Response Act of 1986.

(b) A local educational agency is not liable for any civil penalty under subchapter I of this subchapter for failing or refusing to comply with any rule promulgated or order issued under this subchapter.

(c)(1) In determining the amount of a civil penalty to be assessed under subsection (a) of this section against a local educational agency, the Administrator shall consider—

  (A) the significance of the violation;
  (B) the culpability of the violator, including any history of previous violations under this chapter;
  (C) the ability of the violator to pay the penalty; and
  (D) the ability of the violator to continue to provide educational services to the community.

(2) Any action ordered by a court in fashioning relief under section 2619 of this title shall be consistent with regulations promulgated under section 2643 of this title (or with the requirements of section 2644 of this title if there are no regulations).

(d) Any person may file a complaint with the Administrator or with the Governor of the State in which the school building is located with respect to asbestos-containing material in a school building. If the Administrator or Governor receives a complaint under this subsection containing allegations which provide a reasonable basis to believe that a violation of this chapter has occurred, the Administrator or Governor shall investigate and respond (including taking enforcement action where appropriate) to the complaint within a reasonable period of time.

(e)(1) Any person may petition the Administrator to initiate a proceeding for the issuance, amendment, or repeal of a regulation or order under this subchapter.

  (2) Such petition shall be filed in the principal office of the Administrator and shall set forth the facts which it is claimed establish that it is necessary to issue, amend, or repeal a regulation or order under this subchapter.

  (3) The Administrator may hold a public hearing or may conduct such investigation or proceeding as the Administrator deems appropriate in order to determine whether or not such petition should be granted.

  (4) Within 90 days after filing of a petition described in paragraph (1), the Administrator shall either grant or deny the petition. If the

Administrator grants such petition, the Administrator shall promptly commence an appropriate proceeding in accordance with this sub-chapter. If the Administrator denies such petition, the Administrator shall publish in the Federal Register the Administrator's reasons for such denial. The granting or denial of a petition under this subsection shall not affect any deadline or other requirement of this subchapter.

(f)(1) Any person may commence a civil action without prior notice against the Administrator to compel the Administrator to meet the deadlines in section 2643 of this title for issuing advanced notices of proposed rulemaking, proposing regulations, and promulgating regulations. Any such action shall be brought in the district court of the United States for the District of Columbia.

(2) In any action brought under paragraph (1) in which the court finds the Administrator to be in violation of any deadline in section 2643 of this title, the court shall set forth a schedule for promulgating the regulations required by section 2643 of this title and shall order the Administrator to comply with such schedule. The court may extend any deadline (which has not already occurred) in section 2644(b), 2644(c), or 2644(d) of this title for a period of not more than 6 months, if the court-ordered schedule will result in final promulgation of the pertinent regulations within the extended period. Such deadline extensions may not be granted by the court beginning 720 days after October 22, 1986.

(3) Section 2619 of this title shall apply to civil actions described in this subsection, except to the extent inconsistent with this subsection.

§ 2648. Emergency authority

[Sec. 208] (a)(1) Whenever—

(A) the presence of airborne asbestos or the condition of friable asbestos-containing material in a school building governed by a local educational agency poses an imminent and substantial endangerment to human health or the environment, and

(B) the local educational agency is not taking sufficient action (as determined by the Administrator or the Governor) to respond to the airborne asbestos or friable asbestos-containing material,

the Administrator or the Governor of a State is authorized to act to protect human health or the environment.

(2) The Governor of a State shall notify the Administrator within a reasonable period of time before the Governor plans to take an emergency action under this subsection. After such notification, if the Administrator takes an emergency action with respect to the same hazard, the Governor may not carry out (or continue to carry out, if the action has been started) the emergency action.

(3) The following notification shall be provided before an emergency

action is taken under this subsection:

(A) In the case of a Governor taking the action, the Governor shall notify the local educational agency concerned.

(B) In the case of the Administrator taking the action, the Administrator shall notify both the local educational agency concerned and the Governor of the State in which such agency is located.

(4) The Administrator or the Governor of a State may seek reimbursement for all costs of an emergency action taken under this subsection in the United States District Court for the District of Columbia or for the district in which the emergency action occurred. In any action seeking reimbursement from a local educational agency, the action shall be brought in the United States District Court for the district in which the local educational agency is located.

(b) Upon receipt of evidence that the presence of airborne asbestos-containing material in a school building governed by a local educational agency poses an imminent and substantial endangerment to human health or the environment —

(1) the Administrator may request the Attorney General to bring suit, or

(2) the Governor of a State may bring suit,

to secure relief as may be necessary to respond to the hazard. The district in which the response will be carried out shall have jurisdiction to grant such relief, including injunctive relief.

§ 2649. Preemption

[Sec. 209] (a) Nothing in this subchapter shall be construed, interpreted, or applied to preempt, displace, or supplant any other State or Federal law, whether statutory or common.

(b) Nothing in this subchapter or any standard, regulation, or requirement promulgated pursuant to this subchapter shall be construed or interpreted to preclude any court from awarding costs and damages associated with the abatement, including the removal, of asbestos-containing material, or a portion of such costs, at any time prior to the actual date on which such material is removed.

(c) Nothing in this subchapter shall be construed or interpreted as preempting a State from establishing any additional liability or more stringent requirements with respect to asbestos in school buildings within such State.

(d) Nothing in this subchapter creates a cause of action or in any other way increases or diminishes the liability of any person under any other law.

(e) It is not the intent of Congress that this subchapter or rules, regulations, or orders issued pursuant to this subchapter be interpreted as influencing, in either the plaintiff's or defendant's favor, the disposition of any civil action for damages relating to asbestos. This subsection does not affect the authority of any court to make a determination in an adjudicatory proceeding under applicable State law with respect to the admission into evidence or any other use of this subchapter or rules, regulations, or orders issued pursuant to this subchapter.

§ 2650. Liability insurance for asbestos contractors and local educational agencies

[Sec. 210] (a)(1) The Administrator shall conduct a study on the availability of liability insurance and other forms of assurance against financial loss which are available to local educational agencies and asbestos contractors with respect to actions required under this subchapter. Such study shall examine the following:

(A) The extent to which liabilty insurance and other forms of assurance against financial loss are available to local educational agencies and asbsestos contractors.

(B) The extent to which the cost of insurance or other forms of assurance against financial loss has increased and the extent to which coverage has become less complete.

(C) The extent to which any limitation in the availability of insurance or other forms of assurance against financial loss is the result of factors other than standards of liability in applicable law.

(D) The extent to which the existence of the regulations required by subsections (c) and (d) of section 2643 of this title and the accreditation of contractors under section 2646 of this title has affected the availabilty or cost of insurance or other forms of assurance against financial loss.

(E) The extent to which any limitation on the availability of insurance or other forms of assurance against financial loss is inhibiting inspections for asbestos-containing material or the development or implementation of management plans under this subchapter.

(F) Identification of any other impediments to the timely completion of inspections or the development and implementation of management plans under this subchapter.

(2) Not later than April 1, 1988, the Administrator shall submit to the Congress an interim report on the progress of the study required by this subsection, along with preliminary findings based on information collected to that date.

(3) Not later than October 1, 1990, the Administrator shall submit to the Congress a final report on the study required by this subsection, including final findings based on the information collected.

(b) On the basis of the interim report or the final report of the study required by subsection (a) of this section, a State may enact or amend State law to establish or modify a standard of liability for local educational agencies or asbestos contractors with respect to actions required under this subchapter.

§ 2651. Discrimination by State or local educational agency

[Sec. 211] (a) No State or local educational agency may discriminate against a person in any way, including firing a person who is an employee, because the person provided information relating to a potential violation of this subchapter to any other person, including a State or the Federal Government.

(b) Any public or private employee or representative of employees who believes he or she has been fired or otherwise discriminated against in violation of subsection (a) of this section may within 90 days after the alleged violation occurs apply to the Secretary of Labor for a review of the firing or alleged discrimination. The review shall be conducted in accordance with section 660(c) of Title 29.

§ 2652. Asbestos Ombudsman

[Sec. 212] (a) The Administrator shall appoint an Asbestos Ombudsman, who shall carry out the duties described in subsection (b) of this section.

(b) The duties of the Asbestos Ombudsman are—
(1) to receive complaints, grievances, and requests for information submitted by any person with respect to any aspect of this subchapter,
(2) to render assistance with respect to the complaints, grievances, and requests received, and
(3) to make such recommendations to the Administrator as the Ombudsman considers appropriate.

§ 2653. Study of asbestos-containing material in public buildings

[Sec. 213] Within 360 days after October 22, 1986, the Administrator shall conduct and submit to the Congress the results of a study which shall—
(1) assess the extent to which asbestos-containing materials are present in public and commercial buildings;
(2) assess the condition of asbestos-containing material in commercial buildings and the likelihood that persons occupying such buildings, including service and maintenance personnel, are, or may be, exposed to asbestos fibers;
(3) consider and report on whether public and commercial buildings should be subject to the same inspection and response action requirements that apply to school buildings;
(4) assess whether existing Federal regulations adequately protect the general public, particularly abatement personnel, from exposure to asbestos during renovation and demolition of such buildings; and
(5) include recommendations that explicitly address whether there is a

need to establish standards for, and regulate asbestos exposure in, public and commercial buildings.

§ 2654. Transitional rules

[Sec. 214] Any regulation of the Environmental Protection Agency under subchapter I of this chapter which is inconsistent with this subchapter shall not be in effect after October 22, 1986. Any advanced notice of proposed rulemaking, any proposed rule, and any regulation of the Environmental Protection Agency in effect before October 22, 1986 which is consistent with the regulations required under section 2643 of this title shall remain in effect and may be used to meet the requirements of section 2643 of this title, except that any such regulation shall be enforced under this chapter.

4 • Federal Insecticide, Fungicide, and Rodenticide Act

INTRODUCTION

Initial federal efforts to regulate pesticides began in 1910, with the enactment of what was largely a labeling law intended to prevent the distribution of adulterated or misbranded products. The first pesticide control law was enacted in 1947 and required that pesticide products be registered with the Department of Agriculture. In cases where registration was denied, the manufacturer could still market the product after filing a protest. Although jurisdiction for administering the law first was placed with the Agriculture Department, it was passed to the Environmental Protection Agency (EPA) when that agency was created in 1970.

In 1954, the Food and Drug Administration (FDA) was given authority to establish pesticide residue tolerances—allowable limits for pesticide residues on food and on animal feed. This system has grown into a complicated cooperative scheme under which FDA sets pesticide limits for processed foods, the Department of Agriculture sets limits for edible portions of meat, and the Environmental Protection Agency sets limits for raw, unprocessed meat and agricultural products.

The basic format of the Federal Insecticide, Fungicide, and Rodenticide Act (FIFRA) was conceived in 1972, when Congress created the pesticide regulatory statute as it exists today (PL 92–516). Under the law, no manufacturer or importer may make or sell a product for use to control pests unless the compound is registered with EPA. About 40,000 such products have been registered with the agency, but they contain only about 600 distinct active ingredients.

Congress also required that all pesticides registered before 1972 be reregistered by EPA so that the agency could obtain current toxicological, health, and environmental effects data. Amendments adopted in 1975 tempered some of the reregistration provisions and required EPA to submit proposed pesticide cancellations to a scientific review panel. Additional amendments enacted in 1978 allowed the agency to group products by active ingredients and reregister the products on a generic rather than individual product basis.

Although a number of cancellations followed the 1972 amendments, the agency still is struggling with the reregistration program. Critics say FIFRA needs revision in several areas—most notably in increasing the speed with which EPA reregisters existing pesticides, in expanding the degree to which EPA involves the public in its regulatory process, and revising the way in which it restricts the use of products that officials determine pose potential hazard to people and the environment.

Another area of concern is the statutory scheme for indemnifying manufacturers when previously approved products are pulled off the market through emergency suspensions followed by cancellation of their registrations. Agency officials admitted during 1987 that the cost of indemnification for dinoseb, suspended in October 1986, and other products sometimes affects their decisions about suspending registrations of harmful chemicals.

Critics of FIFRA noted that by mid-1987, EPA had completed its review of only two active ingredients and issued interim registration standards for only 150 of the approximately 600 ingredients needing re-evaluation. With the reviews slated to continue well into the 21st century and regulatory and financial resources being diverted to pay for indemnification of recently canceled products, EPA stepped up its campaign for Congress to repeal the indemnification provision and speed up reregistration. States, meanwhile, began to implement their own pesticide control programs, giving chemical and food industry groups cause to complain about a developing "patchwork quilt" of regulations.

However, the law is so complicated and the interest groups involved in the reauthorization debate are so varied that many observers give the law only 50-50 odds for revision in the 100th Congress. A congressional aide involved in rewriting the statute told food industry representatives in September 1987 that if FIFRA is not reauthorized by March 1988, the presidential election and the need for a new administration to come up to speed on the issues would keep the legislation from being enacted until 1990. By then, he predicted, states will have rewritten pesticide regulatory policy for the federal government by approving 50 different sets of laws and regulations to restrict and ban pesticides.

The danger of such a scenario, according to John A. Moore, EPA assistant administrator for pesticides and toxic substances, is that state governments and legislatures do not have the scientific expertise or the resources to properly examine the real dangers pesticides pose. Moore said he sees salvation in a rewritten FIFRA, which could disentangle the federal agency from the lengthy legal battles it must fight almost every time it moves to control a pesticide under the current statute.

Federal Insecticide, Fungicide, and Rodenticide Act

(P.L. 92–516, approved October 21, 1972; as last amended by P.L. 98–620, approved November 8, 1984)

Subchapter I. Insecticides

§§ 121–134. Repealed

Subchapter II. Environmental Pesticide Control

§ 136. Definitions

[Sec. 2] For purposes of this Act—
(a) The term "active ingredient" means—
(1) in the case of a pesticide other than a plant regulator, defoliant, or desiccant, an ingredient which will prevent, destroy, repel, or mitigate any pest;
(2) in the case of a plant regulator, an ingredient which, through physiological action, will accelerate or retard the rate of growth or rate of maturation or otherwise alter the behavior of ornamental or crop plants or the product thereof;
(3) in the case of a defoliant, an ingredient which will cause the leaves or foliage to drop from a plant; and
(4) in the case of a desiccant, an ingredient which will artificially accelerate the drying of plant tissue.
(b) The term "Administrator" means the Administrator of the Environmental Protection Agency.
(c) The term "adulterated" applies to any pesticide if:
(1) its strength or purity falls below the professed standard of quality as expressed on its labeling under which it is sold;
(2) any substance has been substituted wholly or in part for the pesticide; or
(3) any valuable constituent of the pesticide has been wholly or in part abstracted.

(d) The term "animal" means all vertebrate and invertibrate species, including but not limited to man and other mammals, birds, fish, and shellfish.

(e)(1) The term "certified applicator" means any individual who is certified under section 4 as authorized to use or supervise the use of any pesticide which is classified for restricted use. Any applicator who holds or applies registered pesticides, or use dilutions of registered pesticides consistent with section 2(ee) of this Act, only to provide a service of controlling pests without delivering any unapplied pesticide to any person so served is not deemed to be a seller or distributor of pesticides under this Act.

(2) The term "private applicator" means a certified applicator who uses or supervises the use of any pesticide which is classified for restricted use for purposes of producing any agricultural commodity on property owned or rented by him or his employer or (if applied without compensation other than trading of personal services between producers of agricultural commodities) on the property of another person.

(3) The term "commercial applicator" means an applicator (whether or not he is a private applicator with respect to some uses) who uses or supervises the use of any pesticide which is classified for restricted use for any purpose or on any property other than as provided by paragraph (2).

(4) Unless otherwise prescribed by its labeling, a pesticide shall be considered to be applied under the direct supervision of a certified applicator if it is applied by a competent person acting under the instructions and control of a certified applicator who is available if and when needed, even though such certified applicator is not physically present at the time and place the pesticide is applied.

(f) The term "defoliant" means any substance or mixture of substances intended for causing the leaves or foliage to drop from a plant, with or without causing abscission.

(g) The term "desiccant" means any substance or mixture of substances intended for artificially accelerating the drying of plant tissue.

(h) The term "device" means any instrument or contrivance (other than a firearm) which is intended for trapping, destroying, repelling, or mitigating any pest or any other form of plant or animal life (other than man and other than bacteria, virus, or other microorganism on or in living man or other living animals); but not including equipment used for the application of pesticides when sold separately therefrom.

(i) The term "district court" means a United States district court, the District Court of Guam, the District Court of the Virgin Islands, and the highest court of American Samoa.

(j) The term "environment" includes water, air, land, and all plants and man and other animals living therein, and the interrelationships which exist among these.

(k) The term "fungus" means any non-chlorophyll-bearing thallophyte (that is, any non-chlorophyll-bearing plant of a lower order than mosses and liverworts), as for example, rust, smut, mildew, mold, yeast, and bacteria, except those on or in living man or other animals and those on or in processed food, beverages, or pharmaceuticals.

(l) The term "imminent hazard" means a situation which exists when the continued use of a pesticide during the time required for cancellation proceeding would be likely to result in unreasonable adverse effects on the environment or will involve unreasonable hazard to the survival of a species declared endangered by the Secretary of the Interior under Public Law 91–135.

(m) The term "inert ingredient" means an ingredient which is not active.

(n) The term "ingredient statement" means a statement which contains—

(1) the name and percentage of each active ingredient, and the total percentage of all inert ingredients, in the pesticide; and

(2) if the pesticide contains arsenic in any form, a statement of the percentages of total and water soluble arsenic, calculated as elementary arsenic.

(o) The term "insect" means any of the numerous small invertebrate animals generally having the body more or less obviously segmented, for the most part belonging to the class insecta, comprising six-legged, usually winged forms, as for example, beetles, bugs, bees, flies, and to other allied classes of arthropods whose members are wingless and usually have more than six legs, as for example, spiders, mites, ticks, centipedes, and wood lice.

(p)(1) The term "label" means the written, printed, or graphic matter on, or attached to, the pesticide or device or any of its containers or wrappers.

(2) The term "labeling" means all labels and all other written, printed, or graphic matter—

(A) accompanying the pesticide or device at any time; or

(B) to which reference is made on the label or in literature accompanying the pesticide or device, except to current official publications of the Environmental Protection Agency, the United States Departments of Agriculture and Interior, the Department of Health, Education, and Welfare, State experiment stations, State agricultural colleges, and other similar Federal or State institutions or agencies authorized by law to conduct research in the field of pesticides.

(q)(1) A pesticide is misbranded if—

(A) its labeling bears any statement, design, or graphic representation relative thereto or to its ingredients which is false or misleading in any particular;

(B) it is contained in a package or other container or wrapping which does not conform to the standards established by the Administrator pursuant to section 25(c)(3);

(C) it is an imitation of, or is offered for sale under the name of, another pesticide;

(D) its label does not bear the registration number assigned under section 7 to each establishment in which it was produced;

(E) any word, statement, or other information required by or under authority of this Act to appear on the label or labeling is not prominently placed thereon with such conspicuousness (as compared with other words, statements, designs, or graphic matter in the labeling) and in such terms as to render it likely to be read and understood by the ordinary individual under customary conditions of purchase and use;

(F) the labeling accompanying it does not contain directions for use which are necessary for effecting the purpose for which the product is intended and if complied with, together with any requirements imposed under section 3(d) of this Act, are adequate to protect health and the environment;

(G) the label does not contain a warning or caution statement which may be necessary and if complied with, together with any requirements imposed under section 3(d) of this Act, is adequate to protect health and the environment; or

(H) in the case of a pesticide not registered in accordance with section 3 of this Act and intended for export, the label does not contain, in words prominently placed thereon with such conspicuousness (as compared with other words, statements, designs, or graphic matter in the labeling) as to render it likely to be noted by the ordinary individual under customary conditions of purchase and use, the following: "Not Registered for Use in the United States of America."

(2) A pesticide is misbranded if—

(A) the label does not bear an ingredient statement on that part of the immediate container (and on the outside container or wrapper of the retail package, if there be one, through which the ingredient statement on the immediate container cannot be clearly read) which is presented or displayed under customary conditions of purchase, except that a pesticide is not misbranded under this subparagraph if:

(i) the size of form of the immediate container, or the outside container or wrapper of the retail package, makes it impracticable to place the ingredient statement on the part which is presented or displayed under customary conditions of purchase; and

(ii) the ingredient statement appears prominently on another part of the immediate container, or outside container or wrapper, permitted by the Administrator;

(B) the labeling does not contain a statement of the use classification under which the product is registered;

(C) there is not affixed to its container, and to the outside container or wrapper of the retail package, if there be one, through which the required information on the immediate container cannot be clearly read, a label bearing—

    (i) the name and address of the producer, registrant, or person for whom produced;

    (ii) the name, brand, or trademark under which the pesticide is sold;

    (iii) the net weight or measure of the content: *Provided,* That the Administrator may permit reasonable variations; and

    (iv) when required by regulation of the Administrator to effectuate the purposes of this Act, the registration number assigned to the pesticide under this Act, and the use classification; and

  (D) the pesticide contains any substance or substances in quantities highly toxic to man, unless the label shall bear, in addition to any other matter required by this Act—

    (i) the skull and crossbones;

    (ii) the word "poison" prominently in red on a background of distinctly contrasting color; and

    (iii) a statement of a practical treatment (first aid or otherwise) in case of poisoning by the pesticide.

(r) The term "nematode" means invertebrate animals of the phylum nemathelminthes and class nematoda, that is, unsegmented round worms with elongated, fusiform, or saclike bodies covered with cuticle, and inhabiting soil, water, plants, or plant parts; may also be called nemas or eelworms.

(s) The term "person" means any individual, partnership, association, corporation, or any organized group of persons whether incorporated or not.

(t) The term "pest" means (1) any insect, rodent, nematode, fungus, weed, or (2) any other form of terrestrial or aquatic plant or animal life or virus, bacteria, or other micro-organism (except viruses, bacteria, or other microorganisms on or in living man or other living animals) which the Administrator declares to be a pest under section 25(c)(1).

(u) The term "pesticide" means (1) any substance or mixture of substances intended for preventing, destroying, repelling, or mitigating any pest, and (2) substance or mixture of substances intended for use as a plant regulator, defoliant, or desiccant: *Provided,* That the term "pesticide" shall not include any article (1)(a) that is a "new animal drug" within the meaning of section 201(w) of the Federal Food, Drug, and Cosmetic Act (21 U.S.C. 321(w)), or (b) that has been determined by the Secretary of Health, Education, and Welfare not to be a new animal drug by a regulation establishing conditions of use for the article, or (2) that is an animal feed within the meaning of section 201(x) of such Act (21 U.S.C. 321(x)) bearing or containing an article covered by clause (1) of this proviso.

(v) The term "plant regulator" means any substance or mixture of substances intended, through physiological action, for accelerating or retarding the rate of growth or rate of maturation, or for otherwise altering the behavior of plants or the produce thereof, but shall not include substances to the extent that they are intended as plant nutrients, trace elements, nutritional chemicals, plant inoculants, and soil amendments. Also, the term "plant regulator" shall not be required to include any of such of those nutrient mixtures or soil amendments as are commonly known as vitamin-hormone horticultural products, intended for improvement, maintenance, survival, health, and propagation of plants, and as are not for pest destruction and are nontoxic, nonpoisonous in the undiluted packaged concentration.

(w) The term "producer" means the person who manufactures, prepares, compounds, propagates, or processes any pesticide or device or active ingredient used in producing a pesticide. The term "produce" means to manufacture, prepare, compound, propagate, or process any pesticide or device or active ingredient used in producing a pesticide. The dilution by individuals of formulated pesticides for their own use and according to the directions on registered labels shall not of itself result in such individuals being included in the definition of "producer" for the purposes of this Act.

(x) The terms "protect health and the environment" and "protection of health and the environment" mean protection against any unreasonable adverse effects on the environment.

(y) The term "registrant" means a person who has registered any pesticide pursuant to the provisions of this Act.

(z) The term "registration" includes reregistration.

(aa) The term "State" means a State, the District of Columbia, the Commonwealth of Puerto Rico, the Virgin Islands, Guam, the Trust Territory of the Pacific Islands, and American Samoa.

(bb) The term "unreasonable adverse effects on the environment" means any unreasonable risk to man or the environment, taking into account the economic, social, and environmental costs and benefits of the use of any pesticide.

(cc) The term "weed" means any plant which grows where not wanted.

(dd) The term "establishment" means any place where a pesticide or device or active ingredient used in producing a pesticide is produced, or held, for distribution or sale.

(ee) The term "to use any registered pesticide in a manner inconsistent with its labeling" means to use any registered pesticide in a manner not permitted by the labeling: *Provided*, That the term shall not include (1) applying a pesticide at any dosage, concentration, or frequency less than that specified on the labeling, (2) applying a pesticide against any target pest not specified on the labeling if the application is to the crop, animal, or site specified on the labeling, unless the Administrator has required that the labeling specifically state that the pesticide may be used only for the pests specified on the labeling after the Administrator has determined that the use of the pesticide against other pests would cause an unreasonable adverse effect on the environment, (3) employing any method of application not prohibited by the labeling, or (4) mixing a pesticide or pesticides with a fertilizer when such mixture is not prohibited by the labeling: *Provided further*, That the term also shall not include any use of a pesticide in conformance with section 5, 18, or 24 of this Act, or any use of a pesticide in a manner that the Administrator determines to be consistent with the purposes of this Act: *And provided further*, That after March 31, 1979, the term shall not include the use of a pesticide for agricultural or forestry purposes at a dilution less than label dosage unless before or after that date the Administrator issues a regulation or advisory opinion consistent with the study provided for in section 27(b) of the Federal Pesticide Act of 1978, which regulation or advisory opinion specifically requires the use of definite amounts of dilution.

§ 136a. Registration of pesticides

[Sec. 3] (a) Except as otherwise provided by this Act, no person in any State may distribute, sell, offer for sale, hold for sale, ship, deliver for shipment, or receive and (having so received) deliver or offer to deliver, to any person any pesticide which is not registered with the Administrator.

(b) A pesticide which is not registered with the Administrator may be transferred if—

(1) the transfer is from one registered establishment to another registered establishment operated by the same producer solely for packaging at the second establishment or for use as a constituent part of another pesticide produced at the second establishment; or

(2) the transfer is pursuant to and in accordance with the requirements of an experimental use permit.

(c)(1) Each applicant for registration of a pesticide shall file with the Administrator a statement which includes—

(A) the name and address of the applicant and of any other person whose name will appear on the labeling;

(B) the name of the pesticide;

(C) a complete copy of the labeling of the pesticide, a statement of all claims to be made for it, and any directions for its use;

(D) except as otherwise provided in subsection (c)(2)(D) of this section, if requested by the Administrator, a full description of the tests made and the results thereof upon which the claims are based, or alternatively a citation to data that appear in the public literature or that previously had been submitted to the Administrator and that the Administrator may consider in accordance with the following provisions:

(i) With respect to pesticides containing active ingredients that are initially registered under this Act after the date of enactment of the Federal Pesticide Act of 1978, data submitted to support the application for the original registration of the pesticide, or an application for an amendment adding any new use to the registration and that pertains solely to such new use, shall not, without the written permission of the original data submitter, be considered by the Administrator to support an application by another person during a period of ten years following the date the Administrator first registers the pesticide: *Provided*, That such permission shall not be required in the case of defensive data;

(ii) except as otherwise provided in subparagraph (D)(i) of this paragraph, with respect to data submitted after December 31, 1969, by an applicant or registrant to support an application for registration, experimental use permit, or amendment adding a new use to an existing registration, to support or maintain in effect an existing registration, or for reregistration, the Administrator may, without the permission of the original data submitter, consider any such item of data in support of an application by any other person (hereinafter in this subparagraph referred to as the "applicant") within the fifteen-year period following the date the data were originally submitted only if the applicant has made an offer to compensate the original data submitter and submitted such offer to the Administrator accompanied by evidence of delivery to the original data submitter of the offer. The terms and amount of compensation may be fixed by agreement between the original data submitter and the applicant, or, failing such agreement, binding arbitration under this subparagraph. If, at the end of ninety days after the date of delivery to the original data submitter of the offer to compensate, the original data submitter and the applicant have neither agreed on the amount and terms of compensation nor on a procedure for reaching an agreement on the amount and terms of compensation, either person may initiate binding arbitration proceedings by requesting the Federal Mediation and Conciliation Service to appoint an arbitrator from the roster of arbitrators maintained by such Service. The procedure and rules of the Service shall be applicable to the selection of such arbitrator and to such arbitration proceedings, and the findings and determination of the arbitrator shall be final and conclusive, and no official or court of the United States shall have power or jurisdiction to review any such findings and determination, except for fraud, misrepresentation, or other misconduct by one of the parties to the arbitration or the arbitrator where there is a verified complaint with supporting affidavits attesting to specific instances of such fraud, misrepresentation, or other misconduct. The parties to the arbitration shall share equally in the payment of the fee and expenses of the arbitrator. If the Administrator determines that an original data submitter has failed to participate in a procedure for reaching an agreement or in an arbitration proceeding as required by this subparagraph, or failed to comply with the terms of an agreement or arbitration decision concerning compensation under this subparagraph, the original data submitter shall forfeit the right to compensation for the use of the data in support of the application. Notwithstanding any other provision of this Act, if the Administrator determines that an applicant has failed to participate in a procedure for reaching an agreement or in an arbitration proceeding as required by this subparagraph, or failed to comply with the terms of an agreement or arbitration decision concerning compensation under this subparagraph, the Administrator shall deny the application or cancel the registration of the pesticide in support of which the data were used without further hearing. Before the Administrator takes action under either of the preceding two sentences, the Administrator shall furnish to the affected person, by certified mail, notice of intent to take action and allow fifteen days from the date of delivery of the notice for the affected person to respond. If a registration is denied or canceled under this subparagraph, the Administrator may make such order as the Administrator deems appropriate concerning the continued sale and use of existing stocks of such pesticide. Registration action by the Administrator shall not be delayed pending the fixing of compensation;

(iii) after expiration of any period of exclusive use and any period for which compensation is required for the use of an item of data under subparagraphs (D)(i) and (D)(ii) of this paragraph, the Administrator may consider such item of data in support of an application by any other applicant without the permission of the original data submitter and without an offer having been received to compensate the original data submitter for the use of such item of data;

(E) the complete formula of the pesticide; and

(F) request that the pesticide be classified for general use, for restricted use or for both.

(2)(A) The Administrator shall publish guidelines specifying the kinds of information which will be required to support the registration of a pesticide and shall revise such guidelines from time to time. If thereafter he requires any additional kind of information under subparagraph (B) of this paragraph, he shall permit sufficient time for applicants to obtain such additional information. The Administrator, in establishing standards for data requirements for the registration of pesticides with respect to minor uses, shall make such standards commensurate with the anticipated extent of use, pattern of use, and the level and degree of potential exposure of man and the environment to the pesticide. In the development of these standards, the Administrator shall consider the economic factors of potential national volume of use, extent of distribution, and the impact of the cost of meeting the requirements on the incentives for any potential registrant to undertake the development of the required data. Except as provided by section 10, within 30 days after the Administrator registers a pesticide under this Act he shall make available to the public the data called for in the registration statement together with such other scientific information as he deems relevant to his decision.

(B)(i) If the Administrator determines that additional data are required to maintain in effect an existing registration of a pesticide, the Administrator shall notify all existing registrants of the pesticide to which the determination relates and provide a list of such registrants to any interested person.

(ii) Each registrant of such pesticide shall provide evidence within ninety days after receipt of notification that it is taking appropriate steps to secure the additional data that are required. Two or more registrants may agree to develop jointly, or to share in the cost of developing, such data if they agree and advise the Administrator of their intent within ninety days after notification. Any registrant who agrees to share in the cost of producing the data shall be entitled to examine and rely upon such data in support of maintenance of such registration.

(iii) If, at the end of sixty days after advising the Administrator of their agreement to develop jointly, or share in the cost of developing, data, the registrants have not further agreed on the terms of the data development arrangement or on a procedure for reaching such agreement, any of such registrants may initiate binding arbitration proceedings by requesting the Federal Mediation and Conciliation Service to appoint an arbitrator from the roster of arbitrators maintained by such Service. The procedure and rules of the Service shall be applicable to the selection of such arbitrator and to such arbitration proceedings, and the findings and determination of the arbitrator shall be final and conclusive, and no official or court of the United States shall have power or jurisdiction to review any such findings and determination, except for fraud, misrepresentation, or other misconduct by one of the parties to the arbitration or the arbitrator where there is a verified complaint with supporting affidavits attesting to specific instances of such fraud, misrepresentation, or other misconduct. All parties to the arbitration shall share equally in the payment of the fee and expenses of the arbitrator.

(iv) Notwithstanding any other provision of this Act, if the Administrator determines that a registrant, within the time required by the Administrator, has failed to take appropriate steps to secure the data required under this subparagraph, to participate in a procedure for reaching agreement concerning a joint data development arrangement under this subparagraph or in an arbitration proceeding as required by this subparagraph, or to comply with the terms of an agreement or arbitration decision concerning a joint data development arrangement under this subparagraph, the Administrator may issue a notice of intent to suspend such registrant's registration of the pesticide for which additional data is required. The Administrator may include in the notice of intent to suspend such provisions as the Administrator deems appropriate concerning the continued sale and use of existing stocks of such pesticide. Any suspension proposed under this subparagraph shall become final and effective at the end of thirty days from receipt by the registrant of the notice of intent to suspend, unless during that time a request for hearing is made by a person adversely affected by the notice or the registrant has satisfied the Administrator that the registrant has complied fully with the requirements that served as a basis for the notice of intent to suspend. If a hearing is requested, a hearing shall be conducted under section 6(d) of this Act: *Provided,* That the only matters for resolution at that hearing shall be whether the registrant has failed to take the action that served as the basis for the notice of intent to suspend the registration of the pesticide for which additional data is required, and whether the Administrator's determination with respect to the disposition of existing stocks is consistent with this Act. If a hearing is held, a decision after completion of such hearing shall be final. Notwithstanding any other provision of this Act, a hearing shall be held and a determination made within seventy-five days after receipt of a request for such hearing. Any registration suspended under this subparagraph shall be reinstated by the Administrator if the Administrator determines that the registrant has complied fully with the requirements that served as a basis for the suspension of the registration.

(v) Any data submitted under this subparagraph shall be subject to the provisions of subsection (c)(1)(D) of this section. Whenever such data are submitted jointly by two or more registrants, an agent shall be agreed on at the time of the joint submission to handle any subsequent data compensation matters for the joint submitters of such data.

(C) Within nine months after the date of enactment of this subparagraph, the Administrator shall, by regulation, prescribe simplified procedures for the registration of pesticides, which shall include the provisions of subparagraph (D) of this paragraph.

(D) No applicant for registration of a pesticide who proposes to purchase a registered pesticide from another producer in order to formulate such purchased pesticide into an end-use product shall be required to—

  (i) submit or cite data pertaining to the safety of such purchased product; or

  (ii) offer to pay reasonable compensation otherwise required by paragraph (1)(D) of this subsection for the use of any such data.

(3) The Administrator shall review the data after receipt of the application and shall, as expeditiously as possible, either register the pesticide in accordance with paragraph (5), or notify the applicant of his determination that it does not comply with the provisions of the Act in accordance with paragraph (6).

(4) The Administrator shall publish in the Federal Register, promptly after receipt of the statement and other data required pursuant to paragraphs (1) and (2), a notice of each application for registration of any pesticide if it contains any new active ingredient or if it would entail a changed use pattern. The notice shall provide for a period of 30 days in which any Federal agency or any other interested person may comment.

(5) The Administrator shall register a pesticide if he determines that, when considered with any restrictions imposed under subsection (d)—

(A) its composition is such as to warrant the proposed claims for it;

(B) its labeling and other material required to be submitted comply with the requirements of this Act;

(C) it will perform its intended function without unreasonable adverse effects on the environment; and

(D) when used in accordance with widespread and commonly recognized practice it will not generally cause unreasonable adverse effects on the environment.

The Administrator shall not make any lack of essentiality a criterion for denying registration of any pesticide. Where two pesticides meet the requirements of this paragraph, one should not be registered in preference to the other. In considering an application for the registration of a pesticide, the Administrator may waive data requirements pertaining to efficacy, in which event the Administrator may register the pesticide without determining that the pesticide's composition is such as to warrant proposed claims of efficacy. If a pesticide is found to be efficacious by any State under section 24(c) of this Act, a presumption is established that the Administrator shall waive data requirements pertaining to efficacy for use of the pesticide in such State.

(6) If the Administrator determines that the requirements of paragraph (5) for registration are not satisfied, he shall notify the applicant for registration of his determination and of his reasons (including the factual basis) therefor, and that, unless the applicant corrects the conditions and notifies the Administrator thereof during the 30-day period beginning with the day after the date on which the applicant receives the notice, the Administrator may refuse to register the pesticide. Whenever the Administrator refuses to register a pesticide, he shall notify the applicant of his decision and of his reasons (including the factual basis) therefor. The Administrator shall promptly publish in the Federal Register notice of such denial of registration and the reasons therefor. Upon such notification, the applicant for registration or other interested person with the concurrence of the applicant shall have the same remedies as provided for in section 6.

(7) Notwithstanding the provisions of subsection (c)(5) of this section—

(A) The Administrator may conditionally register or amend the registration of a pesticide if the Administrator determines that (i) the pesticide and proposed use are identical or substantially similar to any currently registered pesticide and use thereof, or differ only in ways that would not significantly increase the risk of unreasonable adverse effects on the environment, and (ii) approving the registration or amendment in the manner proposed by the applicant would not significantly increase the risk of any unreasonable adverse effect on the environment. An applicant seeking conditional registration or amended registration under this subparagraph shall submit such data as would be required to obtain registration of a similar pesticide under subsection (c)(5) of this section: *Provided*, That, if the applicant is unable to submit an item of data because it has not yet been generated, the Administrator may register or amend the registration of the pesticide under such conditions as will require the submission of such data not later than the time such data are required to be submitted with respect to similar pesticides already registered under this Act.

(B) The Administrator may conditionally amend the registration of a pesticide to permit additional uses of such pesticide notwithstanding that data concerning the pesticide may be insufficient to support an unconditional amendment, if the Administrator determines that (i) the applicant has submitted satisfactory data pertaining to the proposed additional use, and (ii) amending the registration in the manner proposed by the applicant would not significantly increase the risk of any unreasonable adverse effect on the environment. Notwithstanding the foregoing provisions of this subparagraph, no registration of a pesticide may be amended to permit an additional use of such pesticide if the Administrator has issued a notice stating that such pesticide, or any ingredient thereof, meets or exceeds risk criteria associated in whole or in part with human dietary exposure enumerated in regulations issued under this Act, and during the pendency of any risk-benefit evaluation initiated by such notice, if (I) the additional use of such pesticide involves a major food or feed crop, or ((II) the additional use of such pesticide involves a minor food or feed crop and the Administrator determines, with the concurrence of the Secretary of Agriculture, there is available an effective alternative pesticide that does not meet or exceed such risk criteria. An applicant seeking amended registration under this subparagraph shall submit such data as would be required to obtain registration of a similar pesticide under subsection (c)(5) of this section: *Provided*, That, if the applicant is unable to submit an item of data (other than data pertaining to the proposed additional use) because it has not yet been generated, the Administrator may amend the registration under such conditions as will require the submission of such data not later than the time such data are required to be submitted with respect to similar pesticides already registered under this Act.

(C) The Administrator may conditionally register a pesticide containing an active ingredient not contained in any currently registered pesticide for a period reasonably sufficient for generation and submission of required data (which are lacking because a period reasonably sufficient for generation of the data has not elapsed since the Administrator first imposed the data requirement) on the condition that by the end of such period the Administrator receives such data and the data do not meet or exceed risk criteria enumerated in regulations issued under this Act, and on such other conditions as the Administrator may prescribe: *Provided*, That a conditional registration under this subparagraph shall be granted only if the Administrator determines that use of the pesticide during such period will not cause any unreasonable adverse effect on the environment, and that use of the pesticides in the public interest.

(8) Notwithstanding any other provision of this Act, the Administrator may not initiate a public interim administrative review process to develop a risk-benefit evaluation of the ingredients of a pesticide or any of its uses prior to initiating a formal action to cancel, suspend, or deny registration of such pesticide, required under this Act, unless such interim administrative process is based on a validated test or other significant evidence raising prudent concerns of unreasonable

adverse risk to man or to the environment. Notice of the definition of the terms "validated test" and "other significant evidence" as used herein shall be published by the Administrator in the Federal Register.

(d)(1)(A) As a part of the registration of a pesticide the Administrator shall classify it as being for general use or for restricted use, provided that if the Administrator determines that some of the uses for which the pesticide is registered should be for general use and that other uses for which it is registered should be for restricted use, he shall classify it for both general use and restricted use. Pesticide uses may be classified by regulation on the initial classification, and registered pesticides may be classified prior to registration. If some of the uses of the pesticide are classified for general use and other uses are classified for restricted use, the direction relating to its general uses shall be clearly separated and distinguished from those directions relating to its restricted uses: *Provided, however*, That the Administrator may require that its packaging and labeling for restricted uses shall be clearly distinguishable from its packaging and labeling for general uses.

(B) If the Administrator determines that the pesticide, when applied in accordance with its directions for use, warnings and cautions and for the uses for which it is registered, or for one or more of such uses, or in accordance with a widespread and commonly recognized practice, will not generally cause unreasonable adverse effects on the environment, he will classify the pesticide, or the particular use or uses of the pesticide to which the determination applies, for general use.

(C) If the Administrator determines that the pesticide, when applied in accordance with its directions for use, warnings and cautions and for the uses for which it is registered, or for one or more of such uses, or in accordance with a widespread and commonly recognized practice, may generally cause, without additional regulatory restrictions, unreasonable adverse effects on the environment, including injury to the applicator, he shall classify the pesticide, or the particular use or uses to which the determination applies, for restricted use:

(i) If the Administrator classifies a pesticide, or one or more uses of such pesticide, for restricted use because of a determination that the acute dermal or inhalation toxicity of the pesticide presents a hazard to the applicator or other persons, the pesticide shall be applied for any use to which the restricted classification applies only by or under the direct supervision of a certified applicator.

(ii) If the Administrator classifies a pesticide, or one or more uses of such pesticide, for restricted use because of a determination that its use without additional regulatory restriction may cause unreasonable adverse effects on the environment, the pesticide shall be applied for any use to which the determination applies only by or under the direct supervision of a certified applicator, or subject to such other restrictions as the Administrator may provide by regulation. Any such regulation shall be reviewable in the appropriate court of appeals upon petition of a person adversely affected filed within 60 days of the publication of the regulation in final form.

(2) If the Administrator determines that a change in the classification of any use of a pesticide from general use to restricted use is necessary to prevent unreasonable adverse effects on the environment, he shall notify the registrant of such pesticide of such determination at least forty-five days before making the change and shall publish the proposed change in the Federal Register. The registrant, or other interested person with the concurrence of the registrant, may seek relief from such determination under section 6(b).

(3) The registrant of any pesticide with one or more uses classified for restricted use may petition the Administrator to change any such classification from restricted to general use. Such petition shall set out the basis for the registrant's position that restricted use classification is unnecessary because classification of the pesticide for general use would not cause unreasonable adverse effects on the environment. The Administrator, within sixty days after receiving such petition, shall notify the registrant whether the petition has been granted or denied. Any denial shall contain an explanation therefor and any such denial shall be subject to judicial review under section 16 of this Act.

(e) Products which have the same formulation, are manufactured by the same person, the labeling of which contains the same claims, and the labels of which bear a designation identifying the product as the same pesticide may be registered as a single pesticide; and additional names and labels shall be added to the registration by supplemental statements.

(f)(1) If the labeling or formulation for a pesticide is changed, the registration shall be amended to reflect such change if the Administrator determines that the change will not violate any provision of this Act.

(2) In no event shall registration of an article be construed as a defense for the commission of any offense under this Act: *Provided*, That as long as no cancellation proceedings are in effect registration of a pesticide shall be prima facie evidence that the pesticide, its labeling and packaging comply with the registration provisions of the Act.

(3) In connection with consideration of any registration or application for registration under this section, the Administrator may consult with any other Federal agency.

(g) The Administrator shall accomplish the reregistration of all pesticides in the most expeditious manner practicable: *Provided*, That, to the extent appropriate, any pesticide that results in a postharvest residue in or on food or feed crops shall be given priority in the reregistration process.

§ 136b. Use of restricted use pesticides; certified applicators

[Sec. 4] (a)(1) In any State for which a State plan for applicator certification has not been approved by the Administrator, the Administrator, in consultation with the Governor of such State, shall conduct a program for the certification of applicators of pesticides: *Provided,* That such program shall conform to the requirements imposed upon the States under the provisions of subsection (a)(2) of this section and shall not require private applicators to take any examination to establish competency in the use of pesticides. Prior to the implementation of the program, the Administrator shall publish in the Federal Register for review and comment a summary of the Federal plan for applicator certification and shall make generally available within the State copies of the plan. The Administrator shall hold public hearings at one or more locations within the State if so requested by the Governor of such State during the thirty days following publication of the Federal Register notice inviting comment on the Federal plan. The hearings shall be held within thirty days following receipt of the request from the Governor. In any State in which the Administrator conducts a certification program, the Administrator may require any person engaging in the commercial application, sale, offering for sale, holding for sale, or distribution of any pesticide one or more uses of which have been classified for restricted use to maintain such records and submit such reports concerning the commercial application, sale, or distribution of such pesticide as the Administrator may by regulation prescribe. Subject to paragraph (2), the Administrator shall prescribe standards for the certification of applicators of pesticides. Such standards shall provide that to be certified, an individual must be determined to be competent with respect to the use and handling of pesticides, or to the use and handling of the pesticide or class of pesticides covered by such individual's certification: *Provided, however,* That the certification standard for a private applicator shall, under a State plan submitted for approval, be deemed fulfilled by his completing a certification form. The Administrator shall further assure that such form contains adequate information and affirmations to carry out the intent of this Act, and may include in the form an affirmation that the private applicator has completed a training program approved by the Administrator so long as the program does not require the private applicator to take, pursuant to a requirement prescribed by the Administrator, any examination to establish competency in the use of the pesticide. The Administrator may require any pesticide dealer participating in a certification program to be licensed under a State licensing program approved by him.

(2) If any State, at any time, desires to certify applicators of pesticides, the Governor of such State shall submit a State plan for such purpose. The Administrator shall approve the plan submitted by any State, or any modification thereof, if such plan in his judgment—

(A) designates a State agency as the agency responsible for administering the plan throughout the State;

(B) contains satisfactory assurances that such agency has or will have the legal authority and qualified personnel necessary to carry out the plan;

(C) gives satisfactory assurances that the State will devote adequate funds to the administration of the plan;

(D) provides that the State agency will make such reports to the Administrator in such form and containing such information as the Administrator may from time to time require; and

(E) contains satisfactory assurances that State standards for the certification of applicators of pesticides conform with those standards prescribed by the Administrator under paragraph (1).

Any State certification program under this section shall be maintained in accordance with the State plan approved under this section.

(b) If the Administrator rejects a plan submitted under this paragraph, he shall afford the State submitting the plan due notice and opportunity for hearing before so doing. If the Administrator approves a plan submitted under this paragraph, then such State shall certify applicators of pesticides with respect to such State. Whenever the Administrator determines that a State is not administering the certification program in accordance with the plan approved under this section, he shall so notify the State and provide for a hearing at the request of the State, and, if appropriate corrective action is not taken within a reasonable time, not to exceed ninety days, the Administrator shall withdraw approval of such plan.

(c) Standards prescribed by the Administrator for the certification of applicators of pesticides under subsection (a), and State plans submitted to the Administrator under subsections (a) and (b), shall include provisions for making instructional materials concerning integrated pest management techniques available to individuals at their request in accordance with the provisions of section 23(c) of this Act, but such plans may not require that any individual receive instruction concerning such techniques or be shown to be competent with respect to the use of such techniques. The Administrator and States implementing such plans shall provide that all interested individuals are notified of the availability of such instructional materials.

§ 136c. Experimental use permits

[Sec. 5] (a) Any person may apply to the Administrator for an experimental use permit for a pesticide. The Administrator shall review the application. After completion of the review, but not later than one hundred and twenty days after receipt of the application and all required supporting data, the Administrator shall either issue the permit or notify the applicant of the Administrator's determination not to issue the permit and the reasons therefor. The applicant may correct the application or request a waiver of the conditions for such permit within thirty days of receipt by the applicant of such notification. The Administrator may issue an experimental use permit only if the Administrator determines that the applicant needs such permit in order to accumulate information necessary to register a pesticide under section 3 of this Act. An application for an experimental use permit may be filed at any time.

(b) If the Administrator determines that the use of a pesticide may reasonably be expected to result in any residue on or in food or feed, he may establish a temporary tolerance level for the residue of the pesticide before issuing the experimental use permit.

(c) Use of a pesticide under an experimental use permit shall be under the supervision of the Administrator, and shall be subject to such terms and conditions and be for such period of time as the Administrator may prescribe in the permit.

(d) When any experimental use permit is issued for a pesticide containing any chemical or combination of chemicals which has not been included in any previously registered pesticide, the Administrator may specify that studies be conducted to detect whether the use of the pesticide under the permit may cause unreasonable adverse effects on the environment. All results of such studies shall be reported to the Administrator before such pesticide may be registered under section 3.

(e) The Administrator may revoke any experimental use permit, at any time, if he finds that its terms or conditions are being violated, or that its terms and conditions are inadequate to avoid unreasonable adverse effects on the environment.

(f) Notwithstanding the foregoing provisions of this section, the Administrator shall, under such terms and conditions as he may by regulations prescribe, authorize any State to issue an experimental use permit for a pesticide. All provisions of section 4 relating to State plans shall apply with equal force to a State plan for the issuance of experimental use permits under this section.

(g) Notwithstanding the foregoing provisions of this section, the Administrator may issue an experimental use permit for a pesticide to any public or private agricultural research agency or educational institution which applies for such permit. Each permit shall not exceed more than a one-year period or such other specific time as the Administrator may prescribe. Such permit shall be issued under such terms and conditions restricting the use of the pesticide as the Administrator may require: *Provided*, That such pesticide may be used only by such research agency or educational institution for purposes of experimentation.

§ 136d. Administrative review; suspension

[Sec. 6] (a)(1) The Administrator shall cancel the registration of any pesticide at the end of the five-year period which begins on the date of its registration (or at the end of any five-year period thereafter) unless the registrant, or other interested person with the concurrence of the registrant, before the end of such period, requests in accordance with regulations prescribed by the Administrator that the registration be continued in effect:

Provided, That the Administrator may permit the continued sale and use of existing stocks of a pesticide whose registration is canceled under this subsection or subsection (b) to such extent, under such conditions, and for such uses as he may specify if he determines that such sale or use is not inconsistent with the purposes of this Act and will not have unreasonable adverse effects on the environment. The Administrator shall publish in the Federal Register, at least 30 days prior to the expiration of such five-year period, notice that the registration will be cancelled if the registrant or other interested person with the concurrence of the registrant does not request that the registration be continued in effect.

(2) If at any time after the registration of a pesticide the registrant has additional factual information regarding unreasonable adverse effects on the environment of the pesticide, he shall submit such information to the Administrator.

(b) If it appears to the Administrator that a pesticide or its labeling or other material required to be submitted does not comply with the provisions of this Act or, when used in accordance with widespread and commonly recognized practice, generally causes unreasonable adverse effect on the environment, the Administrator may issue a notice of his intent either—

(1) to cancel its registration or to change its classification together with the reasons (including the factual basis) for his action, or

(2) to hold a hearing to determine whether or not its registration should be canceled or its classification changed.

Such notice shall be sent to the registrant and made public. In determining whether to issue any such notice. The Administrator shall include among those factors to be taken into account the impact of the action proposed in such notice on production and prices of agricultural commodities, retail food prices, and otherwise on the agricultural economy. At least 60 days prior to sending such notice to the registrant or making public such notice, whichever occurs first, the Administrator shall provide the Secretary of Agriculture with a copy of such notice and an analysis of such impact on the agricultural economy. If the Secretary comments in writing to the Administrator regarding the notice and analysis within 30 days after receiving them, the Administrator shall publish in the Federal Register (with the notice) the comments of the Secretary and the response of the Administrator with regard to the Secretary's comments. If the Secretary does not comment in writing to the Administrator regarding the notice and analysis within 30 days after receiving them, the Administrator may notify the registrant and make public the notice at any time after such 30–day period notwithstanding the foregoing 60–day time requirement. The time requirements imposed by the preceding 3 sentences may be waived or modified to the extent agreed upon by the Administrator and the Secretary. Notwithstanding any other provision of this subsection (b) and section 25(d), in the event that the Administrator determines that suspension of a pesticide registration is necessary to prevent an imminent hazard to human health, then upon such a finding the

Administrator may waive the requirement of notice to and consultation with the Secretary of Agriculture pursuant to subsection (b) and of submission to the Scientific Advisory Panel pursuant to section 25(d) and proceed in accordance with subsection (c). The proposed action shall become final and effective at the end of 30 days from receipt by the registrant, or publication, of a notice issued under paragraph (1), whichever occurs later, unless within that time either (i) the registrant makes the necessary corrections, if possible, or (ii) a request for a hearing is made by a person adversely affected by the notice. In the event a hearing is held pursuant to such a request or to the Administrator's determination under paragraph (2), a decision pertaining to registration or classification issued after completion of such hearing shall be final.

In taking any final action under this subsection, the Administrator shall consider restricting a pesticide's use or uses as an alternative to cancellation and shall fully explain the reasons for these restrictions, and shall include among those factors to be taken into account the impact of such final action on production and prices of agricultural commodities, retail food prices, and otherwise on the agricultural economy, and he shall publish in the Federal Register an analysis of such impact.

(c)(1) If the Administrator determines that action is necessary to prevent an imminent hazard during the time required for cancellation or change in classification proceedings he may, by order, suspend the registration of the pesticide immediately. No order of suspension may be issued unless the Administrator has issued or at the same time issues notice of his intention to cancel the registration or change the classification of the pesticide.

Except as provided in paragraph (3), the Administrator shall notify the registrant prior to issuing any suspension order. Such notice shall include findings pertaining to the question of "imminent hazard". The registrant shall then have an opportunity, in accordance with the provisions of paragraph (2), for an expedited hearing before the Agency on the question of whether an imminent hazard exists.

(2) If no request for a hearing is submitted to the Agency within five days of the registrant's receipt of the notification provided for by paragraph (1), the suspension order may be issued and shall take effect and shall not be reviewable by a court. If a hearing is requested, it shall commence within five days of the receipt of the request for such hearing unless the registrant and the Agency agree that it shall commence at a later time. The hearing shall be held in accordance with the provisions of subchapter II of title 5 of the United States Code, except that the presiding officer need not be a certified administrative law judge. The presiding officer shall have ten days from the conclusion of the presentation of evidence to submit recommended findings and conclusions to the Administrator, who shall then have seven days to render a final order on the issue of suspension.

(3) Whenever the Administrator determines that an emergency exists that

does not permit him to hold a hearing before suspending, he may issue a suspension order in advance of notification to the registrant. In that case, paragraph (2) shall apply except that (i) the order of suspension shall be in effect pending the expeditious completion of the remedies provided by that paragraph and the issuance of a final order on suspension, and (ii) no party other than the registrant and the Agency shall participate except that any person adversely affected may file briefs within the time allotted by the Agency's rules. Any person so filing briefs shall be considered a party to such proceeding for the purpose of section 16(b).

(4) A final order on the question of suspension following a hearing shall be reviewable in accordance with Section 16 of this Act, notwithstanding the fact that any related cancellation proceedings have not been completed. Any order of suspension entered prior to a hearing before the Administrator shall be subject to immediate review in an action by the registrant or other interested person with the concurrence of the registrant in an appropriate district court, solely to determine whether the order of suspension was arbitrary, capricious or an abuse of discretion, or whether the order was issued in accordance with the procedures established by law. The effect of any order of the court will be only to stay the effectiveness of the suspension order, pending the Administrator's final decision with respect to cancellation or change in classification. This action may be maintained simultaneously with any administrative review proceeding under this section. The commencement of proceedings under this paragraph shall not operate as a stay of order, unless ordered by the court.

(d) In the event a hearing is requested pursuant to subsection (b) or determined upon by the Administrator pursuant to subsection (b), such hearing shall be held after due notice for the purpose of receiving evidence relevant and material to the issues raised by the objections filed by the applicant or other interested parties, or to the issues stated by the Administrator, if the hearing is called by the Administrator rather than by the filing of objections. Upon a showing of relevance and reasonable scope of evidence sought by any party to a public hearing, the Hearing Examiner shall issue a subpena to compel testimony or production of documents from any person. The Hearing Examiner shall be guided by the principles of the Federal Rules of Civil Procedure in making any order for the protection of the witness or the content of documents produced and shall order the payment of reasonable fees and expenses as a condition to requiring testimony of the witness. On contest, the subpena may be enforced by an appropriate United States district court in accordance with the principles stated herein. Upon the request of any party to a public hearing and when in the Hearing Examiner's judgment it is necessary or desirable, the Hearing Examiner shall at any time before the hearing record is closed refer to a Committee of the National Academy of Sciences the relevant questions of scientific fact involved in the public hearing. No member of any committee of the National Academy of Sciences established to carry out the functions of this section shall have a financial or other conflict of interest with respect to any matter considered by such committee. The Committee of the National Academy of Sciences shall report in writing to the Hearing Examiner within 60 days after such referral on these questions of scientific fact. The report shall be made public and shall be considered as part of the hearing record. The Administrator shall enter into appropriate arrangements with the National Academy of Sciences to assure an objective and competent scientific review of the questions presented to Committees of the Academy and to provide such other scientific advisory services as may be required by the Administrator for carrying out the purposes of this Act. As soon as practicable after completion of the hearing (including the report of the Academy) but not later than 90 days thereafter, the Administrator shall evaluate the data and reports before him and issue an order either revoking his notice of intention issued pursuant to this section, or shall issue an order either canceling the registration, changing the classification, denying the registration, or requiring modification of the labeling or packaging of the article. Such order shall be based only on substantial evidence of record of such hearing and shall set forth detailed findings of fact upon which the order is based.

(e)(1) The Administrator shall issue a notice of intent to cancel a registration issued under section 3(c)(7) of this Act if (A) the Administrator, at any time during the period provided for satisfaction of any condition imposed, determines that the registrant has failed to initiate and pursue appropriate action toward fulfilling any condition imposed, or (B) at the end of the period provided for satisfaction of any condition imposed, that condition has not been met: *Provided,* That the Administrator may permit the continued sale and use of existing stocks of a pesticide whose conditional registration has been canceled under this subsection to such extent, under such conditions, and for such uses as the Administrator may specify if the Administrator determines that such sale or use is not inconsistent with the purposes of this Act and will not have unreasonable adverse effects on the environment.

(2) A cancellation proposed under this subsection shall become final and effective at the end of thirty days from receipt by the registrant of the notice of intent to cancel unless during that time a request for hearing is made by a person adversely affected by the notice. If a hearing is requested, a hearing shall be conducted under subsection (d) of this section: *Provided,* That the only matters for resolution at that hearing shall be whether the registrant has initiated and pursued appropriate action to comply with the condition or conditions within the time provided or whether the condition or conditions have been satisfied within the time provided, and whether the Administrator's determination with respect to the disposition of existing stocks is consistent with this Act. A decision after completion of such hearing shall be final.

Notwithstanding any other provision of this section, a hearing shall be held and a determination made within seventy-five days after receipt of a request for such hearing.

(f) Final orders of the Administrator under this section shall be subject to judicial review pursuant to section 16.

§ 136e. Registration of establishments

[Sec. 7] (a) No person shall produce any pesticide subject to this Act or active ingredient used in producing a pesticide subject to this Act in any State unless the establishment in which it is produced is registered with the Administrator. The application for registration of any establishment shall include the name and address of the establishment and of the producer who operates such establishment.

(b) Whenever the Administrator receives an application under subsection (a), he shall register the establishment and assign it an establishment number.

(c)(1) Any producer operating an establishment registered under this section shall inform the Administrator within 30 days after it is registered of the types and amounts of pesticides and, if applicable, active ingredients used in producing pesticides—

(A) which he is currently producing;

(B) which he has produced during the past year; and

(C) which he has sold or distributed during the past year.

The information required by this paragraph shall be kept current and submitted to the Administrator annually as required under such regulations as the Administrator may prescribe.

(2) Any such producer shall, upon the request of the Administrator for the purpose of issuing a stop sale order pursuant to section 13, inform him of the name and address of any recipient of any pesticide produced in any registered establishment which he operates.

(d) Any information submitted to the Administrator pursuant to subsection (c) other than the names of the pesticides or active ingredients used in producing pesticides produced, sold, or distributed at an establishment shall be considered confidential and shall be subject to the provisions of section 10.

§ 136f. Books and records

[Sec. 8] (a) The Administrator may prescribe regulations requiring producers to maintain such records with respect to their operations and the pesticides and devices produced as he determines are necessary for the effective enforcement of this Act. No records required under this subsection shall extend to financial data, sales data other than shipment data, pricing data, personnel data, and research data (other than data relating to registered pesticides or to a pesticide for which an application for registration has been filed).

(b) For the purposes of enforcing the provisions of this Act, any producer, distributor, carrier, dealer, or any other person who sells or offers for sale, delivers or offers for delivery any pesticide or device subject to this Act, shall, upon request of any officer or employee of the Environmental Protection Agency or of any State or political subdivision, duly designated by the Administrator, furnish or permit such person at all reasonable times to have access to, and to copy: (1) all records showing the delivery, movement, or holding of such pesticide or device, including the quantity, the date of shipment and receipt, and the name of the consignor and consignee; or (2) in the event of the inability of any person to produce records containing such information, all other records and information relating to such delivery, movement, or holding of the pesticide or device. Any inspection with respect to any records and information referred to in this subsection shall not extend to financial data, sales data other than shipment data, pricing data, personnel data, and research data (other than data relating to registered pesticides or to a pesticide for which an application for registration has been filed). Before undertaking an inspection under this subsection, the officer or employee must present to the owner, operator, or agent in charge of the establishment or other place where pesticides or devices are held for distribution for sale, appropriate credentials and a written statement as to the reason for the inspection, including a statement as to whether a violation of the law is suspected. If no violation is suspected, and alternate and sufficient reason shall be given in writing. Each such inspection shall be commenced and completed with reasonable promptness.

§ 136g.   Inspection of establishments, etc.

[Sec. 9] (a) For purposes of enforcing the provisions of this Act, officers or employees duly designated by the Administrator are authorized to enter at reasonable times, any establishment or other place where pesticides or devices are held for distribution or sale for the purpose of inspecting and obtaining samples of any pesticides or devices, packaged, labeled, and released for shipment, and samples of any containers or labeling for such pesticides or devices.

Before undertaking such inspection, the officers or employees must present to the owner, operator, or agent in charge of the establishment or other place where pesticides or devices are held for distribution or sale, appropriate credentials and a written statement as to the reason for the inspection, including a statement as to whether a violation of the law is suspected. If no violation is suspected, an alternate and sufficient reason shall be given in writing. Each such inspection shall be commenced and completed with reasonable promptness. If the officer or employee obtains any samples, prior to leaving the premises, he shall give to the owner, operator, or agent in charge a receipt describing the samples obtained and, if requested, a portion of each such sample equal in volume or weight to the portion retained. If an analysis is made of such samples, a copy of the results of such analysis shall be furnished promptly to the owner, operator, or agent in charge.

(b) For purposes of enforcing the provisions of this Act and upon a showing to an officer or court of competent jurisdiction that there is reason to believe that the provisions of this Act have been violated, officers or employees duly designated by the Administrator are empowered to obtain and to execute warrants authorizing—

(1) entry for the purpose of this section;

(2) inspection and reproduction of all records showing quantity, date of shipment, and the name of consignor and consignee of any pesticide or device found in the establishment which is adulterated, misbranded, not registered (in the case of a pesticide) or otherwise in violation of this Act and in the event of the inability of any person to produce records containing such information, all other records and information relating to such delivery, movement, or holding of the pesticide or device; and

(3) the seizure of any pesticide or device which is in violation of this Act.

(c)(1) The examination of pesticides or devices shall be made in the Environmental Protection Agency or elsewhere as the Administrator may designate for the purpose of determining from such examinations whether they comply with the requirements of this Act. If it shall appear from any such examination that they fail to comply with the requirements of this Act, the Administrator shall cause notice to be given to the person against whom criminal or civil proceedings are contemplated. Any person so notified shall be given an opportunity to present his views, either orally or in writing, with regard to such contemplated proceedings, and if in the opinion of the Administrator it appears that the provisions of this Act have been violated by such person, then the Administrator shall certify the facts to the Attorney General, with a copy of the results of the analysis or the examination of such pesticide for the institution of a criminal proceeding pursuant to section 14(b) or a civil proceeding under section 14(a), when the Administrator determines that such action will be sufficient to effectuate the purposes of this Act.

(2) The notice of contemplated proceedings and opportunity to present views set forth in this subsection are not prerequisites to the institution of any proceeding by the Attorney General.

(3) Nothing in this Act shall be construed as requiring the Administrator to institute proceedings for prosecution of minor violations of this Act whenever he believes that the public interest will be adequately served by a suitable written notice of warning.

§ 136h. Protection of trade secrets and other information

[Sec. 10] (a) In submitting data required by this Act, the applicant may (1) clearly mark any portions thereof which in his opinion are trade secrets or commercial or financial information and (2) submit such marked material separately from other material required to be submitted under this Act.

(b) Notwithstanding any other provision of this Act and subject to the limitations in subsections (d) and (e) of this section, the Administrator shall not make public information which in his judgment contains or relates to trade secrets or commercial or financial information obtained from a person and privileged or confidential, except that, when necessary to carry out the provisions of this Act, information relating to formulas of products acquired by authorization of this Act may be revealed to any Federal agency consulted and may be revealed at a public hearing or in findings of fact issued by the Administrator.

(c) If the Administrator proposes to release for inspection information which the applicant or registrant believes to be protected from disclosure under subsection (b), he shall notify the applicant or registrant, in writing, by certified mail. The Administrator shall not thereafter make available for inspection such data until thirty days after receipt of the notice by the applicant or registrant. During this period, the applicant or registrant may institute an action in an appropriate district court for a declaratory judgment as to whether such information is subject to protection under subsection (b).

(d)(1) All information concerning the objectives, methodology, results, or significance of any test or experiment performed on or with a registered or previously registered pesticide or its separate ingredients, impurities, or degradation products, and any information concerning the effects of such pesticide on any organism or the behavior of such pesticide in the environment, including, but not limited to, data on safety to fish and wildlife, humans and other mammals, plants, animals, and soil, and studies on persistence, translocation and fate in the environment, and metabolism, shall be available for disclosure to the public: *Provided*, That the use of such data for any registration purpose shall be governed by section 3 of this Act: *Provided further*, That this paragraph does not authorize the disclosure of any information that—

    (A) discloses manufacturing or quality control processes,

    (B) discloses the details of any methods for testing, detecting, or measuring the quantity of any deliberately added inert ingredient of a pesticide, or

    (C) discloses the identity or percentage quantity of any deliberately added inert ingredient of a pesticide.

unless the Administrator has first determined that disclosure is necessary to protect against an unreasonable risk of injury to health or the environment.

(2) Information concerning production, distribution, sale, or inventories of a pesticide that is otherwise entitled to confidential treatment under subsection (b) of this section may be publicly disclosed in connection with a public proceeding to determine whether a pesticide, or any ingredient of a pesticide, causes unreasonable adverse effects on health or the environment, if the Administrator determines that such disclosure is necessary in the public interest.

(3) If the Administrator proposes to disclose information described in clause (A), (B), or (C) of paragraph (1) or in paragraph (2) of this subsection, the Administrator shall notify by certified mail the submitter of such information of the intent to release such information. The Administrator may not release such information, without the submitter's consent, until thirty days after the submitter has been furnished such notice: *Provided*, That where the Administrator finds that disclosure of information described in clause (A), (B), or (C) of paragraph (1) of this subsection is necessary to avoid or lessen an imminent and substantial risk of injury to the public health, the Administrator may set such shorter period of notice (but not less than ten days) and such method of notice as the Administrator finds appropriate. During such period the data submitter may institute an action in an appropriate district court to enjoin or limit the proposed disclosure. The court may enjoin disclosure, or limit the disclosure or the parties to whom disclosure shall be made, to the extent that—

(A) in the case of information described in clause (A), (B), or (C) of paragraph (1) of this subsection, the proposed disclosure is not required to protect against an unreasonable risk of injury to health or the environment; or

(B) in the case of information described in paragraph (2) of this subsection, the public interest in availability of the information in the public proceeding does not outweigh the interests in preserving the confidentiality of the information.

(e) Information otherwise protected from disclosure to the public under subsection (b) of this section may be disclosed to contractors with the United States and employees of such contractors if, in the opinion of the Administrator, such disclosure is necessary for the satisfactory performance by the contractor of a contract with the United States for the performance of work in connection with this Act and under such conditions as the Administrator may specify. The Administrator shall require as a condition to the disclosure of information under this subsection that the person receiving it take such security precautions respecting the information as the Administrator shall by regulation prescribe.

(f)(1) Any officer or employee of the United States or former officer or employee of the United States who, by virtue of such employment or official position, has obtained possession of, or has access to, material the disclosure of which is prohibited by subsection (b) of this section, and who, knowing that disclosure of such material is prohibited by such subsection, willfully discloses the material in any manner to any person not entitled to receive it, shall be fined not more than $10,000 or imprisoned for not more than one year, or both. Section 1905 of title 18 of the United States Code shall not apply with respect to the publishing, divulging, disclosure, or making known of, or making available, information reported or otherwise obtained under this Act. Nothing in this Act shall preempt any civil remedy under State or

Federal law for wrongful disclosure of trade secrets.

(2) For the purposes of this section, any contractor with the United States who is furnished information as authorized by subsection (e) of this section, or any employee of any such contractor, shall be considered to be an employee of the United States.

(g)(1) The Administrator shall not knowingly disclose information submitted by an applicant or registrant under this Act to any employee or agent of any business or other entity engaged in the production, sale, or distribution of pesticides in countries other than the United States or in addition to the United States or to any other person who intends to deliver such data to such foreign or multinational business or entity unless the applicant or registrant has consented to such disclosure. The Administrator shall require an affirmation from any person who intends to inspect data that such person does not seek access to the data for purposes of delivering it or offering it for sale to any such business or entity or its agents or employees and will not purposefully deliver or negligently cause the data to be delivered to such business or entity or its agents or employees and will not purposefully deliver or negligently cause the data to be delivered to such business or entity or its agents or employees. Notwithstanding any other provision of this subsection, the Administrator may disclose information to any person in connection with a public proceeding under law or regulation, subject to restrictions on the availability of information contained elsewhere in this Act, which information is relevant to a determination by the Administrator with respect to whether a pesticide, or any ingredient of a pesticide, causes unreasonable adverse effects on health or the environment.

(2) The Administrator shall maintain records of the names of persons to whom data are disclosed under this subsection and the persons or organizations they represent and shall inform the applicant or registrant of the names and affiliations of such persons.

(3) Section 1001 of title 18 of the United States Code shall apply to any affirmation made under paragraph (1) of this subsection.

§ 136i.   Standards applicable to pesticide applicators

[Sec. 11] (a) No regulations prescribed by the Administrator for carrying out the provisions of this Act shall require any private applicator to maintain any records or file any reports or other documents.

(b) When establishing or approving standards for licensing or certification, the Administrator shall establish separate standards for commercial and private applicators.

§ 136j.   Unlawful acts

[Sec. 12] (a)(1) Except as provided by subsection (b), it shall be unlawful for any person in any State to distribute, sell, offer for sale, hold for sale, ship, deliver for shipment, or receive and (having so received) deliver or offer to deliver, to any person—

(A) any pesticide which is not registered under section 3, except as provided by section 6(a)(1);

(B) any registered pesticide if any claims made for it as a part of its distribution or sale substantially differ from any claims made for it as a part of the statement required in connection with its registration under section 3;

(C) any registered pesticide the composition of which differs at the time of its distribution or sale from its composition as described in the statement required in connection with its registration under section 3;

(D) any pesticide which has not been colored or discolored pursuant to the provisions of section 25(c)(5);

(E) any pesticide which is adulterated or misbranded; or

(F) any device which is misbranded.

(2) It shall be unlawful for any person—

(A) to detach, alter, deface, or destroy, in whole or in part, any labeling required under this Act;

(B) to refuse to keep any records required pursuant to section 8, or to refuse to allow the inspection of any records or establishment pursuant to section 8 or 9, or to refuse to allow an officer or employee of the Environmental Protection Agency to take a sample of any pesticide pursuant to section 9;

(C) to give a guaranty or undertaking provided for in subsection (b) which is false in any particular, except that a person who receives and relies upon a guaranty authorized under subsection (b) may give a guaranty to the same effect, which guaranty shall contain, in addition to his own name and address, the name and address of the person residing in the United States from whom he received the guaranty or undertaking;

(D) to use for his own advantage or to reveal, other than to the Administrator, or officials or employees of the Environmental Protection Agency or other Federal executive agencies, or to the courts, or to physicians, pharmacists, and other qualified persons, needing such information for the performance of their duties, in accordance with such directions as the Administrator may prescribe, any information acquired by authority of this Act which is confidential under this Act;

(E) who is a registrant, wholesaler, dealer, retailer, or other distributor to advertise a produce registered under this Act for restricted use without giving the classification of the product assigned to it under section 3;

(F) to make available for use, or to use, any registered pesticide classified for restricted use for some or all purpose other than in accordance with section 3(d) and any regulations thereunder: *Provided,* That it shall not be unlawful to sell, under regulations issued by the Administrator, a restricted use pesticide to a person who is not a certified applicator for application by a certified applicator;

(G) to use any registered pesticide in a manner inconsistent with its labeling;

(H) to use any pesticide which is under an experimental use permit contrary to the provisions of such permit;

(I) to violate any order issued under section 13;

(J) to violate any suspension order issued under section 6;

(K) to violate any cancellation of registration of a pesticide under section 6, except as provided by section 6(a)(1);

(L) who is a producer to violate any of the provisions of section 7;

(M) to knowingly falsify all or part of any application for registration, application for experimental use permit, any information submitted to the Administrator pursuant to section 7, any records required to be maintained pursuant to section 8, and report filed under this Act, or any information marked as confidential and submitted to the Administrator under any provision of this act;

(N) who is a registrant, wholesaler, dealer, retailer, or other distributor to fail to file reports required by this Act;

(O) to add any substance to, or take any substance from, any pesticide in a manner that may defeat the purpose of this Act; or

(P) to use any pesticide in tests on human beings unless such human beings (i) are fully informed of the nature and purposes of the test and of any physical and mental health consequences which are reasonably foreseeable therefrom, and (ii) freely volunteer to participate in the test.

(b) The penalties provided for a violation of paragraph (1) of subsection (a) shall not apply to—

(1) any person who establishes a guaranty signed by, and containing the name and address of, the registrant or person residing in the United States from whom he purchased or received in good faith the pesticide in the same unbroken package, to the effect that the pesticide was lawfully registered at the time of sale and delivery to him, and that it complies with the other requirements of this Act, and in such case the guarantor shall be subject to the penalties which would otherwise attach to the person holding the guaranty under the provisions of this Act;

(2) any carrier while lawfully shipping, transporting, or delivering for shipment any pesticide or device, if such carrier upon request of any officer or employee duly designated by the Administrator shall permit such officer or employee to copy all of its records concerning such pesticide or device;

(3) any public official while engaged in the performance of his official duties;

(4) any person using or possessing any pesticide as provided by an experimental use permit in effect with respect to such pesticide and such use or possession; or

(5) any person who ships a substance or mixture of substances being put through tests in which the purpose is only to determine its value for pesticide purposes or to determine its toxicity or other properties and from which the user does not expect to receive any benefit in pest control from its use.

§ 136k. Stop sale, use, removal, and seizure

[Sec. 13] (a) Whenever any pesticide or device is found by the Administrator in any State and there is reason to believe on the basis of inspection or tests that such pesticide or device is in violation of any of the provisions of this Act, or that such pesticide or device has been or is intended to be distributed or sold in violation of any such provisions, or when the registration of the pesticide has been canceled by a final order or has been suspended, the Administrator may issue a written or printed "stop sale, use, or removal" order to any person who owns, controls, or has custody of such pesticide or device, and after receipt of such order no person shall sell, use, or remove the pesticide or device described in the order except in accordance with the provisions of the order.

(b) Any pesticide or device that is being transported or, having been transported, remains unsold or in original unbroken packages, or that is sold or offered for sale in any State, or that is imported from a foreign country, shall be liable to be proceeded against in any district court in the district where it is found and seized for confiscation by a process in rem for condemnation if—

(1) in the case of a pesticide—

    (A) it is adulterated or misbranded;

    (B) it is not registered pursuant to the provisions of section 3;

    (C) its labeling fails to bear the information required by this Act;

    (D) it is not colored or discolored any such coloring or discoloring is required under this Act; or

    (E) any of the claims made for it or any of the directions for its use differ in substance from the representations made in connection with its registration;

(2) in the case of a device, it is misbranded; or

(3) in the case of a pesticide or device, when used in accordance with the requirements imposed under this Act and as directed by the labeling, it nevertheless causes unreasonable adverse effects on the environment. In the case of a plant regulator, defoliant, or desiccant, used in accordance with the label claims and recommendations, physical or physiological effects on plants or parts thereof shall not be deemed to be injury, when such effects are the purpose for which the plant regulator, defoliant, or desiccant was applied.

(c) If the pesticide or device is condemned it shall, after entry of the decree, be disposed of by destruction or sale as the court may direct and the proceeds, if sold, less the court costs, shall be paid into the Treasury of the United States, but the pesticide or device shall not be sold contrary to the provisions of this Act or the laws of the jurisdiction in which it is sold: *Provided,* That upon payment of the costs of the condemnation proceedings and the execution and delivery of a good and sufficient bond conditioned that the pesticide or device shall not be sold or otherwise disposed of contrary to the provisions of the Act or the laws of any jurisdiction in which sold, the court may direct that such pesticide or device be delivered to the owner thereof. The proceedings of such condemnation cases shall conform, as near as may be to the proceedings in admiralty, except that either party may demand trial by jury of any issue of fact joined in any case, and all such proceedings shall be at the suit of and in the name of the United States.

(d) When a decree of condemnation is entered against the pesticide or device, court costs and fees, storage, and other proper expenses shall be awarded against the person, if any, intervening as claimant of the pesticide or device.

§ 1361. Penalties

[Sec. 14] (a)(1) Any registrant, commercial applicator, wholesaler, dealer, retailer, or other distributor who violates any provision of this Act may be assessed a civil penalty by the Administrator of not more than $5,000 for each offense.

(2) Any private applicator or other person not included in paragraph (1) who violates any provision of this Act subsequent to receiving a written warning from the Administrator or following a citation for a prior violation, may be assessed a civil penalty by the Administrator of not more than $1,000 for each offense: *Provided,* That any applicator not included under paragraph (1) of this subsection who holds or applies registered pesticides, or uses dilutions of registered pesticides, only to provide a service of controlling pests without delivering any unapplied pesticide to any person so served, and who violates any provision of this Act may be assessed a civil penalty by the Administrator of not more than $500 for the first offense not more than $1,000 for each subsequent offense.

(3) No civil penalty shall be assessed unless the person charged shall have been given notice and opportunity for a hearing on such charge in the county, parish, or incorporated city of the residence of the person charged.

(4) In determining the amount of the penalty, the Administrator shall consider the appropriateness of such penalty to the size of the business of the person charged, the effect on the person's ability to continue in business, and the gravity of the violation. Whenever the Administrator finds that the violation occurred despite the exercise of due care or did

not cause significant harm to health or the environment, the Administrator may issue a warning in lieu of assessing a penalty.

(5) In case of inability to collect such civil penalty or failure of any person to pay all, or such portion of such civil penalty as the Administrator may determine, the Administrator shall refer the matter to the Attorney General, who shall recover such amount by action in the appropriate United States district court.

(b)(1) Any registrant, commercial applicator, wholesaler, dealer, retailer, or other distributor who knowingly violates any provision of this Act shall be guilty of a misdemeanor and shall on conviction be fined not more than $25,000, or imprisoned for not more than one year, or both.

(2) Any private applicator or other person not included in paragraph (1) who knowingly violates any provision of this Act shall be guilty of a misdemeanor and shall on conviction be fined not more than $1,000, or imprisoned for not more than 30 days, or both.

(3) Any person, who, with intent to defraud, uses or reveals information relative to formulas of products acquired under the authority of section 3, shall be fined not more than $10,000 or imprisoned for not more than three years, or both.

(4) When construing and enforcing the provisions of this Act, the act, omission, or failure of any officer, agent, or other person acting for or employed by any person shall in every case be also deemed to be the act, omission, or failure of such person as well as that of the person employed.

§ 136m. Indemnities

[Sec. 15] (a) If—

(1) the Administrator notifies a registrant that he has suspended the registration of a pesticide because such action is necessary to prevent an imminent hazard;

(2) the registration of the pesticide is canceled as a result of a final determination that the use of such pesticide will create an imminent hazard; and

(3) any person who owned any quantity of such pesticide immediately before the notice to the registrant under paragraph (1) suffered losses by reason of suspension or cancellation of the registration,

the Administrator shall make an indemnity payment to such person, unless the Administrator finds that such person (i) had knowledge of facts which, in themselves, would have shown that such pesticide did not meet the requirements of section 3(c)(5) for registration, and (ii) continued thereafter to produce such pesticide without giving timely notice of such facts to the Administrator.

(b)(1) The amount of the indemnity payment under subsection (a) to any person shall be determined on the basis of the cost of the pesticide owned by such person immediately before the notice to the registrant referred to in subsection (a)(1); except that in no event shall an indemnity payment to any person exceed the fair market value of the pesticide owned by such person immediately before the notice referred to in subsection (a)(1).

(2) Notwithstanding any other provision of this Act, the Administrator may provide a reasonable time for use or other disposal of such pesticide. In determining the quantity of any pesticide for which indemnity shall be paid under this subsection, proper adjustment shall be made for any pesticide used or otherwise disposed of by such owner.

§ 136n. Administrative procedure; judicial review

[Sec. 16] (a) Except as is otherwise provided in this Act, Agency refusals to cancel or suspend registrations or change classifications not following a hearing and other final Agency actions not committed to Agency discretion by law are judicially reviewable in the district courts.

(b) In the case of actual controversy as to the validity of any order issued by the Administrator following a public hearing, any person who will be adversely affected by such order and who had been a party to the proceedings may obtain judicial review by filing in the United States court of appeals for the circuit wherein such person resides or has a place of business, within 60 days after the entry of such order, a petition praying that the order be set aside in whole or in part. A copy of the petition shall be forthwith transmitted by the clerk of the court to the Administrator or any officer designated by him for that purpose, and thereupon the Administrator shall file in the court the record of the proceedings on which he based his order, as provided in section 2112 of title 28, United States Code. Upon the filing of such petition the court shall have exclusive jurisdiction to affirm or set aside the order complained of in whole or in part. The court shall consider all evidence of record. The order of the Administrator shall be sustained if it is supported by substantial evidence when considered on the record as a whole. The judgment of the court affirming or setting aside, in whole or in part, any order under this section shall be final, subject to review by the Supreme Court of the United States upon certiorari or certification as provided in section 1254 of title 28 of the United States Code. The commencement of proceedings under this section shall not, unless specifically ordered by the court to the contrary, operate as a stay of an order.

(c) The district courts of the United States are vested with jurisdiction specifically to enforce, and to prevent and restrain violations of, this Act.

(d) The Administrator shall, by publication in such manner as he may prescribe, give notice of all judgments entered in actions instituted under the authority of this Act.

§ 136o. Imports and exports

[Sec. 17] (a) Notwithstanding any other provision of this Act, no pesticide or device or active ingredient used in producing a pesticide intended solely for export to any foreign country shall be deemed in violation of this Act—

(1) when prepared or packed according to the specifications or directions of the foreign purchaser, except that producers of such pesticides and devices and active ingredients used in producing pesticides shall be subject to sections 2(p), 2(q) (1) (A), (C), (D), (E), (G), and (H), 2(q) (2) (A), (B), (C) (i) and (iii), and (D), 7, and 8 of this Act; and

(2) in the case of any pesticide other than a pesticide registered under section 3 or sold under section 6(a)(1) of this Act, if, prior to export, the foreign purchaser has signed a statement acknowledging that the purchaser understands that such pesticide is not registered for use in the United States and cannot be sold in the United States under this Act. A copy of that statement shall be transmitted to an appropriate official of the government of the importing country.

(b) Whenever a registration, or a cancellation or suspension of the registration of a pesticide becomes effective, or ceases to be effective, the Administrator shall transmit through the State Department notification thereof to the governments of other countries and to appropriate international agencies. Such notification shall, upon request, include all information related to the cancellation or suspension of the registration of the pesticide and information concerning other pesticides that are registered under section 3 of this Act and that could be used in lieu of such pesticide.

(c) The Secretary of the Treasury shall notify the Administrator of the arrival of pesticides and devices and shall deliver to the Administrator, upon his request, samples of pesticides or devices which are being imported into the United States, giving notice to the owner or consignee, who may appear before the Administrator and have the right to introduce testimony. If it appears from the examination of a sample that it is adulterated, or misbranded or otherwise violates the provisions set forth in this Act, or is otherwise injurious to health or the environment, the pesticide or device may be refused admission, and the Secretary of the Treasury shall refuse delivery to the consignee and shall cause the destruction of any pesticide or device refused delivery which shall not be exported by the consignee within 90 days from the date of notice of such refusal under such regulations as the Secretary of the Treasury may prescribe: *Provided*, That the Secretary of the Treasury may deliver to the consignee such pesticide or device pending examination and decision in the matter on execution of bond for the amount of the full invoice value of such pesticide or device, together with the duty thereon, and on refusal to return such pesticide or device for any cause to the custody of the Secretary of the Treasury, when demanded, for the purpose of excluding them from the country, or for any other purpose, said consignee shall forfeit the full amount of said bond: *And provided further*, That all charges for storage, cartage, and labor on pesticides or devices which are refused admission or delivery shall be paid by the owner or consignee, and in default of such payment shall constitute a lien against any future importation made by such owner or consignee.

(d) The Administrator shall, in cooperation with the Department of State and any other appropriate Federal agency, participate and cooperate in any international efforts to develop improved pesticide research and regulations.

(e) The Secretary of the Treasury, in consultation with the Administrator, shall prescribe regulations for the enforcement of subsection (c) of this section.

§ 136p. Exemption of federal agencies

[Sec. 18] The Administrator may, at his discretion, exempt any Federal or State agency from any provision of this Act if he determines that emergency conditions exist which require such exemption.

The Administrator, in determining whether or not such emergency conditions exist, shall consult with the Secretary of Agriculture and the Governor of any State concerned if they request such determination.

§ 136q. Disposal and transportation

[Sec. 19] (a) The Administrator shall, after consultation with other interested Federal agencies, establish procedures and regulations for the disposal or storage of packages and containers of pesticides and for disposal or storage of excess amounts of such pesticides, and accept at convenient locations for safe disposal a pesticide the registration of which is canceled under section 6(c) if requested by the owner of the pesticide.

(b) The Administrator shall provide advice and assistance to the Secretary of Transportation with respect to his functions relating to the transportation of hazardous materials under the Department of Transportation Act (49 U.S.C. 1657), the Transportation of Explosives Act (18 U.S.C. 831–835), the Federal Aviation Act of 1958 (49 U.S.C. 1421–1430, 1472 II), and the Hazardous Cargo Act (46 U.S.C. 170, 375, 416)

(c) Notification of cancellation of any pesticide shall include specific provisions for the disposal of the unused quantities of such pesticide.

§ 136r. Research and monitoring

[Sec. 20] (a) The Administrator shall undertake research, including research by grant or contract with other Federal agencies, universities, or others as may be necessary to carry out the purposes of this Act, and he shall conduct research into integrated pest management in coordination with the Secretary of Agriculture.

(b) The Administrator shall formulate and periodically revise, in cooperation with other Federal, State, or local agencies, a national plan for monitoring pesticides.

(c) The Administrator shall undertake such monitoring activities, including, but not limited to monitoring in air, soil, water, man, plants, and animals, as may be necessary for the implementation of this Act and of the

national pesticide monitoring plan, the Administrator shall establish procedures for the monitoring of man and animals and their environment for
incidental pesticide exposure, including, but not limited to, the quantification
of incidental human and environmental pesticide pollution and the secular
trends thereof, and identification of the sources of contamination and their
relationship to human and environmental effects. Such activities shall be
carried out in cooperation with other Federal, State, and local agencies.

§ 136s. Solicitation of comments; notice of public hearings

[Sec. 21] (a) The Administrator, before publishing regulations under this
Act, shall solicit the views of the Secretary of Agriculture in accordance with
the procedure described in section 25(a).

(b) In addition to any other authority relating to public hearings and
solicitation of views, in connection with the suspension or cancellation of a
pesticide registration or any other actions authorized under this Act, the
Administrator may, at his discretion, solicit the views of all interested
persons, either orally or in writing, and seek such advice from scientists,
farmers, farm organizations, and other qualified persons as he deems proper.

(c) In connection with all public hearings under this Act the Administrator shall publish timely notice of such hearings in the Federal Register.

§ 136t. Delegation and cooperation

[Sec. 22](a) All authority vested in the Administrator by virtue of the
provisions of this Act may with like force and effect be executed by such
employees of the Environmental Protection Agency as the Administrator
may designate for the purpose.

(b) The Administrator shall cooperate with the Department of Agriculture, any other Federal agency, and any appropriate agency of any State or
any political subdivision thereof, in carrying out the provisions of this Act,
and in securing uniformity of regulations.

§ 136u. State cooperation, aid, and training

[Sec. 23] (a) The Administrator may enter into cooperative agreements
with States and Indian tribes—

(1) to delegate to any State or Indian tribe the authority to cooperate in
the enforcement of this Act through the use of its personnel or
facilities, to train personnel of the State or Indian tribe to cooperate in
the enforcement of this Act, and to assist States and Indian tribes in
implementing cooperative enforcement programs through grants-in-
aid; and

(2) to assist States in developing and administering State programs, and
Indian tribes that enter into cooperative agreements, to train and

certify applicators consistent with the standards the Administrator prescribes.

Effective with the fiscal year beginning October 1, 1978, there are authorized to be appropriated annually such funds as may be necessary for the Administrator to provide through cooperative agreements an amount equal to 50 percent of the anticipated cost to each State or Indian tribe, as agreed to under such cooperative agreements, of conducting training and certification programs during such fiscal year. If funds sufficient to pay 50 percent of the costs for any year are not appropriated, the share of each State and Indian tribe shall be reduced in a like proportion in allocating available funds.

(b) In addition, the Administrator may enter into contracts with Federal, State, or Indian tribal agencies for the purpose of encouraging the training of certified applicators.

(c) The Administrator shall, in cooperation with the Secretary of Agriculture, use the services of the cooperative State extension services to inform and educate pesticide users about accepted uses and other regulations made under this Act.

§ 136v. Authority of states

[Sec. 24] (a) A State may regulate the sale or use of any federally registered pesticide or device in the State, but only if and to the extent the regulation does not permit any sale or use prohibited by this Act.

(b) Such State shall not impose or continue in effect any requirements for labeling or packaging in addition to or different from those required under this Act.

(c)(1) A State must provide registration for additional uses of federally registered pesticides formulated for distribution and use within that State to meet special local needs in accord with the purposes of this Act and if registration for such use has not previously been denied, disapproved, or canceled by the Administrator. Such registration shall be deemed registration under section 3 for all purposes of this Act, but shall authorize distribution and use only within such State.

(2) A registration issued by a State under this subsection shall not be effective for more than ninety days if disapproved by the Administrator within that period. Prior to disapproval, the Administrator shall, except as provided in paragraph (3) of this subsection, advise the State of the Administrator's intention to disapprove and the reasons therefor, and provide the State time to respond. The Administrator shall not prohibit or disapprove a registration issued by a State under this subsection (A) on the basis of lack of essentiality of a pesticide or (B) except as provided in paragraph (3) of this subsection, if its composition and use patterns are similar to those of a federally registered pesticide.

(3) In no instance may a State issue a registration for a food or feed use unless there exists a tolerance or exemption under the Federal Food,

Drug, and Cosmetic Act that permits the residues of the pesticide on the food or feed. If the Administrator determines that a registration issued by a State is inconsistent with the Federal Food, Drug, and Cosmetic Act, or the use of, a pesticide under a registration issued by a State constitutes an imminent hazard, the Administrator may immediately disapprove the registration.

(4) If the Administrator finds, in accordance with standards set forth in regulations issued under section 25 of this Act, that a State is not capable of exercising adequate controls to assure that State registration under this section will be in accord with the purposes of this Act or has failed to exercise adequate controls, the Administrator may suspend the authority of the State to register pesticides until such time as the Administrator is satisfied that the State can and will exercise adequate controls. Prior to any such suspension, the Administrator shall advise the State of the Administrator's intention to suspend and the reasons therefor and provide the State time to respond.

§ 136w. Authority of Administrator

[Sec. 25] (a)(1) The Administrator is authorized in accordance with the procedure described in paragraph (2), to prescribe regulations to carry out the provisions of this Act. Such regulations shall take into account the difference in concept and usage between various classes of pesticides and differences in environmental risk and the appropriate data for evaluating such risk between agricultural and nonagricultural pesticides.

(2)(A) At least 60 days prior to signing any proposed regulation for publication in the Federal Register, the Administrator shall provide the Secretary of Agriculture with a copy of such regulation. If the Secretary comments in writing to the Administrator regarding any such regulation within 30 days after receiving it, the Administrator shall publish in the Federal Register (with the proposed regulation) the comments of the Secretary and the response of the Administrator with regard to the Secretary's comments. If the Secretary does not comment in writing to the Administrator regarding the regulation within 30 days after receiving it, the Administrator may sign such regulation for publication in the Federal Register any time after such 30-day period notwithstanding the foregoing 60-day time requirement.

(B) At least 30 days prior to signing any regulation in final form for publication in the Federal Register, the Administrator shall provide the Secretary of Agriculture with a copy of such regulation. If the Secretary comments in writing to the Administrator regarding any such final regulation within 15 days after receiving it, the Administrator shall publish in the Federal Register (with the final regulation) the comments of the Secretary, if requested by the Secretary, and the response of the Administrator concerning the Secretary's comments. If the Secretary does not comment in writing to the Administrator regarding the regulation within 15 days after receiving it, the Administrator may sign such regulation for publication in the Federal Register at any time after such 15-day period notwithstanding the foregoing 30-day time requirement. In taking any final action under this subsection, the Administrator shall include among those factors to be taken into account the effect of the regulation on production and prices of agricultural commodities, retail food prices, and otherwise on the agricultural economy, and the Administrator shall publish in the Federal Register an analysis of such effect.

(C) The time requirements imposed by subparagraphs (A) and (B) may be waived or modified to the extent agreed upon by the Administrator and the Secretary.

(D) The Administrator shall, simultaneously with any notification to the Secretary of Agriculture under this paragraph prior to the issuance of any proposed or final regulation, publish such notification in the Federal Register.

(3) At such time as the Administrator is required under paragraph (2) of this subsection to provide the Secretary of Agriculture with a copy of proposed regulations and a copy of the final form of regulations, he shall also furnish a copy of such regulations to the Committee on Agriculture of the House of Representatives and the Committee on Agriculture and Forestry of the Senate.

(4)(A) Notwithstanding any other provision of this Act, simultaneously with promulgation of any rule or regulation under this Act, the Administrator shall transmit a copy thereof to the Secretary of the Senate and the Clerk of the House of Representatives. Except as provided in subparagraph (B), the rule or regulation shall not become effective, if within 90 calendar days of continuous session of Congress after the date of promulgation, both Houses of Congress adopt a concurrent resolution, the matter after the resolving clause of which is as follows: That Congress disapproves the rule or regulation promulgated by the Administrator of the Environmental Protection agency dealing with the matter of ___, which rule or regulation was transmitted to Congress on ___, the blank spaces therein being appropriately filled.

(B) If at the end of 60 calendar days of continuous session of Congress after the date of promulgation of a rule or regulation, no committee of either House of Congress has reported or been discharged from further consideration of a concurrent resolution disapproving the rule or regulation, and neither House has adopted such a resolution, the rule or regulation may go into effect immediately. If, within such 60 calendar days, such a committee has reported or been discharged from further consideration of such a resolution, or either House has adopted such a resolution, the rule or regulation may go into effect not sooner than 90 calendar days of continuous session of Congress after its promulgation unless disapproved as provided in subparagraph (A).

(C) For the purposes of subparagraphs (A) and (B) of this paragraph—

    (i) continuity of session is broken only by an adjournment of Congress sine die; and

    (ii) the days on which either House is not in session because of an adjournment of more than 3 days to a day certain are excluded in the computation of 60 and 90 calendar days of continuous session of Congress.

(D) Congressional inaction on or rejection of a resolution of disapproval shall not be deemed an expression of approval of such rule.

(E)(i) Any interested party, including any person who participated in the rulemaking involved, may institute such actions in the appropriate district court of the United States, including actions for declaratory judgment, as may be appropriate to construe the constitutionality of any provision of this paragraph. The district court immediately shall certify all questions of the constitutionality of this paragraph to the United States court of appeals for the circuit involved, which shall hear the matter sitting en banc.

    (ii) Notwithstanding any other provision of law, any decision on a matter certified under clause (i) of this subparagraph shall be reviewable by appeal directly to the Supreme Court of the United States. Such appeal shall be brought not later than 20 days after the decision of the court of appeals.

(b) The Administrator may exempt from the requirements of this Act by regulation any pesticide which he determines either (1) to be adequately regulated by another Federal agency, or (2) to be of a character which is unnecessary to be subject to this Act in order to carry out the purpose of this Act.

(c) The Administrator, after notice and opportunity for hearing, is authorized—

(1) to declare a pest any form of plant or animal life (other than man and other than bacteria, virus, and other micro-organisms on or in living man or other living animals) which is injurious to health or the environment;

(2) to determine any pesticide which contains any substance or substances in quantities highly toxic to man;

(3) to establish standards (which shall be consistent with those established under the authority of the Poison Prevention Packaging Act (Public Law 91–601)) with respect to the package, container, or wrapping in which a pesticide or device is enclosed for use or consumption, in order

to protect children and adults from serious injury or illness resulting from accidental ingestion or contact with pesticides or devices regulated by this Act as well as to accomplish the other purposes of this Act;

(4) to specify those classes of devices which shall be subject to any provision of paragraph 2(q)(1) or section 7 of this Act upon his determination that application of such provision is necessary to effectuate the purposes of this Act;

(5) to prescribe regulations requiring any pesticide to be colored or discolored if he determines that such requirement is feasible and is necessary for the protection of health and the environment; and

(6) to determine and establish suitable names to be used in the ingredient statement.

(d) The Administrator shall submit to an advisory panel for comment as to the impact on health and the environment of the action proposed in notices of intent issued under section 6(b) and of the proposed and final form of regulations issued under section 25(a) within the same time periods as provided for the comments of the Secretary of Agriculture under such sections. The time requirements for notices of intent and proposed and final forms of regulation may not be modified or waived unless in addition to meeting the requirements of section 6(b) or 25(a), as applicable, the advisory panel has failed to comment on the proposed action within the prescribed time period or has agreed to the modification or waiver. The Administrator shall also solicit from the advisory panel comments, evaluations, and recommendations for operating guidelines to improve the effectiveness and quality of scientific analyses made by personnel of the Environmental Protection Agency that lead to decisions by the Administrator in carrying out the provisions of this Act. The comments, evaluations, and recommendations of the advisory panel submitted under this subsection and the response of the Administrator shall be published in the Federal Register in the same manner as provided for publication of the comments of the Secretary of Agriculture under such sections. The chairman of the advisory panel, after consultation with the Administrator, may create temporary subpanels on specific projects to assist the full advisory panel in expediting and preparing its evaluations, comments, and recommendations. The subpanels may be composed of scientists other than members of the advisory panel, as deemed necessary for the purpose of evaluating scientific studies relied upon by the Administrator with respect to proposed action. Such additional scientists shall be selected by the advisory panel. The panel referred to in this subsection shall consist of seven members appointed by the Administrator from a list of 12 nominees, six nominated by the National Institutes of Health, and six by the National Science Foundation, utilizing a system of staggered terms of appointment. Members of the panel shall be selected on the basis of their professional qualifications to assess the effects of the impact of pesticides on health and the environment. To the extent feasible to insure multidisciplinary representation, the panel membership shall include representation from the disciplines of toxicology, pathology, environmental biology, and related sciences. If a vacancy occurs on the panel due to expiration of a term, resignation, or any other reason, each replacement shall be selected by the Administrator from a group of 4 nominees, 2 submitted by each of the nominating entities named in this subsection. The Administrator may extend the term of a panel member until the new member is appointed to fill the vacancy. If a vacancy occurs due to resignation, or reason other than expiration of a term, the Administrator shall appoint a member to serve during the unexpired term utilizing the nomination process set forth in this subsection. Should the list of nominees provided under this subsection be unsatisfactory, the Administrator may request an additional set of nominees from the nominating entities. The Administrator may require such information from the nominees to the advisory panel as he deems necessary, and he shall publish in the Federal Register the name, address, and professional affiliations of each nominee. Each member of the panel shall receive per diem compensation at a rate not in excess of that fixed for GS-18 of the General Schedule as may be determined by the Administrator, except that any such member who holds another office or position under the Federal Government the compensation for which exceeds such rate may elect to receive compensation at the rate provided for such other office or position in lieu of the compensation provided by this subsection. In order to assure the objectivity of the advisory panel, the Administrator shall promulgate regulations regarding conflicts of interest with respect to the members of the panel. The advisory panel established under this subsection shall terminate September 30, 1987. In performing the functions assigned by this Act, the panel shall consult and coordinate its activities with the Science Advisory Board established under the Environmental Research, Development, and Demonstration Authorization Act of 1978. Whenever the Administrator exercises authority under section 6(c) of this Act to immediately suspend the registration of any pesticide to prevent an imminent hazard, the Administrator shall promptly submit to the advisory panel for comment, as to the impact on health and the environment, the action taken to suspend the registration of such pesticide.

(e) The Administrator shall, by written procedures, provide for peer review with respect to the design, protocols, and conduct of major scientific studies conducted under this Act by the Environmental Protection Agency or by any other Federal agency, any State or political subdivision thereof, or any institution or individual under grant, contract, or cooperative agreement from or with the Environmental Protection Agency. In such procedures, the Administrator shall also provide for peer review, using the advisory panel established under subsection (d) of this section or appropriate experts appointed by the Administrator from a current list of nominees maintained by such panel, with respect to the results of any such scientific studies relied upon by the Administrator with respect to actions the Administrator may take relating to the change in classification, suspension, or cancellation of a pesticide. *Provided*, That whenever the Administrator determines that circumstances do not permit the peer review of the results of any such scientific study prior to the Administrator's exercising authority under section 6(c) of this Act to immediately suspend the registration of any pesticide to prevent an imminent hazard, the Administrator shall promptly thereafter provide for the conduct of peer review as provided in this sentence. The evaluations and relevant documentation constituting the peer review that relate to the proposed scientific studies and the results of the completed scientific studies shall be included in the submission for comment forwarded by the Administrator to the advisory panel as provided in subsection (d). As used in this subsection, the term "peer review" shall mean an independent evaluation by scientific experts, either within or outside the Environmental Protection Agency, in the appropriate disciplines.

§ 136w–1. State primary enforcement responsibility

[Sec. 26] (a) For the purposes of this Act, a State shall have primary enforcement responsibility for pesticide use violations during any period for which the Administrator determines that such State—

(1) has adopted adequate pesticide use laws and regulations; *Provided,* That the Administrator may not require a State to have pesticide use laws that are more stringent than this Act;

(2) has adopted and is implementing adequate procedures for the enforcement of such State laws and regulations; and

(3) will keep such records and make such reports showing compliance with paragraphs (1) and (2) of this subsection as the Administrator may require by regulation.

(b) Notwithstanding the provisions of subsection (a) of this section, any State that enters into a cooperative agreement with the Administrator under section 23 of this Act for the enforcement of pesticide use restrictions shall have the primary enforcement responsibility for pesticide use violations. Any State that has a plan approved by the Administrator in accordance with the requirements of section 4 of this Act that the Administrator determines meets the criteria set out in subsection (a) of this section shall have the primary enforcement responsibility for pesticide use violations. The Administrator shall make such determinations with respect to State plans under section 4 of this Act in effect on the date of enactment of the Federal Pesticide Act of 1978 not later than six months after that date.

(c) The Administrator shall have primary enforcement responsibility for those States that do not have primary enforcement responsibility under this Act. Notwithstanding the provisions of section 2(e)(1) of this Act, during any period when the Administrator has such enforcement responsibility, section 8(b) of this Act shall apply to the books and records of commercial applicators and to any applicator who holds or applies pesticides, or use dilutions of pesticides, only to provide a service of controlling pests without delivering any unapplied pesticide to any person so served, and section 9(a) of this Act shall apply to the establishment or other place where pesticides or devices are held for application by such persons with respect to pesticides or devices held for such application.

§ 136w–2. Failure by the state to assure enforcement of state pesticide use regulations

[Sec. 27] (a) Upon receipt of any complaint or other information alleging or indicating a significant violation of the pesticide use provisions of this Act, the Administrator shall refer the matter to the appropriate State officials for their investigation of the matter consistent with the requirements of this Act. If, within thirty days, the State has not commenced appropriate enforcement action, the Administrator may act upon the complaint or information to the extent authorized under this Act.

(b) Whenever the Administrator determines that a State having primary enforcement responsibility for pesticide use violations is not carrying out (or cannot carry out due to the lack of adequate legal authority) such responsibility, the Administrator shall notify the State. Such notice shall specify those aspects of the administration of the State program that are determined to be inadequate. The State shall have ninety days after receipt of the notice to correct any deficiencies. If after that time the Administrator determines that the State program remains inadequate, the Administrator may rescind, in whole or in part, the State's primary enforcement responsibility for pesticide use violations.

(c) Neither section 26 of this Act nor this section shall limit the authority of the Administrator to enforce this Act, where the Administrator determines that emergency conditions exist that require immediate action on the part of the Administrator and the State authority is unwilling or unable adequately to respond to the emergency.

§ 136w–3. Identification of pests; cooperation with Department of Agriculture's program

[Sec. 28] The Administrator, in coordination with the Secretary of Agriculture, shall identify those pests that must be brought under control. The Administrator shall also coordinate and cooperate with the Secretary of Agriculture's research and implementation programs to develop and improve the safe use and effectiveness of chemical, biological, and alternative methods to combat and control pests that reduce the quality and economical production and distribution of agricultural products to domestic and foreign consumers.

§ 136w–4. Annual report

[Sec. 29] The Administrator shall submit an annual report to Congress before February 16 of each year and the first shall be due February 15, 1979. The report shall include the total number of applications for conditional registration under sections 3(c)(7)(B) and 3(c)(7)(C) of this Act that were filed during the immediately preceding fiscal year, and, with respect to those applications approved, the Administrator shall report the Administrator's findings in each case, the conditions imposed and any modification of such conditions in each case, and the quantities produced of such pesticides.

§ 136x. Severability

[Sec. 30] If any provision of this Act or the application thereof to any person or circumstance is held invalid, the invalidity shall not affect other provisions or applications of this Act which can be given effect without regard to the invalid provision or application, and to this end the provisions of this Act are severable.

§ 136y. Authorization for appropriations

[Sec. 31] There is authorized to be appropriated such sums as may be necessary to carry out the provisions of this Act for each of the fiscal years ending June 30, 1973, June 30, 1974, and June 30, 1975. The amounts authorized to be appropriated for any fiscal year ending after June 30, 1975, shall be the sums hereafter provided by law.

There are hereby authorized to be appropriated to carry out the provisions of this Act for the period beginning October 1, 1975, and ending September 30, 1976, the sum of $47,868,000, and for the period beginning October 1, 1976, and ending September 30, 1977, the sum of $46,636,000, and for the period beginning October 1, 1977, and ending September 30, 1978, the sum of $54,500,000, and for the period beginning October 1, 1978, and ending September 10, 1979, such sums as may be necessary, but not in excess of $70,000,000. There are hereby authorized to be appropriated to carry out the provisions of this Act for the period beginning October 1, 1979, and ending September 30, 1980, such sums as may be necessary, but not in excess of $72,160,000, and for the period beginning October 1, 1980, and ending September 30, 1981, such sums as may be necessary, but not in excess of $77,500,000. There are hereby authorized to be appropriated to carry out the provisions of this Act for the period beginning October 1, 1983, and ending September 30, 1984, such sums as may be necessary, but not in excess of $64,200,000.

5 • The Resource Conservation and Recovery Act

INTRODUCTION

The regulation and cleanup of hazardous wastes in the United States has become one of the most important priorities of the Environmental Protection Agency. The Reagan Administration's proposed budget for fiscal 1988 contained a request for hazardous waste programs, including clean up and management, of almost $1.85 billion, some $400 million more than the 1987 spending level. The proposed budget for fiscal 1988 contained a growing amount of resources directed to enforcement programs as more and more land disposal restrictions and underground storage tank standards are finalized, the agency said. EPA particularly cited a growing emphasis on corrective action remedies for contamination at hazardous waste facilities regulated under the Resource Conservation and Recovery Act, the basic law for regulation of hazardous waste management practices.

EPA estimates that $12 billion in federal funds will be needed to clean up about 2,000 hazardous waste sites. Others say the amount is much higher, with the Office of Technology Assessment predicting that $100 billion could be needed to clean up waste sites over the next 50 years.

The Administration's apparent willingness, in a period of budgetary constraints, to commit large sums of money to the control of hazardous wastes emphasizes the importance of the problem. This was not always the case. Hazardous waste did not really begin to attract the attention of the public and the regulators until after World War II, with the synthetic organic chemical revolution.

Hazardous waste management began at the federal level with the control of solid waste under the Solid Waste Disposal Act of 1965. Carried out by the Department of Health, Education, and Welfare, the law focused on garbage, particularly on restricting open burning, which was considered a fire hazard. In 1970, then-President Nixon signed an amended version of the solid waste law and renamed it the Resource Recovery Act. This law provided funds for collecting and recycling materials and required a comprehensive investigation of hazardous waste management practices in the United States. Administration of the Act was given to the Environmental Protection Agency upon its creation. A Senate staff member said the sentiment at the time was that "we were drowning in our own garbage." Almost overnight, the law spawned an industry to recycle and incinerate waste, laying the foundations for the current waste disposal industry, a Senate staff aide said.

Two former EPA administrators, Douglas M. Costle and William D. Ruckelshaus, said that in the early 1970s some environmental professionals recognized the dangers of the toxic chemicals that were being generated by the chemical industry. But still it was not a particular concern for policy-makers at EPA or for the public, they said.

In 1976, the same year Congress enacted the Toxic Substances Control Act, it passed the Resource Conservation and Recovery Act of 1976 (PL 94-580), which completely replaced the language of the Resource Recovery Act. The new law continued provisions on solid waste and resource recovery, including the disposal of used oil and waste, and it closed most open dumps; it redefined solid waste to include hazardous waste and ordered EPA to require "cradle to grave" tracking of hazardous waste and controls on hazardous waste facilities. The Act required standards to be set for hazardous waste treatment, storage, and disposal facilities to provide for "the maintenance of operation of such facilities and requiring such additional qualifications as to ownership, continuity of operation, training for personnel, and financial responsibility (including financial responsibility for corrective action) as may be necessary or desirable."

The agency gave little attention between 1976 and 1978 to drawing up rules to carry out the law. Steady pressure from the public and Congress focused the agency instead on revising and issuing regulations for the Clean Air Act and the Clean Water Act, Costle said.

That focus changed in August 1978, when then-President Carter declared a state of emergency in a neighborhood near Love Canal, where long-buried chemicals were seeping into homes and high incidences of health effects, from headaches to birth defects, were reported. The event triggered the discovery of thousands of other dumpsites, alarming the public and mobilizing the Administration and the Congress. "The dawning of knowledge in the minds of a few people is not enough to move our political system," Costle told BNA. "What our political system takes to move it is galvanizing events. And when Love Canal came along, bingo, that was a tremendously galvanizing event."

Under a court order, EPA issued the first two portions of the RCRA hazardous waste rules by May 5, 1980, in an attempt to prevent creation of more toxic waste dumps. The regulations define which wastes are hazardous and set standards for treatment, storage, and disposal facilities. Also in 1980, Congress passed what is a logical complement to RCRA, the Comprehensive Environmental Response, Compensation, and Liability Act of 1980 (PL 96–510), also known as the "superfund law," which assures financial responsibility for the long-term maintenance of hazardous waste disposal facilities, and provides for the containment and cleanup of old, abandoned hazardous waste disposal sites that are leaking or endangering the public health.

Regulations governing the transport of hazardous wastes were developed jointly by EPA and the Department of Transportation (DOT). Wastes in transit are regulated by the labeling, packaging, and spill reporting provisions of the Hazardous Materials Transportation Act (HMTA), which is administered by DOT. Shippers must certify that they are in compliance with DOT regulations, and all hazardous wastes regulated by EPA, when shipped, must be accompanied by a uniform hazardous waste manifest. When the waste is received at the disposal facility, the facility must return a copy of the manifest to the generator, thereby letting the generator know that the waste was received. If no copy was received, the generator must notify EPA.

Meanwhile, another perception was surfacing: that the primary method of waste disposal envisioned by the new RCRA rules—land disposal—was going to result in an ever-increasing number of hazardous waste sites.

Major provisions of the 1984 RCRA amendments (PL 98–616) called for banning land disposal of untreated hazardous waste within five and one-half years of passage. Congress set schedules for the bans and made them automatic if the agency failed to act by certain dates.

The new law also closed "loopholes" in previous rules that allowed toxics to be burned in industrial and apartment furnaces. Increasing the breadth of EPA's regulatory program, the amendments require the agency for the first time to regulate an estimated 600,000 generators of small quantities of hazardous substances and petroleum products.

The RCRA amendments and the recently passed Superfund Amendments and Reauthorization Act of 1986 reflect an overriding concern that hazardous substances seep into the earth and contaminate groundwater, which provides more than half of the drinking water in the United States. In large part because of that concern, the 1984 RCRA amendments provided for the regulation of underground storage tanks and the superfund amendments established an underground tank cleanup trust fund.

EPA Administrator Lee M. Thomas said the two major problems in the hazardous waste program are connected to ground water protection: how to impose the land disposal bans with inadequate technical information on hazards posed by the substances over time and how to bring RCRA facilities into compliance with groundwater monitoring rules. J. Clarence Davies, executive vice president of the Conservation Foundation, said the task before EPA and industry is to develop and permit incineration and treatment facilities to replace land disposal. Thomas predicted that in the next few years, alternative technologies will be available to meet the need, but that the process will be "traumatic" for both the hazardous waste industry and business.

The question of how much groundwater contamination must be remedied at superfund sites and what level of groundwater contamination can be allowed under the RCRA program must be addressed, Ruckelshaus said. The task is enormously difficult because no one knows the long-term health effects of exposure to small amounts of most chemicals, according to Ruckelshaus and Costle. "I think it will dawn on us," Ruckelshaus said, that EPA cannot develop risk assessments for every chemical and that the practical solution is to require installation of the best available technology. Costle agreed, continuing that contaminated drinking water will be the next major environmental concern for the public. "I think we'll see a push toward technology as an insurance policy. The issue will be exposure," he told BNA.

The answer to contaminated drinking water supplies may be in finding alternate supplies, he said. Another approach would be development of new technology to treat tap water better, or systems designed to strip trace amounts of chemicals out of water, he suggested. "But if you ask me, 'Does the public health require that?' I don't think we are going to find out any time soon," Costle told BNA. "So it gets back to the question: 'How does a reasonably prudent man act in the face of uncertainty?' He reacts in a reasonably prudent way.

He says, 'Let's limit exposure somehow,' " the former EPA administrator concluded.

Resource Conservation and Recovery Act

**(P.L. 94–580, approved October 21, 1976; as last amended by
P.L. 99–499, approved October 17, 1986)**

Subchapter I. General Provisions

§ 6901. Congressional findings

[Sec. 1002] (a) The Congress finds with respect to solid waste—
(1) that the continuing technological progress and improvement in methods of manufacture, packaging, and marketing of consumer products has resulted in an ever-mounting increase, and in a change in the characteristics, of the mass material discarded by the purchaser of such products;
(2) that the economic and population growth of our Nation, and the improvements in the standard of living enjoyed by our population, have required increased industrial production to meet our needs, and have made necessary the demolition of old buildings, the construction of new buildings, and the provision of highways and other avenues of transportation, which, together with related industrial, commercial, and agricultural operations, have resulted in a rising tide of scrap, discarded, and waste materials;
(3) that the continuing concentration of our population in expanding metropolitan and other urban areas has presented these communities with serious financial, management, intergovernmental, and technical problems in the disposal of solid wastes resulting from the industrial, commercial, domestic, and other activities carried on in such areas;
(4) that while the collection and disposal of solid wastes should continue to be primarily the function of State, regional, and local agencies, the problems of waste disposal as set forth above have become a matter national in scope and in concern and necessitate Federal action through financial and technical assistance and leadership in the development, demonstration, and application of new and improved methods and processes to reduce the amount of waste and unsalvageable materials and to provide for proper and economical solid waste disposal practices.
(b) The Congress finds with respect to the environment and health, that—

(1) although land is too valuable a national resource to be needlessly polluted by discarded materials, most solid waste is disposed of on land in open dumps and sanitary landfills;

(2) disposal of solid waste and hazardous waste in or on the land without careful planning and management can present a danger to human health and the environment;

(3) as a result of the Clean Air Act, the Water Pollution Control Act, and other Federal and State laws respecting public health and the environment, greater amounts of solid waste (in the form of sludge and other pollution treatment residues) have been created. Similarly, inadequate and environmentally unsound practices for the disposal or use of solid waste have created greater amounts of air and water pollution and other problems for the environment and for health;

(4) open dumping is particularly harmful to health, contaminates drinking water from underground and surface supplies, and pollutes the air and the land;

(5) the placement of inadequate controls on hazardous waste management will result in substantial risks to human health and the environment;

(6) if hazardous waste management is improperly performed in the first instance, corrective action is likely to be expensive, complex, and time consuming;

(7) certain classes of land disposal facilities are not capable of assuring long-term containment of certain hazardous wastes, and to avoid substantial risk to human health and the environment, reliance on land disposal should be minimized or eliminated, and land disposal, particularly landfill and surface impoundment, should be the least favored method for managing hazardous wastes; and

(8) alternatives to existing methods of land disposal must be developed since many of the cities in the United States will be running out of suitable solid waste disposal sites within five years unless immediate action is taken.

(c) The Congress finds with respect to materials, that:

(1) millions of tons of recoverable material which could be used are needlessly buried each year;

(2) methods are available to separate usable materials from solid waste; and

(3) the recovery and conservation of such materials can reduce the dependence of the United States on foreign resources and reduce the deficit in its balance of payments.

(d) The Congress finds with respect to energy, that—

(1) solid waste represents a potential source of solid fuel, oil, or gas that can be converted into energy;

(2) the need exists to develop alternative energy sources for public and private consumption in order to reduce our dependence on such

sources as petroleum products, natural gas, nuclear and hydroelectric generation; and
(3) technology exists to produce usable energy from solid waste.

§ 6901a. Congressional findings: used oil recycling

[Sec. 2] The Congress finds and declares that—
(1) used oil is a valuable source of increasingly scarce energy and materials;
(2) technology exists to re-refine, reprocess, reclaim, and otherwise recycle used oil;
(3) used oil constitutes a threat to public health and the environment when reused or disposed of improperly; and
that, therefore, it is in the national interest to recycle used oil in a manner which does not constitute a threat to public health and the environment and which conserves energy and materials.

§ 6902. Objectives

[Sec. 1003] (a) The objectives of this Act are to promote the protection of health and the environment and to conserve valuable material and energy resources by—
(1) providing technical and financial assistance to State and local governments and interstate agencies for the development of solid waste management plans (including resource recovery and resource conservation systems) which will promote improved solid waste management techniques (including more effective organizational arrangements), new and improved methods of collection, separation, and recovery of solid waste, and the environmentally safe disposal of nonrecoverable residues;
(2) providing training grants in occupations involving the design, operation, and maintenance of solid waste disposal systems;
(3) prohibiting future open dumping on the land and requiring the conversion of existing open dumps to facilities which do not pose a danger to the environment or to health;
(4) assuring that hazardous waste management practices are conducted in a manner which protects human health and the environment;
(5) requiring that hazardous waste be properly managed in the first instance thereby reducing the need for corrective action at a future date;
(6) minimizing the generation of hazardous waste and the land disposal of hazardous waste by encouraging process substitution, materials recovery, properly conducted recycling and reuse, and treatment;
(7) establishing a viable Federal-State partnership to carry out the purposes of this Act and insuring that the Administrator will, in carrying

out the provisions of subtitle C of this Act, give a high priority to assisting and cooperating with States in obtaining full authorization of State programs under subtitle C;

(8) providing for the promulgation of guidelines for solid waste collection, transport, separation, recovery, and disposal practices and systems;

(9) promoting a national research and development program for improved solid waste management and resource conservation techniques, more effective organizational arrangements, and new and improved methods of collection, separation, and recovery, and recycling of solid wastes and environmentally safe disposal of nonrecoverable residues;

(10) promoting the demonstration, construction, and application of solid waste management, resource recovery, and resource conservation systems which preserve and enhance the quality of air, water, and land resources; and

(11) establishing a cooperative effort among the Federal, State, and local governments and private enterprise in order to recover valuable materials and energy from solid waste.

(b) The Congress hereby declares it to be the national policy of the United States that, wherever feasible, the generation of hazardous waste is to be reduced or eliminated as expeditiously as possible. Waste that is nevertheless generated should be treated, stored, or disposed of so as to minimize the present and future threat to human health and the environment.

§ 6903. Definitions

[Sec. 1004] As used in this Act:

(1) The term "Administrator" means the Administrator of the Environmental Protection Agency.

(2) The term "construction," with respect to any project of construction under this Act, means (A) the erection or building of new structures and acquisition of lands or interests therein, or the acquisition, replacement, expansion, remodeling, alteration, modernization, or extension of existing structures, and (B) the acquisition and installation of initial equipment of, or required in connection with, new or newly acquired structures or the expanded, remodeled, altered, modernized or extended part of existing structures (including trucks and other motor vehicles, and tractors, cranes, and other machinery) necessary for the proper utilization and operation of the facility after completion of the project; and includes preliminary planning to determine the economic and engineering feasibility and the public health and safety aspects of the project, the engineering, architectural, legal, fiscal, and economic investigations and studies, and any surveys, designs, plans, working drawings, specifications, and other action necessary for the carrying out of the project, and (C) the inspection

and supervision of the process of carrying out the project to completion.

(2)(A) The term "demonstration" means the initial exhibition of a new technology process or practice or a significantly new combination or use of technologies, processes or practices, subsequent to the development stage, for the purpose of proving technological feasibility and cost effectiveness.

(3) The term "disposal" means the discharge, deposit, injection, dumping, spilling, leaking, or placing of any solid waste or hazardous waste into or on any land or water so that such solid waste or hazardous waste or any constituent thereof may enter the environment or be emitted into the air or discharged into any waters, including ground waters.

(4) The term "Federal agency" means any department, agency, or other instrumentality of the Federal Government, any independent agency or establishment of the Federal Government including any Government corporation, and the Government Printing Office.

(5) The term "hazardous waste" means a solid waste, or combination of solid wastes, which because of its quantity, concentration, or physical, chemical, or infectious characteristics may—

(A) cause, or significantly contribute to an increase in mortality or an increase in serious irreversible, or incapacitating reversible, illness; or

(B) pose a substantial present or potential hazard to human health or the environment when improperly treated, stored, transported, or disposed of, or otherwise managed.

(6) The term "hazardous waste generation" means the act or process of producing hazardous waste.

(7) The term "hazardous waste management" means the systematic control of the collection, source separation, storage, transportation, processing, treatment, recovery, and disposal of hazardous wastes.

(8) For purposes of Federal financial assistance (other than rural communities assistance), the term "implementation" does not include the acquisition, leasing, construction, or modification of facilities or equipment or the acquisition, leasing, or improvement of land.

(9) The term "intermunicipal agency" means an agency established by two or more municipalities with responsibility for planning or administration of solid waste.

(10) The term "interstate agency" means an agency of two or more municipalities in different States, or an agency established by two or more States, with authority to provide for the management of solid wastes and serving two or more municipalities located in different States.

(11) The term "long-term contract" means, when used in relation to solid waste supply, a contract of sufficient duration to assure the viability of a resource recovery facility (to the extent that such viability depends

upon solid waste supply).

(12) The term "manifest" means the form used for identifying the quantity, composition, and the origin, routing, and destination of hazardous waste during its transportation from the point of generation to the point of disposal, treatment, or storage.

(13) The term "municipality" (A) means a city, town, borough, county, parish, district, or other public body created by or pursuant to State law, with responsibility for the planning or administration of solid waste management, or an Indian tribe or authorized tribal organization or Alaska Native village or organization, and (B) includes any rural community or unincorporated town or village or any other public entity for which an application for assistance is made by a State or political subdivision thereof.

(14) The term "open dump" means any facility or site where solid waste is disposed of which is not a sanitary landfill which meets the criteria promulgated under section 4004 and which is not a facility for disposal of hazardous waste.

(15) The term "person" means an individual, trust, firm, joint stock company, corporation (including a government corporation), partnership, association, State, municipality, commission, political subdivision of a State, or any interstate body.

(16) The term "procurement item" means any device, good, substance, material, product, or other item whether real or personal property which is the subject of any purchase, barter, or other exchange made to procure such item.

(17) The term "procuring agency" means any Federal agency, or any State agency or agency of a political subdivision of a State which is using appropriated Federal funds for such procurement, or any person contracting with any such agency with respect to work performed under such contract.

(18) The term "recoverable" refers to the capability and likelihood of being recovered from solid waste for a commercial or industrial use.

(19) The term "recovered material" means waste material and byproducts which have been recovered or diverted from solid waste, but such term does not include those materials and byproducts generated from, and commonly reused within, an original manufacturing process.

(20) The term "recovered resources" means material or energy recovered from solid waste.

(21) The term "resource conservation" means reduction of the amounts of solid waste that are generated, reduction of overall resource consumption, and utilization of recovered resources.

(22) The term "resource recovery" means the recovery of material or energy from solid waste.

(23) The term "resource recovery system" means a solid waste management system which provides for collection, separation, recycling, and

recovery of solid wastes, including disposal of nonrecoverable waste residues.

(24) The term "resource recovery facility" means any facility at which solid waste is processed for the purpose of extracting, converting to energy, or otherwise separating and preparing solid waste for reuse.

(25) The term "regional authority" means the authority established or designated under section 4006.

(26) The term "sanitary landfill" means a facility for the disposal of solid waste which meets the criteria published under section 4004.

(26)(A) The term "sludge" means any solid, semisolid or liquid waste generated from a municipal, commercial, or industrial wastewater treatment plant, water supply treatment plant, or air pollution control facility or any other such waste having similar characteristics and effects.

(27) The term "solid waste" means any garbage, refuse, sludge from a waste treatment plant, water supply treatment plant, or air pollution control facility and other discarded material, including solid, liquid, semisolid, or contained gaseous material resulting from industrial, commercial, mining, and agricultural operations, and from community activities, but does not include solid or dissolved material in domestic sewage, or solid or dissolved materials in irrigation return flows or industrial discharges which are point sources subject to permits under section 402 of the Federal Water Pollution Control Act, as amended (86 Stat. 880), or source, special nuclear, or byproduct material as defined by the Atomic Energy Act of 1954, as amended (68 Stat. 923).

(28) The term "solid waste management" means the systematic administration of activities which provide for the collection, source separation, storage, transportation, transfer, processing, treatment, and disposal of solid waste.

(29) The term "solid waste management facility" includes (A) any resource recovery system or component thereof, (B) any system, program, or facility for resource conservation, and (C) any facility for the collection, source separation, storage, transportation, transfer, processing, treatment or disposal of solid wastes including hazardous wastes, whether such facility is associated with facilities generating such wastes or otherwise.

(30) The terms "solid waste planning," "solid waste management," and "comprehensive planning" include planning or management respecting resource recovery and resource conservation.

(31) The term "State" means any of the several States, the District of Columbia, the Commonwealth of Puerto Rico, the Virgin Islands, Guam, American Samoa, and the Commonwealth of the Northern Mariana Islands.

(32) The term "State authority" means the agency established or designated under section 4007.

(33) The term "storage," when used in connection with hazardous waste, means the containment of hazardous waste, either on a temporary basis or for a period of years, in such a manner as not to constitute disposal of such hazardous waste.

(34) The term "treatment," when used in connection with hazardous waste, means any method, technique, or process, including neutralization, designed to change the physical, chemical, or biological character or composition of any hazardous waste so as to neutralize such waste or so as to render such waste nonhazardous, safer for transport, amenable for recovery, amenable for storage, or reduced in volume. Such term includes any activity or processing designed to change the physical form or chemical composition of hazardous waste so as to render it nonhazardous.

(35) The term "virgin material" means a raw material, including previously unused copper, aluminum, lead, zinc, iron, or other metal or metal ore, any undeveloped resource that is, or with new technology will become, a source of raw materials.

(36) The term "used oil" means any oil which has been—

(A) refined from crude oil,

(B) used, and

(C) as a result of such use, contaminated by physical or chemical impurities.

(37) The term "recycled oil" means any used oil which is reused, following its original use, for any purpose (including the purpose for which the oil was originally used). Such term includes oil which is refined, reclaimed, burned, or reprocessed.

(38) The term "lubricating oil" means the fraction of crude oil which is sold for purposes of reducing friction in any industrial or mechanical device. Such term includes re-refined oil.

(39) The term "re-refined oil" means used oil from which the physical and chemical contaminants acquired through previous use have been removed through a refining process.

§ 6904. Government cooperation

[Sec. 1005] (a) The provisions of this Act to be carried out by States may be carried out by interstate agencies and provisions applicable to States may apply to interstate regions where such agencies and regions have been established by the respective States and approved by the Administrator. In any such case, action required to be taken by the Governor of a State, respecting regional designation shall be required to be taken by the Governor of each of the respective States with respect to so much of the interstate region as is within the jurisdiction of that State.

(b) The Consent of the Congress is hereby given to two or more States to negotiate and enter into agreements or compacts, not in conflict with any law or treaty of the United States, for—

(1) cooperative effort and mutual assistance for the management of solid waste or hazardous waste (or both) and the enforcement of their respective laws relating thereto, and

(2) the establishment of such agencies, joint or otherwise, as they may deem desirable for making effective such agreements or compacts.

No such agreement or compact shall be binding or obligatory upon any State a party thereto unless it is agreed upon by all parties to the agreement and until it has been approved by the Administrator and the Congress.

§ 6905. Application of act and integration with other acts

[Sec. 1006] (a) Nothing in this Act shall be construed to apply to (or to authorize any State, interstate, or local authority to regulate) any activity or substance which is subject to the Federal Water Pollution Control Act (33 U.S.C. 1151 and following), the Safe Drinking Water Act (42 U.S.C. 300f and following), the Marine Protection, Research and Sanctuaries Act of 1972 (33 U.S.C. 1401 and following), or the Atomic Energy Act of 1954 (42 U.S.C. 2011 and following) except to the extent that such application (or regulation) is not inconsistent with the requirements of such Acts.

(b)(1) The Administrator shall integrate all provisions of this Act for purposes of administration and enforcement and shall avoid duplication, to the maximum extent practicable, with the appropriate provisions of the Clean Air Act (42 U.S.C. 1857 and following), the Federal Water Pollution Control Act (33 U.S.C. 1151 and following), the Federal Insecticide, Fungicide, and Rodenticide Act (7 U.S.C. 135 and following), the Safe Drinking Water Act (42 U.S.C. 300f and following), the Marine Protection, Research and Sanctuaries Act of 1972 (33 U.S.C. 1401 and following) and such other Acts of Congress as grant regulatory authority to the Administrator. Such integration shall be effected only to the extent that it can be done in a manner consistent with the goals and policies expressed in this Act and in the other acts referred to in this subsection.

(2)(A) As promptly as practicable after the date of the enactment of the Hazardous and Solid Waste Amendments of 1984, the Administrator shall submit a report describing—

    (i) the current data and information available on emissions of polychlorinated dibenzo-p-dioxins from resource recovery facilities burning municipal solid waste;

    (ii) any significant risks to human health posed by these emissions; and

    (iii) operating practices appropriate for controlling these emissions.

(B) Based on the report under subparagraph (A) and on any future information on such emissions, the Administrator may publish advisories or guidelines regarding the control of dioxin emissions from such facilities. Nothing in this paragraph shall be construed to preempt or otherwise affect the authority of the Administrator to promulgate any regulations under the Clean Air Act regarding emissions of polychlorinated dibenzo-p-dioxins.

(3) Notwithstanding any other provisions of law, in developing solid waste plans, it is the intention of this Act that in determining the size of a waste-to-energy facility, adequate provisions shall be given to the present and reasonably anticipated future needs, including those needs created by thorough implementation of section 6002(h), of the recycling and resource recovery interests within the area encompassed by the solid waste plan.

(c) (1) No later than 90 days after the date of enactment of the Solid Waste Disposal Act Amendments of 1980, the Administrator shall review any regulations applicable to the treatment, storage, or disposal of any coal mining wastes or overburden promulgated by the Secretary of the Interior under the Surface Mining and Reclamation Act of 1977. If the Administrator determines that any requirement of final regulations promulgated under any section of subtitle C relating to mining wastes or overburden is not adequately addressed in such regulations promulgated by the Secretary, the Administrator shall promptly transmit such determination, together with suggested revisions and supporting documentation, to the Secretary.

(2) The Secretary of the Interior shall have exclusive responsibility for carrying out any requirement of subtitle C of this Act with respect to coal mining wastes or overburden for which a surface coal mining and reclamation permit is issued or approved under the Surface Mining Control and Reclamation Act of 1977. The Secretary shall, with the concurrence of the Administrator, promulgate such regulations as may be necessary to carry out the purposes of this subsection and shall integrate such regulations with regulations promulgated under the Surface Mining Control and Reclamation Act of 1977.

§ 6906. Financial disclosure

[Sec. 1007] (a) Each officer or employee of the Administrator who—
(1) performs any function or duty under this Act; and
(2) has any known financial interest in any person who applies for or receives financial assistance under this Act shall beginning on February 1, 1977, annually file with the Administrator a written statement concerning all such interests held by such officer or employee during the preceding calendar year. Such statement shall be available to the public.

(b) The Administrator shall—
(1) act within ninety days after the date of enactment of this Act—
  (A) to define the term "known financial interest" for purposes of subsection (a) of this section; and
  (B) to establish the methods by which the requirement to file written statements specified in subsection (a) of this section will be

monitored and enforced, including appropriate provision for the filing by such officers and employees of such statements and the review by the Administrator of such statements; and

(2) report to the Congress on June 1, 1978, and of each succeeding calendar year with respect to such disclosures and the actions taken in regard thereto during the preceding calendar year.

(c) In the rules prescribed under subsection (b) of this section, the Administrator may identify specific positions within the Environmental Protection Agency which are of a nonpolicymaking nature and provide that officers or employees occupying such positions shall be exempt from the requirements of this section.

(d) Any officer or employee who is subject to, and knowingly violates, this section shall be fined not more than $2,500 or imprisoned not more than one year, or both.

§ 6907. Solid waste management information and guidelines

[Sec. 1008] (a) Within one year of enactment of this section, and from time to time thereafter, the Administrator shall, in cooperation with appropriate Federal, State, municipal, and inter-municipal agencies, and in consultation with other interested persons, and after public hearings, develop and publish suggested guidelines for solid waste management. Such suggested guidelines shall—

(1) provide a technical and economic description of the level of performance that can be attained by various available solid waste management practices (including operating practices) which provide for the protection of public health and the environment;

(2) not later than two years after the enactment of this section, describe levels of performance, including appropriate methods and degrees of control, that provide at a minimum for (A) protection of public health and welfare; (B) protection of the quality of ground waters and surface waters from leachates; (C) protection of the quality of surface waters from runoff through compliance with effluent limitations under the Federal Water Pollution Control Act, as amended; (D) protection of ambient air quality through compliance with new source performance standards or requirements of air quality implementation plans under the Clean Air Act, as amended; (E) disease and vector control; (F) safety; and (G) esthetics; and

(3) provide minimum criteria to be used by the States to define those solid waste management practices which constitute the open dumping of solid waste or hazardous waste and are to be prohibited under subtitle D of this Act.

Where appropriate, such suggested guidelines also shall include minimum information for use in deciding the adequate location, design, and construction of facilities associated with solid waste management practices, including the consideration of regional, geographic, demographic, and climatic factors.

(b) The Administrator shall notify the Committee on Public Works of the Senate and the Committee on Interstate and Foreign Commerce of the House of Representatives a reasonable time before publishing any suggested guidelines or proposed regulations under this act of the content of such proposed suggested guidelines or proposed regulations under this Act.

Subchapter II. Office of Solid Waste; Authorities of the Administrator

§ 6911. Office of Solid Waste and Interagency Coordinating Committee

[Sec. 2001] (a) The Administrator shall establish within the Environmental Protection Agency an Office of Solid Waste (hereinafter referred to as the "Office") to be headed by an Assistant Administrator of the Environmental Protection Agency. The duties and responsibilities (other than duties and responsibilities relating to research and development) of the Administrator under this Act (as modified by applicable reorganization plans) shall be carried out through the Office.

(b)(1) There is hereby established an Interagency Coordinating Committee on Federal Resource Conservation and Recovery Activities which shall have the responsibility for coordinating all activities dealing with resource conservation and recovery from solid waste carried out by the Environmental Protection Agency, the Department of Energy, the Department of Commerce, and all other Federal agencies which conduct such activities pursuant to this or any other Act. For purposes of this subsection, the term "resource conservation and recovery activities" shall include, but not be limited to, all research, development and demonstration projects on resource conservation or energy, or material, recovery from solid waste, and all technical or financial assistance for State or local planning for, or implementation of, projects related to resource conservation or energy or material, recovery from solid waste. The Committee shall be chaired by the Administrator of the Environmental Protection Agency or such person as the Administrator may designate. Members of the Committee shall include representatives of the Department of Energy, the Department of Commerce, the Department of the Treasury, and each other Federal agency which the Administrator determines to have programs or responsibilities affecting resource conservation or recovery.

(2) The Interagency Coordinating Committee shall include oversight of the implementation of

(A) the May 1979 Memorandum of Understanding on Energy Recovery from Municipal Solid Waste between the Environmental Protection Agency and the Department of Energy;

(B) the May 30, 1978, Interagency Agreement between the Department of Commerce and the Environmental Protection Agency on the Implementation of the Resource Conservation and Recovery Act; and

(C) any subsequent agreements between these agencies or other Federal agencies which address Federal resource recovery or conservation activities.

(3) The Interagency Coordinating Committee shall submit to the Congress by March 1, 1981, and on March 1 each year thereafter, a five-year action plan for Federal resource conservation or recovery activities which shall identify means and propose programs to encourage resource conservation or material and energy recovery and increase private and municipal investment in resource conservation or recovery systems, especially those which provide for material conservation or recovery as well as energy conservation or recovery. Such plan shall describe, at a minimum, a coordinated and nonduplicatory plan for resource recovery and conservation activities for the Environmental Protection Agency, the Department of Energy, the Department of Commerce, and all other Federal agencies which conduct such activities.

§ 6912. Authorities of administrator

[Sec. 2002] (a) In carrying out this Act, the Administrator is authorized to—

(1) prescribe, in consultation with Federal, State, and regional authorities, such regulations as are necessary to carry out his functions under this Act;

(2) consult with or exchange information with other Federal agencies undertaking research, development, demonstration projects, studies, or investigations relating to solid waste;

(3) provide technical and financial assistance to States or regional agencies in the development and implementation of solid waste plans and hazardous waste management programs;

(4) consult with representatives of science, industry, agriculture, labor, environmental protection and consumer organizations, and other groups, as he deems advisable;

(5) utilize the information, facilities, personnel and other resources of Federal agencies, including the National Bureau of Standards and the National Bureau of the Census, on a reimbursable basis, to perform research and analyses and conduct studies and investigations related to resource recovery and conservation and to otherwise carry out the Administrator's functions under this Act; and

(6) to delegate to the Secretary of Transportation the performance of any inspection or enforcement function under this Act relating to the transportation of hazardous waste where such delegation would avoid

unnecessary duplication of activity and would carry out the objectives of this Act and of the Hazardous Materials Transportation Act.

(b) Each regulation promulgated under this Act shall be reviewed and, where necessary, revised not less frequently than every three years.

(c) In carrying out the provisions of this Act, the Administrator, and duly-designated agents and employees of the Environmental Protection Agency, are authorized to initiate and conduct investigations under the criminal provisions of this Act, and to refer the results of these investigations to the Attorney General for prosecution in appropriate cases.

§ 6913. Resource Conservation and Recovery Panels

[Sec. 2003] The Administrator shall provide teams of personnel, including Federal, State, and local employees or contractors (hereinafter referred to as "Resource Conservation and Recovery Panels") to provide Federal agencies, States and local governments upon request with technical assistance on solid waste management, resource recovery, and resource conservation. Such teams shall include technical, marketing, financial, and institutional specialists, and the services of such teams shall be provided without charge to States or local governments.

§ 6914. Grants for discarded tire disposal

[Sec. 2004] (a) The Administrator shall make available grants equal to 5 percent of the purchase price of tire shredders (including portable shredders attached to tire collection trucks) to those eligible applicants best meeting criteria promulgated under this section. An eligible applicant may be any private purchaser, public body, or public-private joint venture. Criteria for receiving grants shall be promulgated under this section and shall include the policy to offer any private purchaser the first option to receive a grant, the policy to develop widespread geographic distribution of tire shredding facilities, the need for such facilities within a geographic area, and the projected risk and viability of any such venture. In the case of an application under this section from a public body, the Administrator shall first make a determination that there are no private purchasers interested in making an application before approving a grant to a public body.

(b) There is authorized to be appropriated $750,000 for each of the fiscal years 1978 and 1979 to carry out this section.

§ 6914a. Labeling of lubricating oil

[Sec. 2005] For purposes of any provision of law which requires the labeling of commodities, lubricating oil shall be treated as lawfully labeled only if it bears the following statement, prominently displayed:

DON'T POLLUTE—CONSERVE RESOURCES; RETURN USED OIL TO COLLECTION CENTERS.

§ 6915. Annual report

[Sec. 2006] The Administrator shall transmit to the Congress and the President, not later than ninety days after the end of each fiscal year, a comprehensive and detailed report on all activities of the Office during the preceding fiscal year. Each such report shall include—

(1) a statement of specific and detailed objectives for the activities and programs conducted and assisted under this Act;

(2) statements of the Administrator's conclusions as to the effectiveness of such activities and programs in meeting the stated objectives and the purposes of this Act, measured through the end of such fiscal year;

(3) a summary of outstanding solid waste problems confronting the Administrator, in order of priority;

(4) recommendations with respect to such legislation which the Administrator deems necessary or desirable to assist in solving problems respecting solid waste;

(5) all other information required to be submitted to the Congress pursuant to any other provisions of this Act; and

(6) the Administrator's plans for activities and programs respecting solid waste during the next fiscal year.

§ 6916. General authorization

[Sec. 2007] (a) There are authorized to be appropriated to the Administrator for the purpose of carrying out the provisions of this Act, $35,000,000 for the fiscal year ending September 30, 1977, $38,000,000 for the fiscal year ending September 30, 1978, $42,000,000 for the fiscal year ending September 30, 1979, $70,000,000 for the fiscal year ending September 30, 1980, $80,000,000 for the fiscal year ending September 30, 1981, $80,000,000 for the fiscal year ending September 30, 1982, $70,000,000 for the fiscal year ending September 30, 1985, $80,000,000 for the fiscal year ending September 30, 1986, $80,000,000 for the fiscal year ending September 30, 1987, and $80,000,000 for the fiscal year 1988.

(b) Not less than 20 percent of the amount appropriated under subsection (a), or $5,000,000 per fiscal year, whichever is less, shall be used only for purposes of Resource Recovery and Conservation Panels established under section 2003 (including travel expenses incurred by such panels in carrying out their functions under this Act).

(c) Not less than 30 percent of the amount appropriated under subsection (a) shall be used only for purposes of carrying out subtitle C of this Act (relating to hazardous waste) other than section 3011.

(d) Not less than 25 per centum of the total amount appropriated under this title, up to the amount authorized in section 4008(a)(1), shall be used only for purposes of support to State, regional, local, and interstate agencies in accordance with subtitle D of this Act other than section 4008(a)(2) or 4009.

(e) There is authorized to be appropriated to the Administrator $3,246,000 for the fiscal year 1985, $2,408,300 for the fiscal year 1986, $2,529,000 for the fiscal year 1987, and $2,529,000 for the fiscal year 1988 to be used—

(1) for additional officers or employees of the Environmental Protection Agency authorized by the Administrator to conduct criminal investigations (to investigate, or supervise the investigation of, any activity for which a criminal penalty is provided) under this Act; and

(2) for support costs for such additional officers or employees.

(f)(1) There are authorized to be appropriated to the Administrator for the purpose of carrying out the provisions of subtitle I (relating to regulation of underground storage tanks), $10,000,000 for each of the fiscal years 1985 through 1988.

(2) There is authorized to be appropriated $25,000,000 for each of the fiscal years 1985 through 1988 to be used to make grants to the States for purposes of assisting the States in the development and implementation of approved State underground storage tank release detection, prevention, and correction programs under subtitle I.

§ 6917. Office of Ombudsman

[Sec. 2008] (a) The Administrator shall establish an Office of Ombudsman, to be directed by an Ombudsman. It shall be the function of the Office of Ombudsman to receive individual complaints, grievances, requests for information submitted by any person with respect to any program or requirement under this Act.

(b) The Ombudsman shall render assistance with respect to the complaints, grievances, and requests submitted to the Office of Ombudsman, and shall make appropriate recommendations to the Administrator.

(c) The establishment of the Office of Ombudsman shall not affect any procedures for grievances, appeals, or administrative matters in any other provision of this Act, any other provision of law, or any Federal regulation.

(d) The Office of the Ombudsman shall cease to exist 4 years after the date of enactment of the Hazardous and Solid Waste Amendments of 1984.

Subchapter III. Hazardous Waste Management

§ 6921. Identification and listing of hazardous waste

[Sec. 3001] (a) Not later than eighteen months after the date of the enactment of this Act, the Administrator shall, after notice and opportunity for public hearing, and after consultation with appropriate Federal and State agencies, develop and promulgate criteria for identifying the characteristics of hazardous waste, and for listing hazardous waste, which should be subject to the provisions of this subtitle, taking into account toxicity, persistence, and degradability in nature, potential for accumulation in tissue, and other related factors such as flammability, corrosiveness, and other hazardous characteristics. Such criteria shall be revised from time to time as may be appropriate.

(b)(1) Not later than eighteen months after the date of enactment of this section, and after notice and opportunity for public hearing, the Administrator shall promulgate regulations identifying the characteristics of hazardous waste, and listing particular hazardous wastes (within the meaning of section 1004(5)), which shall be subject to the provisions of this subtitle. Such regulations shall be based on the criteria promulgated under subsection (a) and shall be revised from time to time thereafter as may be appropriate. The Administrator, in cooperation with the Agency for Toxic Substances and Disease Registry and the National Toxicology Program, shall also identify or list those hazardous wastes which shall be subject to the provisions of this subtitle solely because of the presence in such wastes of certain constituents (such as identified carcinogens, mutagens, or teratogens) at levels in excess of levels which endanger human health.

(2)(A) Notwithstanding the provisions of paragraph (1) of this subsection, drilling fluids, produced water, and other wastes associated with the exploration, development, or production of crude oil or natural gas or geothermal energy shall be subject only to existing State or Federal regulatory programs in lieu of subtitle C until at least 24 months after the date of enactment of the Solid Waste Disposal Act amendments of 1980 and after promulgation of the regulations in accordance with subparagraphs (B) and (C) of this paragraph. It is the sense of the Congress that such State or Federal programs should include, for waste disposal sites which are to be closed, provisions requiring at least the following:

(i) The identification through surveying, platting, or other measures, together with recordation of such information on the public record, so as to assure that the location where such wastes are disposed of can be located in the future; except however, that no such surveying, platting, or other measure identifying the location of a disposal site for drilling fluids and associated wastes shall be required if the distance from the disposal site to the surveyed or platted location to the associated well is less than two hundred lineal feet; and

(ii) A chemical and physical analysis of a produced water and a composition of a drilling fluid suspected to contain a hazardous material, with such information to be acquired prior to closure and to be placed on the public record.

(B) Not later than six months after completion and submission of the study required by section 8002(m) of this Act, the Administrator shall, after public hearings and opportunity for comment, determine either to promulgate regulations under this subtitle for drilling fluids, produced waters, and other wastes associated with the exploration, development, or production of crude oil or natural gas or geothermal energy or that such regulations are unwarranted. The Administrator shall publish his decision in the Federal Register accompanied by an explanation and justification of the reasons for it. In making the decision under this paragraph, the Administrator shall utilize the information developed or accumulated pursuant to the study required under section 8002(m).

(C) The Administrator shall transmit his decision, along with any regulations, if necessary, to both Houses of Congress. Such regulations shall take effect only when authorized by Act of Congress.

(3)(A) Notwithstanding the provisions of paragraph (1) of this subsection, each waste listed below shall, except as provided in subparagraph (B) of this paragraph, be subject only to regulation under other applicable provisions of Federal or State law in lieu of this subtitle until at least six months after the date of submission of the applicable study required to be conducted under subsection (f), (n), (o), or (p) of section 8002 of this Act and after promulgation of regulations in accordance with subparagraph (C) of this paragraph:

   (i) Fly ash waste, bottom ash waste, slag waste, and flue gas emission control waste generated primarily from the combustion of coal or other fossil fuels.

   (ii) Solid waste from the extraction, beneficiation, and processing of ores and minerals, including phosphate rock and overburden from the mining of uranium ore.

   (iii) Cement kiln dust waste.

(B)(I) Owners and operators of disposal sites for wastes listed in subparagraph (A) may be required by the Administrator, through regulations prescribed under authority of section 2002 of this Act—

   (I) as to disposal sites for such wastes which are to be closed, to identify the locations of such sites through surveying, platting, or other measures, together with recordation of such information on the public record, to assure that the locations where such wastes are disposed of are known and can be located in the future, and

   (II) to provide chemical and physical analysis and composition of such wastes, based on available information, to be placed on the public record.

(ii)(I) In conducting any study under subsection (f), (n), (o), or (p), of section 8002 of this Act, any officer, employee, or authorized representative of the Environmental Protection Agency, duly designated by the Administrator, is authorized, at reasonable times and as reasonably necessary for the purposes of such study, to enter any establishment where any waste subject to such study is generated, stored, treated, disposed of, or transported from; to inspect, take samples, and conduct monitoring and testing; and to have access to and copy records relating to such waste. Each such inspection shall be commenced and completed with reasonable promptness. If the officer, employee, or authorized representative obtains any samples prior to leaving the premises, he shall give to the owner, operator, or agent in charge a receipt describing the sample obtained and if requested a portion of each such sample equal in volume or weight to the portion retained. If any analysis is made of such samples, or monitoring and testing performed, a copy of the results shall be furnished promptly to the owner, operator, or agent in charge.

(II) Any records, reports, or information obtained from any person under subclause (I) shall be available to the public, except that upon a showing satisfactory to the Administrator by any person that records, reports, or information, or particular part thereof, to which the Administrator has access under this subparagraph if made public, would divulge information entitled to protection under section 1905 of title 18 of the United States Code, the Administrator shall consider such information or particular portion thereof confidential in accordance with the purposes of that section, except that such record, report, document, or information may be disclosed to other officers, employees, or authorized representatives of the United States concerned with carrying out this Act. Any person not subject to the provisions of section 1905 of title 18 of the United States Code who knowingly and willfully divulges or discloses any information entitled to protection under this subparagraph shall, upon conviction, be subject to a fine of not more than $5,000 or to imprisonment not to exceed one year, or both.

(iii) The Administrator may prescribe regulations, under the authority of this Act, to prevent radiation exposure which presents an unreasonable risk to human health from the use in construction or land reclamation (with or without revegetation) of (I) solid waste from the extraction, beneficiation, and processing of phosphate rock or (II) overburden from the mining of uranium ore.

(iv) Whenever on the basis of any information the Administrator determines that any person is in violation of any requirement of this subparagraph, the Administrator shall give notice to the violator of his failure to comply with such requirement. If such violation extends beyond the thirtieth day after the Administrator's notification, the Administrator may issue an order requiring compliance within a specified time period or the Administrator may commence a civil action in the United States district court in the district in which the violation occurred for appropriate relief, including a temporary or permanent injunction.

(C) Not later than six months after the date of submission of the applicable study required to be conducted under subsection (f), (n), (o), or (p), of section 8002 of this Act, the Administrator shall, after public hearings and opportunity for comment, either determine to promulgate regulations under this subtitle for each waste listed in subparagraph (A) of this paragraph or determine that such regulations are unwarranted. The Administrator shall publish his determination, which shall be based on information developed or accumulated pursuant to such study, public hearings, and comment, in the Federal Register accompanied by an explanation and justification of the reasons for it.

(c) At any time after the date eighteen months after the enactment of this title, the Governor of any State may petition the Administrator to identify or list a material as a hazardous waste. The Administrator shall act upon such petition within ninety days following his receipt thereof and shall notify the Governor of such action. If the Administrator denies such petition because of financial considerations, in providing such notice to the Governor he shall include a statement concerning such considerations.

(d)(1) By March 31, 1986, the Administrator shall promulgate standards under sections 3002, 3003, and 3004 for hazardous waste generated by a generator in a total quantity of hazardous waste greater than one hundred kilograms but less than one thousand kilograms during a calendar month.

(2) The standards referred to in paragraph (1), including standards applicable to the legitimate use, reuse, recycling, and reclamation of such wastes, may vary from the standards applicable to hazardous waste generated by larger quantity generators, but such standards shall be sufficient to protect human health and the environment.

(3) Not later than two hundred and seventy days after the enactment of the Hazardous and Solid Waste Amendments of 1984 any hazardous waste which is part of a total quantity generated by a generator generating greater than one hundred kilograms but less than one thousand kilograms during one calendar month and which is shipped off the premises on which such waste is generated shall be accompanied by a copy of the Environmental Protection Agency Uniform

Hazardous Waste Manifest form signed by the generator. This form shall contain the following information:

(A) the name and address of the generator of the waste;

(B) the United States Department of Transportation description of the waste, including the proper shipping name, hazard class, and identification number (UN/NA), if applicable;

(C) the number and type of containers;

(D) the quantity of waste being transported; and

(E) the name and address of the facility designated to receive the waste.

If subparagraph (B) is not applicable, in lieu of the description referred to in such subparagraph (B), the form shall contain the Environmental Protection Agency identification number, or a generic description of the waste, or a description of the waste by hazardous waste characteristic. Additional requirements related to the manifest form shall apply only if determined necessary by the Administrator to protect human health and the environment.

(4) The Administrator's responsibility under this subtitle to protect human health and the environment may require the promulgation of standards under this subtitle for hazardous wastes which are generated by any generator who does not generate more than one hundred kilograms of hazardous waste in a calendar month.

(5) Until the effective date of standards required to be promulgated under paragraph (1), any hazardous waste identified or listed under section 3001 generated by any generator during any calendar month in a total quantity greater than one hundred kilograms but less than one thousand kilograms, which is not treated, stored, or disposed of at a hazardous waste treatment, storage, or disposal facility with a permit under section 3005, shall be disposed of only in a facility which is permitted, licensed, or registered by a State to manage municipal or industrial solid waste.

(6) Standards promulgated as provided in paragraph (1) shall, at a minimum, require that all treatment, storage, or disposal of hazardous wastes generated by generators referred to in paragraph (1) shall occur at a facility with interim status or a permit under this subtitle, except that onsite storage of hazardous waste generated by a generator generating a total quantity of hazardous waste greater than one hundred kilograms, but less than one thousand kilograms during a calendar month, may occur without the requirement of a permit for up to one hundred and eighty days. Such onsite storage may occur without the requirement of a permit for not more than six thousand kilograms for up to two hundred and seventy days if such generator must ship or haul such waste over two hundred miles.

(7)(A) Nothing in this subsection shall be construed to affect or impair the validity of regulations promulgated by the Secretary of Transportation pursuant to the Hazardous Materials Transportation Act.

(B) Nothing in this subsection shall be construed to affect, modify, or render invalid any requirements in regulations promulgated prior to January 1, 1983 applicable to any acutely hazardous waste identified or listed under section 3001 which is generated by any generator during any calendar month in a total quantity less than one thousand kilograms.

(8) Effective March 31, 1986, unless the Administrator promulgates standards as provided in paragraph (1) of this subsection prior to such date, hazardous waste generated by any generator in a total quantity greater than one hundred kilograms but less than one thousand kilograms during a calendar month shall be subject to the following requirements until the standards referred to in paragraph (1) of this subsection have become effective:

(A) the notice requirements of paragraph (3) of this subsection shall apply and in addition, the information provided in the form shall include the name of the waste transporters and the name and address of the facility designated to receive the waste;

(B) except in the case of the onsite storage referred to in paragraph (6) of this subsection, the treatment, storage, or disposal of such waste shall occur at a facility with interim status or a permit under this subtitle;

(C) generators of such waste shall file manifest exception reports as required of generators producing greater amounts of hazardous waste per month except that such reports shall be filed by January 31, for any waste shipment occurring in the last half of the preceding calendar year, and by July 31, for any waste shipment occurring in the first half of the calendar year; and

(D) generators of such waste shall retain for three years a copy of the manifest signed by the designated facility that has received the waste.

Nothing in this paragraph shall be construed as a determination of the standards appropriate under paragraph (1).

(9) The last sentence of section 3010(b) shall not apply to regulations promulgated under this subsection.

(e)(1) Not later than 6 months after the date of enactment of the Hazardous and Solid Waste Amendments of 1984, the Administrator shall, where appropriate, list under subsection (b)(1), additional wastes containing chlorinated dioxins or chlorinated-dibenzofurans. Not later than one year after the date of enactment of the Hazardous and Solid Waste Amendments of 1984, the Administrator shall, where appropriate, list under subsection (b)(1) wastes containing remaining halogenated dioxins and halogenated dibenzofurans.

(2) Not later than fifteen months after the date of enactment of the Hazardous and Solid Waste Amendments of 1984, the Administrator

shall make a determination of whether or not to list under subsection (b)(1) the following wastes: Chlorinated Aliphatics, Dioxin, Dimethyl Hydrazine, TDI (toluene diisocyanate), Carbamates, Bromacil, Linuron. Organo-bromines, solvents, refining wastes, chlorinated aromatics, dyes and pigments, inorganic chemical industry wastes, lithium batteries, coke byproducts, paint production wastes, and coal slurry pipeline effluent.

(f)(1) When evaluating a petition to exclude a waste generated at a particular facility from listing under this section, the Administrator shall consider factors (including additional constituents) other than those for which the waste was listed if the Administrator has a reasonable basis to believe that such additional factors could cause the waste to be a hazardous waste. The Administrator shall provide notice and opportunity for comment on these additional factors before granting or denying such petition.

(2)(A) To the maximum extent practicable the Administrator shall publish in the Federal Register a proposal to grant or deny a petition referred to in paragraph (1) within twelve months after receiving a complete application to exclude a waste generated at a particular facility from being regulated as a hazardous waste and shall grant or deny such a petition within twenty-four months after receiving a complete application.

(B) The temporary granting of such a petition prior to the enactment of the Hazardous and Solid Waste Amendments of 1984 without the opportunity for public comment and the full consideration of such comments shall not continue for more than twenty-four months after the date of enactment of the Hazardous and Solid Waste Amendments of 1984. If a final decision to grant or deny such a petition has not been promulgated after notice and opportunity for public comment within the time limit prescribed by the preceding sentence, any such temporary granting of such petition shall cease to be in effect.

(g) Not later than twenty-eight months after the date of enactment of the Hazardous and Solid Waste Amendments of 1984 the Administrator shall examine the deficiencies of the extraction procedure toxicity characteristic as a predictor of the leaching potential of wastes and make changes in the extraction procedure toxicity characteristic, including changes in the leaching media, as are necessary to insure that it accurately predicts the leaching potential of wastes which pose a threat to human health and the environment when mismanaged.

(h) Not later than two years after the date of enactment of the Hazardous and Solid Waste Amendments of 1984, the Administrator shall promulgate regulations under this section identifying additional characteristics of hazardous waste, including measures or indicators of toxicity.

(i) A resource recovery facility recovering energy from the mass burning of municipal solid waste shall not be deemed to be treating, storing, disposing of, or otherwise managing hazardous wastes for the purposes of regulation under this subtitle, if—

(1) such facility—
    (A) receives and burns only—
        (i) household waste (from single and multiple dwellings, hotels, motels, and other residential sources), and
        (ii) solid waste from commercial or industrial sources that does not contain hazardous waste identified or listed under this section, and
    (B) does not accept hazardous wastes identified or listed under this section, and
(2) the owner or operator of such facility has established contractual requirements or other appropriate notification or inspection procedures to assure that hazardous wastes are not received at or burned in such facility.

§ 6922.   Standards applicable to generators of hazardous waste

[Sec. 3002] (a) Not later than eighteen months after the date of the enactment of this section, and after notice and opportunity for public hearings and after consultation with appropriate Federal and State agencies, the Administrator shall promulgate regulations establishing such standards, applicable to generators of hazardous waste identified or listed under this subtitle, as may be necessary to protect human health and the environment. Such standards shall establish requirements respecting—

(1) recordkeeping practices that accurately identify the quantities of such hazardous waste generated, the constituents thereof which are significant in quantity or in potential harm to human health or the environment, and the disposition of such wastes;
(2) labeling practices for any containers used for the storage, transport, or disposal of such hazardous waste such as will identify accurately such waste;
(3) use of appropriate containers for such hazardous waste;
(4) furnishing of information on the general chemical composition of such hazardous waste to persons transporting, treating, storing, or disposing of such wastes;
(5) use of a manifest system and any other reasonable means necessary to assure that all such hazardous waste generated is designated for treatment, storage, or disposal in and arrives at treatment, storage, or disposal facilities (other than facilities on the premises where the waste is generated) for which a permit has been issued as provided in this subtitle, or pursuant to title I of the Marine Protection, Research, and Sanctuaries Act (86 Stat. 1052); and
(6) submission of reports to the Administrator (or the State agency in any

case in which such agency carries out a permit program pursuant to this subtitle) at least once every two years, setting out—

(A) the quantities and nature of hazardous waste identified or listed under this subtitle that he has generated during the year;

(B) the disposition of all hazardous waste reported under subparagraph (A);

(C) the efforts undertaken during the year to reduce the volume and toxicity of waste generated; and

(D) the changes in volume and toxicity of waste actually achieved during the year in question in comparison with previous years, to the extent such information is available for years prior to enactment of the Hazardous and Solid Waste Amendment of 1984.

(b) Effective September 1, 1985, the manifest required by subsection (a)(5) shall contain a certification by the generator that—

(1) the generator of the hazardous waste has a program in place to reduce the volume or quantity and toxicity of such waste to the degree determined by the generator to be economically practicable; and

(2) the proposed method of treatment, storage, or disposal is that practicable method currently available to the generator which minimizes the present and future threat to human health and the environment.

§ 6923. Standards applicable to transporters of hazardous waste

[Sec. 3003] (a) Not later than eighteen months after the date of enactment of this section, and after opportunity for public hearings the Administrator, after consultation with the Secretary of Transportation and the States, shall promulgate regulations establishing such standards, applicable to transporters of hazardous waste identified or listed under this subtitle, as may be necessary to protect human health and the environment. Such standards shall include but need not be limited to requirements respecting—

(1) recordkeeping concerning such hazardous waste transported, and their source and delivery points;

(2) transportation of such waste only if properly labeled;

(3) compliance with the manifest system referred to in section 3002(5); and

(4) transportation of all such hazardous waste only to the hazardous waste treatment, storage, or disposal facilities which the shipper designates on the manifest form to be a facility holding a permit issued under this subtitle, or pursuant to title I of the Marine Protection, Research, and Sanctuaries Act (86 Stat. 1052).

(b) In case of any hazardous waste identified or listed under this subtitle which is subject to the Hazardous Materials Transportation Act (88 Stat. 2156; 49 U.S.C. 1801 and following), the regulations promulgated by the Administrator under this section shall be consistent with the requirements of such Act and the regulations thereunder. The Administrator is authorized to make recommendations to the Secretary of Transportation respecting the regulations of such hazardous waste under the Hazardous Materials Transportation Act and for addition of materials to be covered by such Act.

(c) Not later than two years after the date of enactment of the Hazardous and Solid Waste Amendments of 1984, and after opportunity for public hearing, the Administrator shall promulgate regulations establishing standards, applicable to transporters of fuel produced (1) from any hazardous waste identified or listed under section 3001, or (2) from any hazardous waste identified or listed under section 3001 and any other material, as may be necessary to protect human health and the environment. Such standards may include any of the requirements set forth in paragraphs (1) through (4) of subsection (a) as may be appropriate.

§ 6924. Standards applicable to owners and operators of hazardous waste treatment, storage, and disposal facilities

[Sec. 3004] (a) No later than eighteen months after the date of enactment of this section, and after opportunity for public hearings and after consultation with appropriate Federal and State agencies, the Administrator shall promulgate regulations establishing such performance standards, applicable to owners and operators of facilities for the treatment, storage, or disposal of hazardous waste identified or listed under this subtitle, as may be necessary to protect human health and the environment. In establishing such standards the Administrator shall, where appropriate, distinguish in such standards between requirements appropriate for new facilities and for facilities in existence on the date of promulgation of such regulations. Such standards shall include, but need not be limited to, requirements respecting—

(1) maintaining records of all hazardous wastes identified or listed under this title which is treated, stored, or disposed of, as the case may be, and the manner in which such wastes were treated, stored, or disposed of;

(2) satisfactory reporting, monitoring, and inspection and compliance with the manifest system referred to in section 3002(5);

(3) treatment, storage, or disposal of all such waste received by the facility pursuant to such operating methods, techniques, and practices as may be satisfactory to the Administrator;

(4) the location, design, and construction of such hazardous waste treatment, disposal, or storage facilities;

(5) contingency plans for effective action to minimize unanticipated damage from any treatment, storage, or disposal of any such hazardous waste;

(6) the maintenance of operation of such facilities and requiring such additional qualifications as to ownership, continuity of operation, training for personnel, and financial responsibility (including financial

responsibility for corrective action) as may be necessary or desirable; and

(7) compliance with the requirements of section 3005 respecting permits for treatment, storage, or disposal.

No private entity shall be precluded by reason of criteria established under paragraph (6) from the ownership or operation of facilities providing hazardous waste treatment, storage, or disposal services where such entity can provide assurances of financial responsibility and continuity of operation consistent with the degree and duration of risks associated with the treatment, storage, or disposal of specified hazardous waste.

(b)(1) Effective on the date of the enactment of the Hazardous and Solid Waste Amendments of 1984, the placement of any noncontainerized or bulk liquid hazardous waste in any salt dome formation, salt bed formation, underground mine, or cave is prohibited until such time as—

(A) the Administrator has determined, after notice and opportunity for hearings on the record in the affected areas, that such placement is protective of human health and the environment;

(B) the Administrator has promulgated performance and permitting standards for such facilities under this subtitle, and;

(C) a permit has been issued under section 3005(c) for the facility concerned.

(2) Effective on the date of enactment of the Hazardous and Solid Waste Amendments of 1984, the placement of any hazardous waste other than a hazardous waste referred to in paragraph (1) in a salt dome formation, salt bed formation, underground mine, or cave is prohibited until such time as a permit has been issued under section 3005(c) for the facility concerned.

(3) No determination made by the Administrator under subsection (d), (e), or (g) of this section regarding any hazardous waste to which such subsection (d), (e), or (g) applies shall affect the prohibition contained in paragraph (1) or (2) of this subsection.

(4) Nothing in this subsection shall apply to the Department of Energy Waste Isolation Pilot Project in New Mexico.

(c)(1) Effective 6 months after the date of the enactment of the Hazardous and Solid Waste Amendments of 1984, the placement of bulk or noncontainerized liquid hazardous waste or free liquids contained in hazardous waste (whether or not absorbents have been added) in any landfill is prohibited. Prior to such date the requirements (as in effect on April 30, 1983) promulgated under this section by the Administrator regarding liquid hazardous waste shall remain in force and effect to the extent such requirements are applicable to the placement of bulk or noncontainerized liquid hazardous waste, or free liquids contained in hazardous waste, in landfills.

(2) Not later than fifteen months after the date of the enactment of the Hazardous and Solid Waste Amendments of 1984, the Administrator

shall promulgate final regulations which—

(A) minimize the disposal of containerized liquid hazardous waste in landfills, and

(B) minimize the presence of free liquids in containerized hazardous waste to be disposed of in landfills.

Such regulations shall also prohibit the disposal in landfills of liquids that have been absorbed in materials that biodegrade or that release liquids when compressed as might occur during routine landfill operations. Prior to the date on which such final regulations take effect, the requirements (as in effect on April 30, 1983) promulgated under this section by the Administrator shall remain in force and effect to the extent such requirements are applicable to the disposal of containerized liquid hazardous waste, or free liquids contained in hazardous waste, in landfills.

(3) Effective twelve months after the date of the enactment of the Hazardous and Solid Waste Amendments of 1984, the placement of any liquid which is not a hazardous waste in a landfill for which a permit is required under section 3005(c) or which is operating pursuant to interim status granted under section 3005(e) is prohibited unless the owner or operator of such landfill demonstrates to the Administrator, or the Administrator determines, that—

(A) the only reasonably available alternative to the placement in such landfill is placement in a landfill or unlined surface impoundment, whether or not permitted under section 3005(c) or operating pursuant to interim status under section 3005(e), which contains, or may reasonably be anticipated to contain, hazardous waste; and

(B) placement in such owner or operator's landfill will not present a risk of contamination of any underground source of drinking water.

As used in subparagraph (B), the term "underground source of drinking water" has the same meaning as provided in regulations under the Safe Drinking Water Act (title XIV of the Public Health Service Act).

(4) No determination made by the Administrator under subsection (d), (e), or (g) of this section regarding any hazardous waste to which such subsection (d), (e), or (g) applies shall affect the prohibition contained in paragraph (1) of this subsection.

(d)(1) Effective 32 months after the enactment of the Hazardous and Solid Waste Amendments of 1984 (except as provided in subsection (f) with respect to underground injection into deep injection wells), the land disposal of the hazardous wastes referred to in paragraph (2) is prohibited unless the Administrator determines the prohibition on one or more methods of land disposal of such waste is not required in order to protect human health and the environment for as long as the waste remains hazardous, taking into

account—
  (A) the long-term uncertainties associated with land disposal,
  (B) the goal of managing hazardous waste in an appropriate manner in the first instance, and
  (C) the persistence, toxicity, mobility, and propensity to bioaccumulate of such hazardous wastes and their hazardous constituents.
For the purposes of this paragraph, a method of land disposal may not be determined to be protective of human health and the environment for a hazardous waste referred to in paragraph (2) (other than a hazardous waste which has complied with the pretreatment regulations promulgated under subsection (m)), unless, upon application by an interested person, it has been demonstrated to the Administrator, to a reasonable degree of certainty, that there will be no migration of hazardous constituents from the disposal unit or injection zone for as long as the wastes remain hazardous.
  (2) Paragraph (1) applies to the following hazardous wastes listed or identified under section 3001:
    (A) Liquid hazardous wastes, including free liquids associated with any solid or sludge, containing free cyanides at concentrations greater than or equal to 1,000 mg/l.
    (B) Liquid hazardous wastes, including free liquids associated with any solid or sludge, containing the following metals (or elements) or compounds of these metals (or elements) at concentrations greater than or equal to those specified below:
      (i) arsenic and/or compounds (as As) 500 mg/l;
      (ii) cadmium and/or compounds (as Cd) 100 mg/l;
      (iii) chromium (VI and/or compounds (as Cr VI)) 500 mg/l;
      (iv) lead and/or compounds (as Pb) 500 mg/l;
      (v) mercury and/or compounds (as Hg) 20 mg/l;
      (vi) nickel and/or compounds (as Ni) 134 mg/l;
      (vii) selenium and/or compounds (as Se) 100 mg/l; and
      (viii) thallium and/or compounds (as Th) 130 mg/l.
    (C) Liquid hazardous waste having a pH less than or equal to two (2.0).
    (D) Liquid hazardous wastes containing polychlorinated biphenyls at concentrations greater than or equal to 50 ppm.
    (E) Hazardous wastes containing halogenated organic compounds in total concentration greater than or equal to 1,000 mg/kg.
When necessary to protect human health and the environment, the Administrator shall substitute more stringent concentration levels than the levels specified in subparagraphs (A) through (E).
  (3) During the period ending forty-eight months after the date of the enactment of the Hazardous and Solid Waste Amendments of 1984, this subsection shall not apply to any disposal of contaminated soil or debris resulting from a response action taken under section 104 or 106 of the Comprehensive Environmental Response, Compensation, and

Liability Act of 1980 or a corrective action required under this subtitle.

(e)(1) Effective twenty-four months after the date of enactment of the Hazardous and Solid Waste Amendments of 1984 (except as provided in subsection (f) with respect to underground injection into deep injection wells), the land disposal of the hazardous wastes referred to in paragraph (2) is prohibited unless the Administrator determines the prohibition of one or more methods of land disposal of such waste is not required in order to protect human health and the environment for as long as the waste remains hazardous, taking into account the factors referred to in subparagraph (A) through (C) of subsection (d)(1). For the purposes of this paragraph, a method of land disposal may not be determined to be protective of human health and the environment for a hazardous waste referred to in paragraph (2) (other than a hazardous waste which has complied with the pretreatment regulations promulgated under subsection (m)), unless upon application by an interested person it has been demonstrated to the Administrator, to a reasonable degree of certainty, that there will be no migration of hazardous constituents from the disposal unit or injection zone for as long as the wastes remain hazardous.

(2) The hazardous wastes to which the prohibition under paragraph (1) applies are as follows—

(A) dioxin-containing hazardous wastes numbered F020, F021, F022, and F023 (as referred to in the proposed rule published by the Administrator in the Federal Register for April 4, 1983), and

(B) those hazardous wastes numbered F001, F002, F003, F004, and F005 in regulations promulgated by the Administrator under section 3001 (40 C.F.R. 261.31 (July 1, 1983)), as those regulations are in effect on July 1, 1983.

(3) During the period ending forty-eight months after the date of the enactment of the Hazardous and Solid Waste Amendments of 1984, this subsection shall not apply to any disposal of contaminated soil or debris resulting from a response action taken under section 104 or 106 of the Comprehensive Environmental Response, Compensation, and Liability Act of 1980 or a corrective action required under this subtitle.

(f)(1) Not later than forty-five months after the date of enactment of the Hazardous and Solid Waste Amendments of 1984, the Administrator shall complete a review of the disposal of all hazardous wastes referred to in paragraph (2) of subsection (d) and in paragraph (2) of subsection (e) by underground injection into deep injection wells.

(2) Within forty-five months after the date of the enactment of the Hazardous and Solid Waste Amendments of 1984, the Administrator shall make a determination regarding the disposal by underground injection into deep injection wells of the hazardous wastes referred to in paragraph (2) of subsection (d) and the hazardous wastes referred

to in paragraph (2) of subsection (e). The Administrator shall promulgate final regulations prohibiting the disposal of such wastes into such wells if it may reasonably be determined that such disposal may not be protective of human health and the environment for as long as the waste remains hazardous, taking into account the factors referred to in subparagraphs (A) through (C) of subsection (d)(1). In promulgating such regulations, the Administrator shall consider each hazardous waste referred to in paragraph (2) of subsection (d) or in paragraph (2) of subsection (e) which is prohibited from disposal into such wells by any State.

(3) If the Administrator fails to make a determination under paragraph (2) for any hazardous waste referred to in paragraph (2) of subsection (d) or in paragraph (2) of subsection (e) within forty-five months after the date of enactment of the Hazardous and Solid Waste Amendments of 1984, such hazardous waste shall be prohibited from disposal into any deep injection well.

(4) As used in this subsection, the term "deep injection well" means a well used for the underground injection of hazardous waste other than a well to which section 7010(a) applies.

(g)(1) Not later than twenty-four months after the date of enactment of the Hazardous and Solid Waste Amendments of 1984, the Administrator shall submit a schedule to Congress for—

(A) reviewing all hazardous wastes listed (as of the date of the enactment of the Hazardous and Solid Waste Amendments of 1984) under section 3001 other than those wastes which are referred to in subsection (d) or (e); and

(B) taking action under paragraph (5) of this subsection with respect to each such hazardous waste.

(2) The Administrator shall base the schedule on a ranking of such listed wastes considering their intrinsic hazard and their volume such that decisions regarding the land disposal of high volume hazardous wastes with high intrinsic hazard shall, to the maximum extent possible, be made by the date forty-five months after the date of enactment of the Hazardous and Solid Waste Amendments of 1984. Decisions regarding low volume hazardous wastes with lower intrinsic hazard shall be made by the date sixty-six months after such date of enactment.

(3) The preparation and submission of the schedule under this subsection shall not be subject to the Paperwork Reduction Act of 1980. No hearing on the record shall be required for purposes of preparation or submission of the schedule. The schedule shall not be subject to judicial review.

(4) The schedule under this subsection shall require that the Administrator shall promulgate regulations in accordance with paragraph (5) or make a determination under paragraph (5)—

(A) for at least one-third of all hazardous wastes referred to in paragraph (1) by the date forty-five months after the date of enactment of the Hazardous and Solid Waste Amendments of 1984;

(B) for at least two-thirds of all such listed wastes by the date fifty-five months after the date of enactment of such Amendments; and

(C) for all such listed wastes and for all hazardous wastes identified under 3001 by the date sixty-six months after the date of enactment of such Amendments.

In the case of any hazardous waste identified or listed under section 3001 after the date of enactment of the Hazardous and Solid Waste Amendments of 1984, the Administrator shall determine whether such waste shall be prohibited from one or more methods of land disposal in accordance with paragraph (5) within six months after the date of such identification or listing.

(5) Not later than the date specified in the schedule published under this subsection, the Administrator shall promulgate final regulations prohibiting one or more methods of land disposal of the hazardous wastes listed on such schedule except for methods of land disposal which the Administrator determines will be protective of human health and the environment for as long as the waste remains hazardous, taking into account the factors referred to in subparagraph (A) through (C) of subsection (d)(1). For the purposes of this paragraph, a method of land disposal may not be determined to be protective of human health and the environment (except with respect to a hazardous waste which has complied with the pretreatment regulations promulgated under subsection (m)) unless, upon application by an interested person, it has been demonstrated to the Administrator, to a reasonable degree of certainty, that there will be no migration of hazardous constituents from the disposal unit or injection zone for as long as the wastes remain hazardous.

(6)(A) If the Administrator fails (by the date forty-five months after the date of enactment of the Hazardous and Solid Waste Amendments of 1984) to promulgate regulations or make a determination under paragraph (5) for any hazardous waste which is included in the first one-third of the schedule published under this subsection, such hazardous waste may be disposed of in a landfill or surface impoundment only if—

(i) such facility is in compliance with the requirements of subsection (o) which are applicable to new facilities (relating to minimum technological requirements); and

(ii) prior to such disposal, the generator has certified to the Administrator that such generator has investigated the availability of treatment capacity and has determined that the use of such landfill or surface impoundment is the only practical alternative to treatment currently available to the generator.

The prohibition contained in this subparagraph shall continue to apply until the Administrator promulgates regulations or makes a determination under paragraph (5) for the waste concerned.

(B) If the Administrator fails (by the date 55 months after the date of enactment of the Hazardous and Solid Waste Amendments of 1984) to promulgate regulations or make a determination under paragraph (5) for any hazardous waste which is included in the first two-thirds of the schedule published under this subsection, such hazardous waste may be disposed of in a landfill or surface impoundment only if—

(i) such facility is in compliance with the requirements of subsection (o) which are applicable to new facilities (relating to minimum technological requirements); and

(ii) prior to such disposal, the generator has certified to the Administrator that such generator has investigated the availability of treatment capacity and has determined that the use of such landfill or surface impoundment is the only practical alternative to treatment currently available to the generator.

The prohibition contained in this subparagraph shall continue to apply until the Administrator promulgates regulations or makes a determination under paragraph (5) for the waste concerned.

(C) If the Administrator fails to promulgate regulations, or make a determination under paragraph (5) for any hazardous waste referred to in paragraph (1) within 66 months after the date of enactment of the Hazardous and Solid Waste Amendments of 1984, such hazardous waste shall be prohibited from land disposal.

(h)(1) A prohibition in regulations under subsection (d), (e), (f), or (g) shall be effective immediately upon promulgation.

(2) The Administrator may establish an effective date different from the effective date which would otherwise apply under subsection (d), (e), (f), or (g) with respect to a specific hazardous waste which is subject to a prohibition under subsection (d), (e), (f), or (g) or under regulations under subsection (d), (e), (f), or (g). Any such other effective date shall be established on the basis of the earliest date on which adequate alternative treatment, recovery, or disposal capacity which protects human health and the environment will be available. Any such other effective date shall in no event be later than 2 years after the effective date of the prohibition which would otherwise apply under subsection (d), (e), (f), or (g).

(3) The Administrator, after notice and opportunity for comment and after consultation with appropriate State agencies in all affected States, may on a case-by-case basis grant an extension of the effective date which would otherwise apply under subsection (d), (e), (f), or (g) or under paragraph (2) for up to one year, where the applicant

demonstrates that there is a binding contractual commitment to construct or otherwise provide such alternative capacity but due to circumstances beyond the control of such applicant such alternative capacity cannot reasonably be made available by such effective date. Such extension shall be renewable once for no more than one additional year.

(4) Whenever another effective date (hereinafter referred to as a "variance") is established under paragraph (2), or an extension is granted under paragraph (3), with respect to any hazardous waste, during the period for which such variance or extension is in effect, such hazardous waste may be disposed of in a landfill or surface impoundment only if such facility is in compliance with the requirements of subsection (o).

(i) If the Administrator determines that a method of land disposal will be protective of human health and the environment, he shall promptly publish in the Federal Register notice of such determination, together with an explanation of the basis for such determination.

(j) In the case of any hazardous waste which is prohibited from one or more methods of land disposal under this section (or under regulations promulgated by the Administrator under any provision of this section) the storage of such hazardous waste is prohibited unless such storage is solely for the purpose of the accumulation of such quantities of hazardous waste as are necessary to facilitate proper recovery, treatment or disposal.

(k) For the purposes of this section, the term "land disposal" when used with respect to a specified hazardous waste, shall be deemed to include, but not be limited to, any placement of such hazardous waste in a landfill, surface impoundment, waste pile, injection well, land treatment facility, salt dome formation, salt bed formation, or underground mine or cave.

(l) The use of waste or used oil or other material, which is contaminated or mixed with dioxin or any other hazardous waste identified or listed under section 3001 (other than a waste identified solely on the basis of ignitability), for dust suppression or road treatment is prohibited.

(m)(1) Simultaneously with the promulgation of regulations under subsection (d), (e), (f), or (g) prohibiting one or more methods of land disposal of a particular hazardous waste, and as appropriate thereafter, the Administrator shall, after notice and an opportunity for hearings and after consultation with appropriate Federal and State agencies, promulgate regulations specifying those levels or methods of treatment, if any, which substantially diminish the toxicity of the waste or substantially reduce the likelihood of migration of hazardous constituents from the waste so that short-term and long-term threats to human health and the environment are minimized.

(2) If such hazardous waste has been treated to the level or by a method specified in regulations promulgated under this subsection, such waste or residue thereof shall not be subject to any prohibition promulgated under subsection (d), (e), (f), or (g) and may be disposed of in a land

disposal facility which meets the requirements of this subtitle. Any regulation promulgated under this subsection for a particular hazardous waste shall become effective on the same date as any applicable prohibition promulgated under subsection (d), (e), (f), or (g).

(n) Not later than thirty months after the date of enactment of the Hazardous and Solid Waste Amendments of 1984, the Administrator shall promulgate such regulations for the monitoring and control of air emissions at hazardous waste treatment, storage, and disposal facilities, including but not limited to open tanks, surface impoundments, and landfills, as may be necessary to protect human health and the environment.

(o)(1) The regulations under subsection (a) of this section shall be revised from time to time to take into account improvements in the technology of control and measurement. At a minimum, such regulations shall require, and a permit issued pursuant to section 3005(c) after the date of enactment of the Hazardous and Solid Waste Amendments of 1984 by the Administrator or a State shall require—

(A) for each new landfill or surface impoundment, each new landfill or surface impoundment unit at an existing facility, each replacement of an existing landfill or surface impoundment unit, and each lateral expansion of an existing landfill or surface impoundment unit, for which an application for a final determination regarding issuance of a permit under section 3005(c) is received after the date of enactment of the Hazardous and Solid Waste Amendments of 1984—

(i) the installation of two or more liners and a leachate collection system above (in the case of a landfill) and between such liners; and

(ii) ground water monitoring; and

(B) for each incinerator which receives a permit under section 3005(c) after the date of enactment of the Hazardous and Solid Waste Amendments of 1984, the attainment of the minimum destruction and removal efficiency required by regulations in effect on June 24, 1982.

The requirements of this paragraph shall apply with respect to all waste received after the issuance of the permit.

(2) Paragraph (1)(A)(i) shall not apply if the owner or operator demonstrates to the Administrator, and the Administrator finds for such landfill or surface impoundment, that alternative design and operating practices, together with location characteristics, will prevent the migration of any hazardous constituents into the ground water or surface water at least as effectively as such liners and leachate collection systems.

(3) The double-liner requirement set forth in paragraph (1)(A)(i) may be waived by the Administrator for any monofill, if—

(A) such monofill contains only hazardous wastes from foundry furnace emission control or metal casting molding sand,

(B) such wastes do not contain constituents which would render the wastes hazardous for reasons other than the Extraction Procedure ("EP") toxicity characteristics set forth in regulations under this subtitle, and

(C) such monofill meets the same requirements as are applicable in the case of a waiver under section 3005(j)(2) or (4).

(4)(A) Not later than thirty months after the date of enactment of the Hazardous and Solid Waste Amendments of 1984, the Administrator shall promulgate standards requiring that new landfill units, surface impoundment units, waste piles, underground tanks and land treatment units for the storage, treatment, or disposal of hazardous waste identified or listed under section 3001 shall be required to utilize approved leak detection systems.

(B) For the purposes of subparagraph (A)—

(i) the term "approved leak detection system" means a system or technology which the Administrator determines to be capable of detecting leaks of hazardous constituents at the earliest practicable time; and

(ii) the term "new units" means units on which construction commences after the date of promulgation of regulations under this paragraph.

(5)(A) The Administrator shall promulgate regulations or issue guidance documents implementing the requirements of paragraph (1)(A) within two years after the date of the enactment of the Hazardous and Solid Waste Amendments of 1984.

(B) Until the effective date of such regulations or guidance documents, the requirement for the installation of two or more liners may be satisfied by the installation of a top liner designed, operated, and constructed of materials to prevent the migration of any constituent into such liner during the period such facility remains in operation (including any post-closure monitoring period), and a lower liner designated, operated and constructed to prevent the migration of any constituent through such liner during such period. For the purpose of the preceding sentence, a lower liner shall be deemed to satisfy such requirement if it is constructed of at least a 3-foot thick layer of recompacted clay or other natural material with a permeability of no more than 1×10^{-7} centimeter per second.

(6) Any permit under section 3005 which is issued for a landfill located within the State of Alabama shall require the installation of two or more liners and a leachate collection system above and between such liners, notwithstanding any other provision of this Act.

(7) In addition to the requirements set forth in this subsection, the regulations referred to in paragraph (1) shall specify criteria for the

acceptable location of new and existing treatment, storage, or disposal facilities as necessary to protect human health and the environment. Within 18 months after the enactment of the Hazardous and Solid Waste Amendments of 1984, the Administrator shall publish guidance criteria identifying areas of vulnerable hydrogeology.

(p) The standards under this section concerning ground water monitoring which are applicable to surface impoundments, waste piles, land treatment units, and landfills shall apply to such a facility whether or not—

(1) the facility is located above the seasonal high water table;

(2) two liners and a leachate collection system have been installed at the facility; or

(3) the owner or operator inspects the liner (or liners) which has been installed at the facility.

This subsection shall not be construed to affect other exemptions or waivers from such standards provided in regulations in effect on the date of enactment of the Hazardous and Solid Waste Amendments of 1984 or as may be provided in revisions to those regulations, to the extent consistent with this subsection. The Administrator is authorized on a case-by-case basis to exempt from ground water monitoring requirements under this section (including subsection (o)) any engineered structure which the Administrator finds does not receive or contain liquid waste (nor waste containing free liquids), is designed and operated to exclude liquid from precipitation or other runoff, utilizes multiple leak detection systems within the outer layer of containment, and provides for continuing operation and maintenance of these leak detection systems during the operating period, closure, and the period required for post-closure monitoring and for which the Administrator concludes on the basis of such findings that there is a reasonable certainty hazardous constituents will not migrate beyond the outer layer of containment prior to the end of the period required for post-closure monitoring.

(q)(1) Not later than two years after the date of the enactment of the Hazardous and Solid Waste Amendments of 1984, and after notice and opportunity for public hearing, the Administrator shall promulgate regulations establishing such—

(A) standards applicable to the owners and operators of facilities which produce a fuel—

(i) from any hazardous waste identified or listed under section 3001, or

(ii) from any hazardous waste identified or listed under section 3001 and any other material;

(B) standards applicable to the owners and operators of facilities which burn, for purposes of energy recovery, any fuel produced as provided in subparagraph (A) or any fuel which otherwise contains any hazardous waste identified or listed under section 3001; and

(C) standards applicable to any person who distributes or markets any fuel which is produced as provided in subparagraph (A) or any fuel which otherwise contains any hazardous waste identified or listed under section 3001;

as may be necessary to protect human health and the environment. Such standards may include any of the requirements set forth in paragraphs (1) through (7) of subsection (a) as may be appropriate. Nothing in this subsection shall be construed to affect or impair the provisions of section 3001(b)(3). For purposes of this subsection, the term "hazardous waste listed under section 3001" includes any commercial chemical product which is listed under section 3001 and which, in lieu of its original intended use, is (i) produced for use as (or as a component of) a fuel, (ii) distributed for use as a fuel, or (iii) burned as a fuel.

(2)(A) This subsection, subsection (r), and subsection (s) shall not apply to petroleum refinery wastes containing oil which are converted into petroleum coke at the same facility at which such wastes were generated, unless the resulting coke product would exceed one or more characteristics by which a substance would be identified as a hazardous waste under section 3001.

(B) The Administrator may exempt from the requirements of this subsection, subsection (r), or subsection (s) facilities which burn de minimis quantities of hazardous waste as fuel, as defined by the Administrator, if the wastes are burned at the same facility at which such wastes are generated; the waste is burned to recover useful energy, as determined by the Administrator on the basis of the design and operating characteristics of the facility and the heating value and other characteristics of the waste; and the waste is burned in a type of device determined by the Administrator to be designed and operated at a destruction and removal efficiency sufficient such that protection of human health and environment is assured.

(C)(i) After the date of the enactment of the Hazardous and Solid Waste Amendments of 1984 and until standards are promulgated and in effect under paragraph (2) of this subsection, no fuel which contains any hazardous waste may be burned in any cement kiln which is located within the boundaries of any incorporated municipality with a population greater than five hundred thousand (based on the most recent census statistics) unless such kiln fully complies with regulations (as in effect on the date of the enactment of the Hazardous and Solid Waste Amendments of 1984) under this subtitle which are applicable to incinerators.

(ii) Any person who knowingly violates the prohibition contained in clause (i) shall be deemed to have violated section 3008(d)(2).

(r) Notwithstanding any other provision of law, until such time as the

Administrator promulgates standards under subsection (q) specifically superseding this requirement, it shall be unlawful for any person who is required to file a notification in accordance with paragraph (1) or (3) of section 3010 to distribute or market any fuel which is produced from any hazardous waste identified or listed under section 3001, or any fuel which otherwise contains any hazardous waste identified or listed under section 3001 if the invoice or the bill of sale fails—

    (A) to bear the following statement:
        WARNING: THIS FUEL CONTAINS HAZARDOUS WASTES, and

    (B) to list the hazardous wastes contained therein. Beginning ninety days after the enactment of the Hazardous and Solid Waste Amendments of 1984, such statement shall be located in a conspicuous place on every such invoice or bill of sale and shall appear in conspicuous and legible type in contrast by typography, layouts, or color with other printed matter on the invoice or bill of sale.

  (2) Unless the Administrator determines otherwise as may be necessary to protect human health and the environment, this subsection shall not apply to fuels produced from petroleum refining waste containing oil if—

    (A) such materials are generated and reinserted onsite into the refining process;

    (B) contaminants are removed; and

    (C) such refining waste containing oil is converted along with normal process streams into petroleum-derived fuel products at a facility at which crude oil is refined into petroleum products and which is classified as a number SIC 2911 facility under the Office of Management and Budget Standard Industrial Classification Manual.

  (3) Unless the Administrator determines otherwise as may be necessary to protect human health and the environment, this subsection shall not apply to fuels produced from oily materials, resulting from normal petroleum refining, production and transportation practices, if (A) contaminants are removed; and (B) such oily materials are converted along with normal process streams into petroleum-derived fuel products at a facility at which crude oil is refined into petroleum products and which is classified as a number SIC 2911 facility under the Office of Management and Budget Standard Classification Manual.

(s) Not later than fifteen months after the date of enactment of the Hazardous and Solid Waste Amendments of 1984, the Administrator shall promulgate regulations requiring that any person who is required to file a notification in accordance with subparagraph (1), (2), or (3), of section 3010(a) shall maintain such records regarding fuel blending, distribution, or use as may be necessary to protect human health and the environment.

(t) Financial responsibility required by subsection (a) of this section may be established in accordance with regulations promulgated by the Administrator by any one, or any combination, of the following: insurance, guarantee, surety bond, letter of credit, or qualification as a self-insurer. In promulgating requirements under this section, the Administrator is authorized to specify policy or other contractual terms, conditions, or defenses which are necessary or are unacceptable in establishing such evidence of financial responsibility in order to effectuate the purposes of this Act.

(2) In any case where the owner or operator is in bankruptcy, reorganization, or arrangement pursuant to the Federal Bankruptcy Code or where (with reasonable diligence) jurisdiction in any State court or any Federal Court cannot be obtained over an owner or operator likely to be solvent at the time of judgment, any claim arising from conduct for which evidence of financial responsibility must be provided under this section may be asserted directly against the owner or operator if any action had been brought against the owner or operator by the claimant and which would have been available to the guarantor providing such evidence of financial responsibility. In the case of any action pursuant to this subsection, such guarantor shall be entitled to invoke all rights and defenses which would have been available to the owner or operator if any action had been brought against the owner or operator by the claimant and which would have been available to the guarantor if an action had been brought against the guarantor by the owner or operator.

(3) The total liability of any guarantor shall be limited to the aggregate amount which the guarantor has provided as evidence of financial responsibility to the owner or operator under this Act. Nothing in this subsection shall be construed to limit any other State or Federal statutory, contractual or common law liability of a guarantor to its owner or operator including, but not limited to, the liability of such guarantor for bad faith either in negotiating or in failing to negotiate the settlement of any claim. Nothing in this subsection shall be construed to diminish the liability of any person under section 107 or 111 of the Comprehensive Environmental Response, Compensation and Liability Act of 1980 or other applicable law.

(4) For the purpose of this subsection, the term "guarantor" means any person, other than the owner or operator, who provides evidence of financial responsibility for an owner or operator under this section.

(u) Standards promulgated under this section shall require, and a permit issued after the date of enactment of the Hazardous and Solid Waste Amendments of 1984 by the Administrator or a State shall require, corrective action for all releases of hazardous waste or constituents from any solid waste management unit at a treatment, storage, or disposal facility seeking a permit under this subtitle, regardless of the time at which waste was placed in such unit. Permits issued under section 3005 shall contain schedules of compliance for such corrective action (where such corrective action cannot be completed prior to issuance of the permit) and assurances of financial responsibility for completing such corrective action.

(v) As promptly as practicable after the date of the enactment of the Hazardous and Solid Waste Amendments of 1984, the Administrator shall amend the standards under this section regarding corrective action required at facilities for the treatment, storage, or disposal, of hazardous waste listed or identified under section 3001 to require that corrective action be taken beyond the facility boundary where necessary to protect human health and the environment unless the owner or operator of the facility concerned demonstrates to the satisfaction of the Administrator that, despite the owner or operator's best efforts, the owner or operator was unable to obtain the necessary permission to undertake such action. Such regulations shall take effect immediately upon promulgation, notwithstanding section 3010(b), and shall apply to—

(1) all facilities operating under permits issued under subsection (c), and

(2) all landfills, surface impoundments, and waste pile units (including any new units, replacements of existing units, or lateral expansions of existing units) which receive hazardous waste after July 26, 1982.

Pending promulgation of such regulations, the Administrator shall issue corrective action orders for facilities referred to in paragraphs (1) and (2), on a case-by-case basis, consistent with the purposes of this subsection.

(w) Not later than March 1, 1985, the Administrator shall promulgate final permitting standards under this section for underground tanks that cannot be entered for inspection. Within forty-eight months after the date of the enactment of the Hazardous and Solid Waste Amendments of 1984, such standards shall be modified, if necessary, to cover at a minimum all requirements and standards described in section 9003.

(x) If (1) solid waste from the extraction, beneficiation or processing of ores and minerals, including phosphate rock and overburden from the mining of uranium, (2) fly ash waste, bottom ash waste, slag waste, and flue gas emission control waste generated primarily from the combustion of coal or other fossil fuels, or (3) cement kiln dust waste, is subject to regulation under this subtitle, the Administrator is authorized to modify the requirements of subsections (c), (d), (e), (f), (g), (o), and (u) and section 3005(j), in the case of landfills or surface impoundments receiving such solid waste, to take into account the special characteristics of such wastes, the practical difficulties associated with implementation of such requirements, and site-specific characteristics, including but not limited to the climate, geology, hydrology and soil chemistry at the site, so long as such modified requirements assure protection of human health and the environment.

§ 6925. Permits for treatment, storage, or disposal of hazardous waste

[Sec. 3005] (a) Not later than eighteen months after the date of the enactment of this section, the Administrator shall promulgate regulations requiring each person owning or operating an existing facility or planning to construct a new facility for the treatment, storage, or disposal of hazardous waste identified or listed under this subtitle to have a permit issued pursuant to this section. Such regulations shall take effect on the date provided in section 3010 and upon and after such date the treatment, storage, or disposal of any such hazardous waste and the construction of any new facility for the treatment, storage, or disposal of any such hazardous waste is prohibited except in accordance with such a permit. No permit shall be required under this section in order to construct a facility if such facility is constructed pursuant to an approval issued by the Administrator under section 6(e) of the Toxic Substances Control Act for the incineration of polychlorinated biphenyls and any person owning or operating such a facility may, at any time after operation or construction of such facility has begun, file an application for a permit pursuant to this section authorizing such facility to incinerate hazardous waste identified of listed under this subtitle.

(b) Each application for a permit under this section shall contain such information as may be required under regulations promulgated by the Administrator, including information respecting—

(1) estimates with respect to the composition, quantities, and concentrations of any hazardous waste identified or listed under this subtitle, or combinations of any such hazardous waste and any other solid waste, proposed to be disposed of, treated, transported, or stored, and the time, frequency, or rate of which such waste is proposed to be disposed of, treated, transported, or stored; and

(2) the site at which such hazardous waste or the products of treatment of such hazardous waste will be disposed of, treated, transported to, or stored.

(c)(1) Upon a determination by the Administrator (or a State, if applicable), or compliance by a facility for which a permit is applied for under this section with the requirements of this section and section 3004, the Administrator (or the State) shall issue a permit for such facilities. In the event permit applicants propose modification of their facilities, or in the event the Administrator (or the State) determines that modifications are necessary to conform to the requirements under this section and section 3004, the permit shall specify the time allowed to complete the modifications.

(2)(A)(i) Not later than the date four years after the enactment of the Hazardous and Solid Waste Amendments of 1984, in the case of each application under this subsection for a permit for a land disposal facility which was submitted before such date, the Administrator shall issue a final permit pursuant to such application or issue a final denial of such application.

(ii) Not later than the date five years after the enactment of the Hazardous and Solid Waste Amendments of 1984, in the case of each application for a permit under this subsection for an incinerator facility which was submitted before such date, the Administrator shall issue a final permit pursuant to such application or issue a final denial of such application.

(B) Not later than the date eight years after the enactment of the Hazardous and Solid Waste Amendments of 1984, in the case of each application for a permit under this subsection for any facility (other than a facility referred to in subparagraph (A)) which was submitted before such date, the Administrator shall issue a final permit pursuant to such application or issue a final denial of such application.

(C) The time periods specified in this paragraph shall also apply in the case of any State which is administering an authorized hazardous waste program under section 3006. Interim status under subsection (e) shall terminate for each facility referred to in subparagraph (A)(ii) or (B) on the expiration of the five- or eight-year period referred to in subparagraph (A) or (B), whichever is applicable, unless the owner or operator of the facility applies for a final determination regarding the issuance of a permit under this subsection within—

(i) two years after the date of the enactment of the Hazardous and Solid Waste Amendments of 1984 (in the case of a facility referred to in subparagraph (A)(ii)), or

(ii) four years after such date of enactment (in the case of a facility referred to in subparagraph (B)).

(3) Any permit under this section shall be for a fixed term, not to exceed 10 years in the case of any land disposal facility, storage facility, or incinerator or other treatment facility. Each permit for a land disposal facility shall be reviewed five years after date of issuance or reissuance and shall be modified as necessary to assure that the facility continues to comply with the currently applicable requirements of this section and section 3004. Nothing in this subsection shall preclude the Administrator from reviewing and modifying a permit at any time during its term. Review of any application for a permit renewal shall consider improvements in the state of control and measurement technology as well as changes in applicable regulations. Each permit issued under this section shall contain such terms and conditions as the Administrator (or the State) determines necessary to protect human health and the environment.

(d) Upon a determination by the Administrator (or by a State, in the case of a State having an authorized hazardous waste program under section 3006) of noncompliance by a facility having a permit under this title with the requirements of this section or section 3004, the Administrator (or State, in the case of a State having an authorized hazardous waste program under section 3006) shall revoke such permit.

(e)(1) Any person who—

    (A) owns or operates a facility required to have a permit under this section which facility—
        (i) was in existence on November 19, 1980, or
        (ii) is in existence on the effective date or statutory or regulatory changes under this Act that render the facility subject to the requirement to have a permit under this section.
    (B) has complied with the requirements of section 3010(a), and
    (C) has made an application for a permit under this section shall be treated as having been issued such permit until such time as final administrative disposition of such application is made, unless the Administrator or other plaintiff proves that final administrative disposition of such application has not been made because of the failure of the applicant to furnish information reasonably required or requested in order to process the application.

This paragraph shall not apply to any facility which has been previously denied a permit under this section or if authority to operate the facility under this section has been previously terminated.

  (2) In the case of each land disposal facility which has been granted interim status under this subsection before the date of enactment of the Hazardous and Solid Waste Amendments of 1984, interim status shall terminate on the date twelve months after the date of the enactment of such Amendments unless the owner or operator of such facility—
    (A) applies for a final determination regarding the issuance of a permit under subsection (c) for such facility before the date twelve months after the date of the enactment of such Amendments; and
    (B) certifies that such facility is in compliance with all applicable groundwater monitoring and financial responsibility requirements.

  (3) In the case of each land disposal facility which is in existence on the effective date of statutory or regulatory changes under this Act that render the facility subject to the requirement to have a permit under this section and which is granted interim status under this subsection, interim status shall terminate on the date twelve months after the date on which the facility first becomes subject to such permit requirement unless the owner or operator of such facility—
    (A) applies for a final determination regarding the issuance of a permit under subsection (c) for such facility before the date twelve months after the date on which the facility first becomes subject to such permit requirement; and
    (B) certifies that such facility is in compliance with all applicable groundwater monitoring and financial responsibility requirements.

  (f) Notwithstanding subsection (a) through (e) of this section, any surface coal mining and reclamation permit covering any coal mining wastes or overburden which has been issued or approved under the Surface Mining Control and Reclamation Act of 1977 shall be deemed to be a permit issued pursuant to this section with respect to the treatment, storage, or disposal of such wastes or overburden. Regulations promulgated by the Administrator under this subtitle shall not be applicable to treatment, storage, or disposal of coal mining wastes and overburden which are covered by such a permit.

(g)(1) The Administrator may issue a research, development, and demonstration permit for any hazardous waste treatment facility which proposes to utilize an innovative and experimental hazardous waste treatment technology or process for which permit standards for such experimental activity have not been promulgated under this subtitle. Any such permit shall include such terms and conditions as will assure protection of human health and the environment. Such permits—

(A) shall provide for the construction of such facilities, as necessary, and for operation of the facility for not longer than one year (unless renewed as provided in paragraph (4)), and

(B) shall provide for the receipt and treatment by the facility of only those types and quantities of hazardous waste which the Administrator deems necessary for purposes of determining the efficacy and performance capabilities of the technology or process and the effects of such technology or process on human health and the environment, and

(C) shall include such requirements as the Administrator deems necessary to protect human health and the environment (including, but not limited to, requirements regarding monitoring, operation, insurance or bonding, financial responsibility, closure, and remedial action), and such requirements as the Administrator deems necessary regarding testing and providing of information to the Administrator with respect to the operation of the facility.

The Administrator may apply the criteria set forth in this paragraph in establishing the conditions of each permit without separate establishment of regulations implementing such criteria.

(2) For the purpose of expediting review and issuance of permits under this subsection, the Administrator may, consistent with the protection of human health and the environment, modify or waive permit application and permit issuance requirements established in the Administrator's general permit regulations except that there may be no modification or waiver of regulations regarding financial responsibility (including insurance) or of procedures established under section 7004(b)(2) regarding public participation.

(3) The Administrator may order an immediate termination of all operations at the facility at any time he determines that termination is necessary to protect human health and the environment.

(4) Any permit issued under this subsection may be renewed not more than three times. Each such renewal shall be for a period of not more

than 1 year.

(h) Effective September 1, 1985, it shall be a condition of any permit issued under this section for the treatment, storage, or disposal of hazardous waste on the premises where such waste was generated that the permittee certify, no less often than annually, that—

(1) the generator of the hazardous waste has a program in place to reduce the volume or quantity and toxicity of such waste to the degree determined by the generator to be economically practicable; and

(2) the proposed method of treatment, storage, or disposal is that practicable method currently available to the generator which minimizes the present and future threat to human health and the environment.

(i) The standards concerning ground water monitoring, unsaturated zone monitoring, and corrective action, which are applicable under section 3004 to new landfills, surface impoundments, land treatment units, and waste-pile units required to be permitted under subsection (c) shall also apply to any landfill, surface impoundment, land treatment unit, or waste-pile unit qualifying for the authorization to operate under subsection (e) which receives hazardous waste after July 26, 1982.

(j)(1) Except as provided in paragraph (2), (3), or (4), each surface impoundment in existence on the date of enactment of the Hazardous and Solid Waste Amendments of 1984 and qualifying for the authorization to operate under subsection (e) of this section shall not receive, store, or treat hazardous waste after the date four years after such date of enactment unless such surface impoundment is in compliance with the requirements of section 3004(o)(1)(A) which would apply to such impoundment if it were new.

(2) Paragraph (1) of this subsection shall not apply to any surface impoundment which (A) has at least one liner, for which there is no evidence that such liner is leaking; (B) is located more than one-quarter mile from an underground source of drinking water; and (C) is in compliance with generally applicable ground water monitoring requirements for facilities with permits under subsection (c) of this section.

(3) Paragraph (1) of this subsection shall not apply to any surface impoundment which (A) contains treated waste water during the secondary or subsequent phases of an aggressive biological treatment facility subject to a permit issued under section 402 of the Clean Water Act (or which holds such treated waste water after treatment and prior to discharge); (B) is in compliance with generally applicable ground water monitoring requirements for facilities with permits under subsection (c) of this section; and (C)(i) is part of a facility in compliance with section 301(b)(2) of the Clean Water Act, or (ii) in the case of a facility for which no effluent guidelines required under section 304(b)(2) of the Clean Water Act are in effect and no permit under section 402(a)(1) of such Act implementing section 301(b)(2) of such Act has been issued, is part of a facility in compliance with a

permit under section 402 of such Act, which is achieving significant degradation of toxic pollutants and hazardous constituents contained in the untreated waste stream and which has identified those toxic pollutants and hazardous constituents in the untreated waste stream to the appropriate permitting authority.

(4) The Administrator (or the State, in the case of a State with an authorized program), after notice and opportunity for comment, may modify the requirements of paragraph (1) for any surface impoundment if the owner or operator demonstrates that such surface impoundment is located, designed and operated so as to assure that there will be no migration of any hazardous constituent into ground water or surface water at any future time. The Administrator or the State shall take into account locational criteria established under section 3004(o)(7).

(5) The owner or operator of any surface impoundment potentially subject to paragraph (1) who has reason to believe that on the basis of paragraph (2), (3), or (4) such surface impoundment is not required to comply with the requirements of paragraph (1), shall apply to the Administrator (or the State, in the case of a State with an authorized program) not later than twenty-four months after the date of enactment of the Hazardous and Solid Waste Amendments of 1984 for a determination of the applicability of paragraph (1) (in the case of paragraph (2) or (3)) or for a modification of the requirements of paragraph (1) (in the case of paragraph (4)), with respect to such surface impoundment. Such owner or operator shall provide, with such application, evidence pertinent to such decision, including:

(A) an application for a final determination regarding the issuance of a permit under subsection (c) of this section for such facility, if not previously submitted;

(B) evidence as to compliance with all applicable ground water monitoring requirements and the information and analysis from such monitoring;

(C) all reasonably ascertainable evidence as to whether such surface impoundment is leaking; and

(D) in the case of applications under paragraph (2) or (3), a certification by a registered professional engineer with academic training and experience in ground water hydrology that—

(i) under paragraph (2), the liner of such surface impoundment is designed, constructed, and operated in accordance with applicable requirements, such surface impoundment is more than one-quarter mile from an underground source of drinking water and there is no evidence such liner is leaking; or

(ii) under paragraph (3), based on analysis of those toxic pollutants and hazardous constituents that are likely to be present in the untreated waste stream, such impoundment satisfies the conditions of paragraph (3).

In the case of any surface impoundment for which the owner or operator fails to apply under this paragraph within the time provided by this paragraph or paragraph (6), such surface impoundment shall comply with paragraph (1) notwithstanding paragraph (2), (3), or (4). Within twelve months after receipt of such application and evidence and not later than thirty-six months after such date of enactment, and after notice and opportunity to comment, the Administrator (or, if appropriate, the State) shall advise such owner or operator on the applicability of paragraph (1) to such surface impoundment or as to whether and how the requirements of paragraph (1) shall be modified and applied to such surface impoundment.

(6)(A) In any case in which a surface impoundment becomes subject to paragraph (1) after the date of enactment of the Hazardous and Solid Waste Amendments of 1984 due to the promulgation of additional listings or characteristics for the identification of hazardous waste under section 3001, the period for compliance in paragraph (1) shall be four years after the date of such promulgation, the period for demonstrations under paragraph (4) and for submission of evidence under paragraph (5) shall be not later than twenty-four months after the date of such promulgation, and the period for the Administrator (or if appropriate, the State) to advise such owners or operators under paragraph (5) shall be not later than thirty-six months after the date of promulgation.

(B) In any case in which a surface impoundment is initially determined to be excluded from the requirements of paragraph (1) but due to a change in condition (including the existence of a leak) no longer satisfies the provisions of paragraph (2), (3), or (4) and therefore becomes subject to paragraph (1), the period for compliance in paragraph (1) shall be two years after the date of discovery of such change of condition, or in the case of a surface impoundment excluded under paragraph (3) three years after such date of discovery.

(7)(A) The Administrator shall study and report to the Congress on the number, range of size, construction, likelihood of hazardous constituents migrating into ground water, and potential threat to human health and the environment of existing surface impoundments excluded by paragraph (3) from the requirements of paragraph (1). Such report shall address the need, feasibility, and estimated costs of subjecting such existing surface impoundments to the requirements of paragraph (1).

(B) In the case of any existing surface impoundment or class of surface impoundments from which the Administrator (or the State, in the case of a State with an authorized program) determines hazardous constitutents are likely to migrate into ground water, the Administrator (or if appropriate, the State) is authorized to impose such requirements as may be necessary to protect human health and the environment, including the requirements of section 3004(o) which would apply to such impoundments if they were new.

(C) In the case of any surface impoundment excluded by paragraph (3) from the requirements of paragraph (1) which is subsequently determined to be leaking, the Administrator (or, if appropriate, the State) shall require compliance with paragraph (1), unless the Administrator (or, if appropriate, the State) determines that such compliance is not necessary to protect human health and the environment.

(8) In the case of any surface impoundment in which the liners and leak detection system have been installed pursuant to the requirements of paragraph (1) and in good faith compliance with section 3004(o) and the Administrator's regulations and guidance documents governing liners and leak detection systems, no liner or leak detection system which is different from that which was so installed pursuant to paragraph (1) shall be required for such unit by the Administrator when issuing the first permit under this section to such facility. Nothing in this paragraph shall preclude the Administrator from requiring installation of a new liner when the Administrator has reason to believe that any liner installed pursuant to the requirements of this subsection is leaking.

(9) In the case of any surface impoundment which has been excluded by paragraph (2) on the basis of a liner meeting the definition under paragraph (12)(A)(ii), at the closure of such impoundment the Administrator shall require the owner or operator of such impoundment to remove or decontaminate all waste residues, all contaminated liner material, and contaminated soil to the extent practicable. If all contaminated soil is not removed or decontaminated, the owner or operator of such impoundment shall be required to comply with appropriate post-closure requirements, including but not limited to ground water monitoring and corrective action.

(10) Any incremental cost attributable to the requirements of this subsection or section 3004(o) shall not be considered by the Administrator (or the State, in the case of a State with an authorized program under section 402 of the Clean Water Act)—

(A) in establishing effluent limitations and standards under section 301, 304, 306, 307, or 402 of the Clean Water Act based on effluent limitations guidelines and standards promulgated any time before twelve months after the date of enactment of the Hazardous and Solid Waste Amendments of 1984; or

(B) in establishing any other effluent limitations to carry out the provisions of section 301, 307, or 402 of the Clean Water Act on or before October 1, 1986.

(11)(A) If the Administrator allows a hazardous waste which is prohibited from one or more methods of land disposal under subsection (d), (e), or (g) of section 3004 (or under regulations promulgated by the Administrator under such subsections) to be placed in a surface impoundment (which is operating pursuant to interim status) for storage or treatment, such impoundment shall meet the requirements that are applicable to new surface impoundments under section 3004(o)(1), unless such impoundment meets the requirements of paragraph (2) or (4).

(B) In the case of any hazardous waste which is prohibited from one or more methods of land disposal under subsection (d), (e), or (g) of section 3004 (or under regulations promulgated by the Administrator under such subsection) the placement or maintenance of such hazardous waste in a surface impoundment for treatment is prohibited as of the effective date of such prohibition unless the treatment residues which are hazardous are, at a minimum, removed for subsequent management within one year of the entry of the waste into the surface impoundment.

(12)(A) For the purpose of paragraph (2)(A) of this subsection, the term "liner" means—

    (i) a liner designed, constructed, installed, and operated to prevent hazardous waste from passing into the liner at any time during the active life of the facility; or

    (ii) a liner designed, constructed, installed, and operated to prevent hazardous waste from migrating beyond the liner to adjacent subsurface soil, ground water, or surface water at any time during the active life of the facility.

(B) For the purposes of this subsection, the term "aggressive biological treatment facility" means a system of surface impoundments in which the initial impoundment of the secondary treatment segment of the facility utilizes intense mechanical aeration to enhance biological activity to degrade waste water pollutants and

    (i) the hydraulic retention time in such initial impoundment is no longer than 5 days under normal operating conditions, on an annual average basis;

    (ii) the hydraulic retention time in such initial impoundment is no longer than thirty days under normal operating conditions, on an annual average basis: *Provided,* That the sludge in such impoundment does not constitute a hazardous waste as identified by the extraction procedure toxicity characteristic in effect on the date of enactment of the Hazardous and Solid Waste Amendments of 1984; or

    (iii) such system utilizes activated sludge treatment in the first portion of secondary treatment.

    (C) For the purposes of this subsection, the term "underground source or drinking water" has the same meaning as provided in regulations under the Safe Drinking Water Act (title XIV of the Public Health Service Act).

(13) The Administrator may modify the requirements of paragraph (1) in the case of a surface impoundment for which the owner or operator, prior to October 1, 1984, has entered into, and is in compliance with, a consent order, decree, or agreement with the Administrator or a State with an authorized program mandating corrective action with respect to such surface impoundment that provides a degree of protection of human health and the environment which is at a minimum equivalent to that provided by paragraph (1).

§ 6926. Authorized state hazardous waste programs

[Sec. 3006] (a) Not later than eighteen months after the date of enactment of this Act, the Administrator, after consultation with State authorities, shall promulgate guidelines to assist States in the development of State hazardous waste programs.

(b) Any State which seeks to administer and enforce a hazardous waste program pursuant to this subtitle may develop and, after notice and opportunity for public hearing, submit to the Administrator an application, in such form as he shall require, for authorization of such program. Within ninety days following submission of an application under this subsection, the Administrator shall issue a notice as to whether or not he expects such program to be authorized, and within ninety days following such notice (and after opportunity for public hearing) he shall publish his findings as to whether or not the conditions listed in items (1), (2), and (3) below have been met. Such State is authorized to carry out such program in lieu of the Federal program under this subtitle in such State and to issue and enforce permits for the storage, treatment, or disposal of hazardous waste (and to enforce permits deemed to have been issued under section 3014(d)(1)) unless, within ninety days following submission of the application the Administrator notifies such State that such program may not be authorized and, within ninety days following such notice and after opportunity for public hearing, he finds that (1) such State program is not equivalent to the Federal program under this subtitle, (2) such program is not consistent with the Federal or State programs applicable in other States, or (3) such program does not provide adequate enforcement of compliance with the requirements of this subtitle. In authorizing a State program, the Administrator may base his findings on the Federal program in effect one year prior to submission of a State's application or in effect on January 26, 1983, whichever is later.

(c)(1) Any State which has in existence a hazardous waste program pursuant to State law before the date ninety days after the date of promulgation of regulations under sections 3002, 3003, 3004, and 3005, may submit to the Administrator evidence of such existing program and may request a temporary authorization to carry out such program under this subtitle. The Administrator shall, if the evidence submitted shows the existing State program to be substantially equivalent to the Federal program under this subtitle, grant an interim authorization to the State to carry out such program in lieu of the Federal program pursuant to this subtitle for a period ending no later than January 31, 1986.

(2) The Administrator shall, by rule, establish a date for the expiration of interim authorization under this subsection.

(3) Pending interim or final authorization of a State program for any State which reflects the amendments made by the Hazardous and Solid Waste Amendments of 1984, the State may enter into an agreement with the Administrator under which the State may assist in the administration of the requirements and prohibitions which take effect pursuant to such Amendments.

(4) In the case of a State permit program for any State which is authorized under subsection (b) or under this subsection, until such program is amended to reflect the amendments made by the Hazardous and Solid Waste Amendments of 1984 and such program amendments receive interim or final authorization, the Administrator shall have the authority in such State to issue or deny permits or those portions of permits affected by the requirements and prohibitions established by the Hazardous and Solid Waste Amendments of 1984. The Administrator shall coordinate with States the procedures for issuing such permits.

(d) Any action taken by a State under a hazardous waste program authorized under this section shall have the same force and effect as action taken by the Administrator under this subtitle.

(e) Whenever the Administrator determines after public hearing that a State is not administering and enforcing a program authorized under this section in accordance with requirements of this section, he shall so notify the State and, if appropriate corrective action is not taken within a reasonable time, not to exceed ninety days, the Administrator shall withdraw authorization of such program and establish a Federal program pursuant to this subtitle. The Adminstrator shall not withdraw authorization of any such program unless he shall first have notified the State, and made public, in writing, the reasons for such withdrawal.

(f) No State program may be authorized by the Administrator under this section unless—

(1) such program provides for the public availability of information obtained by the State regarding facilities and sites for the treatment, storage, and disposal of hazardous waste; and

(2) such information, is available to the public in substantially the same manner, and to the same degree, as would be the case if the Administrator was carrying out the provisions of this subtitle in such

State.

(g)(1) Any requirement or prohibition which is applicable to the generation, transportation, treatment, storage, or disposal of hazardous waste and which is imposed under this subtitle pursuant to the amendments made by the Hazardous and Solid Waste Amendments of 1984 shall take effect in each State having an interim or finally authorized State program on the same date as such requirement takes effect in other States. The Administrator shall carry out such requirement directly in each such State unless the State program is finally authorized (or is granted interim authorization as provided in paragraph (2)) with respect to such requirement.

(2) Any State which, before the date of the enactment of the Hazardous and Solid Waste Amendments of 1984 has an existing hazardous waste program which has been granted interim or final authorization under this section may submit to the Administrator evidence that such existing program contains (or has been amended to include) any requirement which is substantially equivalent to a requirement referred to in paragraph (1) and may request interim authorization to carry out that requirement under this subtitle. The Administrator shall, if the evidence submitted shows the State requirement to be substantially equivalent to the requirement referred to in paragraph (1), grant an interim authorization to the State to carry out such requirement in lieu of direct administration in the State by the Administrator of such requirement.

(h) In the case of used oil which is not listed or identified under this subtitle as a hazardous waste but which is regulated under section 3014 of this title, the provisions of this section regarding State programs shall apply in the same manner and to the same extent as such provisions apply to hazardous waste identified or listed under this subtitle.

§ 6927. Inspections

[Sec. 3007] (a) For purposes of developing or assisting in the development of any regulation or enforcing the provisions of this title, any person who generates, stores, treats, transports, disposes of, or otherwise handles or has handled hazardous wastes shall, upon request of any officer, employee or representative of the Environmental Protection Agency, duly designated by the Administrator, or upon request of any duly designated officer, employee or representative of a State having an authorized hazardous waste program, furnish information relating to such wastes and permit such persons at all reasonable times to have access to, and to copy all records relating to such wastes. For the purposes of developing or assisting in the development of any regulation or enforcing the provisions of this title, such officers, employees or representatives are authorized—

(1) to enter at reasonable times any establishment or other place where hazardous wastes are or have been generated, stored, treated, disposed of, or transported from;

(2) to inspect and obtain samples from any person of any such wastes and samples of any containers or labeling for such wastes.

Each such inspection shall be commenced and completed with reasonable promptness. If the officer, employee or representative obtains any samples, prior to leaving the premises, he shall give to the owner, operator, or agent in charge a receipt describing the sample obtained and if requested a portion of each such sample equal in volume or weight to the portion of each such sample equal in volume or weight to the portion retained. If any analysis is made of such samples, a copy of results of such analysis shall be furnished promptly to the owner, operator, or agent in charge.

(b)(1) Any records, reports, or information (including records, reports, or information obtained by representatives of the Environmental Protection Agency) obtained from any person under this section shall be available to the public, except that upon a showing satisfactory to the Administrator (or the State, as the case may be) by any person that records, reports, or information, (including records, reports, or information obtained by representatives of the Environmental Protection Agency) or particular part thereof, to which the Administrator (or the State, as the case may be) or any officer, employee or representative thereof has access under this section if made public, would divulge information (including records, reports, or information obtained by representatives of the Environmental Protection Agency) entitled to protection under section 1905 of title 18 of the United States Code, such information or particular portion thereof shall be considered confidential in accordance with the purposes of that section, except that such record, report, document, or information may be disclosed to other officers, employees, or authorized representatives of the United States concerned with carrying out this Act, or when relevent in any proceeding under this Act.

(2) Any person not subject to the provisions of section 1905 of title 18 of the United States Code who knowingly and willfully divulges or discloses any information (including records, reports, or information obtained by representatives of the Environmental Protection Agency) entitled to protection under this subsection shall, upon conviction, be subject to a fine of not more than $5,000 or to imprisonment not to exceed one year, or both.

(3) In submitting data under this Act, a person required to provide such data may—

(A) designate the data which such person believes is entitled to protection under this subsection, and

(B) submit such designated data separately from other data submitted under this Act.

A designation under this paragraph shall be made in writing and in such manner as the Administrator may prescribe.

(4) Notwithstanding any limitation contained in this section or any other provision of law, all information (including records, reports, or information obtained by representatives of the Environmental Protection Agency) reported to, or otherwise obtained by, the Administrator (or any representative of the Administrator) under this Act shall be made available, upon written request of any duly authorized committee of the Congress, to such committee (including records, reports, or information obtained by representatives of the Environmental Protection Agency).

(c) Beginning twelve months after the date of enactment of the Hazardous and Solid Waste Amendments of 1984, the Administrator shall, or in the case of a State with an authorized hazardous waste program the State may, undertake on an annual basis a thorough inspection of each facility for the treatment, storage, or disposal of hazardous waste which is owned or operated by a Federal agency to enforce its compliance with this subtitle and the regulations promulgated thereunder. The records of such inspections shall be available to the public as provided in subsection (b).

(d) The Administrator shall annually undertake a thorough inspection of every facility for the treatment, storage, or disposal of hazardous waste which is operated by a State or local government for which a permit is required under section 3005 of this title. The records of such inspection shall be available to the public as provided in subsection (b).

(e)(1) The Administrator (or the State in the case of a State having an authorized hazardous waste program under this subtitle) shall commence a program to thoroughly inspect every facility for the treatment, storage, or disposal of hazardous waste for which a permit is required under section 3005 no less often than every two years as to its compliance with this subtitle (and the regulations promulgated under this subtitle). Such inspections shall commence not later than twelve months after the date of enactment of the Hazardous and Solid Waste Amendments of 1984. The Administrator shall, after notice and opportunity for public comment, promulgate regulations governing the minimum frequency and manner of such inspections, including the manner in which records of such inspections shall be maintained and the manner in which reports of such inspections shall be filed. The Administrator may distinguish between classes and categories of facilities commensurate with the risks posed by each class or category.

(2) Not later than six months after the date of enactment of the Hazardous and Solid Waste Amendments of 1984, the Administrator shall submit to the Congress a report on the potential for inspections of hazardous waste treatment, storage, or disposal facilities by nongovernmental inspectors as a supplement to inspections conducted by officers, employees, or representatives of the Environmental Protection Agency or States having authorized hazardous waste programs or operating under a cooperative agreement with the Administrator. Such report shall be prepared in cooperation with the States, insur-

ance companies offering environmental impairment insurance, independent companies providing inspection services, and other other such groups as appropriate. Such report shall contain recommendations on provisions and requirements for a program of private inspections of supplement governmental inspections.

§ 6928. Federal enforcement

[Sec. 3008] (a)(1) Except as provided in paragraph (2), whenever on the basis of any information the Administrator determines that any person has violated or is in violation of any requirement of this subtitle, the Administrator may issue an order assessing a civil penalty for any past or current violation, requiring compliance immediately or within a specified time period, or both, or the Administrator may commence a civil action in the United States district court in the district in which the violation occurred for appropriate relief, including a temporary or permanent injunction.

(2) In the case of a violation of any requirement of this subtitle where such violation occurs in a State which is authorized to carry out a hazardous waste program under section 3006, the Administrator shall give notice to the State in which such violation has occurred prior to issuing an order or commencing a civil action under this section.

(3) Any order issued pursuant to this subsection may include a suspension or revocation of any permit issued by the Administrator or a State under this subtitle and shall state with reasonable specificity the nature of the violation. Any penalty assessed in the order shall not exceed $25,000 per day of noncompliance for each violation of a requirement of this subtitle. In assessing such a penalty, the Administrator shall take into account the seriousness of the violation and any good faith efforts to comply with applicable requirements.

(b) Any order issued under this section shall become final unless, no later than thirty days after the order is served, the person or persons named therein request a public hearing. Upon such request the Administrator shall promptly conduct a public hearing. In connection with any proceeding under this section the Administrator may issue subpoenas for the attendance and testimony of witnesses and the production of relevant papers, books, and documents, and may promulgate rules for discovery procedures.

(c) If a violator fails to take corrective action within the time specified in a compliance order, the Administrator may assess a civil penalty of not more than $25,000 for each day of continued noncompliance with the order and the Administrator may suspend or revoke any permit issued to the violator (whether issued by the Administrator or the State).

(d) Any person who—

(1) knowingly transports or causes to be transported any hazardous waste identified or listed under this subtitle to a facility which does not have

a permit under this subtitle, or pursuant to title I of the Marine Protection, Research, and Sanctuaries Act (86 Stat. 1052).

(2) knowingly treats, stores, or disposes of any hazardous waste identified or listed under this subtitle—

(A) without a permit under this subtitle or pursuant to title I of the Marine Protection, Research, and Sanctuaries Act (86 Stat. 1052); or

(B) in knowing violation of any material condition or requirement of such permit; or

(C) in knowing violation of any material condition or requirement of any applicable interim status regulations or standards;

(3) knowingly omits material information or makes any false material statement or representation in any application, label, manifest, record, report, permit, or other document filed, maintained, or used for purposes of compliance with regulations promulgated by the Administrator (or by a State in the case of an authorized State program) under this subtitle;

(4) knowingly generates, stores, treats, transports, disposes of, exports, or otherwise handles any hazardous waste or any used oil not identified or listed as a hazardous waste under this subtitle (whether such activity took place before or takes place after the date of the enactment of this paragraph) and who knowingly destroys, alters, conceals, or fails to file any record, application, manifest, report, or other document required to be maintained or filed for purposes of compliance with regulations promulgated by the Administrator (or by a State in the case of an authorized State program) under this subtitle;

(5) knowingly transports without a manifest, or causes to be transported without a manifest, any hazardous waste or any used oil not identified or listed as a hazardous waste under this subtitle required by regulations promulgated under this subtitle (or by a State in the case of a State program authorized under this subtitle) to be accompanied by a manifest;

(6) knowingly exports a hazardous waste identified or listed under this subtitle (A) without the consent of the receiving country or, (B) where there exists an international agreement between the United States and the government of the receiving country establishing notice, export, and enforcement procedures for the transportation, treatment, storage, and disposal of hazardous wastes, in a manner which is not in conformance with such agreement; or

(7) knowingly stores, treats, transports, or causes to be transported, disposes of, or otherwise handles any used oil not identified or listed as a hazardous waste under this subchapter—

(A) in knowing violation of any material condition or requirement of a permit under this subchapter; or

(B) in knowing violation of any material condition or requirement of any applicable regulations or standards under this chapter; shall, upon conviction, be subject to a fine of not more than $50,000 for each day of violation, or imprisonment not to exceed two years (five years in the case of a violation of paragraph (1) or (2)), or both. If the conviction is for a violation committed after a first conviction of such person under this paragraph, the maximum punishment under the respective paragraph shall be doubled with respect to both fine and imprisonment.

(e) Any person who knowingly transports, treats, stores, disposes of, or exports any hazardous waste identified or listed under this subtitle or any used oil not identified or listed as a hazardous waste under this subtitle in violation of paragraph (1), (2), (3), (4), (5), (6), or (7) of subsection (d) of this section who knows at that time that he thereby places another person in imminent danger of death or serious bodily injury, shall, upon conviction, be subject to a fine of not more than $250,000 or imprisonment for not more than fifteen years, or both. A defendant that is an organization shall, upon conviction of violating this subsection, be subject to a fine of not more than $1,000,000.

(f) For the purposes of subsection (e)—
(1) A person's state of mind is knowing with respect to—
  (A) his conduct, if he is aware of the nature of his conduct;
  (B) an existing circumstance, if he is aware or believes that the circumstance exists; or
  (C) a result of his conduct, if he is aware or believes that his conduct is substantially certain to cause danger of death or serious bodily injury.
(2) In determining whether a defendant who is a natural person knew that his conduct placed another person in imminent danger of death or serious bodily injury—
  (A) the person is responsible only for actual awareness or actual belief that he possessed; and
  (B) knowledge possessed by a person other than the defendant but not by the defendant himself may not be attributed to the defendant; Provided, That in proving the defendant's possession of actual knowledge, circumstantial evidence may be used, including evidence that the defendant took affirmative steps to shield himself from relevant information.
(3) It is an affirmative defense to a prosecution that the conduct charged was consented to by the person endangered and that the danger and conduct charged were reasonably foreseeable hazards of—
  (A) an occupation, a business, or a profession; or
  (B) medical treatment or medical or scientific experimentation conducted by professionally approved methods and such other person had been made aware of the risks involved prior to giving consent.
The defendant may establish an affirmative defense under this subsec-

tion by a preponderance of the evidence.

(4) All general defenses, affirmative defenses, bars to prosecution that may apply with respect to other Federal criminal offenses may apply under subsection (e) and shall be determined by the courts of the United States according to the principles of common law as they may be interpreted in the light of reason and experience. Concepts of justification and excuse applicable under this section may be developed in the light of reason and experience.

(5) The term "organization" means a legal entity, other than a government, established or organized for any purpose, and such term includes a corporation, company, association, firm, partnership, joint stock company, foundation, institution, trust, society, union, or any other association of persons.

(6) The term "serious bodily injury" means—

    (A) bodily injury which involves a substantial risk of death;

    (B) unconsciousness;

    (C) extreme physical pain;

    (D) protracted and obvious disfigurement; or

    (E) protracted loss or impairment of the function of a bodily member, organ, or mental faculty.

(g) Any person who violates any requirement of this subtitle shall be liable to the United States for a civil penalty in an amount not to exceed $25,000 for each such violation. Each day of such violation shall, for purposes of this subsection, constitute a separate violation.

(h)(1) Whenever on the basis of any information the Administrator determines that there is or has been a release of hazardous waste into the environment from a facility authorized to operate under section 3005(e) of this subtitle, the Administrator may issue an order requiring corrective action or such other response measure as he deems necessary to protect human health or the environment or the Administrator may commence a civil action in the United States district court in the district in which the facility is located for appropriate relief, including a temporary or permanent injunction.

(2) Any order issued under this subsection may include a suspension or revocation of authorization to operate under section 3005(e) of this subtitle, shall state with reasonable specificity the nature of the required corrective action or other response measure, and shall specify a time for compliance. If any person named in an order fails to comply with the order, the Administrator may assess, and such person shall be liable to the United States for, a civil penalty in an amount not to exceed $25,000 for each day of noncompliance with the order.

§ 6929. Retention of state authority

[Sec. 3009] Upon the effective date of regulations under this subtitle no State or political subdivision may impose any requirements less stringent than those authorized under this subtitle respecting the same matter as governed by such regulations, except that if application of a regulation with respect to any matter under this subtitle is postponed or enjoined by the action of any court, no State or political subdivision shall be prohibited from acting with respect to the same aspect of such matter until such time as such regulation takes effect. Nothing in this title shall be construed to prohibit any State or political subdivision thereof from imposing any requirements, including those for site selection, which are more stringent than those imposed by such regulations. Nothing in this title (or in any regulation adopted under this title) shall be construed to prohibit any State from requiring that the State be provided with a copy of each manifest used in connection with hazardous waste which is generated within that State or transported to a treatment, storage, or disposal facility within that State.

§ 6930.   Effective date

[Sec. 3010] (a) Not later than ninety days after promulgation of regulations under section 3001 identifying by its characteristics or listing any substance as hazardous waste subject to this subtitle, any person generating or transporting such substance or owning or operating a facility for treatment, storage, or disposal of such substance shall file with the Administrator (or with States having authorized hazardous waste permit programs under section 3006) a notification stating the location and general description of such activity and the identified or listed hazardous wastes handled by such person.

Not later than fifteen months after the date of enactment of Hazardous and Solid Waste Amendments of 1984—

(1) The owner or operator of any facility which produces a fuel (A) from any hazardous waste identified or listed under section 3001, (B) from such hazardous waste identified or listed under section 3001 and any other material, (C) from used oil, or (D) from used oil and any other material;

(2) The owner or operator of any facility (other than a single- or two-family residence) which burns for purposes of energy recovery any fuel produced as provided in paragraph (1) or any fuel which otherwise contains used oil or any hazardous waste identified or listed under section 3001; and

(3) any person who distributes or markets any fuel which is produced as provided in paragraph (1) or any fuel which otherwise contains used oil or any hazardous waste identified or listed under section 3001

shall file with the Administrator (and with the State in the case of a State with an authorized hazardous waste program) a notification stating the location and general description of the facility, together with a description of the identified or listed hazardous waste involved and, in the case of a facility referred to in paragraph (1) or (2), a description of the production or energy recovery activity carried out at the facility and such other information as the

Administrator deems necessary. For purposes of the preceding provisions, the term "hazardous waste listed under section 3001" also includes any commercial chemical product which is listed under section 3001 and which, in lieu of its original intended use, is (i) produced for use as (or as a component of) a fuel, (ii) distributed for use as a fuel, or (iii) burned as a fuel. Notification shall not be required under the second sentence of this subsection in the case of facilities (such as residential boilers) where the Administrator determines that such notification is not necessary in order for the Administrator to obtain sufficient information respecting current practices of facilities using hazardous waste for energy recovery. Nothing in this subsection shall be construed to affect or impair the provisions of section 3001(b)(3). Nothing in this subsection shall affect regulatory determinations under section 3014. In revising any regulation under section 3001 identifying additional characteristics of hazardous waste or listing any additional substance as hazardous waste subject to this subtitle, the Administrator may require any person referred to in the preceding provisions to file with the Administrator (or with States having authorized hazardous waste permit programs under section 3006) the notification described in the preceding provisions. Not more than one such notification shall be required to be filed with respect to the same substance. No identified or listed hazardous waste subject to this subtitle may be transported, treated, stored, or disposed of unless notification has been given as required under this subsection.

(b) The regulations under this subtitle respecting requirements applicable to the generation, transportation, treatment, storage, or disposal of hazardous waste (including requirements respecting permits for such treatment, storage, or disposal) shall take effect on the date six months after the date of promulgation thereof (or six months after the date of revision in the case of any regulation which is revised after the date required for promulgation thereof). At the time a regulation is promulgated, the Administrator may provide for a shorter period prior to the effective date, or an immediate effective date for:

(1) a regulation with which the Administrator finds the regulated community does not need six months to come into compliance;

(2) a regulation which responds to an emergency situation; or

(3) other good cause found and published with the regulation.

§ 6931. Authorization of assistance to states

[Sec. 3011] (a) There is authorized to be appropriated $25,000,000 for each of the fiscal years 1978 and 1979, $20,000,000 for fiscal year 1980, $35,000,000 for fiscal year 1981, $40,000,000 for the fiscal year 1982, $55,000,000 for the fiscal year 1985, $60,000,000 for the fiscal year 1986, $60,000,000 for the fiscal year 1987, and $60,000,000, for the fiscal year 1988 to be used to make grants to the States for purposes of assisting the States in the development and implementation of authorized State hazardous waste programs.

(b) Amounts authorized to be appropriated under subsection (a) shall be allocated among the States on the basis of regulations promulgated by the Administrator, after consultation with the States, which take into account, the extent to which hazardous waste is generated, transported, treated, stored, and disposed of within such State, the extent of exposure of human beings and the environment within such State to such waste, and such other factors as the Administrator deems appropriate.

(c) State hazardous waste programs for which grants may be made under subsection (a) may include (but shall not be limited to) planning for hazardous waste treatment, storage and disposal facilities, and the development and execution of programs to protect health and the environment from inactive facilities which may contain hazardous waste.

§ 6933. Hazardous waste site inventory

[Sec. 3012] (a) Each State shall, as expeditiously as practicable, undertake a continuing program to compile, publish, and submit to the Administrator an inventory describing the location of each site within such State at which hazardous waste has at any time been stored or disposed of. Such inventory shall contain—

(1) a description of the location of the sites at which any such storage or disposal has taken place before the date on which permits are required under section 3005 for such storage or disposal;

(2) such information relating to the amount, nature, and toxicity of the hazardous waste at each such site as may be practicable to obtain and as may be necessary to determine the extent of any health hazard which may be associated with such site;

(3) the name and address, or corporate headquarters of, the owner of each such site, determined as of the date of preparation of the inventory;

(4) an identification of the types or techniques of waste treatment or disposal which have been used at each such site; and

(5) information concerning the current status of the site, including information respecting whether or not hazardous waste is currently being treated or disposed of at such site (and if not, the date on which such activity ceased) and information respecting the nature of any other activity currently carried out at such site.

For purposes of assisting the States in compiling information under this section, the Administrator shall make available to each State undertaking a program under this section such information as is available to him concerning the items specified in paragraphs (1) through (5) with respect to the sites within such State, including such information as the Administrator is able to obtain from other agencies or departments of the United States and from surveys and studies carried out by any committee or subcommittee of the Congress. Any State may exercise the authority of section 3007 for purposes of this section in the same manner and to the same extent as provided in such section in the case of States having an authorized hazardous waste program, and any State may by order require any person to submit such information as may be necessary to compile the data referred to in paragraphs (1) through (5).

(b) If the Administrator determines that any State program under subsection (a) is not adequately providing information respecting the sites in such State referred to in subsection (a), the Administrator shall notify the State. If within ninety days following such notification, the State program has not been revised or amended in such manner as will adequately provide such information, the Administrator shall carry out the inventory program in such State. In any such case—

(1) the Administrator shall have the authorities provided with respect to State programs under subsection (a);

(2) the funds allocated under subsection (c) for grants to States under this section may be used by the Administrator for carrying out such program in such State; and

(3) no further expenditure may be made for grants to such State under this section until such time as the Administrator determines that such State is carrying out, or will carry out, an inventory program which meets the requirements of this section.

(c)(1) Upon receipt of an application submitted by any State to carry out a program under this section, the Administrator may make grants to the States for purposes of carrying out such a program. Grants under this section shall be allocated among the several States by the Administrator based upon such regulations as he prescribes to carry out the purposes of this section. The Administrator may make grants to any State which has conducted an inventory program which effectively carried out the purposes of this section before the date of the enactment of the Solid Waste Disposal Act Amendments of 1980 to reimburse such State for all, or any portion of, the costs incurred by such State in conducting such program.

(2) There are authorized to be appropriated to carry out this section $25,000,000 for each of the fiscal years 1985 through 1988.

(d) Nothing in this section shall be construed to provide that the Administrator or any State should, pending completion of the inventory required under this section, postpone undertaking any enforcement or remedial action with respect to any site at which hazardous waste has been treated, stored, or disposed of.

§ 6934. Monitoring, analysis, and testing

[Sec. 3013] (a) If the Administrator determines, upon receipt of any information, that—

(1) the presence of any hazardous waste at a facility or site at which hazardous waste is, or has been, stored, treated, or disposed of, or

(2) the release of any such waste from such facility or site may present a substantial hazard to human health or the environment, he may issue

an order requiring the owner or operator of such facility or site to conduct such monitoring, testing, analysis, and reporting with respect to such facility or site as the Administrator deems reasonable to ascertain the nature and extent of such hazard.

(b) In the case of any facility or site not in operation at the time a determination is made under subsection (a) with respect to the facility or site, if the Administrator finds that the owner of such facility or site could not reasonably be expected to have actual knowledge of the presence of hazardous waste at such facility or site and of its potential for release, he may issue an order requiring the most recent previous owner or operator of such facility or site who could reasonably be expected to have such actual knowledge to carry out the actions referred to in subsection (a).

(c) An order under subsection (a) or (b) shall require the person to whom such order is issued to submit to the Administrator within 30 days from the issuance of such order a proposal for carrying out the required monitoring, testing, analysis, and reporting. The Administrator may, after providing such person with an opportunity to confer with the Administrator respecting such proposal, require such person to carry out such monitoring, testing, analysis, and reporting in accordance with such proposal, and such modifications in such proposal as the Administrator deems reasonable to ascertain the nature and extent of the hazard.

(d)(1) If the Administrator determines that no owner or operator referred to in subsection (a) or (b) is able to conduct monitoring, testing, analysis, or reporting satisfactory to the Administrator, if the Administrator deems any such action carried out by an owner or operator to be unsatisfactory, or if the Administrator cannot initially determine that there is an owner or operator referred to in subsection (a) or (b) who is able to conduct such monitoring, testing, analysis, or reporting, he may—

(A) conduct monitoring, testing, or analysis (or any combination thereof) which he deems reasonable to ascertain the nature and extent of the hazard associated with the site concerned, or

(B) authorize a State or local authority or other person to carry out any such action, and require, by order, the owner or operator referred to in subsection (a) or (b) to reimburse the Administrator or other authority or person for the costs of such activity.

(2) No order may be issued under this subsection requiring reimbursement of the costs of any action carried out by the Administrator which confirms the results of an order issued under subsection (a) or (b).

(3) For purposes of carrying out this subsection, the Administrator or any authority or other person authorized under paragraph (1), may exercise the authorities set forth in section 3007.

(e) The Administrator may commence a civil action against any person who fails or refuses to comply with any order issued under this section. Such action shall be brought in the United States district court in which the defendant is located, resides, or is doing business. Such court shall have jurisdiction to require compliance with such order and to assess a civil penalty of not to exceed $5,000 for each day during which such failure or refusal occurs.

§ 6935. Restrictions on recycled oil

[Sec. 3014] (a) Not later than one year after the date of the enactment of this section, the Administrator shall promulgate regulations establishing such performance standards and other requirements as may be necessary to protect the public health and the environment from hazards associated with recycled oil. In developing such regulations, the Administrator shall conduct an analysis of the economic impact of the regulations on the oil recycling industry. The Administrator shall ensure that such regulations do not discourage the recovery or recycling of used oil, consistent with the protection of human health and the environment.

(b) Not later than twelve months after the date of enactment of the Hazardous and Solid Waste Amendments of 1984 the Administrator shall propose whether to list or identify used automobile and truck crankcase oil as hazardous waste under section 3001. Not later than twenty-four months after such date of enactment, the Administrator shall make a final determination whether to list or identify used automobile and truck crankcase oil and other used oil as hazardous wastes under section 3001.

(c)(1) With respect to generators and transporters of used oil identified or listed as a hazardous waste under section 3001, the standards promulgated under section 3001(d), 3002, and 3003 of this subtitle shall not apply to such used oil if such used oil is recycled.

(2)(A) In the case of used oil which is exempt under paragraph(1), not later than twenty-four months after the date of enactment of the Hazardous and Solid Waste Amendments of 1984, the Administrator shall promulgate such standards under this subsection regarding the generation and transportation of used oil which is recycled as may be necessary to protect human health and the environment. In promulgating such regulations with respect to generators, the Administrator shall take into account the effect of such regulations on environmentally acceptable types of used oil recycling and the effect of such regulations on small quantity generators and generators which are small businesses (as defined by the Administrator).

(B) The regulations promulgated under this subsection shall provide that no generator of used oil which is exempt under paragraph (1) from the standards promulgated under section 3001(d), 3002, and 3003 shall be subject to any manifest requirement or any associated recordkeeping and reporting requirement with respect to such used oil if such generator—

(i) either—

(I) enters into an agreement or other arrangement (including an agreement or arrangement with an independent transporter or with an agent of the recycler) for delivery of such used oil to a recycling facility which has a permit under section 3005(c) (or for which a valid permit is deemed to be in effect under subsection (d)), or

(II) recycles such used oil at one or more facilities of the generator which has such a permit under section 3005 of this subtitle (or for which a valid permit is deemed to have been issued under subsection (d) of this section);

(ii) such used oil is not mixed by the generator with other types of hazardous wastes; and

(iii) the generator maintains such records relating to such used oil, including records of agreements or other arrangements for delivery of such used oil to any recycling facility referred to in clause (i)(I), as the Administrator deems necessary to protect human health and the environment.

(3) The regulations under this subsection regarding the transportation of used oil which is exempt from the standards promulgated under section 3001(d), 3002, and 3003 under paragraph (1) shall require the transporters of such used oil to deliver such used oil to a facility which has a valid permit under section 3005 of this subtitle or which is deemed to have a valid permit under subsection (d) of this section. The Administrator shall also establish other standards for such transporters as may be necessary to protect human health and the environment.

(d)(1) The owner or operator of a facility which recycles used oil which is exempt under subsection (c)(1), shall be deemed to have a permit under this subsection for all such treatment or recycling (and any associated tank or container storage) if such owner and operator comply with standards promulgated by the Administrator under section 3004; except that the Administrator may require such owners and operators to obtain an individual permit under section 3005(c) if he determines that an individual permit is necessary to protect human health and the environment.

(2) Notwithstanding any other provision of law, any generator who recycles used oil which is exempt under subsections (c)(1) shall not be required to obtain a permit under section 3005(c) with respect to such used oil until the Administrator has promulgated standards under section 3004 regarding the recycling of such used oil.

§ 6936. Expansion during interim status

[Sec. 3015] (a) The owner or operator of a waste pile qualifying for the authorization to operate under section 3005(e) shall be subject to the same requirements for liners and leachate collection systems or equivalent protection provided in regulations promulgated by the Administrator under section 3004 before October 1, 1982, or revised under section 3004(o) (relating to minimum technological requirements), for new facilities receiving individual permits under subsection (c) of section 3005, with respect to each new unit, replacement of an existing unit, or lateral expansion of an existing unit that is within the waste management area identified in the permit application submitted under section 3005, and with respect to waste received beginning six months after the date of enactment of the Hazardous and Solid Waste Amendments of 1984.

(b)(1) The owner or operator of a landfill or surface impoundment qualifying for the authorization to operate under section 3005(e) shall be subject to the requirements of section 3004(o) (relating to minimum technological requirements), with respect to each new unit, replacement of an existing unit, or lateral expansion of an existing unit that is within the waste management area identified in the permit application submitted under this section, and with respect to waste received beginning 6 months after the date of enactment of the Hazardous and Solid Waste Amendments of 1984.

(2) The owner or operator of each unit referred to in paragraph (1) shall notify the Administrator (or the State, if appropriate) at least sixty days prior to receiving waste. The Administrator (or the State) shall require the filing, within six months of receipt of such notice, of an application for a final determination regarding the issuance of a permit for each facility submitting such notice.

(3) In the case of any unit in which the liner and leachate collection system has been installed pursuant to the requirements of this section and in good faith compliance with the Administrator's regulations and guidance documents governing liners and leachate collection systems, no liner or leachate collection system which is different from that which was so installed pursuant to this section shall be required for such unit by the Administrator when issuing the first permit under section 3005 to such facility, except that the Administrator shall not be precluded from requiring installation of a new liner when the Administrator has reason to believe that any liner installed pursuant to the requirements of this section is leaking. The Administrator may, under section 3004, amend the requirements for liners and leachate collection systems required under this section as may be necessary to provide additional protection for human health and the environment.

§ 6937. Inventory of federal agency hazardous waste facilities

[Sec. 3016] (a) Each Federal agency shall undertake a continuing program to compile, publish, and submit to the Administrator (and to the State in the case of sites in States having an authorized hazardous waste program) an inventory of each site which the Federal agency owns or operates or has owned or operated at which hazardous waste is stored, treated, or disposed of or has been disposed of at any time. The inventory shall be submitted every two years beginning January 31, 1986. Such inventory shall be available to the public as provided in section 3007(b). Information previously submitted by a Federal agency under section 103 of the Comprehensive Environmental

Response, Compensation, and Liability Act of 1980, or under section 3005 or 3010 of this Act, or under this section need not be resubmitted except that the agency shall update any previous submission to reflect the latest available data and information. The inventory shall include each of the following:

(1) A description of the location of each site at which any such treatment, storage, or disposal has taken place before the date on which permits are required under section 3005 for such storage, treatment, or disposal, and where hazardous waste has been disposed, a description of hydrogeology of the site and the location of withdrawal wells and surface water within one mile of the site.

(2) Such information relating to the amount, nature, and toxicity of the hazardous waste in each site as may be necessary to determine the extent of any health hazard which may be associated with any site.

(3) Information on the known nature and extent of environmental contamination at each site, including a description of the monitoring data obtained.

(4) Information concerning the current status of the site, including information respecting whether or not hazardous waste is currently being treated, stored, or disposed of at such site (and if not, the date on which such activity ceased) and information respecting the nature of any other activity currently carried out at such site.

(5) A list of sites at which hazardous waste has been disposed and environmental monitoring data has not been obtained, and the reasons for the lack of monitoring data at each site.

(6) A description of response actions undertaken or contemplated at contaminated sites.

(7) An identification of the types of techniques of waste treatment, storage, or disposal which have been used at each site.

(8) The name and address and responsible Federal agency for each site, determined as of the date of preparation of the inventory.

(b) If the Administrator determines that any Federal agency under subsection (a) is not adequately providing information respecting the sites referred to in subsection (a), the Administrator shall notify the chief official of such agency. If within ninety days following such notification, the Federal agency has not undertaken a program to adequately provide such information, the Administrator shall carry out the inventory program for such agency.

§ 6938. Export of hazardous waste

[Sec. 3017] (a) Beginning twenty-four months after the date of enactment of the Hazardous and Solid Waste Amendments of 1984, no person shall export any hazardous waste identified or listed under this subtitle unless

(1)(A) such person has provided the notification required in subsection (c) of this section.

    (B) the government of the receiving country has consented to accept such hazardous waste,

    (C) a copy of the receiving country's written consent is attached to the manifest accompanying each waste shipment, and

    (D) the shipment conforms with the terms of the consent of the government of the receiving country required pursuant to subsection (e), or

  (2) the United States and the government of the receiving country have entered into an agreement as provided for in subsection (f) and the shipment conforms with the terms of such agreement.

(b) Not later than twelve months after the date of enactment of the Hazardous and Solid Waste Amendments of 1984, the Administrator shall promulgate the regulations necessary to implement this section. Such regulations shall become effective one hundred and eighty days after promulgation.

(c) Any person who intends to export a hazardous waste identified or listed under this subtitle beginning twelve months after the date of enactment of the Hazardous and Solid Waste Amendments of 1984, shall, before such hazardous waste is scheduled to leave the United States, provide notification to the Administrator. Such notification shall contain the following information:

  (1) the name and address of the exporter;

  (2) the types and estimated quantities of hazardous waste to be exported;

  (3) the estimated frequency or rate at which such waste is to be exported; and the period of time over which such waste is to be exported;

  (4) the ports of entry;

  (5) a description of the manner in which such hazardous waste will be transported to and treated, stored, or disposed in the receiving country, and

  (6) the name and address of the ultimate treatment, storage or disposal facility.

(d) Within thirty days of the Administrator's receipt of a complete notification under this section, the Secretary of State, acting on behalf of the Administrator, shall—

  (1) forward a copy of the notification to the government of the receiving country;

  (2) advise the government that United States law prohibits the export of hazardous waste unless the receiving country consents to accept the hazardous waste;

  (3) request the government to provide the Secretary with a written consent or objection to the terms of the notification; and

  (4) forward to the government of the receiving country a description of the Federal regulations which would apply to the treatment, storage, and disposal of the hazardous waste in the United States.

(e) Within thirty days of receipt by the Secretary of State of the receiving country's written consent or objection (or any subsequent communication withdrawing a prior consent or objection), the Administrator shall forward such a consent, objection, or other communication to the exporter.

(f) Where there exists an international agreement between the United States and the government of the receiving country establishing notice, export, and enforcement procedures for the transportation, treatment, storage, and disposal of hazardous wastes, only the requirements of subsection (a)(2) and (g) shall apply.

(g) After the date of enactment of the Hazardous and Solid Waste Amendments of 1984, any person who exports any hazardous waste identified or listed under section 3001 of this subtitle shall file with the Administrator no later than March 1 of each year, a report summarizing the types, quantities, frequency, and ultimate destination of all such hazardous waste exported during the previous calendar year.

(h) Nothing in this section shall preclude the Administrator from establishing other standards for the export of hazardous wastes under section 3002 or section 3003 of this subtitle.

§ 6939. Domestic sewage

[Sec. 3018] (a) The Administrator shall, not later than 15 months after the date of enactment of the Hazardous and Solid Waste Amendments of 1984, submit a report to the Congress concerning those substances identified or listed under section 3001 which are not regulated under the subtitle by reason of the exclusion for mixtures of domestic sewage and other wastes that pass through a sewer system to a publicly owned treatment works. Such report shall include the types, size and number of generators which dispose of such substances in this manner, the types and quantities disposed of in this manner, and the identification of significant generators, wastes, and waste constituents not regulated under existing Federal law or regulated in a manner sufficient to protect human health and the environment

(b) Within eighteen months after submitting the report specified in subsection (a), the Administrator shall revise existing regulations and promulgate such additional regulations pursuant to this subtitle (or any other authority of the Administrator, including section 307 of the Federal Water Pollution Control Act) as are necessary to assure that substances identified or listed under section 3001 which pass through a sewer system to a publicly owned treatment works are adequately controlled to protect human health and the environment.

(c) The Administrator shall, within thirty-six months after the date of the enactment of the Hazardous and Solid Waste Amendments of 1984, submit a report to Congress concerning wastewater lagoons at publicly owned treatment works and their effect on groundwater quality. Such report shall include—

(1) The number and size of such lagoons;

(2) the types and quantities of waste contained in such lagoons;

(3) the extent to which such waste has been or may be released from such

lagoons and contaminate ground water; and

(4) available alternatives for preventing or controlling such releases.

The Administrator may utilize the authority of sections 3007 and 3013 for the purpose of completing such report.

(d) The provisions of sections 3007 and 3010 shall apply to solid or dissolved materials in domestic sewage to the same extent and in the same manner as such provisions apply to hazardous waste.

§ 6939a. Exposure information and health assessments

[Sec. 3019] (a) Beginning on the date nine months after the enactment of the Hazardous and Solid Waste Amendments of 1984, each application for a final determination regarding a permit under section 3005(c) for a landfill or surface impoundment shall be accompanied by information reasonably ascertainable by the owner or operator on the potential for the public to be exposed to hazardous wastes or hazardous constituents through releases related to the unit. At a minimum, such information must address:

(1) reasonably foreseeable potential releases from both normal operations and accidents at the unit, including releases associated with transportation to or from the unit;

(2) the potential pathways of human exposure to hazardous wastes or constituents resulting from the releases described under paragraph (1); and

(3) the potential magnitude and nature of the human exposure resulting from such releases.

The owner or operator of a landfill or surface impoundment for which an application for such a final determination under section 3005(c) has been submitted prior to the date of enactment of the Hazardous and Solid Waste Amendments of 1984 shall submit the information required by this subsection to the Administrator (or the State, in the case of a State with an authorized program) no later than the date nine months after such date of enactment.

(b)(1) The Administrator (or the State, in the case of a State with an authorized program) shall make the information required by subsection (a), together with other relevant information, available to the Agency for Toxic Substances and Disease Registry established by section 104(i) of the Comprehensive Environmental Response, Compensation and Liability Act of 1980.

(2) Whenever in the judgment of the Administrator, or the State (in the case of a State with an authorized program), a landfill or a surface impoundment poses a substantial potential risk to human health, due to the existence of releases of hazardous constituents, the magnitude of contamination with hazardous constituents which may be the result of a release, or the magnitude of the population exposed to such release or contamination, the Administrator or the State (with the concur-

rence of the Administrator) may request the Administrator of the Agency for Toxic Substances and Disease Registry to conduct a health assessment in connection with such facility and take other appropriate action with respect to such risks as authorized by section 104(b) and (i) of the Comprehensive Environmental Response, Compensation and Liability Act of 1980. If funds are provided in connection with such request the Administrator of such Agency shall conduct such health assessment.

(c) Any member of the public may submit evidence of releases of or exposure to hazardous constituents from such a facility, or as to the risks or health effects associated with such releases or exposure, to the Administrator of the Agency for Toxic Substances and Disease Registry, the Administrator, or the State (in the case of a State with an authorized program).

(d) In determining the order in which to conduct health assessments under this subsection, the Administrator of the Agency for Toxic Substances and Disease Registry shall give priority to those facilities or sites at which there is documented evidence of release of hazardous constituents, at which the potential risk to human health appears highest, and for which in the judgment of the Administrator of such Agency existing health assessment data is inadequate to assess the potential risk to human health as provided in subsection (f).

(e) The Administrator of such Agency shall issue periodic reports which include the results of all the assessments carried out under this section. Such assessments or other activities shall be reported after appropriate peer review.

(f) For the purposes of this section, the term "health assessments" shall include preliminary assessments of the potential risk to human health posed by individual sites and facilities subject to this section, based on such factors as the nature and extent of contamination, the existence of potential for pathways of human exposure (including ground or surface water contamination, air emissions, and food chain contamination), the size and potential susceptibility of the community within the likely pathways of exposure, the comparison of expected human exposure levels to the short-term and long-term health effects associated with identified contaminants and any available recommended exposure or tolerance limits for such contaminants, and the comparison of existing morbidity and mortality data on diseases that may be associated with the observed levels of exposure. The assessment shall include an evaluation of the risks to the potentially affected population from all sources of such contaminants, including known point or nonpoint sources other than the site or facility in question. A purpose of such preliminary assessments shall be to help determine whether full-scale health or epidemiological studies and medical evaluations of exposed populations shall be undertaken.

(g) In any case in which a health assessment performed under this section discloses the exposure of a population to the release of a hazardous substance, the cost of such health assessment may be recovered as a cost of response under section 107 of the Comprehensive Environmental Response, Compensation, and Liability Act of 1980 from persons causing or contributing to such release of such hazardous substance or, in the case of multiple releases contributing to such exposure, to all such release.

Subchapter IV. State or Regional Solid Waste Plans

§ 6941. Objectives of subtitle

[Sec. 4001] The objectives of this subtitle are to assist in developing and encouraging methods for the disposal of solid waste which are environmentally sound and which maximize the utilization of valuable resources including energy and materials which are recoverable from solid waste and to encourage resource conservation. Such objectives are to be accomplished through Federal technical and financial assistance to States or regional authorities from comprehensive planning pursuant to Federal guidelines designed to foster cooperation among Federal, State, and local governments and private industry. In developing such comprehensive plans, it is the intention of this Act that in determining the size of the waste-to-energy facility, adequate provision shall be given to the present and reasonably anticipated future needs, including those needs created by thorough implementation of section 6002(h), of the recycling and resource recovery interest within the area encompassed by the planning process.

§ 6942. Federal guidelines for plans

[Sec. 4002] For purposes of encouraging and facilitating the development of regional planning for solid waste management, the Administrator, within one hundred and eighty days after the date of enactment of this section and after consultation with appropriate Federal, State, and local authorities, shall by regulation publish guidelines for the identification of those areas which have common solid waste management problems and are appropriate units for planning regional solid waste management services. Such guidelines shall consider—

(1) the size and location of areas which should be included,
(2) the volume of solid waste which should be included, and
(3) the available means of coordinating regional planning with other related regional planning and for coordination of such regional planning into the State plan.

(b) Not later than eighteen months after the date of enactment of this section and after notice and hearing, the Administrator shall, after consultation with appropriate Federal, State, and local authorities, promulgate regulations containing guidelines to assist in the development and implementation of State solid waste management plans (hereinafter in this title referred to as "State plans"). The guidelines shall contain methods for achieving the objectives specified in section 4001. Such guidelines shall be reviewed from time to time, but not less frequently than every three years, and revised as may be appropriate.

(c) The guidelines promulgated under subsection (b) shall consider—

(1) the varying regional, geologic, hydrologic, climatic, and other circumstances under which different solid waste practices are required in order to insure the reasonable protection of the quality of the ground and surface waters from leachate contamination, the reasonable protection of the quality of the surface waters from surface runoff contamination, and the reasonable protection of ambient air quality;

(2) characteristics and conditions of collection, storage, processing, and disposal operating methods, techniques and practices, and location of facilities where such operating methods, techniques, and practices are conducted, taking into account the nature of the material to be disposed;

(3) methods for closing or upgrading open dumps for purposes of eliminating potential health hazards;

(4) population density, distribution, and projected growth;

(5) geographic, geologic, climatic, and hydrologic characteristics;

(6) the type and location of transportation;

(7) the profile of industries;

(8) the constituents and generation rates of waste;

(9) the political, economic, organizational, financial, and management problems affecting comprehensive solid waste management;

(10) types of resource recovery facilities and resource conservation systems which are appropriate; and

(11) available new and additional markets for recovered material and energy and energy resources recovered from solid waste as well as methods for conserving such materials and energy.

§ 6943. Requirements for approval of plans

[Sec. 4003] (a) In order to be approved under section 4007, each State plan must comply with the following minimum requirements—

(1) The plan shall identify (in accordance with section 4006(b)) (A) the responsibilities of State, local, and regional authorities in the implementation of the State plan, (B) the distribution of Federal funds to the authorities responsible for development and implementation of the State plan, and (C) the means for coordinating regional planning and implementation under the State plan.

(2) The plan shall, in accordance with section 4004(b) and 4005(a), prohibit the establishment of new open dumps within the State, and

contain requirements that all solid waste (including solid waste originating in other States, but not including hazardous waste) shall be (A) utilized for resource recovery or (B) disposed of in sanitary landfills (within the meaning of section 4004(a)) or otherwise disposed of in an environmentally sound manner.

(3) The plan shall provide for the closing or upgrading of all existing open dumps within the State pursuant to the requirements of section 4005.

(4) The plan shall provide for the establishment of such State regulatory powers as may be necessary to implement the plan.

(5) The plan shall provide that no state or local government within the State shall be prohibited under State or local law from negotiating and entering into long-term contracts for the supply of solid waste to resource recovery facilities, from entering into long-term contracts for the operation of such facilities, or from securing long-term markets for material and energy recovered from such facilities or for conserving materials or energy by reducing the volume of waste.

(6) The plan shall provide for such resource conservation or recovery and for the disposal of solid waste in sanitary landfills or any combination of practices so as may be necessary to use or dispose of such waste in a manner that is environmentally sound.

(b) Any State plan submitted under this subtitle may include, at the option of the State, provisions to carry out each of the following:

(1) Encouragement, to the maximum extent feasible and consistent with the protection of the public health and the environment, of the use of recycled oil in all appropriate areas of State and local government.

(2) Encouragement of persons contracting with the State to use recycled oil to the maximum extent feasible, consistent with protection of the public health and the environment.

(3) Informing the public of the uses of recycled oil.

(4) Establishment and implementation of a program (including any necessary licensing of persons and including the use, where appropriate, of manifests) to assure that used oil is collected, transported, treated, stored, reused, and disposed of, in a manner which does not present a hazard to the public health or the environment.

Any plan submitted under this title before the date of the enactment of the Used Oil Recycling Act of 1980 may be amended, at the option of the State, at any time after such date to include any provision referred to in this subsection.

(c)(1) A State which has a plan approved under this subtitle or which has submitted a plan for such approval shall be eligible for assistance under section 4008(a)(3) if the Administrator determines that under such plan the State will—

(A) analyze and determine the economic and technical feasibility of facilities and programs to conserve resources which contribute to the waste stream or to recover energy and materials from municipal waste;

(B) analyze the legal, institutional, and economic impediments to the development of systems and facilities for conservation of energy or materials which contribute to the waste stream or for the recovery of energy and materials from municipal waste and make recommendations to appropriate governmental authorities for overcoming such impediments;

(C) assist municipalities within the State in developing plans, programs, and projects to conserve resources or recover energy and materials from municipal waste; and

(D) coordinate the resource conservation and recovery planning under subparagraph (C).

(2) The analysis referred to in paragraph (1)(A) shall include—

(A) the evaluation of, and establishment of priorities among, market opportunities for industrial and commercial users of all types (including public utilities and industrial parks) to utilize energy and materials recovered from municipal waste;

(B) comparisons of the relative costs of energy recovered from municipal waste in relation to the costs of energy derived from fossil fuels and other sources;

(C) studies of the transportation and storage problems and other problems associated with the development of energy and materials recovery technology, including curbside source separation;

(D) the evaluation and establishment of priorities among ways of conserving energy or materials which contribute to the waste stream;

(E) comparison of the relative total costs between conserving resources and disposing of or recovering such waste; and

(F) studies of impediments to resource conservation or recovery, including business practices, transportation requirements, or storage difficulties.

Such studies and analyses shall also include studies of other sources of solid waste from which energy and materials may be recovered or minimized.

(d) Notwithstanding any of the above requirements, it is the intention of this Act and the planning process developed pursuant to this Act that in determining the size of the waste-to-energy facility, adequate provision shall be given to the present and reasonably anticipated future needs of the recycling and resource recovery interest within the area encompassed by the planning process.

§ 6944. Criteria for sanitary landfills; sanitary landfills required for all disposal

[Sec. 4004] (a) Not later than one year after the date of enactment of this section, after consultation with the States, and after notice and public hearings, the Administrator shall promulgate regulations containing criteria for determining which facilities shall be classified as sanitary landfills and which shall be classified as open dumps within the meaning of this Act. At a minimum, such criteria shall provide that a facility may be classified as a sanitary landfill and not an open dump only if there is no reasonable probability of adverse effects on health or the environment from disposal of solid waste at such facility. Such regulations may provide for the classification of the types of sanitary landfills.

(b) For purposes of complying with section 4003(2), each State plan shall prohibit the establishment of open dumps and contain a requirement that disposal of all solid waste within the State shall be in compliance with such section 4003(2).

(c) The prohibition contained in subsection (b) shall take effect on the date six months after the date of promulgation of regulations under subsection (a) or on the date of approval of the State plan, whichever is later.

§ 6945. Upgrading of open dumps

[Sec. 4005] (a) Upon promulgation of criteria under section 1008(a)(3), any solid waste management practice or disposal of solid waste or hazardous waste which constitutes the open dumping of solid waste or hazardous waste is prohibited, except in the case of any practice or disposal of solid waste under a timetable or schedule for compliance established under this section. The prohibition contained in the preceding sentence shall be enforceable under section 7002 against persons engaged in the act of open dumping. For purposes of complying with section 4003(2) and 4003(3), each State plan shall contain a requirement that all existing disposal facilities or sites for solid waste in such State which are open dumps listed in the inventory under subsection (b) shall comply with such measures as may be promulgated by the Administrator to eliminate health hazards and minimize potential health hazards. Each such plan shall establish, for any entity which demonstrates that it has considered other public or private alternatives for solid waste management to comply with the prohibition on open dumping and is unable to utilize such alternatives to so comply, a timetable or schedule for compliance for such practice or disposal of solid waste which specifies a schedule of remedial measures, including an enforceable sequence of actions or operations, leading to compliance with the prohibition on open dumping solid waste within a reasonable time (not to exceed 5 years from the date of publication of criteria under section 1008(a)(3)).

(b) To assist the States in complying with section 4003(3), not later than one year after promulgation of regulations under section 4004, the Administrator, with the cooperation of the Bureau of the Census shall publish an inventory of all disposal facilities or sites in the United States which are open dumps within the meaning of this Act.

(c)(1)(A) Not later than 36 months after the date of enactment of the Hazardous and Solid Waste Amendments of 1984, each State shall adopt and implement a permit program or other system of prior approval and conditions to assure that each solid waste management facility within such State which may receive hazardous household waste or hazardous waste due to the provision of section 3001(d) for small quantity generators (otherwise not subject to the requirement for a permit under section 3005) will comply with the applicable criteria promulgated under section 4004(a) and section 1008(a)(3).

(B) Not later than eighteen months after the promulgation of revised criteria under subsection 4004(a) (as required by section 4010(c)), each State shall adopt and implement a permit program or other system or prior approval and conditions, to assure that each solid waste management facility within such State which may receive hazardous household waste or hazardous waste due to the provision of section 3001(d)for small quantity generators (otherwise not subject to the requirement for a permit under section 3005) will comply with the criteria revised under section 4004(a).

(C) The Administrator shall determine whether each State has developed an adequate program under this paragraph. The Administrator may make such a determination in conjunction with approval, disapproval or partial approval of a State plan under section 4007.

(2)(A) In any State that the Administrator determines has not adopted an adequate program for such facilities under paragraph (1)(B) by the date provided in such paragraph, the Administrator may use the authorities available under sections 3007 and 3008 of this title to enforce the prohibition contained in subsection (a) of this section with respect to such facilities.

(B) For purposes of this paragraph, the term "requirement of this subtitle" in section 3008 shall be deemed to include criteria promulgated by the Administrator under sections 1008(a)(3) and 4004(a) of this title, and the term "hazardous wastes" in section 3007 shall be deemed to include solid waste at facilities that may handle hazardous household wastes or hazardous wastes from small quantity generators.

§ 6946. Procedure for development and implementation of state plan

[Sec. 4006] (a) Within one hundred and eighty days after publication of guidelines under section 4002(a) (relating to identification of regions), the Governor of each State, after consultation with local elected officials; shall promulgate regulations based on such guidelines identifying the boundaries of each area within the State which, as a result of urban concentrations, geographic conditions, markets, and other factors, is appropriate for carrying out regional solid waste management. Such regulations may be modified from time to time (identifying additional or different regions) pursuant to such guidelines.

(b)(1) Within one hundred and eighty days after the Governor promulgates regulations under subsection (a), for purposes of facilitating the development and implementation of a State plan which will meet the minimum requirements of section 4003, the State, together with appropriate elected officials of general purpose units of local government, shall jointly (A) identify an agency to develop the State plan and identify one or more agencies to implement such plan, and (B) identify which solid waste management activities will, under such State plan, be planned for and carried out by the State and which such management activities will, under such State plan, be planned for and carried out by a regional or local authority or a combination of regional or local and State authorities. If a multi-functional regional agency authorized by State law to conduct solid waste planning and management (the members of which are appointed by the Governor) is in existence on the date of enactment of this Act, the Governor shall identify such authority for purposes of carrying out within such region clause (A) of this paragraph. Where feasible, designation of the agency for the affected area designated under section 208 of the Federal Water Pollution Control Act (86 Stat. 839) shall be considered. A State agency identified under this paragraph shall be established or designated by the Governor of such State. Local or regional agencies identified under this paragraph shall be composed of individuals at least a majority of whom are elected local officials.

(2) If planning and implementation agencies are not identified and designated or established as required under paragraph (1) for any affected area, the governor shall, before the date two hundred and seventy days after promulgation of regulations under subsection (a), establish or designate a State agency to develop and implement the State plan for such area.

(c)(1) In the case of any region which, pursuant to the guidelines published by the Administrator under section 4002(a) (relating to identification of regions), would be located in two or more States, the Governors of the respective States, after consultation with local elected officials, shall consult, cooperate, and enter into agreements identifying the boundaries of such region pursuant to subsection (a).

(2) Within one hundred and eighty days after an interstate region is identified by agreement under paragraph (1), appropriate elected officials of general purpose units of local government within such region shall jointly establish or designate an agency to develop a plan for such region. If no such agency is established or designated within such period by such officials, the Governors of the respective States may, by agreement, establish or designate for such purpose a single

representative organization including elected officials of general purpose units of local government within such region.

(3) Implementation of interstate regional solid waste management plans shall be conducted by units of local government for any portion of a region within their jurisdiction, or by multijurisdictional agencies or authorities designated in accordance with State law, including those designated by agreement by such units of local government for such purpose. If no such unit, agency, or authority is so designated, the respective Governors shall designate or establish a single interstate agency to implement such plan.

(4) For purposes of this subtitle, so much of an interstate regional plan as is carried out within a particular State shall be deemed part of the State plan for such State.

§ 6947. Approval of state plan; federal assistance

[Sec. 4007] (a) The Administrator shall, within six months after a State plan has been submitted for approval, approve or disapprove the plan. The Administrator shall approve a plan if he determines that—

(1) it meets the requirements of paragraphs (1), (2), (3), and (5) of section 4003; and

(2) it contains provision for revision of such plan, after notice and public hearing, whenever the Administrator, by regulation, determines—

(A) that revised regulations respecting minimum requirements have been promulgated under paragraphs (1), (2), (3), and (5) of section 4003 with which the State plan is not in compliance;

(B) that information has become available which demonstrates the inadequacy of the plan to effectuate the purposes of this subtitle; or

(C) that such revision is otherwise necessary.

The Administrator shall review approved plans from time to time and if he determines that revision or corrections are necessary to bring such plan into compliance with the minimum requirements promulgated under section 4003 (including new or revised requirements), he shall, after notice and opportunity for public hearing, withdraw his approval of such plan. Such withdrawal of approval shall cease to be effective upon the Administrator's determination that such complies with such minimum requirements.

(b)(1) The Administrator shall approve a State application for financial assistance under this subtitle, and make grants to such State, if such State and local and regional authorities within such State have complied with the requirements of section 4006 within the period required under such section and if such State has a State plan which has been approved by the Administrator under this subtitle.

(2) The Administrator shall approve a State application for financial assistance under this subtitle, and make grants to such State, for fiscal

years 1978 and 1979 if the Administrator determines that the State plan continues to be eligible for approval under subsection (a) and is being implemented by the State.

(3) Upon withdrawal of approval of a State plan under subsection (a), the Administrator shall withhold Federal financial and technical assistance under this subtitle (other than such technical assistance as may be necessary to assist in obtaining the reinstatement of approval) until such time as such approval is reinstated.

(c) Nothing in this subtitle shall be construed to prevent or affect any activities respecting solid waste planning or management which are carried out by State, regional, or local authorities unless such activities are inconsistent with a State plan approved by the Administrator under this subtitle.

§ 6948. Federal assistance

[Sec. 4008] (a)(1) There are authorized to be appropriated $30,000,000 for fiscal year 1978, $40,000,000 for fiscal 1979, $20,000,000 for fiscal year 1980, $15,000,000 for fiscal year 1981, $20,000,000 for the fiscal year 1982, and $10,000,000 for each of the fiscal years 1985 through 1988 for purposes of financial assistance to States and local, regional, and interstate authorities for the development and implementation of plans approved by the Administrator under this subtitle (other than the provisions of such plans referred to in section 4003(b), relating to feasibility planning for municipal waste energy and materials conservation and recovery).

(2)(A) The Administrator is authorized to provide financial assistance to States, counties, municipalities, and intermunicipal agencies and State and local public solid waste management authorities for implementation of programs to provide solid waste management, resource recovery, and resource conservation services and hazardous waste management. Such assistance shall include assistance for facility planning and feasibility studies; expert consultation; surveys and analyses of market needs; marketing of recovered resources; technology assessments; legal expenses; construction feasibility studies; source separation projects; and fiscal or economic investigations or studies; but such assistance shall not include any other element of construction, or any acquisition of land or interest in land, or any subsidy for the price of recovered resources. Agencies assisted under this subsection shall consider existing solid waste management and hazardous waste management services and facilities as well as facilities proposed for construction.

(B) An applicant for financial assistance under this paragraph must agree to comply with respect to the project or program assisted with the applicable requirements of section 4005 and Subtitle C of this Act and apply applicable solid waste management practices, methods, and levels of control consistent with any guidelines published pursuant to section 1008 of this Act. Assistance under this paragraph shall be available only for programs certified by the State to be consistent with any applicable State or areawide solid waste management plan or program. Applicants for technical and financial assistance under this section shall not preclude or foreclose consideration of programs for the recovery of recyclable materials through source separation or other resource recovery techniques.

(C) There are authorized to be appropriated $15,000,000 for each of the fiscal years 1978 and 1979 for purposes of this section. There are authorized to be appropriated $10,000,000 for fiscal year 1980, $10,000,000 for fiscal year 1981, $10,000,000 for fiscal year 1982, and $10,000,000 for each of the fiscal years 1985 through 1988 for purposes of this paragraph.

(D) There are authorized—

(i) to be made available $15,000,000 out of funds appropriated for fiscal year 1985, and

(ii) to be appropriated for each of the fiscal years 1986 though 1988, $20,000,000

for grants to States (and where appropriate to regional, local, and interstate agencies) to implement programs requiring compliance by solid waste management facilities with the criteria promulgated under section 4004(a) and section 1008(a)(3) and with the provisions of section 4005. To the extent practicable, such programs shall require such compliance not later than thirty-six months after the date of the enactment of the Hazardous and Solid Waste Amendments of 1984.

(3)(A) There is authorized to be appropriated for the fiscal year beginning October 1, 1981, and for each fiscal year thereafter before October 1, 1986, $4,000,000 for purposes of making grants to States to carry out section 4003(b). No amount may be appropriated for such purposes for the fiscal year beginning on October 1, 1986, or for any fiscal year thereafter.

(B) Assistance provided by the Administrator under this paragraph shall be used only for the purposes specified in section 4003(b). Such assistance may not be used for purposes of land acquisition, final facility design, equipment purchase, construction, startup or operation activities.

(C) Where appropriate, any State receiving assistance under this paragraph may make all or any part of such assistance available to municipalities within the State to carry out the activities specified in section 4003(b)(1)(A) and (B).

(b) The sums appropriated in any fiscal year under subsection (a)(1) shall be allotted by the Administrator among all States, in the ratio that the population in each State bears to the population in all of the States, except that no State shall receive less than one-half of 1 per centum of the sums so allotted in any fiscal year. No State shall receive any grant under this section during any fiscal year when its expenditures of non-Federal funds for other than nonrecurrent expenditures for solid waste management control programs will be less than its expenditures were for such programs during fiscal year 1975, except that such funds may be reduced by an amount equal to their proportionate share of any general reduction of State spending ordered by the Governor or legislature of such State. No State shall receive any grant for solid waste management programs unless the Administrator is satisfied that such grant will be so used as to supplement and, to the extent practicable, increase the level of State, local, regional, or other non-Federal funds that would in the absence of such grant be made available for the maintenance of such programs.

(c) The Federal assistance allotted to the States under subsection (b) shall be allocated by the State receiving such funds to State, local, regional, and interstate authorities carrying out planning and implementation of the State plan. Such allocation shall be based upon the responsibilities of the respective parties as determined pursuant to section 4006(b).

(d)(1) The Administrator may provide technical assistance to State and local governments for purposes of developing and implementing State plans. Technical assistance respecting resource recovery and conservation may be provided through resource recovery and conservation panels, established in the Environmental Protection Agency under subtitle B, to assist the State and local governments with respect to particular resource recovery and conservation projects under consideration and to evaluate their effect on the State plan.

(2) In carrying out this subsection, the Administrator may, upon request, provide technical assistance to States to assist in the removal or modification of legal, institutional, economic, and other impediments to the recycling of used oil. Such impediments may include laws, regulations, and policies, including State procurement policies, which are not favorable to the recycling of used oil.

(3) In carrying out this subsection, the Administrator is authorized to provide technical assistance to States, municipalities, regional authorities, and inter-municipal agencies upon request, to assist in the removal or modification of legal, institutional, and economic impediments which have the effect of impeding the development of systems and facilities to recover energy and materials from municipal waste or to conserve energy or materials which contribute to the waste stream. Such impediments may include—

(A) laws, regulations, and policies, including State and local procurement policies, which are not favorable to resource conservation and recovery policies, systems, and facilities;

(B) impediments to the financing of facilities to conserve or recover energy and materials from municipal waste through the exercise of State and local authority to issue revenue bonds and the use of State and local credit assistance; and

(C) impediments to institutional arrangements necessary to undertake

The Resource Conservation and Recovery Act • 363

projects for the conservation or recovery of energy and materials from municipal waste, including the creation of special districts, authorities, or corporations where necessary having the power to secure the supply of waste of a project, to conserve resources, to implement the project, and to undertake related activities.

(e)(1) The Administrator, in cooperation with State and local officials, shall identify local governments within the United States (A) having a solid waste disposal facility (i) which is owned by the unit of local government, (ii) for which an order has been issued by the State to cease receiving solid waste for treatment, storage, or disposal, and (iii) which is subject to a State-approved end-use recreation plan, and (B) which are located over an aquifer which is the source of drinking water for any person or public water system which has serious environmental problems resulting from the disposal of such solid waste, including methane migration.

(2) There is authorized to be appropriated to the Administrator $2,500,000 for the fiscal year 1980 and $1,500,000 for each of the fiscal years 1981 and 1982 to make grants to be used for the containment and stabilization of solid waste located at the disposal sites referred to in paragraph (1). Not more than one community in any State shall be eligible for grants under this paragraph and not more than one project in any State shall be eligible for such grants. No unit of local government shall be eligible for grants under this paragraph with respect to any site which exceeds 65 acres in size.

(f)(1) The Administrator may make grants to States, which have a State plan approved under section 4007, or which have submitted a State plan for approval under such section, if such plan includes the discretionary provisions described in section 4003(b). Grants under this subsection shall be for purposes of assisting the State in carrying out such discretionary provisions. No grant under this subsection may be used for construction or for the acquisition of land or equipment.

(2) Grants under this subsection shall be allotted among the States in the same manner as provided in the first sentence of subsection (b).

(3) No grant may be made under this subsection unless an application therefor is submitted to, and approved by, the Administrator. The application shall be in such form, be submitted in such manner, and contain such information as the Administrator may require.

(4) For purposes of making grants under this subsection, there are authorized to be appropriated $5,000,000 for fiscal year 1982, $5,000,000 for fiscal year 1983, and $5,000,000 for each of the fiscal years 1985 through 1988.

(g)(1) The Administrator is authorized to make grants to municipalities, regional authorities, and intermunicipal agencies to carry out activities described in subparagraphs (A) and (B) of section 4003(b)(1). Such grants may be made only pursuant to an application submitted to the Administrator by the municipality which application has been approved by the State and determined by the State to be consistent with any State plan approved or submitted under this subtitle or any other appropriate planning carried out by the State.

(2) There is authorized to be appropriated for the fiscal year beginning October 1, 1981, and for each fiscal year thereafter before October 1, 1986, $8,000,000 for purposes of making grants to municipalities under this subsection. No amount may be appropriated for such purposes for the fiscal year beginning on October 1, 1986, or for any fiscal year thereafter.

(3) Assistance provided by the Administrator under this subsection shall be used only for the purposes specified in paragraph (1). Such assistance may not be used for purposes of land acquisition, final facility design, equipment purchase, construction, startup or operation activities.

§ 6949. Rural communities assistance

[Sec. 4009] (a) The Administrator shall make grants to States to provide assistance to municipalities with a population of five thousand or less, or counties with a population of ten thousand or less or less than twenty persons per square mile and not within a metropolitan area, for solid waste management facilities (including equipment) necessary to meet the requirements of section 4005 of this Act or restrictions on open burning or other requirements arising under the Clean Air Act or the Federal Water Pollution Control Act. Such assistance shall only be available—

(1) to any municipality or county which could not feasibly be included in a solid waste management system or facility serving an urbanized, multijurisdictional area because of its distance from such systems;

(2) where existing or planned solid wate management services or facilities are unavailable or insufficient to comply with the requirements of section 4005 of this Act; and

(3) for systems which are certified by the State to be consistent with any plans or programs established under any State or areawide planning process.

(b) The Administrator shall allot the sums appropriated to carry out this section in any fiscal year among the States in accordance with regulations promulgated by him on the basis of the average of the ratio which the population of rural areas of each State bears to the total population of rural areas of all the States, the ratio which the population of counties in each State having less than twenty persons per square mile bears to the total population of such counties in all the States, and the ratio which the population of such low-density counties in each State having 33 per centum or more of all families with incomes not in excess of 125 per centum of the poverty level bears to the total population of such counties in all the States.

(c) The amount of any grant under this section shall not exceed 75 per centum of the costs of the project. No assistance under this section shall be available for the acquisition of land or interests in land.

(d) There are authorized to be appropriated $25,000,000 for each of the fiscal years 1978 and 1979 to carry out this section. There are authorized to be appropriated $10,000,000 for the fiscal year 1980 and $15,000,000 for each of the fiscal years 1981 and 1982 to carry out this section.

§ 6949a.   Adequacy of certain guidelines and criteria

[Sec. 4010] (a) The Administrator shall conduct a study of the extent to which the guidelines and criteria under this Act (other than guidelines and criteria for facilities to which subtitle C applies) which are applicable to solid waste management and disposal facilities, including, but not limited to landfills and surface impoundments, are adequate to protect human health and the environment from ground water contamination. Such study shall include a detailed assessment of the degree to which the criteria under section 1008(a) and the criteria under section 4004 regarding monitoring, prevention of contamination, and remedial action are adequate to protect ground water and shall also include recommendation with respect to any additional enforcement authorities which the Administrator, in consultation with the Attorney General, deems necessary for such purposes.

(b) Not later than thirty-six months after the date of enactment of the Hazardous and Solid Waste Amendments of 1984, the Administrator shall submit a report to the Congress setting forth the results of the study required under this section, together with any recommendations made by the Administrator on the basis of such study.

(c) Not later than March 31, 1988, the Administrator shall promulgate revisions of the criteria promulgated under paragraph (1) of section 4004(a) and under section 1008(a)(3) for facilities that may receive hazardous household wastes or hazardous wastes from small quantity generators under section 3001(d). The criteria shall be those necessary to protect human health and the environment and may take into account the practicable capability of such facilities. At a minimum such revisions for facilities potentially receiving such wastes should require ground water monitoring as necessary to detect contamination, establish criteria for the acceptable location of new or existing facilities, and provide for corrective action as appropriate.

Subchapter V. Duties of the Secretary of Commerce in Resource and Recovery

§ 6951.   Functions

[Sec. 5001] The Secretary of Commerce shall encourage greater commercialization of proven resource recovery technology by providing—

(1) accurate specifications for recovered materials;
(2) stimulation of development of markets for recovered materials;
(3) promotion of proven technology; and
(4) a forum for the exchange of technical and economic data relating to resource recovery facilities.

§ 6952. Development of specifications for secondary materials

[Sec. 5002] The Secretary of Commerce, acting through the National Bureau of Standards, and in conjunction with national standards-setting organizations in resource recovery, shall, after public hearings, and not later than two years after September 1, 1979, publish guidelines for the development of specifications for the classification of materials recovered from waste which were destined for disposal. The specifications shall pertain to the physical and chemical properties and characteristics of such materials with regard to their use in replacing virgin materials in various industrial, commercial, and governmental uses. In establishing such guidelines the Secretary shall also, to the extent feasible, provide such information as may be necessary to assist Federal agencies with procurement of items containing recovered materials. The Secretary shall continue to cooperate with national standards-setting organizations, as may be necessary, to encourage the publication, promulgation and updating of standards for recovered materials and for the use of recovered materials in various industrial, commercial, and governmental uses.

§ 6953. Development of markets for recovered materials

[Sec. 5003] The Secretary of Commerce shall within two years after September 1, 1979, take such actions as may be necessary to—
(1) identify the geographical location of existing or potential markets for recovered materials;
(2) identify the economic and technical barriers to the use of recovered materials; and
(3) encourage the development of new uses for recovered materials.

§ 6954. Technology promotion

[Sec. 5004] The Secretary of Commerce is authorized to evaluate the commercial feasibility of resource recovery facilities and to publish the results of such evaluation, and to develop a data base for purposes of assisting persons in choosing such a system.

§ 6955. Nondiscrimination requirement

[Sec. 5005] In establishing any policies which may affect the development of new markets for recovered materials and in making any determination concerning whether or not to impose monitoring or other controls on any marketing or transfer or recovered materials, the Secretary of Commerce may consider whether to establish the same or similar policies or impose the same or similar monitoring or other controls on virgin materials.

§ 6956. Authorization of appropriations

[Sec. 5006] There are authorized to be appropriated to the Secretary of Commerce $5,000,000 for each of fiscal years 1980, 1981 and 1982 and $1,500,000 for each of the fiscal years 1985 through 1988 to carry out the purposes of this subtitle.

Subchapter VI. Federal Responsibilities

§ 6961. Application of federal, state, and local law to federal facilities

[Sec. 6001] Each department, agency, and instrumentality of the executive, legislative, and judicial branches of the Federal Government (1) having jurisdiction over any solid waste management facility or disposal site, or (2) engaged in any activity resulting, or which may result, in the disposal or management of solid waste or hazardous waste shall be subject to, and complying with, all Federal, State, interstate, and local requirements, both substantive and procedural (including any requirement for permits or reporting or any provisions for injunctive relief and such sanctions as may be imposed by a court to enforce such relief), respecting control and abatement of solid waste or hazardous waste disposal in the same manner, and to the same extent, as any person is subject to such requirements, including the payment of reasonable service charges. Neither the United States, nor any agent, employee, or officer thereof, shall be immune or exempt from any process or sanction of any State or Federal Court with respect to the enforcement of any such injunctive relief. The President may exempt any solid waste management facility of any department, agency, or instrumentality in the executive branch from compliance with such a requirement if he determines it to be in the paramount interest of the United States to do so. No such exemption shall be granted due to lack of appropriation unless the President shall have specifically requested such appropriation as a part of the budgetary process and the Congress shall have failed to make available such requested appropriation. Any exemption shall be for a period not in excess of one year, but additional exemptions may be granted for periods not to exceed one year upon the President's making a new determination. The President shall report each January to the Congress all exemptions from the requirements of this section granted during the preceding calendar year, together with his reason for granting each such exemption.

§ 6962. Federal procurement

[Sec. 6002] (a) Except as provided in subsection (b), a procuring agency shall comply with the requirements set forth in this section and any regulations issued under this section, with respect to any purchase or acquisition of a procurement item where the purchase price of the item exceeds $10,000 or where the quantity of such items or of functionally equivalent items purchased or acquired in the course of the preceding fiscal year was $10,000 or more.

(b) Any procurement, by any procuring agency, which is subject to regulations of the Administrator under section 6004 (as promulgated before the date of enactment of this section under comparable provisions of prior law) shall not be subject to the requirements of this section to the extent that such requirements are inconsistent with such regulations.

(c)(1) After the date specified in applicable guidelines prepared pursuant to subsection (e) of this section, each procuring agency which procures any items designated in such guidelines shall procure such items composed of the highest percentage of recovered materials practicable and in the case of paper, the highest percentage of the post consumer recovered materials referred to in subsection (h)(1) practicable consistent with maintaining a satisfactory level of competition, considering such guidelines. The decision not to procure such items shall be based on a determination that such procurement items—

(A) are not reasonably available within a reasonable period of time;

(B) fail to meet the performance standards set forth in the applicable specifications or fail to meet the reasonable performance standards of the procuring agencies; or

(C) are only available at an unreasonable price. Any determination under subparagraph (B) shall be made on the basis of the guidelines of the Bureau of Standards in any case in which such material is covered by such guidelines.

(2) Agencies that generate heat, mechanical, or electrical energy from fossil fuel in systems that have the technical capability of using energy or fuels derived from solid waste as a primary or supplementary fuel shall use such capability to the maximum extent practicable.

(3) After the date specified in any applicable guidelines prepared pursuant to subsection (e) of this section contracting, officers shall require that vendors:

(A) certify that the percentage of recovered materials to be used in the performance of the contract will be at least the amount required by applicable specifications or other contractual requirements and

(B) estimate the percentage of the total material utilized for the performance of the contract which is recovered materials.

(d) All Federal agencies that have the responsibility for drafting or reviewing specifications for procurement items procured by Federal agencies shall—

(1) as expeditiously as possible but in any event no later than eighteen months after the date of enactment of the Hazardous and Solid Waste Amendments of 1984, eliminate from such specifications—
(A) any exclusion of recovered materials and
(B) any requirement that items be manufactured from virgin materials; and
(2) within one year after the date of publication of applicable guidelines under subsection (e), or as otherwise specified in such guidelines, assure that such specifications require the use of recovered materials to the maximum extent possible without jeopardizing the intended end use of the item.

(e) The Administrator, after consultation with the Administrator of General Services, the Secretary of Commerce (acting through the Bureau of Standards), and the Public Printer, shall prepare, and from time to time revise, guidelines for the use of procuring agencies in complying with the requirements of this section. Such guidelines shall—
(1) designate those items which are or can be produced with recovered materials and whose procurement by procuring agencies will carry out the objectives of this section, and in the case of paper, provide for maximizing the use of post consumer recovered materials referred to in subsection (h)(1); and
(2) set forth recommended practices with respect to the procurement of recovered materials and items containing such materials and with respect to certification by vendors of the percentage of recovered materials used,
and shall provide information as to the availability, relative price, and performance of such materials and items and where appropriate shall recommend the level of recovered material to be contained in the procured product. The Administrator shall prepare final guidelines for paper within one hundred and eighty days after the enactment of the Hazardous and Solid Waste Amendments of 1984, and for three additional product categories (including tires) by October 1, 1985. In making the designation under paragraph (1), the Administrator shall consider, but is not limited in his considerations, to—
(A) the availability of such items;
(B) the impact of the procurement of such items by procuring agencies on the volume of solid waste which must be treated, stored or disposed of;
(C) the economic and technological feasibility of producing and using such items; and
(D) other uses for such recovered materials.

(f) A procuring agency shall, to the maximum extent practicable, manage or arrange for the procurement of solid waste management services in a manner which maximizes energy and resource recovery.

(g) The Office of Procurement Policy in the Executive Office of the President, in cooperation with the Administrator, shall implement the requirements of this section. It shall be the responsibility of the Office of Procurement Policy to coordinate this policy with other policies for Federal procurement, in such a way as to maximize the use of recovered resources, and to, every two years beginning in 1984, report to the Congress on actions taken by Federal agencies and the progress made in the implementation of this section, including agency compliance with subsection (d).

(h) As used in this section, in the case of paper products, the term "recovered materials" includes—

    (1) postconsumer materials such as—

        (A) paper, paperboard, and fibrous wastes from retail stores, office buildings, homes, and so forth, after they have passed through their end-usage as a consumer item, including: used corrugated boxes; old newspapers; old magazines; mixed waste paper; tabulating cards; and used cordage; and

        (B) all paper, paperboard, and fibrous wastes that enter and are collected from municipal solid waste, and

    (2) manufacturing, forest residues, and other wastes such as—

        (A) dry paper and paperboard waste generated after completion of the papermaking process (that is, those manufacturing operations up to and including the cutting and trimming of the paper machine reel into smaller rolls or rough sheets) including: envelope cuttings, bindery trimmings, and other paper and paperboard waste, resulting from printing, cutting, forming, and other converting operations; bag, box, and carton manufacturing wastes; and butt rolls, mill wrappers, and rejected unused stock; and

        (B) finished paper and paperboard from obsolete inventories of paper and paperboard manufacturers, merchants, wholesalers, dealers, printers, converters, or others;

        (C) fibrous byproducts of harvesting, manufacturing, extractive, or wood-cutting processes, flax, straw, linters, bagasse, slash, and other forest residues;

        (D) wastes generated by the conversion of goods made from fibrous material (that is, waste rope from cordage manufacture, textile mill waste, and cuttings); and

        (E) fibers recovered from waste water which otherwise would enter the waste stream.

(i)(1) Within one year after the date of publication of applicable guidelines under subsection (e), each procuring agency shall develop an affirmative procurement program which will assure that items composed of recovered materials will be purchased to the maximum extent practicable and which is consistent with applicable provisions of Federal procurement law.

    (2) Each affirmative procurement program required under this subsection

shall, at a minimum, contain—

(A) a recovered materials preference program;
(B) an agency promotion program to promote the preference program adopted under subparagraph (A);
(C) a program for requiring estimates of the total percentage of recovered material utilized in the performance of a contract; certification of minimum recovered material content actually utilized, where appropriate; and reasonable verification procedures for estimates and certifications; and
(D) annual review and monitoring of the effectiveness of an agency's affirmative procurement program.

In the case of paper, the recovered materials preference program required under subparagraph (A) shall provide for the maximum use of the post consumer recovered materials referred to in subsection (h)(1).

(3) In developing the preference program, the following options shall be considered for adoption:

(A) Case-by-Case Policy Development: Subject to the limitations of subsection (c)(1)(A) through (C), a policy of awarding contracts to the vendor offering an item composed of the highest percentage of recovered materials practicable (and in the case of paper, the highest percentage of the post consumer recovered materials referred to in subsection (h)(1)). Subject to such limitations, agencies may make an award to a vendor offering items with less than the maximum recovered materials content.
(B) Minimum Content Standards: Minimum recovered materials content specifications which are set in such a way as to assure that the recovered materials content (and in the case of paper, the content of post consumer materials referred to in subsection (h)(1)) required is the maximum available without jeopardizing the intended end use of the item, or violating the limitations of subsection (c)(1)(A) through (C).

Procuring agencies shall adopt one of the options set forth in subparagraphs (A) and (B) or a substantially equivalent alternative, for inclusion in the affirmative procurement program.

§ 6963. Cooperation with the Environmental Protection Agency

[Sec. 6003] (a) All Federal agencies shall assist the Administrator in carrying out his functions under this Act and shall promptly make available all requested information concerning past or present Agency waste management practices and past or present Agency owned, leased, or operated solid or hazardous waste facilities. This information shall be provided in such format as may be determined by the Administrator.

(b) The Administrator shall collect, maintain, and disseminate information concerning the market potential of energy and materials recovered from solid waste, including materials obtained through source separation, and information concerning the savings potential of conserving resources contributing to the waste stream. The Administrator shall identify the regions in which the increased substitution of such energy for energy derived from fossil fuels and other sources is most likely to be feasible, and provide information on the technical and economic aspects of developing integrated resource conservation or recovery systems which provide for the recovery of source-separated materials to be recycled or the conservation of resources. The Administrator shall utilize the authorities of subsection (a) in carrying out this subsection.

§ 6964. Applicability of solid waste disposal guidelines to executive agencies

[Sec. 6004] (a)(1) If—
- (A) an Executive agency (as defined in section 105 of title 5, United States Code or any unit of the legislative branch of the Federal Government has jurisdiction over any real property or facility the operation or administration of which involves such agency in solid waste management activities, or
- (B) such an agency enters into a contract with any person for the operation by such person of any Federal property or facility, and the performance of such contract involves such person in solid waste management activities,

then such agency shall insure compliance with the guidelines recommended under section 1008 and the purposes of this Act in operation or administration of such property or facility, or the performance of such contract, as the case may be.
- (2) Each Executive agency or any unit of the legislative branch of the Federal Government which conducts any activity—
  - (A) which generates solid waste, and
  - (B) which, if conducted by a person other than such agency, would require a permit or license from such agency in order to dispose of such solid waste,

shall insure compliance with such guidelines and the purposes of this Act in conducting such activity.
- (3) Each Executive agency which permits the use of Federal property for purposes of disposal of solid waste shall insure compliance with such guidelines and the purposes of this Act in the disposal of such waste.
- (4) The President or the Committee on House Administration of the House of Representatives and the Committee on Rules and Administration of the Senate with regard to any unit of the legislative branch of the Federal Government shall prescribe regulations to carry out this subsection.

(b) Each Executive agency which issues any license or permit for disposal of solid waste shall, prior to the issuance of such license or permit, consult with the Administrator to insure compliance with guidelines recommended under section 1008 and the purposes of this Act.

Subchapter VII. Miscellaneous Provisions

§ 6971. Employee protection

[Sec. 7001] (a) No person shall fire, or in any other way discriminate against, or cause to be fired or discriminated against, any employee or any authorized representative of employees by reason of the fact that such employee or representative has filed, instituted, or caused to be filed or instituted any proceeding under this Act or under any applicable implementation plan, or has testified or is about to testify in any proceeding resulting from the administration or enforcement of the provisions of this Act or of any applicable implementation plan.

(b) Any employee or a representative of employees who believes that he has been fired or otherwise discriminated against by any person in violation of subsection (a) of this section may, within thirty days after such alleged violation occurs, apply to the Secretary of Labor for a review of such firing or alleged discrimination. A copy of the application shall be sent to such person who shall be the respondent. Upon receipt of such application, the Secretary of Labor shall cause such investigation to be made as he deems appropriate. Such investigation shall provide an opportunity for a public hearing at the request of any party to such review to enable the parties to present information relating to such alleged violation. The parties shall be given written notice of the time and place of the hearing at least five days prior to the hearing. Any such hearing shall be of record and shall be subject to section 554 of title 5 of the United States Code. Upon receiving the report of such investigation, the Secretary of Labor shall make findings of fact. If he finds that such violation did occur, he shall issue a decision, incorporating an order therein and his findings, requiring the party committing such violation to take such affirmative action to abate the violation as the Secretary of Labor deems appropriate, including, but not limited to, the rehiring or reinstatement of the employee or representative of employees to his former position with compensation. If he finds that there was no such violation, he shall issue an order denying the application. Such order issued by the Secretary of Labor under this subparagraph shall be subject to judicial review in the same manner as orders and decisions of the Administrator or subject to judicial review under this Act.

(c) Whenever an order is issued under this section to abate such violation, at the request of the applicant, a sum equal to the aggregate amount of all costs and expenses (including the attorney's fees) as determined by the Secretary of Labor, to have been reasonably incurred by the applicant for, or in connection with, the institution and prosecution of such proceedings, shall be assessed against the person committing such violation.

(d) This section shall have no application to any employee who, acting without direction from his employer (or his agent) deliberately violates any requirement of this Act.

(e) The Administrator shall conduct continuing evaluations of potential loss or shifts of employment which may result from the administration or enforcement of the provisions of this Act and applicable implementation plans, including, where appropriate, investigating threatened plant closures or reductions in employment allegedly resulting from such administration or enforcement. Any employee who is discharged, or laid off, threatened with discharge or layoff, or otherwise discriminated against by any person because of the alleged results of such administration or enforcement, or any representative of such employee, may request the Administrator to conduct a full investigation of the matter. The Administrator shall thereupon investigate the matter and, at the request of any party, shall hold public hearings on not less than five days' notice, and shall at such hearings require the parties, including the employer involved, to present information relating to the actual or potential effect of such administration or enforcement on employment and on any alleged discharge, layoff, or other discrimination and the detailed reasons or justification therefor. Any such hearing shall be of record and shall be subject to section 554 of title 5 of the United States Code. Upon receiving the report of such investigation, the Administrator shall make findings of fact as to the effect of such administration or enforcement on employment and on the alleged discharge, layoff, or discrimination and shall make such recommendations as he deems appropriate. Such report, findings, and recommendations shall be available to the public. Nothing in this subsection shall be construed to require or authorize the Administrator or any State to modify or withdraw any standard, limitations, or any other requirement of this Act or any applicable implementation plan.

(f) In order to assist the Secretary of Labor and the Director of the National Institute for Occupational Safety and Health in carrying out their duties under the Occupational Safety and Health Act of 1970, the Administrator shall—

(1) provide the following information, as such information becomes available, to the Secretary and the Director:

(A) the identity of any hazardous waste generation, treatment, storage, disposal facility or site where cleanup is planned or underway;

(B) information identifying the hazards to which persons working at a hazardous waste generation, treatment, storage, disposal facility or site or otherwise handling hazardous waste may be exposed, the nature and extent of the exposure, and methods to protect workers from such hazards; and

(C) incidents of worker injury or harm at a hazardous waste generation, treatment, storage or disposal facility or site; and

(2) notify the Secretary and the Director of the Administrator's receipt of

notifications under section 3010 or reports under sections 3002, 3003, and 3004 of this title and make such notifications and reports available to the Secretary and the Director.

§ 6972.   Citizens' suits

[Sec. 7002] (a) Except as provided in subsection (b) or (c) of this section, any person may commence a civil action on his own behalf—

(1)(A) against any person (including (a) the United States, and (b) any other governmental instrumentality or agency, to the extent permitted by the eleventh amendment to the Constitution) who is alleged to be in violation of any permit, standard, regulation, condition, requirement, prohibition, or order which has become effective pursuant to this Act; or

(B) against any person, including the United States and any other governmental instrumentality or agency, to the extent permitted by the eleventh amendment to the Constitution, and including any past or present generator, past or present transporter, or past or present owner or operator of a treatment, storage, or disposal facility, who has contributed or who is contributing to the past or present handling, storage, treatment, transportation, or disposal of any solid or hazardous waste which may present an imminent and substantial endangerment to health or the environment; or

(2) against the Administrator where there is alleged a failure of the Administrator to perform any act or duty under this Act which is not discretionary with the Administrator.

Any action under paragraph (a)(1) of this subsection shall be brought in the district court for the district in which the alleged violation occurred or the alleged endangerment may occur. Any action brought under paragraph (a)(2) of this subsection may be brought in the district court for the distrct in which the alleged violation occurred or in the District Court of the District of Columbia. The district court shall have jurisdiction, without regard to the amount in controversy or the citizenship of the parties, to enforce the permit, standard, regulation, condition, requirement, prohibition, or order, referred to in paragraph (1)(A), to restrain any person who has contributed or who is contributing to the past or present handling, storage, treatment, transportation, or disposal of any solid or hazardous waste referred to in paragraph (1)(B), to order such person to take such other action as may be necessary, or both, or to order the Administrator to perform the act or duty referred to in paragraph (2), as the case may be, and to apply any appropriate civil penalties under section 3008(a) and (g).

(b)(1) No action may be commenced under subsection (a)(1)(A) of this section—

(A) prior to 60 days after the plaintiff has given notice of the violation

to—
(i) the Administrator;
(ii) the State in which the alleged violation occurs; and
(iii) to any alleged violator of such permit, standard, regulation, condition, requirement, prohibition, or order,

except that such action may be brought immediately after such notification in the case of an action under this section respecting a violation of subtitle C of this Act; or

(B) if the Administrator or State has commenced and is diligently prosecuting a civil or criminal action in a court of the United States or a State to require compliance with such permit, standard, regulation, condition, requirement, prohibition, or order.

In any action under subsection (a)(1)(A) in a court of the United States, any person may intervene as a matter of right.

(2)(A) No action may be commenced under subsection (a)(1)(B) of this section prior to ninety days after the plaintiff has given notice of the endangerment to—
(i) the Administrator;
(ii) the State in which the alleged endangerment may occur;
(iii) any person alleged to have contributed or to be contributing to the past or present handling, storage, treatment, transportation, or disposal of any solid or hazardous waste referred to in subsection (a)(1)(B).

except that such action may be brought immediately after such notification in the case of an action under this section respecting a violation of subtitle C of this Act.

(B) No action may be commenced under subsection (a)(1)(B) of this section if the Administrator, in order to restrain or abate acts or conditions which may have contributed or are contributing to the activities which may present the alleged endangerment—
(i) has commenced and is diligently prosecuting an action under section 7003 of this Act or under section 106 of the Comprehensive Environmental Response, Compensation and Liability Act of 1980.
(ii) is actually engaging in a removal action under section 104 of the Comprehensive Environmental Response, Compensation and Liability Act of 1980;
(iii) has incurred costs to initiate a Remedial Investigation and Feasibility Study under section 104 of the Comprehensive Environmental Response, Compensation and Liability Act of 1980 and is diligently proceeding with a remedial action under that Act; or
(iv) has obtained a court order (including a consent decree) or issued an administrative order under section 106 of the Comprehensive Environmental Response, Compensation and Li-

ability Act of 1980 or section 7003 of this Act pursuant to which a responsible party is diligently conducting a removal action, Remedial Investigation and Feasibility Study (RIFS), or proceeding with a remedial action.

In the case of an administrative order referred to in clause (iv), actions under subsection (a)(1)(B) are prohibited only as to the scope and duration of the administrative order referred to in clause (iv).

(C) No action may be commenced under subsection (a)(1)(B) of this section if the State, in order to restrain or abate acts or conditions which may have contributed or are contributing to the activities which may present the alleged endangerment—

    (i) has commenced and is diligently prosecuting an action under subsection (a)(1)(B);

   (ii) is actually engaging in a removal action under section 104 of the Comprehensive Environmental Response, Compensation and Liability Act of 1980; or

  (iii) has incurred costs to initiate a Remedial Investigation and Feasibility Study under section 104 of the Comprehensive Environmental Response, Compensation and Liability Act of 1980 and is diligently proceeding with a remedial action under that Act.

(D) No action may be commenced under subsection (a)(1)(B) by any person (other than a State or local government) with respect to the siting of a hazardous waste treatment, storage, or a disposal facility, nor to restrain or enjoin the issuance of a permit for such facility.

(E) In any action under subsection (a)(1)(B) in a court of the United States, any person may intervene as a matter of right when the applicant claims an interest relating to the subject of the action and he is so situated that the disposition of the action may, as a practical matter, impair or impede his ability to protect that interest, unless the Administrator or the State shows that the applicant's interest is adequately represented by existing parties.

(F) Whenever any action is brought under subsection (a)(1)(B) in a court of the United States, the plaintiff shall serve a copy of the complaint on the Attorney General of the United States and with the Administrator.

(c) No action may be commenced under paragraph (a)(2) of this section prior to sixty days after the plaintiff has given notice to the Administrator that he will commence such action, except that such action may be brought immediately after such notification in the case of an action under this section respecting a violation of subtitle C of the Act. Notice under this subsection shall be given in such manner as the Administrator shall prescribe by regulation. Any action respecting a violation under this Act may be brought under this section only in the judicial district in which such alleged violation occurs.

(d) In any action under this section the Administrator, if not a party, may intervene as a matter of right.

(e) The court, in issuing any final order in any action brought pursuant to this section, or section 7006 may award costs of litigation (including reasonable attorney and expert witness fees) to the prevailing or substantially prevailing party, whenever the court determines such an award is appropriate. The court may, if a temporary restraining order or preliminary injunction is sought, require the filing of a bond or equivalent security in accordance with the Federal Rules of Civil Procedure.

(f) Nothing in this section shall restrict any right which any person (or class of persons) may have under any statute or common law to seek enforcement of any standard or requirement relating to the management of solid waste or hazardous waste, or to seek any other relief (including relief against the Administrator or a State agency).

(g) A transporter shall not be deemed to have contributed or to be contributing to the handling, storage, treatment, or disposal, referred to in subsection (a)(1)(B) taking place after such solid waste or hazardous waste has left the possession or control of such transporter, if the transportation of such waste was under a sole contractual arrangement arising from a published tariff and acceptance for carriage by common carrier by rail and such transporter has exercised due care in the past or present handling, storage, treatment, transportation and disposal of such waste.

§ 6973. Imminent hazard

[Sec. 7003] (a) Notwithstanding any other provision of this Act, upon receipt of evidence that the past or present handling, storage, treatment, transportation or disposal of any solid waste or hazardous waste may present an imminent and substantial endangerment to health or the environment, the Administrator may bring suit on behalf of the United States in the appropriate district court against any person (including any past or present generator, past or present transporter, or past or present owner or operator of a treatment, storage or disposal facility) who has contributed or who is contributing to such handling, storage, treatment, transportation or disposal to restrain such person from such handling, storage, treatment, transportation, or disposal, to order such person to take such other action as may be necessary, or both. A transporter shall not be deemed to have contributed or to be contributing to such handling, storage, treatment, or disposal taking place after such solid waste or hazardous waste has left the possession or control of such transporter if the transportation of such waste was under a sole contractual arrangement arising from a published tariff and acceptance for carriage by common carrier by rail and such transporter has exercised due care in the past or present handling, storage, treatment, transportation and disposal of such waste. The Administrator shall provide notice to the affected State of any such suit. The Administrator may also, after notice to the affected State, take other action under this section including, but not limited to, issuing such orders as may be necessary to protect public health and the environment.

(b) Any person who willfully violates, or fails or refuses to comply with, any order of the Administrator under subsection (a) may, in an action brought in the appropriate United States district court to enforce such order, be fined more than $5,000 for each day in which such violation occurs or such failure to comply continues.

(c) Upon receipt of information that there is hazardous waste at any site which has presented an imminent and substantial endangerment to human health or the environment, the Administrator shall provide immediate notice to the appropriate local government agencies. In addition, the Administrator shall require notice of such endangerment to be promptly posted at the site where the waste is located.

(d) Whenever the United States or the Administrator proposes to covenant not to sue or to forbear from suit or to settle any claim arising under this section, notice, and opportunity for a public meeting in the affected area, and a reasonable opportunity to comment on the proposed settlement prior to is final entry shall be afforded to the public. The decision of the United States or the Administrator to enter into or not to enter into such Consent Decree, covenant or agreement shall not constitute a final agency action subject to judicial review under this Act or the Administrative Procedure Act.

§ 6974. Petition for regulations; public participation

[Sec. 7004] (a) Any person may petition the Administrator for the promulgation, amendment, or repeal of any regulation under this Act. Within a reasonable time following receipt of such petition, the Administrator shall take action with respect to such petition and shall publish notice of such action in the Federal Register together with the reasons therefor.

(b)(1) Public participation in the development, revision, implementation, and enforcement of any regulation, guideline, information, or program under this Act shall be provided for, encouraged, and assisted by the Administrator and the States. The Administrator, in cooperation with the States, shall develop and publish minimum guidelines for public participation in such processes.

(2) Before the issuing of a permit to any person with any respect to any facility for the treatment, storage, or disposal of hazardous wastes under section 3005, the Administrator shall—

(A) cause to be published in major local newspapers of general circulation and broadcast over local radio stations notice of the agency's intention to issue such permit, and

(B) transmit in writing notice of the agency's intention to issue such permit to each unit of local government having jurisdiction over the area in which such facility is proposed to be located and to each State agency having any authority under State law with respect to the construction or operation of such facility.

If within 45 days the Administrator receives written notice of opposition to the agency's intention to issue such permit and a request for a hearing, or if the Administrator determines on his own initiative, he shall hold an informal public hearing (including an opportunity for presentation of written and oral views) on whether he should issue a permit for the proposed facility. Whenever possible the Administrator shall schedule such hearing at a location convenient to the nearest population center to such proposed facility and give notice in the aforementioned manner of the date, time, and subject matter of such hearing. No State program which provides for the issuance of permits referred to in this paragraph may be authorized by the Administrator under section 3006 unless such program provides for the notice and hearing required by the paragraph.

§ 6975. Separability

[Sec. 7005] If any provision of this Act, or the application of any provision of this Act to any person or circumstance, is held invalid, the application of such provision to other persons or circumstances, and the remainder of this Act, shall not be affected thereby.

§ 6976. Judicial review

[Sec. 7006] (a) Any judicial review of final regulations promulgated pursuant to this Act and the Administrator's denial of any petition for the promulgation, amendment, or repeal of any regulation under this Act shall be in accordance with sections 701 through 706 of title 5 of the United States Code, except that—

(1) a petition for review of action of the Administrator in promulgating any regulation, or requirement under this Act or denying any petition for the promulgation, amendment or repeal of any regulation under this Act may be filed only in the United States Court of Appeals for the District of Columbia, and such petition shall be filed within ninety days from the date of such promulgation or denial or after such date if such petition for review is based solely on grounds arising after such ninetieth day; action of the Administrator with respect to which review could have been obtained under this subsection shall not be subject to judicial review in civil or criminal proceedings for enforcement; and

(2) in any judicial proceeding brought under this section in which review is sought of a determination under this Act required to be made on the record after notice and opportunity for hearing, if a party seeking

review under this Act applies to the court for leave to adduce additional evidence, and shows to the satisfaction of the court that the information is material and that there were reasonable grounds for the failure to adduce such evidence in the proceeding before the Administrator, the court may order such additional evidence (and evidence in rebuttal thereof) to be taken before the Administrator, and to be adduced upon the hearing in such manner and upon such terms and conditions as the court may deem proper; the Administrator may modify his findings as to the facts, or make new findings, by reason of the additional evidence so taken, and he shall file with the court such modified or new findings and his recommendation, if any for the modification or setting aside of his original order, with the return of such additional evidence.

(b) Review of the Administrator's action (1) in issuing, denying, modifying or revoking any permit under section 3005, or (2) in granting, denying, or withdrawing authorization or interim authorization under section 3006, may be had by any interested person in the Circuit Court of Appeals of the United States for the Federal judicial district in which such person resides or transacts such business upon application by such person. Any such application shall be made within ninety days from the date of such issuance, denial, modification, revocation, grant, or withdrawal, or after such date only if such application is based solely on grounds which arose after such ninetieth day. Action of the Administrator with respect to which review could have been obtained under this subsection shall not be subject to judicial review in civil or criminal proceedings for enforcement. Such review shall be in accordance with sections 701 through 706 of title 5 of the United States Code.

§ 6977. Grants or contracts for training projects

[Sec. 7007] (a) The Administrator is authorized to make grants to, and contracts with any eligible organization. For purposes of this section the term "eligible organization" means a State or interstate agency, a municipality, educational institution, and any other organization which is capable of effectively carrying out a project which may be funded by grant under subsection (b) of this section.

(b)(1) Subject to the provisions of paragraph (2), grants or contracts may be made to pay all or a part of the costs, as may be determined by the Administrator, of any project operated or to be operated by an eligible organization, which is designed—

    (A) to develop, expand, or carry out a program (which may combine training, education, and employment) for training persons for occupations involving the management, supervision, design, operation, or maintenance of solid waste management and resource recovery equipment and facilities; or

    (B) to train instructors and supervisory personnel to train or supervise persons in occupations involving the design, operation, and maintenance of solid waste management and resource recovery equipment and facilities.

(2) A grant or contract authorized by paragraph (1) of this subsection may be made only upon application to the Administrator at such time or times and containing such information as he may prescribe, except that no such application shall be approved unless it provides for the same procedures and reports (and access to such reports and to other records) as required by section 207(b)(4) and (5) (as in effect before the date of the enactment of Resource Conservation and Recovery Act of 1976) with respect to applications made under such section (as in effect before the date of the enactment of Resource Conservation and Recovery Act of 1976).

(c) The Administrator shall make a complete investigation and study to determine—

(1) the need for additional trained State and local personnel to carry out plans assisted under this Act and other solid waste and resource recovery programs;

(2) means of using existing training programs to train such personnel; and

(3) the extent and nature of obstacles to employment and occupational advancement in the solid waste management and resource recovery field which may limit either available manpower or the advancement of personnel in such field.

He shall report the results of such investigation and study, including his recommendation to the President and the Congress.

§ 6978. Payments

[Sec. 7008] (a) Payments of grants under this Act may be made (after necessary adjustment on account of previously made underpayments or overpayments) in advance or by way of reimbursement, and in such installments and on such conditions as the Administrator may determine.

(b) No grant may be made under this Act to any private profitmaking organization.

§ 6979. Labor standards

[Sec. 7009] No grant for a project of construction under this Act shall be made unless the Administrator finds that the application contains or is supported by reasonable assurance that all laborers and mechanics employed by contractors or subcontractors on projects of the type covered by the Davis-Bacon Act, as amended (40 U.S.C. 276a-276a-5), will be paid wages at rates not less than those prevailing on similar work in the locality as determined by the Secretary of Labor in accordance with that Act; and the Secretary of Labor shall have with respect to the labor standards specified in this section the authority and functions set forth in Reorganization Plan Numbered 14 of 1950 (15 F.R. 3176; 5 U.S.C. 133z–5) and section 2 of the Act of June 13, 1934, as amended (40 U.S.C. 276c).

§ 6979a. Interim control of hazardous waste injection

[Sec. 7010] (a) No hazardous waste may be disposed of by underground injection—
 (1) into a formation which contains (within one-quarter mile of the well used for such underground injection) an underground source of drinking water, or
 (2) above such a formation.
The prohibitions established under this section shall take effect 6 months after the enactment of the Hazardous and Solid Waste Amendments of 1984 except in the case of any State in which identical or more stringent prohibitions are in effect before such date under the Safe Drinking Water Act.

(b) Subsection (a) shall not apply to the injection of contaminated ground water into the aquifer from which it was withdrawn, if—
 (1) such injection is—
  (A) a response action taken under section 104 or 106 of the Comprehensive Environmental Response, Compensation and Liability Act of 1980, or
  (B) part of corrective action required under this title intended to clean up such contamination;
 (2) such contaminated ground water is treated to substantially reduce hazardous constituents prior to such injection; and
 (3) such response action or corrective action will, upon completion, be sufficient to protect human health and the environment.

(c) In addition to enforcement under sections 7002 and 7003 of this Act, the prohibitions established under paragraphs (1) and (2) of subsection (a) shall be enforceable under the Safe Drinking Water Act in any State—
 (1) which has adopted identical or more stringent prohibitions under part C of the Safe Drinking Water Act and which has assumed primary enforcement responsibility under that Act for enforcement of such prohibitions; or
 (2) in which the Administrator has adopted identical or more stringent prohibitions under the Safe Drinking Water Act and is exercising primary enforcement responsibility under that Act for enforcement of such prohibitions.

(d) The terms "primary enforcement responsibility", "underground source of drinking water", "formation" and "well" have the same meanings as provided in regulations of the Administrator under the Safe Drinking Water Act. The term "Safe Drinking Water Act" means title XIV of the Public Health Service Act.

§ 6979b. Law enforcement authority

[Sec. 7012] The Attorney General of the United States shall, at the request of the Administrator and on the basis of a showing of need, deputize qualified employees of the Environmental Protection Agency to serve as special deputy United States marshals in criminal investigations with respect to violations of the criminal provisions of this Act.

Subchapter VIII. Research, Development, Demonstration, and Information

§ 6981. Research, demonstration, training, and other activities

[Sec. 8001] The Administrator, alone or after consultation with the Administrator of the Federal Energy Administration, the Administrator of the Energy Research and Development Administration, or the Chairman of the Federal Power Commission, shall conduct, and encourage, cooperate with, and render financial and other assistance to appropriate public (whether Federal, State, interstate, or local) authorities, agencies, and institutions, private agencies and institutions, and individuals in the conduct of, and promote the coordination of, research, investigations, experiments, training, demonstrations, surveys, public education programs, and studies relating to—

(1) any adverse health and welfare effects of the release into the environment of material present in solid waste, and methods to eliminate such effects;

(2) the operation and financing of solid waste management programs;

(3) the planning, implementation, and operation of resource recovery and resource conservation systems and hazardous waste management systems, including the marketing of recovered resources;

(4) the production of usable forms of recovered resources, including fuel, from solid waste;

(5) the reduction of the amount of such waste and unsalvageable waste materials;

(6) the development and application of new and improved methods of collecting and disposing of solid waste and processing and recovering materials and energy from solid wastes;

(7) the identification of solid waste components and potential materials and energy recoverable from such waste components;

(8) small scale and low technology solid waste management systems, including but limited to, resource recovery source separation systems;

(9) methods to improve the performance characteristics of resources recovered from solid waste and the relationship of such performance

characteristics to available and potentially available markets for such resources;

(10) improvements in land disposal practices for solid waste (including sludge) which may reduce the adverse environmental effects of such disposal and other aspects of solid waste disposal on land, including means for reducing the harmful environmental effects of earlier and existing landfills, means for restoring areas damaged by such earlier or existing landfills, means for rendering landfills safe for purposes of construction and other uses, and techniques of recovering materials and energy from landfills;

(11) methods for the sound disposal of, or recovery of resources, including energy, from, sludge (including sludge from pollution control and treatment facilities, coal slurry pipelines, and other sources);

(12) methods of hazardous waste management, including methods of rendering such waste environmentally safe; and

(13) any adverse effects on air quality (particularly with regard to the emission of heavy metals) which result from solid waste which is burned (either alone or in conjunction with other substances) for purposes of treatment, disposal or energy recovery.

(b)(1)(A) In carrying out his functions pursuant to this Act and any other Federal legislation respecting solid waste or discarded material research, development, and demonstrations, the Administrator shall establish a management program or system to insure the coordination of all such activities and to facilitate and accelerate the process of development of sound new technology (or other discoveries) from the research phase, through development, and into the demonstration phase.

(B) The Administrator shall (i) assist, on the basis of any research projects which are developed with assistance under this Act or without Federal assistance, the construction of pilot plant facilities for the purpose of investigating or testing the technological feasibility of any promising new fuel, energy, or resource recovery or resource conservation method or technology; and (ii) demonstrate each such method and technology that appears justified by an evaluation at such pilot plant stage or at a pilot plant stage developed without Federal assistance. Each such demonstration shall incorporate new or innovative technical advances or shall apply such advances to different circumstances and conditions, for the purpose of evaluating design concepts or to test the performance, efficiency, and economic feasibility of a particular method or technology under actual operating conditions. Each such demonstration shall be so planned and designed that, if successful, it can be expanded or utilized directly as a full-scale operational fuel, energy, or resource recovery or resource conservation facility.

(2) Any energy-related research, development, or demonstration project

for the conversion including bio-conversion, of solid waste carried out by the Environmental Protection Agency or by the Energy Research and Development Administration pursuant to this or any other Act shall be administered in accordance with the May 7, 1976, Interagency Agreement between the Environmental Protection Agency and the Energy Research and Development Administration on the Development of Energy from Solid Wastes and specifically, that in accordance with this agreement, (A) for those energy-related projects of mutual interest, planning will be conducted jointly by the Environmental Protection Agency and the Energy Research and Development Administration, following which project responsibility will be assigned to one agency; (B) energy-related portions of projects for recovery of synthetic fuels or other forms of energy from solid waste shall be the responsibility of the Energy Research and Development Administration; (C) the Environmental Protection Agency shall retain responsibility for the environmental, economic, and institutional aspects of solid waste projects and for assurance that such projects are consistent with any applicable suggested guidelines published pursuant to section 1008, and any applicable State or regional solid waste management plan; and (D) any activities undertaken under provisions of sections 8002 and 8003 as related to energy; as related to energy or synthetic fuels recovery from waste; or as related to energy conservation shall be accomplished through coordination and consultation with the Energy Research and Development Administration.

(c)(1) In carrying out subsection (a) of this section respecting solid waste research, studies, development, and demonstration, except as otherwise specifically provided in section 8004(d), the Administrator may make grants to or enter into contracts (including contracts for construction) with, public agencies and authorities or private persons.

(2) Contracts for research, development, or demonstrations or for both (including contracts for construction) shall be made in accordance with and subject to the limitations provided with respect to research contracts of the military departments in title 10, United States Code, section 2353, except that the determination, approval, and certification required thereby shall be made by the Administrator.

(3) Any invention made or conceived in the course of, or under, any contract under this Act shall be subject to section 9 of the Federal Nonnuclear Energy Research and Development Act of 1974 to the same extent and in the same manner as inventions made or conceived in the course of contracts under such Act, except that in applying such section, the Environmental Protection Agency shall be substituted for the Energy Research and Development Administration and the words "solid waste" shall be substituted for the word "energy" where appropriate.

(4) For carrying out the purpose of this Act the Administrator may detail

personnel of the Environmental Protection Agency to agencies eligible for assistance under this section.

§ 6982. Special studies; plans for research, development, and demonstrations

[Sec. 8002] (a) The Administrator shall undertake a study and publish a report on resource recovery from glass and plastic waste, including a scientific, technological, and economic investigation of potential solutions to implement such recovery.

(b) The Administrator shall undertake a systematic study of the composition of the solid waste stream and of anticipated future changes in the composition of such stream and shall publish a report containing the results of such study and quantitatively evaluating the potential utility of such components.

(c) For purposes of determining priorities for research on recovery of materials and energy from solid waste and developing materials and energy recovery research, development, and demonstration strategies, the Administrator shall review, and make a study of, the various existing and promising techniques of energy recovery from solid waste (including, but not limited to, waterwall furnace incinerators, dry shredded fuel systems, pyrolysis, densified refuse-derived fuel systems, anaerobic digestion, and fuel and feedstock preparation systems). In carrying out such study the Administrator shall investigate with respect to each such technique—

(1) the degree of public need for the potential results of such research development, or demonstration,

(2) the potential for research, development, and demonstration without Federal action, including the degree of restraint on such potential posed by the risks involved, and

(3) the magnitude of effort and period of time necessary to develop the technology to the point where Federal assistance can be ended.

(d) The Administrator shall undertake a comprehensive study and analysis of, and publish a report on, systems of small-scale and low technology solid waste management, including household resource recovery and resource recovery systems which have special application to multiple dwelling units and high density housing and office complexes. Such study and analysis shall include an investigation of the degree to which such systems could contribute to energy conservation.

(e) The Administrator shall undertake research and studies concerning the compatibilty of front-end source separation systems with high technology resource recovery systems and shall publish a report containing the results of such research and studies.

(f) The Administrator, in consultation with the Secretary of the Interior, shall conduct a detailed and comprehensive study on the adverse effects of solid wastes from active and abandoned surface and underground mines on the environment, including, but not limited to, the effects of such wastes on humans, water, air, health, welfare, and natural resources, and on the adequacy of means and measures currently employed by the mining industry, Government agencies, and others to dispose of and utilize such solid wastes and to prevent or substantially mitigate such adverse effects. Such study shall include an analysis of—

(1) the sources and volume of discarded material generated per year from mining;

(2) present disposal practices;

(3) potential dangers to human health and the environment from surface runoff of leachate and air pollution by dust.

(4) alternatives to current disposal methods;

(5) the cost of those alternatives in terms of the impact on mine product costs; and

(6) potential for use of discarded material as a secondary source of the mine product.

Not later than thirty-six months after the date of the enactment of the Solid Waste Disposal Act Amendments of 1980 the Administrator shall publish a report of such study and shall include appropriate findings and recommendations for Federal and non-Federal actions concerning such effects. Such report shall be submitted to the Committee on Environment and Public Works of the United States Senate and the Committee on Interstate and Foreign Commerce of the United States House of Representatives.

(g) The Administrator shall undertake a comprehensive study and publish a report on sludge. Such study shall include an analysis of—

(1) what types of solid waste (including but not limited to sewage and pollution treatment residues and other residues from industrial operations such as extraction of oil from shale, liquefaction and gasification of coal and coal slurry pipeline operations) shall be classified as sludge;

(2) the effects of air and water pollution legislation on the creation of large volumes of sludge;

(3) the amounts of sludge originating in each State and in each industry producing sludge;

(4) methods of disposal of such sludge, including the cost, efficiency and effectiveness of such methods;

(5) alternative methods for the use of sludge, including agricultural applications of sludge and energy recovery from sludge; and

(6) methods to reclaim areas which have been used for the disposal of sludge or which have been damaged by sludge.

(h) The Administrator shall undertake a study and publish a report respecting discarded motor vehicle tires which shall include an analysis of the problems involved in the collection, recovery of resources including energy, and use of such tires.

(i) The Administrator shall conduct research and report on the economics of, and impediments, to the effective functioning of resource recovery facilities.

(j)(1) The Administrator shall serve as Chairman of a Committee composed of himself, the Secretary of Commerce, the Secretary of Labor, the Chairman of the Council on Environmental Quality, the Secretary of Treasury, the Secretary of the Interior, the Secretary of Energy, the Chairman of the Council of Economic Advisors, and a representative of the Office of Management and Budget, which shall conduct a full and complete investigation and study of all aspects of the economic, social and environmental consequences of resource conservation with respect to—

    (A) the appropriateness of recommended incentives and disincentives to foster resource conservation;

    (B) the effect of existing public policies (including subsidies and economic incentives and disincentives, percentage depletion allowances, capital gains treatment and other tax incentives and disincentives) upon resource conservation, and the likely effect of the modification or elimination of such incentives and disincentives upon resource conservation;

    (C) the appropriateness and feasibilty of restricting the manufacture or use of categories of consumer products as a resource conservation strategy;

    (D) the appropriateness and feasibility of employing as a resource conservation strategy the imposition of solid waste management charges on consumer products, which charges would reflect the costs of solid waste management services, litter pickup, the value of recoverable components of such product, final disposal, and any social value associated with the nonrecyclng or uncontrolled disposal of such product; and

    (E) the need for further research, development, and demonstration in the area of resource conservation.

(2) The study required in paragraph (1)(D) may include pilot scale projects, and shall consider and evaluate alternative strategics with respect to—

    (A) the product categories on which such charges would be imposed;

    (B) the appropriate state in the production of such consumer product at which to levy such charge;

    (C) appropriate criteria for establishing such charges for each consumer product category;

    (D) methods for the adjustment of such charges to reflect actions such as recycling which would reduce the overall quantities of solid waste requiring disposal; and

    (E) procedures for amending, modifying, or revising such charges to reflect changing conditions.

(3) The design for the study required in paragraph (1)(D) of this

subsection shall include timetables for the completion of the study. A preliminary report putting forth the study design shall be sent to the President and the Congress within six months following enactment of this section and followup reports shall be sent six months thereafter. Each recommendation resulting from the study shall include at least two alternatives to the proposed recommendation.

(4) The results of such investigation and study, including recommendations, shall be reported to the President and the Congress not later than two years after enactment of this subsection.

(5) There are authorized to be appropriated not to exceed $2,000,000 to carry out this subsection.

(k) The Administrator shall undertake a comprehensive study and analysis of and publish a report on systems to alleviate the hazards to aviation from birds congregating and feeding on landfills in the vicinity of airports.

(l) The Administrator shall complete the research and studies, and submit the reports, required under subsections (b), (c), (d), (e), (f), (g), and (k) not later than October 1, 1978. The Administrator shall complete the research and studies, and submit the reports, required under subsections (a), (h), and (i) not later than October 1, 1979. Upon completion, each study specified in subsections (a) through (k) of this section, the Administrator shall prepare a plan for research, development, and demonstration respecting the findings of the study and shall submit any legislative recommendations resulting from such study to appropriate committees of Congress.

(m)(1) The Administrator shall conduct a detailed and comprehensive study and submit a report on the adverse effects, if any, of drilling fluids, produced waters, and other wastes associated with the exploration, development, or production of crude oil or natural gas or geothermal energy on human health and the environment, including, but not limited to the effects of such wastes on humans, water, air, health, welfare, and natural resources and on the adequacy of means and measures currently employed by the oil and gas and geothermal drilling and production industry, Government agencies, and others to dispose of and utilize such wastes and to prevent or substantially mitigate such adverse effects. Such study shall include an analysis of—

(A) the sources and volume of discarded material generated per year from such wastes;

(B) present disposal practices;

(C) potential danger to human health and the environment from the surface runoff or leachate;

(D) documented cases which prove or have caused danger to human health and the environment from surface runoff or leachate;

(E) alternatives to current disposal methods;

(F) the cost of such alternatives; and

(G) the impact of those alternatives on the exploration for, and development and production of, crude oil and natural gas or geothermal energy.

In furtherance of this study, the Administrator shall, as he deems appropriate, review studies and other actions of other Federal agencies concerning such wastes with a view toward avoiding duplication of effort and the need to expedite such study. The Administrator shall publish a report of such study and shall include appropriate findings and recommendations for Federal and non-Federal actions concerning such effects.

(2) The Administrator shall complete the research and study and submit the report required under paragraph (1) not later than twenty-four months from the date of enactment of the Solid Waste Disposal Act Amendments of 1980. Upon completion of the study, the Administrator shall prepare a summary of the findings of the study, a plan for research, development, and demonstration respecting the findings of the study, and shall submit the findings and the study, along with any recommendations resulting from such study, to the Committee on Environment and Public Works of the United States Senate and the Committee on Interstate and Foreign Commerce of the United States House of Representatives.

(3) There are authorized to be appropriated not to exceed $1,000,000 to carry out the provisions of this subsection.

(n) The Administrator shall conduct a detailed and comprehensive study and submit a report on the adverse effects on human health and the environment, if any, of the disposal and utilization of fly ash waste, bottom ash waste, slag waste, flue gas emission control waste, and other byproduct materials generated primarily from the combustion of coal or other fossil fuels. Such study shall include an analysis of—

(1) the source and volumes of such material generated per year;

(2) present disposal and utilization practices;

(3) potential danger, if any, to human health and the environment from the disposal and reuse of such materials;

(4) documented cases in which danger to human health or the environment from surface runoff or leachate has been proved;

(5) alternatives to current disposal methods;

(6) the costs of such alternatives;

(7) the impact of those alternatives on the use of coal and other natural resources; and

(8) the current and potential utilization of such materials.

In furtherance of this study, the Administrator shall, as he deems appropriate, review studies and other actions of other Federal and State agencies concerning such material and invite participation by other concerned parties, including industry and other Federal and State agencies, with a view toward avoiding duplication of effort. The Administrator shall publish a report on such study, which shall include appropriate findings, not later than twenty-four months after the enactment of the Solid Waste Disposal Act Amendments of 1980. Such study and findings shall be submitted to the Committee on Environment and Public Works of the United States Senate and the Committee on Interstate and Foreign Commerce of the United States House of Representatives.

(o) The Administrator shall conduct a detailed and comprehensive study of the adverse effects on human health and the environment, if any, of the disposal of cement kiln dust waste. Such study shall include an analysis of—

    (1) the source and volumes of such materials generated per year,

    (2) present disposal practices;

    (3) potential danger, if any, to human health and the environment from the disposal of such materials;

    (4) documented cases in which danger to human health or the environment has been proved;

    (5) alternatives to current disposal methods;

    (6) the costs of such alternatives;

    (7) the impact of those alternatives on the use of natural resources; and

    (8) the current and potential utilization of such materials.

In furtherance of this study the Administrator shall, as he deems appropriate, review studies and other actions of other Federal and State agencies concerning such waste or materials and invite participation by other concerned parties, including industry and other Federal and State agencies, with a view toward avoiding duplication of effort. The Administrator shall publish a report of such study, which shall include appropriate findings, not later than thirty-six months after the date of enactment of the Solid Waste Disposal Act Amendments of 1980. Such report shall be submitted to the Committee on Environment and Public Works of the United States Senate and the Committee on Interstate and Foreign Commerce of the United States House of Representatives.

(p) The Administrator shall conduct a detailed and comprehensive study on the adverse effects on human health and the environment, if any, of the disposal and utilization of solid waste from the extraction, beneficiation, and processing of ores and minerals, including phosphate rock and overburden from uranium mining. Such study shall be conducted in conjunction with the study of mining wastes required by subsection (f) of this section and shall include an analysis of—

    (1) the source and volumes of such materials generated per year,

    (2) present disposal and utilization practices;

    (3) potential danger, if any, to human health and the environment from the disposal and reuse of such materials;

    (4) documented cases in which danger to human health or the environment has been proved;

    (5) alternatives to current disposal methods;

    (6) the costs of such alternatives;

    (7) the impact of those alternatives on the use of phosphate rock and

uranium ore, and other natural resources; and

(8) the current and potential utilization of such materials.

In furtherance of this study, the Administrator shall, as he deems appropriate, review studies and other actions of other Federal and State agencies concerning such waste or materials and invite participation by other concerned parties, including industry and other Federal and State agencies, with a view toward avoiding duplication of effort. The Administrator shall publish a report of such study, which shall include appropriate findings, in conjunction with the publication of the report of the study of mining wastes required to be conducted under subsection (f) of this section. Such report and findings shall be submitted to the Committee on Environment and Public Works of the United States Senate and the Committee on Interstate and Foreign Commerce of the United States House of Representatives.

(q) There are authorized to be appropriated not to exceed $8,000,000 for the fiscal years 1978 and 1979 to carry out this section other than subsection (j).

(r) The Administrator shall compile, and not later than October 1, 1986, submit to the Congress, a report on the feasibility and desirability of establishing standards of performance or of taking other additional actions under this Act to require the generators of hazardous waste to reduce the volume or quantity and toxicity of the hazardous waste they generate, and of establishing with respect to hazardous wastes required management practices or other requirements to assure such wastes are managed in ways that minimize present and future risks to human health and the environment. Such report shall include any recommendations for legislative changes which the Administrator determines are feasible and desirable to implement the national policy established by section 1003.

(s) The Administrator shall conduct detailed, comprehensive studies of methods to extend the useful life of sanitary landfills and to better use sites in which filled or closed landfills are located. Such studies shall address—

(1) methods to reduce the volume of materials before placement in landfills;

(2) more efficient systems for depositing waste in landfills;

(3) methods to enhance the rate of decomposition of solid waste in landfills, in a safe and environmentally acceptable manner;

(4) methane production from closed landfill units;

(5) innovative uses of closed landfill sites, including use for energy production such as solar or wind energy and use for metals recovery;

(6) potential for use of sewage treatment sludge in reclaiming landfilled areas; and

(7) methods to coordinate use of a landfill owned by one municipality by nearby municipalities, and to establish equitable rates for such use, taking into account the need to provide future landfill capacity to replace that so used.

The Administrator is authorized to conduct demonstrations in the areas of study provided in this subsection. The Administrator shall periodically report on the results of such studies, with the first such report not later than October 1, 1986. In carrying out this subsection, the Administrator need not duplicate other studies which have been completed and may rely upon information which has previously been compiled.

§ 6983. Coordination, collection, and dissemination of information

[Sec. 8003] (a) The Administrator shall develop, collect, evaluate, and coordinate information on—
(1) methods and costs of the collection of solid waste;
(2) solid waste management practices, including data on the different management methods and the cost, operation, and maintenance of such methods;
(3) the amounts and percentages of resources (including energy) that can be recovered from solid waste by use of various solid waste management practices and various technologies;
(4) methods available to reduce the amount of solid waste that is generated;
(5) existing and developing technologies for the recovery of energy or materials from solid waste and the costs, reliability, and risks associated with such technologies;
(6) hazardous solid waste, including incidents of damage resulting from the disposal of hazardous solid wastes; inherently and potentially hazardous solid wastes; methods of neutralizing or properly disposing of hazardous solid wastes; facilities that properly dispose of hazardous wastes;
(7) methods of financing resource recovery facilities, or sanitary landfills, or hazardous solid waste treatment facilities, whichever is appropriate for the entity developing such facility or landfill (taking into account the amount of solid waste reasonably expected to be available to such entity);
(8) the availability of markets for the purchase of resources, either materials or energy, recovered from solid waste; and
(9) research and development projects respecting solid waste management.

(b)(1) The Administrator shall establish and maintain a central reference library for (A) the materials collected pursuant to subsection (a) of this section and (B) the actual performance and cost effectiveness records and other data and information with respect to—
       (i) the various methods of energy and resource recovery from solid waste,
       (ii) the various systems and means of resource conservation,
       (iii) the various systems and technologies for collection, transport,

storage, treatment, and final disposition of solid waste, and
(iv) other aspects of solid waste and hazardous solid waste
management.

Such central reference library shall also contain, but not be limited to, the model codes and model accounting systems developed under this section, the information collected under subsection (d), and, subject to any applicable requirements of confidentiality, information respecting any aspect of solid waste provided by officers and employees of the Environmental Protection Agency which has been acquired by them in the conduct of their functions under this Act and which may be of value to Federal, State, and local authorities and other persons.

(2) Information in the central reference library shall, to the extent practicable, be collated, analyzed, verified, and published and shall be made available to State and local governments and other persons at reasonable times and subject to such reasonable charges as may be necessary to defray expenses of making such information available.

(c) In order to assist State and local governments in determining the cost and revenues associated with the collection and disposal of solid waste and with resource recovery operations, the Administrator shall develop and publish a recommended model cost and revenue accounting system applicable to the solid waste management functions of State and local governments. Such system shall be in accordance with generally accepted accounting principles. The Administrator shall periodically, but not less frequently than once every five years; review such accounting system and revise it as necessary.

(d) The Administrator is authorized, in cooperation with appropriate State and local agencies, to recommend model codes, ordinances, and statutes, providing for sound solid waste management.

(e)(1) The Administrator shall implement a program for the rapid dissemination of information on solid waste management, hazardous waste management, resource conservation, and methods of resource recovery from solid waste, including the results of any relevant research, investigations, experiments, surveys, studies, or other information which may be useful in the implementation of new or improved solid waste management practices and methods and information on any other technical, managerial, financial, or market aspect of resource conservation and recovery facilities.

(2) The Administrator shall develop and implement educational programs to promote citizen understanding of the need for environmentally sound solid waste management practices.

(f) In collecting and disseminating information under this section, the Administrator shall coordinate his actions and cooperate to the maximum extent possible with State and local authorities.

(g) Upon request, the full range of alternative technologies, programs or processes deemed feasible to meet the resource recovery or resource conservation needs of a jurisdiction shall be described in such a manner as to provide a sufficient evaluative basis from which the jurisdiction can make its decisions, but no officer or employee of the Environmental Protection Agency shall, in an official capacity, lobby for or otherwise represent an agency position in favor of resource recovery or resource conservation, as a policy alternative for adoption into ordinances, codes, regulations, or law by any State or political subdivision thereof.

§ 6984. Full-scale demonstration facilities

[Sec. 8004] (a) The Administrator may enter into contracts with public agencies or authorities or private persons for the construction and operation of a full-scale demonstration facility under this Act, or provide financial assistance in the form of grants to a full-scale demonstration facility under this Act only if the Administrator finds that—

(1) Such facility or proposed facility will demonstrate at full scale a new or significantly improved technology or process, a practical and significant improvement in solid waste management practice, or the technological feasibility and cost effectiveness of an existing, but unproven technology, process, or practice, and will not duplicate any other Federal, State, local, or commercial facility which has been constructed or with respect to which construction has begun (determined as of the date action is taken by the Administrator under this Act),

(2) such contract or assistance meets the requirements of section 8001 and meets other applicable requirements of the Act,

(3) such facility will be able to comply with the guidelines published under section 1008 and with other laws and regulations for the protection of health and the environment,

(4) in the case of a contract for construction or operation, such facility is not likely to be constructed or operated by State, local, or private persons or in the case of an application for financial assistance, such facility is not likely to receive adequate financial assistance from other sources, and

(5) any Federal interest in, or assistance to, such facility will be disposed of or terminated, with appropriate compensation, within such period of time as may be necessary to carry out the basic objectives of this Act.

(b) No obligation may be made by the Administrator for financial assistance under this subtitle for any full-scale demonstration facility after the date ten years after the enactment of this section. No expenditure of funds for any such full-scale demonstration facility under this subtitle may be made by the Administrator after the date fourteen years after such date of enactment.

(c)(1) Wherever practicable, in constructing, operating, or providing financial assistance under this subtitle to a full-scale demonstration facility, the Administrator shall endeavor to enter into agreements and make other arrangements for maximum practicable cost sharing with other Federal, State, and local agencies, private persons, or any combination thereof,

(2) The Administrator shall enter into arrangements, wherever practicable and desirable, to provide monitoring of full-scale solid waste facilities (whether or not constructed or operated under this Act) for purposes of obtaining information concerning the performance, and other aspects, of such facilities. Where the Administrator provides only monitoring and evaluation instruments or personnel (or both) or funds for such instruments or personnel and provides no other financial assistance to a facility, notwithstanding section 8001(c)(3), title to any invention made or conceived of in the course of developing, constructing, or operating such facility shall not be required to vest in the United States and patents respecting such invention shall not be required to be issued to the United States.

(d) After the date of enactment of this section, the Administrator shall not construct or operate any full-scale facility (except by contract with public agencies or authorities or private persons).

§ 6985. Special study and demonstration projects on recovery of useful energy and materials

[Sec. 8005] The Administrator shall conduct studies and develop recommendations for administrative or legislative action on—

(1) means of recovering materials and energy from solid waste, recommended uses of such materials and energy for national or international welfare, including identification of potential markets for such recovered resources, the impact of distribution of such resources on existing markets, and potentials for energy conservation through resource conservation and resource recovery;

(2) actions to reduce waste generation which have been taken voluntarily or in response to governmental action, and those which practically could be taken in the future, and the economic, social, and environmental consequences of such actions;

(3) methods of collection, separation, and containerization which will encourage efficient utilization of facilities and contribute to more effective programs of reduction, reuse, or disposal of wastes;

(4) the use of Federal procurement to develop market demand for recovery resources;

(5) recommended incentives (including Federal grants, loans, and other assistance) and disincentives to accelerate the reclamation or recycling of materials from solid wastes, with special emphasis on motor vehicle hulks;

(6) the effect of existing public policies, including subsidies and economic incentives and disincentives, percentage depletion allowances, capital

gains treatment and other tax incentives and disincentives, upon the recycling and reuse of materials, and the likely effect of the modification or elimination of such incentives and disincentives upon the reuse, recycling and conservation of such materials;

(7) the necessity and method of imposing disposal or other charges on packaging, containers, vehicles, and other manufactured goods, which charges would reflect the cost of final disposal, the value of recoverable components of the item, and any social costs associated with nonrecycling or uncontrolled disposal of such items; and

(8) the legal constraints and institutional barriers to the acquisition of land needed for solid waste management, including land for facilities and disposal sites;

(9) in consultation with the Secretary of Agriculture, agricultural waste management problems and practices, the extent of reuse and recovery of resources in such wastes, the prospects for improvement, Federal, State, and local regulations governing such practices, and the economic, social, and environmental consequences of such practices; and

(10) in consultation with the Secretary of the Interior, mining waste management problems, and practices, including an assessment of existing authorities, technologies, and economics, and the environmental and public health consequences of such practices.

(b) The Administrator is also authorized to carry out demonstration projects to test and demonstrate methods and techniques developed pursuant to subsection (a).

(c) Section 8001 (b) and (c) shall be applicable to investigations, studies, and projects carried out under this section.

§ 6986. Grants for resource recovery systems and improved solid waste disposal facilities

[Sec. 8006] (a) The Administrator is authorized to make grants pursuant to this section to any State, municipal, or interstate or intermunicipal agency for the demonstration of resource recovery systems or for the construction of new or improved solid waste disposal facilities.

(b)(1) Any grant under this section for the demonstration of a resource recovery system may be made only if it (A) is consistent with any plans which meet the requirements of subtitle D of this Act; (B) is consistent with the guidelines recommended pursuant to section 1008 of this Act; (C) is designed to provide area-wide resource recovery systems consistent with the purposes of this Act, as determined by the Administrator, pursuant to regulations promulgated under subsection (d) of this section; and (D) provides an equitable system for distributing the costs associated with the construction, operation, and maintenance of any resource recovery system among the users of such system.

(2) The Federal share for any project to which paragraph (1) applies

shall not be more than 75 percent.

(c)(1) A grant under this section for the construction of a new or improved solid waste disposal facility may be made only if—

    (A) a State or interstate plan for solid waste disposal has been adopted which applies to the area involved, and the facility to be constructed (i) is consistent with such plan, (ii) is included in a comprehensive plan for the area involved which is satisfactory to the Administrator for the purpose of this Act, and (iii) is consistent with the guidelines recommended under section 1008, and

    (B) the project advances the state of the art by applying new and improved techniques in reducing the environmental impact of solid waste disposal, in achieving recovery of energy or resources, or in recycling useful materials.

(2) The Federal share for any project to which paragraph (1) applies shall be not more than 50 percent in the case of a project serving an area which includes only one municipality, and not more than 75 percent in any other case.

(d)(1) The Administrator shall promulgate regulations establishing a procedure for awarding grants under this section which—

    (A) provides that projects will be carried out in communities of varying sizes, under such conditions as will assist in solving the community waste problems of urban-industrial centers, metropolitan regions, and rural areas, under representative geographic and environmental conditions; and

    (B) provides deadlines for submission of, and action on, grant requests.

(2) In taking action on applications for grants under this section, consideration shall be given by the Administrator (A) to the public benefits to be derived by the construction and the propriety of Federal aid in making such grant; (B) to the extent applicable, to the economic and commercial viability of the project (including contractual arrangements with the private sector to market any resources recovered); (C) to the potential of such project for general application to community solid waste disposal problems; and (D) to the use by the applicant of comprehensive regional or metropolitan area planning.

(e) A grant under this section—

(1) may be made only in the amount of the Federal share of (A) the estimated total design and construction costs, plus (B) in the case of a grant to which subsection (b)(1) applies, the first-year operation and maintenance costs;

(2) may not be provided for land acquisition or (except as otherwise provided in paragraph (1)(B)) for operating or maintenance costs;

(3) may not be made until the applicant has made provision satisfactory to

the Administrator for proper and efficient operation and maintenance of the project (subject to paragraph (1)(B)); and

(4) may be made subject to such conditions and requirements, in addition to those provided in this section, as the Administrator may require to properly carry out his functions pursuant to this Act.

For purposes of paragraph (1), the non-Federal share may be in any form, including, but not limited to, lands or interests therein needed for the project or personal property or services, the value of which shall be determined by the Administrator.

(f)(1) Not more than 15 percent of the total of funds authorized to be appropriated for any fiscal year to carry out this section shall be granted under this section for projects in any one State.

(2) The Administrator shall prescribe by regulation the manner in which this subsection shall apply to a grant under this section for a project in an area which includes all or part of more than one State.

§ 6987. Authorization of appropriations

[Sec. 8007] There are authorized to be appropriated not to exceed $35,000,000 for the fiscal year 1978 to carry out the purposes of this subtitle (except for section 8002).

Subchapter IX. Regulation of Underground Storage Tanks

§ 6991. Definitions and exemptions

[Sec. 9001] For the purposes of this subtitle—

(1) The term "underground storage tank" means any one or combination of tanks (including underground pipes connected thereto) which is used to contain an accumulation of regulated substances, and the volume of which (including the volume of the underground pipes connected thereto) is 10 per centum or more beneath the surface of the ground. Such term does not include any—

(A) farm or residential tank of 1,100 gallons or less capacity used for storing motor fuel for noncommercial purposes,

(B) tank used for storing heating oil for consumptive use on the premises where stored,

(C) septic tank,

(D) pipeline facility (including gathering lines) regulated under—

(i) the Natural Gas Pipeline Safety Act of 1968 (49 U.S.C. App.

1671, et seq.),

    (ii) the Hazardous Liquid Pipeline Safety Act of 1979 (49 U.S.C. App. 2001, et seq.), or

    (iii) which is an intrastate pipeline facility regulated under State laws comparable to the provisions of law referred to in clause (i) or (ii) of this subparagraph,

(E) surface impoundment, pit, pond, or lagoon,

(F) storm water or waste water collection system,

(G) flow-through process tank,

(H) liquid trap or associated gathering lines directly related to oil or gas production and gathering operations, or

(I) storage tank situated in an underground area (such as a basement, cellar, mineworking, drift, shaft, or tunnel) if the storage tank is situated upon or above the surface of the floor.

The term "underground storage tank" shall not include any pipes connected to any tank which is described in subparagraphs (A) through (I).

(2) The term "regulated substance" means—

    (A) any substance defined in section 101(14) of the Comprehensive Environmental Response, Compensation, and Liability Act of 1980 (but not including any substance regulated as a hazardous waste under subtitle C), and

    (B) petroleum.

(3) The term "owner" means—

    (A) in the case of an underground storage tank in use on the date of enactment of the Hazardous and Solid Waste Amendments of 1984, or brought into use after that date, any person who owns an underground storage tank used for the storage, use, or dispensing of regulated substances, and

    (B) in the case of any underground storage tank in use before the date of enactment of the Hazardous and Solid Waste Amendments of 1984, but no longer in use on the date of enactment of such Amendments, any person who owned such tank immediately before the discontinuation of its use.

(4) The term "operator" means any person in control of, or having responsibility for, the daily operation of the underground storage tank.

(5) The term "release" means any spilling, leaking, emitting, discharging, escaping, leaching, or disposing from an underground storage tank into ground water, surface water or subsurface soils.

(6) The term "person" has the same meaning as provided in section 1004(15), except that such term includes a consortium, a joint venture, and a commercial entity, and the United States Government.

(7) The term "nonoperational storage tank" means any underground storage tank in which regulated substances will not be deposited or from which regulated substances will not be dispensed after the date of

the enactment of the Hazardous and Solid Waste Amendments of 1984.

(8) The term "petroleum" means petroleum, including crude oil or any fraction thereof which is liquid at standard conditions of temperature and pressure (60 degrees Fahrenheit and 14.7 pounds per square inch absolute).

§ 6991a. Notification

[Sec. 9002] (a)(1) Within 18 months after the date of enactment of the Hazardous and Solid Waste Amendments of 1984, each owner of an underground storage tank shall notify the State or local agency or department designated pursuant to subsection (b)(1) of the existence of such tank, specifying the age, size, type, location, and uses of such tank.

(2)(A) For each underground storage tank taken out of operation after January 1, 1974, the owner of such tank shall, within eighteen months after the date of enactment of the Hazardous and Solid Waste Amendments of 1984, notify the State or local agency, or department designated pursuant to subsection (b)(1) of the existence of such tanks (unless the owner knows the tank subsequently was removed from the ground). The owner of a tank taken out of operation on or before January 1, 1974, shall not be required to notify the State or local agency under this subsection.

(B) Notice under subparagraph (A) shall specify, to the extent known to the owner—

(i) the date the tank was taken out of operation,

(ii) the age of the tank on the date taken out of operation,

(iii) the size, type and location of the tank, and

(iv) the type and quantity of substances left stored in such tank on the date taken out of operation.

(3) Any owner which brings into use an underground storage tank after the initial notification period specified under paragraph (1), shall notify the designated State or local agency or department within thirty days of the existence of such tank, specifying the age, size, type, location and uses of such tank.

(4) Paragraphs (1) through (3) of this subsection shall not apply to tanks for which notice was given pursuant to section 103(c) of the Comprehensive Environmental Response, Compensation, and Liability Act of 1980.

(5) Beginning thirty days after the Administrator prescribes the form of notice pursuant to subsection (b)(2) and for eighteen months thereafter, any person who deposits regulated substances in an underground storage tank shall reasonably notify the owner or operator of

such tank of the owner's notification requirements pursuant to this subsection.

(6) Beginning thirty days after the Administrator issues new tank performance standards pursuant to section 9003(e) of this subtitle, any person who sells a tank intended to be used as an underground storage tank shall notify the purchaser of such tank of the owner's notification requirements pursuant to this subsection.

(b)(1) Within one hundred and eighty days after the enactment of the Hazardous and Solid Waste Amendments of 1984, the Governors of each State shall designate the appropriate State agency or department or local agencies or departments to receive the notifications under subsection (a)(1),(2), or (3).

(2) Within twelve months after the date of enactment of the Hazardous and Solid Waste Amendments of 1984, the Administrator, in consultation with State and local officials designated pursuant to subsection (b)(1), and after notice and opportunity for public comment, shall prescribe the form of the notice and the information to be included in the notifications under subsection (a)(1),(2), or (3). In prescribing the form of such notice, the Administrator shall take into account the effect on small businesses and other owners and operators.

(c) Each State shall make 2 separate inventories of all underground storage tanks in such State containing regulated substances. One inventory shall be made with respect to petroleum and one with respect to other regulated substances. In making such inventories, the State shall utilize and aggregate the data in the notification forms submitted pursuant to subsections (a) and (b) of this section. Each State shall submit such aggregated data to the Administrator not later than 270 days after the enactment of the Superfund Amendments and Reauthorization Act of 1986.

§ 6991b. Release detection, prevention, and correction regulations

[Sec. 9003] (a) The Administrator, after notice and opportunity for public comment, and at least three months before the effective dates specified in subsection (f), shall promulgate release detection, prevention, and correction regulations applicable to all owners and operators of underground storage tanks, as may be necessary to protect human health and the environment.

(b) In promulgating regulations under this section, the Administrator may distinguish between types, classes, and ages of underground storage tanks. In making such distinctions, the Administrator may take into consideration factors, including, but not limited to: location of the tanks, soil and climate conditions, uses of the tanks, history of maintenance, age of the tanks, current industry recommended practices, national consensus codes, hydrogeology, water table, size of the tanks, quantity of regulated substances periodically deposited in or dispensed from the tank, the technical capability of the owners and operators, and the compatibility of the regulated substance and the materials of which the tank is fabricated.

(c) The regulations promulgated pursuant to this section shall include, but need not be limited to, the following requirements respecting all underground storage tanks—

(1) requirements for maintaining a leak detection system, an inventory control system together with tank testing, or a comparable system or method designed to identify releases in a manner consistent with the protection of human health and the environment;

(2) requirements for maintaining records of any monitoring or leak detection system or inventory control system or tank testing or comparable system;

(3) requirements for reporting of releases and corrective action taken in response to a release from an underground storage tank;

(4) requirements for taking corrective action in response to a release from an underground storage tank;

(5) requirements for the closure of tanks to prevent future releases of regulated substances into the environment; and

(6) requirements for maintaining evidence of financial responsibility for taking corrective action and compensating third parties for bodily injury and property damage caused by sudden and nonsudden accidental releases arising from operating an underground storage tank.

(d)(1) Financial responsibility required by this subsection may be established in accordance with regulations promulgated by the Administrator by any one, or any combination, of the following: insurance, guarantee, surety bond, letter of credit, qualification as a self-insurer or any other method satisfactory to the Administrator. In promulgating requirements under this subsection, the Administrator is authorized to specify policy or other contractual terms, conditions, or defenses which are necessary or are unacceptable in establishing such evidence of financial responsibility in order to effectuate the purposes of this subtitle.

(2) In any case where the owner or operator is in bankruptcy, reorganization, or arrangement pursuant to the Federal Bankruptcy Code or where with reasonable diligence jurisdiction in any State court of the Federal Courts cannot be obtained over an owner or operator likely to be solvent at the time of judgment, any claim arising from conduct for which evidence of financial responsibility must be provided under this subsection may be asserted directly against the guarantor providing such evidence of financial responsibility. In the case of any action pursuant to this paragraph such guarantor shall be entitled to invoke all rights and defenses which would have been available to the owner or operator if any action had been brought against the owner or operator by the claimant and which would have been available to the guarantor if an action had been brought against the guarantor by the owner or operator.

(3) The total liability of any guarantor shall be limited to the aggregate amount which the guarantor has provided as evidence of financial

responsibility to the owner or operator under this section. Nothing in this subsection shall be construed to limit any other State or Federal statutory, contractual or common law liability of a guarantor to its owner or operator including, but not limited to, the liability of such guarantor for bad faith either in negotiating or in failing to negotiate the settlement of any claim. Nothing in this subsection shall be construed to diminish the liability of any person under section 107 or 111 of the Comprehensive Environmental Response, Compensation and Liability Act of 1980 or other applicable law.

(4) For the purpose of this subsection, the term "guarantor" means any person, other than the owner or operator, who provides evidence of financial responsibility for an owner or operator under this subsection.

(5)(A) The Administrator, in promulgating financial responsibility regulations under this section, may establish an amount of coverage for particular classes or categories of underground storage tanks containing petroleum which shall satisfy such regulations and which shall not be less than $1,000,000 for each occurrence with an appropriate aggregate requirement.

(B) The Administrator may set amounts lower than the amounts required by subparagraph (A) of this paragraph for underground storage tanks containing petroleum which are at facilities not engaged in petroleum production, refining, or marketing and which are not used to handle substantial quantities of petroleum.

(C) In establishing classes and categories for purposes of this paragraph, the Administrator may consider the following factors:

(i) The size, type, location, storage, and handling capacity of underground storage tanks in the class or category and the volume of petroleum handled by such tanks.

(ii) The likelihood of release and the potential extent of damage from any release from underground storage tanks in the class or category.

(iii) The economic impact of the limits on the owners and operators of each such class or category, particularly relating to the small business segment of the petroleum marketing industry.

(iv) The availability of methods of financial responsibility in amounts greater than the amount established by this paragraph.

(v) Such other factors as the Administrator deems pertinent.

(D) The Administrator may suspend enforcement of the financial responsibility requirements for a particular class or category of underground storage tanks or in a particular State, if the Administrator makes a determination that methods of financial responsibility satisfying the requirements of this subsection are not generally available for underground storage tanks in that class or category, and—

      (i) steps are being taken to form a risk retention group for such class of tanks; or

      (ii) such State is taking steps to establish a fund pursuant to section 9004(c)(1) of this Act to be submitted as evidence of financial responsibility.

A suspension by the Administrator pursuant to this paragraph shall extend for a period not to exceed 180 days. A determination to suspend may be made with respect to the same class or category or for the same State at the end of such period, but only if substantial progress has been made in establishing a risk retention group, or the owners or operators in the class or category demonstrate, and the Administrator finds, that the formation of such a group is not possible and that the State is unable or unwilling to establish such a fund pursuant to clause (ii).

(e) The Administrator shall, not later than three months prior to the effective date specified in subsection (f), issue performance standards for underground storage tanks brought into use on or after the effective date of such standards. The performance standards for new underground storage tanks shall include, but need not be limited to, design, construction, installation, release detection, and compatibility standards.

(f)(1) Regulations issued pursuant to subsections (c) and (d) of this section, and standards issued pursuant to subsection (e) of this section, for underground storage tanks containing regulated substances defined in section 9001(2)(B) (petroleum, including crude oil or any fraction thereof which is liquid at standard conditions of temperature and pressure) shall be effective not later than thirty months after the date of enactment of the Hazardous and Solid Waste Amendments of 1984.

      (2) Standards issued pursuant to subsection (e) of this section (entitled "New Tank Performance Standards") for underground storage tanks containing regulated substances defined in section 9001(2)(A) shall be effective not later than thirty-six months after the date of enactment of the Hazardous and Solid Waste Amendments of 1984.

      (3) Regulations issued pursuant to subsection (c) of this section (entitled "Requirements") and standards issued pursuant to subsection (d) of this section (entitled "Financial Responsibility") for underground storage tanks containing regulated substances defined in section 9001(2)(A) shall be effective not later than forty-eight months after the date of enactment of the Hazardous and Solid Waste Amendments of 1984.

(g)(1) Until the effective date of the standards promulgated by the Administrator under subsection (e) and after one hundred and eighty days after the date of the enactment of the Hazardous and Solid Waste Amendments of 1984, no person may install an underground storage tank for the purpose of storing regulated substances unless such tank (whether of single or double wall construction)—

      (A) will prevent releases due to corrosion or structural failure for the operational life of the tank;

(B) is cathodically protected against corrosion, constructed of noncorrosive material, steel clad with a noncorrosive material, or designed in a manner to prevent the release or threatened release of any stored substance; and

(C) the material used in the construction or lining of the tank is compatible with the substance to be stored.

(2) Notwithstanding paragraph (1), if soil tests conducted in accordance with ASTM Standard G57–78, or another standard approved by the Administrator, show that soil resistivity in an installation location is 12,000 ohm/cm or more (unless a more stringent standard is prescribed by the Administrator by rule), a storage tank without corrosion protection may be installed in that location during the period referred to in paragraph (1).

(h)(1) Before the effective date of regulations under subsection (c), the Administrator (or a State pursuant to paragraph (7) is authorized to—

(A) require the owner or operator of an underground storage tank to undertake corrective action with respect to any release of petroleum when the Administrator (or the State) determines that such corrective action will be done properly and promptly by the owner or operator of the underground storage tank from which the release occurs; or

(B) undertake corrective action with respect to any release of petroleum into the environment from an underground storage tank if such action is necessary, in the judgment of the Administrator (or the State), to protect human health and the environment.

The corrective action undertaken or required under this paragraph shall be such as may be necessary to protect human health and the environment. The Administrator shall use funds in the Leaking Underground Storage Tank Trust Fund for payment of costs incurred for corrective action under subparagraph (B), enforcement action under subparagraph (A), and cost recovery under paragraph (6) of this subsection. Subject to the priority requirements of paragraph (3), the Administrator (or the State) shall give priority in undertaking such actions under subparagraph (B) to cases where the Administrator (or the State) cannot identify a solvent owner or operator of the tank who will undertake action properly.

(2) Following the effective date of regulations under subsection (c), all actions or orders of the Administrator (or a State pursuant to paragraph (7)) described in paragraph (1) of this subsection shall be in conformity with such regulations. Following such effective date, the Administrator (or the State) may undertake corrective action with respect to any release of petroleum into the environment from an underground storage tank only if such action is necessary, in the judgment of the Administrator (or the State), to protect human health and the environment and one or more of the following situations exists:

    (A) No person can be found, within 90 days or such shorter period as may be necessary to protect human health and the environment, who is—

        (i) an owner or operator of the tank concerned,

       (ii) subject to such corrective action regulations, and

     (iii) capable of carrying out such corrective action properly.

    (B) A situation exists which requires prompt action by the Administrator (or the State) under this paragraph to protect human health and the environment.

    (C) Corrective action costs at a facility exceed the amount of coverage required by the Administrator pursuant to the provisions of subsection (c) and (d)(5) of this section and, considering the class or category of underground storage tank from which the release occurred, expenditures from the Leaking Underground Storage Tank Trust Fund are necessary to assure an effective corrective action.

    (D) The owner or operator of the tank has failed or refused to comply with an order of the Administrator under this subsection or section 9006 or with the order of a State under this subsection to comply with the corrective action regulations.

(3) The Administrator (or a State pursuant to paragraph (7)) shall give priority in undertaking corrective actions under this subsection, and in issuing orders requiring owners or operators to undertake such actions, to releases of petroleum from underground storage tanks which pose the greatest threat to human health and the environment.

(4) The Administrator is authorized to issue orders to the owner or operator of an underground storage tank to carry out subparagraph (A) or paragraph (1) or to carry out regulations issued under subsection (c)(4). A State acting pursuant to paragraph (7) of this subsection is authorized to carry out subparagraph (A) of paragraph (1) only until the State's program is approved by the Administrator under section 9004 of this subtitle. Such orders shall be issued and enforced in the same manner and subject to the same requirements as orders under section 9006.

(5) The corrective action undertaken by the Administrator (or a State pursuant to paragraph (7)) under paragraph (1) or (2) may include temporary or permanent relocation of residents and alternative household water supplies. In connection with the performance of any corrective action under paragraph (1) or (2), the Administrator may undertake an exposure assessment as defined in paragraph (10) of this subsection or provide for such an assessment with a State pursuant to paragraph (7) of this subsection. The costs of any such assessment may be treated as corrctive action for purposes of paragraph (6), relating to cost recovery.

(6)(A) Whenever costs have been incurred by the Administrator, or by a State pursuant to paragraph (7), for undertaking corrective action or enforcement action with respect to the release of petroleum from an underground storage tank, the owner or operator of such tank shall be liable to the Administrator or the State for such costs. The liability under this paragraph shall be construed to be the standard of liability which obtains under section 311 of the Federal Water Pollution Control Act.

(B) In determining the equities for seeking the recovery of costs under subparagraph (A), the Administrator (or a State pursuant to paragraph (7) of this subsection) may consider the amount of financial responsibility required to be maintained under subsection (c) and (d)(5) of this section and the factors considered in establishing such amount under subsection (d)(5).

(C)(i) No indemnification, hold harmless, or similar agreement or conveyance shall be effective to transfer from the owner or operator of any underground storage tank or from any person who may be liable for a release or threat of release under this subsection, to any other person the liability imposed under this subsection. Nothing in this subsection shall bar any agreement to insure, hold harmless, or indemnify a party to such agreement for any liability under this section.

(ii) Nothing in this subsection, including the provisions of clause (i) of this subparagraph, shall bar a cause of action that an owner or operator or any other person subject to liability under this section, or a guarantor, has or would have, by reason of subrogation or otherwise against any person.

(D) For purposes of this paragraph, the term "facility" means, with respect to any owner or operator, all underground storage tanks used for the storage of petroleum which are owned or operated by such owner or operator and located on a single parcel of property (or on any contiguous or adjacent property).

(7)(A) A State may exercise the authorities in paragraphs (1) and (2) of this subsection, subject to the terms and conditions of paragraphs (3), (5),(9), (10), and (11), and including the authorities of paragraphs (4), (6), and (8) of this subsection if—

(i) the Administrator determines that the State has the capabilities to carry out effective corrective actions and enforcement activities; and

(ii) the Administrator enters into a cooperative agreement with the State setting out the actions to be undertaken by the State.

The Administrator may provide funds from the Leaking Underground Storage Tank Trust Fund for the reasonable costs of the State's actions under the cooperative agreement.

(B) Following the effective date of the regulations under subsection

(c) of this section, the State shall pay 10 per centum of the cost of corrective actions undertaken either by the Administrator or by the State under a cooperative agreement, except that the Administrator may take corrective action at a facility where immediate action is necessary to respond to an imminent and substantial endangerment to human health or the environment if the State fails to pay the cost share.

(8) Notwithstanding any other provision of law, the Administrator may authorize the use of such emergency procurement powers as he deems necessary.

(9) As used in this subsection, the term "owner" does not include any person who, without participating in the management of an underground storage tank and otherwise not engaged in petroleum production, refining, and marketing, holds indicia of ownership primarily to protect the owner's security interest in the tank.

(10) As used in this subsection, the term "exposure assessment" means an assessment to determine the extent of exposure of, or potential for exposure of, individuals to petroleum from a release from an underground storage tank based on such factors as the nature and extent of contamination and the existence of or potential for pathways of human exposure (including ground or surface water contamination, air emissions, and food chain contamination), the size of the community within the likely pathways of exposure, and the comparison of expected human exposure levels to the short-term and long-term health effects associated with identified contaminants and any available recommended exposure or tolerance limits for such contaminants. Such assessment shall not delay corrective action to abate immediate hazards or reduce exposure.

(11) At any facility where the owner or operator has failed to maintain evidence of financial responsibility in amounts at least equal to the amounts established by subsection (d)(5)(A) of this section (or a lesser amount if such amount is applicable to such facility as a result of subsection (d)(5)(B) of this section) for whatever reason the Administrator shall expend no monies from the Leaking Underground Storage Tank Trust Fund to clean up releases at such facility pursuant to the provisions of paragraph (1) or (2) of this subsection. At such facilities the Administrator shall use the authorities provided in subparagraph (A) of paragraph (1) and paragraph (4) of this subsection and section 9006 of this subtitle to order corrective action to clean up such releases. States acting pursuant to paragraph (7) of this subsection shall use the authorities provided in subparagraph (A) of paragraph (1) and paragraph (4) of this subsection to order corrective action to clean up such releases. Notwithstanding the provisions of this paragraph, the Administrator may use monies from the fund to take the corrective actions authorized by paragraph (5) of this subsection to

protect human health at such facilities and shall seek full recovery of the costs of all such actions pursuant to the provisions of paragraph (6)(A) of this subsection and without consideration of the factors in paragraph (6)(B) of this subsection. Nothing in this paragraph shall prevent the Administrator (or a State pursuant to paragraph (7) of this subsection) from taking corrective action at a facility where there is no solvent owner or operator or where immediate action is necessary to respond to an imminent and substantial endangerment of human health or the environment.

§ 6991c. Approval of state programs

[Sec. 9004] (a) Beginning 30 months after the date of enactment of the Hazardous and Solid Waste Amendments of 1984, any State may submit an underground storage tank release detection, prevention, and correction program for review and approval by the Administrator. The program may cover tanks used to store regulated substances referred to in 9001(A) or (B) or both. A State program may be approved by the Administrator under this section only if the State demonstrates that the State program includes the following requirements and standards and provides for adequate enforcement of compliance with such requirements and standards—

(1) requirements for maintaining a leak detection system, an inventory control system together with tank testing, or a comparable system or method designed to identify releases in a manner consistent with the protection of human health and the environment;
(2) requirements for maintaining records of any monitoring or leak detection system or inventory control system or tank testing system;
(3) requirements for reporting of any releases and corrective action taken in response to a release from an underground storage tank;
(4) requirements for taking corrective action in response to a release from an underground storage tank; and
(5) requirements for the closure of tanks to prevent future releases of regulated substances into the environment;
(6) requirements for maintaining evidence of financial responsibility for taking corrective action and compensating third parties for bodily injury and property damage caused by sudden and nonsudden accidental releases arising from operating an underground storage tank;
(7) standards of performance for new underground storage tanks; and
(8) requirements—
   (A) for notifying the appropriate State agency or department (or local agency or department) designated according to section 9002(b)(1) of the existence of any operational or non-operational underground storage tank; and
   (B) for providing the information required on the form issued pursuant to section 9002(b)(2).

(b)(1) A State program submitted under this section may be approved only if the requirements under paragraphs (1) through (7) of subsection (a) are no less stringent than the corresponding requirements standards promulgated by the Administrator pursuant to section 9003(a).

(2)(A) A State program may be approved without regard to whether or not the requirements referred to in paragraphs (1), (2), (3), and (5) of subsection (a) are less stringent than the corresponding standards under section 9003(a) during the one-year period commencing on the date of promulgation of regulations under section 9003(a) if State regulatory action but no State legislative action is required in order to adopt a State program.

(B) If such State legislative action is required, the State program may be approved without regard to whether or not the requirements referred to in paragraphs (1), (2), (3), and (5) of subsection (a) are less stringent than the corresponding standards under section 9003(a) during the two-year period commencing on the date of promulgation of regulations under section 9003(a) (and during an additional one-year period after such legislative action if regulations are required to be promulgated by the State pursuant to such legislative action).

(c)(1) Corrective action and compensation programs administered by State or local agencies or departments may be submitted for approval under subsection (a)(6) as evidence of financial responsibility.

(2) Financial responsibility required by this subsection may be established in accordance with regulations promulgated by the Administrator by any one, or any combination, of the following: insurance, guarantee, surety bond, letter of credit, qualification as a self-insurer or any other method satisfactory to the Administrator. In promulgating requirements under this subsection, the Administrator is authorized to specify policy or other contractual terms, including the amount of coverage required for various classes and categories of underground storage tanks pursuant to section 9003(d)(5), conditions, or defenses which are necessary or are unacceptable in establishing such evidence of financial responsibility in order to effectuate the purposes of this subtitle.

(3) In any case where the owner or operator is in bankruptcy, reorganization, or arrangement pursuant to the Federal Bankruptcy Code or where with reasonable diligence jurisdiction in any State court of the Federal courts cannot be obtained over an owner or operator likley to be solvent at the time of judgment, any claim arising from conduct for which evidence of financial responsibility must be provided under this subsection may be asserted directly against the guarantor providing such evidence of financial responsibility. In the case of any action pursuant to this paragraph such guarantor shall be entitled to invoke all rights and defenses which would have been available to the owner

or operator if any action had been brought against the owner or operator by the claimant and which would have been available to the guarantor if an action had been brought against the guarantor by the owner or operator.

(4) The total liability of any guarantor shall be limited to the aggregate amount which the guarantor has provided as evidence of financial responsibility to the owner or operator under this section. Nothing in this subsection shall be construed to limit any other State or Federal statutory, contractual or common law liability of a guarantor to its owner or operator including, but not limited to, the liability of such guarantor for bad faith either in negotiating or in failing to negotiate the settlement of any claim. Nothing in this subsection shall be construed to diminish the liability of any person under section 107 or 111 of the Comprehensive Environmental Response, Compensation and Liability Act of 1980 or other applicable law.

(5) For the purpose of this subsection, the term "guarantor" means any person, or other than the owner or operator, who provides evidence of financial responsibility for an owner or operator under this subsection.

(d)(1) Within one hundred and eighty days of the date of receipt of a proposed State program, the Administrator shall, after notice and opportunity for public comment, make a determination whether the State's program complies with the provisions of this section and provides for adequate enforcement of compliance with the requirements and standards adopted pursuant to this section.

(2) If the Administrator determines that a State program complies with the provisions of this section and provides for adequate enforcement of compliance with the requirements and standards adopted pursuant to this section, he shall approve the State program in lieu of the Federal program and the State shall have primary enforcement responsibility with respect to requirements of its program.

(e) Whenever the Administrator determines after public hearing that a State is not administering and enforcing a program authorized under this subtitle in accordance with the provisions of this section, he shall so notify the State. If appropriate action is not taken within a reasonable time, not to exceed one hundred and twenty days after such notification, the Administrator shall withdraw approval of such program and reestablish the Federal program pursuant to this subtitle.

§ 6991d. Inspections, monitoring, testing, and corrective action

[Sec. 9005] (a) For the purposes of developing or assisting in the development of any regulation, conducting any study, taking any corrective action or enforcing the provisions of this subtitle, any owner or operator of an underground storage tank (or any tank subject to study under section 9009 that is used for storing regulated substances) shall, upon request of any officer, employee or representative of the Environmental Protection Agency, duly designated by the Administrator, or upon request of any duly designated officer, employee, or representative of a State acting pursuant to subsection (h)(7) of section 9003 or with an approved program, furnish information relating to such tanks, their associated equipment, their contents, conduct monitoring or testing, permit such officer at all reasonable times to have access to, and to copy all records relating to such tanks and permit such officer to have access for corrective action. For the purposes of developing or assisting in the development of any regulation, conducting any study, taking corrective action, or enforcing the provisions of this subtitle, such officers, employees, or representatives are authorized—

(1) to enter at reasonable times any establishment or other place where an underground storage tank is located;

(2) to inspect and obtain samples from any person of any regulated substances contained in such tank;

(3) to conduct monitoring or testing of the tanks, associated equipment, contents, or surrounding soils, air, surface water or ground water; and

(4) to take corrective action.

Each such inspection shall be commenced and completed with reasonable promptness.

(b)(1) Any records, reports, or information obtained from any persons under this section shall be available to the public, except that upon a showing satisfactory to the Administrator (or the state, as the case may be) by any person that records, reports, or information, or a particular part thereof, to which the Administrator (or the State, as the case may be) or any officer, employee, or representative thereof has access under this section if made public, would divulge information entitled to protection under section 1905 of title 18 of the United States Code, such information or particular portion thereof shall be considered confidential in accordance with the purposes of that section, except that such record, report, document, or information may be disclosed to other officers, employees, or authorized representatives of the United States concerned with carrying out this Act, or when relevent in any proceeding under this Act.

(2) Any person not subject to the provisions of section 1905 of title 18 of the United States Code who knowingly and willfully divulges or discloses any information entitled to protection under this subsection shall, upon conviction, be subject to a fine of not more than $5,000 or to imprisonment not to exceed one year, or both.

(3) In submitting data under this subtitle, a person required to provide such data may—

(A) designate the data which such person believes is entitled to protection under this subsection; and

(B) submit such designated data separately from other data submitted under this subtitle.

A designation under this paragraph shall be made in writing and in such manner as the Administrator may prescribe.

(4) Notwithstanding any limitation contained in this section or any other provision of law, all information reported to, or otherwise obtained, by the Administrator (or any representative of the Administrator) under this Act shall be made available, upon written request of any duly authorized committee of the Congress, to such committee (including records, reports, or information obtained by representatives of the Environmental Protection Agency).

§ 6991e. Federal enforcement

[Sec. 9006] (a)(1) Except as provided in paragraph (2), whenever on the basis of any information, the Administrator determines that any person is in violation of any requirement of this subtitle, the Administrator may issue an order requiring compliance within a reasonable specified time period or the Administrator may commence a civil action in the United States district court in which the violation occurred for appropriate relief, including a temporary or permanent injunction.

(2) In the case of a violation of any requirement of this subtitle where such violation occurs in a State with a program approved under section 9004, the Administrator shall give notice to the State in which such violation has occurred prior to issuing an order or commencing a civil action under this section.

(3) If a violator fails to comply with an order under this subsection within the time specified in the order, he shall be liable for a civil penalty of not more than $25,000 for each day of continued noncompliance.

(b) Any order issued under this section shall become final unless, no later than thirty days after the order is served, the person or persons named therein request a public hearing. Upon such request the Administrator shall promptly conduct a public hearing. In connection with any proceeding under this section the Administrator may issue subpoenas for the attendance and testimony of witnesses and the production of relevant papers, books and documents, and may promulgate rules for discovery procedures.

(c) Any order issued under this section shall state with reasonable specificity the nature of the violation, specify a resonable time for compliance, and assess a penalty, if any, which the Administrator determines is reasonable taking into account the seriousness of the violation and any good faith efforts to comply with the applicable requirements.

(d)(1) Any owner who knowingly fails to notify or submits false information pursuant to section 9002(a) shall be subject to a civil penalty not to exceed $10,000 for each tank for which notification is not given or false information is submitted.

(2) Any owner or operator of an underground storage tank who fails to comply with—

(A) any requirement or standard promulgated by the Administrator under section 9003;

(B) any requirement or standard of a State program approved pursuant to section 9004; or

(C) the provisions of section 9003(g) (entitled "Interim Prohibition") shall be subject to a civil penalty not to exceed $10,000 for each tank for each day of violation.

§ 6991f.   Federal facilities

[Sec. 9007] (a) Each department, agency, and instrumentality of the executive, legislative, and judicial branches of the Federal Government having jurisdiction over any underground storage tank shall be subject to and comply with all Federal, State, interstate, and local requirements, applicable to such tank, both substantive and procedural, in the same manner, and to the same extent, as any other person is subject to such requirements, including payment of reasonable service charges. Neither the United States, nor any agent, employee, or officer thereof, shall be immune or exempt from any process or sanction of any State or Federal court with respect to the enforcement of any such injunctive relief.

(b) The President may exempt any underground storage tanks of any department, agency, or instrumentality in the executive branch from compliance with such a requirement if he determines it to be in the paramount interest of the United States to do so. No such exemption shall be granted due to lack of appropriation unless the President shall have specifically requested such appropriation as a part of the budget process and the Congress shall have failed to make available such requested appropriations. Any exemption shall be for a period not in excess of one year, but additional exemptions may be granted for periods not to exceed one year upon the President's making a new determination. The President shall report each January to the Congress all exemptions from the requirements of this section granted during the preceding calendar year, together with his reason for granting each such exemption.

§ 6991g.   State authority

[Sec. 9008] Nothing in this subtitle shall preclude or deny any right of any State or political subdivision thereof to adopt or enforce any regulation, requirement or standard of performance respecting underground storage tanks that is more stringent than a regulation, requirement, or standard of performance in effect under this subtitle or to impose any additional liability with respect to the release of regulated substances within such State or political subdivision.

§ 6991h. Study of underground storage tanks

[Sec. 9009] (a) Not later than twelve months after the date of enactment of the Hazardous and Solid Waste Amendments of 1984, the Administrator shall complete a study of underground storage tanks used for the storage of regulated substances defined in section 9001(2)(B).

(b) Not later than thirty-six months after the date of enactment of the Hazardous and Solid Waste Amendments of 1984, the Administrator shall complete a study of all other underground storage tanks.

(c) The studies under subsections (a) and (b) shall include an assessment of the ages, types (including methods of manufacture, coatings, protection systems, the compatibility of the construction materials and the installation methods) and locations (including the climate of the locations) of such tanks; soil conditions, water tables, and the hydrogeology of tank locations; the relationship between the foregoing factors and the likelihood of releases from underground storage tanks; the effectiveness and costs of inventory systems, tank testing, and leak detection systems; and such other factors as the Administrator deems appropriate.

(d) Not later than thirty-six months after the date of enactment of the Hazardous and Solid Waste Amendments of 1984, the Administrator shall conduct a study regarding the tanks referred to in section 9001(1)(A) and (B). Such study shall include estimates of the number and location of such tanks and an analysis of the extent to which there may be releases or threatened releases from such tanks into the environment.

(e) Upon completion of the studies authorized by this section, the Administrator shall submit reports to the President and to the Congress containing the results of the studies and recommendations respecting whether or not such tanks should be subject to the preceding provisions of this subtitle.

(f)(1) If any owner or operator (excepting an agency, department, or instrumentality of the United States Government, a State or a political subdivision thereof) shall incur costs, including the loss of business opportunity, due to the closure or interruption of operation of an underground storage tank solely for the purpose of conducting studies authorized by this section, the Administrator shall provide such person fair and equitable reimbursement for such costs.

   (2) All claims for reimbursement shall be filed with the Administrator not later than ninety days after the closure or interruption which gives rise to the claim.

   (3) Reimbursements made under this section shall be from funds appropriated by the Congress pursuant to the authorization contained in section 2007(g).

   (4) For purposes of judicial review, a determination by the Administrator under this subsection shall be considered final agency action.

§ 6991i.   Authorization of appropriations

[Sec. 9010] For authorization of appropriations to carry out this subtitle, see section 2007(g).

6 • Clean Air Act

Recent experience under the Clean Air Act has been characterized by heartening progress in some areas, a discouraging lack of progress in others, and ongoing disputes over the need for the federal government to adopt stricter controls. The major provisions of the Air Act amendments (S 1894) under consideration by the 100th Congress address those areas where the pollution control effort is unfinished. urban ozone compliance, motor vehicle emissions, acid precipitation, and toxic air pollution.d

The difficulty of Congress' task was underscored by its approval December 21, 1987, of legislation delaying sanctions until August 31, 1988, for cities that violate federal ozone and carbon monoxide standards. The 1977 amendments had set December 31, 1987, as the final deadline for attainment, but it became clear that 60 or more cities would miss the deadline for ozone and a comparable number still would exceed the carbon monoxide standard. Ozone pollution is generally considered the more severe long-term attainment problem.

The sanction delay provision, a part of a continuing budget resolution (HJRes 395) signed by President Reagan December 22, 1987, provides: "No restriction or prohibition on construction, permitting, or funding under sections 110(a)(2)(I), 173(4), 176(a), 176(b), or 316 of the Clean Air Act shall be imposed or take effect during the period prior to August 31, 1988, by reason of (1) the failure of any nonattainment area to attain the national primary ambient air quality standard under the Clean Air Act for photochemical oxidants (ozone) or carbon monoxide (or both) by December 31, 1987, (2) the failure of any State to adopt and submit to the Administrator of the Environmental Protection Agency (EPA) an implementation plan that meets the requirements of part D title 1 of such Act and provides for attainment of such standards by December 31, 1987, (3) the failure of any State or designated local government to implement the applicable implementation plan, or (4) any combination of the foregoing. During such period and consistent with the preceding sentence, the issuance of a permit (including required

419

offsets) under section 173 of such Act for the construction or modification of a source in a nonattainment area shall not be denied solely or partially by reason of the reference contained in section 171(1) of such Act to the applicable date established in section 172(a). This subsection shall not apply to any restriction or prohibition in effect under sections 110(a)(2)(I), 173(4), 176(a), 176(b), or 316 of such Act prior to the enactment of this section. Prior to August 31, 1988, the Administrator of the Environmental Protection Agency shall evaluate air quality data and make determinations with respect to which areas throughout the nation have attained, or failed to attain, either or both of the national primary ambient air quality standards referred to in subsection (a) and shall take appropriate steps to designate those areas failing to attain either or both of such standards as nonattainment areas within the meaning of part D of title I of the Clean Air Act."

The eight-month delay was enacted to give Congress enough time to approve S 1894, a bill whose central mission was to clarify the many ambiguities surrounding EPA's enforcement authority over cities that fail to meet the ambient air quality standards.

Title I of the bill would resolve the problem by placing cities in three categories and would require them to attain the standard by 1992, 1997, or 2002, based on the severity of ozone pollution. To avoid sanctions, states would have to submit emission reduction plans for those cities and adopt control measures that would include automobile refueling emission controls, alternative fuel programs for vehicle fleets, adoption of all reasonably available control technologies, and new source compliance with lowest achievable emissions.

Under Title I, EPA would be required to issue control technology guidelines for the following hydrocarbon emission categories: wood furniture coating, auto body refinishing, metal rolling, synthetic organic chemical distillation and batch processing, hazardous waste facilities, bakeries, sewage treatment plants, printing plants, plastic parts coating, and coke oven byproduct plants.

EPA Administrator Lee M. Thomas objected to these provisions in Senate testimony, arguing that not all of the controls are appropriate for many areas.

State and local officials, represented by the State and Territorial Air Pollution Program Administrators and the Association of Local Air Pollution Control Officials, endorse the Senate approach. They feel they lack the clout to implement unpopular control programs on their own and need federal mandates to make further progress.

Environmentalists and their allies in Congress also feel controls on motor vehicles must be tightened for air quality to improve, and S 1894 and its House counterpart, HR 3054, would impose more stringent limits on carbon monoxide, hydrocarbons, and nitrogen oxides. Most of the carbon monoxide, one-half of the hydrocarbons, and one-third of the nitrogen oxides emitted in the United States come from motor vehicles, according to Michael Walsh, former head of EPA's motor vehicle control program. Because automobiles account for so much of the inventory, he said, Congress either must impose tighter controls or tolerate a certain level of pollution.

Automobile manufacturers counter that most emissions have been controlled already, and that a wiser course would be to upgrade vehicle inspection-and-maintenance programs to get the maximum emission reduction from the existing fleet. Automobile hydrocarbon and carbon monoxide emissions have been reduced by 96 percent compared with uncontrolled levels, and nitrogen oxide emissions have been cut 76 percent, according to Richard L. Klimisch, head of environmental activities for the General Motors Corp. Tighter controls would be enormously expensive and would yield no appreciable improvement in air quality, he told the House Energy and Commerce Subcommittee on Health and the Environment July 10, 1987.

Rep. John D. Dingell (D-Mich), who chairs the Energy and Commerce Committee, is expected to oppose the provisions.

The acid rain controls proposed in S 1894 and HR 2666 also have been challenged by the coal and utility industries, EPA, and members of Congress. Sen. Alan K. Simpson (R-Wyo) summarized the problems in a lengthy statement attached to the committee report on S 1894. The first problem is the sulfur dioxide reduction target in the bill: 12 million tons annually. That control level, Simpson said, would more than double the $2.6 billion annual cost of a 10 million ton reduction. The bill's structure also would force most plants to use scrubbers rather than clean coal or emerging control technology, further increasing the cost, he added.

The bill also would cap each state's aggregate sulfur dioxide emissions at the 1980 levels, a provision Simpson said unfairly penalizes Western and gulf states. These states already have low emission rates, meaning the provision either would limit growth or impose extremely costly control measures, he said. These states, moreover, are thought to contribute little to the acid deposition problem threatening forests and lakes in the Northeast and in Canada. Finally, because acid rain is a regional problem and emissions from individual sources are not critical, it makes little sense to require all 40-year-old plants to meet new source performance standards, as S 1894 would do, Simpson said.

Sen. John Breaux (D-La) commented more generally on S 1894 in the report, calling its controls "expensive and distasteful overkill," penalizing small emission sources in areas which had developed control strategies in good faith. The toxic air pollution control provisions would severely impact the petrochemical industry which is so important to Louisiana's economy. Those provisions were criticized by the Chemical Manufacturers Association as overbroad.

Simpson, Breaux, and others warned that adoption of unnecessarily stringent standards could impede final passage of S 1894. "A bill that talks tough but fails to be enacted into law does nothing to improve the quality of our air," Breaux said.

Despite its shortcomings, the Air Act clearly has promoted significant air quality improvements. Concentrations of airborne lead have declined dramatically across the United States, and carbon monoxide pollution now is expected to be a long-term problem only for a few large cities. Many areas have had limited success in their efforts to reduce ozone levels, however, and most observers agree the pollutant is much more difficult to control than previously believed. Meanwhile, proposals to control acid rain precursors and other pollutants have been hampered by a lack of clear scientific evidence that they impair human health or damage the environment.

Lead concentrations declined 79 percent in 53 large urban areas between 1976 and 1985, according to the most recent EPA air quality trends report. Ambient air quality is a concern only near lead smelters, and only a few remain in operation in the United States. Carbon monoxide concentrations declined 21 percent over the same period, and EPA Administrator Lee M. Thomas has said he expects the trend will continue as newer, cleaner automobiles replace older, unregulated vehicles.

Ozone levels, meanwhile, have held relatively constant over the past five years. Because ozone formation is dependent on the presence of volatile organic compounds and nitrogen oxides, control efforts have been concentrated on reduction of these pollutants, particularly VOCs. Despite these efforts, nationwide emissions of both classes of pollutants have held roughly constant over the past five years at about 20 million metric tons annually. EPA and other public and private agencies are studying the role of nitrogen oxide control in ozone reduction programs. EPA also is considering whether to tighten the ozone standard, which now is set at 0.12 parts per million, measured as a one-hour average.

The original Clean Air Act was passed in 1955 (PL 84-159). In 1967 it was wholly replaced by the Air Quality Act of 1967 (PL 90-148), although the name Clean Air Act is still used. Amendments adopted in 1970 (PL 91-604) require EPA to set ambient air quality standards, to control emissions from stationary and mobile sources, to control emissions from new stationary sources, and to control hazardous air pollutants. The 1977 amendments (PL 95-95) adopted a standardized basis for rulemaking regarding criteria for national ambient air quality standards, new source performance standards, hazardous air pollution standards, motor vehicle standards, fuel and fuel-additive provisions, and aircraft emission standards.

Clean Air Act

(P.L. 84-159, approved July 14, 1955; as last amended by P.L. 98-213, approved December 8, 1983)

Subchapter I. Air Pollution Prevention and Control

Part A

Air Quality and Emission Limitations

§ 7401. Congressional findings and declaration of purposes

[Sec. 101] (a) The Congress finds—
(1) that the predominant part of the Nation's population is located in its rapidly expanding metropolitan and other urban areas, which generally cross the boundary lines of local jurisdictions and often extend into two or more States;
(2) that the growth in the amount and complexity of air pollution brought about by urbanization, industrial development, and the increasing use of motor vehicles, has resulted in mounting dangers to the public health and welfare, including injury to agricultural crops and livestock, damage to and the deterioration of property, and hazards to air and ground transportation;
(3) that the prevention and control of air pollution at its source is the primary responsibility of States and local governments; and

(4) that Federal financial assistance and leadership is essential for the development of cooperative Federal, State, regional, and local programs to prevent and control air pollution.

(b) The purposes of this title are—

(1) to protect and enhance the quality of the Nation's air resources so as to promote the public health and welfare and the productive capacity of its population;

(2) to initiate and accelerate a national research and development program to achieve the prevention and control of air pollution;

(3) to provide technical and financial assistance to State and local governments in connection with the development and execution of their air pollution prevention and control programs; and

(4) to encourage and assist the development and operation of regional air pollution control programs.

§ 7402. Cooperative activities

[Sec. 102] (a) The Administrator shall encourage cooperative activities by the States and local governments for the prevention and control of air pollution; encourage the enactment of improved and, so far as practicable in the light of varying conditions and needs, uniform State and local laws relating to the prevention and control of air pollution; and encourage the making of agreements and compacts between States for the prevention and control of air pollution.

(b) The Administrator shall cooperate with and encourage cooperative activities by all Federal departments and agencies having functions relating to the prevention and control of air pollution, so as to assure the utilization in the Federal air pollution control program of all appropriate and available facilities and resources within the Federal Government.

(c) The consent of the Congress is hereby given to two or more States to negotiate and enter into agreements or compacts, not in conflict with any law or treaty of the United States, for (1) cooperative effort and mutual assistance for the prevention and control of air pollution and the enforcement of their respective laws relating thereto, and (2) the establishment of such agencies, joint or otherwise, as they may deem desirable for making effective such agreements or compacts. No such agreement or compact shall be binding or obligatory upon any State a party thereto unless and until it has been approved by Congress. It is the intent of Congress that no agreement or compact entered into between States after the date of enactment of the Air Quality Act of 1967, which relates to the control and abatement of air pollution in an air quality control region, shall provide for participation by a State which is not included (in whole or in part) in such air quality control region.

§ 7403. Research, investigation, training, and other activities

[Sec. 103] (a) The Administrator shall establish a national research and development program for the prevention and control of air pollution and as part of such program shall—

(1) conduct, and promote the coordination and acceleration of, research, investigations, experiments, demonstrations, surveys, and studies relating to the causes, effects, extent, prevention, and control of air pollution;

(2) encourage, cooperate with, and render technical services and provide financial assistance to air pollution control agencies and other appropriate public or private agencies, institutions, and organizations, and individuals in the conduct of such activities;

(3) conduct investigations and research and make surveys concerning any specific problem of air pollution in cooperation with any air pollution control agency with a view to recommending a solution of such problem, if he is requested to do so by such agency or if, in his judgment, such problem may affect any community or communities in a State other than that in which the source of the matter causing or contributing to the pollution is located;

(4) establish technical advisory committees composed of recognized experts in various aspects of air pollution to assist in the examination and evaluation of research progress and proposals and to avoid duplication of research; and

(5) conduct and promote coordination and acceleration of training for individuals relating to the causes, effects, extent, prevention, and control of air pollution.

(b) In carrying out the provisions of the preceding subsection the Administrator is authorized to—

(1) collect and make available, through publications and other appropriate means, the results of and other information, including appropriate recommendations by him in connection therewith pertaining to such research and other activities;

(2) cooperate with other Federal departments and agencies, with air pollution control agencies, with other public and private agencies, institutions, and organizations, and with any industries involved, in the preparation and conduct of such research and other activities;

(3) make grants to air pollution control agencies, to other public or nonprofit private agencies, institutions, and organizations, and to individuals, for purposes stated in subsection (a)(1) of this section;

(4) contract with public or private agencies, institutions, and organizations, and with individuals, without regard to sections 3648 and 3709 of the Revised Statutes (31 U.S.C. 529; 41 U.S.C. 5);

(5) establish and maintain research fellowships, in the Environmental Protection Agency and at public or nonprofit private educational institutions or research organizations;

(6) collect and disseminate, in cooperation with other Federal departments and agencies, and with other public or private agencies,

institutions, and organizations having related responsibilities, basic data on chemical, physical, and biological effects of varying air quality and other information pertaining to air pollution and the prevention and control thereof; and

(7) develop effective and practical processes, methods, and prototype devices for the prevention or control of air pollution.

In carrying out the provisions of subsection (a), the Administrator shall provide training for, and make training grants to, personnel of air pollution control agencies and other persons with suitable qualifications and make grants to such agencies, to other public or nonprofit private agencies, institutions, and organizations for the purposes stated in subsection (a)(5), Reasonable fees may be charged for such training provided to persons other than personnel of air pollution control agencies but such training shall be provided to such personnel of air pollution control agencies without charge.

(c) in carrying out the provisions of subsection (a) of this section the Administrator shall conduct research on, and survey the results of other scientific studies on, the harmful effects to the health or welfare of persons by the various known air pollutants.

(d) The Administrator is authorized to construct such facilities and staff and equip them as he determines to be necessary to carry out his functions under this Act.

(e) If in the judgment of the Administrator, an air pollution problem of substantial significance may result from discharge or discharges into the atmosphere, he may call a conference concerning this potential air pollution problem to be held in or near one or more of the places where such discharge or discharges are occurring or will occur. All interested persons shall be given an opportunity to be heard as such conference, either orally or in writing, and shall be permitted to appear in person or by representative in accordance with procedures prescribed by the Administrator. If the Administrator finds, on the basis of evidence presented at such conference, that the discharge or discharges if permitted to take place or continue are likely to cause or contribute to air pollution subject to abatement under section 115, he shall send such findings, together with recommendations concerning the measures which he finds reasonable and suitable to prevent such pollution, to the person or persons whose actions will result in the discharge or discharges involved; to air pollution agencies of the State or States and of the municipality or municipalities where such discharge or discharges will originate; and to the interstate air pollution control agency, if any, in the jurisdictional area of which any such municipality is located. Such findings and recommendations shall be advisory only, but shall be admitted together with the record of the conference, as part of the proceedings under subsections (b), (c) (d), (e), and (f) of section 115.

(f)(1) In carrying out research pursuant to this Act, the Administrator shall give special emphasis to research on the short- and long-term effects of air pollutants on public health and welfare. In the furtherance of such research, he shall conduct an accelerated research program—

    (A) to improve knowledge of the contribution of air pollutants to the occurrence of adverse effects on health, including, but not limited to, behavioral, physiological, toxicological, and biochemical effects; and

    (B) to improve knowledge of the short- and long-term effects of air pollutants on welfare.

  (2) In carrying out the provisions of this subsection the Administrator may—

    (A) conduct epidemiological studies of the effect of air pollutants on mortality and morbidity;

    (B) conduct clinical and laboratory studies on the immunologic, biochemical, physiological, and the toxicological effects including carcinogenic, teratogenic, and mutagenic effects of air pollutants;

    (C) utilize, on a reimbursable basis, the facilities of existing Federal scientific laboratories and research centers;

    (D) utilize the authority contained in paragraphs (1) through (4) subsection (b); and

    (E) consult with other appropriate Federal agencies to assure that research or studies conducted pursuant to this subsection will be coordinated with research and studies of such other Federal agencies.

  (3) In entering into contracts under this subsection, the Administrator is authorized to contract for a term not to exceed 10 years in duration. For the purposes of this paragraph, there are authorized to be appropriated $15,000,000. Such amounts as are appropriated shall remain available until expended and shall be in addition to any other appropriations under this Act.

§ 7404. Research relating to fuels and vehicles

[Sec. 104] (a) The Administrator shall give special emphasis to research and development into new and improved methods, having industrywide application, for the prevention and control of air pollution resulting from the combustion of fuels. In furtherance of such research and development he shall

  (1) conduct and accelerate research programs directed toward development of improved, low-cost techniques for

    (A) control of combustion byproducts of fuels,

    (B) removal of potential air pollutants from fuels prior to combustion.

    (C) control of emissions from the evaporation of fuels,

    (D) improving efficiency of fuels combustion so as to decrease atmospheric emissions, and

    (E) producing synthetic or new fuels which when used, result in decreased atmospheric emissions,

(2) provide for Federal grants to public or nonprofit agencies, institutions, and organizations and to individuals, and contracts with public or private agencies, institutions, or persons, for payment of (A) part of the cost of acquiring, constructing, or otherwise securing for research and development purposes, new or improved devices or methods having industrywide application of preventing or controlling discharges into the air of various types of pollutants; (B) part of the cost of programs to develop low emission alternatives to the present internal combustion engine; (C) the cost to purchase vehicles and vehicle engines or portions thereof for research, development, and testing purposes; and (D) carrying out the other provisions of this section, without regard to sections 3648 and 3709 of the Revised Statutes (31 U.S.C. 529; 41 U.S.C. 5): *Provided*, That research or demonstration contracts awarded pursuant to this subsection (including contracts for construction) may be made in accordance with, and subject to the limitations provided with respect to research contracts of the military departments in section 2353 of title 10, United States Code, except that the determination, approval, and certification required thereby shall be made by the Administrator: *Provided further*, That no grant may be made under this paragraph in excess of $1,500,000;

(3) determine, by laboratory and pilot plant testing, the results of air pollution research and studies in order to develop new or improved processes and plant designs to the point where they can be demonstrated on a large and practical scale;

(4) construct, operate, and maintain, or assist in meeting the cost of the construction, operation, and maintenance of new or improved demonstration plants or processes which have promise of accomplishing the purposes of this Act;

(5) study new or improved methods for the recovery and marketing or commercially valuable byproducts resulting from the removal of pollutions.

(b) In carrying out the provisions of the section, the Administrator may

(1) conduct and accelerate research and development of low-cost instrumentation techniques to facilitate determination of quantity and quality of air pollutant emissions, including, but not limited to, automotive emissions;

(2) utilize, on a reimbursable basis, the facilities of existing Federal scientific laboratories;

(3) establish and operate necessary facilities and test sites at which to carry on the research, testing, development, and programming necessary to effectuate the purposes of this section;

(4) acquire secret processes, technical data, inventions, patent applications, patents, licenses, and an interest in lands, plants, and facilities, and other property or rights by purchase, license, lease, or donation; and

(5) cause on-site inspections to be made of promising domestic and foreign projects, and cooperate and participate in their development in instances in which the purposes of the Act will be served thereby.

(c) For the purposes of this section there are authorized to be appropriated $75,000,000 for the fiscal year ending June 30, 1971, $125,000,000 for the fiscal year ending June 30, 1972, $150,000,000 for the fiscal year ending June 30, 1973, $150,000,000 for the fiscal year ending June 30, 1974, and $150,000,000 for the fiscal year ending June 30, 1975. Amounts appropriated pursuant to this subsection shall remain available until expended.

§ 7405. Grants for support of air pollution planning and control programs

[Sec. 105] (a)(1)(A) The Administrator may make grants to air pollution control agencies in an amount up to two-thirds of the cost of planning, developing, establishing, or improving, and up to one-half of the cost of maintaining, programs for the prevention and control of air pollution or implementation of national primary and secondary ambient air quality standards.

(B) Subject to subparagraph (C), the Administrator may make grants to air pollution control agencies within the meaning of paragraph (1), (2), or (4) of section 302 (b) in an amount up to three-fourths of the cost of planning, developing, establishing or improving, and up to three-fifths of the cost of maintaining, any program for the prevention and control of air pollution or implementation of national primary and secondary ambient air quality standards in an area that includes two or more municipalities, whether in the same or different States.

(C) With respect to any air quality control region or portion thereof for which there is an applicable implementation plan under section 110, grants under subparagraph (B) may be made only to air pollution control agencies which have substantial responsibilities for carrying out such applicable implementation plan.

(2) Before approving any grant under this subsection to any air pollution control agency within the meaning of sections 302 (b)(2) and 302 (b)(4), the Administrator shall receive assurances that such agency provides for adequate representation of appropriate State, interstate, local, and (when appropriate) international, interests in the air quality control region.

(3) Before approving any planning grant under this subsection to any air pollution control agency within the meaning of section 302(b)(2) and 302(b)(4), the Administrator shall receive assurances that such agency has the capability of developing a comprehensive air quality plan for the air quality control region, which plan shall include (when appro-

priate) a recommended system of alerts to avert and reduce the risk of situations in which there may be imminent and serious danger to the public health or welfare from air pollutants and the various aspects relevant to the establishment of air quality standards for such air quality control region, including the concentration of industries, other commercial establishments, population and naturally occurring factors which shall affect such standards.

(b) From the sums available for the purposes of subsection (a) of this section for any fiscal year, the Administrator shall from time to time make grants to air pollution control agencies upon such terms and conditions as the Administrator may find necessary to carry out the purpose of this section. In establishing regulations for the granting of such funds the Administrator shall, so far as practicable, give due consideration to (1) the population, (2) the extent of the actual or potential air pollution problem, and (3) the financial need of the respective agencies. No agency shall receive any grant under this section during any fiscal year when its expenditures of non-Federal funds for other than non-recurrent expenditures for air pollution control programs will be less than its expenditures were for such programs during the preceding fiscal year, unless the Administrator, after notice and opportunity for public hearing, determines that a reduction in expenditure is attributable to a nonselective reduction in expenditures in the programs of all executive branch agencies of the applicable unit of Government; and no agency shall receive any grant under this section with respect to the maintenance of a program for the prevention and control of air pollution unless the Administrator is satisfied that such grant will be so used as to supplement and, to the extent practicable, increase the level of State, local, or other non-Federal funds that would in the absence of such grant be made available for the maintenance of such program, and will in no event supplant such State, local, or other non-Federal funds. No grant shall be made under this section until the Administrator has consulted with the appropriate official as designated by the Governor or Governors of the State or States affected.

(c) Not more than 10 per centum of the total of funds appropriated or allocated for the purposes of subsection (a) of this section shall be granted for air pollution control programs in any one State. In the case of a grant for a program in an area crossing State boundaries, the Administrator shall determine the portion of such grant that is chargeable to the percentage limitation under this subsection for each State into which such area extends.

In fiscal year 1978 and subsequent fiscal years, subject to the provisions of subsection (b) of this section, no State shall receive less than one-half of 1 per centum of the annual appropriation for grants under this section for grants to agencies within such State.

(d) The Administrator, with the concurrence of any recipient of a grant under this section, may reduce the payments to such recipient by the amount of the pay, allowances, traveling expenses, and any other costs in connection with the detail of any officer or employee to the recipient under section 301 of this Act, when such detail is for the convenience of, and at the request of, such recipient and for the purpose of carrying out the provisions of this Act. The amount by which such payments have been reduced shall be available for payment of such costs by the Administrator, but shall, for the purpose of determining the amount of any grant to a recipient under subsection (a) of this section, be deemed to have been paid to such agency.

(e) No application by a State for a grant under this section may be disapproved by the Administrator without prior notice and opportunity for a public hearing in the affected State, and no commitment or obligation of any funds under any such grant may be revoked or reduced without prior notice and opportunity for a public hearing in the affected State (or in one of the affected States if more than one State is affected).

§ 7406.   Interstate air quality agencies; program cost limitations

[Sec. 106] For the purpose of developing implementation plans for any interstate air quality control region designated pursuant to section 107, the Administrator is authorized to pay, for two years, up to 100 per centum of the air quality planning program costs of any agency designed by the Governors of the affected States, which agency shall be capable of recommending to the Governors plans for implementation of national primary and secondary ambient air quality standards and shall include representation from the States and appropriate political subdivisions within the air quality control region. After the initial two-year period the Administrator is authorized to make grants to such agency in an amount up to three-fourths of the air quality program costs of such agency.

§ 7407.   Air quality control regions

[Sec. 107] (a) Each State shall have the primary responsibility for assuring air quality within the entire geographic area comprising such State by submitting an implementation plan for such State which will specify the manner in which national primary and secondary ambient air quality standards will be achieved and maintained within each air quality control region in such State.

(b) For purposes of developing and carrying out implementation plans under section 110—

(1) an air quality control region designated under this section before the date of enactment of the Clean Air Amendments of 1970, or a region designated after such date under subsection (c), shall be an air quality control region; and

(2) the portion of such State which is not part of any such designated region shall be an air quality control region, but such portion may be subdivided by the State into two or more air quality control regions with the approval of the Administrator.

(c) The Administrator shall, within 90 days after the date of enactment of the Clean Air Amendments of 1970, after consultation with appropriate State and local authorities, designate as an air quality control region any interstate area or major intrastate area which he deems necessary or appropriate for the attainment and maintenance of ambient air quality standards. The Administrator shall immediately notify the governors of the affected States of any designation made under this subsection.

(d)(1) For the purpose of transportation control planning, part D (relating to nonattainment), part C (relating to prevention of significant deterioration of air quality), and for other purposes, each State, within one hundred and twenty days after the date of enactment or the Clean Air Act Amendments of 1977, shall submit to the Administrator a list, together with a summary of the available information, identifying those air quality control regions, or portions thereof, established pursuant to this section in such State which on the date of enactment of the Clean Air Act Amendments of 1977—

   (A) do not meet a national primary ambient air quality standard for any air pollutant other than sulfur dioxide or particulate matter;
   (B) do not meet, or in the judgment of the State may not in the time period required by an applicable implementation plan attain or maintain, any national primary ambient air quality standard for sulfur dioxide or particulate matter;
   (C) do not meet a national secondary ambient air quality standard;
   (D) cannot be classified under subparagraph (B) or (C) of this paragraph on the basis of available information, for ambient air quality levels for sulfur oxides or particulate matter; or
   (E) have ambient air quality levels better than any national primary or secondary air quality standard other than for sulfur dioxide or particulate matter, or for which there is not sufficient data to be classified under subparagraph (A) or (C) of this paragraph.

(2) Not later than sixty days after submittal of the list under paragraph (1) of this subsection the Administrator shall promulgate each such list with such modifications as he deems necessary. Whenever the Administrator proposes to modify a list submitted by a State, he shall notify the State and request all available data relating to such region or portion, and provide such State with an opportunity to demonstrate why any proposed modification is inappropriate.

(3) Any region or portion thereof which is not classified under subparagraph (B) or (C) of paragraph (1) of this subsection for sulfur dioxide or particulate matter within one hundred and eighty days after enactment of the Clean Air Act Amendments of 1977 shall be deemed to be a region classified under subparagraph (D) of paragraph (1) of this subsection.

(4) A State may from time to time review, and as appropriate revise and submit, the list required under this subsection. The Administrator shall consider and promulgate such revised list in accordance with this subsection.

(e)(1) Except as otherwise provided in paragraph (2), the Governor of each State is authorized, with the approval of the Administrator, to redesignate from time to time the air quality control regions within such State for purposes of efficient and effective air quality management. Upon such redesignation the list under subsection (d) shall be modified accordingly.

    (2) In the case of an air quality control region in a State, or part of such region, which the Administrator finds may significantly affect air pollution concentrations in another State, the Governor of the State in which such region, or part of a region, is located may redesignate from time to time the boundaries of so much of such air quality control region as is located within such State only with the approval of the Administrator and with the consent of all Governors of all States which the Administrator determines may be significantly affected.

    (3) No compliance date extension granted under section 113(d)(5) (relating to coal conversion) shall cease to be effective by reason of the regional limitation provided in section 113(d)(5) if the violation of such limitation is due solely to a redesignation of a region under this subsection.

§ 7408. Air quality criteria and control techniques

[Sec. 108] (a)(1) For the purpose of establishing national primary and secondary ambient air quality standards, the Administrator shall within 30 days after the date of enactment of the Clean Air Amendments of 1970 publish, and shall from time to time thereafter revise, a list which includes each air pollutant—

    (A) emissions of which, in his judgment, cause or contribute to air pollution which may reasonably be anticipated to endanger public health or welfare;

    (B) the presence of which in the ambient air results from numerous or diverse mobile or stationary sources; and

    (C) for which air quality criteria had not been issued before the date of enactment of the Clean Air Amendments of 1970, but for which he plans to issue air quality criteria under this section.

    (2) The Administrator shall issue air quality criteria for an air pollutant within 12 months after he has included such pollutant in a list under paragraph (1). Air quality criteria for an air pollutant shall accurately reflect the latest scientific knowledge useful in indicating the kind and extent of all identifiable effects on public health or welfare which may be expected from the presence of such pollutant in the ambient air, in varying quantities. The criteria for an air pollutant, to the extent practicable, shall include information on—

    (A) those variable factors (including atmospheric conditions) which of themselves or in combination with other factors may alter the effects on public health or welfare of such air pollutant;

(B) the types of air pollutants which, when present in the atmosphere, may interact with such pollutant to produce an adverse effect on public health or welfare; and

(C) any known or anticipated adverse effects on welfare.

(b)(1) Simultaneously with the issuance of criteria under subsection (a), the Administrator shall, after consultation with appropriate advisory committees and Federal departments and agencies, issue to the States and appropriate air pollution control agencies information on air pollution control techniques, which information shall include data relating to the cost of installation and operation, energy requirements, emission reduction benefits, and environmental impact of the emission control technology. Such information shall include such data as are available on available technology and alternative methods of prevention and control of air pollution. Such information shall also include data on alternative fuels, processes, and operating methods which will result in elimination or significant reduction of emissions.

(2) In order to assist in the development of information on pollution control techniques, the Administrator may establish a standing consulting committee for each air pollutant included in a list published pursuant to subsection (a)(1), which shall be comprised of technically qualified individuals representative of State and local governments, industry, and the academic community. Each such committee shall submit as appropriate, to the Administrator information related to that required by paragraph (1).

(c) The Administrator shall from time to time review, and, as appropriate, modify, and reissue any criteria or information on control techniques issued pursuant to this section.

Not later than six months after the date of the enactment of the Clean Air Act Amendments of 1977, the Administrator shall revise and reissue criteria relating the concentrations of NO_2 over such period (not more than three hours) as he deems appropriate. Such criteria shall include a discussion of nitric and nitrous acids, nitrites, nitrates, nitrosamines, and other carcinogenic and potentially carcinogenic derivatives of oxides of nitrogen.

(d) The issuance of air quality criteria and information on air pollution control techniques shall be announced in the Federal Register and copies shall be made available to the general public.

(e) The Administrator shall, after consultation with the Secretary of Transportation and the Secretary of Housing and Urban Development and State and local officials and within 180 days after the enactment of this subsection, and from time to time thereafter, publish guidelines on the basic program elements for the planning process assisted under section 175 of part D. Such guidelines shall include information on—

(1) methods to identify and evaluate alternative planning and control activities;

(2) methods of reviewing plans on a regular basis as conditions change or

new information is presented;

(3) identification of funds and other resources necessary to implement the plan, including interagency agreements on providing such funds and resources;

(4) methods to assure participation by the public in all phases of the planning process; and

(5) such other methods as the Administrator determines necessary to carry out a continuous planning process.

(f)(1) The Administrator shall publish and make available to appropriate Federal agencies, States, and air pollution control agencies, including agencies assisted under Section 175 within 6 months after enactment of this subsection for clauses (i), (ii), (iii), and (iv) of subparagraph (A) and within one year after the enactment of this subsection for the balance of this subsection (and from time to time thereafter),

(A) information, prepared, as appropriate, in cooperation with the Secretary of Transportation, regarding processes, procedures, and methods to reduce or control each such pollutant, including but not limited to—

(i) motor vehicle emission inspection and maintenance programs;

(ii) programs to control vapor emissions from fuel transfer and storage operations and operations using solvents;

(iii) programs for improved public transit;

(iv) programs to establish exclusive bus and carpool lanes and areawide carpool programs;

(v) programs to limit portions of road surfaces or certain sections of the metropolitan areas to the use of common carriers, both as to time and place;

(vi) programs for long-range transit improvements involving new transportation policies and transportation facilities or major changes in existing facilities;

(vii) programs to control on-street parking;

(viii) programs to construct new parking facilities and operating existing parking facilities for the purpose of park and ride lots and fringe parking;

(ix) programs to limit portions of road surfaces or certain sections of the metropolitan area to the use of nonmotorized vehicles or pedestrian use, both as to time and place;

(x) provisions for employer participation in programs to encourage carpooling, vanpooling, mass transit, bicycling, and walking;

(xi) programs for secure bicycle storage facilities and other facilities, including bicycle lanes, for the convenience and protection of bicyclists, in both public and private areas;

(xii) programs of staggered hours of work;

(xiii) programs to institute road user charges, tolls, or differential

rates to discourage single occupancy automobile trips;
- (xiv) programs to control extended idling of vehicles;
- (xv) programs to reduce emissions by improvements in traffic flow;
- (xvi) programs for the conversion of fleet vehicles to cleaner engines or fuels, or to otherwise control fleet vehicle operations;
- (xvii) programs for retrofit of emission devices or controls on vehicle and engines, other than light duty vehicles, not subject to regulations under section 202 of title II of this Act; and
- (xviii) programs to reduce motor vehicle emissions which are caused by extreme cold start conditions;
- (B) information or additional methods or strategies that will contribute to the reduction of mobile source related pollutants during periods in which any primary ambient air quality standard will be exceeded and during episodes for which an air pollution alert, warning or emergency has been declared;
- (C) information on other measures which may be employed to reduce the impact on public health or protect the health of sensitive or susceptible individuals or groups; and
- (D) information on the extent to which any process, procedure, or method to reduce or control such air pollutant may cause an increase in the emissions or formation of any other pollutant.
- (2) In publishing such information the Administrator shall also include an assessment of—
  - (A) the relative effectiveness of such processes, procedures, and methods;
  - (B) the potential effect of such processes, procedures, and methods on transportation systems and the provision of transportation services; and
- (c) the environment, energy, and economic impact of such processes, procedures, and methods.

§ 7409. National primary and secondary ambient air quality standards

[Sec. 109] (a)(1) The Administrator—
- (A) within 30 days after the date of enactment of the Clean Air Amendments of 1970, shall publish proposed regulations prescribing a national primary ambient air quality standard and a national secondary ambient air quality standard for each air pollutant for which air quality criteria have been issued prior to such date of enactment; and
- (B) after a reasonable time for interested persons to submit written comments thereon (but no later than 90 days after the initial publication of such proposed standards) shall by regulation promulgate such proposed national primary and secondary ambient

air quality standards with such modifications as he deems appropriate.

(2) With respect to any air pollutant for which air quality criteria are issued after the date of enactment of the Clean Air Amendments of 1970, the Administrator shall publish, simultaneously with the issuance of such criteria and information, proposed national primary and secondary ambient air quality standards for any such pollutant. The procedure provided for in paragraph (1) (B) of this subsection shall apply to the promulgation of such standards.

(b)(1) National primary ambient air quality standards, prescribed under subsection (a) shall be ambient air quality standards the attainment and maintenance of which the judgment of the Administrator, based on such criteria and allowing an adequate margin of safety, are requisite to protect the public health. Such primary standards may be revised in the same manner as promulgated.

(2) Any national secondary ambient air quality standard prescribed under subsection (a) shall specify a level of air quality the attainment and maintenance of which in the judgment of the Administrator, based on such criteria, is requisite to protect the public welfare from any known or anticipated adverse effects associated with the presence of such air pollutant in the ambient air. Such secondary standards may be revised in the same manner as promulgated.

(c) The Administrator shall, not later than one year after the date of the enactment of the Clean Air Act Amendments of 1977, promulgate a national primary ambient air quality standard for NO_2 concentrations over a period of not more than 3 hours unless, based on the criteria issued under section 108(c), he finds that there is no significant evidence that such a standard for such a period is requisite to protect public health.

(d)(1) Not later than December 31, 1980, and at five year intervals thereafter, the Administrator shall complete a thorough review of the criteria published under section 108 and the national ambient air quality standards promulgated under this section and shall make such revisions in such criteria and standards and promulgate such new standards as may be appropriate in accordance with section 108 and subsection (b) of this section. The Administrator may review and revise criteria or promulgate new standards earlier or more frequently than required under this paragraph.

(2)(A) The Administrator shall appoint an independent scientific review committee composed of seven members including at least one member of the National Academy of Sciences, one physician, and one person, representing State air pollution control agencies.

(B) Not later than January 1, 1980, and at five-year intervals thereafter, the committee referred to in subparagraph (A) shall complete a review of the criteria published under section 108 and the national primary and secondary ambient air quality standards promulgated under this section and shall recommend to the

Administrator any new national ambient air quality-standards and revisions of existing criteria and standards as may be appropriate under section 108 and subsection (b) of this section.

(C) Such committee shall also (i) advise the Administrator of areas in which additional knowledge is required to appraise the adequacy and basis of existing, new, or revised national ambient air quality standards, (ii) describe the research efforts necessary to provide the required information, (iii) advise the Administrator on the relative contribution to air pollution concentrations of natural as well as anthropogenic activity, and (iv) advise the Administrator of any adverse public health, welfare, social, economic, or energy effects which may result from various strategies for attainment and maintenance of such national ambient air quality standards.

§ 7410. State implementation plans for national primary and secondary ambient air quality standards

[Sec. 110] (a)(1) Each State shall, after reasonable notice and public hearings, adopt and submit to the Administrator, within nine months after the promulgation of a national primary ambient air quality standard (or any version thereof) under section 109 for any air pollutant, a plan which provides for implementation, maintenance, and enforcement of such primary standard in each air quality control region (or portion thereof) within such State. In addition, such State shall adopt and submit to the Administrator (either as a part of a plan submitted under the preceding sentence or separately) within nine months after the promulgation of a national ambient air quality secondary standard (or revision thereof), a plan which provides for implementation, maintenance, and enforcement of such secondary standard in each air quality control region (or portion thereof) within such State. Unless a separate public hearing is provided, each State shall consider its plan implementing such secondary standard at the hearing required by the first sentence of this paragraph.

(2) The Administrator shall, within four months after the date required for submission of a plan under paragraph (1), approve or disapprove such plan or any portion thereof. The Administrator shall approve such plan, or any portion thereof, if he determines that it was adopted after reasonable notice and hearing and that—

(A) except as may be provided in subparagraph (I), (i), in the case of a plan implementing a national primary ambient air quality standard, it provides for the attainment of such primary standard as expeditiously as practicable but (subject to subsection(e)) in no case later than three years from the date of approval of such plan (or any revision thereof to take account of a revised primary standard); and (ii) in the case of a plan implementing a national secondary ambient air quality standard, it specifies a reasonable time at which such secondary standard will be attained;

(B) it includes emission limitations, schedules, and timetables for compliance with such limitations, and such other measures as may be necessary to insure attainment and maintenance of such primary or secondary standard, including, but not limited to, transportation controls, air quality maintenance plans, and pre-construction review of direct sources of air pollution as provided in subparagraph (D);

(C) it includes provision for establishment and operation of appropriate devices, methods, systems, and procedures necessary to (i) monitor, compile, and analyze data on ambient air quality and, (ii) upon request, make such data available to the Administrator;

(D) it includes a program to provide for the enforcement of emission limitations and regulation of the modification, construction, and operation of any stationary source, including a permit program as required in parts C and D and a permit or equivalent program for any major emitting facility, within such region as necessary to assure (i) that national ambient air quality standards are achieved and maintained, and (ii) a procedure, meeting the requirements of paragraph (4), for review (prior to construction or modification) of the location of new sources to which a standard of performance will apply;

(E) it contains adequate provisions (1) prohibiting any stationary source within the State from emitting any air pollutant in amounts which will (I) prevent attainment or maintenance by any other State of any such national primary or secondary ambient air quality standard or (II) interfere with measures required to be included in the applicable implementation plan for any other State under part C to prevent significant deterioration of air quality or to protect visibility, and (ii) insuring compliance with the requirements of section 126, relating to interstate pollution abatement;

(F) it provides (i) necessary assurances that the State will have adequate personnel, funding, and authority to carry out such implementation plan, (ii) requirements for installation of equipment by owners or operators of stationary sources to monitor emissions from such sources, (iii) for periodic reports on the nature and amounts of such emissions; (iv) that such reports shall be correlated by the State agency with any emission limitations or standards established pursuant to this act, which reports shall be available at reasonable times for public inspection; (v) for authority comparable to that in section 303, and adequate contingency plans to implement such authority; and (vi) requirements that the State comply with the requirements respecting State boards under Section 128;

(G) it provides, to the extent necessary and practicable, for periodic inspection and testing of motor vehicles to enforce compliance with applicable emission standards;

(H) it provides for revision, after public hearings, of such plan (i) from time to time as may be necessary to take account of revisions of such national primary or secondary ambient air quality standard or the availability of improved or more expeditious methods of achieving such primary or secondary standard; or (ii) except as provided in paragraph (3)(C), whenever the Administrator finds on the basis of information available to him that the plan is substantially inadequate to achieve the national ambient air quality primary or secondary standard which it implements or to otherwise comply with any additional requirements established under the Clean Air Act Amendments of 1977; and

(I) it provides that after June 30, 1979, no major stationary source shall be constructed or modified in any nonattainment area (as defined in section 171(2) to which such plan applies, if the emissions from such facility will cause or contribute to concentrations of any pollutant for which a national ambient air quality standard is exceeded in such area, unless, as of the time of application for a permit for such construction or modification, such plan meets the requirements of part D (relating to nonattainment areas);

(J) it meets the requirements of section 121 (relating to consultation), section 127 (relating to public notification), part C (relating to prevention of significant deterioration of air quality and visibility protection); and

(K) it requires the owner or operator or each major stationary source to pay to the permitting authority as a condition of any permit required under this Act a fee sufficient to cover—

　(i) the reasonable costs of reviewing and acting upon any application for such a permit, and

　(ii) if the owner or operator receives a permit for such source, whether before or after the date of enactment of this subparagraph, the reasonable costs (incurred after such date of enactment) of implementing and enforcing the terms and conditions of any such permit (not including any court costs or other costs associated with any enforcement action).

(3)(A) The Administrator shall approve any revision of an implementation plan applicable to an air quality control region if he determines that it meets the requirements of paragraph (2) and has been adopted for the State after reasonable notice and public hearings.

(B) As soon as practicable, the Administrator shall, consistent with the purposes of this Act and the Energy Supply and Environmental Coordination Act of 1974, review each State's applicable implementation plans and report to the State on whether such plans can be revised in relation to fuel burning stationary sources (or persons supplying fuel to such sources) without interfering with the attainment and maintenance of any national ambient air quality standard within the period permitted in this section. If the Administrator determines that any such plan can be revised, he shall notify the State that a plan revision may be submitted by the State. Any plan revision which is submitted by the State shall, after public notice and opportunity for public hearing, be approved by the Administrator if the revision relates only to fuel burning stationary sources (or person supplying fuel to such sources), and the plan as revised complies with paragraph (2) of this subsection. The Administrator shall approve or disapprove any revision no later than three months after its submission.

(C) Neither the State, in the case of a plan (or portion thereof) approved under this subsection, nor the Administrator, in the case of a plan (or portion thereof) promulgated under subsection (c), shall be required to revise an applicable implementation plan because one or more exemptions under section 118 (relating to Federal facilities), enforcement orders under section 113(d), suspensions under section 110(f) or (g) (relating to temporary energy or economic authority), orders under section 119 (relating to primary nonferrous smelters), or extensions of compliance in decrees entered under section 113(e) (relating to iron- and steel-producing operations) have been granted, if such plan would have met the requirements of this section if no such exemptions, orders, or extensions had been granted.

(D) Any applicable implementation plan for which an attainment date later than December 31, 1982, is provided pursuant to section 172(a)(2) shall be revised by July 1, 1979, to include the comprehensive measures and requirements referred to in subsection (c)(5)(B).

(4) The procedure referred to in paragraph (2)(D) for review, prior to construction or modification, of the location of new sources shall (A) provide for adequate authority to prevent the construction or modification of any new source to which a standard of performance under section 111 will apply at any location which the State determines will prevent the attainment or maintenance within any air quality control region (or portion thereof) within such State of a national ambient air quality primary or secondary standard, and (B) require that prior to commencing construction or modification of any such source, the owner or operator thereof shall submit to such State such information as may be necessary to permit the State to make a determination under clause (A).

(5)(A)(i) Any State may include in a State implementation plan, but the Administrator may not require as a condition of approval of such plan under this section, any indirect source review program. The Administrator may approve and enforce, as part of an applicable implementation plan, an indirect source review program which the State chooses to adopt and submit as part of its plan.

(ii) Except as provided in subparagraph (B), no plan promulgated by the Administrator shall include any indirect source review program for any air quality control region, or portion thereof.

(iii) Any State may revise an applicable implementation plan approved under section 110(a) to suspend or revoke any such program included in such plan, provided that such plan meets the requirements of this section.

(B) The Administrator shall have the authority to promulgate, implement and enforce regulations under section 110(c) respecting indirect source review programs which apply only to federally assisted highways, airports, and other major federally assisted indirect sources and federally owned or operated indirect sources.

(C) For purposes of this paragraph, the term "indirect source" means a facility, building, structure, installation, real property, road, or highway which attracts, or may attract, mobile sources of pollution. Such term includes parking lots, parking garages, and other facilities subject to any measure for management of parking supply (within the meaning of section 110(c)(2)(D)(ii)), including regulation of existing off-street parking but such term does not include new or existing on-street parking. Direct emissions sources or facilities at, within, or associated with, any indirect source shall not be deemed indirect sources for the purpose of this paragraph.

(D) For purposes of this section the term "indirect source review program" means the facility-by-facility review of indirect sources of air pollution, including such measures as are necessary to assure, or assist in assuring, that a new or modified indirect source will not attract mobile sources of air pollution, the emissions from which would cause or contribute to air pollution concentrations—

(i) exceeding any national primary ambient air quality standard for a mobile source-related air pollutant after the primary standard attainment date, or

(ii) preventing maintenance of any such standard after such date.

(E) For purposes of this paragraph and paragraph (2)(B), the term "transportation control measure" does not include any measure which is an "indirect source review program".

(6) No State plan shall be treated as meeting the requirements of this section unless such plan provides that in the case of any source which uses a supplemental, or intermittent control system for purposes of meeting the requirements of an order under section 113(d) or section

119 (relating to primary nonferrous smelter orders), the owner or operator of such source may not temporarily reduce the pay of any employee by reason of the use of such supplemental or intermittent or other dispersion dependent control system.

(b) The Administrator may, wherever he determines necessary, extend the period for submission of any plan or portion thereof which implements a national secondary ambient air quality standard for a period not to exceed 18 months from the date otherwise required for submission of such plan.

(c)(1) The Administrator shall, after consideration of any State hearing record, promptly prepare and publish proposed regulations setting forth an implementation plan, or portion thereof, for a State if—

(A) the State fails to submit an implementation plan which meets the requirements of this section.

(B) the plan, or any portion thereof, submitted for such State is determined by the Administrator not to be in accordance with the requirements of this section, or

(C) the State fails, within 60 days after notification by the Administrator or such longer period as he may prescribe, to revise an implementation plan as required pursuant to a provision of its plan referred to in subsection (a)(2)(H).

If such State held no public hearing associated with respect to such plan (or revision thereof), the Administrator shall provide opportunity for such hearing with such State on any proposed regulation. The Administrator shall, within six months after the date required for submission of such plan (or revision thereof), promulgate any such regulations unless, prior to such promulgation, such State has adopted and submitted a plan (or revision) which the Administrator determines to be in accordance with the requirements of this section. Notwithstanding the preceding sentence, any portion of a plan relating to any measure described in the first sentence of section 121 (relating to consultation) or the consultation process required under such section 121 shall not be required to be promulgated before the date eight months after such date required for submission.

(2)(A) The Administrator shall conduct a study and shall submit a report to the Committee on Interstate and Foreign Commerce of the United States House of Representatives and the Committee on Public Works of the United States Senate not later than three months after date of enactment of this paragraph on the necessity of parking surcharge, management of parking supply, preferential bus/carpool lane regulations as part of the applicable implementation plans required under this section to achieve and maintain national primary ambient air quality standards. The study shall include an assessment of the economic impact of such regulations, consideration of alternative means of reducing total vehicle miles traveled, and an assessment of the impact of such regulations on other Federal and State programs dealing with energy or transportation. In the course of such study, the

Administrator shall consult with other Federal officials including, but not limited to, the Secretary of Transportation, the Federal Energy Administrator, and the Chairman of the Council on Environmental Quality.

(B) No parking surcharge regulation may be required by the Administrator under paragraph (1) of this subsection as a part of an applicable implementation plan. All parking surcharge regulations previously required by the Administrator shall be void upon the date of enactment of this subparagraph. This subparagraph shall not prevent the Administrator from approving parking surcharges if they are adopted and submitted by a State as part of an applicable implementation plan. The Administrator may not condition approval of any implementation plan submitted by a State on such plan's including a parking surcharge regulation.

(C) The Administrator is authorized to suspend until January 1, 1975, the effective date or applicability of any regulations for the management of parking supply or any requirement that such regulations be a part of an applicable implementation plan approved or promulgated under this section. The exercise of the authority under this subparagraph shall not prevent the Administrator from approving such regulations if they are adopted and submitted by a State as part of an applicable implementation plan. If the Administrator exercises the authority under this subparagraph, regulations requiring a review or analysis of the impact of proposed parking facilities before construction which take effect on or after January 1, 1975, shall not apply to parking facilities on which construction has been initiated before January 1, 1975.

(D) For purposes of this paragraph—

    (i) The term "parking surcharge regulation" means a regulation imposing or requiring the imposition of any tax, surcharge, fee, or other charge on parking spaces, or any other area used for the temporary storage of motor vehicles.

    (ii) The term "management of parking supply" shall include any requirement providing that any new facility containing a given number of parking spaces shall receive a permit or other prior approval, issuance of which is to be conditioned on air quality considerations.

    (iii) The term "preferential bus/carpool lane" shall include any requirement for the setting aside of one or more lanes of a street or highway on a permanent or temporary basis for the exclusive use of buses or carpools, or both.

(E) No standard, plan, or requirement, relating to management of parking supply or preferential bus/carpool lanes shall be promulgated after the date of enactment of this paragraph by the

Administrator pursuant to this section, unless such promulgation has been subjected to at least one public hearing which has been held in the area affected and for which reasonable notice has been given in such area. If substantial changes are made following public hearings, one or more additional hearings shall be held in such area after such notice.

(3) Upon application of the chief executive officer of any general purpose unit of local government, if the Administrator determines that such unit has adequate authority under State or local law, the Administrator may delegate to such unit the authority to implement and enforce within the jurisdiction of such unit any part of a plan promulgated under this subsection. Nothing in this paragraph shall prevent the Administrator from implementing or enforcing any applicable provision of a plan promulgated under this subsection.

(4) In the case of any applicable implementation plan containing measures requiring—

(A) retrofits on other than commercially owned in-use vehicles,

(B) gas rationing which the Administrator finds would have seriously disruptive and widespread economic or social effects, or

(C) the reduction of the supply of on-street parking spaces, the Governor of the State may, after notice and opportunity for public hearing, temporarily suspend such measures notwithstanding the requirements of this section until January 1, 1979, or the date on which a plan revision under section 110(a)(2)(I) is submitted, whichever is earlier. No such suspension shall be granted unless the State agrees to prepare, adopt, and submit such plan revision as determined by the Administrator.

(5)(A) Any measure in an applicable implementation plan which requires a toll or other charge for the use of a bridge located entirely within one city shall be eliminated from such plan by the Administrator upon application by the Governor of the State, which application shall include a certification by the Governor that he will revise such plan in accordance with subparagraph (B).

(B) In the case of any applicable implementation plan with respect to which a measure has been eliminated under subparagraph (A), such plan shall, not later than one year after the date of the enactment of this subparagraph be revised to include comprehensive measures (including the written evidence required by part D) to:

(i) establish, expand, or improve public transportation measures to meet basic transportation needs, as expeditiously as is practicable; and

(ii) implement transportation control measures necessary to attain and maintain national ambient air quality standards, and such revised plan shall, for the purpose of implementing such comprehensive public transportation measures, include requirements to use (insofar as is necessary) Federal grants, State or local funds, or any combination of such grants and funds as may be consistent with the terms of the legislation providing such grants and funds. Such measures shall, as a substitute for the tolls or charges eliminated under subparagraph (A), provide for emissions reductions equivalent to the reductions which may reasonably be expected to be achieved through the use of the tolls or charges eliminated.

(C) Any revision of an implementation plan for purposes of meeting the requirements of subparagraph (B) shall be submitted in coordination with any plan revision required under part D.

(d) For purposes of this Act, an applicable implementation plan is the implementation plan, or most recent revision thereof, which has been approved under subsection (a) or promulgated under subsection (c) and which implements the requirements of this section.

(e)(1) Upon application of a Governor of a State at the time of submission of any plan implementing a national ambient air quality primary standard, the Administrator may (subject to paragraph (2)) extend the three-year period referred to in subsection (a)(2)(A)(i) for not more than two years for an air quality control region if after review of such plan the Administrator determines that—

(A) one or more emission sources (or classes of moving sources) are unable to comply with the requirements of such plan which implement such primary standard because the necessary technology or other alternatives are not available or will not be available soon enough to permit compliance within such three-year period, and

(B) the State has considered and applied as a part of its plan reasonably available alternative means of attaining such primary standard and has justifiably concluded that attainment of such primary standard within the three years cannot be achieved.

(2) The Administrator may grant an extension under paragraph (1) only if he determines that the State plan provides for—

(A) application of the requirements of the plan which implement such primary standard to all emission sources in such region other than the sources (or classes) described in paragraph (1) (A) within the three-year period, and

(B) such interim measures of control of the sources (or classes) described in paragraph (1) (A) as the Administrator determines to be reasonable under the circumstances.

(f)(1) Upon application by the owner or operator of a fuel burning stationary source, and after notice and opportunity for public hearing, the Governor of the State in which such source is located may petition the President to determine that a national or regional energy emergency exists of such severity that—

(A) a temporary suspension of any part of the applicable implementation plan may be necessary, and

(B) other means of responding to the energy emergency may be inadequate.

Such determination shall not be delegable by the President to any other person. If the President determines that a national or regional energy emergency of such severity exists, a temporary emergency suspension of any part of an applicable implementation plan adopted by the State may be issued by the Governor of any State covered by the President's determination under the conditions specified in paragraph (2) and may take effect immediately.

(2) A temporary emergency suspension under this subsection shall be issued to a source only if the Governor of such State finds that—

(A) there exists in the vicinity of such source a temporary energy emergency involving high levels of unemployment or loss of necessary energy supplies for residential dwellings; and

(B) such unemployment or loss can be totally or partially alleviated by such emergency suspension. Not more than one such suspension may be issued for any source on the basis of the same set of circumstances or on the basis of the same emergency.

(3) A temporary emergency suspension issued by a Governor under this subsection shall remain in effect for a maximum of four months or such lesser period as may be specified in a disapproval order of the Administrator, if any. The Administrator may disapprove such suspension if he determines that it does not meet the requirements of paragraph (2).

(4) This subsection shall not apply in the case of a plan provision or requirement promulgated by the Administrator under subsection (c) of this section, but in any such case the President may grant a temporary emergency suspension for a four month period of any such provision or requirement if he makes the determinations and findings specified in paragraphs (1) and (2).

(5) The Governor may include in any temporary emergency suspension issued under this subsection a provision delaying for a period identical to the period of such suspension any compliance schedule (or increment of progress) to which such source is subject under section 119, as in effect before the date of the enactment of this paragraph or section 113(d) of this Act, upon a finding that such source is unable to comply with such schedule (or increment) solely because of the conditions on the basis of which a suspension was issued under this subsection.

(g)(1) In the case of any State which has adopted and submitted to the Administrator a proposed plan revision which the State determines—

(A) meets the requirements of this section, and

(B) is necessary (i) to prevent the closing for one year or more of any source of air pollution, and (ii) to prevent substantial increases in unemployment which would result from such closing, and which the Administrator has not approved or disapproved under this section within the required four month period, the Governor may issue a temporary emergency suspension of the part of the applicable implementation plan for such State which is proposed to be revised with respect to such source. The determination under subparagraph (B) may not be made with respect to a source which would close without regard to whether or not the proposed plan revision is approved.

(2) A temporary emergency suspension issued by a Governor under this subsection shall remain in effect for a maximum of four months or such lesser period as may be specified in a disapproval order of the Administrator. The Administrator may disapprove such suspension if he determines that it does not meet the requirements of this subsection.

(3) The Governor may include in any temporary emergency suspension issued under this subsection a provision delaying for a period identical to the period of such suspension any compliance schedule (or increment of progress) to which such source is subject under section 119 as in effect before the date of the enactment of this paragraph or section 113(d) upon a finding that such source is unable to comply with such schedule (or increment) solely because of the conditions on the basis of which a suspension was issued under this subsection.

(h)(1) Not later than one year after the date of enactment of the Clean Air Act Amendments of 1977 and annually thereafter, the Administrator shall assemble and publish a comprehensive document for each State setting forth all requirements of the applicable implementation plan for such State and shall publish notice in the Federal Register of the availability of such documents. Each such document shall be revised as frequently as practicable but not less often than annually.

(2) The Administrator may promulgate such regulations as may be reasonably necessary to carry out the purpose of this subsection.

(i) Except for a primary nonferrous smelter order under section 119, a suspension under section 110(f) or (g) (relating to emergency suspensions), an exemption under section 118 (relating to Federal facilities), an order under section 113(d) (relating to compliance orders), a plan promulgation under section 110(c), or a plan revision under section 110(a)(3), no order, suspension, plan revision, or other action modifying any requirement of an applicable implementation plan may be taken with respect to any stationary source by the State or by the Administrator.

(j) As a condition for issuance of any permit required under this title, the owner or operator of each new or modified stationary source which is required to obtain such a permit must show to the satisfaction of the permitting authority that the technological system of continuous emission reduction which is to be used at will enable such source to comply with the standards of performance which are to apply to such source and that the construction or modification and operation of such source will be in compliance with all other requirements of this Act.

§ 7411. Standards of performance for new stationary sources

[Sec. 111] (a) For purposes of this section:

(1) The term "standard of performance" means—

 (A) with respect to any air pollutant emitted from a category of fossil fuel fired stationary sources to which subsection (b) applies, a standard—

   (i) establishing allowable emission limitations for such category of sources, and

   (ii) requiring the achievement of a percentage reduction in the emissions from such category of sources from the emissions which would have resulted from the use of fuels which are not subject to treatment prior to combustion.

 (B) with respect to any air pollution emitted from a category of stationary sources (other than fossil fuel fired sources) to which subsection (b) applies, a standard such as that referred to in subparagraph (A)(i); and

 (C) with respect to any air pollutant emitted from a particular source to which subsection (d) applies, a standard which the State (or the Administrator under the conditions specified in subsection (d)(2)) determines is applicable to that source and which reflects the degree of emission reduction achievable through the application of the best system of continuous emission reduction which (taking into consideration the cost of achieving such emission reduction, and any non-air quality health and environmental impact and energy requirements) the Administrator determines has been adequately demonstrated for that category of sources.

For the purpose of subparagraphs (A)(i) and (ii) and (B), a standard of performance shall reflect the degree of emission limitation and the percentage reduction achievable through application of the best technological system of continuous emission reduction which (taking into consideration the cost of achieving such emission reduction, any non-air quality health and environmental impact and energy requirements) the Administrator determines has been adequately demonstrated. For the purpose of subparagraph (1) (A) (ii), any cleaning of the fuel or reduction in the pollution characteristics of the fuel after extraction and prior to combustion may be credited, as determined under regulations promulgated by the Administrator, to a source which burns such fuel.

(2) The term "new source" means any stationary source, the construction or modification of which is commenced after the publication of regulations (or, if earlier, proposed regulations) prescribing a standard of performance under this section which will be applicable to such source.

(3) The term "stationary source" means any building, structure, facility, or installation which emits or may emit any air pollutant.

(4) The term "modification" means any physical change in, or change in the method of operation of, a stationary source which increases the amount of any air pollutant emitted by such source or which results in the emission of any air pollutant not previously emitted.

(5) The term "owner or operator" means any person who owns, leases, operates, controls, or supervises a stationary source.

(6) The term "existing source" means any stationary source other than a new source.

(7) The term "technological system of continuous emission reduction" means—

   (A) a technological process for production or operation by any source which is inherently lowpolluting or nonpolluting, or

   (B) a technological system for continuous reduction of the pollution generated by a source before such pollution is emitted into the ambient air, including precombustion cleaning or treatment of fuels.

(8) A conversion to coal (A) by reason of an order under section 2(a) of the Energy Supply and Environmental Coordination Act of 1974 or any amendment thereto, or any subsequent enactment which supersedes such Act, or (B) which qualifies under section 113(d)(5)(A)(ii) of this Act, shall not be deemed to be a modification for purposes of paragraphs (2) and (4) of this subsection.

(b)(1)(A) The Administrator shall, within 90 days after the date of enactment of the Clean Air Amendments of 1970, publish (and from time to time thereafter shall revise) a list of categories of stationary sources. He shall include a category of sources in such list if in his judgment he determines it causes, or contributes significantly to air pollution which may reasonably be anticipated to endanger public health or welfare.

   (B) Within 120 days after the inclusion of a category of stationary sources in a list under subparagraph (A), the Administrator shall publish proposed regulations, establishing Federal standards of performance for new sources within such category. The Administrator shall afford interested persons an opportunity for written comment on such proposed regulations. After considering such comments, he shall promulgated, within 90 days after such publication, such standards with such modifications as he deems appropriate. The Administrator shall, at least every four years, review and, if appropriate, revise such standards following the procedure required by this subsection for promulgation of such standards. Standards of performance on revisions thereof shall become effective upon promulgation.

(2) The Administrator may distinguish among classes, types, and sizes within categories of new sources for the purposes of establishing such standards.

(3) The Administrator shall, from time to time, issue information on pollution control techniques for categories of new sources and air pollutants subject to the provisions of this section.

(4) The provisions of this section shall apply to any new source owned or operated by the United States.

(5) Except as otherwise authorized under subsection (h), nothing in this section shall be construed to require, or to authorize the Administrator to require any new or modified source to install and operate any particular technological system of continuous emission reduction to comply with any new source standard of performance.

(6) The revised standards of performance required by enactment of subsection (a)(1)(A)(i) and (ii) shall be promulgated not later than one year after enactment of this paragraph. Any new or modified fossil fuel fired stationary source which commences construction prior .to the date of publication of the proposed revised standards shall not be required to comply with such revised standards.

(c)(1) Each state may develop and submit to the Administrator a procedure for implementing and enforcing standards of performance for new sources located in such State. If the Administrator finds the State procedure is adequate, he shall delegate to such State any authority he has under this Act to implement and enforce such standards.

(2) Nothing in this subsection shall prohibit the Administrator from enforcing any applicable standard of performance under this section.

(d)(1) The Administrator shall prescribe regulations which shall establish a procedure similar to that provided by section 110 under which each State shall submit to the Administrator a plan which (A) establishes standards of performance for any existing source for any air pollutant (i) for which air quality criteria have not been issued or which is not included on a list published under section 108(a) or 112(b) (1)(A) but (ii) to which a standard of performance under this section would apply if such existing source were a new source, and (B) provides for the implementation and enforcement of such standards of performance. Regulations of the Administrator under this paragraph shall permit the State in applying a standard of performance to any particular source under a plan submitted under this paragraph to take into consideration, among other factors, the remaining useful life of the existing source to which such standard applies.

(2) The Administrator shall have the same authority—
  (A) to prescribe a plan for a State in cases where the State fails to submit a satisfactory plan as he would have under section 110(c) in the case of failure to submit an implementation plan, and
  (B) to enforce the provisions of such plan in cases where the State fails to enforce them as he would have under sections 113 and 114 with respect to an implementation plan. In promulgating a standard of performance under a plan prescribed under this

paragraph, the Administrator shall take into consideration, among other factors, remaining useful lives of the sources in the category of sources to which such standard applies.

(e) After the effective date of standards of performance promulgated under this section, it shall be unlawful for any owner or operator of any new source to operate such source in violation of any standard of performance applicable to such source.

(f)(1) Not later than one year after the date of enactment of this subsection, the Administrator shall promulgate regulations listing under subsection (b)(1)(A) the categories of major stationary sources which are not on the date of the enactment of this subsection included on the list required under subsection (b)(1)(A). The Administrator shall promulgate regulations establishing standards of performance for the percentage of such categories of sources set forth in the following table before the expiration of the corresponding period set forth in such table:

Percentage of source categories required to be listed for which standards must be established:	Period by which standards must be promulgated after date list required to be promulgated:
25	2 years
75	3 years
100	4 years

(2) In determining priorities for promulgating standards for categories of major stationary sources for the purpose of paragraph (1), the Administrator shall consider—

(A) the quality of air pollutant emissions which each such category will emit, or will be designed to emit;

(B) the extent to which such pollutant may reasonably be anticipated to endanger public health or welfare; and

(C) the mobility and competitive nature of each such category of sources and the consequent need for nationally applicable new source standards of performance.

(3) Before promulgating any regulations under this subsection or listing any category of major stationary sources as required under this subsection the Administrator shall consult with appropriate representatives of the Governors and of State air pollution control agencies.

(g)(1) Upon application by the Governor of a State showing that the Administrator has failed to specify in regulations under subsection (f)(1) any category of major stationary sources required to be specified under such regulations, the Administrator shall revise such regulations to specify any such category.

(2) Upon application of the Governor of a State, showing that any category of stationary sources which is not included in the list under

subsection (b)(1)(A) contributes significantly to air pollution which may reasonably be anticipated to endanger public health or welfare (notwithstanding that such category is not a category of major stationary sources), the Administrator shall revise such regulations to specify such category of stationary sources.

(3) Upon application of the Governor of a State showing that the Administrator has failed to apply properly the criteria required to be considered under subsection (f)(2), the Administrator shall revise the list under subsection (b)(1)(A) to apply properly such criteria.

(4) Upon application of the Governor of a State showing that—

   (A) a new, innovative, or improved technology or process which achieves greater continuous emission reduction has been adequately demonstrated for any category of stationary sources, and

   (B) as a result of such technology or process, the new source standard of performance in effect under this section for such category no longer reflects the greatest degree of emission limitation achievable through application of the best technological system of continuous emission reduction which (taking into consideration the cost of achieving such emission reduction, and any non-air-quality health and environmental impact and energy requirements) has been adequately demonstrated, the Administrator shall revise such standard of performance for such category accordingly.

(5) Upon application by the Governor of a State showing that the Administrator has failed to list any air pollutant which causes, or contributes to, air pollution which may reasonably be anticipated to result in an increase in mortality or an increase in serious irreversible, or incapacitating reversible, illness as a hazardous air pollutant under section 112, the Administrator shall revise the list of hazardous air pollutants under such section to include such pollutant.

(6) Upon application by the Governor of a State showing that any category of stationary sources of a hazardous air pollutant listed under section 112 is not subject to emission standards under such section, the Administrator shall propose and promulgate such emission standards applicable to such category of sources.

(7) Unless later deadlines for action of the Administrator are otherwise prescribed under this section or section 112, the Administrator shall, not later than three months following the date of receipt of any application by a Governor of a State, either—

   (A) find that such application does not contain the requisite showing and deny such application, or

   (B) grant such application and take the action required under this subsection.

(8) Before taking any action required by subsection (f) or by this subsection, the Administrator shall provide notice and opportunity for public hearing.

(h)(1) For purposes of this section, if in the judgment of the Administrator, it is not feasible to prescribe or enforce a standard of performance, he may instead promulgate a design, equipment, work practice, or operational standard, or combination thereof, which reflects the best technological system of continuous emission reduction which (taking into consideration the cost of achieving such emission reduction, and any nonair quality health and environmental impact and energy requirements) the Administrator determines has been adequately demonstrated. In the event the Administrator promulgates a design or equipment standard under this subsection, he shall include as part of such standard such requirements as will assure the proper operation and maintenance of any such element of design or equipment.

(2) For the purpose of this subsection, the phrase "not feasible to prescribe or enforce a standard of performance" means any situation in which the Administrator determines that (A) a pollutant or pollutants cannot be emitted through a conveyance designed and constructed to emit or capture such pollutant, or that any requirement for, or use of, such a conveyance would be inconsistent with any Federal, State, or local law, or (B) the application of measurement methodology to a particular class of sources is not practicable due to technological or economic limitations.

(3) If after notice and opportunity for public hearing, any person establishes to the satisfaction of the Administrator that an alternative means of emission limitation will achieve a reduction in emission of any air pollutant at least equivalent to the reduction in emissions of such air pollutant achieved under the requirements of paragraph (1), the Administrator shall permit the use of such alternative by the source for purposes of compliance with this section with respect to such pollutant.

(4) Any standard promulgated under paragraph (1) shall be promulgated in terms of standard of performance whenever it becomes feasible to promulgate and enforce such standard in such terms.

(5) Any design, equipment, work practice, or operational standard, or any combination thereof, described in this subsection shall be treated as a standard of performance for purposes of the provisions of this Act (other than the provisions of subsection (a) and this subsection).

(i) Any regulations promulgated by the Administrator under this section applicable to grain elevators shall not apply to country elevators (as defined by the Administrator) which have a storage capacity of less than two million five hundred thousand bushels.

(j)(1)(A) Any person proposing to own or operate a new source may request the Administrator for one or more waivers from the requirements of this section for such source or any portion thereof with respect to any air pollutant to encourage the use of an innovative technological system or systems of continuous emission reduction. The Administrator may, with the consent of the Governor of the State in which the source is to be located, grant a waiver under this paragraph, if the Administrator determines after notice and opportunity for public hearing, that—

> (i) the proposed system or systems have not been adequately demonstrated,
>
> (ii) the proposed system or systems will operate effectively and there is a substantial likelihood that such system or systems will achieve greater continuous emission reduction than that required to be achieved under the standards of performance which would otherwise apply, or achieve at least an equivalent reduction at lower cost in terms of energy, economic, or nonair quality environmental impact,
>
> (iii) the owner or operator of the proposed source has demonstrated to the satisfaction of the Administrator that the proposed system will not cause or contribute to an unreasonable risk to public health, welfare, or safety in its operation, function, or malfunction, and
>
> (iv) the granting of such waiver is consistent with the requirements of subparagraph (C).

In making any determination under clause (ii), the Administrator shall take into account any previous failure of such system or systems to operate effectively or to meet any requirement of the new source performance standards. In determining whether an unreasonable risk exists under clause (iii), the Administrator shall consider, among other factors, whether and to what extent the use of the proposed technological system will cause, increase, reduce, or eliminate emissions of any unregulated pollutants; available methods for reducing or eliminating any risk to public health, welfare, or safety which may be associated with the use of such system; and the availability of other technological systems which may be used to conform to standards under this section without causing or contributing to such unreasonable risk. The Administrator may conduct such tests and may require the owner or operator of the proposed source to conduct such tests and provide such information as is necessary to carry out clause (iii) of this subparagraph. Such requirements shall include a requirement for prompt reporting of the emission of any unregulated pollutant from a system if such pollutant was not emitted, or was emitted in significantly lesser amounts without use of such system.

(B) A waiver under this paragraph shall be granted on such terms and conditions as the Administrator determines to be necessary to assure—

> (i) emissions from the source will not prevent attainment and maintenance of any national ambient air quality standards, and
>
> (ii) proper functioning of the technological system or systems authorized.

Any such term or condition shall be treated as a standard of performance for the purposes of subsection (e) of this section and section 113.

(C) The number of waivers granted under this paragraph with respect to a proposed technological system of continuous emission reduction shall not exceed such number as the Administrator finds necessary to ascertain whether or not such system will achieve the conditions specified in clauses (ii) and (iii) of subparagraph (A).

(D) A waiver under this paragraph shall extend to the sooner of—

(i) the date determined by the Administrator, after consultation with the owner or operator of the source, taking into consideration the design, installation, and capital cost of the technological system or systems being used, or

(ii) the date on which the Administrator determines that such system has failed to—

(I) achieve at least an equivalent continuous emission reduction to that required to be achieved under the standards of performance which would otherwise apply, or

(II) comply with the condition specified in paragraph (1)(A)(iii),

and that such failure cannot be corrected.

(E) In carrying out subparagraph (D)(i), the Administrator shall not permit any waiver for a source or portion thereof to extend beyond the date—

(i) seven years after the date on which any waiver is granted to such source or portion thereof, or

(ii) four years after the date on which such source or portion thereof commences operation, whichever is earlier.

(F) No waiver under this subsection shall apply to any portion of a source other than the portion on which the innovative technological system or systems of continuous emission reduction is used.

(2)(A) If a waiver under paragraph (1) is terminated under clause (ii) of paragraph (1)(D), the Administrator shall grant an extension of the requirements of this section for such source for such minimum period as may be necessary to comply with the applicable standard of performance under this section. Such period shall not extend beyond the date three years from the time such waiver is terminated.

(B) An extension granted under this paragraph shall set forth emission limits and a compliance schedule containing increments of progress which require compliance with the applicable standards of performance as expeditiously as practicable and include such measures as are necessary and practicable in the interim to minimize emissions. Such schedule shall be treated as a standard of performance for purposes of subsection (e) of this section and section 113.

§ 7412. National emission standards for hazardous air pollutants

[Sec. 112] (a) For purposes of this section:

(1) The term "hazardous air pollutant" means an air pollutant to which no ambient air quality standard is applicable and which in the judgment of the Administrator causes, or contributes to, air pollution which may reasonably be anticipated to result in an increase in mortality or an increase in serious irreversible, or incapacitating reversible, illness.

(2) The term "new source" means a stationary source the construction or modification of which is commenced after the Administrator proposes regulations under this section establishing an emission standard which will be applicable to such source.

(3) The terms "stationary source", "modification", "owner' or operator" and "existing source" shall have the same meaning as such terms have under section 111(a).

(b)(1)(A) The Administrator shall, within 90 days after the date of enactment of the Clean Air Amendments of 1970, publish (and shall from time to time thereafter revise) a list which includes each hazardous air pollutant for which he intends to establish an emission standard under this section.

(B) Within 180 days after the inclusion of any air pollutant in such list, the Administrator shall publish proposed regulations establishing emission standards for such pollutant together with a notice of public hearing within 30 days. Not later than 180 days after such publication, the Administrator shall prescribe an emission standard for such pollutant, unless he finds, on the basis of information presented at such hearings, that such pollutant clearly is not a hazardous air pollutant. The Administrator shall establish any such standard at the level which in his judgment provides an ample margin of safety to protect the public health from such hazardous air pollutant.

(C) Any emission standard established pursuant to this section shall become effective upon promulgation.

(2) The Administrator shall, from time to time, issue information on pollutant control techniques for air pollutants subject to the provisions of this section.

(c)(1) After the effective date of any emission standard under this section—

(A) no person may construct any new source or modify any existing source which, in the Administrator's judgment, will emit an air pollutant to which such standard applies unless the Administrator finds that such source if properly operated will not cause emissions in violation of such standard, and

(B) no air pollutant to which such standard applies may be emitted from any stationary source in violation of such standard except that in the case of an existing source—

(i) such standard shall not apply until 90 days after its effective date, and

(ii) the Administrator may grant a waiver permitting such source a period of up to two years after the effective date of a standard to comply with the standard, if he finds that such period is necessary for the installation of controls and that steps will be taken during the period of the waiver to assure that the health of persons will be protected from imminent endangerment.

(2) The President may exempt any stationary source from compliance with paragraphs (1) for a period of not more than two years if he finds that the technology to implement such standards is not available and the operation of such source is required for reasons of national security. An exemption under this paragraph may be extended for one or more additional periods, each period not to exceed two years. The President shall make a report to Congress with respect to each exemption (or extension thereof) made under this paragraph.

(d)(1) Each State may develop and submit to the Administrator a procedure for implementing and enforcing emission standards for hazardous air pollutants for stationary sources located in such State. If the Administrator finds the State procedure is adequate, he shall delegate to such State any authority he has under this Act to implement and enforce such standards.

(2) Nothing in this subsection shall prohibit the Administrator from enforcing any applicable emission standard under this section.

(e)(1) For purposes of this section, if in the judgment of the Administrator, it is not feasible to prescribe or enforce an emission standard for control of hazardous air pollutant or pollutants, he may instead promulgate a design, equipment, work practice, or operational standard, or combination thereof, which in his judgment is adequate to protect the public health from such pollutant or pollutants with an ample margin of safety. In the event the Administrator promulgates a design or equipment standard under this subsection, he shall include as part of such standard such requirements as will assure the proper operation and maintenance of any such element of design or equipment.

(2) For the purpose of this subsection, the phrase "not feasible to prescribe or enforce an emission standard" means any situation in which the Administrator determines that (A) a hazardous pollutant or pollutants cannot be emitted through a conveyance designed and constructed to emit or capture such pollutant, or that any requirement for, or use of, such a conveyance would be inconsistent with any

Federal, State, or local law, or (B) the application of measurement methodology to a particular class of sources is not practicable due to technological or economic limitations.

(3) If after notice and opportunity for public hearing, any person establishes to the satisfaction of the Administrator that an alternative means of emission limitation will achieve a reduction in emissions of any air pollutant at least equivalent to the reduction in emissions of such air pollutant achieved under the requirements of paragraph (1), the Administrator shall permit the use of such alternative by the source for purposes of compliance with this section with respect to such pollutant.

(4) Any standard promulgated under paragraph (1) shall be promulgated in terms of an emission standard whenever it becomes feasible to promulgate and enforce such standard in such terms.

(5) Any design, equipment, work practice, or operational standard, or any combination thereof, described in this subsection shall be treated as an emission standard for purposes of the provisions of this Act (other than the provisions of this subsection).

§ 7413. Federal enforcement procedures

[Sec. 113] (a)(1) Whenever, on the basis of any information available to him, the Administrator finds that any person is in violation of any requirement of an applicable implementation plan, the Administrator shall notify the person in violation of the plan and the State in which the plan applies of such findings. If such violation extends beyond the 30th day after the date of the Administrator's notification, the Administrator may issue an order requiring such person to comply with the requirements of such plan or he may bring a civil action in accordance with subsection (b).

(2) Whenever, on the basis of information available to him, the Administrator finds that violations of an applicable implementation plan are so widespread that such violations appear to result from a failure of the State in which the plan applies to enforce the plan effectively, he shall so notify the State. If the Administrator finds such failure extends beyond the 30th day after such notice, he shall give public notice of such finding. During the period beginning with such public notice and ending when such State satisfies the Administrator that it will enforce such plan (hereafter referred to in this section as "period of Federally assumed enforcement"), the Administrator may enforce any requirement of such plan with respect to any person—

(A) by issuing an order to comply with such requirement, or

(B) by bringing civil action under subsection (b).

(3) Whenever, on the basis of any information available to him, the Administrator finds that any person is in violation of section 111(e) (relating to new source performance standards), 112(c) (relating to

standards for hazardous emissions), or 119(g) (relating to energy-related authorities), or is in violation of any requirement of section 114 (relating to inspections, etc.), he may issue an order requiring such person to comply with such section or requirement, or he may bring a civil action in accordance with subsection (b).

(4) An order issued under this subsection (other than an order relating to a violation of section 112) shall not take effect until the person to whom it is issued has had an opportunity to confer with the Administrator concerning the alleged violation. A copy of any order issued under this subsection shall be sent to the State air pollution control agency of any State in which the violation occurs. Any order issued under this subsection shall state with reasonable specificity the nature of the violation, specify a time for compliance which the Administrator determines is reasonable, taking into account the seriousness of the violation and any good faith efforts to comply with applicable requirements. In any case in which an order under this subsection (or notice to a violator under paragraph (1)) is issued to a corporation, a copy of such order (or notice) shall be issued to appropriate corporate officers.

(5) Whenever, on the basis of information available to him, the Administrator finds that a State is not acting in compliance with any requirement of the regulation referred to in section 129(a)(1) of the Clean Air Act Amendments of 1977 or any plan provisions required under section 110(a)(2)(I) and Part D, he may issue an order prohibiting the construction or modification of any major stationary source in any area to which such provisions apply or he may bring a civil action under subsection (b)(5).

(b) The Administrator shall, in the case of any person which is the owner or operator of a major stationary source, and may, in the case of any other person, commence a civil action for a permanent or temporary injunction, or to assess and recover a civil penalty of not more than $25,000 per day of violation, or both, whenever such person—

(1) violates or fails or refuses to comply with any order issued under subsection (a); or

(2) violates any requirement of an applicable implementation plan (A) during any period of Federally assumed enforcement, or (B) more than 30 days after having been notified by the Administrator under subsection (a)(1) of a finding that such person is violating such requirements; or

(3) violates section 111(e), 112(c), or section 119(g) (as in effect before the date of the enactment of the Clean Air Act Amendments of 1977) subsection (d)(5) (relating to coal conversion), section 324 (relating to cost of certain vapor recovery), section 119 (relating to smelter orders), or any regulation under part B (relating to ozone), or

(4) fails or refuses to comply with any requirement of section 114 or subsection (d); or

(5) attempts to construct or modify a major stationary source in any area with respect to which a finding under subsection (a)(5) has been made.

The Administrator may commence a civil action for recovery of any noncompliance penalty under section 120 or for recovery of any nonpayment penalty for which any person is liable under section 120 or for both.

Any action under this subsection may be brought in the district court of the United States for the district in which the violation occurred or in which the defendant resides or has his principal place of business, and such court shall have jurisdiction to restrain such violation, to require compliance, to assess such civil penalty and to collect any noncompliance penalty (and nonpayment penalty) owed under section 120. In determining the amount of any civil penalty to be assessed under this subsection, the court shall take into consideration (in addition to other factors) the size of the business, the economic impact of the penalty on the business, and the seriousness of the violation.

In the case of any action brought by the Administrator under this subsection, the court may award costs of litigation (including reasonable attorney and expert witness fees) to the party or parties against whom such action was brought in any case where the court finds that such action was unreasonable.

(c)(1) Any person who knowingly—

    (A) violates any requirement of an applicable implementation plan (i) during any period Federally assumed enforcement, (ii) more than 30 days after having been notified by the Administrator under subsection (a)(1) that such person is violating such requirement, or

    (B) violates or fails or refuses to comply with any order under section 119 or under subsection (a) or (d) of this section, or

    (C) violates section 111(e), section 112(c) or

    (D) violates any requirement of section 119(g) (as in effect before the date of the enactment of this Act), subsection (b)(7) or (d)(5) of section 120 (relating to noncompliance penalties), or any requirement of part B (relating to ozone)

shall be punished by a fine of not more than $25,000 per day of violation, or by imprisonment for not more than one year, or by both. If the conviction is for a violation committed after the first conviction of such person under this paragraph, punishment shall be by a fine of not more than $50,000 per day of violation, or by imprisonment for not more than two years or by both.

    (2) Any person who knowingly makes any false statement, representation, or certification in any application, record, report, plan, or other document filed or required to be maintained under this Act or who falsifies, tampers with, or knowingly renders inaccurate any monitoring device or method required to be maintained under this Act, shall upon conviction, be punished by a fine of not more than $10,000, or

by imprisonment for not more than six months, or by both.

(3) For the purpose of this subsection, the term "person" includes, in addition to the entities referred to in section 302(e), any responsible corporate officer.

(d)(1) A State (or, after thirty days notice to the State, the Administrator) may issue to any stationary source which is unable to comply with any requirement of an applicable implementation plan an order which specifies a date for final compliance with such requirement of an applicable implementation plan later than the date for attainment of any national ambient air quality standard specified in such plan if—

(A) such order is issued after notice to the public (and, as appropriate, to the Administrator) containing the content of the proposed order and opportunity for public hearing;

(B) the order contains a schedule and timetable for compliance;

(C) the order requires compliance with applicable interim requirements as provided in paragraph (5)(B) (relating to sources converting to coal), and paragraph (6) and (7) (relating to all sources receiving such orders), and requires the emission monitoring and reporting by the source authorized to be required under sections 110(a)(2)(F) and 114(a)(1);

(D) the order provides for final compliance with the requirement of the applicable implementation plan as expeditiously as practicable, but (except as provided in paragraph (4) or (5)) in no event later than July 1, 1979, or three years after the date for final compliance with such requirement specified in such plan, whichever is later; and

(E) in the case of a major stationary source, the order notifies the source that unless exempted under section 120(a)(2)(B) or (C), it will be required to pay a noncompliance penalty effective July 1, 1979, as provided under section 120 or by such later date as is set forth in the order in accordance with section 120 in the event such source fails to achieve final compliance by July 1, 1979.

(2) In the case of any major stationary source, no such order issued by the State shall take effect until the Administrator determines that such order has been issued in accordance with the requirements of this Act. The Administrator shall determine, not later than 90 days after receipt of notice of the issuance of an order under this subsection with respect to any major stationary source, whether or not any State order under this subsection is in accordance with the requirements of this Act. In the case of any source other than a major stationary source, such order issued by the State shall cease to be effective upon a determination by the Administrator that it was not issued in accordance with the requirements of this Act. If the Administrator so objects, he shall simultaneously proceed to issue an enforcement order in accordance with subsection (a) or an order under this subsection.

Nothing in this section shall be construed as limiting the authority of a State or political subdivision to adopt and enforce a more stringent emission limitation or more expeditious schedule or timetable for compliance than that contained in an order by the Administrator.

(3) If any source not in compliance with any requirement of an applicable implementation plan gives written notification to the State (or the Administrator) that such source intends to comply by means of replacement of the facility, a complete change in production process, or a termination of operation, the State (or the Administrator) may issue an order under paragraph (1) of this subsection permitting the source to operate until July 1, 1979, without any interim schedule of compliance: *Provided,* That as a condition of the issuance of any such order, the owner or operator of such source shall post a bond or other surety in an amount equal to the cost of actual compliance by such facility and any economic value which may accrue to the owner or operator of such source by reason of the failure to comply. If a source for which the bond or other surety required by this paragraph has been posted fails to replace the facility, change the production process, or terminate the operations as specified in the order by the required date, the owner or operator shall immediately forfeit on the bond or other surety and the State (or the Administrator) shall have not discretion to modify the order under this paragraph or to compromise the bond or other surety.

(4) An order under paragraph (1) of this subsection may be issued to an existing stationary source if—

(A) the source will expeditiously use new means of emission limitation which the Administrator determines is likely to be adequately demonstrated (within the meaning of section $111(a)(1)$) upon expiration of the order.

(B) such new means of emission limitation is not likely to be used by such source unless an order is granted under this subsection.

(C) such new means of emission limitation is determined by the Administrator to have a substantial likelihood of—

(i) achieving greater continuous emission reduction than the means of emission limitation which, but for such order would be required; or

(ii) achieving an equivalent continuous reduction at lower cost in terms of energy, economic, or non-air quality environmental impact; and

(D) compliance by the source with the requirement of the applicable implementation plan would be impracticable prior to, or during, the installation of such new means.

Such an order shall provide for final compliance with the requirement in the applicable implementation plan as expeditiously as practicable, but in no event later than five years after the date on which the source would otherwise be required to be in full compliance with the requirement.

(5)(A) In the case of a major stationary source which is burning petroleum products or natural gas, or both and which—

    (i) is prohibited from doing so under an order pursuant to the provisions of section 2(a) of the Energy Supply and Environmental Coordination Act of 1974 or any amendment thereto, or any subsequent enactment which supersedes such provisions, or

    (ii) within one year after enactment of the Clean Air Act Amendments of 1977 gives notice of intent to convert to coal as its primary energy source because of actual or anticipated curtailment of natural gas supplies under any curtailment plan or schedule approved by the Federal Power Commission (or, in the case of intrastate natural supplies, approved by the appropriate State regulatory commission), and which thereby would no longer be in compliance with any requirement under an applicable implementation plan, an order may be issued by the Administrator under paragraph (1) of this subsection for such source which specifies a date for final compliance with such requirement as expeditiously as practicable, but not later than December 31, 1980. The Administrator may issue an additional order under paragraph (1) of this subsection for such source providing an additional period for such source to come into compliance with the requirement in the applicable implementation plan, which shall be expeditiously as practicable, but in no event later than five years after the date required for compliance under the preceding sentence.

(B) In issuing an order pursuant to subparagraph (A), the Administrator shall prescribe (and may from time to time modify) emission limitations, requirements respecting pollution characteristics of coal, or other enforceable measures for control of emissions for each source to which such an order applies. Such limitations, requirements, and measures shall be those which the Administrator determines must be complied with by the source in order to assure (throughout the period before the date for final compliance established in the order) that the burning of coal by such source will not result in emissions which cause or contribute to concentrations of any air pollutant in excess of any national primary ambient air quality standard for such pollutant.

(C) The Administrator may, by regulation, establish priorities under which manufacturers of continuous emission reduction systems necessary to carry out this paragraph shall provide such systems to users thereof, if he finds, after consultation with the States, that priorities must be imposed in order to assure that such systems are first provided to sources subject to order under this paragraph in air quality control regions in which national primary ambient air quality standards have not been achieved. No regulation under this subparagraph may impair the obligation of any contract entered into before the date of enactment of the Clean Air Act Amendments of 1977.

(D) No order issued to a source under this paragraph with respect to an air pollutant shall be effective if the national primary ambient air quality standard with respect to such pollutant is being exceeded at any time in the air quality control region in which such source is located. The preceding sentence shall not apply to a source if, upon submission by any person of evidence satisfactory to the Administrator, the Administrator determines (after notice and public hearing)—

(i) that emissions of such air pollutant from such source will affect only infrequently the air quality concentrations of such pollutant in each portion of the region where such standard is being exceeded at any time;

(ii) that emissions of such air pollutant from such source will have only insignificant effect on the air quality concentrations of such pollutant in each portion of the region where such standard is being exceeded at any time; and

(iii) with reasonable statistical assurance that emissions of such air pollutant from such source will not cause or contribute to air quality concentrations of such pollutant in excess of the national primary ambient air quality standard for such pollutant.

(6) An order issued to a source under this subsection shall set forth compliance schedules containing increments of progress which require compliance with the requirement postponed as expeditiously as practicable.

(7) A source to which an order is issued under paragraph (1),(3),(4) or (5) of this subsection shall use the best practicable system or systems of emission reduction (as determined by the Administrator taking into account the requirement with which the source must ultimately comply) for the period during which such order is in effect and shall comply with such interim requirements as the Administrator determines are reasonable and practicable. Such interim requirements shall include—

(A) such measures as the Administrator determines are necessary to avoid an imminent and substantial endangerment to health of persons, and

(B) a requirement that the source comply with the requirements of the applicable implementation plan during any such period insofar as such source is able to do so (as determined by the Administrator).

(8) Any order under paragraph (1) of this subsection shall be terminated if the Administrator determines on the record, after notice and hearing, that the inability of the source to comply no longer exists. If the owner or operator of the source to which the order is issued demonstrates that prompt termination of such order would result in undue hardship, the termination shall become effective at the earliest practicable date on which such undue hardship would not result, but in no event later than the date required under this subsection.

(9) If the Administrator determines that a source to which an order is issued under this subsection is in violation of any requirement of this subsection, he shall—

(A) enforce such requirement under subsection (a), (b) or (c) of this section,

(B) (after notice and opportunity for public hearing) revoke such order and enforce compliance with the requirement with respect to which such order was granted,

(C) give notice of noncompliance and commence action under section 120, or

(D) take any appropriate combination of such actions.

(10) During the period of the order in effect under this subsection and where the owner or operator is in compliance with the terms of such order, no Federal enforcement action pursuant to this section and no action under section 304 this Act shall be pursued against such owner or operator based upon noncompliance during the period the order is in effect with the requirement for the source covered by such order.

(11) For the purposes of section 110, 304 and 307 of this Act, any order issued by the State in effect pursuant to this subsection shall become part of the applicable implementation plan.

(12) Any enforcement order issued under subsection (a) of this section or any consent decree in an enforcement action which is in effect on the day of enactment of the Clean Air Act Amendments of 1977 shall remain in effect to the extent that such order or consent decree is (A) not inconsistent with the requirements of this subsection and section 119 or (B) the administrative orders on consent issued by the Administrator on November 5, 1975 and February 26, 1976 and requiring compliance with sulfur dioxide emission limitations or standards at least as stringent as those promulgated under section 111. Any such enforcement order issued under subsection (a) of this section or consent decree which provides for an extension beyond July 1, 1979, except such administrative orders on consent, is void unless modified under this subsection within one year after the enactment of the Clean Air Act Amendments of 1977 to comply with the requirements of this subsection.

(e)(1) The Administrator may, in his discretion, in the case of any person which is the owner or operator of a stationary source in an iron- and steel-producing operation not in compliance with the emission limitation requirements of an applicable implementation plan, consent to entry of a Federal judicial decree, or to the modification of an existing Federal judicial decree, with such person establishing a schedule for compliance for such source extending beyond December 31, 1982, but ending not later than December 31, 1985, on the following conditions:

(A) the Administrator finds, on the basis of information submitted by the applicant and other information available to him, that such extension of compliance is necessary to allow such person to make capital investments in its iron- and steel-producing operations to improve their efficiency and productivity;

(B) the Administrator finds, on the basis of information submitted by the applicant and other information available to him, that an amount equal to the funds the expenditure of which would have been required to comply by December 31, 1982, with those requirements of an applicable implementation plan for which such extensions of compliance are granted and whose expenditure for such purposes are being deferred until after December 31, 1982, pursuant to such extensions will be invested prior to two years from the date of enactment of this subsection in additional capital investments in the iron- and steel-producing operations owned or operated by such person, and located in communities which already contain iron- and steel-producing operations, to improve their efficiency and productivity;

(C) the Administrator and such person consent to entry of Federal judicial decree(s) establishing a phased program of compliance to bring each stationary source at all of such person's iron- and steel-producing operations into compliance with the emission limitation requirements of applicable implementation plans (or, with respect to existing stationary sources located in any nonattainment area for which no implementation plan has been approved as meeting the requirements of part D and subject to implementation plan(s) which do not require compliance with emission limitations which represent at least reasonably available control technology, compliance with emission limitations which represent reasonably available control technology) as expeditiously as practicable but no later than December 31, 1982, or, in the case of sources for which extensions of compliance have been granted, no later than December 31, 1985; such decree(s) shall also contain, at a minimum, (i) requirements for interim controls (which may include operation and maintenance procedures); (ii) increments of compliance sufficient to assure compliance by the final compliance deadlines; (iii) requirement(s) that the amount referred to in subparagraph (B) above, is to be invested in projects representing additional capital investments in the iron- and steel-producing operations owned or operated by such person for the purposes specified in such subparagraph and shall contain schedule(s) specifying when each such project (or specified alternative project) is to be commenced and completed, as well as increments of progress toward completion; (iv) stipulated monetary penalties covering completion of the air pollution control projects required by the decree, the projects referred to under (iii) above, and such other items as appropriate; (v) monitoring requirements; (vi) reporting requirements (including provision for periodic reports to be filed with the court); and (vii) provisions for preventing increases of emissions from each stationary source;

(D) the Administrator finds, on the basis of information submitted by the applicant and other information available to him, that such person will have sufficient funds to comply with all applicable requirements by the times set forth in the judicial decree(s) entered into pursuant to subparagraph (C) of this subsection;

(E) the Administrator finds, on the basis of information submitted by the applicant and other information available to him, that the applicant is in compliance with existing Federal judicial decrees (if any) entered under section 113 of this Act applicable to its iron- and steel-producing operations or that any violations of such decrees are de minimus in nature; and

(F) the Administrator finds, on the basis of information submitted by the applicant and other information available to him, that any extension of compliance granted pursuant to this subsection will not result in degradation of air quality during the term of the extension.

(2) For the purpose of this subsection, "iron- and steel-producing operations" include production facilities for iron and steel, as well as associated processing, coke making and sintering facilities. For the purpose of this subsection, "phased program of compliance" means a program assuring, to the extent possible, that capital expenditures for achieving compliance at all sources owned or operated by such person in iron- and steel-producing operations must be made during the second and each succeeding year of the period covered by the decree(s) in an amount such that at the end of each such year the cumulative expenditures under the decree(s) will be at least equal to the amount which would have been spent if the total expenditures to be made under the decree(s) were made in equal increments during each year of the decree(s). For the purpose of this subsection, "additional capital investments in iron- and steel-producing operations" means investments which the Administrator finds would not be made during the same time period if extension(s) of time for compliance with clean air requirements were not granted under this subsection. The decree

entered into pursuant to subparagraph (C) of paragraph (1) of this subsection shall specify the projects which represent additional capital investment in iron- and steel-producing operations, but may also contain specified alternative projects. The decree may also be modified to substitute equivalent projects for those specified. The owner or operator of iron- and steel-producing operations seeking an extension of compliance under this subsection has the burden of satisfying the Administrator with regard to the findings required in paragraphs (A), (B), (D), (E), and (F). A person which is subject to a judicial decree entered or modified pursuant to this subsection shall not be assessed a noncompliance penalty under section 120 of the Act for any source with an extension of compliance under such decree for the period of time covered by the decree only if such source remains in compliance with all provisions and requirements of such decree.

(3) Any records, reports, or information obtained by the Administrator under this subsection shall be available to the public, except that upon a showing satisfactory to the Administrator by any person that records, reports, or information, or particular part thereof (other than emission data) to which the Administrator has access under this section if made public, is likely to cause substantial harm to the person's competitive position, the Administrator shall consider such record, report, or information or particular portion thereof confidential in accordance with the purposes of section 1905 of title 18 of the United States Code, except that such record, report, or information may be disclosed to other officers, employees, or authorized representatives of the United States concerned with carrying out this Act or when relevant in any proceeding under this Act. Any regulations promulgated under section 114 of this Act apply with equal force to this subsection subject, however, to any changes that the Administrator shall determine are necessary. This paragraph does not constitute authority to withhold records, reports, or information from the Congress.

(4) Nothing in this subsection shall preclude or deny the right of any State or political subdivision to enforce any air pollution requirements in any State judicial or administrative forum.

(5) The provisions of this subsection shall be self-executing, and no implementing regulations shall be required.

(6) Upon receipt of an application for an extension of time under this subsection with respect to any stationary source the Administrator shall promptly—

    (i) publish notice of such receipt in the Federal Register;

    (ii) notify the Governor of the State in which the stationary source is located; and

    (iii) notify the chief elected official of the political subdivision in which the source is located.

(7)(A) The Administrator shall publish in the Federal Register notice of any finding made, or other action taken, by him in connection with the entry of any consent decree or modification of an existing consent decree pursuant to this subsection or in connection with the Administrator's failure or refusal to consent to such a decree.

   (B)(i) Except as provided in clause (ii), any finding or other action of the Administrator under this subsection with respect to any stationary source, and any failure or refusal of the Administrator to make any such finding or to take any such action under this subsection, shall be reviewable only by a court in which a civil action under section 113 of this Act is brought against the owner or operator of such stationary source.

   (ii) Where, before the date of the enactment of the Steel Industry Compliance Extension Act of 1981, a civil action was brought under this Act against the owner or operator of such stationary source, any finding or other action of the Administrator under this subsection with respect to such stationary source, and any failure or refusal of the Administrator to make any such finding or to take any such action under this subsection, shall be reviewable only by the court in which the civil action was brought.

(8) The provisions of section 304(b)(1)(B) of this Act shall be applicable to this subsection.

(9) For a source which receives an extension under this subsection, air pollutoin requirements specified in Federal judicial decrees entered into or modified under this subsection that involves such source may not be modified to extend beyond December 31, 1985.

§ 7414. Recordkeeping, inspections, monitoring, and entry

[Sec. 114] (a) For the purpose (i) of developing or assisting in the development of any implementation plan under section 110 or 111(d), any standard or performance under section 111, or any emission standard under section 112, (ii) of determining whether any person is in violation of any such standard or any requirement of such a plan, of (iii) carrying out any provision of this Act (except a provision of Title II with respect to a manufacturer of new motor vehicles or new motor vehicle engines)—

   (1) the Administrator may require any person who owns or operates any emission source or who is subject to any requirements of this Act (other than a manufacturer subject to the provisions of section 206(c) or 208) with respect to a provision of title II to (A) establish and maintain such records, (B) make such reports, (C) install, use, and maintain such monitoring equipment or methods, (D) sample such emissions (in accordance with such methods, at such locations, at such intervals, and in such manner as the Administrator shall prescribe),

and (E) provide such other information, as he may reasonably require; and

(2) the Administrator or his authorized representative, upon presentation of his credentials—

    (A) shall have a right of entry to, upon or through any premises of such person or in which any records required to be maintained under paragraph (1) of this secton are located, and

    (B) may at reasonable times have access to and copy of any records, inspect any monitoring equipment or methods required under paragraph (1), and sample any emissions which such person is required to sample under paragraph (1).

(b)(1) Each State may develop and submit to the Administrator a procedure for carrying out this section in such State. If the Administrator finds the State procedure is adequate, he may delegate to such State any authority he has to carry out this section.

(2) Nothing in this subsection shall prohibit the Administrator from carrying out this section in a State.

(c) Any records, reports or information obtained under subsection (a) shall be available to the public, except that upon a showing satisfactory to the Administrator by any person that records, reports, or information, or particular part thereof, (other than emission data) to which the Administrator has access under this section if made public would divulge methods or processes entitled to protection as trade secrets of such person, the Administrator shall consider such record, report, or information or particular portion thereof confidential in accordance with the purposes of section 1905 of title 18 of the United States Code, except that such record, report, or information may be disclosed to other officers, employees, or authorized representatives of the United States concerned with carrying out this Act or when relevant in any proceeding under this Act.

(d)(1) In the case of any emission standard or limitation or other requirement which is adopted by a State, as part of an applicable implementation plan or as part of an order under section 113(d), before carrying out an entry, inspection, or monitoring under paragraph (2) of subsection (a) with respect to such standard, limitation, or other requirement, the Administrator (or his representatives) shall provide the State air pollution control agency with reasonable prior notice of such action, indicating the purpose of such action. No State agency which receives notice under this paragraph of an action proposed to be taken may use the information contained in the notice to inform the person whose property is proposed to be affected of the proposed action. If the Administrator has reasonable basis for believing that a State agency is so using or will so use such information, notice to the agency under this paragraph is not required until such time as the Administrator determines the agency will no longer so use information contained in a notice under this paragraph. Nothing in this section shall be construed to require notification to any State agency of any action taken by the Administrator with respect to any standard, limitation, or other requirement which is not part of an applicable implementation plan or which was promulgated by the Administrator under section 110(c).

(2) Nothing in paragraph (1) shall be construed to provide that any failure of the Administrator to comply with the requirements of such paragraph shall be defense in any enforcement action brought by the Administrator or shall make inadmissible as evidence in any such action any information or material obtained notwithstanding such failure to comply with such requirements.

§ 7415. International air pollution

[Sec. 115] (a) Whenever the Administrator, upon receipt of reports, surveys or studies from any duly constituted international agency has reason to believe that any air pollutant or pollutants emitted in the United States cause or contribute to air pollution which may reasonably be anticipated to endanger public health or welfare in a foreign country or whenever the Secretary of State requests him to do so with respect to such pollution which the Secretary of State alleges is of such a nature the Administrator shall give formal notification thereof to the Governor of the State in which such emissions originate.

(b) The notice of the Administrator shall be deemed to be a finding under section 110(a)(2)(H)(ii) which requires a plan revision with respect to so much of the applicable implementation plan as is inadequate to prevent or eliminate the endangerment referred to in subsection (a). Any foreign country so affected by such emission of pollutant or pollutants shall be invited to appear at any public hearing associated with any revision of the appropriate portion of the applicable implementation plan.

(c) This section shall apply only to a foreign country which the Administrator determines has given the United States essentially the same rights with respect to the prevention or control of air pollution occurring in that country as is given that country by this section.

(d) Recommendations issued following any abatement conference conducted prior to the enactment of the Clean Air Act Amendments of 1977 shall remain in effect with respect to any pollutant for which no national ambient air quality standard has been established under section 109 of this Act unless the Administrator, after consultation with all agencies which were party to the conference, rescinds any such recommendation on grounds of obsolescence.

§ 7416. Retention of state authority

[Sec. 116] Except as otherwise provided in sections 119(c), (e) and (f) (as in effect before the date of the enactment of the Clean Air Act Amendments of 1977), 209.211(c)(4), and 233 (preempting certain State regulation of moving sources) nothing in this Act shall preclude or deny the right of any State or political subdivision thereof to adopt or enforce (1) any standard or limitation respecting emissions of air pollutants or (2) any requirement respecting control or abatement of air pollution; except that if an emission standard or limitation is in effect under an applicable implementation plan or under section 111 or 112, such State or political subdivision may not adopt or enforce any emission standard and or limitation which is less stringent than the standard or limitation under such plan or section.

§ 7417. Advisory committees

[Sec. 117] (a) In order to obtain assistance in the development and implementation of the purposes of this Act including air quality criteria, recommended control techniques, standards, research and development, and to encourage the continued efforts on the part of industry to improve air quality and to develop economically feasible methods for the control and abatement of air pollution, the Administrator shall from time to time establish advisory committees. Committee members shall include, but not be limited to, persons who are knowledgeable concerning air quality from the standpoint of health, welfare, economics, or technology.

(b) The members of any other advisory committees appointed pursuant to this Act who are not officers or employees of the United States while attending conferences or meeting or while otherwise serving at the request of the Administrator, shall be entitled to receive compensation at a rate to be fixed by the Administrator, but not exceeding $100 per diem, including traveltime, and while away from their homes or regular places of business they may be allowed travel expenses, including per diem in lieu of subsistence, as authorized by section 5703 of title 5 of the United States Code for persons in the Government service employed intermittently.

(c) Prior to—

(1) issuing criteria for an air pollutant under section 108(a)(2),

(2) publishing any list under section 111 (b) (1) (A) or 112 (b)(1)(A),

(3) publishing any standard under section 111 or section 112, or

(4) publishing any regulation under section 202(a),

the Administrator shall, to the maximum extent practicable within the time provided, consult with appropriate advisory committees, independent experts, and Federal departments and agencies.

§ 7418. Control of pollution from federal facilities

[Sec. 118] (a) Each department, agency, and instrumentality of the executive, legislative, and judicial branches of the Federal Government (1) having jurisdiction over any property or facility, or (2) engaged in any activity resulting, or which may result, in the discharge of air pollutants, and each officer, agent, or employee, thereof, shall be subject to, and comply with, all Federal, State, interstate, and local requirements, administrative authority, and process and sanctions respecting the control and abatement of air pollution in the same manner, and to the same extent as any nongovernmental entity. The preceding sentence shall apply (A) to any requirement whether substantive or procedural (including any recordkeeping or reporting requirement, and requirement respecting permits and any other requirement whatsoever), (B) to the exercise of any Federal, State, or local administrative authority, and (C) to any process and sanction, whether enforced in Federal, State, or local courts or any other manner. This subsection shall apply notwithstanding any immunity of such agencies, officers, agents, or employees under any law or rule of law. No officer, agent, or employee of the United States shall be personally liable for any civil penalty for which he is not otherwise liable.

(b) The President may exempt any emission source of any department, agency, or instrumentality in the executive branch from compliance with such a requirement if he determines it to be in the paramount interest of the United States to do so, except that no exemption may be granted from section 111, and an exemption from section 112 may be granted only in accordance with section 112(c). No such exemption shall be granted due to lack of appropriation unless the President shall have specifically requested such appropriation as a part of the budgetary process and the Congress shall have failed to make available such requested appropriation. Any exemption shall be for a period not in excess of one year, but additional exemptions may be granted for periods of not to exceed one year upon the President's making a new determination. In addition to any such exemption of a particular emission source, the President may, if he determines it to be in the paramount interest of the United States to do so, issue regulations exempting from compliance with the requirements of this section any weaponry, equipment, aircraft, vehicles, or other classes or categories of property which are owned or operated by the Armed Forces of the United States (including the Coast Guard) or by the National Guard of any State and which are uniquely military in nature. The President shall reconsider the need for such regulations at three-year intervals. The President shall report each January to the Congress all exemptions from the requirements of this section granted during the preceding calendar year, together with his reason for granting each such exemption.

§ 7419. Primary nonferrous smelter orders

[Sec. 119] (a)(1) Upon application by the owner or operator of a primary nonferrous smelter, a primary nonferrous smelter order under subsection (b) may be issued—

(A) by the Administrator, after thirty days' notice to the State, or

(B) by the State in which such source is located, but no such order issued by the State shall take effect until the Administrator determines that such order has been issued in accordance with the requirements of this Act. Not later than ninety days after submission by the State to the Administrator of notice of the issuance of a primary nonferrous smelter order under this section, the Administrator shall determine whether or not such order has been issued by the State in accordance with the requirements of this Act. If the Administrator determines that such order has not been issued in accordance with such requirements, he shall conduct a hearing respecting the reasonable control technology for primary nonferrous smelters.

(2)(A) An order issued under this section to a primary nonferrous smelter shall be referred to as a "primary nonferrous smelter order". No primary nonferrous smelter may receive both an enforcement order under section 113(d) and a primary nonferrous smelter order under this section.

(B) Before any hearing conducted under this section in the case of an application made by the owner or operator of a primary nonferrous smelter for a second order under this section, the applicant shall furnish the Administrator (or the State as the case may be) with a statement of the grounds on which such application is based (including all supporting documents and information). The statement of the grounds for the proposed order shall be provided by the Administrator or the State in any case in which such State or Administrator is acting on its own initiative. Such statement (including such documents and information) shall be made available to the public for a thirty-day period before such hearing and shall be considered as part of such hearing. No primary nonferrous smelter order may be granted unless the applicant establishes that he meets the conditions required for the issuance of such order (or the Administrator or State establishes the meeting of such conditions when acting on their own initiative).

(C) Any decision with respect to the issuance of a primary nonferrous smelter order shall be accompanied by a concise statement of the findings and of the basis of such findings.

(3) For the purposes of section 110, 304, and 307 of this Act, any order issued by the State and in effect pursuant to this subsection shall become part of the applicable implementation plan.

(b) A primary nonferrous smelter order under this section may be issued to a primary nonferrous smelter if—

(1) such smelter is in existence on the date of the enactment of this section;

(2) the requirement of the applicable implementation plan with respect to which the order is issued is an emission limitation or standard for sulfur oxides which is necessary and intended to be itself sufficient to enable attainment and maintenance of national primary and secondary ambient air quality standards for sulfur oxides, and

(3) such smelter is unable to comply with such requirement by the applicable date for compliance because no means of emission limitation applicable to such smelter which will enable it to achieve compliance with such requirement has been adequately demonstrated

to be reasonably available (as determined by the Administrator, taking into account the cost of compliance, non-air quality health and environmental impact, and energy consideration).

(c)(1) A second order issued to a smelter under this section shall set forth compliance schedules containing increments of progress which require compliance with the requirement postponed as expeditiously as practicable. The increments of progress shall be limited to requiring compliance with subsection (d) and, in the case of a second order, to procuring, installing, and operating the necessary means of emission limitation as expeditiously as practicable after the Administrator determines such means have been adequately demonstrated to be reasonably available within the meaning of subsection (b)(3).

(2) Not in excess of two primary nonferrous smelter orders may be issued under this section to any primary nonferrous smelter. The first such order issued to a smelter shall not result in the postponement of the requirement with respect to which such order is issued beyond January 1, 1983. The second such order shall not result in the postponement of such requirement beyond January 1, 1988.

(d)(1)(A) Each primary nonferrous smelter to which an order is issued under this section shall be required to use such interim measures for the period during which such order is in effect as may be necessary in the judgment of the Administrator to assure attainment and maintenance of the national primary and secondary ambient air quality standards during such period, taking into account the aggregate effect on air quality of such order together with all variances, extensions, waivers, enforcement orders, delayed compliance orders and primary nonferrous smelter orders previously issued under this Act.

(B) Such interim requirements shall include—

(i) a requirement that the source to which the order applies comply with such reporting requirements and conduct such monitoring as the Administrator determines may be necessary, and

(ii) such measures as the Administrator determines are necessary to avoid an imminent and substantial endangerment to health of persons.

(C) Such interim measures shall also, except as provided in paragraph (2), include continuous emission reduction technology. The Administrator shall condition the use of any such interim measures upon the agreement of the owner or operator of the smelter—

(i) to comply with such conditions as the Administrator determines are necessary to maximize the reliability and enforceability of such interim measures, as applied to the smelter, in attaining and maintaining the national ambient air quality standards to which the order relates, and

      (ii) to commit reasonable resources to research and development of appropriate emission control technology.

(2) The requirement of paragraph (1) for the use of continuous emission reduction technology may be waived with respect to a paraticular smelter by the State or the Administrator, after notice and a hearing on the record, and upon a showing by the owner or operator of the smelter that such requirement would be so costly as to necessitate permanent or prolonged temporary cessation of operations of the smelter. Upon application for such waiver, the Administrator shall be notified and shall, within ninety days, hold a hearing on the record in accordance with section 554 of title 5 of the United States Code. At such hearing the Administrator shall require the smelter involved to present information relating to any alleged cessation of operations and the detailed reasons or justifications therefor. On the basis of such hearing the Administrator shall make findings of fact as to the effect of such requirement and on the alleged cessation of operations and shall make recommendations as he deems appropriate. Such report, findings, and recommendations shall be available to the public, and shall be taken into account by the State or the Administrator in making the decision whether or not to grant such waiver.

(3) In order to obtain information for purposes of a waiver under paragraph (2), the Administrator may, on his own motion, conduct an investigation and use the authority under section 321.

(4) In the case of any smelter which on the date of enactment of this section uses continuous emission reduction technology and supplemental controls and which receives an initial primary nonferrous smelter order under this section, no additional continuous emission reduction technology shall be required as a condition of such order unless the Administrator determines, at any time, after notice and public hearing, that such additional continuous emission reduction technology is adequately demonstrated to be reasonably available for the primary nonferrous smelter industry.

(e) At any time during which an order under this section applies, the Administrator may enter upon a public hearing respecting the availability of technology. Any order under this section shall be terminated if the Administrator determines on the record, after notice and public hearing, that the conditions upon which the order was based no longer exist. If the owner or operator of the smelter to which the order is issued demonstrates that prompt termination of such order would result in undue hardship, the termination shall become effective at the earliest practicable date on which such undue hardship would not result, but in no event later than the date required under subsection (c).

(f) If the Administrator determines that a smelter to which an order is issued under this section is in violation of any requirement of subsection (c) or (d), he shall—

(1) enforce such requirement under section 113.

(2) (after notice and opportunity for public hearing) revoke such order and enforce compliance with the requirement with respect to which such order was granted.

(3) give notice of noncompliance and commence action under section 120, or

(4) take any appropriate combination of such actions.

§ 7420.   Noncompliance penalty

[Sec. 120] (a)(1)(A) Not later than 6 months after the date of enactment of this section, and after notice and opportunity for a public hearing, the Administrator shall promulgate regulations requiring the assessment and collection of a noncompliance penalty against persons referred to in paragraph (2)(A).

(B)(i) Each State may develop and submit to the Administrator a plan for carrying out this section in such State. If the Administrator finds that the State plan meets the requirements of this section, he may delegate to such State any authority he has to carry out this section.

(ii) Notwithstanding a delegation to a State under clause (i), the Administrator may carry out this section in such State under the circumstances described in subsection (b)(2)(B).

(2)(A) Except as provided in subparagraph (B) or (C) of this paragraph, the State or the Administrator shall assess and collect a noncompliance penalty against every person who owns or operates—

(i) a major stationary source (other than a primary nonferrous smelter which has received a primary nonferrous smelter order under section 119) which is not in compliance with any emission limitation, emission standard or compliance schedule under any applicable implementation plan (whether or not such source is subject to a Federal or State consent decree), or

(ii) a stationary source which is not in compliance with an emission limitation, emission standard, standard of performance, or other requirement established under section 111 or 112 of this Act, or

(iii) any source referred to in clause (i) or (ii) (for which an extension, order, or suspension referred to in subparagraph (B), or Federal or State consent decree is in effect), or a primary nonferrous smelter which has received a primary nonferrous smelter order under section 119 which is not in compliance with any interim emission control requirement or schedule of compliance under such extension, order, suspension, or consent decree.

For purposes of subsection (d)(2), in the case of a penalty assessed with respect to a source referred to in clause (iii) of this subparagraph, the costs referred to in such subsection (d)(2) shall be the economic value of noncompliance with the interim emission control requirement or the remaining steps in the schedule of compliance referred to in such clause.

(B) Notwithstanding the requirements of subparagraph (A)(i) and (ii), the owner or operator of any source shall be exempted from the duty to pay a noncompliance penalty under such requirements with respect to that source if, in accordance with the procedures in subsection (b)(5), the owner or operator demonstrates that the failure of such source to comply with any such requirement is due solely to—

(i) conversion by such source from the burning of petroleum products or natural gas, or both, as the permanent primary energy source to the burning of coal pursuant to an order under section 113(d)(5) or section 119 (as in effect before the date of enactment of the Clean Air Act Amendments of 1977);

(ii) in the case of a coal-burning source granted an extension under the second sentence of section 119(c)(1) (as in effect before the date of the enactment of the Clean Air Act Amendments of 1977) a prohibition from using petroleum products or natural gas or both, by reason of an order under the provisions of section 2(a) and (b) of the Energy Supply and Environmental Coordination Act of 1974 or under any legislation which amends or supersedes such provisions;

(iii) the use of innovative technology sanctioned by an enforcement order under section 113(d)(4);

(iv) an inability to comply with any such requirement, for which inability the source has received an order under section 113(d) (or order under section 113 issued before the date of enactment of this section) which has the effect of permitting a delay or violation of any requirement of this Act (including a requirement of an applicable implementation plan) which inability results from reasons entirely beyond the control of the owner or operator of such source or of any entity controlling, controlled by, or under common control with the owner or operator of such source, or

(v) the conditions by reason of which a temporary emergency suspension is authorized under section 110(f) or (g).

An exemption under this subparagraph shall cease to be effective if the source fails to comply with the interim emission control requirements or schedules of compliance (including increments of progress) under any such extension, order, or suspension.

(C) The Administrator may, after notice and opportunity for public hearing, exempt any source from the requirements of this section with respect to a particular instance of noncompliance if he finds that such instance of noncompliance is de minimis in nature and in duration.

(b) Regulations under subsection (a) shall—

(1) permit the assessment and collection of such penalty by the State if the State has a delegation of authority in effect under subsection (a)(1)(B)(i);

(2) provide for the assessment and collection of such penalty by the Administrator, if—

    (A) the State does not have a delegation of authority in effect under subsection (a)(1)(B)(i), or

    (B) the State has such a delegation in effect but fails with respect to any particular person or source to assess or collect the penalty in accordance with the requirements of this section;

(3) require the States, or in the event the States fail to do so, the Administrator, to give a brief but reasonably specific notice of noncompliance under this section to each person referred to in subsection (a)(2)(A) with respect to each source owned or operated by such person which is not in compliance as provided in such subsection, not later than July 1, 1979, or thirty days after the discovery of such noncompliance, whichever is later;

(4) require each person to whom notice is given under paragraph (3) to—

    (A) calculate the amount of the penalty owed (determined in accordance with subsection (d)(2) and the schedule of payments (determined in accordance with subsection (d)(3)) for each such source and, within forty-five days after the issuance of such notice or after the denial of a petition under subparagraph (B), to submit that calculation and proposed schedule, together with the information necessary for an independent verification thereof, to the State and to the Administrator, or

    (B) submit a petition, within forty-five days after the issuance of such notice, challenging such notice of noncompliance or alleging entitlement to an exemption under subsection (a)(2)(B) with respect to a particular source;

(5) require the Administrator to provide a hearing on the record (within the meaning of subchapter II of chapter 5 of title 5, United States Code) and to make a decision on such petition (including findings of fact and conclusions of law) not later than ninety days after the receipt of any petition under paragraph (4)(B) unless the State agrees to provide a hearing which is substantially similar to such a hearing on the record and to make a decision on such petition (including such findings and conclusions) within such ninety-day period;

(6)(A) authorize the Administrator on his own initiative to review the decision of the State under paragraph (5) and disapprove it if it is not in accordance with the requirements of this section, and (B) require the Administrator to do so not later than sixty days after receipt of a petition under this subparagraph, notice, and public hearing and a showing by such petitioner that the State decision under paragraph (5) is not in accordance with the requirements of this section;

(7) require payment, in accordance with subsection (d), of the penalty by each person to whom notice of noncompliance is given under paragraph (3) with respect to each noncomplying source for which such notice is given unless there has been a final determination granting a petition under paragraph (4)(B) with respect to such source;

(8) authorize the State or the Administrator to adjust (and from time to time readjust) the amount of the penalty assessment calculated or the payment schedule proposed by such owner or operator under paragraph (4), if the Administrator finds after notice and opportunity for a hearing on the record that the penalty or schedule does not meet the requirements of this section; and

(9) require a final adjustment of the penalty within 180 days after such source comes into compliance in accordance with subsection (d)(4). In any case in which the State establishes a noncompliance penalty under this section, the State shall provide notice thereof to the Administrator.

A noncompliance penalty established by a State under this section shall apply unless the Administrator, within ninety days after the date of receipt of notice of the State penalty assessment under this section, objects in writing to the amount of the penalty as less than would be required to comply with guidelines established by the Administrator. If the Administrator objects under this subsection, he shall immediately establish a substitute noncompliance penalty applicable to such source.

(c) If the owner or operator of any stationary source to whom a notice is issued under subsection (b)(3)—

(1) does not submit a timely petition under subsection (b)(4)(B), or

(2) submits a petition under subsection (b)(4)(B) which is denied, and

fails to submit a calculation of the penalty assessment, a schedule for payment, and the information necessary for independent verification thereof, the State (or the Administrator, as the case may be) may enter into a contract with any person who has no financial interest in the owner or operator of the source (or in any person controlling, controlled by or under common control with such source) to assist in determining the amount of the penalty assessment or payment schedule with respect to such source. The cost of carrying out such contract may be added to the penalty to be assessed against the owner or operator of such source.

(d)(1) All penalties assessed by the Administrator under this section shall be paid to the United States Treasury. All penalties assessed by the State under this section shall be paid to such State.

(2) The amount of the penalty which shall be assessed and collected with respect to any source under this section shall be equal to—

(A) the amount determined in accordance with regulations promulgated by the Administrator under subsection (a), which is no less than the economic value which a delay in compliance beyond July 1, 1979, may have for the owner of such source, including the quarterly equivalent of the capital costs of compliance and debt service over a normal amortization period, not to exceed ten years, operation and maintenance costs forgone as a result of noncompliance, and any additional economic value which such a delay may have for the owner or operator of such source, minus

(B) the amount of any expenditure by the owner or operator of that source during any such quarter for the purpose of bringing that source into, and maintaining compliance with, such requirement to the extent that such expenditures have not been taken into account in the calculation of the penalty under subparagraph (A).

To the extent that any expenditure under subparagraph (B) made during any quarter is not subtracted for such quarter from the costs under subparagraph (A), such expenditure may be subtracted for any subsequent quarter from such costs, except that in no event shall the amount paid be less than the quarterly payment minus the amount attributed to actual cost of construction.

(3)(A) The assessed penalty required under this section shall be paid in quarterly installments for the period of covered noncompliance. All quarterly payments (determined without regard to any adjustment or any subtraction under paragraph (2)(B)) after the first payment shall be equal.

(B) The first payment shall be due on the date six months after the date of issuance of the notice of non-compliance under subsection (b)(3) with respect to any source or on January 1, 1980, whichever is later. Such first payment shall be in the amount of the quarterly installment for the upcoming quarter, plus the amount owed for any preceding period within the period of covered noncompliance for such source.

(C) For the purpose of this section, the term "period of covered noncompliance" means the period which begins—

(i) two years after the date of enactment of this section, in the case of a source for which notice of noncompliance under subsection (b)(3) is issued on or before the date two years after such date of enactment, or

(ii) on the date of issuance of the notice of noncompliance under subsection (b)(3), in the case of a source for which such notice is issued after July 1, 1979,

and ending on the date on which such source comes into (or for the purpose of establishing the schedule of payments, is estimated to come into) compliance with such requirement.

(4) Upon making a determination that a source with respect to which a penalty has been paid under this section is in compliance and is maintaining compliance with the applicable requirement, the State (or

the Administrator as the case may be) shall review the actual expenditures made by the owner or operator of such source for the purpose of attaining and maintaining compliance, and shall within 180 days after such source comes into compliance—

(A) provide reimbursement with interest (to be paid by the State or Secretary of the Treasury, as the case may be) at appropriate prevailing rates (as determined by the Secretary of the Treasury) for any overpayment by such person, or

(B) assess and collect an additional payment with interest at appropriate prevailing rates (as determined by the Secretary of the Treasury) for any underpayment by such person.

(5) Any person who fails to pay the amount of any penalty with respect to any source under this section on a timely basis shall be required to pay in addition a quarterly nonpayment penalty for each quarter during which such failure to pay persists. Such nonpayment penalty shall be in an amount equal to 20 percent of the aggregate amount of such person's penalties and nonpayment penalties with respect to such source which are unpaid as of the beginning of such quarter.

(e) Any action pursuant to this section, including any objection of the Administrator under the last sentence of subsection (b), shall be considered a final action for purposes of judicial review of any penalty under section 307 of this Act.

(f) Any orders, payments, sanctions, or other requirements under this section shall be in addition to any other permits, orders, payments, sanctions, or other requirement established under this Act, and shall in no way affect any civil or criminal enforcement proceedings brought under any provision of this Act or State or local law.

(g) In the case of any emission limitation or other requirement approved or promulgated by the Administrator under this Act after the enactment of the Clean Air Act Amendments of 1977 which is more stringent than the emission limitation or requirement for the source in effect prior to such approval or promulgation, if any, or where there was no emission limitation or requirement approved or promulgated before enactment of the Clean Air Act Amendments of 1977, the date for imposition of the non-compliance penalty under this section, shall be either July 1, 1979, or the date on which the source is required to be in full compliance with such emission limitation or requirement, whichever is later, but in no event later than three years after the approval or promulgation of such emission limitation or requirement.

§ 7421. Consultation

[Sec. 121] In carrying out the requirements of this Act requiring applicable implementation plans to contain—

(1) any transportation controls, air quality maintenance plan requirements or preconstruction review of direct sources of air pollution, or

(2) any measure referred to—

(A) in part D (pertaining to nonattainment requirements), or

(B) in part C (pertaining to prevention of significant deterioration), and in carrying out the requirements of Section 113(d) (relating to certain enforcement orders), the State shall provide a satisfactory process of consultation with general purpose local governments, designated organizations of elected officials of local governments and any Federal land manager having authority over Federal land to which the State plan applies, effective with respect to any such requirement which is adopted more than one year after the date of enactment of the Clean Air Act Amendments of 1977 as part of such plan. Such process shall be in accordance with regulations promulgated by the Administrator to assure adequate consultation. Such regulations shall be promulgated after notice and opportunity for public hearing and not later than 6 months after the date of enactment of the Clean Air Act Amendments of 1977. Only a general purpose unit of local government, regional agency, or council of governments adversely affected by action of the Administrator approving any portion of a plan referred to in this subsection may petition for judicial review of such action on the basis of a violation of the requirements of this section.

§ 7422. Listing of certain unregulated pollutants

[Sec. 122] (a) Not later than one year after date of enactment of this section (two years for radioactive pollutants) and after notice and opportunity for public hearing, the Administrator shall review all available relevant information and determine whether or not emissions of radioactive pollutants (including source material, special nuclear material, and byproduct material), cadmium, arsenic and polycyclic organic matter into the ambient air will cause, or contribute to, air pollution which may reasonably be anticipated to endanger public health. If the Administrator makes an affirmative determination with respect to any such substance, he shall simultaneously with such determination include such substance in the list published under section 108(a)(1) or 112(b)(1)(A) (in the case of a substance which, in the judgment of the Administrator, causes, or contributes to, air pollution which may reasonably be anticipated to result in an increase in mortality or an increase in serious irreversible, or incapacitating reversible, illness), or shall include each category of stationary sources emitting such substance in significant amounts in the list published under section 111(b)(1)(A), or take any combination of such actions.

(b) Nothing in subsection (a) shall be construed to affect the authority of the Administrator to revise any list referred to in subsection (a) with respect to any substance (whether or not enumerated in subsection (a)).

(c)(1) Before listing any source material, special nuclear, or byproduct material (or component or derivative thereof) as provided in subsection (a), the Adminstrator shall consult with the Nuclear Regulatory Commission.

(2) Not later than six months after listing any such material (or component or derivative thereof) the Administrator and the Nuclear Regulatory Commission shall enter into an interagency agreement with respect to those sources or facilities which are under the jurisdiction of the Commission. This agreement shall, to the maximum extent practicable consistent with this Act, minimize duplication of effort and conserve administrative resources in the establishment, implementation, and enforcement of emission limitations, standards of performance, and other requirements and authorities (substantive and procedural) under this Act respecting the emission of such material (or component or derivative thereof) from such sources or facilities.

(3) In case of any standard or emission limitation promulgated by the Administrator, under this Act or by any State (or the Administrator) under any applicable implementation plan under this Act, if the Nuclear Regulatory Commission determines, after notice and opportunity for public hearing that the application of such standard or limitation to a source or facility within the jurisdiction of the Commission would endanger public health or safety, such standard or limitation shall not apply to such facilities or sources unless the President determines otherwise within ninety days from the date of such finding.

§ 7423. Stack heights

[Sec. 123] (a) The degree of emission limitation required for control of any air pollutant under an applicable implementation plan under this title shall not be affected in any manner by—

(1) so much of the stack height of any source as exceeds good engineering practice (as determined under regulations promulgated by the Administrator), or

(2) any other dispersion technique.

The preceding sentence shall not apply with respect to stack heights in existence before the date of enactment of the Clean Air Amendments of 1970 or dispersion techniques implemented before such date. In establishing an emission limitation for coal-fired steam electric generating units which are subject to the provisions of section 118 and which commenced operation before July 1, 1957, the effect of the entire stack height of stacks for which a construction contract was awarded before February 8, 1974, may be taken into account.

(b) For the purpose of this section, the term "dispersion technique" includes any intermittent or supplemental control of air pollutants varying with atmospheric conditions.

(c) No later than six months after the date of enactment of this section, the Administrator, shall after notice and opportunity for public hearing, promulgate regulations to carry out this section. For purposes of this section, good engineering practice means, with respect to stack heights, the height necessary to insure that emissions from the stack do not result in excessive concentrations of any air pollutant in the immediate vicinity of the source as a result of atmospheric downwash, eddies and wakes which may be created by the source itself, nearby structures or nearby terrain obstacles (as determined by the Administrator). For purposes of this section such height shall not exceed two and a half times the height of such source unless the owner or operator of the source demonstrates, after notice and opportunity for public hearing, to the satisfaction of the Administrator, that a greater height is necessary as provided under the preceding sentence. In no event may the Administrator prohibit any increase in any stack height or restrict in any manner the stack height of any source.

§ 7424. Assurance of adequacy of state plans

[Sec. 124] (a) As expeditiously as practicable but not later than one year after date of enactment of this section, each State shall review the provisions of its implementation plan which relate to major fuel burning sources and shall determine—

(1) the extent to which compliance with requirements of such plan is dependent upon the use by major fuel burning stationary sources of petroleum products or natural gas,

(2) the extent to which such plan may reasonably be anticipated to be inadequate to meet the requirements of this Act in such State on a reliable and long-term basis by reason of its dependence upon the use of such fuels, and

(3) the extent to which compliance with the requirements of such plan is dependent upon use of coal or coal derivatives which is not locally or regionally available.

Each State shall submit the results of its review and its determination under this paragraph to the Administrator promptly upon completion thereof.

(b)(1) Not later than eighteen months after the date of enactment of this section, the Administrator shall review the submission of the States under subsection (a) and shall require each State to revise its plan if, in the judgment of the Administrator, such plan revision is necessary to assure that such plan will be adequate to assure compliance with the requirements of this Act in such State on a reliable and long-term basis, taking into account the actual or potential prohibitions on use of petroleum products or natural gas, or both, under any other authority of law.

(2) Before requiring a plan revision under this subsection, with respect to any State the Administrator shall take into account the report of the review conducted by such State under paragraph (1) and shall consult with the Governor of the State respecting such required revision.

§ 7425. Measures to prevent economic disruption or unemployment

[Sec. 125] (a) After notice and opportunity for a public hearing—

(1) the Governor of any State in which a major fuel burning stationary source referred to in this subsection (or class or category thereof) is located,

(2) the Administrator, or

(3) the President (or his designee),

may determine that action under subsection (b) is necessary to prevent or minimize significant local or regional economic disruption or unemployment which would otherwise result from use by such source (or class or category) of—

> (A) coal or coal derivatives other than locally or regionally available coal,
>
> (B) petroleum products,
>
> (C) natural gas, or
>
> (D) any combination of fuels referred to in subparagraphs (A) through (C),

to comply with the requirements of a State implementation plan.

(b) Upon a determination under subsection (a)—

(1) such Governor, with the written consent of the President or his designee,

(2) the President's designee with the written consent of such Governor, or

(3) the President

may by rule or order prohibit any such major fuel burning stationary source (or class or category thereof) from using fuels other than locally or regionally available coal or coal derivatives to comply with implementation plan requirements. In taking any action under this subsection, the Governor, the President, or the President's designee as the case may be, shall take into account, the final cost to the consumer of such an action.

(c) The Governor, in the case of action under subsection (b)(1), or the Administrator, in the case of an action under subsection (b)(2) or (3) shall, by rule or order, require each source to which such action applies to—

(1) enter into long-term contracts of at least ten years in duration (except as the President or his designee may otherwise permit or require by rule or order for good cause) for supplies of locally or regionally available coal or coal derivatives.

(2) enter into contracts to acquire any additional means of emission limitation which the Administrator or the State determines may be necessary to comply with the requirements of this Act while using such coal or coal derivatives as fuel, and

(3) comply with such schedules (including increments of progress), timetables and other requirements as may be necessary to assure compliance with the requirements of this Act.

Requirements under this subsection shall be established simultaneously with, and as a condition of, any action under subsection (b).

(d) This section applies only to existing or new major fuel burning stationary sources—

(1) which have the design capacity to produce 250,000,000 Btu's per hour (or its equivalent), as determined by the Administrator, and

(2) which are not in compliance with the requirements of an applicable implementation plan or which are prohibited from burning oil or

natural gas, or both, under any other authority of law.

(e) Except as may otherwise be provided by rule by the State or the Administrator for good cause, any action required to be taken by a major fuel burning stationary source under this section shall not be deemed to constitute a modification for purposes of section 111(a)(2) and (4) of this Act.

(f) For purposes of sections 113 and 120 a prohibition under subsection (b), and a corresponding rule or order under subsection (c), shall be treated as a requirement of section 113. For purposes of any plan (or portion thereof) promulgated under section 110(c), any rule or order under subsection (c) corresponding to a prohibition under subsection (b), shall be treated as a part of such plan. For purposes of section 113, a prohibition under subsection (b), applicable to any source, and a corresponding rule or order under subsection (c), shall be treated as part of the applicable implementation plan for the State in which subject source is located.

(g) The President may delegate his authority under this section to an officer or employee of the United States designated by him on a case-by-case basis or in any other manner he deems suitable.

(h) For the purpose of this section—the term "locally or regionally available coal or coal derivatives" means coal or coal derivatives which is, or can in the judgment of the State or the Administrator feasibly be, mined or produced in the local or regional area (as determined by the Administrator) in which the major fuel burning stationary source is located.

§ 7426. Interstate pollution abatement

[Sec. 126] (a) Each applicable implementation plan shall—
(1) require each major proposed new (or modified) source—
  (A) subject to part C (relating to significant deterioration of air quality) or
  (B) which may significantly contribute to levels of air pollution in excess of the national ambient air quality standards in any air quality control region outside the State in which such source intends to locate (or make such modification),
  to provide written notice to all nearby States the air pollution levels of which may be affected by such source at least sixty days prior to the date on which commencement of construction is to be permitted by the State providing notice, and
(2) identify all major existing stationary sources which may have the impact described in paragraph (1) with respect to new or modified sources and provide notice to all nearby States of the identity of such sources not later than three months after the date of enactment of the Clean Air Act Amendments of 1977.

(b) Any State or political subdivision may petition the Administrator for a finding that any major source emits or would emit any air pollutant in violation of the prohibition of section 110(a)(2)(E)(i). Within 60 days after receipt of any petition under this subsection and after public hearing, the Administrator shall make such a finding or deny the petition.

(c) Notwithstanding any permit which may have been granted by the State in which the source is located (or intends to locate), it shall be a violation of the applicable implementation plan in such State—

(1) for any major proposed new (or modified) source with respect to which a finding has been made under subsection (b) to be constructed or to operate in violation of the prohibition of section 110(a)(2)(E)(i), or

(2) for any major existing source to operate more than three months after such finding has been made with respect to it.

The Administrator may permit the continued operation of a source referred to in paragraph (2) beyond the expiration of such three-month period if such source complies with such emission limitations and compliance schedules (containing increments of progress) as may be provided by the Administrator to bring about compliance with the requirement contained in section 110(a)(2)(E)(i) as expeditiously as practicable, but in no case later than three years after the date of such finding. Nothing in the preceding sentence shall be construed to preclude any such source from being eligible for an enforcement order under section 113(d) after the expiration of such period during which the Administrator has permitted continuous operation.

§ 7427. Public notification

[Sec. 127] (a) Each State plan shall contain measures which will be effective to notify the public during any calendar year on a regular basis of instances or areas in which any national primary ambient air quality standard is exceeded or was exceeded during any portion of the preceding calendar year to advise the public of the health hazards associated with such pollution, and to enhance public awareness of the measures which can be taken to prevent such standards from being exceeded and the ways in which the public can participate in regulatory and other efforts to improve air quality. Such measures may include the posting of warning signs on interstate highway access points to metropolitan areas or television, radio, or press notices or information.

(b) The Administrator is authorized to make grants to States to assist in carrying out the requirements of subsection (a).

§ 7428. State boards

[Sec. 128] (a) Not later than the date one year after the date of the enactment of this section, each applicable implementation plan shall contain requirements that—

(1) any board or body which approves permits or enforcement orders under this Act shall have at least a majority of members who represent the public interest and do not derive any significant portion of their income from persons subject to permits or enforcement orders under this Act, and

(2) any potential conflicts of interest by members of such board or body or the head of an executive agency with similar power be adequately disclosed.

A state may adopt any requirement respecting conflicts of interest for such boards or bodys or heads of executive agencies, or any other entities which are more stringent than the requirements of paragraph (1) and (2), and the Administrator shall approve any such more stringent requirements submitted as part of an implementation plan.

Part B

Ozone Protection

§ 7450. Congressional declaration of purpose

[Sec. 150] The purposes of this part are (1) to provide for a better understanding of the effects of human actions on the stratosphere, especially the ozone in the stratosphere, (2) to provide for a better understanding of the effects of changes in the stratosphere, especially the ozone in the stratosphere on the public health and welfare, (3) to provide information on the progress of regulation of activities which may reasonably be anticipated to affect the ozone in the stratosphere in such a way as to cause or contribute to endangerment of the public health or welfare, and (4) to provide information on the need for additional legislation in this area, if any.

§ 7451. Congressional findings and definitions

[Sec. 151] (a) The Congress finds, on the basis of presently available information, that—

(1) halocarbon compounds introduced into the environment potentially threaten to reduce the concentration of ozone in the stratosphere;

(2) ozone reduction will lead to increased incidence of solar ultraviolet radiation at the surface of the Earth;

(3) increased incidence of solar ultraviolet radiation is likely to cause increased rates of disease in humans (including increased rates of skin cancer), threaten food crops, and otherwise damage the natural environment;

(4) other substances, practices, processes, and activities may affect the ozone in the stratosphere, and should be investigated to give early warning of any potential problem and to develop the basis for possible future regulatory action; and

(5) there is some authority under existing law, to regulate certain substances, practices, processes, and activities which may affect the ozone in the stratosphere.

§ 7452. "Halocarbon" and "stratosphere" defined

[Sec. 152] For the purposes of this subtitle—
(1) the term "halocarbon" means the chemical compounds $CFCl_3$ and CF_2Cl_2 and such other halogenated compounds as the Administrator determines may reasonably be anticipated to contribute to reductions in the concentration of ozone in the stratosphere.
(2) the term "stratosphere" means that part of the atmosphere above the tropopause.

§ 7453. Studies by Environmental Protection Agency

[Sec. 153] (a) The Administrator shall conduct a study of the cumulative effect of all substances, practices, processes, and activities which may affect the stratosphere, especially ozone in the stratosphere. The study shall include an analysis of the independent effects on the stratosphere especially such ozone in the stratosphere of—
(1) the release into the ambient air of halocarbons,
(2) the release into the ambient air of other sources of chlorine,
(3) the uses of bromine compounds, and
(4) emissions of aircraft and aircraft propulsion systems employed by operational and experimental aircraft.
The study shall also include such physical, chemical, atmospheric, biomedical, or other research and monitoring as may be necessary to ascertain (A) any direct or indirect effects upon the public health and welfare of changes in the stratosphere, especially ozone in the stratosphere, and (B) the probable causes of changes in the stratosphere, especially the ozone in the stratosphere.
(b) The Administrator shall undertake research on—
(1) methods to recover and recycle substances which directly or indirectly affect the stratosphere, especially ozone in the stratosphere.
(2) methods of preventing the escape of such substances,
(3) safe substitutes for such substances, and
(4) other methods to regulate substances, practices, processes, and activities which may reasonably be anticipated to affect the stratosphere, especially ozone in the stratosphere.
(c)(1) The studies and research conducted under this section may be undertaken with such cooperation and assistance from universities and private industry as may be available. Each department, agency, and instrumentality of the United States having the capability to do so is authorized and encouraged to provide assistance to the Administrator in carrying out the

requirements of this section, including (notwithstanding any other provision of law) any services which such department, agency, or instrumentality may have the capability to render or obtain by contract with third parties.

(2) The Administrator shall encourage the cooperation and assistance of other nations in carrying out the studies and research under this section. The Administrator is authorized to cooperate with and support similar research efforts of other nations.

(d)(1) The Administrator shall undertake to contract with the National Academy of Sciences to study the state of knowledge and the adequacy of research efforts to understand (A) the effects of all substances, practices, processes, and activities which may affect the stratosphere, especially ozone in the stratosphere; (B) the health and welfare effects of modifications of the stratosphere, especially ozone in the stratosphere; and (C) methods of control of such substances, practices and activities including alternatives, costs, feasibility, and timing. The Academy shall make a report of its findings by January 1, 1978.

(2) The Administrator shall make available to the Academy such information in the Administrator's possession as is needed for the purposes of the study provided for in this subsection.

(e) The Secretary of Labor shall study and transmit a report to the Administrator and the Congress not later than six months after date of enactment, with respect to the losses and gains to industry and employment which could result from the elimination of the use of halocarbons in aerosol containers and for other purposes. Such report shall include recommended means of alleviating unemployment or other undesirable economic impact, if any, resulting therefrom.

(f)(1) The Administrator shall establish and act as Chairman of a Coordinating Committee for the purpose of insuring coordination of the efforts of other Federal agencies carrying out research and studies related to or supportive of the research provided for in subsections (a) and (b) and section 154.

(2) Members of the Coordinating Committee shall include the appropriate official responsible for the relevant research efforts of each of the following agencies:

(A) the National Oceanic and Atmospheric Administration.

(B) the National Aeronautics and Space Administration.

(C) the Federal Aviation Administration,

(D) the Department of Agriculture

(E) the National Cancer Institute

(F) the National Institute of Environmental Health Sciences,

(G) the National Science Foundation, and the appropriate officials responsible for the relevant research efforts of such other agencies carrying out related efforts as the Chairman shall designate. A representative of the Department of State shall sit on the Coordinating Committee to encourage and facilitate international coordination.

(3) The Coordinating Committee shall review and comment on plans for, and the execution and results of, pertinent research and studies. For this purpose, the agencies named in or designated under paragraph (2) of this subsection shall make appropriate and timely reports to the Coordinating Committee on plans for and the execution and results of such research and studies.

(4) The Chairman may request a report from any Federal Agency for the purpose of determining if that agency should sit on the Coordinating Committee.

(g) Not later than January 1, 1978, and biennially thereafter, the Administrator shall report to the appropriate committees of the House and the Senate, the results of the studies and research conducted under this section and the results of related research and studies conducted by other Federal agencies.

§ 7454. Research and monitoring by other agencies

[Sec. 154] (a) The Administrator of the National Oceanic and Atmospheric Administration shall establish a continuing program of research and monitoring of the stratosphere for the purpose of early detection of changes in the stratosphere and climatic effects of such changes. Such Administrator shall on or before January 1, 1978, and biennially thereafter, transmit such report to the Administrator and the Congress on the findings of such research and monitoring. Such report shall contain any appropriate recommendations for legislation or regulation or both.

(b) The National Aeronautics and Space Administration shall, pursuant to its authority under title IV of the National Aeronautics and Space Act of 1958, continue programs of research, technology, and monitoring of the stratosphere for the purposes of understanding the physics and chemistry of the stratosphere and for the early detection of potentially harmful changes in the ozone in the stratosphere. Such Administration shall transmit reports by January 1, 1978, and biennially thereafter to the Administrator and the Congress on the results of the programs authorized in this subsection, together with any appropriate recommendations for legislation or regulation (or both).

(c) The Director of the National Science Foundation shall encourage and support ongoing stratospheric research programs and continuing research programs that will increase scientific knowledge of the effects of changes in the ozone layer in the stratosphere upon living organisms and ecosystems. Such Director shall transmit reports by January 1, 1978, and biennially thereafter to the Administrator and the Congress on the results of such programs, together with any appropriate recommendations for legislation or regulation (or both).

(d) The Secretary of Agriculture shall encourage and support continuing research programs that will increase scientific knowledge of the effects of changes in the ozone in the stratosphere upon animals, crops, and other plant life. Such Secretary shall transmit reports by January 1, 1978, and biennially thereafter to the Administrator and the Congress on the results of such programs together with any appropriate recommendations for legislation or regulation (or both).

(e) The Secretary of Health, Education, and Welfare shall encourage and support continuing research programs that will increase scientific knowledge of the effects of changes in the ozone in the stratosphere upon human health. Such Secretary shall transmit reports by January 1, 1978, and biennially thereafter, to the Administrator and the Congress on the results of such programs, together with any appropriate recommendations for legislation or regulation (or both).

(f) In carrying out subsections (a) through (e) of this section, the agencies involved (1) shall enlist and encourage cooperation and assistance from other Federal agencies, universities, and private industry, and (2) shall solicit the views of the Administrator with regard to plans for the research involved so that any such research will, if regulatory action by the Administrator is indicated, provide the preliminary information base for such action.

§ 7455. Progress of regulation

[Sec. 155] The Administrator shall provide an interim report to the Congress by January 1, 1978, shall provide a final report within two years after date of enactment, and shall provide follow-up reports annually thereafter on the actions taken by the Environmental Protection Agency and all other Federal agencies to regulate sources of halocarbon emissions, the results of such regulations in protecting the ozone layer, and the need for additional regulatory action, if any. The reports under this section shall also include recommendations for the control of substances, practices, processes, and activities other than those involving halocarbons, which are found to affect the ozone in the stratosphere and which may cause or contribute to harmful effects on public health or welfare.

§ 7456. International cooperation

[Sec. 156] The President shall undertake to enter into international agreements to foster cooperative research which complements studies and research authorized by this part, and to develop standards and regulations which protect the stratosphere consistent with regulations applicable within the United States. For these purposes the President through the Secretary of State and the Assistant Secretary of State for Oceans and International Environmental and Scientific Affairs, shall negotiate multilateral treaties, conventions, resolutions, or other agreements, and formulate, present, or support proposals at the United Nations and other appropriate international forums and shall report to the Congress periodically on efforts to arrive at such agreements.

§ 7457. Regulations

[Sec. 157] (a) If at any time prior to the submission of the final report referred to in section 155 in the Administrator's judgment, any substance, practice, process, or activity may reasonably be anticipated to affect the stratosphere, especially ozone in the stratosphere, and such effect may reasonably be anticipated to endanger public health or welfare, the Administrator shall promptly promulgate regulations respecting the control of such substance, practice, process, or activity, and shall simultaneously submit notice of the promulgation of such regulations to the Congress.

(b) Upon submission of the final report referred to in section 155, and after consideration of the research and study under sections 153 and 154 and, consultation with appropriate Federal agencies and scientific entities, the Administrator shall propose regulations for the control of any substance, practice, process, or activity (or any combination thereof) which in his judgment may reasonably be anticipated to affect the stratosphere, especially ozone in the stratosphere, if such effect in the stratosphere may reasonably be anticipated to endanger public health or welfare. Such regulations shall take into account the feasibility and the costs of achieving such control. Such regulations may exempt medical use products for which the Administrator determines there is no suitable substitute. Not later than three months after proposal of such regulations the Administrator shall promulgate such regulations in final form. From time to time, and under the same procedures, the Administrator may revise any of the regulations submitted under this subsection.

§ 7458. Other provisions unaffected

[Sec. 158] Nothing in this part shall be construed to alter or affect the authority of the Administrator under section 303 (relating to emergency powers), under section 231 (relating to aircraft emission standards), or under any other provision of this Act or to affect the authority of any other department, agency, or instrumentality of the United States under any other provision of law to promulgate or enforce any requirement respecting the control of any substance, practice, process, or activity for purposes of protecting the stratosphere or ozone in the stratosphere. In the case of any proposed rule respecting ozone in the stratosphere which has been published under the Toxic Substances Control Act prior to the date of enactment of this Act notwithstanding section 9(b) of such Act, nothing in this part shall be construed to prohibit or restrict the Administrator from taking any action under the Toxic Substances Control Act respecting the promulgation or enforcement of such rule.

§ 7459. State authority

[Sec. 159] (a) Nothing in this part shall preclude or deny any State or political subdivision thereof from adopting or enforcing any requirement respecting the control of any substance, practice, process, or activity for purposes of protecting the stratosphere or ozone in the stratosphere except as otherwise provided in subsection (b).

(b) If a regulation of any substance, practice, process, or activity is in effect under this part in order to prevent or abate any risk to the stratosphere, or ozone in the stratosphere, no State or political subdivision there of may adopt or attempt to enforce any requirement respecting the control of any such substance, practice, process, or activity to prevent or abate such risk, unless the requirement of the State or political subdivision is identical to the requirement of such regulation. The preceding sentence shall not apply with respect to any law or regulation of any State or political subdivision controlling the use of halocarbons as propellants in aerosol spray containers.

Part C

Prevention of Significant Deterioration of Air Quality

Subpart I. Clean Air

§ 7470. Congressional declaration of purpose

[Sec. 160] The purposes of this part are as follows:

(1) to protect public health and welfare from any actual or potential adverse effect which in the Administrator's judgment may reasonably be anticipated to occur from air pollution (or from exposures to pollutants in other media, which pollutants originate as emissions to the ambient air), notwithstanding attainment and maintenance of all national ambient air quality standards;

(2) to preserve, protect, and enhance the air quality in national parks, national wilderness areas, national monuments, national seashores, and other areas of special national or regional natural recreational, scenic, or historic value;

(3) to insure that economic growth will occur in a manner consistent with the preservation of existing clean air resources;

(4) to assure that emissions from any source in any State will not interfere with any portion of the applicable implementation plan to prevent significant deterioration of air quality for any other State; and

(5) to assure that any decision to permit increased air pollution in any area to which this section applies is made only after careful evaluation of all the consequences of such a decision and after adequate procedural opportunities for informed public participation for the decisionmaking process.

§ 7471. Plan requirements

[Sec. 161] In accordance with the policy of section 101(b)(1), each applicable implementation plan shall contain emission limitations and such other measures as may be necessary, as determined under regulations promulgated under this part, to prevent significant deterioration of air quality in each region (or portion thereof) identified pursuant to section 107(d)(1)(D) or (E).

§ 7472. Initial classifications

[Sec. 162] Upon the enactment of this part, all—
(1) international parks,
(2) national wilderness areas which exceed 5,000 acres in size,
(3) national memorial parks which exceed 5,000 acres in size, and
(4) national parks which exceed six thousand acres in size, and which are in existence on the date of enactment of the Clean Air Act Amendments of 1977 shall be class I areas and may not be redesignated. All areas which were redesignated as class I under regulations promulgated before such date of enactment shall be class I areas which may be redesignated as provided in this part.

(b) All areas in such State identified pursuant to section 107(d)(1)(D) or (E) which are not established as class I under subsection (a) shall be class II areas unless redesignated under section 164.

§ 7473. Increments and ceilings

[Sec. 163] (a) In the case of sulfur oxides and particulates, each applicable implementation plan shall contain measures assuring that maximum allowable increases over baseline concentrations of, and maximum allowable concentrations of, such pollutant shall not be exceeded. In the case of any maximum allowable increase (except an allowable increase specified under 165(d)(2)(C)(iv)) for a pollutant based on concentrations permitted under national ambient air quality standards for any period other than an annual period, such regulations shall permit such maximum allowable increase to be exceeded during one such period per year.

(b)(1) For any class I area, the maximum allowable increase in concentrations of sulfur dioxide and particulate matter over the baseline concentration of such pollutants shall not exceed the following amounts:

Pollutants	Maximum allowable increase (in micrograms per cubic meter)
Particulate matter:	
Annual geometric mean	5
Twenty-four-hour maximum	10
Sulfur dioxide:	
Annual arithmetic mean	2
Twenty-four-hour maximum	5
Three-hour maximum	25

(2) For any class II area, the maximum allowable increase in concentrations of sulfur dioxide and particulate matter over the baseline concentration of such pollutants shall not exceed the following amounts:

Pollutants	Maximum allowable increase (in micrograms per cubic meter)
Particulate matter:	
Annual geometric mean	19
Twenty-four-hour maximum	37
Sulfur dioxide:	
Annual arithmetic mean	20
Twenty-four-hour maximum	91
Three-hour maximum	512

(3) For each class III area, the maximum allowable increase in concentrations of sulfur dioxide and particulate matter over the baseline concentration of such pollutants shall not exceed the following amounts:

Pollutants	Maximum allowable increase (in micrograms per cubic meter)
Particulate matter:	
Annual geometric mean	37
Twenty-four-hour maximum	75
Sulfur dioxide:	
Annual arithmetic mean	40
Twenty-four-hour maximum	182
Three-hour maximum	700

(4) The maximum allowable concentrations of any air pollutant in any areas to which this part applies shall not exceed a concentration for such pollutant for each period of exposure equal to—
   (A) the concentration permitted under the national secondary ambient air quality standards, or
   (B) the concentration permitted under the national primary ambient air quality standard.
      whichever concentration is lowest for such pollutant for such period of exposure.
(c)(1) In the case of any State which has a plan approved by the Administrator for purposes of carrying out this part, the Governor of such

State may, after notice and opportunity for public hearing, issue orders or promulgate rules providing that for purposes of determining compliance with the maximum allowable increases in ambient concentrations of an air pollutant, the following concentrations of such pollutant shall not be taken into account:

(A) concentrations of such pollutant attributable to the increase in emissions from stationary sources which have converted from the use of petroleum products, or natural gas, or both, by reason of an order which is in effect under the provisions of section 2 (a) and (b) of the Energy Supply and Environmental Coordination Act of 1974 (or any subsequent legislation which supersedes such provisions) over the emissions from such sources before the effective date of such order.

(B) the concentrations of such pollutant attributable to the increase in emissions from stationary sources which have converted from using natural gas by reason of a natural gas curtailment pursuant to a natural gas curtailment plan in effect pursuant to the Federal Power Act over the emissions from such sources before the effective date of such plan,

(C) concentrations of particulate matter attributable to the increase in emissions from construction or other temporary emission-related activities, and

(D) the increase in concentrations attributable to new sources outside the United States over the concentrations attributable to existing sources which are included in the baseline concentration determined in accordance with section 169(4).

(2) No action taken with respect to a source under paragraph (1)(A) or (1)(B) shall apply more than five years after the effective date of the order referred to in paragraph (1)(A) or the plan referred to in paragraph (1)(B), whichever is applicable. If both such order and plan are applicable, no such action shall apply more than five years after the later of such effective dates.

(3) No action under this subsection shall take effect unless the Governor submits the order or rule providing for such exclusion to the Administrator and the Administrator determines that such order or rule is in compliance with the provisions of this subsection.

§ 7474. Area redesignation

[Sec. 164] (a) Except as otherwise provided under subsection (c), a State may redesignate such areas as it deems appropriate as class I areas. The following areas may be redesignated only as class I or II:

(1) an area which exceeds ten thousand acres in size and is a national monument, a national primitive area, a national preserve, a national recreation area, a national wild and scenic river, national wildlife refuge, a national lakeshore or seashore, and

(2) a national park or national wilderness area established after the date of enactment of this Act which exceeds ten thousand acres in size.

Any area (other than an areas referred to in paragraph (1) or (2) or an area established as class I under section 162(a)) may be redesignated by the State as class III if—

    (A) such redesignation has been specifically approved by the Governor of the State, after consultation with the appropriate Committees of the legislature if it is in session or with the leadership of the legislature if it is not in session (unless State law provides that such redesignation must be specifically approved by State legislation) and if general purpose units of local government representing a majority of the residents of the area so redesignated enact legislation (including for such units of local government resolutions where appropriate) concurring in the State's redesignation;

    (B) such redesignation will not cause, or contribute to, concentrations of any air pollutant which exceed any maximum allowable increase or maximum allowable concentration permitted under the classification of any other area; and

    (C) such redesignation otherwise meets the requirements of this part.

Subparagraph (A) of this paragraph shall not apply to area redesignations by Indian tribes.

(b)(1)(A) Prior to redesignation of any area under this part, notice shall be afforded and public hearings shall be conducted in areas proposed to be redesignated and in areas which may be affected by the proposed redesignation. Prior to any such public hearing a satisfactory description and analysis of the health, environmental, economic, social, and energy effects of the proposed redesignation shall be prepared and made available for public inspection and prior to any such redesignation, the description and analysis of such effects shall be reviewed and examined by the redesignating authorities.

    (B) Prior to the issuance of notice under subparagraph (A) respecting the redesignation of any area under this subsection, if such area includes any Federal lands, the State shall provide written notice to the appropriate Federal land manager and afford adequate opportunity (but not in excess of 60 days) to confer with the State respecting the intended notice of redesignation and to submit written comments and recommendations with respect to such intended notice of redesignation. In redesignating any area under this section with respect to which any Federal land manager has submitted written comments and recommendations, the State shall publish a list of any inconsistency between such recommendations and an explanation of such inconsistency (together with the reasons for making such redesignation against the recommendation of the Federal land manager).

    (C) The Administrator shall promulgate regulations not later than six months after date of enactment of this part, to assure, insofar as practicable, that prior to any public hearing on redesignation of any area, there shall be available for public inspection any specific plans for any new or modified major emitting facility which may be permitted to be constructed and operated only if the area in question is designated or redesignated as class III.

(2) The Administrator may disapprove the redesignation of any area only if he finds, after notice and opportunity for public hearing, that such redesignation does not meet the procedural requirements of this section or is inconsistent with the requirements of section 162(a) or of subsection (a) of this section. If any such disapproval occurs, the classification of the area shall be that which was in effect prior to the redesignation which was disapproved.

(c) Lands within the exterior boundaries of reservations of federally recognized Indian tribes may be redesignated only by the appropriate Indian governing body. Such Indian governing body shall be subject in all respects to the provisions of subsection (e).

(d) The Federal Land Manager shall review all national monuments, primitive areas, and national preserves, and shall recommend any appropriate areas for redesignation as class I where air quality related values are important attributes of the area. The Federal Land Manager shall report such recommendations, with supporting analysis, to the Congress and the affected States within one year after enactment of this section. The Federal Land Manger shall consult with the appropriate States before making such recommendations.

(e) If any State affected by the redesignation of an area by an Indian tribe or any Indian tribe affected by the redesignation of an area by a State disagrees with such redesignation of any area, or if a permit is proposed to be issued for any new major emitting facility proposed for construction in any State which the Governor of an affected State or governing body of an affected Indian tribe determines will cause or contribute to a cumulative change in air quality in excess of that allowed in this part within the affected State or tribal reservation, the Governor or ruling body may request the Administrator to enter into negotiations with the parties involved to resolve such dispute. If requested by any State or Indian tribe involved, the Administrator shall make a recommendation to resolve the dispute and protect the air quality related values of the lands involved. If the parties involved do not reach agreement, the Administrator shall resolve the dispute and his determination, or the results of agreements reached through other means, shall become part of the applicable plan and shall be enforeable as part of such plan. In resolving such disputes relating to area redesignation, the Administrator shall consider the extent to which the lands involved are of sufficient size to allow effective air quality management or have air quality related values of such an area.

§ 7475. Preconstruction requirements

[Sec. 165] (a) No major emitting facility on which construction is commenced after the date of the enactment of this part may be constructed in any area to which this part applies unless—

(1) a permit has been issued for such proposed facility in accordance with this part setting forth emission limitations for such facility which conform to the requirements of this part;

(2) the proposed permit has been subject to a review in accordance with this section, the required analysis has been conducted in accordance with regulations promulgated by the Administrator, and a public hearing has been held with opportunity for interested persons including representatives of the Administrator to appear and submit written or oral presentations on the air quality impact of such source, alternatives thereto, control technology requirements, and other appropriate considerations;

(3) the owner or operator of such facility demonstrates, as required pursuant to section 110(j), that emissions from construction or operation of such facility will not cause, or contribute to, air pollution in excess of any (A) maximum allowable increase or maximum allowable concentration for any pollutant in any area to which this part applies more than one time per year, (B) national ambient air quality standard in any air quality control region, or (C) any other applicable emission standard or standard of performance under this Act;

(4) the proposed facility is subject to the best available control technology for each pollutant subject to regulation under this Act emitted from, or which results from, such facility;

(5) the provisions of subsection (d) with respect to protection of class I areas have been complied with for such facility;

(6) there has been an analysis of any air quality impacts projected for the area as a result of growth associated with such facility;

(7) the person who owns or operates, or proposes to own or operate, a major emitting facility for which a permit is required under this part agrees to conduct such monitoring as may be necessary to determine the effect which emissions from any such facility may have, or is having, on air quality in any area which may be affected by emissions from such source; and

(8) in the case of a source which proposes to construct in a class III area, emissions from which would cause or contribute to exceeding the maximum allowable increments applicable in a class II area and where no standard under section 111 of this Act has been promulgated subsequent to enactment of the Clean Air Act Amendments of 1977 for such source category, the Administrator has approved the determination of best available technology as set forth in the permit.

(b) The demonstration pertaining to maximum allowable increases required under section (a)(3) shall not apply to maximum allowable increases for class II areas in the case of an expansion or modification of a major emitting facility which is in existence on the date of enactment of the Clean Air Act Amendment of 1977, whose allowable emissions of air pollutants, after compliance with subsection (a)(4), will be less than fifty tons per year and for which the owner or operator of such facility demonstrates that emissions of particulate matter and sulfur oxides will not cause or contribute to ambient air quality levels in excess of the national secondary ambient air quality standard for either of such pollutants.

(c) Any completed permit application under section 100 for a major emitting facility in any area to which this part applies shall be granted or denied not later than one year after the date of filing of such completed application.

(d)(1) Each State shall transmit to the Administrator a copy of each permit application relating to a major emitting facility received by such State and provided notice to the Administrator of every action related to the consideration of such permit.

(2)(A) The Administrator shall provide notice of the permit application to the Federal Land Manager and the Federal official charged with direct responsibility for management of any lands within a class I area which may be affected by emissions from the proposed facility.

(B) The Federal Land Manager and the Federal official charged with direct responsibility for management of such lands shall have an affirmative responsibility to protect the air quality related values (including visibility) of any such lands within a class I area and to consider, in consultation with the Administrator, whether a proposed major emitting facility will have an adverse impact on such values.

(C)(i) In any case where the Federal official charged with direct responsibility for management of any lands within a class I area or the Federal Land Manager of such lands, or the Administrator, or the Governor of an adjacent State containing such a class I area files a notice alleging that emissions from a proposed major emitting facility may cause or contribute to a change in the air quality in such area and identifying the potential adverse impact of such change, a permit shall not be issued unless the owner or operator of such facility demonstrates that emissions of particulate matter and sulfur dioxide will not cause or contribute to concentrations which exceed maximum allowable increases for a class I area.

(ii) In any case where the Federal Land Manager demonstrates to the satisfaction of the State that the emissions from such facility will have an adverse impact on the air quality-related values (including visibility) of such lands, notwithstanding the fact that the change in air quality resulting from emissions from such facility will not cause or contribute to concentrations which exceed the maximum allowable increases for a class I area, a permit shall not be issued.

(iii) In any case where the owner or operator of such facility demonstrates to the satisfaction of the Federal Land Manager, and the Federal Land Manager so certifies, that the emissions from such facility will have no adverse impact on the air quality related values of such lands (including visibility), notwithstanding the fact that the change in air quality resulting from emissions from such facility will cause or contribute to concentrations which exceed the maximum allowable increases for class I areas, the State may issue a permit.

(iv) In the case of a permit issued pursuant to clause (iii), such facility shall comply with such emission limitations under such permit as may be necessary to assure that emissions of sulfur oxides and particulates from such facility, will not cause or contribute to concentrations of such pollutant which exceed the following maximum allowable increases over the baseline concentration for such pollutants.

Pollutants	Maximum allowable increase (in micrograms per cubic meter)
Particulate matter:	
Annual geometric mean	19
Twenty-four-hour maximum	37
Sulfur dioxide;	
Annual arithmetic mean	20
Twenty-four-hour maximum	91
Three-hour maximum	325

(D)(i) In any case where the owner or operator of a proposed major emitting facility who has been denied a certification under subparagraph (C)(iii) demonstrates to the satisfaction of the Governor, after notice and public hearing, and the Governor finds, that the facility cannot be constructed by reason of any maximum allowable increase for sulfur dioxide for periods of 24 hours or less applicable to any class I area and, in the case of Federal mandatory class I areas, that a variance under this clause will not adversely affect the air quality related values of the area (including visibility), the Governor, after consideration of the federal land manager's recommendation (if any) and subject to his concurrence, may grant a variance from such maximum allowable increase. If such variance is granted, a permit may be issued to such source pursuant to the requirements of this subparagraph.

(ii) In any case in which the Governor recommends a variance under this subparagraph in which the Federal land manager does not concur, the recommendations of the Governor and the Federal land manager shall be transmitted to the President. The President may approve the Governor's recommendation if he finds that such variance is in the national interest. No Presidential finding shall be reviewable in any court. The variance shall take effect if the President approves the Governor's recommendations. The President shall approve or disapprove such recommendation within 90 days after his receipt of the recommendations of the Governor and the Federal Land Manager.

(iii) In the case of a permit issued pursuant to this subparagraph, such facility shall comply with such emission limitations under such permit as may be necessary to assure that emissions of sulfur oxides from such facility will not (during any day on which the otherwise applicable maximum allowable increases are exceeded) cause or contribute to concentrations which exceed the following maximum allowable increases for such areas over the baseline concentration for such pollutant and to assure that such emissions will not cause or contribute to concentrations which exceed the otherwise applicable maximum allowable increases for periods of exposure of 24 hours or less on more than 18 days during the annual period:

Maximum Allowable Increase
[In micrograms per cubic meter]

Period of exposure	Low terrain areas	High terrain areas
24-hr maximum	36	62
3-hr maximum	130	221

(iv) For purposes of clause (iii), the term "high terrain area" means with respect to any facility, any area having an elevation of 900 feet or more above the base of the stack of such facility, and the term "low terrain area" means any area other than a high terrain area.

(e)(1) The review provided for in subsection (a) shall be preceded by an analysis in accordance with regulations of the Administrator, promulgated under this subsection, which may be conducted by the State (or any general purpose unit of local government) or by the major emitting facility applying for such permit, of the ambient air quality at the proposed site and in areas which may be affected by emissions from such facility for each pollutant subject to regulation under this Act which will be emitted from such facility.

(2) Effective one year after date of enactment of this part, the analysis required by this subsection shall include continuous air quality monitoring data gathered for purposes of determining whether emis-

sions from such facility will exceed the maximum allowable increases or the maximum allowable concentration permitted under this part. Such data shall be gathered over a period of one calendar year preceding the date of application for a permit under this part unless the State, in accordance with regulations promulgated by the Administrator, determines that a complete and adequate analysis for such purposes may be accomplished in a shorter period. The results of such analysis shall be available at the time of the public hearing on the application for such permit.

(3) The Administrator shall within six months after the date of enactment of this part promulgate regulations respecting the analysis required under this subsection which regulations—

    (A) shall not require the use of any automatic or uniform buffer zone or zones,

    (B) shall require an analysis of the ambient air quality, climate and meteorology, terrain, soils and vegetation, and visibility at the site of the proposed major emitting facility and in the area potentially affected by the emissions from such facility for each pollutant regulated under this Act will be emitted from, or which results from the construction or operation of, such facility, the size and nature of the proposed facility, the degree of continuous emission reduction which could be achieved by such facility, and such other factors as may be relevant in determining the effect of emissions from a proposed facility on any air quality control region.

    (C) shall require the results of such analysis shall be available at the time of the public hearing on the application for such permit, and

    (D) shall specify with reasonable particularity each air quality model or models to be used under specified sets of conditions for purposes of this part.

Any model or models designated under such regulations may be adjusted upon a determination, after notice and opportunity for public hearing, by the Administrator that such adjustment is necessary to take into account unique terrain or meteorological characteristics of an area potentially affected by emissions from a source applying for a permit required under this part.

§ 7476. Other pollutants

[Sec. 166] (a) In the case of the pollutants hydrocarbons, carbon monoxide, photochemical oxidants, and nitrogen oxides, the Administrator shall conduct a study and not later than two years after the date of enactment of this part, promulgate regulations to prevent the significant deterioration of air quality which would result from the emissions of such pollutants. In the case of pollutants for which national ambient air quality standards are promulgated after the date of the enactment of this part, he shall promulgate such regulations not more than 2 years after the date of promulgation of such standards.

(b) Regulations referred to in subsection (a) shall become effective one year after the date of promulgation. Within 21 months after such date of promulgation such plan revision shall be submitted to the Administrator who shall approve or disapprove the plan within 25 months after such date or promulgation in the same manner as required under section 110.

(c) Such regulations shall provide specific numerical measures against which permit applications may be evaluated, a framework for stimulating improved control technology, protection of air quality values, and fulfill the goals and purposes set forth in section 101 and section 160.

(d) The regulations of the Administrator under subsection (a) shall provide specific measures at least as effective as the increments established in section 163 to fulfill such goals and purposes, and may contain air quality increments, emission density requirements, or other measures.

(e) With respect to any air pollutant for which a national ambient air quality standard is established other than sulfur oxides or particulate matter, an area classification plan shall not be required under this section if the implementation plan adopted by the State and submitted for the Administrator's approval or promulgated by the Administrator under section 110(c) contains other provisions which when considered as a whole, the Administrator finds will carry out the purposes in section 160 at least as effectively as an area classification plan for such pollutant. Such other provisions referred to in the preceding sentence need not require the establishment of maximum allowable increases with respect to such pollutant for any area to which this section applies.

§ 7477. Enforcement

[Sec. 167] The Administrator shall, and a State may take such measures, including issuance of an order, or seeking injunctive relief, as necessary to prevent the construction of a major emitting facility which does not conform to the requirements of this part, or which is proposed to be constructed in any area included in the list promulgated pursuant to paragraph (1)(D) or (E) of subsection (d) of section 107 of this Act and which is not subject to an implementation plan which meets the requirements of this part.

§ 7478. Period before plan approval

[Sec. 168] (a) Until such time as an applicable implementation plan is in effect for any area, which plan meets the requirements of this part to prevent significant deterioration of air quality with respect to any air pollutant, applicable regulations under this Act prior to enactment of this part shall remain in effect to prevent significant deterioration of air quality in any such area for any such pollutant except as otherwise provided in subsection (b).

(b) If any regulation in effect prior to enactment of this part to prevent significant deterioration of air quality would be inconsistent with the requirements of section 162(a), section 163(b) or section 164(a), then such regulations shall be deemed amended so as to conform with such requirements. In the case of a facility on which construction was commenced (in accordance with the definition of "commenced" in section 169(2)) after June 1, 1975, and prior to the enactment of the Clean Air Act Amendments of 1977, the review and permitting of such facility shall be in accordance with the regulations for the prevention of significant deterioration in effect prior to the enactment of the Clean Air Act Amendments of 1977.

§ 7479. Definitions

[Sec. 169] For purposes of this part—

(1) The term "major emitting facility" means any of the following stationary sources of air pollutants which emit, or have the potential to emit, one hundred tons per year or more of any air pollutant from the following types of stationary sources: fossil-fuel fired steam electric plants of more than two hundred and fifty million British thermal units per hour heat input, coal cleaning plants (thermal dryers), kraft pulp mills, Portland Cement plants, primary zinc smelters, iron and steel mill plants, primary aluminum ore reduction plants, primary copper smelters, municipal incinerators capable of charging more than two hundred and fifty tons of refuse per day, hydrofluoric, sulfuric, and nitric acid plants, petroleum refineries, lime plants, phosphate rock processing plants, coke oven batteries, sulfur recovery plants, carbon black plants (furnace process), primary lead smelters, fuel conversion plants, sintering plants, secondary metal production facilities, chemical process plants, fossil-fuel boilers of more than two hundred and fifty million British thermal units per hour heat input, petroleum storage and transfer facilities with a capacity exceeding three hundred thousand barrels, taconite ore processing facilities, glass fiber processing plants, charcoal production facilities. Such term also includes any other source with the potential to emit two hundred and fifty tons per year or more of any air pollutant. This term shall not include new or modified facilities which are nonprofit health or education institutions which have been exempted by the State.

(2)(A) The term "commenced" as applied to construction of a major emitting facility means that the owner or operator has obtained all necessary preconstruction approvals or permits required by Federal, State, or local air pollution emissions and air quality laws or regulations and either has (i) begun, or caused to begin, a continuous program of physical on-site construction of the facility or (ii) entered into binding agreements or contractual obligations, which cannot be canceled or modified without substantial loss to the owner or operator, to undertake a program of construction of the facility to be completed within a reasonable time.

(B) The term "necessary preconstruction approvals or permits" means those permits or approvals, required by the permitting authority as a precondition to undertaking any activity under clauses (i) or (ii) of subparagraph (A) of this paragraph.

(C) The term "construction" when used in connection with any source or facility, includes the modification (as defined in section 111(a)) of any source or facility.

(3) The term "best available control technology" means an emission limitation based on the maximum degree of reduction of each pollutant subject to regulation under this Act emitted from or which results from any major emitting facility, which the permitting authority, on a case-by-case basis, taking into account energy, environmental, and economic impacts and other costs, determines is achievable for such facility through application of production, processes and available methods, systems, and techniques, including fuel cleaning or treatment or innovative fuel combustion techniques for control of each such pollutant. In no event shall application of "best available control technology" result in emissions of any pollutants which will exceed the emissions allowed by any applicable standard established pursuant to section 111 or 112 of this Act.

(4) The term "baseline concentration" means, with respect to a pollutant, the ambient concentration levels which exist at the time of the first application for a permit in an area subject to this part, based on air quality data available in the Environmental Protection Agency or a State air pollution control agency and on such monitoring data as the permit applicant is required to submit. Such ambient concentration levels shall take into account all projected emissions in, or which may affect, such area from any major emitting facility on which construction commenced prior to January 6, 1975, but which has not begun operation by the date of the baseline air quality concentration determination. Emissions of sulfur oxides and particulate matter from any major emitting facility on which construction commenced after January 6, 1975, shall not be included in the baseline and shall be counted against the maximum allowable increases in pollutant concentrations established under this part.

Subpart II. Visibility Protection

§ 7491. Visibility protection for federal class I areas

[Sec. 169A] (a)(1) Congress hereby declares as a national goal the prevention of any future, and the remedying of any existing, impairment of visibility in mandatory class I Federal areas which impairment results from manmade air pollution.

(2) Not later than six months after the date of the enactment of this section, the Secretary of the Interior in consultation with other Federal land managers shall review all mandatory class I Federal areas and

identify those where visibility is an important value of the area. From time to time the Secretary of the Interior may revise such identification. Not later than one year after such date of enactment, the Administrator shall, after consultation with the Secretary of the Interior, promulgate a list of mandatory class I Federal areas in which he determines visibility is an important value.

(3) Not later than eighteen months after the date of enactment of this section, the Administrator shall complete a study and report to Congress on available methods for implementing the national goal set forth in paragraph (1). Such report shall include recommendations for—

(A) methods for identifying, characterizing, determining, quantifying, and measuring visibility impairment in Federal areas referred to in paragraph (1), and

(B) modeling techniques (or other methods) for determining the extent to which manmade air pollution may reasonably be anticipated to cause or contribute to such impairment, and

(C) methods for preventing and remedying such manmade air pollution and resulting visibility impairment.

Such report shall also identify the classes or categories of sources and the types of air pollutants which, alone or in conjunction with other sources or pollutants, may reasonably be anticipated to cause or contribute significantly to impairment of visibility.

(4) Not later than twenty-four months after the date of enactment of this section, and after notice and public hearing, the Administrator shall promulgate regulations to assure (A) reasonable progress toward meeting the national goal specified in paragraph (1), and (B) compliance with the requirements of this section.

(b) Regulations under subsection (a)(4) shall—

(1) provide guidelines to the States, taking into account the recommendations under subsection (a)(3) on appropriate techniques and methods for implementing this section (as provided in subparagraphs (A) through (C) of such subsection (a)(3)), and

(2) require each applicable implementation plan for a State in which any area listed by the Administrator under subsection (a)(2) is located (or for a State the emissions from which may reasonably be anticipated to cause or contribute to any impairment of visibility in any such area) to contain such emission limits, schedules of compliance and other measures as may be necessary to make reasonable progress toward meeting the national goal specified in subsection (a), including—

(A) except as otherwise provided pursuant to subsection (c), a requirement that each major stationary source which is in existence on the date of enactment of this section, but which has not been in operation for more than fifteen years as of such date, and which, as determined by the State (or the Administrator in the case of a plan promulgated under section 110(c)) emits any air pollutant which may reasonably be anticipated to cause or contribute to any impairment of visibility in any such area, shall procure, install, and operate, as expeditiously as practicable (and maintain thereafter) the best available retrofit technology, as determined by the State (or the Administrator in the case of a plan promulgated under section 110(c)) for controlling emissions from such source for the purpose of eliminating or reducing any such impairment, and

(B) a long-term (ten to fifteen years) strategy for making reasonable progress toward meeting the national goal specified in subsection (a).

In the case of a fossil-fuel fired generating powerplant having a total generating capacity in excess of 750 megawatts, the emission limitations required under this paragraph shall be determined pursuant to guidelines, promulgated by the Administrator under paragraph (1).

(c)(1) The Administrator may, by rule, after notice and opportunity for public hearing, exempt any major stationary source from the requirement of subsection (b)(2)(A), upon his determination that such source does not or will not, by itself or in combination with other sources, emit any air pollutant which may reasonably be anticipated to cause or contribute to a significant impairment of visibility in any mandatory class I Federal area.

(2) Paragraph (1) of this subsection shall not be applicable to any fossil-fuel fired powerplant with total design capacity of 750 megawatts or more, unless the owner or operator of any such plant demonstrates to the satisfaction of the Administrator that such powerplant is located at such distance from all areas listed by the Administrator under subsection (a)(2) that such powerplant does not or will not, by itself or in combination with other sources, emit any air pollutant which may reasonably be anticipated to cause or contribute to significant impairment of visibility in any such area.

(3) An exemption under this subsection shall be effective only upon concurrence by the appropriate Federal land manager or managers with the Administrator's determination under this subsection.

(d) Before holding the public hearing on the proposed revision of an applicable implementation plan to meet the requirements of this section, the State (or the Administrator, in the case of a plan promulgated under section 110(c)) shall consult in person with the appropriate Federal land manager or managers and shall include a summary of the conclusions and recommendations of the Federal land managers in the notice to the public.

(e) In promulgating regulations under this section, the Administrator shall not require the use of any automatic or uniform buffer zone or zones.

(f) For purposes of section 304(a)(2), the meeting of the national goal specified in subsection (a)(1) by any specific date or dates shall not be considered a "non-discretionary duty" of the Administrator.

(g) For the purpose of this section—

(1) in determining reasonable progress there shall be taken into consideration the costs of compliance, the time necessary for compliance, and the energy and non-air quality environmental impacts of compliance, and the remaining useful life of any existing source subject to such requirements;

(2) in determining best available retrofit technology the State (or the Administrator in determining emission limitations which reflect such technology) shall take into consideration the costs of compliance, the energy and non-air quality environmental impacts of compliance, any existing pollution control technology in use at the source, the remaining useful life of the source, and the degree of improvement in visibility which may reasonably be anticipated to result from the use of such technology;

(3) the term "manmade air pollution" means air pollution which results directly or indirectly from human activities;

(4) the term "as expeditiously as practicable" means as expeditiously as practicable but in no event later than five years after the date of approval of a plan revision under this section (or the date of promulgation of such a plan revision in the case of action by the Administrator under section 110 (c) for purposes of this section);

(5) the term "mandatory class I Federal areas" means Federal areas which may not be designated as other than class I under this part.

(6) the terms "visibility impairment" and "impairment of visibility" shall include reduction in visual range and atmospheric discoloration; and

(7) the term "major stationary source" means the following types of stationary sources with the potential to emit 250 tons or more of any pollutant; fossil-fuel fired steam electric plants of more than 250 million British thermal units per hour heat input, coal cleaning plants (thermal dryers), kraft pulp mills, Portland Cement plants, primary zinc smelters, iron and steel mill plants, primary aluminum ore reduction plants, primary copper smelters, municipal incinerators capable of charging more than 250 tons of refuse per day, hydrofluoric, sulfuric, and nitric acid plants, petroleum refineries, lime plants, phosphate rock processing plants, coke oven batteries, sulfur recovery plants, carbon black plants (furnace process), primary lead smelters, fuel conversion plants, sintering plants, secondary metal production facilities, chemical process plants, fossil-fuel boilers of more than 250 million British thermal units per hour heat input, petroleum storage and transfer facilities with a capacity exceeding 300,000 barrels, taconite ore processing facilities, glass fiber processing plants, charcoal production facilities.

Part D

Plan Requirements for Nonattainment Areas

§ 7501. Definitions

[Sec. 171] For the purpose of this part and section 110 (a) (2) (I)—

(1) The term "reasonable further progress" means annual incremental reductions in emissions of the applicable air pollutant (including substantial reductions in the early years following approval or promulgation of plan provisions under this part and section 110 (a) (2) (I) and regular reductions thereafter) which are sufficient in the judgment of the Administrator, to provide for attainment of the applicable national ambient air quality standard by the date required in section 172 (a).

(2) The term "nonattainment area" means, for any air pollutant an area which is shown by monitored data or which is calculated by air quality modeling (or other methods determined by the Administrator to be reliable) to exceed any national ambient air quality standard for such pollutant. Such term includes any area identified under paragraphs (A) through (C) of section 107 (d) (1).

(3) The term "lowest achievable emission rate" means for any source that rate of emissions which reflects—

(A) the most stringent emission limitation which is contained in the implementation plan of any State for such class or category of source, unless the owner or operator of the proposed source demonstrates that such limitations are not achievable, or

(B) the most stringent emission limitation which is achieved in practice by such class or category of source, whichever is more stringent.

In no event shall the application of this term permit a proposed new or modified source to emit any pollutant in excess of the amount allowable under applicable new source standards of performance.

(4) The terms "modification" and "modified" mean the same as the term "modification" as used in section 111 (a) (4) of this Act.

§ 7502. Nonattainment plan provisions

[Sec. 172] (a) (1) The provisions of an applicable implementation plan for a State relating to attainment and maintenance of national ambient air quality standards in any non-attainment area which are required by section 110 (a) (2) (I) as a precondition for the construction or modification of any major stationary source in any such area after July 1, 1979, shall provide for attainment of each such national ambient air quality standard in each such area as expeditiously as practicable, but, in the case of national primary ambient air quality standards, not later than December 31, 1982.

(2) In the case of the national primary ambient air quality standard for photochemical oxidants or carbon monoxide (or both) if the State demonstrates to the satisfaction of the Administrator (on or before the time required for submission of such plan) that such attainment is not possible in an area with respect to either or both of such pollutants within the period prior to December 31, 1982, despite the implementation of all reasonably available measures, such provisions shall provide for the attainment of the national primary standard for the pollutant (or pollutants) with respect to which such demonstration is made, as expeditiously as practicable but not later than December 31, 1987.

(b) The plan provisions required by subsection (a) shall—

(1) be adopted by the State (or promulgated by the Administrator under section 110(c)) after reasonable notice and public hearing;

(2) provide for the implementation of all reasonably available control measures as expeditiously as practicable;

(3) require, in the interim, reasonable further progress (as defined in section 171(1) including such reduction in emissions from existing sources in the area as may be obtained through the adoption, at a minimum, of reasonably available control technology;

(4) include a comprehensive, accurate, current inventory of actual emissions from all sources (as provided by rule of the Administrator) of each such pollutant for each such area which is revised and resubmitted as frequently as may be necessary to assure that the requirements of paragraph (3) are met and to assess the need for additional reductions to assure attainment of each standard by the date required under subsection (a);

(5) expressly identify and quantify the emissions, if any, of any such pollutant which will be allowed to result from the construction and operation of major new or modified stationary sources for each such area;

(6) require permits for the construction and operation of new or modified major stationary sources in accordance with section 173 (relating to permit requirements);

(7) identify and commit the financial and manpower resources necessary to carry out the plan provisions required by this subsection;

(8) contain emission limitations, schedules of compliance and such other measures as may be necessary to meet the requirements of this section;

(9) evidence public, local government, and State legislative involvement and consultation in accordance with section 174 (relating to planning procedures) and include (A) an identification and analysis of the air quality, health, welfare, economic, energy, and social effects of the plan provisions required by this subsection and of the alternatives considered by the State, and (B) a summary of the public comment on such analysis;

(10) include written evidence that the State, the general purpose local

government or governments, or a regional agency designated by general purpose local governments for such purpose, have adopted by statute, regulation, ordinance, or other legally enforceable document, the necessary requirements and schedules and timetables for compliance, and are committed to implement and enforce the appropriate elements of the plan;

(11) in the case of plans which make a demonstration pursuant to paragraph (2) of subsection (a)—

(A) establish a program which requires, prior to issuance of any permit for construction or modification of a major emitting facility, an analysis of alternative sites, sizes, production processes, and environmental control techniques for such proposed source which demonstrates that benefits of the proposed source significantly outweigh the environmental and social costs imposed as a result of its location, construction, or modification;

(B) establish a specific schedule for implementation of a vehicle emission control inspection and maintenance program; and

(C) identify other measures necessary to provide for attainment of the applicable national ambient air quality standard not later than December 31, 1987.

(c) In the case of a State plan revision required under the Clean Air Act Amendments of 1977 to be submitted before July 1, 1982, by reason of a demonstration under subsection (a)(2), effective on such date such plan shall contain enforceable measures to assure attainment of the applicable standard not later than December 31, 1987.

§ 7503. Permit requirements

[Sec. 173] The permit program required by section 172(b)(6) shall provide that permits to construct and operate may be issued if—

(1) the permitting agency determines that—

(A) by the time the source is to commence operation, total allowable emissions from existing sources in the region, from new or modified sources which are not major emitting facilities, and from the proposed source will be sufficiently less than total emissions from existing sources allowed under the applicable implementation plan prior to the application for such permit to construct or modify so as to represent (when considered together with the plan provisions required under section 172) reasonable further progress (as defined in section 171); or

(B) that emissions of such pollutant resulting from the proposed new or modified major stationary source will not cause or contribute to emissions levels which exceed the allowance permitted for such pollutant for such area from new or modified major stationary sources under section 172(b);

(2) the proposed source is required to comply with the lowest achievable emission rate;

(3) the owner or operator of the proposed new or modified source has demonstrated that all major stationary sources owned or operated by such person (or by any entity controlling, controlled by, or under common control with such person) in such State are subject to emission limitations and are in compliance, or on a schedule' for compliance, with all applicable emission limitations and standards under this Act; and

(4) the applicable implementation plan is being carried out for the nonattainment area in which the proposed source is to be constructed or modified in accordance with the requirements of this part.

Any emission reductions required as a precondition of the issuance of a permit under paragraph (1)(A) shall be legally binding before such permit may be issued.

§ 7504. Planning procedures

[Sec. 174] (a) Within six months after the enactment of the Clean Air Act Amendments of 1977, for each region in which the national primary ambient air quality standard for carbon monoxide or photochemical oxidants will not be attained by July 1, 1979, the State and elected officials of affected local governments shall jointly determine which elements of a revised implementation plan will be planned for and implemented or enforced by the State and which such elements will be planned for and implemented or enforced by local governments or regional agencies, or any combination of local governments, regional agencies, or the State. Where possible within the time required under this subsection, the implementation plan required by this part shall be prepared by an organization of elected officials of local governments designated by agreement of the local governments in an affected area, and certified by the State for this purpose. Where such an organization has not been designated by agreement within six months after the enactment of the Clean Air Act Amendments of 1977, the Governor (or, in the case of an interstate area, Governors), after consultation with elected officials of local governments, and in accordance with the determination under the first sentence of this subparagraph, shall designate an organization of elected officials of local governments in the affected area or a State agency to prepare such plan. Where feasible, such organization shall be the metropolitan planning organization designated to conduct the continuing, cooperative and comprehensive transportation planning process for the area under section 134 of title 23, United States Code, or the organization responsible for the air quality maintenance planning process under regulations implementing this section, or the organization with both responsibilities.

(b) The preparation of implementation plan provisions under this part shall be coordinated with the continuing, cooperative, and comprehensive transportation planning process required under section 134 of title 23, United States Code, and the air quality maintenance planning process required under section 110, and such planning processes shall take into account the requirements of this part.

§ 7505. Environmental Protection Agency grants

[Sec. 175] (a) The Administrator shall make grants to any organization of local elected officials with transportation or air quality maintenance planning responsibilities recognized by the State under section 174(a) for payment of the reasonable costs of developing a plan revision under this part.

(b) The amount granted to any organization under subsection (a) shall be 100 percent of any additional costs of developing a plan revision under this part for the first two fiscal years following receipt of the grant under this paragraph, and shall supplement any funds available under Federal law to such organization for transportation or air quality maintenance planning. Grants under this section shall not be used for construction.

§ 7506. Limitations on certain federal assistance

[Sec. 176] (a) The Administrator shall not approve any projects or award any grants authorized by this Act and the Secretary of Transportation shall not approve any projects or award any grants under title 23, United States Code, other than for safety, mass transit, or transportation improvement projects related to air quality improvement or maintenance, in any air quality control region—

(1) in which any national primary ambient air quality standard has not been attained.

(2) where transportation control measures are necessary for the attainment of such standard, and

(3) where the Administrator finds after July 1, 1979, that the Governor has not submitted an implementation plan which considers each of the elements required by section 172 or that reasonable efforts toward submitting such an implementation plan are not being made (or, after July 1, 1982, in the case of an implementation plan revision required under section 172 to be submitted before July 1, 1982).

(b) In any area in which the State or, as the case may be, the general purpose local government or governments or any regional agency designated by such general purpose local governments for such purpose, is not implementing any requirement of an approved or promulgated plan under section 110, including any requirement for a revised implementation plan under this part, the Administrator shall not make any grants under this Act.

(c) No department, agency, or instrumentality of the Federal Government shall (1) engage in, (2) support in any way or provide financial assistance for, (3) license or permit, or (4) approve, any activity which does not conform to a plan after it has been approved or promulgated under section

110. No metropolitan planning organization designated under section 134 of title 23, United States Code, shall give its approval to any project, program, or plan which does not conform to a plan approved or promulgated under section 110. The assurance of conformity to such a plan shall be an affirmative responsibility of the head of such department, agency, or instrumentality.

(d) Each department, agency, or instrumentality of the Federal Government having authority to conduct or support any program with air-quality related transportation consequences shall give priority in the exercise of such authority, consistent with statutory requirements for allocation among States or other jurisdictions, to the implementation of those portions of plans prepared under this section to achieve and maintain the national primary ambient air quality standards. This paragraph extends to, but is not limited to, authority exercised under the Urban Mass Transportation Act, title 23 of the United States Code, and the Housing and Urban Development Act.

§ 7507. New motor vehicle emission standards in nonattainment areas

[Sec. 177] Notwithstanding section 209(a), any State which has plan provisions approved under this part may adopt and enforce for any model year standards relating to control of emissions from new motor vehicles or new motor vehicle engines and take such other actions as are referred to in section 209(a) respecting such vehicles if—
  (1) such standards are identical to the California standards for which a waiver has been granted for such model year, and
  (2) California and such State adopt such standards at least two years before commencement of such model year (as determined by regulations of the Administrator)

§ 7508. Guidance documents

[Sec. 178] The Administrator shall issue guidance documents under section 108 for purposes of assisting States in implementing requirements of this part respecting the lowest achievable emission rate. Such a document shall be published not later than nine months after the date of enactment of this part and shall be revised at least every two years thereafter.

Subchapter II. Emission Standards for Moving Sources

Part A

Motor Vehicle Emission and Fuel Standards

§ 7521. Emission standards for new motor vehicles or new motor vehicle engines

[Sec. 202] (a) Except as otherwise provided in subsection (b)—

(1) The Administrator shall by regulation prescribe (and from time to time revise) in accordance with the provisions of this section, standards applicable to the emission of any air pollution from any class or classes of new motor vehicles or new motor vehicle engines, which in his judgment cause or contribute to, air pollution which may reasonably be anticipated to endanger public health or welfare. Such standards shall be applicable to such vehicles and engines for their useful life (as determined under subsection (d), relating to useful life of vehicles for purposes of certification), whether such vehicles and engines are designed as complete systems or incorporate devices to prevent or control such pollution.

(2) Any regulation prescribed under paragraph (1) of this subsection (and any revision thereof) shall take effect after such period as the Administrator finds necessary to permit the development and application of the requisite technology, giving appropriate consideration to the cost of compliance within such period.

(3) (A)(i) The Administrator shall prescribe regulations under paragraph (1) of this subsection applicable to emissions of carbon monoxide, hydrocarbons, and oxides of nitrogen from classes or categories of heavy-duty vehicles or engines manufactured during and after model year 1979. Such regulations applicable to such pollutants from such classes or categories of vehicles or engines manufactured during model years 1979 through 1982 shall contain standards which reflect the greatest degree of emission reduction achievable through the application of technology which the Administrator determines will be available for the model year to which such standards apply, giving appropriate consideration to the cost of applying such technology within the period of time available to manufacturers and to noise, energy, and safety factors associated with the application of such technology.

    (ii) Unless a different standard is temporarily promulgated as provided in subparagraph (B) or unless the standard is changed as provided in subparagraph (E), regulations under paragraph (1) of this subsection applicable to emissions from vehicles or engines manufactured during and after model year—

        (I) 1983, in the case of hydrocarbons and carbon monoxide, shall contain standards which require a reduction of at least 90 percent, and

        (II) 1985, in the case of oxides of nitrogen, shall contain standards which require a reduction of at least 75 percent, from the average of the actually measured emissions from heavy-duty gasoline-fueled vehicles or engines, or any class or category thereof, manufactured during the baseline model year.

(iii) The Administrator shall prescribe regulations under paragraph (1) of this subsection applicable to emissions of particulate matter from classes or categories of vehicles manufactured during and after model year 1981 (or during any earlier model year, if practicable). Such regulations shall contain standards which reflect the greatest degree of emission reduction achievable through the application of technology which the Administrator determines will be available for the model year to which such standards apply, giving appropriate consideration to the cost of applying such technology within the period of time available to manufacturers and to noise, energy, and safety factors associated with the application of such technology. Such standards shall be promulgated and shall take effect as expeditiously as practicable taking into account the period necessary for compliance.

(iv) In establishing classes or categories of vehicles or engines for purposes of regulations under this paragraph, the Administrator may base such classes or categories on gross vehicle weight, horsepower, or such other factors as may be appropriate.

(v) For the purpose of this paragraph, the term "base-line model year" means, with respect to any pollutant emitted from any vehicle or engine, or class or category thereof, the model year immediately preceding the model year in which Federal standards applicable to such vehicle or engine, or class or category thereof, first applied with respect to such pollutant.

(B) During the period of June 1 through December 31, 1978, in the case of hydrocarbons and carbon monoxide, or during the period of June 1 through December 31, 1980, in the case of oxides of nitrogen, and during each period of June 1 through December 31 of each year thereafter, the Administrator may, after notice and opportunity for a public hearing promulgate regulations revising any standard prescribed as provided in subparagraph (A) (ii) for any class or category of heavy-duty vehicles or engines. Such standard shall apply only for the period of three model years beginning four model years after the model year in which such revised standard is promulgated. In revising any standard under this subparagraph for any such three model year period, the Administrator shall determine the maximum degree of emission reduction which can be achieved by means reasonably expected to be available for production of such period and shall prescribe a revised emission standard in accordance with such determination. Such revised standard shall require a reduction of emissions from any standard which applies to previous model year.

(C) Action revising any standard for any period may be taken by the Administrator under subparagraph (B) only if he finds—

     (i) that compliance with the emission standards otherwise applicable for such model year cannot be achieved by technology, processes, operating methods, or other alternatives reasonably expected to be available for production for such model year without increasing cost or decreasing fuel economy to an excessive and unreasonable degree; and

    (ii) the National Academy of Sciences has not, pursuant to its study and investigation under subsection (c), issued a report substantially contrary to the findings of the Administrator under clause (i).

(D) A report shall be made to the Congress with respect to any standard revised under subparagraph (B) which shall contain—

     (i) a summary of the health effects found, or believed to be associated with, the pollutant covered by such standard,

    (ii) an analysis of the cost-effectiveness of other strategies for attaining and maintaining national ambient air quality standards and carrying out regulations under part C of title I (relating to significant deterioration) in relation to the cost-effectiveness for such purposes of standards which, but for such revision, would apply.

    (iii) a summary of the research and development efforts and progress being made by each manufacturer for purposes of meeting the standards promulgated as provided in subparagraph (A) (ii) or, if applicable, subparagraph (E), and

    (iv) specific findings as to the relative costs of compliance, and relative fuel economy, which may be expected to result from the application for any model year of such revised standard and the application for such model year of the standard, which, but for such revision, would apply.

(E)(i) The Administrator shall conduct a continuing pollutant-specific study concerning the effects of each air pollutant emitted from heavy-duty vehicles or engines and from other sources of mobile source related pollutants on the public health and welfare. The results of such study shall be published in the Federal Register and reported to the Congress not later than June 1, 1978, in the case of hydrocarbons and carbon monoxide, and June 1, 1980, in the case of oxides of nitrogen, and before June 1 of each third year thereafter.

    (ii) On the basis of such study and such other information as is available to him (including the studies under section 214, the Administrator may, after notice and opportunity for a public hearing, promulgate regulations under paragraph (1) of this subsection changing any standard prescribed in subparagraph (AA) (ii) (or revised under subparagraph (B) or previously changed under this subparagraph). No such changed standard shall apply for any model year before the model year four years after the model year during which regulations containing such changed standard are promulgated.

(F) For purposes of this paragraph, motorcycles and motorcycle engines shall be treated in the same manner as heavy-duty vehicles and engines (except as otherwise permitted under section 206 (f)(1)) unless the Administrator promulgates a rule reclassifying motorcycles as light-duty vehicles within the meaning of this section or unless the Administrator promulgates regulations under subsection (a) applying standards applicable to the emission of air pollutants from motorcycles as a separate class or category. In any case in which such standards are promulgated for such emissions from motorcycles as a separate class or category, the Administrator, in promulgating such standards, shall consider the need to achieve equivalency of emission reductions between motorcycles and other vehicles to the maximum extent practicable.

(4)(A) Effective with respect to vehicles and engines manufactured after model year 1978, no emission control device, system, or element of design shall be used in a new motor vehicle or new motor vehicle engine for purposes of complying with standards prescribed under this subsection if such device, system, or element of design will cause or contribute to an unreasonable risk to public health, welfare, or safety in its operation or function.

(B) In determining whether an unreasonable risk exists under subparagraph (A), the Administrator shall consider, among other factors, (i) whether and to what extent the use of any device, system, or element of design causes, increases, reduces, or eliminates emissions of any unregulated pollutants; (ii) available methods for reducing or eliminating any risk to public health, welfare, or safety which may be associated with the use of such device, system, or element of design, and (iii) the availability of other devices, systems, or elements of design which may be used to conform to standards prescribed under this subsection without causing or contributing to such unreasonable risk. The Administrator shall include in the consideration required by this paragraph all relevant information developed pursuant to section 214.

(5)(A) If the Administrator promulgates final regulations which define the degree of control required and the test procedures by which compliance could be determined for gasoline vapor recovery of uncontrolled emissions from the fueling of motor vehicles, the Administrator shall, after consultation with the Secretary of Transportation with respect to motor vehicle safety prescribe, by regulation, fill pipe standards for new motor vehicles in order to insure effective connection between such fill pipe and any vapor recovery system which the Administrator determines may be required to comply with such vapor recovery regulations. In promulgating such standards the Administrator shall take into consideration limits on fill pipe diameter, minimum design criteria for nozzle retainer lips, limits on the location of the unleaded fuel restrictors, a minimum access zone surrounding a fill pipe, a minimum fill pipe or nozzle insertion angle, and such other factors as he deems pertinent.

(B) Regulations prescribing standards under subparagraph (A) shall not become effective until the introduction of the model year for which it would be feasible to implement such standards, taking into consideration the restraints of an adequate leadtime for design and production.

(C) Nothing in subparagraph (A) shall (i) prevent the Administrator from specifying different nozzle and fill neck sizes for gasoline with additives and gasoline without additives or (ii) permit the Administrator to require a specific location, configuration, modeling, or styling of the motor vehicle body with respect to the fuel tank fill neck or fill nozzle clearance envelope.

(D) For the purpose of this paragraph, the term "fill pipe" shall include the fuel tank fill pipe, fill neck, fill inlet, and closure.

(6) The Administrator shall determine the feasibility and desirability of requiring new motor vehicles to utilize onboard hydrocarbon control technology which would avoid the necessity of gasoline vapor recovery of uncontrolled emissions emanating from the fueling of motor vehicles. The Administrator shall compare the costs and effectiveness of such technology to that of implementing and maintaining vapor recovery systems (taking into consideration such factors as fuel economy, economic costs of such technology, administrative burdens, and equitable distribution of costs). If the Administrator finds that it is feasible and desirable to employ such technology, he shall, after consultation with the Secretary of Transportation with respect to motor vehicle safety, prescribe, by regulation, standards requiring the use of onboard hydrocarbon technology which shall not become effective until the introduction to the model year for which it would be feasible to implement such standards, taking into consideration compliance costs and the restraints of an adequate leadtime for design and production.

(b)(1)(A) The regulations under subsection (a) applicable to emissions of carbon monoxide and hydrocarbons from light-duty vehicles and engines manufactured during model years 1977 through 1979 shall contain standards which provide that such emissions from such vehicles and engines may not exceed 1.5 grams per vehicle mile of hydrocarbons and 15.0 grams per vehicle mile of carbon monoxide. The regulations under subsection (a) applicable to emissions of carbon monoxide from light-duty vehicles and engines manufactured during the model year 1980 shall contain standards which provide that such emissions may not exceed 7.0 grams per vehicle mile. The regulations under subsection (a) applicable to emissions of hydrocarbons from light-duty vehicles and engines manufactured during or after model year 1980 shall contain standards which require a reduction of at least 90 percent from emissions of such pollutant allowable under the standards under this section applicable to light-duty vehicles and engines manufactured in model year 1970. Unless waived as provided in paragraph (5), regulations under subsection (a) applicable to emissions of carbon monoxide from light-duty vehicles and engines manufactured during or after the model year 1981 shall contain standards which require a reduction of at least 90 percent from emissions of such pollutants allowable under the standards under this section applicable to light-duty vehicles and engines manufactured in model year 1970.

(B) The regulations under subsection (a) applicable to emissions of oxides of nitrogen from light-duty vehicles and engines manufactured during model years 1977 through 1980 shall contain standards which provide that such emissions from such vehicles and engines may not exceed 2.0 grams per vehicle mile. The regulations under subsection (a) applicable to emissions of oxides or nitrogen from light-duty vehicles and engines manufactured during the model year 1981 and thereafter shall contain standards which provide that such emissions from such vehicles and engines may not exceed 1.0 gram per vehicle mile. The Administrator shall prescribe standards in lieu of those required by the preceding sentence, which provide that emissions of oxides of nitrogen may not exceed 2.0 grams per vehicle mile for any light-duty vehicle manufactured during model years 1981 and 1982 by any manufacturer whose production, by corporate identity, for calendar year 1976 was less than 300,000 light-duty motor vehicles worldwide if the Administrator determines that—

(i) the ability of such manufacturer to meet emission standards in the 1975 and subsequent model years was, and is, primarily dependent upon technology developed by other manufacturers and purchased from such manufacturers; and

(ii) such manufacturer lacks the financial resources and technological ability to develop such technology.

(C) Effective with respect to vehicles and engines manufactured after model year 1978 (or in the case of heavy-duty vehicles or engines, such later model year as the Administrator determines is the earliest feasible model year), the test procedure promulgated under paragraph (2) for measurement of evaporative emissions of hydrocarbons shall require that such emissions be measured from the vehicle or engine as a whole. Regulations to carry out this subparagraph shall be promulgated not later than two hundred and seventy days after date of enactment of this subparagraph.

(2) Emission standards under paragraph (1), and measurement techniques on which such standards are based (if not promulgated prior to the date of enactment of the Clean Air Amendments of 1970, shall be prescribed by regulation within 180 days after such date.

(3) For purposes of this part

(A)(i) The term "model year" with reference to any specific calendar year means the manufacturer's annual production period (as determined by the Administrator) which includes January 1 of such calendar year. If the manufacturer has no annual production period, the term "model year" shall mean the calendar year.

    (ii) For the purpose of assuring that vehicles and engines manufactured before the beginning of a model year were not manufactured for purposes of circumventing the effective date of a standard required to be prescribed by subsection (b), the Administrator may prescribe regulations defining "model year" otherwise than as provided in clause (i).

(B) The term "light duty vehicles and engines" means new light duty motor vehicles and new light duty motor vehicle engines, as determined under regulations of the Administrator.

(C) The term "heavy duty vehicle" means a truck, bus, or other vehicle manufactured primarily for use on the public streets, roads, and highways (not including any vehicle operated exclusively on a rail or rails) which has a gross vehicle weight (as determined under regulations promulgated by the Administrator) in excess of six thousand pounds. Such term includes any such vehicle which has special features enabling off-street or off-highway operation and use.

(4) On July 1 of 1971, and of each year thereafter, the Administrator shall report to the Congress with respect to the development of systems necessary to implement the emission standards established pursuant to this section. Such reports shall include information regarding the continuing effects of such air pollutants subject to standards under this section on the public health and welfare, the extent and progress of efforts being made to develop the necessary systems, the costs associated with development and application of such systems, and following such hearings as he may deem advisable, any recommendations for additional congressional action necessary to achieve the purposes of this Act. In gathering information for the purposes of this paragraph and in connection with any hearing, the provisions of section 307(a) (relating to subpoenas) shall apply.

(5)(A)At any time after August 31, 1978, any manufacturer may file an application requesting the waiver for model years 1981 and 1982 of the effective date of the emission standard required by paragraph (1) (A) for carbon monoxide applicable to any model (as determined by the Administrator) of light-duty motor vehicles and engines manufactured in such model years. The Administrator shall make his determination with respect to any such application within 60 days after such application is filed with respect to such model. If he determines, in accordance with the provisions of this paragraph, that such waiver should be granted, he shall simultaneously with such determination prescribe by regulation emission standards which shall apply (in lieu of the standards required to be prescribed by paragraph (1) (A) of this subsection) to emissions of carbon monoxide from such class or category of vehicles or engines manufactured during model years 1981 and 1982.

(B) Any standards prescribed under this paragraph shall not permit emissions of carbon monoxide from vehicles and engines to which such waiver applies to exceed 7.0 grams per vehicle per mile.

(C) Within 60 days after receipt of the application for any such waiver and after public hearing, the Administrator shall issue a decision granting or refusing such waiver. The Administrator may grant such waiver if he finds that protection of the public health does not require attainment of such 90 percent reduction for carbon monoxide for the model years to which such waiver applies in the case of such vehicles and engines and if he determines that—

(i) such waiver is essential to the public interest or the public health and welfare of the United States;

(ii) all good faith efforts have been made to meet the standards established by this subsection:

(iii) the applicant has established that effective control technology, processes, operating methods, or other alternatives are not available or have not been available with respect to the model in question for a sufficient period of time to achieve compliance prior to the effective date of such standards, taking into consideration costs, driveability, and fuel economy; and

(iv) studies and investigations of the National Academy of Sciences conducted pursuant to subsection (c) and other information available to him has not indicated that technology, processes, or other alternatives are available (within the meaning of clause (iii) to meet such standards.

(6)(A) Upon the petition of any manufacturer, the Administrator, after notice and opportunity for public hearing, may waive the standard required under subparagraph (B) of paragraph (1) to not exceed 1.5 grams of oxides of nitrogen per vehicle mile for any class or category of light-duty vehicles or engines manufactured by such manufacturer during any period of up to four model years beginning after the model year 1980 if the manufacturer demonstrates that such waiver is necessary to permit the use of an innovative power train technology, or innovative emission control device or system, in such class or category of vehicles or engines and that such technology or system was not utilized by more than 1 percent of the light-duty vehicles sold in the United States in the 1975 model year. Such waiver may be granted only if the Administrator determines—

(i) that such waiver would not endanger public health,

(ii) that there is a substantial likelihood that the vehicles or engines will be able to comply with the applicable standard under this section at the expiration of the waiver, and

(iii) that the technology or system has a potential for long-term air quality benefit and has the potential to meet or exceed the average fuel economy standard applicable under the Energy Policy and Conservation Act upon the expiration of the waiver.

No waiver under this subparagraph granted to any manufacturer shall apply to more than 5 percent of such manufacturer's production or 50,000 vehicles or engines, whichever is greater.

(B) Upon the petition of any manufacturer, the Administrator, after notice and opportunity for public hearing, may waive the standard required under subparagraph (B) of paragraph (1) to not exceed 1.5 grams of oxides of nitrogen per vehicle mile for any class or category of light-duty vehicles and engines manufactured by such manufacturer during the four model year period beginning with the model year 1981 if the manufacturer can show that such waiver is necessary to permit the use of diesel engine technology in such class or category of vehicles or engines. Such waiver may be granted if the Administrator determines—

(i) that such waiver will not endanger public health,

(ii) that such waiver will result in significant fuel savings at least equal to the fuel economy standard applicable in each year under the Energy Policy and Conservation Act, and

(iii) that the technology has a potential for long-term air quality benefit and has the potential to meet or exceed the average fuel economy standard applicable under the Energy Policy and Conservation Act at the expiration of the waiver.

(7) The Congress hereby declares and establishes as a research objective, the development of propulsion systems and emission control technology to achieve standards which represent a reduction of at least 90 per centum from the average emissions of oxides of nitrogen actually measured from light duty motor vehicles manufactured in model year 1971 not subject to any Federal or State emission standard for oxides of nitrogen. The Administrator shall, by regulations promulgated within one hundred and eighty days after enactment of the Clean Air Act Amendments of 1977, require each manufacturer whose sales represent at least 0.5 per centum of light duty motor vehicle sales in the United States, to build and, on a regular basis, demonstrate the

operation of light duty motor vehicles that meet this research objective, in addition to any other applicable standards or requirements for other pollutants under this Act. Such demonstration vehicles shall be submitted to the Administrator no later than the end of model year 1979 and in each model year thereafter. Such demonstration shall, in accordance with applicable regulations, to the greatest extent possible, (A) be designed to encourage the development of new power-plant and emission control technologies that are fuel efficient, (B) assure that the demonstration vehicles are or could reasonably be expected to be within the productive capability of the manufacturers, and (C) assure the utilization of optimum engine, fuel, and emission control systems.

(c)(1) The Administrator shall undertake to enter into appropriate arrangements with the National Academy of Sciences to conduct a comprehensive study and investigation of the technology feasibility of meeting the emissions standards required to be prescribed by the Administrator by subsection (b) of this section.

(2) Of the funds authorized to be appropriated to the Administrator by this Act, such amounts as are required shall be available to carry out the study and investigation authorized by paragraph (1) of this subsection.

(3) In entering into any arrangement with the National Academy of Sciences for conducting the study and investigation authorized by paragraph (1) of this subsection, the Administrator shall request the National Academy of Sciences to submit semiannual reports on the progress of its study and investigation to the Administrator and the Congress, beginning not later than July 1, 1971, and continuing until such study and investigation is completed.

(4) The Administrator shall furnish to such Academy at its request any information which the Academy deems necessary for the purpose of conducting the investigation and study authorized by paragraph (1) of this subsection. For the purpose of furnishing such information, the Administrator may use any authority he has under this Act (A) to obtain information from any person, and (B) to require such person to conduct such tests, keep such records, and make such reports respecting research or other activities conducted by such person as may be reasonably necessary to carry out this subsection.

(d) The Administrator shall prescribe regulations under which the useful life of vehicles and engines shall be determined for purposes of subsection (a)(1) of this section and section 207. Such regulations shall provide that useful life shall—

(1) in the case of light duty vehicles and light duty vehicle engines, be a period of use of five years or of fifty thousand miles (or the equivalent), whichever first occrs;

(2) in the case of any other motor vehicle or motor vehicle engine (other than motorcycles or motorcycle engines) be a period of use set forth in

paragraph (1) unless the Administrator determines that a period of use of greater duration or mileage is appropriate in lieu thereof; and

(3) in the case of any motorcycle or motorcycle engine, be a period of use the Administrator shall determine.

(e) In the event a new power source or propulsion system for new motor vehicles or new motor vehicle engines is submitted for certification pursuant to section 206(a), the Administrator may postpone certification until he has prescribed standards for any air pollutants emitted by such vehicle or engine which in his judgment cause, or contribute to, air pollution which may reasonably be anticipated to endanger the public health or welfare but for which standards have not been prescribed under subsection (a).

(f)(1) The high altitude regulation in effect with respect to model year 1977 motor vehicles shall not apply to the manufacture, distribution, or sale of 1978 and later model year motor vehicles. Any future regulation affecting the sale or distribution of motor vehicles or engines manufactured before the model year 1984 in high altitude areas of the country shall take effect no earlier than model year 1981.

(2) Any future regulation applicable to high altitude vehicles or engines shall not require a percentage of reduction in the emissions of such vehicles which is greater than the required percentage of reduction in emissions from motor vehicles as set forth in section 202(b). This percentage reduction shall be determined by comparing any proposed high altitude emission standards to high altitude emissions from vehicles manufactured during model year 1970. In no event shall regulations applicable to high altitude vehicles manufactured before the model year 1984 establish a numerical standard which is more stringent than that applicable to vehicles certified under non-high altitude conditions.

(3) Section 307(d) shall apply to any high altitude regulation referred to in paragraph (2) and before promulgating any such regulation, the Administrator shall consider and make a finding with respect to—

(A) the economic impact upon consumers, individual high altitude dealers, and the automobile industry of any such regulation, including the economic impact which was experienced as a result of the regulation imposed during model year 1977 with respect to high altitude certification requirements:

(B) the present and future availability of emission control technology capable of meeting the applicable vehicle and engine emission requirements without reducing model availability; and

(C) the likelihood that the adoption of such a high altitude regulation will result in any significant improvement in air quality in any area to which it shall apply, be used to conform to standards prescribed under this subsection without causing or contributing to such unreasonable risk. The Administrator shall include in the consideration required by this paragraph all relevant information developed pursuant to section 214.

§ 7522. Prohibited acts

[Sec. 203] (a) The following acts and the causing thereof are prohibited—

(1) in the case of a manufacturer of new motor vehicles or new motor vehicle engines for distribution in commerce, the sale, or the offering for sale, or the introduction, or delivery for introduction, into commerce, or (in the case of any person, except as provided by regulation of the Administrator), the importation into the United States, of any new motor vehicle or new motor vehicle engine, manufactured after the effective date of regulations under this part which are applicable to such vehicle or engine unless such vehicle or engine is covered by a certificate of conformity issued (and in effect) under regulations prescribed under this part (except as provided in subsection (b));

(2) for any person to fail or refuse to permit access to or copying of records or to fail to make reports or provide information, required under section 208 or for any person to fail or refuse to permit entry, testing, or inspection authorized under section 206(c).

(3)(A) for any person to remove or render inoperative any device or element of design installed on or in a motor vehicle or motor vehicle engine in compliance with regulations under this title prior to its sale and delivery to the ultimate purchaser, or for any manufacturer or dealer knowingly to remove or render inoperative any such device or element of design after such sale and delivery to the ultimate purchaser; or

   (B) for any person engaged in the business or repairing, servicing, selling, leasing, or trading motor vehicles or motor vehicle engines, or who operates a fleet of motor vehicles knowingly to remove or render inoperative any device or element of design installed on or in a motor vehicle or motor vehicle engine in compliance with regulations under this title following its sale and delivery to the ultimate purchaser, or

(4) for any manufacturer of a new motor vehicle or new motor vehicle engine subject to standards prescribed under section 202—

   (A) to sell or lease any such vehicle or engine unless such manufacturer has complied with the requirements of section 207(a) and (b) with respect to such vehicle or engine, and unless a label or tag is affixed to such vehicle or engine in accordance with section 207(c)(3),

   (B) to fail or refuse to comply with the requirements of section 207(c) or (e).

   (C) except as provided in subsection (c)(3) of section 207, to provide directly or indirectly in any communication to the ultimate purchaser or any subsequent purchaser that the coverage of any warranty under this Act is conditioned upon use of any part, component, or system manufactured by such manufacturer or any person acting for such manufacturer or under his control, or conditioned upon service performed by any such person, or

(D) to fail or refuse to comply with the terms and conditions of the warranty under section 207(a) or (b) with respect to any vehicle.

No action with respect to any element of design referred to in paragraph (3) (including any adjustment or alteration of such element) shall be treated as a prohibited act under such paragraph (3) if such action is in accordance with section 215.

Nothing in paragraph (3) shall be construed to require the use of manufacturer parts in maintaining or repairing any motor vehicle or motor vehicle engine. For the purpose of the preceding sentence, the term "manufacturer parts" means, with respect to a motor vehicle engine, parts produced or sold by the manufacturer of the motor vehicle or motor vehicle engine.

(b)(1) The Administration may exempt any new motor vehicle or new motor vehicle engine, from subsection (a) upon such terms and conditions as he may find necessary for the purpose of research, investigations, studies, demonstrations, or training, or for reasons of national security.

(2) A new motor vehicle or new motor vehicle engine offered for importation or imported by any person in violation of subsection (a) shall be refused admission into the United States, but the Secretary of the Treasury and the Administrator may, by joint regulation, provide for deferring final determination as to admission and authorizing the delivery of such a motor vehicle or engine offered for import to the owner or consignee thereof upon such terms and conditions (including the furnishing of a bond) as may appear to them appropriate to insure that any such motor vehicle or engine will be brought into conformity with the standards, requirements, and limitations applicable to it under this title. The Secretary of the Treasury shall, if a motor vehicle or engine is finally refused admission under this paragraph, cause disposition thereof in accordance with the customs laws unless it is exported, under regulations prescribed by such Secretary, within ninety days of the date of notice of such refusal or such additional time as may be permitted pursuant to such regulations, except that disposition in accordance with the customs laws may not be made in such manner as may result, directly or indirectly, in the sale, to the ultimate consumer, of a new motor vehicle or new motor vehicle engine that fails to comply with applicable standards of the Administrator under this part.

(3) A new motor vehicle or new motor vehicle engine intended solely for export, and so labeled or tagged on the outside of the container and on the vehicle or engine itself, shall be subject to the provisions of subsection (a), except that if the country which is to receive such vehicle or engine has emission standards which differ from the

standards prescribed under section 202, then such vehicle or engine shall comply with the standards of such country which is to receive such vehicle or engine.

(c) Upon application therefor, the Administrator may exempt from section 203(a)(3) any vehicles (or class thereof) manufactured before the 1974 model year from section 203(a)(3) for the purpose of permitting modifications to the emission control device or system of such vehicle in order to use fuels other than those specified in certification testing under section 206(a)(1), if the Administrator, on the basis of information submitted by the applicant, finds that such modification will not result in such vehicle or engine not complying with standards under section 202 applicable to such vehicle or engine. Any such exemption shall identify (1) the vehicle or vehicles so exempted, (2) the specific nature of the modification, and (3) the person or class of persons to whom the exemption shall apply.

§ 7523. Actions to restrain violations

[Sec. 204] (a) The district courts of the United States shall have jurisdiction to restrain violations of section 203(a).

(b) Actions to restrain such violations shall be brought by and in the name of the United States. In any such action, subpoenas for witnesses who are required to attend a district court in any district may run into another district.

§ 7524. Penalties

[Sec. 205] Any person who violates paragraph (1), (2), or (4) of section 203(a) or any manufacturer, dealer, or other person who violates paragraph (3)(A) of section 203(a) shall be subject to a civil penalty of not more than $10,000. Any person who violates paragraph (3)(B) of such section 203(a) shall be subject to a civil penalty of not more than $2,500. Any such violation with respect to paragraph (1), (3), or (4) of section 203(a) shall constitute a separate offense with respect to each motor vehicle or motor vehicle engine.

§ 7525. Motor vehicle and motor vehicle engine compliance testing and certification

[Sec. 206] (a)(1) The Administrator shall test, or require to be tested in such manner as he deems appropriate, any new motor vehicle or new motor vehicle engine submitted by a manufacturer to determine whether such vehicle or engine conforms with the regulations prescribed under section 202 of this Act. If such vehicle or engine conforms to such regulations, the Administrator shall issue a certificate of conformity upon such terms, and for such period (not in excess of one year), as he may prescribe.

In the case of any manufacturer of vehicles or vehicle engines whose projected sales in the United States for any model year (as determined by the Administrator) will not exceed three hundred, the regulations prescribed by the Administrator concerning testing by the manufacturer for purposes of determining compliance with regulations under section 202 for the useful life of the vehicle or engine shall not require operation of any vehicle or engine manufactured during such model year for more than five thousand miles or one hundred and sixty hours, respectively, but the Administrator shall apply such adjustment factors as he deems appropriate to assure that each such vehicle or engine will comply during its useful life (as determined under section 202(d)) with the regulations prescribed under section 202 of the Act.

(2) The Administrator shall test any emission control system incorporated in a motor vehicle or motor vehicle engine submitted to him by any person, in order to determine whether such system enables such vehicle or engine to conform to the standards required to be prescribed under section 202(b) of this Act. If the Administrator finds on the basis of such tests that such vehicle or engine conforms to such standards, the Administrator shall issue a verification of compliance with emission standards for such system when incorporated in vehicles of a class of which the tested vehicle is representative. He shall inform manufacturers and the National Academy of Sciences, and make available to the public, the results of such tests. Tests under this paragraph shall be conducted under such terms and conditions (including requirements for preliminary testing by qualified independent laboratories) as the Administrator may prescribe by regulations.

(3)(A) A certificate of conformity may be issued under this section only if the Administrator determines that the manufacturer (or in the case of vehicle or engine for import, any person) has established to the satisfaction of the Administrator that any emission control device, system, or element of design installed on, or incorporated in, such vehicle or engine conforms to applicable requirements of section 202(a)(4).

(B) The Administrator may conduct such tests and may require the manufacturer (or any such person) to conduct such tests and provide such information as is necessary to carry out subparagraph (A) of this paragraph. Such requirements shall include a requirement for prompt reporting of the emission of any unregulated pollutant from a system, device, or element of design if such pollutant was not emitted, or was emitted in significantly lesser amounts, from the vehicle or engine without use of the system, device, or element of design.

(b)(1) In order to determine whether new motor vehicles or new motor vehicle engines being manufactured by a manufacturer do in fact conform with the regulations with respect to which the certificate of conformity was issued, the Administrator is authorized to test such vehicles or engines. Such tests may be conducted by the Administrator directly or, in accordance with conditions specified by the Administrator, by the manufacturer.

(2)(A)(i) If, based on tests conducted under paragraph (1) on a sample of new vehicles or engines covered by a certificate of conformity, the

Administrator determines that all or part of the vehicles or engines so covered do not conform with the regulations with respect to which the certificate of conformity was issued and with the requirements of section 202(a)(4), he may suspend or revoke such certificate in whole or in part, and shall so notify the manufacturer. Such suspension or revocation shall apply in the case of any new motor vehicles or new motor vehicle engines manufactured after the date of such notification (or manufactured before such date if still in the hands of the manufacturer), and shall apply until such time as the Administrator finds that vehicles and engines manufactured by the manufacturer do conform to such regulations and requirements. If, during any period of suspension or revocation, the Administrator finds that a vehicle or engine actually conforms to such regulations and requirements, he shall issue a certificate of conformity applicable to such vehicle or engine.

   (ii) If, based on tests conducted under paragraph (1) on any new vehicle or engine, the Administrator determines that such vehicle or engine does not conform with such regulations and requirements, he may suspend or revoke such certificate insofar as it applies to such vehicle or engine until such time as he finds such vehicle or engine actually so conforms with such regulations and requirements, and he shall so notify the manufacturer.

(B)(i) At the request of any manufacturer the Administrator shall grant such manufacturer a hearing as to whether the tests have been properly conducted or any sampling methods have been properly applied, and make a determination on the record with respect to any suspension or revocation under subparagraph (A); but suspension or revocation under subparagraph (A) shall not be stayed by reason of such hearing.

   (ii) In any case of actual controversy as to the validity of any determination under clause (i), the manufacturer may at any time prior to the 60th day after such determination is made file a petition with the United States court of appeals for the circuit wherein such manufacturer resides or has his principal place of business for a judicial review of such determination. A copy of the petition shall be forthwith transmitted by the clerk of the court to the Administrator or other officer designated by him for that purpose. The Administrator thereupon shall file in the court record of the proceedings on which the Administrator based his determination, as provided in section 2112 of title 28 of the United States Code.

   (iii) If the petitioner applies to the court for leave to adduce additional evidence, and shows to the satisfaction of the court that such additional evidence is material and that there were reasonable grounds for the failure to adduce such evidence in the proceeding before the Administrator, the court may order such additional evidence (and evidence in rebuttal thereof) to be taken before the Administrator, in such manner and upon such terms and conditions as the court may deem proper. The Administrator may modify his findings as to the facts, or make new findings, by reason of the additional evidence so taken and he shall file such modified or new findings, and his recommendation, if any, for the modification or setting aside of his original determination, with the return of such additional evidence.

(iv) Upon the filing of the petition referred to in clause (ii), the court shall have jurisdiction to review the order in accordance with chapter 7 of title 5, United States Code, and to grant appropriate relief as provided in such chapter.

(c) For purposes of enforcement of this section, officers or employees duly designated by the Administrator, upon presenting appropriate credentials to the manufacturer or person in charge, are authorized (1) to enter, at reasonable times, any plant or other establishment of such manufacturer, for the purpose of conducting tests of vehicles or engines in the hands of the manufacturer, or, (2) to inspect at reasonable times, records, files, papers, processes, controls, and facilities used by such manufacturer in conducting tests under regulations of the Administrator. Each such inspection shall be commenced and completed with reasonable promptness.

(d) The Administrator shall by regulation establish methods and procedures for making tests under this section.

(e) The Administrator shall announce in the Federal Register and make available to the public the results of his tests of any motor vehicle or motor vehicle engine submitted by a manufacturer under subsection (a) as promptly as possible after the enactment of the Clean Air Act Amendments of 1970 and at the beginning of each model year which begins thereafter. Such results shall be described in such nontechnical manner as will reasonably disclose to prospective ultimate purchasers of new motor vehicles and new motor vehicle engines the comparative performance of the vehicle and engines tested in meeting the standards prescribed under section 202 of this Act.

(f)(1) All light duty vehicles and engines manufactured during or after model year 1984 shall comply with the requirements of section 202 of this Act regardless of the altitude at which they are sold.

(2) By October 1, 1978, the Administrator shall report to the Congress on the economic impact and technological feasibility of the requirements found in subparagraph (1) of this subsection. The report is also to evaluate the technological feasibility and the health consequences of separate proportional emission standards for light duty vehicles and engines in high altitude areas that would reflect a comparable percent-

age of reduction in emissions to that achieved by light duty vehicles and engines in low altitude areas.

(g)(1) In the case of any class or category of heavy duty vehicles or engines to which a standard promulgated under section 202(a) of this Act applies, except as provided in paragraph (2), a certificate of conformity shall be issued under subsection (a) and shall not be suspended or revoked under subsection (b) for such vehicles or engines manufactured by a manufacturer notwithstanding the failure of such vehicles or engines to meet such standard if such manufacturer pays a noncomformance penalty as provided under regulations promulgated by the Administrator after notice and opportunity for public hearing. In the case of motorcycles to which such standard applies, such a certificate may be issued notwithstanding such failure if the manufacturer pays such a penalty.

(2) No certificate of conformity may be issued under paragraph (1) with respect to any class or category of vehicle or engine if the degree by which the manufacturer fails to meet any standard promulgated under section 202(a) with respect to such class or category exceeds the percentage determined under regulations promulgated by the Administrator to be practicable. Such regulations shall require such testing of vehicles or engines being produced as may be necessary to determine the percentage of the classes or categories of vehicles or engines which are not in compliance with the regulations with respect to which a certifcate of conformity was issued and shall be promulgated not later than one year after the date of enactment of the Clean Air Act Amendments of 1977.

(3) The regulations promulgated under paragraph (1) shall, not later than one year after the date of enactment of the Clean Air Act Amendments of 1977, provide for noncomformance penalties in amounts determined under a formula established by the Administrator. Such penalties under such formula—

(A) may vary from pollutant-to-pollutant;

(B) may vary by class or category of vehicle or engine;

(C) shall take into account the extent to which actual emissions of any air pollutant exceed allowable emissions under the standards promulgated under section 202;

(D) shall be increased periodically in order to create incentives for the development of production vehicles or engines which achieve the required degree of emission reduction; and

(E) shall remove any competitive disadvantage to manufacturers whose engines or vehicles achieve the required degree of emission reduction (including any such disadvantage arising from the application of paragraph (4)).

(4) In any case in which a certificate of conformity has been issued under this subsection, any warranty required under section 207(b)(2) and any action under section 207(c) shall be required to be effective only

for the emission levels which the Administrator determines that such certificate was issued and not for the emission levels required under the applicable standard.

(5) The authorities of section 208(a) shall apply, subject to the conditions of section 208(b), for purposes of this subsection.

§ 7541. Compliance by vehicles and engines in actual use

[Sec. 207] (a)(1) Effective with respect to vehicles and engines manufactured in model years beginning more than 60 days after the date of the enactment of the Clean Air Act Amendments of 1970, the manufacturer of each new motor vehicle and new motor vehicle engine shall warrant to the ultimate purchaser and each subsequent purchaser that such vehicle or engine is (A) designed, built, and equipped so as to conform at the time of sale with applicable regulations under section 202, and (B) free from defects in materials and workmanship which cause such vehicle or engine to fail to conform with applicable regulations for its useful life (as determined under section 202(d)).

(2) In the case of a motor vehicle part or motor vehicle engine part, the manufacturer or rebuilder of such part may certify that use of such part will not result in a failure of the vehicle or engine to comply with emission standards promulgated under section 202. Such certification shall be made only under such regulations as may be promulgated by the Administrator to carry out the purposes of subsection (b). The Administrator shall promulgate such regulations no later than two years following the date of the enactment of this paragraph.

(3) The cost of any part, device, or component of any light-duty vehicle that is designed for emission control and which in the instructions issued pursuant to subsection (c)(3) of this section is scheduled for replacement during the useful life of the vehicle in order to maintain compliance with regulations under section 202 of this Act, the failure of which shall not interfere with the normal performance of the vehicle, and the expected retail price of which, including installation costs, is greater than 2 percent of the suggested retail price of such vehicle, shall be borne or reimbursed at the time of replacement by the vehicle manufacturer and such replacement shall be provided without cost to the ultimate purchaser, subsequent purchaser, or dealer. The term "designed for emission control" as used in the preceding sentence means a catalytic converter, thermal reactor, or other component installed on or in a vehicle for the sole or primary purpose of reducing vehicle emissions (not including those vehicle components which were in general use prior to model year 1968 and the primary function of which is not related to emission control).

(b) If the Administrator determines that (i) there are available testing methods and procedures to ascertain whether, when in actual use throughout its useful life (as determined under section 202(d)), each vehicle and engine to which regulations under section 202 apply complies with the emission standards of such regulations, (ii) such methods and procedures are in accordance with good engineering practices, and (iii) such methods and procedures are reasonably capable of being correlated with tests conducted under section 206(a)(1), then—

(1) he shall establish such methods and procedures by regulation, and

(2) at such time as he determines that inspection facilities or equipment are available for purposes of carrying out testing methods and procedures established under paragraph (1), he shall prescribe regulations which shall require manufacturers to warrant the emission control device or system of each motor vehicle or new motor vehicle engine to which a regulation under section 202 applies and which is manufactured in a model year beginning after the Administrator first prescribes warranty regulations under this paragraph (2). The warranty under such regulations shall run to the ultimate purchaser and each subsequent purchaser and shall provide that if—

(A) the vehicle or engine is maintained and operated in accordance with instructions under subsection (c)(3),

(B) it fails to conform at any time during its useful life (as determined under section 202(d) to the regulations prescribed under section 202, and

(C) such nonconformity results in the ultimate purchaser (or any subsequent purchaser) of such vehicle or engine having to bear any penalty or other sanction (including the denial of the right to use such vehicle or engine) under State or Federal law, then such manufacturer shall remedy such nonconformity under such warranty with the cost thereof to be borne by the manufacturer.

No such warranty shall be invalid on the basis of any part used in the maintenance or repair of a vehicle or engine if such part was certified as provided under subsection (a)(2).

For purposes of the warranty under this subsection, for the period after 24 months or 24,000 miles (whichever first occurs) the term "emission control device or system" means a catalytic converter, thermal reactor, or other component installed on or in a vehicle for the sole or primary purpose of reducing vehicle emissions. Such term shall not include those vehicle components which were in general use prior to model year 1968.

(c) Effective with respect to vehicles and engines manufactured during model year beginning more than 60 days after the date of enactment of the Clean Air Amendments of 1970—

(1) if the Administrator determines that a substantial number of any class or category of vehicles or engines, although properly maintained and used, do not conform to the regulations prescribed under section 202, when in actual use throughout their useful life (as determined under section 202(d)), he shall immediately notify the manufacturer to submit a plan for remedying the nonconformity of the vehicles or

engines with respect to which such notification is given. The plan shall provide that the nonconformity of any such vehicles or engines which are properly used and maintained will be remedied at the expense of the manufacturer. If the manufacturer disagrees with such determination of nonconformity and so advises the Administrator, the Administrator shall afford the manufacturer and other interested persons an opportunity to present their views and evidence in support thereof at a public hearing. Unless, as a result of such hearing the Administrator withdraws such determination of nonconformity, he shall, within 60 days after completion of such hearing, order the manufacturer to provide prompt notification of such nonconformity in accordance with paragraph (2).

(2) Any notification required by paragraph (1) with respect to any class or category of vehicles or engines shall be given to dealers, ultimate purchasers, and subsequent purchasers (if known) in such manner and containing such information as the Administrator may by regulations require.

(3)(A) The manufacturer shall furnish with each new motor vehicle or motor vehicle enginer written instructions for the proper maintenance and use of the vehicle or engine by the ultimate purchaser and such instructions shall correspond to regulations which the Administrator shall promulgate. The manufacturer shall provide in bold-face type on the first page of the written maintenance instructions notice that maintenance, replacement, or repair of the emission control evices and systems may be performed by any automotive repair establishment or individual using any automotive part which has been certified as provided in susbsection (a)(2).

(B) The instruction under subparagraph (A) of this paragraph shall not include any condition on the ultimate purchaser's using, in connection with such vehicle or engine, any component or service (other than a component or service provided without charge under the terms of the purchase agreement) which is identified by brand, trade, or corporate name; or directly or indirectly distinguishing between service performed by the franchised dealers of such manufacturer or any other service establishments with which such manufacturer has a commercial relationship, and service performed by independent automotive repair facilities with which such manufacturer has no commercial relationships; except that the prohibition of this subsection may be waived by the Administrator if—

(i) the manufacturer satisfies the Administrator that the vehicle or engine will function properly only if the component or service so identified is used in connection with such vehicle or engine, and

(ii) the Administrator finds that such a waiver is in the public interest.

(C) In addition, the manufacturer shall indicate by means of a label or tag permanently affixed to such vehicle or engine that such vehicle or engine is covered by a certificate of conformity issued for the purpose of assuring achievement of emissions standards prescribed under section 202 of this Act. Such label or tag shall contain such other information relating to control of motor vehicle emissions as the Administrator shall prescribe by regulation.

(d) Any cost obligation of any dealer incurred as a result of any requirement imposed by subsection (a), (b), or (c) shall be borne by the manufacturer. The transfer of any such cost obligation from a manufacturer to any dealer through franchise or other agreement is prohibited.

(e) If a manufacturer includes in any advertisement a statement respecting the cost or value of emission control devics or systems, such manufacturer shall set forth in such statement the cost or value attributed to such devices or systems by the Secretary of Labor (through the Bureau of Labor Statistics). The Secretary of Labor, and his representatives, shall have the same access for this purpose to the books, documents, papers, and records of a manufacturer as the Comptroller General has to those of a recipient of assistance for the purposes of section 311.

(f) Any inspection of a motor vehicle or a motor vehicle engine for purposes of subsection (c)(1), after its sale to the ultimate purchaser, shall be made only if the owner of such vehicle or engine voluntarily permits such inpsection to be made, except as may be provided by any State or local inspection program.

(g)(1) Upon the sale of each new light-duty motor vehicle by a dealer, the dealer shall furnish to the purchaser a certificate that such motor vehicle conforms to the applicable regulations under section 202 including notice of the purchaser's rights under paragraph (2).

(2) If at any time during the period for which the warranty applies under subsection (b), a motor vehicle fails to conform to the applicable regulations under section 202 as determined under subsection (b) of this section such nonconformity shall be remedied by the manufacturer at the cost of the manufacturer pursuant to such warranty as provided in section 207(b)(2) (without regard to subparagraph (C) thereof).

(3) Nothing in section 209(a) shall be construed to prohibit a State from testing, or requiring testing of, a motor vehicle after the date of sale of such vehicle to the ultimate purchaser (except that no new motor vehicle manufacturer or dealer may be required to conduct testing under this paragraph).

(h) For the purposes of this section, the owner of any motor vehicle or motor vehicle engine warranted under this section is responsible in the proper maintenance of such vehicle or engine to replace and to maintain, at his expense at any service establishment or facility of his choosing, such items as spark plugs, points, condensors, and any other part, item, or device related to emission control (but not designed for emission control under the terms of the last three sentences of section 207(a)(1)), unless such part, item, or device is covered by any warranty not mandated by this Act.

§ 7542. Records and reports

[Sec. 208] (a) Every manufacturer shall establish and maintain such records, make such reports, and provide such information as the Administrator may reasonably require to enable him to determine whether such manufacturer has acted or is acting in compliance with this title and regulations thereunder and shall, upon request of an officer or employee duly designated by the Administrator, permit such officer or employee at reasonable times to have access to and copy such records.

(b) Any records, reports or information obtained under subsection (a) shall be available to the public, except that upon a showing satisfactory to the Administrator by any person that records, reports, or information, or particular part thereof (other than emission data), to which the Administrator has access under this section if made public, would divulge methods or processes entitled to protection as trade secrets of such persons, the Administrator shall consider such record, report, or information or particular portion thereof confidential in accordance with the purposes of section 1905 of title 18 of the Untied States Code, except that such record, report, or information may be disclosed to other officers, employees, or authorized representatives of the United States concerned with carrying out this Act or when relevant in any proceeding under this Act. Nothing in this section shall authorize the withholding of information by the Administrator or any officer or employee under his control from the duly authorized committees of Congress.

§ 7543. State standards

[Sec. 209] (a) No State or any political subdivision thereof shall adopt or attempt to enforce any standard relating to the control of emissions from new motor vehicles or new motor vehicle engines subject to this part. No State shall require certification, inspection, or any other approval relating to the control of emissions from any new motor vehicle or new motor vehicle engine as conditions precedent to the initial retail sale, titling (if any), or registration of such motor vehicle, motor vehicle engine or equipment.

(b)(1) The Administrator shall, after notice and opportunity for public hearing, waive application of this section to any State which has adopted standards (other than crankcase emission standards) for the control of emissions from new motor vehicles or new motor vehicle engines prior to March 30, 1966, if the State determines that the State standards will be, in the aggregate, at least as protective of public health and welfare as applicable Federal standards. No such waiver shall be granted if the Administrator finds that—

    (A) the determination of the State is arbitrary and capricious,

    (B) such State does not need such State standards to meet compelling and extraordinary conditions, or

    (C) such State standards and accompanying enforcement procedures are not consistent with section 202(a) of this part.

(2) If each State standard is at least as stringent as the comparable applicable Federal standard, such State standards shall be deemed to be at least as protective of health and welfare as such Federal standards for purposes of paragraph (1).

(3) In the case of any new motor vehicle or new motor vehicle engine to which State standards apply pursuant to a waiver granted under paragraph (1), compliance with such State standards shall be treated as compliance with applicable Federal standards for purposes of this title.

    (c)(1) Whenever a regulation with respect to any motor vehicle part or motor vehicle engine part is in effect under section 207(a)(2), no State or political subdivision thereof shall adopt or attempt to enforce any standard or any requirement of certification, inspection or approval which relates to motor vehicle emissions and is applicable to the same aspect of such part. The preceding sentence shall not apply in the case of a State with respect to which a waiver is in effect under subsection (b).

    (d) Nothing in this part shall preclude or deny to any State or political subdivision thereof the right otherwise to control, regulate, or restrict the use, operation, or movement of registered or licensed motor vehicles.

§ 7544. State grants

[Sec. 210] The Administrator is authorized to make grants to appropriate State agencies in an amount up to two-thirds of the cost of developing and maintaining effective vehicle emission devices and systems inspection and emission testing and control programs, except that—

    (1) no such grant shall be made for any part of any State vehicle inspection program which does not directly relate to the cost of the air pollution control aspects of such a program;

    (2) no such grant shall be made unless the Secretary of Transportation has certified to the Administrator that such program is consistent with any highway safety program developed pursuant to section 402 of title 23 of the United States Code; and

    (3) no such grant shall be made unless the program includes provisions designed to insure that emission control devices and systems on vehicles in actual use have not been discontinued or rendered inoperative.

Grants may be made under this section by way of reimbursement in any case in which amounts have been expended by the State before the date on which any such grant was made.

§ 7545. Regulation of fuels

[Sec. 211] (a) The Administrator may by regulation designate any fuel or fuel additive and, after such date or dates as may be prescribed by him, no manufacturer or processor of any such fuel or additive may sell, offer for sale, or introduce into commerce such fuel or additive unless the Administrator has registered such fuel or additive in accordance with subsection (b) of this section.

(b)(1) for the purpose of registration of fuels and fuel additives, the Administrator shall require—

    (A) the manufacturer of any fuel to notify him as to the commercial identifying name and manufacturer of any additive contained in such fuel; the range of concentration of any additive in the fuel; and the purpose-in-use of any such additive; and

    (B) the manufacturer of any additive to notify him as to the chemical composition of such additive.

(2) For the purpose of registration of fuels and fuel additives, the Administrator may also require the manufacturer of any fuel or fuel additive—

    (A) to conduct tests to determine potential public health effects of such fuel or additive (including, but not limited to, carcinogenic, teratogenic, or mutagenic effects), and

    (B) to furnish the description of any analytical technique that can be used to detect and measure any additive in such fuel, the recommended range of concentration of such additive, and the recommended purpose-in-use of such additive, and such other information as is reasonable and necessary to determine the emissions resulting from the use of the fuel or additive contained in such fuel, the effect of such fuel or additive on the emission control performance of any vehicle or vehicle engine, or the extent to which such emissions affect the public health or welfare.

Tests under subparagraph (A) shall be conducted in conformity with test procedures and protocols established by the Administrator. The result of such tests shall not be considered confidential.

(3) Upon compliance with the provision of this subsection, including assurances that the Administrator will receive changes in the information required, the Administrator shall register such fuel or fuel additive.

(c)(1) The Administrator may, from time to time on the basis of information obtained under subsection (b) of this section or other information available to him, by regulation, control or prohibit the manufacture, introduction into commerce, offering for sale, or sale of any fuel additive for use in a motor vehicle or motor vehicle engine (A) if in the judgment of the Administrator any emission product of such fuel or fuel additives causes, or contributes to, air pollution which may reasonably be anticipated to endanger the public health or welfare, or (B) if emission products of such fuel or fuel additive will impair to a significant degree the performance of any emission control device or system which is in general use, or which the Administrator finds has been developed to a point where in a reasonable time it would be in general use were such regulation to be promulgated.

(2)(A) No fuel, class of fuels, or fuel additive may be controlled or prohibited by the Administrator pursuant to clause (A) of paragraph (1) except after consideration of all relevant medical and scientific evidence available to him, including consideration of other technologically or economically feasible means of achieving emission standards under section 202.

(B) No fuel or fuel additive may be controlled or prohibited by the Administrator pursuant to clause (B) of paragraph (1) except after consideration of available scientific and economic data, including a cost benefit analysis comparing emission control devices or systems which are or will be in general use and require the proposed control or prohibition with emission control devices or systems which are or will be in general use and do not require the proposed control or prohibition. On request of a manufacturer of motor vehicles, motor vehicle engines, fuels, or fuel additives submitted within 10 days of notice of proposed rulemaking, the Administrator shall hold a public hearing and publish his findings with respect to any matter he is required to consider under this subparagraph. Such findings shall be published at the time of promulgation of final regulations.

(C) No fuel or fuel additive may be prohibited by the Administrator under paragraph (1) unless he finds, and publishes such finding, that in his judgment such prohibition will not cause the use of any other fuel or fuel additive which will produce emissions which will endanger the public health or welfare to the same or greater degree than the use of the fuel or fuel additive proposed to be prohibited.

(3)(A) For the purpose of obtaining evidence and data to carry out paragraph (2), the Administrator may require the manufacturer of any motor vehicle engine to furnish any information which has been developed concerning the emissions from motor vehicles resulting from the use of any fuel additive, or the effect of such use on the performance of any emission control device system.

(B) In obtaining information under subparagraph (A), section 307(a) (relating to subpoenas) shall be applicable.

(4)(A) Except as otherwise provided in subparagraph (B) or (C), no State (or political subdivision thereof) may prescribe or attempt to enforce, for purposes of motor vehicle emission control, any control or prohibition respecting use of a fuel or fuel additive in a motor vehicle or motor vehicle engine—

(i) if the Administrator has found that no control or prohibition under paragraph (1) is necessary and has published his finding in the Federal Register, or

(ii) if the Administrator has prescribed under paragraph (1) a control or prohibition applicable to such fuel or fuel additive, unless State prohibition or control is identical to the prohibition or control prescribed by the Administrator.

(B) Any State for which application of section 209(a) has at anytime been waived under section 209(b) may at any time prescribe and enforce, for the purpose of motor vehicle emission control, a control or prohibition respecting any fuel or fuel additive.

(C) A State may prescribe and enforce, for the purposes of motor vehicle emission control, a control or prohibition respecting the use of a fuel or fuel additive in a motor vehicle or motor vehicle engine if an applicable implementation plan for such State under section 110 so provides. The Administrator may approve such provision in an implementation plan, or promulgate an implementation plan containing such a provision, only if he finds that the State control or prohibition is necessary to achieve the national primary or secondary ambient air quality standard which the plan implements.

(d) Any person who violates subsection (a) or (f) or the regulations prescribed under subsection (c) or who fails to furnish any information required by the Administrator under subsection (b) shall forfeit and pay to the United States a civil penalty of $10,000 for each and every day of the continuance of such violation, which shall accrue to the United States and be recovered in a civil suit in the name of the United States, brought in the district where such person has his principal office of in any district in which he does business. The Administrator may, upon application therefor, remit or mitigate any forfeiture provided for in this subsection and he shall have authority to determine the facts upon all such applications.

(e)(1) Not later than one year after the date of enactment of this subsection and after notice and opportunity for a public hearing, the Administrator shall promulgate regulations which implement the authority under subsection (b) (2) (A) and (B) with respect to each fuel or fuel additive which is registered on the date of promulgation of such regulations and with respect to each fuel or fuel additive for which an application for registration is filed thereafter.

(2) Regulations under subsection (b) to carry out this subsection shall require that the requisite information be provided to the Administrator by each such manufacturer—

(A) prior to registration, in the case of any fuel or fuel additive which is not registered on the date of promulgation of such regulations; or

(B) not later than three years after the date of promulgation of such regulations, in the case of any fuel or fuel additive which is registered on such date.

(3) In promulgating such regulations, the Administrator may—
  (A) exempt any small business (as defined in such regulations) from or defer or modify the requirements of, such regulations with respect to any such small business;
  (B) provide for cost-sharing with respect to the testing of any fuel or fuel additive which is manufactured or processed by two or more persons or otherwise provide for shared responsibility to meet the requirements of this section without duplication; or
  (C) exempt any person from such regulations with respect to a particular fuel or fuel additive upon a finding that any additional testing of such fuel or fuel additive would be duplicative of adequate existing testing.

(f)(1) Effective upon March 31, 1977, it shall be unlawful for any manufacturer of any fuel or fuel additive to first introduce into commerce, or to increase the concentration in use of, any fuel or fuel additive for general use in light duty motor vehicles manufactured after model year 1974 which is not substantially similar to any fuel or fuel additive utilized in the certification of any model year 1975, or subsequent model year, vehicle or engine under section 206.

(2) Effective November 30, 1977, it shall be unlawful for any manufacturer of any fuel to introduce into commerce any gasoline which contains a concentration of manganese in excess of .0625 grams per gallon of fuel, except as otherwise provided pursuant to a waiver under paragraph (4).

(3) Any manufacturer of any fuel or fuel additive which prior to March 31, 1977, and after January 1, 1974, first introduced into commerce or increased the concentration in use of a fuel or fuel additive that would otherwise have been prohibited under paragraph (1) if introduced on or after March 31, 1977 shall, not later than September 15, 1978, cease to distribute such fuel or fuel additive in commerce. During the period beginning 180 days after the date of the enactment of this subsection and before September 15, 1978, the Administrator shall prohibit or restrict the concentration of any fuel additive which he determines will cause or contribute to the failure of any emission control device or system (over the useful life of any vehicle in which such device or system is used) to achieve compliance by the vehicle with the emission standards with respect to which it has been certified under section 206.

(4) The Administrator, upon application of any manufacturer of any fuel or fuel additive, may waive the prohibitions established under paragraph (1) or (3) of this subsection or the limitation specified in paragraph (2) of this subsection, if he determines that the applicant has established that such fuel or fuel additive or specified concentration thereof, and the emission products of such fuel or additive or specified concentration thereof, will not cause or contribute to a failure

of any emission control device or system (over the useful life of any vehicle in which such device or system is used) to achieve compliance by the vehicle with the emission standards with respect to which it has been certified pursuant to section 206. If the Administrator has not acted to grant or deny an application under this paragraph within one hundred and eighty days of receipt of such application, the waiver authorized by this paragraph shall be treated as granted.

(5) No action of the Administrator under this section may be stayed by any court pending judicial review of such action.

(g)(1) For the purpose of this subsection:

(A) The terms "gasoline" and "refinery" have the meaning provided under regulations of the Administrator promulgated under this section.

(B) The term "small refinery" means a refinery or a portion of a refinery producing gasoline—

(i) the gasoline producing capacity of which was in operation or under construction at any time during the one-year period immediately preceding October 1, 1976, and

(ii) which has a crude oil or bona fide feed stock capacity (as determined by the Administrator) of 50,000 barrels per day or less, and

(iii) which is owned or controlled by a refiner with a total combined crude oil or bona fide feed stock capacity (as determined by the Administrator) of 137,500 barrels per day or less.

(2) No regulations of the Administrator under this section (or any amendment or revision thereof) respecting the control or prohibition of lead additives in gasoline shall require a small refinery prior to October 1, 1982, to reduce the average lead content per gallon of gasoline line refined as such refinery below the applicable amount specified in the table below:

If the average gasoline production of the small refinery for the immediately preceding calendar year (or, in the case of refineries under construction, half the designed crude oil capacity was barrels per day):	The applicable amount is (in grams per gallon)
5,000 or under	2.65
5,001 to 10,000	2.15
10,001 to 15,000	1.65
15,001 to 20,000	1.30
20,001 to 25,000	0.80
25,001 or over	as prescribed by the Administrator, but not greater than 0.80

The Administrator may promulgate such regulations as he deems
appropriate with respect to the reduction of the average lead content of
gasoline refined by small refineries on and after October 1, 1982,
taking into account the experience under the preceding provisions of
this paragraph.

(3) Effective on the date of the enactment of this subsection, the regulations of the Administrator under this section respecting fuel additives
(40 CFR part 80) shall be deemed amended to comply with the
requirement contained in paragraph (2).

(4) Nothing in this section shall be construed to preempt the right of any
State to take action as permitted by section 211(c)(4) of this Act.

§ 7546. Low-emission vehicles

[Sec. 212] (a) For the purpose of this section—

(1) The term "Board" means the Low-Emission Vehicle Certification
Board.

(2) The term "Federal Government" includes the legislative, executive,
and judicial branches of the Government of the United States, and the
government of the District of Columbia.

(3) The term "motor vehicle" means any self-propelled vehicle designed
for use in the United States on the highways, other than a vehicle
designed or used for military field training, combat, or tactical
purposes.

(4) The term "low-emission vehicle" means any motor vehicle which—
   (A) emits any air pollutant in amounts significantly below new motor
       vehicle standards applicable under section 202 at the time of
       procurement to that type of vehicle; and
   (B) with respect to all other air pollutants meets the new motor
       vehicle standards applicable under section 202 at the time of
       procurement to that type of vehicle.

(5) The term "retail price" means (A) the maximum statutory price
applicable to any class or model of motor vehicle; or (B) in any case
where there is no applicable maximum statutory price, the most recent
procurement price paid for any class or model of motor vehicle.

(b)(1) There is established a Low-Emission Vehicle Certification Board to
be composed of the Administrator or his designee, the Secretary of Transportation or his designee, the Chairman of the Council on Environmental
Quality or his designee, the Director of the National Highway Safety
Bureau in the Department of Transportation, the Administrator of General
Services, and two members appointed by the President. The President shall
designate one member of the Board as Chairman.

(2) Any member of the Board not employed by the United States may
receive compensation at the rate of $125 for each day such member is
engaged upon work of the Board. Each member of the Board shall be

reimbursed for travel expenses, including per diem in lieu of subsistence as authorized by section 5703 of title 5, United States Code, for persons in the Government service employed intermittently.

(3)(A) The Chairman, with the concurrence of the members of the Board, may employ and fix the compensation of such additional personnel as may be necessary to carry out the functions of the Board, but no individual so appointed shall receive compensation in excess of the rate authorized for GS-18 by section 5332 of title 5, United States Code.

(B) The Chairman may fix the time and place of such meetings as may be required, but a meeting of the Board shall be called whenever a majority of its members so request.

(C) The Board is granted all other powers necessary for meeting its responsibilities under this section.

(c) The Administrator shall determine which models or classes of motor vehicles qualify as low-emission vehicles in accordance with the provisions of this section.

(d)(1) The Board shall certify any class or model of motor vehicles—

(A) for which a certification application has been filed in accordance with paragraph (3) of this subsection;

(B) which is a low-emission vehicle as determined by the Administrator; and

(C) which it determines is suitable for use as a substitute for a class or model of vehicles at that time in use by agencies of the Federal Government.

The Board shall specify with particularity the class or model of vehicles for which the class or model of vehicles described in the application is a suitable substitute. In making the determination under this subsection the Board shall consider the following criteria:

(i) the safety of the vehicle;

(ii) its performance characteristics;

(iii) its reliability potential;

(iv) its serviceability;

(v) its fuel availability

(vi) its noise level; and

(vii) its maintenance costs as compared with the class or model of motor vehicle for which it may be a suitable substitute.

(2) Certification under this section shall be effective for a period of one year from the date of issuance.

(3)(A) Any party seeking to have a class or model of vehicle certified under this section shall file a certification application in accordance with regulations prescribed by the Board.

(B) The Board shall publish notice of each application received in the Federal Register.

(C) The Administrator and the Board shall make determinations for the purposes of this section in accordance with procedures prescribed by regulation by the Administrator and the Board, respectively.

(D) The Administrator and the Board shall conduct whatever investigation is necessary, including actual inspection of the vehicle at a place designated in regulations prescribed under subparagraph (A).

(E) The Board shall receive and evaluate written comments and documents from interested parties in support of, or in opposition to, certification of the class or model of vehicle under consideration.

(F) Within 90 days after the receipt of a properly filed certification application, the Administrator shall determine whether such class or model of vehicle is a low-emission vehicle, and within 180 days of such determination, the Board shall reach a decision by majority vote as to whether such class or model of vehicle, having been determined to be a low-emission vehicle, is a suitable substitute for any class or classes of vehicle presently being purchased by the Federal Government for use by its agencies.

(G) Immediately upon making any determination or decision under subparagraph (F), the Administrator and the Board shall each publish in the Federal Register notice of such determination or decision, including reasons therefor and in the case of the Board any dissenting views.

(e)(1) Certified low-emission vehicles shall be acquired by purchase or lease by the Federal Government for use by the Federal Government in lieu of other vehicles if the Administrator of General Services determines that such certified vehicles have procurement costs which are no more than 150 per centum of the retail price of the least expensive class or model of motor vehicle for which they are certified substitutes.

(2) In order to encourage development of inherently low-pollution propulsion technology, the Board may, at its discretion, raise the premium set forth in paragraph (1) of this subsection to 200 per centum of the retail price of any class or model of motor vehicle for which a certified low-emission vehicle is a certified substitute, if the Board determines that the certified low-emission vehicle is powered by an inherently low-polluting propulsion system.

(3) Data relied upon by the Board and the Administrator in determining that a vehicle is a certified low-emission vehicle shall be incorporated in any contract for the procurement of such vehicle.

(f) The procuring agency shall be required to purchase available certified low-emission vehicles which are eligible for purchase to the extent they are available before purchasing any other vehicles for which any low-emission vehicle is a certified substitute. In making purchasing selection between competing eligible certified low-emission vehicles, the procuring agency shall give priority to (1) any class or model which does not require extensive periodic maintenance to retain its low-polluting qualities or which does not require the use of fuels which are more expensive than those of the classes or models of vehicles for which it is a certified substitute; and (2) passenger vehicles other than buses.

(g) For the purpose of procuring certified low-emission vehicles any statutory price limitations shall be waived.

(h) The Administrator shall, from time to time as the Board deems appropriate, test the emissions from certified low-emission vehicles purchased by the Federal Government. If at any time he finds that the emission rates exceed the rates on which certification under this section was based, the Administrator shall notify the Board. Thereupon the Board shall give the supplier of such vehicles written notice of this finding, issue public notice of it, and give the supplier an opportunity to make necessary repairs, adjustments, or replacements. If no such repairs, adjustments, or replacements are made within a period to be set by the Board, the Board may order the supplier to show cause why the vehicle involved should be eligible for certification.

(i) There are authorized to be appropriated for paying additional amounts for motor vehicles pursuant to, and for carrying out the provisions of, this section, $5,000,000 for the fiscal year ending June 30, 1971, and $25,000,000 for each of the four succeeding fiscal years.

(j) The Board shall promulgate the procedures required to implement this section within one hundred and eighty days after the date of enactment of the Clean Air Amendments of 1970.

§ 7547. Fuel economy improvement from new motor vehicles

[Sec. 213] (a)(1) The Administrator and the Secretary of Transportation shall conduct a joint study, and shall report to the Committee on Interstate and Foreign Commerce of the United States House of Representatives and the Committees on Public Works and Commerce of the United States Senate within one hundred and twenty days following the date of enactment of this section, concerning the practicability of establishing a fuel economy improvement standard of 20 per centum for new motor vehicles manufactured during and after model year 1980. Such study and report shall include, but not be limited to, the technological problems of meeting any such standard, including the leadtime involved; the test procedures required to determine compliance; the economic costs associated with such standard, including any beneficial economic impact; the various means of enforcing such standard; the effect on consumption of natural resources, including energy consumed; and the impact of applicable safety and emission standards. In the course of performing such study, the Administrator and the Secretary of Transportation shall utilize the research previously performed in the Department of

Transportation, and the Administrator and the Secretary shall consult with the Federal Energy Administrator, the Chairman of the Council on Environmental Quality, and the Secretary of the Treasury. The Office of Management and Budget may review such report before its submission to such committees of the Congress, but such Office may not revise the report or delay its submission beyond the date prescribed for its submission, and may submit to Congress its comments respecting such report. In connection with such study, the Administrator may utilize the authority provided in section 307(a) of this Act to obtain necessary information.

(2) For the purpose of this section, the term "fuel economy improvement standard" means a requirement of a percentage increase in the number of miles of transportation provided by a manufacturer's entire annual production of new motor vehicles per unit of fuel consumed, as determined for each manufacturer in accordance with test procedures established by the Administrator pursuant to this Act. Such term shall not include any requirement for any design standard or any other requirement specifying or otherwise limiting the manufacturer's discretion in deciding how to comply with the fuel economy improvement standard by any lawful means.

§ 7548. Study of particulate emissions from motor vehicles

[Sec. 214] (a)(1) The Administrator shall conduct a study concerning the effects on health and welfare of particulate emissions from motor vehicles or motor vehicle engines to which section 202 applies. Such study shall characterize and quantify such emissions and analyze the relationship of such emissions to various fuels and fuel additives.

(2) The study shall also include an analysis of particulate emissions from mobile sources which are not related to engine emissions (including, but not limited to tire debris, and asbestos from brake lining).

(b) The Administrator shall report to the Congress the findings and results of the study conducted under subsection (a) not later than two years after the date of the enactment of the Clean Air Act Amendments of 1977. Such report shall also include recommendations for standards or methods to regulate particulate emissions described in paragraph (2) of subsection (a).

§ 7549. High altitude performance adjustments

[Sec. 215] (a)(1) Any action taken with respect to any element of design installed on or in a motor vehicle or motor vehicle engine in compliance with regulations under this title (including any alteration or adjustment of such element), shall be treated as not in violation of section 203(a) if such action is performed in accordance with high altitude adjustment instructions provided by the manufacturer under subsection (b) and approved by the Administrator.

(2) If the Administrator finds that adjustments or modifications made pursuant to instructions of the manufacturer under paragraph (1) will not insure emission control performance with respect to each standard under section 202 at least equivalent to that which would result if no such adjustments or modifications were made, he shall disapprove such instructions. Such finding shall be based upon minimum engineering evaluations consistent with good engineering practice.

(b)(1) Instructions respecting each class or category of vehicles or engines to which this title applies providing for such vehicle and engine adjustments and modifications as may be necessary to insure emission control performance at different altitudes shall be submitted by the manufacturer to the Administrator pursuant to regulations promulgated by the Administrator.

(2) Any knowing violation by a manufacturer of requirements of the Administrator under paragraph (1) shall be treated as a violation by such manufacturer of section 203(a)(3) for purposes of the penalties contained in section 205.

(3) Such instructions shall provide, in addition to other adjustments, for adjustments for vehicles moving from high altitude areas to low altitude areas after the initial registration of such vehicles.

(c) No instructions under this section respecting adjustments or modifications may require the use of any manufacturer parts (as defined in section (203(a))) unless the manufacturer demonstrates to the satisfaction of the Administrator that the use of such manufacturer parts is necessary to insure emission control performance.

(d) Before January 1, 1981 the authority provided by this section shall be available in any high altitude State (as determined under regulations of the Administrator under regulations promulgated before the date of the enactment of this Act) but after December 31, 1980, such authority shall be available only in any such State in which an inspection and maintenance program for the testing of motor vehicle emissions has been instituted for the portions of the State where any national ambient air quality standard for auto-related pollutants has not been attained.

§ 7550. Definitions for Part A

[Sec. 216] As used in this title—

(1) The term "manufacturer" as used in sections 202, 203, 206, 207, and 208 means any person engaged in the manufacturing or assembling of new motor vehicles or new motor vehicle engines, or importing such vehicles or engines for resale, or who acts for and is under the control of any such person in connection with the distribution of new motor vehicles or new motor vehicle engines, but shall not include any dealer with respect to new motor vehicles or new motor vehicle engines received by him in commerce.

(2) The term "motor vehicle" means any self-propelled vehicle designed for transporting persons or property on a street or highway.

(3) Except with respect to vehicles or engines imported or offered for importation, the term "new motor vehicle" means a motor vehicle the equitable or legal title to which has never been transferred to an ultimate purchaser; and the term "new motor vehicle engine" means an engine in a new motor vehicle or a motor vehicle engine the equitable or legal title to which has never been transferred to the ultimate purchaser; and with respect to imported vehicles or engines, such terms mean a motor vehicle and engine, respectively, manufactured after the effective date of a regulation issued under section 202 which is applicable to such vehicle or engine (or which would be applicable to such vehicle or engine had it been manufactured for importation into the United States).

(4) The term "dealer" means any person who is engaged in the sale or the distribution of new motor vehicles or new motor vehicle engines to the ultimate purchaser.

(5) The term "ultimate purchaser" means, with respect to any new motor vehicle or new motor vehicle engine, the first person who in good faith purchases such new motor vehicle or new engine for purposes other than resale.

(6) The term "commerce" means (A) commerce between any place in any State and any place outside thereof; and (B) commerce wholly within the District of Columbia.

Part B

Aircraft Emission Standards

§ 7571. Establishment of standards

[Sec. 231] (a)(1) Within 90 days after the date of enactment of the Clean Air Amendments of 1970, the Administrator shall commence a study and investigation of emissions of air pollutants from aircraft in order to determine—

(A) the extent to which such emissions affect air quality in air quality control regions throughout the United States, and

(B) the technological feasibility of controlling such emissions.

(2) The Administrator shall, from time to time, issue proposed emission standards applicable to emissions of any air pollution from any class or classes of aircraft or aircraft engines which in his judgment causes, or contributes to, air pollution which may reasonably be anticipated to endanger the public health or welfare.

(3) The Administrator shall hold public hearings with respect to such proposed standards. Such hearings shall, to the extent practicable, be held in air quality control regions which are most seriously affected by aircraft emissions. Within 90 days after the issuance of such proposed

regulations, he shall issue such regulations with such modifications as he deems appropriate. Such regulations may be revised from time to time.

(b) Any regulation prescribed under this section (and any revision thereof) shall take effect after such period as the Administrator finds necessary (after consultation with the Secretary of Transportation) to permit the development and application of the requisite technology, giving appropriate consideration to the cost of compliance within such period.

(c) Any regulations in effect under this section on date of enactment of the Clean Air Act Amendments of 1977 or proposed or promulgated thereafter, or amendments thereto, with respect to aircraft shall not apply if disapproved by the President, after notice and opportunity for public hearing, on the basis of a finding by the Secretary of Transportation that any such regulation would create a hazard to aircraft safety. Any such finding shall include a reasonably specific statement of the basis upon which the finding was made.

§ 7572. Enforcement of standards

[Sec. 232](a) The Secretary of Transportation, after consultation with the Administrator, shall prescribe regulations to insure compliance with all standards prescribed under section 231 by the Administrator. The regulations of the Secretary of Transportation shall include provisions making such standards applicable in the issuance, amendment, modification, suspension, or revocation of any certificate authorized by the Federal Aviation Act or the Department of Transportation Act. Such Secretary shall insure that all necessary inspections are accomplished, and, may execute any power or duty vested in him by any other provision of law in the execution of all powers and duties vested in him under this section.

(b) In any action to amend, modify, suspend, or revoke a certificate in which violation of an emission standard prescribed under section 231 or of a regulation prescribed under subsection (a) is at issue, the certificate holder shall have the same notice and appeal rights as are prescribed for such holders in the Federal Aviation Act of 1958 or the Department of Transportation Act, except that in any appeal to the National Transportation Safety Board, the Board may amend, modify, or revoke the order of the Secretary of Transportation only if it finds no violation of such standard or regulation and that such amendment, modification, or revocation is consistent with safety in air transportation.

§ 7573. State standards and controls

[Sec. 233] No State or political subdivision thereof may adopt or attempt to enforce any standard respecting emissions of any air pollutant from any aircraft or engine thereof unless such standard is identical to a standard applicable to such aircraft under this part.

§ 7574. Definitions

[Sec. 234] Terms used in this part (other than Administrator) shall have the same meaning as such terms have under section 101 of the Federal Aviation Act of 1985.

Subchapter III. General Provisions

§ 7601. Administration

[Sec. 301] (a)(1) The Administrator is authorized to prescribe such regulations as are necessary to carry out his functions under this Act. The Administrator may delegate to any officer or employee of the Environmental Protection Agency such of his powers and duties under this Act, except the making of regulations, as he may deem necessary or expedient.

(2) Not later than one year after the date of enactment of this paragraph, the Administrator shall promulgate regulations establishing general applicable procedures and policies for regional officers and employees (including the Regional Administrator) to follow in carrying out a delegation under paragraph (1), if any. Such regulations shall be designed—

(A) to assure fairness and uniformity in the criteria, procedures, and policies applied by the various regions implementing and enforcing the Act;

(B) to assure at least an adequate quality audit of each State's performance and adherence to the requirements of this Act in implementing and enforcing the Act, particularly in the review of new sources and in enforcement of the Act; and

(C) to provide a mechanism for identifying and standardizing inconsistent or varying criteria, procedures, and policies being employed by such officers and employees in implementing and enforcing the Act.

(b) Upon the request of an air pollution control agency, personnel of the Environmental Protection Agency may be detailed to such agency for the purpose of carrying out the provisions of this Act.

(c) Payments under grants made under this Act may be made in installments, and in advance or by way of reimbursement, as may be determined by the Administrator.

§ 7602. Definitions

[Sec. 302] When used in this Act—

(a) The term "Administrator" means the Administrator of the Environmental Protection Agency.

(b) The term "air pollution control agency" means any of the following:

(1) A single State agency designated by the Governor of that State as the official State air pollution control agency for purposes of this Act;

(2) An agency established by two or more States and having substantial powers or duties pertaining to the prevention and control of air pollution;

(3) A city, county, or other local government health authority, or, in the case of any city, county, or other local government in which there is an agency other than the health authority charged with responsibility for enforcing ordinances or laws relating to the prevention and control of air pollution, such other agency; or

(4) An agency of two or more municipalities located in the same State or in different States and having substantial powers or duties pertaining to the prevention and control of air pollution.

(c) The term "interstate air pollution control agency" means—

(1) an air pollution control agency established by two or more States, or

(2) an air pollution control agency of two or more municipalities located in different States.

(d) The term "State" means a State, the District of Columbia, the Commonwealth of Puerto Rico, the Virgin Islands, Guam, and American Samoa and includes the Commonwealth of the Northern Mariana Islands.

(e) The term "person" includes an individual, corporation, partnership, association, State, municipality, political subdivision of a State, and any agency, department, or instrumentality of the United States and any officer, agent, or employee thereof.

(f) The term "municipality" means a city, town, borough, county, parish, district, or other public body created by or pursuant to State law.

(g) The term "air pollutant" means any air pollution agent or combination of such agents, including any physical, chemical, biological, radioactive (including source material, special nuclear material, and by-product material) substance or matter which is emitted into or otherwise enters the ambient air.

(h) All language referring to effects on welfare includes, but is not limited to, effects on soils, water, crops, vegetation, manmade materials, animals, wildlife, weather, visibility, and climate, damage to and deterioration of property, and hazards to transportation, as well as effects on economic values and on personal comfort and well-being.

(i) The term "Federal land manager" means with respect to any lands in the United States the Secretary of the department with authority over such lands.

(j) Except as otherwise expressly provided, the terms "major stationary source" and "major emitting facility" mean any stationary facility or source of air pollutants which directly emits, or has the potential to emit, one hundred tons per year or more of any air pollutant (including any major emitting facility or source of fugitive emissions of any such pollutant, as determined by rule by the Administrator).

(k) The terms "emission limitation" and "emission standard" mean a requirement established by the State or the Administrator which limits the quantity, rate, or concentration of emissions of air pollutants on a continuous basis including any requirement relating to the operation or maintenance of a source to assure continuous emission reduction.

(l) The term "standard of performance" means a requirement of continuous emission reduction, including any requirement relating to the operation or maintenance of a source to assure continuous emission reduction.

(m) The term "means of emission limitation" means a system of continuous emission reduction (including the use of specific technology or fuels with specified pollution characteristics).

(n) The term "primary standard attainment date" means the date specified in the applicable implementation plan for the attainment of a national primary ambient air quality standard for any air pollutant.

(o) The term "delayed compliance order" means an order issued by the State or by the Administrator to an existing stationary source, postponing the date required under an applicable implementation plan for compliance by such source with any requirement of such plan.

(p) The term "schedule and timetable of compliance" means a schedule of remedial measures including an enforceable sequence of actions or operations leading to compliance with an emission limitation, other limitation, prohibition, or standard.

§ 7603. Emergency powers

[Sec. 303] (a) Notwithstanding any other provision of this Act, the Administrator, upon receipt of evidence that a pollution source or combination of sources (including moving sources) is presenting an imminent and substantial endangerment to the health of persons, and that appropriate State or local authorities have not acted to abate such sources, may bring suit on behalf of the United States in the appropriate United States district court to immediately restrain any person causing or contributing to the alleged pollution to stop the emission of air pollutants causing or contributing to such pollution or to take such other action as may be necessary. If it is not practicable to assure prompt protection of the health of persons solely by commencement of such a civil action, the Administrator may issue such orders as may be necessary to protect the health of persons who are, or may be, affected by such pollution source (or sources). Prior to taking any action under this section, the Administrator shall consult with the State and local authorities in order to confirm the correctness of the information on which action proposed to be taken is based and to ascertain the action which such authorities are or will be taking. Such order shall be effective for a period of not more than twenty-four hours unless the Administrator brings an action under the first sentence of this subsection before the expiration of such period. Whenever the Administrator brings such an action within such period, such order shall be effective for a period of forty-eight hours or such longer period as may be authorized by the court pending litigation or thereafter.

(b) Any person who willfully violates or fails or refuses to comply with any order issued by the Administrator under subsection (a) may, in an action brought in the appropriate United States district court to enforce such order, be fined not more than $5,000 for each day during which such violation occurs or failure to comply continues.

§ 7604. Citizen suits

[Sec. 304] (a) Except as provided in subsection (b), any person may commence a civil action on his own behalf—

(1) against any person (including (i) the United States, and (ii) any other governmental instrumentality or agency to the extent permitted by the Eleventh Amendment to the Constitution) who is alleged to be in violation of (A) an emission standard or limitation under this Act or (B) an order issued by the Administrator or a State with respect to such a standard or limitation,

(2) against the Administrator where there is alleged a failure of the Administrator to perform any act or duty under this Act which is not discretionary with the Administrator, or

(3) against any person who proposes to construct or constructs any new or modified major emitting facility without a permit required under part C of title I (relating to significant deterioration of air quality) or part D of title I (relating to nonattainment) or who is alleged to be in violation of any condition of such permit.

The district courts shall have jurisdiction, without regard to the amount in controversy or the citizenship of the parties, to enforce such an emission standard or limitation, or such an order, or to order the Administrator to perform such act or duty, as the case may be.

(b) No action may be commenced—

(1) under subsection (a)(1)—

(A) prior to 60 days after the plaintiff has given notice of the violation (i) to the Administrator, (ii) to the State in which the violation occurs, and (iii) to any alleged violator of the standard, limitation, or order, or

(B) if the Administrator or State has commenced and is diligently prosecuting a civil action in a court of the United States or a State to require compliance with the standard, limitation, or order, but in any such action in a court of the United States any person may intervene as a matter of right.

(2) under subsection (a)(2) prior to 60 days after the plaintiff has given notice of such action to the Administrator, except that such action may be brought immediately after such notification in the case of an action under this section respecting a violation of section 112(c)(1)(B) or an

order issued by the Administrator pursuant to section 113(a). Notice under this subsection shall be given in such manner as the Administrator shall prescribe by regulation.

(c)(1) Any action respecting a violation by a stationary source of an emission standard or limitation or an order respecting such standard or limitation may be brought only in the judicial district in which such source is located.

(2) In such action under this section, the Administrator, if not a party, may intervene as a matter of right.

(d) The court, in issuing any final order in any action brought pursuant to subsection (a) of this section, may award costs of litigation (including reasonable attorney and expert witness fees) to any party, whenever the court determines such award is appropriate. The court may, if a temporary restraining order or preliminary injunction is sought, require the filing of a bond or equivalent security in accordance with the Federal Rules of Civil Procedure.

(e) Nothing in this section shall restrict any right which any person (or class of persons) may have under any statute or common law to seek enforcement of any emission standard or limitation or to seek any other relief (including relief against the Administrator or a State agency). Nothing in this section or in any other law of the United States shall be construed to prohibit, exclude, or restrict any State, local, or interstate authority from—

(1) bringing any enforcement action or obtaining any judicial remedy or sanction in any State or local court, or

(2) bringing any administrative enforcement action or obtaining any administrative remedy or sanction in any State or local administrative agency, department or instrumentality, against the United States, any department, agency, or instrumentality thereof, or any officer, agent, or employee thereof under State or local law respecting control and abatement of air pollution. For provisions requiring compliance by the United States, departments, agencies, instrumentalities, officers, agents, and employees in the same manner as nongovernmental entities, see section 118.

(f) For purposes of this section, the term "emission standard or limitation under this Act" means—

(1) a schedule or timetable of compliance, emission limitation, standard of performance or emission standard,

(2) a control or prohibition respecting a motor vehicle fuel or fuel additive, which is in effect under this Act (including a requirement applicable by reason of section 118) or under an applicable implementation plan, or

(3) any condition or requirement of a permit under part C of title I (relating to significant deterioration of air quality) or part D of title I (relating to nonattainment), any condition or requirement of section 113(d) (relating to certain enforcement orders), 119 (relating to

primary nonferrous smelter orders), any condition or requirement under an applicable implementation plan relating to transportation control measures, air quality maintenance plans, vehicle inspection and maintenance programs, or vapor recovery requirements, section 211(e) and (f) (relating to fuels and fuel additives), section 169A (relating to visibility protection), any condition or requirement under part B of title I (relating to ozone protection), or any requirement under section 111 or 112 (without regard to whether such requirement is expressed as an emission standard or otherwise).

§ 7605. Representation in litigation

[Sec. 305](a) The Administrator shall request the Attorney General to appear and represent him in any civil action instituted under this Act to which the Administrator is a party. Unless the Attorney General notifies the Administrator that he will appear in such action, within a reasonable time, attorneys appointed by the Administrator shall appear and represent him.

(b) In the event the Attorney General agrees to appear and represent the Administrator in any such action, such representation shall be conducted in accordance with, and shall include participation by attorneys appointed by the Administrator to the extent authorized by, the memorandum of understanding between the Department of Justice and the Environmental Protection Agency, dated June 13, 1977, respecting representation of the agency by the department in civil litigation.

§ 7606. Federal procurement

[Sec. 306](a) No Federal agency may enter into any contract with any person who is convicted of any offense under section 113(c)(1) for the procurement of goods, material, and services to perform such contract at any facility at which the violation which gave rise to such conviction occurred if such facility is owned, leased, or supervised by such person. The prohibition in the preceding sentence shall continue until the Administrator certifies that the condition giving rise to such a conviction has been corrected.

(b) The Administrator shall establish procedures to provide all Federal agencies with the notification necessary for the purposes of subsection (a).

(c) In order to implement the purposes and policy of this Act to protect and enhance the quality of the Nation's air the President shall, not more than 180 days after enactment of the Clean Air Amendments of 1970 cause to be issued an order (1) requiring each Federal agency authorized to enter into contracts and each Federal agency which is empowered to extend Federal assistance by way of grant, loan, or contract to effectuate the purpose and policy of this Act in such contracting or assistance activities, and (2) setting forth procedures, sanctions, penalties, and such other provisions, as the President determines necessary to carry out such requirement.

(d) The President may exempt any contract, loan, or grant from all or part of the provisions of this section where he determines such exemption is necessary in the paramount interest of the United States and he shall notify the Congress of such exemption.

(e) The President shall annually report to the Congress on measures taken toward implementing the purpose and intent of this section, including but not limited to the progress and problems associated with implementation of this section.

§ 7607. Administrative proceedings and judicial review

[Sec. 307] (a)(1) In connection with any determination under section 110(f) or section 202(b)(5), or for purposes of obtaining information under section 202(b)(4) or 211(c)(3), the Administrator may issue subpoenas for the attendance and testimony of witnesses and the production of relevant papers, books, and documents, and he may administer oaths. Except for emission data, upon a showing satisfactory to the Administrator by such owner or operator that such papers, books, documents, or information or particular part thereof, if made public, would divulge trade secrets or secret processes of such owner or operator, the Administrator shall consider such record, report, or information or particular portion thereof confidential in accordance with the purposes of section 1905 of title 18 of the United States Code, except that such paper, book, document, or information may be disclosed to other officers, employees, or authorized representatives of the United States concerned with carrying out this Act, to persons carrying out the National Academy of Sciences study and investigation provided for in section 202(c), or when relevant in any proceeding under this Act. Witnesses summoned shall be paid the same fees and mileage that are paid witnesses in the courts of the United States. In case of contumacy or refusal to obey a subpoena served upon any person under this subparagraph, the district court of the United States for any district in which such person is found or resides or transactions business, upon application by the United States and after notice to such person, shall have jurisdiction to issue an order requiring such person to appear and give testimony before the Administrator to appear and produce papers, books, and documents before the Administrator, or both, and any failure to obey such order of the court may be punished by such court as a contempt thereof.

(b)(1) A petition for review of action of the Administrator in promulgating any national primary or secondary ambient air quality standard, any emission standard or requirement under section 112, any standard of performance or requirement under section 111; any standard under section 202 (other than a standard required to be prescribed under section 202(b)(1)), any determination under section 202(b)(5), any control or prohibition under section 211, any standard under section 231 or any rule issued under section 113, 119, or under section 120 or any other nationally applicable regulations promulgated, or final action taken, by the Administrator under this Act may be filed only in the United States Court of Appeals for the District of Columbia. A petition for review of the Administrator's action in approving or promulgating any implementation plan under section 110 or section 111(d), any order under section 111(j), under section 112(c), under section 113(d), under section 119, or under section 120, or his action under section 119(c) (2) (A), (B), or (C) (as in effect before the enactment of the Clean Air Act Amendment of 1977) or under regulations thereunder, or any other final action of the Administrator under this (including any denial or disapproval by the Administrator under Title I) Act which is locally or regionally applicable may be filed only in the United States Court of Appeals for the appropriate circuit. Any petition for review under this subsection shall be filed within sixty days from the date notice of such promulgation, approval, or action appears in the Federal Register, except that if such petition is based solely on grounds arising after such sixtieth day, then any petition for review under this subsection shall be filed within sixty days after such grounds arise. Notwithstanding the preceding sentence a petition for review of any action referred to in such sentence may be filed only in the United States Court of Appeals for the District of Columbia if such action is based on a determination of nationwide scope or effect and if in taking such action the Administrator finds and publishes that such action is based on such a determination;

    (2) Action of the Administrator with respect to which review could have been obtained under paragraph (1) shall not be subject to judicial review in civil or criminal proceedings for enforcement.

    (c) In any judicial proceeding in which review is sought of a determination under this Act required to be made on the record after notice and opportunity for hearing, if any party applies to the court for leave to adduce additional evidence, and shows to the satisfaction of the court that such additional evidence is material and that there were reasonable grounds for the failure to adduce such evidence in the proceeding before the Administrator the court may order such additional evidence (and evidence in rebuttal thereof) to be taken before the Administrator, in such manner and upon such terms and conditions as to the court may deem proper. The Administrator may modify his findings as to the facts, or make new findings, by reason of the additional evidence so taken and he shall file such modified or new findings, and his recommendation, if any, for the modification or setting aside of his original determination, with the return of such additional evidence.

    (d)(1) This subsection applies to—

        (A) the promulgation or revision of any national ambient air quality standard under section 109,

        (B) the promulgation or revision of an implementation plan by the Administrator under section 110(c),

        (C) the promulgation or revision of any standard of performance under section 111 or emission standard under section 112,

        (D) the promulgation or revision of any regulation pertaining to any fuel or fuel additive under section 211,

        (E) the promulgation or revision of any aircraft emission standard under section 231,

    (F) promulgation or revision of regulations pertaining to orders for coal conversion under section 113(d)(5) (but not including orders granting or denying any such orders),

    (G) promulgation or revision of regulations pertaining to primary nonferrous smelter orders under section 119 (but not including the granting or denying of any such order),

    (H) promulgation or revision of regulations under subtitle B of title I (relating to stratosphere and ozone protection),

    (I) promulgation or revision of regulations under subtitle C of title I (relating to prevention of significant deterioration of air quality and protection of visibility),

    (J) promulgation or revision of regulations under section 202 and test procedures for new motor vehicles or engines under section 206, and the revision of a standard, under section 202(a)(3),

    (K) promulgation or revision of regulations for noncompliance penalties under section 120,

    (L) promulgation or revision of any regulations promulgated under section 207 (relating to warranties and compliance by vehicles in actual use),

    (M) action of the Administrator under section 126 (relating to interstate pollution abatement), and

    (N) Such other actions as the Administrator may determine. The provisions of section 553 through 557 and section 706 of title 5 of the United States Code shall not, except as expressly provided in this subsection, apply to actions to which this subsection applies. This subsection shall not apply in the case of any rule or circumstance referred to in subparagraphs (A) or (B) of subsection 553 (b) of title 5 of the United States Code;

(2) Not later than the date of proposal of any action to which this subsection applies, the Administrator shall establish a rulemaking docket for such action (hereinafter in this subsection referred to as a "rule"). Whenever a rule applies only within a particular State, a second (identical) docket shall be simultaneously established in the appropriate regional office of the Environmental Protection Agency.

(3) In the case of any rule to which this subsection applies, notice of proposed rulemaking shall be published in the Federal Register, as provided under section 553(b) of title 5, United States Code, shall be accompanied by a statement of its basis and purpose and shall specify the period available for public comment (hereinafter referred to as the "comment period"). The notice of proposed rulemaking shall also state the docket number, the location or locations of the docket, and the times it will be open to public inspection. The statement of basis and purpose shall include a summary of—

    (A) the factual data on which the proposed rule is based;

(B) the methodology used in obtaining the data and in analyzing the data; and

(C) the major legal interpretations and policy considerations underlying the proposed rule. The statement shall also set forth or summarize and provide a reference to any pertinent findings, recommendations, and comments by the Scientific Review Committee established under section 109(d) and the National Academy of Sciences, and, if the proposed differs in any important respect from any of these recommendations, an explanation of the reasons for such differences. All data, information, and documents referred to in this paragraph on which the proposed rule relies shall be included in the docket on the date of publication of the proposed rule.

(4)(A) The rulemaking docket required under paragraph (2) shall be open for inspection by the public at reasonable times specified in the notice of proposed rulemaking. Any person may copy documents contained in the docket. The Administrator shall provide copying facilities which may be used at the expense of the person seeking copies, but the Administrator may waive or reduce such expenses in such instances as the public interest requires. Any person may request copies by mail if the person pays the expenses, including personnel costs to do the copying.

(B)(i) Promptly upon receipt by the agency, all written comments and documentary information on the proposed rule received from any person for inclusion in the docket during the comment period shall be placed in the docket. The transcript of public hearings, if any, on the proposed rule shall also be included in the docket promptly upon receipt from the person who transcribed such hearings. All documents which become available after the proposed rule has been published and which the Administrator determines are of central relevance to the rulemaking shall be placed in the docket as soon as possible after their availability.

(ii) The drafts of proposed rules submitted by the Administrator to the Office of Management and Budget for any interagency review process prior to proposal of any such rule, all documents accompanying such drafts, and all written comments thereon by other agencies and all written responses to such written comments by the Administrator shall be placed in the docket no later than the date of proposal of the rule. The drafts of the final rule submitted for such review process prior to promulgation and all such written comments thereon, all documents accompanying such drafts, and written responses thereto shall be placed in the docket no later than the date of promulgation.

(5)(A) In promulgating a rule to which this subsection applies (i) the

Administrator shall allow any person to submit written comments, data, or documentary information; (ii) the Administrator shall give interested persons an opportunity for the oral presentation of data, views, or arguments, in addition to an opportunity to make written submissions; (iii) a transcript shall be kept of any oral presentation; and (iv) the Administrator shall keep the record of such proceeding open for thirty days after completion of the proceeding to provide an opportunity for submission of rebuttal and supplementary information.

(6)(A) The promulgated rule shall be accompanied by (i) a statement of basis and purpose like that referred to in paragraph (3) with respect to a proposed rule and (ii) an explanation of the reasons for any major changes in the promulgated rule from the proposed rule.

(B) The promulgated rule shall also be accompanied by a response to each of the significant comments, criticisms, and new data submitted, in written or oral presentations during the comment period.

(C) The promulgated rule may not be based (in part or whole) on any information or data which has not been placed in the docket as of the date of such promulgation.

(7)(A) The record for judicial review shall consist exclusively of the material referred to in paragraph (3), clause (i) of paragraph (4)(B), and subparagraphs (A) and (B) of paragraph (6).

(B) Only an objection to a rule or procedure which was raised with reasonable specificity during the period for public comment (including any public hearing) may be raised during judicial review. If the person raising an objection can demonstrate to the Administrator that it was impracticable to raise such objection within such time or if the grounds for such objection arose after the period for public comment (but within the time specified for judicial review) and if such objection is of central relevance to the outcome of the rule, the Administrator shall convene a proceeding for reconsideration of the rule and provide the same procedural rights as would have been afforded had the information been available at the time the rule was proposed. If the Administrator refuses to convene such a proceeding, such person may seek review of such refusal in the United States court of appeals for the appropriate circuit (as provided in subsection (b)). Such reconsideration shall not postpone the effectiveness of the rule. The effectiveness of the rule may be stayed during such reconsideration, however, by the Administrator or the court for a period not to exceed three months.

(8) The sole forum for challenging procedural determinations made by the Administrator under this subsection shall be in the United States court of appeals for the appropriate circuit (as provided in subsection

(b)) at the time of the substantive review of the rule. No interlocutory appeals shall be permitted with respect to such procedural determinations. In reviewing alleged procedural errors, the court may invalidate the rule only if the errors were so serious and related to matters of such central relevance to the rule that there is a substantial likelihood that the rule would have been significantly changed if such errors had not been made.

(9) In the case of review of any action of the Administrator to which this subsection applies, the court may reverse any such action found to be—

    (A) arbitrary, capricious, an abuse of discretion, or otherwise not in accordance with law;

    (B) contrary to constitutional right, power, privilege, or immunity;

    (C) in excess of statutory jurisdiction, authority, or limitations, or short of statutory right; or

    (D) without observance of procedure required by law if (i) such failure to observe such procedure is arbitrary or capricious, (ii) the requirement of paragraph (7)(B) has been met, and (iii) the condition of the last sentence of paragraph (8) is met.

(10) Each statutory deadline for promulgation of rules to which this subsection applies which requires promulgation less than six months after date of proposal may be extended to not more than six months after date of proposal by the Administrator upon a determination that such extension is necessary to afford the public, and the agency, adequate opportunity to carry out the purposes of this subsection.

(11) The requirements of this subsection shall take effect with respect to any rule the proposal of which occurs after ninety days after the date of enactment of the Clean Air Act Amendments of 1977.

(e) Nothing in this Act shall be construed to authorize judicial review of regulations or orders of the Administrator under this Act, except as provided in this section.

(f) In any judicial proceeding under this section, the court may award costs of litigation (including reasonable attorney and expert witness fees) whenever it determines that such award is appropriate.

(g) In any action respecting the promulgation of regulations under section 120 or the administration or enforcement of section 120 no court shall grant any stay, injunctive, or similar relief before final judgment by such court in such action.

§ 7608. Mandatory licensing

[Sec. 308] Whenever the Attorney General determines, upon application of the Administrator—

(1) that—

    (A) in the implementation of the requirements of section 111, 112, or 202 of this Act, a right under any United States letters patent, which is being used or intended for public or commercial use and not otherwise reasonably available, is necessary to enable any person required to comply with such limitation to so comply, and

(B) there are no reasonable alternative methods to accomplish such purpose, and

(2) that the unavailability of such right may result in a substantial lessening of competition or tendency to create monopoly in any line of commerce in any section of the country, the Attorney General may so certify to a district court of the United States, which may issue an order requiring the person who owns such patent to license it on such reasonable terms and conditions as the court, after hearing, may determine. Such certification may be made to the district court for the district in which the person owning the patent resides, does business, or is found.

§ 7609. Policy review

[Sec. 309] (a) The Administrator shall review and comment in writing on the environmental impact of any matter relating to duties and responsibilities granted pursuant to this Act or other provisions of the authority of the Administrator, contained in any (1) legislation proposed by any Federal department or agency, (2) newly authorized Federal projects for construction and any major Federal agency action (other than a project for construction) to which section 102(2)(C) of Public Law 91–190 applies and (3) proposed regulations published by any department or agency of the Federal Government. Such written comment shall be made public at the conclusion of any such review.

(b) In the event the Administrator determines that any such legislation, action, or regulation is unsatisfactory from the standpoint of public health or welfare or environmental quality he shall publish his determination and the matter shall be referred to the Council on Environmental Quality.

§ 7610. Other authority not affected

[Sec. 310] (a) Except as provided in subsection (b) of this section, this Act shall not be construed as superseding or limiting the authorities and responsibilities, under any other provision of law, of the Administrator or any other Federal officer, department, or agency.

(b) No appropriation shall be authorized or made under section 301, 311, or 314 of the Public Health Service Act for any fiscal year after the fiscal year ending June 30, 1964, for any purpose for which appropriations may be made under authority of this Act.

§ 7611. Records and audit

[Sec 311] (a) Each recipient of assistance under this Act shall keep records as the Administrator shall prescribe, including records which fully disclose the amount and disposition by such recipient of the records of such assistance, the total cost of the project or undertaking in connection with which such assistance is given or used, and the amount of that portion of the cost of the project or undertaking supplied by other sources, and such other records as will facilitate an effective audit.

(b) The Administrator and the Comptroller General of the United States, or any of their duly authorized representatives, shall have access for the purpose of audit and examinations to any books, documents, papers, and records of the recipients that are pertinent to the grants received under this Act.

§ 7612. Cost studies

[Sec. 312](a) In order to provide the basis for evaluating programs authorized by this Act and the development of new programs and to furnish the Congress with the information necessary for authorization of appropriations by fiscal years beginning after June 30, 1969, the Administrator, in cooperation with State, interstate, and local air pollution control agencies shall make a detailed estimate of the cost of carrying out the provisions of this Act; a comprehensive study of the cost of program implementation by affected units of government; and a comprehensive study of the economic impact of air quality standards on the Nation's industries, communities, and other contributing sources of pollution, including an analysis of the national requirements for the cost of controlling emissions to attain such standards of air quality as may be established pursuant to this Act or applicable State law. The Administrator shall submit such detailed estimate and the results of such comprehensive study of cost for the five-year period beginning July 1, 1969, and the results of such other studies, to the Congress not later than January 10, 1969, and shall submit a reevaluation of such estimate and studies annually thereafter.

(b) The Administrator shall also make a complete investigation and study to determine (1) the need for additional trained State and local personnel to carry out programs assisted pursuant to this Act and other programs for the same purpose as this Act: (2) means of using existing Federal training programs to train such personnel; and (3) the need for additional trained personnel to develop, operate and maintain those pollution control facilities designed and installed to implement air quality standards. He shall report the results of such investigation and study to the President and the Congress not later than July 1, 1969.

(c) Not later than January 1, 1979, the Administrator shall study the possibility of increased use for cost-effectiveness analyses in devising strategies for the control of air pollution and shall report its recommendations to the Congress, including any recommendations for revisions in any provision of this Act. Such study shall also include an analysis and report to Congress concerning whether or not existing air pollution control strategies are adequate to achieve the purposes of this Act.

§ 7613. Additional reports to Congress

[Sec. 313] Not later than six months after the effective date of this section and not later than January 10 of each calendar year beginning after such date, the Administrator shall report to Congress on measures taken toward implementing the purpose and intent of this Act including, but not limited to, (1) the progress and problems associated with control of automotive exhaust emissions and the research efforts related thereto, (2) the development of air quality criteria and recommended emission control requirements; (3) the status of enforcement actions taken pursuant to this Act; (4) the status of State ambient air standards setting, including such plans for implementation and enforcement as have been developed; (5) the extent of development and expansion of air pollution monitoring systems; (6) progress and problems related to development of new and improved control techniques; (7) the development of quantitative and qualitative instrumentation to monitor emissions and air quality; (8) standards set or under consideration pursuant to title II of this Act; (9) the status of State, interstate, and local pollution control programs established pursuant to and assisted by this Act; (10) the reports and recommendations made by the President's Air Quality Advisory Board; and (11) (A) the status of plan provisions developed by States as required under section 110(a)(2)(F)(v), and an accounting of States failing to develop suitable plans; (B) the number of annual incidents of air pollution reaching or exceeding levels determined to present an imminent and substantial endangerment to health (within the meaning of section 303) by location, date, pollution source, and the duration of the emergency; (C) measures taken pursuant to section 110(a)(2)(F)(v), and an evaluation of their effectiveness in reducing pollution, and (D) an accounting of those instances in which an air pollution alert, warning, or emergency is declared as required under regulations of this Administrator and in which no action is taken by either the Administrator, State, or local officials, together with an explanation for the failure to take action.

§ 7614. Labor standards

[Sec. 314] The Administrator shall take such action as may be necessary to insure that all laborers and mechanics employed by contractors or subcontractors on projects assisted under this Act shall be paid wages at rates not less than those prevailing for the same type of work on similar construction in the locality as determined by the Secretary of Labor, in accordance with the Act of March 3, 1931, as amended, known as the Davis-Bacon Act (46 Stat. 1494; 40 U.S.C. 276a–276a-5). The Secretary of Labor shall have, with respect to the labor standards specified in this subsection, the authority and functions set forth in Reorganization Plan Numbered 14 of 1950 (15 F.R. 3176; 64 Stat. 1267) and section 2 of the Act of June 13, 1934, as amended (48 Stat. 948; 40 U.S.C. 276c).

§ 7615. Separability of provisions

[Sec. 315] If any provision of this Act, or the application of any provision of this Act to any person or circumstance, is held invalid, the application of such provision to other persons or circumstances, and the remainder of this Act, shall not be affected thereby.

§ 7616. Sewage treatment grants

[Sec. 316] (a) No grant which the Administrator is authorized to make to any applicant for construction of sewage treatment works in any area in any State may be withheld, conditioned, or restricted by the Administrator on the basis of any requirement of this Act except as provided in subsection (b).

(b) The Administrator may withhold, condition, or restrict the making of any grant for construction referred to in subsection (a) only if he determines that—

(1) such treatment works will not comply with applicable standards under section 111 or 112,

(2) the State does not have in effect, or is not carrying out, a State implementation plan approved by the Administrator which expressly quantifies and provides for the increase in emissions of each air pollutant (from stationary and mobile sources in any area to which either part C or part D of title I applies for such pollutant) which increase may reasonably be anticipated to result directly or indirectly from the new sewage treatment capacity which would be created by such construction,

(3) the construction of such treatment works would create new sewage treatment capacity which—

    (A) may reasonably be anticipated to cause or contribute to, directly or indirectly, an increase in emissions of any air pollutant in excess of the increase provided for under the provisions referred to in paragraph (2) for any such area, or

    (B) would otherwise not be in conformity with the applicable implementation plan, or

(4) such increase in emissions would interfere with, or be inconsistent with, the applicable implementation plan for any other State.

In the case of construction of a treatment works which would result, directly or indirectly, in an increase in emissions of any air pollutant from stationary and mobile sources in an area to which part D of title I applies, the quantification of emissions referred to in paragraph (2) shall include the emissions of any such pollutant resulting directly or indirectly from areawide and nonmajor stationary source growth (mobile and stationary) for each such area.

(c) Nothing in this section shall be construed to amend or alter any provision of the National Environmental Policy Act or to affect any determination as to whether or not the requirements of such Act have been met in the case of the construction of any sewage treatment works.

§ 7617. Economic impact assessment

[Sec. 317] (a) This section applies to action of the Administrator in promulgating or revising—

(1) any new source standard of performance under section 111.

(2) any regulation under section 111(d),

(3) any regulation under part B of title I (relating to ozone and stratosphere protection),

(4) any regulation under Part C of title I (relating to prevention of significant deterioration of air quality),

(5) any regulation establishing emission standards under section 202 and any other regulation promulgated under that section,

(6) any regulation controlling or prohibiting any fuel or fuel additive under section 211(c), and

(7) any aircraft emission standard under section 231.

Nothing in this section shall apply to any standard or regulation described in paragraphs (1) through (7) of this subsection unless the notice of proposed rulemaking in connection with such standard or regulation is published in the Federal Register after the date ninety days after the date of enactment of this section. In the case of revisions of such standards or regulations, this section shall apply only to revisions which the Administrator determines to be substantial revisions.

(b) Before publication of notice of proposed rulemaking with respect to any standard or regulation to which this section applies, the Administrator shall prepare an economic impact assessment respecting such standard or regulation. Such assessment shall be included in the docket required under section 307 (d)(2) and shall be available to the public as provided in section 307(d)(4). Notice of proposed rulemaking shall include notice of such availability together with an explanation of the extent and manner in which the Administrator has considered the analysis contained in such economic impact assessment in proposing the action. The Administrator shall also provide such an explanation in his notice of promulgation of any regulation or standard referred to in subsection (a). Each such explanation shall be part of the statements of basis and purpose required under sections 307(d)(3) and 307(d)(6).

(c) Subject to subsection (d), the assessment required under this section with respect to any standard or regulation shall contain an analysis of—

(1) the costs of compliance with any such standard or regulation, including extent to which the costs of compliance will vary depending on (A) the effective date of the standard or regulation, and (B) the development of less expensive, more efficient means or methods of compliance with the standard or regulation;

(2) the potential inflationary or recessionary effects of the standard or regulation;

(3) the effects on competition of the standard or regulation with respect to small business;

(4) the effects of the standard or regulation on consumer costs; and

(5) the effects of the standard or regulation on energy use.

Nothing in this section shall be construed to provide that the analysis of the factors specified in this subsection affects or alters the factors which the Administrator is required to consider in taking any action referred to in subsection (a).

(d) The assessment required under this section shall be as extensive as practicable, in the judgment of the Administrator taking into account the time and resources available to the Environmental Protection Agency and other duties and authorities which the Administrator is required to carry out under this Act.

(e) Nothing in this section shall be construed—

(1) to alter the basis on which a standard or regulation is promulgated under this Act;

(2) to preclude the Administrator from carrying out his responsibility under this Act to protect public health and welfare; or

(3) to authorize or require any judicial review of any such standard or regulation, or any stay or injunction of the proposal, promulgation, or effectiveness of such standard or regulation on the basis of failure to comply with this section.

(f) The requirements imposed on the Administrator under this section shall be treated as nondiscretionary duties for purposes of section 304 (a)(2), relating to citizen suits. The sole method for enforcement of the Administrator's duty under this section shall be by bringing a citizen suit under such section 304 (a)(2) for a court order to compel the Administrator to perform such duty. Violation of any such order shall subject the Administrator to penalties for contempt of court.

(g) In the case of any provision of this Act in which costs are expressly required to be taken into account, the adequacy or inadequacy of any assessment required under this section may be taken into consideration, but shall to be treated for purposes of judicial review of any such provision as conclusive with respect to compliance or noncompliance with the requirement of such provision to take cost into account.

§ 7618. Financial disclosure; conflicts of interest

[Sec. 318] (a) Each person who—

(1) has any known financial interest in (A) any person subject to this Act, or (B) any person who applies for or receives any grant, contract, or other form of financial assistance pursuant to this Act, and

(2) is (A) an officer or employee of the Environmental Protection Agency who performs any function of duty under this Act, (B) a member of

the National Commission on Air Quality appointed as a member of the public, or (C) a member of the Scientific Review Committee under section 109(d)

shall, beginning six months after the date of enactment of this section, annually file with the Administrator a written statement concerning all such interests held by such officer, employee, or member during the preceding calendar year. Such statement shall be available to the public.

(b) The Administrator shall—

(1) act within ninety days after the date of enactment of the Clean Air Act Amendments of 1977—

    (A) to define the term "known financial interest" for purposes of subsection (a) of this section;

    (B) to establish the methods by which the requirement to file written statements specified in subsection (a) of this section will be monitored and enforced, including appropriate provisions for the filing by such officers, employees and members of such statements and the review by the Administrator (or the commission in the case of members of the Commission) of such statements; and

(2) report to the Congress on June 1 of each calendar year with respect to such statements to the Administrator and the actions taken in regard thereto during the preceding calendar year.

(c) After the date one year after the date of the enactment of this section, no person who—

(1) is employed by, serves as attorney for, acts as a consultant for, or holds any other official or contractual relationship to—

    (A) the owner or operator of any major stationary source or any stationary source which is subject to a standard of performance or emission standard under section 111 or 112.

    (B) any manufacturer of any class or category of mobile sources if such mobile sources are subject to regulation under this Act.

    (C) any trade or business association of which such owner or operator referred to in subparagraph (A) or such manufacturer referred to in subparagraph (B) is a member, or

    (D) any organization (whether or not nonprofit) which is a party to litigation, or engaged in political, educational, or informational activities, relating to air quality, or

(2) owns, or has any financial interest in, any stock, bonds, or other financial interest which ownership or interest may be inconsistent with a position as an officer or employee of the Environmental Protection Agency, as determined under regulations of the Administrator, may concurrently serve as such an officer or employee of the Environmental Protection Agency.

(d) The Administrator shall promulgate rules for purposes of subsections (b) and (c) which—

(1) identify specific offices or positions within such agency which are of a

nonregulatory or nonpolicy-making nature and provide that officers or employees occupying such positions shall be exempt from the requirements of this section, and

(2) identify the ownership or financial interests which may be inconsistent with particular regulatory or policy making offices or positions within the Environmental Protection Agency.

(c) Any officer or employee of the Environmental Protection Agency or member of the National Commission on Air Quality or of the Scientific Review Committee under section 109 (d) who is subject to, and knowingly violates, this section or any regulation issued thereunder, shall be fined not more than $2,500 or imprisoned not more than one year, or both.

(f) Nothing in this section shall be construed to affect or impair any other federal statutory requirements respecting disclosure or conflict of interest applicable to the Environmental Protection Agency. Subsections (c) and (d) of this section shall not apply after the effective date of any such requirements respecting conflicts of interest which are generally applicable to departments, agencies, and instrumentalities of the United States.

§ 7619. Air quality monitoring

[Sec. 319] Not later than one year after the date of enactment of the Clean Air Act Amendments of 1977 and after notice and opportunity for public hearing, the Administrator shall promulgate regulations establishing an air quality monitoring system throughout the United States which—

(1) utilizes uniform air quality monitoring criteria and methodology and measures such air quality according to a uniform air quality index.

(2) provides for air quality monitoring stations in major urban areas and other appropriate areas throughout the United States to provide monitoring such as will supplement (but not duplicate) air quality monitoring carried out by the States required under any applicable implementation plan.

(3) provides for daily analysis and reporting of air quality based upon such uniform air quality index, and

(4) provides for recordkeeping with respect to such monitoring data and for periodic analysis and reporting to the general public by the Administrator with respect to air quality based upon such data.

The operation of such air quality monitoring system may be carried out by the Administrator or by such other departments, agencies, or entities of the Federal Government (including the National Weather Service) as the President may deem appropriate. Any air quality monitoring system required under any applicable implementation plan under section 110 shall, as soon as practicable following promulgation of regulations under this section, utilize the standard criteria and methodology, and measure air quality according to the standard index, established under such regulations.

§ 7620. Standardized air quality modeling

[Sec. 320] (a) Not later than six months after the date of the enactment of the Clean Air Act Amendments of 1977, and at least every three years thereafter, the Administrator shall conduct a conference on air quality modeling. In conducting such conference, special attention shall be given to appropriate modeling necessary for carrying out part C of title I (relating to prevention of significant deterioration of air quality).

(b) The conference conducted under this section shall provide for participation by the National Academy of Sciences, representatives of state and local air pollution control agencies, and appropriate Federal agencies, including the National Science Foundation; the National Oceanic and Atmospheric Administration, and the National Bureau of Standards.

(c) Interested persons shall be permitted to submit written comments and a verbatim transcript of the conference proceedings shall be maintained.

(d) The comments submitted and the transcript maintained pursuant to subsection (c) shall be included in the docket required to be established for purposes of promulgating or revising any regulation relating to air quality modeling under part C of title I.

§ 7621. Employment effects

[Sec. 321] (a) The Administrator shall conduct continuing evaluations of potential loss or shifts of employment which may result from the administration or enforcement of the provision of this Act and applicable implementation plans, including where appropriate, investigating threatened plant closures or reductions in employment allegedly resulting from such administration or enforcement.

(b) Any employee, or any representative of such employee, who is discharged or laid off, threatened with discharge or layoff, or whose employment is otherwise adversely affected or threatened to be adversely affected because of the alleged results of any requirement imposed or proposed to be imposed under this Act, including any requirement applicable to Federal facility and any requirement imposed by a State or political subdivision thereof, may request the Administrator to conduct a full investigation of the matter. Any such request shall be reduced to writing, shall set forth with reasonable particularity the grounds for the request, and shall be signed by the employee, or representative of such employee, making the request. The Administrator shall thereupon investigate the matter and, at the request of any party, shall hold public hearings on not less than five days notice. At such hearings, the Administrator shall require the parties, including the employer involved, to present information relating to the actual or potential effect of such requirements on employment and the detailed reasons or justification therefor. If the Administrator determines that there are no reasonable grounds for conducting a public hearing he shall notify (in writing), the party requesting such hearing of such determination and the reasons therefor. If the Administrator does convene such a hearing, the hearing shall be on the record. Upon receiving the report of such investigation, the Administrator shall make findings of fact as to the effect of such requirements on employment and on the alleged actual or potential discharge, layoff, or other adverse effect on employment, and shall make such recommendations as he deems appropriate. Such report, findings, and recommendations shall be available to the public.

(c) In connection with any investigation or public hearing conducted under subsection (b) of this section or as authorized in section 119 (relating to primary nonferrous smelter orders), the Administrator may issue subpoenas for the attendance and testimony of witnesses and the production of relevant papers, books, and documents, and he may administer oaths. Except for emission data, upon a showing satisfactory to the Administrator by such owner or operator that such papers, books, documents, or information or particular part thereof, if made public, would divulge trade secrets or secret processes of such owner, or operator, the Administrator shall consider such record, report, or information or particular portion thereof confidential in accordance with the purposes of section 1905 of title 18 of the United States Code, except that such paper, book, document, or information may be disclosed to other officers, employees, or authorized representatives of the United States concerned with carrying out this Act, or when relevant in any proceeding under this Act. Witnesses summoned shall be paid the same fees and mileage that are paid witnesses in the courts of the United States. In cases of contumacy or refusal to obey a subpoena served upon any person under this subparagraph, the district court of the United States for any district in which such person is found or resides or transacts business, upon application by the United States and after notice to such person, shall have jurisdiction to issue an order requiring such person to appear and give testimony before the Administrator, to appear and produce papers, books and documents before the Administrator, or both, and any failure to obey such order of the court may be punished by such court as a contempt thereof.

(d) Nothing in this section shall be construed to require or authorize the Administrator, the States, or political subdivisions thereof, to modify or withdraw any requirement imposed or proposed to be imposed under this Act.

§ 7622. Employee protection

[Sec. 322] (a) No employer may discharge any employee or otherwise discriminate against any employee with respect to his compensation, terms, conditions, or privileges of employment because the employee (or any person acting pursuant to a request of the employee)—

(1) commenced, caused to be commenced, or is about to commence or cause to be commenced a proceeding under this Act or a proceeding for the administration or enforcement of any requirement imposed under this Act or under any applicable implementation plan,

(2) testified or is about to testify in such proceeding, or

(3) assisted or participated or is about to assist or participate in any manner in such a proceeding or in any other action to carry out the purposes of this Act.

(b)(1) Any employee who believes that he has been discharged or otherwise discriminated against by any person in violation of subsection (a) may, within thirty days after such violation occurs, file (or have any person file on his behalf) a complaint with the Secretary of Labor (hereinafter in this subsection referred to as the "Secretary") alleging such discharge or discrimination. Upon receipt of such a complaint, the Secretary shall notify the person named in the complaint of the filing of the complaint.

(2)(A) Upon receipt of a complaint filed under paragraph (1), the Secretary shall conduct an investigation of the violation alleged in the complaint. Within thirty days of the receipt of such complaint, the Secretary shall complete such investigation and shall notify in writing the complainant (and any person acting in his behalf) and the person alleged to have committed such violation of the results of the investigation conducted pursuant to this subparagraph. Within ninety days of the receipt of such complaint the Secretary shall, unless the proceeding on the complaint is terminated by the Secretary on the basis of a settlement entered into by the Secretary and the person alleged to have committed such violation, issue an order either providing the relief prescribed by subparagraph (B) or denying the complaint. An order of the Secretary shall be made on the record after notice and opportunity for public hearing. The Secretary may not enter into a settlement terminating a proceeding on a complaint without the participation and consent of the complainant.

(B) If, in response to a complaint filed under paragraph (1), the Secretary determines that a violation of subsection (a) has occurred, the Secretary shall order the person who committed such violation to (i) take affirmative action to abate the violation, and (ii) reinstate the complainant to his former position together with the compensation (including back pay), terms, conditions, and privileges of his employment, and the Secretary may order such person to provide compensatory damages to the complainant. If an order is issued under this paragraph, the Secretary, at the request of the complainant, shall assess against the person against whom the order is issued a sum equal to the aggregate amount of all costs and expenses (including attorneys' and expert witness fees) reasonably incurred, as determined by the Secretary, by the complainant for, or in connection with, the bringing of the complaint upon which the order was issued.

(c)(1) Any person adversely affected or aggrieved by an order issued under subsection (b) may obtain review of the order in the United States court of appeals for the circuit in which the violation, which respect to which the order was issued, allegedly occurred. The petition for review must be filed within sixty days from the issuance of the Secretary's order. Review shall conform to chapter 7 of title 5 of the United States Code. The commencement of proceedings under this subparagraph shall not, unless ordered by the court, operate as a stay of the Secretary's order.

(2) An order of the Secretary with respect to which review could have been obtained under paragraph (1) shall not be subject to judicial review in any criminal or other civil proceeding.

(d) Whenever a person has failed to comply with an order issued under subsection (b) (2), the Secretary may file a civil action in the United States district court for the district in which the violation was found to occur to enforce such order. In actions brought under this subsection, the district courts shall have jurisdiction to grant all appropriate relief including, but not limited to, injunctive relief, compensatory, and exemplary damages.

(e)(1) Any person on whose behalf an order was issued under paragraph (2) of subsection (b) may commence a civil action against the person to whom such order was issued to require compliance with such order The appropriate United States district court shall have jurisdiction, without regard to the amount in controversy or the citizenship of the parties, to enforce such order.

(2) The court, in issuing any final order under this subsection, may award costs of litigation (including reasonable attorney and expert witness fees) to any party whenever the court determines such award is appropriate.

(f) Any nondiscretionary duty imposed by this section shall be enforceable in a mandamus proceeding brought under section 1361 of title 28 of the United States Code.

(g) Subsection (a) shall not apply with respect to any employee who, acting without direction from his employer (or the employer's agent), deliberately causes a violation of any requirement of this Act.

§ 7624.   Cost of vapor recovery equipment

[Sec. 324] (a) The regulations under this Act applicable to vapor recovery with respect to mobile source fuels at retail outlets of such fuels shall provide that the cost of procurement and installation of such vapor recovery shall be borne by the owner of such outlet (as determined under such regulations). Except as provided in subsection (b), such regulations shall provide that no lease of a retail outlet by the owner thereof which is entered into or renewed after the date of enactment of the Clean Air Act Amendments of 1977 may provide for a payment by the lessee of the cost of procurement and installation of vapor recovery equipment. Such regulations shall also provide that the cost of procurement and installation of vapor recovery equipment may be recovered by the owner of such outlet by means of price increases in the cost of any product sold by such owner, notwithstanding any provision of law.

(b) The regulations of the Administrator referred to in subsection (a) shall permit a lease of a retail outlet to provide for payment by the lessee of the cost of procurement and installation of vapor recovery equipment over a reasonable period (as determined in accordance with such regulations), if the owner of such outlet does not sell, trade in, or otherwise dispense any product at wholesale or retail at such outlet.

§ 7625. Vapor recovery for small business marketers of petroleum products

[Sec. 326] (a) The regulations under this Act applicable to vapor recovery from fueling of motor vehicles at retail outlets of gasoline shall not apply to any outlet owned by an independent small business marketer of gasoline having monthly sales of less than 50,000 gallons. In the case of any other outlet owned by an independent small business marketer, such regulations shall provide, with respect to independent small business marketers of gasoline, for a three-year phase-in period for the installation of such vapor recovery equipment at such outlets under which such marketers shall have—

(1) 33 percent of such outlets in compliance at the end of the first year during which such regulations apply to such marketers,

(2) 66 percent at the end of such second year, and

(3) 100 percent at the end of the third year.

(b) Nothing in subsection (a) shall be construed to prohibit any State from adopting or enforcing, with respect to independent small business marketers of gasoline having monthly sales of less than 50,000 gallons, any vapor recovery requirements for mobile source fuels at retail outlets. Any vapor recovery requirement which is adopted by a State and submitted to the Administrator as part of its implementation plan may be approved and enforced by the Administrator as part of the applicable implementation plan for that State.

(c) For purposes of this section, an independent small business marketer of gasoline is a person engaged in the marketing of gasoline who would be required to pay for procurement and installation of vapor recovery equipment under section 324 of this Act or under regulations of the Administrator, unless such person—

(1)(A) is a refiner, or

(B) controls, is controlled by, or is under common control with, a refiner,

(C) is otherwise directly or indirectly affiliated (as determined under the regulations of the Administrator) with a refiner or with a person who controls, is controlled by, or is under a common control with a refiner (unless the sole affiliation referred to herein is by means of a supply contract or an agreement or contract to use a trademark, trade name, service mark, or other identifying symbol or name owned by such refiner or any such person), or

(2) receives less than 50 percent of his annual income from refining or marketing of gasoline.

For the purpose of this section, the term "refiner" shall not include any refiner whose total refinery capacity (including the refinery capacity of any person who controls, is controlled by, or is under common control with, such refiner) does not exceed 65,000 barrels per day. For purposes of this section, "control" of a corporation means ownership of more than 50 percent of its stock.

§ 7625–1. Exemptions for certain territories

[Sec. 325] (a)(1) Upon petition by the governor of Guam, American Samoa, or the Commonwealth of the Northern Mariana Islands, the Administrator is authorized to exempt any person or source or class of persons or sources in such territory from any requirement under this Act other than section 112 or any requirement under section 110 or part D necessary to attain or maintain a national primary ambient air quality standard. Such exemption may be granted if the Administrator finds that compliance with such requirement is not feasible or is unreasonable due to unique geographical, meteorological, or economic factors of such territory, or such other local factors as the Administrator deems significant. Any such petition shall be considered in accordance with section 307(d) and any exemption under this subsection shall be considered final action by the Administrator for the purposes of section 307(b).

(2) The Administrator shall promptly notify the Committees on Energy and Commerce and on Interior and Insular Affairs of the House of Representatives and the Committees on Environment and Public Works and on Energy and Natural Resources of the Senate upon receipt of any petition under this subsection and of the approval or rejection of such petition and the basis for such action.

(b) Notwithstanding any other provision of this Act, any fossil fuel fired steam electric power plant operating within Guam as of the date of enactment of this section is hereby exempted from:

(1) any requirement of the new source performance standards relating to sulfur dioxide promulgated under section 111 as of such date of enactment; and

(2) any regulation relating to sulfur dioxide standards or limitations contained in a State implementation plan approved under section 110 as of such date of enactment: *Provided,* That such exemption shall expire eighteen months after such date of enactment unless the Administrator determines that such plant is making all emissions reductions practicable to prevent exceedances of the national ambient air quality standards for sulfur dioxide.

§ 7625a. Statutory construction

[Sec. 327] The parenthetical cross-references in any provision of this Act to other provisions of the Act, or other provisions of law, where the words "relating to" or "pertaining to" are used, are made only for convenience, and shall be given no legal effect.

§ 7626. Authorization of appropriations

[Sec. 328] (a) There are authorized to be appropriated to carry out this Act (other than provisions for which amounts are authorized under subsection (b)), $200,000,000 for the fiscal year 1978 and for each of the three fiscal years beginning thereafter.

(b)(1) There are authorized to be appropriated to carry out section 175 beginning in fiscal year 1978, $75,000,000 to be available until expended.

(2) There are authorized to be appropriated for use in carrying out section 323 (relating to National Commission on Air Quality), not to exceed $10,000,000 beginning in fiscal year 1978. For the study authorized under Section 323 there shall be available by contract to the National Commission on Air Quality from the appropriation to the Environmental Protection Agency for fiscal year 1977 the sum of $1,000,000.

(3) There are authorized to be appropriated to carry out section 127 (relating to grants for public notification) $4,000,000 for the fiscal year 1978 and each of the three succeeding fiscal years.

(4) For purposes of section 103(a)(5), there are authorized to be appropriated $7,500,000 for the fiscal year 1978 and each of the three fiscal years beginning after the date of enactment of the Clean Air Act Amendments of 1977.

(5) For the purpose of carrying out the provisions of part B of title I relating to studies and reports, there are authorized to be appropriated—

(A) to the National Aeronautics and Space Administration, the National Science Foundation, and the Department of State, such sums as may be necessary for the fiscal year ending September 30, 1977, and the fiscal year ending September 30, 1978;

(B) to the Environmental Protection Agency, $157,000,000 for fiscal year 1978; and

(C) to all other agencies such sums as may be necessary.

(6) There are authorized to be appropriated for carrying out research, development and demonstration under sections 103 and 104 of this Act $120,000,000 for fiscal year 1978.

Subchapter IV. Noise Pollution

§ 7641. Noise abatement

[Sec. 402] (a) The Administrator shall establish within the Environmental Protection Agency an Office of Noise Abatement and Control, and shall carry out through such Office a full and complete investigation and study of noise and its effect on the public health and welfare in order to (1) identify and classify causes and sources of noise, and (2) determine—

    (A) effects at various levels;

    (B) projected growth of noise levels in urban areas through the year 2000;

    (C) the psychological and physiological effect on humans;

    (D) effects of sporadic extreme noise (such as jet noise near airports) as compared with constant noise;

    (E) effect on wildlife and property (including values);

    (F) effect of sonic booms on property (including values); and

    (G) such other matters as may be of interest in the public welfare.

(b) In conducting such investigation, the Administrator shall hold public hearings, conduct research, experiments, demonstrations, and studies. The Administrator shall report the results of such investigation and study, together with his recommendations for legislation or other action, to the President and the Congress not later than one year after the date of enactment of this title.

(c) In any case where any Federal department or agency is carrying out or sponsoring any activity resulting in noise which the Administrator determines amounts to a public nuisance or is otherwise objectionable, such department or agency shall consult with the Administrator to determine possible means of abating such noise.

§ 7642. Authorization of appropriations

[Sec. 403] There is authorized to be appropriated such amount not to exceed $30,000,000 as may be necessary for the purposes of this title.

7 • Clean Water Act

INTRODUCTION

The Clean Water Act's roots stretch back to 1948, when Congress provided the first trickle of money to help municipalities construct sewage treatment facilities. However, the 1948 law contained no federal requirements concerning the control of water pollution. Its stated policy was simply "to recognize, preserve, and protect the primary responsibilities and rights of the states in controlling water pollution."

The next two decades saw numerous amendments to the 1948 law. But it was not until 1972, when Congress passed the Federal Water Pollution Control Act Amendments of 1972 (PL 92-500), which essentially rewrote federal water pollution law.

The 1972 law set optimistic and ambitious goals. By 1983, Congress envisioned fishable, swimmable waters throughout the nation. By 1985, it was the act's goal that the discharge of pollutants to waterways be eliminated. The law embodied two major strategies for achieving these objectives. First, it expanded the limited federal assistance of the past into a giant, $5 billion per year federal grants program to finance construction of local sewage treatment systems.

Second, the Act required all municipal and industrial waste water to be treated before being discharged into waterways. The Environmental Protection Agency was required to establish federal limits on the amounts of specific pollutants that could be released by municipal and industrial facilities. These "effluent limitations" were to be based on the level of cleanup that could be achieved using existing technologies and were to take into account costs to the regulated community. The limits were to be written into "national pollutant discharge elimination system" permits issued to all dischargers.

The technology-based approach of the 1972 Clean Water Act is regarded as a success. Discharges of pollutants from industrial facilities have largely been brought under control, and while more work is needed to bring municipalities into compliance, substantial progress was made.

Nevertheless, many waterways, notably marine estuaries, lakes, and rivers in heavily populated areas, still suffer from degradation. In amending the Clean Water Act in 1987, the basic issue lawmakers had to confront was that after most technology standards called for in the 1970s had been issued, and the final push to get cities to provide a minimum of secondary treatment for sewage was at hand, some stubborn water pollution problems still remained. The most serious of these remaining problems are excessive levels of toxic pollutants in some waters—even where dischargers have installed required pollution control technologies—and contaminated runoff from "non-point" sources such as farmland and city streets.

The Water Quality Act of 1987, passed by Congress over a presidential veto on February 4, 1987, seeks to correct these problems. The amendments direct EPA and state officials to supplement existing, nationwide technology-based standards with a water-quality-based approach to control persistent pollution problems. Essentially, Congress said, regulators should identify waterways that are still polluted and do what is needed to restore them.

For example, under non-point source pollution control provisions in the 1987 amendments, states are required to identify waters that are not expected to meet water quality standards because of non-point source pollution and develop programs for reducing the polluted runoff. In similar toxic control provisions, states must identify waters that are not expected to meet water quality standards, even after technology-based controls have been put into effect, because of the presence of toxic pollutants. States must identify the sources responsible for the toxic pollution and propose strategies for reducing discharges of toxic pollutants from these facilities.

According to Rebecca Hanmer, EPA deputy assistant administrator for water, Congress, in the process of drafting the 1987 Water Act amendments, recognized that "a huge base program has now been established, and said, 'Now, on top of that base...let's see if we can try the water-quality-based approach again'" to address remaining problems. Hanmer told BNA in July 1987 that, although the 1972 law put control of water pollution firmly in the hands of the federal government, the 1987 amendments give many new responsibilities to the states: "From my perspective, those are the two things about the Water Quality Act that we think are quite special: There are many requirements that speak to the states, and...it is, generally speaking, a water-quality-based law."

The other major change made by the 1987 amendments involves

the phase-out of federal assistance for municipal waste water treatment plant construction. Under the new law, the existing construction grants program is reauthorized through fiscal year 1990 at a total level of $9.6 billion. Afterwards, the grants program is to be replaced by a new federal program that will provide a total of $8.4 billion through fiscal year 1994 in seed money for states to establish permanent, state-run revolving loan fund programs. The revolving funds, which states must also contribute to, will be used to provide loans and other forms of non-grant assistance to local areas for construction of sewage treatment systems, with loan repayments to be channeled back into the state funds and reused.

This $18 billion funding scheme was seen as accomplishing two desired purposes. It eventually will end the federal government's role in financing the construction of local sewage treatment plants, but at the same time will provide a continuing source of money for construction of those facilities, thereby ensuring progress toward the Clean Water Act's goal of fishable, swimmable waters.

In other important provisions, the 1987 amendments add a new section to the law directing EPA to solve pollution problems in estuaries, the coastal water bodies where fresh river water and salty ocean water meet. EPA is authorized $60 million over five years for the program aimed at improving water quality and restoring fish, wildlife, and economic and recreational opportunities in U.S. estuaries.

Another new section bolsters U.S. efforts to comply with the 1978 Great Lakes Water Quality Agreement. Under the agreement, the United States and Canada made a commitment "to eliminate or reduce to the maximum extent practicable the discharge of pollutants into the Great Lakes system." Specific steps called for in the agreement include construction of sewage treatment facilities and control of pesticide runoff and toxic industrial discharges. So far, however, little progress has been made in implementing the agreement, according to a 1985 report by the National Academy of Sciences and the Royal Society of Canada.

Other provisions of the amendments build upon and strengthen an existing program to improve water quality in lakes, with authorizations totaling $85 million, including $15 million to aid lakes that have been damaged by acid rain.

In other key changes, the amendments:

▶ Require permits for all discharges of storm water from industrial facilities, and set deadlines for cities to obtain permits for storm water discharges;

▶ Limit the ability of industrial facilities to get exemptions, or "variances," from federal pollution control regulations;

▶ Prohibit, except in certain narrowly defined circumstances, "backsliding" on permits, or the weakening of treatment requirements when industrial and municipal discharge permits are renewed or reissued;

▶ Extend deadlines for industries to comply with national pollution control standards to account for the fact that EPA has not yet finished issuing some of these regulations;

▶ Specify deadlines for EPA to issue remaining needed industrial effluent limitations;

▶ Require EPA to promulgate regulations to control toxic pollutants in sewage sludge; and

▶ Limit availability of modifications of federal treatment standards for nonconventional pollutants to five well-understood substances.

Federal Water Pollution Control Act, as amended by the Clean Water Act of 1977 (commonly referred to as Clean Water Act)

(P.L. 92–500, approved October 18, 1972; as last amended by P.L. 100-4, approved February 4, 1987)

Subchapter I. Research and Related Programs

§ 1251. Congressional declaration of goals and policy

[Sec. 101] (a) The objective of this Act is to restore and maintain the chemical, physical, and biological integrity of the Nation's waters. In order to achieve this objective it is hereby declared that, consistent with the provisions of this Act—

(1) it is the national goal that the discharge of pollutants into the navigable waters be eliminated by 1985;

(2) it is the national goal that wherever attainable, an interim goal of water quality which provides for the protection and propagation of

fish, shellfish, and wildlife and provides for recreation in and on the water be achieved by July 1, 1983;

(3) it is the national policy that the discharge of toxic pollutants in toxic amounts be prohibited;

(4) it is the national policy that Federal financial assistance be provided to construct publicly owned waste treatment works;

(5) it is the national policy that areawide waste treatment management planning processes be developed and implemented to assure adequate control of sources of pollutants in each State;

(6) it is the national policy that a major research and demonstration effort be made to develop technology necessary to eliminate the discharge of pollutants into the navigable waters, waters of the contiguous zone, and the oceans; and

(7) it is the national policy that programs for the control of nonpoint sources of pollution be developed and implemented in an expeditious manner so as to enable the goals of this Act to be met through the control of both point and nonpoint sources of pollution.

(b) It is the policy of the Congress to recognize, preserve, and protect the primary responsibilities and rights of States to prevent, reduce, and eliminate pollution, to plan the development and use (including restoration, preservation, and enhancement) of land and water resources, and to consult with the Administrator in the exercise of his authority under this Act. It is the policy of Congress that the States manage the construction grant program under this Act and implement the permit programs under sections 402 and 404 of this Act. It is further the policy of the Congress to support and aid research relating to the prevention, reduction, and elimination of pollution, and to provide Federal technical services and financial aid to State and interstate agencies and municipalities in connection with the prevention, reduction, and elimination of pollution.

(c) It is further the policy of Congress that the President, acting through the Secretary of State and such national and international organizations as he determines appropriate, shall take such action as may be necessary, to insure that to the fullest extent possible all foreign countries shall take meaningful action for the prevention, reduction, and elimination of pollution in their waters and in international waters and for the achievement of goals regarding the elimination of discharge of pollutants and the improvement of water quality to at least the same extent as the United States does under its laws.

(d) Except as otherwise expressly provided in this Act, the Administrator of the Environmental Protection Agency (hereinafter in this Act called "Administrator") shall administer this Act.

(e) Public participation in the development, revision, and enforcement of any regulation, standard, effluent limitation, plan, or program established by the Administrator or any State under this Act shall be provided for, encouraged, and assisted by the Administrator and the States. The Administrator, in cooperation with the States, shall develop and publish regulations specifying minimum guidelines for public participation in such processes.

(f) It is the national policy that to the maximum extent possible the procedures utilized for implementing this Act shall encourage the drastic minimization of paperwork and interagency decision procedures, and the best use of available manpower and funds, so as to prevent needless duplication and unnecessary delays at all levels of government.

(g) It is the policy of Congress that the authority of each State to allocate quantities of water within its jurisdiction shall not be superseded, abrogated or otherwise impaired by this Act. It is the further policy of Congress that nothing in this Act shall be construed to supersede or abrogate rights to quantities of water which have been established by any State. Federal agencies shall co-operate with State and local agencies to develop comprehensive solutions to prevent, reduce and eliminate pollution in concert with programs for managing water resources.

§ 1252. Comprehensive programs for water pollution control

[Sec. 102] (a) The Administrator shall, after careful investigation, and in cooperation with other Federal agencies, State water pollution control agencies, interstate agencies, and the municipalities and industries involved, prepare or develop comprehensive programs for preventing, reducing, or eliminating the pollution of the navigable waters and ground waters and improving the sanitary condition of surface and underground waters. In the development of such comprehensive programs due regard shall be given to the improvements which are necessary to conserve such waters for the protection and propagation of fish and aquatic life and wildlife, recreational purposes, and the withdrawal of such waters for public water supply, agricultural, industrial and other purposes. For the purpose of this section, the Administrator is authorized to make joint investigations with any such agencies of the condition of any waters in any State or States, and of the discharges of any sewage, industrial wastes, or substance which may adversely affect such waters.

(b)(1) In the survey of planning of any reservoir by the Corps of Engineers, Bureau of Reclamation, or other Federal agency, consideration shall be given to inclusion of storage for regulation of streamflow, except that any such storage and water releases shall not be provided as a substitute for adequate treatment or other methods of controlling waste at the source.

(2) The need for and the value of storage or regulation of streamflow (other than for water quality) including but not limited to navigation, salt water intrusion, recreation, esthetics, and fish and wildlife, shall be determined by the Corps of Engineers, Bureau of Reclamation, or other Federal agencies.

(3) The need for, the value of, and the impact of, storage for water quality control shall be determined by the Administrator, and his views on

these matters shall be set forth in any report or presentation to Congress proposing authorization or construction of any reservoir including such storage.

(4) The value of such storage shall be taken into account in determining the economic value of the entire project of which it is a part, and costs shall be allocated to the purpose of regulation of streamflow in a manner which will insure that all project purposes, share equitably in the benefits of multiple-purpose construction.

(5) Costs of regulation of streamflow features incorporated in any Federal reservoir or other impoundment under the provisions of this Act shall be determined and the beneficiaries identified and if the benefits are widespread or national in scope, the costs of such features shall be nonreimbursable.

(6) No license granted by the Federal Power Commission for a hydroelectric power project shall include storage for regulation of streamflow for the purpose of water quality control unless the Administrator shall recommend its inclusion and such reservoir storage capacity shall not exceed such proportion of the total storage required for the water quality control plan as the drainage area of such reservoir bears to the drainage area of the river basin or basins involved in such water quality control plan.

(c)(1) The Administrator shall, at the request of the Governor of a State, or a majority of the Governors when more than one State is involved, make a grant to pay not to exceed 50 per centum of the administrative expenses of a planning agency for a period not to exceed three years, which period shall begin after the date of enactment of the Federal Water Pollution Control Act Amendments of 1972, if such agency provides for adequate representation of appropriate State, interstate, local, or (when appropriate) international interests in the basin or portion thereof involved and is capable of developing an effective, comprehensive water quality control plan for a basin or portion thereof.

(2) Each planning agency receiving a grant under this subsection shall develop a comprehensive pollution control plan for the basin or portion thereof which—

(A) is consistent with any applicable water quality standards, effluent and other limitations, and thermal discharge regulations established pursuant to current law within the basin;

(B) recommends such treatment works as will provide the most effective and economical means of collection, storage, treatment, and elimination of pollutants and recommends means to encourage both municipal and industrial use of such works;

(C) recommends maintenance and improvement of water quality within the basin or portion thereof and recommends methods of adequately financing those facilities as may be necessary to implement the plan; and

(D) as appropriate, is developed in cooperation with, and is consistent with any comprehensive plan prepared by the Water Resources Council, any areawide waste management plans developed pursuant to section 208 of this Act, and any State plan developed pursuant to section 303(e) of this Act.

(3) For the purposes of this subsection the term "basin" includes, but is not limited to, rivers and their tributaries, streams, coastal waters, sounds, estuaries, bays, lakes, and portions thereof, as well as the lands drained thereby.

(d) The Administrator, after consultation with the States, and River Basin Commissions established under the Water Resources Planning Act, shall submit a report to Congress on or before July 1, 1978, which analyzes the relationship between programs under this Act, and the programs by which State and Federal agencies allocate quantities of water. Such report shall include recommendations concerning the policy in section 101(g) of the Act to improve coordination of efforts to reduce and eliminate pollution in concert with programs for managing water resources.

§ 1253. Interstate cooperation and uniform laws

[Sec. 103] (a) The Administrator shall encourage cooperative activities by the States for the prevention, reduction, and elimination of pollution, encourage the enactment of improved and, so far as practicable, uniform State laws relating to the prevention, reduction, and elimination of pollution; and encourage compacts between States for the prevention and control of pollution.

(b) The consent of the Congress is hereby given to two or more States to negotiate and enter into agreements or compacts, not in conflict with any law or treaty of the United States, for (1) cooperative effort and mutual assistance for the prevention and control of pollution and the enforcement of their respective laws relating thereto, and (2) the establishment of such agencies, joint or otherwise, as they may deem desirable for making effective such agreements and compacts. No such agreement or compact shall be binding or obligatory upon any State a party thereto unless and until it has been approved by the Congress.

§ 1254. Research, investigations, training, and information

[Sec. 104] (a) The Administrator shall establish national programs for the prevention, reduction, and elimination of pollution and as part of such programs shall—

(1) in cooperation with other Federal, State, and local agencies, conduct and promote the coordination and acceleration of, research, investiga-

tions, experiments, training, demonstrations, surveys, and studies relating to the causes, effects, extent, prevention, reduction, and elimination of pollution;

(2) encourage, cooperate with, and render technical services to pollution control agencies and other appropriate public or private agencies, institutions, and organizations, and individuals, including the general public, in the conduct of activities referred to in paragraph (1) of this subsection;

(3) conduct, in cooperation with State water pollution control agencies and other interested agencies, organizations and persons, public investigations concerning the pollution of any navigable waters, and report on the results of such investigations;

(4) establish advisory committees composed of recognized experts in various aspects of pollution and representatives of the public to assist in the examination and evaluation of research progress and proposals and to avoid duplication of research;

(5) in cooperation with the States, and their political subdivisions, and other Federal agencies establish, equip, and maintain a water quality surveillance system for the purpose of monitoring the quality of the navigable waters and ground waters and the contiguous zone and the oceans and the Administrator shall, to the extent practicable, conduct such surveillance by utilizing the resources of the National Aeronautics and Space Administration, the National Oceanic and Atmospheric Administration, the Geological Survey, and the Coast Guard, and shall report on such quality in the report required under subsection (a) of section 516; and

(6) initiate and promote the coordination and acceleration of research designed to develop the most effective practicable tools and techniques for measuring the social and economic costs and benefits of activities which are subject to regulation under this Act; and shall transmit a report on the results of such research to the Congress not later than January 1, 1974.

(b) In carrying out the provisions of subsection (a) of this section the Administrator is authorized to—

(1) collect and make available, through publications and other appropriate means, the results of and other information, including appropriate recommendations by him in connection therewith, pertaining to such research and other activities referred to in paragraph (1) of subsection (a);

(2) cooperate with other Federal departments and agencies, State water pollution control agencies, interstate agencies, other public and private agencies, institutions, organizations, industries involved, and individuals, in the preparation and conduct of such research and other activities referred to in paragraph (1) of subsection (a);

(3) make grants to State water pollution control agencies, interstate

agencies, other public or nonprofit private agencies, institutions, organizations, and individuals, for purposes stated in paragraph (1) of subsection (a) of this section;

(4) contract with public or private agencies, institutions, organizations, and individuals, without regard to sections 3648 and 3709 of the Revised Statutes (31 U.S.C. 529; 41 U.S.C. 5), referred to in paragraph (1) of subsection (a);

(5) establish and maintain research fellowships at public or nonprofit private educational institutions or research organizations;

(6) collect and disseminate, in cooperation with other Federal departments and agencies, and with other public or private agencies, institutions, and organizations having related responsibilities, basic data on chemical, physical, and biological effects of varying water quality and other information pertaining to pollution and the prevention, reduction, and elimination thereof; and

(7) develop effective and practical processes, methods, and prototype devices for the prevention, reduction, and elimination of pollution.

(c) In carrying out the provisions of subsection (a) of this section the Administrator shall conduct research on, and survey the results of other scientific studies on, the harmful effects on the health or welfare of persons caused by pollutants. In order to avoid duplication of effort, the Administrator shall, to the extent practicable, conduct such research in cooperation with and through the facilities of the Secretary of Health, Education, and Welfare.

(d) In carrying out the provisions of this section the Administrator shall develop and demonstrate under varied conditions (including conducting such basic and applied research, studies, and experiments) as may be necessary:

(1) practicable means of treating municipal sewage, and other waterborne wastes to implement the requirements of section 201 of this Act;

(2) improved methods and procedures to identify and measure the effects of pollutants, including those pollutants created by new technological developments; and

(3) methods and procedures for evaluating the effects on water quality of augmented streamflows to control pollution not susceptible to other means of prevention, reduction, or elimination.

(e) The Administrator shall establish, equip, and maintain field laboratory and research facilities, including, but not limited to, one to be located in the northeastern area of the United States, one in the Middle Atlantic area, one in the southeastern area, one in the midwestern area, one in the southwestern area, one in the Pacific Northwest, and one in the State of Alaska, for the conduct of research, investigations, experiments, field demonstrations and studies, and training relating to the prevention, reduction and elimination of pollution. Insofar as practicable, each such facility shall be located near institutions of higher learning in which graduate training in such research might be carried out. In conjunction with the development of criteria under section 403 of this Act, the Administrator shall construct the facilities authorized for the National Marine Water Quality Laboratory established under this subsection.

(f) The Administrator shall conduct research and technical development work, and make studies, with respect to the quality of the waters of the Great Lakes, including an analysis of the present and projected future water quality of the Great Lakes under varying conditions of waste treatment and disposal, an evaluation of the water quality needs of those to be served by such waters, an evaluation of municipal, industrial, and vessel waste treatment and disposal practices with respect to such waters, and a study of alternate means of solving pollution problems (including additional waste treatment measures) with respect to such waters.

(g)(1) For the purpose of providing an adequate supply of trained personnel to operate and maintain existing and future treatment works and related activities, and for the purpose of enhancing substantially the proficiency of those engaged in such activities, the Administrator shall finance pilot programs, in cooperation with State and interstate agencies, municipalities, educational institutions, and other organizations and individuals, of manpower development and training and retraining of persons in, on entering into, the field of operation and maintenance of treatment works and related activities. Such program and any funds expended for such a program shall supplement, not supplant, other manpower and training programs and funds available for the purposes of this paragraph. The Administrator is authorized under such terms and conditions as he deems appropriate, to enter into agreements with one or more States, acting jointly or severally, or with other public or private agencies or institutions for the development and implementation of such a program.

(2) The Administrator is authorized to enter into agreements with public and private agencies and institutions, and individuals to develop and maintain an effective system for forecasting the supply of, and demand for, various professional and other occupational categories needed for the prevention, reduction, and elimination of pollution in each region, State, or area of the United States and, from time to time, to publish the results of such forecasts.

(3) In furtherance of the purposes of this Act, the Administrator is authorized to—

(A) make grants to public or private agencies and institutions and to individuals for training projects, and provide for the conduct of training by contract with public or private agencies and institutions and with individuals without regard to sections 3648 and 3709 of the Revised Statutes;

(B) establish and maintain research fellowships in the Environmental Protection Agency with such stipends and allowances, including traveling and subsistence expenses, as he may deem necessary to procure the assistance of the most promising research fellows; and

    (C) provide, in addition to the program established under paragraph (1) of this subsection, training in technical matters relating to the causes, prevention, reduction, and elimination of pollution for personnel of public agencies and other persons with suitable qualifications.

  (4) The Administrator shall submit, through the President, a report to the Congress not later than December 31, 1973, summarizing the actions taken under this subsection and the effectiveness of such actions, and setting forth the number of persons trained, the occupational categories for which training was provided, the effectiveness of other Federal, State, and local training programs in this field, together with estimates of future needs, recommendations on improving training programs, and such other information and recommendations, including legislative recommendations, as he deems appropriate.

(h) The Administrator is authorized to enter into contracts with, or make grants to, public or private agencies and organizations and individuals for (A) the purpose of developing and demonstrating new or improved methods for the prevention, removal, reduction, and elimination of pollution in lakes, including the undesirable effects of nutrients and vegetation, and (B) the construction of publicly owned research facilities for such purpose.

(i) The Administrator, in cooperation with the Secretary of the department in which the Coast Guard is operating, shall—

  (1) engage in such research, studies, experiments, and demonstrations as he deems appropriate, relative to the removal of oil from any waters and to the prevention, control, and elimination of oil and hazardous substances pollution;

  (2) publish from time to time the results of such activities; and

  (3) from time to time, develop and publish in the Federal Register specifications and other technical information on the various chemical compounds used in the control of oil and hazardous substances spills.

In carrying out this subsection, the Administrator may enter into contracts with, or make grants to, public or private agencies and organizations and individuals.

(j) The Secretary of the department in which the Coast Guard is operating shall engage in such research, studies, experiments, and demonstrations as he deems appropriate relative to equipment which is to be installed on board a vessel and is designed to receive, retain, treat, or discharge human body wastes and the wastes from toilets and other receptacles intended to receive or retain body wastes with particular emphasis on equipment to be installed on small recreational vessels. The Secretary of the department in which the Coast Guard is operating shall report to Congress the results of such research, studies, experiments, and demonstrations prior to the effective date of any regulations established under section 312 of this Act. In carrying out this subsection the Secretary of the department in which the Coast Guard is operating may enter into contracts with, or make grants to, public or private organizations and individuals.

(k) In carrying out the provisions of this section relating to the conduct by the Administrator of demonstration projects and the development of field laboratories and research facilities, the Administrator may acquire land and interests therein by purchase, with appropriated or donated funds, by donation, or by exchange for acquired or public lands under his jurisdiction when he classifies as suitable for disposition. The values of the properties so exchanged either shall be approximately equal, or if they are not approximately equal, the values shall be equalized by the payment of cash to the grantor or to the Administrator as the circumstances require.

(l)(1) The Administrator shall, after consultation with appropriate local, State, and Federal agencies, public and private organizations, and interested individuals, as soon as practicable but not later than January 1, 1973, develop and issue to the States for the purpose of carrying out this Act the latest scientific knowledge available in indicating the kind and extent of effects on health and welfare which may be expected from the presence of pesticides in the water in varying quantities. He shall revise and add to such information whenever necessary to reflect developing scientific knowledge.

(2) The President shall, in consultation with appropriate local, State, and Federal agencies, public and private organizations, and interested individuals, conduct studies and investigations of methods to control the release of pesticides into the environment which study shall include examination of the persistency of pesticides in the water environment and alternatives thereto. The President shall submit reports, from time to time, on such investigations to Congress together with his recommendations for any necessary legislation.

(m)(1) The Administrator shall, in an effort to prevent degradation of the environment from the disposal of waste oil, conduct a study of (A) the generation of used engine, machine, cooling, and similar waste oil, including quantities generated, the nature and quality of such oil, present collecting methods and disposal practices, and alternate uses of such oil; (B) the long-term, chronic biological effects of the disposal of such waste oil; and (C) the potential market for such oils, including the economic and legal factors relating to the sale of products made from such oils, the level of subsidy, if any, needed to encourage the purchase by public and private nonprofit agencies of products from such oil, and the practicability of Federal procurement, on a priority basis, of products made from such oil. In conducting such study, the Administrator shall consult with affected industries and other persons.

(2) The Administrator shall report the preliminary results of such study to Congress within six months after the date of enactment of the Federal Water Pollution Control Act Amendments of 1972, and shall submit a final report to Congress within 18 months after such date of

enactment.

(n)(1) the Administrator shall, in cooperation with the Secretary of the Army, the Secretary of Agriculture, the Water Resources Council, and with other appropriate Federal, State, interstate, or local public bodies and private organizations, institutions, and individuals, conduct and promote, encourage contributions to, continuing comprehensive studies of the effects of pollution, including sedimentation, in the estuaries and estuarine zones of the United States on fish and wildlife, on sport and commercial fishing, on recreation, on water supply and water power, and on other beneficial purposes. Such studies shall also consider the effect of demographic trends, the exploitation of mineral resources and fossil fuels, land and industrial development, navigation, flood and erosion control, and other uses of estuaries and estuarine zones upon the pollution of the waters therein.

(2) In conducting such studies, the Administrator shall assemble, coordinate, and organize all existing pertinent information on the Nation's estuaries and estuarine zones; carry out a program of investigations and surveys to supplement existing information in representative estuaries and estuarine zones; and identify the problems and areas where further research and study are required.

(3) The Administrator shall submit to Congress, from time to time, reports of the studies authorized by this subsection but at least one such report during any six-year period. Copies of each such report shall be made available to all interested parties, public and private.

(4) For the purpose of this subsection, the term "estuarine zones" means an environmental system consisting of an estuary and those transitional areas which are consistently influenced or affected by water from an estuary such as, but not limited to, salt marshes, coastal and intertidal areas, bays, harbors, lagoons, inshore waters, and channels, and the term "estuary" means all or part of the mouth of a river or stream or other body of water having unimpaired natural connection with open sea and within which the sea water is measurably diluted with fresh water derived from land drainage.

(o)(1) The Administrator shall conduct research and investigations on devices, systems, incentives, pricing policy, and other methods of reducing the total flow of sewage, including, but not limited to, unnecessary water consumption in order to reduce the requirements for, and the costs of, sewage and waste treatment services. Such research and investigations shall be directed to develop devices, systems, policies, and methods capable of achieving the maximum reduction of unnecessary water consumption.

(2) The Administrator shall report the preliminary results of such studies and investigations to the Congress within one year after the date of enactment of the Federal Water Pollution Control Act Amendments of 1972, and annually thereafter in the report required under subsection (a) of section 516. Such report shall include recommendations for any legislation that may be required to provide for the adoption and use of

devices, systems, policies, or other methods of reducing water consumption and reducing the total flow of sewage. Such report shall include an estimate of the benefits to be derived from adoption and use of such devices, systems, policies, or other methods and also shall reflect estimates of any increase in private, public, or other cost that would be occasioned thereby.

(p) In carrying out the provisions of subsection (a) of this section the Administrator shall, in cooperation with the Secretary of Agriculture, other Federal agencies, and the States, carry out a comprehensive study and research program to determine new and improved methods and the better application of existing methods of preventing, reducing, and eliminating pollution from agriculture, including the legal, economic, and other implications of the use of such methods.

(q)(1) The Administrator shall conduct a comprehensive program of research and investigation and pilot project implementation into new and improved methods of preventing, reducing, storing, collecting, treating, or otherwise eliminating pollution from sewage in rural and other areas where collection of sewage in conventional, community-wide sewage collection systems is impractical, uneconomical, or otherwise infeasible, or where soil conditions or other factors preclude the use of septic tank and drainage field systems.

(2) The Administrator shall conduct a comprehensive program of research and investigation and pilot project implementation into new and improved methods for the collection and treatment of sewage and other liquid wastes combined with the treatment and disposal of solid wastes.

(3) The Administrator shall establish, either within the Environmental Protection Agency, or through contract with an appropriate public or private non-profit organization, a national clearinghouse which shall (A) receive reports and information resulting from research, demonstrations, and other projects funded under this Act related to paragraph (1) of this subsection and to subsection (e)(2) of section 105; (B) coordinate and disseminate such reports and information for use by Federal and State agencies, municipalities, institutions, and persons in developing new and improved methods pursuant to this subsection; and (C) provide for the collection and dissemination of reports and information relevant to this subsection from other Federal and State agencies, institutions, universities, and persons.

(4) Notwithstanding section 205(d) of this Act, from amounts that are set aside for a fiscal year under section 205(i) of this Act and are not obligated by the end of the 24-month period of availability for such amounts under section 205(d), the Administrator shall make available $1,000,000 or such unobligated amount, whichever is less, to support a national clearinghouse within the Environmental Protection Agency to collect and disseminate information on small flows of sewage and

innovative or alternative wastewater treatment processes and techniques, consistent with paragraph (3). This paragraph shall apply with respect to amounts set aside under section 205(i) for which the 24-month period of availability referred to in the preceding sentence ends on or after September 30, 1986.

(r) The Administrator is authorized to make grants to colleges and universities to conduct basic research into the structure and function of fresh water aquatic ecosystems, and to improve understanding of the ecological characteristics necessary to the maintenance of the chemical, physical, and biological integrity of freshwater acquatic ecosystems.

(s) The Administrator is authorized to make grants to one or more institutions of higher education (regionally located and to be designated as "River Study Centers") for the purpose of conducting and reporting on interdisciplinary studies on the nature of river systems, including, hydrology, biology, ecology, economics, the relationship between river uses and land uses, and the effects of development within river basins on river systems and on the value of water resources and water related activities. No such grant in any fiscal year shall exceed $1,000,000.

(t) The Administrator shall, in cooperation with State and Federal agencies and public and private organizations, conduct continuing comprehensive studies of the effects and methods of control of thermal discharges. In evaluating alternative methods of control the studies shall consider (1) such data as are available on the latest available technology, economic feasibility including cost-effectiveness analysis, and (2) the total impact on the environment, considering not only water quality but also air quality, land use, and effective utilization and conservation of fresh water and other natural resources. Such studies shall consider methods of minimizing adverse effects and maximizing beneficial effects of thermal discharges. The results of these studies shall be reported by the Administrator as soon as practicable, but not later than 270 days after enactment of this subsection, and shall be made available to the public and the States, and considered as they become available by the Administrator in carrying out section 316 of this Act and by the States in proposing thermal water quality standards.

(u) There is authorized to be appropriated (1) not to exceed $100,000,000 per fiscal year for the fiscal year ending June 30, 1973, the fiscal year ending June 30, 1974 and the fiscal year ending June 30, 1975, not to exceed $14,039,000 for the fiscal year ending September 30, 1980, not to exceed $20,697,000 for the fiscal year ending September 30, 1981, not to exceed $22,770,000 for the fiscal year ending September 30, 1982, such sums as may be necessary for fiscal years 1983 through 1985, and not to exceed $22,770,000 per fiscal year for each of the fiscal years 1986 through 1990, for carrying out the provisions of this section, other than subsections (g)(1) and (2), (p),(r), and (t), except that such authorizations are not for any research, development, or demonstration activity pursuant to such provisions; (2) not to exceed $7,500,000 for fiscal years 1973, 1974 and 1975,

$2,000,000 for fiscal year 1977, $3,000,000 for fiscal year 1978, $3,000,000 for fiscal year 1979, $3,000,000 for fiscal year 1980, $3,000,000 for fiscal year 1981, $3,000,000 for fiscal year 1982, such sums as may be necessary for fiscal years 1983 through 1985, and $3,000,000 per fiscal year for each of the fiscal years 1986 through 1990, for carrying out the provisions of subsection (g)(1); (3) not to exceed $2,500,000 for fiscal year 1973, 1974, and 1975. $1,000,000 for fiscal year 1977, $1,500,000 for fiscal year 1978, $1,500,000 for fiscal year 1979, $1,500,000 for fiscal year 1980, $1,500,000 for fiscal year 1981, $1,500,000 for fiscal year 1982, such sums as may be necessary for fiscal years 1983 through 1985, and $1,500,000 per fiscal year for each of the fiscal years 1986 through 1990, for carrying out the provisions of subsection (g)(2); (4) not to exceed $10,000,000 for each of the fiscal years ending June 30, 1973, June 30, 1974, and June 30, 1975, for carrying out the provisions of subsection (p); (5) not to exceed $15,000,000 per fiscal year for the fiscal years ending June 30, 1973, June 30, 1974, and June 30, 1975, for carrying out the provisions of subsection (r); and (6) not to exceed $10,000,000 per fiscal year for the fiscal years ending June 30, 1973, June 30, 1974, and June 30, 1975, for carrying out the provisions of subsection (t).

§ 1255. Grants for research and development

[Sec. 105](a) The Administrator is authorized to conduct in the Environmental Protection Agency, and to make grants to any State, municipality, or intermunicipal or interstate agency for the purpose of assisting in the development of—

(1) any project which will demonstrate a new or improved method of preventing, reducing, and eliminating the discharge into any waters of pollutants from sewers which carry storm water or both storm water and pollutants; or

(2) any project which will demonstrate advanced waste treatment and water purification methods (including the temporary use of new or improved chemical additives which provide substantial immediate improvement to existing treatment processes), or new or improved methods or joint treatment systems for municipal and industrial wastes; and to include in such grants such amounts as are necessary for the purpose of reports, plans, and specifications in connection therewith.

(b) The Administrator is authorized to make grants to any State or States or interstate agency to demonstrate, in river basins or portions thereof, advanced treatment and environmental enhancement techniques to control pollution from all sources, within such basins or portions thereof, including nonpoint sources, together with in stream water quality improvement techniques.

(c) In order to carry out the purposes of section 301 of this Act, the Administrator is authorized to (1) conduct in the Environmental Protection Agency, (2) make grants to persons, and (3) enter into contracts with persons, for research and demonstration projects for prevention of pollution of any waters by industry including, but not limited to, the prevention, reduction, and elimination of the discharge of pollutants. No grant shall be made for any project under this subsection unless the Administrator determines that such project will develop or demonstrate a new or improved method of treating industrial wastes or otherwise prevent pollution by industry, which method shall have industrywide application.

(d) In carrying out the provisions of this section, the Administrator shall conduct, on a priority basis, an accelerated effort to develop, refine, and achieve practical application of:

(1) waste management methods applicable to point and nonpoint sources of pollutants to eliminate the discharge of pollutants, including, but not limited to, elimination of runoff of pollutants and the effects of pollutants from inplace or accumulated sources;

(2) advanced waste treatment methods applicable to point and nonpoint sources, including inplace or accumulated sources of pollutants, and methods for reclaiming and recycling water and confining pollutants so they will not migrate to cause water or other environmental pollution; and

(3) improved methods and procedures to identify and measure the effects of pollutants on the chemical, physical, and biological integrity of water, including those pollutants created by new technological developments.

(e)(1) The Administrator is authorized to (A) make, in consultation with the Secretary of Agriculture, grants to persons for research and demonstration projects with respect to new and improved methods of preventing, reducing, and eliminating pollution from agriculture, and (B) disseminate, in cooperation with the Secretary of Agriculture, such information obtained under this subsection, section 104(p), and section 304 as will encourage and enable the adoption of such methods in the agricultural industry.

(2) The Administrator is authorized, (A) in consultation with other interested Federal agencies, to make grants for demonstration projects with respect to new and improved methods of preventing, reducing, storing, collecting, treating, or otherwise eliminating pollution from sewage in rural and other areas where collection of sewage in conventional, community-wide sewage collection systems is impractical, uneconomical, or otherwise infeasible, or where soil conditions or other factors preclude the use of septic tank and drainage field systems, and (B) in cooperation with other interested Federal and State agencies, to disseminate such information obtained under this subsection as will encourage and enable the adoption of new and improved methods developed pursuant to this subsection.

(f) Federal grants under subsection (a) of this section shall be subject to the following limitations:

(1) No grant shall be made for any project unless such project shall have been approved by the appropriate State water pollution control agency or agencies and by the Administrator;

(2) No grant shall be made for any project in an amount exceeding 75 per centum of cost thereof as determined by the Administrator; and

(3) No grant shall be made for any project unless the Administrator determines that such project will serve as a useful demonstration for the purpose set forth in clause (1) or (2) of subsection (a).

(g) Federal grants under subsections (c) and (d) of this section shall not exceed 75 per centum of the cost of the project.

(h) For the purpose of this section there is authorized to be appropriated $75,000,000 per fiscal year for the fiscal year ending June 30, 1973, the fiscal year ending June 30, 1974, and the fiscal year ending June 30, 1975, and from such appropriations at least 10 per centum of the funds actually appropriated in each fiscal year shall be available only for the purposes of subsection (e).

(i) The Administrator is authorized to make grants to a municipality to assist in the costs of operating and maintaining a project which received a grant under this section, section 104, or section 113 of this Act prior to the date of enactment of this subsection so as to reduce the operation and maintenance costs borne by the recipients of services from such project to costs comparable to those for projects assisted under title II of this Act.

(j) The Administrator is authorized to make a grant to any grantee who received an increased grant pursuant to section 202(a)(2) of this Act. Such grant may pay up to 100 per centum of the costs of technical evaluation of the operation of the treatment works, costs of training of persons (other than employees of the grantee), and costs of disseminating technical information on the operation of the treatment works.

§ 1256. Grants for pollution control programs

[Sec. 106](a) There are hereby authorized to be appropriated the following sums, to remain available until expended, to carry out the purposes of this section—

(1) $60,000,000 for the fiscal year ending June 30, 1973; and

(2) $75,000,000 for the fiscal year ending June 30, 1974, and the fiscal year ending June 30, 1975, $100,000,000 per fiscal year for the fiscal years 1977, 1978, 1979, 1980, $75,000,000 per fiscal year for the fiscal years 1981 and 1982, such sums as may be necessary for fiscal years 1983 through 1985, and $75,000,000 per fiscal year for each of the fiscal years 1986 through 1990; for grants to States and to interstate agencies to assist them in administering programs for the prevention, reduction, and elimination of pollution, including enforce-

ment directly or through appropriate State law enforcement officers or agencies.

(b) From the sums appropriated in any fiscal year, the Administrator shall make allotments to the several States and interstate agencies in accordance with regulations promulgated by him on the basis of the extent of the pollution problem in the respective States.

(c) The Administrator is authorized to pay each State and interstate agency each fiscal year either—

(1) the allotment of such State or agency for such fiscal year under subsection (b), or

(2) the reasonable costs as determined by the Administrator of developing and carrying out a pollution program by such State or agency during such fiscal year, whichever amount is the lesser.

(d) No grant shall be made under this section to any State or interstate agency for any fiscal year when the expenditure of non-Federal funds by such State or interstate agency during such fiscal year for the recurrent expenses of carrying out its pollution control program are less than the expenditure by such State or interstate agency or non-Federal funds for such recurrent program expenses during the fiscal year ending June 30, 1971.

(e) Beginning in fiscal year 1974 the Administrator shall not make any grant under this section to any State which has not provided or is not carrying out as a part of its program—

(1) the establishment and operation of appropriate devices, methods, systems, and procedures necessary to monitor, and to compile and analyze data on (including classification according to eutrophic condition), the quality of navigable waters and to the extent practicable, ground waters including biological monitoring; and provision for annually updating such data and including it in the report required under section 305 of this Act:

(2) authority comparable to that in section 504 of this Act and adequate contingency plans to implement such authority.

(f) Grants shall be made under this section on condition that—

(1) Such State (or interstate agency) filed with the Administrator within one hundred and twenty days after the date of enactment of this section:

(A) a summary report of the current status of the State pollution control program, including the criteria used by the State in determining priority of treatment works; and

(B) such additional information, data, and reports as the Administrator may require.

(2) No federally assumed enforcement as defined in section 309(a)(2) is in effect with respect to such State or interstate agency.

(3) Such State (or interstate agency) submits within one hundred and twenty days after the date of enactment of this section and before October 1 of each year thereafter for the Administrator's approval of

its program for the prevention, reduction, and elimination of pollution in accordance with purposes and provisions of this Act in such form and content as the Administrator may prescribe.

(g) Any sums allotted under subsection (b) in any fiscal year which are not paid shall be reallotted by the Administrator in accordance with regulations promulgated by him.

§ 1257. Mine water pollution control demonstrations

[Sec. 107] (a) The Administrator in cooperation with the Appalachian Regional Commission and other Federal agencies is authorized to conduct, to make grants for, or to contract for, projects to demonstrate comprehensive approaches to the elimination or control of acid or other mine water pollution resulting from active or abandoned mining operations and other environmental pollution affecting water quality within all or part of a watershed or river basin, including siltation from surface mining. Such projects shall demonstrate the engineering and economic feasibility and practicality of various abatement techniques which will contribute substantially to effective and practical methods of acid or other mine water pollution elimination or control, and other pollution affecting water quality, including techniques that demonstrate the engineering and economic feasibility and practicality of using sewage sludge materials and other municipal wastes to diminish or prevent pollution affecting water quality from acid, sedimentation, or other pollutants and in such projects to restore affected lands to usefulness for forestry, agriculture, recreation, or other beneficial purposes.

(b) Prior to undertaking any demonstration project under this section in the Appalachian region (as defined in section 403 of the Appalachian Regional Development Act of 1965, as amended), the Appalachian Regional Commission shall determine that such demonstration project is consistent with the objectives of the Appalachian Regional Development Act of 1965, as amended.

(c) The Administrator, in selecting watersheds for the purposes of this section, shall be satisfied that the project area will not be affected adversely by the influx of acid or other mine water pollution from nearby sources.

(d) Federal participation in such projects shall be subject to the conditions—

(1) that the State shall acquire any land or interests therein necessary for such project; and

(2) that the State shall provide legal and practical protection to the project area to insure against any activities which will cause future acid or other mine water pollution.

(e) There is authorized to be appropriated $30,000,000 to carry out the provisions of this section, which sum shall be available until expended.

§ 1258. Pollution control in Great Lakes

[Sec. 108] (a) The Administrator, in cooperation with other Federal departments, agencies, and instrumentalities is authorized to enter into agreements with any State, political subdivision, interstate agency, or other public agency, or combination thereof, to carry out one or more projects to demonstrate new methods and techniques and to develop preliminary plans for the elimination or control of pollution, within all or any part of the watersheds of the Great Lakes. Such projects shall demonstrate the engineering and economic feasibility and practicality of removal of pollutants and prevention of any polluting matter from entering into the Great Lakes in the future and other reduction and remedial techniques which will contribute substantially to effective and practical methods of pollution prevention, reduction, or elimination.

(b) Federal participation in such projects shall be subject to the condition that the State, political subdivision, interstate agency, or other public agency, or combination thereof, shall pay not less than 25 per centum of the actual project costs, which payment may be in any form, including, but not limited to, land or interests therein that is needed for the project, and personal property or services the value of which shall be determined by the Administrator.

(c) There is authorized to be appropriated $20,000,000 to carry out the provisions of subsections (a) and (b) of this section, which sum shall be available until expended.

(d)(1) In recognition of the serious conditions which exist in Lake Erie, the Secretary of the Army, acting through the Chief of Engineers, is directed to design and develop a demonstration waste water management program for the rehabilitation and environmental repair of Lake Erie. Prior to the initiation of detailed engineering and design, the program, along with the specific recommendations shall be submitted to the Congress for statutory approval. This authority is in addition to, and not in lieu of, other waste water studies aimed at eliminating pollution emanating from select sources around Lake Erie.

(2) This program is to be developed in cooperation with the Environmental Protection Agency, other interested departments, agencies, and instrumentalities of the Federal Government, and the States and their political subdivisions. This program shall set forth alternative systems for managing waste water on a regional basis and shall provide local and State governments with a range of choice as to the type of system to be used for the treatment of waste water. These alternative systems shall include both advanced waste treatment technology and land disposal systems including aerated treatment spray irrigation technology and will also include provisions for the disposal of solid wastes, including sludge.

Such program should include measures to control point sources of pollution, area sources of pollution, including acid-mine drainage, urban runoff and rural runoff, and in place sources of pollution, including bottom loads, sludge banks, and polluted harbor dredgings.

(e) There is authorized to be appropriated $5,000,000 to carry out the provisions of subsection (d) of this section, which sum shall be available until expended.

§ 1259. Training grants and contracts

[Sec. 109] (a) The Administrator is authorized to make grants to or contracts with institutions of higher education, or combinations of such institutions, to assist them in planning, developing, strengthening, improving, or carrying out programs or projects for the preparation of undergraduate students to enter an occupation which involves the design, operation, and maintenance of treatment works, and other facilities whose purpose is water quality control. Such grants or contracts may include payment of all or part of the cost of programs or projects such as—

    (A) planning for the development or expansion of programs or projects for training persons in the operation and maintenance of treatment works:

    (B) training and retraining of faculty members;

    (C) conduct of short-term or regular session institutes for study by persons engaged in, or preparing to engage in, the preparation of students preparing to enter an occupation involving the operation and maintenance of treatment works;

    (D) carrying out innovative and experimental programs of cooperative education involving alternative periods of full-time or part-time academic study at the institution and periods of full-time or part-time employment involving the operation and maintenance of treatment works; and

    (E) research into, and development of, methods of training students or faculty, including the preparation of teaching materials and the planning of curriculum.

(b)(1) The Administrator may pay 100 per centum of any additional cost of construction of treatment works required for a facility to train and upgrade waste treatment works operation and maintenance personnel and for the costs of other State treatment works operator training programs, including mobile training units, classroom rental, specialized instructors, and instructional material.

    (2) The Administrator shall make no more than one grant for such additional construction in any State (to serve a group of States, where, in his judgment, efficient training programs require multi-State programs), and shall make such grant after consultation with and approval by the State or States or the basis of (A) the suitability of

such facility for training operation and maintenance personnel for treatment works throughout such State or States; and (B) a commitment by the State agency or agencies to carry out at such facility a program of training approved by the Administrator. In any case where a grant is made to serve two or more States, the Administrator is authorized to make an additional grant for a supplemental facility in each such State.

(3) The Administrator may make such grant out of the sums allocated to a State under section 205 of this Act, except that in no event shall the Federal cost of any such training facilities exceed $500,000.

(4) The Administrator may exempt a grant under this section from any requirement under section 204(a)(3) of this Act. Any grantee who received a grant under this section prior to enactment of the Clean Water Act of 1977 shall be eligible to have its grant increased by funds made available under such Act.

§ 1260. Application for training grant or contract; allocation of grants or contracts

[Sec. 110] (1) A grant or contract authorized by section 109 may be made only upon application to the Administrator at such time or times and containing such information as he may prescribe, except that no such application shall be approved unless it—

(A) sets forth programs, activities, research, or development for which a grant is authorized under section 109 and describes the relation to any program set forth by the applicant in an application, if any, submitted pursuant to section 111;

(B) provides such fiscal control and fund accounting procedures as may be necessary to assure proper disbursement of and accounting for Federal funds paid to the applicant under this section; and

(C) provides for making such reports, in such form and containing such information, as the Administrator may require to carry out his functions under this section, and for keeping such records and for affording such access thereto as the Administrator may find necessary to assure the correctness and verification of such reports.

(2) The Administrator shall allocate grants or contracts under section 109 in such manner as will most nearly provide an equitable distribution of the grants or contracts throughout the United States among institutions of higher education which show promise of being able to use funds effectively for the purpose of this section.

(3)(A) Payments under this section may be used in accordance with regulations of the Administrator, and subject to the terms and conditions set forth in an application approved under paragraph (1), to pay part of the compensation of students employed in connection with the operation and maintenance of treament works, other than as an employee in connection with the operation and maintenance of treatment works or as an employee in any branch of the Government of the United States, as part of a program for which a grant has been approved pursuant to this section.

(B) Departments and agencies of the United States are encouraged, to the extent consistent with efficient administration, to enter into arrangements with institutions of higher education for the full-time, part-time, or temporary employment, whether in the competitive or excepted service, of students enrolled in programs set forth in applications approved under paragraph (1).

§ 1261.   Award of scholarships

[Sec. 111] (1) The Administrator is authorized to award scholarships in accordance with the provisions of this section for undergraduate study by persons who plan to enter an occupation involving the operation and maintenance of treatment works. Such scholarships shall be awarded for such periods as the Administrator may determine but not to exceed four academic years.

(2) The Administrator shall allocate scholarships under this section among institutions of higher education with programs approved under the provisions of this section for the use of individuals accepted into such programs, in such manner and accordance to such plan as will insofar as practicable—

(A) provide an equitable distribution of such scholarships throughout the United States; and

(B) attract recent graduates of secondary schools to enter an occupation involving the operation and maintenance of treatment works.

(3) The Administrator shall approve a program of any institution of higher education for the purposes of this section only upon application by the institution and only upon his finding—

(A) that such program has a principal objective the education and training of persons in the operation and maintenance of treatment works;

(B) that such program is in effect and of high quality or can be readily put into effect and may reasonably be expected to be of high quality;

(C) that the application describes the relation of such program to any program, activity, research, or development set forth by the applicant in any application, if any, submitted pursuant to section 110 of this Act; and

(D) that the application contains satisfactory assurances that (i) the institution will recommend to the Administrator for the award of scholarships under this section, for study in such program, only persons who have demonstrated to the satisfaction of the institution a serious intent, upon completing the program, to enter an occupation involving the operation and maintenance of treatment works, and (ii) the institution will make reasonable continuing efforts to encourage recipients of scholarships under this section, enrolled in such program, to enter occupations involving the operation and maintenance of treatment works upon completing the program.

(4)(A) The Administrator shall pay to persons awarded scholarships under this section such stipends (including such allowances for subsistence and other expenses for such persons and their dependents) as he may determine to be consistent with prevailing practices under comparable federally supported programs.

(B) The Administrator shall (in addition to the stipends paid to persons under paragraph (1)) pay to the institution of higher education at which such person is pursuing his course of study such amount as he may determine to be consistent with prevailing practices under comparable federally supported programs.

(5) A person awarded a scholarship under the provisions of this section shall continue to receive the payments provided in this section only during such periods as the Administrator finds that he is maintaining satisfactory proficiency and devoting full time to study or research in the field in which such scholarship was awarded in an institution of higher education, and is not engaging in gainful employment other than employment approved by the Administrator by or pursuant to regulation.

(6) The Administrator shall by regulation provide that any person awarded a scholarship under this section shall agree in writing to enter and remain in an occupation involving the design, operation, or maintenance of treatment works for such period after completion of this course of studies as the Administrator determines appropriate.

§ 1262. Definitions and authorizations

[Sec. 112](a) As used in sections 109 through 112 of this Act—

(1) The term "institution of higher education" means an educational institution described in the first sentence of section 1201 of the Higher Education Act of 1965 (other than an institution of any agency of the United States) which is accredited by a nationally recognized accrediting agency or association approved by the Administrator for this purpose. For purposes of this subsection, the Administrator shall publish a list of nationally recognized accrediting agencies or associations which he determines to be reliable authority as to the quality of training offered.

(2) The term "academic year" means an academic year or its equivalent,

as determined by the Administrator.

(b) The Administrator shall annually report his activities under section 109 through 112 of this Act, including recommendations for needed revisions in the provisions thereof.

(c) There are authorized to be appropriated $25,000,000 per fiscal year for the fiscal years ending June 30, 1973, June 30, 1974, and June 30, 1975, $6,000,000 for the fiscal year ending September 30, 1977, $7,000,000 for the fiscal year ending September 30, 1978, $7,000,000 for the fiscal year ending September 30, 1979, $7,000,000 for the fiscal year ending September 30, 1980, $7,000,000 for the fiscal year ending September 30, 1981, $7,000,000 for the fiscal year ending September 30, 1982, such sums as may be necessary for fiscal years 1983 through 1985, and $7,000,000 per fiscal year for each of the fiscal years 1986 through 1990, to carry out sections 109 through 112 of this Act.

§ 1263. Alaska village demonstration projects

[Sec. 113](a) The Administrator is authorized to enter into agreements with the State of Alaska to carry out one or more projects to demonstrate methods to provide for central community facilities for safe water and elimination or control of pollution in those native villages of Alaska without such facilities. Such project shall include provisions for community safe water supply systems, toilets, bathing and laundry facilities, sewage disposal facilities, and other similar facilities, and educational and informational facilities and programs relating to health and hygiene. Such demonstration projects shall be for the further purpose of developing preliminary plans for providing such safe water and such elimination or control of pollution for all native villages in such State.

(b) In carrying out this section the Administrator shall cooperate with the Secretary of Health, Education, and Welfare for the purpose of utilizing such of the personnel and facilities of that Department as may be appropriate.

(c) The Administrator shall report to Congress not later than July 1, 1973, the results of the demonstration projects authorized by this section together with his recommendations, including any necessary legislation, relating to the establishment of a statewide program.

(d) There is authorized to be appropriated not to exceed $2,000,000 to carry out this section. In addition, there is authorized to be appropriated to carry out this section not to exceed $200,000 for the fiscal year ending September 30, 1978 and $220,000 for the fiscal year ending September 30, 1979.

(e) The Administrator is authorized to coordinate with the Secretary of the Department of Health, Education, and Welfare, the Secretary of the Department of Housing and Urban Development, the Secretary of the Department of the Interior, the Secretary of the Department of Agriculture, and the heads of any other departments or agencies he may deem appropriate to conduct a joint study with representatives of the State of Alaska and the appropriate Native organizations (as defined in Public Law 92–203) to develop a comprehensive program for achieving adequate sanitation services in Alaska villages. This study shall be coordinated with the programs and projects authorized by sections 104(q) and 105(e)(2) of this Act. The Administrator shall submit a report of the results of the study, together with appropriate supporting data and such recommendations as he deems desirable, to the Committee on Environment and Public Works of the Senate and to the Committee on Public Works and Transportation of the House of Representatives not later than December 31, 1979. The Administrator shall also submit recommended administrative actions, procedures, and any proposed legislation necessary to implement the recommendations of the study no later than June 30, 1980.

(f) The Administrator is authorized to provide technical, financial and management assistance for operation and maintenance of the demonstration projects constructed under this section, until such time as the recommendations of subsection (e) are implemented.

(g) For the purpose of this section, the term "village" shall mean an incorporated or unincorporated community with a population of ten to six hundred people living within a two-mile radius. The term "sanitation services" shall mean water supply, sewage disposal, solid waste disposal and other services necessary to maintain generally accepted standards of personal hygiene and public health.

§ 1264.   Lake Tahoe study

[Sec. 114] (a) The Administrator, in consultation with the Tahoe Regional Planning Agency, the Secretary of Agriculture, other Federal agencies, representatives of State and local governments, and members of the public, shall conduct a thorough and complete study on the adequacy of and need for extending Federal oversight and control in order to preserve the fragile ecology of Lake Tahoe.

(b) Such study shall include an examination of the interrelationships and responsibilities of the various agencies of the Federal Government and State and local governments with a view to establishing the necessity for redefinition of legal and other arrangements between these various governments, and making specific legislative recommendations to Congress. Such study shall consider the effect of various actions in terms of their environmental impact on the Tahoe Basin, treated as an ecosystem.

(c) The Administrator shall report on such study to Congress not later than one year after the date of enactment of this subsection.

(d) There is authorized to be appropriated to carry out this section not to exceed $500,000.

§ 1265. In-place toxic pollutants

[Sec. 115] The Administrator is directed to identify the location of in-place pollutants with emphasis on toxic pollutants in harbors and navigable waterways and is authorized, acting through the Secretary of the Army, to make contracts for the removal and appropriate disposal of such materials from critical port and harbor areas. There is authorized to be appropriated $15,000,000 to carry out the provisions of this section, which sum shall be available until expended.

§ 1266. Hudson River PCB reclamation demonstration project

[Sec. 116] (a) The Administrator is authorized to enter into contracts and other agreements with the State of New York to carry out a project to demonstrate methods for the selective removal of polychlorinated biphenyls contaminating bottom sediments of the Hudson River, treating such sediments as required, burying such sediments in secure landfills, and installing monitoring systems for such landfills. Such demonstration project shall be for the purpose of determining the feasibility of indefinite storage in secure landfills of toxic substances and of ascertaining the improvement of the rate of recovery of a toxic contaminated national waterway. No pollutants removed pursuant to this paragraph shall be placed in any landfill unless the Administrator first determines that disposal of the pollutants in such landfill would provide a higher standard of protection of the public health, safety, and welfare than disposal of such pollutants by any other method including, but not limited to, incineration or a chemical destruction process.

(b) The Administrator is authorized to make grants to the State of New York to carry out this section from funds allotted to such State under section 205(a) of this Act, except that the amount of any such grant shall be equal to 75 per centum of the cost of the project and such grant shall be made on condition that non-Federal sources provide the remainder of the cost of such project. The authority of this section shall be available until September 30, 1983. Funds allotted to the State of New York under section 205(a) shall be available under this subsection only to the extent that funds are not available, as determined by the Administrator, to the State of New York for the work authorized by this section under section 115 or 311 of this Act or a comprehensive hazardous substance response and clean up fund. Any funds used under the authority of this subsection shall be deducted from any estimate of the needs of the State of New York prepared under section 626(b) of this Act. The Administrator may not obligate or expend more than $20,000,000 to carry out this section.

§ 1267. Chesapeake Bay

[Sec. 117] (a) The Administrator shall continue the Chesapeake Bay Program and shall establish and maintain in the Environmental Protection Agency an office, division, or branch of Chesapeake Bay Programs to

(1) collect and make available, through publications and other appropriate means, information pertaining to the environmental quality of the Chesapeake Bay (hereinafter in this subsection referred to as the "Bay");

(2) coordinate Federal and State efforts to improve the water quality of the Bay;

(3) determine the impact of sediment deposition in the Bay and identify the sources, rates, routes, and distribution patterns of such sediment deposition; and

(4) determine the impact of natural and man-induced environmental changes on the living resources of the Bay and the relationships among such changes, with particular emphasis placed on the impact of pollutant loadings of nutrients, chlorine, acid precipitation, dissolved oxygen, and toxic pollutants, including organic chemicals and heavy metals, and with special attention given to the impact of such changes on striped bass.

(b)(1) The Administrator shall, at the request of the Governor of a State affected by the interstate management plan developed pursuant to the Chesapeake Bay Program (hereinafter in this section referred to as the "plan"), make a grant for the purpose of implementing the management mechanisms contained in the plan if such State has, within 1 year after the date of the enactment of this section, approved and committed to implement all or substantially all aspects of the plan. Such grants shall be made subject to such terms and conditions as the Administrator considers appropriate.

(2) A State or combination of States may elect to avail itself of the benefits of this subsection by submitting to the Administrator a comprehensive proposal to implement management mechanisms contained in the plan which shall include (A) a description of proposed abatement actions which the State or combination of States commits to take within a specified time period to reduce pollution in the Bay and to meet applicable water quality standards, and (B) the estimated cost of the abatement actions proposed to be taken during the next fiscal year. If the Administrator finds that such proposal is consistent with the national policies set forth in section 101(a) of this Act and will contribute to the achievement of the national goals set forth in such section, the Administrator shall approve such proposal and shall finance the costs of implementing segments of such proposal.

(3) Grants under this subsection shall not exceed 50 percent of the costs of implementing the management mechanisms contained in the plan in any fiscal year and shall be made on condition that non-Federal sources provide the remainder of the cost of implementing the management mechanisms contained in the plan during such fiscal year.

(4) Administrative costs in the form of salaries, overhead, or indirect costs for services provided and charged against programs or projects supported by funds made available under this subsection shall not exceed

in any one fiscal year 10 percent of the annual Federal grant made to a State under this subsection.

(c) Any State or combination of States that receives a grant under subsection (b) shall, within 18 months after the date of receipt of such grant and biennially thereafter, report to the Administrator on the progress made in implementing the interstate management plan developed pursuant to the Chesapeake Bay Program. The Administrator shall transmit each such report along with the comments of the Administrator on such report to Congress.

(d) There are hereby authorized to be appropriated the following sums, to remain available until expended, to carry out the purposes of this section:
(1) $3,000,000 per fiscal year for each of the fiscal years 1987, 1988, 1989, and 1990, to carry out subsection (a); and
(2) $10,000,000 per fiscal year for each of the fiscal years 1987, 1988, 1989, and 1990, for grants to States under subsection (b).

§ 1268. Great Lakes

[Sec. 118] (a)(1)The Congress finds that—
(A) the Great Lakes are a valuable national resource, continuously serving the people of the United States and other nations as an important source of food, fresh water, recreation, beauty, and enjoyment;
(B) the United States should seek to attain the goals embodied in the Great Lakes Water Quality Agreement of 1978 with particular emphasis on goals related to toxic pollutants; and
(C) the Environmental Protection Agency should take the lead in the effort to meet those goals, working with other Federal agencies and State and local authorities.
(2) It is the purpose of this section to achieve the goals embodied in the Great Lakes Water Quality Agreement of 1978 through improved organization and definition of mission on the part of the Agency, funding of State grants for pollution control in the Great Lakes area, and improved accountability for implementation of such agreement.
(3) For purposes of this section, the term—
(A) "Agency" means the Environmental Protection Agency;
(B) "Great Lakes" means Lake Ontario, Lake Erie, Lake Huron (including Lake St. Clair), Lake Michigan, and Lake Superior, and the connecting channels (Saint Mary's River, Saint Clair River, Detroit River, Niagara River, and Saint Lawrence River to the Canadian Border);
(C) "Great Lakes System" means all the streams, rivers, lakes, and other bodies of water within the drainage basin of the Great Lakes;
(D) "Program Office" means the Great Lakes National Program

Office established by this section; and
(E) "Research Office" means the Great Lakes Research Office established by subsection (d).

(b) The Great Lakes National Program Office (previously established by the Administrator) is hereby established within the Agency. The Program Office shall be headed by a Director who, by reason of management experience and technical expertise relating to the Great Lakes, is highly qualified to direct the development of programs and plans on a variety of Great Lakes issues. The Great Lakes National Program Office shall be located in a Great Lakes State.

(c)(1) The Program Office shall—
(A) in cooperation with appropriate Federal, State, tribal, and international agencies, and in accordance with section 101(e) of this Act, develop and implement specific action plans to carry out the responsibilities of the United States under the Great Lakes Water Quality Agreement of 1978;
(B) establish a Great Lakes system-wide surveillance network to monitor the water quality of the Great Lakes, with specific emphasis on the monitoring of toxic pollutants;
(C) serve as the liaison with, and provide information to, the Canadian members of the International Joint Commission and the Canadian counterpart to the Agency;
(D) coordinate actions of the Agency (including actions by headquarters and regional offices thereof) aimed at improving Great Lakes water quality; and
(E) coordinate actions of the Agency with the actions of other Federal agencies and State and local authorities, so as to ensure the input of those agencies and authorities in developing water quality strategies and obtain the support of those agencies and authorities in achieving the objectives of such agreement.
(2) The Program Office shall develop, in consultation with the States, a five-year plan and program for reducing the amount of nutrients introduced into the Great Lakes. Such program shall incorporate any management program for reducing nutrient runoff from nonpoint sources established under section 319 of this Act and shall include a program for monitoring nutrient runoff into, and ambient levels in, the Great Lakes.
(3) The Program Office shall carry out a five-year study and demonstration projects relating to the control and removal of toxic pollutants in the Great Lakes, with emphasis on the removal of toxic pollutants from bottom sediments. In selecting locations for conducting demonstration projects under this paragraph, priority consideration shall be given to projects at the following locations: Saginaw Bay, Michigan; Sheboygan Harbor, Wisconsin; Grand Calumet River, Indiana; Ashtabula River, Ohio; and Buffalo River, New York.

(4) The Administrator shall ensure that the Program Office enters into agreements with the various organizational elements of the Agency involved in Great Lakes activities and the appropriate State agencies specifically delineating—

    (A) the duties and responsibilities of each such element in the Agency with respect to the Great Lakes;

    (B) the time periods for carrying out such duties and responsibilities; and

    (C) the resources to be committed to such duties and responsibilities.

(5) The Administrator shall, in the Agency's annual budget submission to Congress, include a funding request for the Program Office as a separate budget line item.

(6) Within 90 days after the end of each fiscal year, the Administrator shall submit to Congress a comprehensive report which—

    (A) describes the achievements in the preceding fiscal year in implementing the Great Lakes Water Quality Agreement of 1978 and shows by categories (including judicial enforcement, research, State cooperative efforts, and general administration) the amounts expended on Great Lakes water quality initiatives in such preceding fiscal year;

    (B) describes the progress made in such preceding fiscal year in implementing the system of surveillance of the water quality in the Great Lakes System, including the monitoring of groundwater and sediment, with particular reference to toxic pollutants;

    (C) describes the long-term prospects for improving the condition of the Great Lakes; and

    (D) provides a comprehensive assessment of the planned efforts to be pursued in the succeeding fiscal year for implementing the Great Lakes Water Quality Agreement of 1978, which assessment shall—

        (i) show by categories (including judicial enforcement, research, State cooperative efforts, and general administration) the amount anticipated to be expended on Great Lakes water quality initiatives in the fiscal year to which the assessment relates; and

        (ii) include a report of current programs administered by other Federal agencies which make available resources to the Great Lakes water quality management efforts.

(d)(1)There is established within the National Oceanic and Atmospheric Administration the Great Lakes Research Office.

(2) The Research Office shall identify issues relating to the Great Lakes resources on which research is needed. The Research Office shall submit a report to Congress on such issues before the end of each fiscal year which shall identify any changes in the Great Lakes system with respect to such issues.

(3) The Research Office shall identify and inventory Federal, State, university, and tribal environmental research programs (and, to the extent feasible, those of private organizations and other nations) relating to the Great Lakes system, and shall update that inventory every four years.

(4) The Research Office shall establish a Great Lakes research exchange for the purpose of facilitating the rapid identification, acquisition, retrieval, dissemination, and use of information concerning research projects which are ongoing or completed and which affect the Great Lakes System.

(5) The Research Office shall develop, in cooperation with the Coordination Office, a comprehensive environmental research program and data base for the Great Lakes system. The data base shall include, but not be limited to, data relating to water quality, fisheries, and biota.

(6) The Research Office shall conduct, through the Great Lakes Environmental Research Laboratory, the National Sea Grant College program, other Federal laboratories, and the private sector, appropriate research and monitoring activities which address priority issues and current needs relating to the Great Lakes.

(7) The Research Office shall be located in a Great Lakes State.

(e)(1)Before October 1 of each year, the Program Office and the Research Office shall prepare a joint research plan for the fiscal year which begins in the following calendar year.

(2) Each plan prepared under paragraph (1) shall—

(A) identify all proposed research dedicated to activities conducted under the Great Lakes Water Quality Agreement of 1978;

(B) include the Agency's assessment of priorities for research needed to fulfill the terms of such Agreement; and

(C) identify all proposed research that may be used to develop a comprehensive environmental data base for the Great Lakes System and establish priorities for development of such data base.

(f) The head of each department, agency, or other instrumentality of the Federal Government which is engaged in, is concerned with, or has authority over programs relating to research, monitoring, and planning to maintain, enhance, preserve, or rehabilitate the environmental quality and natural resources of the Great Lakes, including the Chief of Engineers of the Army, the Chief of the Soil Conservation Service, the Commandant of the Coast Guard, the Director of the Fish and Wildlife Service, and the Administrator of the National Oceanic and Atmospheric Administration, shall submit an annual report to the Administrator with respect to the activities of that agency or office affecting compliance with the Great Lakes Water Quality Agreement of 1978.

(g) Nothing in this section shall be construed to affect the jurisdiction, powers, or prerogatives of any department, agency, or officer of the Federal Government or of any State government, or of any tribe, nor any powers, jurisdiction, or prerogatives of any international body created by treaty with authority relating to the Great Lakes.

(h) There are authorized to be appropriated to the Administrator to carry out this section not to exceed $11,000,000 per fiscal year for the fiscal years 1987, 1988, 1989, 1990, and 1991. Of the amounts appropriated each fiscal year—

(1) 40 percent shall be used by the Great Lakes National Program Office on demonstration projects on the feasibility of controlling and removing toxic pollutants;

(2) 7 percent shall be used by the Great Lakes National Program Office for the program of nutrient monitoring; and

(3) 30 percent shall be transferred to the National Oceanic and Atmospheric Administration for use by the Great Lakes Research Office.

Subchapter II. Grants for Construction of Treatment Works

§ 1281. Congressional declaration of purpose

[Sec. 201](a) It is the purpose of this title to require and to assist the development and implementation of waste treatment management plans and practices which will achieve the goals of this Act.

(b) Waste treatment management plans and practices shall provide for the application of the best practicable waste treatment technology before any discharge into receiving waters, including reclaiming and recycling of water, and confined disposal of pollutants so they will not migrate to cause water or other environmental pollution and shall provide for consideration of advanced waste treatment techniques.

(c) To the extent practicable, waste treatment management shall be on an areawide basis and provide control or treatment of all point and nonpoint sources of pollution, including in place or accumulated pollution sources.

(d) The Administrator shall encourage waste treatment management which results in the construction of revenue producing facilities providing for—

(1) the recycling of potential sewage pollutants through the production of agriculture, silviculture, or aquaculture products, or any combination thereof;

(2) the confined and contained disposal of pollutants not recycled;

(3) the reclamation of wastewater; and

(4) the ultimate disposal of sludge in a manner that will not result in environmental hazards.

(e) The Administrator shall encourage waste treatment management which results in integrating facilities for sewage treatment and recycling with facilities to treat, dispose of, or utilize other industrial and municipal wastes, including but not limited to solid waste and waste heat and thermal discharges. Such integrated facilities shall be designed and operated to produce revenues in excess of capital and operation and maintenance costs and such revenues shall be used by the designated regional management agency to aid in financing other environmental improvement programs.

(f) The Administrator shall encourage waste treatment management which combines "open space" and recreational considerations with such management.

(g)(1) The Administrator is authorized to make grants to any State, municipality, or intermunicipal or interstate agency for the construction of publicly owned treatment works. On and after October 1, 1984, grants under this title shall be made only for projects for secondary treatment or more stringent treatment, or any cost effective alternative thereto, new interceptors and appurtenances, and infiltration-in-flow correction. Notwithstanding the preceding sentences, the Administrator may make grants on and after October 1, 1984, for (A) any project within the definition set forth in section 212(2) of this Act, other than for a project referred to in the preceding sentence, and (B) any purpose for which a grant may be made under sections 319 (h) and (i) of this Act (including any innovative and alternative approaches for the control of nonpoint sources of pollution), except that not more than 20 per centum (as determined by the Governor of the State) of the amount allotted to a State under section 205 of this Act for any fiscal year shall be obligated in such State under authority of this sentence.

(2)The Administrator shall not make grants from funds authorized for any fiscal year beginning after June 30, 1974, to any State, municipality, or intermunicipal or interstate agency for the erection, building, acquisition, alteration, remodeling, improvement, or extension of treatment works unless the grant applicant has satisfactorily demonstrated to the Administrator that—

  (A) alternative waste management techniques have beeen studied and evaluated and the works proposed for grant assistance will provide for the application of the best practicable waste treatment technology over the life of the works consistent with the purposes of this title; and

  (B) as appropriate, the works proposed for grant assistance will take into account and allow to the extent practicable the application of technology at a later date which will provide for the reclaiming or recycling of water or otherwise eliminate the discharge of pollutants.

(3) The Administrator shall not approve any grant after July 1, 1973, for treatment works under this section unless the applicant shows to the satisfaction of the Administrator that each sewer collection system discharging into such treatment works is not subject to excessive infiltration.

(4) The Administrator is authorized to make grants to applicants for

treatment works grants under this section for such sewer system evaluation studies as may be necessary to carry out the requirements of paragraph (3) of this subsection. Such grants shall be made in accordance with rules and regulations promulgated by the Administrator. Initial rules and regulations shall be promulgated under this paragraph not later than 120 days after the date of enactment of the Federal Water Pollution Control Act Amendments of 1972.

(5) The Administrator shall not make grants from funds authorized for any fiscal year beginning after September 30, 1978, to any State, municipality, or intermunicipal or interstate agency for the erection, building, acquisition, alteration, remodeling, improvement, or extension of treatment works unless the grant applicant has satisfactorily demonstrated to the Administrator that innovative and alternative wastewater treatment processes and techniques which provide for the reclaiming and reuse of water, otherwise eliminate the discharge of pollutants, and utilize recycling techniques, land treatment, new or improved methods of waste treatment management for municipal and industrial waste (discharged in municipal systems) and the confined disposal of pollutants, so that pollutants will not migrate to cause water or other environmental pollution, have been fully studied and evaluated by the applicant taking into account section 201(d) of this Act and taking into account and allowing to the extent practicable the more efficient use of energy and resources.

(6) The Administrator shall not make grants from funds authorized for any fiscal year beginning after September 30, 1978, to any State, municipality, or intermunicipal or interstate agency for the erection, building, acquisition, alteration, remodeling, improvement, or extension of treatment works unless the grant applicant has satisfactorily demonstrated to the Administrator that the applicant has analyzed the potential recreation and open space opportunities in the planning of the proposed treatment works.

(h) A grant may be made under this section to construct a privately owned treatment works serving one or more principal residences or small commercial establishments constructed prior to, and inhabited on the date of enactment of this subsection where the Administrator finds that—

(1) a public body otherwise eligible for a grant under subsection (g) of this section has applied on behalf of a number of such units and certified that public ownership of such works is not feasible;

(2) such public body has entered into an agreement with the Administrator which guarantees that such treatment works will be properly operated and maintained and will comply with all other requirements of section 204 of this Act and includes a system of charges to assure that each recipient of waste treatment services under such a grant will pay its proportionate share of the cost of operation and maintenance (including replacement); and

(3) the total cost and environmental impact of providing waste treatment services to such residences or commercial establishments will be less than the cost of providing a system of collection and central treatment of such wastes.

(i) The administrator shall encourage waste treatment management methods, processes, and techniques which will reduce total energy requirements.

(j) The Administrator is authorized to make a grant for any treatment works utilizing processes and techniques meeting the guidelines promulgated under section 304(d)(3) of this Act, if the Administrator determines it is in the public interest and if in the cost effectiveness study made of the construction grant application for the purpose of evaluating alternative treatment works, the life cycle cost of the treatment works for which the grant is to be made does not exceed the life cycle cost of the most effective alternative by more than 15 per centum.

(k) No grant made after November 15, 1981, for a publicly owned treatment works, other than for facility planning and the preparation of construction plans and specifications, shall be used to treat, store, or convey the flow of any industrial user into such treatment works in excess of a flow per day equivalent to fifty thousand gallons per day of sanitary waste. This subsection shall not apply to any project proposed by a grantee which is carrying out an approved project to prepare construction plans and specifications for a facility to treat wastewater, which received its grant approval before May 15, 1980. This subsection shall not be in effect after November 15, 1981.

(l)(1) After the date of enactment of this subsection, Federal grants shall not be made for the purpose of providing assistance solely for facility plans, or plans, specifications, and estimates for any proposed project for the construction of treatment works. In the event that the proposed project receives a grant under this section for construction, the Administrator shall make an allowance in such grant for non-Federal funds expended during the facility planning and advanced engineering and design phase at the prevailing Federal share under section 202(a) of this Act, based on the percentage of total project costs which the Administrator determines is the general experience for such projects.

(2)(A) Each State shall use a portion of the funds allotted to such State each fiscal year, but not to exceed 10 per centum of such funds, to advance to potential grant applicants under this title the costs of facility planning or the preparation of plans, specifications, and estimates.

(B) Such an advance shall be limited to the allowance for such costs which the Administrator establishes under paragraph (1) of this subsection, and shall be provided only to a potential grant applicant which is a small community and which in the judgment of the State would otherwise be unable to prepare a request for a grant for construction costs under this section.

(C) In the event a grant for construction costs is made under this section for a project for which an advance has been made under this paragraph, the Administrator shall reduce the amount of such grant by the allowance established under paragraph (1) of this subsection. In the event no such grant is made, the State is authorized to seek repayment of such advance on such terms and conditions as it may determine.

(m)(1) Notwithstanding any other provisions of this title, the Administrator is authorized to make a grant from any funds otherwise allotted to the State of California under section 205 of this Act to the project (and in the amount) specified in Order WQG 81-1 of the California State Water Resources Control Board.

(2) Notwithstanding any other provision of this Act, the Administrator shall make a grant from any funds otherwise allotted to the State of California to the city of Eureka, California, in connection with project numbered C–06–2772, for the purchase of one hundred and thirty-nine acres of property as environmental mitigation for siting of the proposed treatment plant.

(3) Notwithstanding any other provision of this Act, the Administrator shall make a grant from any funds otherwise allotted to the State of California to the city of San Diego, California, in connection with that city's aquaculture sewage process (total resources recovery system) as an innovative and alternative waste treatment process.

(n)(1) On and after October 1, 1984, upon the request of the Governor of an affected State, the Administrator is authorized to use funds available to such State under section 205 to address water quality problems due to the impacts of discharges from combined storm water and sanitary sewer overflows, which are not otherwise eligible under this subsection, where correction of such discharge is a major priority for such State.

(2) Beginning fiscal year 1983, the Administrator shall have available $200,000,000 per fiscal year in addition to those funds authorized in section 207 of this Act to be utilized to address water quality problems of marine bays and estuaries subject to lower levels of water quality due to the impacts of discharges from combined storm water and sanitary sewer overflows from adjacent urban complexes, not otherwise eligible under this subsection. Such sums may be used as deemed appropriate by the Administrator as provided in paragraphs (1) and (2) of this subsection, upon the request of and demonstration of water quality benefits by the Governor of an affected State.

(o) The Administrator shall encourage and assist applicants for grant assistance under this title to develop and file with the Administrator a capital financing plan which, at a minimum—

(1) projects the future requirements for waste treatment services within

the applicant's jurisdiction for a period of no less than ten years;

(2) projects the nature, extent, timing, and costs of future expansion and reconstruction of treatment works which will be necessary to satisfy the applicant's projected future requirements for waste treatment services; and

(3) sets forth with specificity the manner in which the applicant intends to finance such future expansion and reconstruction.

(p) In any case in which a dispute arises with respect to the awarding of a contract for construction of treatment works by a grantee of funds under this title and a party to such dispute files an appeal with the Administrator under this title for resolution of such dispute, the Administrator shall make a final decision on such appeal within 90 days of the filing of such appeal.

§ 1282. Federal share

[Sec. 202] (a)(1) The amount of any grant for treatment works made under this Act from funds authorized for any fiscal year beginning after June 30, 1971, and ending before October 1, 1984, shall be 75 per centum of the cost of construction thereof (as approved by the Administrator), and for any fiscal year beginning on or after October 1, 1984, shall be 55 per centum of the cost of construction thereof (as approved by the Administrator), unless modified to a lower percentage rate uniform throughout a State by the Governor of that State with the concurrence of the Administrator. Within ninety days after the enactment of this sentence the Administrator shall issue guidelines for concurrence in any such modification, which shall provide for the consideration of the unobligated balance of sums allocated to the State under section 205 of this Act, the need for assistance under this title in such State, and the availability of State grant assistance to replace the Federal share reduced by such modification. The payment of any such reduced Federal share shall not constitute an obligation on the part of the United States or a claim on the part of any State or grantee to reimbursement for the portion of the Federal share reduced in any such State. Any grant (other than for reimbursement) made prior to the date of enactment of the Federal Water Pollution Control Act Amendments of 1972 from any funds authorized for any fiscal year beginning after June 30, 1971, shall, upon the request of the applicant, be increased to the applicable percentage under this section. Notwithstanding the first sentence of this paragraph, in any case where a primary, secondary, or advanced waste treatment facility or its related interceptors or a project for infiltration-in-flow correction has received a grant for erection, building, acquisition, alteration, remodeling, improvement, extension, or correction before October 1, 1984, all segments and phases of such facility, interceptors, and project for infiltration-in-flow correction shall be eligible for grants at 75 per centum of the cost of construction thereof for any grant made pursuant to a State obligation which obligation occurred before October 1, 1990. Notwithstanding the first sentence of this paragraph, in the case of a project for which an application for a grant under this title has been made to the Administrator before October 1, 1984, and which project is under judicial injunction on such date prohibiting its construction, such project shall be eligible for grants at 75 percent of the cost of construction thereof. Notwithstanding the first sentence of this paragraph, in the case of the Wyoming Valley Sanitary Authority project mandated by judicial order under a proceeding begun prior to October 1, 1984, and a project for wastewater treatment for Altoona, Pennsylvania, such projects shall be eligible for grants at 75 percent of the cost of construction thereof.

(2) The amount of any grant made after September 30, 1978, and before October 1, 1981, for any eligible treatment works or significant portion thereof utilizing innovative or alternative wastewater treatment processes and techniques referred to in section 201(g)(5) shall be 85 per centum of the cost of construction thereof unless modified by the Governor of the State with the concurrence of the Administrator to a percentage rate no less than 15 percentum greater than the modified uniform percentage rate in which the Administrator has concurred pursuant to paragraph (1) of this subsection. The amount of any grant made after September 30, 1981, for any eligible treatment works or unit processes and techniques thereof utilizing innovative or alternative wastewater treatment processes and techniques referred to in section 201(g)(5) shall be a percentage of the cost of construction thereof equal to 20 per centum greater than the percentage in effect under paragraph (1) of this subsection for such works or unit processes and techniques, but in no event greater than 85 per centum of the cost of construction thereof. No grant shall be made under this paragraph for construction of a treatment works in any State unless the proportion of the State contribution to the non-Federal share of construction costs for all treatment works in such State receiving a grant under this paragraph is the same as or greater than the proportion of the State contribution (if any) to the non-Federal share of construction costs for all treatment works receiving grants in such State under paragraph (1) of this subsection.

(3) In addition to any grant made pursuant to paragraph (2) of this subsection, the Administrator is authorized to make a grant to fund all of the costs of the modification or replacement of any facilities constructed with a grant made pursuant to paragraph (2) if the Administrator finds that such facilities have not met design performance specifications unless such failure is attributable to negligence on the part of any person and if such failure has significantly increased capital or operating and maintenance expenditures. In addition, the Administrator is authorized to make a grant to fund all of the costs of the modification or replacement of biodisc equipment (rotating biological contactors) in any publicly owned treatment works if the Administrator finds that such equipment has failed to meet design

performance specifications, unless such failure is attributable to negligence on the part of any person, and if such failure has significantly increased capital or operating and maintenance expenditures.

(4) For the purposes of this section, the term "eligible treatment works" means those treatment works in each State which meet the requirements of section 201(g)(5) of this Act and which can be fully funded from funds available for such purpose in such State.

(b) The amount of the grant for any project approved by the Administrator after January 1, 1971, and before July 1, 1971, for the construction of treatment works, the actual erection, building or acquisition of which was not commenced prior to July 1, 1971, shall, upon the request of the applicant, be increased to the applicable percentage under subsection (a) of this section for grants for treatment works from funds for fiscal years beginning after June 30, 1971, with respect to the cost of such actual erection, building, or acquisition. Such increased amount shall be paid from any funds allocated to the State in which the treatment works is located without regard to the fiscal year for which such funds were authorized. Such increased amount shall be paid for such project only if—

(1) a sewage collection system that is a part of the same total waste treatment system as the treatment works for which such grant was approved is under construction or is to be constructed for use in conjunction with such treatment works, and if the cost of such sewage collection system exceeds the cost of such treatment works, and

(2) the State water pollution control agency or other appropriate State authority certifies that the quantity of available ground water will be insufficient, inadequate, or unsuitable for public use, including the ecological preservation and recreational use of surface water bodies, unless effluents from publicly owned treatment works after adequate treatment are returned to the ground water consistent with acceptable technological standards.

§ 1283. Plans, specifications, estimates, and payments

[Sec. 203] (a)(1) Each applicant for a grant shall submit to the Administrator for his approval, plans, specifications, and estimates for each proposed project for the construction of treatment works for which a grant is applied for under section 201(g)(1) from funds allotted to the State under section 205 and which otherwise meets the requirements of this Act. The Administrator shall act upon such plans, specifications, and estimates as soon as practicable after the same have been submitted, and his approval of any such plans, specifications, and estimates shall be deemed a contractual obligation of the United States for the payment of its proportional contribution to such project.

(2)(A) Before taking final action on any plans, specifications, and estimates submitted under this subsection after the 60th day following the date of the enactment of the Water Quality Act of 1987, the Administrator shall enter into a written agreement with the applicant which establishes and specifies which items of the proposed project are eligible for Federal payments under this section. The Administrator may not later modify such eligibility determinations unless they are found to have been made in violation of applicable Federal statutes and regulations.

(B) Eligibility determinations under this paragraph shall not preclude the Administrator from auditing a project pursuant to section 501 of this Act, or other authority, or from withholding or recovering Federal funds for costs which are found to be unreasonable, unsupported by adequate documentation, or otherwise unallowable under applicable Federal cost principles, or which are incurred on a project which fails to meet the design specifications or effluent limitations contained in the grant agreement and permit pursuant to section 402 of this Act for such project.

(3) In the case of a treatment works that has an estimated total cost of $8,000,000 or less (as determined by the Administrator), and the population of the applicant municipality is twenty-five thousand or less (according to the most recent United States census), upon completion of an approved facility plan, a single grant may be awarded for the combined Federal share of the cost of preparing construction plans and specifications, and the building and erection of the treatment works.

(b) The Administrator shall, from time to time as the work progresses, make payments to the recipient of a grant for costs of construction incurred on a project. These payments shall at no time exceed the Federal share of the cost of construction incurred to the date of the voucher covering such payment plus the Federal share of the value of the materials which have been stockpiled in the vicinity of such construction in conformity to plans and specifications for the project.

(c) After completion of a project and approval of the final voucher by the Administrator, he shall pay out of the appropriate sums the unpaid balance of the Federal share payable on account of such project.

(d) Nothing in this Act shall be construed to require, or to authorize the Administrator to require, that grants under this Act for construction of treatment works be made only for projects which are operable units usable for sewage collection, transportation, storage, waste treatment, or for similar purposes without additional construction.

(e) At the request of a grantee under this title, the Administrator is authorized to provide technical and legal assistance in the administration and enforcement of any contract in connection with treatment works assisted under this title, and to intervene in any civil action involving the enforcement of such a contract.

(f)(1) Consistent with State law, an applicant who proposes to construct waste water treatment works may enter into an agreement with the Administrator under this subsection providing for the preparation of construction plans and specifications and the erection of such treatment works, in lieu of proceeding under the other provisions of this section.

(2) Agreements under this subsection shall be limited to projects under an approved facility plan which projects are—

(A) treatment works that have an estimated total cost of $8,000,000 or less; and

(B) any of the following types of waste water treatment systems: aerated lagoons, trickling filters, stabilization ponds, land application systems, sand filters, and subsurface disposal systems.

(3) An agreement entered into under this subsection shall—

(A) set forth an amount agreed to as the maximum Federal contribution to the project, based upon a competitively bid document of basic design data and applicable standard construction specifications and a determination of the federally eligible costs of the project at the applicable Federal share under section 202 of this Act;

(B) set forth dates for the start and completion of construction of the treatment works by the applicant and a schedule of payments of the Federal contribution to the project;

(C) contain assurances by the applicant that (i) engineering and management assistance will be provided to manage the project; (ii) the proposed treatment works will be an operable unit and will meet all the requirements of this title; and (iii) not later than 1 year after the date specified as the date of completion of construction of the treatment works, the treatment works will be operating so as to meet the requirements of any applicable permit for such treatment works under section 402 of this Act;

(D) require the applicant to obtain a bond from the contractor in an amount determined necessary by the Administrator to protect the Federal interest in the project; and

(E) contain such other terms and conditions as are necessary to assure compliance with this title (except as provided in paragraph (4) of this subsection).

(4) Subsections (a), (b), and (c) of this section shall not apply to grants made pursuant to this subsection.

(5) The Administrator shall reserve a portion of the grant to assure contract compliance until final project approval as defined by the Administrator. If the amount agreed to under paragraph (3)(A) exceeds the cost of designing and constructing the treatment works, the Administrator shall reallot the amount of the excess to the State in which such treatment works are located for the fiscal year in which such audit is completed.

(6) The Administrator shall not obligate more than 20 percent of the amount allotted to a State for a fiscal year under section 205 of this

Act for grants pursuant to this subsection.

(7) The Administrator shall determine an allowance for facilities planning for projects constructed under this subsection in accordance with section 201(l).

(8) In no event shall the Federal contribution for the cost of preparing construction plans and specifications and the building and erection of treatment works pursuant to this subsection exceed the amount agreed upon under paragraph (3).

(9) In any case in which the recipient of a grant made pursuant to this subsection does not comply with the terms of the agreement entered into under paragraph (3), the Administrator is authorized to take such action as may be necessary to recover the amount of the Federal contribution to the project.

(10) A recipient of a grant made pursuant to this subsection shall not be eligible for any other grants under this title for the same project.

§ 1284. Limitations and conditions

[Sec. 204] (a) Before approving grants for any project for any treatment works under section 201(g)(1) the Administrator shall determine—

(1) that any required areawide waste treatment management plan under section 208 of this Act (A) is being implemented for such area and the proposed treatment works are included in such plan, or (B) is being developed for such area and reasonable progress is being made toward its implementation and the proposed treatment works will be included in such plan;

(2) that (A) the State in which the project is to be located (i) is implementing any required plan under section 303(e) of this Act and the proposed treatment works are in conformity with such plan, or (ii) is developing such a plan and the proposed treatment works will be in conformity with such plan, and (B) such State is in compliance with section 305(b) of this Act;

(3) that such works have been certified by the appropriate State water pollution control agency as entitled to priority over such other works in the State in accordance with any applicable State plan under section 303(e) of this Act, except that any priority list developed pursuant to section 303(e)(3)(H) may be modified by such State in accordance with regulations promulgated by the Administrator to give higher priority for grants for the Federal share of the cost of preparing construction drawings and specifications for any treatment works utilizing processes and techniques meeting the guidelines promulgated under section 304(d)(3) of this Act and for grants for the combined Federal share of the cost of preparing construction drawings and specifications and the building and erection of any treatment works meeting the requirements of the next to the last sentence of section

203(a) of this Act which utilizes processes and techniques meeting the guidelines promulgated under section 304(d)(3) of this Act;

(4) that the applicant proposing to construct such works agrees to pay the non-Federal costs of such works and has made adequate provisions satisfactory to the Administrator for assuring proper and efficient operation, including the employment of trained management and operations personnel, and the maintenance of such works in accordance with a plan of operation approved by the State water pollution control agency or, as appropriate, the interstate agency, after construction thereof;

(5) that the size and capacity of such works relate directly to the needs to be served by such works, including sufficient reserve capacity. The amount of reserve capacity provided shall be approved by the Administrator on the basis of a comparison of the cost of constructing such reserves as a part of the works to be funded and the anticipated cost of providing expanded capacity at a date when such capacity will be required after taking into account, in accordance with regulations promulgated by the Administrator, efforts to reduce total flow of sewage and unnecessary water consumption. The amount of reserve capacity eligible for a grant under this title shall be determined by the Administrator taking into account the projected population and associated commercial and industrial establishments within the jurisdiction of the applicant to be served by such treatment works as identified in an approved facilities plan, an areawide plan under section 208; or an applicable municipal master plan of development. For the purpose of this paragraph, section 208, and any such plan, projected population shall be determined on the basis of the latest information available from the United States Department of Commerce or from the States as the Administrator, by regulation, determines appropriate. Beginning October 1, 1984, no grant shall be made under this title to construct that portion of any treatment works providing reserve capacity in excess of existing needs (including existing needs of residential, commercial, industrial, and other users) on the date of approval of a grant for the erection, building, acquisition, alteration, remodeling, improvement, or extension of a project for secondary treatment or more stringent treatment or new interceptors and appurtenances, except that in no event shall reserve capacity of a facility and its related interceptors to which this subsection applies be in excess of existing needs on October 1, 1990. In any case in which an applicant proposes to provide reserve capacity greater than that eligible for Federal financial assistance under this title, the incremental costs of the additional reserve capacity shall be paid by the applicant;

(6) that no specification for bids in connection with such works shall be written in such a manner as to contain proprietary, exclusionary, or discriminatory requirements other than those based upon perfor-

mance, unless such requirements are necessary to test or demonstrate a specific thing or to provide for necessary interchangeability of parts and equipment. When in the judgment of the grantee, it is impractical or uneconomical to make a clear and accurate description of the technical requirements, a "brand name or equal" description may be used as a means to define the performance or other salient requirements of a procurement, and in doing so the grantee need not establish the existence of any source other than the brand or source so named.

(b)(1) Notwithstanding any other provision of this title, the Administrator shall not approve any grant for any treatment works under section 201(g)(1) after March 1, 1973, unless he shall first have determined that the applicant (A) has adopted or will adopt a system of charges to assure that each recipient of waste treatment services within the applicant's jurisdiction, as determined by the Administrator, will pay its proportionate share (except as otherwise provided in this paragraph) of the costs of operation and maintenance (including replacement) of any waste treatment services provided by the applicant; and (B) has legal, institutional, managerial, and financial capability to insure adequate construction, operation, and maintenance of treatment works throughout the applicant's jurisdiction, as determined by the Administrator. In any case where an applicant which, as of the date of enactment of this sentence, uses a system of dedicated ad valorem taxes and the Administrator determines that the applicant has a system of charges which results in the distribution of operation and maintenance costs for treatment works within the applicant's jurisdiction, to each user class, in proportion to the contribution to the total cost of operation and maintenance of such works by each user class (taking into account total waste water loading of such works, the constituent elements of the waste, and other appropriate factors) and such applicant is otherwise in compliance with clause (A) of this paragraph with respect to each industrial user, then such dedicated ad valorem tax system shall be deemed to be the user charge system meeting the requirements of clause (A) of this paragraph for the residential user class and such small non-residential user classes as defined by the Administrator. In defining small non-residential users, the Administrator shall consider the volume of wastes discharged into the treatment works by such users and the constituent elements of such wastes as well as such other factors as he deems appropriate. A system of user charges which imposes a lower charge for low-income residential users (as defined by the Administrator) shall be deemed to be a user charge system meeting the requirements of clause (A) of this paragraph if the Administrator determines that such system was adopted after public notice and hearing.

(2) The Administrator shall, within one hundred and eighty days after the date of enactment of the Federal Water Pollution Control Act Amendments of 1972, and after consultation with appropriate State, interstate, municipal, and intermunicipal agencies, issue guidelines applicable to payment of waste treatment costs by industrial and

nonindustrial recipients of waste treatment services which shall establish (A) classes of users of such services, including categories of industrial users; (B) criteria against which to determine the adequacy of charges imposed on classes and categories of users reflecting all factors that influence the cost of waste treatment, including strength, volume, and delivery flow rate characteristics of waste; and (C) model systems and rates of user charges typical of various treatment works serving municipal-industrial communities.

(3) Approval by the Administrator of a grant to an interstate agency established by interstate compact for any treatment works shall satisfy any other requirement that such works be authorized by Act of Congress.

(4) A system of charges which meets the requirement of clause (A) of paragraph (1) of this subsection may be based on something other than metering the sewage or water supply flow of residential recipients of waste treatment services, including ad valorem taxes. If the system of charges is based on something other than metering the Administrator shall require (A) the applicant to establish a system by which maintenance of the treatment works; and (B) the applicant to establish a procedure under which the residential user will be notified as to that portion of his total payment which will be allocated to the costs of the waste treatment services.

(c) The next to the last sentence of paragraph (5) of subsection (a) of this section shall not apply in any case where a primary, secondary or advanced waste treatment facility or its related interceptors has received a grant for erection, building, acquisition, alteration, remodeling, improvement, or extension before October 1, 1984, and all segments and phases of such facility and interceptors shall be funded based on a 20-year reserve capacity in the case of such facility and a 20-year reserve capacity in the case of such interceptors, except that, if a grant for such interceptors has been approved prior to the date of enactment of the Municipal Wastewater Treatment Construction Grant Amendments of 1981, such interceptors shall be funded based on the approved reserve capacity not to exceed 40 years.

(d)(1) A grant for the construction of treatment works under this title shall provide that the engineer or engineering firm supervising construction or providing architect engineering services during construction shall continue its relationship to the grant applicant for a period of one year after the completion of construction and initial operation of such treatment works. During such period such engineer or engineering firm shall supervise operation of the treatment works, train operating personnel, and prepare curricula and training material for operating personnel. Costs associated with the implementation of this paragraph shall be eligible for Federal assistance in accordance with this title.

(2) On the date one year after the completion of construction and initial operation of such treatment works, the owner and operator of such

treatment works shall certify to the Administrator whether or not such treatment works meet the design specifications and effluent limitations contained in the grant agreement and permit pursuant to section 402 of the Act for such works. If the owner or operator of such treatment works cannot certify that such treatment works meet such design specifications and effluent limitations, any failure to meet such design specifications and effluent limitations shall be corrected in a timely manner, to allow such affirmative certification, at other than Federal expense.

(3) Nothing in this section shall be construed to prohibit a grantee under this title from requiring more assurances, guarantees, or indemnity or other contractual requirements from any party to a contract pertaining to a project assisted under this title, than those provided under this subsection.

§ 1285. Allotment of grant funds

[Sec. 205] (a) Sums authorized to be appropriated pursuant to section 207 for each fiscal year beginning after June 30, 1972, and before September 30, 1977, shall be allotted by the Administrator not later than the January 1st immediately preceding the beginning of the fiscal year for which authorized, except that the allotment for fiscal year 1973 shall be made not later than 30 days after the date of enactment of the Federal Water Pollution Control Act Amendments of 1972. Such sums shall be allotted among the States by the Administrator in accordance with regulations promulgated by him, in the ratio that the estimated cost of constructing all needed publicly owned treatment works in each State bears to the estimated cost of construction of all needed publicly owned treatment works in all of the States. For the fiscal years ending June 30, 1973, and June 30, 1974, such ratio shall be determined on the basis of the table III of House Public Works Committee Print No. 92–50.

For the fiscal year ending June 30, 1975, such ratio shall be determined one-half on the basis of table I of House Public Works Committee Print Numbered 93–28 and one-half on the basis of table II of such print, except that no State shall receive an allotment less than that which it received for the fiscal year ending June 30, 1972, as set forth in table III of such print. Allotments for fiscal years which begin after the fiscal year ending June 30, 1975 shall be made only in accordance with a revised cost estimate made and submitted to Congress in accordance with section 516(b) of this Act and only after such revised cost estimate shall have been approved by law specifically enacted hereafter.

(b)(1) Any sums allotted to a State under subsection (a) shall be available for obligation under section 203 on and after the date of such allotment. Such sums shall continue available for obligation in such State for a period of one year after the close of the fiscal year for which such sums are authorized. Any amount so allotted which are not obligated by the end of such one-year period shall be immediately reallotted by the Administrator, in accordance with regulations promulgated by him, generally on the basis of the ratio used in making the last allotment of sums under this section. Such reallotted sums shall be added to the last allotments made to the States. Any sum made available to a State by reallotment under this subsection shall be in addition to any funds otherwise allotted to such State for grants under this title during any fiscal year.

(2) Any sums which have been obligated under section 203 and which are released by the payment of the final voucher for the project shall be immediately credited to the State to which such sums were last allotted. Such released sums shall be added to the amounts last allotted to such State and shall be immediately available for obligation in the same manner and to the same extent as such last allotment.

(c)(1) Sums authorized to be appropriated pursuant to section 207 for the fiscal years during the period beginning October 1, 1977, and ending September 30, 1981, shall be allotted for each such year by the Administrator not later than the tenth day which begins after the date of enactment of the Clean Water Act of 1977. Notwithstanding any other provision of law, sums authorized for the fiscal years ending September 30, 1978, September 30, 1979, September 30, 1980, and September 30, 1981, shall be allotted in accordance with table 3 of Committee Print Numbered 95-30 of the Committee on Public Works and Transportation of the House of Representatives.

(2) Sums authorized to be appropriated pursuant to section 207 for the fiscal years 1982, 1983, 1984, and 1985 shall be allotted for each such year by the Administrator not later than the tenth day which begins after the date of enactment of the Municipal Wastewater Treatment Construction Grant Amendments of 1981. Notwithstanding any other provision of law, sums authorized for the fiscal year ending September 30, 1982, shall be allotted in accordance with table 3 of Committee Print Numbered 95-30 of the Committee on Public Works and Transportation of the House of Representatives. Sums authorized for the fiscal years ending September 30, 1983, September 30, 1984, September 30, 1985, and September 30, 1986, shall be allotted in accordance with the following table:

States:	Fiscal years 1983 through 1985
Alabama	.011398
Alaska	.006101
Arizona	.006885
Arkansas	.006668
California	.072901
Colorado	.008154
Connecticut	.012487

Delaware	.004965
District of Columbia	.004965
Florida	.034407
Georgia	.017234
Hawaii	.007895
Idaho	.004965
Illinois	.046101
Indiana	.024566
Iowa	.013796
Kansas	.009201
Kentucky	.012973
Louisiana	.011205
Maine	.007788
Maryland	.024653
Massachusetts	.034608
Michigan	.043829
Minnesota	.018735
Mississippi	.009184
Missouri	.028257
Montana	.004965
Nebraska	.005214
Nevada	.004965
New Hampshire	.010186
New Jersey	.041654
New Mexico	.004965
New York	.113097
North Carolina	.018396
North Dakota	.004965
Ohio	.057383
Oklahoma	.008235
Oregon	.011515
Pennsylvania	.040377
Rhode Island	.006750
South Carolina	.010442
South Dakota	.004965
Tennessee	.014807
Texas	.038726
Utah	.005371
Vermont	.004965
Virginia	.020861
Washington	.017726
West Virginia	.015890
Wisconsin	.027557
Wyoming	.004965
Samoa	.000915

Guam	.000662
Northern Marianas	.000425
Puerto Rico	.013295
Pacific Trust Territories	.001305
Virgin Islands	.000531
United States totals	.999996

(3) Sums authorized to be appropriated pursuant to section 207 for the fiscal years 1987, 1988, 1989, and 1990 shall be allotted for each such year by the Administrator not later than the 10th day which begins after the date of the enactment of this paragraph. Sums authorized for such fiscal years shall be allotted in accordance with the following table:

States:	**Fiscal years 1987 through 1990**
Alabama	.011309
Alaska	.006053
Arizona	.006831
Arkansas	.006616
California	.072333
Colorado	.008090
Connecticut	.012390
Delaware	.004965
District of Columbia	.004965
Florida	.034139
Georgia	.017100
Hawaii	.007833
Idaho	.004965
Illinois	.045741
Indiana	.024374
Iowa	.013688
Kansas	.009129
Kentucky	.012872
Louisiana	.011118
Maine	.007829
Maryland	.024461
Massachusetts	.034338
Michigan	.043487
Minnesota	.018589
Mississippi	.009112
Missouri	.028037
Montana	.004965
Nebraska	.005173
Nevada	.004965
New Hampshire	.010107

New Jersey	.041329
New Mexico	.004965
New York	.111632
North Carolina	.018253
North Dakota	.004965
Ohio	.056936
Oklahoma	.008171
Oregon	.0125
Pennsylvania	.040062
Rhode Island	.006791
South Carolina	.010361
South Dakota	.004965
Tennessee	.014692
Texas	.046226
Utah	.005329
Vermont	.004965
Virginia	.020698
Washington	.017588
West Virginia	.015766
Wisconsin	.027342
Wyoming	.004965
American Samoa	.000908
Guam	.000657
Northern Marianas	.000422
Puerto Rico	.013191
Pacific Trust Territories	.001295
Virgin Islands	.000527
United States totals	.999996

(d) Sums allotted to the States for a fiscal year shall remain available for obligation for the fiscal year for which authorized and for the period of the next succeeding twelve months. The amount of any allotment not obligated by the end of such twenty-four-month period shall be immediately reallotted by the Administrator on the basis of the same ratio as applicable to sums allotted for the then current fiscal year, except that none of the funds reallotted by the Administrator for fiscal year 1978 and for fiscal years thereafter shall be allotted to any State which failed to obligate any of the funds being reallotted. Any sum made available to a State by reallotment under this subsection shall be in addition to any funds otherwise allotted to such State for grants under this title during any fiscal year.

(e) For the fiscal years 1978, 1979, 1980, 1981, 1982, 1983, 1984, 1985, 1986, 1987, 1988, 1989, and 1990, no State shall receive less than one-half of 1 per centum of the total allotment under subsection (c) of this section, except that in the case of Guam, Virgin Islands, American Samoa, and the Trust Territories not more than thirty-three one-hundredths of 1 per centum on the aggregate shall be allotted to all four of these jurisdictions. For the purpose of carrying out this subsection there are authorized to be appropriated, subject to such amounts as are provided in appropriation Acts, not to exceed $75,000,000 for each of fiscal years 1978, 1979, 1980, 1981, 1982, 1983, 1984, 1985, 1986, 1987, 1988, 1989, and 1990. If for any fiscal year the amount appropriated under authority of this subsection is less than the amount necessary to carry out this subsection, the amount each State receives under this subsection for such year shall bear the same ratio to the amount such State would have received under this subsection in such year if the amount necessary to carry it out had been appropriated as the amount appropriated for such year bears to the amount necessary to carry out this subsection for such year.

(f) Notwithstanding any other provision of this section, sums made available between January 1, 1975, and March 1, 1975, by the Administrator for obligation shall be available for obligation until September 30, 1978.

(g)(1) The Administrator is authorized to reserve each fiscal year not to exceed 2 percentum of the amount authorized under section 207 of this title for purposes of the allotment made to each State under this section on or after October 1, 1977, except in the case of any fiscal year beginning on or after October 1, 1981, and ending before October 1, 1994, in which case the percentage authorized to be reserved shall not exceed 4 per centum, or $400,000 whichever amount is the greater. Sums so reserved shall be available for making grants to such State under paragraph (2) of this subsection for the same period as sums are available from such allotment under subsection (d) of this section, and any such grant shall be available for obligation only during such period. Any grant made from sums reserved under this subsection which has not been obligated by the end of the period for which available shall be added to the amount last allotted to such State under this section and shall be immediately available for obligation in the same manner and to the same extent as such last allotment. Sums authorized to be reserved by this paragraph shall be in addition to and not in lieu of any other funds which may be authorized to carry out this subsection.

(2) The Administrator is authorized to grant to any State from amounts reserved to such State under this subsection, the reasonable costs of administering any aspects of sections 201, 203, 204, and 212 of this Act the responsibility for administration of which the Administrator has delegated to such State. The Administrator may increase such grant to take into account the reasonable costs of administering an approved program under section 402 or 404, administering a statewide waste treatment management planning program under section 208(b)(4), and managing waste treatment construction grants for small communities.

(h) The Administrator shall set aside from funds authorized for each fiscal year beginning on or after October 1, 1978, a total (as determined by the Governor of the State) of not less than 4 percent nor more than 7 1/2 percent of the sums allotted to any State with a rural population of 25 per centum or more of the total population of such State, as determined by the Bureau of the Census. The Administrator may set aside no more than 7 1/2 percent of the sums allotted to any other State for which the Governor requests such action. Such sums shall be available only for alternatives to conventional sewage treatment works for municipalities having a population of three thousand five hundred or less, or for the highly dispersed sections of larger municipalities, as defined by the Administrator.

(i) Not less than 1/2 of 1 percent of funds allotted to a State for each of the fiscal years ending September 30, 1979, through September 30, 1990, under subsection (c) of this section shall be expended only for increasing the Federal share of grants for construction of treatment works utilizing innovative processes and techniques pursuant to section 202(a)(2) of this Act. Including the expenditures authorized by the preceding sentence, a total of 2 percent of the funds allotted to a State for each of the fiscal years ending September 30, 1979, and September 30, 1980, and 3 percent of the funds allotted to a State for the fiscal year ending September 30, 1981, under subsection (c) of this section shall be expended only for increasing grants for construction of treatment works pursuant to section 202(a)(2) of this Act. Including the expenditures authorized by the first sentence of this subsection, a total (as determined by the Governor of the State) of not less than 4 percent nor more than 7 1/2 percent of the funds allotted to such State under subsection (c) of this section for each of the fiscal years ending September 30, 1982, through September 30, 1990, shall be expended only for increasing the Federal share of grants for construction of treatment works pursuant to section 202(a)(2) of this Act.

(j)(1) The Administrator shall reserve each fiscal year not to exceed 1 per centum of the sums allotted and available for obligation to each State under this section for each fiscal year beginning on or after October 1, 1981, or $100,000, whichever amount is the greater.

(2) Such sums shall be used by the Administrator to make grants to the States to carry out water quality management planning, including, but not limited to—

(A) identifying most cost effective and locally acceptable facility and non-point measures to meet and maintain water quality standards;

(B) developing an implementation plan to obtain State and local financial and regulatory commitments to implement measures developed under subparagraph (A);

(C) determining the nature, extent, and causes of water quality problems in various areas of the State and interstate region, and reporting on these annually; and

(D) determining those publicly owned treatment works which should be constructed with assistance under this title, in which areas and in what sequence, taking into account the relative degree of effluent reduction attained, the relative contributions to water quality of other point or nonpoint sources, and the consideration of alternatives to such construction, and implementing section 303(e) of this Act.

(3) In carrying out planning with grants made under paragraph (2) of this subsection, a State shall develop jointly with local, regional, and interstate entities, a plan for carrying out the program and give funding priority to such entities and designated or undesignated public comprehensive planning organizations to carry out the purposes of this subsection. In giving such priority, the State shall allocate at least 40 percent of the amount granted to such State for a fiscal year under paragraph (2) of this subsection to regional public comprehensive planning organizations in such State and appropriate interstate organizations for the development and implementation of the plan described in this paragraph. In any fiscal year for which the Governor, in consultation with such organizations and with the approval of the Administrator, determines that allocation of at least 40 percent of such amount to such organizations will not result in significant participation by such organizations in water quality management planning and not significantly assist in development and implementation of the plan described in this paragraph and achieving the goals of this Act, the allocation to such organization may be less than 40 percent of such amount.

(4) All activities undertaken under this subsection shall be in coordination with other related provisions of this Act.

(5) In addition to the sums reserved under paragraph (1), the Administrator shall reserve each fiscal year for each State 1 percent of the sums allotted and available for obligation to such State under this section for each fiscal year beginning on or after October 1, 1986, or $100,000, whichever is greater, for the purpose of carrying out section 319 of this Act. Sums so reserved in a State in any fiscal year for which such State does not request the use of such sums, to the extent such sums exceed $100,000, may be used by such State for other purposes under this title.

(k) The Administrator shall allot to the State of New York from sums authorized to be appropriated for the fiscal year ending September 30, 1982, an amount necessary to pay the entire cost of conveying sewage from the Convention Center of the city of New York to the Newtown sewage treatment plant, Brooklyn-Queens area, New York. The amount allotted under this subsection shall be in addition to and not in lieu of any other amounts authorized to be allotted to such state under this Act.

(l)(1)(A) Prior to making allotments among the States under subsection (c) of this section, the Administrator shall reserve funds from sums appropriated pursuant to section 207 for each fiscal year beginning after September 30, 1986.

(B) For each of fiscal years 1987 and 1988 the reservation shall be 1 percent of the sums appropriated pursuant to section 207 for such fiscal year.

(C) For each of fiscal years 1989 and 1990 the reservation shall be 1 1/2 percent of the funds appropriated pursuant to section 207 for such fiscal year.

(2) Of the sums reserved under this subsection, two-thirds shall be available to address water quality problems of marine bays and estuaries subject to lower levels of water quality due to the impacts of discharges from combined storm water and sanitary sewer overflows from adjacent urban complexes, and one-third shall be available for the implementation of section 320 of this Act, relating to the national estuary program.

(3) Sums reserved under this subsection shall be subject to the period of availability for obligation established by subsection (d) of this section.

(4) For purposes of this section and section 201(n), Newark Bay, New Jersey, and the portion of the Passaic River up to Little Falls, in the vicinity of Beatties Dam, shall be treated as a marine bay and estuary.

(m)(1) In addition to any amounts deposited in a water pollution control revolving fund established by a State under title VI, upon request of the Governor of such State, the Administrator shall make available to the State for deposit, as capitalization grants, in such fund in any fiscal year beginning after September 30, 1986, such portion of the amounts allotted to such State under this section for such fiscal year as the Governor considers appropriate; except that (A) in fiscal year 1987, such deposit may not exceed 50 percent of the amounts allotted to such State under this section for such fiscal year, and (B) in fiscal year 1988, such deposit may not exceed 75 percent of the amounts allotted to such State under this section for this fiscal year.

(2) The Governor of a State may make a request under paragraph (1) for a deposit into the water pollution control revolving fund of such State—

(A) in fiscal year 1987 only if no later than 90 days after the date of the enactment of this subsection, and

(B) in each fiscal year thereafter only if 90 days before the first day of such fiscal year, the State provides notice of its intent to make such deposit.

(3) Sums reserved under section 205(j) of this Act shall not be available for obligation under this subsection.

§ 1286. Reimbursement and advanced construction

[Sec. 206] (a) Any publicly owned treatment works in a State on which construction was initiated after June 30, 1966, but before July 1, 1973, which was approved by the appropriate State water pollution control agency and which the Administrator finds meets the requirements of section 8 of this Act in effect at the time of the initiation of construction shall be reimbursed a total amount equal to the difference between the amount of Federal financial assistance, if any, received under such section 8 for such project and 50 per centum of the cost of such project, or 55 per centum of the project cost where the Administrator also determines that such treatment works was constructed in conformity with a comprehensive metropolitan treatment plan as described in section 8(f) of the Federal Water Pollution Control Act as in effect immediately prior to the date of enactment of the Federal Water Pollution Control Act Amendments of 1972. Nothing in this subsection shall result in any such works receiving Federal grants from all sources in excess of 80 per centum of the cost of such project.

(b) Any publicly owned treatment works constructed with or eligible for Federal financial assistance under this Act in a State between June 30, 1956, and June 30, 1966, which was approved by the State water pollution control agency and which the Administrator finds meets the requirements of section 8 of this Act prior to the date of enactment of the Federal Water Pollution Control Act Amendments of 1972 but which was constructed without assistance under such section 8 or which received such assistance in an amount less than 30 per centum of the cost of such project shall qualify for payments and reimbursement of State or local funds used for such project from sums allocated to such State under this section in an amount which shall not exceed the difference between the amount of such assistance, if any, received for such project and 30 per centum of the cost of such project.

(c) No publicly owned treatment works shall receive any payment or reimbursement under subsection (a) or (b) of this section unless an application for such assistance is filed with the Administrator within the one year period which begins on the date of enactment of the Federal Water Pollution Control Act Amendments of 1972. Any application filed within such one year period may be revised from time to time, as may be necessary.

(d) The Administrator shall allocate to each qualified project under subsection (a) of this section each fiscal year for which funds are appropriated under subsection (e) of this section an amount which bears the same ratio to the unpaid balance of the reimbursement due such project as the total of such funds for such year bears to the total unpaid balance of reimbursement due all such approved projects on the date of enactment of such appropriations. The Administrator shall allocate to each qualified project under subsection (b) of this section each fiscal year for which funds are appropriated under subsection (e) of this section an amount which bears the same ratio to the unpaid balance of the reimbursement due such project as the total of such funds for such years bears to the total unpaid balance of reimbursement due all such approved projects on the date of enactment of such appropriation.

(e) There is authorized to be appropriated to carry out subsection (a) of this section not to exceed $2,600,000,000 and to carry out subsection (b) of this section, not to exceed $750,000,000. The authorizations contained in this subsection shall be the sole source of funds for reimbursements authorized by this section.

(f)(1) In any case where a substantial portion of the funds allotted to a State for the current fiscal year under this title have been obligated under section 201(g), or will be so obligated in a timely manner (as determined by the Administrator), and there is construction of any treatment work project without the aid of Federal funds and in accordance with all procedures and all requirements applicable to treatment works projects, except those procedures and requirements which limit construction of projects to those constructed with the aid of previously allotted Federal funds, the Administrator, upon his approval of an application made under this subsection therefor, is authorized to pay the Federal share of the cost of construction of such project when additional funds are allotted to the State under this title if prior to the construction of the project the Administrator approves plans, specifications, and estimates therefor in the same manner as other treatment works projects. The Administrator may not approve an application under this subsection unless an authorization is in effect for the first fiscal year in the period for which the application requests payment and such requested payment for that fiscal year does not exceed the State's expected allotment from such authorization. The Administrator shall not be required to make such requested payment for any fiscal year—

  (A) to the extent that such payment would exceed such State's allotment of the amount appropriated for such fiscal year; and

  (B) unless such payment is for a project which, on the basis of an approved funding priority list of such State, is eligible to receive such payment based on the allotment and appropriation for such fiscal year.

To the extent that sufficient funds are not appropriated to pay the full Federal share with respect to a project for which obligations under the provisions of this subsection have been made, the Administrator shall reduce the Federal share to such amount less than 75 per centum as such appropriations do provide.

  (2) In determining the allotment for any fiscal year under this title, any treatment works project constructed in accordance with this section and without the aid of Federal funds shall not be considered completed until an application under the provisions of this subsection with respect to such project has been approved by the Administrator, or the availability of funds from which this project is eligible for reimbursement has expired, whichever first occurs.

§ 1287. Authorization of appropriations

[Sec. 207] There is authorized to be appropriated to carry out this title, other than sections 206(e), 208 and 209, for the fiscal year ending June 30, 1973, not to exceed $5,000,000,000, for the fiscal year ending June 30, 1974, not to exceed $6,000,000,000, and for the fiscal year ending June 30, 1975, not to exceed $7,000,000,000, and, subject to such amounts as are provided in appropriation Acts, for the fiscal year ending September 30, 1977, $1,000,000,000 for the fiscal year ending September 30, 1978, $4,500,000,000 and for the fiscal years ending September 30, 1979, September 30, 1980, not to exceed $5,000,000,000; for the fiscal year ending September 30, 1981, not to exceed $2,548,837,000; and for the fiscal years ending September 30, 1982, September 30, 1983, September 30, 1984, and September 30, 1985, not to exceed $2,400,000,000 per fiscal year; and for each of the fiscal years ending September 30, 1986, September 30, 1987, and September 30, 1988, not to exceed $2,400,000,000; and for each of the fiscal years ending September 30, 1989, and September 30, 1990, not to exceed $1,200,000,000.

§ 1288. Areawide waste treatment management

[Sec. 208] (a) For the purpose of encouraging and facilitating the development and implementation of areawide waste treatment management plans—

(1) The Administrator, within ninety days after the date of enactment of this Act and after consultation with appropriate Federal, State, and local authorities, shall by regulation publish guidelines for the identification of those areas which, as a result of urban-industrial concentrations or other factors, have substantial water quality control problems.

(2) The Governor of each State, within sixty days after publication of the guidelines issued pursuant to paragraph (1) of this subsection, shall identify each area within the State which, as a result of urban-industrial concentrations or other factors, has substantial water quality control problems. Not later than one hundred and twenty days following such identification and after consultation with appropriate elected and other officials of local governments having jurisdiction in such areas, the Governor shall designate (A) the boundaries of each such area, and (B) a single representative organization, including elected officials from local governments or their designees, capable of developing effective areawide waste treatment management plans for such area. The Governor may in the same manner at any later time identify any additional area (or modify an existing area) for which he determines areawide waste treatment management to be appropriate, designate the boundaries of such area, and designate an organization capable of developing effective areawide waste treatment management plans for such area.

(3) With respect to any area which, pursuant to the guidelines published under paragraph (1) of this subsection, is located in two or more States, the Governors of the respective States shall consult and cooperate in carrying out the provisions of paragraph (2), with a view toward designating the boundaries of the interstate area having common water quality control problems and for which areawide waste

treatment management plans would be most effective, and toward designating, within one hundred and eighty days after publication of guidelines issued pursuant to paragraph (1) of this subsection, of a single representative organization capable of developing effective areawide waste treatment management plans for such area.

(4) If a Governor does not act, either by designating or determining not to make a designation under paragraph (2) of this subsection, within the time required by such paragraph, or if, in the case of an interstate area, the Governors of the States involved do not designate a planning organization within the time required by paragraph (3) of this subsection, the chief elected officials of local governments within an area may by agreement designate (A) the boundaries for such an area, and (B) a single representative organization including elected officials from such local governments, or their designees, capable of developing an areawide waste treatment management plan for such area.

(5) Existing regional agencies may be designated under paragraphs (2), (3), and (4) of this subsection.

(6) The State shall act as a planning agency for all portions of such State which are not designated under paragraphs (2), (3), or (4) of this subsection.

(7) Designations under this subsection shall be subject to the approval of the Administrator.

(b)(1)(A) Not later than one year after the date of designation of any organization under subsection (a) of this section such organization shall have in operation a continuing areawide waste treatment management planning process consistent with section 201 of this Act. Plans prepared in accordance with this process shall contain alternatives for waste treatment management, and be applicable to all wastes generated within the area involved. The initial plan prepared in accordance with such process shall be certified by the Governor and submitted to the Administrator not later than two years after the planning process is in operation.

(B) For any agency designated after 1975 under subsection (a) of this section and for all portions of a State for which the State is required to act as the planning agency in accordance with subsection (a)(6), the initial plan prepared in accordance with such process shall be certified by the Governor and submitted to the Administrator not later than three years after the receipt of the initial grant award authorized under subsection (f) of this section.

(2) Any plan prepared under such process shall include, but not be limited to—

(A) the identification of treatment works necessary to meet the anticipated municipal and industrial waste treatment needs of the area over a twenty-year period, annually updated (including an analysis of alternative waste treatment systems), including any requirements for the acquisition of land for treatment purposes; the necessary waste water collection and urban storm water runoff systems; and a program to provide the necessary financial arrangements for the development of such treatment works, and an identification of open space and recreation opportunities that can be expected to result from improved water quality, including consideration of potential use of lands associated with treatment works and increased access to water-based recreation;

(B) the establishment of construction priorities for such treatment works and time schedules for the initiation and completion of all treatment works;

(C) the establishment of a regulatory program to—

    (i) implement the waste treatment management requirements of section 201(c),

   (ii) regulate the location, modification, and construction of any facilities within such area which may result in any discharge in such area, and

  (iii) assure that any industrial or commercial waste discharged into any treatment works in such area meet applicable pretreatment requirements;

(D) the identification of those agencies necessary to construct, operate, and maintain all facilities required by the plan and otherwise to carry out the plan;

(E) the identification of the measures necessary to carry out the plan (including financing), the period of time necessary to carry out the plan, the costs of carrying out the plan within such time, and the economic, social and environmental impact of carrying out the plan within such time;

(F) a process to (i) identify, if appropriate, agriculturally and silviculturally related nonpoint sources of pollution, including return flows from irrigated agriculture, and their cumulative effects, runoff from manure disposal areas, and from land used for livestock and crop production, and (ii) set forth procedures and methods (including land use requirements) to control to the extent feasible such sources;

(G) a process of (i) identify, if appropriate, mine-related sources of pollution including new, current, and abandoned surface and underground mine runoff, and (ii) set forth procedures and methods (including land use requirements) to control to the extent feasible such sources;

(H) a process to (i) identify construction activity related sources of pollution, and (ii) set forth procedures and methods (including land use requirements) to control to the extent feasible such sources;

(I) a process to (i) identify, if appropriate, salt water intrusion into rivers, lakes, and estuaries resulting from reduction of fresh water flow from any cause, including irrigation, obstruction, ground water extraction, and diversion, and (ii) set forth procedures and methods to control such intrusion to the extent feasible where such procedures and methods are otherwise a part of the waste treatment management plan;

(J) a process to control the disposition of all residual waste generated in such area which could affect water quality; and

(K) a process to control the disposal of pollutants on land or in subsurface excavations within such area to protect ground and surface water quality.

(3) Areawide waste treatment management plans shall be certified annually by the Governor or his designee (or Governors or their designees, where more than one State is involved) as being consistent with applicable basin plans and such areawide waste treatment management plans shall be submitted to the Administrator for his approval.

(4)(A) Whenever the Governor of any State determines (and notifies the Administrator) that consistency with a statewide regulatory program under section 303 so requires, the requirements of clauses (F) through (K) of paragraph (2) of this subsection shall be developed and submitted by the Governor to the Administrator for approval for application to a class or category of activity throughout each State.

(B) Any program submitted under subparagraph (A) of this paragraph which, in whole or in part, is to control the discharge or other placement of dredged or fill material into the navigable waters shall include the following:

(i) A consultation process which includes the State agency with primary jurisdiction over fish and wildlife resources.

(ii) A process to identify and manage the discharge or other placement of dredged or fill material which adversely affects navigable waters, which shall complement and be coordinated with a State program under section 404 conducted pursuant to this Act.

(iii) A process to assure that any activity conducted pursuant to a best management practice will comply with the guidelines established under section 404(b)(1), and sections 307 and 403 of this Act.

(iv) A process to assure that any activity conducted pursuant to a best management practice can be terminated or modified for cause including, but not limited to, the following:

(I) violation of any condition of the best management practice;

(II) change in any activity that requires either a temporary or permanent reduction or elimination of the discharge pursuant to the best management practice.

(v) A process to assure continued coordination with Federal and

Federal-State water-related planning and reviewing processes, including the National Wetlands Inventory.

(C) If the Governor of a State obtains approval from the Administrator of a statewide regulatory program which meets the requirements of subparagraph (B) of this paragraph and if such State is administering a permit program under section 404 of this Act, no person shall be required to obtain an individual permit pursuant to such section, or to comply with a general permit issued pursuant to such section, with respect to any appropriate activity within such State for which a best management practice has been approved by the Administrator under the program approved by the Administrator pursuant to this paragraph.

(D)(i) Whenever the Administrator determines after public hearing that a State is not administering a program approved under this section in accordance with the requirements of this section, the Administrator shall so notify the State, and if appropriate corrective action is not taken within a reasonable time, not to exceed ninety days, the Administrator shall withdraw approval of such program. The Administrator shall not withdraw approval of any such program unless he shall first have notified the State, and made public, in writing, the reasons for such withdrawal.

(ii) In the case of a State with a program submitted and approved under this paragraph, the Administrator shall withdraw approval of such program under this subparagraph only for a substantial failure of the State to administer its program in accordance with the requirements of this paragraph.

(c)(1) The Governor of each State, in consultation with the planning agency designated under subsection (a) of this section, at the time a plan is submitted to the Administrator, shall designate one or more waste treatment management agencies (which may be an existing or newly created local, regional or State agency or potential subdivision) for each area designated under subsection (a) of this section and submit such designations to the Administrator.

(2) The Administrator shall accept any such designation, unless, within 120 days of such designation, he finds that the designated management agency (or agencies) does not have adequate authority—

(A) to carry out appropriate portions of an areawide waste treatment management plan developed under subsection (b) of this section;

(B) to manage effectively waste treatment works and related facilities serving such area in conformance with any plan required by subsection (b) of this section;

(C) directly or by contract, to design and construct new works, and to operate and maintain new and existing works as required by any plan developed pursuant to subsection (b) of this section;

(D) to accept and utilize grants, or other funds from any source, for waste treatment management purposes;

(E) to raise revenues, including the assessment of waste treatment charges;

(F) to incur short- and long-term indebtedness;

(G) to assure in implementation of an areawide waste treatment management plan that each participating community pays its proportionate share of treatment costs;

(H) to refuse to receive any wastes from any municipality or subdivision thereof, which does not comply with any provisions of an approved plan under this section applicable to such area; and

(I) to accept for treatment industrial wastes.

(d) After a waste treatment management agency having the authority required by subsection (c) has been designated under such subsection for an area and a plan for such area has been approved under subsection (b) of this section, the Administrator shall not make any grant for construction of a publicly owned treatment works under section 201(g)(1) within such area except to such designated agency and for works in conformity with such plan.

(e) No permit under section 402 of this Act shall be issued for any point source which is in conflict with a plan approved pursuant to subsection (b) of this section.

(f)(1) The Administrator shall make grants to any agency designated under subsection (a) of this section for payment of the reasonable costs of developing and operating a continuing areawide waste treatment management planning process under subsection (b) of this section.

(2) For the two-year period beginning on the date the first grant is made under paragraph (1) of this subsection to an agency, if such first grant is made before October 1, 1977, the amount of each such grant to such agency shall be 100 per centum of the costs of developing and operating a continuing areawide waste treatment management planning process under subsection (b) of this section, and thereafter the amount granted to such agency shall not exceed 75 per centum of such costs in each succeeding one-year period. In the case of any other grant made to an agency under such paragraph (1) of this subsection, the amount of such grant shall not exceed 75 per centum of the costs of developing and operating a continuing areawide waste treatment management planning process in any year.

(3) Each applicant for a grant under this subsection shall submit to the Administrator for his approval each proposal for which a grant is applied for under this subsection. The Administrator shall act upon such proposal as soon as practicable after it has been submitted, and his approval of that proposal shall be deemed a contractual obligation of the United States for the payment of its contribution to such proposal, subject to such amounts as are provided in appropriation Acts. There is authorized to be appropriated to carry out this

subsection not to exceed $50,000,000 for the fiscal year ending June 30, 1973, not to exceed $100,000,000 for the fiscal year ending June 30, 1974, not to exceed $150,000,000 per fiscal year for the fiscal years ending June 30, 1975, September 30, 1977, September 30, 1978, September 30, 1979, and September 30, 1980, not to exceed $100,000,000 per fiscal year for the fiscal years ending September 30, 1981, and September 30, 1982, and such sums as may be necessary for fiscal years 1983 through 1990.

(g) The Administrator is authorized, upon request of the Governor or the designated planning agency, and without reimbursement, to consult with, and provide technical assistance to, any agency designated under subsection (a) of this section in the development of areawide waste treatment management plans under subsection (b) of this section.

(h)(1) The Secretary of the Army, acting through the Chief of Engineers, in cooperation with the Administrator is authorized and directed, upon request of the Governor or the designated planning organization, to consult with, and provide technical assistance to, any agency designed under subsection (a) of this section in developing and operating a continuing areawide waste treatment management planning process under subsection (b) of this section.

(2) There is authorized to be appropriated to the Secretary of the Army, to carry out this subsection, not to exceed $50,000,000 per fiscal year for the fiscal years ending June 30, 1973, and June 30, 1974.

(i)(1) The Secretary of the Interior, acting through the Director of the United States Fish and Wildlife Service, shall, upon request of the Governor of a State, and without reimbursement, provide technical assistance to such State in developing a statewide program for submission to the Administrator under subsection (b)(4)(B) of this section and in implementing such program after its approval.

(2) There is authorized to be appropriated to the Secretary of the Interior $6,000,000 to complete the National Wetlands Inventory of the United States, by December 31, 1981, and to provide information from such Inventory to States as it becomes available to assist such States in the development and operation of programs under this Act.

(j)(1) The Secretary of Agriculture, with the concurrence of the Administrator, and acting through the Soil Conservation Service and such other agencies of the Department of Agriculture as the Secretary may designate, is authorized and directed to establish and administer a program to enter into contracts of not less than five years nor more than ten years with owners and operators having control of rural land for the purpose of installing and maintaining measures incorporating best management practices to control nonpoint source pollution for improved water quality in those States or areas for which the Administrator has approved a plan under subsection (b) of this section where the practices to which the contracts apply are certified by the management agency designated under subsection (c)(1) of this section to be consistent with such plans and will result in improved water quality. Such contracts may be entered into during the period ending not later than September 31, 1988. Under such contracts the land owner or operator shall agree—

(i) to effectuate a plan approved by a soil conservation district, where one exists, under this section for his farm, ranch, or other land substantially in accordance with the schedule outlined therein unless any requirement thereof is waived or modified by the Secretary;

(ii) to forfeit all rights to further payments or grants under the contract and refund to the United States all payments and grants received thereunder, with interest, upon his violation of the contract at any stage during the time he has control of the land if the Secretary, after considering the recommendations of the soil conservation district where one exists, and the Administrator, determines that such violation is of such a nature as to warrant termination of the contract, or to make refunds or accept such payment adjustments as the Secretary may deem appropriate if he determines that the violation by the owner or operator does not warrant termination of the contract;

(iii) upon transfer of his right and interest in the farm, ranch, or other land during the contract period to forfeit all rights to further payments or grants under the contract and refund to the United States all payments or grants received thereunder, with interest, unless the transferee of any such land agrees with the Secretary to assume all obligations of the contract;

(iv) not to adopt any practice specified by the Secretary on the advice of the Administrator in the contract as a practice which would tend to defeat the purposes of the contract;

(v) to such additional provisions as the Secretary determines are desirable and includes in the contract to effectuate the purposes of the program or to facilitate the practical administration of the program.

(2) In return for such agreement by the landowner or operator the Secretary shall agree to provide technical assistance and share the cost of carrying out those conservation practices and measures set forth in the contract for which he determines that cost sharing is appropriate and in the public interest and which are approved for cost sharing by the agency designated to implement the plan developed under subsection (b) of this section. The portion of such cost (including labor) to be shared shall be that part which the Secretary determines is necessary and appropriate to effectuate the installation of the water quality management practices and measures under the contract, but not to exceed 50 per centum of the total cost of the measures set forth in the contract; except the Secretary may increase the matching cost share

where he determines that (1) the main benefits to be derived from the measures are related to improving offsite water quality, and (2) the matching share requirement would place a burden on the landowner which would probably prevent him from participating in the program.

(3) The Secretary may terminate any contract with a landowner or operator by mutual agreement with the owner or operator if the Secretary determines that such termination would be in the public interest, and may agree to such modification of contracts previously entered into as he may determine to be desirable to carry out the purposes of the program or facilitate the practical administration thereof or to accomplish equitable treatment with respect to other conservation, land use, or water quality programs.

(4) In providing assistance under this subsection the Secretary will give priority to those areas and sources that have the most significant effect upon water quality. Additional investigations or plans may be made, where necessary, to supplement approved water quality management plans, in order to determine priorities.

(5) The Secretary shall, where practicable, enter into agreements with soil conservation districts, State soil and water conservation agencies, or State water quality agencies to administer all or part of the program established in this subsection under regulations developed by the Secretary. Such agreements shall provide for the submission of such reports as the Secretary deems necessary, and for payment by the United States of such portion of the costs incurred in the administration of the program as the Secretary may deem appropriate.

(6) The contracts under this subsection shall be entered into only in areas where the management agency designated under subsection (c)(1) of this section assures an adequate level of participation by owners and operators having control of rural land in such areas. Within such areas the local soil conservation district, where one exists, together with the Secretary of Agriculture, will determine the priority of assistance among individual landowners and operators to assure that the most critical water quality problems are addresssed.

(7) The Secretary, in consultation with the Administrator and subject to section 304(k) of this Act, shall, not later than September 30, 1978, promulgate regulations for carrying out this subsection and for support and cooperation with other Federal and non-Federal agencies for implementation of this subsection.

(8) This program shall not be used to authorize or finance projects that would otherwise be eligible for assistance under the terms of Public Law 83–566.

(9) There are hereby authorized to be appropriated to the Secretary of Agriculture $200,000,000 for fiscal year 1979, $400,000,000 for fiscal year 1980, $100,000,000 for fiscal year 1981, $100,000,000 for fiscal year 1982, and such sums as may be necessary for fiscal years 1983

through 1990, to carry out this subsection. The program authorized under this subsection shall be in addition to, and not in substitution of, other programs in such area authorized by this or any other public law.

§ 1289.   Basin planning

[Sec. 209](a) The President, acting through the Water Resources Council, shall, as soon as practicable, prepare a Level B plan under the Water Resources Planning Act for all basins in the United States. All such plans shall be completed not later than January 1, 1980, except that priority in the preparation of such plans shall be given to those basins and portions thereof which are within those areas designated under paragraphs (2), (3), and (4) of subsection (a) of section 208 of this Act.

(b) The President, acting through the Water Resources Council, shall report annually to Congress on progress being made in carrying out this section. The first such report shall be submitted not later than January 31, 1973.

(c) There is authorized to be appropriated to carry out this section not to exceed $200,000,000.

§ 1290.   Annual survey

[Sec. 210] The Administrator shall annually make a survey to determine the efficiency of the operation and maintenance of treatment works constructed with grants made under this Act, as compared to the efficiency planned at the time the grant was made. The results of such annual survey shall be included in the report required under section 516(a) of this Act.

§ 1291.   Sewage collection systems

[Sec. 211](a) No grant shall be made for a sewage collection system under this title unless such grant (1) is for replacement or major rehabilitation of an existing collection system and is necessary to the total integrity and performance of the waste treatment works servicing such community, or (2) is for a new collection system in an existing community with sufficient existing or planned capacity adequately to treat such collected sewage and is consistent with section 201 of this Act.

(b) If the Administrator uses population density as a test for determining the eligibility of a collector sewer for assistance it shall be only for the purpose of evaluating alternatives and determining the needs for such system in relation to ground or surface water quality impact.

(c) No grant shall be made under this title from funds authorized for any fiscal year during the period beginning October 1, 1977, and ending September 30, 1990, for treatment works for control of pollutant discharges from separate storm sewer systems.

§ 1292. Definitions

[Sec. 212] As used in this title—

(1) The term "construction" means any one or more of the following: preliminary planning to determine the feasibility of treatment works, engineering, architectural, legal, fiscal, or economic investigations or studies, surveys, designs, plans, working drawings, specifications, procedures, field testing of innovative or alternative waste water treatment processes and techniques meeting guidelines promulgated under section 304(d)(3) of this Act, or other necessary actions, erection, building, acquisition, alteration, remodeling, improvement, or extension of treatment works, of the inspection or supervision of any of the foregoing items.

(2)(A) The term "treatment works" means any devices and systems used in the storage, treatment, recycling, and reclamation of municipal sewage or industrial wastes of a liquid nature to implement section 201 of this act, or necessary to recycle or reuse water at the most economical cost over the estimated life of the works, including intercepting sewers, outfall sewers, sewage collection systems, pumping, power, and other equipment, and their appurtenances; extensions, improvements, remodeling, additions, and alterations thereof; elements essential to provide a reliable recycled supply such as standby treatment units and clear well facilities; and any works, including site acquisition of the land that will be an integral part of the treatment process (including land use for the storage of treated wastewater in land treatment systems prior to land application) or is used for ultimate disposal of residues resulting from such treatment.

(B) In addition to the definition contained in subparagraph (A) of this paragraph, "treatment works" means any other method or system for preventing, abating, reducing, storing, treating, separating, or disposing of municipal waste, including storm water runoff, or industrial waste, including water in combined storm water and sanitary sewer systems. Any application for construction grants which includes wholly or in part such methods or systems shall, in accordance with guidelines published by the Administrator pursuant to subparagraph (C) of this paragraph, contain adequate data and analysis demonstrating such proposal to be, over the life of such works, the most cost efficient alternative to comply with sections 301 or 302 of this Act, or the requirements of section 201 of this Act.

(C) For the purposes of subparagraph (B) of this paragraph, the Administrator shall, within one hundred and eighty days after the date of enactment of this title, publish and thereafter revise no less often than annually, guidelines for the evaluation of methods, including cost effective analysis, described in subparagraph (B) of this paragraph.

(3) The term "replacement" as used in this title means those expenditures for obtaining and installing equipment, accessories, or appurtenances during the useful life of the treatment works necessary to maintain the capacity and performance for which such works are designed and constructed.

§ 1293. Loan guarantees for construction of treatment works

[Sec. 213](a) Subject to the conditions of this section and to such terms and conditions as the Administrator determines to be necessary to carry out the purposes of this title, the Administrator is authorized to guarantee, and to make commitments to guarantee, the principal and interest (including interest accruing between the date of default and the date of the payment in full of the guarantee) of any loan, obligation, or participation therein of any State, municipality, or intermunicipal or interstate agency issued directly and exclusively to the Federal Financing Bank to finance that part of the cost of any grant-eligible project for the construction of publicly owned treatment works not paid for with Federal financial assistance under this title (other than this section), which project the Administrator has determined to be eligible for such financial assistance under this title, including, but not limited to, projects eligible for reimbursement under section 206 of this title.

(b) No guarantee, or commitment to make a guarantee, may be made pursuant to this section—

(1) unless the Administrator certifies that the issuing body is unable to obtain on reasonable terms sufficient credit to finance its actual needs without such guarantee; and

(2) unless the Administrator determines that there is a reasonable assurance of repayment of the loan, obligation, or participation therein.

A determination of whether financing is available at reasonable rates shall be made by the Secretary of the Treasury with relationship to the current average yield on outstanding marketable obligations of municipalities of comparable maturity.

(c) The Administrator is authorized to charge reasonable fees for the investigation of an application for a guarantee and for the issuance of a commitment to make a guarantee.

(d) The Administrator, in determining whether there is a reasonable assurance of repayment, may require a commitment which would apply to such repayment. Such commitment may include, but not be limited to, any funds received by such grantee from the amounts appropriated under section 206 of this Act.

§ 1294. Public information and education on recycling and reuse of wastewater, use of land treatment, and reduction of wastewater volume

[Sec. 214] The Administrator shall develop and operate within one year of the date of enactment of this section, a continuing program of public information and education on recycling and reuse of wastewater (including sludge), the use of land treatment, and methods for the reduction of wastewater volume.

§ 1295. Requirements for American materials

[Sec. 215] Notwithstanding any other provision of law, no grant for which application is made after February 1, 1978, shall be made under this title for any treatment works unless only such unmanufactured articles, materials, and supplies as have been mined or produced in the United States, and only such manufactured articles, materials, and supplies as have been manufactured in the United States, substantially all from articles, materials, or supplies mined, produced, or manufactured, as the case may be, in the United States will be used in such treatment works. This section shall not apply in any case where the Administrator determines, based upon those factors the Administrator deems relevant, including the available resources of the agency, it to be inconsistent with the public interest (including multilateral government procurement agreements) or the cost to be unreasonable, or if articles, materials, or supplies of the class or kind to be used or the articles, material, or supplies from which they are manufactured are not mined, produced, or manufactured, as the case may be, in the United States in sufficient and reasonably available commercial quantities and of a satisfactory quality.

§ 1296. Determination of priority of projects

[Sec. 216] Notwithstanding any other provision of this Act, the determination of the priority to be given each category of projects for construction of publicly owned treatment works within each State shall be made solely by that State, except that if the Administrator, after a public hearing, determines that a specific project will not result in compliance with the enforceable requirements of this Act, such project shall be removed from the State's priority list and such State shall submit a revised priority list. These categories shall include, but not be limited to (A) secondary treatment, (B) more stringent treatment, (C) infiltration-in-flow correction, (D) major sewer system rehabilitation, (E) new collector sewers and appurtenances, (F) new interceptors and appurtenances, and (G) correction of combined sewer overflows. Not less than 25 per centum of funds allocated to a State in any fiscal year under this title for construction of publicly owned treatment works in such State shall be obligated for those types of projects referred to in clauses (D), (E), (F), and (G) of this section, if such projects are on such State's priority list for that year and are otherwise eligible for funding in that fiscal year. It is the policy of Congress that projects for wastewater treatment and management undertaken with Federal financial assistance under this Act by any State, municipality, or intermunicipal or interstate agency shall be projects which, in the estimation of the State, are designed to achieve optimum water quality management, consistent with the public health and water quality goals and requirements of the Act.

§ 1297. Guidelines for cost-effectiveness analysis

[Sec. 217] Any guidelines for cost-effectiveness analysis published by the Administrator under this title shall provide for the identification and selection of cost effective alternatives to comply with the objective and goals of this Act and sections 201(b), 201(d), 201(g)(2)(A), and 301(b)(2)(B) of this Act.

§ 1298. Cost effectiveness

[Sec. 218](a) It is the policy of Congress that a project for waste treatment and management undertaken with Federal financial assistance under this Act by any State, municipality, or intermunicipal or interstate agency shall be considered as an overall waste treatment system for waste treatment and management, and shall be that system which constitutes the most economical and cost-effective combination of devices and systems used in the storage, treatment, recycling, and reclamation of municipal sewage or industrial wastes of a liquid nature to implement section 201 of this Act, or necessary to recycle or reuse water at the most economical cost over the estimated life of the works, including intercepting sewers, outfall sewers, sewage collection systems, pumping power, and other equipment, and their appurtenances; extension, improvements, remodeling, additions, and alterations thereof; elements essential to provide a reliable recycled supply such as standby treatment units and clear well facilities; and any works, including site acquisition of the land that will be an integral part of the treatment process (including land use for the storage of treated wastewater in land treatment systems prior to land application) or which is used for ultimate disposal of residues resulting from such treatment; water efficiency measures and devices; and any other method or system for preventing, abating, reducing, storing, treating, separating, or disposing of municipal waste, including storm water runoff, or industrial waste, including waste in combined storm water and sanitary sewer systems; to meet the requirements of this Act.

(b) In accordance with the policy set forth in subsection (a) of this section, before the Administrator approves any grant to any State, municipality, or intermunicipal or interstate agency for the erection, building, acquisition, alteration, remodeling, improvement, or extension of any treatment works the Administrator shall determine that the facilities plan of which such treatment works are a part constitutes the most economical and cost-effective combination of treatment works over the life of the project to meet the requirements of this Act, including, but not limited to, consideration of construction costs, operation, maintenance, and replacement costs.

(c) In furtherance of the policy set forth in subsection (a) of this section, the Administrator shall require value engineering review in connection with any treatment works, prior to approval of any grant for the erection, building, acquisition, alteration, remodeling, improvement, or extension of such treatment works, in any case in which the cost of such erection, building, acquisition, alteration, remodeling, improvement, or extension is projected to be in excess of $10,000,000. For purposes of this subsection, the term "value engineering review" means a specialized cost control technique which uses a systematic and creative approach to identify and to focus on unnecessarily high cost in a project in order to arrive at a cost saving without sacrificing the reliability or efficiency of the project.

(d) This section applies to projects for waste treatment and management for which no treatment works including a facilities plan for such project have received Federal financial assistance for the preparation of construction plans and specifications under this Act before the date of enactment of this section.

§ 1299. State certification of projects

[Sec. 219] Whenever the Governor of a State which has been delegated sufficient authority to administer the construction grant program under this title in that State certifies to the Administrator that a grant application meets applicable requirements of Federal and State law for assistance under this title, the Administrator shall approve or disapprove such application within 45 days of the date of receipt of such application. If the Administrator does not approve or disapprove such application within 45 days of receipt, the application shall be deemed approved. If the Administrator disapproves such application the Administrator shall state in writing the reasons for such disapproval. Any grant approved or deemed approved under this section shall be subject to amounts provided in appropriation Acts.

Subchapter III. Standards and Enforcement

§ 1311. Effluent limitations

[Sec. 301] (a) Except as in compliance with this section and sections 302, 306, 307, 318, 402, and 404 of this Act, the discharge of any pollutant by any person shall be unlawful.

(b) In order to carry out the objective of this Act there shall be achieved—

(1)(A) not later than July 1, 1977, effluent limitations for point sources, other than publicly owned treatment works, (i) which shall require the application of the best practicable control technology currently available as defined by the Administrator pursuant to section 304(b) of this Act, or (ii) in the case of a discharge into a publicly owned treatment works which meets the requirements of subparagraph (B) of this paragraph, which shall require compliance with any applicable pretreatment requirements and any requirements under section 307 of this Act; and

(B) for publicly owned treatment works in existence on July 1, 1977, or approved pursuant to section 203 of this Act prior to June 30, 1974 (for which construction must be completed within four years of approval), effluent limitations based upon secondary treatment as defined by the Administrator pursuant to section 304(d)(1) of this Act; or,

(C) not later than July 1, 1977, any more stringent limitation, including those necessary to meet water quality standards, treatment standards, or schedule of compliance, established pursuant to any State law or regulations, (under authority preserved by section 510) or any other Federal law or regulation, or required to implement any applicable water quality standard established pursuant to this Act.

(2)(A) for pollutants identified in subparagraphs (C), (D), and (F) of this paragraph, effluent limitations for categories and classes of point sources, other than publicly owned treatment works, which (i) shall require application of the best available technology economically achievable for such category or class, which will result in reasonable further progress toward the national goal of eliminating the discharge of all pollutants, as determined in accordance with regulations issued by the Administrator pursuant to section 304(b)(2) of this Act, which such effluent limitations shall require the elimination of discharges of all pollutants if the Administrator finds, on the basis of information available to him (including information developed pursuant to section 315), that such elimination is technologically and economically achievable for category or class of point sources as determined in accordance with regulations issued by the Administrator pursuant to section 304(b)(2) of this Act or (ii) in the case of the introduction of a pollutant into a publicly owned treatment works which meets the requirements of subparagraph (b) of this paragraph, shall require compliance with any applicable pretreatment requirements and any other requirement under section 307 of this Act;

(B) [Repealed]

(C) with respect to all toxic pollutants referred to in table 1 of Committtee Print Number 95–30 of the Committee on Public Works and Transportation of the House of Representatives compliance with effluent limitations in accordance with subparagraph (A) of this paragraph as expeditiously as practicable but in no case later than three years after the date such limitations are promulgated under section 304(b), and in no case later than March 31, 1989;

(D) for all toxic pollutants listed under paragraph (1) of subsection (a) of section 307 of this Act which are not referred to in subparagraph (C) of this paragraph compliance with effluent limitation in accordance with subparagraph (A) of this paragraph as expeditiously as practicable but in no case later than three years after the date such limitations are promulgated under section 304(b), and in no case later than March 31, 1989;

(E) as expeditiously as practicable but in no case later than three years after the date such limitations are promulgated under section 304(b), and in no case later than March 31, 1989, compliance with effluent limitations for categories and classes of point sources, other than publicly owned treatment works, which in the case of pollutants identified pursuant to section 304(a)(4) of this Act shall require application of the best conventional pollutant control technology as determined in accordance with regulations issued by the Administrator pursuant to section 304(b)(4) of this Act; and

(F) for all pollutants (other than those subject to subparagraphs (C), (D), or (E) of this paragraph) compliance with effluent limitations in accordance with subparagraph (A) of this paragraph as expeditiously as practicable but in no case later than 3 years after the date such limitations are promulgated under section 304(b), and in no case later than March 31, 1989.

(3)(A) for effluent limitations under paragraph (1)(A)(i) of this subsection promulgated after January 1, 1982, and requiring a level of control substantially greater or based on fundamentally different control technology than under permits for an industrial category issued before such date, compliance as expeditiously as practicable but in no case later than three years after the date such limitations are promulgated under section 304(b), and in no case later than March 31, 1989; and

(B) for any effluent limitation in accordance with paragraph (1)(A)(i), (2)(A)(i), or (2)(E) of this subsection established only on the basis of section 402(a)(1) in a permit issued after enactment of the Water Quality Act of 1987, compliance as expeditiously as practicable but in no case later than three years after the date such limitations are established, and in no case later than March 31, 1989.

(c) The Administrator may modify the requirements of subsection (b)(2)(A) of this section with respect to any point source for which a permit application is filed after July 1, 1977, upon a showing by the owner or operator of such point source satisfactory to the Administrator that such modified requirements (1) will represent the maximum use of technology within the economic capability of the owner or operator; and (2) will result in reasonable further progress toward the elimination of the discharge of pollutants.

(d) Any effluent limitation required by paragraph (2) of subsection (b) of this section shall be reviewed at least every five years and, if appropriate, revised pursuant to the procedure established under such paragraph.

(e) Effluent limitations established pursuant to this section or section 302 of this Act shall be applied to all point sources of discharge of pollutants in accordance with the provisions of this Act.

(f) Notwithstanding any other provisions of this Act it shall be unlawful to discharge any radiological, chemical, or biological warfare agent or high-level radioactive waste into the navigable waters.

(g)(1) The Administrator, with the concurrence of the State, may modify the requirements of subsection (b)(2)(A) of this section with respect to the discharge from any point source of ammonia, chlorine, color, iron, and total phenols (4AAP) (when determined by the Administrator to be a pollutant covered by subsection (b)(2)(F)) and any other pollutant which the Administrator lists under paragraph (4) of this subsection).

(2) A modification under this subsection shall be granted only upon a showing by the owner or operator of such point source satisfactory to the Administrator that—

(A) such modified requirements will result at a minimum in accordance with the requirements of subsection (b)(1)(A) or (C) of this section, whichever is applicable;

(B) such modified requirements will not result in any additional requirements on any other point or nonpoint source; and

(C) such modification will not interfere with the attainment of maintenance of that water quality which shall assure protection of public water supplies, and the protection and propagation of a balanced population of shellfish, fish, and wildlife, and allow recreational activities, in and on the water and such modification will not result in the discharge of pollutants in quantities which may reasonably be anticipated to pose an unacceptable risk to human health or the environment because of bioaccumulation, persistency in the environment, acute toxicity, chronic toxicity (including carcinogenicity, mutagenicity or teratogenicity), or synergistic propensities.

(3) If an owner or operator of a point source applies for a modification under this subsection with respect to the discharge of any pollutant, such owner or operator shall be eligible to apply for modification under subsection (c) of this section with respect to such pollutant only during the same time-period as he is eligible to apply for a modifica-

tion under this subsection.

(4)(A) Upon petition of any person, the Administrator may add any pollutant to the list of pollutants for which modification under this section is authorized (except for pollutants identified pursuant to section 304(a)(4) of this Act, toxic pollutants subject to section 307(a) of this Act, and the thermal component of discharges) in accordance with the provisions of this paragraph.

(B)(i) The person petitioning for listing of an additional pollutant under this subsection shall submit to the Administrator sufficient information to make the determinations required by this subparagraph.

(ii) The Administrator shall determine whether or not the pollutant meets the criteria for listing as a toxic pollutant under section 307(a) of this Act.

(iii) If the Administrator determines that the pollutant meets the criteria for listing as a toxic pollutant under section 307(a), the Administrator shall list the pollutant as a toxic pollutant under section 307(a).

(iv) If the Administrator determines that the pollutant does not meet the criteria for listing as a toxic pollutant under such section and determines that adequate test methods and sufficient data are available to make the determinations required by paragraph (2) of this subsection with respect to the pollutant, the Administrator shall add the pollutant to the list of pollutants specified in paragraph (1) of this subsection for which modifications are authorized under this subsection.

(C) A petition for listing of a pollutant under this paragraph—

(i) must be filed not later than 270 days after the date of promulgation of an applicable effluent guideline under section 304;

(ii) may be filed before promulgation of such guideline; and

(iii) may be filed with an application for a modification under paragraph (1) with respect to the discharge of such pollutant.

(D) A decision to add a pollutant to the list of pollutants for which modifications under this subsection are authorized must be made within 270 days after the date of promulgation of an applicable effluent guideline under section 304.

(E) The burden of proof for making the determinations under subparagraph (B) shall be on the petitioner.

(5) The Administrator may remove any pollutant from the list of pollutants for which modifications are authorized under this subsection if the Administrator determines that adequate test methods and sufficient data are no longer available for determining whether or not modifications may be granted with respect to such pollutant under

paragraph (2) of this subsection.

(h) The Administrator, with the concurrence of the State, may issue a permit under section 402 which modifies the requirements of subsection (b)(1)(B) of this section with respect to the discharge of any pollutant from a publicly owned treatment works into marine waters, if the applicant demonstrates to the satisfaction of the Administrator that—

(1) there is an applicable water quality standard specific to the pollutant for which the modification is requested, which has been identified under section 304(a)(6) of this Act;

(2) such modified requirements will not interfere with the attainment or maintenance of that water quality which assures protection of public water supplies and protection and propagation of a balanced, indigenous population of shellfish, fish and wildlife, and allows recreational activities, in and on the water;

(3) the applicant has established a system for monitoring the impact of such discharge on a representative sample of aquatic biota, to the extent practicable, and the scope of such monitoring is limited to include only those scientific investigations which are necessary to study the effects of the proposed discharge;

(4) such modified requirements will not result in any additional requirements on any other point or nonpoint source;

(5) all applicable pretreatment requirements for sources introducing waste into such treatment works will be enforced;

(6) in the case of any treatment works serving a population of 50,000 or more, with respect to any toxic pollutant introduced into such works by an industrial discharger for which pollutant there is no applicable pretreatment requirement in effect, sources introducing waste into such works are in compliance with all applicable pretreatment requirements, the applicant will enforce such requirements, and the applicant has in effect a pretreatment program which, in combination with the treatment of discharges from such works, removes the same amount of such pollutant as would be removed if such works were to apply secondary treatment discharges and if such works had no pretreatment program with respect to such pollutant;

(7) to the extent practicable, the applicant has established a schedule of activities designed to eliminate the entrance of toxic pollutants from nonindustrial sources into such treatment works;

(8) there will be no new or substantially increased discharges from the point source of the pollutant to which the modification applies above that volume of discharge specified in the permit;

(9) the applicant at the time such modification becomes effective be discharging effluent which has received at least primary or equivalent treatment and which meets the criteria established under section 304(a)(1) of this Act after initial mixing in the waters surrounding or adjacent to the point at which such effluent is discharged.

For the purposes of this subsection, the phrase "the discharge of any pollutant into marine waters" refers to a discharge into deep waters of the territorial sea or the waters of the contiguous zone, or into saline estuarine waters where there is strong tidal movement and other hydrological and geological characteristics which the Administrator determines necessary to allow compliance with paragraph (2) of this subsection, and section 101(a)(2) of this Act. For the purposes of paragraph (9), "primary or equivalent treatment" means treatment by screening, sedimentation, and skimming adequate to remove at least 30 percent of the biological oxygen demanding material and of the suspended solids in the treatment works influent, and disinfection, where appropriate. A municipality which applies secondary treatment shall be eligible to receive a permit pursuant to this subsection which modifies the requirements of subsection (b)(1)(B) of this section with respect to the discharge of any pollutant from any treatment works owned by such municipality into marine waters. No permit issued under this subsection shall authorize the discharge of sewage sludge into marine waters. In order for a permit to be issued under this subsection for the discharge of a pollutant into marine waters, such marine waters must exhibit characteristics assuring that water providing dilution does not contain significant amounts of previously discharged effluent from such treatment works. No permit issued under this subsection shall authorize the discharge of any pollutant into saline estuarine waters which at the time of application do not support a balanced indigenous population of shellfish, fish and wildlife, or allow recreation in and on the waters or which exhibit ambient water quality below applicable water quality standards adopted for the protection of public water supplies, shellfish, fish and wildlife or recreational activities or such other standards necessary to assure support and protection of such uses. The prohibition contained in the preceding sentence shall apply without regard to the presence or absence of a causal relationship between such characteristics and the applicant's current or proposed discharge. Notwithstanding any other provisions of this subsection, no permit may be issued under this subsection for discharge of a pollutant into the New York Bight Apex consisting of the ocean waters of the Atlantic Ocean westward of 73 degrees 30 minutes west longitude and northward of 40 degrees 10 minutes north latitude.

(i)(1) Where construction is required in order for a planned or existing publicly owned treatment works to achieve limitations under subsection (b)(1)(B) or (b)(1)(C) of this section, but (A) construction cannot be completed within the time required in such subsection, or (B) the United States has failed to make financial assistance under this Act available in time to achieve such limitations by the time specified in such subsection, the owner or operator of such treatment works may request the Administrator (or if appropriate the State) to issue a permit pursuant to section 402 of this Act or to modify a permit issued pursuant to that section to extend such time for compliance. Any such request shall be filed with the Administrator (or if appropriate the State) within 180 days after the date of enactment of the Water Quality Act of 1987. The Administrator (or if appropriate the State) may grant such request and issue or modify such a permit, which shall contain a schedule of compliance for the publicly owned treatment works based on the earliest date by which such financial assistance will be available from the United States and construction can be completed, but in no event later than July 1, 1988, and shall contain such other terms and conditions, including those necessary to carry out subsections (b) through (g) of section 201 of this Act, section 307 of this Act, and such interim effluent limitations applicable to that treatment works as the Administrator determines are necessary to carry out the provisions of this Act.

 (2)(A) Where a point source (other than a publicly owned treatment works) will not achieve the requirements of subsections (b)(1)(A) and (b)(1)(C) of this section and—

  (i) if a permit issued prior to July 1, 1977, to such point source is based upon a discharge into a publicly owned treatment works; or

  (ii) if such point source (other than a publicly owned treatment works) had before July 1, 1977, a contract (enforceable against such point source) to discharge into a publicly owned treatment works; or

  (iii) if either an application made before July 1, 1977, for a construction grant under this Act for a publicly owned treatment works, or engineering or architectural plans or working drawings made before July 1, 1977, for a publicly owned treatment works, show that such point source was to discharge into such publicly owned treatment works, and such publicly owned treatment works is presently unable to accept such discharge without construction, and in the case of a discharge to an existing publicly owned treatment works, such treatment works has an extension pursuant to paragraph (1) of this subsection, the owner or operator of such point source may request the Administrator (or if appropriate the State) to issue or modify such a permit pursuant to such section 402 to extend such time for compliance. Any such request shall be filed with the Administrator (or if appropriate the State) within 180 days after the date of enactment of this subsection or the filing of a request by the appropriate publicly owned treatment works under paragraph (1) of this subsection, whichever is later. If the Administrator (or if appropriate the State) finds that the owner or operator of such point source has acted in good faith, he may grant such request and issue or modify such a permit, which shall contain a schedule of compliance for the point source to achieve the requirements of subsections (b)(1)(A) and (C) of this section and shall contain such other terms and conditions, including pretreatment and interim effluent limitations and water conservation requirements applicable to that point source, as the Administrator determines are necessary to carry out the provisions of this Act.

(B) No time modification granted by the Administrator (or if appropriate the State) pursuant to paragraph (2)(A) of this subsection shall extend beyond the earliest date practicable for compliance or beyond the date of any extension granted to the appropriate publicly owned treatment works pursuant to paragraph (1) of this subsection, but in no event shall it extend beyond July 1, 1988; and no such time modification shall be granted unless (i) the publicly owned treatment works will be in operation and available to the point source before July 1, 1988, and will meet the requirements to subsections (b)(1)(B) and (C) of this section after receiving the discharge from that point source; and (ii) the point source and the publicly owned treatment works have entered into an enforceable contract requiring the point source to discharge into the publicly owned treatment works, the owner or operator of such point source to pay the costs required under section 204 of this Act, and the publicly owned treatment works to accept the discharge from the point source; and (iii) the permit for such point source requires point source to meet all requirements under section 307(a) and (b) during the period of such time modification.

(j)(1) Any application filed under this section for a modification of the provisions of—

(A) subsection (b)(1)(B) under subsection (h) of this section shall be filed not later than the 365th day which begins after the date of enactment of the Municipal Wastewater Treatment Construction Grant Amendments of 1981, except that a publicly owned treatment works which prior to December 31, 1982, had a contractual arrangement to use a portion of the capacity of an ocean outfall operated by another publicly owned treatment works which has applied for or received modification under subsection (h), may apply for a modification of subsection (h) in its own right not later than 30 days after the date of the enactment of the Water Quality Act of 1987;

(B) subsection (b)(2)(A) as it applies to pollutants identified in subsection (b)(2)(F) shall be filed not later than 270 days after the date of promulgation of an applicable effluent guideline under section 304 or not later than 270 days after the date of enactment of the Clean Water Act of 1977, whichever is later.

(2) Any application for a modification filed under subsection (g) of this section shall not operate to stay any requirement under this Act, unless in the judgment of the Administrator such a stay or the

modification sought will not result in the discharge of pollutants in quantities which may reasonably be anticipated to pose an unacceptable risk to human health or the environment because of bioaccumulation, persistency in the environment, acute toxicity, chronic toxicity (including carcinogenicity, mutagenicity or teratogenicity), or synergistic propensities, and that there is a substantial likelihood that the applicant will succeed on the merits of such application. In the case of an application filed under subsection (g) of this section, the Administrator may condition any stay granted under this paragraph on requiring the filing of a bond or other appropriate security to assure timely compliance with the requirements from which a modification is sought.

(3)(A)An application for a modification under subsection (g) and a petition for listing of a pollutant as a pollutant for which modifications are authorized under such subsection shall not stay the requirement that the person seeking such modification or listing comply with effluent limitations under this Act for all pollutants not the subject of such application or petition.

(B) Disapproval of an application for a modification under subsection (g) shall not stay the requirement that the person seeking such modification comply with all applicable effluent limitations under this Act.

(4) An application for a modification with respect to a pollutant filed under subsection (g) must be approved or disapproved not later than 365 days after the date of such filing; except that in any case in which a petition for listing such pollutant as a pollutant for which modifications are authorized under such subsection is approved, such application must be approved or disapproved not later than 365 days after the date of approval of such petition.

(k) In the case of any facility subject to a permit under section 402 which proposes to comply with the requirements of subsection (b)(2)(A) or (b)(2)(E) of this section by replacing existing production capacity with an innovative production process which will result in an effluent reduction significantly greater than that required by the limitation otherwise applicable to such facility and moves toward the national goal of eliminating the discharge of all pollutants, or with the installation of an innovative control technique that has a substantial likelihood for enabling the facility to comply with the applicable effluent limitation by achieving a significantly greater effluent reduction than that required by the applicable effluent limitation and moves toward the national goal of eliminating the discharge of all pollutants, or by achieving the required reduction with an innovative system that has the potential for significantly lower costs than the systems which have been determined by the Administrator to be economically achievable, the Administrator (or the State with an approved program under section 402, in consultation with the Administrator) may establish a date for compliance under subsection (b)(2)(A) or (b)(2)(E) of this section no later than two years after the date for compliance with such effluent limitation which would otherwise be applicable under such subsection, if it is also determined that such innovative system has the potential for industrywide application.

(l) Other than as provided in subsection (n) of this section, the Administrator may not modify any requirement of this section as it applies to any specific pollutant which is on the toxic pollutant list under section 307(a) (1) of this Act.

(m)(1) The Administrator, with the concurrence of the State, may issue a permit under section 402 which modifies the requirements of subsections (b)(1)(A) and (b)(2)(E) of this section, and of section 403, with respect to effluent limitations to the extent such limitations relate to biochemical oxygen demand and pH from discharges by an industrial discharger in such State into deep waters of the territorial seas, if the applicant demonstrates and the Administrator finds that—

    (A) the facility for which modification is sought is covered at the time of the enactment of this subsection by National Pollutant Discharge Elimination System permit number CA0005894 or CA0005282;

    (B) the energy and environmental costs of meeting such requirements of subsections (b)(1)(A) and (b)(2)(E) and section 403 exceed by an unreasonable amount the benefits to be obtained, including the objectives of this Act;

    (C) the applicant has established a system for monitoring the impact of such discharges on a representative sample of aquatic biota;

    (D) such modified requirements will not result in any additional requirements on any other point or nonpoint source;

    (E) there will be no new or substantially increased discharges from the point source of the pollutant to which the modification applies above that volume of discharge specified in the permit;

    (F) the discharge is into waters where there is strong tidal movement and other hydrological and geological characteristics which are necessary to allow compliance with this subsection and section 101(a)(2) of this Act;

    (G) the applicant accepts as a condition to the permit a contractual obligation to use funds in the amount required (but not less than $250,000 per year for ten years) for research and development of water pollution control technology, including but not limited to closed cycle technology;

    (H) the facts and circumstances present a unique situation which, if relief is granted, will not establish a precedent or the relaxation of the requirements of this Act applicable to similarly situated discharges; and

    (I) no owner or operator of a facility comparable to that of the applicant situated in the United States has demonstrated that it would be put at a competitive disadvantage to the applicant (or the parent company or any subsidiary thereof) as a result of the issuance of a permit under this subsection.

(2) The effluent limitations established under a permit issued under paragraph (1) shall be sufficient to implement the applicable State water quality standards, to assure the protection of public water supplies and protection and propagation of a balanced, indigenous population of shellfish, fish, fauna, wildlife, and other aquatic organisms, and to allow recreational activities in and on the water. In setting such limitations, the Administrator shall take into account any seasonal variations and the need for an adequate margin of safety, considering the lack of essential knowledge concerning the relationship between effluent limitations and water quality and the lack of essential knowledge of the effects of discharges on beneficial uses of the receiving waters.

(3) A permit under this subsection may be issued for a period not to exceed five years, and such a permit may be renewed for one additional period not to exceed five years upon a demonstration by the applicant and a finding by the Administrator at the time of application for any such renewal that the provisions of this subsection are met.

(4) The Administrator may terminate a permit issued under this subsection if the Administrator determines that there has been a decline in ambient water quality of the receiving waters during the period of the permit even if a direct cause and effect relationship cannot be shown: *Provided*, That if the effluent from a source with a permit issued under this subsection is contributing to a decline in ambient water quality of the receiving waters, the Administrator shall terminate such permit.

(n)(1) The Administrator, with the concurrence of the State, may establish an alternative requirement under subsection (b)(2) or section 307(b) for a facility that modifies the requirements of national effluent limitation guidelines or categorical pretreatment standards that would otherwise be applicable to such facility, if the owner or operator of such facility demonstrates to the satisfaction of the Administrator that—

(A) the facility is fundamentally different with respect to the factors (other than cost) specified in section 304(b) or 304(g) and considered by the Administrator in establishing such national effluent limitation guidelines or categorical pretreatment standards;

(B) the application—

(i) is based solely on information and supporting data submitted to the Administrator during the rulemaking for establishment of the applicable national effluent limitation guidelines or categorical pretreatment standard specifically raising the factors that are fundamentally different for such facility; or

    (ii) is based on information and supporting data referred to in clause (i) and information and supporting data the applicant did not have a reasonable opportunity to submit during such rulemaking;

  (C) the alternative requirement is no less stringent than justified by the fundamental difference; and

  D) the alternative requirement will not result in a non-water quality environmental impact which is markedly more adverse than the impact considered by the Administrator in establishing such national effluent limitation guideline or categorical pretreatment standard.

(2) An application for an alternative requirement which modifies the requirements of an effluent limitation or pretreatment standard under this subsection must be submitted to the Administrator within 180 days after the date on which such limitation or standard is established or revised, as the case may be.

(3) The Administrator shall approve or deny by final agency action an application submitted under this subsection within 180 days after the date such application is filed with the Administrator.

(4) The Administrator may allow an applicant under this subsection to submit information and supporting data until the earlier of the date the application is approved or denied or the last day that the Administrator has to approve or deny such application.

(5) For the purposes of this subsection, an application for an alternative requirement based on fundamentally different factors which is pending on the date of the enactment of this subsection shall be treated as having been submitted to the Administrator on the 180th day following such date of enactment. The applicant may amend the application to take into account the provisions of this subsection.

(6) An application for an alternative requirement under this subsection shall not stay the applicant's obligation to comply with the effluent limitation guideline or categorical pretreatment standard which is the subject of the application.

(7) If an application for an alternative requirement which modifies the requirements of an effluent limitation or pretreatment standard under this subsection is denied by the Administrator, the applicant must comply with such limitation or standard as established or revised, as the case may be.

(8) Every 6 months after the date of the enactment of this subsection, the Administrator shall submit to the Committee on Environment and Public Works of the Senate and the Committee on Public Works and Transportation of the House of Representatives a report on the status of applications for alternative requirements which modify the requirements of effluent limitations under section 301 or 304 of this Act or

any national categorical pretreatment standard under section 307(b) of this Act filed before, on, or after such date of enactment.

(o) The Administrator shall prescribe and collect from each applicant fees reflecting the reasonable administrative costs incurred in reviewing and processing applications for modifications submitted to the Administrator pursuant to subsections (c), (g), (i), (k), (m), and (n) of section 301, section 304(d)(4), and section 316(a) of this Act. All amounts collected by the Administrator under this subsection shall be deposited into a special fund of the Treasury entitled "Water Permits and Related Services" which shall thereafter be available for appropriation to carry out activities of the Environmental Protection Agency for which such fees were collected.

(p)(1) Subject to paragraphs (2) through (4) of this subsection, the Administrator, or the State in any case which the State has an approved permit program under section 402(b), may issue a permit under section 402 which modifies the requirements of subsection (b)(2)(A) of this section with respect to the pH level of any pre-existing discharge, and with respect to pre-existing discharges of iron and manganese from the remined area of any coal remining operation or with respect to the pII level or level of iron or manganese in any pre-existing discharge affected by the remining operation. Such modified requirements shall apply the best available technology economically achievable on a case-by-case basis, using best professional judgment, to set specific numerical effluent limitations in each permit.

(2) The Administrator or the State may only issue a permit pursuant to paragraph (1) if the applicant demonstrates to the satisfaction of the Administrator or the State, as the case may be, that the coal remining operation will result in the potential for improved water quality from the remining operation but in no event shall such a permit allow the pH level of any discharge, and in no event shall such a permit allow the discharges of iron and manganese, to exceed the levels being discharged from the remined area before the coal remining operation begins. No discharge from, or affected by, the remining operation shall exceed State water quality standards established under section 303 of this Act.

(3) For purposes of this subsection—
   (A) The term "coal remining operation" means a coal mining operation which begins after the date of the enactment of this subsection at a site on which coal mining was conducted before the effective date of the Surface Mining Control and Reclamation Act of 1977.
   (B) The term "remined area" means only that area of any coal remining operation on which coal mining was conducted before the effective date of the Surface Mining Control and Reclamation Act of 1977.
   (C) The term "pre-existing discharge" means any discharge at the time of permit application under this subsection.

(4) Nothing in this subsection shall affect the application of the Surface Mining Control and Reclamation Act of 1977 to any coal remining operation, including the application of such Act to suspended solids.

§ 1312. Water quality related effluent limitations

[Sec. 302] (a) Whenever, in the judgment of the Administrator or as identified under section 304(l) discharges of pollutants from a point source or group of point sources, with the application of effluent limitations required under section 301(b)(2) of this Act, would interfere with the attainment or maintenance of that water quality in a specific portion of the navigable waters which shall assure protection of public health, public water supplies, agricultural and industrial uses, and the protection and propagation of a balanced population of shellfish, fish and wildlife, and allow recreational activities in and on the water, effluent limitations (including alternative effluent control strategies) for such point source or sources shall be established which can reasonably be expected to contribute to the attainment or maintenance of such water quality.

(b)(1) Prior to establishment of any effluent limitation pursuant to subsection (a) of this section, the Administrator shall publish such proposed limitation and within 90 days of such publication hold a public hearing.

(2)(A) The Administrator, with the concurrence of the State, may issue a permit which modifies the effluent limitations required by subsection (a) of this section for pollutants other than toxic pollutants if the applicant demonstrates at such hearing that (whether or not technology or other alternative control strategies are available) there is no reasonable relationship between the economic and social costs and the benefits to be obtained (including attainment of the objective of this Act) from achieving such limitation.

(B) The Administrator, with the concurrence of the State, may issue a permit which modifies the effluent limitations required by subsection (a) of this section for toxic pollutants for a single period not to exceed 5 years if the applicant demonstrates to the satisfaction of the Administrator that such modified requirements (i) will represent the maximum degree of control within the economic capability of the owner and operator of the source, and (ii) will result in reasonable further progress beyond the requirements of section 301(b)(2) toward the requirements of subsection (a) of this section.

(c) The establishment of effluent limitations under this section shall not operate to delay the application of any effluent limitation established under section 301 of this Act.

§ 1313. Water quality standards and implementation plans

[Sec. 303] (a)(1) In order to carry out the purpose of this Act, any water quality standard applicable to interstate waters which was adopted by any State and submitted to, and approved by, or is awaiting approval by, the Administrator pursuant to this Act as in effect immediately prior to the date of enactment of the Federal Water Pollution Control Act Amendments of 1972, shall remain in effect unless the Administrator determined that such standard is not consistent with the applicable requirements of this Act as in effect immediately prior to the date of enactment of the Federal Water Pollution Control Act Amendments of 1972. If the Administrator makes such a determination he shall, within three months after the date of enactment of the Federal Water Pollution Control Act Amendments of 1972, notify the State and specify the changes needed to meet such requirements. If such changes are not adopted by the State within ninety days after the date of such notification, the Administrator shall promulgate such changes in accordance with subsection (b) of this section.

(2) Any State which, before the date of enactment of the Federal Water Pollution Control Act Amendments of 1972, has adopted pursuant to its own law, water quality standards applicable to intrastate waters shall submit such standards to the Administrator within thirty days after the date of enactment of the Federal Water Pollution Control Act Amendments of 1972. Each such standard shall remain in effect, in the same manner and to the same extent as any other water quality standard established under this Act unless the Administrator determines that such standard is inconsistent with the applicable requirements of this Act as in effect immediately prior to the date of enactment of the Federal Water Pollution Control Act Amendments of 1972. If the Administrator makes such a determination he shall not later than the one hundred and twentieth day after the date of submission of such standards, notify the State and specify the changes needed to meet such requirements. If such changes are not adopted by the State within ninety days after such notification, the Administrator shall promulgate such changes in accordance with subsection (b) of this section.

(3)(A) Any State which prior to the date of enactment of the Federal Water Pollution Control Act Amendments of 1972 has not adopted pursuant to its own laws water quality standards applicable to intrastate waters shall, not later that one hundred and eighty days after the date of enactment of the Federal Water Pollution Control Act Amendments of 1972, adopt and submit such standards to the Administrator.

(B) If the Administrator determines that any such standards are consistent with the applicable requirements of this Act as in effect immediately prior to the date of enactment of the Federal Water Pollution Control Act Amendments of 1972, he shall approve such standards.

(C) If the Administrator determines that any such standards are not consistent with the applicable requirements of this Act as in effect immediately prior to the date of enactment of the Federal Water Pollution Control Act Amendments of 1972, he shall, not later than the ninetieth day after the date of submission of such standards, notify the State and specify the changes to meet such requirements. If such changes are not adopted by the State within ninety days after the date of notification, the Administrator shall promulgate such standards pursuant to subsection (b) of this section.

(b)(1) The Administrator shall promptly prepare and publish proposed regulations setting forth water quality standards for a State in accordance with the applicable requirements of this Act as in effect immediately prior to the date of enactment of the Federal Water Pollution Control Act Amendments of 1972, if—

 (A) the State fails to submit water quality standards within the times prescribed in subsection (a) of this section,

 (B) a water quality standard submitted by such State under subsection (a) of this section is determined by the Administrator not to be consistent with the applicable requirements of subsection (a) of this section.

(2) The Administrator shall promulgate any water quality standard published in a proposed regulation not later than one hundred and ninety days after the date he publishes any such proposed standard, unless prior to such promulgation, such State has adopted a water quality standard which the Administrator determines to be in accordance with subsection (a) of this section.

(c)(1) The Governor of a State or the State water pollution control agency of such State shall from time to time (but at least once each three year period beginning with the date of enactment of the Federal Water Pollution Control Act Amendments of 1972) hold public hearings for the purpose of reviewing applicable water quality standards and, as appropriate, modifying and adopting standards. Results of such review shall be made available to the Administrator.

(2)(A) Whenever the State revises or adopts a new standard, such revised or new standard shall be submitted to the Administrator. Such revised or new water quality standard shall consist of the designated uses of the navigable waters involved and the water quality criteria for such waters based upon such uses. Such standards shall be such as to protect the public health or welfare, enhance the quality of water and serve the purposes of this Act. Such standards shall be established taking into consideration their use and value for public water supplies, propagation of fish and wildlife, recreational purposes, and agricultural, industrial, and other purposes, and also taking into consideration their use and value for navigation.

(B) Whenever a State reviews water quality standards pursuant to paragraph (1) of this subsection, or revises or adopts new standards pursuant to this paragraph, such State shall adopt criteria for all toxic pollutants listed pursuant to section 307(a)(1) of this Act for which criteria have been published under section 304(a), the discharge or presence of which in the affected waters could reasonably be expected to interfere with those designated uses adopted by the State, as necessary to support such designated uses. Such criteria shall be specific numerical criteria for such toxic pollutants. Where such numerical criteria are not available, whenever a State reviews water quality standards pursuant to paragraph (1), or revises or adopts new standards pursuant to this paragraph, such State shall adopt criteria based on biological monitoring or assessment methods consistent with information published pursuant to section 304(a)(8). Nothing in this section shall be construed to limit or delay the use of effluent limitations or other permit conditions based on or involving biological monitoring or assessment methods or previously adopted numerical criteria.

(3) If the Administrator, within sixty days after the date of submission of the revised or new standard, determines that such standard meets the requirements of this Act, such standard shall thereafter be the water quality standard for the applicable waters of that State. If the Administrator determines that any such revised or new standard is not consistent with the applicable requirements of this Act, he shall not later than the ninetieth day after the date of submission of such standard notify the State and specify the changes to meet such requirements. If such changes are not adopted by the State within ninety days after the date of notification, the Administrator shall promulgate such standard pursuant to paragraph (4) of this subsection.

(4) The Administrator shall promptly prepare and publish proposed regulations setting forth a revised or new water quality standard for the navigable waters involved—

(A) If a revised or new water quality standard submitted by such State under paragraph (3) of this subsection for such waters is determined by the Administrator not to be consistent with the applicable requirements of this Act, or

(B) In any case where the Administrator determines that a revised or new standard is necessary to meet the requirements of this Act.

The Administrator shall promulgate any revised or new standard under this paragraph not later than ninety days after he publishes such proposed standards, unless prior to such promulgation, such State has adopted a revised or new water quality standard which the Administrator determines to be in accordance with this Act.

(d)(1)(A) Each state shall identify those waters within its boundaries for which the effluent limitations required by section 301(b)(1)(A) and section 301(b)(1)(B) are not stringent enough to implement any water quality standard applicable to such waters. The State shall establish a priority ranking for such waters, taking into account the severity of the pollution and the uses to be made of such waters.

(B) Each State shall identify those waters or parts thereof within its boundaries for which controls on thermal discharges under section 301 are not stringent enough to assure protection and propagation of a balanced indigenous population of shellfish, fish, and wildlife.

(C) Each State shall establish for the waters identified in paragraph (1)(A) of this subsection, and in accordance with the priority ranking, the total maximum daily load, for those pollutants which the Administrator identifies under section 304(a)(2) as suitable for such calculation. Such load shall be established at a level necessary to implement the applicable water quality standards with seasonal variations and a margin of safety which takes into account any lack of knowledge concerning the relationship between effluent limitations and water quality.

(D) Each State shall estimate for the waters identified in paragraph (1)(D) of this subsection the total maximum daily thermal load required to assure protection and propagation of a balanced, indigenous population of shellfish, fish and wildlife. Such estimates shall take into account the normal water temperatures, flow rates, seasonal variations, existing sources of heat input, and the dissipative capacity of the identified waters or parts thereof. Such estimates shall include a calculation of the maximum heat input that can be made into each such part and shall include a margin of safety which takes into account any lack of knowledge concerning the development of thermal water quality criteria for such protection and propagation in the identified waters or parts thereof.

(2) Each State shall submit to the Administrator from time to time, with the first such submission not later than one hundred and eighty days after the date of publication of the first identification of pollutants under section 304(a)(2)(D), for his approval the waters identified and the loads established under paragraphs (1)(A), (1)(B), (1)(C), and (1)(D) of this subsection. The Administrator shall either approve or disapprove such identification and load not later than thirty days after the date of submission. If the Administrator approves such identification and load, such State shall incorporate them into its current plan under subsection (e) of this section. If the Administrator disapproves such identification and load, he shall not later than thirty days after the date of such disapproval identify such waters in such State and

establish such loads for such waters as he determines necessary to implement the water quality standards applicable to such waters and upon such identification and establishment the State shall incorporate them into its current plan under subsection (e) of this section.

(3) For the specific purpose of developing information, each State shall identify all waters within its boundaries which it has not identified under paragraph (1)(A) and (1)(B) of this subsection and estimate for such waters the total maximum daily load with seasonal variations and margins of safety, for those pollutants which the Administrator identifies under section 304(a)(2) as suitable for such calculation and for thermal discharges, at a level that would assure protection and propagation of a balanced indigenous population of fish, shellfish and wildlife.

(4)(A) For waters identified under paragraph (1)(A) where the applicable water quality standard has not yet been attained, any effluent limitation based on a total maximum daily load or other waste load allocation established under this section may be revised only if (i) the cumulative effect of all such revised effluent limitations based on such total maximum daily load or waste load allocation will assure the attainment of such water quality standard, or (ii) the designated use which is not being attained is removed in accordance with regulations established under this section.

(B) For waters identified under paragraph (1)(A) where the quality of such waters equals or exceeds levels necessary to protect the designated use for such waters or otherwise required by applicable water quality standards, any effluent limitation based on a total maximum daily load or other waste load allocation established under this section, or any water quality standard established under this section, or any other permitting standard may be revised only if such revision is subject to and consistent with the antidegradation policy established under this section.

(e)(1) Each State shall have a continuing planning process approved under paragraph (2) of this subsection which is consistent with this Act.

(2) Each State shall submit not later than 120 days after the date of the enactment of the Water Pollution Control Amendments of 1972 to the Administrator for his approval a proposed continuing planning process which is consistent with this Act. Not later than thirty days after the date of submission of such a process the Administrator shall either approve or disapprove such process. The Administrator shall from time to time review each State's approved planning process for the purpose of insuring that such planning process is at all times consistent with this Act. The Administrator shall not approve any State permit program under title IV of this Act for any State which does not have an approved continuing planning process under this section.

(3) The Administrator shall approve any continuing planning process

submitted to him under this section which will result in plans for all navigable waters within such State which include, but are not limited to, the following:

(A) effluent limitations and schedules of compliance at least as stringent as those required by section 301(b)(1), section 301(b)(2), section 306, and section 307, and at least as stringent as any requirements contained in any applicable water quality standard in effect under authority of this section;

(B) the incorporation of all elements of any applicable areawide waste management plans under section 208, and applicable basin plans under section 209 of this Act;

(C) total maximum daily load for pollutants in accordance with subsection (d) of this section;

(D) procedures for revision;

(E) adequate authority for intergovernmental cooperation;

(F) adequate implementation, including schedules of compliance, for revised or new water quality standards, under subsection (c) of this section;

(G) controls over the disposition of all residual waste from any water treatment processing;

(H) an inventory and ranking, in order of priority, of needs for construction of waste treatment works required to meet the applicable requirements of sections 301 and 302.

(f) Nothing in this section shall be construed to affect any effluent limitation, or schedule of compliance required by any State to be implemented prior to the dates set forth in sections 301(b)(1) and 301(b)(2) nor to preclude any State from requiring compliance with any effluent limitation or schedule of compliance at dates earlier than such dates.

(g) Water quality standards relating to heat shall be consistent with the requirements of section 316 of this Act.

(h) For the purposes of this Act the term "water quality standards" includes thermal water quality standards.

§ 1314. Information and guidelines

[Sec. 304] (a)(1) The Administrator, after consultation with appropriate Federal and State agencies and other interested persons, shall develop and publish, within one year after the date of enactment of this title (and from time to time thereafter revise) criteria for water quality accurately reflecting the latest scientific knowledge (A) on the kind and extent of all identifiable effects on health and welfare including, but not limited to, plankton, fish, shellfish, wildlife, plant life, shorelines, beaches, esthetics, and recreation which may be expected from the presence of pollutants in any body of water, including ground water; (B) on the concentration and dispersal of pollutants, or their byproducts, through biological, physical, and chemical processes; and

(C) on the effects of pollutants on biological community diversity, productivity, and stability, including information on the factors affecting rates of eutrophication and rates of organic and inorganic sedimentation for varying types of receiving waters.

(2) The Administrator, after consultation with appropriate Federal and State agencies and other interested persons, shall develop and publish, within one year after the date of enactment of this title (and from time to time thereafter revise) information (A) on the factors necessary to restore and maintain the chemical, physical, and biological integrity of all navigable waters, ground waters, waters of the contiguous zone, and the oceans; (B) on the factors necessary for the protection and propagation of shellfish, fish, and wildlife for classes and categories of receiving waters and to allow recreational activities in and on the water; and (C) on the measurement and classification of water quality; and (D) for the purpose of section 303, on and the identification of pollutants suitable for maximum daily load measurement correlated with the achievement of water quality objectives.

(3) Such criteria and information and revisions thereof shall be issued to the States and shall be published in the Federal Register and otherwise made available to the public.

(4) The Administrator shall, within 90 days after the date of enactment of the Clean Water Act of 1977 and from time to time thereafter, publish and revise as appropriate information identifying conventional pollutants, including but not limited to, pollutants classified as biological oxygen demanding, suspended solids, fecal coliform, and pH. The thermal component of any discharge shall not be identified as a conventional pollutant under this paragraph.

(5)(A) The Administrator, to the extent practicable before consideration of any request under section 301(g) of this Act and within six months after the date of enactment of the Clean Water Act of 1977, shall develop and publish information on the factors necessary for the protection of public water supplies, and the protection and propagation of a balanced population of shellfish, fish and wildlife, and to allow recreational activities, in and on the water.

(B) The Administrator, to the extent practicable before consideration of any application under section 301(h) of this Act and within six months after the date of enactment of the Clean Water Act of 1977, shall develop and publish information on the factors necessary for the protection of public water supplies, and the protection and propagation of a balanced indigenous population of shellfish, fish and wildlife, and to allow recreational activities, in and on the water.

(6) The Administrator shall, within three months after enactment of the Clean Water Act of 1977 and annually thereafter, for purposes of section 301(h) of this Act publish and revise as appropriate informa-

tion identifying each water quality standard in effect under this Act [or] State law, the specific pollutants associated with such water quality standard, and the particular waters to which such water quality standard applies.

(7) The Administrator, after consultation with appropriate State agencies and on the basis of criteria and information published under paragraphs (1) and (2) of this subsection, shall develop and publish, within 9 months after the date of the enactment of the Water Quality Act of 1987, guidance to the States on performing the identification required by section 304(l)(1) of this Act.

(8) The Administrator, after consultation with appropriate State agencies and within 2 years after the date of the enactment of the Water Quality Act of 1987, shall develop and publish information on methods for establishing and measuring water quality criteria for toxic pollutants on other bases than pollutant-by-pollutant criteria, including biological monitoring and assessment methods.

(b) For the purpose of adopting or revising effluent limitations under this Act the Administrator shall, after consultation with appropriate Federal and State agencies and other interested persons, publish within one year of enactment of this title, regulations, providing guidelines for effluent limitations, and, at least annually thereafter, revise, if appropriate, such regulations. Such regulations shall—

(1)(A) identify, in terms of amounts of constituents and chemical, physical, and biological characteristics of pollutants, the degree of effluent reduction attainable through the application of the best practicable control technology currently available for classes and categories of point sources (other than publicly owned treatment works); and

(B) specify factors to be taken into account in determining the control measures and practices to be applicable to point sources (other than publicly owned treatment works) within such categories or classes. Factors relating to the assessment of best practicable control technology currently available to comply with subsection (b)(1) of section 301 of this Act shall include consideration of the total cost of application of technology in relation to the effluent reduction benefits to be achieved from such application, and shall also take into account the age of equipment and facilities involved, the process employed, the engineering aspects of the application of various types of control techniques, process changes, non-water quality environmental impact (including energy requirements), and such other factors as the Administrator deems appropriate;

(2)(A) identify in terms of amounts of constituents and chemical, physical, and biological characteristics of pollutants, the degree of effluent reduction attainable through the application of the best control measures and practices achievable including treatment techniques, process and procedure innovations, operating methods, and other alternatives for classes and categories of point sources (other than publicly owned treatment works); and

(B) specify factors to be taken into account in determining the best measures and practices available to comply with subsection (b)(2) of section 301 of this Act to be applicable to any point source (other than publicly owned treatment works) within such categories of classes. Factors relating to the assessment of best available technology shall take into account the age of equipment and facilities involved, the process employed, the engineering aspects of the application of various types of control techniques, process changes, the cost of achieving such effluent reduction, non-water quality environmental impact (including energy requirements), and such other factors as the Administrator deems appropriate;

(3) identify control measures and practices available to eliminate the discharge of pollutants from categories and classes of point sources, taking into account the cost of achieving such elimination of the discharge of pollutants; and

(4)(A) identify, in terms of amounts of constituents and chemical, physical, and biological characteristics of pollutants, the degree of effluent reduction attainable through the application of the best conventional pollutant control technology (including measures and practices) for classes and categories of point sources (other than publicly owned treatment works); and

(B) specify factors to be taken into account in determining the best conventional pollutant control technology measures and practices to comply with section 301(b)(2)(E) of this Act to be applicable to any point source (other than publicly owned treatment works) within such categories or classes. Factors relating to the assessment of best conventional pollutant control technology (including measures and practices) shall include consideration of the reasonableness of the relationship between the costs of attaining a reduction in effluents and the effluent reduction benefits derived, and the comparison of the cost and level of reduction of such pollutants from the discharge from publicly owned treatment works to the cost and level of reduction of such pollutants from a class or category of industrial sources, and shall take into account the age of equipment and facilities involved, the process employed, the engineering aspects of the application of various types of control techniques, process changes, non-water quality environmental impact (including energy requirements), and such other factors as the Administrator deems appropriate.

(c) The Administrator, after consultation, with appropriate Federal and State agencies and other interested persons, shall issue to the States and appropriate water pollution control agencies within 270 days after enactment of this title (and from time to time thereafter) information on the processes, procedures, or operating methods which result in the elimination or reduction of the discharge of pollutants to implement standards of performance under section 306 of this Act. Such information shall include technical and other data, including costs, as are available on alternative methods of elimination or reduction of the discharge of pollutants. Such information, and revisions thereof, shall be published in the Federal Register and otherwise shall be made available to the public.

(d)(1) The Administrator, after consultation with appropriate Federal and State agencies and other interested persons, shall publish within sixty days after the date of enactment of this title (and from time to time thereafter) information, in terms of amounts of constituents and chemical, physical, and biological characteristics of pollutants, on the degree of effluent reduction attainable through the application of secondary treatment.

(2) The Administrator, after consultation with appropriate Federal and State agencies and other interested persons, shall publish within nine months after the date of enactment of this title (and from time to time thereafter) information on alternative waste treatment management techniques and systems available to implement section 201 of this Act.

(3) The Administrator, after consultation with appropriate Federal and State agencies and other interested persons, shall promulgate within one hundred and eighty days after the date of enactment of this subsection guidelines for identifying and evaluating innovative and alternative wastewater treatment processes and techniques referred to in section 201(g)(5) of this Act.

(4) For the purposes of this subsection, such biological treatment facilities as oxidation ponds, lagoons, and ditches and trickling filters shall be deemed the equivalent of secondary treatment. The Administrator shall provide guidance under paragraph (1) of this subsection on design criteria for such facilities, taking into account pollutant removal efficiencies and, consistent with the objective of the Act, assuring that water quality will not be adversely affected by deeming such facilities as the equivalent of secondary treatment.

(e) The Administrator, after consultation with appropriate Federal and State agencies and other interested persons, may publish regulations, supplemental to any effluent limitations specified under subsection (b) and (c) of this section for a class or category of point sources, for any specific pollutant which the Administrator is charged with a duty to regulate as a toxic or hazardous pollutant under section 307(a)(1) or 311 of this Act, to control plant site runoff, spillage or leaks, sludge or waste disposal, and drainage from raw material storage which the Administrator determines are associated with or ancillary to the industrial manufacturing or treatment process within such class or category of point sources and may contribute significant amounts of such pollutants to navigable waters. Any applicable controls established under this subsection shall be included as a requirement for the purposes of section 301, 302, 306, 307, or 403, as the case may be, in any permit issued to a point source pursuant to section 402 of this Act.

(f) The Administrator, after consultation with appropriate Federal and State agencies and other interested persons, shall issue to appropriate Federal agencies, the States, water pollution control agencies, and agencies designated under section 208 of this Act, within one year after the effective date of this subsection (and from time to time thereafter) information including (1) guidelines for identifying and evaluating the nature and extent of nonpoint sources of pollutants, and (2) processes, procedures, and methods to control pollution resulting from—

    (A) agricultural and silvicultural activities, including runoff from fields and crop and forest lands;

    (B) mining activities, including runoff and siltation from new, currently operating, and abandoned surface and underground mines;

    (C) all construction activity, including runoff from the facilities resulting from such construction;

    (D) the disposal of pollutants in wells or in subsurface excavations;

    (E) salt water intrusion resulting from reductions of fresh water flow from any cause, including extraction of ground water, irrigation, obstruction, and diversion; and

    (F) changes in the movement, flow, or circulation of any navigable waters or ground waters, including changes caused by the construction of dams, levees, channels, causeways, or flow diversion facilities.

Such information and revisions thereof shall be published in the Federal Register and otherwise made available to the public.

(g)(1) For the purpose of assisting States in carrying out programs under section 402 of this Act, the Administrator shall publish, within one hundred and twenty days after the date of enactment of this title, and review at least annually thereafter and, if appropriate, revise guidelines for pretreatment of pollutants which he determines are not suspectible to treatment by publicly owned treatment works. Guidelines under this subsection shall be established to control and prevent the discharge into the navigable waters, the contiguous zone, or the ocean (either directly or through publicly owned treatment works) of any pollutant which interferes with, passes through, or otherwise is incompatible with such works.

    (2) When publishing guidelines under this subsection, the Administrator shall designate the category or categories of treatment works to which the guidelines shall apply.

(h) The Administrator shall, within one hundred and eighty days from the date of enactment of this title, promulgate guidelines establishing test procedures for the analysis of pollutants that shall include the factors which must be provided in any certification pursuant to section 401 of this Act or permit application pursuant to section 402 of this Act.

(i) The Administrator shall (1) within sixty days after the enactment of this title promulgate guidelines for the purpose of establishing uniform application forms and other minimum requirements for the acquisition of information from owners and operators of point-sources of discharge subject to any State program under section 402 of this Act, and (2) within sixty days from the date of enactment of this title promulgate guidelines establishing the minimum procedural and other elements of any State program under section 402 of this Act which shall include:

(A) monitoring requirements;

(B) reporting requirements (including procedures to make information available to the public);

(C) enforcement provisions; and

(D) funding, personnel qualifications, and manpower requirements (including a requirement that no board or body which approves permit applications or portions thereof shall include, as a member, any person who receives, or has during the previous two years received, a significant portion of his income directly or indirectly from permit holders or applicants for a permit).

(j) The Administrator shall, within 1 year after the date of the enactment of the Water Quality Act of 1987 and biennially thereafter, publish and disseminate a lake restoration guidance manual describing methods, procedures, and processes to guide State and local efforts to improve, restore, and enhance water quality in the Nation's publicly owned lakes.

(k)(1) The Administrator shall enter into agreements with the Secretary of Agriculture, the Secretary of the Army, and the Secretary of the Interior, and the heads of such other departments, agencies, and instrumentalities of the United States as the Administrator determines, to provide for the maximum utilization of other Federal laws and programs for the purpose of achieving and maintaining water quality through appropriate implementation of plans approved under section 208 of this Act and nonpoint source pollution management programs approved under section 319 of this Act.

(2) The Administrator is authorized to transfer to the Secretary of Agriculture, the Secretary of the Army, and the Secretary of the Interior and the heads of such other departments, agencies, and instrumentalities of the United States as the Administrator determines, any funds appropriated under paragraph (3) of this subsection to supplement funds otherwise appropriated to programs authorized pursuant to any agreement under paragraph (1).

(3) There is authorized to be appropriated to carry out the provisions of this subsection, $100,000,000 per fiscal year for the fiscal years 1979 through 1983 and such sums as may be necessary for fiscal years 1984 through 1990.

(l)(1) Not later than 2 years after the date of the enactment of this subsection, each State shall submit to the Administrator for review, approval, and implementation under this subsection—

(A) a list of those waters within the State which after the application of effluent limitations required under section 301(b)(2) of this Act cannot reasonably be anticipated to attain or maintain (i) water quality standards for such waters reviewed, revised, or adopted in accordance with section 303(c)(2)(B) of this Act, due to toxic pollutants, or (ii) that water quality which shall assure protection of public health, public water supplies, agricultural and industrial uses, and the protection and propagation of a balanced population of shellfish, fish and wildlife, and allow recreational activities in and on the water;

(B) a list of all navigable waters in such State for which the State does not expect the applicable standard under section 303 of this Act will be achieved after the requirements of sections 301(b), 306, and 307(b) are met, due entirely or substantially to discharges from point sources of any toxic pollutants listed pursuant to section 307(a);

(C) for each segment of the navigable waters included on such lists, a determination of the specific point sources discharging any such toxic pollutant which is believed to be preventing or impairing such water quality and the amount of each such toxic pollutant discharged by each such source; and

(D) for each such segment, an individual control strategy which the State determines will produce a reduction in the discharge of toxic pollutants from point sources identified by the State under this paragraph through the establishment of effluent limitations under section 402 of this Act and water quality standards under section 303(c)(2)(B) of this Act, which reduction is sufficient, in combination with existing controls on point and nonpoint sources of pollution, to achieve the applicable water quality standard as soon as possible, but not later than 3 years after the date of the establishment of such strategy.

(2) Not later than 120 days after the last day of the 2-year period referred to in paragraph (1), the Administrator shall approve or disapprove the control strategies submitted under paragraph (1) by any State.

(3) If a State fails to submit control strategies in accordance with paragraph (1) or the Administrator does not approve the control strategies submitted by such State in accordance with paragraph (1), then, not later than 1 year after the last day of the period referred to in paragraph (2), the Administrator, in cooperation with such State and after notice and opportunity for public comment, shall implement the requirements of paragraph (1) in such State. In the implementation of such requirements, the Administrator shall, at a minimum, consider for listing under this subsection any navigable waters for which any person submits a petition to the Administrator for listing not later than 120 days after such last day.

(m)(1) Within 12 months after the date of the enactment of the Water Quality Act of 1987, and biennially thereafter, the Administrator shall publish in the Federal Register a plan which shall—

    (A) establish a schedule for the annual review and revision of promulgated effluent guidelines, in accordance with subsection (b) of this section;

    (B) identify categories of sources discharging toxic or nonconventional pollutants for which guidelines under subsection (b)(2) of this section and section 306 have not previously been published; and

    (C) establish a schedule for promulgation of effluent guidelines for categories identified in subparagraph (B), under which promulgation of such guidelines shall be no later than 4 years after such date of enactment for categories identified in the first published plan or 3 years after the publication of the plan for categories identified in later published plans.

  (2) The Administrator shall provide for public review and comment on the plan prior to final publication.

§ 1315. State reports on water quality; transmittal to Congress

[Sec. 305] (a) The Administrator, in cooperation with the States and with the assistance of appropriate Federal agencies shall prepare a report to be submitted to the Congress on or before January 1, 1974, which shall—

  (1) describe the specific quality, during 1973, with appropriate supplemental descriptions as shall be required to take into account seasonal, tidal, and other variations, of all navigable waters and the waters of the contiguous zone;

  (2) include an inventory of all point sources of discharge (based on a qualitative and quantitative analysis of discharges) of pollutants, into all navigable waters and the waters of the contiguous zone; and

  (3) identify specifically those navigable waters, the quality of which—

    (A) is adequate to provide for the protection and propagation of a balanced population of shellfish, fish, and wildlife and allow recreational activities in and on the water;

    (B) can reasonably be expected to attain such level by 1977 or 1983; and

    (C) can reasonably be expected to attain such level by any later date.

(b)(1) Each State shall prepare and submit to the Administrator by April 1, 1975, and shall bring up to date by April 1, 1976, and biennially thereafter, a report which shall include—

    (A) a description of the water quality of all navigable waters in such State during the preceding year, with appropriate supplemental descriptions as shall be required to take into account seasonal, tidal, and other variations, correlated with the quality of water required by the objective of this Act (as identified by the Administrator pursuant to criteria published under section 304(a) of this Act) and the water quality described in subparagraph (B) of this paragraph;

(B) an analysis of the extent to which all navigable waters of such State provide for the protection and propagation of a balanced population of shellfish, fish, and wildlife, and allow recreational activities in and on the water;

(C) an analysis of the extent to which the elimination of the discharge of pollutants and a level of water quality which provides for the protection and propagation of a balanced population of shellfish, fish, and wildlife and allows recreational activities in and on the water, have been or will be achieved by the requirements of this Act, together with recommendations as to additional action necessary to achieve such objectives and for what waters such additional action is necessary;

(D) an estimate of (i) the environmental impact, (ii) the economic and social costs necessary to achieve the objective of this Act in such State, (iii) the economic and social benefits of such achievement, and (iv) an estimate of the date of such achievement; and

(E) a description of the nature and extent of nonpoint sources of pollutants, and recommendations as to the programs which must be undertaken to control each category of such sources, including an estimate of the costs of implementing such programs.

(2) The Administrator shall transmit such State reports, together with an analysis thereof, to Congress on or before October 1, 1975, and October 1, 1976, and biennially thereafter.

§ 1316. National standards of performance

[Sec. 306] (a) For purposes of this section:

(1) The term "standard of performance" means a standard for the control of the discharge of pollutants which reflects the greatest degree of effluent reduction which the Administrator determines to be achievable through application of the best available demonstrated control technology, processes, operating methods, or other alternatives, including, where practicable, a standard permitting no discharge of pollutants.

(2) The term "new source" means any source, the construction of which is commenced after the publication of proposed regulations prescribing a standard of performance under this section which will be applicable to such source, if such standard is thereafter promulgated in accordance with this section.

(3) The term "source" means any building, structure, facility, or installation from which there is or may be the discharge of pollutants.

(4) The term "owner or operator" means any person who owns, leases,

operates, controls, or supervises a source.

(5) The term "construction" means any placement, assembly, or installation of facilities or equipment (including contractual obligations to purchase such facilities or equipment) at the premises where such equipment will be used, including preparation work at such premises.

(b)(1)(A) The Administrator shall, within ninety days after the date of enactment of this title publish (and from time to time thereafter shall revise) a list of categories of sources, which shall, at the minimum, include:

pulp and paper mills;
paperboard, builders paper and board mills;
meat product and rendering processing;
dairy product processing;
grain mills;
canned and preserved fruits and vegetables processing;
canned and preserved seafood processing;
sugar processing;
textile mills;
cement manufacturing;
feedlots;
electroplating;
organic chemicals manufacturing;
inorganic chemicals manufacturing;
plastic and synthetic materials manufacturing;
soap and detergent manufacturing;
fertilizer manufacturing;
petroleum refining;
iron and steel manufacturing;
nonferrous metals manufacturing;
phosphate manufacturing;
steam electric powerplants;
ferroalloy manufacturing;
leather tanning and finishing;
glass and asbestos manufacturing;
rubber processing; and
timber products processing.

(B) As soon as practicable, but in no case more than one year, after a category of sources is included in a list under subparagraph (A) of this paragraph, the Administrator shall propose and publish regulations establishing Federal standards of performance for new sources within such category. The Administrator shall afford interested persons an opportunity for written comment on such proposed regulations. After considering such comments, he shall promulgate, within one hundred and twenty days after publication of such proposed regulations, such standards with such adjustments as he deems appropriate. The Administrator shall, from time to time, as technology and alternatives change, revise such standards following the procedure required by this subsection for promulgation of such standards. Standards of performance, or revisions thereof, shall become effective upon promulgation. In establishing or revising Federal standards of performance for new sources under this section, the Administrator shall take into consideration the cost of achieving such effluent reduction, and any non-water quality environmental impact and energy requirements.

(2) The Administrator may distinguish among classes, types, and sizes within categories of new sources for the purpose of establishing such standards and shall consider the type of process employed (including whether batch or continuous).

(3) The provisions of this section shall apply to any new source owned or operated by the United States.

(c) Each State may develop and submit to the Administrator a procedure under State law for applying and enforcing standards of performance for new sources located in such State. If the Administrator finds that the procedure and the law of any State require the application and enforcement of standards of performance to at least the same extent as required by this section, such State is authorized to apply and enforce such standards of performance (except with respect to new sources owned or operated by the United States).

(d) Notwithstanding any other provision of this Act, any point source the construction of which is commenced after the date of enactment of the Federal Water Pollution Control Act Amendments of 1972 and which is so constructed as to meet all applicable standards of performance shall not be subject to any more stringent standard of performance during a ten-year period beginning on the date of completion of such construction or during the period of depreciation or amortization of such facility for the purposes of section 167 or 169 (or both) of the Internal Revenue Code of 1954, whichever period ends first.

(e) After the effective date of standards of performance promulgated under this section, it shall be unlawful for any owner or operator of any new source to operate such source in violation of any standard of performance applicable to such source.

§ 1317. Toxic and pretreatment effluent standards

[Sec. 307] (a)(1) On and after the date of enactment of the Clean Water Act of 1977, the list of toxic pollutants or combination of pollutants subject to this Act shall consist of those toxic pollutants listed in table 1 of Committee Print Numbered 95–30 of the Committee on Public Works and Transportation of the House of Representatives, and the Administrator shall publish, not later than the thirtieth day after the date of enactment of the Clean Water Act of 1977, that list. From time to time thereafter, the Administrator may revise such list and the Administrator is authorized to add to or remove from such list any pollutant. The Administrator in publishing any revised list, including the addition or removal of any pollutant from such list, shall take into account the toxicity of the pollutant, its persistence, degradability, the usual or potential presence of the affected organisms in any waters, the importance of the affected organisms, and the nature and extent of the effect of the toxic pollutant on such organisms. A determination of the Administrator under this paragraph shall be final except that if, on judicial review, such determination was based on arbitrary and capricious action of the Administrator, the Administrator shall make a redetermination.

(2) Each toxic pollutant listed in accordance with paragraph (1) of this subsection shall be subject to effluent limitations resulting from the application of the best available technology economically achievable for the applicable category or class of point sources established in accordance with section 301(b)(2)(A) and 304(b)(2) of this Act. The Administrator, in his discretion, may publish in the Federal Register a proposed effluent standard (which may include a prohibition) establishing requirements for a toxic pollutant which, if an effluent limitation is applicable to a class or category of point sources, shall be applicable to such category or class only if such standard imposes more stringent requirements. Such published effluent standard (or prohibition) shall take into account the toxicity of the pollutant, its persistence, degradability, the usual or potential presence of the affected organisms in any waters, the importance of the affected organisms and the nature and extent of the effect of the toxic pollutant on such organisms, and the extent to which effective control is being or may be achieved under other regulatory authority. The Administrator shall allow a period of not less than sixty days following publication of any such proposed effluent standard (or prohibition) for written comment by interested persons on such proposed standard. In addition, if within thirty days of publication of any such proposed effluent standard (or prohibition) any interested person so requests, the Administrator shall hold a public hearing in connection therewith. Such a public hearing shall provide an opportunity for oral and written presentations, such cross-examination as the Administrator determines is appropriate on disputed issues of material fact, and the transcription of a verbatim record which shall be available to the public. After consideration of such comments and any information and material presented at any public hearing held on such proposed standard or prohibition, the Administrator shall promulgate such standards (or prohibition) with such modifications as the Administrator finds are justified. Such promulgation by the Administrator shall be made within two hundred and seventy days after publication of proposed standard (or prohibition). Such standard (or prohibition) shall be final except that if, on judicial review, such standard was not based on substantial evidence,

the Administrator shall promulgate a revised standard. Effluent limitations shall be established in accordance with sections 301(b)(2)(A) and 304(b)(2) for every toxic pollutant referred to in table 1 of Committee Print Numbered 95–30 of the Committee on Public Works and Transportation of the House of Representatives as soon as practicable after the date of enactment of the Clean Water Act of 1977, but no later than July 1, 1980. Such effluent limitations or effluent standards (or prohibitions) shall be established for every other toxic pollutant listed under paragraph (1) of this subsection as soon as practicable after it is so listed.

(3) Each such effluent standard (or prohibition) shall be revised and, if appropriate, revised at least every three years.

(4) Any effluent standard promulgated under this section shall be at that level which the Administrator determines provides an ample margin of safety.

(5) When proposing or promulgating any effluent standard (or prohibition) under this section, the Administrator shall designate the category or categories of sources to which the effluent standard (or prohibition) shall apply. Any disposal of dredged material may be included in such a category of sources after consultation with the Secretary of the Army.

(6) Any effluent standard (or prohibition) established pursuant to this section shall take effect on such date or dates as specified in the order promulgating such standard, but in no case, more than one year from the date of such promulgation. If the Administrator determines that compliance within one year from the date of promulgation is technologically infeasible for a category of sources, the Administrator may establish the effective date of the effluent standard (or prohibition) for such category at the earliest date upon which compliance can be feasibly attained by sources within such category, but in no event more than three years after the date of such promulgation.

(7) Prior to publishing any regulations pursuant to this section the Administrator shall, to the maximum extent practicable within the time provided, consult with appropriate advisory committees, States, independent experts, and Federal departments and agencies.

(b)(1) The Administrator shall, within one hundred and eighty days after the date of enactment of this title and from time to time thereafter, publish proposed regulations establishing pretreatment standards for introduction of pollutants into treatment works (as defined in section 212 of this Act) which are publicly owned for those pollutants which are determined not to be susceptible to treatment by such treatment works or which would interfere with the operation of such treatment works. Not later than ninety days after such publication, and after opportunity for public hearing, the Administrator shall promulgate such pretreatment standards. Pretreatment standards under this subsection shall specify a time for compliance not to exceed three years from the date of promulgation and shall be established to prevent the discharge of any pollutant through treatment works (as defined in section 212 of this Act) which are publicly owned, which pollutant interferes with, passes through, or otherwise is incompatible with such works. If, in the case of any toxic pollutant under subsection (a) of this section introduced by a source into a publicly owned treatment works, the treatment by such works removes all or any part of such toxic pollutant and the discharge from such works does not violate that effluent limitation or standard which would be applicable to such toxic pollutant if it were discharged by such source other than through a publicly owned treatment works, and does not prevent sludge use or disposal by such works in accordance with section 405 of this Act, then the pretreatment requirements for the sources actually discharging such toxic pollutant into such publicly owned treatment works may be revised by the owner or operator of such works to reflect the removal of such toxic pollutant by such works.

(2) The Administrator shall, from time to time, as control technology, processes, operating methods, or other alternative[s] change, revise such standards following the procedure established by this subsection for promulgation of such standards.

(3) When proposing or promulgating any pretreatment standard under this section, the Administrator shall designate the category or categories of sources to which such standard shall apply.

(4) Nothing in this subsection shall affect any pretreatment requirement established by any State or local law not in conflict with any pretreatment standard established under this subsection.

(c) In order to insure that any source introducing pollutants into a publicly owned treatment works, which source would be a new source subject to section 306 if it were to discharge pollutants, will not cause a violation of the effluent limitations established for any such treatment works, the Administrator shall promulgate pretreatment standards for the category of such sources simultaneously with the promulgation of standards of performance under section 306 for the equivalent category of new sources. Such pretreatment standards shall prevent the discharge of any pollutant into such treatment works, which pollutant may interfere with, pass through, or otherwise be incompatible with such works.

(d) After the effective date of any effluent standard or prohibition or pretreatment standard promulgated under this section, it shall be unlawful for any owner or operator of any source to operate any source in violation of any such effluent standard or prohibition or pretreatment standard.

(e) In the case of any existing facility that proposes to comply with the pretreatment standards of subsection (b) of this section by applying an innovative system that meets the requirements of section 301(k) of this Act, the owner or operator of the publicly owned treatment works receiving the treated effluent from such facility may extend the date for compliance with the applicable pretreatment standard established under this section for a period not to exceed 2 years—

(1) if the Administrator determines that the innovative system has the potential for industrywide application, and

(2) if the Administrator (or the State in consultation with the Administrator, in any case in which the State has a pretreatment program approved by the Administrator)—

(A) determines that the proposed extension will not cause the publicly owned treatment works to be in violation of its permit under section 402 or of section 405 or to contribute to such a violation, and

(B) concurs with the proposed extension.

§ 1318. Records and reports; inspections

[Sec. 308] (a) Whenever required to carry out the objective of this Act, including but not limited to (1) developing or assisting in the development of any effluent limitation, or other limitation, prohibition, or effluent standard, pretreatment standard, or standard of performance under this Act; (2) determining whether any person is in violation of any such effluent limitation, or other limitation, prohibition or effluent standard, pretreatment standard, or standard of performance; (3) any requirement established under this section; or (4) carrying out sections 305, 311, 402, 404 (relating to State permit programs), 405, and 504 of this Act—

(A) the Administrator shall require the owner or operator of any point source to (i) establish and maintain such records, (ii) make such reports, (iii) install, use and maintain such monitoring equipment or methods (including where appropriate, biological monitoring methods), (iv) sample such effluents (in accordance with such methods, at such locations, at such intervals, and in such manner as the Administrator shall prescribe), and (v) provide such other information as he may reasonably require; and

(B) the Administrator or his authorized representative (including an authorized contractor acting as a representative of the Administrator), upon presentation of his credentials—

(i) shall have a right of entry to, upon, or through any premises in which an effluent source is located or in which any records required to be maintained under clause (A) of this subsection are located, and

(ii) may at reasonable times have access to and copy any records, inspect any monitoring equipment or method required under clause (A), and sample any effluents which the owner or operator of such source is required to sample under such clause.

(b) Any records, reports, or information obtained under this section (1) shall, in the case of effluent data, be related to any applicable effluent limitations, toxic, pretreatment, or new source performance standards, and (2) shall be available to the public, except that upon a showing satisfactory to the Administrator by any person that records, reports, or information, or particular part thereof (other than effluent data), to which the Administrator has access under this section, if made public would divulge methods or processes entitled to protection as trade secrets of such person, the Administrator shall consider such record, report, or information, or particular portion thereof confidential in accordance with the purposes of section 1905 of title 18 of the United States Code. Any authorized representative of the Administrator (including an authorized contractor acting as a representative of the Administrator) who knowingly or willfully publishes, divulges, discloses, or makes known in any manner or to any extent not authorized by law any information which is required to be considered confidential under this subsection shall be fined not more than $1,000 or imprisoned not more than 1 year, or both. Nothing in this subsection shall prohibit the Administrator or an authorized representative of the Administrator (including any authorized contractor acting as a representative of the Administrator) from disclosing records, reports, or information to other officers, employees, or authorized representatives of the United States concerned with carrying out this Act or when relevant in any proceeding under this Act.

(c) Each State may develop and submit to the Administrator procedures under State law for inspection, monitoring, and entry with respect to point sources located in such State. If the Administrator finds that the procedures and the law of any State relating to inspection, monitoring, and entry are applicable to at least the same extent as those required by this section, such State is authorized to apply and enforce its procedures for inspection, monitoring, and entry with respect to point sources located in such State (except with respect to point sources owned or operated by the Untied States).

(d) Notwithstanding any limitation contained in this section or any other provision of law, all information reported to or otherwise obtained by the Administrator (or any representative of the Administrator) under this Act shall be made available, upon written request of any duly authorized committee of Congress, to such committee.

§ 1319. Enforcement

[Sec. 309] (a)(1) Whenever, on the basis of any information available to him, the Administrator finds that any person is in violation of any condition or limitation which implements section 301, 302, 306, 307, 308, 318, or 405 of this Act in a permit issued by a State under an approved permit program under section 402 or 404 of this Act, he shall proceed under his authority in paragraph (3) of this subsection or he shall notify the person in alleged violation and such State of such finding. If beyond the thirtieth day after the Administrator's notification the State has not commenced appropriate enforcement action, the Administrator shall issue an order requiring such person to comply with such condition or limitation or shall bring a civil action in accordance with subsection (b) of this section.

(2) Whenever, on the basis of information available to him, the Administrator finds that violations of permit conditions or limitations as set forth in paragraph (1) of this subsection are so widespread that such violations appear to result from a failure of the State to enforce such permit conditions or limitations effectively, he shall so notify the State. If the Administrator finds such failure extends beyond the thirtieth day after such notice, he shall give public notice of such finding. During the period beginning with such public notice and ending when such State satisfies the Administrator that it will enforce such conditions and limitations (hereafter referred to in this section as the period of "federally assumed enforcement"), except where an extension has been granted under paragraph (5)(B) of this subsection, the Administrator shall enforce any permit condition or limitation with respect to any person—

(A) by issuing an order to comply with such condition or limitation, or

(B) by bringing a civil action under subsection (b) of this section.

(3) Whenever on the basis of any information available to him the Administrator finds that any person is in violation of section 301, 302, 306, 307, 308, 318, or 405 of this Act, or is in violation of any permit condition or limitation implementing any of such sections in a permit issued under section 402 of this Act by him or by a State or in a permit issued under section 404 of this Act by a State, he shall issue an order requiring such person to comply with such section or requirement, or he shall bring a civil action in accordance with subsection (b) of this section.

(4) A copy of any order issued under this subsection shall be sent immediately by the Administrator to the State in which the violation occurs and other affected States. In any case in which an order under this subsection (or notice to a violator under paragraph (1) of this subsection) is issued to a corporation, a copy of such order (or notice) shall be served on any appropriate corporate officers. An order issued under this subsection relating to a violation of section 308 of this Act shall not take effect until the person to whom it is issued has had an opportunity to confer with the Administrator concerning the alleged violation.

(5)(A) Any order issued under this subsection shall be by personal service, shall state with reasonable specificity the nature of the violation, and shall specify a time for compliance not to exceed thirty days in the case of a violation of an interim compliance schedule or operation and maintenance requirement and not to exceed a time the Administrator determines to be reasonable in the case of a violation of a final deadline, taking into account the seriousness of the violation and any good faith efforts to comply with applicable requirements.

    (B) The Administrator may, if he determines (i) that any person who is a violator of, or any person who is otherwise not in compliance with, the time requirements under this Act or in any permit issued under this Act, has acted in good faith, and has made a commitment (in the form of contracts or other securities) of necessary resources to achieve compliance by the earliest possible date after July 1, 1977, but not later than April 1, 1979; (ii) that any extension under this provision will not result in the imposition of any additional controls on any other point or nonpoint source; (iii) that an application for a permit under section 402 of this Act was filed for such person prior to December 31, 1974; and (iv) that the facilities necessary for compliance with such requirements are under construction, grant an extension of the date referred to in section 301(b)(1)(A) to a date which will achieve compliance at the earliest time possible but not later than April 1, 1979.

  (6) Whenever, on the basis of information available to him, the Administrator finds (A) that any person is in violation of section 301(b)(1)(A) or (C) of this Act, (B) that such person cannot meet the requirements for a time extension under section 301(i)(2) of this Act, and (C) that the most expeditious and appropriate means of compliance with this Act by such person is to discharge into a publicly owned treatment works, then, upon request of such person, the Administrator may issue an order requiring such person to comply with this Act at the earliest date practicable, but not later than July 1, 1983, by discharging into a publicly owned treatment works if such works concur with such order. Such order shall include a schedule of compliance.

(b) The Administrator is authorized to commence a civil action for appropriate relief, including a permanent or temporary injunction, for any violation for which he is authorized to issue a compliance order under subsection (a) of this section. Any action under this subsection may be brought in the district court of the United States for the district in which the defendant is located or resides or is doing business, and such court shall have jurisdiction to restrain such violation and to require compliance. Notice of the commencement of such action shall be given immediately to the appropriate State.

  (c)(1) Any person who—

    (A) negligently violates section 301, 302, 306, 307, 308, 318, or 405 of this Act, or any permit condition or limitation implementing any of such sections in a permit issued under section 402 of this Act by the Administrator or by a State, or any requirement imposed in a pretreatment program approved under section 402(a)(3) or 402(b)(8) of this Act or in a permit issued under section 404 of this Act by the Secretary of the Army or by a State; or

(B) negligently introduces into a sewer system or into a publicly owned treatment works any pollutant or hazardous substance which such person knew or reasonably should have known could cause personal injury or property damage or, other than in compliance with all applicable Federal, State, or local requirements or permits, which causes such treatment works to violate any effluent limitation or condition in any permit issued to the treatment works under section 402 of this Act by the Administrator or a State; shall be punished by a fine of not less than $2,500 nor more than $25,000 per day of violation, or by imprisonment for not more than 1 year, or by both. If a conviction of a person is for a violation committed after a first conviction of such person under this paragraph, punishment shall be by a fine of not more than $50,000 per day of violation, or by imprisonment of not more than 2 years, or by both.

(2) Any person who—

(A) knowingly violates section 301, 302, 306, 307, 308, 318, or 405 of this Act, or any permit condition or limitation implementing any of such sections in a permit issued under section 402 of this Act by the Administrator or by a State, or any requirement imposed in a pretreatment program approved under section 402(a)(3) or 402(b)(8) of this Act or in a permit issued under section 404 of this Act by the Secretary of the Army or by a State; or

(B) knowingly introduces into a sewer system or into a publicly owned treatment works any pollutant or hazardous substance which such person knew or reasonably should have known could cause personal injury or property damage or, other than in compliance with all applicable Federal, State, or local requirements or permits, which causes such treatment works to violate any effluent limitation or condition in a permit issued to the treatment works under section 402 of this Act by the Administrator or a State; shall be punished by a fine of not less than $5,000 nor more than $50,000 per day of violation, or by imprisonment for not more than 3 years, or by both. If a conviction of a person is for a violation committed after a first conviction of such person under this paragraph, punishment shall be by a fine of not more than $100,000 per day of violation, or by imprisonment of not more than 6 years, or by both.

(3)(A) Any person who knowingly violates section 301, 302, 303, 306, 307, 308, 318, or 405 of this Act, or any permit condition or limitation implementing any of such sections in a permit issued under section 402 of this Act by the Administrator or by a State, or in a permit issued under section 404 of this Act by the Secretary of the Army or by a State, and who knows at that time that he thereby places another person in imminent danger of death or serious bodily injury, shall, upon conviction, be subject to a fine of not more than $250,000 or imprisonment of not more than 15 years, or both. A person which is an organization shall, upon conviction of violating this subparagraph, be subject to a fine of not more than $1,000,000. If a conviction of a person is for a violation committed after a first conviction of such person under this paragraph, the maximum punishment shall be doubled with respect to both fine and imprisonment.

(B) For the purpose of subparagraph (A) of this paragraph—

    (i) in determining whether a defendant who is an individual knew that his conduct placed another person in imminent danger of death or serious bodily injury—

        (I) the person is responsible only for actual awareness or actual belief that he possessed; and

        (II) knowledge possessed by a person other than the defendant but not by the defendant himself may not be attributed to the defendant; except that in proving the defendant's possession of actual knowledge, circumstantial evidence may be used, including evidence that the defendant took affirmative steps to shield himself from relevant information;

    (ii) it is an affirmative defense to prosecution that the conduct charged was consented to by the person endangered and that the danger and conduct charged were reasonably foreseeable hazards of—

        (I) an occupation, a business, or a profession; or

        (II) medical treatment or medical or scientific experimentation conducted by professionally approved methods and such other person had been made aware of the risks involved prior to giving consent; and such defense may be established under this subparagraph by a preponderance of the evidence;

    (iii) the term "organization" means a legal entity, other than a government, established or organized for any purpose, and such term includes a corporation, company, association, firm, partnership, joint stock company, foundation, institution, trust, society, union, or any other association of persons; and

    (iv) the term "serious bodily injury" means bodily injury which involves a substantial risk of death, unconsciousness, extreme physical pain, protracted and obvious disfigurement, or protracted loss or impairment of the function of a bodily member, organ, or mental faculty.

(4) Any person who knowingly makes any false material statement, representation, or certification in any application, record, report, plan, or other document filed or required to be maintained under this Act or who knowingly falsifies, tampers with, or renders inaccurate any

monitoring device or method required to be maintained under this Act, shall upon conviction, be punished by a fine of not more than $10,000, or by imprisonment for not more than 2 years, or by both. If a conviction of a person is for a violation committed after a first conviction of such person under this paragraph, punishment shall be by a fine of not more than $20,000 per day of violation, or by imprisonment of not more than 4 years, or by both.

(5) For purposes of this subsection, a single operational upset which leads to simultaneous violations of more than one pollutant parameter shall be treated as a single violation.

(6) For the purpose of this subsection, the term "person" means, in addition to the definition contained in section 502(5) of this Act, any responsible corporate officer.

(7) For the purpose of this subsection, the term "hazardous substance" means (A) any substance designated pursuant to section 311(b)(2)(A) of this Act, (B) any element, compound, mixture, solution, or substance designated pursuant to section 102 of the Comprehensive Environmental Response, Compensation, and Liability Act of 1980, (C) any hazardous waste having the characteristics identified under or listed pursuant to section 3001 of the Solid Waste Disposal Act (but not including any waste the regulation of which under the Solid Waste Disposal Act has been suspended by Act of Congress), (D) any toxic pollutant listed under section 307(a) of this Act, and (E) any imminently hazardous chemical substance or mixture with respect to which the Administrator has taken action pursuant to section 7 of the Toxic Substances Control Act.

(d) Any person who violates section 301, 302, 306, 307, 308, 318, or 405 of this Act, or any permit condition or limitation implementing any of such sections in a permit issued under section 402 of this Act by the Administrator, or by a State, or in a permit issued under section 404 of this Act by a State, or any requirement imposed in a pretreatment program approved under section 402(a)(3) or 402(b)(8) of this Act, and any person who violates any order issued by the Administrator under subsection (a) of this section, shall be subject to a civil penalty not to exceed $25,000 per day for each violation. In determining the amount of a civil penalty the court shall consider the seriousness of the violation or violations, the economic benefit (if any) resulting from the violation, any history of such violations, any good-faith efforts to comply with the applicable requirements, the economic impact of the penalty on the violator, and such other matters as justice may require. For purposes of this subsection, a single operational upset which leads to simultaneous violations of more than one pollutant parameter shall be treated as a single violation.

(e) Whenever a municipality is a party to a civil action brought by the United States under this section, the State in which such municipality is located shall be joined as a party. Such State shall be liable for payment of any judgment, or any expenses incurred as a result of complying with any judgment, entered into against the municipality in such action to the extent that the laws of that State prevent the municipality from raising revenues needed to comply with such judgment.

(f) Whenever, on the basis of any information available to him, the Administrator finds that an owner or operator of any source is introducing a pollutant into a treatment works in violation of subsection (d) of section 307, the Administrator may notify the owner or operator of such treatment works and the State of such violation. If the owner or operator of the treatment works does not commence appropriate enforcement action within 30 days of the date of such notification, the Administrator may commence a civil action for appropriate relief including but not limited to, a permanent or temporary injunction, against the owner or operator of such treatment works. In any such civil action the Administrator shall join the owner or operator of such source as a party to the action. Such action shall be brought in the district court of the United States in the district in which the treatment works is located. Such court shall have jurisdiction to restrain such violation and to require the owner or operator of the treatment works and the owner or operator of the source to take such action as may be necessary to come into compliance with this Act. Notice of commencement of any such action shall be given to the State. Nothing in this subsection shall be construed to limit or prohibit any other authority the Administrator may have under this Act.

(g)(1) Whenever on the basis of any information available—

(A) the Administrator finds that any person has violated section 301, 302, 306, 307, 308, 318, or 405 of this Act, or has violated any permit condition or limitation implementing any of such sections in a permit issued under section 402 of this Act by the Administrator or by a State, or in a permit issued under section 404 by a State, or

(B) the Secretary of the Army (hereinafter in this subsection referred to as the "Secretary") finds that any person has violated any permit condition or limitation in a permit issued under section 404 of this Act by the Secretary, the Administrator or Secretary, as the case may be, may, after consultation with the State in which the violation occurs, assess a class I civil penalty or a class II civil penalty under this subsection.

(2)(A) The amount of a class I civil penalty under paragraph (1) may not exceed $10,000 per violation, except that the maximum amount of any class I civil penalty under this subparagraph shall not exceed $25,000. Before issuing an order assessing a civil penalty under this subparagraph, the Administrator or the Secretary, as the case may be, shall give to the person to be assessed such penalty written notice of the Administrator's or Secretary's proposal to issue such order and the opportunity to request, within 30 days of the date the notice is received by such person, a hearing on the proposed order. Such hearing shall not be subject to section 554 or 556 of title 5, United States Code, but shall provide a reasonable opportunity to be heard and to present evidence.

(B) The amount of a class II civil penalty under paragraph (1) may not exceed $10,000 per day for each day during which the violation continues; except that the maximum amount of any class II civil penalty under this subparagraph shall not exceed $125,000. Except as otherwise provided in this subsection, a class II civil penalty shall be assessed and collected in the same manner, and subject to the same provisions, as in the case of civil penalties assessed and collected after notice and opportunity for a hearing on the record in accordance with section 554 of title 5, United States Code. The Administrator and the Secretary may issue rules for discovery procedures for hearings under this subparagraph.

(3) In determining the amount of any penalty assessed under this subsection, the Administrator or the Secretary, as the case may be, shall take into account the nature, circumstances, extent and gravity of the violation, or violations, and, with respect to the violator, ability to pay, any prior history of such violations, the degree of culpability, economic benefit or savings (if any) resulting from the violation, and such other matters as justice may require. For purposes of this subsection, a single operational upset which leads to simultaneous violations of more than one pollutant parameter shall be treated as a single violation.

(4)(A) Before issuing an order assessing a civil penalty under this subsection the Administrator or Secretary, as the case may be, shall provide public notice of and reasonable opportunity to comment on the proposed issuance of such order.

(B) Any person who comments on a proposed assessment of a penalty under this subsection shall be given notice of any hearing held under this subsection and of the order assessing such penalty. In any hearing held under this subsection, such person shall have a reasonable opportunity to be heard and to present evidence.

(C) If no hearing is held under paragraph (2) before issuance of an order assessing a penalty under this subsection, any person who commented on the proposed assessment may petition, within 30 days after the issuance of such order, the Administrator or Secretary, as the case may be, to set aside such order and to provide a hearing on the penalty. If the evidence presented by the petitioner in support of the petition is material and was not considered in the issuance of the order, the Administrator or Secretary shall immediately set aside such order and provide a hearing in accordance with paragraph (2)(A) in the case of a class I civil penalty and paragraph (2)(B) in the case of a class II civil penalty. If the Administrator or Secretary denies a hearing under this subparagraph, the Administrator or Secretary shall provide to the petitioner, and publish in the Federal Register, notice of and the reasons for such denial.

(5) An order issued under this subsection shall become final 30 days after its issuance unless a petition for judicial review is filed under paragraph (8) or a hearing is requested under paragraph (4)(C). If such a hearing is denied, such order shall become final 30 days after such denial.

(6)(A) Action taken by the Administrator or the Secretary, as the case may be, under this subsection shall not affect or limit the Administrator's or Secretary's authority to enforce any provision of this Act; except that any violation—

    (i) with respect to which the Administrator or the Secretary has commenced and is diligently prosecuting an action under this subsection,

   (ii) with respect to which a State has commenced and is diligently prosecuting an action under a State law comparable to this subsection, or

  (iii) for which the Administrator, the Secretary, or the State has issued a final order not subject to further judicial review and the violator has paid a penalty assessed under this subsection, or such comparable State law, as the case may be, shall not be the subject of a civil penalty action under subsection (d) of this section or section 311(b) or section 505 of this Act.

(B) The limitations contained in subparagraph (A) on civil penalty actions under section 505 of this Act shall not apply with respect to any violation for which—

    (i) a civil action under section 505(a)(1) of this Act has been filed prior to commencement of an action under this subsection, or

   (ii) notice of an alleged violation of section 505(a)(1) of this Act has been given in accordance with section 505(b)(1)(A) prior to commencement of an action under this subsection and an action under section 505(a)(1) with respect to such alleged violation is filed before the 120th day after the date on which such notice is given.

(7) No action by the Administrator or the Secretary under this subsection shall affect any person's obligation to comply with any section of this Act or with the terms and conditions of any permit issued pursuant to section 402 or 404 of this Act.

(8) Any person against whom a civil penalty is assessed under this subsection or who commented on the proposed assessment of such penalty in accordance with paragraph (4) may obtain review of such assessment—

(A) in the case of assessment of a class I civil penalty, in the United

States District Court for the District of Columbia or in the district in which the violation is alleged to have occurred, or

(B) in the case of assessment of a class II civil penalty, in United States Court of Appeals for the District of Columbia Circuit or for any other circuit in which such person resides or transacts business, by filing a notice of appeal in such court within the 30-day period beginning on the date the civil penalty order is issued and by simultaneously sending a copy of such notice by certified mail to the Administrator or the Secretary, as the case may be, and the Attorney General. The Administrator or the Secretary shall promptly file in such court a certified copy of the record on which the order was issued. Such court shall not set aside or remand such order unless there is not substantial evidence in the record, taken as a whole, to support the finding of a violation or unless the Administrator's or Secretary's assessment of the penalty constitutes an abuse of discretion and shall not impose additional civil penalties for the same violation unless the Administrator's or Secretary's assessment of the penalty constitutes an abuse of discretion.

(9) If any person fails to pay an assessment of a civil penalty—

(A) after the order making the assessment has become final, or

(B) after a court in an action brought under paragraph (8) has entered a final judgment in favor of the Administrator or the Secretary, as the case may be, the Administrator or the Secretary shall request the Attorney General to bring a civil action in an appropriate district court to recover the amount assessed (plus interest at currently prevailing rates from the date of the final order or the date of the final judgment, as the case may be). In such an action, the validity, amount, and appropriateness of such penalty shall not be subject to review. Any person who fails to pay on a timely basis the amount of an assessment of a civil penalty as described in the first sentence of this paragraph shall be required to pay, in addition to such amount and interest, attorneys fees and costs for collection proceedings and a quarterly nonpayment penalty for each quarter during which such failure to pay persists. Such nonpayment penalty shall be in an amount equal to 20 percent of the aggregate amount of such person's penalties and nonpayment penalties which are unpaid as of the beginning of such quarter.

(10) The Administrator or Secretary, as the case may be, may issue subpoenas for the attendance and testimony of witnesses and the production of relevant papers, books, or documents in connection with hearings under this subsection. In case of contumacy or refusal to obey a subpoena issued pursuant to this paragraph and served upon any person, the district court of the United States for any district in which

such person is found, resides, or transacts business, upon application by the United States and after notice to such person, shall have jurisdiction to issue an order requiring such person to appear and give testimony before the administrative law judge or to appear and produce documents before the administrative law judge, or both, and any failure to obey such order of the court may be punished by such courrt as a contempt thereof.

(11) Nothing in this subsection shall change the procedures existing on the day before the date of the enactment of the Water Quality Act of 1987 under other subsections of this section for issuance and enforcement of orders by the Administrator.

§ 1320. International pollution abatement

[Sec. 310] (a) Whenever the Administrator, upon receipts of reports, surveys, or studies from any duly constituted international agency, has reason to believe that pollution is occurring which endangers the health or welfare of persons in a foreign country, and the Secretary of State requests him to abate such pollution, he shall give formal notification thereof to the State water pollution control agency of the State or States in which such discharge or discharges originate and to the appropriate interstate agency, if any. He shall also promptly call such a hearing, if he believes that such pollution is occurring in sufficient quantity to warrant such action, and if such foreign country has given the United States essentially the same rights with respect to the prevention and control of pollution occurring in that country as is given that country by this subsection. The Administrator, through the Secretary of State, shall invite the foreign country which may be adversely affected by the pollution to attend and participate in the hearing, and the representative of such country shall, for the purpose of the hearing and any further proceeding resulting from such hearing, have all the rights of a State water pollution control agency. Nothing in this subsection shall be construed to modify, amend, repeal, or otherwise affect the provisions of the 1909 Boundary Waters Treaty between Canada and the United States or the Water Utilization Treaty of 1944 between Mexico and the United States (59 Stat. 1219), relative to the control and abatement of pollution in waters covered by those treaties.

(b) The calling of a hearing under this section shall not be construed by the courts, the Administrator, or any person as limiting, modifying, or otherwise affecting the functions and responsibilities of the Administrator under this section to establish and enforce water quality requirements under this Act.

(c) The Administrator shall publish in the Federal Register a notice of a public hearing before a hearing board of five or more persons appointed by the Administrator. A majority of the members of the board and the chairman who shall be designated by the Administrator shall not be officers or employees of Federal, State, or local governments. On the basis of the evidence presented at such hearing, the board shall within sixty days after completion of the hearing make findings of fact as to whether or not such pollution is occurring and shall thereupon by decision, incorporating its findings therein, make such recommendations to abate the pollution as may be appropriate and shall transmit such decision and the record of the hearings to the Administrator. All such decisions shall be public. Upon receipt of such decision, the Administrator shall promptly implement the board's decision in accordance with the provisions of this Act.

(d) In connection with any hearing called under this subsection, the board is authorized to require any person whose alleged activities result in discharges causing or contributing to pollution to file with it in such forms as it may prescribe, a report based on existing data, furnishing such information as may reasonably be required as to the character, kind, and quantity of such discharges and the use of facilities or other means to prevent or reduce such discharges by the person filing such a report. Such report shall be made under oath or otherwise, as the board may prescribe, and shall be filed with the board within such reasonable period as it may prescribe, unless additional time is granted by it. Upon a showing satisfactory to the board by the person filing such report that such report or portion thereof (other than effluent data), to which the Administrator has access under this section, if made public would divulge trade secrets or secret processes of such person, the board shall consider such report or portion thereof confidential for the purposes of section 1905 of title 18 of the United States Code. If any person required to file any report under this paragraph shall fail to do so within the time fixed by the board for filing the same, and such failure shall continue for thirty days after notice of such default, such person shall forfeit to the United States the sum of $1,000 for each and every day of the continuance of such failure, which forfeiture shall be payable into the Treasury of the United States, and shall be recoverable in a civil suit in the name of the United States in the district court of the United States where such person has his principal office or in any district in which he does business. The Administrator may upon application therefor remit or mitigate any forfeiture provided for under this subsection.

(e) Board members, other than officers or employees of Federal, State, or local governments, shall be for each day (including travel-time) during which they are performing board business, entitled to receive compensation at a rate fixed by the Administrator but not in excess of the maximum rate of pay for grade GS-18, as provided in the General Schedule under section 5332 of title 5 of the United States Code, and shall, notwithstanding the limitations of sections 5703 and 5704 of title 5 of the United States Code, be fully reimbursed for travel, subsistence, and related expenses.

(f) When any such recommendation adopted by the Administrator involves the institution of enforcement proceedings against any person to obtain the abatement of pollution subject to such recommendation, the

Administrator shall institute such proceedings if he believes that the evidence warrants such proceedings. The district court of the United States shall consider and determine de novo all relevant issues, but shall receive in evidence the record of the proceedings before the conference or hearing board. The court shall have jurisdiction to enter such judgment and orders enforcing such judgment as it deems appropriate or to remand such proceedings to the Administrator for such further action as it may direct.

§ 1321.   Oil and hazardous substance liability

[Sec. 311] (a) For the purpose of this section, the term—
(1) "oil" means oil of any kind or in any form, including, but not limited to, petroleum, fuel oil, sludge, oil refuse, and oil mixed with wastes other than dredged spoil;
(2) "discharge" includes, but is not limited to, any spilling, leaking, pumping, pouring, emitting, emptying or dumping, but excludes (A) discharges in compliance with a permit under section 402 of this Act, (B) discharges resulting from circumstances identified and reviewed and made a part of the public record with respect to a permit issued or modified under section 402 of this Act, and subject to a condition in such permit, and (C) continuous or anticipated intermittent discharges from a point source, identified in a permit or permit application under section 402 of this Act, which are caused by events occurring within the scope of relevant operating or treatment systems.
(3) "vessel" means every description of watercraft or other artificial contrivance used, or capable of being used, as a means of transportation on water other than a public vessel;
(4) "public vessel" means a vessel owned or bare-boat-chartered and operated by the United States, or by a State or political subdivision thereof, or by a foreign nation, except when such vessel is engaged in commerce;
(5) "United States" means the States, the District of Columbia, the Commonwealth of Puerto Rico, the Commonwealth of the Northern Mariana Islands, Guam, American Samoa, the Virgin Islands, and the Trust Territory of the Pacific Islands;
(6) "owner or operator" means (A) in the case of a vessel, any person owning, operating, or chartering by demise, such vessel, and (B) in the case of an onshore facility, and an offshore facility, any person owning or operating such onshore facility or offshore facility, and (C) in the case of any abandoned offshore facility, the person who owned or operated such facility immediately prior to such abandonment;
(7) "person" includes an individual, firm, corporation, association, and a partnership;
(8) "remove" or "removal" refers to removal of the oil or hazardous substances from the water and shorelines or the taking of such other

actions as may be necessary to minimize or mitigate damage to the public health or welfare, including, but not limited to, fish, shellfish, wildlife, and public and private property, shorelines, and beaches;

(9) "contiguous zone" means the entire zone established or to be established by the United States under article 24 of the Convention on the Territorial Sea and the Contiguous Zone;

(10) "onshore facility" means any facility (including, but not limited to, motor vehicles and rolling stock) of any kind located in, on, or under, any land within the United States other than submerged land;

(11) "offshore facility" means any facility of any kind located in, on, or under, any of the navigable waters of the United States, and any facility of any kind which is subject to the jurisdiction of the United States and is located in, on, or under any other waters, other than a vessel or a public vessel;

(12) "act of God" means an act occasioned by an unanticipated grave natural disaster;

(13) "barrel" means 42 United States gallons at 60 degrees Fahrenheit;

(14) "hazardous substance" means any substance designated pursuant to subsection (b)(2) of this section;

(15) "inland oil barge" means a non-self propelled vessel carrying oil in bulk as cargo and certificated to operate only in the inland waters of the United States, while operating in such waters;

(16) "inland waters of the United States" means those waters of the United States lying inside the baseline from which the territorial sea is measured and those waters outside such baseline which are a part of the Gulf Intracoastal Waterway.

(17) "Otherwise subject to the jurisdiction of the United States" means subject to the jurisdiction of the United States by virtue of United States citizenship, United States vessel documentation or numbering, or as provided for by international agreement to which the United States is a party.

(b)(1) The Congress hereby declares that it is the policy of the United States that there should be no discharges of oil or hazardous substances into or upon the navigable waters of the United States, adjoining shorelines, or into or upon the waters of the contiguous zone, or in connection with activities under the Outer Continental Shelf Lands Act or the Deepwater Port Act of 1977, or which may affect natural resources belonging to, appertaining to, or under the exclusive management authority of the United States (including resources under the Magnuson Fishery Conservation and Management Act of 1976).

(2)(A) The Administrator shall develop, promulgate, and revise as may be appropriate, regulations designating as hazardous substances, other than oil as defined in this section, such elements and compounds which, when discharged in any quantity into or upon the navigable waters of the United States or adjoining shorelines or the waters of the contiguous zone or in connection with activities under the Outer Continental Shelf Lands Act or the Deepwater Port Act of 1974, or which may affect natural resources belonging to appertaining to, or under the exclusive management authority of the United States (including resources under the Magnuson Fishery Conservation and Management Act of 1976), present an imminent and substantial danger to the public health or welfare, including, but not limited to, fish, shellfish, wildlife, shorelines, and beaches.

(B) The Administrator shall within 18 months after the date of enactment of this paragraph, conduct a study and report to the Congress on methods, mechanisms, and procedures to create incentives to achieve a higher standard of care in all aspects of the management and movement of hazardous substances on the part of owners, operators, or persons in charge of onshore facilities, offshore facilities or vessels. The Administrator shall include in such study (1) limits of liability, (2) liability for third party damages, (3) penalties and fees, (4) spill prevention plans, (5) current practices in the insurance and banking industries, and (6) whether the penalty enacted in subclause (bb) of clause (iii) of subparagraph (B) of subsection (b)(2) of section 311 of Public Law 92–500 should be enacted.

(3) The discharge of oil or hazardous substances (i) into or upon the navigable waters of the United States, adjoining shorelines, or into or upon the waters of the contiguous zone, or (ii) in connection with activities under the Outer Continental Shelf Lands Act or the Deepwater Port Act of 1974, or which may affect natural resources belonging to, appertaining to, or under the exclusive management authority of the United States (including resources under the Magnuson Fishery Conservation and Management Act of 1976), in such quantities as may be harmful as determined by the President under paragraph (4) of this subsection, is prohibited, except (A) in the case of such discharges into the waters of the contiguous zone or which may affect natural resources belonging to, appertaining to, or under the exclusive management authority of the United States (including resources under the Magnuson Fishery Conservation and Management Act of 1976), where permitted under the Protocol of 1978 Relating to the International Convention for the Prevention of Pollution from Ships, 1973 and (B) where permitted in quantities and at times and locations or under such circumstances or conditions as the President may, by regulation, determine not to be harmful. Any regulations issued under this subsection shall be consistent with maritime safety and with marine and navigation laws and regulations and applicable water quality standards.

(4) The President shall by regulation determine for the purposes of this section those quantities of oil and any hazardous substances the

discharge of which may be harmful to the public health or welfare of the United States, including but not limited to fish, shellfish, wildlife, and public and private property, shorelines, and beaches.

(5) Any person in charge of a vessel or of an onshore facility or an offshore facility shall, as soon as he has knowledge of any discharge of oil or a hazardous substance from such vessel or facility in violation of paragraph (3) of this subsection, immediately notify the appropriate agency of the United States Government of such discharge. Any such person (A) in charge of a vessel from which oil or a hazardous substance is discharged in violation of paragraph (3)(i) of this subsection, or (B) in charge of a vessel from which oil or a hazardous substance is discharged in violation of paragraph (3)(ii) of this subsection and who is otherwise subject to the jurisdiction of the United States at the time of the discharge, or (C) in charge of an onshore facility or an offshore facility, who fails to notify immediately such agency of such discharge shall, upon conviction, be fined not more than $10,000, or imprisoned for not more than one year or both. Notification received pursuant to this paragraph or information obtained by the exploitation of such notification shall not be used against any such person in any criminal case, except a prosecution for perjury or for giving a false statement.

(6)(A) Any owner or operator, or person in charge of any onshore facility or offshore facility from which oil or a hazardous substance is discharged in violation of paragraph (3) of this subsection shall be assessed a civil penalty by the Secretary of the department in which the Coast Guard is operating of not more than $5,000 for each offense. Any owner, operator, or person in charge of any vessel from which oil or a hazardous substance is discharged in violation of paragraph (3)(i) of this subsection, and any owner, operator, or person in charge of a vessel from which oil or a hazardous substance is discharged in violation of paragraph (3)(ii) who is otherwise subject to the jurisdiction of the United States at the time of the discharge, shall be assessed a civil penalty by the Secretary of the department in which the Coast Guard is operating of not more than $5,000 for each offense. No penalty shall be assessed unless the owner or operator charged shall have been given notice and opportunity for a hearing on such charge. Each violation is a separate offense. Any such civil penalty may be compromised by such Secretary. In determining the amount of the penalty, or the amount agreed upon in compromise, the appropriateness of such penalty to the size of the business of the owner or operator charged, the effect on the owner or operator's ability to continue in business, and the gravity of the violation, shall be considered by such Secretary. The Secretary of the Treasury shall withhold at the request of such Secretary the clearance required by section 4197 of the Revised Statutes of the United States, as amended (46 U.S.C. 91), of any vessel the owner or operator of which is subject to the foregoing penalty. Clearance may be granted in such cases upon the filing of a bond or other surety satisfactory to such Secretary.

(B) The Administrator, taking into account the gravity of the offense, and the standard of care manifest by the owner, operator or person in charge, may commence a civil action against any such person subject to the penalty under subparagraph (A) of this paragraph to impose a penalty based on consideration of the size of the business of the owner or operator, the effect on the ability of the owner or operator to continue in business, the gravity of the violation, and the nature, extent, and degree of success of any efforts made by the owner, operator, or person in charge to minimize or mitigate the effects of such discharge. The amount of such penalty shall not exceed $50,000, except that where the United States can show that such discharge was the result of willful negligence or willful misconduct within the privity and knowledge of the owner, operator, or person in charge, such penalty shall not exceed $250,000. Each violation is a separate offense.

Any action under this subparagraph may be brought in the district court of the United States for the district in which the defendant is located or resides or is doing business, and such court shall have jurisdiction to assess such penalty. No action may be commenced under this clause where a penalty has been assessed under clause (A) of this paragraph.

(C) In addition to establishing a penalty for the discharge of a hazardous substance, the Administrator may act to mitigate the damage to the public health or welfare caused by such discharge. The cost of such mitigation shall be deemed a cost incurred under subsection (c) of this section for the removal of such substance by the United States Government.

(D) Any cost of removal incurred in connection with a discharge excluded by subsection (a)(2)(C) of this section shall be recoverable from the owner or operator of the source of the discharge in an action brought under section 309(b) of this Act.

(E) Civil penalties shall not be assessed under both this section and section 309 for the same discharge.

(c)(1) Whenever any oil or a hazardous substance is discharged, or there is a substantial threat of such discharge, into or upon the navigable waters of the United States, adjoining shorelines, or into or upon the waters of the contiguous zone, or in connection with activities under the Outer Continental Shelf Lands Act or the Deepwater Port Act of 1974, or which may affect natural resources belonging to, appertaining to, or under the exclusive management authority of the United States (including resources under the Magnuson Fishery Conservation and Management Act of 1976) the President is authorized to act to remove or arrange for the removal of such oil or substance at any time, unless he determines such removal will be done properly by the owner or operator of the vessel, onshore facility, or offshore facility from which the discharge occurs.

(2) Within sixty days after the effective date of this section, the President shall prepare and publish a National Contingency Plan for removal of oil and hazardous substances, pursuant to this subsection. Such National Contingency Plan shall provide for efficient, coordinated, and effective action to minimize damage from oil and hazardous substance discharges, including containment, dispersal, and removal of oil and hazardous substances, and shall include, but not be limited to—

(A) assignment of duties and responsibilities among Federal departments and agencies in coordination with State and local agencies, including, but not limited to, water pollution control, conservation, and port authorities;

(B) identification, procurement, maintenance, and storage of equipment and supplies;

(C) establishment or designation of a strike force consisting of personnel who shall be trained, prepared, and available to provide necessary services to carry out the Plan, including the establishment at major ports, to be determined by the President, of emergency task forces of trained personnel, adequate oil and hazardous substance pollution control equipment and material, and a detailed oil and hazardous substance pollution prevention and removal plan;

(D) a system of surveillance and notice designed to insure earliest possible notice of discharges of oil and hazardous substances and imminent threats of such discharges to the appropriate State and Federal agencies;

(E) establishment of a national center to provide coordination and direction for operation in carrying out the Plan;

(F) procedures and techniques to be employed in identifying, containing, dispersing, and removing oil and hazardous substances;

(G) a schedule, prepared in cooperation with the State, identifying (i) dispersants and other chemicals, if any, that may be used in carrying out the Plan, (ii) the waters in which such dispersants and chemicals may be used, and (iii) the quantities of such dispersant or chemical which can be used safely in such waters, which schedule shall provide in the case of any dispersant, chemical, or waters not specifically identified in such schedule that the President, or his delegate, may, on a case-by-case basis, identify the dispersants and other chemicals which may be used, the waters in which they may be used, and the quantities which can be used safely in such waters; and

(H) a system whereby the State or States affected by a discharge of oil or hazardous substance may act where necessary to remove such discharge and such State or States may be reimbursed from the fund established under subsection (k) of this section for the reasonable costs incurred in such removal.

The President may, from time to time, as he deems advisable revise or otherwise amend the National Contingency Plan. After publication of the National Contingency Plan, the removal of oil and hazardous substances and actions to minimize damage from oil and hazardous substance discharges shall, to the greatest extent possible, be in accordance with the National Contingency Plan.

(d) Whenever a marine disaster in or upon the navigable waters of the United States has created a substantial threat of a pollution hazard to the public health or welfare of the United States, including, but not limited to, fish, shellfish, and wildlife and the public and private shorelines and beaches of the United States, because of a discharge, or an imminent discharge, of large quantities of oil, or a hazardous substance from a vessel the United States may (A) coordinate and direct all public and private efforts directed at the removal or elimination of such threat; and (B) summarily remove, and, if necessary, destroy such vessel by whatever means are available without regard to any provisions of law governing the employment of personnel or the expenditure of appropriated funds. Any expense incurred under this subsection or under the Intervention on the High Seas Act (or the convention defined in section 2(3) thereof) shall be a cost incurred by the United States Government for the purposes of subsection (f) in the removal of oil or hazardous substance.

(e) In addition to any other action taken by a State or local government, when the President determines there is an imminent and substantial threat to the public health or welfare of the United States, including, but not limited to, fish, shellfish, and wildlife and public and private property, shorelines, and beaches within the United States, because of an actual or threatened discharge of oil or hazardous substance into or upon the navigable waters of the United States from an onshore or offshore facility, the President may require the United States attorney of the district in which the threat occurs to secure such relief as may be necessary to abate such threat, and the district courts of the United States shall have jurisdiction to grant such relief as the public interest and the equities of the case may require.

(f)(1) Except where an owner or operator can prove that a discharge was caused solely by (A) an act of God, (B) an act of war, (C) negligence on the part of the United States Government, or (D) an act or omission of a third party without regard to whether any such act or omission was or was not negligent, or any combination of the foregoing clauses, such owner or operator of any vessel from which oil or a hazardous substance is discharged in violation of subsection (b)(3) of this section shall, notwithstanding any other provision of law, be liable to the United States Government for the actual costs incurred under subsection (c) for the removal of such oil or substance by the United States Government in an amount not to exceed, in the case of an inland oil barge $125 per gross ton of such barge, or $125,000, whichever is greater, and in the case of any other vessel, $150 per gross ton of such vessel (or, for a vessel carrying oil or hazardous substances as cargo, $250,000), whichever is greater, except that where the United States can show that such discharge was the result of willful negligence or willful misconduct within the privity and knowledge of the owner, such owner or operator shall be liable to the United States Government for the full amount of such costs. Such costs shall constitute a maritime lien on such vessel which may be recovered in an action in rem in the district court of the United States for any district within which any vessel may be found. The United States may also bring an action against the owner or operator of such vessel in any court of competent jurisdiction to recover such costs.

(2) Except where an owner or operator of an onshore facility can prove that a discharge was caused solely by (A) an act of God, (B) an act of war, (C) negligence on the part of the United States Government, or (D) an act or omission of a third party without regard to whether any such act or omission was or was not negligent, or any combination of the foregoing clauses, such owner or operator of any such facility from which oil or a hazardous substance is discharged in violation of subsection (b)(3) of this section shall be liable to the United States Government for the actual costs incurred under subsection (c) for the removal of such oil or substance by the United States Government in an amount not to exceed $50,000,000, except that where the United States can show that such discharge was the result of willful negligence or willful misconduct within the privity and knowledge of the owner, such owner or operator shall be liable to the United States Government for the full amount of such costs. The United States may bring an action against the owner or operator of such facility in any court of competent jurisdiction to recover such costs. The Administrator is authorized, by regulation, after consultation with the Secretary of Commerce and the Small Business Administration, to establish reasonable and equitable classifications of those onshore facilities having a total fixed storage capacity of 1,000 barrels or less which he determines because of size, type, and location do not present a substantial risk of the discharge of oil or a hazardous substance in violation of subsection (b)(3) of this section, and apply with respect to such classifications differing limits of liability which may be less than the amount contained in this paragraph.

(3) Except where an owner or operator of an offshore facility can prove that a discharge was caused solely by (A) an act of God, (B) an act of war, (C) negligence on the part of the United States Government, or (D) an act or omission of a third party without regard to whether any such act or omission was or was not negligent, or any combination of the foregoing clauses, such owner or operator of any such facility from

which oil or a hazardous substance is discharged in violation of subsection (b)(3) of this section shall, notwithstanding any other provision of law, be liable to the United States Government for the actual costs incurred under subsection (c) for the removal of such oil or substance by the United States Government in an amount not to exceed $50,000,000, except that where the United States can show that such discharge was the result of willful negligence or willful misconduct with the privity and knowledge of the owner, such owner or operator shall be liable to the United States Government for the full amount of such costs. The United States may bring an action against the owner or operator of such a facility in any court of competent jurisdiction to recover such costs.

(4) The costs of removal of oil or a hazardous substance for which the owner or operator of a vessel or onshore or offshore facility is liable under subsection (f) of this section shall include any costs or expenses incurred by the Federal Government or any State government in the restoration or replacement of natural resources damaged or destroyed as a result of a discharge of oil or a hazardous substance in violation of subsection (b) of this section.

(5) The President, or the authorized representative of any State, shall act on behalf of the public as trustee of the natural resources to recover the costs of replacement or restoring such resources. Sums recovered shall be used to restore, rehabilitate, or acquire the equivalent of such natural resources by the appropriate agencies of the Federal Government, or the State government.

(g) Where the owner or operator of a vessel (other than an inland oil barge) carrying oil or hazardous substances as cargo or an onshore or offshore facility which handles or stores oil or hazardous substances in bulk, from which oil or a hazardous substance is discharged in violation of subsection (b) of this section, alleges that such discharge was caused solely by an act or omission of a third party, such owner or operator shall pay to the United States Government the actual costs incurred under subsection (c) for removal of such oil or substance and shall be entitled by subrogation to all rights of the United States Government to recover such costs from such third party under this subsection. In any case where an owner or operator of a vessel, of an onshore facility, or of an offshore facility, from which oil or a hazardous substance is discharged in violation of subsection (b)(3) of this section, proves that such discharge of oil or hazardous substance was caused solely by an act or omission of a third party, or was caused solely by such an act or omission in combination with an act of God, an act of war, or negligence on the part of the United States Government, such third party shall, notwithstanding any other provision of law, be liable to the United States Government for the actual costs incurred under subsection (c) for removal of such oil or substance by the United States Government, except where such third party can prove that such discharge was caused solely by

(A) an act of God, (B) an act of war, (C) negligence on the part of the United States Government, or (D) an act or omission of another party without regard to whether such act or omission was or was not negligent, or any combination of the foregoing clauses. If such third party was the owner or operator of a vessel which caused the discharge of oil or a hazardous substance in violation of subsection (b)(3) of this section, the liability of such third party under this subsection shall not exceed, in the case of an inland oil barge, $125 per gross ton of such barge, $125,000, whichever is greater, and in the case of any other vessel, $150 per gross ton of such vessel (or, for a vessel carrying oil or hazardous substances as cargo, $250,000), whichever is greater. In any other case the liability of such third party shall not exceed the limitation which would have been applicable to the owner or operator of the vessel or the onshore or offshore facility from which the discharge actually occurred if such owner or operator were liable. If the United States can show that the discharge of oil or a hazardous substance in violation of subsection (b)(3) of this section was the result of willful negligence or willful misconduct within the privity and knowledge of such third party, such third party shall be liable to the United States Government for the full amount of such removal costs. The United States may bring an action against the third party in any court of competent jurisdiction to recover such removal costs.

(h) The liabilities established by this section shall in no way affect any rights which (1) the owner or operator of a vessel or of an onshore facility or an offshore facility may have against any third party whose acts may in any way have caused or contributed to such discharge, or (2) the United States Government may have against any third party whose actions may in any way have caused or contributed to the discharge of oil or hazardous substance.

(i)(1) In any case where an owner or operator of a vessel or an onshore facility or an offshore facility from which oil or a hazardous substance is discharged in violation of subsection (b)(3) of this section acts to remove such oil or substance in accordance with regulations promulgated pursuant to this section, such owner or operator shall be entitled to recover the reasonable costs incurred in such removal upon establishing, in a suit which may be brought against the United States Government in the United States Claims Court, that such discharge was caused solely by (A) an act of God, (B) an act of war, (C) negligence on the part of the United States Government or (D) an act or omission of a third party without regard to whether such act or omission was or was not negligent, or of any combination of the foregoing clauses.

(2) The provisions of this subsection shall not apply in any case where liability is established pursuant to the Outer Continental Shelf Lands Act, or the Deepwater Port Act of 1974.

(3) Any amount paid in accordance with a judgment of the United States Claims Court pursuant to this section shall be paid from the funds established pursuant to subsection (k).

(j)(1) Consistent with the National Contingency Plan required by subsection (c)(2) of this section, as soon as practicable after the effective date of this section and from time to time thereafter, the President shall issue regulations consistent with maritime safety and with marine and navigation laws (A) establishing methods and procedures for removal of discharged oil and hazardous substances, (B) establishing criteria for the development and implementation of local and regional oil and hazardous substance removal contingency plans, (C) establishing procedures, methods, and equipment and other requirements for equipment to prevent discharges of oil and hazardous substances from vessels and from onshore facilities and offshore facilities, and to contain such discharges, and (D) governing the inspection of vessels carrying cargoes of oil and hazardous substances and the inspection of such cargoes in order to reduce the likelihood of discharges of oil from vessels in violation of this section.

(2) Any owner or operator of a vessel or an onshore facility or an offshore facility and any other person subject to any regulation issued under paragraph (1) of this subsection who fails or refuses to comply with the provisions of any such regulations, shall be liable to a civil penalty of not more than $5,000 for each such violation. This paragraph shall not apply to any owner or operator of any vessel from which oil or a hazardous substance is discharged in violation of paragraph (3)(ii) of subsection (b) unless such owner, operator, or person in charge is otherwise subject to the jurisdiction of the United States. Each violation shall be a separate offense. The President may assess and compromise such penalty. No penalty shall be assessed until the owner, operator, or other person charged shall have been given notice and an opportunity for a hearing on such charge. In determining the amount of the penalty, or the amount agreed upon in compromise, the gravity of the violation, and the demonstrated good faith of the owner, operator, or other person charged in attempting to achieve rapid compliance after notification of a violation, shall be considered by the President.

(k)(1) There is hereby authorized to be appropriated to a revolving fund to be established in the Treasury such sums as may be necessary to maintain such fund at a level of $35,000,000 to carry out the provisions of subsections (c), (d), (i), and (l) of this section. Any other funds received by the United States under this section shall also be deposited in said fund for such purposes. All sums appropriated to or deposited in, said fund shall remain available until expended.

(2) The Secretary of Transportation shall notify the Congress whenever the unobligated balance of the fund is less than $12,000,000, and shall include in such notification a recommendation for a supplemental appropriation relating to the sums that are needed to maintain the fund at the level provided in paragraph (1).

(l) The President is authorized to delegate the administration of this section to the heads of those Federal departments, agencies, and instrumentalities which he determines to be appropriate. Any moneys in the fund established by subsection (k) of this section shall be available to such Federal departments, agencies, and instrumentalities to carry out the provisions of subsections (c) and (i) of this section. Each such department, agency, and instrumentality, in order to avoid duplication of effort, shall, whenever appropriate, utilize the personnel, services, and facilities of other Federal departments, agencies, and instrumentalities.

(m) Anyone authorized by the President to enforce the provisions of this section may, except as to public vessels, (A) board and inspect any vessel upon the navigable waters of the United States or the waters of the contiguous zone, (B) with or without a warrant arrest any person who violates the provisions of this section or any regulation issued thereunder in his presence or view, and (C) execute any warrant or other process issued by an officer or court of competent jurisdiction.

(n) The several district courts of the United States are invested with jurisdiction for any actions, other than actions pursuant to subsection (i)(1), arising under this section. In the case of Guam and the Trust Territory of Pacific Islands, such actions may be brought in the district court of Guam, and in the case of the Virgin Islands such actions may be brought in the district court of the Virgin Islands. In the case of America Samoa and the Trust Territory of the Pacific Islands, such actions may be brought in the District Court of the United States for the District of Hawaii and such court shall have jurisdiction of such actions. In the case of the Canal Zone, such actions may be brought in the United States District for the District of the Canal Zone.

(o)(1) Nothing in this section shall affect or modify in any way the obligations of any owner or operator of any vessel, or of any owner or operator of any onshore facility or offshore facility to any person or agency under any provision of law for damages to any publicly owned or privately owned property resulting from a discharge of any oil or hazardous substance or from the removal of any such oil or hazardous substance.

(2) Nothing in this section shall be construed as preempting any State or political subdivision thereof from imposing any requirement or liability with respect to the discharge of oil or hazardous substance into any waters within such State.

(3) Nothing in this section shall be construed as affecting or modifying any other existing authority of any Federal department, agency, or instrumentality, relative to onshore or offshore facilities under this Act or any other provision of law, or to affect any State or local law not in conflict with this section.

(p)(1) Any vessel over three hundred gross tons, including any barge of equivalent size, but not including any barge that is not self-propelled and that does not carry oil or hazardous substances as cargo or fuel, using any port or place in the United States or the navigable waters of the United

States for any purpose shall establish and maintain under regulations to be prescribed from time to time by the President, evidence of financial responsibility of, in the case of an inland oil barge $125 per gross ton of such barge, or $125,000, whichever is greater, and in the case of any other vessel, $150 per gross ton of such vessel (or, for a vessel carrying oil or hazardous substances as cargo, $250,000), whichever is greater, to meet the liability to the United States which such vessel could be subjected under this section. In cases where an owner or operator owns, operates, or charters more than one such vessel, financial responsibility need only be established to meet the maximum liability to which the largest of such vessels could be subjected. Financial responsibility may be established by any one of, or a combination of, the following methods acceptable to the President: (A) evidence of insurance, (B) surety bonds, (C) qualification as a self-insurer, or (D) other evidence of financial responsibility. Any bond filed shall be issued by a bonding company authorized to do business in the United States.

(2) The provisions of paragraph (1) of this subsection shall be effective April 3, 1971, with respect to oil and one year after the date of enactment of this section with respect to hazardous substances. The President shall delegate the responsibility to carry out the provisions of this subsection to the appropriate agency within sixty days after the date of enactment of this section. Regulations necessary to implement this subsection shall be issued within six months after the date of enactment of this section.

(3) Any claim for costs incurred by such vessel may be brought directly against the insurer or any other person providing evidence of financial responsibility as required under this subsection. In the case of any action pursuant to this subsection such insurer or other person shall be entitled to invoke all rights and defenses which would have been available to the owner or operator if an action had been brought against him by the claimant, and which would have been available to him if an action had been brought against him by the owner or operator.

(4) Any owner or operator of a vessel subject to this subsection, who fails to comply with the provisions of this subsection or any regulation issued thereunder, shall be subject to a fine of not more than $10,000.

(5) The Secretary of the Treasury may refuse the clearance required by section 4197 of the Revised Statutes of the United States, as amended (4 U.S.C. 91), to any vessel subject to this subsection, which does not have evidence furnished by the President that the financial responsibility provisions of paragraph (1) of this subsection have been complied with.

(6) The Secretary of the Department in which the Coast Guard is operated may (A) deny entry to any port or place in the United States or the navigable waters of the United States, to, and (B) detain at the port or place in the United States from which it is about to depart for

any other port or place in the United States, any vessel subject to this subsection, which upon request, does not produce evidence furnished by the President that the financial responsibility provisions of paragraph (1) of this subsection have been complied with.

(q) The President is authorized to establish, with respect to any class or category of onshore or offshore facilities, a maximum limit of liability under subsections (f)(2) and (3) of this section of less than $50,000,000, but not less that $8,000,000.

(r) Nothing in this section shall be construed to impose or authorize the imposition of any limitation on liability under the Outer Continental Shelf Lands Act or the Deepwater Port Act of 1974.

§ 1322.   Marine sanitation devices

[Sec. 312] (a) For the purpose of this section, the term—

(1) "new vessel" includes every description of watercraft or other artificial contrivance used, or capable of being used, as a means of transportation on the navigable waters, the construction of which is initiated after promulgation of standards and regulation under this section;

(2) "existing vessel" includes every description of watercraft or other artificial contrivance used, or capable of being used, as a means of transportation on the navigable waters, the construction of which is initiated before promulgation of standards and regulations under this section;

(3) "public vessel" means a vessel owned or bare-boat-chartered and operated by the United States, by a State or political subdivision thereof, or by a foreign nation, except when such vessel is engaged in commerce;

(4) "United States" includes the States, the District of Columbia, the Commonwealth of Puerto Rico, the Virgin Islands, Guam, American Samoa, the Canal Zone, and the Trust Territory of the Pacific Islands;

(5) "marine sanitation device" includes any equipment for installation on board a vessel which is designed to receive, retain, treat, or discharge sewage, and any process to treat such sewage;

(6) "sewage" means human body wastes and the wastes from toilets and other receptacles intended to receive or retain body wastes except that, with respect to commercial vessels on the Great Lakes such term shall include graywater;

(7) "manufacturer" means any person engaged in the manufacturing, assembling, or importation of marine sanitation devices or of vessels subject to standards and regulations promulgated under this section;

(8) "person" means an individual, partnership, firm, corporation, or association, but does not include an individual on board a public vessel;

(9) "discharge" includes, but is not limited to, any spilling, leaking,

pumping, pouring, emitting, emptying or dumping;

(10) "commercial vessels" means those vessels used in the business of transporting property for compensation or hire, or in transporting property in the business of the owner, lessee, or operator of the vessel;

(11) "graywater" means galley, bath, and shower water.

(b)(1) As soon as possible, after the enactment of this section and subject to the provisions of section 101(j) of this Act, the Administrator, after consultation with the Secretary of the department in which the Coast Guard is operating, after giving appropriate consideration to the economic costs involved, and within the limits of available technology, shall promulgate Federal standards of performance for marine sanitation devices (hereafter in this section referred to as "standards") which shall be designed to prevent the discharge of untreated or inadequately treated sewage into or upon the navigable waters from new vessels and existing vessels, except vessels not equipped with installed toilet facilities. Such standards and standards established under subsection (c)(1)(B) of this section shall be consistent with maritime safety and the marine and navigation laws and regulations and shall be coordinated with the regulations issued under this subsection by the Secretary of the department in which the Coast Guard is operating. The Secretary of the department in which the Coast Guard is operating shall promulgate regulations, which are consistent with standards promulgated under this subsection and subsection (c) of this section and with maritime safety and the marine and navigation laws and regulations governing the design, construction, installation, and operation of any marine sanitation device on board such vessels.

(2) Any existing vessel equipped with a marine sanitation device on the date of promulgation of initial standards and regulations under this section, which device is in compliance with such initial standards and regulations, shall be deemed in compliance with this section until such time as the device is replaced or is found not to be in compliance with such initial standards and regulations.

(c)(1)(A) Initial standards and regulations under this section shall become effective for new vessels two years after promulation; and for existing vessels five years after promulgation. Revisions of standards and regulations shall be effective upon promulgation, unless another effective date is specified, except that no revision shall take effect before the effective date of the standard or regulation being revised.

(B) The Administrator shall, with respect to commercial vessels on the Great Lakes, establish standards which require at a minimum the equivalent of secondary treatment as defined under section 304(d) of this Act. Such standards and regulations shall take effect for existing vessels after such time as the Administrator determines to be reasonable for the upgrading of marine sanitation devices to attain such standard.

(2) The Secretary of the department in which the Coast Guard is

operating with regard to his regulatory authority established by this section, after consultation with the Administrator, may distinguish among classes, types, and sizes of vessels as well as between new and existing vessels, and may waive applicability of standards and regulations as necessary or appropriate for such classes, types, and sizes of vessels (including existing vessels equipped with marine sanitation devices on the date of promulgation of the initial standards required by this section), and, upon application, for individual vessels.

(d) The provisions of this section and the standards and regulations promulgated hereunder apply to vessels owned and operated by the United States unless the Secretary of Defense finds that compliance would not be in the interest of national security. With respect to vessels owned and operated by the Department of Defense, regulations under the last sentence of subsection (b)(1) of this section and certifications under subsection (g)(2) of this section shall be promulgated and issued by the Secretary of Defense.

(e) Before the standards and regulations under his section are promulgated, the Administrator and the Secretary of the department in which the Coast Guard is operating shall consult with the Secretary of State; the Secretary of Health, Education, and Welfare; the Secretary of Defense; the Secretary of the Treasury; the Secretary of Commerce; other interested Federal agencies; and the States and industries interested; and otherwise comply with the requirements of section 553 of title 5 of the United States Code.

(f)(1)(A) Except as provided in subparagraph (B), after the effective date of the initial standards and regulations promulgated under this section, no State or political subdivision thereof shall adopt or enforce any statute or regulation of such State or political subdivision with respect to the design, manufacture, or installation or use of any marine sanitation device on any vessel subject to the provisions of this section.

> (B) A State may adopt and enforce a statute or regulation with respect to the design, manufacture, or installation or use of any marine sanitation device on a houseboat, if such statute or regulation is more stringent than the standards and regulations promulgated under this section. For purposes of this paragraph, the term "houseboat" means a vessel which, for a period of time determined by the State in which the vessel is located, is used primarily as a residence and is not used primarily as a means of transportation.

> (2) If after promulgation of the initial standards and regulations and prior to their effective date, a vessel is equipped with a marine sanitation device in compliance with such standards and regulations and the installation and operation of such device is in accordance with such standards and regulations, such standards and regulations shall, for the purposes of paragraph (1) of this subsection, become effective with

respect to such vessel on the date of such compliance.

(3) After the effective date of the initial standards and regulations promulgated under this section, if any State determines that the protection and enhancement of the quality of some or all of the waters within such State require greater environmental protection, such State may completely prohibit the discharge from all vessels of any sewage, whether treated or not, into such waters, except that no such prohibition shall apply until the Administrator determines that adequate facilities for the safe and sanitary removal and treatment of sewage from all vessels are reasonably available for such water to which such prohibition would apply. Upon application of the State, the Administrator shall make such determination within 90 days of the date of such application.

(4)(A) If the Administrator determines upon application by a State that the protection and enhancement of the quality of specified waters within such State requires such a prohibition, he shall by regulation completely prohibit the discharge from a vessel of any sewage (whether treated or not) into such waters.

(B) Upon application by a State, the Administrator shall, by regulation, establish a drinking water intake zone in any waters within such State and prohibit the discharge of sewage from vessels within that zone.

(g)(1) No manufacturer of a marine sanitation device shall sell, offer for sale, or introduce or deliver for introduction in interstate commerce, or import into the United States for sale or resale any marine sanitation device manufactured after the effective date of the standards and regulations promulgated under this section unless such device is in all material respects substantially the same as a test device certified under this subsection.

(2) Upon application of the manufacturer, the Secretary of the department in which the Coast Guard is operating shall so certify a marine sanitation device if he determines, in accordance with the provisions of this paragraph, that it meets the appropriate standards and regulations promulgated under this section. The Secretary of the department in which the Coast Guard is operating shall test or require such testing of the device in accordance with procedures set forth by the Administrator as to standards of performance and for such other purposes as may be appropriate. If the Secretary of the department in which the Coast Guard is operating determines that the device is satisfactory from the standpoint of safety and any other requirements of maritime law or regulation, and after consideration of the design, installation, operation, material, or other appropriate factors, he shall certify the device. Any device manufactured by such manufacturer which is in all material respects substantially the same as the certified test device shall be deemed to be in conformity with the appropriate standards and regulations established under this section.

(3) Every manufacturer shall establish and maintain such records, make such reports, and provide such information as the Administrator or the Secretary of the department in which the Coast Guard is operating may reasonably require to enable him to determine whether such manufacturer has acted or is acting in compliance with this section and regulations issued thereunder and shall, upon request of an officer or employee duly designated by the Administrator or the Secretary of the department in which the Coast Guard is operating, permit such officer or employee at reasonable times to have access to and copy such records. All information reported to or otherwise obtained by the Administrator or the Secretary of the department in which the Coast Guard is operating or their representatives pursuant to this subsection which contains or relates to a trade secret or other matter referred in section 1905 of title 18 of the United States Code shall be considered confidential for the purpose of that section, except that such information may be disclosed to other officers or employees concerned with carrying out this section. This paragraph shall not apply in the case of the construction of a vessel by an individual for his own use.

(h) After the effective date of standards and regulations promulgated under this section, it shall be unlawful—

(1) for the manufacturer of any vessel subject to such standards and regulations to manufacture for sale, to sell or offer for sale, or to distribute for sale or resale any such vessel unless it is equipped with a marine sanitation device which is in all material respects substantially the same as the appropriate test device certified pursuant to this section;

(2) for any person, prior to the sale or delivery of a vessel subject to such standards and regulations to the ultimate purchaser, wrongfully to remove or render inoperative any certified marine sanitation device or element of design of such device installed in such vessel;

(3) for any person to fail or refuse to permit access to or copying of records or to fail to make reports or provide information required under this section; and

(4) for a vessel subject to such standards and regulations to operate on the navigable waters of the United States, if such vessel is not equipped with an operable marine sanitation device certified pursuant to this section.

(i) The district courts of the United States shall have jurisdictions to restrain violations of subsection (g)(1) of this section and subsections (h)(1) through (3) of this section. Actions to restrain such violations shall be brought by, and in, the name of the United States. In case of contumacy or refusal to obey a subpena served upon any person under this subsection, the district court of the United States for any district in which such person is found or resides or transacts business, upon application by the United States and after notice to such person, shall have jurisdiction to issue an order requiring such person to appear and give testimony or to appear and produce documents, and any failure to obey such order of the court may be punished by such court as a contempt thereof.

(j) Any person who violates subsection (g)(1) of this section or clause (1) or (2) of subsection (h) of this section shall be liable to a civil penalty of not more than $5,000 for each violation. Any person who violates clause (4) of subsection (h) of this section or any regulation issued pursuant to this section shall be liable to a civil penalty of not more than $2,000 for each violation. Each violation shall be a separate offense. The Secretary of the department in which the Coast Guard is operating may assess and compromise any such penalty. No penalty shall be assessed until the person charged shall have been given notice and an opportunity for a hearing on such charge. In determining the amount of the penalty, or the amount agreed upon in compromise, the gravity of the violation, and the demonstrated good faith of the person charged in attempting to achieve rapid compliance, after notification of a violation, shall be considered by said Secretary.

(k) The provisions of this section shall be enforced by the Secretary of the department in which the Coast Guard is operating and he may utilize by agreement, with or without reimbursement, law enforcement officers or other personnel and facilities of the Administrator, other Federal agencies, or the States to carry out the provisions of this section. The provisions of this section may also be enforced by a State.

(l) Anyone authorized by the Secretary of the department in which the Coast Guard is operating to enforce the provisions of this section may, except as to public vessels, (1) board and inspect any vessel upon the navigable waters of the United States and (2) execute any warrant or other process issued by an officer or court of competent jurisdiction.

(m) In the case of Guam and the Trust Territory of the Pacific Islands, actions arising under this section may be brought in the district court of Guam, and in the case of the Virgin Islands such actions may be brought in the district court of the Virgin Islands. In the case of American Samoa and the Trust Territory of the Pacific Islands, such actions may be brought in the District Court of the United States for the District of Hawaii and such court shall have jurisdiction of such actions. In the case of the Canal Zone, such action may be brought in the District Court for the District of the Canal Zone.

§ 1323. Federal facilities pollution control

[Sec. 313] (a) Each department, agency, or instrumentality of the executive, legislative, and judicial branches of the Federal Government (1) having jurisdiction over any property or facility, or (2) engaged in any activity resulting, or which may result, in the discharge of runoff of pollutants, and each officer, agent, or employee thereof in the performance of his official duties, shall be subject to, and comply with, all Federal, State, interstate, and local requirements, administrative authority, and process and sanctions respecting the control and abatement of water pollution in the same manner, and to the same extent as any nongovernment entity including the payment of reasonable service charges. The preceding sentence shall apply (A) to any requirement whether substantive or procedural (including any recordkeeping or reporting requirement, any requirement respecting permits and any other requirement, whatsoever), (B) to the exercise of any Federal, State, or local administrative authority, and (C) to any process and sanction, whether enforced in Federal, State, or local courts or in any other manner. This subsection shall apply notwithstanding any immunity of such agencies, officers, agents, or employees under any law or rule of law. Nothing in this section shall be construed to prevent any department, agency, or instrumentality of the Federal Government, or any officer, agent, or employee thereof in the performance of his official duties, from reporting to the appropriate Federal district court any proceeding to which the department, agency, or instrumentality or officer, agent, or employee thereof is subject pursuant to this section, and any such proceeding may be removed in accordance with 28 U.S.C. 1441 et seq. No officer, agent, or employee of the United States shall be personally liable for any civil penalty arising from the performance of his official duties, for which he is not otherwise liable, and the United States shall be liable only for those civil penalties arising under Federal law or imposed by a State or local court to enforce an order or the process of such court. The President may exempt any effluent source of any department, agency, or instrumentality in the executive branch from compliance with any such a requirement if he determines it to be in the paramount interest of the United States to do so; except that no exemption may be granted from the requirements of section 306 or 307 of this Act. No such exemptions shall be granted due to lack of appropriation unless the President shall have specifically requested such appropriation as a part of the budgetary process and the Congress shall have failed to make available such requested appropriation. Any exemption shall be for a period not in excess of one year, but additional exemptions may be granted for periods of not to exceed one year upon the President's making a new determination. The President shall report each January to the Congress all exemptions from the requirements of this section granted during the preceding calendar year, together with his reason for granting such exemption. In addition to any such exemption of a particular effluent source, the President may, if he determines it to be in the paramount interest of the United States to do so, issue regulations exempting from compliance with the requirements of this section any weaponry, equipment, aircraft, vessel, vehicles, or other classes or categories of property, and access to such property, which are owned or operated by the Armed Forces of the United States (including the Coast Guard) or by the National Guard of any State and which are uniquely military in nature. The President shall reconsider the need for such regulations at three-year intervals.

(b)(1) The Administrator shall coordinate with the head of each department, agency, or instrumentality of the Federal Government having jurisdiction over any property or facility utilizing federally owned wastewater facilities to develop a program of cooperation for utilizing wastewater control systems utilizing those innovative treatment processes and techniques for which guidelines have been promulgated under section 304(d)(3). Such program shall include an inventory of property and facilities which could utilize such processes and techniques.

(2) Construction shall not be initiated for facilities for treatment of wastewater at any Federal property or facility after September 30, 1979, if alternative methods for wastewater treatment at such property or facility utilizing innovative treatment processes and techniques, including but not limited to methods utilizing recycle and reuse techniques and land treatment are not utilized, unless the life cycle cost of the alternative treatment works exceeds the life cycle cost of the most cost effective alternative by more than 15 per centum. The Administrator may waive the application of this paragraph in any case where the Administrator determines it to be in the public interest, or that compliance with this paragraph would interfere with the orderly compliance with conditions of a permit issued pursuant to section 402 of this Act.

§ 1324. Clean lakes

[Sec. 314] (a)(1) Each State shall on a biennial basis prepare and submit to the Administrator for his approval—

(A) an identification and classification according to eutrophic condition of all publicly owned lakes in such State;

(B) a description of procedures, processes, and methods (including land use requirements), to control sources of pollution of such lakes;

(C) a description of methods and procedures, in conjunction with appropriate Federal agencies, to restore the quality of such lakes;

(D) methods and procedures to mitigate the harmful effects of high acidity, including innovative methods of neutralizing and restoring buffering capacity of lakes and methods of removing from lakes toxic metals and other toxic substances mobilized by high acidity;

(E) a list and description of those publicly owned lakes in such State for which uses are known to be impaired, including those lakes which are known not to meet applicable water quality standards or which require implementation of control programs to maintain compliance with applicable standards and those lakes in which water quality has deteriorated as a result of high acidity that may reasonably be due to acid deposition; and

(F) an assessment of the status and trends of water quality in lakes in such State, including but not limited to, the nature and extent of pollution loading from point and nonpoint sources and the extent to which the use of lakes is impaired as a result of such pollution, particularly with respect to toxic pollution.

(2) The information required under paragraph (1) shall be included in the report required under section 305(b)(1) of this Act, beginning with the report required under such section by April 1, 1988.

(3) Not later than 180 days after receipt from the States of the biennial information required under paragraph (1), the Administrator shall submit to the Committee on Public Works and Transportation of the House of Representatives and the Committee on Environment and Public Works of the Senate a report on the status of water quality in lakes in the United States, including the effectiveness of the methods and procedures described in paragraph (1)(D).

(4) Beginning after April 1, 1988, a State must have submitted the information required under paragraph (1) in order to receive grant assistance under this section.

(b) The Administrator shall provide financial assistance to States in order to carry out methods and procedures approved by him under subsection (a) of this section. The Administrator shall provide financial assistance to States to prepare the identification and classification surveys required in subsection (a)(1) of this section.

(c)(1) The amount granted to any State for any fiscal year under subsection (b) of this section shall not exceed 70 per centum of the funds expended by such State in such year for carrying out approved methods and procedures under subsection (a) of this section.

(2) There is authorized to be appropriated $50,000,000 for the fiscal year ending June 30, 1973; $100,000,000 for the fiscal year 1974; $150,000,000 for the fiscal year 1975, $50,000,000 for fiscal year 1977, $60,000,000 for fiscal year 1978, $60,000,000 for fiscal year 1979, $60,000,000 for fiscal year 1980, $30,000,000 for fiscal year 1981, $30,000,000 for fiscal year 1982, such sums as may be necessary for fiscal years 1983 through 1985, and $30,000,000 per fiscal year for each of the fiscal years 1986 through 1990 for grants to States under subsection (b) of this section which sums shall remain available until expended. The Administrator shall provide for an equitable distribution of such sums to the States with approved methods and procedures under subsection (a) of this section.

(d)(1) The Administrator is authorized and directed to establish and conduct at locations throughout the Nation a lake water quality demonstration program. The program shall, at a minimum—

(A) develop cost effective technologies for the control of pollutants to preserve or enhance lake water quality while optimizing multiple lakes uses;

(B) control nonpoint sources of pollution which are contributing to the degradation of water quality in lakes;

(C) evaluate the feasibility of implementing regional consolidated pollution control strategies;

(D) demonstrate environmentally preferred techniques for the removal and disposal of contaminated lake sediments;

(E) develop improved methods for the removal of silt, stumps, aquatic growth, and other obstructions which impair the quality of lakes;

(F) construct and evaluate silt traps and other devices or equipment to prevent or abate the deposit of sediment in lakes; and

(G) demonstrate the costs and benefits of utilizing dredged material from lakes in the reclamation of despoiled land.

(2) Demonstration projects authorized by this subsection shall be undertaken to reflect a variety of geographical and environmental conditions. As a priority, the Administrator shall undertake demonstration projects at Lake Houston, Texas; Beaver Lake, Arkansas; Greenwood Lake and Belcher Creek, New Jersey; Deal Lake, New Jersey; Alcyon Lake, New Jersey; Gorton's Pond, Rhode Island; Lake Washington, Rhode Island; Lake Bomoseen, Vermont; Sauk Lake, Minnesota; and Lake Worth, Texas.

(3) The Administrator shall report annually to the Committee on Public Works and Transportation of the House of Representatives and the Committee on Environment and Public Works of the Senate on work undertaken pursuant to this subsection. Upon completion of the program authorized by this subsection, the Administrator shall submit to such committees a final report on the results of such program, along with recommendations for further measures to improve the water quality of the Nation's lakes.

(4)(A) There is authorized to be appropriated to carry out this subsection not to exceed $40,000,000 for fiscal years beginning after September 30, 1986, to remain available until expended.

(B)(i) There is authorized to be appropriated to carry out subsection (b) with respect to subsection (a)(1)(D) not to exceed $15,000,000 for fiscal years beginning after September 30, 1986, to remain available until expended.

(ii) The Administrator shall provide for an equitable distribution of sums appropriated pursuant to this subparagraph among States carrying out approved methods and procedures. Such distribution shall be based on the relative needs of each such State for the mitigation of the harmful effects on lakes and other surface waters of high acidity that may reasonably be due to acid deposition or acid mine drainage.

(iii) The amount of any grant to a State under this subparagraph shall be in addition to, and not in lieu of, any other Federal financial assistance.

§ 1325. National Study Commission

[Sec. 315] (a) There is established a National Study Commission, which shall make a full and complete investigation and study of all of the technological aspects of achieving, and all aspects of the total economic, social, and environmental effects of achieving or not achieving, the effluent limitations and goals set forth for 1983 in section 301(b)(2) of this Act.

(b) Such Commission shall be composed of fifteen members, including five members of the Senate, who are members of the Public Works committee, appointed by the President of the Senate, five members of the House, who are members of the Public Works committee appointed by the Speaker of the House, and five members of the public appointed by the President. The Chairman of such Commission shall be elected from among its members.

(c) In the conduct of such study, the Commission is authorized to contract with the National Academy of Sciences and the National Academy of Engineering (acting through the National Research Council), the National Institute of Ecology, Brookings Institution, and other nongovernmental entities, for the investigation of matters within their competence.

(d) The heads of the departments, agencies and instrumentalities of the executive branch of the Federal Government shall cooperate with the Commission in carrying out the requirements of this section, and shall furnish to the Commission such information as the Commission deems necessary to carry out this section.

(e) A report shall be submitted to the Congress of the results of such investigation and study, together with recommendations, not later than three years after the date of enactment of this title.

(f) The members of the Commission who are not officers or employees of the United States, while attending conferences or meetings of the Commission or while otherwise serving at the request of the Chairman shall be entitled to receive compensation at a rate not in excess of the maximum rate of pay for grade GS–18, as provided in the General Schedule under section 5332 of title V of the United States Code, including traveltime and while away from their homes or regular places of business they may be allowed travel expenses, including per diem in lieu of subsistence as authorized by law (5 U.S.C. 73b–2) for persons in the Government service employed intermittently.

(g) In addition to authority to appoint personnel subject to the provisions of title 5, United States Code, governing appointments in the competitive service, and to pay such personnel in accordance with the provisions of chapter 51 and subchapter III of chapter 53 of such title relating to classification and General Schedule pay rates, the Commission shall have authority to enter into contracts with private or public organizations who shall furnish the Commission with such administrative and technical personnel as may be necessary to carry out the purpose of this section. Personnel furnished by such organizations under this subsection are not, and shall not be considered to be, Federal employees for any purposes, but in the performance of their duties shall be guided by the standards which apply to employees of the legislative branches under rules 41 and 43 of the Senate and House of Representatives, respectively.

(h) There is authorized to be appropriated, for use in carrying out this section, not to exceed $17,250,000.

§ 1326. Thermal discharges

[Sec. 316] (a) With respect to any point source otherwise subject to the provisions of section 301 or section 306 of this Act, whenever the owner or operator of any such source, after opportunity for public hearing, can demonstrate to the satisfaction of the Administrator (or, if appropriate, the State) that any effluent limitation proposed for the control of the thermal component of any discharge from such source will require effluent limitations more stringent than necessary to assure the protection and propagation of a balanced, indigenous population of shellfish, fish, and wildlife in and on the body of water into which the discharge is to be made, the Administrator (or, if appropriate, the State) may impose an effluent limitation under such sections for such plant, with respect to the thermal component of such discharge (taking into account the interaction of such thermal component with other pollutants), that will assure the protection and propagation of a balanced, indigenous population of shellfish, fish, and wildlife in and on that body of water.

(b) Any standard established pursuant to section 301 or section 306 of this Act and applicable to a point source shall require that the location, design, construction, and capacity of cooling water intake structures reflect the best technology available for minimizing adverse environmental impact.

(c) Notwithstanding any other provision of this Act, any point source of a discharge having a thermal component, the modification of which point source is commenced after October 18, 1972 and which, as modified, meets effluent limitations established under section 301, or, if more stringent, effluent limitations established under section 303 and which effluent limitations will assure protection and propagation of a balanced, indigenous population of shellfish, fish, and wildlife in or on the water into which the discharge is made, shall not be subject to any more stringent effluent limitation with respect to the thermal component of its discharge during a ten year period beginning on the date of completion of such modification or during the period of depreciation or amortization of such facility for the purpose of section 167 of 169 (or both) of the Internal Revenue Code of 1954, whichever period ends first.

§ 1327. Financing study

[Sec. 317] (a) The Administrator shall continue to investigate and study the feasibility of alternate methods of financing the cost of preventing, controlling and abating pollution as directed in the Water Quality Improvement Act of 1970 (Public Law 91-224), including, but not limited to, the feasibility of establishing a pollution abatement trust fund. The results of such investigation and study shall be reported to the Congress not later than two years after enactment of this title, together with recommendations of the Administrator for financing the programs for preventing, controlling and abating pollution for the fiscal years beginning after fiscal year 1976, including any necessary legislation.

(b) There is autorized to be appropriated for use in carrying out this section, not to exceed $1,000,000.

§ 1328. Aquaculture

[Sec. 318] (a) The Administrator is authorized, after public hearings, to permit the discharge of a specific pollutant or pollutants under controlled conditions associated with an approved aquaculture project under Federal or State supervision pursuant to section 402 of this Act.

(b) The Administrator shall by regulation establish any procedures and guidelines which the Administrator deems necessary to carry out this section. Such regulations shall require the application to such discharge of each criterion, factor, procedure, and requirement applicable to a permit issued under section 402 of this title, as the Administrator determines necessary to carry out the objective of this Act.

(c) Each State desiring to administer its own permit program within its jurisdiction for discharge of a specific pollutant or pollutants under controlled conditions associated with an approved aquaculture project may do so if upon submission of such program the Administrator determines such program is adequate to carry out the objective of this Act.

§ 1329. Nonpoint Source Management Programs

[Sec. 319] (a)(1) The Governor of each State shall, after notice and opportunity for public comment, prepare and submit to the Administrator for approval, a report which—

   (A) identifies those navigable waters within the State which, without additional action to control nonpoint sources of pollution, cannot reasonably be expected to attain or maintain applicable water quality standards or the goals and requirements of this Act;
   (B) identifies those categories and subcategories of nonpoint sources or, where appropriate, particular nonpoint sources which add significant pollution to each portion of the navigable waters identified under subparagraph (A) in amounts which contribute to such portion not meeting such water quality standards or such goals and requirements;
   (C) describes the process, including intergovernmental coordination and public participation, for identifying best management prac-

tices and measures to control each category and subcategory of nonpoint sources and, where appropriate, particular nonpoint sources identified under subparagraph (B) and to reduce, to the maximum extent practicable, the level of pollution resulting from such category, subcategory, or source; and

(D) identifies and describes State and local programs for controlling pollution added from nonpoint sources to, and improving the quality of, each such portion of the navigable waters, including but not limited to those programs which are receiving Federal assistance under subsections (h) and (i).

(2) In developing the report required by this section, the State (A) may rely upon information developed pursuant to sections 208, 303(e), 304(f), 305(b), and 314, and other information as appropriate, and (B) may utilize appropriate elements of the waste treatment management plans developed pursuant to sections 208(b) and 303, to the extent such elements are consistent with and fulfill the requirements of this section.

(b)(1) The Governor of each State, for that State or in combination with adjacent States, shall, after notice and opportunity for public comment, prepare and submit to the Administrator for approval a management program which such State proposes to implement in the first four fiscal years beginning after the date of submission of such management program for controlling pollution added from nonpoint sources to the navigable waters within the State and improving the quality of such waters.

(2) Each management program proposed for implementation under this subsection shall include each of the following:

(A) An identification of the best management practices and measures which will be undertaken to reduce pollutant loadings resulting from each category, subcategory, or particular nonpoint source designated under paragraph (1)(B), taking into account the impact of the practice on ground water quality.

(B) An identification of programs (including, as appropriate, nonregulatory or regulatory programs for enforcement, technical assistance, financial assistance, education, training, technology transfer, and demonstration projects) to achieve implementation of the best management practices by the categories, subcategories, and particular nonpoint sources designated under subparagraph (A).

(C) A schedule containing annual milestones for (i) utilization of the program implementation methods identified in subparagraph (B), and (ii) implementation of the best management practices identified in subparagraph (A) by the categories, subcategories, or particular nonpoint sources designated under paragraph (1)(B). Such schedule shall provide for utilization of the best management practices at the earliest practicable date.

(D) A certification of the attorney general of the State or States (or the chief attorney of any State water pollution control agency which has independent legal counsel) that the laws of the State or States, as the case may be, provide adequate authority to implement such management program or, if there is not such adequate authority, a list of such additional authorities as will be necessary to implement such management program. A schedule and commitment by the State or States to seek such additional authorities as expeditiously as practicable.

(E) Sources of Federal and other assistance and funding (other than assistance provided under subsections (h) and (i)) which will be available in each of such fiscal years for supporting implementation of such practices and measures and the purposes for which such assistance will be used in each of such fiscal years.

(F) An identification of Federal financial assistance programs and Federal development projects for which the State will review individual assistance applications or development projects for their effect on water quality pursuant to the procedures set forth in Executive Order 12372 as in effect on September 17, 1983, to determine whether such assistance applications or development projects would be consistent with the program prepared under this subsection; for the purposes of this subparagraph, identification shall not be limited to the assistance programs or development projects subject to Executive Order 12372 but may include any programs listed in the most recent Catalog of Federal Domestic Assistance which may have an effect on the purposes and objectives of the State's nonpoint source pollution management program.

(3) In developing and implementing a management program under this subsection, a State shall, to the maximum extent practicable, involve local public and private agencies and organizations which have expertise in control of nonpoint sources of pollution.

(4) A State shall, to the maximum extent practicable, develop and implement a management program under this subsection on a watershed-by-watershed basis within such State.

(c)(1) Any report required by subsection (a) and any management program and report required by subsection (b) shall be developed in cooperation with local, substate regional, and interstate entities which are actively planning for the implementation of nonpoint source pollution controls and have either been certified by the Administrator in accordance with section 208, have worked jointly with the State on water quality management planning under section 205(j), or have been designated by the State legislative body or Governor as water quality management planning agencies for their geographic areas.

(2) Each report and management program shall be submitted to the Administrator during the 18-month period beginning on the date of

the enactment of this section.

(d)(1) Subject to paragraph (2), not later than 180 days after the date of submission to the Administrator of any report or management program under this section (other than subsections (h), (i), and (k)), the Administrator shall either approve or disapprove such report or management program, as the case may be. The Administrator may approve a portion of a management program under this subsection. If the Administrator does not disapprove a report, management program, or portion of a management program in such 180-day period, such report, management program, or portion shall be deemed approved for purposes of this section.

(2) If, after notice and opportunity for public comment and consultation with appropriate Federal and State agencies and other interested persons, the Administrator determines that—

(A) the proposed management program or any portion thereof does not meet the requirements of subsection (b)(2) of this section or is not likely to satisfy, in whole or in part, the goals and requirements of this Act;

(B) adequate authority does not exist, or adequate resources are not available, to implement such program or portion;

(C) the schedule for implementing such program or portion is not sufficiently expeditious; or

(D) the practices and measures proposed in such program or portion are not adequate to reduce the level of pollution in navigable waters in the State resulting from nonpoint sources and to improve the quality of navigable waters in the State; the Administrator shall within 6 months of the receipt of the proposed program notify the State of any revisions or modifications necessary to obtain approval. The State shall thereupon have an additional 3 months to submit its revised management program and the Administrator shall approve or disapprove such revised program within three months of receipt.

(3) If a Governor of a State does not submit the report required by subsection (a) within the period specified by subsection (c)(2), the Administrator shall, within 30 months after the date of the enactment of this section, prepare a report for such State which makes the identifications required by paragraphs (1)(A) and (1)(B) of subsection (a). Upon completion of the requirement of the preceding sentence and after notice and opportunity for comment, the Administrator shall report to Congress on his actions pursuant to this section.

(e) If a State fails to submit a management program under subsection (b) or the Administrator does not approve such a management program, a local public agency or organization which has expertise in, and authority to, control water pollution resulting from nonpoint sources in any area of such State which the Administrator determines is of sufficient geographic size may, with approval of such State, request the Administrator to provide, and the Administrator shall provide, technical assistance to such agency or organization in developing for such area a management program which is described in subsection (b) and can be approved pursuant to subsection (d). After development of such management program, such agency or organization shall submit such management program to the Administrator for approval. If the Administrator approves such management program, such agency or organization shall be eligible to receive financial assistance under subsection (h) for implementation of such management program as if such agency or organization were a State for which a report submitted under subsection (a) and a management program submitted under subsection (b) were approved under this section. Such financial assistance shall be subject to the same terms and conditions as assistance provided to a State under subsection (h).

(f) Upon request of a State, the Administrator may provide technical assistance to such State in developing a management program approved under subsection (b) for those portions of the navigable waters requested by such State.

(g)(1) If any portion of the navigable waters in any State which is implementing a management program approved under this section is not meeting applicable water quality standards or the goals and requirements of this Act as a result, in whole or in part, of pollution from nonpoint sources in another State, such State may petition the Administrator to convene, and the Administrator shall convene, a management conference of all States which contribute significant pollution resulting from nonpoint sources to such portion. If, on the basis of information available, the Administrator determines that a State is not meeting applicable water quality standards or the goals and requirements of this Act as a result, in whole or in part, of significant pollution from nonpoint sources in another State, the Administrator shall notify such States. The Administrator may convene a management conference under this paragraph not later than 180 days after giving such notification, whether or not the State which is not meeting such standards requests such conference. The purpose of such conference shall be to develop an agreement among such States to reduce the level of pollution in such portion resulting from nonpoint sources and to improve the water quality of such portion. Nothing in such agreement shall supersede or abrogate rights to quantities of water which have been established by interstate water compacts, Supreme Court decrees, or State water laws. This subsection shall not apply to any pollution which is subject to the Colorado River Basin Salinity Control Act. The requirement that the Administrator convene a management conference shall not be subject to the provisions of section 505 of this Act.

(2) To the extent that the States reach agreement through such conference, the management programs of the States which are parties to such agreements and which contribute significant pollution to the navigable waters or portions thereof not meeting applicable water

quality standards or goals and requirements of this Act will be revised to reflect such agreement. Such management programs shall be consistent with Federal and State law.

(h)(1) Upon application of a State for which a report submitted under subsection (a) and a management program submitted under subsection (b) is approved under this section, the Administrator shall make grants, subject to such terms and conditions as the Administrator considers appropriate, under this subsection to such State for the purpose of assisting the State in implementing such management program. Funds reserved pursuant to section 205(j)(5) of this Act may be used to develop and implement such management program.

(2) An application for a grant under this subsection in any fiscal year shall be in such form and shall contain such other information as the Administrator may require, including an identification and description of the best management practices and measures which the State proposes to assist, encourage, or require in such year with the Federal assistance to be provided under the grant.

(3) The Federal share of the cost of each management program implemented with Federal assistance under this subsection in any fiscal year shall not exceed 60 percent of the cost incurred by the State in implementing such management program and shall be made on condition that the non-Federal share is provided from non-Federal sources.

(4) Notwithstanding any other provision of this subsection, not more than 15 percent of the amount appropriated to carry out this subsection may be used to make grants to any one State, including any grants to any local public agency or organization with authority to control pollution from nonpoint sources in any area of such State.

(5) For each fiscal year beginning after September 30, 1987, the Administrator may give priority in making grants under this subsection, and shall give consideration in determining the Federal share of any such grant, to States which have implemented or are proposing to implement management programs which will—

(A) control particularly difficult or serious nonpoint source pollution problems, including, but not limited to, problems resulting from mining activities;

(B) implement innovative methods or practices for controlling nonpoint sources of pollution, including regulatory programs where the Administrator deems appropriate;

(C) control interstate nonpoint source pollution problems; or

(D) carry out ground water quality protection activities which the Administrator determines are part of a comprehensive nonpoint source pollution control program, including research, planning, ground water assessments, demonstration programs, enforcement, technical assistance, education, and training to protect ground water quality from nonpoint sources of pollution.

(6) The funds granted to each State pursuant to this subsection in a fiscal year shall remain available for obligation by such State for the fiscal year for which appropriated. The amount of any such funds not obligated by the end of such fiscal year shall be available to the Administrator for granting to other States under this subsection in the next fiscal year.

(7) States may use funds from grants made pursuant to this section for financial assistance to persons only to the extent that such assistance is related to the costs of demonstration projects.

(8) No grant may be made under this subsection in any fiscal year to a State which in the preceding fiscal year received a grant under this subsection unless the Administrator determines that such State made satisfactory progress in such preceding fiscal year in meeting the schedule specified by such State under subsection (b)(2).

(9) No grant may be made to a State under this subsection in any fiscal year unless such State enters into such agreements with the Administrator as the Administrator may require to ensure that such State will maintain its aggregate expenditures from all other sources for programs for controlling pollution added to the navigable waters in such State from nonpoint sources and improving the quality of such waters at or above the average level of such expenditures in its two fiscal years preceding the date of enactment of this subsection.

(10) The Administrator may request such information, data, and reports as he considers necessary to make the determination of continuing eligibility for grants under this section.

(11) Each State shall report to the Administrator on an annual basis concerning (A) its progress in meeting the schedule of milestones submitted pursuant to subsection (b)(2)(C) of this section, and (B) to the extent that appropriate information is available, reductions in nonpoint source pollutant loading and improvements in water quality for those navigable waters or watersheds within the State which were identified pursuant to subsection (a)(1)(A) of this section resulting from implementation of the management program.

(12) For purposes of this subsection, administrative costs in the form of salaries, overhead, or indirect costs for services provided and charged against activities and programs carried out with a grant under this subsection shall not exceed in any fiscal year 10 percent of the amount of the grant in such year, except that costs of implementing enforcement and regulatory activities, education, training, technical assistance, demonstration projects, and technology transfer programs shall not be subject to this limitation.

(i)(1) Upon application of a State for which a report submitted under subsection (a) and a plan submitted under subsection (b) is approved under this section, the Administrator shall make grants under this subsection to such State for the purpose of assisting such State in carrying out ground-water quality protection activities which the Administrator determines will advance the State toward implementation of a comprehensive nonpoint source pollution control program. Such activities shall include, but not be limited to, research, planning, groundwater assessments, demonstration programs, enforcement, technical assistance, education and training to protect the quality of groundwater and to prevent contamination of groundwater from nonpoint sources of pollution.

    (2) An application for a grant under this subsection shall be in such form and shall contain such information as the Administrator may require.

    (3) The Federal share of the cost of assisting a State in carrying out groundwater protection activities in any fiscal year under this subsection shall be 50 percent of the costs incurred by the State in carrying out such activities, except that the maximum amount of Federal assistance which any State may receive under this subsection in any fiscal year shall not exceed $150,000.

    (4) The Administrator shall include in each report transmitted under subsection (m) a report on the activities and programs implemented under this subsection during the preceding fiscal year.

    (j) There is authorized to be appropriated to carry out subsections (h) and (i) not to exceed $70,000,000 for fiscal year 1988, $100,000,000 per fiscal year for each of fiscal years 1989 and 1990, and $130,000,000 for fiscal year 1991; except that for each of such fiscal years not to exceed $7,500,000 may be made available to carry out subsection (i). Sums appropriated pursuant to this subsection shall remain available until expended.

    (k) The Administrator shall transmit to the Office of Management and Budget and the appropriate Federal departments and agencies a list of those assistance programs and development projects identified by each State under subsection (b)(2)(F) for which individual assistance applications and projects will be reviewed pursuant to the procedures set forth in Executive Order 12372 as in effect on September 17, 1983. Beginning not later than sixty days after receiving notification by the Administrator, each Federal department and agency shall modify existing regulations to allow States to review individual development projects and assistance applications under the identified Federal assistance programs and shall accommodate, according to the requirements and definitions of Executive Order 12372, as in effect on September 17, 1983, the concerns of the State regarding the consistency of such applications or projects with the State nonpoint source pollution management program.

    (l) The Administrator shall collect and make available, through publications and other appropriate means, information pertaining to management practices and implementation methods, including, but not limited to, (1) information concerning the costs and relative efficiencies of best management practices for reducing nonpoint source pollution; and (2) available data concerning the relationship between water quality and implementation of various management practices to control nonpoint sources of pollution.

(m)(1) Not later than January 1, 1988, and each January 1 thereafter, the Administrator shall transmit to the Committee on Public Works and Transportation of the House of Representatives and the Committee on Environment and Public Works of the Senate, a report for the preceding fiscal year on the activities and programs implemented under this section and the progress made in reducing pollution in the navigable waters resulting from nonpoint sources and improving the quality of such waters.

(2) Not later than January 1, 1990, the Administrator shall transmit to Congress a final report on the activities carried out under this section. Such report, at a minimum, shall—

(A) describe the management programs being implemented by the States by types and amount of affected navigable waters, categories and subcategories of nonpoint sources, and types of best management practices being implemented;

(B) describe the experiences of the States in adhering to schedules and implementing best management practices;

(C) describe the amount and purpose of grants awarded pursuant to subsections (h) and (i) of this section;

(D) identify, to the extent that information is available, the progress made in reducing pollutant loads and improving water quality in the navigable waters;

(E) indicate what further actions need to be taken to attain and maintain in those navigable waters (i) applicable water quality standards, and (ii) the goals and requirements of this Act;

(F) include recommendations of the Administrator concerning future programs (including enforcement programs) for controlling pollution from nonpoint sources; and

(G) identify the activities and programs of departments, agencies, and instrumentalities of the United States which are inconsistent with the management programs submitted by the States and recommend modifications so that such activities and programs are consistent with and assist the States in implementation of such management programs.

(n) Not less than 5 percent of the funds appropriated pursuant to subsection (j) for any fiscal year shall be available to the Administrator to maintain personnel levels at the Environmental Protection Agency at levels which are adequate to carry out this section in such year.

§ 1330. National Estuary Program

[Sec. 320] (a)(1) The Governor of any State may nominate to the Administrator an estuary lying in whole or in part within the State as an estuary of national significance and request a management conference to develop a comprehensive management plan for the estuary. The nomination shall document the need for the conference, the likelihood of success, and information relating to the factors in paragraph (2).

(2)(A) In any case where the Administrator determines, on his own initiative or upon nomination of a State under paragraph (1), that the attainment or maintenance of that water quality in an estuary which assures protection of public water supplies and the protection and propagation of a balanced, indigenous population of shellfish, fish, and wildlife, and allows recreational activities, in and on the water, requires the control of point and nonpoint sources of pollution to supplement existing controls of pollution in more than one State, the Administrator shall select such estuary and convene a management conference.

(B) The Administrator shall give priority consideration under this section to Long Island Sound, New York and Connecticut; Narragansett Bay, Rhode Island; Buzzards Bay, Massachusetts; Puget Sound, Washington; New York-New Jersey Harbor, New York and New Jersey; Delaware Bay, Delaware and New Jersey; Delaware Inland Bays, Delaware; Albemarle Sound, North Carolina; Sarasota Bay, Florida; San Francisco Bay, California; Santa Monica Bay, California; and Galveston Bay, Texas.

(3) In any case in which a boundary between two States passes through an estuary and such boundary is disputed and is the subject of an action in any court, the Administrator shall not convene a management conference with respect to such estuary before a final adjudication has been made of such dispute.

(b) The purposes of any management conference convened with respect to an estuary under this subsection shall be to—

(1) assess trends in water quality, natural resources, and uses of the estuary;

(2) collect, characterize, and assess data on toxics, nutrients, and natural resources within the estuarine zone to identify the causes of environmental problems;

(3) develop the relationship between the inplace loads and point and nonpoint loadings of pollutants to the estuarine zone and the potential uses of the zone, water quality, and natural resources;

(4) develop a comprehensive conservation and management plan that recommends priority corrective actions and compliance schedules addressing point and nonpoint sources of pollution to restore and maintain the chemical, physical, and biological integrity of the estuary, including restoration and maintenance of water quality, a balanced indigenous population of shellfish, fish and wildlife, and recreational activities in the estuary, and assure that the designated uses of the estuary are protected;

(5) develop plans for the coordinated implementation of the plan by the States as well as Federal and local agencies participating in the conference;

(6) monitor the effectiveness of actions taken pursuant to the plan; and

(7) review all Federal financial assistance programs and Federal development projects in accordance with the requirements of Executive Order 12372, as in effect on September 17, 1983, to determine whether such assistance program or project would be consistent with and further the purposes and objectives of the plan prepared under this section.

For purposes of paragraph (7), such programs and projects shall not be limited to the assistance programs and development projects subject to Executive Order 12372, but may include any programs listed in the most recent Catalog of Federal Domestic Assistance which may have an effect on the purposes and objectives of the plan developed under this section.

(c) The members of a management conference convened under this section shall include, at a minimum, the Administrator and representatives of—

(1) each State and foreign nation located in whole or in part in the estuarine zone of the estuary for which the conference is convened;

(2) international, interstate, or regional agencies or entities having jurisdiction over all or a significant part of the estuary;

(3) each interested Federal agency, as determined appropriate by the Administrator;

(4) local governments having jurisdiction over any land or water within the estuarine zone, as determined appropriate by the Administrator; and

(5) affected industries, public and private educational institutions, and the general public, as determined appropriate by the Administrator.

(d) In developing a conservation and management plan under this section, the management conference shall survey and utilize existing reports, data, and studies relating to the estuary that have been developed by or made available to Federal, interstate, State, and local agencies.

(e) A management conference convened under this section shall be convened for a period not to exceed 5 years. Such conference may be extended by the Administrator, and if terminated after the initial period, may be reconvened by the Administrator at any time thereafter, as may be necessary to meet the requirements of this section.

(f)(1) Not later than 120 days after the completion of a conservation and management plan and after providing for public review and comment, the Administrator shall approve such plan if the plan meets the requirements of this section and the affected Governor or Governors concur.

(2) Upon approval of a conservation and management plan under this section, such plan shall be implemented. Funds authorized to be appropriated under titles II and VI and section 319 of this Act may be used in accordance with the applicable requirements of this Act to

assist States with the implementation of such plan.

(g)(1) The Administrator is authorized to make grants to State, interstate, and regional water pollution control agencies and entities, State coastal zone management agencies, interstate agencies, other public or nonprofit private agencies, institutions, organizations, and individuals.

(2) Grants under this subsection shall be made to pay for assisting research, surveys, studies, and modeling and other technical work necessary for the development of a conservation and management plan under this section.

(3) The amount of grants to any person (including a State, interstate, or regional agency or entity) under this subsection for a fiscal year shall not exceed 75 percent of the costs of such research, survey, studies, and work and shall be made on condition that the non-Federal share of such costs are provided from non-Federal sources.

(h) Any person (including a State, interstate, or regional agency or entity) that receives a grant under subsection (g) shall report to the Administrator not later than 18 months after receipt of such grant and biennially thereafter on the progress being made under this section.

(i) There are authorized to be appropriated to the Administrator not to exceed $12,000,000 per fiscal year for each of fiscal years 1987, 1988, 1989, 1990, and 1991 for—

(1) expenses related to the administration of management conferences under this section, not to exceed 10 percent of the amount appropriated under this subsection;

(2) making grants under subsection (g); and

(3) monitoring the implementation of a conservation and management plan by the management conference or by the Administrator, in any case in which the conference has been terminated.

The Administrator shall provide up to $5,000,000 per fiscal year of the sums authorized to be appropriated under this subsection to the Administrator of the National Oceanic and Atmospheric Administration to carry out subsection (j).

(j)(1) In order to determine the need to convene a management conference under this section or at the request of such a management conference, the Administrator shall coordinate and implement, through the National Marine Pollution Program Office and the National Marine Fisheries Service of the National Oceanic and Atmospheric Administration, as appropriate, for one or more estuarine zones—

(A) a long-term program of trend assessment monitoring measuring variations in pollutant concentrations, marine ecology, and other physical or biological environmental parameters which may affect estuarine zones, to provide the Administrator the capacity to determine the potential and actual effects of alternative management strategies and measures;

(B) a program of ecosystem assessment assisting in the development of (i) baseline studies which determine the state of estuarine zones and the effects of natural and anthropogenic changes, and (ii) predictive models capable of translating information on specific discharges or general pollutant loadings within estuarine zones into a set of probable effects on such zones;

(C) a comprehensive water quality sampling program for the continuous monitoring of nutrients, chlorine, acid precipitation dissolved oxygen, and potentially toxic pollutants (including organic chemicals and metals) in estuarine zones, after consultation with interested State, local, interstate, or international agencies and review and analysis of all environmental sampling data presently collected from estuarine zones; and

(D) a program of research to identify the movements of nutrients, sediments and pollutants through estuarine zones and the impact of nutrients, sediments, and pollutants on water quality, the ecosystem, and designated or potential uses of the estuarine zones.

(2) The Administrator, in cooperation with the Administrator of the National Oceanic and Atmospheric Administration, shall submit to the Congress no less often than biennially a comprehensive report on the activities authorized under this subsection including—

(A) a listing of priority monitoring and research needs;

(B) an assessment of the state and health of the Nation's estuarine zones, to the extent evaluated under this subsection;

(C) a discussion of pollution problems and trends in pollutant concentrations with a direct or indirect effect on water quality, the ecosystem, and designated or potential uses of each estuarine zone, to the extent evaluated under this subsection; and

(D) an evaluation of pollution abatement activities and management measures so far implemented to determine the degree of improvement toward the objectives expressed in subsection (b)(4) of this section.

(k) For purposes of this section, the terms "estuary" and "estuarine zone" have the meanings such terms have in section 104(n)(4) of this Act, except that the term "estuarine zone" shall also include associated aquatic ecosystems and those portions of tributaries draining into the estuary up to the historic height of migration of anadromous fish or the historic head of tidal influence, whichever is higher.

Subchapter IV. Permits and Licenses

§ 1341. Certification

[Sec. 401](a)(1) Any applicant for a Federal license or permit to conduct any activity including but not limited to, the construction or operation of facilities, which may result in any discharge into the navigable waters, shall provide the licensing or permitting agency a certification from the State in which the discharge originates or will originate, or, if appropriate, from the interstate water pollution control agency having jurisdiction over the navigable waters at the point where the discharge originates or will originate, that any such discharge will comply with the applicable provisions of sections 301, 302, 303, 306, and 307 of this Act. In the case of any such activity for which there is not an applicable effluent limitation or other limitation under sections 301(b) and 302, and there is not an applicable standard under sections 306 and 307, the State shall so certify, except that any such certification shall not be deemed to satisfy section 511(c) of this Act. Such State or interstate agency shall establish procedures for public notice in the case of all applications for certification by it and, to the extent it deems appropriate, procedures for public hearings in connection with specific applications. In any case where a State or interstate agency has no authority to give such a certification, such certification shall be from the Administrator. If the State, interstate agency, or Administrator, as the case may be, fails or refuses to act on a request for certification, within a reasonable period of time (which shall not exceed one year) after receipt of such request, the certification requirements of this subsection shall be waived with respect to such Federal application. No license or permit shall be granted until the certification required by this section has been obtained or has been waived as provided in the preceding sentence. No license or permit shall be granted if certification has been denied by the State, interstate agency, or the Administrator, as the case may be.

(2) Upon receipt of such application and certification the licensing or permitting agency shall immediately notify the Administrator of such application and certification. Whenever such a discharge may affect, as determined by the Administrator, the quality of the waters of any other State, the Administrator within thirty days of the date of notice of application for such Federal license or permit shall so notify such other State, the licensing or permitting agency, and the applicant. If, within sixty days after receipt of such notification, such other State determines that such discharge will affect the quality of its waters so as to violate any water quality requirement in such State, and within such sixty-day period notifies the Administrator and the licensing or permitting agency in writing of its objection to the issuance of such license or permit and requests a public hearing on such objection, the licensing or permitting agency shall hold such a hearing. The Administrator shall at such hearing submit his evaluation and recommendations with respect to any such objection to the licensing or permitting agency. Such agency, based upon the recommendations of such State, the Administrator, and upon any additional evidence, if any, presented to the agency at the hearing, shall condition such license or permit in such manner as may be necessary to insure compliance with applicable water quality requirements. If the imposition of conditions cannot

insure such compliance such agency shall not issue such license or permit.

(3) The certification obtained pursuant to paragraph (1) of this subsection with respect to the construction of any facility shall fulfill the requirements of this subsection with respect to certification in connection with any other Federal license or permit required for the operation of such facility unless, after notice to the certifying State, agency, or Administrator, as the case may be, which shall be given by the Federal agency to whom application is made for such operating license or permit, the State, or if appropriate, the interstate agency or the Administrator, notifies such agency within sixty days after receipt of such notice that there is no longer reasonable assurance that there will be compliance with the applicable provisions of setions 301, 302, 303, 306, and 307 of this Act because of changes since the construction license or permit certification was issued in (A) the construction or operation of the facility, (B) the characteristics of the waters into which such discharge is made, (C) the water quality criteria applicable to such waters or (D) applicable effluent limitations or other requirements. This paragraph shall be inapplicable in any case where the applicant for such operating license or permit has failed to provide the certifying State, or, if appropriate, the interstate agency or the Administrator, with notice of any proposed changes in the construction or operation of the facility with respect to which a construction license or permit has been granted, which changes may result in violation of section 301, 302, 303, 306, or 307 of this Act.

(4) Prior to the initial operation of any federally licensed or permitted facility or activity which may result in any discharge into the navigable waters and with respect to which a certification has been obtained pursuant to paragraph (1) of this subsection, which facility or activity is not subject to a Federal operating license or permit, the licensee or permittee shall provide an opportunity for such certifying State, or, if appropriate, the interstate agency or the Administrator to review the manner in which the facility or activity shall be operated or conducted for the purposes of assuring that applicable effluent limitations or other limitations or other applicable water quality requirements will not be violated. Upon notification by the certifying State, or if appropriate, the interstate agency or the Administrator that the operation of any such federally licensed or permitted facility or activity will violate applicable effluent limitations or other limitations or other water quality requiremetns such Federal agency may, after public hearing, suspend such license or permit. If such license or permit is suspended, it shall remain suspended until notification is received from the certifying State, agency, or Administrator, as the case may be, that there is reasonable assurance that such facility or activity will not violate the applicable provisions of section 301, 302, 303, 306, or

307 of this Act.

(5) Any Federal license or permit with respect to which a certification has been obtained under paragraph (1) of this subsection may be suspended or revoked by the Federal agency issuing such license or permit upon the entering of a judgment under this Act that such facility or activity has been operated in violation of the applicable provisions of section 301, 302, 303, 306, or 307 of this Act.

(6) Except with respect to a permit issued under section 402 of this Act, in any case where actual construction of a facility has been lawfully commenced prior to April 3, 1970, no certification shall be required under this subsection for a license or permit issued after April 3, 1970, to operate such facility, except that any such license or permit issued without certification shall terminate April 3, 1973, unless prior to such termination date the person having such license or permit submits to the Federal agency which issued such license or permit a certification and otherwise meets the requirements of this section.

(b) Nothing in this section shall be construed to limit the authority of any department or agency pursuant to any other provision of law to require compliance with any applicable water quality requirements. The Administrator shall, upon the request of any Federal department or agency, or State or interstate agency, or applicant, provide, for the purpose of this section, any relevant information on applicable effluent limitations, or other limitations, standards, regulations or requirements, or water quality criteria, and shall, when requested by any such department or agency or State or interstate agency, or applicant, comment on any methods to comply with such limitations, standards, regulations, requirements, or criteria.

(c) In order to implement the provisions of this section, the Secretary of the Army, acting through the Chief of Engineers, is authorized, if he deems it to be in the public interest, to permit the use of spoil disposal areas under his jurisdiction by Federal licensees or permittees, and to make an appropriate charge for such use. Moneys received from such licensees or permittees shall be deposited in the Treasury as miscellaneous receipts.

(d) Any certification provided under this section shall set forth any effluent limitations and other limitations, and monitoring requirements necessary to assure that any applicant for a Federal license or permit will comply with any applicable effluent limitations and other limitations under section 301 or 302 of this Act, standard of performance under section 306 of this Act, or prohibition, effluent standard, or pretreatment standard under section 307 of this Act, and with any other appropriate requirement of State law set forth in such certification, and shall become a condition on any Federal license or permit subject to the provisions of this section.

§ 1342. National pollutant discharge elimination system

[Sec. 402] (a)(1) Except as provided in sections 318 and 404 of this Act, the Administrator may, after opportunity for public hearing, issue a permit for the discharge of any pollutant, or combination of pollutants, notwithstanding section 301(a), upon condition that such discharge will meet either (A) all applicable requirements under sections 301, 302, 306, 307, 308, and 403 of this Act, or (B) prior to the taking of necessary implementing actions relating to all such requirements, such conditions as the Administrator determines are necessary to carry out the provisions of this Act.

(2) The Administrator shall prescribe conditions for such permits to assure compliance with the requirements of paragraph (1) of this subsection, including conditions on data and information collection, reporting, and such other requirements as he deems appropriate.

(3) The permit program of the Administrator under paragraph (1) of this subsection, and permits issued thereunder, shall be subject to the same terms, conditions, and requirements as apply to a State permit program and permits issued thereunder under subsection (b) of this section.

(4) All permits for discharges into the navigable waters issued pursuant to section 13 of the Act of March 3, 1899, shall be deemed to be permits issued under this title, and permits issued under this title shall be deemed to be permits issued under section 13 of the Act of March 3, 1899, and shall continue in force and effect for their term unless revoked, modified, or suspended in accordance with the provisions of this Act.

(5) No permit for a discharge into the navigable waters shall be issued under section 13 of the Act of March 3, 1899, after the date of enactment of this title. Each application for a permit under section 13 of the Act of March 3, 1899, pending on the date of enactment of this Act shall be deemed to be an application for a permit under this section. The Administrator shall authorize a State, which he determines has the capability of administering a permit program which will carry out the objective of this Act, to issue permits for discharges into the navigable waters within the jurisdiction of such State. The Administrator may exercise the authority granted him by the preceding sentence only during the period which begins on the date of enactment of this Act and ends either on the ninetieth day after the date of the first promulgation of guidelines required by section 304(h)(2) of this Act, or the date of approval by the Administrator of a permit program for such State under subsection (b) of this section, whichever date first occurs, and no such authorization to a State shall extend beyond the last day of such period. Each such permit shall be subject to such conditions as the Administrator determines are necessary to carry out the provisions of this Act. No such permit shall issue if the Administrator objects to such issuance.

(b) At any time after the promulgation of the guidelines required by subsection (h)(2) of section 304 of this Act, the Governor of each State desiring to administer its own permit program for discharges into navigable waters within its jurisdiction may submit to the Administrator a full and complete description of the program it proposes to establish and administer under State law or under an interstate compact. In addition, such State shall submit a statement from the attorney general (or the attorney for those State water pollution control agencies which have independent legal counsel), or from the chief legal officer in the case of an interstate agency, that the laws of such State, or the interstate compact, as the case may be, provide adequate authority to carry out the described program. The Administrator shall approve each such submitted program unless he determines that adequate authority does not exist:

(1) To issue permits which—
    (A) apply, and insure compliance with, any applicable requirements of sections 301, 302, 306, 307, and 403;
    (B) are for fixed terms not exceeding five years; and
    (C) can be terminated or modified for cause including, but not limited to, the following:
        (i) violation of any condition of the permit;
        (ii) obtaining a permit by misrepresentation, or failure to disclose fully all relevant facts;
        (iii) change in any condition that requires either a temporary or permanent reduction or elimination of the permitted discharge;
    (D) control the disposal of pollutants into wells;

(2)(A) To issue permits which apply, and insure compliance with, all applicable requirements of section 308 of this Act, or
    (B) To inspect, monitor, enter, and require reports to at least the same extent as required in section 308 of this Act;

(3) To insure that the public, and any other State the waters of which may be affected, receive notice of each application for a permit and to provide an opportunity for public hearing before a ruling on each such application;

(4) To insure that the Administrator receives notice of each application (including a copy thereof) for a permit;

(5) To insure that any State (other than the permitting State), whose waters may be affected by the issuance of a permit may submit written recommendations to the permitting State (and the Administrator) with respect to any permit application and, if any part of such written recommendations are not accepted by the permitting State, that the permitting State will notify such affected State (and the Administrator) in writing of its failure to so accept such recommendations together with its reasons for so doing;

(6) To insure that no permit will be issued if, in the judgment of the Secretary of the Army acting through the Chief of Engineers, after consultation with the Secretary of the department in which the Coast Guard is operating, anchorage and navigation of any of the navigable waters would be substantially impaired thereby;

(7) To abate violations of the permit or the permit program, including civil and criminal penalties and other ways and means of enforcement;

(8) To insure that any permit for a discharge from a publicly owned treatment works includes conditions to require the identification in terms of character and volume of pollutants of any significant source introducing pollutants subject to pretreatment standards under section 307(b) of this Act into such works and a program to assure compliance with such pretreatment standards by each such source, in addition to adequate notice to the permitting agency of (A) new introductions into such works of pollutants from any source which would be a new source as defined in section 306 if such source were discharging pollutants. (B) new introductions of pollutants into such works from a source which would be subject to section 301 if it were discharging such pollutants, or (C) a substantial change in volume or character of pollutants being introduced into such works by a source introducing pollutants into such works at the time of issuance of the permit. Such notice shall include information on the quality and quantity of effluent to be introduced into such treatment works and any anticipated impact of such change in the quantity or quality of effluent to be discharged from such publicly owned treatment works; and

(9) To insure that any industrial user of any publicly owned treatment works will comply with sections 204(b), 307, and 308.

(c)(1) Not later than ninety days after the date on which a State has submitted a program (or revision thereof) pursuant to subsection (b) of this section, the Administrator shall suspend the issuance of permits under subsection (a) of this section as to those discharges subject to such program unless he determines that the State permit program does not meet the requirements of subsection (b) of this section or does not conform to the guidelines issued under section 304 (i)(2) of this Act. If the Administrator so determines, he shall notify the State of any revisions or modifications necessary to conform to such requirements or guidelines.

(2) Any State permit program under this section shall at all times be in accordance with this section and guidelines promulgated pursuant to section 304 (h)(2) of this Act.

(3) Whenever the Administrator determines after public hearing that a State is not administering a program approved under this section in accordance with requirements of this section, he shall so notify the State and, if appropriate corrective action is not taken within a reasonable time, not to exceed ninety days, the Administrator shall withdraw approval of such program. The Administrator shall not withdraw approval of any such program unless he shall first have notified the State, and made public, in writing, the reasons for such withdrawal.

(4) A State may return to the Administrator administration, and the Administrator may withdraw under paragraph (3) of this subsection

approval, of—

(A) a State partial permit program approved under subsection (n)(3) only if the entire permit program being administered by the State department or agency at the time is returned or withdrawn; and

(B) a State partial permit program approved under subsection (n)(4) only if an entire phased component of the permit program being administered by the State at the time is returned or withdrawn.

(d)(1) Each State shall transmit to the Administrator a copy of each permit application received by such State and provide notice to the Administrator of every action related to the consideration of such permit application, including each permit proposed to be issued by such State.

(2) No permit shall issue (A) if the Administrator within ninety days of the date of his notification under subsection (b)(5) of this section objects in writing to the issuance of such permit, or (B) if the Administrator within ninety days of the date of transmittal of the proposed permit by the State objects in writing to the issuance of such permit as being outside the guidelines and requirements of this Act. Whenever the Administrator objects to the issuance of a permit under this paragraph such written objection shall contain a statement of the reasons for such objection and the effluent limitations and conditions which such permit would include if it were issued by the Administrator.

(3) The Administrator may, as to any permit application, waive paragraph (2) of this subsection.

(4) In any case where, after the date of enactment of this paragraph, the Administrator, pursuant to paragraph (2) of this subsection, objects to the issuance of a permit, or request of the State, a public hearing shall be held by the Administrator on such objection. If the State does not resubmit such permit revised to meet such objection within 30 days after completion of the hearing, or, if no hearing is requested within 90 days after the date of such objection, the Administrator may issue the permit pursuant to subsection (a) of this section for such source in accordance with the guidelines and requirements of this Act.

(e) In accordance with guidelines promulgated pursuant to subsection (h)(2) of section 304 of this Act, the Administrator is authorized to waive the requirements of subsection (d) of this section at the time he approves a program pursuant to subsection (b) of this section for any category (including any class, type, or size within such category) of point sources within the State submitting such program.

(f) The Administrator shall promulgate regulations establishing categories of point sources which he determines shall not be subject to the requirements of subsection (d) of this section in any State with a program approved pursuant to subsection (b) of this section. The Administrator may distinguish among classes, types, and sizes within any category of point sources.

(g) Any permit issued under this section for the discharge of pollutants into the navigable waters from a vessel or other floating craft shall be subject to any applicable regulations promulgated by the Secretary of the Department in which the Coast Guard is operating, establishing specifications for safe transportation, handling, carriage, storage, and stowage of pollutants.

(h) In the event any condition of a permit for discharges from a treatment works (as defined in section 212 of this Act) which is publicly owned is violated, a State with a program approved under subsection (b) of this section or the Administrator, where no State program is approved or where the Administrator determines pursuant to section 309(a) of this Act that a State with an approved program has not commenced appropriate enforcement action with respect to such permit, may proceed in a court of competent jurisdiction to restrict or prohibit the introduction of any pollutant into such treatment works by a source not utilizing such treatment works prior to the finding that such condition was violated.

(i) Nothing in this section shall be construed to limit the authority of the Administrator to take action pursuant to section 309 of this Act.

(j) A copy of each permit application and each permit issued under this section shall be available to the public. Such permit application or permit, or portion thereof, shall further be available on request for the purpose of reproduction.

(k) Compliance with a permit issued pursuant to this section shall be deemed compliance, for purposes of sections 309 and 505, with sections 301, 302, 306, 307, and 403, except any standard imposed under section 307 for a toxic pollutant injurious to human health. Until December 31, 1974, in any case where a permit for discharge has been applied for pursuant to this section, but final administrative disposition of such application has not been made, such discharge shall not be a violation of (1) section 301, 306, and 402, of this Act, or (2) section 13 of the Act of March 3, 1899, unless the Administrator or other plaintiff proves that final administrative disposition of such application has not been made because of failure of the applicant to furnish information reasonably required or requested in order to process the application. For the 180-day period beginning on the date of enactment of the Federal Water Pollution Control Act Amendments of 1972, in the case of any point source discharging any pollutant or combination of pollutants immediately prior to such date of enactment which source is not subject to section 13 of the Act of March, 3, 1899, the discharge by such source shall not be a violation of this Act if such a source applies for a permit for discharge pursuant to this section within such 180-day period.

(l)(1) The Administrator shall not require a permit under this section, for discharge composed entirely of return flows from irrigated agriculture, nor shall the Administrator directly or indirectly, require any State to require such a permit.

(2) The Administrator shall not require a permit under this section, nor shall the Administrator directly or indirectly require any State to

require a permit, for discharges of stormwater runoff from mining operations or oil and gas exploration, production, processing, or treatment operations or transmission facilities, composed entirely of flows which are from conveyances or systems of conveyances (including but not limited to pipes, conduits, ditches, and channels) used for collecting and conveying precipitation runoff and which are not contaminated by contact with, or do not come into contact with, any overburden, raw material, intermediate products, finished product, byproduct, or waste products located on the site of such operations.

(m) To the extent a treatment works (as defined in section 212 of this Act) which is publicly owned is not meeting the requirements of a permit issued under this section for such treatment works as a result of inadequate design or operation of such treatment works, the Administrator, in issuing a permit under this section, shall not require pretreatment by a person introducing conventional pollutants identified pursuant to section 304(a)(4) of this Act into such treatment works other than pretreatment required to assure compliance with pretreatment standards under subsection (b)(8) of this section and section 307(b)(1) of this Act. Nothing in this subsection shall affect the Administrator's authority under sections 307 and 309 of this Act, affect State and local authority under sections 307(b)(4) and 510 of this Act, relieve such treatment works of its obligations to meet requirements established under this Act, or otherwise preclude such works from pursuing whatever feasible options are available to meet its responsibility to comply with its permit under this section.

(n)(1) The Governor of a State may submit under subsection (b) of this section a permit program for a portion of the discharges into the navigable waters in such State.

   (2) A partial permit program under this subsection shall cover, at a minimum, administration of a major category of the discharges into the navigable waters of the State or a major component of the permit program required by subsection (b).

   (3) The Administrator may approve a partial permit program covering administration of a major category of discharges under this subsection if—

     (A) such program represents a complete permit program and covers all of the discharges under the jurisdiction of a department or agency of the State; and

     (B) the Administrator determines that the partial program represents a significant and identifiable part of the State program required by subsection (b).

   (4) The Administrator may approve under this subsection a partial and phased permit program covering administration of a major component (including discharge categories) of a State permit program required by subsection (b) if—

     (A) the Administrator determines that the partial program represents a significant and identifiable part of the State program required by subsection (b); and

(B) the State submits, and the Administrator approves, a plan for the State to assume administration by phases of the remainder of the State program required by subsection (b) by a specified date not more than 5 years after submission of the partial program under this subsection and agrees to make all reasonable efforts to assume such administration by such date.

(o)(1) In the case of effluent limitations established on the basis of subsection (a)(1)(B) of this section, a permit may not be renewed, reissued, or modified on the basis of effluent guidelines promulgated under section 304(b) subsequent to the original issuance of such permit, to contain effluent limitations which are less stringent than the comparable effluent limitations in the previous permit. In the case of effluent limitations established on the basis of section 301(b)(1)(C) or section 303 (d) or (e), a permit may not be renewed, reissued, or modified to contain effluent limitations which are less stringent than the comparable effluent limitations in the previous permit except in compliance with section 303(d)(4).

(2) A permit with respect to which paragraph (1) applies may be renewed, reissued, or modified to contain a less stringent effluent limitation applicable to a pollutant if—

(A) material and substantial alterations or additions to the permitted facility occurred after permit issuance which justify the application of a less stringent effluent limitation;

(B)(i) information is available which was not available at the time of permit issuance (other than revised regulations, guidance, or test methods) and which would have justified the application of a less stringent effluent limitation at the time of permit issuance; or

(ii) the Administrator determines that technical mistakes or mistaken interpretations of law were made in issuing the permit under subsection (a)(1)(B);

(C) a less stringent effluent limitation is necessary because of events over which the permittee has no control and for which there is no reasonably available remedy;

(D) the permittee has received a permit modification under section 301(c), 301(g), 301(h), 301(i), 301(k), 301(n), or 316(a); or

(E) the permittee has installed the treatment facilities required to meet the effluent limitations in the previous permit and has properly operated and maintained the facilities but has nevertheless been unable to achieve the previous effluent limitations, in which case the limitations in the reviewed, reissued, or modified permit may reflect the level of pollutant control actually achieved (but shall not be less stringent than required by effluent guidelines in effect at the time of permit renewal, reissuance, or modification).

Subparagraph (B) shall not apply to any revised waste load allocations or any alternative grounds for translating water quality standards into effluent limitations, except where the cumulative effect of such revised allocations results in a decrease in the amount of pollutants discharged into the concerned waters, and such revised allocations are not the result of a discharger eliminating or substantially reducing its discharge of pollutants to complying with the requirements of this Act or for reasons otherwise unrelated to water quality.

(3) In no event may a permit with respect to which paragraph (1) applies be renewed, reissued, or modified to contain an effluent limitation which is less stringent than required by effluent guidelines in effect at the time the permit is renewed, reissued, or modified. In no event may such a permit to discharge into waters be renewed, reissued, or modified to contain a less stringent effluent limitation if the implementation of such limitation would result in a violation of a water quality standard under section 303 applicable to such waters.

(p)(1) Prior to October 1, 1992, the Administrator or the State (in the case of a permit program approved under section 402 of this Act) shall not require a permit under this section for discharges composed entirely of stormwater.

(2) Paragraph (1) shall not apply with respect to the following stormwater discharges:

(A) A discharge with respect to which a permit has been issued under this section before the date of the enactment of this subsection.

(B) A discharge associated with industrial activity.

(C) A discharge from a municipal separate storm sewer system serving a population of 250,000 or more.

(D) A discharge from a municipal separate storm sewer system serving a population of 100,000 or more but less than 250,000.

(E) A discharge for which the Administrator or the State, as the case may be, determines that the stormwater discharge contributes to a violation of a water quality standard or is a significant contributor of pollutants to waters of the United States.

(3)(A) Permits for discharges associated with industrial activity shall meet all applicable provisions of this section and section 301.

(B) Permits for discharges from municipal storm sewers—

(i) may be issued on a system- or jurisdiction-wide basis;

(ii) shall include a requirement to effectively prohibit non-stormwater discharges into the storm sewers; and

(iii) shall require controls to reduce the discharge of pollutants to the maximum extent practicable, including management practices, control techniques and system, design and engineering methods, and such other provisions as the Administrator or the State determines appropriate for the control of such pollutants.

(4)(A) Not later than 2 years after the date of the enactment of this subsection, the Administrator shall establish regulations setting forth the permit application requirements for stormwater discharges described in paragraphs (2)(B) and (2)(C). Applications for permits for such discharges shall be filed no later than 3 years after such date of enactment. Not later than 4 years after such date of enactment, the Administrator or the State, as the case may be, shall issue or deny each such permit. Any such permit shall provide for compliance as expeditiously as practicable, but in no event later than 3 years after the date of issuance of such permit.

(B) Not later than 4 years after the date of the enactment of this subsection, the Administrator shall establish regulations setting forth the permit application requirements for stormwater discharges described in paragraph (2)(D). Applications for permits for such discharges shall be filed no later than 5 years after such date of enactment. Not later than 6 years after such date of enactment, the Administrator or the State, as the case may be, shall issue or deny each such permit. Any such permit shall provide for compliance as expeditiously as practicable, but in no event later than 3 years after the date of issuance of such permit.

(5) The Administrator, in consultation with the States, shall conduct a study for the purposes of—
   (A) identifying those stormwater discharges or classes of stormwater discharges for which permits are not required pursuant to paragraphs (1) and (2) of this subsection;
   (B) determining, to the maximum extent practicable, the nature and extent of pollutants in such discharges; and
   (C) establishing procedures and methods to control stormwater discharges to the extent necessary to mitigate impacts on water quality.
   Not later than October 1, 1988, the Administrator shall submit to Congress a report on the results of the study described in subparagraphs and (B). Not later than October 1, 1989, the Administrator shall submit to Congress a report on the results of the study described in subparagraph (C).

(6) Not later than October 1, 1992, the Administrator, in consultation with State and local officials, shall issue regulations (based on the results of the studies conducted under paragraph (5)) which designate stormwater discharges, other than those discharges described in paragraph (2), to be regulated to protect water quality and shall establish a comprehensive program to regulate such designated sources. The program shall, at a minimum, (A) establish priorities, (B) establish requirements for State stormwater management programs, and (C) establish expeditious deadlines. The program may include perform-

ance standards, guidelines, guidance, and management practices and treatment requirements, as appropriate.

§ 1343. Ocean discharge criteria

[Sec. 403] (a) No permit under section 402 of this Act for a discharge into the territorial sea, the waters of the contiguous zone, or the oceans shall be issued, after promulgation of guidelines established under subsection (c) of this section, except in compliance with such guidelines. Prior to the promulgation of such guidelines, a permit may be issued under such section 402 if the Administrator determines it to be in the public interest.

(b) The requirements of subsection (d) of section 402 of this Act may not be waived in the case of permits for discharges into the territorial sea.

(c)(1) The Administrator shall, within one hundred and eighty days after enactment of this Act (and from time to time thereafter), promulgate guidelines for determining the degradation of the waters of the territorial seas, the contiguous zone, and the oceans, which shall include:

(A) the effect of disposal of pollutants on human health or welfare, including but not limited to plankton, fish, shellfish, wildlife, shorelines, and beaches;

(B) the effect of disposal of pollutants on marine life including the transfer, concentration, and dispersal of pollutants or their by-products trough biological, physical, and chemical processes; changes in marine ecosystem diversity, productivity, and stability; and species and community population changes;

(C) the effect of disposal, of pollutants on esthetic, recreation, and economic values;

(D) the persistence and permanence of the effects of disposal of pollutants;

(E) the effect of the disposal at varying rates, of particular volumes and concentrations of pollutants;

(F) other possible locations and methods of disposal or recycling of pollutants including land-based alternatives; and

(G) the effect on alternate uses of the oceans, such as mineral exploitation and scientific study.

(2) In any event where insufficient information exists on any proposed discharge to make a reasonable judgment on any of the guidelines established pursuant to this subsection no permit shall be issued under section 402 of this Act.

§ 1344. Permits for dredged or fill material

[Sec. 404] (a) The Secretary may issue permits, after notice and opportunity for public hearings for the discharge of dredged or fill material into the navigable waters at specified disposal sites. Not later than the fifteenth day after the date an applicant submits all the information required to complete an application for a permit under this subsection, the Secretary shall publish the notice required by this subsection.

(b) Subject to subsection (c) of this section, each such disposal site shall be specified for each such permit by the Secretary (1) through the application of guidelines developed by the Administrator, in conjunction with the Secretary, which guidelines shall be based upon criteria comparable to the criteria applicable to the territorial seas, the contiguous zones, and the ocean under section 403(c), and (2) in any case where such guidelines under clause (1) alone would prohibit the specification of a site, through the application additionally of the economic impact of the site on navigation and anchorage.

(c) The Administrator is authorized to prohibit the specification (including the withdrawal of specification) of any defined area as a disposal site, and he is authorized to deny or restrict the use of any defined area for specification (including the withdrawal of specification) as a disposal site, whenever he determines, after notice and opportunity for public hearings, that the discharge of such materials into such area will have an unacceptable adverse effect on municipal water supplies, shellfish beds and fishery areas (including spawning and breeding areas), wildlife, or recreational areas. Before making such determination, the Administrator shall consult with the Secretary. The Administrator shall set forth in writing and make public his findings and his reasons for making any determination under this subsection.

(d) The term "Secretary" as used in this section means the Secretary of the Army, acting through the Chief of Engineers.

(e)(1) In carrying out his functions relating to the discharge of dredged or fill material under this section, the Secretary may, after notice and opportunity for public hearing, issue general permits on a State, regional, or nationwide basis for any category of activities involving discharges of dredged or fill material if the Secretary determines that the activities in such category are similar in nature, will cause only minimal adverse effect on the environment. Any general permit issued under this subsection shall (A) be based on the guidelines described in subsection (b)(1) of this section, and (B) set forth the requirements and standards which shall apply to any activity authorized by such general permit.

(2) No general permit issued under this subsection shall be for a period of more than five years after the date of its issuance and such general permit may be revoked or modified by the Secretary if, after opportunity for public hearing, the Secretary determines that the activities authorized by such general permit have and adverse impact on the environment or such activities are more appropriately authorized by individual permits.

(f)(1) Except as provided in paragraph (2) of this subsection, the discharge of dredge or fill material—

(A) from normal farming, silviculture, and ranching activities such as plowing, seeding, cultivating, minor drainage, harvesting for the production of food, fiber, and forest products, or upland soil and water conservation practices;

(B) for the purpose of maintenance, including emergency reconstruction of recently damaged parts, of currently serviceable structures such as dikes, dams, levees, groins, riprap, breakwaters, causeways, and bridge abutments or approaches, and transportation structure;

(C) for the purpose of construction or maintenance of farm or stock ponds or irrigation ditches, or the maintenance of drainage ditches;

(D) for the purpose of construction of temporary sedimentation basins on a construction site which does not include placement of fill material into the navigable waters;

(E) for the purpose of construction or maintenance of farm roads or forest roads, or temporary roads for moving mining equipment, where such roads are constructed and maintained, in accordance with best management practices, to assure that flow and circulation patterns and chemical and biological characteristics of the navigable waters are not impaired, that the reach of the navigable waters is not reduced, and that any adverse effect on the aquatic environment will be otherwise minimized;

(F) resulting form any activity with respect to which a State has an approved program under section 208(b)(4) which meets the requirements of subparagraphs (B) and (C) of such section, is not prohibited by or otherwise subject to regulation under this section or section 301(a) or 402 of this Act (except for effluent standards or prohibitions under section 307).

(2) Any discharge of dredged or fill material into the navigable waters incidental to any activity having as its purpose bringing an area of the navigable waters into a use to which it was not previously subject, where the flow or circulation of navigable waters may be impaired or the reach of such waters be reduced, shall be required to have a permit under this section.

(g)(1) The Governor of any State desiring to administer its own individual and general permit program for the discharge of dredged or fill material into the navigable waters (other than those waters which are presently used, or are susceptible to use in their natural condition or by reasonable improvement as a means to transport interstate or foreign commerce shoreward to their ordinary high water mark, including all waters which are subject to the ebb and flow of the tide shoreward to their mean high water mark, or mean higher high water mark on the west coast, including wetlands adjacent thereto), within its jurisdiction may submit to the Administrator a full and complete description of the program it proposes to establish and administer under State law or under an interstate compact. In addition, such State shall submit a statement from the attorney general (or the attorney for those State agencies which have independent legal counsel), or from the chief legal officer in the case of an interstate agency, that the laws of such State, or the interstate compact, as the case may be, provide adequate authority to carry out the described program.

(2) Not later than the tenth day after the date of the receipt of the program and statement submitted by any State under paragraph (1) of this subsection, the Administrator shall provide copies of such program and statement to the Secretary and the Secretary of the Interior, acting through the Director of the United States Fish and Wildlife Service.

(3) Not later than the ninetieth day after the date of the receipt by the Administrator of the program and statement submitted by any State, under paragraph (1) of this subsection, the Secretary and the Secretary of the Interior, acting through the Director of the United States Fish and Wildlife Service, shall submit any comments with respect to such program and statement to the Administrator in writing.

(h)(1) Not later than the one-hundred-twentieth day after the date of the receipt by the Administrator of a program and statement submitted by any State under paragraph (1) of this subsection, the Administrator shall determine, taking into account any comments submitted by the Secretary and the Secretary of the Interior, acting through the Director of the United States Fish and Wildlife Service, pursuant to subsection (g) of this section, whether such State has the following authority with respect to the issuance of permits pursuant to such program:

(A) To issue permits which—
    (i) apply and assure compliance with, any applicable requirements of this section, including, but not limited to, the guidelines established under section (b)(1) of this section, and sections 307 and 403 of this Act;
    (ii) are for fixed terms not exceeding five years; and
    (iii) can be terminated or modified for cause including, but not limited to, the following:
     (I) violation of any condition of the permit;
    (II) obtaining a permit by misrepresentation, or failure to disclose fully all relevant facts;
    (III) change in any condition that requires either a temporary or permanent reduction or elimination of the permitted discharge.

(B) To issue permits which apply, and assure compliance with, all applicable requirements of section 308 of this Act, or to inspect, monitor, enter, and require reports to at least the same extent as required in section 308 of this Act.

(C) To assure that the public, and any other State the waters of which may be affected, receive notice of each application for a permit and to provide an opportunity for public hearing before a ruling on each such application.

(D) To assure that the administrator receives notice of each application (including a copy thereof) for a permit.

(E) To assure that any State (other than the permitting State), whose waters may be affected by the issuance of a permit may submit written recommendation to the permitting State (and the Administrator) with respect to any permit application and, if any part of such written recommendations are not accepted by the permitting State, that the permitting State will notify such affected State (and the Administrator) in writing of its failure to so accept such recommendations together with its reasons for so doing.

(F) To assure than no permit will be issued if, in the judgment of the Secretary, after consultation with the Secretary of the department in which the Coast Guard is operation, anchorage and navigation of any of the navigable water would be substantially impaired thereby.

(G) To abate violations of the permit or the permit program, including civil and criminal penalties and other ways and means of enforcement.

(H) To assure continued coordination with Federal and Federal-State water-related planning and review processes.

(2) If, with respect to a State program submitted under subsection (g)(1) of this section, the Administrator shall approve the program and so notify (i) such State, and (ii) the Secretary, who upon subsequent notification form such State that it is administering such program, shall suspend the issuance of permits under subsections (a) and (e) of this section for activities with respect to which a permit may be issued pursuant to such State program; or

(B) does not have the authority set forth in paragraph (1) of this subsection, the Administrator shall so notify such State, which notification shall also describe the revisions or modifications necessary so that such State may resubmit such program for a determination by the Administrator under this subsection.

(3) If the Administrator fails to make a determination with respect to any program submitted by a State under subsection (g)(1) of this section within one-hundred-twenty days after the date of the receipt of such program, such program shall be deemed approved pursuant to paragraph (2)(A) of this subsection and the Administrator shall so notify such State and the Secretary who, upon subsequent notification form such State that it is administering such program, shall suspend the issuance of permits under subsections (a) and (e) of this section for activities with respect to which a permit may be issued by such State.

(4) After the Secretary receives notification from the Administrator under paragraph (2) or (3) of this subsection that a State permit program has been approved, the Secretary shall transfer any applications for

permits before the Secretary for activities with respect to which a permit may be issued pursuant to such State program to such State for appropriate action.

(5) Upon notification from a State with a permit program approved under this subsection that such State intends to administer and enforce the terms and conditions of a general permit issued by the Secretary under subsection (e) of this section with respect to activities in such State to which such general permit applies, the Secretary shall suspend the administration and enforcement of such general permit with respect to such activities.

(i) Whenever the Administrator determines after public hearing that a State is not administering a program approved under section (h)(2)(A) of this section, in accordance with this section, including, but not limited to, the guidelines established under subsection (b)(1) of this section, the Administrator shall so notify the State, and, if appropriate corrective action is not taken within a reasonable time, not to exceed ninety days after the date of the receipt of such notification, the Administrator shall (1) withdraw approval of such program until the Administrator determines such corrective action has been taken, and (2) notify the Secretary that the Secretary shall resume the program for the issuance of permits under subsections (a) and (e) of this section for activities with respect to which the State was issuing permits and that such authority of the Secretary shall continue in effect until such time as the Administrator makes the determination described in clause (1) of this subsection and such State again has an approved program.

(j) Each State which is administering a permit program pursuant to this section shall transmit to the Administrator (1) a copy of each permit application received by such State and provide notice to the Administrator of every action related to the consideration of such permit application, including each permit proposed to be issued by such State, and (2) a copy of each proposed general permit which such State intends to issue. No later than the tenth day after the date of the receipt of such permit application or such proposed general permit, the Administrator shall provide copies of such permit application or such proposed general permit to the Secretary and the Secretary of the Interior, acting through the Director of the United States Fish and Wildlife Service. If the Administrator intends to provide written comments to such State with respect to such permit application or such proposed general permit, he shall so notify such State not later than the thirtieth day after the date of the receipt of such application or such proposed general permit and provide such written comments to such State, after consideration of any comments made in writing with respect to such application or such proposed general permit by the Secretary and the Secretary of the Interior, acting through the Director of the United States Fish and Wildlife Service, not later than the ninetieth day after the date of such receipt. If such State is so notified by the Administrator, it shall not issue the proposed permit until after the receipt of such comments from the

Administrator, or after such ninetieth day, whichever first occurs. Such State shall not issue such proposed permit after such ninetieth day if it has received such written comments in which the Administrator objects (A) to the issuance of such proposed permit and such proposed permit is one that has been submitted to the Administrator pursuant to subsection (h)(1)(E), or (B) to the issuances of such proposed permit as being outside the requirements of this section, including, but not limited to, the guidelines developed under subsection (b)(1) of this section unless it modifies such proposed permit in accordance with such comments. Whenever the Administrator objects to the issuance of a permit under the preceding sentence such written objection shall contain a statement of the reasons for such objection and the conditions which such permit would include if it were issued by the Administrator. In any case where the Administrator objects to the issuance of a permit, on request of the State, a public hearing shall be held by the Administrator on such objection. If the State does not resubmit such permit revised to meet such objection within 30 days after completion of the hearing or, if no hearing is requested within 90 days after the date of such objection, the Secretary may issue the permit pursuant to subsection (a) or (e) of this section, as the case may be, for such source in accordance with the guidelines and requirements of this Act.

(k) In accordance with guidelines promulgated pursuant to subsection (h)(2) of section 304 of this Act, the Administrator is authorized to waive the requirements of subsection (j) of this section at the time of the approval of a program pursuant to subsection (h)(2)(A) of this section for any category (including any class, type, or size within such category) of discharge within the State submitting such program.

(l) The Administrator shall promulgate regulations establishing categories of discharges which he determines shall not be subject to the requirements of subsection (j) of this section in any State with a program approved pursuant to subsection (h)(2)(A) of this section. The Administrator may distinguish among classes, types, and sizes within any category of discharges.

(m) Not later than the ninetieth day after the date on which the Secretary notifies the Secretary of the Interior, acting through the Director of the United States Fish and Wildlife Service that (1) an application for a permit under subsection (a) of this section has been received by the Secretary, or (2) the Secretary proposes to issue a general permit under subsection (e) of this section, the Secretary of the Interior, acting through the Director of the United States Fish and Wildlife Service, shall submit any comments with respect to such application or such proposed general permit in writing to the Secretary.

(n) Nothing in this section shall be construed to limit the authority of the Administrator to take action pursuant to section 309 of this Act.

(o) A copy of each permit application and each permit issued under this section shall be available to the public. Such permit application or portion thereof, shall further be available on request for the purpose of reproduction.

(p) Compliance with a permit issued pursuant to this section, including any activity carried out pursuant to a general permit issued under this section, shall be deemed compliance, for purposes of sections 309 and 505, with sections 301, 307, and 403.

(q) Not later than the one-hundred-eightieth day after the date of enactment of this subsection, the Secretary shall enter into agreements with the Administrator, the Secretaries of the Departments of Agriculture, Commerce, Interior, and Transportation, and the heads of other appropriate Federal agencies to minimize, to the maximum extent practicable, duplication, needless paperwork, and delays in the issuance of permits under this section. Such agreements shall be developed to assure that, to the maximum extent practicable, a decision with respect to an application for a permit under subsection (a) of this section will be made not later than the ninetieth day after the date the notice of such application is published under subsection (a) of this section.

(r) The discharge of dredged or fill material as part of the construction of a Federal project specifically authorized by Congress, whether prior to or on or after the date of enactment of this subsection, is not prohibited by or otherwise subject to regulation under this section, or a State program approved under this section, or section 301(a) or 402 of the Act (except for effluent standards or prohibitions under section 307), if information on the effects of such discharge, including consideration of the guidelines developed under subsection (b)(1) of this section, is included in an environmental impact statement for such project pursuant to the National Environmental Policy Act of 1969 and such environmental impact statement has been submitted to Congress before the actual discharge of dredged or fill material in connection with the construction of such project and prior to either authorization of such project or an appropriation of funds for each construction.

(s)(1) Whenever on the basis of any information available to him the Secretary finds that any person is in violation of any condition or limitation set forth in a permit issued by the Secretary under this section, the Secretary shall issue an order requiring such persons to comply with such condition or limitation, or the Secretary shall bring a civil action in accordance with paragraph (3) of this subsection.

(2) A copy of any order issued under this subsection shall be sent immediately by the Secretary to the State in which the violation occurs and other affected States. Any order issued under this subsection shall be by personal service and shall state with reasonable specificity the nature of the violation, specify a time for compliance, not to exceed thirty days, which the Secretary determines is reasonable, taking into account the seriousness of the violation and any good faith efforts to comply with applicable requirements. In any case in which an order under this subsection is issued to a corporation, a copy of such order

shall be served on any appropriate corporate officers.

(3) The Secretary is authorized to commence a civil action for appropriate relief, including a permanent or temporary injunction for any violation for which he is authorized to issue a compliance order under paragraph (1) of this subsection. Any action under this paragraph may be brought in the district court of the United States for the district in which the defendant is located or resides or is doing business, and such court shall have jurisdiction to restrain such violation and to require compliance. Notice of the commencement of such action shall be given immediately to the appropriate State.

(4) Any person who violates any condition or limitation in a permit issued by the Secretary under this section, and any person who violates any order issued by the Secretary under paragraph (1) of this subsection, shall be subject to a civil penalty not to exceed $25,000 per day for each violation. In determining the amount of a civil penalty the court shall consider the seriousness of the violation or violations, the economic benefit (if any) resulting from the violation, any history of such violations, any good-faith efforts to comply with the applicable requirements, the economic impact of the penalty on the violator, and such other matters as justice may require.

(t) Nothing in this section shall preclude or deny the right of any State or interstate agency to control the discharge of dredged or fill material in any portion of the navigable waters within the jurisdiction of such State, including any activity of any Federal agency, and each such agency shall comply with such State or interstate requirements both substantive and procedural to control the discharge of dredged or fill material to the same extent that any person is subject to such requirements. This section shall not be construed as affecting or impairing the authority of the Secretary to maintain navigation.

§ 1345. Disposal or use of sewage sludge

[Sec. 405] (a) Notwithstanding any other provision of this Act or of any other law, in the case where the disposal of sewage sludge resulting from the operation of a treatment works as defined in section 212 of this Act (including the removal of in-place sewage sludge from one location and its deposit at another location) would result in any pollutant from such sewage sludge entering the navigable waters, such disposal is prohibited except in accordance with a permit issued by the Administrator under section 402 of this Act.

(b) The Administrator shall issue regulations governing the issuance of permits for the disposal of sewage sludge subject to subsection (a) of this section and section 402 of this Act. Such regulations shall require the application to such disposal of each criterion, factor, procedure, and requirement applicable to a permit issued under section 402 of this title.

(c) Each State desiring to administer its own permit program for disposal of sewage sludge subject to subsection (a) of this section within its jurisdiction may do so in accordance with section 402 of this Act.

(d)(1) The Administrator, after consultation with appropriate Federal and State agencies and other interested persons, shall develop and publish, within one year after the date of enactment of this subsection and from time to time thereafter, regulations providing guidelines for the disposal of sludge and the utilization of sludge for various purposes. Such regulations shall—

(A) identify uses of sludge, including disposal;

(B) specify factors to be taken into account in determining the measures and practices applicable to each such use or disposal (including publication of information on costs);

(C) identify concentrations of pollutants which interfere with each such use or disposal.

The Administrator is authorized to revise any regulation issued under this subsection.

(2)(A)(i) Not later than November 30, 1986, the Administrator shall identify those toxic pollutants which, on the basis of available information on their toxicity, persistence, concentration, mobility, or potential for exposure, may be present in sewage sludge in concentrations which may adversely affect public health or the environment, and propose regulations specifying acceptable management practices for sewage sludge containing each such toxic pollutant and establishing numerical limitations for each such pollutant for each use identified under paragraph (1)(A).

(ii) Not later than August 31, 1987, and after opportunity for public hearing, the Administrator shall promulgate the regulations required by subparagraph (A)(i).

(B)(i) Not later than July 31, 1987, the Administrator shall identify those toxic pollutants not identified under subparagraph (A)(i) which may be present in sewage sludge in concentrations which may adversely affect public health or the environment, and propose regulations specifying acceptable management practices for sewage sludge containing each such toxic pollutant and establishing numerical limitations for each pollutant for each such use identified under paragraph (1)(A).

(ii) Not later than June 15, 1988, the Administrator shall promulgate the regulations required by subparagraph (B)(i).

(C) From time to time, but not less often than every 2 years, the Administrator shall review the regulations promulgated under this paragraph for the purpose of identifying additional toxic pollutants and promulgating regulations for such pollutants consistent with the requirements of this paragraph.

(D) The management practices and numerical criteria established under subparagraphs (A), (B), and (C) shall be adequate to protect public health and the environment from any reasonably anticipated adverse effects of each pollutant. Such regulations shall require compliance as expeditiously as practicable but in no case later than 12 months after their publication, unless such regulations require the construction of new pollution control facilities, in which case the regulations shall require compliance as expeditiously as practicable but in no case later than two years from the date of their publication.

(3) For purposes of this subsection, if, in the judgment of the Administrator, it is not feasible to prescribe or enforce a numerical limitation for a pollutant identified under paragraph (2), the Administrator may instead promulgate a design, equipment, management practice, or operational standard, or combination thereof, which in the Administrator's judgment is adequate to protect public health and the environment from any reasonably anticipated adverse effects of such pollutant. In the event the Administrator promulgates a design or equipment standard under this subsection, the Administrator shall include as part of such standard such requirements as will assure the proper operation and maintenance of any such element of design or equipment.

(4) Prior to the promulgation of the regulations required by paragraph (2), the Administrator shall impose conditions in permits issued to publicly owned treatment works under section 402 of this Act or take such other measures as the Administrator deems appropriate to protect public health and the environment from any adverse effects which may occur from toxic pollutants in sewage sludge.

(5) Nothing in this section is intended to waive more stringent requirements established by this Act or any other law.

(e) The determination of the manner of disposal or use of sludge is a local determination, except that it shall be unlawful for any person to dispose of sludge from a publicly owned treatment works or any other treatment works treating domestic sewage for any use for which regulations have been established pursuant to subsection (d) of this section, except in accordance with such regulations.

(f)(1) Any permit issued under section 402 of this Act to a publicly owned treatment works or any other treatment works treating domestic sewage shall include requirements for the use and disposal of sludge that implement the regulations established pursuant to subsection (d) of this section, unless such requirements have been included in a permit issued under the appropriate provisions of subtitle C of the Solid Waste Disposal Act, part C of the Safe Drinking Water Act, the Marine Protection, Research, and Sanctuaries Act of 1972, or the Clean Air Act, or under State permit programs approved by the Administrator, where the Administrator determines that such programs assure compliance with any applicable requirements of this section. Not later than December 15, 1986, the Administrator shall promulgate procedures for approval of State programs pursuant to this paragraph.

(2) In the case of a treatment works described in paragraph (1) that is not subject to section 402 of this Act and to which none of the other above listed permit programs nor approved State permit authority apply, the Administrator may issue a permit to such treatment works solely to impose requirements for the use and disposal of sludge that implement the regulations established pursuant to subsection (d) of this section. The Administrator shall include in the permit appropriate requirements to assure compliance with the regulations established pursuant to subsection (d) of this section. The Administrator shall establish procedures for issuing permits pursuant to this paragraph.

(g)(1) The Administrator is authorized to conduct or initiate scientific studies, demonstration projects, and public information and education projects which are designed to promote the safe and beneficial management or use of sewage sludge for such purposes as aiding the restoration of abandoned mine sites, conditioning soil for parks and recreation areas, agricultural and horticultural uses, and other beneficial purposes. For the purposes of carrying out this subsection, the Administrator may make grants to State water pollution control agencies, other public or nonprofit agencies, institutions, organizations, and individuals. In cooperation with other Federal departments and agencies, other public and private agencies, institutions, and organizations, the Administrator is authorized to collect and disseminate information pertaining to the safe and beneficial use of sewage sludge.

(2) For the purposes of carrying out the scientific studies, demonstration projects, and public information and education projects authorized in this section, there is authorized to be appropriated for fiscal years beginning after September 30, 1986, not to exceed $5,000,000.

Subchapter V. General Provisions

§ 1361. Administration

[Sec. 501] (a) The Administrator is authorized to prescribe such regulations as are necessary to carry out his functions under this Act.

(b) The Administrator, with the consent of the head of any other agency of the United States, may utilize such officers and employees of such agency as may be found necessary to assist in carrying out the purposes of this Act.

(c) Each recipient of financial assistance under this Act shall keep such records as the Administrator shall prescribe, including records which fully disclose the amount and disposition by such recipient of the proceeds of such assistance, the total cost of the project or undertaking in connection with which such assistance is given or used, and the amount of that portion of the cost of the project or undertaking supplied by other sources, and such other records as will facilitate an effective audit.

(d) The Administrator and the Comptroller General of the United States, or any of their duly authorized representatives, shall have access, for the purpose of audit and examination, to any books, documents, papers, and records of the recipients that are pertinent to the grants received under this Act. For the purpose of carrying out audits and examinations with respect to recipients of Federal assistance under this Act, the Administrator is authorized to enter into noncompetitive procurement contracts with independent State audit organizations, consistent with chapter 75 of title 31, United States Code. Such contracts may only be entered into to the extent and in such amounts as may be provided in advance in appropriation Acts

(e)(1) It is the purpose of this subsection to authorize a program which will provide official recognition by the United States Government to those industrial organizations and political subdivisions of States which during the preceding year demonstrated an outstanding technological achievement or an innovative process, method, or device in their waste treatment and pollution abatement programs. The Administrator shall, in consultation with the appropriate State water pollution control agencies, establish regulations under which such recognition may be applied for and granted, except that no applicant shall be eligible for an award under this subsection if such applicant is not in total compliance with all applicable water quality requirements under this Act, or otherwise does not have a satisfactory record with respect to environmental quality.

(2) The Administrator shall award a certificate or plaque of suitable design to each industrial organization or political subdivision which qualifies for such recognition under regulations established under this subsection.

(3) The President of the United States, the Governor of the appropriate State, the Speaker of the House of Representatives, and the President pro tempore of the Senate shall be notified of the award by the Administrator and the awarding of such recognition shall be published in the Federal Register.

(f) Upon the request of a State water pollution control agency, personnel of the Environmental Protection Agency may be detailed to such agency for the purpose of carrying out the provisions of this Act.

§ 1362. Definitions

[Sec. 502] Except as otherwise specifically provided, when used in this Act:

(1) The term "State water pollution control agency" means the State agency designated by the Governor having responsibility for enforcing State laws relating to the abatement of pollution.

(2) The term "interstate agency" means an agency of two or more States established by or pursuant to an agreement of compact approved by

the Congress, or any other agency of two or more States, having substantial powers or duties pertaining to the control of pollution as determined and approved by the Administrator.

(3) The term "State" means a State, the District of Columbia, the Commonwealth of Puerto Rico, the Virgin Islands, Guam, American Samoa, the Commonwealth of the Northern Mariana Islands, and the Trust Territory of the Pacific Islands.

(4) The term "municipality" means a city, town, borough, county, parish, district, association, or other public body created by or pursuant to State law and having jurisdiction over disposal of sewage, industrial wastes, or other wastes, or an Indian tribe or an authorized Indian tribal organization, or a designated and approved management agency under section 208 of this Act.

(5) The term "person" means an individual, corporation, partnership, association, State, municipality, commission, or political subdivision of a State, or any interstate body.

(6) The term "pollutant" means dredged spoil, solid waste, incinerator residue, sewage, garbage, sewage sludge, munitions, chemical wastes, biological materials, radioactive materials, heat, wrecked or discarded equipment, rock, sand, cellar dirt and industrial, municipal, and agricultural waste discharged into water. This term does not mean (A) "sewage from vessels" within the meaning of section 312 of this Act; or (B) water, gas, or other material which is injected into a well to facilitate production of oil or gas, or water derived in association with oil or gas production and disposed of in a well, if the well used either to facilitate production or for disposal purposes is approved by authority of the State in which the well is located, and if such State determines that such injection or disposal will not result in the degradation of ground or surface water resources.

(7) The term "navigable waters" means the waters of the United States, including the territorial seas.

(8) The term "territorial seas" means the belt of the seas measured from the line of ordinary low water along that portion of the coast which is in direct contract with the open sea and the line marking the seaward limit of inland waters, and extending seaward a distance of three miles.

(9) The term "contiguous zone" means the entire zone established or to be established by the United States under article 24 of the Convention of the Territorial Sea and the Contiguous Zone.

(10) The term "ocean" means any portion of the high seas beyond the contiguous zone.

(11) The term "effluent limitation" means any restriction established by a State or the Administrator on quantities, rates, and concentrations of chemical, physical, biological, and other constituents which are discharged from point sources into navigable waters, the waters of the

contiguous zone, or the ocean, including schedules of compliance.

(12) The term "discharge of a pollutant" and the term "discharge of pollutants" each means (A) any addition of any pollutant to navigable waters from any point source, (B) any addition of any pollutant to the waters of the contiguous zone or the ocean from any point source other than a vessel or other floating craft.

(13) The term "toxic pollutant" means those pollutants, or combinations of pollutants, including disease-causing agents, which after discharge and upon exposure, ingestion, inhalation or assimilation into any organism, either directly from the environment or indirectly by ingestion through food chains, will, on the basis of information available to the Administrator, cause death, disease, behavioral abnormalities, cancer, genetic mutations, physiological malfunctions (including malfunctions in reproduction) or physical deformations, in such organisms or their offspring.

(14) The term "point source" means any discernible, confined and discrete conveyance, including but not limited to any pipe, ditch, channel, tunnel, conduit, well, discrete fissure, container, rolling stock, concentrated animal feeding operation, or vessel or other floating craft, from which pollutants are or may be discharged. This term does not include agricultural stormwater discharges and return flows from irrigated agriculture.

(15) The term "biological monitoring" shall mean the determination of the effects on aquatic life, including accumulation of pollutants in tissue, in receiving waters due to the discharge of pollutants (A) by techniques and procedures, including sampling of organisms representative of appropriate levels of the food chain appropriate to the volume and the physical, chemical, and biological characteristics of the effluent, and (B) at appropriate frequencies and locations.

(16) The term "discharge" when used without qualification includes a discharge of a pollutant, and a discharge of pollutants.

(17) The term "schedule of compliance" means a schedule of remedial measures including an enforceable sequence of actions or operations leading to compliance with an effluent limitation, other limitation, prohibition, or standard.

(18) The term "industrial user" means those industries identified in the Standard Industrial Classification Manual, Bureau of the Budget, 1967, as amended and supplemented, under the category "Division D—Manufacturing" and such other classes of significant waste products as, by regulation, the Administrator deems appropriate.

(19) The term "pollution" means the man-made or man-induced alteration of the chemical, physical, biological and radiological integrity of water.

§ 1363. Water Pollution Control Advisory Board

[Sec. 503] (a)(1) There is hereby established in the Environmental

Protection Agency a Water Pollution Control Advisory Board, composed of the Administrator or his designee, who shall be Chairman, and nine members appointed by the President, none of whom shall be Federal officers or employees. The appointed members, having due regard for the purposes of this Act, shall be selected from among representatives of various State, interstate, and local governmental agencies, of public or private interests contributing to, affected by, or concerned with pollution, and of other public and private agencies, organizations, or groups demonstrating an active interest in the field of pollution prevention and control, as well as other individuals who are expert in this field.

    (2)(A) Each member appointed by the President shall hold office for a term of three years, except that (i) any member appointed to fill a vacancy occurring prior to the expiration of the term for which his predecessor was appointed shall be appointed for the remainder of such term, and (ii) the terms of office of the members first taking office after June 30, 1956, shall expire as follows: three at the end of one year after such date, three at the end of two years after such date, and three at the end of three years after such date, as designated by the President at the time of appointment, and (iii) the term of any member under the preceding provisions shall be extended until the date on which his successor's appointment is effective. None of the members appointed by the President shall be eligible for reappointment within one year after the end of his preceding term.

    (B) The members of the Board who are not officers or employees of the Untied States, while attending conferences or meetings of the Board or while otherwise serving at the request of the Administrator, shall be entitled to receive compensation at a rate to be fixed by the Administrator, but not exceeding $100 per diem, including travel-time, and while away from their homes or regular places of business they may be allowed travel expenses, including per diem in lieu of subsistence, as authorized by law (5 U.S.C. 73b–2) for persons in the Government service employed intermittently.

  (b) The Board shall advise, consult with, and make recommendations to the Administrator on matters of policy relating to the activities and functions of the Administrator under this Act.

  (c) Such clerical and technical assistance as may be necessary to discharge the duties of the Board shall be provided from the personnel of the Environmental Protection Agency.

§ 1364. Emergency powers

[Sec. 504] (a) Notwithstanding any other provision of this Act, the Administrator upon receipt of evidence that a pollution source or combination of sources is presenting an imminent and substantial endangerment to the health of persons or to the welfare of persons where such endangerment is to the livelihood of such persons, such as inability to market shellfish, may bring suit on behalf of the United States in the appropriate district court to immediately restrain any person causing or contributing to the alleged pollution to stop the discharge of pollutants causing or contributing to such pollution or to take such other action as may be necessary.

§ 1365. Citizens' suits

[Sec. 505] (a) Except as provided in subsection (b) of this section and section 309(g)(6), any citizen may commence a civil action on his own behalf—

   (1) against any person (including (i) the United States, and (ii) any other governmental instrumentality or agency to the extent permitted by the eleventh amendment to the Constitution) who is alleged to be in violation of (A) an effluent standard of limitation under this Act or (B) an order issued by the Administrator or a State with respect to such a standard or limitation, or

   (2) against the Administrator where there is alleged a failure of the Administrator to perform any act or duty under this Act which is not discretionary with the Administrator.

The district courts shall have jurisdiction, without regard to the amount in controversy or the citizenship of the parties, to enforce such an effluent standard or limitation, or such an order, or to order the Administrator to perform such act or duty, as the case may be, and to apply any appropriate civil penalties under section 309(d) of this Act.

   (b) No action may be commenced—

   (1) under subsection (a)(1) of this section—

      (A) prior to sixty days after the plaintiff has given notice of the alleged violation (i) to the Administrator, (ii) to the State in which the alleged violation occurs, and (iii) to any alleged violator of the standard, limitation, or order, or

      (B) if the Administrator or State has commenced and is diligently prosecuting a civil or criminal action in a court of the United States, or a State to require compliance with the standard, limitation, or order, but in any such action in a court of the United States any citizen may intervene as a matter of right.

   (2) under subsection (a)(2) of this section prior to sixty days after the plaintiff has given notice of such action to the Administrator.

except that such action may be brought immediately after such notification in the case of an action under this section respecting a violation of sections 306 and 307(a) of this Act. Notice under this subsection shall be given in such manner as the Administrator shall prescribe by regulation.

   (c)(1) Any action respecting a violation by a discharge source of an effluent standard or limitation or an order respecting such standard or limitation may be brought under this section only in the judicial district in which such source is located.

(2) In such action under this section, the Administrator, if not a party, may intervene as a matter of right.

(3) Whenever any action is brought under this section in a court of the United States, the plaintiff shall serve a copy of the complaint on the Attorney General and the Administrator. No consent judgment shall be entered in an action in which the United States is not a party prior to 45 days following the receipt of a copy of the proposed consent judgment by the Attorney General and the Administrator.

(d) The court, in issuing any final order in any action brought pursuant to this section, may award costs of litigation (including reasonable attorney and expert witness fees) to any prevailing or substantially prevailing party, whenever the court determines such award is appropriate. The court may, if a temporary restraining order or preliminary injunction is sought, require the filing of a bond or equivalent security in accordance with the Federal Rules of Civil Procedure.

(e) Nothing in this section shall restrict any right which any person (or class of persons) may have under any statute or common law to seek enforcement of any effluent standard or limitation or to seek any other relief (including relief against the Administrator or a State agency).

(f) For purposes of this section, the term "effluent standard or limitation under this Act" means (1) effective July 1, 1973, an unlawful act under subsection (a) of section 301 of this Act; (2) an effluent limitation or other limitation under section 301 or 302 of this Act; (3) standard of performance under section 306 of this Act; (4) prohibition, effluent standard or pretreatment standards under section 307 of this Act; (5) certification under section 401 of this Act; (6) a permit or condition thereof issued under section 402 of this Act, which is in effect under this Act (including a requirement applicable by reason of section 313 of this Act); or (7) a regulation under section 405(d) of this Act.

(g) For the purpose of this section the term "citizen" means a person or persons having an interest which is or may be adversely affected.

(h) A Governor of a State may commence a civil action under subsection (a), without regard to the limitations of subsection (b) of this section, against the Administrator where there is alleged a failure of the Administrator to enforce an effluent standard or limitation under this Act the violation of which is occurring in another State and is causing an adverse effect on the public health or welfare in his State, or is causing a violation of any water quality requirement in his State.

§ 1366. Appearance

[Sec. 506] The Administrator shall request the Attorney General to appear and represent the United States in any civil or criminal action instituted under this Act to which the Administrator is a party. Unless the Attorney General notifies the Administrator within a reasonable time, that he will appear in a civil action, attorneys who are officers or employees of the Environmental Protection Agency shall appear and represent the United States in such action.

§ 1367. Employee protection

[Sec. 507] (a) No person shall fire, or in any other way discriminate against, or cause to be fired or discriminated against, any employee or any authorized reprsentative of employees by reason of the fact that such employee or representative has filed, instituted, or caused to be filed or instituted any proceeding under this Act, or has testified or is about to testify in any proceeding resulting from the administration or enforcement of the provisions of this Act.

(b) Any employee or a representative of employees who believe that he has been fired or otherwise discriminated against by any person in violation of subsection (a) of this section may, within thirty days after such alleged violation occurs, apply to the Secretary of Labor for a review of such firing or alleged discrimination. A copy of the application shall be sent to such person who shall be the respondent. Upon receipt of such application, the Secretary of Labor shall cause such investigation to be made as he deems appropriate. Such investigation shall provide an opportunity for a public hearing at the request of any party to such review to enable the parties to present information relating to such alleged violation. The parties shall be given written notice of the time and place of the hearing at least five days prior to the hearing. Any such hearing shall be of record and shall be subject to section 554 of title 5 of the United States Code. Upon receiving the report of such investigation, the Secretary of Labor shall make findings of fact. If he finds that such violation did occur, he shall issue a decision, incorporating an order therein and his findings, requiring the party committing such violation to take such affirmative action to abate the violation as the Secretary of Labor deems appropriate, including, but not limited to, the rehiring or reinstatement of the employee or represenative of employees to his former position with compensation. If he finds that there was no such violation, he shall issue an order denying the application. Such order issued by the Secretary of Labor under this subparagraph shall be subject to judicial review in the same manner as orders and decisions of the Administrator are subject to judicial review under this Act.

(c) Whenever an order is issued under this section to abate such violation, at the request of the applicant, a sum equal to the aggregate amount of all costs and expenses (including the attorney's fees), as determined by the Secretary of Labor, to have been reasonably incurred by the applicant for, or in connection with, the institution and prosecution of such proceedings, shall be assessed against the person committing such violation.

(d) This section shall have no application to any employee who, acting without direction from his employer (or his agent) deliberately violates any prohibition of effluent limitation or other limitation under section 301 or 302 of this Act, standards of performance under section 306 of this Act, effluent standard, prohibition or pretreatment standard under section 307 of this Act, or any other prohibition or limitation established under this Act.

(e) The Administrator shall conduct continuing evaluations of potential loss or shifts of employment which may result from the issuance of any effluent limitation or order under this Act, including, where appropriate, investigating threatened plant closures or reductions in employment allegedly resulting from such limitation or order. Any employee who is discharged or laid off, threatened with discharge or lay-off, or otherwise discriminated against by any person because of the alleged results of any effluent limitation or order issued under this Act, or any representative of such employee, may request the Administrator to conduct a full investigation of the matter. The Administrator shall thereupon investigate the matter and, at the request of any party, shall hold public hearings on not less than five days notice, and shall at such hearing require the parties, including the employer involved, to present information relating to the actual or potential effect of such limitation or order on employment and on any alleged discharge, layoff, or other discrimination and the detailed reasons or justification therefor. Any such hearing shall be of record and shall be subject to section 554 of title 5 of the United States Code. Upon receiving the report of such investigation, the Administrator shall make findings of fact as to the effect of such effluent limitation or order on employment and on the alleged discharge, lay-off, or discrimination and shall make such recommendations as he deems appropriate. Such report, findings, and recommendations shall be available to the public. Nothing in this subsection shall be construed to require or authorize the Administrator to modify or withdraw any effluent limitation or order issued under this Act.

§ 1368.   Federal procurement

[Sec. 508] (a) No Federal agency may enter into any contract with any person, who has been convicted of any offense under section 309(c) of this Act, for the procurement of goods, materials, and services if such contract is to be performed at any facility at which the violation which gave rise to such conviction occurred, and if such facility is owned, leased, or supervised by such person. The prohibition in the preceding sentence shall continue until the Administrator certifies that the condition giving rise to such conviction has been corrected.

(b) The Administrator shall establish procedures to provide all Federal agencies with the notification necessary for the purposes of subsection (a) of this section.

(c) In order to implement the purposes and policy of this Act to protect and enhance the quality of the Nation's water, the President shall, not more than one hundred and eighty days after enactment of this Act, cause to be issued an order (1) requiring each Federal agency authorized to enter into contracts and each Federal agency which is empowered to extend Federal assistance by way of grant, loan, or contract to effectuate the purpose and policy of this Act in such contracting or assistance activities, and (2) setting forth procedures, sanctions, penalties, and such other provisions, as the President determines necessary to carry out such requirement.

(d) The President may exempt any contract, loan, or grant from all or part of the provisions of this section where he determines such exemption is necessary in the paramount interest of the United States and he shall notify the Congress of such exemption.

(e) The President shall annually report to the Congress on measures taken in compliance with the purpose and intent of this section, including, but not limited to, the progress and problems associated with such compliance.

§ 1369. Administrative procedure and judicial review

[Sec. 509] (a)(1) For the purposes of obtaining information under section 305 of this Act, or carrying out section 507(e) of this Act, the Administrator may issue subpenas for the attendance and testimony of witnesses and the production of relevant papers, books, and documents, and he may administer oaths. Except for effluent data, upon a showing satisfactory to the Administrator that such papers, books, documents, or information or particular part thereof, if made public, would divulge trade secrets or secret processes, the Administrator shall consider such record, report, or information or particular portion thereof confidential in accordance with the purposes of section 1905 of title 18 of the United States Code, except that such paper, book, document, or information may be disclosed to other officers, employees, or authorized representatives of the United States concerned with carrying out this Act, or when relevant in any proceeding under this Act. Witnesses summoned shall be paid the same fees and mileage that are paid witnesses in the courts of the United States. In case of contumacy or refusal to obey a subpena served upon any person under this subsection, the district court of the United States for any district in which such person is found or resides or transacts business, upon application by the United States and after notice to such person, shall have jurisdiction to issue an order requiring such person to appear and give testimony before the Administrator, to appear and produce papers, books, and documents before the Administrator, or both, and any failure to obey such order of the court may be punished by such court as a contempt thereof.

(2) The district courts of the United States are authorized, upon application by the Administrator, to issue subpenas for attendance and testimony of witnesses and the production of relevant papers, books, and documents, for purposes of obtaining information under sections 304(b) and (c) of this Act. Any papers, books, documents, or other information or part thereof, obtained by reason of such a subpena

shall be subject to the same requirements as are provided in paragraph (1) of this subsection.

(b)(1) Review of the Administrator's action (A) in promulgating any standard of performance under section 306, (B) in making any determination pursuant to section 306(b)(1)(C), (C) in promulgating any effluent standard, prohibition, or pretreatment standard under section 307, (D) in making any determination as to a State permit program submitted under section 402(b), (E) in approving or promulgating any effluent limitation or other limitation under sections 301, 302, 306, or 405, (F) in issuing or denying any permit under section 402, and (G) in promulgating any individual control strategy under section 304(l), may be had by any interested person in the Circuit Court of Appeals of the United States for the Federal judicial district in which such person resides or transacts business which is directly affected by such action upon application by such person. Any such application shall be made within 120 days from the date of such determination, approval, promulgation, issuance or denial, or after such date only if such application is based solely on grounds which arose after such 120th day.

(2) Action of the Administrator with respect to which review could have been obtained under paragraph (1) of this subsection shall not be subject to judicial review in any civil or criminal proceeding for enforcement.

(3)(A) If applications for review of the same agency action have been filed under paragraph (1) of this subsection in 2 or more Circuit Courts of Appeals of the United States and the Administrator has received written notice of the filing of one or more applications within 30 days or less after receiving written notice of the filing of the first application, then the Administrator shall promptly advise in writing the Administrative Office of the United States Courts that applications have been filed in 2 or more Circuit Courts of Appeals of the United States, and shall identify each court for which he has written notice that such applications have been filed within 30 days or less of receiving written notice of the filing of the first such application. Pursuant to a system of random selection devised for this purpose, the Administrative Office thereupon shall, within 3 business days of receiving such written notice from the Administrator, select the court in which the record shall be filed from among those identified by the Administrator. Upon notification of such selection, the Administrator shall promptly file the record in such court. For the purpose of review of agency action which has previously been remanded to the Administrator, the record shall be filed in the Circuit Court of Appeals of the United States which remanded such action.

(B) Where applications have been filed under paragraph (1) of this subsection in two or more Circuit Courts of Appeals of the United States with respect to the same agency action and the record has been filed in one of such courts pursuant to subparagraph (A), the other courts in which such applications have been filed shall promptly transfer such applications to the Circuit Court of Appeals of the United States in which the record has been filed. Pending selection of a court pursuant to subparagraph (A), any court in which an application has been filed under paragraph (1) of this subsection may postpone the effective date of the agency action until 15 days after the Administrative Office has selected the court in which the record shall be filed.

(C) Any court in which an application with respect to any agency action has been filed under paragraph (1) of this subsection, including any court selected pursuant to subparagraph (A), may transfer such application to any other Circuit Court of Appeals of the United States for the convenience of the parties or otherwise in the interest of justice.

(4) In any judicial proceeding under this subsection, the court may award costs of litigation (including reasonable attorney and expert witness fees) to any prevailing or substantially prevailing party whenever it determines that such award is appropriate.

(c) In any judicial proceeding brought under subsection (b) of this section in which review is sought of a determination under this Act required to be made on the record after notice and opportunity for hearing, if any party applies to the court for leave to adduce additional evidence, and shows to the satisfaction of the court that such additional evidence is material and that there were reasonable grounds for the failure to adduce such evidence in the proceeding before the Administrator, the court may order such additional evidence (and evidence in rebuttal thereof) to be taken before the Administrator in such manner and upon such terms and conditions as the court may deem proper. The Administrator may modify his findings as to the facts, or make new findings, by reason of the additional evidence so taken and he shall file such modified or new findings, and his recommendation, if any, for the modification or setting aside of his original determination, with the return of such additional evidence.

§ 1370. State authority

[Sec. 510] Except as expressly provided in this Act, nothing in this Act shall (1) preclude or deny the right of any State or political subdivision thereof or interstate agency to adopt or enforce (A) any standard or limitation respecting discharges of pollutants, or (B) any requirement respecting control or abatement of pollution; except that if an effluent limitation, or other limitation, effluent standard, prohibition, pretreatment standard, or standard of performance is in effect under this Act, such State or political subdivision or interstate agency may not adopt or enforce any effluent limitation, or other limitation, effluent standard, prohibition, pretreatment standard, or standard of performance which is less stringent than the effluent limitation, or other limitation, effluent standard, prohibition, pretreatment standard, or standard of performance under this Act; or (2) be construed as impairing or in any manner affecting any right or jurisdiction of the States with respect to the waters (including boundary waters) of such States.

§ 1371. Authority under other laws and regulations

[Sec. 511] (a) This Act shall not be construed as (1) limiting the authority or functions of any officer or agency of the United States under any other law or regulation not inconsistent with this Act; (2) affecting or impairing the authority of the Secretary of the Army (A) to maintain navigation or (B) under the Act of March 3, 1899 (30 Stat. 1112); except that any permit issued under section 404 of this Act shall be conclusive as to the effect on water quality of any discharge resulting from any activity subject to section 10 of the Act of March 3, 1899, or (3) affecting or impairing the provisions of any treaty of the United States.

(b) Discharges of pollutants into the navigable waters subject to the Rivers and Harbors Act of 1910 (36 Stat. 593; 33 U.S.C. 421) and the Supervisory Harbors Act of 1888 (25 Stat. 209; 33 U.S.C. 441–451b) shall be regulated pursuant to this Act, and not subject to such Act of 1910 and the Act of 1888 except as to effect on navigation and anchorage.

(c)(1) Except for the provision of Federal financial assistance for the purpose of assisting the construction of publicly owned treatment works as authorized by section 201 of this Act, and the issuance of a permit under section 402 of this Act for the discharge of any pollutant by a new source as defined in section 306 of this Act, no action of the Administrator taken pursuant to this Act shall be deemed a major Federal action significantly affecting the quality of the human environment within the meaning of the National Environmental Policy Act of 1969 (83 Stat. 852); and

(2) Nothing in the National Environmental Policy Act of 1969 (83 Stat. 852) shall be deemed to—

   (A) authorize any Federal agency authorized to license or permit the conduct of any activity which may result in the discharge of a pollutant into the navigable waters to review any effluent limitation or other requirement established pursuant to this Act or the adequacy of any certification under section 401 of this Act; or

   (B) authorize any such agency to impose, as a condition precedent to the issuance of any license or permit, any effluent limitation other than any such limitation established pursuant to this Act.

(d) Notwithstanding this Act or any other provision of law, the Administrator (1) shall not require any State to consider in the development of the ranking in order of priority of needs for the construction of treatment works (as defined in title II of this Act), any water pollution control agreement which may have been entered into between the United States and any other nation, and (2) shall not consider any such agreement in the approval of any such priority ranking.

§ 1372. Labor standards

[Sec. 513] The Administrator shall take such action as may be necessary to insure that all laborers and mechanics employed by contractors or subcontractors on treatment works for which grants are made under this Act shall be paid wages at rates not less than those prevailing for the same type of work on similar construction in the immediate locality, as determined by the Secretary of Labor, in accordance with the Act of March 3, 1931, as amended, known as the Davis-Bacon Act (46 Stat. 1494; 40 U.S.C., sec. 276a through 276a-5). The Secretary of Labor shall have, with respect to the labor standards specified in this subsection, the authority and functions set forth in Reorganization Plan Numbered 14 of 1950 (15 F.R. 3176) and section 2 of the Act of June 13, 1934, as amended (48 Stat. 948; 40 U.S.C. 276c).

§ 1373. Public health agency coordination

[Sec. 514] The permitting agency under section 402 shall assist the applicant for a permit under such section in coordinating the requirements of this Act with those of the appropriate public health agencies.

§ 1374. Effluent standards and Water Quality Information Advisory Committee

[Sec. 515] (a)(1) There is established an Effluent Standards and Water Quality Information Advisory Committee, which shall be composed of a Chairman and eight members who shall be appointed by the Administrator within sixty days after the date of enactment of this Act.

(2) All members of the Committee shall be selected from the scientific community, qualified by education, training, and experience to provide, assess, and evaluate scientific and technical information on effluent standards and limitations.

(3) Members of the Committee shall serve for a term of four years, and may be reappointed.

(b)(1) No later than one hundred and eighty days prior to the date on which the Administrator is required to publish any proposed regulations required by section 304(b) of this Act, any proposed standard of performance for new sources required by section 306 of this Act, or any proposed toxic effluent standard required by section 307 of this Act, he shall transmit to the Committee a notice of intent to propose such regulations. The Chairman of the Committee within ten days after receipt of such notice may publish a notice of a public hearing by the Committee, to be held within thirty days.

(2) No later than one hundred and twenty days after receipt of such notice, the Committee shall transmit to the Administrator such scienti-

fic and technical information as is in its possession, including that presented at any public hearing, related to the subject matter contained in such notice.

(3) Information so transmitted to the Administrator shall constitute a part of the administrative record and comments on any proposed regulations or standards as information to be considered with other comments and information in making any final determinations.

(4) In preparing information for transmittal, the Committee shall avail itself of the technical and scientific services of any Federal agency, including the United States Geological Survey and any national environmental laboratories which may be established.

(c)(1) The Committee shall appoint and prescribe the duties of a Secretary, and such legal counsel as it deems necessary to exercise and fulfill its powers and responsibilities. The compensation of all employees appointed by the Committee shall be fixed in accordance with chapter 51 and subchapter III of chapter 53 of title V of the United States Code.

(2) Members of the Committee shall be entitled to receive compensation at a rate to be fixed by the President but not in excess of the maximum rate of pay for GS-18, as provided in the General Schedule under section 5332 of title V of the United States Code.

(d) Five members of the Committee shall constitute a quorum, and official actions of the Committee shall be taken only on the affirmative vote of at least five members. A special panel composed of one or more members upon order of the Committee shall conduct any hearing authorized by this section and submit the transcript of such hearing to the entire Committee for its action thereon.

(e) The Committee is authorized to make such rules as are necessary for the orderly transaction of its business.

§ 1375. Reports to Congress

[Sec. 516] (a) Within ninety days following the convening of each session of Congress, the Administrator shall submit to the Congress a report, in addition to any other report required by this Act, on measures taken toward implementing the objective of this Act, including, but not limited to, (1) the progress and problems associated with developing comprehensive plans under section 102 of this Act, area-wide plans under section 208 of this Act, basin plans under section 209 of this Act, and plans under section 303(e) of this Act; (2) a summary of actions taken and results achieved in the field of water pollution control research, experiments, studies, and related matters by the Administrator and other Federal agencies and by other persons and agencies under Federal grants or contracts; (3) the progress and problems associated with the development of effluent limitations and recommended control techniques; (4) the status of State programs, including a detailed summary of the progress obtained as compared to that planned under State program plans for development and enforcement of water quality requirements; (5) the identification and status of enforcement actions pending or completed under such Act during the preceding year; (6) the status of State, interstate, and local pollution control programs established pursuant to, and assisted by, this Act; (7) a summary of the results of the survey required to be taken under section 210 of this Act; (8) his activities including recommendations under sections 109 through 111 of this Act; and (9) all reports and recommendations made by the Water Pollution Control Advisory Board.

(b)(1) The Administrator, in cooperation with the States, including water pollution control agencies and other water pollution control planning agencies, shall make (A) a detailed estimate of the cost of carrying out the provisions of this Act; (B) a detailed estimate, biennially revised, of the cost of construction of all needed publicly owned treatment works in all of the States and of the cost of construction of all needed publicly owned treatment works in each of the States; (C) a comprehensive study of the economic impact on affected units of government of the cost of installation of treatment facilities; and (D) a comprehensive analysis of the national requirements for and the cost of treating municipal, industrial, and other effluent to attain the water quality objectives as established by this Act or applicable State law. The Administrator shall submit such detailed estimate and such comprehensive study of such cost to the Congress no later than February 10 of each odd-numbered year. Whenever the Administrator, pursuant to this subsection, requests and receives an estimate of cost from a State, he shall furnish copies of such estimate together with such detailed estimate to Congress.

(2) Notwithstanding the second sentence of paragraph (1) of this subsection, the Administrator shall make a preliminary detailed estimate called for by subparagraph (B) of such paragraph and shall submit such preliminary detailed estimate to the Congress no later than September 3, 1974. The Administrator shall require each State to prepare an estimate of cost for such State, and shall utilize the survey form EPA-1, O.M.B. No. 158-R0017, prepared for the 1973 detailed estimate, except that such estimate shall include all costs of compliance with section 201(g)(2)(A) of this Act and water quality standards established pursuant to section 303 of this Act, and all costs of treatment works as defined in section 212(2), including all eligible costs of constructing sewage collection systems and correcting excessive infiltration or inflow and all eligible costs of correcting combined storm and sanitary sewer problems and treating storm water flows. The survey form shall be distributed by the Administrator to each State no later than January 31, 1974.

(c) The Administrator shall submit to the Congress by October 1, 1978, a report on the status of combined sewer overflows in municipal treatment works operations. The report shall include (1) the status of any projects funded under this Act to address combined sewer overflows, (2) a listing by State of combined sewer overflow needs identified in the 1977 State priority listing, (3) an estimate for each applicable municipality of the number of years necessary, assuming an annual authorization and appropriation for the construction grant program of $5,000,000,000 to correct combined sewer overflow problems, (4) an analysis using representative municipalities faced with major combined sewer overflow needs, of the annual discharges of pollutants from overflows in comparison to treated effluent discharges, (5) an analysis of the technological alternatives available to municipalities to correct major combined sewer overflow problems, and (6) any recommendations of the Administrator for legislation to address the problem of combined sewer overflows, including whether a separate authorization and grant program should be established by the Congress to address combined sewer overflows.

(d) The Administrator shall submit to the Congress by October 1, 1978, a report on the status of the use of municipal secondary effluent and sludge for agricultural and other purposes that utilize the nutrient value of treated wastewater effluent. The report shall include (1) a summary of results of research and development programs, grants, and contracts carried out by the Environmental Protection Agency pursuant to sections 104 and 105 of this Act, regarding alternatives to disposal, landfill, or incineration of secondary effluent of sludge, (2) an estimate of the amount of sludge generated by public treatment works and its disposition, including an estimate of annual energy costs to incinerate sludge, (3) an analysis of current technologies for the utilization, reprocessing, and other uses of sludge to utilize the nutrient value of sludge, (4) legal, institutional, public health, economic, and other impediments to the greater utilization of treated sludge, and (5) any recommendations of the Administrator for legislation to encourage or require the expanded utilization of sludge for agricultural and other purposes. In carrying out this subsection, the Administrator shall consult with, and use the services of the Tennessee Valley Authority and other departments, agencies and instrumentalities of the United States, to the extent it is appropriate to do so.

(e) The Administrator, in cooperation with the States, including water pollution control agencies, and other water pollution control planning agencies, and water supply and water resources agencies of the States and the United States shall submit to Congress, within two years of the date of enactment of this section, a report with recommendations for legislation on a program to require coordination between water supply and wastewater control plans as a condition to grants for construction of treatment works under this Act. No such report shall be submitted except after opportunity for public hearings on such proposed report.

(g)(1) Not later than February 10, 1990, the Administrator shall submit to Congress a report on the financial status and operations of water pollution control revolving funds established by the States under title VI of this Act. The Administrator shall prepare such report in cooperation with the States, including water pollution control agencies and other water pollution control planning and financing agencies.

(2) The report under this subsection shall also include the following:

(A) an inventory of the facilities that are in significant noncompliance with the enforceable requirements of this Act;

(B) an estimate of the cost of construction necessary to bring such facilities into compliance with such requirements;

(C) an assessment of the availability of sources of funds for financing such needed construction, including an estimate of the amount of funds available for providing assistance for such construction through September 30, 1999, from the water pollution control revolving funds established by the States under title VI of this Act;

(D) an assessment of the operations, loan portfolio, and loan conditions of such revolving funds;

(E) an assessment of the effect on user charges of the assistance provided by such revolving funds compared to the assistance provided with funds appropriated pursuant to section 207 of this Act; and

(F) an assessment of the efficiency of the operation and maintenance of treatment works constructed with assistance provided by such revolving funds compared to the efficiency of the operation and maintenance of treatment works constructed with assistance provided under section 201 of this Act.

§ 1376. Authorization of appropriations

[Sec. 517] There are authorized to be appropriated to carry out this Act, other than sections 104, 105, 106(a), 107, 108, 112, 113, 114, 115, 206, 207, 208(f) and (h), 209, 304, 311(c), (d), (i), (l), and (k), 314, 315, and 317, $250,000,000 for the fiscal year ending June 30, 1973, $300,000,000 for the fiscal year ending June 30, 1974, $350,000,000 for the fiscal year ending June 30, 1975, $100,000,000 for the fiscal year ending September 30, 1977, $150,000,000 for the fiscal year ending September 30, 1978, $150,000,000 for the fiscal year ending September 30, 1979, $150,000,000 for the fiscal year ending September 30, 1980, $150,000,000 for the fiscal year ending September 30, 1981, $161,000,000 for the fiscal year ending September 30, 1982, such sums as may be necessary for fiscal years 1983 through 1985, and $135,000,000 per fiscal year for each of the fiscal years 1986 through 1990.

§ 1377. Indian tribes

[Sec. 518](a) Nothing in this section shall be construed to affect the application of section 101(g) of this Act, and all of the provisions of this section shall be carried out in accordance with the provisions of such section 101(g). Indian tribes shall be treated as States for purposes of such section 101(g).

(b) The Administrator, in cooperation with the Director of the Indian Health Service, shall assess the need for sewage treatment works to serve Indian tribes, the degree to which such needs will be met through funds allotted to States under section 205 of this Act and priority lists under section 216 of this Act, and any obstacles which prevent such needs from being met. Not later than one year after the date of the enactment of this section, the Administrator shall submit a report to Congress on the assessment under this subsection, along with recommendations specifying (1) how the Administrator intends to provide assistance to Indian tribes to develop waste treatment management plans and to construct treatment works under this Act, and (2) methods by which the participation in and administration of programs under this Act by Indian tribes can be maximized.

(c) The Administrator shall reserve each fiscal year beginning after September 30, 1986, before allotments to the States under section 205(e), one-half of one percent of the sums appropriated under section 207. Sums reserved under this subsection shall be available only for grants for the development of waste treatment management plans and for the construction of sewage treatment works to serve Indian tribes.

(d) In order to ensure the consistent implementation of the requirements of this Act, an Indian tribe and the State or States in which the lands of such tribe are located may enter into a cooperative agreement, subject to the review and approval of the Administrator, to jointly plan and administer the requirements of this Act.

(e) The Administrator is authorized to treat an Indian tribe as a State for purposes of title II and sections 104, 106, 303, 305, 308, 309, 314, 319, 401, 402, and 404 of this Act to the degree necessary to carry out the objectives of this section, but only if—

(1) the Indian tribe has a governing body carrying out substantial governmental duties and powers;

(2) the functions to be exercised by the Indian tribe pertain to the management and protection of water resources which are held by an Indian tribe, held by the United States in trust for Indians, held by a member of an Indian tribe if such property interest is subject to a trust restriction on alienation, or otherwise within the borders of an Indian reservation; and

(3) the Indian tribe is reasonably expected to be capable, in the Administrator's judgment, of carrying out the functions to be exercised in a manner consistent with the terms and purposes of this Act and of all applicable regulations.

Such treatment as a State may include the direct provision of funds reserved under subsection (c) to the governing bodies of Indian tribes, and the determination of priorities by Indian tribes, where not determined by the Administrator in cooperation with the Director of the Indian Health Service. The Administrator, in cooperation with the Director of the Indian Health Service, is authorized to make grants under title II of this Act in an amount not to exceed 100 percent of the cost of a project. Not later than 18 months after the date of the enactment of this section, the Administrator shall, in consultation with Indian tribes, promulgate final regulations which specify how Indian tribes shall be treated as States for purposes of this Act. The Administrator shall, in promulgating such regulations, consult affected States sharing common water bodies and provide a mechanism for the resolution of any unreasonable consequences that may arise as a result of differing water quality standards that may be set by States and Indian tribes located on common bodies of water. Such mechanism shall provide for explicit consideration of relevant factors including, but not limited to, the effects of differing water quality permit requirements on upstream and downstream dischargers, economic impacts, and present and historical uses and quality of the waters subject to such standards. Such mechanism should provide for the avoidance of such unreasonable consequences in a manner consistent with the objective of this Act.

(f) The Administrator shall make grants to an Indian tribe under section 319 of this Act as though such tribe was a State. Not more than one-third of one percent of the amount appropriated for any fiscal year under section 319 may be used to make grants under this subsection. In addition to the requirements of section 319, an Indian tribe shall be required to meet the requirements of paragraphs (1), (2), and (3) of subsection (d) of this section in order to receive such a grant.

(g) No provision of this Act shall be construed to—
(1) grant, enlarge, or diminish, or in any way affect the scope of the governmental authority, if any, of any Alaska Native organization, including any federally-recognized tribe, traditional Alaska Native council, or Native council organized pursuant to the Act of June 18, 1934 (48 Stat. 987), over lands or persons in Alaska;
(2) create or validate any assertion by such organization or any form of governmental authority over lands or persons in Alaska; or
(3) in any way affect any assertion that Indian country, as defined in section 1151 of title 18, United States Code, exists or does not exist in Alaska.

(h) For purposes of this section, the term—
(1) "Federal Indian reservation" means all land within the limits of any Indian reservation under the jurisdiction of the United States Government, notwithstanding the issuance of any patent, and including rights-of-way running through the reservation; and
(2) "Indian tribe" means any Indian tribe, band, group, or community recognized by the Secretary of the Interior and exercising governmental authority over a Federal Indian reservation.

Subchapter VI. Title VI—State Water Pollution Control Revolving Funds

§ 1381. Grants to States for establishment of revolving funds

[Sec. 601] (a) Subject to the provisions of this title, the Administrator shall make capitalization grants to each State for the purpose of establishing a water pollution control revolving fund for providing assistance (1) for construction of treatment works (as defined in section 212 of this Act) which are publicly owned, (2) for implementing a management program under section 319, and (3) for developing and implementing a conservation and management plan under section 320.

(b) The Administrator and each State shall jointly establish a schedule of payments under which the Administrator will pay to the State the amount of each grant to be made to the State under this title. Such schedule shall be based on the State's intended use plan under section 606(c) of this Act, except that—
  (1) such payments shall be made in quarterly installments, and
  (2) such payments shall be made as expeditiously as possible, but in no event later than the earlier of—
     (A) 8 quarters after the date such funds were obligated by the State, or
     (B) 12 quarters after the date such funds were allotted to the State.

§ 1382. Capitalization grant agreements

[Sec. 602] (a) To receive a capitalization grant with funds made available under this title and section 205(m) of this Act, a State shall enter into an agreement with the Administrator which shall include but not be limited to the specifications set forth in subsection (b) of this section.

(b) The Administrator shall enter into an agreement under this section with a State only after the State has established to the satisfaction of the Administrator that—
  (1) the State will accept grant payments with funds to be made available under this title and section 205(m) of this Act in accordance with a payment schedule established jointly by the Administrator under section 601(b) of this Act and will deposit all such payments in the water pollution control revolving fund established by the State in accordance with this title;
  (2) the State will deposit in the fund from State moneys an amount equal to at least 20 percent of the total amount of all capitalization grants which will be made to the State with funds to be made available under this title and section 205(m) of this Act on or before the date on which

each quarterly grant payment will be made to the State under this title;

(3) the State will enter into binding commitments to provide assistance in accordance with the requirements of this title in an amount equal to 120 percent of the amount of each such grant payment within 1 year after the receipt of such grant payment;

(4) all funds in the fund will be expended in an expeditious and timely manner;

(5) all funds in the fund as a result of capitalization grants under this title and section 205(m) of this Act will first be used to assure maintenance of progress, as determined by the Governor of the State, toward compliance with enforceable deadlines, goals, and requirements of this Act, including the municipal compliance deadline;

(6) treatment works eligible under section 603(c)(1) of this Act which will be constructed in whole or in part before fiscal year 1995 with funds directly made available by capitalization grants under this title and section 205(m) of this Act will meet the requirements of, or otherwise be treated (as determined by the Governor of the State) under sections 201(b), 201(g)(1), 201(g)(2), 201(g)(3), 201(g)(5), 201(g)(6), 201(n)(1), 201(o), 204(a)(1), 204(a)(2), 204(b)(1), 204(d)(2), 211, 218, 511(c)(1), and 513 of this Act in the same manner as treatment works constructed with assistance under title II of this Act;

(7) in addition to complying with the requirements of this title, the State will commit or expend each quarterly grant payment which it will receive under this title in accordance with laws and procedures applicable to the commitment or expenditure of revenues of the State;

(8) in carrying out the requirements of section 606 of this Act, the State will use accounting, audit, and fiscal procedures conforming to generally accepted government accounting standards;

(9) the State will require as a condition of making a loan or providing other assistance, as described in section 603(d) of this Act, from the fund that the recipient of such assistance will maintain project accounts in accordance with generally accepted government accounting standards; and

(10) the State will make annual reports to the Administrator on the actual use of funds in accordance with section 606(d) of this Act.

§ 1383. Water pollution control revolving loan funds

[Sec. 603] (a) Before a State may receive a capitalization grant with funds made available under this title and section 205(m) of this Act, the State shall first establish a water pollution control revolving fund which complies with the requirements of this section.

(b) Each State water pollution control revolving fund shall be administered by an instrumentality of the State with such powers and limitations as may be required to operate such fund in accordance with the requirements and objectives of this Act.

(c) The amounts of funds available to each State water pollution control revolving fund shall be used only for providing financial assistance (1) to any municipality, intermunicipal, interstate, or State agency for construction of publicly owned treatment works (as defined in section 212 of this Act), (2) for the implementation of a management program established under section 319 of this Act, and (3) for development and implementation of a conservation and management plan under section 320 of this Act. The fund shall be established, maintained, and credited with repayments, and the fund balance shall be available in perpetuity for providing such financial assistance.

(d) Except as otherwise limited by State law, a water pollution control revolving fund of a State under this section may be used only—

(1) to make loans, on the condition that—

    (A) such loans are made at or below market interest rates, including interest free loans, at terms not to exceed 20 years;

    (B) annual principal and interest payments will commence not later than 1 year after completion of any project and all loans will be fully amortized not later than 20 years after project completion;

    (C) the recipient of a loan will establish a dedicated source of revenue for repayment of loans; and

    (D) the fund will be credited with all payments of principal and interest on all loans;

(2) to buy or refinance the debt obligation of municipalities and intermunicipal and interstate agencies within the State at or below market rates, where such debt obligations were incurred after March 7, 1985;

(3) to guarantee, or purchase insurance for, local obligations where such action would improve credit market access or reduce interest rates;

(4) as a source of revenue or security for the payment of principal and interest on revenue or general obligation bonds issued by the State if the proceeds of the sale of such bonds will be deposited in the fund;

(5) to provide loan guarantees for similar revolving funds established by municipalities or intermunicipal agencies;

(6) to earn interest on fund accounts; and

(7) for the reasonable costs of administering the fund and conducting activities under this title, except that such amounts shall not exceed 4 percent of all grant awards to such fund under this title.

(e) If a State makes, from its water pollution revolving fund, a loan which will finance the cost of facility planning and the preparation of plans, specifications, and estimates for construction of publicly owned treatment works, the State shall ensure that if the recipient of such loan receives a grant under section 201(g) of this Act for construction of such treatment works and an allowance under section 201(l)(1) of this Act for non-Federal funds expended for such planning and preparation, such recipient will promptly repay such loan to the extent of such allowance.

(f) A State may provide financial assistance from its water pollution control revolving fund only with respect to a project which is consistent with plans, if any, developed under sections 205(j), 208, 303(e), 319, and 320 of this Act.

(g) The State may provide financial assistance from its water pollution control revolving fund only with respect to a project for construction of a treatment works described in subsection (c)(1) if such project is on the State's priority list under section 216 of this Act. Such assistance may be provided regardless of the rank of such project on such list.

(h) A State water pollution control revolving fund may provide assistance (other than under subsection (d)(1) of this section) to a municipality or intermunicipal or interstate agency with respect to the non-Federal share of the costs of a treatment works project for which such municipality or agency is receiving assistance from the Administrator under any other authority only if such assistance is necessary to allow such project to proceed.

§ 1384. Allotment of funds

[Sec. 604] (a) Sums authorized to be appropriated to carry out this section for each of fiscal years 1989 and 1990 shall be allotted by the Administrator in accordance with section 205(c) of this Act.

(b) Each State shall reserve each fiscal year 1 percent of the sums allotted to such State under this section for such fiscal year, or $100,000, whichever amount is greater, to carry out planning under sections 205(j) and 303(e) of this Act.

(c) (1) Sums allotted to a State under this section for a fiscal year shall be available for obligation by the State during the fiscal year for which sums are authorized and during the following fiscal year.

(2) The amount of any allotment not obligated by the State by the last day of the 2-year period of availability established by paragraph (1) shall be immediately reallotted by the Administrator on the basis of the same ratio as is applicable to sums allotted under title II of this Act for the second fiscal year of such 2-year period. None of the funds reallotted by the Administrator shall be reallotted to any State which has not obligated all sums allotted to such State in the first fiscal year of such 2-year period.

§ 1385. Corrective action

[Sec. 605] (a) If the Administrator determines that a State has not complied with its agreement with the Administrator under section 602 of this Act or any other requirement of this title, the Administrator shall notify the State of such noncompliance and the necessary corrective action.

(b) If a State does not take corrective action within 60 days after the date a State receives notification of such action under subsection (a), the Administrator shall withhold additional payments to the State until the Administrator is satisfied that the State has taken the necessary corrective action.

(c) If the Administrator is not satisfied that adequate corrective actions have been taken by the State within 12 months after the State is notified of such actions under subsection (a), the payments withheld from the State by the Administrator under subsection (b) shall be made available for reallotment in accordance with the most recent formula for allotment of funds under this title.

§ 1386. Audit, reports, and fiscal controls: intended use plan

[Sec. 606] (a) Each State electing to establish a water pollution control revolving fund under this title shall establish fiscal controls and accounting procedures sufficient to assure proper accounting during appropriate accounting periods for—

(1) payments received by the fund;

(2) disbursements made by the fund; and

(3) fund balances at the beginning and end of the accounting period.

(b) The Administrator shall, at least on an annual basis, conduct or require each State to have independently conducted reviews and audits as may be deemed necessary or appropriate by the Administrator to carry out the objectives of this section. Audits of the use of funds deposited in the water pollution revolving fund established by such State shall be conducted in accordance with the auditing procedures of the General Accounting Office, including chapter 75 of title 31, United States Code.

(c) After providing for public comment and review, each State shall annually prepare a plan identifying the intended uses of the amounts available to its water pollution control revolving fund. Such intended use plan shall include, but not be limited to—

(1) a list of those projects for construction of publicly owned treatment works on the State's priority list developed pursuant to section 216 of this Act and a list of activities eligible for assistance under sections 319 and 320 of this Act;

(2) a description of the short- and long-term goals and objectives of its water pollution control revolving fund;

(3) information on the activities to be supported, including a description of project categories, discharge requirements under titles III and IV of this Act, terms of financial assistance, and communities served;

(4) assurances and specific proposals for meeting the requirements of paragraphs (3), (4), (5), and (6) of section 602(b) of this Act; and

(5) the criteria and method established for the distribution of funds.

(d) Beginning the first fiscal year after the receipt of payments under this title, the State shall provide an annual report to the Administrator describing how the State has met the goals and objectives for the previous fiscal year as identified in the plan prepared for the previous fiscal year pursuant to subsection (c), including identification of loan recipients, loan amounts, and loan terms and similar details on other forms of financial assistance provided from the water pollution control revolving fund.

(e) The Administrator shall conduct an annual oversight review of each State plan prepared under subsection (c), each State report prepared under subsection (d), and other such materials as are considered necessary and appropriate in carrying out the purposes of this title. After reasonable notice by the Administrator to the State or the recipient of a loan from a water pollution control revolving fund, the State or loan recipient shall make available to the Administrator such records as the Administrator reasonably requires to review and determine compliance with this title.

(f) Except to the extent provided in this title, the provisions of title II shall not apply to grants under this title.

§ 1387. Authorization of appropriations

[Sec. 607] There is authorized to be appropriated to carry out the purposes of this title the following sums:
(1) $1,200,000,000 per fiscal year for each of fiscal years 1989 and 1990;
(2) $2,400,000,000 for fiscal year 1991;
(3) $1,800,000,000 for fiscal year 1992;
(4) $1,200,000,000 for fiscal year 1993; and
(5) $600,000,000 for fiscal year 1994.

8 • Emergency Planning and Community Right-To-Know Act of 1986

INTRODUCTION

Before the passage of the Emergency Planning and Community Right-to-Know Act of 1986, enacted as Title III of the Superfund Amendments and Reauthorization Act, several states had already approved legislation requiring public notification of the types of hazardous substances used by business and industry.

Most of the first "right-to-know" laws were designed to inform workers of the types of hazards they might be exposed to in the workplace. After several highly publicized industrial accidents, however, the emphasis began to shift to include the right of the community to know what dangers it faced from manufacturing facilities, chemical plants, and other such industries.

Perhaps the most notable of these events was the catastrophic leak of methyl isocyanate from a Union Carbide Corp. subsidiary in Bhopal, India. On the night of December 3, 1984, a massive leak of the toxic MIC, used as an intermediate in the manufacture of various agricultural chemicals, swept over a densely populated area near the plant, causing hundreds of thousands of screaming men, women, and children to attempt to flee the area. When it was over, nearly 2,000 people had died and another 200,000 had been injured. No emergency plans had been made to deal with such a disaster.

And an accident in 1986 had perhaps an even more profound effect on the public and lawmakers in the states and in Washington, D.C. That disaster was the explosion and fire at the Chernobyl nuclear power station in the Soviet Union. Added to the United States' own brush with nuclear disaster at the Three Mile Island nuclear power plant in Pennsylvania in 1979, the event at Chernobyl deeply exacerbated fears of nuclear power and caused communities throughout the United States to wonder how prepared they would be to deal with such a disaster.

Sen. Frank Lautenberg (D-NJ), one of the chief authors of EPCRA, said the act "will be critical to communities — in alerting them to the dangerous chemicals present in their communities, and in laying the foundation for effective emergency response management. The right to know means public information about what hazardous substances are being stored and released into the environment in our communities. It means planning for emergency releases before they happen. It means our citizens and our emergency response personnel will be safer and better prepared for the threats from chemical releases. It means that this nation will not tolerate Bhopal- or Chernobyl-type tragedies."

Under the law, the governor of each state must appoint a "state emergency response commission," which in turn appoints local emergency planning committees. Members of the local committees must include state and local officials; law enforcement, fire-fighting, civil defense, first aid, health, local environmental, hospital, and transportation personnel; representatives from news media; community groups; and owners and operators of facilities covered by the law.

As required by the law, the Environmental Protection Agency on November 17, 1986, published a list of 402 "extremely hazardous substances" (51 FR 41570). EPA also set threshold levels for those substances, and any facility that has any of the 402 substances in excess of the threshold amount is subject to the act's reporting requirements. The agency's emergency planning and notification rules were issued in April 1987 (40 CFR 355).

Two basic emissions reporting requirements were established by EPCRA. One requires covered facilities to report any unexpected release of an extremely hazardous substance.

The other requires that owners and operators of facilities annually prepare "toxic chemical release forms," providing information about the chemicals that were used on-site, and the quantities of chemicals that were released into the environment via routes such as waste streams or air emissions. EPA told BNA January 19, 1988, that the agency plans to have its routine-emissions-reporting regulations under Section 313 published by the end of January 1988.

Some owners and operators of facilities must prepare or have available Material Safety Data Sheets (MSDSs) under the Occupational Safety and Health Act. Under Section 311 of the right-to-know law, these owners and operators must provide these MSDSs, or a list of the chemicals they cover, to the local emergency planning committee, the state commission, and to the local fire departments. If the facility provides only a list of the chemicals covered by the MSDSs, it must make the data sheets available on demand.

These same owners and operators must, under Section 312 of the law, prepare emergency and hazardous chemical inventory forms. Again, the local committee, the state commission, and the local fire department must be provided with this form by the facility.

EPA issued its Section 311 and Section 312 regulations in October 1987 (40 CFR 370).

Much about EPCRA has generated considerable interest and controversy, but some of the most spirited discussion has centered around what information that must be reported can qualify for a trade secret exemption. In general, the law permits the withholding of the specific chemical identity of a hazardous substance if the information has never before been disclosed to others, if the information need not be disclosed under any federal law, if the disclosure of the information would be likely to cause substantial competitive harm, and if the chemical identity of the substance cannot be readily ascertained through reverse engineering. EPA's complicated trade secret rules are not expected to be issued in final form before June 1988.

Emergency Planning and Community Right-To-Know Act of 1986

(P.L. 99-499, approved October 17, 1986)

Subchapter I. Emergency Planning and Notification

§ 11001. Establishment of State commissions, planning districts, and local committees

[Sec. 301] (a) Not later than six months after the date of the enactment of this title, the Governor of each State shall appoint a State emergency response commission. The Governor may designate as the State emergency response commission one or more existing emergency response organizations that are State-sponsored or appointed. The Governor shall, to the extent practicable, appoint persons to the State emergency response commission who have technical expertise in the emergency response field. The State emergency response commission shall appoint local emergency planning committees under subsection (c) and shall supervise and coordinate the activities of such committees. The State emergency response commission shall establish procedures for receiving and processing requests from the public for information under section 324, including tier II information under section 312. Such procedures shall include the designation of an official to serve as coordinator for information. If the Governor of any State does not designate a State emergency response commission within such period, the Governor shall operate as the State emergency response commission until the Governor makes such designation.

(b) Not later than nine months after the date of the enactment of this title, the State emergency response commission shall designate emergency planning districts in order to facilitate preparation and implementation of emergency plans. Where appropriate, the State emergency response commission may designate existing political subdivisions or multijurisdictional planning organizations as such districts. In emergency planning areas that involve more than one State, the State emergency response commissions of all potentially affected States may designate emergency planning districts and local emergency planning committees by agreement. In making such designation, the State emergency response commission shall indicate which facilities subject to the requirements of this subtitle are within such emergency planning district.

(c) Not later than 30 days after designation of emergency planning districts or 10 months after the date of the enactment of this title, whichever is earlier, the State emergency response commission shall appoint members of a local emergency planning committee for each emergency planning district. Each committee shall include, at a minimum, representatives from each of the following groups or organizations: elected State and local officials; law enforcement, civil defense, firefighting, first aid, health, local environmental, hospital, and transportation personnel; broadcast and print media; community groups; and owners and operators of facilities subject to the requirements of this subtitle. Such committee shall appoint a chairperson and shall establish rules by which the committee shall function. Such rules shall include provisions for public notification of committee activities, public meetings to discuss the emergency plan, public comments, response to such comments by the committee, and distribution of the emergency plan. The local emergency planning committee shall establish procedures for receiving and processing requests from the public for information under section 324, including tier II information under section 312. Such procedures shall include the designation of an official to serve as coordinator for information.

(d) A State emergency response commission may revise its designations and appointments under subsections (b) and (c) as it deems appropriate. Interested persons may petition the State emergency response commission to modify the membership of a local emergency planning committee.

§ 11002. Substances and facilities covered and notification

[Sec. 302] (a)(1) A substance is subject to the requirements of this subtitle if the substance is on the list published under paragraph (2).

(2) Within 30 days after the date of the enactment of this title, the Administrator shall publish a list of extremely hazardous substances. The list shall be the same as the list of substances published in November 1985 by the Administrator in Appendix A of the "Chemical Emergency Preparedness Program Interim Guidance."

(3)(A) At the time the list referred to in paragraph (2) is published the Administrator shall—

    (i) publish an interim final regulation establishing a threshold planning quantity for each substance on the list, taking into account the criteria described in paragraph (4), and

    (ii) initiate a rulemaking in order to publish final regulations establishing a threshold planning quantity for each substance on the list.

(B) The threshold planning quantities may, at the Administrator's discretion, be based on classes of chemicals or categories of facilities.

(C) If the Administrator fails to publish an interim final regulation establishing a threshold planning quantity for a substance within 30 days after the date of the enactment of this title, the threshold planning quantity for the substance shall be 2 pounds until such time as the Administrator publishes regulations establishing a threshold for the substance.

(4) The Administrator may revise the list and thresholds under paragraphs (2) and (3) from time to time. Any revisions to the list shall take into account the toxicity, reactivity, volatility, dispersibility, combustibility, or flammability of a substance. For purposes of the preceding sentence, the term "toxicity" shall include any short- or long-term health effect which may result from a short-term exposure to the substance.

(b)(1) Except as provided in section 304, a facility is subject to the requireof this subtitle if a substance on the list referred to in subsection (a) is present at the facility in an amount in excess of the threshold planning quantity established for such substance.

(2) For purposes of emergency planning, a Governor or a State emergency response commission may designate additional facilities which shall be subject to the requirements of this subtitle, if such designation is made after public notice and opportunity for comment. The Governor or State emergency response commission shall notify the facility concerned of any facility designation under this paragraph.

(c) Not later than seven months after the date of the enactment of this title, the owner or operator of each facility subject to the requirements of this subtitle by reason of subsection (b)(1) shall notify the State emergency response commission for the State in which such facility is located that such facility is subject to the requirements of this subtitle. Thereafter, if a substance on the list of extremely hazardous substances referred to in subsection (a) first becomes present at such facility in excess of the threshold planning quantity established for such substance, or if there is a revision of such list and the facility has present a substance on the revised list in excess of the threshold planning quantity established for such substance, the owner or operator of the facility shall notify the State emergency response commission and the local emergency planning committee within 60 days after such acquisition or revision that such facility is subject to the requirements of this subtitle.

(d) The State emergency response commission shall notify the Administrator of facilities subject to the requirements of this subtitle by notifying the Administrator of—

(1) each notification received from a facility under subsection (c), and

(2) each facility designated by the Governor or State emergency response commission under subsection (b)(2).

§ 11003. Comprehensive emergency response plans

[Sec. 303] (a) Each local emergency planning committee shall complete preparation of an emergency plan in accordance with this section not later than two years after the date of the enactment of this title. The committee shall review such plan once a year, or more frequently as changed circumstances in the community or at any facility may require.

(b) Each local emergency planning committee shall evaluate the need for resources necessary to develop, implement, and exercise the emergency plan, and shall make recommendations with respect to additional resources that may be required and the means for providing such additional resources.

(c) Each emergency plan shall include (but is not limited to) each of the following:

(1) Identification of facilities subject to the requirements of this subtitle that are within the emergency planning district, identification of routes likely to be used for the transportation of substances on the list of extremely hazardous substances referred to in section 302(a), and identification of additional facilities contributing or subjected to additional risk due to their proximity to facilities subject to the requirements of this subtitle, such as hospitals or natural gas facilities.

(2) Methods and procedures to be followed by facility owners and operators and local emergency and medical personnel to respond to any release of such substances.

(3) Designation of a community emergency coordinator and facility emergency coordinators, who shall make determinations necessary to implement the plan.

(4) Procedures providing reliable, effective, and timely notification by the facility emergency coordinators and the community emergency coor-

dinator to persons designated in the emergency plan, and to the public, that a release has occurred (consistent with the emergency notification requirements of section 304).

(5) Methods for determining the occurrence of a release, and the area or population likely to be affected by such release.

(6) A description of emergency equipment and facilities in the community and at each facility in the community subject to the requirements of this subtitle, and an identification of the persons responsible for such equipment and facilities.

(7) Evacuation plans, including provisions for a precautionary evacuation and alternative traffic routes.

(8) Training programs, including schedules for training of local emergency response and medical personnel.

(9) Methods and schedules for exercising the emergency plan.

(d) For each facility subject to the requirements of this subtitle:

(1) Within 30 days after establishment of a local emergency planning committee for the emergency planning district in which such facility is located, or within 11 months after the date of the enactment of this title, whichever is earlier, the owner or operator of the facility shall notify the emergency planning committee (or the Governor if there is no committee) of a facility representative who will participate in the emergency planning process as a facility emergency coordinator.

(2) The owner or operator of the facility shall promptly inform the emergency planning committee of any relevant changes occurring at such facility as such changes occur or are expected to occur.

(3) Upon request from the emergency planning committee, the owner or operator of the facility shall promptly provide information to such committee necessary for developing and implementing the emergency plan.

(e) After completion of an emergency plan under subsection (a) for an emergency planning district, the local emergency planning committee shall submit a copy of the plan to the State emergency response commission of each State in which such district is located. The commission shall review the plan and make recommendations to the committee on revisions of the plan that may be necessary to ensure coordination of such plan with emergency response plans of other emergency planning districts. To the maximum extent practicable, such review shall not delay implementation of such plan.

(f) The national response team, as established pursuant to the National Contingency Plan as established under section 9605 of the Comprehensive Environmental Response, Compensation, and Liability Act of 1980 (42 U.S.C. 9601 et seq.), shall publish guidance documents for preparation and implementation of emergency plans. Such documents shall be published not later than five months after the date of the enactment of this title.

(g) The regional response teams, as established pursuant to the National Contingency Plan as established under section 9605 of the Comprehensive

Environmental Response, Compensation, and Liability Act of 1980 (42 U.S.C. 9601 et seq.), may review and comment upon an emergency plan or other issues related to preparation, implementation, or exercise of such a plan upon request of a local emergency planning committee. Such review shall not delay implementation of the plan.

§ 11004. Emergency notification

[Sec. 304] (a)(1) If a release of an extremely hazardous substance referred to in section 302(a) occurs from a facility at which a hazardous chemical is produced, used, or stored, and such release requires a notification under section 9603(a) of the Comprehensive Environmental Response, Compensation, and Liability Act of 1980 (hereafter in this section referred to as "CERCLA") (42 U.S.C. 9601 et seq.), the owner or operator of the facility shall immediately provide notice as described in subsection (b).

(2) If a release of an extremely hazardous substance referred to in section 302(a) occurs from a facility at which a hazardous chemical is produced, used, or stored, and such release is not subject to the notification requirements under section 9603(a) of CERCLA, the owner or operator of the facility shall immediately provide notice as described in subsection (b), but only if the release—

(A) is not a federally permitted release as defined in section 9601(10) of CERCLA,

(B) is in an amount in excess of a quantity which the Administrator has determined (by regulation) requires notice, and

(C) occurs in a manner which would require notification under section 9603(a) of CERCLA.

Unless and until superseded by regulations establishing a quantity for an extremely hazardous substance described in this paragraph, a quantity of 1 pound shall be deemed that quantity the release of which requires notice as described in subsection (b).

(3) If a release of a substance which is not on the list referred to in section 302(a) occurs at a facility at which a hazardous chemical is produced, used, or stored, and such release requires notification under section 9603(a) of CERCLA, the owner or operator shall provide notice as follows:

(A) If the substance is one for which a reportable quantity has been established under section 9602(a) of CERCLA, the owner or operator shall provide notice as described in subsection (b).

(B) If the substance is one for which a reportable quantity has not been established under section 9602(a) of CERCLA—

(i) Until April 30, 1988, the owner or operator shall provide, for releases of one pound or more of the substance, the same notice to the community emergency coordinator for the local emergency planning committee, at the same time and in the same form, as notice is provided to the National Response Center under section 9603(a) of CERCLA.

(ii) On and after April 30, 1988, the owner or operator shall provide, for releases of one pound or more of the substance, the notice as described in subsection (b).

(4) This section does not apply to any release which results in exposure to persons solely within the site or sites on which a facility is located.

(b)(1) Notice required under subsection (a) shall be given immediately after the release by the owner or operator of a facility (by such means as telephone, radio, or in person) to the community emergency coordinator for the local emergency planning committees, if established pursuant to section 301(c), for any area likely to be affected by the release and to the State emergency planning commission of any State likely to be affected by the release. With respect to transportation of a substance subject to the requirements of this section, or storage incident to such transportation, the notice requirements of this section with respect to a release shall be satisfied by dialing 911 or, in the absence of a 911 emergency telephone number, calling the operator.

(2) Notice required under subsection (a) shall include each of the following (to the extent known at the time of the notice and so long as no delay in responding to the emergency results):

(A) The chemical name or identity of any substance involved in the release.

(B) An indication of whether the substance is on the list referred to in section 302(a).

(C) An estimate of the quantity of any such substance that was released into the environment.

(D) The time and duration of the release.

(E) The medium or media into which the release occurred.

(F) Any known or anticipated acute or chronic health risks associated with the emergency and, where appropriate, advice regarding medical attention necessary for exposed individuals.

(G) Proper precautions to take as a result of the release, including evacuation (unless such information is readily available to the community emergency coordinator pursuant to the emergency plan).

(H) The name and telephone number of the person or persons to be contacted for further information.

(c) As soon as practicable after a release which requires notice under subsection (a), such owner or operator shall provide a written followup emergency notice (or notices, as more information becomes available) setting forth and updating the information required under subsection (b), and including additional information with respect to—

(1) actions taken to respond to and contain the release,

(2) any known or anticipated acute or chronic health risks associated with

the release, and

(3) where appropriate, advice regarding medical attention necessary for exposed individuals.

(d) The exemption provided in section 327 (relating to transportation) does not apply to this section.

§ 11005. Emergency training and review of emergency systems

[Sec. 305] (a)(1) Officials of the United States Government carrying out existing Federal programs for emergency training are authorized to specifically provide training and education programs for Federal, State, and local personnel in hazard mitigation, emergency preparedness, fire prevention and control, disaster response, long-term disaster recovery, national security, technological and natural hazards, and emergency processes. Such programs shall provide special emphasis for such training and education with respect to hazardous chemicals.

(2) There is authorized to be appropriated to the Federal Emergency Management Agency for each of the fiscal years 1987, 1988, 1989, and 1990, $5,000,000 for making grants to support programs of State and local governments, and to support university-sponsored programs, which are designed to improve emergency planning, preparedness, mitigation, response, and recovery capabilities. Such programs shall provide special emphasis with respect to emergencies associated with hazardous chemicals. Such grants may not exceed 80 percent of the cost of any such program. The remaining 20 percent of such costs shall be funded from non-Federal sources.

(3) Nothing in this section shall affect the availability of appropriations to the Federal Emergency Management Agency for any programs carried out by such agency other than the programs referred to in paragraph (2).

(b)(1) The Administrator shall initiate, not later than 30 days after the date of the enactment of this title, a review of emergency systems for monitoring, detecting, and preventing releases of extremely hazardous substances at representative domestic facilities that produce, use, or store extremely hazardous substances. The Administrator may select representative extremely hazardous substances from the substances on the list referred to in section 302(a) for the purposes of this review. The Administrator shall report interim findings to the Congress not later than seven months after such date of enactment, and issue a final report of findings and recommendations to the Congress not later than 18 months after such date of enactment. Such report shall be prepared in consultation with the States and appropriate Federal agencies.

(2) The report required by this subsection shall include the Administra-

tor's findings regarding each of the following:

(A) The status of current technological capabilities to (i) monitor, detect, and prevent, in a timely manner, significant releases of extremely hazardous substances, (ii) determine the magnitude and direction of the hazard posed by each release, (iii) identify specific substances, (iv) provide data on the specific chemical composition of such releases, and (v) determine the relative concentrations of the constituent substances.

(B) The status of public emergency alert devices or systems for providing timely and effective public warning of an accidental release of extremely hazardous substances into the environment, including releases into the atmosphere, surface water, or groundwater from facilities that produce, store, or use significant quantities of such extremely hazardous substances.

(C) The technical and economic feasibility of establishing, maintaining, and operating perimeter alert systems for detecting releases of such extremely hazardous substances into the atmosphere, surface water, or groundwater, at facilities that manufacture, use, or store significant quantities of such substances.

(3) The report required by this subsection shall also include the Administrator's recommendations for—

(A) initiatives to support the development of new or improved technologies or systems that would facilitate the timely monitoring, detection, and prevention of releases of extremely hazardous substances, and

(B) improving devices or systems for effectively alerting the public in a timely manner, in the event of an accidental release of such extremely hazardous substances.

Subchapter II. Reporting Requirements

§ 11021. Material safety data sheets

[Sec. 311] (a)(1) The owner or operator of any facility which is required to prepare or have available a material safety data sheet for a hazardous chemical under the Occupational Safety and Health Act of 1970 and regulations promulgated under that Act (15 U.S.C. 651 et seq.) shall submit a material safety data sheet for each such chemical, or a list of such chemicals as described in paragraph (2), to each of the following:

(A) The appropriate local emergency planning committee.

(B) The State emergency response commission.

(C) The fire department with jurisdiction over the facility.

(2)(A) The list of chemicals referred to in paragraph (1) shall include each of the following:

    (i) A list of the hazardous chemicals for which a material safety data sheet is required under the Occupational Safety and Health Act of 1970 and regulations promulgated under that Act, grouped in categories of health and physical hazards as set forth under such Act and regulations promulgated under such Act, or in such other categories as the Administrator may prescribe under subparagraph (B).

    (ii) The chemical name or the common name of each such chemical as provided on the material safety data sheet.

    (iii) Any hazardous component of each such chemical as provided on the material safety data sheet.

(B) For purposes of the list under this paragraph, the Administrator may modify the categories of health and physical hazards as set forth under the Occupational Safety and Health Act of 1970 and regulations promulgated under that Act by requiring information to be reported in terms of groups of hazardous chemicals which present similar hazards in an emergency.

(3) An owner or operator may meet the requirements of this section with respect to a hazardous chemical which is a mixture by doing one of the following:

(A) Submitting a material safety data sheet for, or identifying on a list, each element or compound in the mixture which is a hazardous chemical. If more than one mixture has the same element or compound, only one material safety data sheet, or one listing, of the element or compound is necessary.

(B) Submitting a material safety data sheet for, or identifying on a list, the mixture itself.

(b) The Administrator may establish threshold quantities for hazardous chemicals below which no facility shall be subject to the provisions of this section. The threshold quantities may, in the Administrator's discretion, be based on classes of chemicals or categories of facilities.

(c)(1) If an owner or operator of a facility submits a list of chemicals under subsection (a)(1), the owner or operator, upon request by the local emergency planning committee, shall submit the material safety data sheet for any chemical on the list to such committee.

(2) A local emergency planning committee, upon request by any person, shall make available a material safety data sheet to the person in accordance with section 324. If the local emergency planning committee does not have the requested material safety data sheet, the committee shall request the sheet from the facility owner or operator and then make the sheet available to the person in accordance with section 324.

(d)(1) The initial material safety data sheet or list required under this section with respect to a hazardous chemical shall be provided before the later of—

(A) 12 months after the date of the enactment of this title, or

(B) 3 months after the owner or operator of a facility is required to prepare or have available a material safety data sheet for the chemical under the Occupational Safety and Health Act of 1970 and regulations promulgated under that Act.

(2) Within 3 months following discovery by an owner or operator of significant new information concerning an aspect of a hazardous chemical for which a material safety data sheet was previously submitted to the local emergency planning committee under subsection (a), a revised sheet shall be provided to such person.

(e) For purposes of this section, the term "hazardous chemical" has the meaning given such term by section 1910.1200(c) of title 29 of the Code of Federal Regulations, except that such term does not include the following:

(1) Any food, food additive, color additive, drug, or cosmetic regulated by the Food and Drug Administration.

(2) Any substance present as a solid in any manufactured item to the extent exposure to the substance does not occur under normal conditions of use.

(3) Any substance to the extent it is used for personal, family, or household purposes, or is present in the same form and concentration as a product packaged for distribution and use by the general public.

(4) Any substance to the extent it is used in a research laboratory or a hospital or other medical facility under the direct supervision of a technically qualified individual.

(5) Any substance to the extent it is used in routine agricultural operations or is a fertilizer held for sale by a retailer to the ultimate customer.

§ 11022. Emergency and hazardous chemical inventory forms

[Sec. 312] (a)(1) The owner or operator of any facility which is required to prepare or have available a material safety data sheet for a hazardous chemical under the Occupational Safety and Health Act of 1970 and regulations promulgated under that Act shall prepare and submit an emergency and hazardous chemical inventory form (hereafter in this chapter referred to as an "inventory form") to each of the following:

(A) The appropriate local emergency planning committee.

(B) The State emergency response commission.

(C) The fire department with jurisdiction over the facility.

(2) The inventory form containing tier I information (as described in subsection (d)(1)) shall be submitted on or before March 1, 1988, and annually thereafter on March 1, and shall contain data with respect to the preceding calendar year. The preceding sentence does not apply if an owner or operator provides, by the same deadline and with respect

to the same calendar year, tier II information (as described in subsection (d)(2)) to the recipients described in paragraph (1).

(3) An owner or operator may meet the requirements of this section with respect to a hazardous chemical which is a mixture by doing one of the following:

(A) Providing information on the inventory form on each element or compound in the mixture which is a hazardous chemical. If more than one mixture has the same element or compound, only one listing on the inventory form for the element or compound at the facility is necessary.

(B) Providing information on the inventory form on the mixture itself.

(b) The Administrator may establish threshold quantities for hazardous chemicals covered by this section below which no facility shall be subject to the provisions of this section. The threshold quantities may, in the Administrator's discretion, be based on classes of chemicals or categories of facilities.

(c) A hazardous chemical subject to the requirements of this section is any hazardous chemical for which a material safety data sheet or a listing is required under section 311.

(d)(1)(A) An inventory form shall provide the information described in subparagraph (B) in aggregate terms for hazardous chemicals in categories of health and physical hazards as set forth under the Occupational Safety and Health Act of 1970 and regulations promulgated under that Act.

(B) The information referred to in subparagraph (A) is the following:

(i) An estimate (in ranges) of the maximum amount of hazardous chemicals in each category present at the facility at any time during the preceding calendar year.

(ii) An estimate (in ranges) of the average daily amount of hazardous chemicals in each category present at the facility during the preceding calendar year.

(iii) The general location of hazardous chemicals in each category.

(C) For purposes of reporting information under this paragraph, the Administrator may—

(i) modify the categories of health and physical hazards as set forth under the Occupational Safety and Health Act of 1970 and regulations promulgated under that Act by requiring information to be reported in terms of groups of hazardous chemicals which present similar hazards in an emergency, or

(ii) require reporting on individual hazardous chemicals of special concern to emergency response personnel.

(2) An inventory form shall provide the following additional information for each hazardous chemical present at the facility, but only upon request and in accordance with subsection (e):

(A) The chemical name or the common name of the chemical as

provided on the material safety data sheet.

(B) An estimate (in ranges) of the maximum amount of the hazardous chemical present at the facility at any time during the preceding calendar year.

(C) An estimate (in ranges) of the average daily amount of the hazardous chemical present at the facility during the preceding calendar year.

(D) A brief description of the manner of storage of the hazardous chemical.

(E) The location at the facility of the hazardous chemical.

(F) An indication of whether the owner elects to withhold location information of a specific hazardous chemical from disclosure to the public under section 324.

(e)(1) Upon request by a State emergency planning commission, a local emergency planning committee, or a fire department with jurisdiction over the facility, the owner or operator of a facility shall provide tier II information, as described in subsection (d), to the person making the request. Any such request shall be with respect to a specific facility.

(2) A State or local official acting in his or her official capacity may have access to tier II information by submitting a request to the State emergency response commission or the local emergency planning committee. Upon receipt of a request for tier II information, the State commission or local committee shall, pursuant to paragraph (1), request the facility owner or operator for the tier II information and make available such information to the official.

(3)(A) Any person may request a State emergency response commission or local emergency planning committee for tier II information relating to the preceding calendar year with respect to a facility. Any such request shall be in writing and shall be with respect to a specific facility.

(B) Any tier II information which a State emergency response commission or local emergency planning committee has in its possession shall be made available to a person making a request under this paragraph in accordance with section 324. If the State emergency response commission or local emergency planning committee does not have the tier II information in its possession, upon a request for tier II information the State emergency response commission or local emergency planning committee shall, pursuant to paragraph (1), request the facility owner or operator for tier II information with respect to a hazardous chemical which a facility has stored in an amount in excess of 10,000 pounds present at the facility at any time during the preceding calendar year and make such information available in accordance with section 324 to the person making the request.

(C) In the case of tier II information which is not in the possession of a State emergency response commission or local emergency planning committee and which is with respect to a hazardous chemical which a facility has stored in an amount less than 10,000 pounds present at the facility at any time during the preceding calendar year, a request from a person must include the general need for the information. The State emergency response commission or local emergency planning committee may, pursuant to paragraph (1), request the facility owner or operator for the tier II information on behalf of the person making the request. Upon receipt of any information requested on behalf of such person, the State emergency response commission or local emergency planning committee shall make the information available in accordance with section 324 to the person.

(D) A State emergency response commission or local emergency planning committee shall respond to a request for tier II information under this paragraph no later than 45 days after the date of receipt of the request.

(f) Upon request to an owner or operator of a facility which files an inventory form under this section by the fire department with jurisdiction over the facility, the owner or operator of the facility shall allow the fire department to conduct an on-site inspection of the facility and shall provide to the fire department specific location information on hazardous chemicals at the facility.

(g) The Administrator shall publish a uniform format for inventory forms within three months after the date of the enactment of this title. If the Administrator does not publish such forms, owners and operators of facilities subject to the requirements of this section shall provide the information required under this section by letter.

§ 11023. Toxic chemical release forms

[Sec. 313] (a) The owner or operator of a facility subject to the requirements of this section shall complete a toxic chemical release form as published under subsection (g) for each toxic chemical listed under subsection (c) that was manufactured, processed, or otherwise used in quantities exceeding the toxic chemical threshold quantity established by subsection (f) during the preceding calendar year at such facility. Such form shall be submitted to the Administrator and to an official or officials of the State designated by the Governor on or before July 1, 1988, and annually thereafter on July 1 and shall contain data reflecting releases during the preceding calendar year.

(b)(1)(A) The requirements of this section shall apply to owners and operators of facilities that have 10 or more full-time employees and that are in Standard Industrial Classification Codes 20 through 39 (as in effect on July 1, 1985) and that manufactured, processed, or otherwise used a toxic chemical listed under subsection (c) in excess of the quantity of that toxic chemical established under subsection (f) during the calendar year for which a release form is required under this section.

    (B) The Administrator may add or delete Standard Industrial Classification Codes for purposes of subparagraph (A), but only to the extent necessary to provide that each Standard Industrial Code to which this section applies is relevant to the purposes of this section.

    (C) For purposes of this section—

        (i) The term "manufacture" means to produce, prepare, import, or compound a toxic chemical.

        (ii) The term "process" means the preparation of a toxic chemical, after its manufacture, for distribution in commerce—

            (I) in the same form or physical state as, or in a different form or physical state from, that in which it was received by the person so preparing such chemical, or

            (II) as part of an article containing the toxic chemical.

  (2) The Administrator, on his own motion or at the request of a Governor of a State (with regard to facilities located in that State), may apply the requirements of this section to the owners and operators of any particular facility that manufactures, processes, or otherwise uses a toxic chemical listed under subsection (c) if the Administrator determines that such action is warranted on the basis of toxicity of the toxic chemical, proximity to other facilities that release the toxic chemical or to population centers, the history of releases of such chemical at such facility, or such other factors as the Administrator deems appropriate.

  (c) The toxic chemicals subject to the requirements of this section are those chemicals on the list in Committee Print Number 99–169 of the Senate Committee on Environment and Public Works, titled "Toxic Chemicals Subject to Section 313 of the Emergency Planning and Community Right-To-Know Act of 1986" (including any revised version of the list as may be made pursuant to subsection (d) or (e)).

  (d)(1) The Administrator may by rule add or delete a chemical from the list described in subsection (c) at any time.

  (2) A chemical may be added if the Administrator determines, in his judgment, that there is sufficient evidence to establish any one of the following:

    (A) The chemical is known to cause or can reasonably be anticipated to cause significant adverse acute human health effects at concentration levels that are reasonably likely to exist beyond facility site boundaries as a result of continuous, or frequently recurring, releases.

    (B) The chemical is known to cause or can reasonably be anticipated to cause in humans—

        (i) cancer or teratogenic effects, or

   (ii) serious or irreversible—
      (I) reproductive dysfunctions,
      (II) neurological disorders,
      (III) heritable genetic mutations, or
      (IV) other chronic health effects.
   (C) The chemical is known to cause or can reasonably be anticipated
      to cause, because of—
      (i) its toxicity,
      (ii) its toxicity and persistence in the environment, or
      (iii) its toxicity and tendency to bioaccumulate in the environment,
         a significant adverse effect on the environment of sufficient
         seriousness, in the judgment of the Administrator, to warrant
         reporting under this section. The number of chemicals included
         on the list described in subsection (c) on the basis of the preceding
         sentence may constitute in the aggregate no more than 25 percent
         of the total number of chemicals on the list.
   A determination under this paragraph shall be based on generally
   accepted scientific principles or laboratory tests, or appropriately
   designed and conducted epidemiological or other population studies,
   available to the Administrator.
   (3) A chemical may be deleted if the Administrator determines there is not
      sufficient evidence to establish any of the criteria described in para-
      graph (2).
   (4) Any revision made on or after January 1 and before December 1 of
      any calendar year shall take effect beginning with the next calendar
      year. Any revision made on or after December 1 of any calendar year
      and before January 1 of the next calendar year shall take effect
      beginning with the calendar year following such next calendar year.

   (e)(1) Any person may petition the Administrator to add or delete a
chemical from the list described in subsection (c) on the basis of the criteria
in subparagraph (A) or (B) of subsection (d)(2). Within 180 days after
receipt of a petition, the Administrator shall take one of the following
actions:
      (A) Initiate a rulemaking to add or delete the chemical to the list, in
         accordance with subsection (d)(2) or (d)(3).
      (B) Publish an explanation of why the petition is denied.
   (2) A State Governor may petition the Administrator to add or delete a
      chemical from the list described in subsection (c) on the basis of the
      criteria in subparagraph (A), (B), or (C) of subsection (d)(2). In the
      case of such a petition from a State Governor to delete a chemical, the
      petition shall be treated in the same manner as a petition received
      under paragraph (1) to delete a chemical. In the case of such a petition
      from a State Governor to add a chemical, the chemical will be added to
      the list within 180 days after receipt of the petition, unless the
      Administrator—

(A) initiates a rulemaking to add the chemical to the list, in accordance with subsection (d)(2), or

(B) publishes an explanation of why the Administrator believes the petition does not meet the requirements of subsection (d)(2) for adding a chemical to the list.

(f)(1) The threshold amounts for purposes of reporting toxic chemicals under this section are as follows:

(A) With respect to a toxic chemical used at a facility, 10,000 pounds of the toxic chemical per year.

(B) With respect to a toxic chemical manufactured or processed at a facility—

(i) For the toxic chemical release form required to be submitted under this section on or before July 1, 1988, 75,000 pounds of the toxic chemical per year.

(ii) For the form required to be submitted on or before July 1, 1989, 50,000 pounds of the toxic chemical per year.

(iii) For the form required to be submitted on or before July 1, 1990, and for each form thereafter, 25,000 pounds of the toxic chemical per year.

(2) The Administrator may establish a threshold amount for a toxic chemical different from the amount established by paragraph (1). Such revised threshold shall obtain reporting on a substantial majority of total releases of the chemical at all facilities subject to the requirements of this section. The amounts established under this paragraph may, at the Administrator's discretion, be based on classes of chemicals or categories of facilities.

(g)(1) Not later than June 1, 1987, the Administrator shall publish a uniform toxic chemical release form for facilities covered by this section. If the Administrator does not publish such a form, owners and operators of facilities subject to the requirements of this section shall provide the information required under this subsection by letter postmarked on or before the date on which the form is due. Such form shall—

(A) provide for the name and location of, and principal business activities at, the facility;

(B) include an appropriate certification, signed by a senior official with management responsibility for the person or persons completing the report, regarding the accuracy and completeness of the report; and

(C) provide for submission of each of the following items of information for each listed toxic chemical known to be present at the facility:

(i) Whether the toxic chemical at the facility is manufactured, processed, or otherwise used, and the general category or categories of use of the chemical.

(ii) An estimate of the maximum amounts (in ranges) of the toxic chemical present at the facility at any time during the preceding calendar year.

(iii) For each wastestream, the waste treatment or disposal methods employed, and an estimate of the treatment efficiency typically achieved by such methods for that wastestream.

(iv) The annual quantity of the toxic chemical entering each environmental medium.

(2) In order to provide the information required under this section, the owner or operator of a facility may use readily available data (including monitoring data) collected pursuant to other provisions of law, or, where such data are not readily available, reasonable estimates of the amounts involved. Nothing in this section requires the monitoring or measurement of the quantities, concentration, or frequency of any toxic chemical released into the environment beyond that monitoring and measurement required under other provisions of law or regulation. In order to assure consistency, the Administrator shall require that data be expressed in common units.

(h) The release forms required under this section are intended to provide information to the Federal, State, and local governments and the public, including citizens of communities surrounding covered facilities. The release form shall be available, consistent with section 324(a), to inform persons about releases of toxic chemicals to the environment; to assist governmental agencies, researchers, and other persons in the conduct of research and data gathering; to aid in the development of appropriate regulations, guidelines, and standards; and for other similar purposes.

(i)(1) The Administrator may modify the frequency of submitting a report under this section, but the Administrator may not modify the frequency to be any more often than annually. A modification may apply, either nationally or in a specific geographic area, to the following:

(A) All toxic chemical release forms required under this section.

(B) A class of toxic chemicals or a category of facilities.

(C) A specific toxic chemical.

(D) A specific facility.

(2) A modification may be made under paragraph (1) only if the Administrator—

(A) makes a finding that the modification is consistent with the provisions of subsection (h), based on—

(i) experience from previously submitted toxic chemical release forms, and

(ii) determinations made under paragraph (3), and

(B) the finding is made by a rulemaking in accordance with section 553 of Title 5, United States Code.

(3) The Administrator shall make the following determinations with respect to a proposed modification before making a modification under

paragraph (1):

(A) The extent to which information relating to the proposed modification provided on the toxic chemical release forms has been used by the Administrator or other agencies of the Federal Government, States, local governments, health professionals, and the public.

(B) The extent to which the information is (i) readily available to potential users from other sources, such as State reporting programs, and (ii) provided to the Administrator under another Federal law or through a State program.

(C) The extent to which the modification would impose additional and unreasonable burdens on facilities subject to the reporting requirements under this section.

(4) Any modification made under this subsection shall be reviewed at least once every 5 years. Such review shall examine the modification and ensure that the requirements of paragraphs (2) and (3) still justify continuation of the modification. Any change to a modification reviewed under this paragraph shall be made in accordance with this subsection.

(5) The Administrator shall notify Congress of an intention to initiate a rulemaking for a modification under this subsection. After such notification, the Administrator shall delay initiation of the rulemaking for at least 12 months, but no more than 24 months, after the date of such notification.

(6) In any judicial review of a rulemaking which establishes a modification under this subsection, a court may hold unlawful and set aside agency action, findings, and conclusions found to be unsupported by substantial evidence.

(7) A modification under this subsection may apply to a calendar year or other reporting period beginning no earlier than January 1, 1993.

(8) Any modification made on or after January 1 and before December 1 of any calendar year shall take effect beginning with the next calendar year. Any modification made on or after December 1 of any calendar year and before January 1 of the next calendar year shall take effect beginning with the calendar year following such next calendar year.

(j) The Administrator shall establish and maintain in a computer data base a national toxic chemical inventory based on data submitted to the Administrator under this section. The Administrator shall make these data accessible by computer telecommunication and other means to any person on a cost reimbursable basis.

(k) Not later than June 30, 1991, the Comptroller General, in consultation with the Administrator and appropriate officials in the States, shall submit to the Congress a report including each of the following:

(1) A description of the steps taken by the Administrator and the States to implement the requirements of this section, including steps taken to

make information collected under this section available to and accessible by the public.

(2) A description of the extent to which the information collected under this section has been used by the Environmental Protection Agency, other Federal agencies, the States, and the public, and the purposes for which the information has been used.

(3) An identification and evaluation of options for modifications to the requirements of this section for the purpose of making information collected under this section more useful.

(l)(1) The Administrator shall arrange for a mass balance study to be carried out by the National Academy of Sciences using mass balance information collected by the Administrator under paragraph (3). The Administrator shall submit to Congress a report on such study no later than 5 years after the date of the enactment of this title.

(2) The purposes of the study are as follows:

(A) To assess the value of mass balance analysis in determining the accuracy of information on toxic chemical releases.

(B) To assess the value of obtaining mass balance information, or portions thereof, to determine the waste reduction efficiency of different facilities, or categories of facilities, including the effectiveness of toxic chemical regulations promulgated under laws other than this title.

(C) To assess the utility of such information for evaluating toxic chemical management practices at facilities, or categories of facilities, covered by this section.

(D) To determine the implications of mass balance information collection on a national scale similar to the mass balance information collection carried out by the Administrator under paragraph (3), including implications of the use of such collection as part of a national annual quantity toxic chemical release program.

(3)(A) The Administrator shall acquire available mass balance information from States which currently conduct (or during the 5 years after the date of enactment of this title initiate) a mass balance-oriented annual quantity toxic chemical release program. If information from such States provides an inadequate representation of industry classes and categories to carry out the purposes of the study, the Administrator also may acquire mass balance information necessary for the study from a representative number of facilities in other States.

(B) Any information acquired under this section shall be available to the public, except that upon a showing satisfactory to the Administrator by any person that the information (or a particular part thereof) to which the Administrator or any officer, employee, or representative has access under this section if made public would divulge information entitled to protection under section 1905 of Title 18, United States Code, such information or part shall be considered confidential in accordance with the purposes of that section, except that such information or part may be disclosed to other officers, employees, or authorized representatives of the United States concerned with carrying out this section.

(C) The Administrator may promulgate regulations prescribing procedures for collecting mass balance information under this paragraph.

(D) For purposes of collecting mass balance information under subparagraph (A), the Administrator may require the submission of information by a State or facility.

(4) For purposes of this subsection, the term "mass balance" means an accumulation of the annual quantities of chemicals transported to a facility, produced at a facility, consumed at a facility, used at a facility, accumulated at a facility, released from a facility, and transported from a facility as a waste or as a commercial product or byproduct or component of a commercial product or byproduct.

Subchapter III. General Provisions

§ 11041. Relationship to other law

[Sec. 321] (a) Nothing in this title shall—

(1) preempt any State or local law,

(2) except as provided in subsection (b), otherwise affect any State or local law or the authority of any State or local government to adopt or enforce any State or local law, or

(3) affect or modify in any way the obligations or liabilities of any person under other Federal law.

(b) Any State or local law enacted after August 1, 1985, which requires the submission of a material safety data sheet from facility owners or operators shall require that the data sheet be identical in content and format to the data sheet required under subsection (a) of section 311. In addition, a State or locality may require the submission of information which is supplemental to the information required on the data sheet (including information on the location and quantity of hazardous chemicals present at the facility), through additional sheets attached to the data sheet or such other means as the State or locality considers appropriate.

§ 11042. Trade secrets

[Sec. 322] (a)(1)(A) With regard to a hazardous chemical, an extremely hazardous substance, or a toxic chemical, any person required under section 303(d)(2), 303(d)(3), 311, 312, or 313 to submit information to any other person may withhold from such submittal the specific chemical identity (including the chemical name and other specific identification), as defined in regulations prescribed by the Administrator under subsection (c), if the person complies with paragraph (2).

(B) Any person withholding the specific chemical identity shall, in the place on the submittal where the chemical identity would normally be included, include the generic class or category of the hazardous chemical, extremely hazardous substance, or toxic chemical (as the case may be).

(2)(A) A person is entitled to withhold information under paragraph (1) if such person—

    (i) claims that such information is a trade secret, on the basis of the factors enumerated in subsection (b),

    (ii) includes in the submittal referred to in paragraph (1) an explanation of the reasons why such information is claimed to be a trade secret, based on the factors enumerated in subsection (b), including a specific description of why such factors apply, and

    (iii) submits to the Administrator a copy of such submittal, and the information withheld from such submittal.

(B) In submitting to the Administrator the information required by subparagraph (A)(iii), a person withholding information under this subsection may—

    (i) designate, in writing and in such manner as the Administrator may prescribe by regulation, the information which such person believes is entitled to be withheld under paragraph (1), and

    (ii) submit such designated information separately from other information submitted under this subsection.

(3) The authority under this subsection to withhold information shall not apply to information which the Administrator has determined, in accordance with subsection (c), is not a trade secret.

(b) No person required to provide information under this title may claim that the information is entitled to protection as a trade secret under subsection (a) unless such person shows each of the following:

(1) Such person has not disclosed the information to any other person, other than a member of a local emergency planning committee, an officer or employee of the United States or a State or local government, an employee of such person, or a person who is bound by a confidentiality agreement, and such person has taken reasonable measures to protect the confidentiality of such information and intends to continue to take such measures.

(2) The information is not required to be disclosed, or otherwise made available, to the public under any other Federal or State law.

(3) Disclosure of the information is likely to cause substantial harm to the

competitive position of such person.

(4) The chemical identity is not readily discoverable through reverse engineering.

(c) As soon as practicable after the date of enactment of this title, the Administrator shall prescribe regulations to implement this section. With respect to subsection (b)(4), such regulations shall be equivalent to comparable provisions in the Occupational Safety and Health Administration Hazard Communication Standard (29 C.F.R. 1910.1200) and any revisions of such standard prescribed by the Secretary of Labor in accordance with the final ruling of the courts of the United States in United Steelworkers of America, AFL–CIO–CLC v. Thorne G. Auchter.

(d)(1) Any person may petition the Administrator for the disclosure of the specific chemical identity of a hazardous chemical, an extremely hazardous substance, or a toxic chemical which is claimed as a trade secret under this section. The Administrator may, in the absence of a petition under this paragraph, initiate a determination, to be carried out in accordance with this subsection, as to whether information withheld constitutes a trade secret.

(2) Within 30 days after the date of receipt of a petition under paragraph (1) (or upon the Administrator's initiative), the Administrator shall review the explanation filed by a trade secret claimant under subsection (a)(2) and determine whether the explanation presents assertions which, if true, are sufficient to support a finding that the specific chemical identity is a trade secret.

(3)(A) If the Administrator determines pursuant to paragraph (2) that the explanation presents sufficient assertions to support a finding that the specific chemical identity is a trade secret, the Administrator shall notify the trade secret claimant that he has 30 days to supplement the explanation with detailed information to support the assertions.

(B) If the Administrator determines, after receipt of any supplemental supporting detailed information under subparagraph (A), that the assertions in the explanation are true and that the specific chemical identity is a trade secret, the Administrator shall so notify the petitioner and the petitioner may seek judicial review of the determination.

(C) If the Administrator determines, after receipt of any supplemental supporting detailed information under subparagraph (A), that the assertions in the explanation are not true and that the specific chemical identity is not a trade secret, the Administrator shall notify the trade secret claimant that the Administrator intends to release the specific chemical identity. The trade secret claimant has 30 days in which he may appeal the Administrator's determination under this subparagraph to the Administrator. If the Administrator does not reverse his determination under this subparagraph in such an appeal by the trade secret claimant, the trade secret claimaint may seek judicial review of the determination.

(4)(A) If the Administrator determines pursuant to paragraph (2) that the explanation presents insufficient assertions to support a finding that the specific chemical identity is a trade secret, the Administrator shall notify the trade secret claimant that he has 30 days to appeal the determination to the Administrator, or, upon a showing of good cause, amend the original explanation by providing supplementary assertions to support the trade secret claim.

(B) If the Administrator does not reverse his determination under subparagraph (A) after an appeal or an examination of any supplementary assertions under subparagraph (A), the Administrator shall so notify the trade secret claimant and the trade secret claimant may seek judicial review of the determination.

(C) If the Administrator reverses his determination under subparagraph (A) after an appeal or an examination of any supplementary assertions under subparagraph (A), the procedures under paragraph (3) of this subsection apply.

(e) Nothing in this section, or regulations adopted pursuant to this section, shall authorize any person to withhold information which is required to be provided to a health professional, a doctor, or a nurse in accordance with section 323.

(f) Any information submitted to the Administrator under subsection (a)(2) or subsection (d)(3) (except a specific chemical identity) shall be available to the public, except that upon a showing satisfactory to the Administrator by any person that the information (or a particular part thereof) to which the Administrator has access under this section if made public would divulge information entitled to protection under section 1905 of Title 18, United States Code, such information or part shall be considered confidential in accordance with the purposes of that section, except that such information or part may be disclosed to other officers, employees, or authorized representatives of the United States concerned with carrying out this title.

(g) Upon request by a State, acting through the Governor of the State, the Administrator shall provide to the State any information obtained under subsection (a)(2) and subsection (d)(3).

(h)(1) In any case in which the identity of a hazardous chemical or an extremely hazardous substance is claimed as a trade secret, the Governor or State emergency response commission established under section 301 shall identify the adverse health effects associated with the hazardous chemical or extremely hazardous substance and shall assure that such information is provided to any person requesting information about such hazardous chemical or extremely hazardous substance.

(2) In any case in which the identity of a toxic chemical is claimed as a trade secret, the Administrator shall identify the adverse health and

environmental effects associated with the toxic chemical and shall assure that such information is included in the computer database required by section 313(j) and is provided to any person requesting information about such toxic chemical.

(i) Notwithstanding any limitation contained in this section or any other provision of law, all information reported to or otherwise obtained by the Administrator (or any representative of the Administrator) under this title shall be made available to a duly authorized committee of the Congress upon written request by such a committee.

§ 11043. Provision of information to health professionals, doctors, and nurses

[Sec. 323] (a) An owner or operator of a facility which is subject to the requirements of section 311, 312, or 313 shall provide the specific chemical identity, if known, of a hazardous chemical, extremely hazardous substance, or a toxic chemical to any health professional who requests such information in writing if the health professional provides a written statement of need under this subsection and a written confidentiality agreement under subsection (d). The written statement of need shall be a statement that the health professional has a reasonable basis to suspect that—
  (1) the information is needed for purposes of diagnosis or treatment of an individual,
  (2) the individual or individuals being diagnosed or treated have been exposed to the chemical concerned, and
  (3) knowledge of the specific chemical identity of such chemical will assist in diagnosis or treatment.
Following such a written request, the owner or operator to whom such request is made shall promptly provide the requested information to the health professional. The authority to withhold the specific chemical identity of a chemical under section 322 when such information is a trade secret shall not apply to information required to be provided under this subsection, subject to the provisions of subsection (d).

(b) An owner or operator of a facility which is subject to the requirements of section 311, 312, or 313 shall provide a copy of a material safety data sheet, an inventory form, or a toxic chemical release form, including the specific chemical identity, if known, of a hazardous chemical, extremely hazardous substance, or a toxic chemical, to any treating physician or nurse who requests such information if such physician or nurse determines that—
  (1) a medical emergency exists,
  (2) the specific chemical identity of the chemical concerned is necessary for or will assist in emergency or first-aid diagnosis or treatment, and
  (3) the individual or individuals being diagnosed or treated have been

exposed to the chemical concerned.

Immediately following such a request, the owner or operator to whom such request is made shall provide the requested information to the physician or nurse. The authority to withhold the specific chemical identity of a chemical from a material safety data sheet, an inventory form, or a toxic chemical release form under section 322 when such information is a trade secret shall not apply to information required to be provided to a treating physician or nurse under this subsection. No written confidentiality agreement or statement of need shall be required as a precondition of such disclosure, but the owner or operator disclosing such information may require a written confidentiality agreement in accordance with subsection (d) and a statement setting forth the items listed in paragraphs (1) through (3) as soon as circumstances permit.

(c)(1) An owner or operator of a facility subject to the requirements of section 311, 312, or 313 shall provide the specific chemical identity, if known, of a hazardous chemical, an extremely hazardous substance, or a toxic chemical to any health professional (such as a physician, toxicologist, or epidemiologist)—

   (A) who is a local government employee or a person under contract with the local government, and

   (B) who requests such information in writing and provides a written statement of need under paragraph (2) and a written confidentiality agreement under subsection (d).

Following such a written request, the owner or operator to whom such request is made shall promptly provide the requested information to the local health professional. The authority to withhold the specific chemical identity of a chemical under section 322 when such information is a trade secret shall not apply to information required to be provided under this subsection, subject to the provisions of subsection (d).

(2) The written statement of need shall be a statement that describes with reasonable detail one or more of the following health needs for the information:

   (A) To assess exposure of persons living in a local community to the hazards of the chemical concerned.

   (B) To conduct or assess sampling to determine exposure levels of various population groups.

   (C) To conduct periodic medical surveillance of exposed population groups.

   (D) To provide medical treatment to exposed individuals or population groups.

   (E) To conduct studies to determine the health effects of exposure.

   (F) To conduct studies to aid in the identification of a chemical that may reasonably be anticipated to cause an observed health effect.

(d) Any person obtaining information under subsection (a) or (c) shall, in accordance with such subsection (a) or (c), be required to agree in a written confidentiality agreement that he will not use the information for any purpose other than the health needs asserted in the statement of need, except as may otherwise be authorized by the terms of the agreement or by the person providing such information. Nothing in this subsection shall preclude the parties to a confidentiality agreement from pursuing any remedies to the extent permitted by law.

(e) As soon as practicable after the date of the enactment of this title, the Administrator shall promulgate regulations describing criteria and parameters for the statement of need under subsection (a) and (c) and the confidentiality agreement under subsection (d).

§ 11044. Public availability of plans, data sheets, forms, and follow-up notices

[Sec. 324] (a) Each emergency response plan, material safety data sheet, list described in section 311(a)(2), inventory form, toxic chemical release form, and followup emergency notice shall be made available to the general public, consistent with section 322, during normal working hours at the location or locations designated by the Administrator, Governor, State emergency response commission, or local emergency planning committee, as appropriate. Upon request by an owner or operator of a facility subject to the requirements of section 312, the State emergency response commission and the appropriate local emergency planning committee shall withhold from disclosure under this section the location of any specific chemical required by section 312(d)(2) to be contained in an inventory form as tier II information.

(b) Each local emergency planning committee shall annually publish a notice in local newspapers that the emergency response plan, material safety data sheets, and inventory forms have been submitted under this section. The notice shall state that followup emergency notices may subsequently be issued. Such notice shall announce that members of the public who wish to review any such plan, sheet, form, or followup notice may do so at the location designated under subsection (a).

§ 11045. Enforcement

[Sec. 325] (a) The Administrator may order a facility owner or operator (except an owner or operator of a facility designated under section 302(b)(2)) to comply with section 302(c) and section 303(d). The United States district court for the district in which the facility is located shall have jurisdiction to enforce the order, and any person who violates or fails to obey such an order shall be liable to the United States for a civil penalty of not more than $25,000 for each day in which such violation occurs or such failure to comply continues.

(b)(1)(A) A civil penalty of not more than $25,000 per violation may be assessed by the Administrator in the case of a violation of the requirements of section 304.

(B) No civil penalty may be assessed under this subsection unless the person accused of the violation is given notice and opportunity for a hearing with respect to the violation.

(C) In determining the amount of any penalty assessed pursuant to this subsection, the Administrator shall take into account the nature, circumstances, extent and gravity of the violation or violations and, with respect to the violator, ability to pay, any prior history of such violations, the degree of culpability, economic benefit or savings (if any) resulting from the violation, and such other matters as justice may require.

(2) A civil penalty of not more than $25,000 per day for each day during which the violation continues may be assessed by the Administrator in the case of a violation of the requirements of section 304. In the case of a second or subsequent violation the amount of such penalty may be not more than $75,000 for each day during which the violation continues. Any civil penalty under this subsection shall be assessed and collected in the same manner, and subject to the same provisions, as in the case of civil penalties assessed and collected under section 16 of the Toxic Substances Control Act. In any proceeding for the assessment of a civil penalty under this subsection the Administrator may issue subpoenas for the attendance and testimony of witnesses and the production of relevant papers, books, and documents and may promulgate rules for discovery procedures.

(3) The Administrator may bring an action in the United States District court for the appropriate district to assess and collect a penalty of not more than $25,000 per day for each day during which the violation continues in the case of a violation of the requirements of section 304. In the case of a second or subsequent violation, the amount of such penalty may be not more than $75,000 for each day during which the violation continues.

(4) Any person who knowingly and willfully fails to provide notice in accordance with section 304 shall, upon conviction, be fined not more than $25,000 or imprisoned for not more than two years, or both (or in the case of a second or subsequent conviction, shall be fined not more than $50,000 or imprisoned for not more than five years, or both).

(c)(1) Any person (other than a governmental entity) who violates any requirement of section 312 or 313 shall be liable to the United States for a civil penalty in an amount not to exceed $25,000 for each such violation.

(2) Any person (other than a governmental entity) who violates any requirement of section 311 or 323(b), and any person who fails to furnish to the Administrator information required under section

322(a)(2) shall be liable to the United States for a civil penalty in an amount not to exceed $10,000 for each such violation.

(3) Each day a violation described in paragraph (1) or (2) continues shall, for purposes of this subsection, constitute a separate violation.

(4) The Administrator may assess any civil penalty for which a person is liable under this subsection by administrative order or may bring an action to assess and collect the penalty in the United States district court for the district in which the person from whom the penalty is sought resides or in which such person's principal place of business is located.

(d)(1) If the Administrator determines—

(A)(i) under section 322(d)(4) that an explanation submitted by a trade secret claimant presents insufficient assertions to support a finding that a specific chemical identity is a trade secret, or (ii) after receiving supplemental supporting detailed information under section 322(d)(3)(A), that the specific chemical identity is not a trade secret; and

(B) that the trade secret claim is frivolous,

the trade secret claimant is liable for a penalty of $25,000 per claim. The Administrator may assess the penalty by administrative order or may bring an action in the appropriate district court of the United States to assess and collect the penalty.

(2) Any person who knowingly and willfully divulges or discloses any information entitled to protection under section 322 shall, upon conviction, be subject to a fine of not more than $20,000 or to imprisonment not to exceed one year, or both.

(e) Whenever any facility owner or operator required to provide information under section 323 to a health professional who has requested such information fails or refuses to provide such information in accordance with such section, such health professional may bring an action in the appropriate United States district court to require such facility owner or operator to provide the information. Such court shall have jurisdiction to issue such orders and take such other action as may be necessary to enforce the requirements of section 323.

(f)(1) Any person against whom a civil penalty is assessed under this section may obtain review thereof in the appropriate district court of the United States by filing a notice of appeal in such court within 30 days after the date of such order and by simultaneously sending a copy of such notice by certified mail to the Administrator. The Administrator shall promptly file in such court a certified copy of the record upon which such violation was found or such penalty imposed. If any person fails to pay an assessment of a civil penalty after it has become a final and unappealable order or after the appropriate court has entered final judgment in favor of the United States, the Administrator may request the Attorney General of the United States to institute a civil action in an appropriate district court of the United States to collect the penalty, and such court shall have jurisdiction to hear and decide any such action. In hearing such action, the court shall have authority to review the violation and the assessment of the civil penalty on the record.

(2) The Administrator may issue subpoenas for the attendance and testimony of witnesses and the production of relevant papers, books, or documents in connection with hearings under this section. In case of contumacy or refusal to obey a subpoena issued pursuant to this paragraph and served upon any person, the district court of the United States for any district in which such person is found, resides, or transacts business, upon application by the United States and after notice to such person, shall have jurisdiction to issue an order requiring such person to appear and give testimony before the administrative law judge or to appear and produce documents before the administrative law judge, or both, and any failure to obey such order of the court may be punished by such court as a contempt thereof.

§ 11046. Civil actions

[Sec. 326] (a)(1) Except as provided in subsection (e), any person may commence a civil action on his own behalf against the following:

(A) An owner or operator of a facility for failure to do any of the following:
   (i) Submit a followup emergency notice under section 304(c).
   (ii) Submit a material safety data sheet or a list under section 311(a).
   (iii) Complete and submit an inventory form under section 312(a) containing tier I information as described in section 312(d)(1) unless such requirement does not apply by reason of the second sentence of section 312(a)(2).
   (iv) Complete and submit a toxic chemical release form under section 313(a).

(B) The Administrator for failure to do any of the following:
   (i) Publish inventory forms under section 312(g).
   (ii) Respond to a petition to add or delete a chemical under section 313(e)(1) within 180 days after receipt of the petition.
   (iii) Publish a toxic chemical release form under section 313(g).
   (iv) Establish a computer database in accordance with section 313(j).
   (v) Promulgate trade secret regulations under section 322(c).
   (vi) Render a decision in response to a petition under section 322(d) within 9 months after receipt of the petition.

(C) The Administrator, a State Governor, or a State emergency response commission, for failure to provide a mechanism for public availability of information in accordance with section 324(a).

(D) A State Governor or a State emergency response commission for failure to respond to a request for tier II information under section 312(e)(3) within 120 days after the date of receipt of the request.

(2)(A) Any State or local government may commence a civil action against an owner or operator of a facility for failure to do any of the following:

(i) Provide notification to the emergency response commission in the State under section 302(c).

(ii) Submit a material safety data sheet or a list under section 311(a).

(iii) Make available information requested under section 311(c).

(iv) Complete and submit an inventory form under section 312(a) containing tier I information unless such requirement does not apply by reason of the second sentence of section 312(a)(2).

(B) Any State emergency response commission or local emergency planning committee may commence a civil action against an owner or operator of a facility for failure to provide information under section 303(d) or for failure to submit tier II information under section 312(e)(1).

(C) Any State may commence a civil action against the Administrator for failure to provide information to the State under section 322(g).

(b)(1) Any action under subsection (a) against an owner or operator of a facility shall be brought in the district court for the district in which the alleged violation occurred.

(2) Any action under subsection (a) against the Administrator may be brought in the United States District Court for the District of Columbia.

(c) The district court shall have jurisdiction in actions brought under subsection (a) against an owner or operator of a facility to enforce the requirement concerned and to impose any civil penalty provided for violation of that requirement. The district court shall have jurisdiction in actions brought under subsection (a) against the Administrator to order the Administrator to perform the act or duty concerned.

(d)(1) No action may be commenced under subsection (a)(1)(A) prior to 60 days after the plaintiff has given notice of the alleged violation to the Administrator, the State in which the alleged violation occurs, and the alleged violator. Notice under this paragraph shall be given in such manner as the Administrator shall prescribe by regulation.

(2) No action may be commenced under subsection (a)(1)(B) or (a)(1)(C) prior to 60 days after the date on which the plaintiff gives notice to the Administrator, State Governor, or State emergency response commission (as the case may be) that the plaintiff will commence the action.

Notice under this paragraph shall be given in such manner as the Administrator shall prescribe by regulation.

(e) No action may be commenced under subsection (a) against an owner or operator of a facility if the Administrator has commenced and is diligently pursuing an administrative order or civil action to enforce the requirement concerned or to impose a civil penalty under this Act with respect to the violation of the requirement.

(f) The court, in issuing any final order in any action brought pursuant to this section, may award costs of litigation (including reasonable attorney and expert witness fees) to the prevailing or the substantially prevailing party whenever the court determines such an award is appropriate. The court may, if a temporary restraining order or preliminary injunction is sought, require the filing of a bond or equivalent security in accordance with the Federal Rules of Civil Procedure.

(g) Nothing in this section shall restrict or expand any right which any person (or class of persons) may have under any Federal or State statute or common law to seek enforcement of any requirement or to seek any other relief (including relief against the Administrator or a State agency).

(h)(1) In any action under this section the United States or the State, or both, if not a party, may intervene as a matter of right.

(2) In any action under this section, any person may intervene as a matter of right when such person has a direct interest which is or may be adversely affected by the action and the disposition of the action may, as a practical matter, impair or impede the person's ability to protect that interest unless the Administrator or the State shows that the person's interest is adequately represented by existing parties in the action.

§ 11047. Exemption

[Sec. 327] Except as provided in section 304, this title does not apply to the transportation, including the storage incident to such transportation, of any substance or chemical subject to the requirements of this title, including the transportation and distribution of natural gas.

§ 11048. Regulations

[Sec. 328] The Administrator may prescribe such regulations as may be necessary to carry out this title.

§ 11049. Definitions

[Sec. 329] For purposes of this title—

(1) The term "Administrator" means the Administrator of the Environ-

mental Protection Agency.

(2) The term "environment" includes water, air, and land and the interrelationship which exists among and between water, air, and land and all living things.

(3) The term "extremely hazardous substance" means a substance on the list described in section 302(a)(2).

(4) The term "facility" means all buildings, equipment, structures, and other stationary items which are located on a single site or on contiguous or adjacent sites and which are owned or operated by the same person (or by any person which controls, is controlled by, or under common control with, such person). For purposes of section 304, the term includes motor vehicles, rolling stock, and aircraft.

(5) The term "hazardous chemical" has the meaning given such term by section 311(e).

(6) The term "material safety data sheet" means the sheet required to be developed under section 1910.1200(g) of Title 29 of the Code of Federal Regulations, as that section may be amended from time to time.

(7) The term "person" means any individual, trust, firm, joint stock company, corporation (including a government corporation), partnership, association, State, municipality, commission, political subdivision of a State, or interstate body.

(8) The term "release" means any spilling, leaking, pumping, pouring, emitting, emptying, discharging, injecting, escaping, leaching, dumping, or disposing into the environment (including the abandonment or discarding of barrels, containers, and other closed receptacles) of any hazardous chemical, extremely hazardous substance, or toxic chemical.

(9) The term "State" means any State of the United States, the District of Columbia, the Commonwealth of Puerto Rico, Guam, American Samoa, the United States Virgin Islands, the Northern Mariana Islands, and any other territory or possession over which the United States has jurisdiction.

(10) The term "toxic chemical" means a substance on the list described in section 313(c).

§ 11050. Authorization of appropriations

[Sec. 330] There are authorized to be appropriated for fiscal years beginning after September 30, 1986, such sums as may be necessary to carry out this title.

9 • The Endangered Species Act

SUMMARY ─────────────────────────────────────

(P.L. 93–205, approved December 28, 1973; as last amended by
P.L. 98–327, approved June 25, 1984)

§ 1531. Congressional findings and declaration of purposes and policy

Summary: The purpose of the Endangered Species Act is to provide a program for the conservation of threatened and endangered species of plants and animals, and the habitats in which they are found. The Act provides the legislative authority to implement the treaties and conventions on endangered species to which the United States is signatory.

§ 1532. Definitions

Summary: Terms having a specific meaning for the Act are defined. The Secretary of Interior is responsible for land animals and freshwater fish; the Secretary of Commerce, for marine mammals and fish; and the Secretary of Agriculture, for the import or export of land plants.

§ 1533. Determination of endangered species and threatened species

Summary: The procedures and criteria for determining what species to list as endangered or threatened are described. The proper authority shall designate, solely on the basis of the best available scientific data, species to be listed, removed, or have their status changed. Regulations may be issued to implement protection of listed species, set aside critical habitat, or initiate recovery plans. Petitions must be acted on within 90 days and determinations made within one year, although extensions are allowed if the information available is insufficient. The status of listed species must be reviewed every five years. Species that cannot be distinguished from listed species may also be protected. Written explanations must be given to state authorities for regulations contrary to the stated position of the state.

§ 1534. Land acquisition

Summary: The appropriate authority may acquire lands to protect listed species. Funds are provided under the Land and Water Conservation Fund Act of 1965.

§ 1535. Cooperation with states

Summary: Federal officials must consult and cooperate with state officials in the implementation of the Act. Agreements may be made with states for the establishment and management of programs implementing the Act. Assistance may be given to state programs consistent with the Act. Financial assistance is limited to 75 percent of the cost of a program, except for programs involving more than one state, when the federal share may be 90 percent. Programs under this section must be reviewed at least annually. State actions are superseded if they provide less protection than under federal law. State laws may provide stronger protection.

§ 1536. Interagency cooperation

Summary: All federal agencies must ensure that their actions are not likely to jeopardize a listed species. Interagency consultations are provided for. Biological assessments must be made to determine if an agency action will adversely affect a listed or proposed species. No commitment of resources that would preclude an alternative measure may be made during the consultation. An Endangered Species Committee is established to consider exemptions of agency actions. The manner and timing of the consideration of applications, the reporting of findings to the committee, and the granting or denying of the exemption are described. Actions of the committee are subject to review by the Secretary of State for assessment of consistency with international treaty or other obligations. Exemptions may be granted for national security reasons. Decisions on exemptions are not considered major federal actions if an environmental impact statement has been prepared. Those exempted must include the costs of any mitigation and enhancement measures as part of the cost of the proposed action. A report must be submitted to the Council on Environmental Quality within one year, describing compliance with required measures. Annual reports will be continued until the measures are completed. Decisions of the Endangered Species Committee are subject to judicial review. Taking of listed species under an exemption is not considered taking with respect to the Act. The President may grant exemptions in disaster areas.

§ 1537. International cooperation

Summary: Foreign currency reserves may be used to provide assistance to foreign countries in implementing programs furthering the purposes of the Act. Appropriated funds may be used if foreign currencies on hand are insufficient. Foreign conservation efforts are encouraged. Personnel and financial assistance may be provided for foreign programs and the training of foreign personnel. Enforcement investigations and research abroad are permitted.

§ 1537a. Convention implementation

Summary: The Secretary of the Interior, acting through the Fish and Wildlife Service is designated to implement the CITES treaty. If the United States votes against the inclusion of any species in the CITES Appendix I or II and does not enter an official reservation under the treaty, a written report explaining the reasons for not entering a reservation must be submitted to Congress within 90 days. The secretary is required to discharge U.S. responsibilities in the Western Hemisphere under the Western Convention, and report to Congress by September, 30, 1985, describing actions taken and those remaining to be taken under its provisions.

§ 1538. Prohibited acts

Summary: The import, export, or taking of endangered species, their possession or sale, or the violation of any regulation pertaining to them or to a threatened species is prohibited. Animals taken captive prior to regulation under this Act and their still captive progeny are not included in the prohibitions of this section. The selling of animals protected under the CITES treaty is prohibited. The import or export of fish or wildlife without a permit or at a nondesignated port is prohibited. It is unlawful for importers or exporters to fail to keep required records or file a required report. It is unlawful to attempt to commit, solicit another to commit, or cause to be committed, any offense defined in this section.

§ 1539. Exceptions

Summary: Permits for taking prohibited species for scientific purposes, to enhance propagation or survival, or taking incidental to a lawful activity may be granted if the application is found to be in good faith and consistent with protection of the species and the purposes of the Act. The applicant must submit a conservation plan specifying the impact, mitigating steps, alternatives considered and the reasons for not using them, and any other information or measures required. A permit may be revoked if its provisions are not complied with. Exemptions may be granted for one year in the case of undue economic hardship to those involved in the taking of a species before it was proposed for listing, except for commercial exploitation of a species listed in Appendix I of the CITES treaty. Subsistence taking and the sale of handicrafts by indigenous peoples of Alaska is exempt from the Act, although taking may be regulated if it adversely affects the survival of the species. Sperm whale oil and scrimshaw legally in the United States before December 28, 1973, may be exempted from the commercial prohibitions of the Act. Applications for exemptions must be filed within one year of the effective date of regulatory action. If an exemption is granted, a certificate outlining the conditions of the exemption must be issued. A report reviewing the implementation of the exemption process must be submitted to Congress, and revised regulations adopted by Oct. 1, 1983, to ensure the exemption process does not result in illegal products being marketed. After January 31, 1984, no one may sell pre-Act scrimshaw unless it has been held before October 13, 1982, and a certificate of exemption has been obtained. Artifacts more than 100 years old, made from listed species, are excepted unless they have been repaired or modified after December 28, 1973. All imports must meet applicable customs restrictions. Legally taken wildlife may be trans-shipped through the United States. Experimental populations of listed species may be released.

§ 1540. Penalties and enforcement

Summary: Civil penalties for violation of the Act may be up to $10,000 per violation. Hearings on civil penalties may be held, with subpoena power. Penalties for criminal violations go up to $20,000 and one year in prison, per violation. Permits or licenses under the Act held by persons convicted of criminal violations may be revoked. District courts have jurisdiction over cases involving the Act. Rewards may be given to informers other than public officials. Confiscation of endangered species and property used in their taking is permitted. Enforcing regulations may be promulgated. Citizen suits against violations (including government agencies) are permitted. District courts may, in response to such suits, order enforcement actions or issue injunctions. Sixty days notice must be given for citizens suits, which may not proceed if action on the complaint is under way or initiated within the notice period. The 60-day period may be waived for emergencies posing risk to a species. The Act must be coordinated with animal quarantine laws.

§ 1541. Endangered plants

Summary: The Secretary of the Smithsonian Institution is directed to review plants for inclusion on the Endangered Species List, and to report findings, including conservation measures, to Congress by December 28, 1974.

§ 1542. Authorization of appropriations

Summary: Appropriations to the Department of the Interior are $27 million for each of 1983, 1984, and 1985; to the Department of Commerce $3.5 million per year; and to the Department of Agriculture $1.85 million per year. For cooperation with the states, $6 million per year is appropriated; for the Endangered Species Committee $600,000; and for implementation of the CITES treaty $150,000 each year for 1983 and 1984, and $300,000 for 1985, the funds to be retained until expended.

§ 1543. Construction with Marine Mammal Protection Act of 1972

Summary: This Act does not take precedence over more restrictive provisions of the Marine Mammal Protection Act of 1972.

10 • Marine Mammal Protection Act

SUMMARY _____

(P.L. 92–522, approved October 21, 1972; as last amended by
P.L. 98–364, approved July 17, 1984)

Subchapter I. Generally

§ 1361.   Congressional findings and declaration of policy

Summary: The purpose of the Act is to protect, conserve, and encourage
international research on marine mammals.

§ 1362.   Definitions

Summary: Terms having a specific meaning under the Act are defined.
The Secretary of Commerce is given responsibility for cetaceans and pin-
nipeds other than walruses. The Secretary of the Interior is given responsibility for all other marine mammals.

Subchapter II. Conservation and Protection of Marine Mammals

§ 1371.   Moratorium on taking and importing marine mammals and marine mammal products

Summary: A moratorium is imposed on the taking and import of marine
mammals and products made from them. Permits may be issued for scientific
research or public display, and for incidental taking during commercial
fishing operations. Guidelines must be issued for the monitoring of incidental
taking. Import of fish or fish products may be banned if they are caught in a
manner resulting in taking of marine mammals in excess of U.S. standards.
Taking or import may be allowed if it does not threaten the species involved.
Programs for such taking must be certified to be consistent with the purpose
and provisions of the Act. Permits may not be issued for species designated as
depleted, except for research. Citizens may be permitted to incidentally take

832

marine mammals during specified activities in specified areas for up to five years, if this will not have an impact on the species taken. Coastal indigenous Alaskans are exempted from the Act for subsistence and handicraft purposes. Regulations may limit this take if the species is threatened. Exemptions may be granted for undue economic hardship until October 21, 1973.

§ 1372. Prohibitions

Summary: The taking of marine mammals on the high seas is unlawful for any person or vessel under U.S. jurisdiction. Except if permitted under international treaty, the taking or import of marine mammals or their products in any area under U.S. jurisdiction is forbidden. Possession or trade in illegally taken marine mammals or their products, or commercial fishing by means in contravention of regulations or limitations, is unlawful. Import of pregnant or lactating females, or their young that are nursing or less than eight months old, or of animals from depleted stocks, or those taken inhumanely is unlawful except under a research permit. Import of illegally taken marine mammals or their products or fish caught in a manner illegal under the Act is forbidden. Commercial whaling in waters under U.S. jurisdiction is unlawful.

§ 1373. Regulations on taking of marine mammals

Summary: Regulations shall be made to protect marine mammals and control their take and import. In promulgating regulations, the following must be considered: population levels, international treaty obligations, environmental factors, fishery resources, and economic and technological feasibility. Regulations may restrict the number, sex, age, or size of animals, season, manner and location of taking, and fishing techniques. Population estimates, the impact of the regulation, and the evidence and studies that decisions were based on must be part of the record. Regulations must be periodically reviewed. An annual report must be sent to Congress on actions taken or planned under the Act.

§ 1374. Permits

Summary: Permits must be consistent with regulations and specify the number and kind of animals to be taken, the location and manner of taking, the period of the permit, and any necessary conditions. Permits for display or research must also specify the care to be given subsequent to capture. Transplanting must be considered in the case of permits for reducing overpopulation. Procedures shall be developed for permitting. Judicial review of permit refusal is permitted. Permits may be modified, suspended, or revoked, either to update them to subsequent regulations, or for noncompliance. Such action may be appealed by the permit holder. The permit must be in the possession of the holder or an agent, and a copy must be attached to the enclosure of the marine mammal taken under it. Permit fees may be charged. General permits and regulations for their use may be issued.

§ 1375. Penalties

Summary: Civil penalties may be up to $10,000 per violation. If imported for personal use, forfeiture of the animal or product at the port of entry may be accepted rather than initiating a civil suit. Knowingly violating the Act, or regulations under it, may be punished by a fine of up to $20,000 and one year in prison per violation.

§ 1376. Seizure and forfeiture of cargo

Summary: The cargo of any vessel or conveyance employed in a violation may be confiscated. Any vessel so involved may be fined up to $25,000, and the vessel held until payment is made. Up to $2,500 may be paid as reward to informers other than government employees.

§ 1377. Enforcement

Summary: The personnel, services, and facilities of other federal or state agencies may be used for enforcing the Act. Any animals or products controlled under the Act may be forfeited upon conviction of violation.

§ 1378. International program

Summary: Negotiations shall be initiated in international agreements for the conservation and protection of animals covered by the Act, including control of harmful commercial fishing operations, and protections of environments. A report to Congress on these efforts must be made by October 21, 1972. A study of the Northern fur seal shall be undertaken for the purpose of possible modification of the North Pacific Fur Seal Convention. A report must be submitted to Congress by October 21, 1973.

§ 1379. Transfer of management authority

Summary: States may enforce the Act if authority is transferred to them and they have developed a program that is consistent with the Act and international treaty obligations and that includes standards protecting animals that are below their optimum sustainable population. Transfer of management authority may be revoked for nonimplementation. Transfer to Alaska must be preceded by state regulation of subsistence hunting or other consumptive use. Actions under this section do not require an environmental impact statement. Taking of animals by government officials as part of their duties is exempt from the Act. Regulations may be issued mandating marking, tagging, and record keeping for animals taken for subsistence. The federal government may make grants of up to 50 percent of the cost to states to develop and administer programs under this section. Appropriations for this purpose are $400,000 to the Department of the Interior and $225,000 to the Department of Commerce for each of the years 1979, 1980, and 1981.

§ 1380. Marine mammal research grants

Summary: Grants may be made for research into methods of fishing for yellowfin tuna without incidental taking of marine mammals. Conditions may be set for such grants. Appropriations are $2.5 million for each of the years from 1973 to 1977; $1.4 million for 1978; $4 million for 1979; $4.2 million for 1980; and $4.8 million for 1981.

§ 1381. Commercial fisheries gear development

Summary: Research and development of fishing methods and gear to reduce incidental taking of marine mammals during commercial fishing shall be accomplished. Research and monitoring may take place aboard U.S. fishing vessels. A report must be made to Congress by October 21, 1974. An appropriation of $1 milion is made for this purpose for each of 1973 and 1974, to remain available until expended. Regulations limiting incidental takes during commercial fishing in 1973 and 1974 shall be issued. Implementation will be delayed for up to four months. The United States will negotiate with the Inter-American Tropical Tuna Commission to effect compliance with these regulations.

§ 1382. Regulations and administration

Summary: Federal agencies will coordinate and cooperate in developing and implementing regulations under the Act. Programs in which the United States participates in the taking of marine mammals on land shall be reviewed annually. Suspension of programs will take place if they can not be conducted on federal land in compliance with the Act.

§ 1383. Application to other treaties and conventions

Summary: The provisions of the Act are in addition to, not in contradiction to, treaty obligations. Commercial fishing operations controlled under international agreements are exempt from the provisions of the Act.

§ 1384. Authorization of appropriations

Summary: Appropriations for the Department of Commerce are $7.223 million for 1982, $8 million for 1983, and $8.8 million for 1984. Appropriations for the Department of Interior are $1.6 million for 1982, $1.76 million for 1983, and $2 million for 1984.

Subchapter III. Marine Mammal Commission

§ 1401. Establishment

Summary: The Marine Mammal Commission is established, composed of three members appointed by the President, effective September 1, 1982. No member of the commission may also be a government employee. Terms of office shall be staggered. No member may serve consecutive full terms. The President shall designate the chairman. The chairman shall appoint an executive director.

§ 1402. Duties of commission

Summary: The commission shall review U.S. activities under existing laws and treaties relating to marine mammals, the conditions of marine mammals, methods for their protection, conservation, and humane taking, research programs under the Act, and permit applications. It shall undertake or commission studies, make recommendations for actions, treaties, policies, revisions to the endangered species list, and the protection of native Alaskan subsistence hunters, and compile the annual report for submission to Congress. Recommendations to federal officials shall be responded to within 120 days, and explanation given of the reasons for rejecting any recommendation.

§ 1403. Committee of scientific advisors on marine mammals

Summary: The commission shall establish, within 90 days of its creation, a committee of scientific advisors on marine mammals, consisting of nine marine scientists. The commission shall consult with the committee on all studies, recommendations, and permits. Any committee recommendations not accepted by the commission must be forwarded to the appropriate federal agency with an explanation of the reasons for not adopting them.

§ 1404. Reports

Summary: The commission must transmit a report to Congress by January 31 of each year describing, for the previous year, its activities and findings, and recommendations made to or by it, along with responses to the recommendations.

§ 1405. Coordination with other federal agencies

Summary: The commission shall have access to all relevant studies and data compiled by the federal government. The commission may, with the permission of the appropriate official, use the facilities or services of any federal agency, and take steps to avoid duplication of research.

§ 1406. Administration

Summary: The commission may hire and pay people, equip offices, enter into contracts, and procure the services of experts, and take other actions to implement its responsibilities under the Act.

§ 1407. Authorization of appropriations

Summary: Appropriations to the commission are $672,000 for 1982, $1 million for 1983, and $1.1 million for 1984.

11 • Port and Tanker Safety Act

SUMMARY ───────────────────────────────────

(P.L. 95–474, approved October 17, 1978)

§ 391a(1). Statement of policy

Summary: The purpose of the Act is to authorize increased supervision of vessel and port operations and to set safety standards for vessel operation and for the handling of dangerous substances.

§ 391a(2). Definitions

Summary: Terms having a specific meaning for the Act are defined. The Secretary of Transportation is authorized to administer the Act.

§ 391a(3). Applicability

Summary: The Act applies to all vessels that transport oil or hazardous materials in bulk in a U.S. jurisdiction.

§ 391a(4). Exceptions

Summary: Public vessels; oil exploration vessels of less than 500 gross tons that are not tankers; fishing vessels or less than 500 gross tons used in salmon or crab fisheries of Washington, Oregon, or Alaska; and foreign vessels not destined for or departing from a port under U.S. jurisdiction are excepted from the Act.

§ 391a(5). Fish processing vessels

Summary: Fish processing vessels of less than 5,000 gross tons used in fisheries of Washington, Oregon, or Alaska are excepted from the Act.

§ 391a(6). Regulatory authority

Summary: Regulation of the design, construction, alteration, repair, maintenance, operation, equipping, personnel qualification, or manning of vessels to which the Act applies is permitted. Procedures to consult with federal, state, and local governments, port officials, the maritime community, environmental groups, or knowledgeable interested parties are to be established.

§ 391a(7). Minimum standards

Summary: Self-propelled vessels are subject to minimum standards. They must have segregated ballast tanks, crude oil washing systems, and/or cargo tank protection systems, by varying compliance dates, depending on size (for vessels of at least 20,000 deadweight tons), age, and vessel type. Navigational and safety systems are required on all vessels of at least 10,000 deadweight tons.

§ 391a(8). Evidence of compliance

Summary: Vessels must have on board a Certificate of Inspection (if U.S.) or Compliance (if foreign) showing that they meet the requirements of the Act. Certificates must be renewed every two years.

§ 391a(9). Personnel and manning standards for vessels of the United States

Summary: Standards for the manning of U.S. vessels are mandated outlining the duties, qualifications, and training required of officers and crew. Necessary instruction and licensing qualifications are to be set.

§ 391a(10). Tankerman requirements

Summary: The number of crew certified as tankermen must be specified, and standards for certification set by DOT.

§ 391a(11). Personnel and manning standards for foreign vessels

Summary: An evaluation of foreign manning standards is to be made, followed by a determination of the comparability of each country's standards to those of the United States.

§ 391a(12). Modifications

Summary: U.S. regulations may be modified to meet the requirements of international agreements ratified by the United States.

§ 391a(13). Prohibited acts

Summary: The violation of the provisions of the Act or its regulations is prohibited, including refusal of inspection. It is unlawful for vessels to operate in an area under U.S. jurisdiction while not in compliance with the requirements of the Act.

§ 391a(14). Enforcement

Summary: Civil penalties for violation of the Act provide for fines of up to $25,000 per violation. Criminal penalties are up to $50,000 and five years imprisonment per violation.

§ 391a(15). Inspection

Summary: A national program for annual inspection of vessels subject to the Act is mandated, as are regulations setting fees. Documents are required showing the amount and type of cargo carried, the shipper, and the consignee.

§ 391a(16). Marine safety information system

Summary: A marine safety information system is established. Vessels may be required to supply information necessary for this system.

§ 391a(17). Lightering

Summary: The regulation of lightering operating conditions, spill prevention and cleanup, location, and communications is mandated. Vessels used for such transfers must have the same certificate as is required for transport vessels.

§ 391a(18). Tank washings

Summary: Any vessel that discharges tank washings containing oil or hazardous materials in violation of U.S. law or international treaty may not transfer cargo in a U.S. port.

12 • Safe Drinking Water Act

SUMMARY _____

(P.L. 93–523, approved December 16, 1974; as last amended by P.L. 99–339, approved June 19, 1986)

Subchapter XII. Safety of Public Water Systems

Part A
Definitions

§ 300f. Definitions

Summary: Terms having a specific meaning under the Act are defined. The Environmental Protection Agency (EPA) is given responsibility for administering the Act.

Part B
Public Water Systems

§ 300g. Coverage

Summary: Regulations under the Act apply to all public water systems except those consisting only of storage and distribution facilities, those obtaining all their water from a covered system, and those not selling water. See Sections 300g–4 and 300–5 for other exemptions.

§ 300g–1. National drinking water regulations

Summary: Effective June 19, 1986, national interim or revised primary drinking water regulations and recommended maximum contaminant levels previously promulgated became national primary drinking water regulations and maximum contaminant levels. After that date drinking water regulations and maximum contaminant levels must be proposed simultaneously. Contamination levels shall be set allowing a margin of safety for no adverse health effects. Treatment techniques may be mandated instead of a maximum level if that level cannot be achieved. Filtration and disinfection criteria must be set. Revisions to regulations will take effect 18 months after their promulgation. Regulations may not require addition of substances for preventive health care unrelated to drinking water contamination.

§ 300g–2. State primary enforcement responsibility; regulations; notice and hearing; publication in Federal Register; applications

Summary: States will have primary enforcement responsibility if they have adopted drinking water regulations no less stringent than federal regulations.

§ 300g–3. Failure of state to ensure enforcement of drinking water regulations

Summary: If a public water system in a state having enforcement responsibility is out of compliance with regulations under the Act, EPA shall notify the state and provide assistance to bring the facility into compliance, including public hearings. If the problem is not corrected and the state fails to report the steps being taken to achieve compliance or fails to take steps to achieve compliance or find an alternative safe water supply in a timely fashion, a civil action may be taken. In cases in states without enforcement responsibility, a civil action may be filed as soon as noncompliance is discovered. Such cases shall be heard in a federal district court, which may require actions to meet requirements or, in cases of willful violation, impose a fine of up to $25,000 per day of violation. Public water systems subject to a variance or exemption or failing to comply with regulations must notify their customers. Failure to do so may result in a $25,000 fine.

§ 300g–4. Variances

Summary: Variances may be granted by a state program (or by EPA when there is no state program) when available water sources cannot be brought into compliance using the best available technology, if there is no unreasonable health risk. A compliance schedule must be prescribed. Variances may also be granted where a specified treatment is unnecessary. Notice and public hearings must be provided before a variance can be issued. EPA may veto variances. Variances must be reviewed by EPA at least every three years. If a state is found to abuse its variance powers, variances may be revoked. Revocations shall not take effect if the problem is corrected.

§ 300g–5. Exemptions

Summary: Exemptions may be granted by a state program (or by EPA when there is no state program), when available water sources cannot be brought into compliance, the problem predated the regulations, no alternative water supply is available, and there is no unreasonable health risk. A compliance schedule must be prescribed and may permit the exemption for no more than 12 months after the effective date of the requirement. Notice and public hearings must be provided before an exemption can be issued. Exemptions must be reviewed by EPA at least every three years. If a state is found to abuse its exemption powers, exemptions may be revoked. Revocations shall not take effect if the problem is corrected.

§ 300g–6. Prohibitions on use of lead pipes, solder, or flux

Summary: Pipe, solder, or flux used after June 19, 1986, in the construction or repair of any public water system or building providing drinking water connected to a public system shall be lead free. Joints necessary for the repair of cast iron pipe are excepted. Public water systems must give notice to the public of lead contamination in their systems. States must enforce these provisions within two years after June 19, 1986. Up to five percent of Federal funds for program grants under section 300j-2(a) may be withheld from states not enforcing these provisions.

Part C

Protection of Underground Sources of Drinking Water

§ 300h. Regulations for state programs

Summary: Regulations shall be made for state underground injection control programs, in consultation with the National Drinking Water Advisory Council. Regulations shall contain minimum requirements for an effective program to prevent injection that will endanger drinking water sources. Injection not covered by state permit will be forbidden, and permits must ensure that no injection will endanger drinking water sources. State programs must include inspection, monitoring, record-keeping, and reporting requirements. The federal government is not exempt from the provisions of underground injection regulations under the Act, but injections for recovery of oil and natural gas are, except where they will endanger underground drinking water supplies. Regulations shall not disrupt ongoing state programs. EPA may authorize temporary permits until December 16, 1978.

§ 300h–1. State primary enforcement responsibility

Summary: EPA will make a list of states needing an underground injection control program. A listed state must submit an application showing it has adopted a program and will meet record-keeping and reporting requirements. The agency will approve, disapprove, or approve in part the state program. EPA may prescribe a program for any listed state not having an approved program. Indian tribes may also assume primary enforcement responsibility.

§ 300h-2. Enforcement of program

Summary: EPA shall notify states with programs, and the person not complying, of violations. If the problem is not corrected and the state fails to report the steps being taken to achieve compliance or fails to take steps to achieve compliance, a civil action may be taken. In cases in states without programs, a civil action may be filed as soon as noncompliance is discovered. Such cases shall be heard in a federal district court, which may require actions to meet requirements or impose a fine of up to $25,000 per day of violation. In cases of willful violation, up to three years in prison may also result.

§ 300h-3. Interim regulation of underground injections

Summary: Areas may be designated in which new underground injection wells will not be allowed without an EPA permit until a state program is in operation. A permit may be issued if the injection well will not contaminate the aquifer and create a significant health hazard. A fine of up to $5,000 per day of violation ($10,000 for willful violations) may be imposed on anyone violating a permit. Injunctions may be sought to stop violations. No federal monies may go to a project that may endanger an aquifer that is the principal drinking water supply for an area and create a significant public health hazard, except for a plan to assure that the project will not contaminate the aquifer.

§ 300h-4. Optional demonstration by states relating to oil or natural gas

Summary: States may demonstrate that injections for oil and gas production or gas storage meet the requirements of the state plan to prevent endangering drinking water sources.

§ 300h-5. Regulation of state programs

Summary: EPA shall modify regulations to modify monitoring methods for Class I injection wells within 18 months of June 19, 1986. EPA shall report results of state surveys of injection wells to Congress by September 1987.

§ 300h-6. Sole source aquifer demonstration program

Summary: EPA shall establish procedures and criteria for demonstration programs for critical aquifer protection areas. States or local governments may apply for inclusion of an identified area in a demonstration program. A comprehensive management plan must be part of any application. States must report on the impact of programs by the end of 1989. EPA must summarize the state reports for Congress by Sept. 30, 1990.

§ 300h-7. State programs to establish wellhead protection areas

Summary: States shall adopt programs to protect wellhead areas from contamination within three years of June 19, 1986. Public participation of such plans is required. EPA must approve the plans. States having more than 2,500 active injection wells as of the start of 1986 must certify the effectiveness of their programs.

Part D

Emergency Powers

§ 300i. Emergency powers

Summary: EPA may supersede state programs in emergencies if local authorities do not act. The agency may issue orders to protect consumers and commence civil action for relief. Willful noncompliance with such orders may result in fines up to $5,000 per day of violation.

§ 300i-1. Tampering with public water systems

Summary: Any person who tampers with a public water system may be fined up to $50,000 and/or imprisoned for up to five years. Any person who attempts to tamper with a public water system may be fined up to $20,000 and/or imprisoned for up to three years.

Part E

General Provisions

§ 300j. Assurances of availability of adequate supplies of chemicals necessary for treatment of water

Summary: If sufficient water treatment chemicals are not available to a public water system before October 1, 1982, this may be certified by the agency. EPA may decide the form of applications for certification of need, and the conditions for issuance or denial. Upon certification, provision of the necessary chemicals shall be ordered within seven days. Certifications or orders are limited to one year. Such orders may not apply to those who manufacture, produce, or process such chemicals solely for their own use. Orders shall be equitably apportioned taking into account geography and production. Compliance with such order is a defense for breach of contract to supply the substance subject to an order. Noncompliance with such an order is punishable by a fine of up to $2,500 per violation and $5,000 per knowing violation. Court orders may be obtained for enforcement of orders.

§ 300j-1. Research, technical assistance, information, training of personnel

Summary: EPA may conduct research into the health effects of drinking water contaminants or the provision of safe supplies, including methods to identify and measure contaminants and their sources and health effects, treat raw water, and protect aquifers from contamination. It may also provide technical assistance to local programs or help alleviate emergency situations endangering public health. Grants may be supplied only if the action to prevent a health hazard would not be taken without it. Reports shall be made to Congress on the cost of carrying out national drinking water regulations, available water supplies, alternative methods of compliance, methods of paying the costs of public water system compliance, and the costs to different classes of consumers of different size sources. A survey of waste disposal that may endanger drinking water supplies, injection methods that will not contaminate underground water sources, methods of dealing with spills, and control of viral contamination shall be conducted. A study shall also be made of surface contamination and abandoned wells. EPA may also make available information and research facilities and grants for program development and training.

§ 300j-2. Grants for state programs

Summary: Grants to states for supervision of programs may be made, but for only one year unless the state program assumes primary enforcement. Grants may be for up to 75 percent of program costs. No state may receive less than one percent of the annual appropriation, except Guam, American Samoa, and the Virgin Islands. Grants may be made for up to 75 percent of the cost of underground water supply protection if the state has an approved program within two years after regulations for injection control programs are in force.

§ 300j-3. Special project grants and guaranteed loans

Summary: Grants may be made for projects on new ways to provide drinking water supplies, investigate health effects of recycling wastewater, and prepare safe drinking water. Grants are limited to two-thirds of capital costs and 75 percent of operating expenses. Projects must be approved by the state and determined to serve a useful purpose under the Act. Priority is to be given for advanced technology to remove particles that are health hazards and are too small to be removed by ordinary treatment. Loans by private lenders to small public water systems to meet national primary drinking standards may be guaranteed for 1975 and 1976. Limits are $50,000 per loan and $50 million total.

§ 300j-3a. Grants to public sector agencies

Summary: Grants to public agencies may be made for the same purposes as in Section 300j-3. Grants are limited to two-thirds of capital costs and 75 percent of operating expenses. Projects must be approved by the state and determined to serve a useful purpose under the Act.

§ 300j-3b. Contaminant standards or treatment technique guidelines

Summary: Guidelines shall establish supplemental standards or treatments for microbiological, viral, radiological, organic, and inorganic contaminants and as conditions for projects under the two previous sections involving direct human consumption of treated wastewater. These conditions shall provide adequate protection to human health. Projects receiving grants must comply with national primary drinking water regulations, the guidelines of this section, and provide safe drinking water. Guidelines may vary according to project conditions.

§ 300j-4. Records and inspections

Summary: All suppliers of water, those subject to either national primary drinking water or underground injection regulations, and those receiving financial support under the Act must comply with the record-keeping, reporting, and monitoring provisions required under the Act or its regulations. Following written notice, agency officials may enter any regulated premises for inspection of facilities and records or for testing. In states having primary enforcement responsibility, EPA shall consult with the state regulatory agency. States may not inform those to be inspected. Anyone refusing to allow an inspection or audit is subject to a fine of up to $25,000. Confidentiality of information will be respected.

§ 300j-5. National Drinking Water Advisory Council

Summary: A National Drinking Water Advisory Council of 15 members is established. Terms of members are for three years. One-third of the members will come from each of the general public, state and local water agencies, and private water supply and hygiene organizations. The Council shall advise EPA on matters relating to the Act. Compensation shall be at the GS–18 level.

§ 300j–6. Federal agencies

Summary: Federal agencies with jurisdiction over water supplies or engaging in underground injection are subject to the Act. No federal employee may be held personally responsible for civil penalties with respect to official duties. Waivers may be granted for national security matters. Records will be maintained of the basis for such waivers, and shall be available for examination by the courts. Indian lands and water rights are not affected by the Act.

§ 300j–7. Judicial review

Summary: Petitions for review of national primary drinking water, underground injection, or state primary enforcement responsibility regulations may be filed in the U.S. Court of Appeals for the District of Columbia, within 45 days of promulgation or effect. District Courts may review other regulations, variances, and exemptions within the same time constraints.

§ 300j–8. Citizen's civil action

Summary: Civil actions may be brought against violators or government agencies failing to perform duties under the Act. Sixty days notice must be given for citizens suits, which may not proceed if action on the complaint is under way or initiated within the notice period. The court may order court costs to be paid or bonds to be filed.

§ 300j–9. General provisions

Summary: Regulations may be prescribed to carry out the functions of the Act. Personnel of other agencies may be seconded to assist in administering the Act. Methods of payment of grants may be determined. Labor practices under the act will comply with the Davis-Bacon Act (40 USC 276a–276a5). Employers may not discharge or discriminate against employees taking part in proceedings under the Act. EPA must report to Congress by April 1 of each year on activities under the Act. The report will include a statement on the costs of compliance to public water systems in each state.

The Office of Management and Budget (OMB) may comment on but not revise such reports.

§ 300j–10. Appointment of scientific, etc., personnel by administrator of EPA for implementation of responsibilities; compensation

Summary: Up to 30 persons may be appointed to EPA positions up to GS–18 to discharge functions under the Act.

§ 300j–11. Indian tribes

Summary: Indian tribes may be treated as states, and primary enforcement responsibility may be delegated to them, as well as grant and contract assistance. EPA shall promulgate regulations within 18 months of June 19, 1986 specifying for what provisions of the Act recognized Indian tribes may be treated as states. EPA may regulate administration of provisions for which Indian tribes cannot act as states.

13 • Noise Control Act

SUMMARY ───────────────────────────────

(P.L. 92–574, approved October 18, 1972; as last amended by
P.L. 95–609, approved November 8, 1978)

§ 4901. Congressional findings and statement of policy

Summary: Congress finds that uncontrolled noise from transportation
vehicles and equipment, machinery, appliances, and other products of
commerce presents a danger to the population. The policy of the United
States is to promote an environment free from noise harmful to health or
welfare. The Act coordinates research and control activities, establishes
standards, and provides for the dissemination of information on noise
emissions.

§ 4902. Definitions

Summary: Terms having a specific meaning under the Act are defined.
The Environmental Protection Agency (EPA) is given responsibility for
administration of the Act.

§ 4903. Federal programs

Summary: All government agencies shall comply with noise abatement
requirements. The President may exempt executive branch activities from
some requirements of the Act if it is in the national interest. Exemptions may
be for up to one year, and may be renewed once. Exemptions and the reasons
for granting them must be reported to Congress annually, EPA shall
coordinate federal noise programs, make regulations in consultation with
other agencies, and report on federal agency noise control programs.

§ 4904. Identification of major noise sources

Summary: EPA shall develop and publish noise criteria for the health
effects of different types and amounts of noise on public health or welfare,
information on safe noise levels and products that are major sources of noise,
and techniques and costs of noise control.

850

§ 4905. Noise emission standards for products distributed in commerce

Summary: EPA shall regulate products that are major sources of noise, such as construction, transportation, or electronic equipment, or motors and engines. Regulations shall be promulgated within 24 months of identification of a major noise source. Regulations shall include noise emission performance standards sufficient to protect public health or welfare. Regulations may contain testing procedures for verifying compliance with standards and mandate inclusion of instructions with regulated products. Manufacturers of regulated products must warrant them to be in compliance with applicable regulations. Transfer of costs of warranting products is prohibited. Advertising including the cost or value of noise reduction devices must use Labor Department figures. To establish figures, the Department of Labor shall have access to manufacturers' records. Local governments cannot set noise emission limits different from federal ones. They may petition EPA to set more stringent standards.

§ 4906. [Omitted]

§ 4907. Labeling

Summary: The EPA may designate products that effectively reduce noise or are capable of adversely affecting public health or welfare. Regulations may require information on noise levels to be attached to products and/or their packaging. States may do likewise if they do not conflict with federal regulations.

§ 4908. Imports

Summary: The Treasury Department may regulate imports of new products under the provisions of the Act.

§ 4909. Prohibited acts

Summary: It is prohibited to sell any new product not in compliance with regulations, to remove noise reduction equipment mandated by regulation from a product before sale or use a product not in compliance, to remove a notice pursuant to regulations, to import new products not complying with regulations, or to fail to comply with a requirement of a court enforcement order or request for records, information, or products for testing. Exemptions may be made for research, testing, or training, or for products specifically manufactured and labeled to prevent their use in any state.

§ 4910. Enforcement

Summary: Anyone willfully committing a prohibited act may be fined up to $25,000 for each day of violation, imprisoned for one year, or both. Penalties are doubled for repeat offenders. Civil penalties are fines up to $10,000 per day of violation. District courts shall hear actions to restrain violations. EPA may issue orders specifying relief from violators (other than federal agencies) necessary to protect public health or welfare. Notice and hearing opportunity must precede orders.

§ 4911. Citizens' suits

Summary: Citizens' suits may be brought in federal district court against any violators or federal agencies failing to carry out duties under the Act. Sixty days notice must be given for citizens' suits, which may not proceed if action on the complaint is under way or initiated within the notice period. The court may order court costs to be paid.

§ 4912. Records, reports, and information

Summary: Manufacturers of regulated products must comply with requirements for records, information, or products for testing. Confidentiality of information shall be respected. Falsification of records or impairment of monitoring devices is punishable by a fine of up to $10,000 and imprisonment for up to six months.

§ 4913. Quiet communities, research, and public information

Summary: EPA shall develop and disseminate information on noise effects and control, support research on the effects of noise on humans, animals, and property, noise control technology, monitoring equipment, and economic impact of both noise and noise control. It shall also administer a "Quiet Communities Program" including grants to local government agencies to determine local noise problems, establish control programs, develop abatement plans for transportation facilities, evaluate noise control techniques, and demonstrate best available techniques; loan equipment to local jurisdictions to implement noise control programs; develop quality assurance programs for monitoring procedures for local jurisdiction; study personnel needs for noise abatement and control programs; and develop training programs. The agency shall implement a national noise environmental assessment program, establish regional technical assistance centers, and provide technical assistance to local government programs. Maximum use should be made of senior citizens eligible under the Older Americans Act.

§ 4914. Development of low-noise-emission products

EPA shall determine and certify low-noise-emission products under regulations it shall develop. Certification shall be for one year. A low-noise-emission product advisory committee may be established to assist in determining qualified products. Members may be paid at GS-18 level. Products certified shall be purchased for federal use whenever they are available, if they cost no more than 125 percent of the products they would replace. Preference shall be given to products with lower operating and maintenance costs. Appropriations for payment of higher prices for certified products are $1 million in 1973, $2 million for each of 1974 and 1975, $2.2 million for 1976, and $2.97 million for 1977. Certification data shall be used in procurement contracts. Certified products used by the federal government shall be tested. If they fail the tests, the manufacturer shall be provided with an opportunity to rectify the situation. Failure to do so may result in refusal to recertify.

§ 4915. Judicial review

Summary: Petitions for review of regulations may be filed in the U.S. Court of Appeals for the District of Columbia within 90 days of promulgation or effect. EPA may subpoena witnesses and information and administer oaths for hearings to obtain information necessary for the administration of the Act.

§ 4916. Railroad noise emission standards

Summary: EPA and the Department of Transportation shall make regulations, in consultation, setting noise emission standards and ensuring compliance for interstate commerce by railroad. Standards shall be based on best available technology, considering cost of compliance. Local governments cannot set standards different from federal regulations.

§ 4917. Motor carrier noise emission standards

Summary: EPA and DOT shall make regulations in consultation, setting noise emission standards and ensuring compliance for interstate commerce by motor carriers. Standards shall be based on the best available technology, considering cost of compliance. Local governments cannot set standards conflicting with federal regulations.

§ 4918. Authorization of appropriations

Summary: Appropriation under the Act for activities other than research and development is $15 million for 1979.

14 • Intervention on the High Seas Act

SUMMARY ⸻

**(P.L. 93–248, approved February 5, 1974; as last amended by
P.L. 97–164, approved October 1, 1982)**

§ 1471. Definitions

Summary: Terms having a specific meaning under the Act are defined.
The Commerce Department is given responsibility for administering the
Act.

§ 1472. Grave and imminent danger from oil pollution casualties to coastline or related interests of United States; federal non-liability for federal preventive measures on the high seas

Summary: The Commerce Department may take action on the high seas
under the international convention relating to intervention on the high seas
in cases of oil pollution casualties to prevent, mitigate, or eliminate the
danger from damage, or the imminent threat of damage, to a ship that may
result in pollution affecting the coast of the United States, without liability
for damages to the ship.

§1473. Consultations and determinations respecting creation of hazards to human health, etc.; criteria for determinations respecting grave and imminent dangers of major harmful consequences to the United States coastline or related interests

Summary: The Commerce Department, in consultation with the Environmental Protection Agency (EPA), shall determine when substances not
covered by the convention may cause damage to U.S. interests. Interests
include human health, living marine resources, wildlife, costs and estuaries,
and public and private shorelines and beaches.

§ 1474. Federal intervention actions

Summary: When there is a grave and imminent danger, the department
may coordinate and direct removal or elimination of pollution damage;
undertake salvage operations; or remove or destroy ships or cargo that are
the source of danger.

§ 1475. Consultation procedure

Summary: Before acting, the department shall consult, via the State Department, with foreign countries affected by the marine casualty and the flag country of the ship involved; notify the EPA and others who may be affected by the action; and consider the views of those consulted or notified.

§ 1476. Emergencies

Summary: The Commerce Department may act without consultation or notice in cases of extreme urgency.

§ 1477. Responsible measures; considerations

Summary: Measures taken shall be proportional to the damage or threat present. The extent or probability of damage if measures are not taken, the likely effectiveness of those measures, and the extent of possible damage from the action must be considered.

§ 1478. Personal, flag state, and foreign state considerations

Summary: Measures should avoid risk to human life, aid distressed persons, and not interfere unnecessarily with the rights or interests of other persons or foreign states.

§ 1479. Federal liability for unreasonable damages

Summary: The United States may be held liable for damages caused by unreasonable measures. Actions seeking compensation may be brought in U.S. courts. The United States will have the burden of proving a substance not covered by the convention posed a grave and imminent danger equal to a substance listed under the convention.

§ 1480. Notification by Secretary of State

Summary: The Secretary of State must notify foreign countries affected by measures taken under the Act, as well as the International Maritime Organization.

§ 1481. Violations; penalties

Summary: Violations of the Act or regulations under it, failure to comply with an order pursuant to Act, or willful obstruction of those acting in compliance with the Act is punishable by a fine of up to $10,000 and one year in prison. Proof that compliance would have endangered human life shall be a defense in criminal proceedings.

§ 1482. Consultation for nomination and nomination of experts, negotiators, etc.; proposal of amendments to list of substances other than convention oil; presidential acceptance of amendments

Summary: The department, in consultation with the State Department and EPA, may nominate persons to the list of experts and propose amendments to the list of substances under the convention. The President may accept amendments to the list of substances. The State Department, in consultation with Commerce, shall nominate negotiators, arbitrators, or conciliators under the convention.

§ 1483. Foreign government ships; immunity

Summary: No measures may be taken against ships owned by any government and used for noncommercial purposes.

§ 1484. Interpretation and administration; other right, duty, privilege or immunity, and other remedy unaffected

Summary: The Act must be administered in accordance with the convention.

§ 1485. Rules and regulations

Summary: The department may make rules and regulations to implement the Act.

§ 1486. Revolving fund for federal actions and activities

Summary: The revolving fund established under the Water Pollution Control Act may be used for intervention actions under the Act.

§ 1487. Effective date

Summary: The Act shall be in effect on the later of February 5, 1974, or the date the convention comes into effect in regard to the United States.

15 • National Ocean Pollution Planning Act

SUMMARY ─────────────────────────────────────

(P.L. 95–273, approved May 8, 1978; as last amended by P.L. 97–375, approved December 21, 1982)

§ 1701. Findings and purposes

Summary: Congress finds there is a need for comprehensive federal planning for research and development and monitoring of ocean pollution. The purpose of the Act is to establish a five-year plan for federal programs in this field and to develop an information base for policy making. The National Oceanic and Atmospheric Administration (NOAA) is given responsibility for preparation and enforcement of the plan.

§ 1702. Definitions

Summary: Terms having a specific meaning under the Act are defined.

§ 1703. Comprehensive federal plan relating to ocean pollution

Summary: NOAA shall prepare a five-year plan for federal ocean pollution research and development and monitoring. The plan shall be revised every three years, and submitted to Congress and the President by September 15 of each revision year. The plan shall identify and establish priorities for national needs and problems related to ocean pollution and explain the reasons for changes in previous plans. It shall list all existing federal ocean pollution programs, including a catalog of personnel, facilities, and equipment, and a description of the goals and costs of each program; and analyze how well each program will meet the priorities of the plan. The plan shall recommend changes to enable programs to better carry out the priorities set. Recommendations may include changes in goals and funding, proposals for interagency cooperation, and suggestions for new legislation. The plan shall describe actions taken to coordinate budget review to ensure interagency cooperation in carrying out programs and elimination of duplication of efforts. The plan period is the five-year period beginning the year before a revision year.

§ 1704. Comprehensive ocean pollution program in the administration

Summary: NOAA shall establish a comprehensive, coordinated, and effective program for ocean pollution research and development and monitoring. Activities under the program must be consistent with the plan. The program will include all projects and activities under the Act, and those under the Marine Protection, Research, and Sanctuaries Act; projects and activities addressing the priorities set by the plan; and financial assistance under section 1705.

§ 1705. Financial assistance

Summary: NOAA may provide grants and contracts for activities to meet plan priorities when federal programs do not address them. Applications may be made and proposals invited. NOAA shall determine the form of applications. Activities under grants or contracts will be administered by existing federal programs when possible. NOAA shall decide on applications within six months. Up to 100 percent of project costs may be paid. Recipients of financial assistance must keep records as prescribed. Records must be retained for three years after project completion and be available for audit and examination.

§ 1706. Interagency cooperation

Summary: The head of each federal entity involved in programs under the Act shall cooperate with NOAA and make available facilities, personnel, and data on written request.

§ 1707. Dissemination of information

Summary: NOAA shall disseminate information gathered by programs under the Act to government agencies and others interested in ocean pollution research and development and monitoring.

§ 1708. Effect on other laws

Summary: Nothing in the Act affects the authority of other federal entities to conduct ocean pollution research and development and monitoring.

§ 1709. Authorization of appropriations

Summary: Appropriations are $5 million for 1979, $4.3 million for 1980, $3 million for 1981, and $4 million for 1982.

16 • Marine Protection, Research, and Sanctuaries Act

SUMMARY ————————————————————————

(P.L. 92–532, approved October 23, 1972; as last amended by
P.L. 99–499, approved October 17, 1986)

Chapter 27. Ocean Dumping

§ 1401. Congressional finding, policy, and declaration of purpose

Summary: Congress finds that ocean dumping endangers the environment.
U.S. policy is to regulate the dumping of material in U.S. waters to protect
the marine environment.

§ 1402. Definitions

Summary: Terms having a specific meaning under the Act are defined.
The Environmental Protection Agency (EPA) is given responsibility for
enforcement of the Act.

Subchapter I. Regulation

§ 1411. Prohibited acts

Summary: Dumping of material in U.S. territorial waters, or within 12
miles of the territorial waters if it may affect them, is prohibited unless
authorized by permit.

§ 1412. Dumping permit program

Summary: EPA may issue permits for materials other than dredging
spoils, highly radioactive waste, and agents of biological, chemical, radiological warfare. The agency must determine that such dumping will not harm

859

the environment, and develop criteria for evaluating permit applications. EPA may decide where dumping may be allowed. No permit is required for fish waste except in areas where it may threaten health or the environment. Permits issued by countries that are parties to the Convention on the Prevention of Marine Pollution by Dumping of Wastes and Other Matter will be honored by the United States.

§ 1412a. Dumping of sewage sludge and industrial waste

Summary: The dumping of sewage sludge and industrial waste will be halted under the Act. After December 31, 1981, dumping of small amounts of industrial waste may be permitted only for research purposes or in emergencies.

§ 1413. Dumping permit program for dredged material

Summary: Ocean dumping permit for dredged material may be issued by the Secretary of the Army. EPA may veto such permit grants. The Secretary may issue regulations covering dumping of dredged materials from federal projects.

§ 1414. Permit conditions

Summary: Permits must designate the amount and type of waste to be dumped and the location and permit of validity of the permit, plus any other provisions deemed necessary. Permit fees and reporting requirements may be mandated. General permits may be issued. Permits shall be reviewed periodically. Permit information shall be available to the public. From January 6, 1983, to January 5, 1985, no dumping of low level radioactive waste shall be permitted except for small amounts for research purposes. After that period no permits may be issued unless a Radioactive Material Disposal Impact Assessment is completed. A copy of the assessment must be sent to the House Committee on Merchant Marine and Fisheries and the Senate Committee on Environment and Public Works. Permits must be approved by Congress.

§ 1415. Penalties

Summary: Violations of the Act are subject to a civil penalty of up to $50,000 per violation. Knowing violations are subject to fines up to $50,000 and one year imprisonment. Each day of violation is considered a separate violation. Vessels may be held for payment of fines. Permits may be suspended or revoked for violation of permit conditions. Civil suits may be brought by private citizens. Actions in emergencies to safeguard life must be reported but are not violations.

§ 1416. Relationship to other laws

Summary: Permits for dumping except under the Rivers and Harbors Act issued before this Act becomes effective are invalid. No permits will be granted that may interfere with navigation. State programs must be consistent with the Act. Nothing in the Act affects the provisions of the Fish and Wildlife Coordination Act or the rights of any person to seek damages or enforcement under State or Federal law. Dumping of dredged material in Long Island Sound must comply with permit criteria.

§ 1417. Enforcement

Summary: Other governmental agencies may be used in enforcing the Act. The Coast Guard will conduct surveillance and enforcement activities.

§ 1418. Regulations

Summary: Appropriate regulations may be issued by EPA, the Army, or the Coast Guard.

§ 1419. International cooperation

Summary: The Secretary of State shall seek international cooperation to protect the marine environment.

§ 1420. Authorization of appropriations

Summary: Appropriations are $3.6 million for 1973; $5.5 million each for 1974 and 1975; $5.3 million for 1976; $1.325 million for the transition period July 1 to September 30, 1976; $4.8 million each for 1977 and 1978; $2 million each for 1980 and 1981; and $4.213 million for 1982.

§ 1421. Annual report to Congress

Summary: Every year a report on the previous year shall be submitted to Congress by February 1.

Subchapter II. Research

§ 1441. Monitoring and research program; reports to Congress

Summary: A monitoring program is mandated on the effects of dumping on ocean, coastal, and Great Lakes basin waters. Annual reports must be made to Congress.

§ 1442. Research program respecting possible long-range effects of pollution, overfishing, and man-induced changes of ocean ecosystems

Summary: A research program is mandated on the long-range effects of pollution, overfishing, and manmade changes in the ocean ecosystem, including oil spills. Such studies may be undertaken in cooperation with other nations. An annual report on the previous fiscal year's activities must be submitted to Congress each March.

§ 1443. Cooperation with public authorities, agencies, and institutions, and private agencies and institutions, and individuals

Summary: EPA shall conduct research into means of minimizing or ending ocean dumping and coordinate or assist the efforts of others.

§ 1444. Authorization of appropriations

Summary: Appropriations are $6 million each for 1972 to 1976; $1.5 million for the transition period July 1 to September 30, 1976; $5.6 million for 1977; $6.5 million for 1978; $11.396 million for 1981; and $12 million for 1982.

§ 1445. Removal of heavy metals and other toxic organic materials from sewage sludge of city of New York; study, etc.

Summary: EPA may assist New York City in assessing options for the removal of heavy metals and toxic organics from its sewage sludge and the reduction of pollutants entering the system. The study must be completed by July 1, 1981.

Chapter 32. Marine Sanctuaries

§ 1431. Definitions

Summary: Terms having a specific meaning under the Act are defined. The Commerce Department is given responsibility for enforcement of the Act.

§ 1432. Designation of sanctuaries

Summary: The department may designate marine sanctuaries in consultation with contiguous states. Designations may be vetoed by Congress or the governor of a contiguous state. The department may negotiate with other countries to form international sanctuaries. A biennial report must be submitted to Congress by March 1 of even numbered years. Public hearings must be held in coastal areas before designation of a sanctuary. The department may issue and enforce regulations.

§ 1433. Penalties

Summary: Violations of regulations are punishable by a civil fine of up to $50,000 per violation. Each day of violation is considered a separate violation. Vessels may be held for payment of fines.

§ 1434. Authorization of appropriations

Summary: Appropriations are $10 million each for 1973 to 1975; $6.2 million for 1976; $1.55 million for the transition period July 1 to September 30, 1976; $0.5 million each for 1977 and 1978; $2.25 million for 1981; and $2.235 million for 1982 and 1983.

17 • Outer Continental Shelf Lands Act

SUMMARY

(Chapter 345, Section 2, 67 Stat. 462, approved August 7, 1953; as last amended by P.L. 97–212, approved June 30, 1982)

Chapter 29

Subchapter III. Outer Continental Shelf Lands

§ 1331. Definitions

Summary: Terms having a specific meaning under the Act are defined. The Secretary of the Interior is given primary responsibility under the Act.

§ 1332. Congressional declaration of policy

Summary: The purpose of the Act is to assert control by the federal government over the development of mineral resources in the outer continental shelf, and to ensure that operations there do not harm the environment.

§ 1333. Laws and regulations governing lands

Summary: The jurisdiction of the United States is extended to the subsoil and seabed of the outer continental shelf and all installations on it. The President shall establish procedures for resolving border disputes by September 18, 1979. Death or disability occurring during exploitation of natural resources on the outer continental shelf is covered by the Longshoreman's and Harbor Workers' Compensation Act. The National Labor Relations Act applies to labor practices occurring on installations. The Coast Guard may make safety regulations. The Army may prevent obstruction of navigation.

§ 1334. Administration of leasing

Summary: The leasing provisions of the Act shall be administered and regulated by the Department of the Interior. Leases may be suspended, or canceled after being suspended, if activities would be harmful to the environment, aquatic life, mineral resources, or national security. Lessees must comply with all applicable regulations. Nonproducing leases may be canceled by the department for failure to comply; producing leases may be canceled only by a district court. Pipeline rights-of-way may be granted for transport of mineral resources. Pipelines must provide access to nonowners; expansion of capacity must be approved by the Federal Energy Regulatory Commission (FERC). The commission may exempt pipelines feeding facilities which first process oil or gas. Production of oil or gas must be at approved rates. Unapproved flaring of natural gas is not permitted after September 18, 1978, except to alleviate an emergency or during testing.

§ 1335. Validation and maintenance of prior leases

Summary: State leases, issued before December 21, 1948, and effective on August 7, 1953, are covered by this section and may continue operations. Sulfur rights are continued only for as long as production continues.

§ 1336. Controversies over jurisdiction; agreements; payments; final settlement or adjudication; approval of notice concerning oil and gas operations in Gulf of Mexico

Summary: The department may enter into agreements with states to resolve whether, and under what conditions, previously leased state lands are covered under the Act. The notice of December 11, 1950, on oil and gas exploration in the Gulf of Mexico is still in force.

§ 1337. Grant of leases by Secretary

Summary: Leases may be granted to the highest qualified bidder in competitive sealed bidding. Bidding procedures and royalties shall be established by regulation. Bidding systems must be submitted to Congress, which may veto them. In order to obtain information on the utility of different bidding systems, bidders may be required to submit bids using several systems until September 18, 1983. Information on lease sales must be reported to Congress annually. Oil and gas leases shall be no larger than 5,760 acres unless a larger area is needed for economic feasibility, and for no more than 10 years, which may be renewed if exploration or production is ongoing. Leases are subject to the provisions prescribed in regulations, and 20 percent of production must be offered for sale at market value to small or independent refiners. Lease sales must be reviewed for antitrust violations. Bids may not be submitted by those not meeting due diligence requirements of other leases. Transfer of leases requires approval. Leases within three miles of shore must be notified to the governor of the state, along with information enabling the state to decide whether to negotiate an agreement for revenue sharing. Separate sulfur leases may be granted. Royalties must be no less than 5 percent of gross value. Leases for other minerals may also be granted.

§ 1338. Disposition of revenues

Summary: Funds received from leases go into the Treasury.

§ 1339. Refunds; filing time limitation; certification of repayment; necessity of report to Congress

Summary: Lease overpayments will be refunded without interest, if a request is filed within two years. Payments may not be made until 30 days after notification to Congress.

§ 1340. Geological and geophysical explorations

Summary: Federal agencies may conduct geophysical studies if they do not interfere with lease operations or harm aquatic life. All explorations by lessees must be in accordance with the provisions of this section. Exploration plans must be approved in advance. They must include a schedule of exploration, a description of equipment that will be used, and the location of operations. Necessary modifications to meet the requirements of the Act must be made, or the plan will not be approved, and the lease may be canceled. If a plan is revised, the revision must also be approved. States must approve of plans affecting coastal zone management programs. A drilling permit may be required for each well. Permits issued before November 17, 1978, are considered in compliance, but a temporary suspension of activities may be ordered pending a revision. Permits may be issued only when the applicant is qualified, and the exploration will not interfere with other leased activities or endanger aquatic life, cause pollution, or disturb historical objects. No lease or permits may be granted within 15 miles of the Point Reyes Wilderness unless approved by California.

§ 1341. Reservation of lands and rights

Summary: The President may withdraw unleased lands from the program. During war the United States will have right of first refusal for all mineral production. Operations under leases may be suspended with compensation, and areas restricted, for national security reasons. The United States gets all materials essential to the production of fissionable materials, and all helium produced under lease.

§ 1342.   Prior claims as unaffected

Summary: The rights to land covered by the Act but acquired previous to it are unaffected.

§ 1343.   Annual report by Secretary to Congress

Summary: A report to Congress must be made annually, within six months of the end of the fiscal year. It must describe moneys received and spent, activities under leases, a summary of management and enforcement activities, recommendations for improvements in administration, and a list of shut-in and flaring wells. A second report prepared in consultation with the Attorney General shall include an evaluation of competitive bidding systems, alternative bidding systems, measures to encourage competition and distribution of oil and gas to independents, and recommendations for administrative changes.

§ 1344.   Outer continental shelf leasing program

Summary: A leasing program shall be established, including schedules indicating the size, timing, and location of leases meeting energy needs for the following five years. Management of the shelf must take into account economic, social, and environmental values of its resources and the impact of exploration on the environment. Timing and location of exploration must be based on existing geological and environmental information, sharing of risks and benefits among regions, energy markets, other uses of the sea and seabed, producer interest, state laws, and environmental sensitivity and productivity. Leasing shall ensure receipt of fair market value by the government. The leasing program must include estimates of the appropriations and staff required to run the program in accordance with the Act. Suggestions from federal agencies and states shall be solicited and considered. A copy of the proposed program must be submitted to the state affected. Comments must be included when the proposal is submitted to Congress within nine months of September 18, 1978. Leasing may continue under previous rules until approval of the program. Regulations shall establish procedures for management of the leasing program. Information may be obtained from public, private, and federal sources for preparing environmental impact statements or evaluations required by the Act. Confidentiality of information will be maintained.

§ 1345.   Coordination and consultation with affected state and local governments

Summary: State or local governments may comment on leases affecting them within 60 days of notification. Acceptance or rejection or recommendations must be made in writing. Cooperative agreements with affected states are permitted.

§ 1346. Environmental studies

Summary: Studies must be done to determine the environmental effects of development. Studies must be started at least six months before lease sales. Effects on marine life and coastal areas of pollution should be assessed. Necessary additional studies to provide long-term information on effects must be conducted after leasing and development. Regulations shall establish procedures for such studies. These studies must be considered in decision making. A report on the cumulative effect of activities under the Act must be submitted to Congress annually. The Departments of Interior and Commerce shall cooperate in administering the Act.

§ 1347. Safety and health regulations

Summary: On September 18, 1978, the Departments of Interior and Commerce and any other appropriate federal agencies shall begin a study of the adequacy of health and safety regulations pertaining to activities under the Act and submit the results to the President, who shall submit a plan to Congress to promote health and safety in the activities controlled by the Act. Operations must use the best available and safest economically feasible technologies. The Commerce Department shall promulgate regulations applying to hazardous working conditions. This will not affect the authority of the Labor Department, the Transportation Department (DOT), or the Environment Protection Agency (EPA) in their respective areas. Commerce and the National Institute of Occupational Safety and Health (NIOSH) shall study diving techniques and equipment to improve their safety and efficiency. An annual compilation of safety and other regulations under the Act will be published.

§ 1348. Enforcement of safety and environmental regulations

Summary: Commerce, Interior, and the Army shall enforce regulations promulgated under the Act. The holder of a lease or permit must maintain workplaces in compliance with occupational safety and health regulations to protect persons, property, and the environment in the area, and must allow inspections. Regulations for inspection procedures shall be promulgated. Investigations of deaths, serious injuries, fires, or oil spills shall be made and a report published. Allegations of regulatory violations may be made, with the power to call witnesses and obtain records. Violations, investigations, and subsequent actions, plus diving studies must be included in the annual report to Congress.

§ 1349. Citizens' suits, jurisdiction, and judicial review

Summary: Citizens' suits against violators (including government agencies) are permitted. District courts may, in response to such suits, order enforcement actions or issue injunctions. Sixty days notice must be given for citizens' suits, which may not proceed if action on the complaint is under way or initiated within the notice period. The 60-day period may be waived for emergencies posing a risk to public health and safety. Judicial review of leasing programs can be heard only in the Court of Appeals for the District of Columbia.

§ 1350. Remedies and penalties

Summary: The government may institute civil action for a temporary injunction to enforce the Act. Civil penalties for violation of the Act may be up to $10,000 per day of violation. Hearings on civil penalties may be held, with subpoena power. Penalties for criminal violations go up to $100,000 per day of violation and 10 years in prison. Corporate officers guilty of criminal violations are subject to the same penalties as their corporation. Penalties are concurrent and cumulative.

§ 1351. Oil and gas development and production

Summary: The lease holder must submit a development and production plan for approval before beginning operations for any lease outside the Gulf of Mexico. The plan must describe all shore facilities and operations, including environmental and safety protection measures. The plan shall be made available to state and local officials. Affected states with coastal management plans must approve any plan before activities may begin. If approval of a plan is a major federal action, copies of the draft environmental impact statement must be made available to affected state and local governments and the public. The plan may be approved, disapproved, or approved after modification by the lessee. If a plan is disapproved due to noncompliance with the Act, the lessee will not be compensated. Five years are allowed for modifications to a plan. Failure to submit a plan or to comply with an approved plan may result in loss of the lease. Any part of a plan dealing with natural gas must be approved by FERC. A plan may also be required for the Florida coast of the Gulf of Mexico.

§ 1352. Oil and gas information program

Summary: The lease holder must provide all data and information from lease operations to the government. The agency will pay the reproduction and processing costs. Regulations shall be made to protect confidentiality of information supplied. Such information may be passed on to affected states, so they may plan for onshore impacts of development, only with permission of the lessee. State officials may, however, inspect confidential information. Civil suits may be brought against any government involved for failure to maintain confidentiality.

§ 1353. Federal purchase and disposition of oil and gas

Summary: The United States may purchase or receive as royalties up to one-sixth of production under a lease. The United States may sell or distribute any oil or gas received under this section and may limit bidding to small refiners or regional distributors, if they do not have other access to supplies. The lessee must buy back any oil or gas the government is unable to sell.

§ 1354. Limitations on export of oil or gas

Summary: Production is subject to the Export Administration Act of 1969 unless it is being exchanged with foreign oil for ease of transport to U.S. markets or pursuant to international agreement. The President must certify exports as being in accordance with the export law.

§ 1355. Restrictions on employment of former officers or employees of the Department of the Interior

Summary: No one administering this Act at GS–16 level or above may act for a private concern dealing with a government action involving the Act for two years after leaving government service, or one year in the case of Interior Department actions.

§ 1356. Documentary, registry, and manning requirements

Summary: Regulations shall be promulgated requiring documentation that equipment used in lease activities meet design and construction standards and be manned by U.S. citizens or resident aliens, except for equipment built or personnel hired before September 18, 1978, or when sufficient qualified Americans are not available, or the equipment is more than 50 percent foreign owned and the foreign government has adequate protection for those manning its equipment.

Chapter 36

Subchapter I. Offshore Oil Spill Pollution Fund

§ 1811. Definitions

Summary: Terms having a specified meaning under the Act are defined. The Department of Transportation (DOT) is given responsibility for administering this subchapter of the Act.

§ 1812. Offshore oil pollution compensation fund

Summary: An offshore oil pollution compensation fund is established using funds from the fee levied on oil obtained from the outer continental shelf. The fund may be used to clean up oil spills, settle claims, and administer the fund. A civil penalty of up to $10,000 will be imposed on anyone failing to pay a required fee. Anyone falsifying records is liable to criminal prosecution. DOT may borrow money from the Treasury if the fund is insufficient to meet obligations.

§ 1813. Claims for economic loss from oil pollution

Summary: Claims may be made for cleanup costs or for damages due to oil pollution. Those causing an incident may only make claims for damage that was not their fault or that is above their limit of liability.

§ 1814. Scope of liability

Summary: Sources of oil pollution shall be liable for cleanup costs and payment of claims up to $35 million, except in cases of war, natural disaster, or negligence by another party.

§ 1815. Financial responsibility

Summary: Owners of vessels using offshore facilities must demonstrate ability to meet the financial responsibilities of liability. DOT may deny entry or exit at port for vessels not certified. Inspections to verify certification are permitted. A study shall be made to determine whether adequate insurance is available.

§ 1816. Notification, designation, and advertisement

Summary: Those involved in oil spills must notify DOT immediately. DOT shall designate the source of pollution, and advertise procedures for filing claims.

§ 1817. Claims settlement

Summary: Claims may be presented to the owner, insurer, or the fund. If the claim is not settled, the claimant may sue. Claims in excess of the limit of liability may be presented to the fund. DOT shall determine procedures for appraisal and settlement of claims.

§ 1818. Subrogation

Summary: Anyone, including the fund, that pays a claim may be substituted as a creditor to those responsible for the incident.

§ 1819. Jurisdiction and venue

Summary: District courts have jurisdiction over controversies under the Act. The venue shall be the district in which the injury occurred or the defendant resides. For the fund, this is the District of Columbia.

§ 1820. Relationship to other state or federal laws

Summary: Those compensated by the fund may not collect under other state or federal laws, and vice versa. The Act does not prevent states from imposing additional requirements or liability.

§ 1821. Oil discharge prohibition

Summary: The discharge of oil in harmful quantities from an offshore facility or vessel is prohibited.

§ 1822. Penalties

Summary: Anyone not complying with the financial responsibility requirements of the Act is subject to a civil penalty up to $10,000. Anyone failing to give notice of an oil spill is subject to a fine up to $10,000 and one year in prison.

§ 1823. Authorization of appropriations

Summary: Appropriations for administration of the Act are $10 million for 1979 and $5 million for each of 1980 and 1981. Additional appropriations to the fund may be made.

§ 1824. Annual report

Summary: DOT shall report to Congress annually on the administration of the fund and recommendations for legislative changes.

Subchapter II. Fishermen's Contingency Fund

§ 1841. Definitions

Summary: Terms having a specific meaning under the Act are defined. The Department of Commerce is given responsibility for administering this subchapter of the Act.

§ 1842. Fishermen's contingency fund

Summary: A fishermen's contingency fund is established, using fees from holders of permits and licenses, to compensate losses.

§ 1843. Duties and powers of Secretary

Summary: The Commerce Department shall identify potential hazards to commercial fishing under the Act, prescribe regulations for procedures for filing claims, and make payments for losses resulting from activities under the Act.

§ 1844. Burden of proof

Summary: It is presumed that damages were due to activities under the Act when a report on damage occurring in a lease area is filed, no notice of danger was given, no record of hazards are found on nautical charts, and there were no surface markers or lighted buoys.

§ 1845. Claims procedure

Summary: Claims must be filed in the form prescribed within 60 days and lease holders notified. The Commerce Department will decide the merits of the claim and make payments when necessary. Decisions may be reviewed in court.

§ 1846. Annual report

Summary: The department shall make an annual report to Congress on the number and types of damages suffered, and the compensation awarded.

§ 1847.   Repealed

Subchapter III. Miscellaneous Provisions

§ 1861.   Report to Comptroller General on shut-in and flaring oil and gas wells; submission of findings and recommendations to Congress

Summary: The Department of the Interior must include in its annual report to Congress a list of all shut-in or flaring wells.

§ 1862.   Natural gas distribution

Summary: The Federal Energy Regulatory Commission (FERC) shall establish a policy encouraging the participation of local distributors in the leasing and development of natural gas resources under the Act.

§ 1863.   Unlawful employment practices; regulations

Summary: Regulations under the Act shall ensure that no unlawful or discriminatory employment practices are permitted.

§ 1864.   Disclosure of financial interests by officers and employees of the Department of the Interior

Summary: Officers or employees of the Interior Department who administer the Act and have a financial interest in a lease or other activity under the Act must annually file a written statement of those interests. Anyone who knowingly violates this requirement is subject to a fine of up to $2,500 and one year in prison.

§ 1865.   Investigation of reserves of oil and gas in outer continental shelf

Summary: The Interior Department shall conduct a continuing study of the availability of oil and natural gas on the outer continental shelf and report periodically to the Congress on its findings.

§ 1866.   Relationship to existing law

Summary: Except as specifically provided, nothing in the Act affects any provisions of other laws.